HELPS TO THE
STUDY OF THE BIBLE

SECOND EDITION

WITH MANY CORRECTIONS, ALTERA-
TIONS AND ADDITIONS

BY

THE BISHOP OF BRADFORD
G. H. BOX, C. H. DODD, G. BUCHANAN GRAY
HUGH LAST, R. H. MALDEN
THE BISHOP OF OXFORD
H. WHEELER ROBINSON, G. ADAM SMITH
AND A. SOUTER

LONDON

OXFORD UNIVERSITY PRESS

HUMPHREY MILFORD

1931

OXFORD UNIVERSITY PRESS
AMEN HOUSE, E.C. 4
LONDON EDINBURGH GLASGOW
LEIPZIG NEW YORK TORONTO
MELBOURNE CAPETOWN BOMBAY
CALCUTTA MADRAS SHANGHAI
HUMPHREY MILFORD
PUBLISHER TO THE
UNIVERSITY

PRINTED IN GREAT BRITAIN AT THE UNIVERSITY PRESS, OXFORD
BY JOHN JOHNSON, PRINTER TO THE UNIVERSITY

SUMMARY OF CONTENTS

PART I

GENERAL INTRODUCTION

THE BIBLE

PART II

THE OLD TESTAMENT

Summary of Contents

Summary of Contents

PART V

PALESTINE, ITS INHABITANTS, PHYSICAL GEOGRAPHY, CUSTOMS, ETC.

Summary of Contents

EDITORIAL NOTE

A NEW EDITION of the *Oxford Helps to the Study of the Bible* has long been due. Since the first edition was issued, biblical study has very largely changed in character. Not only has a great deal of new light been thrown on the Bible story by archaeological discovery, by researches into comparative religion, by the growth of historical and ethnological knowledge ; not only has the science of biblical criticism passed in regard to many matters beyond the stage of tentative suggestion towards that of established conclusion; but, as a result of all this, the proportion of interest in the biblical records has greatly changed. The Bible used formerly to be studied in the main as a literature in isolation ; and the Bible student made it his chief ambition to know fully the details of the stories which the Bible itself told, the events of Abraham's life, the sequence of David's career, the exact items of the Tabernacle furniture, and so on. Nowadays, the Bible has been brought into relation with the story of the world beyond the Hebrew people, and the Bible student concerns himself not so much with the biblical accounts by themselves, but far more with those narratives in their relation to the life of the larger world of which the events of Hebrew history formed but a part. This change of interest is of course especially noticeable in the study of the Old Testament, but it has taken place also in that of the New, though here in a less degree, inasmuch as the history of New Testament times had always been better known than that of the pre-Christian world. Then too, the process of biblical criticism has immensely enlarged our knowledge of the processes by which the books of the Bible came to be formed, and has raised many problems, and solved some, as to the authorship and date of the several books or of parts of those books. Thus this edition, in which, while unproved hypotheses are not taken into account, the results of the new knowledge are frankly faced and the new interest is frankly catered for, is bound to be in many respects very different from its predecessor. As much as was serviceable in the old edition has been retained, though sometimes in abbreviated form, but in the historical, critical, and archaeological sections re-editing has practically involved complete re-writing. It is hoped that in its new form this volume will provide a handy and useful book of reference for this generation of students, as the former edition had done for an earlier generation.

To index a book which is in some respects itself an index, and is in every respect a book of reference, has not been an easy task.

Limitations of space and convenience, and the consideration of the general purposes for which this book might be useful, prescribed that the Index should not be too elaborate and unwieldy, and that unnecessary duplication of references should as far as possible be avoided. Those using the book will find that the best way to look up any general topic will be to turn to the Summary of Contents, which has been made more detailed than is usually considered necessary. The General Index has been compiled so as to include the chief mentions of individual names and subjects. Thus the reader will turn rather to it for the references to particular words, names, and allusions. In one or the other of these two it is hoped that every subject of major, and all significant mentions of minor importance, have been incorporated, so that the student may not have to search long before finding the reference for which he is seeking.

It remains to be added that the work of re-editing has been parcelled out among several scholars, each being directly responsible only for his own contribution. But the initials of the writers have not been appended to their several contributions, as the work was greatly subdivided, and the book is less a work of theory or suggestion than a record of the facts and results which are the common property of biblical scholarship as a whole, and are not the mere hypotheses of one individual scholar, or group of scholars, more than of another.

General Index

BIBLIOGRAPHY

*Books marked with an asterisk (*) are those which are more suitable for
the general reader or the non-specialist student.*

COMMENTARIES

One volume : *Ed. A. S. Peake. Jack. 12s. 6d.
          *Ed. C. Gore. S.P.C.K. 16s.
Separate volumes : The International Critical Commentary. Clark.
          Westminster Commentaries. Methuen.
          Macmillan's series.
          Expositor's Bible. Hodder.
          *Cambridge Bible for Schools and Colleges. C.U.P.
          *Century Bible. Nelson.
          *Clarendon Bible. O.U.P.

GENERAL

*J. BAIKIE.	Lands and Peoples of the Bible. Black. 5s.
C. BRIGGS.	General Introduction to the Study of Holy Scripture. Scribner's.
*H. E. FOSDICK.	The Modern Use of the Bible. S.C.M. 6s.
H. J. MACKINDER.	Wall Map of Palestine. Stanford. 21s.
J. MOFFATT	A New Translation of the Bible. Hodder. 20s.
*J. PATERSON SMYTH.	Our Bible in the Making. Low. 3s. 6d.
A. S. PEAKE.	The Bible, its Origin, its Significance, and its Abiding Worth. Hodder. 7s. 6d.
*W. B. SELBIE.	The Nature and Message of the Bible. Clarke. 2s. 6d.
G. A. SMITH.	Historical Geography of the Holy Land. Hodder. 20s.
——	Atlas of the Historical Geography of the Holy Land. Hodder. 25s.
	The Legacy of Israel, ed. E. R. BEVAN and C. SINGER. O.U.P. 10s.
	The People and the Book, ed. A. S. PEAKE. O.U.P. 10s.

OLD TESTAMENT AND APOCRYPHA
1. General

*W. H. BENNETT.	An Introduction to the Old Testament. Methuen. 5s.
*G. H. BOX.	A Short Introduction to the Literature of the Old Testament. Rivingtons. 2s. 6d.
S. R. DRIVER.	Introduction to the Literature of the Old Testament. Clark. 15s.
G. B. GRAY.	A Critical Introduction to the Old Testament. Duckworth. 3s. 6d.
*H. MARTIN.	The Meaning of the Old Testament. S.C.M. 2s. 6d.
*A. NAIRNE.	Everyman's Story of the Old Testament. Mowbray. 4s.6d.
*J. W. POVAH.	A Study of the Old Testament. S.C.M. 2s. 6d.
E. B. REDLICH.	An Introduction to Old Testament Study. Macmillan. 6s.
*P. C. SANDS.	The Literary Genius of the Old Testament. O.U.P. 4s. 6d.
E. SELLIN.	Introduction to the Old Testament. Hodder. 10s. 6d.
W. R. SMITH.	The Old Testament in the Jewish Church. Black. 6s.
	The Apocrypha and Pseudepigrapha of the Old Testament. Ed. R. H. CHARLES. 2 vols. O.U.P. 84s.

2. Special Sections

W. E. ADDIS.	Documents of the Hexateuch. 2 vols. Nutt. 10s.6d. each.
*A. W. F. BLUNT.	The Prophets of Israel. O.U.P. 2s. 6d.
CARPENTER and HARFORD.	The Composition of the Hexateuch. Longmans. 18s.
*A. T. CHAPMAN.	An Introduction to the Pentateuch. C.U.P. 4s.
*W. A. L. ELMSLIE.	Studies in Life from Jewish Proverbs. Clarke. 6s.
*A. R. GORDON.	The Poets of the Old Testament. Hodder. 6s.
W. O. E. OESTERLEY.	The Books of the Apocrypha. Scott. 21s.
*T. H. ROBINSON.	Prophecy and Prophets in Ancient Israel. Duckworth. 3s. 6d.
D. C. SIMPSON.	Pentateuchal Criticism. O.U.P. 6s.
J. SKINNER.	Prophecy and Religion (Jeremiah). C.U.P. 12s. 6d.
*G. A. SMITH.	The Early Poetry of Israel. O.U.P. 3s.
W. R. SMITH.	The Prophets of Israel. Black. 7s. 6d.
*V. F. STORR.	The Prophets of the Old Testament and their Message. S.P.C.K. 2s. 6d.
P. J. WADDY.	The Homes of the Psalms. S.P.C.K. 6s.
A. WELCH.	Jeremiah, his time and his work. O.U.P. 6s.
A. WELCH.	The Psalms in Life, Worship, and History. O.U.P. 5s.

3. Old Testament History

N. H. BAYNES.	Israel among the Nations. S.C.M. 5s.
*E. R. BEVAN.	Jerusalem under the High Priests. Arnold. 8s. 6d.
*A. W. F. BLUNT.	Israel in World-History. O.U.P. 2s. 6d.
J. H. BREASTED.	Ancient Times. Ginn. 10s. 6d.
L. E. BROWNE.	Early Judaism. C.U.P. 15s.
C. F. BURNEY.	Israel's Settlement in Canaan. O.U P. 3s. 6d.
*W. FAIRWEATHER.	From the Exile to the Advent. Clark. 3s.
A. H. GODBEY.	The Lost Tribes a Myth. Duke University Press. 34s.
H. R. HALL.	The Ancient History of the Near East. Methuen. 7s.
P. S. P. HANDCOCK.	The Archaeology of the Holy Land. Fisher Unwin. 10s.
*D. G. HOGARTH.	The Ancient East. Thornton Butterworth. 2s. 6d.
C. F. KENT.	History of the Hebrew People. Murray. 2 vols. 9s. each.
————	A History of the Jewish People during the Babylonian, Persian, and Greek Periods. Murray. 6s.
*J. L MYRES.	The Dawn of History. Thornton Butterworth. 2s. 6d.
*R. L. OTTLEY.	A Short History of the Hebrews. C.U.P. 6s. 6d.
J. S. RIGGS.	A History of the Jewish People during the Maccabean and Roman Periods. Murray. 6s.
T. H. ROBINSON, J. W. HUNKIN, and F. C. BURKITT.	Palestine in General History. O.U.P. 6s.
*M. SARSON and E. A. PHILLIPS.	The History of the People of Israel. Longmans. 6s.
*J. SKINNER.	The Historical Connection between the Old and New Testaments. Clark. 1s.
H. P. SMITH.	Old Testament History. Clark. 14s.
W. L. WARDLE.	Israel and Babylon. Holborn Publishing House. 5s.

4. Old Testament Theology and Religion

*A. W. F. BLUNT.	Israel before Christ (Social and Religious Development.) O.U.P. 2s. 6d.
*C. F. BURNEY.	Israel's Hope of Immortality. O.U.P. 2s. 6d.

*C. F. Burney.	Outlines of Old Testament Theology. Rivingtons. 2s.6d.
R. H. Charles.	A Critical History of the Doctrine of a Future Life. Black. 15s.
* ———	Religious Development between the Old and New Testaments. Williams and Norgate. 2s.
W. Fairweather.	The Background of the Gospels. Clark. 12s.
J. G. Frazer.	Folk-lore in the Old Testament. (Abridged in 1 vol.) Macmillan. 18s.
H. F. Hamilton.	The People of God. O.U.P. 10s. 6d.
*K. Marti.	The Religion of the Old Testament. Williams and Norgate. 4s. 6d.
W. O. E. Oesterley.	Immortality and the Unseen World. S.P.C.K. 12s. 6d.
H. P. Smith.	The Religion of Israel. Clark. 10s.
W. R. Smith.	The Religion of the Semites. Black. 12s. 6d.
A. Welch.	The Religion of Israel under the Kingdom. Clark. 10s.
H. Wheeler Robinson.	The Religious Ideas of the Old Testament. Duckworth. 3s. 6d.

NEW TESTAMENT

1. General

W. F. Adeney.	An Introduction to the New Testament. Methuen. 5s.
A. Deissmann.	Light from the Ancient East. Hodder. 42s.
A. Harnack.	The Origin of the New Testament. Williams and Norgate. 6s.
M. Jones.	The New Testament in the 20th Century. Macmillan. 12s. 6d.
*K. Lake.	The Text of the New Testament. Rivingtons. 2s.
A. H. McNeile.	An Introduction to the New Testament. O.U.P. 18s.
R. H. Malden.	Religion and the New Testament. O.U.P. 6s.
J. Moffatt.	Introduction to the Literature of the New Testament. Clark. 15s.
———	The Approach to the New Testament. Hodder. 8s. 6d.
*A. Nairne.	Everyman's Story of the New Testament. Mowbray. 4s. 6d.
*A. S. Peake.	A Critical Introduction to the New Testament. Duckworth. 3s. 6d.
*A. Souter.	The Text and Canon of the New Testament. Duckworth. 3s. 6d.

2. The Gospels

F. C. Burkitt.	The Gospel History and its Transmission. Clark. 12s.
J. Denney.	Jesus and the Gospel. Hodder. 12s.
A. C. Headlam.	The Life and Teaching of Jesus the Christ. Murray. 12s.
*M. Jones.	The Four Gospels. S.P.C.K. 4s.
J. Klausner.	Jesus of Nazareth. Allen and Unwin. 18s.
*J. Moffatt.	Theology of the Gospels. Duckworth. 3s. 6d.
*L. Pullan.	The Gospels. Longmans. 5s.
A. E. J. Rawlinson.	The New Testament Doctrine of the Christ. Longmans. 12s. 6d.
*J. A. Robinson.	The Study of the Gospels. Longmans. 3s. 6d.
W. Sanday.	Outlines of the Life of Christ. Clark. 8s.

E. F. Scott.	The Fourth Gospel, its Purpose and Theology. Clark. 10s.
A. Schweitzer.	The Quest of the Historical Jesus. Black. 12s. 6d.
V. H. Stanton.	The Gospels in Historical Documents. C.U.P. 3 Parts, 12s. 6d., 16s., and 20s.
B. H. Streeter.	The Four Gospels. Macmillan. 21s.

3. St. Paul

A. Deissmann.	St. Paul: a Study in Social and Religious History. Hodder. 10s. 6d.
F. J. Foakes-Jackson.	The Life of St. Paul. Cape. 10s.
P. Gardner.	The Religious Experience of St. Paul. Williams and Norgate. 6s.
*T. R. Glover.	Paul of Tarsus. S.C.M. 9s.
*H. A. A. Kennedy.	The Theology of the Epistles. Duckworth. 3s. 6d.
K. Lake.	The Earlier Epistles of St. Paul. Rivingtons. 18s.
*W. Lock.	St. Paul—the Master-Builder. Methuen. 5s.
W. Morgan.	The Religion and Theology of Paul. Clark. 10s.
W. M. Ramsay.	St. Paul—the Traveller and the Roman Citizen. Hodder. 12s.
C. A. A. Scott.	Christianity according to St. Paul. C.U.P. 12s. 6d.
*J. Paterson Smyth.	The Life and Letters of St. Paul. Low. 3s. 6d.

4. History

*S. Angus.	The Environment of Early Christianity. Duckworth. 3s. 6d.
C. Bigg.	The Church's Task under the Roman Empire. O.U.P. 7s. 6d.
T. R. Glover.	The Conflict of Religions in the Early Roman Empire. Methuen. 7s. 6d.
W. J. Lightley.	Jewish Sects and Parties in the Time of Christ. Epworth Press. 8s. 6d.
W. M. Ramsay.	Luke, the Physician. Hodder. 12s.
*F. Richards.	The World to which Christ came. Epworth Press. 5s.
*J. H. Roper.	The Apostolic Age in the Light of Modern Criticism. Hodder. 6s.

5. New Testament Ethics

*C. Gore.	The Sermon on the Mount. Murray. 5s.
*H. Rashdall.	Conscience and Christ. Duckworth. 5s.
*C. A. A. Scott.	New Testament Ethics: an Introduction. C.U.P. 5s.
E. F. Scott.	The Ethical Teaching of Jesus. Macmillan. 6s.

DICTIONARIES

Hastings' Dictionary of the Bible. 5 vols. Clark. 26s. each.
Hastings' Dictionary of the Bible. 1 vol. Clark. 24s.
Encyclopaedia Biblica. 4 vols. Black. 80s.
Encyclopaedia of Religion and Ethics. 12 vols. Clark. 35s. each.
Hastings' Dictionary of Christ and the Gospels. 2 vols. Clark. 26s. each.
Hastings' Dictionary of the Apostolic Church. 2 vols. Clark. 26s. each.
Moulton and Geden. Concordance to the Greek Testament. Clark. 26s.
Souter. Pocket Lexicon of the Greek New Testament. O.U.P. 3s. 6d.
Abbott-Smith. Manual Greek Lexicon of the New Testament. Clark. 21s.

HELPS TO THE STUDY OF THE BIBLE

PART I

GENERAL INTRODUCTION

THE BIBLE

I. THE TITLE OF THE BIBLE

1. The Bible. The word Bible came into English from the
Greek through the Latin. Byblus, which properly meant the rind
of a stem of the papyrus plant (a gigantic sedge which grew
mainly in Egypt), came to be used also for the pith which
constituted the real writing material. This use originated the
Greek name βίβλος, βιβλίον for a book (Matt. 1¹, Luke 4¹⁷). The
Sacred Books, which were read in their Churches, were naturally
called by the Greek Christians τὰ βιβλία, the Books, though this
usage has not been traced higher than the fourth century, when it
is found in Chrysostom. In process of time this name, with many
others of Greek origin, passed into the vocabulary of the Western
Church. Here another term, first used by Jerome, *bibliotheca divina*,
'the divine library', had also been in use, appearing in Old English
in the form *bibliopéce*. In the thirteenth century the neuter
plural 'Biblia' came to be regarded as a feminine singular, and
'the Books' became by common consent 'the Book' (*Biblia* sing.).
This gradually displaced the term *bibliopéce*, and was adopted into
our language in the form Bible.*

2. The Scriptures. The Bible is also called αἱ γραφαί, *the
Scriptures*, or the *Holy Scriptures*, i. e. the Sacred Writings.
St. Paul speaks of ἱερὰ γράμματα, i. e. the Old Testament (literally
Holy Writings) as being able to make wise unto salvation through
faith in Christ Jesus (2 Tim. 3¹⁵, ¹⁶). In the Gospels and the
Acts of the Apostles αἱ γραφαί is employed (Matt. 21⁴², Luke 24³²,
John 5³⁹, Acts 18²⁴). The corresponding singular term ἡ γραφή—the
Scripture—is generally used in the New Testament for a special
passage (Mark 12¹⁰, Luke 4²¹, James 2⁸, &c.). Now the term

* See Bp. Westcott's *Bible in the Church*, p. 5.

'Scripture', 'Holy Writ', the early English rendering of the Latin word, is used alike for the part and for the whole.

3. The Old and New Testaments. St. Paul, in a notable passage, calls the Books of Moses, if not the whole of the Hebrew Canon, 'the Old Covenant' ('at the reading of the Old Covenant', 2 Cor. 3¹⁴, R.V.). In the same context he describes himself and his fellow-labourers as 'Ministers of a New Covenant' (2 Cor. 3⁶). These terms ἡ παλαιὰ διαθήκη *the Old Covenant*, and ἡ καινὴ διαθήκη *the New Covenant*, were employed at the close of the second century by ecclesiastical writers to denote the Jewish and Christian Scriptures respectively. The Latin rendering of διαθήκη fluctuated at first between *instrumentum* and *testamentum*, but *testamentum* prevailed. Hence in the languages of the West the two collections of writings, which make up the Bible, came to be called 'the Old Testament' and 'the New Testament'. But the original idea of a Covenant, i. e. of an agreement between God and man, must never be lost sight of. Jeremiah (31³¹⁻⁴) speaks of a new and better Covenant which God will make : and though it is probable that he had in mind Israel only, as purified by the Exile, the idea was accepted and extended by our Lord at the Last Supper (Matt. 26²⁸).

II. THE CANON OF SCRIPTURE

1. The Canon. The word *Canon* signifies properly in classical Greek *a straight rod*, especially *a carpenter's rule*. Thus it came to be used figuratively of a *testing rule* in art, logic, grammar, and ethics. In the sense of a 'rule of life' it occurs in Gal. 6¹⁶. In the early ages of Christianity, the term was used generally to denote a standard of opinion and practice. The word was also used in the sense of a list or catalogue, such as a list of books permitted to be read in the public services of the Church. Its first direct application to the Holy Scriptures occurs in the 'imprimatur' appended by Amphilochius to his Catalogue (A. D. 380); though Origen seems to have termed those books *Canonical* which Christians regard as genuine and of Divine authority. *Uncanonical* books are those not specified in the Canon. Apocryphal books derive their name from the Greek ἀπόκρυφος, which signifies (1) *hidden*, (2) *of unknown authority*, (3) *spurious*. The majority of these books were not written in Hebrew, and the Jewish Church did not rank them with the Old Testament. They are found in MSS., as well as in printed Bibles, in company with the Canonical Books, and are

2

read for historical purposes, and for 'instruction of manners'. The week-day lessons from Oct. 27–Nov. 19 are taken from Wisdom, Ecclesiasticus, and Baruch. Portions of these books rise very high : but as a whole the Church has endorsed the secondary position assigned to them by the Jews.

2. **The Jewish Canon.** The Canon of the Old Testament contains a number of different writings, covering a period of many centuries. It is probable that some collection of them had begun to be made before the capture of Jerusalem in 586 B.C. Some works (e. g. the Book of Jashar, 2 Samuel 1[18]) may have disappeared in that catastrophe. The re-collection of older books was probably begun soon after the Return, and the existing Canon was formed by a gradual process of accretion, in three successive collections (Law, Prophets, and Writings), from the latter part of the fifth century B. C. onwards. It was largely stereotyped by the persecution of Antiochus Epiphanes (*c.* 176 B. C.), when the Jews had to decide definitely what books were so sacred as to be dearer than life itself.

3. **The first Notice of the Old Testament** as a collection of writings is in the Prologue to the Greek translation of Ecclesiasticus (132 B. C.), which specifies 'the Law and the Prophets and the other Books'; cp. Luke 24[44]. Philo, a learned Jewish philosopher of Alexandria (*c.* 20 B. C.–A. D. 40), regards the Pentateuch as of the highest Divine authority and considers its legislation to be of supreme permanent value. A number of passages illustrating his view have been collected by H. E. Ryle, *Philo and Holy Scripture*, Intr. pp. xvi–xx. Josephus (A. D. 38— *c.* 100) enumerates twenty-two books as 'divine', viz. *five* of Moses, *thirteen* of Prophets (in which Job was probably included), and *four* of 'hymns and directions of life'. He mentions all the books of the Old Testament as canonical except Job, Proverbs, Ecclesiastes, and the Song of Solomon, to which he does not allude, as none of them furnished any materials for his work. He also adds that, since the death of Artaxerxes (B. C. 424), no one had dared, up to this day, 'to add anything to them, to take anything from them, or to make any change in them' (*Against Apion*, i. 8). This, however, is not accurate. Zechariah 9–14, Daniel 7–12, and many other portions are of later date than this. When the Jewish Canon was finally fixed in the second century B. C. its contents were as they are now : our thirty-nine books were, however, grouped so as to accord with the twenty-two letters of the Hebrew alphabet, the

twelve minor prophets counting as one, Ruth being coupled with Judges, Ezra with Nehemiah, Lamentations with Jeremiah, while the two Books of Samuel, Kings, and Chronicles were reckoned as one each.

4. **The Evidence of the New Testament.** The Books of the Old Testament are referred to in the New without any trace of hesitation. Sometimes they are alluded to under such collective titles as 'the Scriptures', 'the writings' (Matt. 22^{29}, Acts 17^{11}); sometimes under the fuller phrase 'the Law and the Prophets' (Matt. 7^{12}, Rom. 3^{21}), 'the Law of Moses, the Prophets, the Psalms' (Luke 24^{44}): and the records, to which the names are applied, are assumed to contain the truth of the Divine Revelation. Again and again we have also express quotations made from the books of the Hebrew Bible by our Lord and His Apostles, and, with the exceptions of Judges, Ecclesiastes, the Song of Solomon, Esther, Ezra, and Nehemiah, every book of the Old is quoted in the New Testament. The Christian Church accepted the Jewish Canon *en bloc* as a matter of course ; and for a generation at least possessed no other Bible.

5. **The New Testament Canon.** The New Testament was gradually added to the Old. But it was some considerable time after our Lord's Ascension before any of the books contained in it were actually written. The first and most important work of the Apostles was to deliver a personal testimony to the chief facts of the Gospel History (Luke 24^{48}, Acts $1^{21, 22}$). Their teaching was at first *oral*, and it was no part of their intention to create a permanent literature. A cycle of selected representative facts sufficed to form the groundwork of the *oral Gospel* (1 Cor. 15^{1-10}). But in the course of time, many endeavoured to commit to *writing* this oral Gospel (Luke 1^{1-4}). So long as the Apostles were still living, the necessity for written records of the words and actions of our Lord was not so pressing, especially as His Second Coming was regarded as imminent (1 Thess. 4^{15}). But when the time came for their removal from this world, it became extremely important that authoritative records should be put forth. Thus the Gospels came into existence, two bearing the names of Apostles, and two by friends and close companions of Apostles. But already had arisen another kind of composition. Founders of Churches, often unable to visit them personally, desired to communicate with their converts for purposes of counsel, reproof, or instruction. Thus arose the Epistles, which were put forth from time to time to meet special wants and emergencies.

4

6. **Quotations.** The existence and authority of the several Books of the New Testament, which thus gradually arose, are attested by quotations in a series of Christian writers, which begins with the immediate successors of the Apostles. Clement of Rome, for example, at the end of the first century refers expressly to 1 Corinthians as the work of St. Paul, and gives evidence of his acquaintance with the writings of St. James and St. John. Polycarp of Smyrna, who was martyred A. D. 166, and had heard St. John, does not quote the sacred writers by name, but his Epistle contains many references to their writings, especially to the Pastoral Epistles of St. Paul. Justin Martyr, about the middle of the second century, was so well acquainted with the writings of the first three Evangelists that it would be almost possible to rewrite from his works a considerable portion of the records of the life of Christ. Irenaeus, who became Bishop of Lyons in 177 or 178, quotes almost every book of the New Testament and often names the writers. So do Tertullian and Clement of Alexandria in the next generation. Origen (*c.* 185–251) not only bears testimony by quotation, but speaks definitely on the subject of authorship. He mentions that the genuineness of 2 Peter and 2 and 3 John was not unquestioned; and with regard to the Epistle to the Hebrews, he attributes the thoughts to Paul and the actual authorship to some unknown writer.

7. **Collections of Books.** But besides quotations we have collections or lists of books known to be Apostolic and authoritative. Of such collections we possess a remarkable specimen in the famous Muratorian *Fragment on the Canon*, so called as being first published by Muratori in A. D. 1740 from a MS. in the Ambrosian Library at Milan, which had originally belonged to the Irish Monastery at Bobbio. The date of this fragment cannot be much later than A. D. 170. It was probably written at Rome, and may be taken to represent the Canon in use among Western Churches at the time of its composition. It includes in its catalogue St. Luke's and St. John's Gospels, the Acts, thirteen Epistles of St. Paul, 1 and 2 John, Jude, and the Apocalypse, but omits the Epistles of James, 3 John, 1 and 2 Peter, and the Epistle to the Hebrews, which is possibly due to the fragmentary and corrupt state of the MS., which begins in the middle of an account of St. Mark. It may therefore be presumed that it included St. Matthew. Almost contemporary with it is the Old Latin Version, the Bible of the North African Churches. It contains all the New Testament except Hebrews, 2 Peter, and James.

8. **Testimony of Eusebius.** The persecution of Diocletian, A. D. 303, brought to the front the question of the sacred literature of the Church. The persecutors demanded that the Scriptures should be given up; and Christians refused to give them up; hence the question became urgent—what books were Apostolic? The answer lies in our New Testament. Eusebius, who wrote his *Ecclesiastical History* early in the fourth century, discusses the question of the Canon. He divides what claimed to be sacred writings into three classes: (1) *Those universally acknowledged;* (2) *Disputed books;* (3) *Spurious writings, usually composed by heretics.* (1) The first class included definitely the Four Gospels, the Acts, the thirteen Epistles of Paul, 1 John, and 1 Peter; while he speaks with some hesitation about the Epistle to the Hebrews and the Revelation. (2) The second class included the Epistles of James, Jude, 2 Peter, 2 and 3 John. (3) The third class comprised spurious books like the Apocryphal Gospels, the Acts of Paul, the Shepherd of Hermas, the Apocalypse of Peter. The language of Eusebius illustrates the great care and caution exercised in the admittance of books into the Canon. At length a decree was issued respecting the contents of the Sacred Books at the Council of Carthage A. D. 397, and the books of the New Testament, as we now have them, were settled by the authority of the Christian Church.

III. LANGUAGE OF THE OLD AND NEW TESTAMENTS

1. **The Language** in which the Old Testament is written is Hebrew. The only exceptions are Ezra 4^8-6^{18}, 7^{12-26}, Jer. 10^{11}, Dan. 2^4-7^{28}. These particular portions are written in an Aramaic dialect which is transitional, and presents various points of difference from the later Aramaic, in which the Targums were written, though its linguistic character shews that it is not earlier than the fourth century B. C.

2. **Hebrew.** The Hebrew language is a branch of the great Semitic family of languages, viz. the Eastern (Accadian, the language of Babylonia and Assyria) and the Western (Aramaic, Canaanite, Arabic, and Ethiopic). Hebrew belongs to the Canaanite branch of the Western group, and is most closely related to Moabite and Phoenician. The word *Shibboleth* and the

question of its pronunciation (Judges 12[6]) shew how it was liable, like all languages, to tribal provincialisms. Similar provincialisms occur in the Hebrew of some of the historical and poetical books; but still, when used for sacred purposes, it remained comparatively unchanged from the days of Moses to the Captivity. After the Captivity, however, the language was considerably affected by the intercourse of the Jews with foreign nations. The Hebrew language referred to several times in the New Testament (e. g. Acts 21[40]) was really Aramaic, since Hebrew was no longer generally spoken.

3. **The Language of the New Testament is Greek.** It is not, however, the Greek of the classical writers, but a more or less literary form of the cosmopolitan spoken Greek of the Roman Empire at the time. Such elements in the Greek Bible as do not belong to this are traceable to the Hebrew original of the Old Testament and the Hebrew nationality of its translators on the one hand and of the majority of the writers of the New Testament on the other. But the great bulk of the Greek of both the Old and the New Testament is quite ordinary. For the study of the *sayings* in the Gospels a knowledge of the underlying Aramaic is invaluable.

IV. AUTHENTICITY OF THE BIBLE

(i) THE OLD TESTAMENT.

1. **General Character.** The Bible is the only collection of writings to which the Christian Church has given the title *Inspired*. Now we cannot tell of our own knowledge what manner of thing inspired writing is likely to be. We can only discover by examining the actual books whose title to Inspiration the Church does not question. If we assume that an inspired writer can necessarily deal only in facts, we are making an assumption which further study may establish or may destroy. Careful study of the Old Testament has revealed first that it is the work of more hands than appears at first sight: secondly that it contains much beside facts. Myth and legend are interwoven with its history: poetry is mingled with its prose. The story of the Flood—to take one single example—is based on a legend common to all the Semitic peoples. The Holy Spirit is not confined to any one method of teaching. He can use imagination as well as memory and conscience. The studies of recent years have shewn that Inspiration is a much larger and richer thing than had sometimes

7

been supposed. The Inspiration of the Old Testament will never be doubted by those who respond to it. But it does not admit of any proof which can carry conviction to those who do not.

2. Permanent Value. (*a*) It shews us how the world was prepared for Christ by shewing how God gradually educated one people to believe in His Unity, Goodness, and Care for Mankind. Until these three great truths had been firmly grasped, the very idea of the Incarnation of the Son of God would have been almost unthinkable and all but meaningless.

(*b*) It gives us what the Jews knew of their own early history, and what they believed about the origins of the world and of human society, regarded as a revelation of the Goodness, Power, and Justice of God. His Presence pervades everything : nothing which happens is outside His Knowledge or can be understood without reference to Him. No other people has ever treated its national history in this way, or been able to recognize the Hand of God in its disasters no less than in its triumphs (cf. Isaiah 42^{24}).

(*c*) It shews us how to clothe great ideas with form sufficiently vivid and dramatic to make them widely effective.* In this respect the Old Testament writers have no rivals.

(ii) The New Testament.

1. External Evidence. That Christian writers during the first three centuries, belonging to all parts of the world, testify to the incidents told or implied in the Gospel narrative, is notorious. It is not to be expected that references in pagan writers should be abundant. But some of the earliest and best known are worth recording.

(1) In A. D. 57 Pomponia Graecina, wife of Aulus Plautius, the conqueror of Britain, was accused of 'foreign superstition'. But this does not necessarily mean that she had become a Christian (Tacitus, *Annals*, xiii. 32).

(2) Referring to the torture inflicted upon those 'commonly called Christians' by the Emperor Nero (A. D. 64), Tacitus says that Christ was put to death by Pontius Pilate during the reign of Tiberius, and that the 'abominable superstition' which had thereby been checked for the moment broke out again and had spread even to Rome (ib. xv. 44).

---

* For a fuller discussion of the general character of the Old Testament see *The Old Testament : Its Meaning and Value for the Church to-day*, by R. H. Malden (Macmillan 1919).

(3) Suetonius, in his life of Nero, referring to the same event, describes Christians as ' a race of men of new and baneful superstition' (c. 16).

(4) When Pliny became governor of Bithynia on the southern shore of the Black Sea in or about A. D. 111, Christians were so numerous in his province that he had to ask advice of Trajan how to deal with them. The most definite thing which he could discover about them was that they were accustomed to meet before daybreak on a certain day and sing hymns to Christ as to a God (Plin. *Ep. ad Trai.* 96).

2. **Internal Evidence.** The language of the New Testament, as we have seen, was the chief language of the civilized world at the era of the Advent. But Palestine was at this time under a peculiar system of double government, partly Jewish and partly Roman. The closest analogy in the world to-day is in the native states of our Indian Empire. This arrangement came to an end in A. D. 70 when Jerusalem was destroyed. But it appears in the Gospels in a way which is perfectly natural if they are what they profess to be, but would be beyond the compass of any forger.

3. **Circumstantiality.** Again, the records of the New Testament, like those of the Old, contain histories and biographies of the most varied character. We find mentioned the names of Roman emperors, as Augustus, Tiberius, and Claudius. We have Roman governors, as Quirinius, Pontius Pilate, Felix, Festus, Sergius Paulus, and Gallio. We have Jewish kings, as Herod the Great, Archelaus, Antipas, Agrippa I, Agrippa II. Classical history and the writings of Josephus attest that they existed at the time specified, that they bore the offices assigned to them in the sacred story, and in the chronological order in which their names occur. The actions, moreover, ascribed to them are either such as these writers tell us they performed, or are at least in perfect keeping with their known characters.

4. **Undesigned Coincidences.** The same records contain allusions to places as varied as Antioch, Cyprus, Iconium, Thessalonica, Philippi, Athens, Corinth, Rome ; to senatorial provinces and imperial provinces ; to Roman procurators and proconsuls ; to ' politarchs ' of Thessalonica and ' Asiarchs ' of Ephesus ; to natives of heathen districts like Lycaonia, and of islands like Malta ; to soldiers of the imperial guard, and the members of Caesar's household ; to the great goddess Artemis, the recorder, the craftsmen, the assizes, the 'regular assembly' at Ephesus. And every

addition to our knowledge arising from archaeological exploration in Palestine, Asia Minor, Cyprus, or Greece serves to illustrate the minute accuracy with which every particular respecting them is recorded, even in reference to facts apparently the most insignificant. Indeed, it may be said that ancient literature has preserved few, if any, pictures of Asiatic towns and Roman colonies comparable for lifelike truthfulness to the narrative of St. Luke in the Acts.* But the strongest testimony to the truth of the New Testament is to be found in the existence of the Church. If we dismiss Gospels and Acts as works of fiction, the Church of History becomes an absolutely inexplicable phenomenon.

V. INTEGRITY OF THE TEXT

(i) The Old Testament.

1. **The Times of Ezra.** After the settlement of the Pentateuch in its present form, scrupulous care was taken to preserve the text of this and the other books which were subsequently received into the Canon. The ancient Hebrew, in which nearly the whole of the Old Testament was written, gradually gave way to Aramaic, the popular, commercial language, closely related to Hebrew. For a time both were in use, but, about the date of the return from the Exile, it is evident that Hebrew was no longer *universally* understood by the people ; and hence arose the custom of reciting in the synagogues an Aramaic translation, after the reading of the Hebrew original. (Neh. 8[8] perhaps refers to the beginning of the practice.) This was at first delivered orally, and the translator was not allowed to use a book. On these translations see § 5.

2. **Manuscripts.** There are no very ancient MSS. of the Hebrew Bible, and of such as have come down to us, all belong to the same family or recension. The earliest *dated* Hebrew manuscript known was written in A. D. 916: another, undated, in the British Museum, is probably a little older. Many were destroyed in the Middle Ages, and others were buried through the pious, if mistaken, reverence of the Jews. That other recensions were at one time in existence is shewn by the variations in the ancient versions. The Septuagint was in places evidently made from a Hebrew text which differed widely from that crystallized by Masorah (see

* See Bp. Lightfoot's *Essays on Supernatural Religion*, p. 292. Also Sir W. M. Ramsay's *St. Paul the Traveller and the Roman Citizen.*

§ 6). In many cases a conjectural restoration of the original reading is possible.

3. **The Synagogue Rolls.** Such Hebrew MSS. as exist, consist of the Synagogue Rolls, and copies for private reading. The former were written, as Josephus tells us, on fine skins, some of which, found in the Crimea, are preserved in the Library at Leningrad. The care with which they were transcribed is evident from the rules laid down in the Talmud.* The text consisted of the letters (i. e. consonants) alone, no addition such as vowel-points (which were not known before the sixth century), or accents, was allowed, and any inaccuracy rendered the copy unfit for use in the synagogue. The rolls contained (1) the *Tôrâh*, ('Law', i. e. Pentateuch); (2) *Megillôth* ('rolls'); and (3) the *Haphtârôth* (prophetical lessons). It is from this Hebrew text, compared with the various versions, that a correct copy of the Scriptures must be derived; and the English Authorized Version was formed from the best recensions known at the time of its preparation.

4. **Various Readings.** Although the 'various readings' in the MSS. and printed editions of the Hebrew Bible are very numerous, being estimated at 30,000, and even by some scholars at 200,000, they are very unimportant. The Talmudic literature states that a standard copy of the Bible was kept in the Temple Court for purposes of reference, and that there were paid correctors of the text amongst the regular Temple officials. And that some such arrangement was in force is supported by the fact that there appear to have been no differences as to readings between the Pharisees and the Sadducees. We may therefore conclude that the text, of as much at least as belonged to the canon, had become fixed by 200 B.C. or even earlier. The Hebrew Bible of the present day is therefore substantially the same as that which was the 'Received Text' about our Lord's time. In it, however, the older phraseology has been occasionally simplified, obscure expressions explained by glosses, and the chronologies and genealogies have suffered, especially through the errors of transcribers. Thus there are many alterations in the *language*, yet few in the *meaning* of the original writers. We have no autographs and no perfect MSS. of either Hebrew or Greek Scriptures, neither have

* The immense body of oral interpretation of the Scriptures which grew up in the rabbinic schools of Palestine and Babylon between the third and fifth centuries A.D. According to tradition it was finally completed by Rabina, who died A.D. 499. It is uncertain when it was committed to writing. But the process may have been begun soon after his death.

we of any Greek or Latin classic author; on the contrary, there is no ancient book, sacred or secular, of which the text is not more or less imperfect. In this respect the Hebrew Scriptures stand in the same position as all other writings of antiquity.

5. **Targums.** As mentioned above (§ 1), the Jewish people, from the time of Ezra, no longer universally understood the sacred language. Those who read the Law to them had 'to read distinctly, and give the sense' (Neh. 8[8]), which is often taken, on the authority of the Talmud, to mean that they translated, or paraphrased the law in Aramaic, or (as some call it) Chaldee, the language of ordinary intercourse. It became the business of a particular class of persons to prepare these versions or explanations; they are called Targumists, from their paraphrases, which were called Targums. The present form of the Targums is much later than the original paraphrases, but they give an idea both of the way in which the work was done and of the dialect of those times. In the course of centuries the oral translation, which had become traditional in Palestine, was adopted by the Jews of Babylon as their 'authorized version', and reduced to writing there. The most notable Targums are (i) that ascribed, by a mistake, to Onkelos (Aquila) on the Pentateuch, and (2) that ascribed to Jonathan Ben Uzziel on the Prophets, viz. Joshua, Judges, Samuel, Kings, Isaiah, Jeremiah, Ezekiel, and the twelve Minor Prophets. The former appears to have been composed in Palestine during the second century A. D. and to have been 'authorized' by the Babylonian school. (See note on *Talmud* in § 3.) The latter appears also to have originated in Palestine and subsequently to have been adapted to the vernacular of Babylonia. Its date is uncertain, but it was regarded as of ancient authority by the beginning of the fourth century A. D.

6. **The Talmudists.** The Talmudists undertook a highly critical recension of the many divergent texts of the Old Testament writings, which, however, they interpreted by a great mass of traditional commentary; but they collected together all that was known and approved (both written and oral) respecting the sacred books, rejecting what was not, in their opinion, supported by a considerable weight of testimony. In the sixth century A. D., the Jewish Doctors at Tiberias, known as the 'Massoretes', extracted from the Talmud the *traditional* comments (*Masorah*) of criticism and grammatical emendations, in order to form a 'fence' or protection to the genuine text of the Hebrew Scriptures. The text, as so fixed by them, became the one and only recognized

standard from which others were multiplied, so that it is with difficulty that the readings of any earlier text can now be recovered. In the eleventh century a collation was made of the Massoretic text of Tiberias, known as the Palestine Codex, with the Babylonian text, and between the two there were found to be eight hundred differences of reading, none of them, however, in any way affecting the sense of the subject-matter.

7. **The Samaritan Pentateuch.** The Samaritans, while rejecting the rest of the Canon of the Old Testament, have preserved the Pentateuch independently of the orthodox Jews. The date at which they received it is disputed, but they have preserved the archaic form of the Hebrew letters. While substantially agreeing with the Hebrew Textus Receptus, it contains readings which vary from it. Several of these may have existed in the copy originally received by the Samaritans, but some are perhaps alterations introduced to support the Samaritan Schism.* They possess also a Targum of their own, which bears much resemblance to that of Onkelos. Their 'Book of Joshua' is nothing but a comparatively late chronicle in Arabic.

(ii) THE NEW TESTAMENT.

The Evidence for the Text of the New Testament comes to us from three sources : (1) MSS. of the whole or portions of the New Testament ; (2) Quotations by the Fathers ; (3) Ancient Versions.

(1) *Manuscripts.*

No work that has come down to us from classical writers presents so many valuable MSS. of ancient date by which to establish its text as the New Testament. There are several MSS. of Virgil which claim an antiquity as high as the fourth or fifth century, but generally the MSS. of the Classics belong to periods between the ninth and fifteenth centuries. The earliest of the MSS. of the New Testament are called Uncial † MSS., because they were written in large letters, on fine vellum, or the prepared skins of calves or kids. Later on than these, come Minuscule MSS., so called from being written in smaller letters.

(*a*) *Uncial MSS.* Of the Greek Uncial MSS. the most important are the following :

(1) **Sinaitic**, known to critics as ℵ (Cent. iv), in the *Leningrad Museum and Library.* It was found by Tischendorf in the convent

---

* Prof. Kirkpatrick's *Divine Library of the Old Testament*, pp. 62, 63.
† From the Latin Uncialis (Uncia = *an Inch*), large, applied to letters. Skeat's *Etymological Dict.*

of St. Catherine on Mount Sinai in 1859. The New Testament is entire; and is followed by the Epistle of Barnabas, and part of the 'Shepherd' of Hermas.

(2) **Alexandrian**, known as A (Cent. v), in the *British Museum*; given by Cyril Lucar, Patriarch of Constantinople, to Charles I in 1627. Some parts of the New Testament are missing (Matt. 1^1–25^6; John 6^{50}–8^{52}; 2 Cor. 4^{13}–12^6). At the end stands the First Epistle of Clement, and part of the Second.

(3) **Vatican**, known as B (Cent. iv), in the *Vatican Library*. The First and Second Epistles to Timothy and the Epistles to Titus and Philemon are wanting. Heb. 9^{14} to the end, and Revelation, have been supplied by a later hand (Cent. xv).

(4) **Ephrem's**, known as C (Cent. v), a palimpsest (i. e. a MS. from which the original writing has been erased so that the pages can be used afresh. It is generally possible to make the original legible again by means of chemical treatment) in the *Paris Library*. It contains fragments of the LXX, and about three-fifths of the New Testament, including parts of almost every book. The original writing was effaced in the twelfth century, and Greek translations from the works of Ephrem of Edessa, a Syrian saint of the fourth century, were written over it.

(5) **Beza's**, known as D (Cent. v or vi), in the *Cambridge Library*; found by Beza in the monastery of St. Irenaeus at Lyons in 1562, and presented by him to the University of Cambridge. It is a Graeco-Latin MS. of the Gospels and Acts, with a small fragment of 3 John.

(6) **Clermont**, known as D_2 (Cent. vi), in the *Paris Library*; once in Beza's possession. It is a Graeco-Latin MS. of Paul's Epistles.

(7) **Laudian**, known as E_2 (Cent. vii), in the *Bodleian Library*. It is a Graeco-Latin MS. of the Acts.

(8) **Parisian**, known as L (Cent. ix), in the *Paris Library*; one of the most important of the later Uncial MSS. It contains the four Gospels (except Matt. 4^{22}–5^{14}, 28^{17-20}, Mark 10^{16-20}, John 21^{15-25}). It agrees in a remarkable manner with the quotations found in Origen, and with the Vatican MS.

(9) **Washington (Freer)**, known as W (Cent. iv or v), either already or presently to be placed in the *Smithsonian Institution, Washington*, U.S.A., by the gift of its owner, C. L. Freer, Esq., of Detroit, Michigan, an important uncial MS., containing the Gospels, in the 'Western' order, Matthew, John, Luke, Mark (John 14^{25}–16^7 and Mark 15^{13-38} have perished). The manuscript was found in Egypt and was probably written there. The text is not uniform

14

in character throughout, but is of the utmost importance as providing the oldest known Greek testimony for many readings hitherto known only from versions (particularly Old Latin) or quotations in the Fathers. A number of its readings remain unique.

(b) *Minuscule MSS.* Minuscule MSS. date from the ninth century onwards, and whereas of Uncials we have somewhat more than a hundred, of Minuscules there are some 3,600 accessible to scholars. They are mostly denoted by numerals. While the readings of all the Uncials may be considered to be satisfactorily determined, of the Minuscules not all have been thoroughly collated. It is quite possible for a comparatively modern MS. to possess a high value, as, for example, if a scribe of the fifteenth century had copied in Minuscule hand direct from the Vatican MS. B. For this and other reasons some Minuscules are very important evidence. If we bear in mind that ten or twelve manuscripts, and these generally modern, are all we have for ascertaining the text of most classical authors, it will help us to understand what a mass of MS. evidence is available for the New Testament.

(2) *Patristic Quotations.*

The materials for this branch of evidence have been much improved of recent years by the appearance of good critical editions of early Christian writers.* We are now often in a position to say definitely what a given writer read in his copy of the Bible. But while this testimony may be very valuable it is to be remembered that ancient writers did not as a rule attach as much importance as we do to verbal accuracy in quotation.

(3) *Ancient Versions.*

By a *Version* is meant a translation into some other language than the original, and the most important versions of the Scriptures are enumerated in the next section. The versions of the New Testament are of varying critical value. The oldest of them have been handed down to us in MS. as the Greek original has been, and in some languages we have a large number of MSS., while in others the total number is very scanty. It is obvious that the versions afford valuable testimony as to the prevalence of the readings which they employ : and that in the case of the earliest versions this may be of the highest importance.

* Many of the Latin Fathers have now been thus edited, in the series undertaken by the Vienna Academy, *Corpus Scriptorum Ecclesiasticorum Latinorum.* A similar series for the Ante-Nicene Greek writers is in process under the direction of the Prussian Academy.

VI. ANCIENT VERSIONS OF THE SCRIPTURES

(i) THE OLD TESTAMENT.

Greek Versions. At least seven Greek versions, at any rate of some parts of the Old Testament, were known to Origen of Alexandria (*c.* A. D. 185–251). 1. Of these the oldest and most important is known as *the Septuagint.* The title is derived from the Latin word *septuaginta,* meaning *seventy,* because of the legend that seventy translators working independently produced seventy verbally identical versions. In fact, it is the work of a number of different hands. It was begun about 250 B. C. for the benefit of the Jews of Alexandria. It contains all the books of the Apocrypha except 2 Esdras and the Prayer of Manasses, and is the source from which most of the quotations of the Old Testament in the New are taken.* There are important variations from, as well as additions to, the Hebrew, notably in the Books of Kings and Proverbs : while the version of the Book of Daniel varied so much from the Hebrew and Aramaic as to be disused altogether, and is not found in any of the early MSS., Theodotion's version being substituted for it.

2. *Aquila's Version.* Aquila was a native of Pontus, and became a Jewish proselyte. His version was undertaken in the second century, and was intended to furnish a literal rendering, word by word, of the Hebrew text. A second edition of his work was published even more literal than the first. In places the translation is so literal that it is unintelligible. It was supposed by some to have been made to be used controversially against the Christians who had accepted the LXX version ; but there seems to be little ground for this. Aquila is by some identified with the Onkelos of the Targum on the Pentateuch.

3. *The Version of Theodotion.* This translation was made about the same time as Aquila's. Its character is that rather of a revision of the LXX than of an independent version : though in his translation of Daniel he must have worked upon material differing entirely from that underlying the LXX version which it superseded. He is said to have been a native of Ephesus, and an Ebionite.

4. *The Version of Symmachus.* Symmachus, also said to have been an Ebionite, published his version a few years later than

* An edition by Brooke and McLean is being prepared at the Cambridge University Press. See also *Introduction to the Old Testament in Greek*, by H. B. Swete (Cambridge University Press, 1900).

Theodotion. He aimed at being literal, but at the same time at greater purity and elegance in style and language.

These four versions, arranged in columns parallel to the Hebrew, and to a transliterated Hebrew in Greek characters, formed the *Hexapla*, i. e. *The Sixfold* of Origen, of which unfortunately only fragments remain. Origen also quoted in a few places three other versions, of which nothing is known as to their authors or their dates.

(ii) ANCIENT VERSIONS OF THE OLD AND NEW TESTAMENTS.

1. Syriac. (1) The most important of all the Syriac versions of the Scriptures is the *Pĕshîttâ*, 'the simple' or 'plain version'. This name was in use as early as the ninth or tenth century. Neither the time nor the place of its translation is known, but it seems to be the work of several hands, and the evidence points to the conclusion that it was produced in the second century. The influence of the Septuagint can be traced, but the translators were well acquainted with Hebrew, a language akin to their own ; and, on the whole, the books of the Old and of the New Testament are rendered with great exactness. The New Testament appears to belong to the early years of the fifth century, and to be, at least so far as the Gospels are concerned, a revision of (3). This version has always been accepted by all sections of the Syrian Church as authentic, and from it several Arabic translations have been made. It contains all the Canonical Books of the Old Testament, as well as those of the New, except the Second and Third Epistles of John, 2 Peter, the Epistle of Jude, and the Revelation.

(2) In the beginning of the seventh century the Syriac New Testament was revised by Thomas of Harkel. The *Harcleian Syriac*, like Aquila's Version, is remarkable for its extreme literality.

(3) The Gospels are also found in a Syriac Version which, from the discoverers of the MSS., has been called the *Curetonian-Lewis Syriac*. It appears to belong to the latter part of the second century, and is closely allied to the *Old Latin Version*.

(4) The *Palestinian Syriac* (of which only fragments are extant) is a version quite independent of those already named, and intended, apparently, for 'Hebrew' Christians, as distinguished from the Hellenists (Acts 6[1]). It is a good and very ancient version, in language approximating to Aramaic.

(5) About A. D. 170 Tatian, who had produced a harmony of the Gospels in Greek, translated it into Syriac. Of the original text

c

of this work very little is known, but the arrangement is known to us. The *Diatessaron*, as it was called, exercised a very great influence, particularly in the Syrian Church. The relation of its text to that of (3) is a subject of much dispute.

2. **The Old-Latin Versions.** Fragments of an Old-Latin Version of the Bible are found in ancient Christian writers, but the history of its origin is lost in complete obscurity. There was certainly an Old-Latin Version current in North Africa, where the Church was Latin-speaking from the first, as early as the latter half of the second century. At the same time, or perhaps somewhat later, a Latin translation appeared in Europe ; but whether the two arose independently, or whether the *European* text was revised from the *African*, cannot be decided. The author of the Epistle of the Churches of Lyons and Vienne, which was written in A. D. 177 to the Churches of Asia describing the sufferings of the Christians of southern Gaul, appears to have possessed a Latin version of the Bible. He was living in a part of the world where Latin was in wider use than Greek. Later, the *European* was superseded in Italy by a revised text usually termed the *Italian*. In the Old Testament these versions were made from the unrevised edition of the LXX ; in the New the Epistle to the Hebrews, James, and 2 Peter were absent from the canon.

3. **The Vulgate.** The *Italian* Version was superseded in turn by the *Vulgate* (i. e. the *current* text), made by one of the greatest Biblical scholars of his day, Eusebius Hieronymus, better known as St. Jerome. Jerome revised the current Latin Version of the New Testament (begun A. D. 383). He also translated the Old Testament into Latin from the Hebrew. For this work he took up his residence at Bethlehem, and was occupied upon it for twenty-one years. Although at first the reverence for the LXX militated against its reception, from the time of Gregory the Great it became the authorized version of the Western Church. This translation, however, was gradually corrupted by intermixture with the older Latin versions. The discordance of the copies in use was noticed by the Council of Trent in one of its decrees, and Sixtus V gave to the world a revised text in A. D. 1590. Two years later the present standard edition was issued by Clement VIII. This edition was an improvement on its predecessor, but it is by no means faultless. A new edition is in process at Rome. The labours of Jerome were very important. His work is a witness to the Hebrew text at a very early period,

for he had probably MSS. before him of great antiquity, and even in its present state it is a valuable aid in the criticism of the Hebrew text.

4. **Other Versions.** Besides the Syriac and the Latin, there are many other versions, made at different times, and in different countries; as (1) the famous Gothic Version of Ulfilas, which was made *c.* 388. It is said to have contained all the Scriptures except the books of Kings, which were thought to be too warlike. Only fragments of it exist to-day. (2) The Armenian, made in the fifth century, which contains some apocryphal additions. (3) The Ethiopic, made for the Church of Abyssinia in the fourth or fifth century. (4) The Coptic, which belongs probably to the third century. It is still used in the native church of Egypt, though it has long been unintelligible to the congregations. All these have their value in elucidating the sacred text. They are for the most part independent testimonies, and not mere copies of some one common original, as their verbal differences sufficiently attest; but their complete agreement in all essential points demonstrates the care with which the sacred books have been preserved, while it establishes their integrity more satisfactorily than that of any other ancient book is established.

VII. ANGLO-SAXON AND ENGLISH VERSIONS OF THE SCRIPTURES

ALDHELM, Bishop of Sherborne, †709, is said to have translated the Psalter into Anglo-Saxon verse. There is nothing unlikely in the tradition; Aldhelm is known to have been a master in our native minstrelsy; and some critics have thought that the poetical version of Pss. 52-150 in the Paris MS. (Bibl. Nat. Fonds Latin 8824) might be by Aldhelm. This, however, probably belongs to the tenth century. Aldhelm's version would be in West-Saxon.

Bede, †735, was at the very time of his death engaged on an Anglo-Saxon translation of St. John's Gospel. Unhappily, not even a fragment of it survives. The dialect would of course be Northumbrian.

Of Alfred the Great, †901, William of Malmesbury says, ' he began to translate the Psalter, but died when he had barely finished the first part '. There is nothing improbable in this notice. Asser tells us of the care with which Alfred had his children taught the Psalter. And it is not impossible that the prose version of

Pss. 1–51 in the Paris MS. cited above may be, if not Alfred's work, at any rate based upon it. Alfred's dialect would be West-Saxon.

The famous Vespasian Psalter (MS. Cotton. Vespasian A. 1), may be dated *c.* 900. It is in the Kentish dialect, but it is rather a word-for-word interlinear gloss than a genuine translation.

The same may be said of the Northumbrian gloss made by Aldred the priest in the tenth century, in the famous Lindisfarne Gospels (Cotton. Nero D. iv).

To the same period belongs the gloss in the Rushworth Gospels (Bodleian, Auct. D. ii. 19). This for the three last Gospels closely follows the Lindisfarne Version. But the gloss on St. Matthew is Mercian in dialect, and is freer in character, approaching more nearly to a genuine translation.

At the end of the ninth century (about 900), Ælfric, the author of the Homilies, using to some extent earlier materials, gave a version of the Pentateuch and Joshua (Judges is probably by a later hand). But he dealt very freely with his texts, omitting whatever he thought unsuitable for the general reader. Of the six books, Genesis keeps closest to its original. The dialect is West-Saxon.

The West-Saxon version of the four Gospels was made *c.* 900. Of the origin and author of this translation nothing unfortunately is known ; and a list which begins with 'them that have left a name', like Aldhelm, Bede, and Alfred, ends with one who has ' no memorial', beyond the work which he bequeathed to his country-men.

Glosses on the Canticles and other parts of Scripture used in the services of the Church are found in various MSS., e. g. the Rituale Ecclesiae Dunelmensis, &c. A careful reading of the Anglo-Saxon Homilies would furnish a native version of many passages of Scripture ; which might, if collected, throw light on the history of the Bible in this country prior to the Norman Conquest.

The influx of foreign influences at and after the Conquest, and the growing tendency of the Roman Church to withdraw the Bible from the laity, checked the translation of the Scriptures into the native tongue ; so that between 1066 and Wyclif there is com-paratively little to record. Exception was made in favour of the Psalter. Accordingly, Richard Rolle of Hampole, †1349, in his Commentary on the Psalms, translates the Latin Psalter into English, verse by verse, and comments upon it in the same language. The dialect is Yorkshire. Other versions of the whole or parts of the Psalter are found. Recently, Miss Anna C. Paues has published (Cambridge University Press) a great part of a fourteenth-century version of the New Testament. To the end of the same century, probably, belongs a version of the Pauline epistles (edited by Miss M. J. Powell, 1916).

1384. Nicholas Hereford and some followers of John Wyclif translated the whole Bible into English from the Vulgate. This translation is commonly known as *Wyclif's Bible*. It was revised about twelve years afterwards by Purvey and others. (This work was first printed at the Clarendon Press in 1850, edited by Forshall and Madden.)

1525. *Tindale's New Testament*. The printing of the 4to edition with glosses was begun at Cologne by Quentel ; but, the press being stopped by the city authorities, Tindale fled to Worms, where Peter Schoeffer printed for him an 8vo edition without notes. There is no evidence that the first 4to was ever completed. Many copies of early editions were burned by the order of Cuthbert Tunstall, Bishop of London, who was offended by Tindale's rendering of various ecclesiastical terms, such as 'Congregation' for Church, 'Seniour' for Priest or Elder, &c.

1530. *Tindale's Pentateuch* was printed in five separate 8vo books by Hans Luft at Malborow in the land of Hesse. Genesis was revised and reprinted in 1534. Genesis (1530) and Numbers are printed in black letter, the other books and the reprint of Genesis in neat Roman type.

1534-5. Tindale's last revision was published at Antwerp by Godfridus Dumaeus. The printer's name is not positively known ; but most likely this edition came from the press of Martin de Keyser, who in books printed in English adopted the name of Marten Emperowr. This is the true primary version of the English New Testament.

1535. *Miles Coverdale* translated the Bible principally from Luther's Bible and the Vulgate, the Zürich (Swiss-German) and Pagninus. Coverdale was employed by others, by whom 'the coste and charges' were borne. It was printed at Antwerp by Jacob von Meteren, and brought to England in sheets by James Nicolson of Southwark, by whom it was published. This was the first version of the English printed Bible.

1537. *Matthew's Bible*. This was made up of Tindale's translation to the end of the Second Book of Chronicles, and Tindale's New Testament of 1534-5 ; all the rest is taken from Coverdale's Bible of 1535. It was edited by John Rogers, and probably printed at the same press as the 1535 Bible. It was published under the name of Thomas Matthew by Grafton and

Whitchurch of London with the King's licence, and was the first 'Authorized Version'.

1539. *Taverner's Bible.* This is partly a revision of Matthew's Bible and partly an original rendering by Taverner.

1539. *The Great Bible.* A new edition of Coverdale's Bible, revised from the Hebrew and Greek by the original translator at the instigation of Thomas Cromwell. Often called Cranmer's Bible ; but the archbishop had no connexion with it, except that he wrote a prologue to the second of the seven editions.

1557. *Whittingham's New Testament.* This was the first English Testament divided into verses. It was printed at Geneva in 12mo by Conrad Badius in 1557.

1560. *The Geneva Bible.* Printed by Rouland Hall, Geneva, for the refugee reformers. It was the first Bible divided into verses and printed in Roman letter. For more than half a century it was the most popular of all English versions, especially with the Puritan party. The New Testament of this version was practically superseded by Tomson's version of Beza in 1576. It is commonly known as the 'Breeches' Bible, from its rendering of Gen. 3^7.

1568. *The Bishops' Bible.* A revision of the Great Bible made at the suggestion of Archbishop Parker by nine bishops and other theologians. A very handsome large folio volume. The second edition, extensively revised, appeared in 4to in 1569.

1582. *The Rheims Version of the New Testament.* An accurate and literal translation of the Vulgate made by the refugees at Rheims in 1582, 4to size. A translation of the Old Testament was made at the same time ; but from their 'poor estate in banishment' they were unable to print it. When the English College had removed to Douai, the Old Testament was brought out in two volumes, 1609–10.

1611. Commonly called the *Authorized Version.* There is no evidence that it was ever formally authorized in spite of the statement on the title-page 'Appointed to be read in Churches'. It supplanted the Bishops' Bible by its intrinsic merit.

The textual value of these successive editions may be briefly stated thus. The style, tone, and to a great extent the phraseology of the English Bible were settled once for all by William Tindale. The only proof of this required is to read a Gospel in the Revised Version side by side with the Fry facsimile of the 1525 Tindale, and Genesis in the Revised Version side by side with the 1534 Pentateuch. Next in order of importance comes Matthew's Bible, giving the results of Tindale's latest work. In the Great Bible of 1539 Coverdale is seen at his best, as for that edition he very carefully revised and improved his 1535 Bible. The Bishops' of 1568 exerted little influence upon subsequent revisions ; but in the preparation of the Authorized Version the Bishops' text as printed in the 1602 edition was taken as the basis. A very powerful influence was exerted on King James's translators by two very opposite versions : first, the Geneva Bible of 1560 ; and second, the Rheims New Testament of 1582.

THE REVISED VERSION.

1881, 1885 ; Apocrypha, 1895. *The Revised Version* originated in a resolution of the Convocation of the Province of Canterbury in February, 1870. The work of revision was entrusted to two companies, of tried Biblical scholarship, one for the Old, the other for the New Testament, in co-operation with two similar American companies. The Revised *New Testament* was issued in 1881, the Revised *Bible* in 1885, the Apocrypha in 1895. The changes effected by the Revisers may be thus classified :—

(a) *Emendations of the Text.* It was the great aim of the Revisers, by a comparison of early MSS., ancient versions, and early quotations, to obtain a text approximating as near as possible to the original documents. But there is a great difference between the Old and New Testaments in respect to the design. The Received, or, as it is commonly called, the Massoretic Text of the Old Testament, has come down in MSS. of no very great antiquity, the earliest of which the age is certainly known bearing date A. D. 916. But in view of the lack of material necessary for a scientific revision of the Massoretic Text it was thought most prudent to adopt it as the basis of the work, and to depart from it only in exceptional cases.* In respect, however, to the New Testament, there are many MSS. and translations to be dealt with. The number of changes, therefore, made by the Revisers in the text on the authority of the best MSS. is very considerable ; but while they give a more faithful rendering, they leave unchanged every doctrine found in the Old Version.

(b) *Modification of Language.* It was intended that the modern reader should be enabled to understand the meaning of the original writers, while losing as little as possible the sacred associations which have gathered round the familiar language of our English Bible. Antique, or archaic, words were therefore only altered,

* See the Revisers' Preface.

where they had become misleading or unintelligible; and whatever changes were introduced, they were made as far as possible
to conform to the language of the time when the Authorized Version was made. In some cases Hebrew words of a technical or
personal character are retained instead of being translated. Thus
'goat for Azazel' replaces 'scapegoat' in Lev. 16; the word
Ashêrah, with its plurals Asherim and Asheroth, denoting the
wooden symbol of some goddess, takes the place of 'grove' in
Judges 3[7], 6[25], and other passages. In rendering technical terms
and names of places and persons greater uniformity has been
observed, and greater accuracy in the rendering of names of plants,
animals, and precious stones.

(c) *Changes of Form.* The old divisions of chapters and verses
are so retained as to be still available for reference, but the books
are divided into paragraphs, and sometimes, especially in the Old
Testament, the transition to a new subject is marked by a space.
Poetical books, or short poetical passages, are printed in lines like
the verses of modern poetry. The New Testament quotations
from the prophetical books are given in lines. The English headings to the chapters are omitted throughout, as involving questions
of interpretation. Only such titles are retained as already existed
in the Hebrew, such as we find in many of the Psalms, the new
translation of which and the marginal explanations are very
instructive. The whole collection of the Psalms is divided into
five books, corresponding to the arrangement of the Hebrew
Psalter.

(d) *Mistranslations*, again, have been corrected where necessary.
This is naturally more noticeable in the New than in the Old
Testament. Thus, to quote one or two instances: in Luke 23[15]
the substitution of 'for he sent him back unto us' for 'I sent you to
him', gives a meaning to a clause which is otherwise not only
wrong but meaningless. Again, in Acts 26[28] the translation
'With but little persuasion thou wouldest fain make me a Christian'
is far more accurate than the 'Almost thou persuadest me to be a
Christian' of the A.V. In Acts 27[14] the A.V. rendering, 'not
long after there arose against it a tempestuous wind', introduces a
geographical confusion, which disappears before the R.V. rendering, 'there beat down from it a tempestuous wind'. The marginal
references are here of special importance as justifying a better
rendering of various clauses.

PART II

THE OLD TESTAMENT

VIII. SUMMARY OF THE BOOKS OF THE OLD TESTAMENT

Divisions of the Hebrew Bible. The Hebrew Bible consists of three parts, which, like the two parts (Old Testament and New Testament) of the Christian Bible, represent stages in its growth. The three parts are :—

1. 'THE LAW' (*Tôrâh*), comprising Genesis, Exodus, Leviticus, Numbers, and Deuteronomy.
2. 'THE PROPHETS' (*Nebiim*), comprising the Books of Joshua, Judges, Samuel, Kings, Isaiah, Jeremiah, Ezekiel, and the Twelve (Prophets, commonly but unfortunately styled 'Minor').
3. 'THE SCRIPTURES OR WRITINGS' (*Këthubim*). Under this title were placed :—
   (1) Psalms, Proverbs, Job.
   (2) Song of Solomon, Ruth, Lamentations, Ecclesiastes, Esther.
   (3) Daniel, Ezra, Nehemiah, Chronicles.

The third stage in the growth of the Hebrew Bible, i. e. the addition of other books to a Bible already consisting of the Law and the Prophets, had already begun, though perhaps it was not yet complete, c. 132 B.C., at which date the Sacred Scriptures were spoken of as 'the Law, and the prophecies (or the prophets), and the rest of the books' (*Prologue* to Ecclesiasticus). This second stage was probably complete when Ecclesiasticus was written (about 180 B. C.), for that book (49[10]) implies that the last book of the second part of the Hebrew Bible was already known by the title of 'The Twelve (Prophets)'. The first stage must be dated at latest not long after 444 B.C., and in that year itself if 'the Law of Moses' solemnly read to and accepted by the people in that year (Neh. 8–9) was identical with the Pentateuch, i. e. the first part of the Hebrew Bible, in its entirety. A still earlier stage in the growth of the Bible, when it consisted of something much less than even one only of the three parts above defined, is marked by the acceptance in 621 B.C. of the 'Book of the Law' found in the Temple (2 Kings 22[8]). This book, as Jerome long ago perceived, was not the Pentateuch, but rather (part of) Deuteronomy. Before this date, though much of the literature now contained in the Old Testament was written, it was custom or the spoken words or decisions of prophets or priests rather than a book that constituted the religious standard or authority.

The canonical books of the Old Testament according to Jewish reckoning, which did not recognize the division of Samuel, Kings, and Chronicles each into two books, and also regarded (*a*) Ezra and Nehemiah, and (*b*) The Twelve Prophets, each as a single book, numbered twenty-four (2 Esdras 14$^{48ff.}$).

The New Testament refers to three divisions of the Jewish Scriptures (Luke 24^{44}), and to some of the twenty-four books by name (e. g. Luke 4^{17}), and very occasionally defines the section of a book by number (Acts 13^{33}) or name (Acts 2^{16}, Mark 12^{26}).

Divisions of the Text. The Law and the Prophets were at an early period regularly read on the sabbaths in the synagogues (Acts 13^{15}, 15^{21}, Luke 4$^{16, 17}$), and the Talmud recognizes a division of 'The Law' into fifty-four portions, one for each sabbath of the intercalary year. These were called *Pârâshiôth*. The Prophets also were subdivided into Sabbath Lessons. These portions were called *Haphtârôth* ('dismissals'), because they were read immediately before the close of the service.

Early also is the division of the Hebrew text into a much larger number of sense divisions or paragraphs. They were also called *Parashioth* and were classed under two heads, viz. 'Open' (*Pĕthuchoth*), which marked a change of subject, like the modern paragraph, and began with a *fresh line* in the MSS. ; and 'Shut' (*Sĕthumoth*), corresponding to minor divisions, like sentences, marked only by a *space* in the line. These breaks in the text were marked by the initials 'P' or 'S' to catch the reader's eye ; and often, though not always, coincide with the ¶ placed before certain verses in the Authorized Version.

The Talmud is also familiar with the division into Verses (*Pĕsukim*), the termination of each in the Hebrew MSS. being marked by a colon (:), which is retained in the Prayer-book version of the Psalms to point them for chanting. On the other hand the division into Chapters is neither ancient nor in origin Jewish, but is ascribed to Stephen Langton (thirteenth century), or Hugh of St. Cher ; it was first adopted in the Latin Vulgate to facilitate reference to the text, and only considerably later introduced into Hebrew Bibles.

DIVISIONS OF THE ENGLISH BIBLE

Very different from the arrangement of the Hebrew is that of the English Bible, which has been much influenced by the arrangement of the books in the Greek and Latin (Vulgate) Versions. Whereas the arrangement of the Hebrew Bible seems due to historical reasons, i. e. to the gradual growth of the Jewish Canon, the arrangement of the English Bible is more affected by regard for similarity of subject: thus all the historical books are brought together: and Daniel is included among the prophets. We may consider the books in the order in which they stand:—

i. THE PENTATEUCH.

ii. THE (OTHER) HISTORICAL BOOKS, from Joshua to the end of Esther.

iii. THE POETICAL OR DEVOTIONAL BOOKS, from Job to the Song of Solomon.

iv. THE PROPHETICAL BOOKS, from Isaiah to Malachi.

(i) *THE PENTATEUCH*

The first five books of the Old Testament—Genesis, Exodus, Leviticus, Numbers, Deuteronomy—were never separate works, but are five parts of a single work, as the Greek term PENTATEUCH, *the five-volume book*, correctly indicates. The Hebrew term for the whole is *the Law*, or with reference to its division into five parts, 'the five-fifths of the Law'.

The A.V. gives as alternative titles to the several divisions of the Pentateuch 'the first Book of Moses', 'the second Book of Moses' and so forth; but these titles have no place in the Hebrew text, nor in the ancient Greek and Latin Versions, though alternatively to 'The Law' as a title of the whole we sometimes find such expressions as 'the Law of Moses' or 'Moses' (2 Cor. 3^{14}); and *parts* of the work are attributed in the Pentateuch itself to the authorship of Moses (see Exod. 17^{14}, 24^4, Num. 33^2, Deut. 31^{9-11}). On the other hand, from the Pentateuch itself it is obvious that the work as a whole is not the work of Moses, for it closes with a description of his death and burial and a statement that at a time (long) subsequent to his death the place of his tomb was unknown; and many other passages no less clearly imply a writer to whom the times of Moses are a long past age (e. g. Gen. 12^6, 13^7, 36^{31}, Deut. 2^{22} 3^{14}). A simple way of meeting these immediately obvious features of the work would be to suppose that a work in the main by Moses was subsequently expanded and annotated by much later writers, but other features of the work suggest that it had a far more complex origin and history.

The Pentateuch consists in the main of these two classes of material: (*a*) historical narratives, (*b*) laws and legal matter. Now in the historical narratives the same events or episodes are recorded more than once; and in the legal parts laws on the same subject recur more than once (see pp. 35–36). It is also found that these different narratives of the same event and these different laws on the same subject are accompanied by differences of style. The conclusion suggested by these facts is that the Pentateuch is a work not merely based on, but actually in large part incorporating, different documents or sources. Three such sources stand out most distinctly: one is nearly coextensive with chapters 1–31 of the book of Deuteronomy and is commonly distinguished as D: another comprises Leviticus and parts of the remaining books, and is known as the Priestly Code or P; the third comprises most of the remainder of the Pentateuch, and itself appears to have arisen from the union of two still earlier sources which can still to some extent be distinguished from one another: the combined source is known by the symbol JE, the separate sources as J and E.

The parts of the Pentateuch which appear to be derived from P are:—

Gen. 1^1–2^{4a}, $5^{1-28,\ 30-2}$, 6^{9-22}, $7^{6,\ 11,\ 13-16a,\ 17a,\ 18-21,\ 24}$, $8^{1,\ 2a,\ 3b-5,\ 13a,\ 14-19}$, $9^{1-17,\ 28,\ 29}$, $10^{1-7,\ 20,\ 22,\ 23,\ 31,\ 33}$, $11^{10-27,\ 31,\ 32}$, $12^{4b,\ 5}$, $13^{6,\ 11b,\ 12a}$, $16^{1a,\ 3,\ 15,\ 16}$, 17, 19^{29}, $21^{1b,\ 2b-5}$, 23, $25^{7-11a,\ 12-17,\ 19,\ 20,\ 26b}$, $26^{34,\ 35}$, 27^{46}–28^9, 29^{24-39}, 31^{18b}, 33^{18a}, $34^{1,\ 2a,\ 4,\ 6,\ 8-10,\ 13-18,\ 20-4,\ 25,\ 27-9}$, $35^{9-13,\ 15,\ 22b,\ 29}$, 36 (mostly), 37^{1-2a}, 41^{46}, 46^{6-27}, $47^{5,\ 6a,\ 7-11,\ 27b,\ 28}$, $48^{3,\ 6,\ 7}$, $49^{1a,\ 28b-33}$, $50^{12,\ 13}$.

Exod. $1^{1-5,\ 7,\ 13,\ 14}$, 2^{23b-5}, 6^2–$7^{13,\ 19,\ 20a,\ 21b,\ 22}$, $8^{5-7,\ 15b-19}$, 9^{8-12}, 11^{9-10}, $12^{1-20,\ 28,\ 37a,\ 40,\ 41,\ 43,\ 51}$, $13^{1,\ 2,\ 20}$, $14^{1-4,\ 8,\ 9,\ 15-18,\ 21a,\ 21c-23,\ 26,\ 27a,\ 28a,\ 29}$, $16^{1-3,\ 6-24,\ 31-6}$, 17^{1a}, $19^{1,\ 2a}$, 24^{15-18a}, 25^1–31^{18a}, $34^{29,\ 35}$, $35-40$.

Lev.

Num. 1^1–$10^{28,\ 34}$, $13^{1-17a,\ 21,\ 25,\ 26a,\ 32a}$, $14^{1,\ 2,\ 5,\ 7,\ 10,\ 26-30,\ 34-8}$, 15, $16^{1a,\ 2b-7a,\ (7b-11),\ (16,\ 17),\ 18-24,\ 27a,\ 32b,\ 35,\ (36-40),\ 41-50}$, $17-19$, $20^{1a,\ 2,\ 3b,\ 4,\ 6,\ 13,\ 22-9}$, $21^{4a,\ 10,\ 11}$, 22^1, 25^{6-18}, $26-31$, $32^{18,\ 19,\ 28,\ 32,\ 33-36}$.

Deut. 1^3, 32^{48-52}, $34^{1a,\ 5b,\ 7a,\ 29}$.

Of these documents D is commonly assigned to the seventh century B.C., and J and E are both regarded as prior to D, J being commonly referred to the ninth, E to the eighth century. P, which was at one time held to be the earliest of the sources, is now more commonly assigned to about 500 B.C. In all cases these approximate dates must be taken as referring to the age of the written books; all the sources alike incorporate laws and customs far older than these written records of them, and some of them contain ancient poems, or give written form to narratives that had for generations been told and retold orally. Within P there may be distinguished (*a*) certain parts somewhat older than the main work, in particular much of Lev. 17–26 ('the law of holiness') and (*b*) also certain later additions (e. g. the verses in Num. 16 bracketed above).

1. GENESIS

1. Genesis is a Greek word signifying *origin* or *beginning*. It is given to the first book of the Pentateuch in the LXX Version, and is very suitable to a document which contains an account of the origin of the heaven and the earth, of the human race, and the Israelitish nation.

2. Contents. The book may be thus divided :—Part I containing the early history of mankind gives (*a*) (1–5) an account of the Creation, Fall, and antediluvian history including the first Covenant, and (*b*) (6–11) an account of the Deluge, the second Covenant (with Noah), the re-peopling of the earth, the Dispersion, and confusion of tongues, concluding with the genealogy of Shem down to Terah and Abraham. Part II. The special history of the patriarchs, or 'fathers' of the Jewish people. In chapters 12–28 Abraham is the prominent figure, and we have the history of his call, and graphic accounts of the patriarchal age, down to the emigration of Jacob to Padan-Aram. Chapters 29–50 give the history of Jacob and Joseph down to the death of the latter in Egypt. Thus the book has a character of its own. It embraces the world and the entire human race, but its real design is to shew how God revealed Himself to the first fathers of the Jewish nation in order that He might make to Himself a people who should be His witnesses on the earth.

3. The Creation. Genesis opens with two different accounts of Creation. In one (1¹–2⁴ᵃ) man is the crowning act of Creation, man and woman being both created together on the sixth and last day of the Creation week: in the other (2⁴ᵇ ff.) man is created first, and then, after an interval in which plants and animals are created, woman is created last of all. In neither account does the *order* of Creation agree with that inferred by modern science: on the other hand the recovery during the last century of Babylonian stories of Creation has shewn that between the Hebrew and Babylonian conceptions of Creation there are striking resemblances, and that much in the Hebrew is ultimately derived from the Babylonian accounts. But the religious standpoint of the Babylonian and Hebrew stories is markedly different; whereas the Babylonian is polytheistic, the Hebrew story in Genesis is strikingly monotheistic: the Bible thus opens with an impressive presentation of the fundamental religious truth that all that is owes its existence to the One God.

4. The Deluge. Of the Deluge also, Genesis contains two stories; but these are not placed one after the other as are the stories of Creation, but are interwoven with one another. The two stories when unravelled are found to be each nearly though not quite complete. One of these stories is found in those parts of chapters 6-9, given above on p. 28 as belonging to P; the remainder of the same chapters contains the other and earlier story. Like the stories of Creation, these stories of the Deluge differ from one another in many details, such as the duration of the flood and the number of each species of animals taken into the ark. Again the stories in Genesis in many striking details resemble the yet earlier Babylonian stories; e. g. the hero of the Babylonian Flood story is, like Noah, warned to take refuge in a vessel which he is instructed to build of particular dimensions, with a given number of storeys and to make watertight with bitumen. But again, as in the case of the Creation stories, the obvious polytheistic setting of the Babylonian disappears in the Hebrew stories.

5. The Patriarchs. Unlike much of Gen. 1-11, the stories of the patriarchs in 12-39 are not anticipated by corresponding Babylonian stories. A single incident in the story of Joseph, his temptation by Potiphar's wife, finds a striking parallel in the ancient Egyptian story of 'The Two Brothers'. The *name* Abram —applied to altogether other persons than the Hebrew patriarch— has been found on very early Babylonian tablets (before 2000 B. C.); and on an Egyptian monument of the tenth century B. C. a place in southern Palestine is named 'Field of Abram'. Jacob-el, of which Jacob might be an abbreviation, occurs as the name of a place in Canaan in an Egyptian monument of about 1480 B. C.

6. Poetry in the Book of Genesis. This Book contains not a little poetry all of which appears to belong to an early period of Hebrew history, and to be older than the prose narratives in which it is now embedded. The longest of these poems (c. 49) describes characteristic features of the twelve tribes and should be compared with the similar but somewhat later poem in Deut. 33. Other poems and poetical fragments occur in $4^{23f.}$, 9^{25-7}, 25^{23}, $27^{27-9, 39-40}$.

2. EXODUS

1. **Title.** The name *Exodus* is derived from the Greek word in the Septuagint Version, and signifies *Departure* (see Heb. 11^{22}, R.V.) or *Going out*, viz. of the descendants of Abraham from bondage in Egypt to the Promised Land.

2. **Contents.** The Book gives a sketch of the early history of Israel as a nation, (1) enslaved, (2) redeemed, (3) set apart through the blending of its religious and political life and consecrated to the service of God. The narrative of events extends from the birth of Moses to the erection of the Tabernacle. (*a*) Part I (1–19) is *historical*. It gives an account of the oppression of Israel in Egypt, the early life of Moses, his call to be the deliverer of Israel, the ten plagues, the institution of the Passover, the passage of the Red Sea, the leading incidents on the way to Sinai, the arrival at Sinai and the preparations for receiving the Law. (*b*) Part II (20–24) is *legislative*. In it we have the promulgation of the Law, and the ratification of the Mosaic Covenant. (*c*) Part III (25–40) is mainly *constructive*; it gives the orders for making the Tabernacle, the consecration of the family of Aaron to the priesthood, and of their vestments; and records the sin and punishment of Israel for making the golden calf; and the setting up of the Tabernacle by Bezaleel and Aholiab, and its dedication.

3. **Poetry.** The Book contains two poems (c. $15^{1-18, 21}$), celebrating the deliverance of Israel from the pursuit of the Egyptians.

4. **Law.** In Exodus we reach the first of those collections of Law which constitute one of the two chief elements of the Pentateuch and have given to the entire work its Hebrew title, the Law. The Laws are mainly grouped together in $20–23^{19}$: there are also a Law of Passover in 12^{2-20}, and a small group of ritual laws in 34^{17-28}. In 20-23 we may distinguish two types: (*a*) absolute commands such as the Ten words or commandments in chapter 20 and others in $22^{18}–23^{19}$, (*b*) conditional decisions: $21^2–22^{17}$. The second type seems to have been called 'judgements' (cp. 21^2), and in form they closely resemble the laws collected in the famous Babylonian code of Hammurabi, which is earlier by several centuries than the age of Moses. On the subject of these laws and their relation to other orders of law in the Pentateuch, see under Deuteronomy.

3. LEVITICUS

1. Title. The name *Leviticus* is taken from the Greek title given in the Septuagint to the third book of the Pentateuch. A term used by the Jews to describe the book, viz. 'the Priests' Law' would have been a better title, for the book consists mainly of laws for the priests (who indeed formed *part* of the tribe of Levi), but with the remainder of the tribe of Levi, commonly called Levites, it has nothing to do.

2. Distinctive Character. The book has a distinctive character in the general exclusion from it of historical narrative, with the exception of the sections relating to the consecration of the priests Lev. 8, 9), the death of Nadab and Abihu (Lev. 10^{1-7}), and the stoning of the blasphemer (Lev. 24^{10-16}). It embraces the history of only one month, viz. the first month of the second year of the Exodus ; and the scene of the whole book is Sinai: the arrival at Sinai is recorded in Exod. 19, the departure from it in Num. 10. While the order for the consecration of the priests is given in Exodus, the ceremony itself is recorded in Leviticus.

3. Contents. The book gives—(i) (1–7) The laws concerning the different kinds of sacrifices. (ii) (8–10) The consecration of Aaron and his four sons ; the punishment of two of them, Nadab and Abihu, for offering unbidden incense. (iii) (11–16) Laws concerning clean and unclean food, personal purity, and leprosy ; the ordinance of the Day of Atonement. (iv) (17–26) 'The Law of Holiness'. Among the subjects referred to in this section in which peculiar stress is laid on holiness 'as a quality distinguishing Israel, demanded of Israel by Jehovah, and regulating the Israelite's life' are the slaughter of animals ; unlawful marriages and lusts ; the priests ; sacred times, seasons, and festivals ; the lights of the sanctuary and the shewbread ; the episode respecting a blasphemer and his punishment ; the Sabbatical Year and the Jubilee ; the section concludes with promises and warnings. (v) (27) Vows, tithes, and offerings to Jehovah.

4. References. There are frequent references to many of the ceremonies and customs mentioned in Leviticus in the subsequent writings of the Old Testament, especially those of the priest-prophet Ezekiel. In the New Testament we find our Lord referring to the rites connected with the cleansing of the leper (Matt. 8^4, Mark 1^{44}), and quoting the second great commandment (Lev. 19^{18}, Mark 12^{31}) ; while the special ceremonies of the Day of Atonement and their fulfilment by Christ are commented on with great fullness in the Epistle to the Hebrews (Heb. 9^{1-15}).

4. NUMBERS

1. Title. The appellation *Numbers* is a translation of the word Ἀριθμοί in the LXX, and is derived from two numberings of the people at the beginning (c. 1) and the end of the wanderings (c. 26). It comprises a period of thirty-eight years and three months, from the completion of the Law-giving, 'the first day of the second month of the second year' of the Exodus, to the first day of the fifth month of the fortieth year.

2. The Contents may be thus summarized :—(i) *The last days at Sinai*; first census; arrangement of the army; the service of the Levites, with an inventory of their charge; various laws (5, 6); the cloudy pillar; the silver trumpets (1–10^{10}). (ii) *The march from Sinai to the borders of Canaan*, including the appeal of Moses to Hobab; the burning at Taberah; the giving of the quails; the sedition of Aaron and Miriam and her leprosy; the sending of the spies, their report, and the murmuring of the people; the rash attack on the Canaanites and its repulse (10$^{10-14}$). (iii) *The thirty-eight years' wandering.* Various laws (15); the rebellion of Korah, Dathan, and Abiram and its punishment (16–17); Dues payable to the Levites (18). Defilement by the dead (19). (iv) *The last year.* The death of Miriam; the sin of Moses and Aaron; the circuit round Edom; the death of Aaron; the conquest of the Amorites; the episode of Balaam; the sin of Baal-peor and its consequences; Phinehas; the second census; law of inheritance, offerings, and vows; the war against the Midianites; settlement of Gad, Reuben, and Manasseh; summary of journeys; Levitical cities and cities of refuge (20–36).

3. Poetical Fragments. The Book of Numbers is rich in fragments of ancient poetry, some of them of great beauty, and all throwing an interesting light on the character of the times in which they were composed. Such are the chants, which were the signal for the Ark to move when the people journeyed, and for it to rest when they were about to encamp (10$^{35, 36}$); the song from 'the Book of the wars of Jehovah (21$^{14f.}$), the poem commemorating the victory of the Israelites over Moab (21$^{27-30}$), and 'the Song of the Well', afterwards no doubt used by those who came to draw water (21$^{17, 18}$). Peculiarly interesting is the group of poems assigned to Balaam in 22–4.

4. The Writer's Candour. It is impossible to read the narrative contained in this book without being struck by the writer's candour. He freely exposes the faults not only of the people, but of Aaron and Miriam; and while he does full justice to the

D

generosity of Moses (11^{29}), his meekness (12^3), and his self-efface-
ment (14^{13}), he notes also his liability to despondency (11^{15}), and
relates fully the offence which excluded him from the Promised
Land (20^{9-12}).

5. **References in the New Testament.** It is to be noted that
besides references to some of the incidents recorded in this book
in the later Scriptures of the Old Testament, we have in the New
our Lord making special reference to that of the brazen serpent
lifted up by Moses (John 3^{14}); while St. Paul mentions the
serpents which destroyed the people (1 Cor. 10^9), and the sin of
Baal-peor (1 Cor. 10^8), and St. Peter in his Epistle (2 Pet. $2^{15,\ 16}$)
and St. John in the Apocalypse both refer to the sin of Balaam
(Rev. 2^{14}).

5. DEUTERONOMY

1. **The name Deuteronomy** comes from the LXX (cp. 17^{18}) and
signifies 'Repetition of the Law' or second law-giving. The
suggestion of this title is only broadly correct: the book contains
a body of law given in the fortieth year of the Exodus: the chief
bodies of law (Exod. 20—Num. 10) previously given were given
at Sinai in the second year, but other laws were given in the
interval, and in particular those in Num. 30–6 are ascribed to the
same year as those in Deuteronomy. Again, while some laws in
Deuteronomy are a repetition of laws previously given, far more
either deal with the same or similar cases in a different way, or
with cases not dealt with at all elsewhere in the Pentateuch (see
below, pp. 35–6).

2. **Contents.** The book consists mainly of three addresses
given by Moses in the fortieth year of the Exodus and the last
year of his own life. Of the three addresses, the *first* ($1–4^{40}$)
is introductory, reminding the people of their deliverance from
bondage, of God's guidance and protection in their wanderings,
and their frequent ingratitude, closing with a warning from the
past, and an exhortation to obedience in the future, so as to secure
the inheritance now within reach. The *second* address, starting
with the Ten Commandments, consists of a hortatory and retro-
spective introduction (5–11) followed by (12–26) the Laws in three
main groups, viz. (1) laws concerning religion; (2) concerning
administration of justice; (3) concerning private and social rights.
The conclusion to this address is probably to be found in the solemn
appeal and warning of chapter 28. The *third* address (29, 30) is
the solemn renewal of the Covenant, with an impressive recital of
the blessings upon observance, and the curses on neglect of the

Law.   At the close of these addresses we have an account of the delivery of the Law to the Levites, a Song of Moses recited in the ears of the people, the final benediction of the twelve tribes, and the closing scenes of Moses' life (31–4).

3. The following table will illustrate the scope and arrangement of the code and the extent to which the same law or laws on the same subject occur elsewhere in the Pentateuch, and the subjects treated only in Deuteronomy.   The differences between laws on the same subject can be seen only on an examination of the parallel passages : the most striking differences will be found in the laws of place of sacrifice, tithes, year of release, slaves, festivals, revenues of the Levites. Of the three columns the centre contains a brief indication of the subject of the law with the passage in Deuteronomy where it is to be found, the left-hand column the reference to the corresponding law in the Book of the Covenant and other early laws, the right-hand column the reference to the Priestly Code, now commonly held to be later than Deuteronomy (see p. 28), though according to the chronology of the Pentateuch the laws of the third column were given not more than forty years nor less than eight or ten previously to the laws of Deuteronomy.

Book of the Covenant, &c.	Deuteronomy.	Priestly Laws.
Exod. 20^{24}	12^{1-28} Place of sacrifice.	Lev. 17^{1-9}
,, 23^{24}, $34^{12, 15f.}$	12^{29-31} Canaanite rites.	Num. 33^{52}
	13 Instigators to idolatry.	
	$14^{1f.}$ Rites for the dead.	Lev. 19^{28}
	14^{3-20} Clean and unclean animals.	,, 11^{2-22}, 20^{25}
,, 22^{21}, 23^{19b}, 34^{26b}	14^{21} Forbidden foods.	,, $11^{39f.}$, 17^{15}
	14^{22-9} Tithes.	,, 27^{30-3}, Num. 18^{21-32}
,, $23^{10f.}$	15^{1-11} Year of release.	,, 25^{1-7}
,, 21^{2-11}	15^{12-18} Slaves.	,, 25^{39-46}
,, 22^{30}, $13^{11, 12}$, 34^{19}	15^{19-23} Firstlings.	Exod. 13^2, Num. $18^{17f.}$
,, 23^{14-17}, 34^{15}, $20, 22-5$	16^{1-17} Annual feasts.	Lev. 23, Num. 28, 29
,, $23^{1-3, 6-8}$	16^{18-20} Judges and justice.	,, 19^{15}
	$16^{21, 22}$ Asherahs and pillars.	,, 26^1
	17^1 Unblemished sacrifices.	,, 22^{17-24}
22^{20}	17^{2-7} Idolatry : death penalty : two witnesses.	
	17^{8-13} Tribunals.	
	17^{14-20} The king.	
	18^{1-8} Revenues, &c. of the Levites.	,, 7^{32-4}, Num. 18^{1-20}
,, 22^{18}	18^{9-14} Divinations, &c.	,, $19^{26, 31}, 20^{6, 27}$
	18^{15-22} The prophet.	

Exod. 21¹²⁻¹⁴	19¹⁻¹³ Manslaughter: cities of refuge.	Num. 35, Lev. 24¹⁷, ²¹
,, 23¹	19¹⁴ Boundary stones.	
	19¹⁵⁻²¹ Witnesses.	
	20 Military service and warfare.	
	21¹⁻⁹ Untraced murder.	
	21¹⁰⁻¹⁴ Female captives of war.	
	21¹⁵⁻¹⁷ Primogeniture.	
	21¹⁸⁻²¹ Unruly sons.	
,, 23⁴ᶠ.	21²²ᶠ. Criminal's corpse.	
	22¹⁻⁴ Lost property.	
	22⁵ Interchange of men's and women's clothing.	
	22⁶, ⁷ Bird's nest.	
	22⁸ Safe roofs.	
	22⁹⁻¹¹ Forbidden mixtures.	Lev. 19¹⁹
	22¹² Tassels.	Num. 15³⁷⁻⁴¹
	22¹³⁻²¹ Slandering a bride.	
	22²²⁻⁷ Adultery.	Lev. 18²⁰, 20¹⁰
,, 22¹⁶ᶠ.	22²⁸ᶠ. Seduction.	
	22³⁰ Incest.	,, 18⁸, 20¹¹
	23¹⁻⁸ Persons excluded from the community.	
	23⁹⁻¹⁴ Holiness of the camp.	
	23¹⁵, ¹⁶ Escaped slaves.	
	23¹⁷, ¹⁸ Prostitution.	
,, 22²⁵	23¹⁹ ²⁰ Interest on loans.	,, 25³⁵⁻⁷
	23²¹⁻³ Vows.	Num. 30² ᶠᶠ.
	23²⁴, ²⁵ Plucking grapes and ears of corn.	
	24¹⁻⁴ Divorce.	
,, 22²⁶, ²⁷	24⁶, ¹⁰⁻¹³ Pledges.	
	24⁷ Man-stealing.	
	24⁸, ⁹ Leprosy.	Lev. 13, 14
	24¹⁴, ¹⁵ Hired servant.	,, 19¹³
	24¹⁶ Individual responsibility.	
,, 22²¹⁻⁴, 23⁹	24¹⁷ᶠ. Strangers, widows, and orphans.	,, 19³³ᶠ.
	24¹⁹⁻²³ Gleanings.	,, 19⁹, ¹⁰, 23²²
	25¹⁻³ Forty stripes.	
	25⁴ Ox unmuzzled while threshing.	
	25⁵⁻¹⁰ Levirate marriage.	
	25¹¹, ¹² Immodesty.	
	25¹³⁻¹⁶ Weights and measures.	,, 19³⁵, ³⁶
,, 17¹⁴	25¹⁷⁻¹⁹ Amalek.	
,, 22²⁹, 23¹⁹, 34²⁶	26¹⁻¹¹ Ritual of firstfruits.	Num. 18¹³
	26¹²⁻¹⁵ Ritual of tithe.	

4. **New and old elements in Deuteronomy.** To a large extent Deuteronomy is a restatement of old written law; where it may be a first statement it is yet a statement of very long-established law and custom. The greater part of the laws in Exod. 20–23 are here repeated with or without modification—the Ten Commandments (Exod. 20) in Deut. 5 and most of the remainder as indicated in the first column of the foregoing table. The old element in

all probability also includes very many of the laws in 20-25, although to but few of these are there parallels in Exodus. But there is also unmistakable novelty in the code: and the novelty consists primarily in requiring all sacrifices to be offered, not as hitherto at many places, but at one place only (12). It was the aim of the Reformation of Josiah (2 Kings 22, 23) to give effect to this novel requirement of Deuteronomy, and, as already remarked, the Book of the Law, the discovery of which led to that Reformation, is probably contained in the Book of Deuteronomy.

Not only does the legal part of the book reproduce or rest on old laws, but the hortatory and historical introductions rest on and often reproduce the phraseology of older narratives, in particular of those parts of the preceding books which are not assigned in the table on p. 28 to P.

5. **Special character—literary, ethical, and religious—of the Book.** Though even in Exodus, Leviticus, and Numbers much takes the form of words spoken by Moses, the sustained addresses of Deuteronomy have a marked rhetorical character of their own. Though a book of law, it is penetrated through and through by a religious and ethical spirit and warmth. It is dominated by the fundamental belief in the unity of God and the conviction of the consequent necessity of a whole-hearted devotion on the part of Israel to God ($6^{4, 5}$). It is also permeated by the conviction that God above all requires of men kindness and consideration towards their fellows: this may be seen in the reasons assigned for some of the Ten Commandments and in the frequent regard in the laws for weak and helpless classes.

6. **Poetry.** Deuteronomy contains two long poems, known respectively as the Song (32), and the Blessing (33) of Moses.

7. **References in the New Testament.** The declaration in $6^{4, 5}$ is quoted by our Lord as the chief of all the commandments (Matt. $22^{37, 38}$), and it is with three sentences ($6^{13, 16}$, 8^3) from this book that He defeats the three temptations of the Evil One (Matt. 4^{1-10}). The Law of Divorce ($24^{1 \text{ff.}}$) is referred to in Matt. 5^{31}, 19^7. Other noticeable references are that in Rom. 10^{6-8} to 30 $^{12-14}$, the double reference (1 Cor. 9^9, 1 Tim. 5^{18}) to the law against muzzling the ox, and the references to the Song of Moses ($32^{21, 35, 36, 43}$) in Rom. 10^{19}, 12^{19}, Heb. $10^{30, 16}$.

(ii) *THE HISTORICAL BOOKS*

With the Book of Joshua, which carries on the history from the point reached at the close of the Pentateuch, commence what may be termed (in contrast to the Pentateuch, which contains both history and law, but is named in Hebrew from the latter element) the Historical Books. They contain the history of the Israelite people during the three great periods of their national life: (1) as a confederation of independent tribes united by religion and blood; (2) as a monarchy, separated after three generations into two distinct kingdoms; (3) as tributary to foreign invaders.

THE BOOK OF JOSHUA

1. The name Joshua (*Jehovah is salvation*) was substituted by Moses for Joshua's earlier name Hoshea on the occasion of sending out the twelve spies (Num. 13^{16}). In later times the name Joshua, modified to Jeshua (Neh. 8^{17}), took in the LXX and in later Greek the form Ἰησοῦς, *Jesus* (Acts 7^{45}, Heb. 4^8), which has become indelibly impressed on history as the greatest of all names.

2. Joshua was born in Egypt during the bondage of the Israelites. He first appears as a military captain at Rephidim (Exod. 17$^{9-14}$) on the occasion of the attack of the Amalekites; he is Moses' minister at the giving of the Law (Exod. 24^{13}); he is sent to spy out the land of Canaan as representative of the tribe of Ephraim (Num. 13^8), and is appointed on the death of Moses his successor as leader of the people (Num. 27$^{18-23}$), and to him is entrusted the task of settling them in Canaan.

3. Date and Authorship. In the title the name Joshua defines of course, not the author, but the subject of the book. The author of Joshua, as of most books of the Old Testament, is unknown: the date of the book in its present form is not earlier than 500 B. C. Behind the book in its present form can be traced the main sources drawn upon by it; and these appear to be largely the same as those utilized in the Pentateuch. Thus, from P (see p. 28) are derived 4$^{13,\ 15-17,\ 19}$, 5$^{10-12}$, 7^1, 8$^{15b,\ 17-21}$, 13$^{15-32}$, 14$^{1-5}$, 15$^{1-13,\ 20-44,\ 48-62}$, 16$^{4-8}$, 17$^{1a,\ 3,\ 4,\ 7,\ 9a-10a}$, 18$^{1,\ 11-28}$, 19$^{1-8,\ 10-46,\ 48-51}$, 20$^{1-3,\ 6a,\ 7-9}$, 21$^{1-42}$, 22$^{9-34}$. Another considerable part of the book seems to be derived from a writer influenced by Deuteronomy, viz. 1, 2$^{10-11}$, 3$^{2-4,\ 6-9}$, 4$^{11b,\ 12,\ 14,\ 21-24}$, 5$^{1,\ 4-7}$, 8$^{30-5}$, 9$^{1,\ 2,\ 9b,\ 10, 24,\ 25,\ 27b}$, 10$^{8,\ 12a,\ 14b,\ 25,\ 28-43}$, 11$^{10-23}$, 12, 20$^{4-6}$, 21$^{43-5}$, 22$^{1-6}$, 23, 24$^{11b,\ 13,\ 31}$. Most of the remainder is derived (sometimes with modifications) from JE.

4. Contents of the Book. i. The conquest of Canaan west of the Jordan. (1) The preparations for the conquest (1–5^{12}); (2) the

conquest of (*a*) the South (5^{13}–10), (*b*) the Centre (implied in 8^{30-5}), (*c*) the North (11); (3) summary (12).   ii. The partition of the land east and west of the Jordan (13–22).   iii. The close of Joshua's career, and his death (23, 24).   The general impression conveyed by the book of Joshua is of a complete conquest of Canaan by all Israel acting together under Joshua within a period of a few years.   A few scattered notices (e. g. 13^{13}, 15^{63}, 16^{10}, 17^{11-18}, 19^{47}) suggest (as also does Judges 1) that the conquest and occupation of Canaan by the Israelites was a more gradual process and not altogether due to the united action of the whole people.

JUDGES

1. **The Book of the Judges**, Κριταί (Acts 13^{20}), receives its title from those who after the death of Joshua were raised up to be the 'deliverers' of the people from their enemies around.   The Hebrew words used for these deliverers, *Shôphêṭ*, plur. *Shôphêṭim*, which we have translated *Judge*, bear a marked resemblance to the *Suffes*, *Suffetes* of the Carthaginians at the time of the Punic wars (Livy, xxx. 7).   These Suffetes at Carthage were sometimes styled by the Romans *reges*, sometimes *consules* or *dictatores*.

2. **Contents.**   The book may be divided thus:—(i) *Part I* (1–2^5) is introductory, and gives an account of the conquest of certain portions of the land by different tribes.   (ii) *Part II* (2^5–16) contains stories of Ehud, Deborah, and Barak, Gideon and his son Abimelech, Jephthah, Samson, with briefer accounts or notices of Othniel, Shamgar, Tola, Jair, Ibzan, Elon, and Abdon, preceded by an introduction (2^6–3^6) conveying the writer's view of the age as consisting of successive periods of national sin, punishment, penitence, deliverance, and peace, and interspersed with comments reiterating the same point of view and supplying a chronology. (iii) *Part III* (17–21) contains a record of two remarkable incidents, (*a*) that of Micah and the Danites (17, 18), and (*b*) ' the deed of shame' performed at Gibeah, and the consequent war which led nearly to the extermination of the tribe of Benjamin (19–21).   This portion forms a kind of appendix recording events antecedent to some at least of those related in the body of the book, and illustrating the demoralized condition of some of the families of Israel.   The earliness of the period described is indicated by the mention as living of Phinehas, the grandson of Aaron (20^{28}), and of Jonathan, the son of Gershom, and the grandson of Moses, in 18^{30} (R.V.).

3. **Date.**   The song of Deborah and Barak (5) affords, it has

been remarked, abundant proof of having been composed shortly after the date of the event commemorated (*c.* 1100 B. C.); but the reference in 18^{30} to the 'captivity of the land' seems to mark a date posterior to the Assyrian captivity of Israel (722 B. C.). Thus Judges, like other books, contains material of more periods than one. Part II probably represents a work of the seventh century B. C. based on earlier stories. Parts I and III also contain much early material. Some of the earlier material in all three parts has some similarity of style and outlook with those parts of the Pentateuch termed JE (p. 28). The book scarcely attained its present form and extent prior to *c.* 400 B. C.

4. Chronology. According to Part II the Judges were con- secutive rulers of *all* Israel; and the period of the Judges covered 410 years. But there are indications that the activity of the Judges was often limited to some tribe or tribes, and that the chronology, which cannot be harmonized with other statements in the Old Testament, unduly lengthens the period, which in fact may not have exceeded two centuries.

5. Poetry. In addition to the long and ancient poem in 5, Samson's riddles in 14, 15 are specimens of brief popular snatches of verse.

RUTH

1. The Book of Ruth, named from its heroine, is a story of the times of the Judges, and so in the English, though not in the Hebrew, Bible it immediately follows the Book of Judges. No certain date can be assigned to it, but it must have been written after the time of David (4^{22}), and probably not long before, if not indeed after, the Exile.

2. Summary. During a period of famine two Ephrathites of Beth-lehem-Judah, Elimelech and Naomi, go forth with their two sons, Mahlon and Chilion, to seek a home in the land of Moab (1^2). Here Elimelech dies, and after about ten years his sons, who have married two of the daughters of Moab, Orpah and Ruth, die also (1$^{3-5}$). Naomi prepares to return to her native town, and Ruth, who cannot be dissuaded, accompanies her (1$^{8-18}$). Reaching Beth-lehem Ruth goes to glean in the fields of Boaz, a wealthy kinsman of Elimelech (2^1). Struck by her simple fidelity, he permits her to share in the provision made for his servants. By the advice of her mother-in-law Ruth claims kinship with him (3), and he is not slow to acknowledge it. But there is a nearer kinsman, who is first asked to discharge a kinsman's duties (4$^{1-8}$). When he declines, Boaz readily performs them, and marries Ruth,

by whom he becomes the father of Obed, the grandfather of King David (4^{13-17}).

3. **Value of the Book.** The book illustrates several important points. (1) It brings out the pious character of the good Boaz, and the friendly relations between him and his reapers; (2) it illustrates the Jewish land-system, and the method of transferring property from one person to another; (3) it records the brave love and unshaken trustfulness of her who, though not of the chosen race, was privileged to become the ancestress of David and so of 'great David's greater Son' (Ruth 4^{18-22}, Matt. 1^{5-16}); and (4) by the adoption of the Moabitess Ruth into the Church of God and her acceptance as a mother in Israel it anticipates the words of Christ that 'many should come from the east and west, and should sit down with Abraham, and Isaac, and Jacob, in the kingdom of heaven' (Matt. 8^{11}).

THE BOOKS OF SAMUEL

1. **The two Books of Samuel** are so called, not because Samuel was the author, but because that prophet is the most prominent actor in the opening portion, and the great instrument in the establishment of the kingdom of Israel. The two books are in reality a single work, and are so regarded in the Hebrew Canon. The LXX translators divided the Book of Samuel and the Book of Kings into four books, which they named first, second, third and fourth *Books of the Kingdoms* respectively. This division is followed in the Vulgate, only the title is altered to *Books of the Kings*; hence the alternative titles of the four books in the Authorized Version of the English Bible.

2. **The Subject-Matter** of the books may be best studied as forming three biographies—those of Samuel (1 Sam. 1–12), Saul (1 Sam. 13–2 Sam. 1), and David (1 Sam. 16^{11}–2 Sam. 24). The period covered is practically coextensive with these lives and covered about eighty years, from about 1050–970 B.C. As in the history of the patriarchs, so in these biographies, no reader can fail to notice the remarkable candour of the writers, who hide nothing and forget nothing. They are no mere hero-worshippers; they do not dissemble the sins of kings; they depict the miseries which follow the forsaking of the path of righteousness, and the blessings which accompany adherence thereto.

3. **Samuel** is the connecting link by which the judgeship passes on to monarchy. To his personal character, administrative skill, and intellectual ability is attributed the reformation of the people

from unbridled licentious anarchy to a peaceful acquiescence in a monarchy and a respect for justice. It is easy to see why he became one of the 'Heroes of Hebrew History'; why, as the last representative of the Judges, the first of the regular succession of prophets, the inaugurator of the kingdom, he could be associated with Moses and Aaron in the Psalms (see Ps. 99[6], and cp. Jer. 15[1]).

4. **Saul**, as he appears in the existing books of Samuel, began well and ended badly. Nothing could be more promising than his first acts (1 Sam. 10, 11), but his elevation soon makes him self-willed and self-assertive. Hence his fits of melancholy and jealousy, his bitter persecution of David, his moments of remorse, and his final defection exhibited in his consulting the witch of En-dor, just before the disastrous battle of Mount Gilboa. Proud, selfish, reserved, obstinately stiffnecked and profane, as he appears in parts of the books, he sought to govern absolutely, instead of as the vicegerent of God. But he was never sovereign of more than the central part of the country. Indeed, he was rather the pastoral chief of amalgamated tribes than the monarch of a kingdom.

5. **David.** In David, for the first time, we see a true monarch. With him the sceptre came into the house of Judah, and he became the founder of a dynasty, which lasted upwards of four centuries. In his career we note (i) his early life as a preparation for his subsequent career; (ii) his life at court and as an outlaw; (iii) his elevation to the throne after long and varied discipline; (iv) his devotion to Jonathan and his magnanimity towards Saul, his valour, his musical and poetical gifts; (v) the depths into which he fell when he gave way to the temptations of passion, the seriousness of his contrition, and the severity of the punishment which followed the great sin of his life.

6. **Date.** Like Judges, Samuel is a book of much old material brought to its present state and extent at a relatively recent date. Here it must suffice to refer to two of the older masses of material. One of these is derived from a work probably not later than the ninth century B.C., which regarded the monarchy as a gift bestowed by Jehovah unasked on Israel (see 1 Sam. 9[1]–10[16], 10[27b] (R.V. Marg.), 11[1–11, 15], 13, 14; to the same or related works belong, e.g. 1 Sam. 16[14–23], 18[5–11, 20–30], 20[1–4, 18–39], 22, 23–25 (mostly), 27–31 (mostly), 2 Sam. 1–6 (mostly) and a large part of 9–20). The other work, somewhat later (about the eighth century B.C.), regarded the monarchy as yielded by Yahweh to the demands of the people for which Samuel gravely rebuked them (see 1 Sam.

8, 10^{17-27a}, 12; other passages derived from this or related works are most of 1 Sam. 1–7, 15, 17, $18^{1-4, \; 12-19}$, 19, 26, 2 Sam. 7).

7. **Poetry.** In addition to the Psalm (18) in 2 Sam. 22, the books contain several poems (in 1 Sam. 2, 2 Sam. 1, 3, and 23) and the women's chant, 1 Sam. 18^7.

THE BOOKS OF KINGS

1. **First and Second Kings** formed originally in the Hebrew Canon one book, called 'The Book of Kings'. It was broken into two parts by the Greek translators of the LXX, and the Vulgate followed this division, which has been adopted by the whole Western Church.

2. **Date.** The second book concludes with a notice of the release of Jehoiachin in 561 B.C. and his subsequent life. The Books of Kings in their present extent therefore are not earlier than the middle of the sixth century B.C. But it is commonly held that a book of somewhat less extent was compiled between the Reformation of Josiah (621 B.C.) and the Fall of Jerusalem (586 B.C.) to which the record of later events was subsequently added. The compiler refers to three sources of his narrative: (1) the Book of the Acts of Solomon (1 Kings 11^{41}); (2) the Book of the Chronicles of the Kings of Judah (1 Kings 14^{29}), quoted *fifteen* times; (3) the Book of the Chronicles of the Kings of Israel (1 Kings 14^{19}), quoted *seventeen* times. These annals have perished, but the selection from them, intended to exhibit God's dealings with His people, has survived. In addition to these royal annals, which he names, the compiler also seems to have drawn upon, and in large part incorporated in his work, certain early stories of prophets; possibly, too, he made use of Temple records.

3. **Subject-Matter.** The books embrace the regal period of Israelite history from the death of David to the Captivity, i.e. from c. 970 B.C. to 586 B.C. with the later notices already referred to. The narrative falls into three parts :— (i) The reign of Solomon, portraying the undivided kingdom at its greatest height of power (1 Kings 1–11). (ii) A parallel account of the two divided kingdoms, Judah and Israel, until the captivity of Israel (1 Kings 12– 2 Kings 17). (iii) The history of the kingdom of Judah down to the Babylonian conquest of Jerusalem by Nebuchadnezzar and the captivity of the people (2 Kings 18–25).

4. **The Prophetical Office** assumed throughout this period special prominence. The Guilds of the Prophets, founded by Samuel, bore abundant fruit, and the value of the Prophetic Order

was incalculable. 'The prophets were the privy-councillors of kings, the historians of the nation, the instructors of the people.' It was their function to maintain the religion of Jehovah against the idolatrous tendency so rife in their times, to defend and interpret the Moral Law, to denounce oppression and covetousness, injustice and profligacy, cruelty and wrong dealing, and to lift up their voice with fearless courage for God against the vicious practices of kings and people. The concluding chapters of 2 Kings (15–25) should be read in the light of the successive contemporary prophets—Hosea, Amos, Isaiah, Micah, Zephaniah, Jeremiah, Nahum.

THE BOOKS OF THE CHRONICLES

1. Title. The First and Second Chronicles form one work in the Hebrew, and are entitled *The Acts or Annals of the Days*, from which our title, 'Chronicles', arises. The Greek title in the LXX translation is *Paraleipomena*, or 'the things omitted'; a name intended to imply that Chronicles is supplementary to the Books of Samuel and Kings, and supplies the omissions of the earlier history. The Latin has followed the LXX in dividing the work into two books, but has retained the name *Paraleipomenon* *.

2. Contents. The books are naturally divided into four parts. (i) Part I (1 Chron. 1–9) consists of genealogies from Adam, and we trace (*a*) the line from Adam to Abraham ; (*b*) the line of Judah to Elishama ; (*c*) the kingly line of David through Zerubbabel ; (*d*) the line of priests to the Captivity ; and (*e*) the three leading families of singers, one of which represented the line of Samuel. (ii) Part II (1 Chron. 10–29) gives the history of David, and is remarkable both for the omissions which are found in the narrative, and also for many new facts which are not given in the Books of the Kings. (iii) Part III contains the reign of Solomon (2 Chron. 1–9). (iv) Part IV (2 Chron. 10–36) gives the history of the kings of Judah up to the Captivity.

3. Date, Extent, and Sources of the Work. The Books of Chronicles together with Ezra and Nehemiah probably formed originally a single work (the concluding verses of Chronicles, 2 Chron. $36^{22, 23}$, are identical with the opening verses of Ezra, 1^{1-3}). The whole work extends from Adam to the secret visit of Nehemiah to Jerusalem in 432 B.C., and incidentally takes account of persons living even later than this, viz. of the descendants of David (1 Chron. 3^{19-24}) several generations later than Zerubbabel (fl. 520–518 B.C.),

* The genitive plural after *Liber* understood.

and of the high priests to the third generation beyond Nehemiah (Neh. 13²⁸). Thus the work was scarcely compiled earlier than about 300 B.C. ; and perhaps somewhat later.

The work has a peculiar interest in as much as it shows us the methods adopted by a Jewish compiler of a historical work : for to a large extent the sources used by the compiler of the works still lie before us in the Books of Samuel and Kings. Thus by comparing Chronicles with Samuel and Kings we can see how the later compiler sometimes incorporates the earlier material practically unaltered, sometimes abbreviates it, sometimes expands it, and how he modifies it, for example, by substituting one divine name for another, or by correcting its theology, as when he attributes to Satan (1 Chron. 21¹) instead of to Jehovah (2 Sam. 24¹) the instigating of David to number the people. Accordingly, the value of Chronicles for us consists less in such additional information as it may afford us for the period covered by the books of Samuel and Kings than in its revelation of the interests, ideas, and temper of certain Jewish circles about 300 B.C. On the other hand the latter part of the work, i. e. the books of Ezra and Nehemiah, are almost our sole source of knowledge for the period covered by them.

4. **Characteristics of the Book.** As compared with the parallel histories of Samuel and Kings, we notice (*a*) a great tendency to dwell on the details of the Temple worship, the arrangement of the courses of the priests, and the like ; (*b*) a marked bias for genealogical tables, and for assigning names to persons engaged in any of the events narrated ; (*c*) a constant desire to ascribe all the events narrated to the Divine agency, and to represent the Divine favour as directly dependent on the faithfulness of rulers and people to the original Covenant, and Divine punishment as the natural result of unfaithfulness. Hence the history of Chronicles has been called 'ecclesiastical', that of Samuel and Kings 'political'.

5. **Additions and Omissions.** Chronicles was evidently not intended to supersede the histories written earlier, for a knowledge of the history contained in those books is in several places presupposed,* while many sections agree almost verbally with those of Samuel and Kings. Others are peculiar to Chronicles. The most important of these are (i) certain songs at the bringing up of the ark by David (1 Chron. 16) ; (ii) the account of the

---

* Thus in 2 Chron. 21¹²⁻¹⁶ Elijah is spoken of in a way which assumes that the reader is acquainted with his history ; and in 2 Chron. 22⁷, ⁸ a knowledge is presupposed of the sayings of Elijah and the acts of Elisha. Apart from Genesis, 1 Chron. 1¹⁻⁴ would be unintelligible.

organization of the Temple ritual and the Levitical Order, as also of many of the civil officers of Solomon's kingdom (1 Chron. 21–9); (iii) various incidents in the history of the kings, in connexion with which the mission of certain prophets is introduced (see 2 Chron. 24, 25); (iv) the account of the great Passover Feasts kept by Hezekiah and Josiah (2 Chron. 29, 30, and 35). Important matters related in Samuel and Kings and not reproduced in Chronicles are (i) almost all incidents relating to the northern kingdom; it was not the aim of the chronicler as it was of the earlier historians to relate the history of the whole people, but of Judah only ; (ii) in the history of the southern kingdom all record of the sinful acts and consequent misfortunes of David's reign, viz. the affairs of Uriah and Bath-sheba, Amnon, Absalom, Sheba, Adonijah ; (iii) Solomon's judgement, administration, and sin ; (iv) the matters connected with Hadad and Rezin.

EZRA

1. **Ezra** (*help*) was the son of Seraiah, and was probably born at Babylon. He was a scribe (Ezra 7⁶), who went up to Jerusalem with a later body of returning captives.

2. **The Book of Ezra**, originally with Nehemiah and his conclusion of Chronicles (see above), was in the Hebrew Canon, through a breach, separated from Chronicles, still united with the Book of Nehemiah as a single book ; so in the LXX these two books of the English Bible formed but one, viz. Second Esdras; in the Vulgate they are called First and Second Esdras. Ezra is written partly in Hebrew, and partly in Aramaic. The parts in Aramaic (cc. 4⁸–6¹⁸, and 7¹¹⁻²⁶) consist mainly of letters and other public documents taken from the archives, and are probably quoted in the original language, instead of being translated, to mark their authenticity.

3. **Analysis.** The book falls into two sections with a considerable interval between the two. (i) Part I (1–6) gives an account of the return of the captives from Babylon at the beginning of the reign of Cyrus, 538 B.C., and the rebuilding of the Temple, interrupted by the Samaritans, but renewed at the preaching of Haggai and Zechariah, and accomplished in the sixth year of Darius, 516 B.C.; chapter 4⁶⁻²³, referring to the reigns of Xerxes (486–465) and his successor Artaxerxes, is chronologically out of place. (ii) Part II (7–10), separated by more than half a century from the period dealt with in Part I (apart from 4⁶⁻²³), gives an account of the second return of exiles in the seventh year of Artaxerxes (i. e. probably

Artaxerxes Longimanus, whose seventh year was 458, 457 B.C.), which was led by Ezra himself, who carries out a reformation of the people, and forbids the intermarriage of the Jews with heathen wives. Thus the whole period covered by the book extends over seventy-nine years, from 538 B.C. to 457 B.C.

4. **Ezra's Memoirs.** The book of Ezra is part of a larger work, the books of Chronicles, written scarcely earlier than 380 B.C., but it appears to contain in 7^{27}–9^{15} practically unaltered extracts from memoirs written by Ezra himself; and in 7^{1-26}, 10 we may have further extracts from these memoirs but modified by the compiler, just as in Chronicles many passages from Samuel and Kings are not cited verbatim but with modifications.

NEHEMIAH

1. **The Book of Nehemiah** was, as we have seen, anciently united with the Book of Ezra, and in the Vulgate it is called 2 Esdras. It is closely connected with the later chapters of Ezra, and carries on the history from about twelve years after the close of the book of Ezra to 432 B.C.

2. **Nehemiah** (*the Lord comforts*) was a Jew (Neh. 1^2), and was acting as cupbearer to the King of Persia at Shushan, his winter residence, when he received intelligence of the deplorable condition of Jerusalem and of the residents in Judæa. Filled with sorrow he prays to God, and God opens the heart of Artaxerxes to give him a commission to rebuild the walls of his ancestral city. Zerubbabel had rebuilt the Temple, but not the city walls. These Nehemiah endeavoured to re-erect, and amidst the opposition of many enemies, within and without, he employs the whole body of the people of every rank and order, by night as well as by day, in carrying out the operation, and in fifty-two days accomplishes his work.

3. **Analysis.** The book falls into three main divisions. (i) Part I (1–7) describes (*a*) Nehemiah's sorrow for his country while at the court of Persia, and his return (1, 2); and (*b*) his plans for rebuilding the walls amidst the opposition of many enemies (cc. 3–6); (*c*) the seventh chapter, an extract from Ezra 2, 3, apparently inserted as containing the names of the original immigrants a century earlier. (ii) Part II (8–10), introduction and acceptance of the Law. (iii) Part III (11–12) relates the arrangements made for the occupation of the city, and contains various lists. (iv) Part IV (13): After holding the position of Governor or Satrap of Jerusalem, Nehemiah returned to the

court of Artaxerxes. During his absence the old abuses began to creep in, and being informed of this, he once more (432 B. C.) obtained leave of absence from the Persian court, and as Tirshatha was invested with renewed powers. He employed his time in diligently putting down abuses, introducing measures for the prevention of traffic on the Sabbath, denouncing mixed marriages, and carrying out a second reformation.

4. **Nehemiah's Memoirs.** Large parts of the books ($1-7^{73}$, 13^{4-31}) are related in the first person and appear to be extracts from memoirs written by Nehemiah himself; and 11, 12 are perhaps based on his memoirs. In 8–10 both Ezra and Nehemiah are referred to in the third person, but the narrative seems based on some contemporary record which according to some was the memoirs of Ezra (see above).

ESTHER

1. **Esther** (*star*). This little book contains an episode in the history of those Israelites who did not return from the Captivity. It opens in the third year of Ahasuerus, i. e. Xerxes, who reigned 486–465 B. C.; and tells the story of a Jewess, whose Hebrew name was Hadassah (*myrtle*), but who except in 2^7 is called Esther, which has been explained as the Persian word for 'star' or the name of the Babylonian goddess Ishtar. Brought by her kinsman Mordecai, one of the captives carried away from Jerusalem (2^6) in 597 B. C., and now in 482 B. C. occupied in the palace at Shushan, she is selected in place of Vashti to become the favourite wife of the Persian despot. Mordecai as one of those who 'sat in the king's gate' (Esther 2^{21}) discovers a plot of the eunuchs to assassinate the king. This he divulges, and the record of his services is entered in the royal chronicles. But he has a rival for the royal favour, Haman, an Agagite, a descendant of the ancient Amalekite kings. The new favourite, hating Mordecai, forms a plot for the wholesale destruction of the Jewish exiles (chap. 3). Mordecai discovering this informs Esther, and she, putting her life in her hands, intercedes with the king in behalf of her nation, and Haman is hanged on the very gallows he had designed for Mordecai, while the latter is advanced to high honour in the Persian court (cc. 7, 8). The Jews, saved from peril themselves, make a great slaughter of their enemies, and thereafter keep a feast which was subsequently repeated year by year under the name of Purim (9^{26}).

2. **The Feast of Purim** (*lots*) is still kept up amongst the Jews in ironical commemoration of their great enemy, who had resorted

to the augury by lots to find a lucky day on which to slay the Jews (3⁷). Preceded by a strict fast on the thirteenth of Adar, or March, the festival is celebrated with great rejoicings. The Book of Esther is recited in the synagogue, and when the reader comes to the name of Haman, the entire assembly shout in execration, and the conclusion of the service is followed by feasting and merriment. It is no doubt on account of its giving the story of the origin of an annual festival, and not on account of any high moral or religious value, that the book found its place in the Jewish and consequently in the Christian Canon. That this story of the origin of the festival is strictly historical is scarcely to be maintained.

3. The Author of the Book is unknown, and the date at which it was written—perhaps about 300 B.C.—cannot be closely defined. It was written in Hebrew, but the LXX version contains considerable additions to the narrative, which appear by themselves in the English apocrypha ; these additions amply supply a curious defect of the original work, viz. that it nowhere mentions God, and that 'the point of view is throughout purely secular'.

(iii) *THE POETICAL BOOKS*

As pointed out under the several books already considered, not a little poetry is contained in the preceding books of the Old Testament. With Job we reach the first of the books that are mainly or entirely poetry ; Psalms and Proverbs which follow are entirely poetry, Ecclesiastes less so, Song of Songs again entirely so. Outside this group of five books, the whole of Lamentations is also poetry, as also are large parts of the prophetical books.

JOB

1. The Story of Job is told in prose at the beginning (1, 2) and end (42⁷⁻¹⁷) of the book which bears his name. He appears on the scene as a wealthy God-fearing man, living in patriarchal style in the land of Uz, which lay E. of Canaan and probably in the NE. of Arabia Deserta (1¹). Suddenly he is prostrated by a succession of calamities, and is stripped of goods, of children, of health (1¹³⁻²²). His friends visit him, and a discussion (in poetry) between them ensues (3–31). At length God speaks to Job, and puts a series of questions intended to illustrate the unfathomable wisdom and power of the Most High as compared with the littleness of man (38–41). Thus Job is brought to realize and confess that

E

he had in the discussion spoken beyond his knowledge. Then the blessing of God is once more shed forth upon His servant, and the latter end of Job is more prosperous than the beginning (42).

2. **Opinions respecting the Book.** The most varied opinions have been held respecting the book. Ancient Jewish conjectures generally ascribed the book to the Patriarchal age, and regarded it as historical. Much more rarely the book was regarded as a parable or a philosophical fiction. Modern scholars generally regard it as a great imaginative poem resting upon a traditional basis.

3. **The Age depicted in the Book.** One of the most striking things about the book is that in all its forty-two chapters there is not a single reference to Israelite history. There are references it is thought to Adam and the Fall (c. 31^{33}), possibly to the Flood (c. 22^{16}); but no explicit reference to any subsequent event recorded in Scripture, unless we except c. 20^{23}, which has some resemblance to the punishment connected with the sending quails in the desert (comp. Ps. $78^{30, 31}$). When we add to this the long life attributed to Job (c. 42^{16}), the patriarchal customs and forms of worship which meet us, the absence of all explicit allusion to the Mosaic Law from the speeches, and of the national Hebrew name for God (Jehovah), we must conclude that the author conceives of the events he describes as occurring in patriarchal times outside the sphere of God's peculiar revelation to Israel. This is appropriate : for the problem discussed is of the widest human reference and interest.

4. **The Age in which the Book** was written is quite another question, and more uncertain. Earlier conjectures which assigned it to the pre-Mosaic, the Mosaic or the Solomonic age have been generally abandoned, and it has been increasingly recognized that a book turning, as this does, on the question of individual responsibility was written after the age of Jeremiah and Ezekiel, who did so much to secure recognition for this (see e. g. Ezek. 18^{33}). If we particularize more closely we may surmise a date towards the end of the fifth century B. C.

5. **Analysis.** The book itself may be thus analysed : (i) *The Introduction* (1, 2) consists of a prose narrative of the cause and extent of Job's sufferings, and his patient endurance of them ; it affirms that Job is righteous, and that sin is not the cause of his calamities; (ii) *The Colloquies* between Job and his friends is poetry, the theme of which is the cause in particular of Job's, and more generally of human suffering. His friends affirm it to be *sin,* and

exhort Job to repentance. He denies their accusations, claims to have been righteous, and also that other righteous men suffer, while some wicked men prosper. This portion consists of three series of speeches; (a) Job's complaint (c. 3), followed by the speeches of Eliphaz, Bildad, and Zophar, each being successively answered by Job (cc. 4–14); (b) a further speech of each of these three, with Job's answer thereto (cc. 15–21); (c) a speech of Eliphaz and Bildad, with the answer to each (cc. 22–31). But this third series of speeches is probably in some disorder; and $27^{7-10, 13-23}$ now assigned to Job belonged rather to a speech of Bildad or Zophar. Chapter 28 is also probably out of place. (iii) *The Argument* of Elihu that sufferings are remedial and for the good of the one afflicted, followed by a reproof to Job for his self-justification, and a defence of God's government, with a magnificent description of His wonderful works in the world of Nature (cc. 32–7); this section also, which now interrupts Job's appeal to God at the close of chapter 31 and God's response in 38–41 is probably out of place—a later addition to the original poem. (iv) An address of the Almighty Himself out of the whirlwind, revealing His power and wisdom, concluding with Job's confession ($38–42^6$) that he had spoken beyond his limited knowledge. (v) A prose *Conclusion*, reaffirming Job's righteousness and condemning the friends for their ungrounded accusations, and narrating the end of Job's life in peace and prosperity (42^{7-17}). Job himself, it is to be remembered, is named by Ezekiel (Ezek. 14^{14}), as well as by St. James (James 5^{11}), and is classed by them with other holy men.

THE PSALMS

1. The Book of Psalms occupies in the Hebrew Canon the first place in the third of the great divisions into which the Canonical Books were divided—*Law, Prophets, Hagiographa*. It is the product of the Jewish Church, but 'in its spiritual fullness it belongs to no special time', and the old words are 'fulfilled' in Christ. Its growth was gradual, and its composition extends over many centuries.

2. Names of the Psalter. The title of the book in the Hebrew Bible is *Sêpher Tĕhillim*, the *Book of Praises*, or simply *Praises*. The Septuagint translators use the word ψαλμός *, *psalm*, to render the Hebrew word for a song with musical accompaniment; and the entire collection was entitled *Psalms*, Ψαλμοί (Luke 24^{44}), or the

---

* Ψαλμός denotes (1) the music of a stringed instrument; (2) a song sung to the accompaniment of such music.

Book of Psalms (Luke 20^{42}). Later came the word Ψαλτήριον, *Psalter,* a *Collection of Psalms,* which has come down to us from the Greek through the Latin.

3. **Divisions of the Psalter.** The *completed* Psalter was divided by the Jews into five books (1–41, 42–72, 73–89, 90–106,107–150), answering to the Five Books of Moses. More interesting are the indications of earlier and smaller Psalters incorporated in our present collection. There are (1) the statement at the end of 72 that the prayers of David are ended, though as a matter of fact in the existing Psalter another prayer of David follows in 86 ; (2) the occurrence of certain Psalms or parts of Psalms twice (e. g. Ps. 14= 53); (3) the grouping in masses of Psalms with a common heading; thus 3–41 (with the exception of 10, a continuation of 9, and 33) are all headed 'of David' ; so with few exceptions are 51–70 ; 42–9 (except 43 which is a continuation of 42) are headed 'of the sons of Korah', and 73–83 (also 50) 'of Asaph'. We may believe that collections of Psalms with these headings existed before our Psalter, and were wholly or in part incorporated in the larger work.

4. **Alphabetic Psalms.** Psalm 119 is divided into sections of eight verses. In the Hebrew every verse of each section begins with the letter of the alphabet inscribed over it, which is evidently intended to help the memory in reciting it. Other alphabetic Psalms not indicated as such in E.V. are 9 and 10 (imperfect), 25, 34, 37, 111, 112, 145. In these the sections are shorter than in 119, and consist of half a verse, a verse or two verses to each letter.

5. **The Bible Version of the Psalms** was made direct from the Hebrew in 1611. It is more accurate, but less melodious than the version in the Prayer Book. The latter is taken from Cranmer's Bible of 1539. It is pointed for chanting, and is admirably adapted for that purpose ; but the rendering is not so close to the existing Hebrew text, and has been to some degree influenced by the LXX through the Latin, and so in some cases, where the LXX preserves an earlier reading than the Hebrew, is nearer to the original text.

6. **Universal Adaptation of the Psalter.** 'The Psalter has been through all the centuries, and will ever continue to be, the one unique and inexhaustible treasury of devotion for the individual and for the Church.' The product of one, it is the property of two Dispensations, Jewish and Christian. There is no other Book of Praise so pregnant with expressions of the heart's deepest emotions under all the vicissitudes of life, or so adapted to all climes and ages as to be the universal medium of praise for all nations of the world. No country but such a 'museum-country' as Palestine,

varying as it does from the arid desert to the mountains capped with snow, could have furnished such a combination of subjects for poetical imagery; its vines and fruits; its valleys thick with corn and shining with lilies; its mountains, torrents, rivers, lakes; its wild and domestic animals, and its beasts of prey—all are pictured in the Psalms with a noble simplicity to which we find no parallel elsewhere. 'The Psalms are as living as when they were written. . . . They were composed in an age at least as immature as that of the singers of the Veda; but they are now what they have been for thirty centuries, the very life of spiritual religion —they suit the needs, they express, as nothing else can express, the deepest religious ideas of "the foremost in the files of time.*"'

7. **Age and Authorship.** When we speak of the Psalms of David, we use a popular and general form of expression. That the great king was also a poet there can be no doubt (see 2 Sam. 1), and some of the Psalms may be due to his authorship, though the headings 'Of David' cannot be taken as proof of his authorship in particular cases. Other Psalms, though later than David, were written before the Exile: many Psalms are certainly later than that event and possibly some Psalms are to be referred to the Maccabaean period, though this is a question on which opinion is divided.

8. **Headings.** The Latin headings, which are prefixed to the Psalms in the Prayer Book, are the first few words of the particular Psalm in the Vulgate, and are a survival and reminder of the time when the Psalms were 'said' or 'sung' in Latin. They are only valuable for purposes of designation. The Hebrew titles and inscriptions, as they are translated or merely transliterated in our version, are very obscure, and their meanings often can only be matters of conjecture. As they are translated in the Authorized Version, these notes, apart from those like 'Of David', 'Of the sons of Korah' already referred to, indicate a traditional belief as to (i) the style or character of the Psalm, or (ii) its musical setting, or (iii) its liturgical use, or (iv) the occasion of its composition.

(i) *The Style or Character of the Psalms :—*

1. *Mizmor*, rendered 'Psalm', is prefixed to fifty-seven Psalms, and denotes a Psalm accompanied with instrumental music.

2. *Shir*, a song, sometimes preceded and sometimes followed by *Mizmor*, is the general term for a song or canticle. It occurs thirty times in the titles.

3. *Maskil*, prefixed to thirteen Psalms, has been held to denote either (1)

---

* Dean Church, *The Sacred Poetry of Early Religions*, pp. 12, 38.

an instruction, or *a poem of a didactic nature* (see titles of Pss. 32 and 74); or (2) *a skilful Psalm* (see the R.V. of Ps. 47[7]).

4. *Michtam* occurs in the title of six Psalms (Pss. 16, 56–60). The meaning is very obscure. Some would explain it as meaning ' engraven in gold ', ' a golden Psalm', with reference to the value and popularity of the Psalm as an outpouring of thankfulness ; others understand it to mean a poem of epigrammatic character. But none of these are very probable guesses.

5. *Shiggaion* (Ps. 7), 'wandering', ' erratic', seems to denote a poem in wild irregular rhythm.

6. The expression 'A Prayer' stands as the title of five Psalms (Pss. 17, 86, 90, 102, 142).

(ii) *Musical Setting*, or *accompanying instruments :*—

1. *Negīnōth*, R.V. ' *on stringed instruments* ', occurs six times (Pss. 4, 6, 54, 55, 67, 76).

2. *Nehīlōth*, R.V. *with the Nehiloth*, or (marg.) 'wind instruments '. It occurs in Ps. 5 only ; and the meaning is very doubtful.

3. *Alāmōth*, R.V. *set to Alamoth*, Ps. 46, precariously conjectured to mean ' for maidens' voices, soprano '.

4. *Shemīnīth*, R.V. *set to the Sheminith*, i. e. in marg. 'the eighth ' (Pss. 6 and 12), or the lower octave, for bass voices. Doubtful.

5. *Gittith*, R.V. *set to the Gittith* (Pss. 8, 81, 84), may denote some Gittite instrument, or a Gittite tune, brought by David from Gath.

6. *To Jeduthun*, R.V. *after the manner of Jeduthun* (Pss. 39, 62, 77); this has been supposed to mean that the Psalm was set to some melody called after or composed by David's chief musician (1 Chron. 16[41]).

7. Certain titles seem to indicate the melody to which the Psalm was to be sung, as Ps. 22, *set to Aiyéleth hash-Shahar*, i. e. 'the hind of the morning ' ; Pss. 45, 69, 80, *set to Shoshannim*, R.V. 'the tune of the Lilies ' ; Ps. 56, *Yonath-elem-Reḥoḳim*, 'the silent dove of them that are far off'; Pss. 57–9, 75, *set to Al-tashcheth* = ' Do not destroy' ; Ps. 9, *set to Muth-labben*, R.V. = ' Die for the son' (?).

8. *For the Chief Musician* is prefixed to fifty-five Psalms, of which most bear the name of David. It has been supposed to denote the destination of the Psalm for the precentor or conductor of the choir in the Temple services ; but the preposition in Hebrew is the same as that rendered ' Of' in ' Of David ' &c., and this note may be of the same nature as the notes 'Of David ', ' Of the sons of Korah ', &c.

9. *Selah* is not a title, but a musical expression, which occurs seventy-one times in the Psalter, is rendered by the LXX διάψαλμα (*diapsalma*), and is supposed to have been an instruction to the orchestra to strike up either with a louder note, or while the singing ceased with a softer accompaniment.

(iii) *Liturgical Use :*—

In the Second Temple each day had its special Psalm, and so Ps. 3 is a morning Psalm, Ps. 4 an evening Psalm, Ps. 92 is entitled *A Psalm or Song for the Sabbath Day*, and in the LXX Pss. 24, 48, 82, 94, 81 (?), 103 are assigned to the first and following days of the week respectively. Pss. 38 and 70 are entitled *to bring to remembrance*, or R.V. marg. ' to make memorial '. This may indicate that they were sung at the offer-

• ing of incense. Ps. 100, entitled *a Psalm of Thanksgiving*, R.V. marg. 'for the thank-offering', may have been sung at the oblation of thank-offerings.

Fifteen Psalms, 120-34, bear the title of *Songs of Degrees*, or *Songs of Goings up, Ascents.* There is much difference of opinion as to the meaning of this title. It seems most probable that they were either (i) the songs sung by the Jewish exiles on their return from Babylon (Ezra 7^9), or (ii) those sung by the Jewish pilgrims on their journeys up to the Holy City to keep the annual feasts (Ps. 42^4; Isa. 30^{29}).

(iv) *Occasion of Composition :—*

Notes describing this are prefixed to thirteen Psalms, all headed 'Of David'. (*a*) Pss. 7, 34, 52, 54, 56, 57, 59, 142, refer to the time of his persecution by Saul; (*b*) 18 to the day of his deliverance from the hands of all his enemies; (*c*) 60 to Joab's victory over Edom in 'the valley of Salt'; (*d*) 51 to David's sin with Bath-sheba; (*e*) 3 and 63 to his flight from Absalom.

9. **The Imprecatory Psalms** constitute one of the 'moral difficulties *' of the Old Testament. They are the 7th, 35th, 69th, and the 109th. They startle us because they are not merely prophetic of the downfall of the sinner, but express a real desire, a passionate prayer that God's vengeance may take its course and that good may triumph over evil. The writers regard sins against God as personal injuries, and sometimes they regard mischief wrought undeservedly against themselves as wrought against the Most High. In forming an opinion respecting them we must bear in mind (i) that there is a marked difference between the Old and New Testament as regards the reception of injuries and the treatment of enemies. Our Lord distinctly declared that the old Dispensation, based upon the rule of retaliation, was inferior to the new, which is animated by the principle of love (Matt. 5$^{43,\ 44}$); that actions were allowable under that Dispensation which could not be permitted to His followers. (ii) It is important to observe that these imprecations are not to be regarded as the expressions of vindictive hatred against mere personal enemies, or as a mere personal thirst for revenge. They are directed against those who, by wicked words of falsehood, and acts of injustice and cruelty, had made themselves the enemies of God; and they express a desire for the realization of the Divine government of the world by the active intervention of Him to whom 'vengeance belongeth' (Ps. 94$^{1-4}$). (iii) They are to be regarded in the light of prayers to God that He will vindicate Himself against those who have outraged His attributes of justice, mercy, and truth; and they are put up by those who had a keen sense of the great conflict going on between good and evil, between Israel and the enemies of

* Professor Kirkpatrick, Introd. to *Psalms*, p. xxxv.

Israel, who were the enemies of Israel's God (cf. Judges 5[31]). (iv) These utterances belong to an age which, as Professor Mozley has pointed out,* had but an imperfect conception of the rights of the individual. They belong to the Old Testament and not to the New; and it is to be remembered that even He, who came to expand what was rudimentary and imperfect in the Law, could utter terrible denunciations against hardened and impenitent sinners (cf. Matt. 23[37-9]).

10. **The Messianic Psalms.** The term Messiah, or Messiah of Jehovah, i. e. 'the anointed', or 'the anointed of Jehovah', was a term applied to actual Jewish kings. For this reason any of the Psalms referring to a Jewish king (2, 18, 20, 21, 45, 60, 61, 72, 89, 110) might in a certain sense be termed Messianic. But in several of these Psalms the king is idealized; and it is this ideal element rather than any historical description that is commonly contemplated when a Psalm is termed Messianic, or when we speak of the Messianic element in the Psalter. And in particular those Psalms have come to be called Messianic which contain an ideal that can be seen to have been fulfilled by Christ, or which contain passages applied to Christ in the New Testament, though much else in the same Psalm may be very inapplicable to Him. In this wider sense the Messianic Psalms include many that contained no actual reference to any one whom the writer would have termed Messiah; thus they include not merely Royal but Passion Psalms (22, 69, 109, 35, 41, 55). If in the 45th Psalm, applied to Christ in Heb. 1[8, 9], we have allusions to a King 'fairer than the children of men', 'anointed with the oil of gladness above His fellows', whose 'throne is for ever and ever'; if the 110th Psalm sets before us distinctly a Person, combining, as no sovereign of Judah ever combined, the priesthood of Melchizedek with the royalty of David, 'ruling out of Zion in the midst of his enemies', and seated as Adonai at the right hand of Jehovah; so also in the 22nd Psalm we have a marvellous description of a sufferer from which more than one passage is in the New Testament applied to Christ (Matt. 27[46], John 19[24], Heb. 2[12]). 'Passages are often *applied* to Christ though they do not primarily refer either to Him, or even to a Jewish Messiah, because they describe a situation similar to one in which He was placed, or because they are true of Him in a fuller and more comprehensive sense than they are of those of whom they were originally spoken. Thus Ps. 41[9] is said in John 13[18] to be

* Mozley's *Lectures on the Old Testament*, pp. 87 sqq.

"fulfilled" by Christ. The verse, where it stands, in Psalm 41, refers actually to the false friend of the author of the Psalm and to no one else. Christ cannot, as is sometimes strangely supposed, be the speaker in the Psalm, because of the confession of sin in v. 4, and because of the unchristian prayer in v. 10. Psalm 35[19] is quoted similarly in John 15[25], but the Psalm cannot as a whole be referred to Christ, because it contains much (including imprecations, vv. 8, 26) which would be quite unsuitable in his mouth. Ps. 40[8-10] again, is in Hebrews 10[5-7] quoted as referring to Christ. But it must be obvious that this Psalm, in its original intention, has no reference to Christ. But the ideal of obedience, expressed in vv. 8–10, is *applied* to Christ, as a fitting expression of His perfect conformity to His Father's Will' (Driver, *Studies in the Psalter*, pp. 24–6).

11. **Classification of the Psalms according to Subjects.**

1. *Instructive.* On the perfection of God's law : 19, 119. On the blessing of piety, misery of vice : 1, 5, 7, 9–12, 14, 15, 17, 24, 25, 32, 34, 36, 37, 50, 52, 53, 58, 73, 75, 84, 91, 92, 94, 112, 119, 121, 125, 127, 128, 133. On vanity of human life : 39, 49, 90. On duty of rulers : 82, 101.

2. *Devotional.* (a) Prayer.—Penitence : 6, 32, 38, 51, 102, 130, 143. Resignation : 3, 16, 27, 31, 54, 56, 57, 61, 62, 71, 86. Contrition : 13, 22, 69, 77, 88, 143. In severe trouble : 4, 5, 11, 28, 41, 55, 59, 64, 70, 109, 120, 140, 141, 143. In affliction : 44, 60, 74, 79, 80, 83, 89, 94, 102, 129, 137. When deprived of public worship : 42, 43, 63, 84. Intercession : 20, 67, 122, 132, 144.

(b) Praise.—For God's providential care : 23, 34, 35, 91, 100, 103, 107, 117, 121, 145, 146. Of God's attributes : 8, 19, 24, 29, 33, 47, 50, 65, 66, 76, 77, 93, 95-7, 99, 104, 111, 113–15, 134, 139, 147, 148, 150.

(c) Thanksgiving.—For individual mercies : 9, 18, 22, 30, 34, 40, 75, 103, 108, 116, 118, 138, 144. For general or national mercies : 46, 48, 65, 66, 68, 76, 81, 85, 98, 105, 124, 126, 129, 135, 136, 149.

3. Messianic : see above.

4. *Historical :* 78, 105, 106.

12. **Alphabetical Table of the First Line of each Psalm.**

THE PROVERBS

1. Title. The Book of Proverbs opens with the words 'The proverbs of Solomon the son of David, king of Israel', whence the abbreviated title in the Hebrew Bible, *Mishlê*, i. e. 'the proverbs of'. The Hebrew word *Mashal* has amongst other significations that of a *representation* or *similitude*. In the LXX the title is Παροιμίαι Σαλομῶνος, and in the Vulgate *Proverbia Salomonis*, whence comes our English title.

2. Design. The book is a manual of practical rules for daily life, as the Psalms are a manual of daily devotion, the former guiding the actions, the latter the thoughts. It is a book of daily lessons for all ages and states of men and women. In it 'wisdom' is religion, and 'folly' is irreligion.

3. Contents. The book may be divided as follows:— (i) A preface setting forth the general character of the contents (1^{1-6}). (ii) Several introductory discourses treating of the characteristics and value of wisdom (1^7–9). (iii) A collection of 'the proverbs of Solomon' (10–22). (iv) A second introduction on the study of wisdom (22^{17}–24^{22}), with an appendix headed 'These also are (sayings) of the wise' 24^{23-34}. (v) A second volume of proverbs of Solomon, copied by 'the men of Hezekiah, king of Judah'. (vi) An appendix containing the instructions of 'Agur the son of Jakeh', and the words of King Lemuel (31^{1-9}). (vii) A poem of great beauty in praise of a virtuous wife (31^{10-31}) ; this last is alphabetic, like certain Psalms (see Psalms 9, 25, 37, 145 &c., and see p. 52).

4. **Authorship.** As the Psalms go by the name of David because he was deemed the author of many of them, so the Proverbs are called after Solomon for a similar reason. To him, as already indicated, two parts of the book are assigned. Yet even these parts contain proverbs, such as those which speak of the king from the standpoint of a subject, that were scarcely coined by Solomon himself. In I Kings 4[32] Solomon is credited with having *spoken* 3,000 proverbs, but the relation of these to the much smaller number *written* in the Book of proverbs is not clear. The other portions, it is thought, were collected and added to the rest in the time of Hezekiah, while the original title was preserved for the whole of the compilation, just as was done for the Psalms. The Egyptian 'Teaching of Amenophis' is the source of Prov. 22[17]–24[22].

5. **The Date** of individual proverbs cannot be determined : according to 25[1] many of them are older than the eighth century B. C., but this title betrays its late origin, and much of the Book (e. g. 1–9) is later than this, and not a little probably post-exilic. Ecclesiasticus reminds us that literature of the same general character was certainly still being written in the second century B.C.

ECCLESIASTES

1. **Title.** The title of this book is taken from the LXX, and answers to the Hebrew *Kohéleth*, which the Authorized Version renders 'Preacher', but the Revised Version (margin) the 'Great Orator'. The idea conveyed by the Hebrew may be that of a person calling together an assembly of people with the intention of addressing them, an action applied to Wisdom personified (Prov. 1[20], 8[1], &c.).

2. **Author and Date.** The book is written in the person of Solomon (who is intended by 'Koheleth'), son of David, king in Jerusalem (1 [1, 12]), and was for long supposed to have been actually written by Solomon at the close of his life, after his fall (1 Kings 11[1–13]), and to contain the expression of his penitence for his worldliness and backsliding, when his heathen wives had turned away his heart from following God. Yet as a matter of fact the book is not the work of a penitent, nor of one who had been the prosperous king of an independent people ; but the language and the subject-matter of the book—the expression of misery under a tyrannical government, the sudden vicissitudes of fortune alluded to, the tone of despondency, the moral and religious declension, and the condition of literature—all point to the book being the work of a writer (whose name is unknown), living long after the

Exile, when his people were the subjects of a foreign government, whether Persian or Greek. The book can scarcely have been written before the middle of the fourth century B.C. and may well be later.

3. **Contents and Character.** The book consists in the main of reflections upon and illustrations of the theme stated at the beginning and (with the exception of an appendix) at the close ($1^1, 12^8$) of the book, viz. the complete vanity of life. Man gets nothing new or satisfying out of all his toil. The lot of men is not equitably affected by their conduct in this life, and there is no life beyond death for man any more than there is for beast : the righteous may meet with calamity, the unrighteous with prosperity (see e. g. $3^{19,20}$, 7^{15}, $8^{14f.}$, $9^{2f.,11f.}$, 12^7). Mingled with such reflections are others of an opposite nature in which the certainty of a judgement discriminating between the righteous and the unrighteous is insisted upon, and the fear of God commended (e. g. 3^{17}, 8^{11-13}, 11^9, 12^{14}). This combination within the book of opposite standpoints has been attributed either to a single writer presenting the conflict between a higher and a lower self, or to the work of the writer having been modified by the additions of another.

THE SONG OF SOLOMON

1. **Title.** The book is called in the Hebrew title *The Song of Songs*, i. e. the best of them all, and is said in 1^1 to be Solomon's (cp. 1 Kings 4^{32}). The old popular title 'Cantica', 'Canticles', may be more exact in so far as it suggests a collection of poems, rather than a single poem.

2. **The Canonicity of the Song,** not wholly unchallenged, was secured by the fact that the book had come to be treated in Jewish circles, as it was subsequently in the Christian Church, as allegorical throughout.

3. **Contents and Character.** The book obviously consists in large part of *dialogue,* of words exchanged between two or more persons, one a woman. The theme is love and marriage. Since the allegorical interpretation has been increasingly abandoned, two theories of the Book have been put forward : (1) that the book is a *drama* whether with two or three chief characters. This theory, to render the book intelligible, requires elaborate stage directions, of which the text contains no hint, to be supplied ; (2) that the book is a collection of popular Hebrew songs, of a simple dramatic nature ; to such songs modern Syria would supply interesting analogies.

4. **Date.** The traditional ascription of the book to Solomon is now, like that of Ecclesiastes, though for different reasons, commonly given up. The date cannot be very certainly or closely determined : the age of David and Solomon seems to be regarded as one that is long past. By some the style is regarded as relatively early, while others find features in the language of the book, particularly the presence of Persian words, which point to a much later date, perhaps not earlier than the third century B.C.

(iv) *THE PROPHETICAL BOOKS*

From the middle of the eighth century B.C. the development of prophecy exhibited a new phase. The prophetic spirit, which received a new impulse through Samuel, became yet more active during the later period of Jewish history ; and of this activity we have a record in the sixteen books which in the English Bible bear the names of prophets. These prophets may be arranged chronologically as follows :—(i) *Those of the eighth century* B.C. : Amos, Hosea, Isaiah, Micah. (ii) *Those living during the half-century before the Exile* : Nahum, Zephaniah, Habakkuk, Jeremiah. (iii) *Prophets active during the Exile* : Ezekiel, the authors of Isaiah xl–lv and certain other parts of Isaiah. (iv) *Those after the return from the Captivity*: Haggai, Zechariah, and Malachi.

With regard to the prophetical books in general, it should be observed : (1) that in some cases certainly, and perhaps in all, the books were not entirely written by the prophets mentioned in the several titles : thus, some of these books contain extracts from the Books of Kings, or other biographical notices written by disciples or others about the prophets ; the same prophecies sometimes occur in two different books, while on the other hand in some books, e. g. Isaiah, Zechariah, the works of more than one prophet are included within the same books ; (2) much of the words of the prophets consists of poetry ; (3) most of the prophetic utterances are brief, commonly not extending beyond a few verses, e. g. the prophetic poem which occurs in both Isa. 2^{2-4}, Mic. 4^{1-4}. The chapter divisions of the English Bible are useless for distinguishing the several prophecies: chapters frequently contain more than one utterance (e. g. Isa. 1, 9).

ISAIAH

1. **Isaiah** (*Jah is salvation*), the son of Amoz, was called to prophesy in the year that King Uzziah died (about 740 B.C.), and continued his work at least as late as 701 B.C. Of his personal

history we know little. His wife, 'the prophetess' (8³), and his sons, whose names bear witness to his prophetic announcements (7³, 8³), are mentioned; and his access to the kings of his time (Uzziah, Jotham, Ahaz, and Hezekiah) is indicated.

2. **The Epoch** in which he prophesied was critical. The state of the nation is painted in sombre colours alike by Amos, who lived somewhat earlier, by Isaiah himself, and the contemporary prophets, Hosea and Micah. Luxury, oppression, idolatry, immorality, vain confidence in man, lack of confidence in God, together with zealous attendance to the ceremonials of religious worship, were the characteristics alike of Israel and Judah. Outside the Holy Land, Assyria, after a period of relative quiescence, with the accession of Tiglath-Pileser in 745 entered on the period of its greatest power and expansion, and Syria and Palestine were at once exposed to its severity. Babylon was subject to Assyria, though ready to seize any favourable opportunity to reassert itself; Syria was approaching its end; Egypt after a period of weakness and disunion obtained a more vigorous dynasty from about 712 B.C. onwards; Tyre and Sidon were at the head of commercial enterprise; Moab, Ammon, Philistia, and Edom—Israel's nearest neighbours—like Israel itself, suffered from the Assyrian advance. The destinies of all these kingdoms are touched upon by Isaiah, though the people of Israel are foremost in his thoughts; behind all alike he sees the activity of God.

The Book of Isaiah consists of two entirely distinct parts (1–39, 40–66), the first closing with the narratives (36–9) derived from 2 Kings 18–20, which record the events of the last great period of Isaiah's career. The last part of the book (40–66) never mentions and has nothing whatever to do with Isaiah, but belongs to a quite different age.

Chapters 1–39 is a combination of various collections of prophecies or prophetic narratives mostly, but not wholly, belonging to the age of Isaiah. The prophetic narratives occur mostly in chapters 6, 7, 8, 20, 36–9; those like 36–9 (= 2 Kings 18–20) do not purport to have been written by Isaiah; but it is Isaiah himself who records his call in chapter 6, and certain other experiences of his earlier life down to shortly before 732 B.C. in 7, 8. Chapter 20, referring to the years 713–711, appears like 36–9 to be a narrative about the prophet written by some one else. The prophecies (almost all of them poems) in these chapters fall into groups—1, 2–5 (with a fresh title, 2¹), 8¹⁹–12, 13–23 (with a fresh title, 13¹) mainly consisting of prophecies concerning foreign nations, 24–7, 28–35. The prophecies of Isaiah can in some, though not in all cases; be referred to particular periods of his life: thus 6, as already remarked, describes his call to be a prophet (*c.* 740 B. C.), 2^{5-21} may be dated about 739 B. C., 9^7-10^4, 5^{26-9} about 737 B.C., 7^1-8^{18} are records of what he did and said about 735 and before 732 B.C., 17^{1-11} a prophecy not long before 732 B.C. fulfilled by the fall of Damascus in that year, 10^{5-15} after 717 B. C.; much of the remainder of Isaiah's prophecies belongs to the period (702–701 B. C.) described in 36–9, viz. 18, 22^{1-14}, a good deal of 28–31, and part probably of 1.

Prophecies in 1–39, later than the age of Isaiah, include 13, 14^{1-22}, 21 (written towards the close of the Exile, *c.* 550 B. C.), and 24–7, which is an apocalypse.

Chapters 40–66. This part of the book falls into two main divisions, 40–55, 56–66. The prophecies in 40–55 are the work of a prophet who was the contemporary of Cyrus, and had already, when he spoke or wrote, witnessed part of his victorious career, and predicts that he will make yet further conquests and will release the Jews now in exile in Babylon. The prophecies were most probably made a year or two before the capture of Babylon by Cyrus in 539. Convinced himself of this coming deliverance of his people and of God's purposes bound up with it, the prophet sets himself to rouse the Exiles from their unbelief and despondency; he does this by laying stress on certain aspects of God's nature: he insists on the uniqueness of God, that there is no other God, that other gods, those of Babylon for example, are no gods: he also insists on the power and might of God and His consequent ability to carry out His gracious purpose of delivering Israel and restoring them to their land. Equally distinctive is this prophet's conception of Israel as destined to be a missionary people bringing their religion to the nations. The age of the last part of the book (56–66) is less clear than that of the prophecies of Isaiah in 1–39, or of the prophet of the Exile (46–55), but for the most part 56–66 appears to be post-exilic and perhaps belongs to the middle of the fifth century B. C.

JEREMIAH

1. Jeremiah (*Jehovah shoots* (?) or *hurls* (?)) was the son of Hilkiah and a priest of the priestly city of Anathoth, three miles north of Jerusalem. He was called to prophesy when but a youth, in the thirteenth year of King Josiah (*c.* 626 B. C.), and he continued to prophesy in Jerusalem and other cities of Judah for forty years, until the final capture of the city (586 B. C.). After this event a remnant gathered round him at Mizpah with Gedaliah, the governor of the land, and he warned them in vain against

going down into Egypt. But he was carried off thither by his countrymen ($43^{6ff.}$), where to the last he protested against their idolatry. According to a late tradition, he was stoned to death at Tahpanhes.

2. **Character and Style of the Book.** No prophet reveals to us the inmost recesses of his mind more than Jeremiah. Naturally of a shy and timid disposition, subject to despondency and sadness (15^{10}, 20^7), he was called to a work requiring undaunted resolution and rare courage. Belonging to the orders both of priest and prophet, he was compelled to witness against each, when these offices had sunk into the lowest state of degradation. From the first moment of his call he was 'alone amidst a hostile world', but devoted to his duty he maintained his work to the end; and the promise that he should be a 'brazen wall', made at the time of his call, and renewed later (1^8, 15^{20}), never failed him. His style reflects the sadness of his mission. He lays aside all unnecessary ornament, and in an effective form of poetry expresses the painful imagery which ever interprets his thoughts. The book varies between prose and poetry, and contains history mingled with prophecy. The prophetic utterances are often broken by outbursts of prayer or complaint, and the bitter opposition of his enemies wrings from him occasionally words of indignation and cries for vengeance.

3. **Origin and History of the Book.** Jeremiah is not the author of the book that bears his name, but was the author, as we are told in a narrative casting very valuable light on the origin of prophetic literature (36), of a book which in all probability is in larger part incorporated in that book. According to this narrative, in the year 604, i. e. more than twenty years after his call to prophesy, Jeremiah was directed to prepare a book containing what he had been saying these twenty years past. This he did; but the book was destroyed by King Jehoiakim. He prepared another book in the following year, and it is of this book that a large part probably survives in chapters 1–25 of our existing Book of Jeremiah. Parts, however, even of 1–25 cannot have formed part of that book, for they are prophecies delivered later than 603 (e. g. 22^{20-37}, 24). But, whether earlier or later, most of 1–25 seems to come, not indeed without modifications and expansions, directly from Jeremiah; this is true not only of the prophetic poems, but also of the narratives which, within 1–25, are for the most part told in the first person (see, e. g. 1^{4-19}, 13). On every ground this first part of the book (1–25) has a character

F 2

of its own which distinguishes it from the rest, viz. *Part II*, chapters 26–45, which consist mainly of narratives *about* Jeremiah and his life subsequently to 604 B. C. : these narrative chapters have often been supposed to be (in the main) the work of his disciple Baruch ; embedded in this mainly narrative section of the book are additional prophecies, some of which may be later than the age of Jeremiah (30–3). *Part III* consists of a collection of prophecies concerning foreign nations (46–51 : cp. Isa. 13–23), and *Part IV* is an extract from the Book of Kings (52 = 2 Kings 25: cp. Isa. 36–9). It is due to the independent origin of the several parts of the book that some chapters which are closely connected are widely separated from one another: e. g. 7 and 26 refer to the same occasion.

LAMENTATIONS

1. **Title.** The name 'Lamentations' corresponds to that under which this book appears in the Latin Vulgate, and which is a translation of the Septuagint *Threnoi*, itself a rendering of the Hebrew word *Kînôth*, which is the plural of the term applied to David's funeral song over Saul and Jonathan. The E.V. without any warrant in the Hebrew text introduces the name of Jeremiah into the title. It should also be observed that in the Hebrew Bible the book does not as in the E.V. stand next to Jeremiah.

2. **Authorship and Date.** That the book is the work of the prophet Jeremiah was long commonly believed, and the earliest extant translation, the Septuagint, already ascribes to him, scarcely indeed the whole book, but certainly one of the dirges or lamentations contained in it ; in a note prefixed to the first chapter it records : '*And it came to pass after Israel was taken captive and Jerusalem made desolate, Jeremiah sat weeping, and lamented with this lamentation over Jerusalem, and said.*' This assertion is repeated in the Latin Vulgate. Yet it is uncertain whether Jeremiah was the author of any part, improbable that he was the author of the whole book. Certain features in the language and still more the standpoint, which (in 2 and 4) is rather that of the party upon whom the fall of Jerusalem came with a shock of surprise than of the prophet who had long expected and foretold it, suggest that even those parts of the book which appear to be the work of one who had actually passed through the siege of Jerusalem are not the work of Jeremiah. Chapters 2 and 4 were written probably before 560 B. C., 1, 3, and 5 later.

3. **Analysis.** The book is not a single poem, but five distinct poems. The twenty-two verses of chapters 1, 2, 4 begin with the

twenty-two letters of the Hebrew alphabet; and the sixty-six verses of chapter 3 are arranged in groups of threes (see Revised Version), the first group beginning with *a* (א), the second with *b* (ב), and so on. The fifth chapter, though consisting of twenty-two verses, has no alphabetical arrangement. Chapter 1 dwells on the desolation and grief of the city; 2 describes her destruction, and acknowledges that it is the result of sin; 3 complains of the bitter cup which God's people have to drink, but traces a Merciful Hand in the infliction of their miseries; 4 describes the horrors of the siege and capture of the city; 5 repeats many of the painful details, and concludes with a prayer for deliverance. It is to be noticed that chapter 3^{45} is applied by St. Paul (1 Cor. 4^{13}) to the despised condition of himself and his fellow Apostles.

EZEKIEL

1. Ezekiel (*God strengthens*) was the son of Buzi, and of priestly descent. He was carried away with King Jehoiachin at the time of Nebuchadnezzar's second attack on Jerusalem (597 B. C.), and was settled with a Jewish colony on the banks of the river Chebar, i. e. the great river or Grand Canal (*Nār Kabarir*), in Babylonia, where he saw visions. He continued to prophesy for twenty-two years, beginning five years after he went into captivity.

2. Canonicity of his Prophecy. The great obscurity of parts of the book (11, 40–48), and the apparent discrepancy between it and the Pentateuch (e. g., cp. 18^{20} and Exod. 20^5), led to a Jewish rule that no one might read the obscure portions before the age of thirty; and to the raising of the question whether it should be used for public reading in the synagogue. But on no other ground has its canonicity been disputed, nor has its genuineness been seriously impugned.

3. Style. Large portions of the book are prose, but it also contains some fine poems, such as the dirge over the princes of Israel (19) and the poems on Tyre in 26–8. A good many of the chapters are dated, and the very day of the month is usually mentioned, and the years are reckoned from Jehoiachin's captivity.

4. Summary. The book may be thus divided: *Part I* contains those prophecies which were uttered before the destruction of Jerusalem to disabuse the people of all false hope of succour from Egypt, and to exhort them to sincere repentance in the prospect of certain judgement. It comprises Ezekiel's call; the general carrying out of his commission; the rejection of the people on account of their idolatry; the sins of the age in detail; the nature

of the judgement and the guilt which caused it (1–24). *Part II (a)* announces God's judgements on the seven heathen nations around, Ammon, Moab, Edom, Philistia, Tyre, Zidon, Egypt (25–32). This was largely written between the commencement of Nebu-chadnezzar's siege of Jerusalem and the news of its fall ; *(b)* foretells the re-creation of the land and people of Israel (33–9) ; *(c)* contains a vision of the restored temple, city, and country (40–8). There are no direct quotations from the book in the New Testament.

DANIEL

1. **Title.** The book bears as its title simply the name of the chief person in the stories that constitute the first half (1–6), who is also the recipient of the visions that constitute the last half of the book (7–12).

2. **Character of the Book.** In the Hebrew Bible Daniel stands quite apart from the prophetical books, forming one of the mis-cellaneous writings that constitute the third part of the Hebrew Canon. In the English Bible, which in this follows the LXX, it stands among the prophetical books. The position in the English Bible has helped to obscure the difference in character between Daniel and the prophetical books. Daniel, in virtue more par-ticularly of the contents of the second half of the book, belongs to a class of literature which was greatly cultivated during the three or four centuries immediately preceding the Apocalypse of John, and following the Christian era ; and which has contributed to the New as to the Old Testament. The greater number of the works of this Vision or Apocalyptic literature, however, failed to gain a place either in the Old (though 2 Esdras stands in the Apocrypha) or in the New Testament. A common method of writers of this school is to select some figure of ancient times as the recipient of the vision or revelation which, so far as it refers to matters between the time of the recipient of the vision and the author of the book, is, while in form prediction, in reality a survey of a history, and so far as it contemplates things beyond the time of the author is prediction alike in form and reality. Thus an apocalypse written between 170 and 160 B.C. is attributed to Enoch, an apoca-lypse written in the first century A.D. to Baruch, the disciple of Jeremiah, and an apocalypse and the second book of Esdras written at the beginning of the second century A.D. to Ezra. So the visions of the canonical book of Daniel, though written about 165 B.C., are ascribed to Daniel, a captive in Babylon, in the fifth century B.C. The narratives with which the book opens do not

purport to have been written by Daniel, but to be stories of which he is the leading character. These stories, which are didactic in character, have their parallels in other Jewish and Biblical literature, e.g. Esther. The first part of the book is in various ways linked with the second ; for example, both are written partly in Aramaic, partly in Hebrew ; and the first part contains in the interpretation of Nebuchadnezzar's dream (c. 2) an apocalyptic element.

3. **Date and Purpose.** The date of the book is defined by the point at which historical survey under the form of prediction passes over into actual prediction ; this is shortly before the death of Antiochus Epiphanes in 164 B.C., for the defilement of the Temple, the cessation of the Jewish daily service, and the erection in the Temple of an altar to Zeus Olympius (Dan. 11^{31}, 8^{14}, 2 Macc. 6^2, 1 Macc. $1^{54,\,59}$) seem to belong to the historical survey, whereas the death of Antiochus still appears to belong to the future and to be a matter of actual prediction (11^{45}). The Book written under these circumstances had as its purpose the encouragement of the Jews, sorely tried by Antiochus' attack on their religion as described in the Books of Maccabees ; and the author sought to achieve this purpose (1) partly by the stories of those who stood firm to their religion under severe trials, like the three youths cast into the fiery furnace for refusing to bow down to the image set up by Nebuchadnezzar, or Daniel cast into the den of lions for maintaining his daily habit of prayer to God ; and partly (2) by contrasting the power of the Most High with the impotence of the most exalted and proud earthly monarchs and (c. 4) the everlasting Kingdom of God which is to be given to His saints with the passing empires of men (2, 6–12).

4. The traditional view was that the entire book was written not merely about but by Daniel in the sixth century B.C., and this view has found defenders down to the present time. Into the various details which, apart from the general character of the book (see above), have led to an increasing recognition of the untenability of this theory, and into the explanations offered in defence of them it is impossible to enter fully ; it may suffice to refer to two : Belshazzar is addressed by the queen both as king and as son of Nebuchadnezzar (5^{10-11}) ; it is urged that Babylonian tablets shew that Belshazzar is a historical figure and was in the last days of Babylon admitted to a share of the government : but the inscriptions also shew (1) that Nabonidus, not Belshazzar, was the last king of Babylon ; and (2) that Belshazzar was the son of Nabonidus, and neither the son nor, so far as is known, even a

descendant of Nebuchadnezzar. Again, the last 'Chaldæan king' —Nabonidus, as we have seen and not Belshazzar by name—yielded his kingdom not to Darius the Mede (5^{30}, 6^1) but to Cyrus the Persian. It now seems to most more probable that these inaccuracies, which do not really in any way interfere with the purpose of the book, are due to the remoteness of the writer from the time he describes than that a Babylonian queen was unaware which king of Babylon was her husband's father, and that a contemporary writer should give the wrong name and description of the king who overthrew the Babylonian empire.

5. **Daniel and the New Testament.** The influence of Daniel over the New Testament is far greater than is represented by one explicit reference to it (Matt. 24^{15} = Mark 13^{14} = Dan. 12^{11}). Its influence may for example be traced in the description of the Son of Man (cp. e. g. Matt. 26^{64} with Dan. 7^{15}). The explicit reference to a resurrection and the naming of angels (Michael 10^{13}, Gabriel 8^{16}: cp. Rev. 12^7, Luke 1^{19}) illustrate important transitions from the beliefs of the earlier parts of the Old Testament to those of the New Testament.

HOSEA

1. **Hosea** (*He hath saved*) belonged to the northern kingdom. He began to prophesy towards the close of the reign of Jeroboam II, i.e. before the overthrow of the house of Jehu (1^4), which took place about 746 B.C., and continued to do so during the anarchic period of the kings that followed till perhaps about 735 B.C. In spite of the external prosperity of the reign of Jeroboam II, there were corrupting influences at work, and these asserted themselves during the anarchy which succeeded his death. The kings were profligate ; the priests had failed to teach the knowledge of God, with the moral results indicated in chapter 4 ; God was forgotten, and the rulers looked to Assyria or to Egypt for help in their misfortunes.

2. **Style.** The illustrations employed by Hosea are taken from rural and domestic pursuits, such as the snaring of birds, sowing, reaping, threshing, and baking bread. He gives us an insight into the modes of life of that day. The women are decked with ear-rings and jewels ; the feasts and Sabbaths are days of mirth ; the people sacrifice on mountain tops, and burn incense on hills 'under oaks and poplars and elms'; while the priests, forgetful of their functions, 'lie in wait as troops of robbers' and murder in the way towards Shechem (6^9). With the exception of the narratives in 1^1–2^3, 3 the book consists of prophetic poems.

3. The Contents fall into two main divisions :—*Part I* (1–3) gives us the key to the imagery which colours all the prophet's language afterwards. The unfaithfulness of his wife, who had borne him two sons and one daughter, was a symbol of the idolatry of the nation in the sight of God. Degraded as she had been, so should ' the nation be many days without king, without prince, and without sacrifice, and without ephod or teraphim, till the day that they returned, and sought the Lord their God ' (3⁴, ⁵). *Part II* (4–14) consists, under the most vivid imagery, of accusations general and special against Israel for their sins, which the prophet denounces unsparingly; their dishonesty, idolatry, distrust of God, and unwillingness to return to Him.

4. The Quotations from the book in the New Testament are important. Our Lord quotes the words, ' I will have mercy and not sacrifice' (6⁶, Matt. 9¹³) ; and refers (Luke 23³⁰), as does also St. John (Rev. 6¹⁶, 9⁶), to the striking metaphor, ' They shall say to the mountains, Cover us, and to the hills, Fall on us' (10⁸). St. Matthew applies Hos. 11¹, ' I called my son out of Egypt', to the return of the Holy Child from Egypt (Matt. 2¹⁵); and St. Paul applies, in Rom. 9²⁵, ²⁶, in a very striking manner the names which the prophet gives to his children (Hos. 2²³).

JOEL

1. Joel (*Jehovah is God*), the son of Pethuel (1¹), prophesied at a date not directly stated in the book or elsewhere. Some have placed him in the ninth century, so making him the earliest of the prophets whose writings have survived. More probably he prophesied after the Dispersion of the Jews (3²), perhaps about 400 B.C.

2. The Contents range themselves under two main divisions. (*a*) In *Part I* (1–2¹⁷) the prophet describes an impending visitation of locusts and drought, which may be regarded as a figurative picture of threatened invasions ; and he exhorts the people of Judah to repentance, fasting, and prayer to avert these calamities. (*b*) In *Part II* (2¹⁸–3²¹) he promises a blessing in their stead, and the outpouring of the Spirit on all flesh ; and declares that while there shall be a judgement of the heathen in the valley of Jehoshaphat, there shall be a blessing reserved for Judah, and while Edom and Egypt shall be wasted, ' Judah shall abide for ever, and Jerusalem from generation to generation ' (3²⁰, R.V.).

3. Quotations. St. Peter (Acts 2¹⁶⁻²¹) on the day of Pentecost alludes to the promised outpouring of the Spirit upon old and young, servants and handmaids (Joel 2²⁸, ²⁹) ; and St. Paul in his

Epistle to the Romans (10^{13}) quotes the promise of the call of the Gentiles (Joel 2^{32}).

AMOS

1. Amos (a derivative from the word meaning *to bear a burden*) was a native of Tekoa in Judah, about twelve miles from Jerusalem, a 'herdsman and a dresser of sycomore trees' (7^{14}). In the reign of Jeroboam II, king of Israel, and Uzziah, king of Judah, he was sent to Beth-el to prophesy against Israel. Accordingly he presented himself in the royal sanctuary of Beth-el, to encounter not the king, but the priest Amaziah, who warned him off the sacred precincts. Thereupon Amos denounced to Amaziah the coming of a day, when, captured by the Assyrian invaders, his wife should be reduced to earning her living by infamy (7^{17}), his sons and daughters should be slain by the sword, and Israel should go into captivity, and the priest himself should die in a polluted land. After delivering his message at Beth-el in rebuke of the prevalent vices (extreme luxury, revelry, and debauchery, combined with cruelty and oppression of the poor), he returned to Tekoa, and there, as we may suppose, committed to writing the prophecies which he had spoken at Beth-el.

2. Style. The peasant-prophet and tree-dresser is a true 'child of nature'. The imagery of his visions is full of country life. We have the 'lion roaring in the forest' (3^4); the shepherd rescuing 'out of the mouth of the lion two legs, or a piece of an ear' (3^{12}); the 'bird falling into a snare' (3^5); 'blasting and mildew' (4^9); the 'hooks' of the fisher (4^2); 'rain within three months of the harvest' (4^7); dangers from 'lions and bears' (5^{19}); 'the king's mowings' and 'the latter growth' (7^1); 'corn sifted in a sieve' (9^9); 'the plowman, the reaper, and the treader of grapes' (9^{13}); 'a cart pressed that is full of sheaves' (2^{13}, R.V. marg.). The prophet shews also a knowledge of the great historical movements not only of his own, but of other nations ($1, 2, 9^7$). The narrative in 7^{10-17} is prose : most of the remainder of the book, poetry.

3. Summary. I. ($1, 2$) A long prophetic poem with refrains in which the prophet denounces the sins, especially the inhumanity, of the nations bordering on Israel and Judah—Syria, Philistia, Tyre, Edom, Ammon, and Moab—and at greater length, of Israel itself. II. ($3-6$) The iniquities of Israel, the elect people of God (3^2), and the coming punishment of them. III. (7^1-9^{10}) In five striking visions ($7^{1,4,7}, 8^1, 9^1$) he sketches the impending punishment of Israel which he predicted to Amaziah. IV. (9^{11-15}) Words of hope and promise, depicting the raising up of the fallen tabernacle

of David, and the final restoration of God's people (cp. Amos 9^{12} with Acts 15^{15-17})—possibly later than the age of Amos.

OBADIAH

1. **Obadiah** (*worshipper of Jehovah*) bears the same name as the minister of Ahab, who protected the prophets of the Lord (1 Kings 18), and many other persons mentioned in the Old Testament. Of his personal history we know absolutely nothing.

2. **Date.** A considerable part of this brief book reappears in Jeremiah : Obad.$^{1-4,\ 5,\ 6,\ 8}$ = Jer. $49^{14-16,\ 9,\ 10a,\ 7}$. This has caused a doubt which of the two prophets repeated the denunciations of the other; and therefore the exact date of Obadiah is rendered uncertain, some advocating its priority to that of Jeremiah, others ascribing it to a later date. Dr. Pusey maintains that the Hebrew future determines the question in favour of the priority of the Book of Obadiah. Those who take the opposite view conjecture that the occasion of this prophecy was the hostility shown by the sons of Esau to their brethren the Israelites at the time of the Babylonish invasion. They seem to have rejoiced in the downfall of Jerusalem, and to have cut off those Jews who attempted to fly through Idumæa into Egypt. Hence arose the prayer of the Jewish captives in Babylon (Ps. 137^7), and the answer to it in the denunciations of Obadiah, who predicts the Divine retribution on Edom, and the future glory of Israel in the occupation of Idumæa. It is possible that the literary problems of this brief prophecy call for a more complex theory, but this cannot be considered here.

3. **Summary.** The prophecy contains two parts. (i) The first part denounces destruction to Edom, sketching its punishment and the guilt that had called down that punishment (vv. 1–16) ; (ii) the second part predicts the future restoration of Israel, who, after their return, should possess the land of Edom and Philistia, and rejoice in the establishment of the kingdom of Jehovah (vv. 17–21).

JONAH

1. **Jonah** (*dove*), the son of Amittai, who was born at Gath-hepher, a village in Zebulun, is said to have been sent as prophet to Jeroboam II to announce the victories which should cast a gleam of prosperity over his reign (2 Kings 14^{25}).

2. **Nature and Date of the Book.** But the prophecies referred to in 2 Kings are not contained in the Book of Jonah, which indeed contains no prophecy beyond the brief prediction in 3^4.

Thus the book, unlike those with which it is grouped, is not a book of prophecies, but a story about a prophet. Neither the author of the story nor the age when it was written is defined ; but it may be inferred that it was not written before the fifth century B. C. ; the overthrow of Nineveh (612 B. C.) seems already past, and language and other considerations point to a relatively late date.

3. Summary of the Book. I. Commissioned to proceed to Nineveh, the capital of Assyria, Jonah hastens to Joppa, and takes ship for Tarshish, or Tartessus, on the south coast of Spain. A furious storm arises, and the mariners at his own request fling him into the sea. Here a great fish swallows him, and he remains in its belly three days and three nights (c. 1). II. He prays earnestly, and the sea-monster casts him forth on land (c. 2). III. Bidden a second time to go to Nineveh he dares not disobey, and proclaims there his message, 'Yet forty days, and Nineveh shall be overthrown'. King and people repent. Their penitence is accepted, and the judgement is deferred (c. 3). IV. Disappointed and angry, the prophet sits in a booth of woven boughs outside the city, waiting in vain for the judgement he had denounced, and the book closes with an exhibition of his petulance and God's tender mercy even towards the heathen (c. 4).

4. The Value of the Book consists in the nobility of the ideas conveyed by means of the story. 'The Book of Jonah is not actual history, but the enforcement of a profound religious truth nearer to the level of the New Testament than anything else in the Old, and cast in the form of Christ's own parables. . . . The purpose of the parable, and it is patent from first to last, is to illustrate the mission of prophecy to the Gentiles, God's care for them, and their susceptibility to His word ' (G. A. Smith).

5. Allusions in the New Testament. Twice does our Lord allude to incidents recorded in this book. In reply to the Pharisees asking for 'a sign from heaven', He gives them a sign from beneath, and declares that the swallowing up of Jonah by the sea-monster and his restoration to life after apparently certain destruction was a figure of His own resurrection from the grave (Matt. 12⁴⁰, 16⁴). He also declares that the repentant Ninevites shall stand up in the judgement and condemn 'the children of the kingdom', who had so many privileges and improved them not (Matt. 12⁴¹).*

---

* See Bishop Ellicott's *Christus Comprobator*, pp. 166, 167.

MICAH

1. Micah (*who is like* (*unto Jehovah ?*)) was a native of Moresheth-gath, in the Shephelah or low-lying plain of Philistia (Mic. 1^{14}). He flourished in the latter part of the eighth century B. C., during the reigns of Jotham, Ahaz, and Hezekiah, and was contemporary with Isaiah. Jeremiah expressly refers to him, and tells us how on one occasion, when in danger of his own life on account of his announcement that the Temple and Jerusalem would be destroyed, he was saved by an appeal to the precedent of 'Micaiah the Morashtite', who was spared by Hezekiah in spite of a similar bold testimony (Jer. 26^{8-24}, R.V.).

2. Summary. The prophecies in this book fall into three sections, each opening with 'Hear ye'. (*a*) In Section I (1–3) *threatening* predominates. The advent of Jehovah is denounced for judgement of the sins of Israel and Judah, and the guilt which rendered it necessary is described, especially that of the false prophets. (*b*) In Section II (4, 5) *promise* predominates: restoration is promised of Zion, of its temple, and of its people, with a gathering in of all nations under the sovereignty of the Messiah. (*c*) In Section III (6, 7) *the sadder tone* again prevails: we have a magnificent colloquy between Jehovah and His people; a justification of His government of the nation, and an assurance that in the midst of judgement He will remember mercy. Much in Sections II and III may be of later date than Micah, and 4^{1-4} = Is. 2^{2-4}.

3. The Chief Quotations in the New Testament from the book are (i) the prediction of Beth-lehem Ephratah as the birthplace of the Messiah (5^2), quoted to Herod by the Jewish rulers (Matt. $2^{5,\ 6}$) and elsewhere by some of the multitude (John 7^{42}); (ii) the strife in families (7^6), quoted Matt. 10^{36}, Mark 13^{12}.

NAHUM

1. Nahum (*consoler*), 'the Elkoshite', was a native of Elkosh, a little village in Galilee, or according to some commentators, identical with Alkosh about thirty miles to the north of Môsul. He prophesied after 667 B. C., the date of the sack of Thebes (No-Amon), to which he refers, and before, probably immediately before, the fall of Nineveh in 612 B. C.

2. Scope of his Prophecies. Whatever his precise date, he comes forward as a *consoler* from Jehovah, foretelling the overthrow of Assyria. It is the peculiarity of his prophecy that it is

devoted to a single theme, the coming destruction of Nineveh, the capital of Assyria, which was not yet deprived of its long dominance, and from which Judah for a century past had suffered so severely. Directly of Judah he has scarcely anything to say.

3. **The Prophet's Country.** Those who identify Elkosh with Alkosh consider him to have been the son of an Israelite captive. They hold that the prophet could not have described the doom of Nineveh in language so pictorially vivid if he had not drawn the scenes from personal observation, and point to the interspersion of Assyrian words in his book as indicating that country to have been the scene of his prophecies. But others deny that internal evidence favours any other than a Palestinian origin of the work, which accords with the greatest weight of external evidence.

4. **Summary.** On Nineveh, notorious for brutal violence, cruelty, and bloodshed, its blasphemy and hostility against God, Nahum pronounces sentence. Its destruction was near, and would be swift and complete. There are three very distinct predictions : (i) A general description of God in judgement, containing parts of an alphabetic poem (c. 1) ; (ii) the certain fall of Nineveh, with a vivid picture of the siege and sack of the city, aided by the sudden inundation of the Tigris (2) ; (iii) its utter destruction and desolation (3) — a desolation so complete that Nineveh vanished entirely from view, and Alexander could march over it, ' not knowing that a world-empire was buried under his feet ' ; nor was the city ever seen again till in modern times the labours of Botta, Layard, and others revealed to the world the wrecks of its former splendour.

HABAKKUK

1. **Habakkuk** (*close embrace ?*). Of the prophet himself we know nothing ; from the musical directions attached to chapter 3, a Psalm, like so many in the Psalter, ' of the chief musician ', it has been precariously conjectured that he was a Levite. He prophesied not earlier than the last quarter of the seventh century B.C.

2. **Scope of the Prophecy.** Writing after the great reformation in the days of Josiah, the prophet had to sustain hope and to teach patience under difficult circumstances. Sincere repentance and earnest turning to God, the removal of the high places, the great national fast, had not brought the removal of the scourge of invasion which threatened the kingdom of Judah. The suffering of the chosen people of God from cruel, ruthless oppressors, ' fiercer even than evening wolves ', was a mysterious trial.

3. **Summary.** (i) In chapter 1 the prophet appeals to God, and asks how long the Most High will suffer His own people to suffer : in verses 5 ff. he describes the fierceness of the Chaldæans. (ii) In chapter 2 he stands upon his watch and waits for an answer ; and while he is told that 'the just shall live by his faithfulness', he is assured that the scourge shall be removed and the oppressor shall perish. Verses 9 ff., a series of 'woes'. (iii) In chapter 3 the prophet (if we follow the heading of the Psalm) breaks forth into a note of prayer, which introduces the great hymn of faith, recounting the miraculous deliverances of old as earnests of future ones, and closing with the vision of God's enemies prostrate, but faith exultant in the God of salvation.

4. **Quotations in the New Testament.** To Habakkuk belongs the special distinction of having furnished (2^4) to the Apostle Paul the text which in a different sense forms the keynote of the Epistles to the Romans and Galatians, ' the just shall live by his faith' (Rom. 1^{17}, Gal. 3^{11}). He is also quoted by the writer of the Epistle to the Hebrews (10^{38}), and in Acts 13^{41}.

ZEPHANIAH

1. **Zephaniah** (*Jehovah hath hidden*) was a great-grandson of Hezekiah (1^1). He tells us himself that he prophesied 'in the days of Josiah, the son of Amon, king of Judah'. We may fix the date of his prophecy at about the time of Jeremiah's call, i. e. about 626 B.C., before Josiah's reformation in 621 B.C. had suppressed Baalism, and ' the worship of the host of heaven upon the housetops' ($1^{4,5}$), which Zephaniah denounces.

2. **Summary.** The prophecy may be divided into three parts : (i) A denunciation of the idolatry of Judah and a description of the day of Jehovah (c. 1); (ii) a call to repent and so escape the judgement which is to fall on the Philistines, Moab, Ammon, Ethiopia, and Nineveh ($2^{1-3,7}$); (iii) promises to Zion of a day of restoration when the judgement of wicked nations is overpast (3^{8-20}).

HAGGAI

1. **Haggai** (*born at the feast ?*), the first of the prophets after the Exile, was a contemporary of Zerubbabel and Joshua, who led those that returned from Babylon, and of the prophet Zechariah, with whom he is mentioned in Ezra 5^1, 6^{14}. He was inspired by God to rouse the people to support Zerubbabel and Joshua in building the Temple.

2. **Date.** His prophecies consist of two chapters, and he has carefully preserved, even to the very day, the date of their com-

mencement. They all belong to the second year of Darius Hystaspes, 520 B. C., and were delivered in the sixth, seventh, and ninth months of that year, very probably orally in the hearing of the people at the festivals of the New Moon, and of Tabernacles, and the season of the autumn rains. They have all one object in view, to reprove the lethargy of the people and encourage the completion of the Temple.

3. **Summary.** The book divides itself into four sections : (*a*) *The First* (c. 1) rebukes the apathy of the people in not devoting themselves in earnest to the great work of restoration, and in listening to those who sought to persuade them that the time was not opportune for continuing the enterprise ; his words took effect, and on the twenty-fourth of the same month the people 'did work in the house of the Lord' (1^{12-15}). (*b*) *The Second* (2^{1-9}) encourages them with the assurance that the glory of the latter Temple shall be greater than that of the former. (*c*) *The Third* (2^{10-19}) promises them that from the day they commence in earnest the work of restoration, the defective harvests shall cease, and the years of drought and famine be changed into blessing. (*d*) *The Fourth* (2^{20-3}) contains a special word of encouragement for Zerubbabel to be up and doing in rebuilding the Temple. The key-words of his prophecies are worth noting. They are, *Be strong, be strong, be strong* (2^4) ; *Consider your ways, consider, consider* ($1^{5, 7}$, $2^{15, 18}$).

4. **Quotations in the New Testament.** Two passages of Haggai's prophecies are brought to mind by the New Testament. His words concerning 'the shaking of the heavens and the earth' are quoted in Heb. 12^{26}, and the promise to Zerubbabel that he should be as a signet-ring on the right hand, was accomplished when his name stood enshrined in both the genealogies of our Lord as one through whom 'the sure mercies of David' were preserved to the house of David (Matt. 1^{12}, Luke 3^{27}).

ZECHARIAH

1. **Zechariah** (*Jehovah hath remembered*) was the son of Berechiah and grandson of Iddo (Ezra 5^1, 6^{14}). Iddo was the head of one of the priestly houses (Neh. 12^{4-16}), and as he returned from the Exile with Zechariah, the prophet must have been a young man when he commenced his work. A contemporary of Haggai, he began to prophesy (Zech. 1^1) two months after Haggai's first prophecy, and continued during two years, encouraging the Jews to prosecute the erection of the National Sanctuary.

2. **Style of his Prophecies.** The object he has in view is the same as that which Haggai proposed to himself, the rousing of

the people from their lethargy. But his style is very different. In a series of *night-visions* received while the building of the Temple is going on, he seeks to rouse in the people a national enthusiasm for the great work.

3. Summary. The book consists of two distinct parts: 1–8 Zechariah's prophecies and visions; 9–14 anonymous prophecies. The first part, Zechariah's prophecies and visions, consists of (*a*) 1^{1-7} a call to repentance; (*b*) a series of visions. Vision i. *The four horse-men of Jehovah* (1^{7-17}). Vision ii. *Four horns and four smiths*, symbolizing the approaching judgement of the heathen (1^{18-21}, R.V.). Vision iii. *A man with a measuring line enlarging the boundaries of Jerusalem*, symbolizing the inclusion of the Gentiles (2^{1-9}). Vision iv. *The cleansing of the Priesthood*, and *the Advent of 'the Branch'* (3). Vision v. *The golden candelabrum*, symbolizing the restored com-munity, *fed by two olive trees*, representing the two heads of the com-munity, Joshua and Zerubbabel; possibly verses 6^b–10^a are mis-placed (4^{1-14}). Vision vi. *The flying roll*, or vengeance on the ungodly (5^{1-4}). Vision vii. *The woman pressed in the ephah and borne eastward*, symbolizing the departure of guilt from Judah (5^{5-11}). Vision viii. *The four chariots issuing from two brazen mountains*, or the course of Divine Providence (6^{1-8}). This section concludes with a command to make a crown for the 'Branch', i. e. Joshua, according to the present text, but originally perhaps Zerubbabel.

(*c*) After the last vision there is a pause of two years in Zechariah's prophetic activity. But in the fourth year of Darius, 518 B.C., the word of the Lord again comes to him. Certain people put a question about continuing to fast as they had done in the fifth month, on the tenth day of which the Chaldæans had set fire to Jerusalem. To them the prophet by the word of the Lord expounds the nature of a true fast (7), and the conversion of fasts into feasts of joy and gladness, when many nations shall encourage each other to go and worship at Jerusalem (8).

The Anonymous Prophecies (9–14) present greater difficulties than the rest of the book. On the questions of unity, date, and interpretation there have been many opinions. Many hold that there are two distinct prophecies (9–11 with 13^{7-9}, and 12–14), separated from one another by the formula in 12^1, which recurs in Mal. 1^1 and has preceded in Zech. 9^1; others maintain the unity of 9–14. As to date, Matt. $27^{9\,f.}$ cites Zech. $11^{10\,f.}$ as from *Jeremiah*; and many have sought for part at least of Zech. 9–14 a pre-exilic date, some placing it as early as the eighth century B.C. But the reference to Greece in 9^{13} implies a date later than Alexander (332 B.C.), and the probability that Zech. 9–14 contains at least a large post-exilic element is great. In general, like most post-exilic but unlike much pre-exilic prophecy, these chapters are chapters of promise; Judah, now subject to foreign rulers, is promised its own native king; now a despised and subject people, it is to become supreme with Jerusalem as the religious centre of the whole world.

4. **The References in the New Testament** to this prophet are numerous and important. The lowly king who comes riding on an ass (Zech. 9^9) is quoted in Matt. $21^{4,\,5}$, John 12^{14-16}; the betrayal of the Good Shepherd ($11^{12,\,13}$) for thirty pieces of silver, in Matt. 27^9; 'they shall look unto me whom they have pierced' (12^{10}, R.V.) in John 19^{37}; the fate of the Shepherd of the sheep (13^{7-9}), in Matt. 26^{31}, Mark 14^{27}.

MALACHI

1. **Malachi** ('*my messenger*', cp. 3^1, from which the name may be an inference), though his book stands last in order of the prophetical books, was not the latest prophet whose writings survive. Of his life and personal history no single fact is recorded. It seems probable that he was of the priestly order, or had close relations with the priesthood.

2. **Time of Composition.** Internal evidence is conclusive in favour of his having written in the period after the Exile. The indications have been held to point in particular to the days when Nehemiah was absent for twelve years at the court of Artaxerxes, and the abuses which that governor had sought to check had broken out afresh, and the mixed marriages and profanity of the priests had again become conspicuous. (Cp. Mal. 2^8 with Neh. $13^{15,\,29}$, Mal. 2^{10-16} with Neh. 13^{23-7}.) We should in this case place the beginning of his prophecy about 435 B. C. Others date the prophecy about 460, shortly before the arrival of Ezra.

3. **Summary.** In the LXX and Vulgate the book consists of four chapters, as in our Version, but in the Hebrew chapters 3 and 4 form but one. The prophecy divides itself into three sections: I. After dwelling on the affection of God for Judah as a loving father and ruler of His people, he rebukes the priests as the leaders of the spiritual defection ($1-2^9$). II. He rebukes the mixed marriages and divorces, portrayed by the deserted wives weeping at the altar (2^{10-16}). III. He predicts the coming of a faithful Messenger, who shall carry out a sifting of the true ore from the dross in Israel, purge their silver and gold as in a furnace; and bids them *remember* the Law of Moses, and *look forward* to the advent of Elijah before 'the great and dreadful day of the Lord' ($2^{17}-4^6$).

4. In the New Testament we have three prominent references to the prophecy of Malachi. His prediction (1) of the Messenger of the Covenant (3^1), in Mark 1^2, Luke 1^{76}, 7^{27} ; (2) of the coming of the prophet Elijah (4^5), in Matt. 11^{14}, 17^{12} ; (3) of the approach of the Day of the Lord (4^{1-3}), in Matt. 3^{12}. Also, the love of God for Jacob in preference to Esau ($1^{2,\ 3}$), in Rom. 9^{13}. The last prophetic book of the Old Testament closes with the promise of the forerunner of the New.

IX. THE CHIEF PERIODS OF OLD TESTAMENT HISTORY

1. The Primeval Period.

THE Book of Genesis opens (cc. 1–11) with Hebrew stories (largely as we now know derived from Babylon and not to be regarded as history) of the Creation of the World, of the increase of mankind, of the origin of cities and of human crafts, of the Deluge, of the descendants of Noah, and of the distribution of mankind into various races and families and their dispersion over the earth. All this according to the Biblical chronology occurred within a little over two thousand years (see below, pp. 92 ff.).

2. The Patriarchal Period.

From Genesis 12 onwards Biblical history becomes primarily the history of the chosen people, Israel. But before the history of the nation lay the history of certain individuals from whom the Hebrews traced the descent of the whole or parts of the nation—Abraham, Isaac, Jacob and his sons, especially Joseph. How great the element of actual history of individuals in the stories of the patriarchs may be is uncertain; to some extent an idealizing element has to be recognized, to some extent also the fortunes or movements of tribes rather than of individuals. In Gen. 14 Abraham appears as a contemporary of Amraphel, king of Shinar (i. e. Babylon); if Amraphel is identical with Hammurabi, king of Babylon, c. 2100, this fixes the date of the beginning of the patriarchal period, which as described in Genesis extends over four generations. The age of Joseph cannot be independently determined, for the king or Pharaoh of Egypt with whom he was contemporary is not defined. Between Joseph and the beginning of the Mosaic period there elapsed, according to certain statements, three generations (four from Jacob): see Gen. 15^{16} and the genealogy of Levi (see p. 92).

3. The Mosaic Period.

The history of the Hebrew *nation* first clearly opens in the age of Moses, and with the Exodus from Egypt of those Hebrews who for a period that cannot be closely determined had been resident there. The Exodus which, on the older chronology, was placed in the sixteenth century B.C. is now more commonly placed towards the end of the thirteenth century B.C. For a period, regarded in the Hebrew narratives as a generation, the Hebrews under Moses are nomads in the desert country between Egypt and Palestine; two centres stand out in particular, Sinai and Kadesh, the latter being some 50 miles south of Beersheba.

4. The Period of Settlement in Canaan, and of the Judges.

To the nomadic period of Hebrew history succeeds the period of conquest and settlement in Canaan; this was not a brief process as the Book of Joshua suggests, but prolonged (Judges 1). Gradually various sections of the people made good their footing in various parts of the country, but not in all cases remaining permanently where they first attempted to settle (Dan); and in course of time they obtained the upper hand over and absorbed the Canaanites with whom at first they merely shared the country; and indeed, it was not until the reign of David, who had to expel the Jebusites from Jerusalem before he could make it his own capital, that the conquest was complete. Throughout this period, covering perhaps about two centuries, there was an absence of any sustained national unity, the 'Judges' being rather leaders of individual tribes, or combinations of tribes, than governors of all Israel.

5. The Period of the United Monarchy.

For a period of nearly a century, and under three kings, Saul, David, and Solomon (from about 1020–930 B.C.), the Hebrew people were united, though even within this period a cleavage between North and South, or Israel and Judah, more than once threatened or for a time took place—when after Saul's death Ish-bosheth reigned at Mahanaim and David at Hebron (2 Sam. 2$^{8ff.}$–3), and, again, later in David's reign (2 Sam. 19^{41}–20).

6. The Period of the Two Kingdoms.

After Solomon's death (*c.* 930 B.C.) this cleavage became permanent; the Hebrew people became divided into two distinct communities, the people of the South, mainly consisting of the tribe of, and commonly called, Judah, under kings of the line of David, the people of the North under kings of several different lines, chiefly those of the house of Jeroboam, the first king, of Omri (c. 885–842), and of Jehu (c. 842–746). As the southern kingdom throughout its history was ruled by a single line of kings, so it had but a single capital—Jerusalem; but the northern kingdom had at different times several, Samaria, the most famous, being the creation of Omri. The northern kingdom came to an end in 722 B. C., when it became a province of the Assyrian Empire.

7. PERIOD OF THE SOLE KINGDOM OF JUDAH.

Judah, after the fall of the northern kingdom (722 B. C.), retained its separate and native government, though it was tributary to Assyria and subsequently to Babylon. The kingdom of Judah came to an end with the destruction of Jerusalem and the captivity of a large part of the population of Judah in 586 B. C.

8. PERIOD OF THE EXILE.

Even after 586 B. C. a considerable Jewish population remained in Judah, but the religious and political leaders of the people were exiles in Babylon. This state of things continued till the capture of Babylon by Cyrus (539 B. C.).

9. PERIOD OF PERSIAN DOMINION.

By permission of Cyrus a considerable body of Jews, including Zerubbabel, a descendant of David, returned to Judah. Many of the children and grandchildren of the exiles of 586 B. C., however, preferred to remain behind in Babylonia; and from now onwards Jewish history continues to be the history of the Jews in Palestine and the history of the Jews abroad. Alike in Babylon and in Palestine, the Jews were during this period subjects of the Persian Empire. Within this period of some two centuries we have detailed information for two brief periods only—for the years 520–516 B. C., which witnessed the activity of Zerubbabel, of the high priest Joshua, and the prophets Haggai and Zechariah, and the rebuilding of the Temple, and for the years—on the more commonly accepted view of the chronology—458–432 B. C., which witnessed the activity of Ezra and Nehemiah and the acceptance of the Law as described in Nehemiah (8 f.). The period of Persian dominion over the Jews came to an end with the overthrow of the Persian Empire by Alexander in 333 B. C. Parts of the Old Testament belong to this 'Greek' period.

X. ITINERARY OF THE ISRAELITES TO THE LAND OF CANAAN

The Itinerary of the Israelites, as indicated in various places throughout the Pentateuch, or as given consecutively in Num. 33, may be divided into four parts:—

(*a*) The Exodus; (*b*) The Journey from the Red Sea to Sinai; (*c*) From Sinai to Kadesh; (*d*) From Kadesh to the borders of the Jordan.

It must, however, be remembered that there are some differences of view implied in different passages, and that the identifications, especially in (*b*), are for the most part quite uncertain.

(*a*) *The Exodus.*

Ex. 12[37] Num. 33[3]	1.	At **Rameses** the march begins on the fifteenth day of the first month, and the first halt is at
Ex. 12[37–39]	2.	**Succoth** (*Tell el-Maskhutah*), and so down the *Wady Tumilât* to
Ex. 13[20]	3.	**Etham** 'in the edge of the wilderness'. Thence, instead of proceeding N. and NE. towards Philistia, they are ordered to turn SE. to
Ex. 14[1–9] 1 Cor. 10[1, 2]	4.	**Pi-hahiroth**, between Migdol and the sea, over against Baal-Zephon. Here Pharaoh overtakes them, and they pass through the Red Sea to a spot often but not certainly identified with '*Ayûn Mûsa* ('The Fountains of Moses').

(*b*) *The Route to Sinai.*

Ex. 15[23–25] Num. 33[8]	1.	**Marah** ('*Ain-Hawwârah*) is the first halting-place in the Wilderness of Shur (Ex.) or Etham (Num.). Here the bitter waters are sweetened. Thence they proceed to
Ex. 15[27]	2.	**Elim** (*Wady Gharandel*). Here they find 12 wells and 70 palm-trees, and pass on to
Ex. 16 John 6[31, 49] Rev. 2[17]	3.	The **Wilderness of Sin**, and obtain the miraculous supply of quails and manna. Thence passing Dophkah and Alush, the sites of which are doubtful, they reach
Ex. 17[1–8] 1 Cor. 10[4] Ex. 17[13]	4.	**Rephidim** in the Horeb region, where occurs the murmuring of Massah and Meribah; water given from the rock in Horeb; the battle with the Amalekites, and the victory of Joshua. Leaving this station, they enter
Ex. 19[1] Ex. 18[5] Ex. 20 Ex. 32 1 Cor. 10[7] Ex. 40	5.	The **Wilderness of Sinai**, and encamp before 'the Mount of God' (*Jebel Mûsa*), where Jethro visits Moses. Here the Decalogue is given; the worship of the 'molten calf' takes place; the people are numbered; the 'Tent of Meeting' is erected, and the second Passover celebrated.

(c) *From Sinai to Kadesh-barnea.*

Ex. 19[1]		After a stay of nearly a year at Sinai, from the fifteenth day of the third month of the first year
Num. 10[11, 12]		after leaving Egypt until the twentieth day of
Num. 10[33]		the second month of the second year, they move three days' journey to
Num. 11[1–3]	1.	Tab'erah (*burning*), where their complainings bring down fire from heaven; and next to
Num. 11[1–34]	2.	Kibroth-hattá'ávah (*the graves of lust*), where the people are smitten, while the flesh of the quails is yet in their mouths. Thence they proceed to
Num. 11[35]	3.	Hazeroth. Here Aaron and Miriam sin, and Miriam is smitten with leprosy. The next station is
Num. 13[26]	4.	Kadesh-barnea. Hence twelve spies are sent to Canaan; ten bring back an evil report; Caleb
Num. 14[1–39]		and Joshua alone remain faithful. The people
1 Cor. 10[10]		murmur, and are condemned to wander forty
Num. 16		years in the Wilderness of Paran. Rebellion of Korah; earthquake; fire and plague inflicted.

(d) *From Kadesh-barnea to the Border of the Jordan.*

Num. 20[14–21]	1.	At the close of the 'forty' years Moses smites the
Num. 27[14]		rock at Kadesh; Miriam dies; Edom refuses the people a passage through Mount Seir, and they pass along the border of his territory to
Num. 20[24–29]	2.	Mount Hor, near Selah or Petra (Jos. Ant. iv. 4. 7). Here Aaron dies and is buried. Thence they pass down
Deut. 2[8] (R.V.)	3.	The Arabah by way of Elath and Ezion-geber (at
Num. 21[5–9]		the head of the Gulf of 'Akabah) round Mount
John 3[14]		Seir. The people murmur; the plague of ser-
1 Cor. 10[9]		pents; the setting up of the brazen serpent. Nothing is now known of their halting-places till they reach
Num. 21[12, 16, 18]	4.	Zared, and Beer-Elim (*the well of heroes*), celebrated for 'the song of the well'. Proceeding thence to
Num. 21[23, 24]	5.	Jahaz, they defeat Sihon, king of the Amorites, and at
Num. 21[33]	6.	Edrei, Og, the king of Bashan. These two victories give to Israel possession of the whole country east of Jordan, from the river Arnon to Mount Hermon. They next encamp at
Num. 33[49]	7.	Abel-Shittim (*the meadow* or *oasis of the acacias*), in the *plains of Moab*, i. e. the level country at the foot of the hills of Moab, east of Jordan over
Num. 22[4]		against Jericho. Here the Moabites, Ammonites,
Num. 23, 24		and Midianites under Balak ally themselves
Num. 25		against Israel; Balaam attempts in vain to curse
1 Cor. 10[9]		the people; apostasy of Israel; sensual rites of
Num. 31		Baal-peor; 24,000 slain by a plague; zeal of
Num. 31[8]		Phinehas; defeat of Midian; death of Balaam

Num. 31[12] Deut. 1[5] Deut. 32 Deut. 34[6]	on the battle-field. Expounding of the Law by Moses to the new generation of Israel. Moses delivers his last charge; recites his song; ascends Mount Nebo to view the land of Canaan; his death and burial.

XI. MIRACLES IN THE OLD TESTAMENT

Miracles.	*References.*
In Egypt.	
Aaron's rod turned into a serpent	Exod. 7[10—12]
The ten plagues :—	
1. Water made blood	—— 7[20—25]
2. Frogs	—— 8[5—14]
3. Lice	—— 8[16—18]
4. Flies	—— 8[20—24]
5. Murrain	—— 9[3—6]
6. Boils and blains	—— 9[8—11]
7. Thunder and hail	—— 9[22—26]
8. Locusts	—— 10[12—19]
9. Darkness	—— 10[21—23]
10. Firstborn slain	—— 12[29, 30]
Parting of the Red Sea	—— 14[21—31]
In the Wilderness.	
The curing of the waters of Marah . .	—— 15[23—25]
Feeding with manna	—— 16[14—35]
Water from the rock, at Rephidim . .	—— 17[5—7]
Death of Nadab and Abihu	Lev. 10[1, 2]
Burning of the congregation at Taberah .	Num. 11[1—3]
Death of Korah, Dathan, and Abiram, &c. .	—— 16[31—35]
Budding of Aaron's rod, at Kadesh . .	—— 17[8]
Water from the rock, at Meribah . . .	—— 20[7—11]
The brazen serpent	—— 21[8, 9]
Stoppage of the Jordan stream . . .	Joshua 3[14—17]
In Canaan.—Under Joshua.	
Fall of Jericho	—— 6[6—25]
Staying of sun and moon	—— 10[12—14]
Under the Kings.	
Death of Uzzah	2 Sam. 6[7]
Withering of Jeroboam's hand, and destruction of the altar at Beth-el	1 Kings 13[4—6]
By Elijah.	
The staying of the cruse of oil and meal at Zarephath	—— 17[14—16]
The raising of the widow's son at Zarephath .	—— 17[17—24]
The burning of the sacrifice on Mount Carmel .	—— 18[30—38]
Burning of the captains and their companies .	2 Kings 1[10—12]
Dividing of Jordan	—— 2[7, 8]

Miracles.	References
By Elisha.	
Dividing of Jordan	—— 2^{14}
Cure of waters of Jericho	—— $2^{21,\ 22}$
Destruction of mocking children at Beth-el . .	—— 2^{24}
Supply of water to the allied armies in Moab .	—— 3^{16-20}
Increase of the widow's oil	—— 4^{2-7}
Raising the Shunammite's son . . .	—— 4^{32-37}
Healing the deadly pottage	—— 4^{38-41}
Feeding one hundred men with twenty loaves .	—— 4^{42-44}
Cure of Naaman's leprosy, and its transfer to Gehazi	—— $5^{10-14,\ 27}$
Making an iron axe swim	—— 6^{5-7}
Smiting the Syrian army	—— 6^{18-20}
Resurrection of dead man by touching Elisha's bones	—— 13^{21}
Recorded by Isaiah.	
Destruction of Sennacherib's army . . .	—— 19^{35}
Return of sun by the dial of Ahaz . . .	—— 20^{9-11}
During Captivity.	
Deliverance of the Three Children from the fiery furnace	Dan. 3^{19-27}
Deliverance of Daniel from the lions . .	—— 6^{16-23}
Miscellaneous.	
Smiting of Philistines, and fall of Dagon . .	1 Sam. 5^{3-12}
Smiting of Uzziah with leprosy . . .	2 Chron. 26^{16-21}
Deliverance of Jonah from the great fish .	Jonah 2^{1-10}

XII. PARABLES IN THE OLD TESTAMENT

Parables.	By whom spoken.	References.
The ewe lamb . . .	Nathan to David . .	2 Sam. 12^{1-4}
The two brethren, and avengers of blood . .	Widow of Tekoah . .	—— 14^{1-11}
Escaped captive . .	Man of the sons of the prophets to Ahab . .	1 Kings 20^{35-40}
Vineyard and grapes . .	Isaiah to Judah and Jerusalem . . .	Isaiah 5^{1-7}
Eagles and vine . .	Ezekiel to Israel . .	Ezek. 17^{2-10}
Lions' whelps . . .	,, ,, . .	—— 19^{2-9}
The boiling pot . . .	,, ,, . .	—— 24^{3-5}
Parabolic Fables.		
Trees choosing a king .	Jotham to Shechemites .	Judges 9^{7-15}
Micaiah's vision . .	. . . . .	1 Kings 22^{19-23}
Thistle and cedar . .	Jehoash to Amaziah . .	2 Kings 14^9

XIII. SPECIAL PRAYERS IN THE OLD TESTAMENT

Of whom recorded.	*References.*	*Subjects.*
Aaron and priests	Num. 6$^{22-26}$	The Aaronic blessing of Israel.
Abraham	Gen. 15^2	For a son.
Abraham	—— 17$^{17,\ 18}$	For Ishmael's acceptance.
Abraham	—— 18^{23}	For mercy on Sodom.
Abraham's servant	—— 24^{12}	Success in his mission, when sent to find a wife for Isaac.
Agur	Prov. 30^1	For moderation in his desires.
Asa	2 Chron. 14^{11}	When going to battle with Zerah the Ethiopian.
Daniel	Dan. 9^4	For restoration of Jerusalem.
David	2 Sam. 7^{18}	Prayer for blessing on his house.
David	Ps. 51	After his sin with Bath-sheba.
David	2 Sam. 24^{17}	After numbering the people.
David	1 Chron. 29$^{10-19}$	Thanksgiving at close of life.
Elijah	1 Kings 17^{20}	For the restoration of the widow's son.
Elijah	—— 18^{36}	For Divine attestation of his mission.
Elijah	—— 19^4	For death.
Elisha	2 Kings 6^{17}	For his servant's eyes to be opened.
Elisha	—— 6^{18}	That the army sent to take him may be blinded.
Ezekiel	Ezek. 9^8	Intercession for his people.
Ezra	Ezra 9^6	Confession of sin in the people's alliances with the heathen.
Habakkuk	Hab. 3$^{1-16}$	For revival of God's work.
Hannah	1 Sam. 1^{11}	For the gift of a son.
Hezekiah	2 Kings 19^{15}; Is. 37^{16}	For protection against Sennacherib.
Hezekiah	—— 20^3; Is. 38^3	When dangerously ill.
Hezekiah	2 Chron. 30^{18}	For the unprepared who had eaten of the Passover.
Israel	Deut. 21$^{6-8}$	Expiation of undiscovered murder.
Israel	—— 26$^{5-10}$	Confession on presenting first-fruits.
Israel	—— 26$^{13-15}$	The prayer of the tithing year.
Jabez	1 Chron. 4^{10}	For the Divine blessing.
Jacob	Gen. 32^9	For deliverance from Esau.
Jehoshaphat	2 Chron. 20^6	For protection against armies of Moabites and Ammonites.
Jeremiah	Jer. 14^7	In a great famine.
Jeremiah	—— 15$^{15-18}$	For comfort.
Jonah	Jonah 2^2	For deliverance from the great fish.
Joshua	Joshua 7$^{7-9}$	After Achan's sin.
Levites	Neh. 9^5	Confession of God's goodness, and their nation's sins.

Of whom recorded.	References.	Subjects.
Manoah . . .	Judges 13[8, 9] . .	For Divine guidance in training his child.
Moses . . .	Exod. 32[11] ; Deut. 9[26]	Forgiveness for the people's idolatry.
Moses . . .	—— 33[12] . .	For the Divine presence.
Moses . . .	Num. 10[35, 36] . .	At the setting forth and stopping of the ark.
Moses . . .	—— 11[11–15] . .	For Divine help to govern the Israelites.
Moses . . .	—— 12[13] . .	For Miriam, for cure from leprosy.
Moses . . .	—— 14[13–19] . .	For the people disappointed at the spies' report.
Moses . . .	—— 27[15] . .	For a successor.
Moses . . .	Deut. 3[24] . .	To enter Canaan.
Nehemiah . .	Neh. 1[5] . . .	For the remnant in captivity.
Nehemiah . .	—— 4[4] . . .	For protection against Sanballat and Tobiah.
Samson . . .	Judges 16[28] . .	To be avenged on his enemies.
Solomon . .	1 Kings 3[5–9] . .	For wisdom to govern Israel.
Solomon . .	1 Kings 8[23] ; 2 Chr. 6[14]	Dedication of the Temple.

XIV. THE PATRIARCHS AND THEIR DESCENDANTS

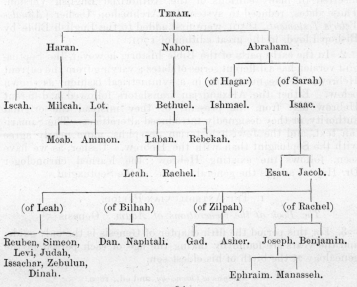

91

XV. LEVI AND THE PRIESTHOOD

XVI. CHRONOLOGY OF THE EARLY PERIOD OF OLD TESTAMENT HISTORY

Introductory.

1. The Chronology of the Old Testament, as given in the Hebrew text, is represented with much accuracy by the marginal dates inserted in many editions of the Authorized English Version. These dates, reduced to system by Archbishop Ussher (*Annales Veteris Testamenti*, 1650), were first added to the English Bible by Bishop Lloyd, in the great edition of 1701.

2. In the early parts of the Bible history, however, the Septuagint version has a different series of dates ; varying from the current Hebrew, for the most part, in a symmetrical fashion, as shown below.   Either the Alexandrian translators followed a different Hebrew text from the present, or they misread the original authority, or they designedly introduced alterations.   The Samaritan text, and the Jewish historian Josephus, more nearly agree with the Septuagint than with the Hebrew.   Ussher, as we have seen, follows the existing Hebrew ; the learned chronologer Dr. Hales * adopts the general scheme of the Septuagint.

I. The Antediluvian Period.
The Book of the Generations of Adam.   Genesis 5[1].

3. For this period the fifth chapter of Genesis is the only guide, and the years are found by taking the age of each person in the genealogy at the birth of his eldest son.

---

* *New Analysis of Chronology*, 2nd ed., 1830.

| | Age at birth of eldest son. | |
	HEBREW.	SEPTUAGINT.
Adam	130	230
Seth	105	205
Enos	90	190
Cainan	70	170
Mahalaleel	65	165
Jared	162	162
Enoch	65	165
Methuselah	187	167 *
Lamech	182	188
(Noah's age at Deluge)	600	600
Year from Adam (generally termed *Anno Mundi*) of the Deluge . . .	1656	2242

4. The reduction of these dates to the years B.C. (or A.C., *Ante Christum*) is found by reckoning backwards from dates to be here-after established ; as e. g. the division of the Hebrew monarchies. But owing to the uncertainties of the intervening period opinions of chronologers as to the 'era of Creation', implied by the Old Testament data, vary by many centuries (Ussher 4004 B.C., Hales 5411, Jewish reckoning 3760, Alexandrian 5503, &c.). The actual origin of the world is now recognized to be innumerable millennia earlier than the earliest of these dates.

2. FROM THE DELUGE TO THE CALL OF ABRAHAM.

The Generations of Shem. Genesis 11[10].

| | Age at birth of Firstborn. | |
5.	HEBREW.	SEPTUAGINT.
(Two years after the Deluge)	2	2
Arphaxad	35	135
Cainan (only in LXX †)		130
Salah . . . . :	30	130
Eber	34	134
Peleg	30	130
Reu	32	132
Serug	30	130
Nahor	29	179 ‡
Terah at Birth of Abram §	130	130
Abraham's age at his entrance into Canaan .	75	75
	427	1307

* Another reading gives 187. † And in Luke 3[37].
‡ Another reading gives 79.
§ According to the direct statement of Gen. 11[26], Terah was 70 years old at the birth of Abram : the figure in the table is obtained by deducting 75, Abram's age on leaving Haran, from 205, the age, according to the Hebrew text and the Septuagint, of Terah at his death in Haran : the Samaritan text gives Terah's age as 145 ; Gen. 11[32] ; 12[4].

6. Adding these results to those of the preceding Table we have the date, *anno mundi*, of Abraham's call, according to the Hebrew, 2083; according to the Septuagint, 3549. The date 2083 is Ussher's (Eng. Bible, marg. 1921 B.C.=2083 A.M.); the LXX date, on the other hand, is shortened by Hales to 3333 by computations which need not here be noted.

3. FROM THE CALL OF ABRAHAM TO THE EXODUS.

The sojourning of the children of Israel, which they sojourned in Egypt, was four hundred and thirty years. Exodus 12[40], R.V., according to Heb.

The sojourning of the children of Israel, which they sojourned in the land of Egypt, and in the land of Canaan, was four hundred and thirty years. Ib., LXX.

7. In the earlier dates of this series the Hebrew and Septuagint agree.

	HEBREW.	LXX.
Abraham in Canaan to birth of Isaac . .	25	25
Age of Isaac at birth of Esau and Jacob . .	60	60
Age of Jacob at the migration to Egypt . .	130	130
The sojourning in Egypt	430	215 (inferential)
Total for the period	645	430

Both Ussher and Hales here follow the Septuagint, which, however, is scarcely original. The Hebrew text in Exod. 12[40] agrees substantially with the 400 years mentioned in Gen. 15[13], and also with the statement (Gen. 15[16]) that the Exodus was to be 'in the fourth generation' after the migration into Egypt, if a patriarchal generation be reckoned at 100 years. The four generations from Jacob to Moses, if of normal length, would be far too few to fill up even the 215 years of the LXX.

4. FROM THE EXODUS TO THE FOUNDING OF THE TEMPLE.

In the four hundred and eightieth year after the children of Israel were come out of the land of Egypt, in the fourth year of Solomon's reign . . . he began to build the house of the Lord. 1 Kings 6[1].

8. This is a most difficult period in which to harmonize the several chronological references in Scripture with one another, or with other known facts. In general it may be said that the number of years mentioned in Kings is considerably in excess of the actual lapse of time between the Exodus and Solomon, and yet less than the sum of the separate numbers mentioned elsewhere in the Old Testament.

These separate numbers are:

Wanderings in the Wilderness	40 years
Sum of years mentioned in Judges 3^8, ^{11}, ^{14}, ^{30}, 4^2, 5^{31}, 6^1, 8^{28}, 9^{22}, 10^2, ^{3}, ^{8}, 12^7, ^{9}, ^{11}, ^{14}, 13^1, 15^{20}, 16^{31}	410 ,,
Eli's judgeship (1 Sam. 4^{18})	40 ,,
David's reign (1 Kings 2^{11})	40 ,,
To the fourth year of Solomon	4 ,,
	534 ,,

Apart from these numbered years, which are by themselves 54 years in excess of the 480 of 1 Kings 6^1, there are two considerable periods to which no length is assigned, viz. from the close of the wanderings to the death of Joshua, and from the death of Eli to the death of Saul (i.e. the greater part of the lifetime of Samuel and Saul). Two considerations serve to shew that for this period no exact chronological tradition survived: (1) the recurrence of the round number 40 (or $80 = 40 \times 2$, or $20 = \frac{40}{2}$), and (2) that the chronology assumes that the Judges were *successive* rulers of *all* Israel, which few, if any, of them were (see p. 40). If the Exodus took place in the reign of the Egyptian king Merneptah towards the end of the thirteenth century B.C., the actual period from the Exodus to Solomon scarcely exceeded 250 years.

XVII. CHRONOLOGY OF THE KINGS OF JUDAH AND ISRAEL

The Biblical data for this period are the explicit chronological statements chiefly in the Books of Kings and Chronicles. These assign to each reign its duration ; and, after the division of the kingdom, give cross-references to the times of the contemporary kings. But the lists of Israel and Judah do not agree. From the accession of Rehoboam to the sixth year of Hezekiah, the year of the destruction of Samaria, 260 years appear to be enumerated in the line of Judah, 241 in that of Israel. To meet this difficulty it has been suggested either (i) that there were in the Israelite line intervals of interregnum, so *lengthening* the period ; or, (ii) that in the line of David there were times of associated sovereignty— father with son—the years in the annals being counted to both, so *shortening* the period. Both interregna and co-regnancies there may have been; but no data exist for determining when they were, or for how long they continued ; and the hypothesis fails to meet all the difficulties presented by the Biblical data even when considered by themselves, still less when considered in connexion with the fixed dates now obtained within this period from the Assyro-Babylonian chronology. The first accurately determined date in the history of Israel is 854, in which year Shalmaneser King of Assyria records that Ahab King of Israel was defeated by him at Karkar: Ahab, then, was reigning in the year 854, and other Assyrian inscriptions shew that Jehu was king in 842, Menahem in 738, Ahaz in 734. It is further known that Samaria fell in 722, and that Sennacherib's retreat from Jerusalem took place in 701, and consequently that the interval between the two events was 21, and not as 2 Kings 18^{10,13} suggests, only 8 years.

In the following chronological table, which includes a few events prior to the monarchy in Israel, and the chief events of interest in connexion with the history of the Jews after the fall of the monarchy down to the age of Alexander, the dates which can be accurately determined are shewn in heavy type; the kings of Israel and Judah are mentioned mainly in groups with the number of years assigned to the reign of each in Kings added in brackets.

CHRONOLOGICAL TABLES

[The dates, except those printed in heavy type, are only approximate; the number in brackets following the name of a king of Israel or Judah is that given in the Books of Kings for the years of his reign.]

	Hebrew History.	*Foreign Nations.*
2100	(Abraham)	Hammurabi (? = Amraphel. Gen. 14), King of Babylon.
1479–1459	. . . .	Thothmes III of Egypt conquers Palestine.
1411–1375	. . . .	Reigns of Amenophis III and IV: decline of Egyptian power in Palestine. Tel-el-Amarna letters. Ḥabiri in Palestine.
1292–1225	Hebrews in Egypt	Rameses II builder of Raamses (Exod. 1^{11}): his campaigns in Palestine, and treaty with the Hittites.
1225–1215	(Moses. The Exodus) . . .	Merneptah, King of Egypt, 'desolates' Israel (in Palestine).
	Settlement of Hebrews in Canaan. 'The Judges.'	
1020	Saul.	
1010–970	David (40).	
970–930	Solomon (40).	

	Israel.	Judah.	Foreign.
930–854	Jeroboam I (22), Nadab (2), Baasha (12), Elah (2), Zimri (Tibri), Omri (12), Ahab (22).	Rehoboam (17), Abijah (3), Asa (40), Jehoshaphat (25).	Shishak, King of Egypt (about 945–924) invades Judah in the reign of Rehoboam.
854	Ahab and Benhadad of Damascus defeated by Shalmaneser II of Assyria at Ḳarkar.		
853–842	Ahaziah (2)	Jehoram (8).	
842	Jehoram (12)	Ahaziah (1).	
842	Accession of Jehu and Jehu pays tribute to Shalmaneser.	Athaliah	Syria and Palestine tributary to Assyria.
842–786	Jehu (28), Jehoahaz (17), Jehoash (6).	Athaliah (6), Joash (40), Amaziah (29).	
786–746	Jeroboam II (41).	Uzziah (52).	
746–736	Zechariah ($\frac{1}{2}$), Shallum ($\frac{1}{12}$), Menahem (10), Pekahiah (1).	Uzziah, Jotham (16).	
745	. . .	. . .	Tiglath-Pileser III, King of Assyria.
738	Menahem pays tribute to Tiglath-Pileser.		
735	Pekah (20)	Ahaz (16) .	Syro-Ephraimite attack on Judah.
734	. . . .	Ahaz pays tribute to Tiglath-Pileser.	
733	Hoshea (9).		
732	. . . .	. . .	Assyrians capture Damascus : end of the kingdom of Damascus.
727	. . . .	. . .	Shalmaneser V, King of Assyria.
727–698 (or 715–686)	. . . .	Hezekiah (29).	
722	Fall of Samaria : end of the kingdom of Israel.	. . .	Sargon, King of Assyria.

97

H

	Israel.	*Judah.*	*Foreign.*
712	. . . .		Sabako, first king of the 'Ethiopian' Dynasty (xxx) in Egypt.
711	. . . .	Judah, Egypt, Ashdod, &c. against Assyria.	Assyrians capture Ashdod (Isa. 20).
705	. . . . . .		Sennacherib, King of Assyria.
701	. . . .	Sennacherib's retreat from Jerusalem.	
		Judah.	
698 (or 686)	Manasseh (55).		
694	. . . .		Tirhakah, King of Egypt.
681	. . . .		Esar-haddon, King of Assyria.
671	. . . . . .		Assyrians capture Memphis.
668	. . . . . .		Asshurbanipal, King of Assyria.
667	. . . . . .		Assyrians capture Thebes (= No-ammon, Nah. 3^8).
641	Amon (2).		
639	Josiah (31).		
626	. . . . . .		Nabopolassas, King of Babylon.
621	Reformation of Josiah.		
609	Josiah slain at Megiddo by	. .	Pharaoh-Necho, King of Egypt.
608	Jehoahaz ($\frac{1}{4}$).		
612	Capture of Nineveh: and fall of the Assyrian Empire.		
607	Jehoiakim (11).		
605	. . . . . .		Nebuchadnezzar defeats Pharaoh-Necho at Carchemish. Nebuchadnezzar II, King of Babylon.
597	Jehoiachin ($\frac{1}{4}$). First siege of Jerusalem and deportation of Jews.		
596	Zedekiah (11).		
586	Destruction of Jerusalem by Nebuchadnezzar: second deportation of Jews.		
561	. . . . . .		Evil-Merodach releases Jehoiachin from prison (2 Kings 25^{27}).
556	. . . . . .		Nabonidus, last king of Babylon (till 539).

	Judah.	Foreign.
550	. . . .	Median Empire overthrown by Cyrus, King of Persia.
547	. . . .	Cyrus defeats Croesus, and destroys the Lydian Empire.
539	Return of Jewish exiles in Babylon to Judah.	Capture of Babylon by Cyrus.
529	. . . .	Cambyses, King of Persia.
525	. . . .	Cambyses in Egypt.
522	. . . .	Darius I, King of Persia.
520–516	Rebuilding of the Temple : Zerubbabel and Joshua.	
486	. . . .	Xerxes, King of Persia.
465	. . . .	Artaxerxes I, ,, ,,
458	Ezra comes to Jerusalem.	
444	Nehemiah's first visit to Jerusalem. Walls of Jerusalem rebuilt.	
432	Nehemiah's second visit to Jerusalem.	
425	Eliashib, high-priest (Neh. 13^{28}) .	Xerxes II, King of Persia.
424	. . . .	Darius II, ,, ,,
405	. . . .	Artaxerxes II, ,, ,,
359	. . . .	Artaxerxes III, ,, ,,
351–331	Jaddua, high-priest (Neh. 12^{11}).	
333	. . . .	Persian Empire overthrown by Alexander.

XVIII. CHRONOLOGICAL TABLE OF THE PROPHETS

The four Prophets placed first in our Bibles are called 'Major', the remaining twelve 'Minor', not because of their comparative importance, but because of their respective length. This classification being entirely conventional, and apt to mislead, may be disregarded. Daniel, as we have seen above, p. 70, was not reckoned by the Jews among the Prophets, but was placed in the Hagiographa between Esther and Ezra (including Nehemiah).

	Approximate Date B. C.	*Kings under whom they are said to have prophesied.*
(i) *Before the Babylonian Captivity.*		
Amos . . .	760	Jeroboam II of Israel ; Uzziah of Judah.
Hosea . . .	745–735	Jeroboam II (and successors).
Isaiah . . .	740–700	Uzziah, Jotham, Ahaz, Hezekiah.
Micah . . .	725–700	Jotham, Ahaz, Hezekiah.

	Approximate Date B. C.	Kings under whom they are said to have prophesied.
(ii) *Near to and during the Captivity.*		
Nahum . . .	613	
Zephaniah . .	630–620	Josiah.
Habakkuk . .	620–610	
Jeremiah . .	628–586	Josiah to Zedekiah.
Obadiah . . .	587	Soon after the destruction of Jerusalem.
Ezekiel . . .	592–572	Among the Jewish exiles : before and after the destruction of Jerusalem.
Isaiah 40–55 . .	540	
(iii) *After the Return from Captivity.*		
Haggai . . .	520	Rebuilding of the Temple.
Zechariah . .	520–518	Rebuilding and Dedication of the Temple.
Malachi . . .	460	

XIX. MODERN DISCOVERIES AND THE OLD TESTAMENT

1. The past century has been remarkable for the discovery and decipherment of monuments, and the exploration of Eastern lands, which have thrown much unexpected light on the Biblical narratives. Much has been won from discoveries particularly (i) in Egypt; (ii) in the valleys of the Euphrates and Tigris; (iii) in Palestine, and in the Sinaitic peninsula.

(1) EGYPTIAN RESEARCHES.

2. Until the Beginning of the Last Century our knowledge of the history of Egypt and its people was limited to what could be learned from the Bible, and from classical authors such as Herodotus and Diodorus Siculus, for though from the sixteenth to the end of the eighteenth century many attempts were made by learned men all over Europe to read the Egyptian inscriptions, copies of which had been published by such men as Kircher, they all failed. Each student professed to have discovered the key to the locked secret, but the translations which each gave to the world shewed at once that the patient and learned worker had not even found out what the problem to be solved really was, much less the solution thereof. The first good piece of work done in deciphering Egyptian inscriptions was that of Zoëga the Dane, who shewed that the hieroglyphs were

letters, and that each cartouche (i. e. the oval in which the name of a royal person is enclosed) contained a name. In the year 1799 a French officer named Boussard discovered a large black basalt stone at Fort St. Julien, near Rosetta, or the ancient Bolbitane, which from this circumstance has always been known by the name of the 'Rosetta Stone'. It was inscribed in hieroglyphics, Greek, and a third class of writing which is now called *demotic*, because it was the common writing of the people as opposed to the hieroglyphic which was the writing of the priests. The Greek inscription upon the stone was easily made out, and it was found to consist of a decree drawn up by the priests of Memphis in honour of Ptolemy V Epiphanes, who reigned about 198 B.C. It was at once evident that the Greek inscription on this stone was a translation of the hieroglyphics, and here, at last, the key of the secret was found. By the fortunes of war the Rosetta Stone was surrendered by the French to General Hutchinson, and it was subsequently presented to the British Museum. Accurate copies of the text were made forthwith, and distributed among the scholars of Europe. Among the earliest workers at the inscriptions were Silvestre de Sacy and Akerblad the Swede ; the former was able to identify in the demotic version the equivalents of the proper names in the Greek, and the latter succeeded in giving phonetic values to several of the demotic characters. In 1818 Thomas Young published the results of his labours on the hieroglyphic inscription on the Rosetta Stone, in which he assigned correct values to several hieroglyphics, and identified the hieroglyphic names of Ptolemy and Berenice. About the same time Champollion was engaged upon the decipherment of the hieroglyphics, and as he was better equipped than Young (e. g. in possessing a good working knowledge of Coptic), he succeeded in making out an alphabet of hieroglyphic signs, and in identifying a large number of cartouches : it is to him in particular that we must ascribe the honour of founding the science of Egyptology. His system was adopted by Lepsius in Germany and Birch in England, and the subsequent labours of Brugsch, De Rougé, and Chabas proved that it was based upon a sound method of induction and work. When it was once shewn that the Egyptian inscriptions could be read, the most important results were anticipated, and a new impetus was given to excavations in Egypt. The political representatives of the great countries of Europe made collections of antiquities in Egypt, and travellers spent much time and money in opening tombs and digging out ruins. The tombs have given up not only their dead, but with them the books which the Egyptians read, the furniture which they used in their houses, the ornaments and articles of the toilet of the Egyptian lady, the weapons of the warrior, the tools of the handicraftsman and labourer, the dice of the gambler, the toys of the child, and the portrait statues and figures of the men and women for whom they were made. The many-lined inscriptions upon the tombs give us their (often inconsistent) ideas about the future world, the judgement of the dead, the paradise of happy souls, and the transmigration of souls ; and they enable us to control the statements of those Greek writers who professed to understand and to describe with accuracy the difficult religion of the educated Egyptian. Briefly, the Egyptians believed that man possessed a soul (*ba*), a genius or 'double' (*ka*), and an intelligence (*khu*). The soul returned to the body after a long period of years, and the body was carefully preserved by means of bitumen, spices, and drugs, and laid in the tomb to await its arrival. After death the conscience, symbolized by the heart, was taken into the judgement-hall of Osiris, the god of the underworld and of the dead, to be weighed in a balance against righteousness or the Law. There were present at the weighing on behalf of the deceased his soul, his luck, and the goddesses who presided over his infancy. The weighing was watched by Anubis, the god of the tomb, and by the god Thoth, who reported the result to Osiris. On the centre of the beam of the balance sat the cynocephalus or dog-headed ape, whose duty it was to take care that the beam was exactly and evenly balanced. Near Thoth stood a monster, part crocodile, part lion, and part hippopotamus, called the 'Devourer', ready to make away with the heart in the event of its being condemned by the weighing. When the heart exactly balanced the Law this result was proclaimed by Thoth, and the deceased was decreed to be 'justified' or 'triumphant' and passed into everlasting life.

(2) BABYLONIAN AND ASSYRIAN RESEARCHES.

3. The Decipherment of the Cuneiform Inscriptions is due to Professors Grotefend, Lassen, and Sir Henry Rawlinson. Professor Grotefend deciphered the names of Cyrus, Darius, Xerxes, and Hystaspes, and thus obtained the true determination of nearly one-third of the entire Persian cuneiform alphabet. The results of his labours were announced at Göttingen in 1802, but not published till 1893. Professor Lassen assigned accurate values to twelve characters, and an account of his work was published at Bonn in 1836. In 1835 Major Rawlinson began to copy the cuneiform inscriptions at Hamadân, and having no access to the works of previous writers on the subject he deciphered independently the

names of Hystaspes, Darius, and Xerxes. In 1836 and 1837 he gave much time to copying the great trilingual inscription cut in the rock of Behistun, and in 1837 sent translations of the first two paragraphs, which recorded the titles and genealogy of Darius Hystaspes, to the Royal Asiatic Society. As these paragraphs would have been untranslatable by the systems of Grotefend and Lassen, and as subsequent investigations have proved beyond all doubt the general accuracy of the translation of the two hundred lines of the monument of Darius at Behistun, and of the values assigned to the characters of the Persian cuneiform alphabet, the credit of the decipherment of the cuneiform inscriptions is mainly due to Sir Henry Rawlinson. The Babylonian and 'Scythic' (Susian) versions of the trilingual inscription at Behistun subsequently formed the subject of the labours of Norris, Hincks, and Oppert ; and although each of these scholars was able to make philological discoveries in the course of his inquiries, and to supply information on points of detail, the net result of their work only proved the accuracy of Sir Henry Rawlinson's system of decipherment, which he had also applied to these versions. In the year 1842 M. Botta began to make excavations at Kouyunjik, the site of the ancient Nineveh, but meeting with little success here, he decided to excavate at Khorsabad. In 1845 Mr. (afterwards Sir Henry) Layard undertook excavations at Kouyunjik for the Trustees of the British Museum, and succeeded in uncovering the palaces of Sennacherib, Esar-haddon, and Assur-bani-pal, and in bringing to light the terra-cotta tablets which formed the great library founded by these kings at Nineveh, and of which some twenty-two thousand are now preserved in the British Museum. An examination of these tablets soon shewed that they consisted of historical inscriptions, astronomical reports and calculations, grammatical lists, &c., and scholars began to apply Sir Henry Rawlinson's system of decipherment of the Babylonian version of the Behistun inscription to the texts inscribed upon these tablets. Certain sceptics having stated that no genuine progress had been made in cuneiform decipherment, Sir Henry Rawlinson, Hincks, Oppert, and Fox Talbot determined to translate independently the historical inscription of Tiglath-Pileser I, inscribed on a cylinder found at Kal'at Sherkât, and to submit their versions to a committee for examination. The translations were at length made, and as there could be no suspicion of collusion, and as the translation of each scholar bore the marks of the individuality of the author, and as the general meaning given to the inscription by each scholar was the same, and as the general accuracy of this fourfold translation has been established by subsequent researches, it is proved once and for all that the system of cuneiform decipherment now in use is based upon a sure foundation. A large portion of the history of Babylonia and Assyria is now revealed to us, and the knowledge of the language of these countries has thrown much light upon the language, literature, history, and learning of the Jews. The excavations which have been carried on in Mesopotamia for the last eighty years have yielded the most valuable results; and the inscribed slabs, monolithic stelae, boundary stones, gate-sockets, bricks, seal-cylinders, and tablets, now preserved in the British Museum, afford an abundant supply of material from which Bible customs and language may be freely explained and illustrated. The cuneiform writing is, at least, as old as 3500 B.C., and there is evidence to shew that it was in use as late as 80 B.C. It is generally believed now that cuneiform writing was introduced into Mesopotamia by the Sumerians at a very remote period, and that it was adopted by the Semitic inhabitants of the country, who wrote their own language in it. Cuneiform writing was originally pictorial, but the modifications in the forms of the pictures which were necessary when inscriptions were carved in stone or impressed upon clay, caused the characters to assume the forms now familiar to us.

How widely the influence of Babylon extended and the Babylonian script was employed are strikingly illustrated by the discovery at Tel-el-Amarna in Egypt in 1887 of an extensive series of letters written in Babylonian and addressed to the Egyptian kings Amenophis III and Amenophis IV (c. 1414–1365 B.C.) by the rulers of various states in communication with Egypt or more largely by the governors of towns in Palestine appointed by the Egyptian government. Another great monument of early Babylonian civilization found outside Babylonia itself is the great block discovered at Susa in 1901 by M. de Morgan which contains a code of Babylonian laws comprising some 250 sections and dealing with a great variety of subjects (*Code of Hammurabi*).

(3) PALESTINE AND THE SINAITIC PENINSULA.

4. In the early part of last Century comparatively little was accurately known about Palestine. The student indeed had the Bible, Josephus, certain itineraries composed in early times, and the narratives of pilgrimages and crusades in the Middle Ages and the works of more recent travellers. But while sacred places were multiplied, comparatively few sites were identified on

intelligible principles, and there were no scientific inquiries into the physical geography of the land or into the ways of the people who inhabited it. But within the last century the writings of many distinguished travellers have awakened a keen interest in everything connected with Sinai and Palestine, and made the natural history and antiquities of the East a special pursuit. In 1865 the Palestine Exploration Fund was opened and excavations were begun in Jerusalem ; subsequently many other sites have been excavated under the same fund (Lachish, Gezer, Beth-shemesh, Ashkelon) or others (Jericho, Megiddo, Samaria). These excavations have brought to light comparatively little written material (among the more important Hebrew inscriptions being the Siloam inscription, a list of monks (Gezer) and a group of names of the age of Ahab from Samaria), but have revealed the implements and utensils used at various periods, the size and nature of the ancient cities, the external influences (Babylonian, Egyptian, Aegean) operating in ancient Palestinian life, and the burial and sacrificial customs &c. of the ancient inhabitants.

Geological investigations have also been made, natural history collections have been formed, inquiries into modern customs carried out, and above all a complete trigonometrical survey of Western Palestine set on foot by officers of the Royal Engineers, who have enabled us to localize towns, villages, hills, valleys, watercourses, wells, cisterns, notable trees, and other landmarks and remains. In 1868 a party of engineering officers and other experts left England to make a scientific survey of the Sinaitic Peninsula. This they effected, making plans and models, taking 300 photographs and 3,000 copies of inscriptions, with collections of specimens bearing on the zoology, botany, and geology of the country. The results of the enterprise were published in 1872, by authority of the Treasury, in five massive folio volumes.

(4) Other Fields.

Among other discoveries brief reference may be made to (1) The Sabaean and Minaean inscriptions discovered (since 1811), principally in South Arabia, and in largest numbers by J. Halévy (1869) and E. Glaser (from 1882) ; to (2) Aramaic inscriptions, scattered widely over the area of the ancient world, and ranging in date from the ninth century B.C. downwards, and Aramaic papyri from Egypt, especially an important collection of documents (fifth century B.C.) of a Jewish community in Elephantine at the southern extremity of Egypt ; (3) Phoenician and other Semitic inscriptions ; (4) the remains of Hittite civilization, especially the discoveries of Hugo Winckler (from 1906) at Boghaz-köi in Asia Minor. The Hittite inscriptions still await complete decipherment.

(5) RESULTS.

The results of the foregoing researches and discoveries may now be briefly indicated :

(i) *The Primeval Period.*

For this period the discoveries have been nothing short of revolutionary, revealing highly developed civilizations both in the Nile and the Euphrates valleys long before the date suggested by the Biblical chronology as that of the creation of the world. These discoveries have also shewn that much of the Hebrew narrative of the primeval period rests on earlier stories current in Babylonia ; and that alike the Biblical and the Babylonian stories are not history of the primeval period but simply very ancient stories of the beginnings of things (cp. above, pp. 29-30).

(ii) *The Patriarchal Age.*

Clearer knowledge has been obtained as to the position of Abraham's native place, *Ur of the Chaldees,* now represented by the Mound of Mugayyar in Southern Babylonia, about six miles from the Euphrates on its western bank ; and *Haran* or Kharran has been recovered, its important position recognized, its religious condition investigated. Of the patriarchs themselves, however, the inscriptions contain no record, though *names* identical or nearly identical with some of them (Abraham, Jacob-el) have been recovered, and if Amraphel in Gen. 14 be identical with Hammurabi, King of Babylon, the era of Abraham according to that document is fixed at about 2100 B.C. Egyptian monuments have also furnished numerous illustrations of the manners and customs implied in the story of Joseph in Egypt, as also of the internal and external history, the religious and civil observances of the times ; and mummies of the most ancient kings—some anterior to the patriarchal age—have been discovered. Not only is the history of Egypt and Babylonia during the patriarchal period (say about 2100-1250 B.C.) now known, but also in some important respects that of Palestine. Thus the letters discovered at Tel-el-Amarna in Egypt in 1887 and written (about 1400 B.C.) to the Egyptian court mainly from Palestine shew (1) from the fact that they are written in the Babylonian script and language that Palestine must before this time have been deeply affected by Babylonia, and (2) directly the relation at this period of Palestine with its numerous little city-kingdoms to Egypt. Excavations in Palestine have thrown light on early intercourse between that country and Egypt, the Aegean and Babylonia.

(iii) *Moses and the Exodus, and the Settlement in Canaan.*

For this period again the discoveries have (with one exception) yielded no fresh direct record of the people of Israel as a whole or Israelite individuals. The one exception is an inscription (discovered 1896) in which Merneptah, King of Egypt about 1225–1215, records that 'Ysirael is desolated, its seed is not'. For the rest, light has been thrown on sites mentioned in connexion with the residence of the Hebrews in Egypt or the Exodus (e. g. Goshen, Pithom). So, too, the position of the places and the boundaries of the tribes in Canaan have been more nearly ascertained. Moreover it is now known that a large number of the names of places in Canaan are more ancient than the Hebrew settlement in the country.

(iv) *The Period of the Kings.*

Monumental Inscriptions throw considerable light upon this period. Not only are the dynasties of the Egyptian kings at this epoch ascertained, but we find the invasion of Judah by Shishak recorded on the walls of Karnak, and we are enabled to trace the movements of Sabako (? = So, 2 Kings 17^{3-5}), Tirhakah (2 Kings 19^9), Necho (2 Kings 23^9), and Hophra (Jer. 44^{30}). The Moabite Stone, discovered in 1868 among the ruins of ancient Dibon, now in the Museum of the Louvre at Paris, is a monument erected by Mesha King of Moab in which he speaks of Omri and, as contemporary with himself, Ahab. But it is from Assyria and Babylonia that most light has fallen on this period.

The Assyrian Kings and their dealings with the kings of Israel and Judah are amply illustrated by the Assyrian monuments. *Assur-nasir-pal* (884–859 B.C.) ruled from Elam to Syria, and from Armenia to the Persian Gulf. *Shalmaneser III* (859–824 B.C.) records a victory in 854 B.C. over, amongst others, Dad'idri (i.e. Hadadezer) of Damascus and Ahab of the land of Israel : and in 842 over Hazael of Damascus : he also mentions receiving tribute in 842 B.C. from 'Jehu, the son of Omri'. *Adad-niran III* (810–782 B.C.) imposed taxes on various kingdoms, including the land of Omri (i.e. Israel). *Pul* (2 Kings 15^{19}) has been shewn to be the same as Tiglath-Pileser III. *Tiglath-Pileser III* (745–727 B.C.) mentions taking tribute from Rezin of Syria, Menahem of Samaria, Pekah, and Hoshea. *Sargon* (722–705 B.C.), named in Isa. 20^1, records his capture of Samaria (cp. 2 Kings 17^6) in 722 B.C. and his carrying away captive of the inhabitants of the kingdom of Israel: and his conquest of Ashdod in 711, and its allies, including Judah; he also reduced Merodach-baladan, King of Babylonia. Khorsabad was built by him. *Sennacherib* (Sargon's son, 705–681 B.C.) relates how, in a campaign undertaken to suppress a concerted revolt of Phoenicia, Philistia, and Judah, he attacked Hezekiah, took forty-six of his cities, shut him up in Jerusalem like a caged bird, built towers against him, gave his cities to the Philistines, imposed on him a tribute of thirty talents of gold and 800 of silver, and sent his daughters and his treasures to Nineveh (cp. 2 Kings 18$^{14-16}$). Sennacherib also warred against *Merodach-baladan*, incited the Babylonians and Elamites to revolt. Clay cylinders give an account of the reign of *Esar-haddon* (681–669 B.C.), and mention that he demanded of twenty-two kings of the Hittite country, including Manasseh, King of Judah, building materials for a new palace; he conquered the son of Merodach-baladan, and, invading Egypt, captured Memphis and defeated Tirhakah. *Assurbani-pal* (668–626 B.C.) again subdued Tirhakah and captured Thebes (No-ammon, Nahum 3^6); he also gained victories over his rebellious brother Shamash-shum-ukin, subject-king of Babylon, and over the armies of Elam and the surrounding regions. After his time the glory of Assyria faded, and with the fall of Nineveh, 612 B.C., perished.

The Neo-Babylonian Empire now comes to the front. This was founded by Nabopolassar and attained the climax of its magnificence and power under Nebuchadnezzar. Many inscriptions of these kings of Babylon survive, and serve to illustrate the terms in which Nebuchadnezzar and his city and empire are referred to in the Old Testament, though unlike the Assyrian inscriptions they contain no direct references to Jewish affairs.

(v) *The Persian Empire.*

Passing to the Persian Empire, we have first a tablet of the age of Nabonidus telling us that in his seventeenth year (539), on the third of Marchesvan (October), *Cyrus* entered Babylon and appointed Gobryas to be governor; secondly, a fragment of a cylinder of Cyrus, giving his own account of the taking of Babylon and also giving his ancestry, through his grandfather Cyrus, back to his great-grandfather Teispes. His forces are described as marching like the waters of a river; opposition comes to nothing before him—' he (Marduk) suffered him (Cyrus) without battle and conflict to enter Babylon . . . Nabonidus the king he delivered into his hand '; the gods are favourable to Cyrus, especially Merodach, Bel, and Nebo, and he shews himself devoted to them. The inscriptions shew clearly that there can have been no reign of *Darius the Mede* between those of Nabonidus and Cyrus, but that the kingship of Babylon passed immediately from Nabonidus to Cyrus. There is a large trilingual inscription of *Darius the son of Hystaspes* (the second king in succession *after* Cyrus) in whose reign the rebuilding of the Temple at Jerusalem was completed, at Behistun; in this Darius records the various revolts, including two on the part of Babylon, with the suppression of which the first year or two of his reign was occupied. Light has been cast on the large Jewish population that remained in Babylonia after the time of Cyrus by the discovery of quantities of business documents (especially at Nippur) which include a large number of Jewish names.

XX. ETHNOLOGY OF THE JEWS AND THE SURROUNDING NATIONS

1. The Hebrews were Semites, and are the accepted type of that race, whereto belonged also the Canaanites, Phoenicians, Syrians, Moabites, Ammonites, Arabs, Assyrians, and Babylonians. We know the languages of these races, and find them similar in their grammatical structure, and closely allied in their vocabularies. Western Asia (excluding Asia Minor), eastwards from the coasts of the Mediterranean and the Red Sea to the Zagros mountain-chain, which bounds Mesopotamia on the east, was anciently peopled, in the main, by peoples speaking a Semitic language, and at least for the most part, also belonging to the Semitic stock. Most important of the non-Semitic peoples of this region were the Sumerians, the pre-Semitic inhabitants of Babylonia, and the Hittites, who with their chief centres at Boghaz-keui in Asia Minor, east of the Halys, and Carchemish on the Euphrates, at times also settled in, or exercised influence far southwards into, Syria.

2. In Palestine excavations have traced in the earliest period the presence of a non-Semitic people at Gezer before *c.* 2600 B.C. In the Old Testament we hear of Rephaim, Horim, Avim, Emim, Anakim, Zuzim, as old inhabitants of Palestine displaced by later intruders. There are no means of determining with any certainty the ethnic character of the peoples so named, or, except approximately and in a general way, their habitats; for in dealing with the ancient races and tribes of the East we cannot speak of frontiers in the modern sense of the term, but at best of limits only. Ethnic names, too, are by no means decisive factors in determining race. In the case of some of the above names we

must leave it undetermined whether they were those of Semitic or of non-Semitic races. Their geographical connexions are indicated in Scripture as follows: The REPHAIM dwelt on the east of Jordan (Deut. 3[11—13]). The term, identical with that used by the Hebrews for ghosts or the shades of the departed, was comprehensive and included the ZAMZUMMIM (Deut. 2[20]) (sometimes identified with the Zuzim of Gen. 14[5]), and the EMIM (Deut. 2[10]). The HORIM inhabited Mount Seir, i.e. the land of Edom (Gen. 14[6]; Deut. 2[22]). The AVIM held a portion of the Philistine country (Deut. 2[23]; Joshua 13[3]) and the ANAKIM possessed the region about Hebron (Num. 13[22]).

3. Whatever may have been the racial affinities of the inhabitants of Canaan in a remote period and in spite of the connexion of Canaan not with Shem but with Ham in Gen. 10, the population, apart from such Hittite centres in the north as are referred to in Judges 1[26], had been thoroughly Semitized long before the Hebrew settlement, and the language generally spoken, as the place-names recorded, for example, in Thothmes inscriptions (*c.* 1470 B.C.) and the Canaanite vocabulary appearing in the Tel-el-Amarna letters testify, was Semitic, and indeed scarcely distinguishable from the Hebrew of the Old Testament. As a general term to describe this population comprehensively the Old Testament in different parts employs Amorite (e. g. Amos 2[9, 10]; Judges 1[34], 6[10]; Joshua 24[15]; Gen. 48[22]) or Canaanite (e. g. Gen.10[19], 12[6]; Exod. 13[11]). At times Canaanite is used in a more limited way of the inhabitants of the sea-coast, and the Jordan valley (e. g. Num. 13[29]). Other terms— Girgashite, Hivite, Perizzite, Jebusite (e. g. Deut. 7)—used for pre-Israelite inhabitants of Canaan were of more local application; thus the Jebusites were centred at Jerusalem (Joshua 18[28], 2 Samuel 5[6]). This pre-Israelite population continued long after the Hebrew settlement to share the country with the Hebrews (cp. Judges 1, 2 Samuel 5[6ff.]), being at times intimately associated with them in the same towns (cp. Judges 9).

THE PHILISTINES may be distinguished from the pre-Israelite inhabitants of Canaan just mentioned (1) as at the time of the Hebrew settlement relatively recent settlers: (2) as maintaining throughout Hebrew history a distinct national existence in their cities situated in the coastal region south of Joppa, from which their name was extended by the Greeks to cover the whole of Palestine; and (3) as of non-Semitic origin, though they also appear to have adopted the Semitic language of the country in which they settled. The Philistines are the Palusabi of the Egyptian inscriptions: and the records of Rameses III (*c.* 1193 B. C.) suggest that the movement which led to their settlement on the southern stretch of the Palestinian coast-land was already in progress. Hebrew tradition regarded them as immigrants from Caphtor (Amos 9[7]; Jer. 47[4]: cp. Deut. 2[23]), which has been by many identified with Crete: but a connexion of the Philistines with the southern parts of the mainland of Asia Minor seems to be on archaeological grounds probable.

4. The **Deserts** bordering **Palestine** on the south and east, as well as the peninsula of Sinai, were in ancient as in modern times the homes of nomads. Among the nomadic peoples mentioned in the Old Testament and connected genealogically with the Hebrews are the Amalekites, with whom the Kenites (1 Sam. 15[6]) are closely associated, mainly connected with the south (e. g. Exod. 17[8−16]), the Ishmaelites divided into many tribes, including Kedar and Nebaioth (Gen. 25[12ff.]), and the Midianites associated mainly with the east (e. g. Gen. 25[6]) or south-east.

5. **Eastward** were certain **peoples** connected in Hebrew tradition with the family of Abraham, the most important of which were the Moabites and Ammonites, descendants of Abraham's nephew, Lot (Gen. 19[37, 38]) and to the south the Edomites, descendants of Jacob's elder brother Esau. We know little, comparatively speaking, of the AMMONITES, who have left no records. They worshipped Moloch or Milcom, the name being identical with or derived from the Semitic word for 'king'; and their capital city was Rabbath-Ammon, or 'Great Ammon', again a Semitic name. With their kindred, the MOABITES, we are better acquainted, both from the prophecies of Isaiah (cc. 15 and 16) and Jeremiah (c. 48), and from the 'stone' erected by Mesha at Dibon in Moab. This 'stone' shews that the Moabite language was, in the ninth century B. C., almost identical with the Hebrew, and that the modes of expression in the two countries were similar. The differences of language are merely dialectal, such as *anak* for *anoki*, 'I', and the like. The numerals are the same; and a common element in the names of towns is *Beth*. The Moabites and Ammonites were *settled* races, like the Hebrews; the cities, at least of the Moabites, were many and strong; they cultivated the vine (Isa. 16[8−10]), and were graziers also upon a large scale (2 Kings 3[4]). The distinction is very marked between them and the nomads, whom they adjoined, who dwelt in tents and wandered freely over the desert. The Edomites (later in Greek form Idumaeans) occupied 'Mount Seir', a country largely barren

though with some fruitful valleys. Bitterly hostile for centuries, Jews and Edomites later coalesced and in Herod the Idumaeans furnished the Jews with a royal house.

6. On the North, the principal neighbours of the Jews were the Phoenicians and the Aramaeans or Syrians. The PHOENICIANS were the inhabitants of the coast towns of Palestine, of which Sidon and Tyre were the most celebrated. In the Old Testament (e. g. 1 Kings 16[31]) as in Phoenician inscriptions they are called, after the former of these two cities, the Sidonians. The Semitic character of the Phoenicians in historical times is obvious and undisputed. The inscriptions, few of which are much earlier than 600 B. C., shew the Phoenician form of speech to be closely akin to the Hebrew. The Phoenicians shewed a remarkable aptitude for trade and commerce: while, on the other hand, they had the character of being unscrupulous and untrustworthy. They were famous for their manufacture of glass and of purple stuffs, and were the greatest traders and navigators of antiquity in Western Asia.

7. Nothing certain is known of the original home of the SYRIANS or ARAMAEANS, for Kir (Amos 9[7]) cannot be safely identified. 'Aram' appears at an early period as a designation of certain districts in Syria and Mesopotamia. The language of the Aramaeans gradually occupied all Syria, and 'last of all, Palestine became Aramaized. Towards the east this language was spoken on the Euphrates, and throughout the districts of the Tigris south and west of the Armenian and Kurdish mountains. In Babylonia and Assyria, a large, or perhaps the larger, portion of the population were most probably Aramaeans, even at a very early date, whilst Assyrian was the language of the Government' (Nöldeke).

8. If, from these immediate Neighbours of the Jews, we pass to those more distant ones with whom the circumstance of war, invasion, and conquest from time to time brought them into contact, we find that, on the south, they were liable to attack from two great nations, the Egyptians and the Ethiopians; on the east they had dealings, military and other, with four—the Assyrians, the Babylonians, the Elamites, and the Persians; while, on the north, they came into collision, in their later history, with four races—the Scythians, the Greeks, the Romans, and the Parthians. A few words must therefore be said, in order to complete this sketch, concerning the ethnic character and affinities of these ten remoter nations.

9. THE EGYPTIANS. According to Gen. 10[6] Mizraim was 'the son of Ham'. Egypt is called repeatedly in Scripture ' *the* land

of Ham' (Ps. 105$^{23, 27}$; 106^{22}). Its own native name was *Kêmet*, which has been explained as 'the Black Land'. The physique of the Egyptians was very marked and striking: they were tall and thin, with reddish brown skin and dark hair. They offered a marked contrast to their Semitic neighbours upon the east. Their language, however, had certain Semitic analogies, and received through contact and immigration a not inconsiderable infusion of Semitic words into it.

10. THE ETHIOPIANS (CUSHITE) with dark complexions were distinct from the Egyptians, by whom they were designated negroes. Their descent from Ham is distinctly asserted in Genesis (10^6). They occupied the country south of the first cataract. Egyptian civilization was readily received among them, but suffered deterioration in the process. From early times generally subject to Egypt, in the eighth and seventh centuries the Cushites became dominant, and the three kings of the Egyptian XXVth dynasty (712–663) were Cushites.

11. THE ASSYRIANS were pure Semites, as appears both from the Book of Genesis (10^{22}) and from the native inscriptions. Their physiognomy, physical type, and manners are also clearly Semitic, and render any doubt upon the subject impossible. In features, as represented in the sculptures, they closely resemble the Jews, in general ethnic character they are not dissimilar. They were pre-eminently a fighting race. Their civilization was largely derived from Babylonia.

12. THE BABYLONIANS. The oldest inhabitants of Babylonia of whom there are records were the Sumerians and Akkadians; of these the latter were Semites, the former a non-Semitic race. The Sumerians appear to have been the earlier inhabitants: to them the cuneiform writing, later employed alike by the Semitic Babylonians and the Assyrians, and many other elements of Babylonian civilization are due; and from them many non-Semitic words passed over into the languages of Babylon and Assyria. Linguistically Sumerian is entirely distinct from Assyrian or Babylonian: on the other hand, these latter languages, i. e. the languages spoken by Sennacherib and Nebuchadnezzar respectively, differed less than Spanish and Portuguese; the Babylonians and Assyrians had an almost identical religion; and their physical type was not very different. The Babylonians were somewhat shorter and clumsier in figure, their noses more depressed, their foreheads lower, and their expression altogether more commonplace.

I

13. THE ELAMITES (so called from Elam, i. e. Highlands) were the inhabitants of Susiana, which extended east of the Lower Tigris and north of the Persian Gulf to the mountains in the north and east, and was watered by the rivers Choaspes and Eulaeus. They were a non-Semitic race and enjoyed well-regulated political institutions. According to the Babylonian inscriptions, they subdued Babylonia as early as *c.* 2280 B. C., but their domination was brought to an end by Hammurabi (*c.* 2000). Their chief city was Susa (Shushan), which subsequently became the residence of the kings of Persia.

14. With the PERSIANS we come upon an entirely new and distinct nationality. The Persians belonged to the Aryan (or Indo-European) family, as Darius Hystaspes emphatically asserts in the inscription upon his tomb. Indeed the word 'Iran', which is the native name for the country ruled by the Shah, is the actual word 'Aryan' in another form. The language of the Persians exists in four stages, and can be traced from the age of the earliest portions of the Avesta to the present day. It appears as Avestan—or, more correctly, Old Bactrian—in the Avesta; as Achaemenian Persian in the inscriptions of (Cyrus), Darius, Xerxes, and Artaxerxes; as Pehlevi (with a large admixture of Aramaean words) in the inscriptions of the Sassanians and the Pehlevi version of the Zend-Avesta; and in the poems of Firdausi and his contemporaries, about A. D. 1000, it enters at once on its modern stage of development. In due course it has received a considerable accession of Arabic (more recently also of Turkish) words. In its most ancient form Persian is closely akin to Sanskrit, in its most modern to Hindustani; in all its forms it has close analogy with the tongues of the West. And the ethnic character of the people was in many respects Western. They were lively, enterprising, spirited, worshippers of the god Ormazd, tasteful in their architecture, possessed of a considerable power of organization. Their physique was decidedly what has been called 'Caucasian'—a high forehead, a well-formed nose, large eyes, a short upper lip, a well-rounded chin. Their limbs were slighter than those of their Semitic neighbours the Assyrians and Babylonians, but were well knit and muscular.

15. The name of SCYTHIANS was given by the Greeks to a race of the Indo-European (Aryan) family closely allied to the Iranians (Müllenhoff) and settled on the northern shores of the Black Sea. They are the same race that Herodotus denominates

Scolotes, who were probably only a Scythian tribe. They are called Sakas by the Persians, and are mentioned by that name in the cuneiform inscriptions of Darius. They themselves came from the east and drove out the Kimmerians from the northern shores of the Pontus Euxinus about the eighth century B.C. With later historians they appear to have lost their individuality; by them all the rude tribes of the Sarmatian plains are called Scythians irrespective of nationality, and they are credited with the most cruel habits and rites. They were probably the rudest of all the races with which the 'chosen people' came into contact; and it was fortunate for that people that the contact was once only in their history, and for a short time.

16. The ethnic character of the GREEKS and ROMANS is too well known to need many words in this place. The Hellenic and Italic races are universally recognized as two main branches of the great Aryan stock, and the two which in the ancient world carried Aryan civilization to the highest point. Possessing languages nearly akin to each other and not remotely allied to Sanskrit and Avestan, possessing moreover vast energy and high intellectual power, they became respectively the masters of the East and West. The Jewish nationality narrowly escaped absorption into the Greek at the time of Antiochus Epiphanes, and both in Egypt and in Palestine received permanent Hellenic impressions. Before Rome it refused to bend, and the refusal led to its destruction.

17. As with the SCYTHIANS, so with the PARTHIANS, there was one occasion only when the 'chosen people' came into contact with them. In 40 B.C., not long after the defeat of Crassus, a Parthian army crossed the Euphrates, and, defeating the Romans under Decidius Saxa, occupied and ravaged the whole of Syria and Palestine. Jerusalem itself was plundered by them, and Antigonus placed upon the throne as Parthian viceroy, a position which he occupied for three years.

PART III

THE APOCRYPHA*

XXI. SUMMARY OF THE BOOKS OF THE APOCRYPHA

Introductory.

1. These Books form part of the sacred literature of the Alexandrian Jews, and with the exception of the Second Book of Esdras are found interspersed with the Hebrew Scriptures in the ancient copies of the Septuagint, or Greek Version of the Old Testament. They are the product of the era subsequent to the Captivity, having their origin partly in Babylonia, partly in Palestine and Egypt, and perhaps other countries. Most of them belong to the last three centuries B.C., when prophecy, oracles, and direct revelation had ceased. Some of them form an historical link between the Old and New Testament, others have a linguistic value in connexion with the Hellenistic phraseology of the latter ; others, again, throw important light upon the growth of the Palestinian Canon (Ecclesiasticus, 2 Esdras). The narratives of the Apocrypha are partly historical records, and partly allegorical. The religious poetry is to a large extent a paraphrase upon the poetical and prophetical books of the Hebrew Canon. In the paraphrases upon the latter there is often a near approach to New Testament teaching, especially upon God's care for the heathen world. Only one purely apocalyptic book (2 Esdras) is included in the Apocrypha.

2. As to their **Canonical Authority,** Josephus seems to reject it as a whole, but appears from his use of 1 Esdras rather than our canonical Ezra to have accepted the authenticity of at least that work. The early Christians differed in opinion respecting them, but received them as part of the sacred literature of Israel. Several of the books of the Apocrypha were more generally accepted than

---

* For larger works in English dealing with the Apocrypha generally and in detail, the reader may be referred to *The Books of the Apocrypha : Their Origin, Teaching, and Contents*, by W. O. E. Oesterley, D.D. (London, 1914) ; and *The Apocrypha and Pseudepigrapha of the Old Testament*, ed. by R. H. Charles, D.D., 2 vols. (Oxford, 1913) ; Vol. I, *The Apocrypha.* Cf. also *An Introduction to the Old Testament in Greek*, by H. B. Swete (new ed. by R. R. Ottley) ; and *A Handbook to the LXX* by R. R. Ottley (Methuen), a good popular account.

the disputed books of the New Testament Canon. Melito (c. 170), referring to the Hebrew Canon, separated them from the authoritative and Divine records; while Origen (c. 230), following the LXX, included in Daniel (and so among the canonical books) the history of Susanna; and speaks ambiguously about the Books of the Maccabees. Jerome, a century and a half later, called them 'apocryphal' (hidden, secret, and so of uncertain origin and authority), affirming (when speaking of Wisdom and Ecclesiasticus) that 'the Church doth read them for example of life and instruction of manners; but yet doth it not apply them to establish any doctrine'. In the Western Church they gradually rose in esteem, until the Council of Trent affirmed the canonicity of the greater part; but they are treated by the more critical Roman divines as 'deutero-canonical', who thus make some distinction between them and the books of the Hebrew Canon.

It must be remembered that the Bible of the early Christian Church was the LXX, which included the apocryphal books as Sacred Scripture. Jerome appears to have been the first to draw any distinction clearly between Old Testament books which are recognized in the Hebrew Canon, and the Greek books of the Apocrypha.

(i) THE BOOKS OF ESDRAS

The first of these Books is quoted largely by Josephus and by Athanasius, and the second by some other early Christian writers, but they were not included in the Canon of the Council of Trent.

(a) The First Book.

The contents of the apocryphal Ezra (= 1 Esdras) can best be seen in a table showing the parallel sections in the Hebrew Ezra–Nehemiah of our English Bible. They are as follows:

1 Esdras.	Hebrew Bible (and E.V.).
1	= 2 Chron. 35–36.
2^{1-15}	= Ezra 1.
2^{16-30}	= Ezra 4^{7-24}.
3^1-5^6	= not in Hebrew (in English Bible).
5^{7-73}	= Ezra 2^1-4^5.
6–7	= Ezra 5–6.
7^1-9^{36}	= Ezra 7–10.
9^{37-55}	= Neh. $7^{72}-8^{12}$.

Thus 1 Esdras embraces not only our canonical Ezra, but parts of Chronicles and Nehemiah as well, and also a section (3^1-5^6,

containing the famous story of the Three Youths) which has no
parallel in the Hebrew (and English) Bible. The old explanation
of these phenomena was that it was a Greek 'compilation' made
from the canonical books. But the special object of such a
'compilation' is not obvious. The researches of Howorth, Torrey,
and other scholars have demonstrated that the true explanation
is to regard 1 Esdras as a fragment from the old Greek version
of the Chronicler's complete work (= 1 and 2 Chron. + Ezra,
Nehemiah), representing an older recension of the text. The
canonical books, Ezra and Nehemiah, represent a revision of this
older text which was made before the books were accepted as part
of the Hebrew Bible. Only Greek and Latin versions of the book
are known to exist.

(b) The Second Book.

The more ancient Title of this Book was the 'Revelation of
Ezra', or 'Esdras the Prophet', but it is more commonly known
as the 'Fourth Book of Ezra'. The original text was probably
Hebrew (entirely lost), from which a Greek version was made, but,
with the exception of a few verses found in quotations, the Greek
text also is entirely lost. From it a Latin, Ethiopic, and two
Arabic translations have been made; but the English version, as
also an Armenian, was entirely taken from the Latin. The book,
which forms no part of the Greek Bible, owes its place in our
Apocrypha to the fact that it was included in Latin Biblical MSS.,
and was regarded as a sort of appendix to the Vulgate. This
Latin text contains certain interpolations (cc. 1, 2, 15, 16), which
are evidently of Christian origin, and omits in the later MSS.—
which our version followed—a long passage after chapter 7[35], on the
'intermediate state' and 'intercession of departed souls'. The
omission arose from the accidental loss of a leaf in a ninth-century
MS., which leaf is now recovered. This omitted passage is given
in the Oriental versions, and has been restored in the R.V. The
Oriental versions also do not recognize chapters 1-2 and 15-16. In
them the Apocalypse appears in its true form, i.e. it embraces
chapters 3-14 only of our 2 Esdras. The Apocalypse itself appears
to be a composite work which was reduced to its present form by an
editor about the year A.D. 120. The material used by him, and
embodied in the book, consists of a Salathiel Apocalypse (cf. 3[1])
which is contained mainly in chapters 3-10 of 2 Esdras. This
work, originally written in the name of Salathiel (= Shealtiel),
the father of Zerubbabel, who lived through the Exile, is embodied
in practically a complete form in our Apocalypse. It seems to

have been written and published in Hebrew about the year A.D. 100. To it the final editor appended three pieces derived from other sources, viz. (1) the famous Eagle-Vision (cc. 11–12), (2) the Son of Man Vision (c. 13)—both extracted apparently from a Book of Dream-Visions—and (3) the Ezra-Legend (c. 14, mainly). There are, naturally, traces of the final editor's hand throughout in redactional links and adjustments. The whole compilation is parallel with the twin (Syriac) Apocalypse of Baruch, which is not included in our Apocrypha, and which may have been edited in its final form somewhat later. The importance of both Apocalypses for the study of Jewish and Christian theology is very great. In its present form 2 Esdras 3–14 consists of angelic revelations in a series of visions, teaching some of the mysteries of the moral world, and the final triumph of the righteous. It may be divided as follows into seven visions, which contain dialogues between the Seer and the Angel (representing God):

1. *Vision I* (3^1–5^{19}). Whence the sin and misery of the world? and the divine reply.

2. *Vision II* (5^{20}–6^{34}). Ezra's Prayer and its Answer. How the plan of Providence progresses in spite of man's difficulties in understanding it, and good finally triumphs over evil in judgement.

3. *Vision III* (6^{35}–9^{25}). The Problem is debated: If the world was created for Israel, why is Israel disinherited? The narrow limits of Israel necessitated by Adam's sin; and the paucity of the redeemed explained by natural analogies. The section contains also an account of the state after death and final judgement. (Between 7^{35} and 7^{36} is inserted the 'missing fragment'; cf. R.V.)

4. *Vision IV* (9^{26}–10^{59}). Sion and the Heavenly Jerusalem. A woman (Sion) lamenting the death of her only son (i.e. the city of Solomon) on his bridal day; but her sorrow is turned into joy at the appearance of a newly-built city.

5. *Vision V*: The Eagle-Vision (10^{60}–12^{3a}). An eagle (the fourth kingdom of Daniel), rising from the sea, spreads its wings over the earth, undergoes various transformations, is rebuked by a lion (Messiah), and is burnt up (11^1–12^{39}).

6. *Vision VI*: The Man from the Sea (13^{1-58}). A Man (the Son of Man), flying on the clouds, destroys by the blast of His mouth the opposing powers of the world, gathers the lost tribes of Israel, and gives them the City of Sion.

7. *Vision VII*: The Ezra-Legend (c. 14). The appearance of

the Lord in a burning bush, with a promise to Ezra of a restoration of the books of the Law which had been burnt. Ezra's Commission and Prayer (14^{1-26}).

Ezra dictates to the scribes the whole of the Law ' to be published openly ', and seventy books of secret mysteries which are not to be divulged (14^{27-48}).

(ii) THE BOOK OF ESTHER

This Book consists of certain interpolated passages found in many copies of the Septuagint version of Esther, which are not in the original Hebrew copy. Their object was partly to supplement the narrative of the canonical Esther, partly to give it a more distinctly religious tone by pointing to God as the Prime Mover in the events, whereas His Name nowhere occurs in the original. These interpolated passages are supposed to have been inserted at a later date by the Alexandrian Jews. Jerome removed them from the text, and placed them in the order in which we now have them in the English text among the uncanonical books. The disconnected fragments were arranged consecutively, as if they formed a complete continuation of the canonical book, whereas the first alone followed directly after the conclusion of our canonical Esther. The dream of Mardocheus (Mordecai), chapter 2, and the conspiracy of the two eunuchs (c. 12), were introduced at the beginning of the book; the copy of the letters of Artaxerxes (c. 13^{1-7}) after 3^{13}; the prayers of Mordecai and Esther (c. 13^8-14^{19}) at the end of chapter 4. The description of Esther's entrance before the king (c. 15) is an expansion of chapter $5^{1, 2}$; and the letter of Artaxerxes (c. 16) was added after 8^{12}. These fragments are usually assigned to some period of the first or second century B.C.

(iii) THE BOOK OF WISDOM

1. The original Book seems to have been in Greek, and is contained in the chief Biblical MSS.; but there is an ancient Latin version older than the time of Jerome, and translations in Armenian, Syriac, and Arabic, of which the last two are paraphrastic.

2. Summary. It consists of two main parts: I. The praise of wisdom in its moral and intellectual aspects: 1st, as the source of immortality in contradiction to the theory of sensualists; 2nd, as the practical guide of moral and intellectual life (c. 1-9). II. The doctrine of wisdom in its historical aspect: (1) an illustration of the influence of wisdom in the reward of the virtuous and

the punishment of the vicious, both in the case of individuals (from Adam to Moses), and of nations, e.g. the Egyptians and Canaanites (cc. 10–12); followed by (2) a description of the origin of idolatry, its folly and its sin; and an estimate of its demoralizing influence upon life (cc. 13–15); and (3) a contrast between the fortunes of idolatrous and religious people (cc. 16–19). The harmony pervading the whole book contradicts the opinion that it is a compilation from several authors who wrote at different times, though some have attributed the two sections to separate authors. It is widely held that the book falls into two distinct parts (cc. 1–11^1 and 11^2–19), which are marked by certain differences of style and thought, and suggest the combination of two originally distinct compositions. An attractive view regards 11^5–19^{21} as an extract from a Hellenistic Passover Haggadah, i. e. the Greek Home-service, which was intended to be recited on the Eve of the Passover (cf. *Wisdom* 18$^{6-9}$). The Solomonic Book of Wisdom may be regarded as ending at 9^{18}, and chapter 10 may be looked upon as the connecting-link between this Wisdom Book and the Passover Haggadah. It possesses the highest literary excellence, and is comparable for sublimity of thought, rhetorical power, and command of language with some of the finest productions of classical antiquity.

3. Its Diction, as well as its doctrine, points to a Greek original, unfettered by Hebrew idioms. Its date is variously conjectured, from 217 B.C. to A.D. 40; the probable date of composition is, perhaps, some time in the first century B.C. We find in it the doctrine of the creation of the world from uncreated matter, of the pre-existence of souls, of the pervading influence of the Divine Spirit throughout the universe; but there is no mention of the Christian doctrine of the resurrection of the body, nor any reference to the regeneration of humanity by the Messiah, while immortality is vividly depicted as the reward and consequence of wisdom. These facts all point to Alexandria as the place of its composition, and to a period anterior to Christianity, in which Hebrew thought and Greek philosophy of various schools had become fused together. Moreover, its style and diction seem to point to an earlier date than that of Philo, to whom it has been sometimes ascribed. Some passages in the Epistle to the Hebrews suggest that the writer was acquainted with this book, but no direct quotation from it is found earlier than the first half of the second century A.D., when it seems to be treated as inspired Scripture. The doctrine concerning wisdom already found in Proverbs, Job, and Ecclesiastes is here still further developed; it is treated as an existence

co-eternal with the Creator, acting on created matter, as the source of life, and continuing in the land of spirits. And so the foundation is laid for the Christian doctrine of the existence and influence of the Divine Word and Holy Spirit.[*]

(iv) ECCLESIASTICUS

1. This Book is so called in the Vulgate and A.V. from its local name in the African Church, and was originally so designated from its practical use as a book of instruction in the Church. Its earlier titles were ' Proverbs ' and ' The Wisdom of Jesus the Son of Sirach '. Both internal evidence and the testimony of Jerome sufficiently attested the existence of a Hebrew original,[†] which was subsequently translated, with some additions, by a descendant, probably the grandson of the author, resident in Alexandria, in the reign of Euergetes II (see the Prologues). The date of this translation is fixed by the reference in the Prologue to the thirty-eighth year 'of (under) Euergetes the King ', i. e. Ptolemy Physcon, Euergetes II = 132 B. C. The original work was probably written about 190 B. C. The Simon mentioned in chapter 50^1 as High Priest (and a contemporary of Sirach) will thus be Simon II (flourished 200 B.C. and following years).

2. The Hebrews did not place the Book among the canonical Scriptures, nor is it so classed by Jerome ; but it is quoted as such, and even attributed to Solomon, by many Christian writers after the second century. The text of the Greek translation is found in the LXX, and from it were derived, with a few apparent exceptions, the Vulgate and the Authorized Version. On the other hand, the Syriac version is an independent translation of the original Hebrew, and of great value in restoring the text and explaining obscurities. Quotations from the original Hebrew, and others translated into Aramaic, are found in the Jerusalem and Babylonian Talmuds. There is considerable difference both of the text and of the order in the several authorities. The book

---

[*] See the Introductions to *The Book of Wisdom*, by A. T. S. Goodrick (Rivingtons, 1913), and *The Wisdom of Solomon*, by J. A. F. Gregg (Cambridge Bible, 1909).

[†] Now conclusively proved by the discovery of a considerable fragment of the original text. (See *The Original Hebrew of Ecclesiasticus* 39^{15}–49^{11}, *with Early Versions and English Translation*, by A. E. Cowley and Ad. Neubauer (Clarendon Press, 1897). Other fragments of the Hebrew original have been recovered. For a full account of these and the value of the recovered texts, see the Introduction to 'Sirach' in Vol. I of Charles's *Apocrypha and Pseudepigrapha*, pp. 272 ff.

is half philosophical, half ethical in its character, and belongs to what is called the Wisdom literature of the Jews. In its view of wisdom it is transitional between books like Proverbs and Job and the later Alexandrian Book of the Wisdom of Solomon.

3. **The Tone of the Book** is mainly Palestinian, with but few traces of Greek philosophy. Such traces as there are, however, as a comparison with the Syriac shows, are mainly the additions of the translator. God is the Creator, Preserver, and Governor of the universe; the hope of a future life is dim and uncertain. A good name and grateful remembrance by posterity are the reward of the righteous. It contains, however, some sublime passages on the works of creation and on the praise of wisdom (cc. 24, 42, 43), and its testimony to the Hebrew Canon from Genesis to the latest prophet is of great value. The contents of the book may broadly be summarized under the following heads: (1) 1^1-16^{23}, The nature and essence of Wisdom; (2) 16^{24}-23^{27}, God and Creation: various precepts and warnings; (3) 24^1-33^{31}, Wisdom and the Law; (4) 34-36^{17}, Wisdom in relation to various states and experiences of life; (5) 36^{18}-39^{35}, Wisdom applied to various social and professional relationships, with an Appendix (39^{12-35}) in praise of Creation; (6) 40^1-42^{14}, The goods and evils of humanity; (7) 42^{15}-43^3, In praise of God; (8) 44^1-50^{29}, In praise of the Fathers of old (culminating in the eulogy of Simon the High Priest); (9) 51^{1-30}; a Prayer, a Psalm, and a Poem, forming an Appendix to the book. [Between verses 12 and 13 falls a psalm which is extant only in the Hebrew text.] A notable feature which distinguishes Sirach from the Book of Proverbs is the prominence it gives to the Law and the priesthood. Its standpoint reflects that of the conservative (Sadducean) priesthood of the earlier (pre-Maccabean) period.

(v) THE BOOK OF BARUCH

1. **This Book,** which bears the name of the companion of Jeremiah, is found in a Greek version in all our editions of the LXX. No reference is made to it in the New Testament, or by the Apostolic Fathers; but subsequently Christian writers refer to it as the work of Jeremiah. In its present form the book was probably compiled after the destruction of Jerusalem in A.D. 70 (to which event it alludes in veiled language). It is, however, composite in character, and contains much earlier material. The so-called **Epistle of Jeremiah** (c. 6) is an entirely independent production, composed in Greek, probably by an Alexandrian Jew,

to warn his countrymen against heathen idolatry. The date of composition is uncertain. It may be as early as the first century B.C. (Dr. C. J. Ball in the Oxford *Corpus* has argued for a Hebrew original and a much earlier date—*c.* 306 B.C.).

2. The Book of Baruch contains paraphrases upon Jeremiah and Daniel and other prophetical writings. Like Ecclesiasticus it dwells upon the temporal promises of God and national restoration, and there are no traces of those hopes of immortality which were awakened in the Maccabean period. In this respect it differs from the later Syriac treatise, 'the Apocalypse of Baruch'.

3. The First Part (1–3^8) consists of an introduction, followed by a confession and prayer on the part of the captive exiles. This was probably compiled in its present form about A.D 75, but it contains in 1^{15}–3^8 a long liturgical piece, which is probably much older and may have been derived from the Temple liturgy. The Second Part (3^9–4^4), which is in poetical form, contains a gentle rebuke of Israel for their sins, and a sublime passage on the condescension of God in manifesting His Law and His Presence to them. It is modelled on the Wisdom Books of the Old Testament (Job and Proverbs), and is addressed to the Jews in exile. The Third Part (4^5–5^9) is a further piece of exhortation and consolation. Parts 1 and 2 were probably composed originally in Hebrew (or Aramaic), Part 3 in Greek. The book may have been redacted and put into its present form at the beginning of the second century A.D.

(vi) APOCRYPHAL ADDITIONS TO DANIEL

These Three Fragments are not found in the original text of the Book of Daniel, but have a place in the LXX Version, and seem to embody certain popular traditions embellishing historical facts. They are probably all (except the last piece, 'Bel and the Dragon') derived from Hebrew sources.

1. THE SONG OF THE THREE CHILDREN.

This Book supplements the narrative in Daniel 3, and gives a supposed prayer of Azarias for deliverance from the fiery furnace, and an account of the means by which the Three Children were saved, followed by a hymn of thanksgiving, sung by them in the fire, which has been used in Christian worship, under the name of the 'Hymn of the Three', ever since the fourth century A.D. Accordingly, it is found in the Appendix to the Alexandrian Psalter. Expansions of this story are common in Talmudic literature, and it is probable that this came originally from some early Midrash.

2. THE HISTORY OF SUSANNA.

This Narrative is usually prefixed to the Hebrew Book of Daniel in the copies of the Septuagint and other Greek versions. There are also Syriac and other versions, differing widely from the Greek text and giving additional details. It is the subject of a Latin poem by Hildebert of Tours, A. D. 1100. According to Origen it is connected with the history of Ahab and Zedekiah in Jer. 29[22]. A similar story is found in early Jewish literature. The writer's object was to censure the judges of Israel, in his own day, by a comparison of the guilty elders with the virtuous youth Daniel. The piece was probably composed (in Hebrew) within the first century B.C. (after the time of Simon b. Shetach, *c.* 100–67 B. C.). It was perhaps attached to the Book of Daniel to illustrate the meaning of Daniel's name (*Daniel* = 'my Judge is 'El').

3. BEL AND THE DRAGON.

This Book, called in the LXX 'Part of the Prophecy of Habakkuk, the son of Joshua, of the tribe of Levi' (cf. verses 33–39a, which, however, are probably a later addition to the story), contains the history of the destruction of two objects of Babylonian worship, with an account of Daniel's deliverance from the lions. The event is placed in the time of Cyrus, and Jewish tradition regarded it as a distinct incident from that recorded in the canonical Book of Daniel. The composition is a philippic against idolatry. It may have originated about 100 B. C. and was probably composed in Greek for propaganda purposes (cf. the Sibylline oracles).

(vii) THE PRAYER OF MANASSES

The original Prayer of the penitent king of Judah existed when the Book of Chronicles was written in two distinct documents (2 Chron. 33[18, 19]). This version is found in some copies of the LXX, and in the *Apostolic Constitutions*, with a legend of his miraculous deliverance from captivity, but it appears to be no true part of the LXX text. Its date and authorship are both uncertain. It is cast in a poetical form, and is based upon the prophetical Scriptures, and was probably of Hebrew or Aramaic origin. It is, perhaps, of Palestinian origin, the work of a pious Pharisee (? first century B. C.). In its original form it probably had no special reference to Manasses, but was adapted later for this special purpose by slight modifications. It is a fine specimen of liturgical composition, and reflects real religious feeling.

(viii) TOBIT

1. The Original of this Book was perhaps in Hebrew or Aramaic (more probably the latter), though the extant Hebrew versions are later than the Greek book in the Septuagint. The Vulgate was translated by Jerome from an Aramaic version done for his special benefit into Hebrew ; but this version differed from the Aramaic (Chaldee) Tobit now in the Bodleian Library in Oxford, which is based upon the LXX. The LXX text itself is extant in different recensions, of which that of Codex Sinaiticus (א) is markedly the superior. The author's purpose was, apparently, to impart moral and religious instruction rather than to record an historical event. The scene of the story is laid in Nineveh and Media. The book itself falls into three main divisions: (1) chapters 1–3 ; here Tobit relates how he, his wife Anna, and his son Tobias had been carried captive to Nineveh in the days of Shalmaneser. Loyalty to the Law (especially the duty of almsgiving and burial of the dead) is insisted upon: (2) chapters 4–11, relating the journey of Tobias to Media. Tobias marries Sarah (escaping death through the Demon) and returns to Nineveh: (3) chapters 12–14 form the conclusion. There is much concerning the angel Raphael, and Tobit's prayer is given. The angelology of the book is notable, and an interesting literary problem arises in connexion with the references to the story of Aḥikar (cf. Tobit 1²¹, ²²).

2. From internal Evidence the writer, it has been conjectured, must have been a Jew, resident in Egypt (but this is not certain). The book is almost certainly pre-Maccabean and may have been originally composed between 190 and 170 B.C. It has been more highly esteemed by Christians than by Jews. It presents a most vivid and pleasing picture of domestic life, and of the influence of religion upon it, among the captive Jews, and in this respect it bears a strong affinity to the historical part of the Book of Job.

(ix) JUDITH

It is practically certain that the Greek text of this book is derived from a Hebrew or Aramaic original. As in the case of Tobit, Jerome made his Vulgate translation of the book with the help of an Aramaic version translated for the purpose into Hebrew. But the carelessness with which this was confessedly done makes it extremely difficult to decide which of the two texts, the Greek or Aramaic, is closer to the original, or what is their relation to each other. The Greek form of the story exists in three recensions, which vary not inconsiderably. But besides this, a much shorter form of the story is extant in Hebrew (Codex Gaster and *Megillôth Ta'anith*), which probably represents a more original shape. In this form Seleucus takes the place of Nebuchadnezzar, Judith is pictured as a maiden (not a widow), and the scene is laid in Jerusalem (not Bethulia).

The geographical and historical references in the book are so irreconcilable with known facts that there is little doubt that the book is an historical fiction. The later (Greek) form of the book contains many references to ceremonial customs which were developed by Pharisaism. The only time which will suit the historical allusions is 63 B.C. (when Pompey approached Jerusalem). The shorter form may be somewhat earlier. It is probable that the leading characters were taken from historical personages of the period, disguised under fictitious names, though some have regarded them as purely allegorical.

(x) MACCABEES

There are Four Books bearing this Title, but only the First and Second have been regarded as worthy of a place among the sacred writings, because they supply the Hebrew history of the second century B.C., written after the model of the Books of Chronicles. The origin of the name is doubtful, but is probably derived from *Makkâbâh*, 'a hammer'.

1. The First Book of Maccabees.

Date and Place of Writing. Both ancient testimony and internal evidence point to a Hebrew original, written in Palestine, probably between 100 and 90 B.C.; but the English version is taken from the Greek translation annexed to the Alexandrian version of the Old Testament. It consists of an introduction, containing a brief sketch of Alexander's conquests, followed by an account of the invasion and oppression of Antiochus Epiphanes, culminating in his attempt to extirpate Hebrew nationality and worship. The main body of the work narrates the struggle for independence, beginning with Mattathias, and ending with Simon. It comprises a period of thirty-three years (168–135 B.C.). After an enumeration of the Maccabean family, it relates the exploits of Mattathias and his five sons, by whom the struggle is carried on to a successful issue. The history divides itself into three distinct epochs, each stamped with the individuality of its leader —first, Judas; second, Jonathan; third, Simon—each of whom fell a victim to his patriotism. The antiquity of the book is inferred from the praises bestowed upon the Roman Senate and people in chapter 8, which no Jewish patriot of the age of Pompey or Crassus could have written. Hence the book has a special value as a first-class source for an important period.

The author, who was a patriotic and pious Jew, seems rather to represent a Sadducean than a Pharisaic religious standpoint. There is no reference to a belief in life after death. The book was apparently compiled from different sources, which included some important letters. He may also have utilized oral accounts of events by eye-witnesses.

2. The Second Book of Maccabees.

1. This Book is in no sense a continuation of the First, but seems to be a compilation, made from some extant materials furnished to the compiler at Alexandria. The main portion of the book is derived from a previous work, called the 'Five Books of Jason of Cyrene', probably the son of Eleazar (cf. 2 Macc. 2^{19-32}). From internal evidence this latter work appears to have been written in Greek, about 125 B.C. or a little later. The source from which the first two chapters are taken is very doubtful; their value and authenticity have been much debated. They may have been derived from a good source and prepared by the epitomist himself. Possibly they have been translated from Hebrew or Aramaic originals. These two chapters form the main source from which the history anterior to the Maccabees is derived, comprising a period of twenty-five years from 185 (?)–161 B.C., so that a portion of the narrative is chronologically anterior to 1 Maccabees, another is contemporaneous with it, and a third is supplementary.

2. Summary. It may be thus divided: 1. The two introductory chapters, addressed by the Council at Jerusalem to the Jews at Alexandria. 2. The history of Heliodorus (3). 3. The beginning and course of the great persecution (4–7). 4. The fortunes of Judas to the restoration of the Temple service (8–10^9). 5. Reign of Antiochus Eupator (10^{10}–13). 6. From the treachery of Alcimus to the final triumph of Judas (14–15).

3. The main Features of the Book are its high religious tone and its very oratorical style. In it are depicted the Divine influence over human events, retributive justice, the connexion between the visible and spiritual world, and the doctrine of a future resurrection. Holding these opinions, the compiler seems to have used historical events in support of them rather than to have adhered

to strict accuracy of detail; hence there are many discrepancies between this book and 1 Maccabees which are otherwise inexplicable.*

The compiler, or epitomist, probably put the book into its present shape shortly before the Christian era. He is essentially an apologist, using the history to glorify the Jews, and commending with special emphasis such things as martyrdom for a good cause. Specially noticeable are his references to the doctrine of the resurrection ($7^{11, 12, 23}$, 14^{46}), prayers for the dead ($12^{43, 45}$), and intercession of departed saints (15^{11-16}). His standpoint is rather polemical and Pharisaic, in contrast with the sober Sadducean orthodoxy of 1 Maccabees.

XXII. HISTORICAL SKETCH OF THE PERIOD BETWEEN THE OLD AND NEW TESTAMENTS

During the Period between the Old and New Testaments the Jews were influenced by the rule of four different dynasties: (i) The Dominion of Persia, 539–333 B.C.; (ii) of Greece, 333–167 B.C.; (iii) of the Asmonaeans, 167–63 B.C.; (iv) of the Idumaean Antipater, and Herod, 63–4 B.C.

(i) *The Dominion of Persia*, 539–333 B.C.

The Persian period properly dates from the fall of Babylon, 536 B.C. It was from Babylon, in 538, that the little band of exiles, led by Zerubbabel, 'Prince of Judah', started for the land of their fathers. From Babylon also, nearly a century later (458 B.C.), Ezra led a second band of pilgrims to reinforce the small community at Jerusalem (Ezra 7^6). In fact, many indications show that the Babylonian community continued throughout the Persian era to be the most important centre of Jewish life and thought. The 'Great Scribe' himself (Ezra) was the head of a school that had grown up in Babylon, which no doubt continued to exercise a large influence over religious affairs in Palestine, at least till the rise of new political conditions after the death of Alexander the Great (323 B.C.).

1. Did Persian ideas and beliefs at all influence Jewish religious thought during this period? This important question can receive here only the barest consideration, and it is necessary to speak with caution; but it seems probable that on such subjects as the

---

* See the *Speaker's Commentary on the Books of Maccabees*; Schürer's *Jewish People in the Time of Jesus Christ*, Div. I, vol. i, pp. 36–46; Oesterley, *op. cit.*, pp. 479 ff.; Moffatt in Charles, vol. i, pp. 125 ff.

number and personality of angels, and the existence of demons, Jewish beliefs were directly indebted to Persia; while it is possible that the Jewish development of the doctrine of future retribution *may* have received an impulse from the noblest elements of Iranian religion. It seems certain that one of the later Jewish festivals (Purim) has a Persian origin.

The closing days of the decaying Persian Empire were marked by commotions, the effects of which must have been felt by the Jews. During the reigns of both Artaxerxes Mnemon (404-362 B.C.) and Artaxerxes Ochus (361-338 B.C.), the Persian forces were constantly engaged in suppressing insurrections in Egypt. The frequent passage of troops along the Syrian coast must have involved the Judaeans in many of the burdens of war. It is not improbable, indeed, that the growing corruption and oppression of the Persian régime (witness the defilement of the temple by the satrap Bagoses, perhaps 483 B.C.) at last drove the Jews themselves to join other nations in open revolt.

2. **Form of Government.** From the time of Ezra onwards the internal affairs of the Jewish community were controlled by the high priests assisted by a body of aristocratic ‘elders’. This body, which underwent successive modifications, ultimately developed into the Sanhedrin, which was presided over by the high priest as its official head and was the chief domestic power in Judaea in the Roman epoch. There is no evidence that it was ever designated the Great Synagogue.

3. **The Great Synagogue.** According to Jewish tradition ‘The Great Synagogue’ was a permanent council of scribes, founded by Ezra (the Great Scribe), which directed and decided all matters of religious concern down to about 300 B.C. But neither in the canonical Scriptures, the Apocrypha, nor the writings of Josephus or Philo, is there any mention of such an institution (certainly 1 Macc. 7[12], 14[28] do not presuppose it). The story, in fact, is ‘due to the attempt to read into earlier times the synagogue system which prevailed in the Talmudic period’ (Ryle), and must be given up as unhistorical. While, however, no such sacred senate as the Great Synagogue of Jewish legend existed, there was undoubtedly, during the whole of this period, a body of men, who may fitly be described as Ezra’s successors, the Sopherim (scribes, students of the Law), whose unobtrusive but most effective labours left an indelible mark upon the Jewish people and religion. These earlier Sopherim were members of the priesthood like Ezra (‘scribe and priest’). For a good description of these earlier ‘scribes’, cf. Ecclus. 38[24ff.]

(ii) *The Dominion of Greece*, 333–167 B.C.

1. The Victories of Alexander. The Persian Empire, to which the Jews had so long owed allegiance, crumbled to pieces before the armies of Alexander the Great. Victorious over the Persian forces at the Granicus, 334 B.C., and again at Issus in the following year, the conqueror captured Damascus, and having taken Sidon, laid siege to Tyre, 332 B.C. In the next year he is said to have marched against Jerusalem, to punish the people for refusing to transfer their allegiance from the Persians to himself. His visit is described with characteristic colouring by Josephus (*Antiq.* II. 8³). He tells us that when Alexander approached Jerusalem with hostile intent, Jaddua, the high priest, in conformity with a dream, awaited his approach, clad in his priestly robes of hyacinth and gold, and accompanied by a train of priests and citizens arrayed in white. Alexander, moved by the novel spectacle, did reverence to the high priest, and kissed the sacred inscription on his mitre, alleging that he had seen in a dream that same venerable form, who had promised him success in his Eastern campaign. Thus Jerusalem was spared.

2. Importance of Alexander's Conquests. Jerusalem, however, was not only spared, but the Jews there and throughout Palestine received from the conqueror peculiar privileges, which they continued to enjoy under his successors. When Alexander had subdued Egypt, and built the new capital, Alexandria, he invited a great number of Jews to settle there, and granted them many privileges and immunities. Alexander's conquests were of great importance. They broke down the barrier separating one kingdom from another, and especially those between the Asiatic and European states. Men learned to understand each other's thoughts, while Greek literature and intelligence spread over the East, and the Greek language became almost universal.

3. After the Death of Alexander, 323 B.C., Palestine came into the possession of Laomedon, one of his generals. But it was soon afterwards (320 B.C.) wrested from him by Ptolemy Soter, King of Egypt, who gained possession of all Syria and Phoenicia, and captured Jerusalem. He transported ten thousand of the inhabitants to Egypt, and granted them equal privileges with the Macedonians themselves, and shortly afterwards removed another large body of them to Libya and Cyrene. In the year 314 B.C. Antigonus, King of Syria, one of the most turbulent of Alexander's generals, took possession of Palestine ; but after he had lost his life at the battle of Ipsus, 301 B.C., the country reverted to the Ptolemies (under whose dominion it remained for the next hundred years), and became a kind of neutral territory between the rival empires of Syria and Egypt.

4. **Under the Ptolemies** the condition of the Jews was peaceful and happy. The Egyptian monarchs bestowed upon them many privileges, allowed them to build synagogues in all their settlements, and thus spread them and their religion over all the countries subject to their sway. Thus the Greek language gradually became the language of the scattered Jews, 'the Jews of the Dispersion' (1 Pet. 1¹), and they derived from this circumstance the name of 'Hellenists', and became a connecting link between Judaism and heathenism. Hence arose the want of a Greek version of the Old Testament, which Ptolemy Philadelphus is said to have inaugurated by causing to be made, for the large library which he had founded at Alexandria, a translation of the Pentateuch, which was later gradually extended by the addition of the prophetic and other writings, and became known as the Septuagint (284–247 B.C.). Henceforward Alexandria exercised a greater influence on Judaism in its relation to other nations than even Jerusalem itself, as being from its situation the point of contact between Eastern and Western thought. Judaea, also, during its connexion with Egypt, appears to have enjoyed a large measure of internal freedom and prosperity. The head of the community was the high priest. One of the most notable of the high priests was Simon I (*c.* 300–270 B.C.), who succeeded his father Onias I, and was the grandson of Jaddua. This Simon was surnamed 'the Just'. Simon the Just was succeeded by his brother Eleazar, and the latter by his uncle Manasseh, who in turn was succeeded by Onias II (a son of Simon the Just). The son and successor of Onias II was Simon II (? 200–190 B.C.), to whom Sirach pays so eloquent a tribute (Ecclus. 50). Onias III, son of the preceding, was contemporary with Antiochus Epiphanes (175 B.C.) and is the high priest referred to in the early period of the Maccabean struggles. He distinguished himself as an opponent of the Hellenizers.

5. **The Centres of Judaism.** The two great centres of Judaism were now Jerusalem and Alexandria, the latter the capital of the Hellenist, or Greek-speaking Jew, who mingled Greek culture and independence with Jewish autonomy and Oriental contemplation and allegory, and fostered an alliance between Jewish revelation and Greek philosophy.

A parallel case to Alexandria is that of Antioch, the capital city of Seleucus I (died 280 B.C.). Seleucus conferred citizen rights upon the Jews in this city, and in all the cities founded by himself in Syria and Asia Minor.

The Jewish Dispersion (Diaspora) became very widespread. It embraced settlements all over the Eastern and Western world. Besides those in Syria (e. g. Damascus) and Asia Minor (e. g. Ephesus), there were Jewish communities in the valley of the Euphrates, and in Greece and other Mediterranean lands. It is curious to note the presence of Samaritans as well as Jews in Rome and Alexandria during the Empire.

6. **The Seleucidae.** The battle of Ipsus elevated another of Alexander's generals, Seleucus, to the command of a great empire, extending from the Euxine to the confines of Arabia. He founded as his Eastern capital Seleucia, on the banks of the Tigris, and for his Western metropolis Antioch, on the banks of the Orontes. The power of the Seleucidae thus became very great, and for several decades of years they contested with the Ptolemies the possession of Palestine. Eventually Antiochus the Great captured Jerusalem in 198 B.C., granted the Jews many privileges, and amply secured to them their religious liberty. Imitating the examples of Alexander and Seleucus, he removed two thousand Jewish families from Babylon to Lydia and Phrygia, assigning them land and exempting them from tribute.

7. **Antiochus Epiphanes.** His son, however, Seleucus Philopator, plundered the temple of Jerusalem, and his successor, Antiochus Epiphanes, took the city by storm, 170 B.C., slew vast numbers of the inhabitants, and sold many into slavery. At the same time, in pursuance of his Hellenizing policy—which aimed at welding together the motley mass of nationalities that made up his empire by imposing upon his subjects a common form of faith —he determined to stamp out Judaism, and with this end in view he profaned the Temple, dedicating it to Jupiter Olympius, burnt the sacred writings, and used every kind of torture to compel the Jews to renounce the religion and customs of their fathers. Thus was 'the abomination of desolation' spoken of by Daniel (11^{31}), i.e. an idol altar, set up on the altar of burnt offering (1 Macc. 1^{54}), and the daily sacrifice was 'taken away'.

(iii) *The Dominion of the Asmonaeans*, 167–63 B.C.

1. **The Chasidim.** The reign of Antiochus marked a great crisis in the history of the Jews. In Jerusalem itself the Hellenizing party, with their strong taste for Grecian manners and Grecian

arts, gained a great hold of the people, and exercised a powerful influence on the national life; but another party resisted these tendencies to the utmost, protested against all declension from the Mosaic law, and were known by the name of 'the Chasidim' or 'the pious', being opposed to all change, and zealous for the traditions of their fathers. The time was now come when an outward struggle alone could decide whether Judaism should degenerate into a rationalized Paganism or rise from the conflict more rigorous and more pure. The determination of Antiochus to stamp out Judaism provoked the struggle which now began.

2. **Mattathias.** The spirited resistance of the Chasidim to the efforts of Antiochus to Hellenize the people roused the national temper, and one noble-minded family raised the Jews from their prostrate misery to a height of power which recalled the splendour even of the reign of David. At Modin, on the road between Jerusalem and Joppa, lived a priest named Mattathias, the father of five heroic sons, and head of the Asmonaean family (so called from his great-grandfather Asmonai). When an apostate Jew approached a heathen altar at Modin to offer idolatrous sacrifice, he struck him down, and then slew Apelles, the commissioner of Antiochus, who had set up the altar. Aided by his five sons, he next rallied the faithful round him, and after throwing down the altar, fled to the mountains and raised the standard of liberty (1 Macc. 2^15, &c.).

3. **Judas Maccabaeus.** Mattathias died 166 B.C., and was succeeded by his son Judas, who displayed the greatest heroism, and was known as Maccabaeus, or the 'Hammer', like Charles Martel in later times. Alert of foot and quick of brain, in a few months of service he changed his rabble of zealots into an army of solid troops, and succeeded after a rapid and victorious career in winning a series of brilliant victories against overwhelming odds, which ended in the expulsion of the Syrians, and the re-dedication of the Temple on the 25th of the winter month Chisleu in the year 165 B.C. In commemoration of this event the Feast of the Dedication was instituted (John 10^22), and in the following year, 164 B.C., Antiochus Epiphanes died of an incurable disorder, while the brave Maccabee continued to lead the patriot forces till his death in battle at Eleasa, 161 B.C.

4. **Jonathan and Simon Maccabaeus.** Judas was succeeded by his brother Jonathan, who attained considerable success, and conducted the affairs of the country with vigour and prudence. He was assassinated 144 B.C., and was succeeded by his brother

Simon, who, favoured by the disorders of the time, at length was enabled, 141 B.C., to capture the citadel of Jerusalem (the Acra), which had hitherto been occupied by the Syrians, and to secure independence for his people. He gained for the Jews the active support of Rome (1 Macc. 15^{16-21}), and encouraged trade and agriculture. But he was murdered at a banquet, 135 B.C., by his son-in-law Ptolemaeus, the governor of Jericho, and his successful sway came to an end.

5. John Hyrcanus, his son and successor, reduced Idumaea, or Edom, conquered Samaria, and destroyed the temple on Mount Gerizim. He compelled the Idumaeans to unite with the Jewish people by submitting to circumcision. Escaping the fate of all the older members of his family, he died in peace, 106 B.C., and his son Aristobulus I was the first who assumed the kingly power. After this period the Asmonaean house suffered a complete moral collapse, and gradually declined in power, retaining none of the religious faith or moral purity of their ancestors. The grandsons of Aristobulus contended with each other for the sovereignty, and their internal disputes and jealousy paved the way for the intervention of the Romans. Unable to settle their respective claims themselves, they both appeared in Damascus before the Roman general Pompeius, who had lately seized that city. Pompeius postponed his decision, and shortly afterwards, 63 B.C., took Jerusalem, threw down the walls, and entered the Temple itself, but left its treasures untouched. He then nominated Hyrcanus II to the high priesthood, who, weak and indolent, permitted the artful Idumaean, Antipater, the father of Herod the Great, to administer affairs and assume the supreme power.

6. Pharisees and Sadducees. The *Assidaeans* ('Chasidim'), so long as religious liberty was at stake, fought side by side with the national party, led by the Asmonaeans. The alliance, however, did not last, the essential diversity of aim between the two soon becoming apparent. From the time of Judas Maccabaeus till the closing days of John Hyrcanus the Asmonaeans and the national party worked in close alliance with the priestly aristocracy who controlled the Sanhedrin. It is during the reign of John Hyrcanus that we first hear of the conflicting parties of Sadducees (= 'Zadokites') and Pharisees. The latter appear to have grown out of the ranks of a body of laymen, who were zealous for the teaching of the Law during the period of stress, when the old system of priestly scribal schools had broken down. The Pharisees (='separated ones') may have derived their name

from a split in the Sanhedrin, from which body, it appears, the Pharisaic members were expelled. More probably, however, the name was given because of their separatist rigour. The Pharisaic Party, who inherited the rigid ideals of the ' Chasidim ', abhorred Hellenism, and looked with suspicion upon the growing material greatness of the State. They came into violent conflict at this period with the Sadducees, which reached its climax in the reign of Alexander Jannaeus (104–78 B.C.), and the result of this internal strife, ultimately, was Roman intervention (63 B. C.), the Pharisees triumphing.

(iv) *The Dominion of the Idumaean Antipater, and Herod,* 63–4 B.C.

1. **Rise of the Herods.** Antipater made good use of the power he had acquired, and managed to keep in favour with the Roman authorities. . When Julius Caesar arrived in Egypt to carry on the Alexandrian war, Antipater espoused his cause, and was rewarded in 47 B.C. with the privilege of Roman citizenship and the procuratorship of Judaea. In this capacity he appointed his younger son Herod governor of Galilee, and when he himself was poisoned in 43 B. C., Herod, though left alone, was equal to the occasion, and managed to ingratiate himself with Mark Antony and Octavian, and in 40 B. C. was appointed king of all Judaea. In 37 B. C., with the aid of Roman troops, he captured Jerusalem, deposed the last Asmonaean prince, Antigonus, married his niece Mariamne, granddaughter of Hyrcanus the high priest, and became nominal sovereign, subject to Rome. ' By birth an Idumaean, by profession a Jew, by necessity a Roman, by culture and by choice a Greek ', he sought by every means in his power to reconcile his Jewish and Greek subjects to each other. He laid out a new palace on Sion ; he raised the city walls, and strengthened them in every part ; he rebuilt the Temple on the most gorgeous scale, and while he left the erection of the sanctuary to the care of the priests, he exhausted all his skill on the Court of the Gentiles, which he adorned with cloisters and rows of columns, with a marble pavement and many noble gates, one called 'Solomon's Porch' (John 10^{23}), and another 'the Beautiful Gate' (Acts 3^2).

2. **Cruelties of Herod.** But though he tried every means in his power he could not conciliate his heathen and Jewish subjects. His personal life alienated from him the sympathies of all good men. Household murder stained his hearth again and again. His nearest relatives, friends, companions, aged men, unoffending women, were slain, one in one way, another in another. As he

grew older, and the dream of founding a great independent empire faded away, the slightest suspicion provoked an order for a massacre. When he died at Jericho, 4 B.C., of internal ulcers and putrid sores, he had made use of his position to betray his country to the Roman power by fostering immorality, cultivating alien customs, sapping religious faith, corrupting the priesthood, massacring the nobles, and enacting such cruelties that it is not surprising that Josephus should have omitted to mention the swoop of his soldiers on a few babes at Bethlehem (Matt. 2^{16-18}).

3. **Effect on the Jews.** The loss of political liberty had a serious effect on the Jewish people. While on the one hand it filled them with exasperation against their oppressors, and the fiscal system, customs, and excise which foreign governors brought with them, on the other it drove them into greater and greater exclusiveness. The extraordinary energy and zeal of the Pharisees expended itself in the building up of the synagogue system and worship, and extending popular religious education. The Rabbinical schools flourished, and the synagogue and its allied institutions overshadowed the Temple itself. Pharisees, scribes, and lawyers were in greater esteem than priests and Levites, and the teaching became rhetorical and disputatious rather than dogmatic and authoritative.[*]

Appended Note. Much light is thrown upon the better and more spiritual elements in Pharisaic religion by the so-called *Psalms of Solomon* (perhaps written *c.* 63–40 B.C.), which exhibit a noble conception of the Messianic ideal.

The centuries immediately preceding the Christian era produced an extensive Jewish literature. This fruitful time is remarkable for the development of *Apocalyptic Writings*, the most notable example of which is the *Book of Enoch*. Apparently a whole literature of Enochic writings was at one time in existence. Such writings, too, as the *Book of Jubilees*, the *Assumption of Moses*, *Testaments of the Twelve Patriarchs* (in its original form) were produced at this period. The *Book of Daniel* is itself an apocalyptic writing (produced at the time of the Maccabaean crisis), and exercised a great influence on subsequent apocalyptic literature.

---

[*] For this period, see Lewin's *Fasti Sacri*, pp. 8–62 ; Schürer's *The Jewish People in the Time of Jesus Christ*, Div. I, vol. i, pp. 371–462 ; Dean Milman's *History of the Jews*, vol. ii ; Grätz, *History of the Jews* (English Translation), vols. i and ii ; Edwyn Bevan, *Jerusalem under the High Priests* ; and W. D. Morrison, *The Jews under Roman Rule*.

XXIII. CHRONOLOGICAL TABLE OF THE PERIOD

B.C.	Jews in Palestine and Egypt.	Contemporary Events.
350	Jaddua, High Priest.	Egypt a Persian province.
336	. . . .	Darius Codomannus, King of Persia : era of Alexander the Great.
334	. . . .	Alexander invades Persia. Victory at the Granicus.
333	. . . .	Battle of Issus.
332	Alexander visits Jerusalem.	Foundation of Alexandria.
331	Settlement of Jews at Alexandria.	Battle of Arbela.
330	Onias I, High Priest.	Death of Darius : end of the Persian Empire.
323	. . . .	Death of Alexander. The Ptolemies take the Egyptian kingdom ; the Seleucidae the Syrian.
320	Ptolemy Soter captures Jerusalem.	Colonies of Jews in Egypt and Cyrene.
	Palestine subject to Egypt.	
314	Palestine subject to Syria.	
310	Simon the Just, High Priest.	
301	Palestine reverts to Egypt.	Battle of Ipsus.
284	Beginning of the LXX translation of the Old Testament.	Ptolemy Philadelphus.
264	. . . .	First Punic War.
219	. . . .	Second Punic War.
201	. . . .	Colonies of Jews from Babylon transplanted to Asia Minor.
198	Antiochus the Great becomes master of Palestine.	Palestine subject to Syria.
175– 164	Antiochus Epiphanes.	
170	Tyranny of Antiochus Epiphanes.	
168	Revolt of Mattathias.	
167	Rise of the Maccabees.	
166	Judas Maccabaeus.	
165	Battles of Beth-horon and Emmaus. Re-dedication of the Temple.	
161	Judas killed in battle at Eleasa : Jonathan succeeds him. Asmonaean line of priestly rulers established.	
149	. . . .	Third Punic War.
146	. . . .	Fall of Carthage and Corinth. Greece a Roman province.
144	Murder of Jonathan Maccabaeus.	
141	Simon Maccabaeus completes the deliverance of Palestine.	

B.C.	Jews in Palestine and Egypt.	Contemporary Events.
135	Murder of Simon Maccabaeus: John Hyrcanus succeeds him.	
130	Hyrcanus destroys the temple on Mount Gerizim.	
109	First mention of Pharisees and Sadducees.	
107	Accession of Aristobulus, under the title of 'king'.	
106	Alexander Jannaeus. First mention of the Essenes.	
79	Alexandra, queen.	
69	Aristobulus II.	
63	Pompey subjugates Judaea.	Conspiracy of Catiline.
60	. . . . .	The first triumvirate.
58	. . . . .	Caesar in Gaul.
54	The Temple plundered by Crassus.	
48	. . . . .	Battle of Pharsalia: death of Pompey.
	Hyrcanus II restored.	
47	Antipater the Idumaean appointed by Caesar procurator of Judaea. Herod made governor of Galilee.	
44	. . . . .	Assassination of Caesar.
43	Death of Antipater.	
40	Hyrcanus banished; Antigonus succeeds: last of the Asmonaean priestly line. Herod at Rome. Herod appointed King of Judaea.	
37	Herod captures Jerusalem.	
31	. . . . .	Battle of Actium.
30	. . . . .	Egypt conquered by Octavian. Line of the Ptolemies ends.
29	. . . . .	Temple of Janus closed.
27	. . . . .	Augustus made emperor.
19	Herod begins to rebuild the Temple.	
16	Herod goes to meet Agrippa and invites him to Judaea.	Agrippa sent to settle the affairs of Syria.
15	Agrippa visits Judaea.	
14	He confirms the privileges of the Jews.	
11	The Outer Temple finished.	
4	Herod dies at Jericho after the NATIVITY OF OUR LORD.	

PART IV

THE NEW TESTAMENT

XXIV. SUMMARY OF THE BOOKS OF THE NEW TESTAMENT

1. Divisions of the New Testament. The Books of the New Testament may be grouped as follows:

i. *Historical Books.*

    (a) **The Four Gospels,** two bearing the names of Apostles, two by close friends and companions of Apostles.

    (b) **The Acts of the Apostles,** a sequel to the Third Gospel, forming the link of connexion between the historical and didactic portions.

ii. *Didactic.*

    (a) **The Pauline Epistles.**

        (1) *Doctrinal*: addressed to Churches, viz. Romans, Corinthians, Galatians, Ephesians, Philippians, Colossians, Thessalonians, Hebrews.

        (2) *Pastoral*: addressed to Timothy and Titus.

        (3) *Special*: addressed to an individual (Philemon).

    (b) **The General Epistles,** addressed to the Church at large.

        (1) One of St. James.

        (2) Two of St. Peter.

        (3) Three of St. John.

        (4) One of St. Jude.

iii. *Prophetic.*

The Revelation of St. John.

I. THE FIVE HISTORICAL BOOKS.

1. The name **Gospel** is applied to the four inspired histories, which contain the 'good tidings' of salvation through the life, death, and resurrection of Jesus Christ. The word Gospel is the Old English translation of the Greek word Εὐαγγέλιον, *Evangelium*. It is used by euphony for 'Godspel', that is 'News (spelian = *to tell*) about God'. It became current from Wyclif's translation.

2. One Gospel under Four Aspects. But though four in number the inspired histories really constitute one Gospel, as presented to the minds of four different writers. The first three give a combined and, for the most part, harmonious view of our Lord's life and teaching, and so are called 'Synoptic', from a Greek word which means *Taking the Same View* ; the fourth is supplementary and doctrinal. The four Gospels have often been supposed to have been prefigured by the four cherubim seen by Ezekiel in his vision (c. 1): St. Matthew as a *Man* ; St. Mark as a *Lion* ; St. Luke as an *Ox* ; St. John as an *Eagle*. The *first* emphasizes the kingly and human aspect of the life of Christ ; the *second*, the power and fullness of His living energy ; the *third*, His priestly and mediatorial character ; the *fourth*, His Divinity.

(i) ST. MATTHEW

1. St. Matthew was the son of Alphaeus, and a Hebrew. Before his conversion he was named Levi, and had been a 'publican', that is, a collector of tolls and customs imposed on persons and goods crossing the lake of Gennesaret at Capernaum. The Gospels, not excepting the one which bears his name, record nothing respecting him except his occupation, his call, and his farewell feast (Matt. 9^9, Luke 5^{29}). No saying of his is recorded in the Gospels, and he appears for the last time in Acts 1^{13}, after which he vanishes from our sight.

2. **Design.** Papias, who was Bishop of Hierapolis in Phrygia in the first half of the second century, says that Matthew wrote his Gospel in Hebrew, i. e. in Aramaic (Eusebius iii. 39). But as it is certain that our Gospel was originally written in Greek, and is in part a copy of St. Mark and of another Greek document which has disappeared, we cannot reconcile it with Papias's statement. The first Evangelist nowhere professes to have been an eye-witness of the events : and we cannot identify him. Writing for the Jews, his great object is to portray our Lord as the Fulfiller of the Old Testament promises—the Son of David, and therefore Heir to the Jewish Kingdom—the Son of Abraham, and therefore the Promised Seed, in whom all nations should be blessed (Matt. 1^1). In Him the Old Testament passes into the New ; the prohibitions of the Law into the encouragements of the Gospel ; Sinai into the Mount of Beatitudes ; the prophetic into the teaching office ; priesthood into redemption by suffering ; kingship into the supremacy of Almighty grace restoring a fallen world.

3. **Time, Place, and Characteristics.** The time and place of

writing are uncertain, but it is extremely probable that the Gospel was written in Palestine some time between A.D. 68 and 75. One of its special characteristics is its constant citations from the Old Testament, which amount to no less than sixty-five. This is significant of the writer's purpose. The authority of the books of the Old Covenant is always taken for granted, and made the basis of all teaching concerning the kingdom of heaven. The Law of Moses is represented as not done away but completely fulfilled, and the great discourses, which are such a peculiar feature of the Gospel, all bear on the work of the Messiah, as Lawgiver, Judge, and King.

4. Summary. The arrangement of the Gospel is not chronological, but in groups, showing how Jesus, the offspring of Abraham, fulfils the promises of the Old Testament. His doctrine and life disappoint the false aspirations of degenerate Judaism. The conflict provoked by this disappointment apparently terminates against Him; really it completes His triumph and establishes His kingdom, since His death reconciles the world to God. Thus, fulfilling the Old Covenant, He is the true Christ—eternal Prophet, Priest, and King.

The true character of the Messiah is attested :

1. By His lineal descent, and Divine revelation at His birth (1-4).

2. By the manifestation of His triple office (Prophet, Priest, and King), in conflict with the popular ideas (5-16).

3. By unfolding the true nature of His kingdom and its future history, in contrast with that of the ancient world (16-20).

4. By His self-sacrifice and humiliation (21-4).

5. By prophetic revelations of the judgement on the Jewish nation and on the world (24, 25).

6. By His sacerdotal presentation of Himself as the atoning sacrifice (26, 27).

7. By His glorification at the right hand of power (28).

(ii) ST. MARK

1. St. Mark. Marcus was the Latin surname of the writer of the second Gospel. His Hebrew name was John. He was the son of Mary, whose house at Jerusalem became the refuge and earliest church of the Christian community (Acts 12[12]). He was nephew or cousin of Barnabas, and the attendant of the Apostles Barnabas and Paul on their first mission (Acts 13[5]); but returned home from Perga (Acts 13[13]), and was not allowed by St. Paul to join them on their second mission. Upon this he

attached himself to Barnabas, but was afterwards reconciled to St. Paul (Col. 4[10]), who charges Timothy to bring him with him to Rome, during his second imprisonment, as one who was 'profitable unto him for ministering'. We have traces of him also in 1 Peter 5[13], and he is the reputed founder of the Alexandrian Church.

2. **Design of the Gospel.** Eusebius iii. 39, quoting Papias, whose authority was 'John the Elder', says that St. Mark was the 'interpreter of St. Peter', and it is possible that the Apostle in some way superintended the composition of the Gospel, which was written primarily for Gentiles. This is made probable by internal evidence. For St. Mark (i) omits all reference to the Jewish Law; (ii) he gives no genealogy of our Lord; (iii) he explains words which could not be understood by Gentile readers, as *Boanerges* (3[17]), *Talitha cumi* (5[41]), *Corban* (7[11]); (iv) he appends explanations which Jews would not require (1[5], 2[18], 13[3]); (v) he uses several Latin words which do not occur in the other Gospels.

3. **Time, Place, and Characteristics.** According to primitive tradition the place where the Gospel was written was Rome, and the date was clearly before the destruction of Jerusalem, probably between A.D. 50 and 60. St. Mark abounds in graphic touches; event succeeds event in rapid succession; his favourite word is 'straightway', which occurs no less than forty-one times; he prefers the present tense, supplies, as above noted, the very vernacular words used in the occurrences he narrates (3[17, 22], 5[41]), and often notices the very looks, and accents, and gestures (3[5, 34], 5[32], 10[23], 11[11]) of the Lord. All this suggests strongly that the Gospel has behind it the testimony of an eyewitness. It is what we should expect to find if after St. Peter's death St. Mark had written down the story, as he had been accustomed to hear the Apostle tell it.

4. **Summary.** The book may be thus divided: (i) The Preparation (1[1–13]). (ii) The works of Christ in Eastern Galilee (1[14]–7[23]). (iii) The works of Christ in Northern Galilee (7[24]-9[50]). (iv) The works of Christ in Peraea (10[1–31]). (v) The last journey to Jerusalem and the Passion (10[32]–15[47]). (vi) The Resurrection and Ascension (16).

(iii) ST. LUKE

1. **St. Luke** was in all probability a Gentile, and perhaps a native of Antioch. He was a physician (Col. 4[14]), and the faithful companion of St. Paul. He first appears by the Apostle's side in Acts 16[10], on the eve of the voyage to Europe, and after a

considerable stay at Philippi accompanied him to Jerusalem (Acts $21^{15, 18}$), and shared his imprisonment at Caesarea. From thence he sailed with him on the disastrous voyage to Rome, remained by his side during his first imprisonment, and was with him on the eve of his martyrdom (2 Tim. 4^{11}).

2. **Time and Place of Writing.** Tradition asserts that he wrote his Gospel under the influence of St. Paul, and from Acts 1^1 it is clear that it was written before the Acts of the Apostles. The opinion has been held that it was written about A.D. 60, but a later date is more probable.

3. **The Superior Education of the Evangelist** is proved by the literary excellence of his writings, viz. his Gospel and the Acts of the Apostles, which constitute but two volumes of one work. His preface, in pure Greek, asserts a careful study of documentary and other evidence. He speaks of 'other attempts' to write a life of Christ, which were unsatisfactory. Though it is the same Gospel, it is narrated with peculiar independence, containing additional matter, more accuracy in preserving the chronological order of events, and complying with the requirements of history. He tested tradition by documentary records (e. g. 1^5, 2^2, 3^1); by comparing the oral testimony of living witnesses ($1^{2, 3}$); and only when he had 'perfect understanding of all things from the very first', ventured to compile a 'Life of Christ' as a perfect man, restoring human nature, and offering Himself a sacrifice for all mankind.

4. **Special Features.** Writing according to common belief for Greeks, the Evangelist presents our Lord to us in the widest and most universal aspect as the Redeemer of the entire human race. His Gospel is (i) *The Gospel of the Infancy*, and to him we are indebted for the account of the birth and childhood of Jesus and His Forerunner, and for the Song of Zacharias, of the Blessed Virgin, and of Simeon (1, 2). (ii) *It is the Gospel for the Gentiles.* He traces our Lord's genealogy to Adam (3^{38}), and specially records the parallels of Elijah being sent to the woman of Sarepta ($4^{25, 26}$), and of Elisha healing the heathen Naaman (4^{27}), and the Mission of the Seventy (10^{1-16}). (iii) *It is the Gospel for the outcast and the despised.* He gives the parables of the lost sheep, the lost coin, and the prodigal son (15^{3-32}); the prayer of our Lord for those who crucified Him (23^{34}); and the promise to the penitent malefactor (23^{43}).

5. **Summary.** The general outline runs as follows: (i) The Introduction, the birth of Jesus and His Forerunner, His manifestation in Childhood, and growth to Manhood (1, 2). (ii) The

Baptism and Temptation (3–4¹³). (iii) The early Ministry in Galilee (4¹⁴–8). (iv) Incidents and Teachings in Peraea and the North (9–18). (v) The Passion, Death, and Burial (19–23). (v) The Resurrection and Ascension (24).

6. **The Synoptic Problem.** The study of the problem of the literary relation between the first, second, and third Gospels, which has exercised the minds of scholars for the past century, has led to two conclusions, the first of which is almost universally accepted, and the second only less so. These are (a) that the Gospel of Mark was employed as a leading source both by the writer of the first and the writer of the third Gospel; (b) that when the Markan matter has been separated from the first and third Gospels, the common matter which remains is derived from a lost work, commonly called Q (*Quelle*, German for ' source '), which consisted mainly of sayings of our Lord which had been translated from Aramaic into Greek, and were handled by the first and third evangelists in this Greek dress. (See Sir John Hawkins's *Horae Synopticae*, 2nd ed., Clarendon Press, *Studies in the Synoptic Problem*, by Members of the University of Oxford, edited by W. Sanday, Clarendon Press, and *The Four Gospels*, by Canon Streeter).

(iv) ST. JOHN

1. **The Fourth Gospel** has always borne the name of John and has always been ascribed to the son of Zebedee. Irenaeus in his letter to Florinus, which was written before A.D. 180, says that Polycarp, Bishop of Smyrna (d. 156), had told him that it was the work of the Apostle. As Polycarp had been a disciple of St. John, it is very difficult to set this testimony aside.

There is no doubt that the Gospel is the work of an eye-witness, or at least rests upon the testimony of an eye-witness, and its historical value need not be called in question. But it presents certain features which make it difficult to believe that the author was a Galilean fisherman. Not only is the style very unlike that of the other evangelists, but the author seems to have known what passed at a private meeting of the Sanhedrin (11⁴⁷⁻⁵³), and to have had unrestricted right of entry into the high priest's palace, where he was well known (18¹⁵, ¹⁶). It must be a matter of opinion whether such considerations as these outweigh the testimony of Polycarp or not.

It has been suggested that ' the beloved disciple ' who wrote the Gospel was a constant companion of our Lord, but not one of the Twelve. If this were so he might have been some years younger than any of the Apostles, and might have lived until the end of the first century without having attained an abnormal age.[*]

2. **Time and Place of Writing.** Tradition is unanimous that he composed his Gospel at the request of the elders of the Christian Churches of Asia, most probably at Ephesus towards the close of the first century, as the summary of his oral teaching upon the life of Christ. 'The contents of the Gospel', says Bishop Westcott, 'go far to support this view of its relatively late date. It assumes a knowledge of the substance of the Synoptic narratives. It deals with later aspects of Christian life and opinion than these. It corresponds with the circumstances of a new world.'[†]

3. **The Object.** What his purpose was in composing it he tells us plainly himself. '*These are written*', he says, '*that ye may believe that Jesus is the Christ, the Son of God; and that believing ye may have life in His name*' (20³¹). Therefore the evangelist carefully selects and arranges certain scenes from the life of his Divine Master, which all lead up, step by step, to the confession of St. Thomas, 'My Lord and my God'. But, on the other side, there is a development also of the unbelief and hatred which rejected and ultimately slew the Lord of Glory.

4. **Characteristics.** From the earliest times the fourth Gospel has been distinguished as 'the spiritual Gospel'. While the Synoptists give us mainly the external acts of the Son of Man, St. John gives us glimpses of His very inner life. His subject is the Eternal Word made flesh, (i) as pre-existent, (ii) as incarnate, (iii) as revealing the Father, (iv) as connecting humanity with Divinity through His own incarnation. Hence his Gospel contains a much larger proportion of Christ's discourses than we find in the others. He assumes that the contents of his predecessors' Gospels are known to his readers, and abstains from traversing the same ground. St. John only narrates one miracle which is common to all the four Gospels (the feeding of the five thousand), but gives us four others not mentioned elsewhere, viz. (i) the change of water into wine, (ii) the healing of the impotent man, (iii) the cure of one born blind, and (iv) the raising of Lazarus. While the events narrated by the Synoptists are mainly those which took place in Galilee, St. John's Gospel is almost wholly occupied with Christ's ministry in Judaea, and one-third of it is devoted to the sayings and doings of the last twenty-four hours of His life. He omits all parables.

[*] See *The Criticism of the Fourth Gospel*, by W. Sanday (Clarendon Press, 1905), especially pp. 97–108.

[†] *Introduction to St. John's Gospel*, p. xxxvi.

5. Summary. The following analysis may be helpful: We have in the Gospel (i) *The Prologue.* The pre-existent and Incarnate Word (1^{1-18}). (ii) *The revelation of Himself to the world* (*a*) by the preaching of the Baptist (1^{19-34}), and the first-called disciples (1^{35-51}); (*b*) by His own 'signs' and 'works' at Cana (2^{1-11}), Jerusalem ($2^{13}-3$), Samaria ($4^{1, 42}$), Galilee (4^{43-54}). (iii) *Development of Antagonism* (*a*) after the miracle at the pool of Bethesda (5); (*b*) after the feeding of the five thousand (6); (*c*) at the Feast of Tabernacles (7, 8); (*d*) after the healing of the man born blind (9, 10); (*e*) after the resurrection of Lazarus (11); (*f*) after the triumphal entry (12). (iv) *Christ's revelation of Himself in the last Discourses*: (*a*) He washes His disciples' feet (13^{1-30}); (*b*) reveals His approaching departure to the Father and the coming of the Paraclete (14^{1-31}); (*c*) declares Himself to be the true Vine, and the true source of union with the Church (15^{1}-16); (*d*) offers up His last high-priestly prayer to His Father (17). (v) *The Passion and Resurrection,* resulting in belief in Him as the risen Lord by Mary Magdalene, St. John, the Ten, St. Thomas (18-20). (vi) *Epilogue.* The manifestation by the lake, the restoration of St. Peter, the attestation of the Ephesian elders (21).

(v) THE ACTS OF THE APOSTLES

1. The Acts of the Apostles is described as 'a second treatise' by St. Luke, and it commences with an inscription to the same Theophilus whom the evangelist addresses in his Gospel. It is a continuation of the life of our Lord, who through the promised Spirit is manifested on earth in the deeds and preaching of the Apostles. Hence it has been called 'the Gospel of the Spirit'.

2. Time and Place of Writing. These points we are left to gather from indirect notices. But it is most probable that St. Luke wrote it at Rome, whither he accompanied St. Paul (Acts 28). As the narrative terminates about the year A.D. 62, its composition may have been soon after that date, and possibly not later than A.D. 63.

3. Special Features. The book is a 'Book of Origins'. It is the earliest sketch of the formation and spread of the Christian Church. It tells of 'the first Apostolic miracle, the first Apostolic sermon, the first rise of ecclesiastical organization, the first persecution, the first martyr, the first Gentile convert, the first European Church'. In the Codex Sinaiticus it is entitled simply Πράξεις, '*Acts*'; and this, or 'Acts of Apostles', is a more correct title than '*the* Acts of *the* Apostles', for it really contains a detailed account of only two Apostles, St. Peter and St. Paul.

4. **Contents.** The best analysis, therefore, of the book, is that which divides it into (*a*) *the Acts of St. Peter* (cc. 1–13³), and (*b*) *the Acts of St. Paul* (13⁴–28).

(*a*) *The Acts of St. Peter*: Birth of the Christian Church and its spread to Samaria, comprising (i) Foundation and Progress of the Church in Jerusalem and Judaea (1–8); (ii) First Persecution, and Extension to Samaria and to the Gentile family of Cornelius (8–11¹⁸); (iii) Second Persecution, and Foundation of the Church at Antioch (11¹⁹–13³).

(*b*) *The Acts of St. Paul*: Extension of the Church to the Gentiles. (i) St. Paul's Call, and first Apostolic journey (13⁴–15⁵); (ii) Council of Jerusalem, fixing terms of admission (15); (iii) Second Apostolic journey (15³⁶–18²²); (iv) Third Apostolic journey (18²³–21¹⁷); (5) St. Paul's imprisonment at Caesarea, and voyage to Rome (21¹⁸–28).

5. Thus we trace the Progress of the Christian Society from a small Jewish sect to a Universal Church. The same marks of Catholicity as regards the offer of the Glad Tidings to the entire human race, which we notice in the third Gospel, are maintained in the Acts; and though the book touches in all directions upon contemporary events, politics, and topography, yet 'no ancient work', to use the words of Bishop Lightfoot, 'affords at so many points so many tests of veracity'.*

II. Didactic.

(1) *THE PAULINE EPISTLES*

Introductory.

1. **The Epistles.** The twenty-one letters contained in the New Testament form a unique collection amongst the sacred books of the world. The Bibles of the world, the Vedas, the Koran, the Zend-Avesta, the writings of Confucius, contain no letters. They are poems, philosophical discourses, or legendary histories, but they never assume the epistolary form.†

The fact that a large part of the New Testament consists of letters is of real importance.

(*a*) Genuine letters are the least 'studied' of all forms of literary composition; therefore their historical value is very great. More

---

* See also Sir W. Ramsay, *St. Paul the Traveller and the Roman Citizen* (Hodder and Stoughton, 1895). For an exposition of the book, see *The Acts of the Apostles*, R. B. Rackham (Methuen, 1901).

† Archdeacon Farrar's *The Message of the Books*, p. 143.

formal documents may lie under the suspicion of having been composed with a view to impressing posterity, and in order to uphold some particular point of view. But genuine letters are spontaneous productions. They are intended for contemporaries, who are probably in a position to check many of the author's statements out of their own knowledge. The author says what he really thinks, and is dealing with matters of which he really knows. Therefore what he says, and still more what he implies, may generally be accepted as true history without demur.

We may sometimes regret that the apostolic letters are so few and so brief. But no other form of documentary evidence as to the beliefs and practices of the first generation of Christians which could have come down to us could be of equal value.

(*b*) It is to be remembered that the Epistles are letters. Therefore they are not to be read as if they were formal theological treatises. Romans, Ephesians, and (within narrower limits) Hebrews answer most nearly to this description (see below, pp. 150, 155, 161). But they too are letters. The Epistles furnish us with a very vivid sketch of Christian principles as they concern the life of the community and that of the individual. They were never intended to provide an exhaustive table of doctrinal and ecclesiastical precedents. The exact method in which the principles are to be applied to daily life is the task which the Church has to take up for itself in every generation.

2. **General Characteristics.** The Epistles are all more or less ' occasional '. They were originally written in view of some special set of circumstances and intended for a limited circle of readers only. (This applies less to James and to 1 John than to any others. But it is, within limits, true of them.) Therefore, while the structure of them all is much the same, the contents differ widely. But one most noteworthy feature is common to them all. Expediency and compromise have no place in them. Everything is a matter of principle. Every difficulty, whether small or great, which can possibly arise is to be settled by reference to the eternal principles which the Life, Death, and Resurrection of Christ have brought to the knowledge of mankind. For this reason the apostolic letters can never become obsolete. The Church has acted rightly in raising them to the rank of Scripture.

It is also to be remembered that the majority of the Epistles are older than any written Gospel which we now possess.* They

---

* 1 and 2 Timothy and Titus may be later than St. Mark. 2 Peter, Jude, and the three epistles of John are almost certainly later than the first three Gospels.

reveal to us what the first generation of Christians really believed, and how they tried to live. The Gospels show us *why* the first Christians believed what they did, and the source from which they drew the courage and resolution needed for the supremely difficult undertaking of walking in *The Way*.

3. **The Chronological Order of the Pauline Epistles** is of great importance. As generally arranged, their chronological order is not noted. The letters to the Romans and Corinthians are put first, apparently because of the size and importance of Rome and Corinth ; while the letters to the Ephesians and Colossians precede the Epistles to the Thessalonians, though the latter were without doubt composed some years before. Many scholars, for instance, hold that the Epistles to the Thessalonians are the earliest. There is some doubt about one or two separate Epistles, but the following is probably the true order :

I. Before Imprisonment at Rome.

Galatians, A. D. 50	1 Corinthians, A. D. 55
1 Thessalonians,* A. D. 51	2 Corinthians, A. D. 55
2 Thessalonians, A. D. 51	Romans, A. D. 56

II. During the Roman Imprisonment.

Philippians, *c.* A. D. 60	Philemon, *c.* A. D. 61
Colossians, *c.* A. D. 61	Ephesians, *c.* A. D. 61

III. After the Roman Imprisonment.†

1 Timothy	Titus
2 Timothy ‡	

(a) Doctrinal.

(i) THE EPISTLE TO THE ROMANS

1. **The Church of Rome** was probably founded by Jews and proselytes from Jerusalem, who had been converted by St. Peter on the Day of Pentecost (Acts 2[10]), and on returning to Rome became the nucleus of a Christian congregation. Others would be added on the return of the Jews who had been banished from Rome in the time of Claudius, and had, in not a few instances, become Christians (Acts 18[2]). It is probable that the letter is in reality an 'encyclical', i. e. that it was intended for all churches and not exclusively for Rome. If so, the personal salutations in

---

* The subscriptions to the Epistles in the Authorized Version are destitute of authority.

† Contain genuine fragments, but compiled by another writer.

‡ See the Chronological Table below, p. 196.

chapter 16 may have belonged originally to the copy intended for Ephesus, where St. Paul had many friends.*

2. **Occasion, Place, and Date of the Epistle.** Though in the first instance the members of the Church were probably Jews, it had received considerable accessions from the Gentiles, and they were apparently in a large majority. There was much to draw the Apostle's thoughts towards the great capital of the West, and he had planned a visit to it, but his intention had been frustrated (Rom. 1¹³). During, however, his stay at Corinth, A. D. 56, the departure of Phoebe, a deaconess of Cenchreae, for Rome, seemed to present a favourable opportunity for writing to the Church there, and this he accordingly did.

3. **Object.** (i) In view of the composition of the Church the thoughts of St. Paul would naturally be directed towards the *true doctrine of Justification*, and he resolved to state and explain in all its bearings the Divine plan of salvation for Jews and Gentiles alike. (ii) The failure of the Jews to attain righteousness has been no less signal than that of the Gentiles. Salvation cannot be secured by the accident of birth ; nor can it be earned as a right by the performance of prescribed duties. It is the gift of God, and can be received only through faith in Jesus Christ. It is open to all who show themselves morally worthy, but is not bestowed upon any other terms. (iii) Ceremonial details are of no importance in themselves. They are of value only in so far as they help to build up character (c. 14).

4. **Summary.** The Epistle falls into two great divisions, (i) *doctrinal* and (ii) *practical*. I. *Doctrinal*. (i) After a greeting and thanksgiving (1¹⁻¹⁵), the Apostle sets forth his fundamental thesis, the condemnation of the Jew and Gentile alike as involved in the guilt of sin (1¹⁸–3). (ii) He shows how both are justified by the work of Christ through faith, which is contrasted with that of Adam, through whose transgression came death (4, 5) ; and how (iii) free grace does not multiply sin or discredit the Law (6–8). (iv) He next dwells on the sad condition and rejection of Israel, and shows that it is not final but temporary, that their future restoration will involve the blessing of the Gentiles (9–11). II. *The Practical* portion now commences, and in it he (i) exhorts the Roman Christians to the steady cultivation of various Christian graces (12), to obedience to civil authority (13), to mutual forbearance especially as regards the question of foods (14, 15), and

---

* See D. Smith's *The Life and Letters of St. Paul*, pp. 373-8.

(ii) closes with a long list of greetings and salutations, and a final blessing (16).

(ii) THE FIRST EPISTLE TO THE CORINTHIANS

1. **The Church of Corinth,** to which St. Paul addressed at least two Epistles, included not only the Corinthians, but those who lived in the adjacent district of Achaia, i.e. the upper portion of the Morea, along the coast of the gulf of Lepanto. Corinth was the great centre of commercial traffic on the overland route from Rome to the East, and also between Upper and Lower Greece. It possessed the only good harbour in that quarter, and, as it was the shortest and safest route, small vessels were dragged across the isthmus, larger ones transhipped their cargoes, and hence most of the trade of the Mediterranean flowed through it, so that 'a perpetual fair was held there from year's end to year's end'; to which were added the great annual gatherings of Greeks at the 'Isthmian Games' (alluded to by St. Paul, 1 Cor. 9^{24-7}). Hence, also, it was proverbial for wealth, luxury, and profligacy. Its population, and that of Achaia, was in great part foreign, formed of descendants of colonists from Julius Caesar's army and of manumitted slaves (e.g. Tertius, Quartus, Achaicus, Fortunatus, etc.), settlers from Asia Minor, returned exiles from the islands, and at this time a large influx of Jews lately expelled from Rome (Acts 18^2).

2. **Foundation of the Church.** The Apostle first visited Corinth in A. D. 50, and his preaching in the synagogues was acceptable, till he boldly testified that Jesus was the Messiah. Then persecution set in; the Jews set upon him, and dragged him before the judgement-seat of Gallio, the Roman governor (Acts 18^{12}). Yet he was successful in founding a Church. His disciples were mostly of the lower orders of society, partly Jews, but mainly Roman freedmen and heathen Greeks, who became enthusiastic admirers of the Apostle. The natural jealousy between these two bodies, repressed during the Apostle's presence, burst out on his departure, and divided the Church into various parties. (i) Some professed fidelity solely to Paul himself (1^{12}, 3^4); (ii) a second party, probably the Jewish section, to Peter and 'the brethren of the Lord' (1^{12}, 9^5); (iii) a third, enthralled by the eloquence of Apollos, had attached themselves to him (1^{12}); (iv) while a fourth styled themselves the Christ party (1^{12}). Some did not shrink from bringing their disputes before heathen tribunals. And there was apparently a section which held that nothing which was done in the body

could defile the soul. This had naturally led to a complete disregard of all moral obligation, and had scandalized even pagan public opinion (5, 6).

3. **Occasion and Date of Epistle.** Amidst such corruption, during three years, factions attained a formidable height. The Apostle was defamed by the Jewish party, and rumours of alarming disputes reached him, followed by a letter brought by a deputation of freedmen, full of inquiries on matters of morality and doctrine. He had already dispatched Timothy to Corinth. Now, instead of going thither as he had intended, he writes the first Epistle to the Church there from Ephesus, in the spring of A. D. 55.

4. **Summary.** After a salutation and thanksgiving (1^{1-9}), (i) he severely reproves the spirit of faction, contrasts his own simple preaching with the assumptions of his followers, and sets forth the proper relation of teachers and disciples ($1^{10}-4^{21}$). (ii) He then proceeds to deal with the moral disorders in the Corinthian Church, the case of incest, going to law in heathen courts, and gives advice concerning marriage and celibacy, and instructions concerning the marriage of virgins (5–7). (iii) He next treats of food offered to idols and the heathen sacrificial feasts, comments on the conduct and dress of women at the public services of the Church, rebukes the disorders at the Holy Eucharist, deals with spiritual gifts, and shows that love is the greatest of all gifts, and that the gift of prophecy is superior to that of tongues (8–14). (iv) Then in an immortal chapter he establishes the doctrine of the Resurrection (15), and (v) concludes with sundry practical directions, salutations, and the Apostolic benediction (16).

(iii) THE SECOND EPISTLE TO THE CORINTHIANS

1. **The Second Epistle** as we have it now is thought by some scholars to be composite. The change of tone after the end of chapter 9 is so marked that chapters 10, 11, 12, and 13 to the end of verse 10 are held by them to constitute a separate letter. On this theory this document is the 'severe letter' referred to in 10^{10} and, somewhat less explicitly, in 2^4; or at least a part of it. It was written before 2 Cor. 1–9, and the riot at Ephesus and St. Paul's flight (Acts 19) intervened between them. These incidents are referred to in 2 Cor. 1^{8-11}. The last four verses of chapter 13 must then belong to chapter 9, and must have been removed to their present position when the two letters were run together.* This hypothesis is plausible and in many ways attractive ; but it must be admitted

---

* See D. Smith's *The Life and Letters of St. Paul*, pp. 655-6.

that it rests on internal evidence only. It assumes that St. Paul *could* not have changed his tone so abruptly and completely in the course of a single letter. This is surely an assumption. It is not supported by any MS. which we possess, or by any external testimony of any kind. It also presupposes a considerable degree of carelessness in the handling of documents on the part of the primitive Church. This presupposition often affords a convenient support for some critical theories; but apart from its manifest convenience we have no real warrant for postulating it.

We can only say that while certain considerations point to our 2 Corinthians being compounded of two letters of St. Paul, which have got out of order, other considerations point in the opposite direction.

2. **News from Corinth.** This had been unfavourable. The disorders which had evoked 1 Cor. still continued, and the Apostle's personal character and authority were being impugned (11^7, 12^{20}). Therefore he dispatched a stern letter, probably by the lad Titus, from Ephesus or Macedonia in the summer of A. D. 55. This was effective, and led to the third joyful letter (2 Cor. 1–9), probably in the following year.

3. **Summary.** (A). Vindication of his own motives and apostleship, which consists principally of an unvarnished narrative of his sufferings for Christ's sake (11^{23-33}) and of the revelations which had been vouchsafed to him (12^{1-13}).

(B). (i) Thankfulness for his own escape from imminent danger, and for the good news which he has at last received from Corinth (1^1–6^{13}). (ii) Warnings as to the moral dangers arising from the heathen society surrounding them. (iii) Recognition of the effect produced by the stern epistle (6^5, ^{16}). (iv) The arrangements for the collection for the benefit of the poor Christians of Jerusalem which was being made in the churches of Macedonia and Achaia (8, 9).

(iv) THE EPISTLE TO THE GALATIANS

1. **Galatia**, 'the Gaul of the East', was the name given by the Greeks to a comparatively small district of Asia Minor, occupied by the descendants of the Gauls, who had poured down into Italy and Greece in the third century B.C. Driven thence, they forced their way into Asia Minor, and were pent up in a strip of land amidst the central mountain fastnesses. The people were first barbarian, then mingling with the Greeks became tempered by Greek civilization, and were finally subjugated by the Romans

(189 B.C.). In 25 B.C. the name was given by the Romans to a 'province' which included, in addition to the original Galatia, (a) a large part of Phrygia, (b) Pisidia, (c) Isaurica, (d) part of Lycaonia, (e) Pontus Galaticus, (f) Paphlagonia. It is almost certain that it is in this wider sense that St. Paul uses the term Galatia, and that the churches of Galatia are Pisidian Antioch, Iconium, Lystra, and Derbe.

2. **Foundation of the Church.** St. Paul visited the country in A.D. 44 on his first missionary journey, and, while detained there by illness (Gal. 4$^{13, 14}$), converted many Jews and Gentiles (3$^{27, 28}$). He visited it again on his third journey (Acts 18^{23}). Originally worshippers of those who were 'no gods' (4^8), some of the Galatians were converted to Judaism, then, welcoming the Apostle with peculiar fervour (4^{14}), they received his announcement of a crucified Saviour with corresponding gladness.

3. **Occasion and Date of Epistle.** But the Apostle's enemies, the Judaisers, interfered. They insisted on the necessity of circumcision and the observance of the Mosaic Law. They impugned his credit and represented him as nothing compared with James, Peter, and John, 'the pillars' of the Church (2^9). This teaching completely 'fascinated' the impressionable Galatians (3^1), and many relapsed into Judaism with the same alacrity with which they had before accepted the Apostle's doctrine. This induced him to write the present Epistle in A.D. 50, for the purpose of stopping this falling away into Judaism and expounding the contrast between 'the righteousness of the Law' and 'Justification by faith', as more fully set forth afterwards in the Epistle to the Romans.

4. **Summary.** The Epistle begins with words of severity, and then parts under three heads. (i) *Personal.* The Apostle complains of the fickleness of the Galatians, and vindicates his own independence of (a) the twelve Apostles, and (b) Peter, the Apostle of the Circumcision (1–2^{21}). (ii) *Doctrinal.* He shows from the Old Testament how the Law was not final but preparatory to the Gospel Dispensation, which was its fulfilment (3–4^{31}). (iii) *Practical.* He then dwells on the nature of Christian freedom, warns the Galatians against its abuse, and exhorts them to let faith work by love, and to walk in the Spirit (5, 6).

(v) THE EPISTLE TO THE EPHESIANS

1. The words 'at Ephesus' are not found in some of the best MSS., and from the absence of personal greetings and any indications of personal intimacy, it has been thought to have been a circular

letter, of which copies were sent to several adjacent Churches in the province of Roman Asia (*see* Col. 4[16]). It might be entitled *On the Church.*

2. **Ephesus was to Asia,** as Corinth to Greece, the great port, to which flowed the commerce of the East and West. The inhabitants were noted for their licentious and luxurious life, for the cultivation of magical arts, and the fanatical worship of the Asiatic Artemis, the personification of natural fertility. Her temple, owing to its magnificent structure and extravagant enrichment, was one of the wonders of the world and the centre of worship and nationality, as that of Solomon was to the Jews; but the three years' sojourn there of the Apostle broke its power, till the annual Pan-Ionic festival brought about a temporary reaction (Acts 19).

3. **Date and Object.** The letter belongs to the period of St. Paul's Roman imprisonment, and was written from Rome about A.D. 61. It was not evoked by any relapse or special errors on the part of the members of the Ephesian Church, but was written to establish those who had left heathenism, and been made partakers of the fore-ordained election of all members of the Universal Church, in their holy faith, to contrast their present higher life with their former state of degradation, and to exhort them to walk in a way worthy of their calling.

4. **Summary.** Like the Epistle to the Colossians, which it greatly resembles, the letter falls into two clearly marked divisions. *Three* chapters are doctrinal; *three* are moral and practical. I. *Doctrinal.* (*a*) The Apostle thanks God for the glorious inheritance to which the Ephesians had been called, and which had been manifested in the death, resurrection, and exaltation of His Son (1); (*b*) he enlarges on the mystery of the call of the Gentiles to participation in Christian privileges (2); (*c*) he dwells on the union of Christians with God and with each other in Christ, and prays that the Ephesians may be strengthened by the indwelling of Christ, and may more and more realize their high vocation and its responsibilities (3). II. *Practical.* In this section he exhorts them (*a*) to unity (4[1-16]); (*b*) to a higher Christian walk in conformity with the mind of God and in the steps of Christ (4[17-32]); (*c*) to consecrate to Him all their actions in the various relationships of life, as husbands, wives, children, parents, slaves (5[6, 10]); and (*d*) to put on the whole armour of God as the only safeguard against evil in themselves and in the world around (6[10-24]).

(vi) THE EPISTLE TO THE PHILIPPIANS

1. **Philippi,** so named from the great Macedonian king who founded it, was situated in Macedonia, north of the archipelago, on the great high road between Europe and Asia. It was the scene of the last struggle of the Roman republic against despotism, where Brutus and Cassius, defeated by Octavian and Antony, committed suicide. It was then made a Roman 'colony' or garrison city of Roman citizen soldiers, governed by Roman magistrates and laws—a miniature of the imperial city. The Jews were few, and had no synagogue, but were allowed 'a place of prayer' outside the city gate on the banks of the Gangites.

2. **Foundation of the Church there.** St. Paul first visited Philippi in A.D. 49–50, and at 'the place of prayer' (Acts 16¹³) converted Lydia, a proselyte of Thyatira. Here, too, through healing a damsel possessed with ventriloquistic power, he came into collision with paganism, and was brought before the magistrates on a charge of creating a disturbance in the colony, and with his companion Silas was scourged and imprisoned. During the night, however, they were miraculously delivered, the jailer was converted, and a faithful Christian community was founded. Twice again he visited his grateful converts—first awaiting at Philippi in an agony of suspense the arrival of Titus from Corinth (2 Cor. 2¹³, 7⁵, ⁶), then afterwards lingering behind there to keep with them the paschal feast on his way to Asia Minor in A. D. 57 (Acts 20⁵, ⁶).

3. **Occasion and Date of Epistle.** The members of the Church of Philippi always retained the greatest gratitude and affection for the Apostle (Phil. 4¹⁰). One of them, Epaphroditus, arrived at Rome in A. D. 60, during St. Paul's imprisonment, with a generous contribution to his necessities, which had been sent by that loving Church (Phil. 4¹⁸). Here the devoted messenger was laid low by a dangerous illness, and almost lost his life. On his recovery he was filled with anxiety to return to his friends at Philippi, who were in much distress at the news of his sickness. St. Paul also was anxious that he should rejoin them in order to quiet their alarm ; and so Epaphroditus returned, bearing a letter from the Apostle, in which he pours forth his warm affection to a grateful Church.

4. **Analysis.** In it (i) the Apostle expresses his heartfelt thankfulness for all he had heard of the constancy of the Philippians under persecution, and for their liberality towards himself (1¹⁻¹²).

(ii) He then dwells on his own personal circumstances, and on the results of his imprisonment as tending to the spread of the Church (1^{13-30}). (iii) He exhorts the Philippians to unity, and dwells on the humility of Christ as the great exemplar (2^{1-18}), expresses his intention of shortly sending Timothy to them, and refers to the recent illness of Epaphroditus (2^{19-30}). (iv) He then digresses into a warning against Judaising teachers and evil workers (3^{1-21}). (v) He urges two female converts of distinction, who had fallen into strife, to reconciliation (4^{1-3}), exhorts all members of the church to a holy and consistent life (4^{4-13}), and concludes with an allusion to his personal position and a salutation from the Christians in Caesar's household (4^{14-23}).

(vii) THE EPISTLE TO THE COLOSSIANS

1. Colossae, or Colassae, was a chief city of Phrygia, situated in the valley of the Lycus, close to Hierapolis and Laodicea. Nothing is known for certain of the foundation of the church there. St. Paul *may* have visited the place during his tour in 'the Phrygian and Galatian country' (Acts 16^6), but it is hardly probable, especially as he speaks of the Colossians and those of Laodicea as 'not having seen his face in the flesh' (Col. 2^1).

2. Occasion of Epistle. The Colossian Epaphras had more probably been the instrument of their conversion during the Apostle's long sojourn at Ephesus. Two incidents brought Colossae before St. Paul's notice during his imprisonment at Rome, a visit of Epaphras (4^{12}), and the coming of the runaway slave, Onesimus, who had left his Colossian master, Philemon, and fled to Rome. Epaphras could speak favourably of the faith of the Colossians and their works of love (1^{4-8}); but he had to announce the appearance amongst them of a dangerous form of heresy, half Jewish half Oriental, tending to corrupt the simplicity of their faith, and to obscure the dignity of Christ by a spurious union of Jewish observances with a worshipping of angels and an extravagant asceticism. Theosophy offers the closest parallel in our world to-day.

3. Date and Place. Tychicus and Onesimus were now, A. D. 61, on the point of leaving Rome for the East (4^{7-9}), and the Apostle resolved to avail himself of the opportunity to address a special letter to the Colossians to warn them to be on their guard against the vain deceit of a false philosophy, and exhort them to constancy to their one and only Lord.

4. Summary. Accordingly, after the opening salutation and thanksgiving (1^{1-15}), he proceeds to dwell (i) on the pre-eminent and surpassing dignity of Christ as pre-existent through all eternity, the Head of the natural Creation, and the Head of the new moral Creation, the Church, who by His Resurrection and Ascension had reconciled humanity to God the Father (1^{16-29}). (ii) He warns them not to be led astray by any strange philosophy, and urges them to fix their attention on Him whose all-perfect Sacrifice had freed them from all ritual prohibitions (2^8-3^4). (iii) He applies practically the effects of their participation in Christ's Resurrection to various social relations, as husbands, wives, children, fathers, mothers, slaves (3^5-4^6). (iv) He refers them to Tychicus and Onesimus for information respecting his condition, and requests them to forward this epistle to the Laodiceans, and to read that addressed to Laodicea (4^{7-18}).

(viii) THE FIRST EPISTLE TO THE THESSALONIANS

1. Thessalonica (*Saloniki*), anciently called Therma, but renamed after the sister of Alexander the Great by her husband Cassander, who restored it, was one of the chief cities of Macedonia, the greatest and most populous port of that division of Europe. It was to the West what Ephesus was to the East, and Corinth to Southern Greece. Situated half-way between the Adriatic and the Hellespont, at the entrance of the pass into the Macedonian plains, it was a busy commercial centre, with a constant tide of traffic ebbing and flowing through it, and thus a fit centre of evangelization, whence the Word of the Lord could sound forth 'not only in Macedonia and Achaia, but also in every place' (1 Thess. 1^8).

2. Foundation of the Church. Thessalonica was first visited by Paul and Silas, in A. D. 49–50, and here in the synagogue of the Jews for three Sabbaths they preached Jesus as the promised Messiah (Acts $17^{2, 3}$). Failing in controversy, the Jews resorted to violence, set the city in an uproar, assailed the house where the Apostle was lodging, and so compelled him to leave, but not before he had gained here two of his most attached friends, Jason (Rom. 16^{21}) and Aristarchus (Col. 4^{10}). On turning to the Gentiles he met with more success, for the Gentile element predominated in the Thessalonian Church (1 Thess. 1^9 ; 2^{14}).

3. Occasion and Date of Writing. While the Apostle was at Corinth, in A. D. 51, Silas and Timothy returned from Macedonia, and informed him of the continued faith and love of the Thessalonians, and their fond remembrance of himself (1 Thess. 3⁶). But they had adopted certain mistaken notions which needed correction. Since the Apostle's visit several of their friends and relatives had died, and it was feared that these would lose the happiness of witnessing the Lord's second coming, which they believed to be close at hand. Consequently many had abandoned their lawful callings, and thinking it unnecessary to work, claimed the support of the richer members of the Church, and evinced a lack of order and self-control which called for amendment.

4. **Summary.** The Epistle falls into two main divisions: (i) The Apostle expresses his gratitude for their eager acceptance of the Gospel (1^{1-10}), encourages them under trial by his own example (2^{1-12}), thanks God for their constancy (2^{13-16}), sends several messages, and prays for their continuance in the faith (3^{1-13}). (ii) He exhorts them to purity and diligence in their several callings (4^{1-12}), comforts those bereaved by unfolding the triumph of the resurrection and the transformation to a glorified body (4^{13}–5^{11}), and gives some final cautions on the respect due to those who laboured amongst them, and on the necessity of watchfulness and prayer and following the leadings of the Spirit (5^{12-28}).

(ix) THE SECOND EPISTLE TO THE THESSALONIANS

1. **The Second Epistle** was written, like the first, from Corinth, probably in A. D. 51. The first letter had produced much good, but it had not abated the excitement connected with the expectation of the Second Advent. A fanatical section had even laboured to increase it, claiming imaginary revelations from the Spirit (2^2), and a rumoured letter from the Apostle himself in support of their views, that 'the day of the Lord' had arrived, and He must be looked for immediately.

2. **Summary.** To discourage such ideas the Apostle wrote his second letter, in which, after an affectionate greeting and thanksgiving for their progress in the faith (1^{1-12}), he explains why so speedy a consummation was impossible. The Second Advent, he affirms, cannot be realized before the coming of the 'Man of Sin' or 'Lawlessness' (2^3, R.V. marg.), whom 'the Lord shall destroy with the brightness of His coming' (2^{1-12}). He then deals with certain practical points, and exhorts them to perseverance, to diligence in their daily callings (3^{6-15}), and ends with the autographic salutation and benediction, which he now for the first time appends to his letters (3^{16-18}).

160

(x) THE EPISTLE TO THE HEBREWS

1. The Epistle to the Hebrews occupies a peculiar place in the New Testament. The writer, whoever he is, conceals his name. He begins without any address, though he closes with a brief salutation (Heb. 13²⁴). It is not surprising, therefore, that opinion is divided as to its authorship, and that it has been ascribed to St. Paul, to St. Luke, to St. Clement, to Apollos, and to St. Barnabas. It has recently been conjectured that it is the work of Prisca, wife of Aquila.

2. As to the Place whence and the Time when the Epistle was written, we have little to guide us. In the closing chapter the writer says, 'they of Italy salute you' (13²⁴). Hence it has been inferred that it was written from some place in Italy; but the words 'may describe Italian Christians in their own country, or Italian Christians in a foreign land'.* In the same chapter the writer intimates his hope of coming to see those whom he addresses, with Timothy, 'the brother', who had just been released from imprisonment (13²³). Nothing, however, is known of this event, and no argument can be drawn from it as to the place of the writing of the Epistle. The facts, however, that the Temple worship is spoken of as still going on, that there is no allusion to the tragic event of the destruction of Jerusalem, and that a generation of Christians had clearly already passed away (2³; 13⁷), as also the indication by the writer of severe trials in store for the Church (12⁴; 13¹³), may point to some date between A. D. 64 and 67, when the Jewish war commenced, as the most probable. But it may be later and meant for Hellenistic Christians, as the thought is Alexandrian and the title is not original.

3. The Persons Addressed. The title suggests that the letter was addressed to 'Hebrews'; that is, probably, Hebrew Christians either of Palestine or of Rome. They were at this time exposed to severe persecution from their fellow-countrymen, and needed comfort under the difficulties of their position. For a time it had seemed to be possible for Christians of Jewish race to hold both religions together (Acts 6⁷). Now it had become necessary to choose definitely between them. The writer's object is to shew that the Law was never intended to be permanent. It has done its work and has now been superseded by Christ. CHRIST, the Son of God, is now our Mediator and Intercessor, superior to Angels because nearer to the Father, and partaker of the same nature with the Father; superior to Moses, because a Son, not a servant;

---

* Bishop Westcott's *Introduction to the Epistle to the Hebrews*, p. xliii.

M

superior to the Jewish High Priest, because more powerful in intercession, seeing that His Priesthood is eternal, and His intercession is the constant display before the Father of the sacrifice which He offered once for all upon the Cross. Thus :—

   (i) The *exceptional* ministration of angels is superseded by the *continuous* ministration of the God-man.

   (ii) The *legislative* ministration of Moses is perfected by the *Divine* Lawgiver.

   (iii) The *typical* sacrifice of the High Priest is replaced by a *real* sacrifice of a higher order.

   (iv) The *indirect* communion with God is supplanted by the *direct* union of God and man in Christ, and the communion of the Head with His Body, the Church.

4. Summary. The epistle, then, having this object, presents two main divisions : (i) *Doctrinal* (1–10^{18}) ; (ii) *Practical* (10^{19}–13^{25}). In Part I the writer, first stating his grand thesis (a) that ' God, having of old time spoken unto the fathers in the prophets by divers portions and in divers manners ', hath now 'spoken unto us in His Son' (1^1, R. V.), proceeds to shew that Christ in His exalted Humanity is superior (i) to *Angels* (1–2^{18}) ; (ii) to *Moses*, being the Builder, Son, Master of the House, while Moses was only a servant in it (3–4^{13}) ; (iii) to the *Aaronic Priesthood* in respect to His office, nature, and vocation (4^{14}–5^{10}) ; then, after a digression of practical exhortation (5^{11}–6^{12}), (iv) to the primaeval High Priest *Melchizedek* (7^{1-28}). Next (b) the writer shews how the New Covenant is the fulfilment of the Old, which was imperfect in itself, and incapable of making its members perfect (8^{1-13}); how its sacrifices were types and shadows of Christ's one perfect Sacrifice ; its earthly sanctuary a figure of the true sanctuary in heaven (9–10^{18}). In Part II he exhorts the Hebrew Christians (a) to constancy in the faith, of the principle of which he gives a magnificent description (10^{19}–11) ; (b) to moral steadfastness in spite of trials (12^{1-13}) ; (c) to mutual kindness, hospitality, sympathy, and remembrance of their departed teachers (12^{14}–13^9) ; and (d) ends with a few affectionate exhortations, a brief message, and a benediction (13^{10-25}).

(b) *The Pastoral Epistles.*

General Introduction. The epistles to Timothy and Titus are known collectively as *The Pastoral Epistles* because they are ostensibly addressed to individuals whom St. Paul had definitely placed in charge of particular churches. They are therefore concerned with directions for the shepherding of Christ's flock.

Of late years doubt has been cast upon them, and they have been thought to be forgeries of the second century, whereby an unknown writer has tried to secure the authority of St. Paul for his own opinions, though it is admitted that 2 Timothy contains some fragments of a genuine work of the Apostle.

The reasons advanced for this view may be summarized as follows :—

1. The style is unlike that of St. Paul. It is stiff and formal, and the vocabulary is very different from that of his genuine writings.

2. The stress laid upon intellectual orthodoxy, and upon ecclesiastical organization, are foreign to the mind of St. Paul and conclusive proofs of a later date.

As against these contentions it may be urged :—

1. The difference of style is not more than may be reasonably accounted for by the fact that the Apostle was approaching the end of an exceptionally arduous and harassing life. It is natural that his literary powers should have lost something of their vigour and freshness. If his vocabulary is somewhat different from that of his earlier writings, so is his theme.

2. The emphasis on intellectual orthodoxy, to the exclusion of other elements in Christian life, is not really so great as may be thought at first sight, or as the A.V. rendering of one or two phrases suggests. And as the letters profess to be addressed to young men who had been given responsible administrative positions in the Church, it is natural that matters ecclesiastical should loom larger than in St. Paul's earlier writings.

It is to be remembered that these letters were originally entirely private. They were addressed to intimate friends who were well acquainted with his general mind.

We should only be entitled to dismiss the letters as forgeries if it could be shewn :—

(*a*) That there is no period of St. Paul's life during which they *could* have been written.

(*b*) That Timothy and Titus *could* not really have held the positions assigned to them.

As regards (*a*), Acts ends with St. Paul in prison at Rome awaiting trial. The tone of the narrative makes it inconceivable that this trial resulted in his condemnation and death. We may therefore assume that he was acquitted and released. There was, in fact, no charge against him of which the Roman Government could take cognizance. St. Paul was probably restored to liberty early in the year 62. In the Second Epistle to Timothy he is again a prisoner, and is convinced that his execution is imminent (4^{6-8} and $^{16-18}$). The most probable date for his martyrdom is 67.

There is therefore a period of five years during which we know nothing of his movements. There is reason for thinking that his projected expedition to Spain (Romans 15^{24}) was accomplished: and it is possible that he visited the island of Crete. In any case there is a period of his life during which these epistles could have been written.

As regards (*b*), the position of Timothy and Titus is admittedly, so far as we know, without parallel. We do not know whether their office was intended to be permanent and of independent authority; or whether they were merely St. Paul's temporary lieutenants. But the assertion that the situation implied by these epistles never could have existed in fact can be maintained only by those who have made up their minds as to what the Apostolic Church must have been like, and are therefore unwilling to admit any evidence which traverses their theory.

We may therefore conclude that there is no adequate ground for refusing to accept the Pastoral Epistles as genuine works of St. Paul, at least in part.

(i) THE FIRST EPISTLE TO TIMOTHY

1. **Timothy**, the son of a Greek father and a Jewish mother, Eunice, was converted by St. Paul after his visit to the region of Lycaonia, A. D. 44, became his 'own son in the faith' (1 Tim. 1^2), and his constant companion in his missionary journeys. After he was circumcised by St. Paul, 'because of the Jews', we lose sight of him during the Apostle's confinement at Caesarea; nor does he seem to have shared the perilous voyage to Italy. But he joined him soon after his arrival at Rome, and was with him during his imprisonment (Phil. 1^1; 2^{19}; Col. 1^1; Philem. 1).

2. **Date and Place of the Epistle.** When the Apostle was liberated from this first imprisonment, he and Timothy appear to have revisited proconsular Asia, the scene of so many of the missionary efforts of St. Paul. Here Timothy was placed in charge of the Church at Ephesus, a position of responsibility, peril, and difficulty. On leaving Asia Minor for Macedonia the Apostle addressed this letter to him. The place from which it was written is uncertain, but it was probably somewhere in Macedonia, or the neighbouring district, and the date about A. D. 63.

3. **Object.** The Apostle wished to encourage Timothy amidst the difficulties of his position at Ephesus, owing to the licentiousness connected with the worship of Artemis (Diana), and the lax

discipline and moral disorder which heretical teaching had brought with it. He desired also to give him some practical advice as to the way in which he should deal with the various classes of persons he would meet in the capital of Roman Asia; to lay down certain principles of Church organization, and to aid him in his struggle with teachers like Hymenaeus, Philetus, Alexander (1 Tim. 1²⁰; 2 Tim. 2¹⁷), who were perverting the minds of the disciples, and blending with the simplicity of the faith the subtleties of Greek philosophy, Jewish superstition, and wild Oriental speculation.

4. **Summary.** (i) *Controversial.* After the greeting (1¹, ²) the Apostle recalls the charge committed to Timothy, claims his allegiance, and contrasts the truth with the false teaching of Judaisers (1³⁻²⁰). (ii) *Practical Rules.* He then lays down certain rules for his guidance respecting (*a*) the regulation of public worship generally, as regarded both men and women (2); (*b*) he specifies the qualifications of Christian ministers, and the demeanour that should characterize their wives and families (3); (*c*) he then gives some special advice to Timothy himself relative to his conduct in the ministry (4); (*d*) how he should bear himself towards elders and communities of widows, aged and young (5¹⁻¹⁶); how presbyters should be maintained, offenders punished (5¹⁷⁻²⁵); how slaves should behave towards their masters (6¹, ²). (iii) *Personal Directions.* He then reverts to Timothy's relationship towards the heretical teachers (6³⁻¹⁰), adjures him to continue steadfast himself (6¹¹⁻¹⁶), to remind the rich of their duties in respect to almsgiving (6¹⁷⁻¹⁹), and diligently to guard the faith committed to his trust against all heretical teaching (6²⁰, ²¹).

(ii) THE SECOND EPISTLE TO TIMOTHY

1. The Second Epistle was written from Rome during the Apostle's second imprisonment. After his release from his first confinement, he was arrested again through the restless activity of his many enemies, and sent to Rome to be tried a second time for his life. This imprisonment was much more severe than the former. Not only was he chained to a soldier, but he was treated as a malefactor (2 Tim. 2⁹), and after a while was put upon his trial.

2. On this Occasion no Friend or Advocate stood by him to cheer and encourage (2 Tim. 4¹⁶). Alone and unaided he pleaded his cause, and was delivered 'out of the mouth of the lion' (4¹⁷). Remanded back to his dungeon to await the second hearing of his case, and convinced that his death was at hand, the Apostle longed for the society of Timothy, and he resolved to

write to him for the last time, and bid him come to him with all speed and receive his parting injunctions, before the winter storms had closed the Mediterranean (4^{21}).

3. **Summary.** In this Epistle, written A. D. 64, the Apostle, after greeting and thanksgiving (1^{1-5}), (i) exhorts his 'own son' to steadfastness in the Gospel (1^{6-15}), and a willingness to share in the sufferings of the saints (2^{1-13}); (ii) he urges upon him certain duties of pastoral conduct (2^{14-26}), and warns him against false teachers (3^{1-17}); (iii) he exhorts him with all possible solemnity to be faithful to all the duties of his office (4^{1-8}); (iv) bids him come quickly, describes his loneliness and desertion, and sends his last salutations to several dear friends (4^{9-22}).

4. **Special Features.** One or two points deserve special notice in this Epistle, the last written by St. Paul. (i) It furnishes a noble view of the consolation afforded by Christian faith in the midst of suffering and face to face with death (4^{6-8}). (ii) It contains what seems to be undoubtedly a fragment of a very early Christian hymn (2^{10-13}). (iii) It gives us some details unrecorded elsewhere respecting Timothy, the names of his mother and grandmother, his ordination by St. Paul ($1^{5,\ 6}$), and his presence with him on his first journey ($3^{10,\ 11}$). (iv) It mentions some otherwise unknown incidents of the Apostle's life between his two imprisonments: (*a*) the falling away from him of some Asiatic converts of note (1^{15}); (*b*) the injury done to him by Alexander (4^{14}); (*c*) the lapse of Demas (4^{10}); (*d*) the Apostle's reconciliation to St. Mark (4^{11}); (*e*) an unrecorded visit to Corinth and Miletus (4^{20}), and Troas (4^{13}).

(iii) THE EPISTLE TO TITUS

1. **Titus, a Greek by birth, and** addressed by Paul as his 'own son after the common faith' (Tit. 1^4), was probably converted by St. Paul during his first missionary journey. He was the first Christian convert who was not circumcised, and was taken by the Apostle to Jerusalem to try the matter, when the Council decided against its necessity (Acts 15; Gal. 2^3). More than once he had been sent to Corinth to order matters there (2 Cor. 7, 8), and his vigour and practical efficiency now qualified him to preside over the Church in Crete.

2. **Object of the Epistle.** It is not known when the Church in that island was founded, but the position of Titus was one of peculiar difficulty, for the people were notorious for immorality, instability, and lying (Titus 1^{12}). The Apostle, therefore, desires

to encourage him in confronting the opposition he was likely to encounter, and writes, A. D. 64, giving a condensed code of instruction on doctrine, morals, and discipline, which much resembles that in the First Epistle to Timothy.

3. **Summary.** After an earnest Apostolic salutation (1^{1-4}), he advises Titus (i) on several points of Church organization, the qualifications of elders, with special reference to the bad reputation of the Cretans, and the Judaic errors to be combated (1^{5-16}). (ii) He next lays down certain Christian precepts for aged men and women, the young of both sexes, and slaves (2). (iii) He urges on Titus some personal advice as to exemplifying gentleness in his dealings with his people (3^{1-7}); and (iv) concludes by insisting on his devoting himself to practical duties instead of tuning aside to idle and profitless speculations, and by sending a few personal messages and salutations (3^{8-15}).

(c) Special (to an Individual).

THE EPISTLE TO PHILEMON

1. **The Epistle to Philemon**, says Bishop Lightfoot, 'holds a unique place among the writings of St. Paul. It is the only strictly private letter of his which has been preserved. The Pastoral Epistles indeed are addressed to individuals, but they discuss important matters of Church discipline and government. On the other hand, the letter before us does not touch upon any question of public interest. It is wholly occupied with an incident of domestic life.'

2. **The Occasion** which called it forth was apparently accidental. Amongst the converts whom the Apostle had won to Christ while 'in bonds' at Rome, was one Onesimus, once a slave, who had run away from the house of Philemon, a Christian of Colossae, and had fled to Rome. Falling into the Apostle's hands, he had been baptized, and become 'the freedman of Christ'. But the Apostle did not forget that Onesimus was still the slave of Philemon, and justly liable to punishment for desertion, and possibly misappropriation of his master's goods. He therefore decided that Onesimus must return and submit again to the servitude from which he had escaped. Tychicus, the bearer of the letter to Colossae, was on the point of starting, and to help him to plead in person the cause of the penitent slave the Apostle resolved to write a short letter, which should prove how deeply he felt the case of Onesimus. The date therefore is probably the same as that of the Epistle to the Colossians, A. D. 61.

167

3. **Summary.** The Epistle is remarkable for its delicacy, generosity, and justice. After (i) a brief thanksgiving for what he had heard of Philemon's charitable deeds (vv. 1–7), the Apostle (ii) prefers his petition in behalf of one who, though once 'unprofitable', was now, he says (playing on the word 'Onesimus '), 'profitable' and a dearly beloved brother (vv. 8–11). (iii) He then begs Philemon to receive him as he would receive himself, and offers to be responsible for any damage Onesimus had caused by absconding (vv. 12–20); and (iv) in the full confidence that Philemon will do all that he asks of him, begs him to provide him (Paul) a lodging when he should be liberated from imprisonment (v. 22).

It is not too much to say that owing to the fact that we possess thirteen letters by his hand, as well as the account of him which is supplied by Acts, St. Paul is more intimately known to us than any figure of ancient history, with the possible exception of Cicero. We do really know what manner of man he was ; what he believed, hoped, dreaded, and hated. And the more closely we study him the more clearly do we see the baselessness of the theory that the religion which he propagated was a distorted travesty of the simple Gospel of Jesus. Christ has never had a more faithful interpreter than the Apostle to the Gentiles.*

(2) *THE GENERAL EPISTLES*

The Epistles of St. James, St. Peter, St. John, and St. Jude are called 'General' or 'Catholic' Epistles, i. e. 'universal', or 'pertaining to the whole Church ', as being addressed not to one Christian community specially, but generally to all. Clement of Alexandria applies the term 'Catholic' to the letter contained in Acts 15[23ff.], and it was appropriately applied at the close of the second century to the letters of James, 1 Peter, 1 John, and was then extended to 2 Peter and Jude, which are quite general in their address, and so, less accurately, to 2, 3 John.*

* The student who desires to make a fuller study of St. Paul may be referred to the following works amongst others. *Galatians*, Lightfoot (Macmillan, 1874) ; *Philippians*, Lightfoot (Macmillan, 1868) ; *Colossians and Philemon*, Lightfoot (Macmillan, 1892) ; *Ephesians*, J. Armitage Robinson (Macmillan, 1903) ; *Romans*, Sanday and Headlam (T. and T. Clark, 1895) ; 1 *Corinthians*, Robertson and Plummer (T. and T. Clark, 1911) ; 2 *Corinthians*, Plummer (T. and T. Clark, 1915) ; 1 and 2 *Thessalonians*, Frame (T. and T. Clark, 1912). These last four belong to the *International Critical Commentary* series. *The Pastoral Epistles*, Parry (Cambridge University Press, 1920) ; *The Earlier Epistles of St. Paul*, Lake (Rivingtons, 1911) ; *The Life and Letters of St. Paul*, Smith (Hodder and Stoughton, 1919) ; *St. Paul the Traveller and the Roman Citizen*, Ramsay (Hodder and Stoughton, 1895).

† See Bp. Westcott's *Introduction to the Epistles of St. John*, pp. xxviii, xxix.

(a) THE EPISTLE OF ST. JAMES

1. The St. James to whom the first of these Epistles is attributed was 'James, the Lord's brother' (Gal. 1^{19}), and first Overseer of the Church at Jerusalem (Acts 15^{13}). During the lifetime of our Lord he and his brothers 'did not believe on Him' (John 7^5). But immediately after the Ascension we find him and them with the Apostles in the Upper Room (Acts $1^{13, 14}$), and the appearance of the risen Lord to St. James (1 Cor. 15^7) wrought, we may believe, the great change. Seven or eight years afterwards he met St. Paul at Jerusalem on his return from Damascus (Gal. 1^{19}), and there he seems to have remained until his martyrdom in A.D. 63.

2. Occasion of the Epistle. A rigid observer of the Mosaic ritual, a Nazirite and an ascetic, he was pre-eminently suited to rebuke sternly the sins which became so terribly prominent during the closing days of Jerusalem—hypocrisy, presumption, censoriousness, love of riches, contempt of the poor, 'feuds and factions, wars and fightings', the vices which culminated in and precipitated the destruction of Jerusalem. This he does in his Epistle addressed to the 'twelve tribes which are of the Dispersion', that is, Jewish Christians scattered throughout the Roman world, and written, according to some, shortly before his martyrdom A. D. 63, according to others, as early as A. D. 52. Yet others put the work in the second century, and believe it has no connexion with the Lord's brother.

3. Summary. The Epistle is remarkable for its eminently practical character, the homeliness and aptness of its illustrations, and its bold, plain-spoken rebuke of the wealthy oppressors of the poor. (i) The first section treats of sincerity and patience under afflictions (1^{1-15}). (ii) The second declaims against hypocrisy and self-deceit (1^{16-27}). (iii) The third against adulation of the rich and contempt of the poor; against false charity and spurious faith (2^{1-26}). (iv) The next treats of the duty of ruling the tongue, and cultivating peace (3). (v) To this succeed warnings against strife and evil-speaking; against the corruption of the world, pride, luxury, and oppression; against the attempt to serve both God and Mammon (4). (vi) Then follow warnings against covetousness (5^{1-11}), profane and rash oaths (5^{12}), exhortations to prayer, especially in sickness (5^{13-18}), and a declaration of the blessedness of converting a sinner from the error of his ways ($5^{19, 20}$).

(*b*) THE FIRST EPISTLE OF ST. PETER

1. **Simon Peter**, son of Johanan or John (*the grace of God*), a fisherman of Bethsaida (John 1⁴²; Matt. 16¹⁷), was one of the foremost of the Apostles, who flung open the gates of the Church to three thousand of his own countrymen on the Day of Pentecost (Acts 2⁴¹), and admitted the first Gentile family by baptism into the same fold (Acts 10⁴⁷, ⁴⁸). Later, his work as an 'Apostle of the Circumcision' took him eastward to his own countrymen scattered through Pontus, Galatia, Cappadocia, Roman Asia, and Bithynia, and to them he addressed this letter, probably after the death of St. Paul.

2. **Occasion of the Epistle.** He was apparently induced to write it because, through Silvanus (5¹²), he had learnt that the Christians in these countries were exposed to a cruel persecution, and were accused of being evil-doers, and of preaching revolutionary doctrines (2¹⁵, ¹⁶). A wave of fanatical hatred against the very name of 'Christian' (4¹⁶) was at this time passing over the Roman Empire. Accordingly the Apostle felt bound to comfort the members of these Churches suffering from the storm of fiery trials, and to encourage them to stand fast in the faith.

3. **Summary.** (i) After a brief salutation he dilates on the necessity and transitory nature of earthly trials (1¹⁻¹²). (ii) He exhorts them by a holy life to follow the example of Christ, who died to purchase their glorification (1¹³⁻2¹⁰). (iii) He then gives them practical advice as to their duty as citizens, slaves, husbands, wives (2¹³⁻3⁷). (iv) He then earnestly exhorts them to unity, peaceableness, sanctification, with a warning of the second Advent and a reference to the previous judgements of God on those who neglected the preaching of Noah (3⁸⁻4⁶). (v) In view of the future Judgement he bids them love one another, and regard the fiery trial they may be called upon to undergo as no strange thing, but a cause of joy and ready surrender to the will of God (4⁷⁻¹⁹). (vi) Finally, he exhorts those bearing office in the Church to feed the flock of God, the younger to submit to their elders, and all to be on the watch against the great Enemy of souls (5¹⁻⁹); and he ends with a prayer for their preservation and perfection (5¹⁰⁻¹⁴).

THE SECOND EPISTLE OF ST. PETER

1. **This Epistle** was placed by Eusebius among the 'Disputed Books', but it was received into the Canon by the Councils of Laodicea (A.D. 372) and Third Carthage (A.D. 397).

2. **Characteristics.** The style is quite unlike that of 1 Peter, and of the Apostle's speeches as reported in Acts. The reference to the Epistles of St. Paul as a generally recognized authority is a mark of late date. We may therefore conclude that the Epistle is not by St. Peter himself but is the work of a group which produced several other works under the Apostle's name * at the end of the first century or very early in the second.

3. **Summary.** After a greeting ($1^{1,\ 2}$), the author (i) exhorts his readers to advance in holiness, and to aim at attaining more and more knowledge of Divine things (1^{3-11}). (ii) Speaking in the person of the Apostle he declares that his own end is near, and appeals to the Transfiguration in support of what he has taught about the Person of Christ (1^{12-21}). (iii) He next warns his readers of the certainty of punishment on impenitent sinners, by reference to past history, e.g. the Flood and the overthrow of Sodom and Gomorrah (2^{1-10}), and urges them to beware of false teachers by the example of Balaam (2^{11-22}). (iv) Lastly, he dwells in solemn tones on the certainty of the Future Judgement, and exhorts all to endurance and long-suffering, founded on the teaching of the Apostle Paul, the difficulties of whose Epistles he affirms had been perverted by many ; and ends, as he had begun, by calling on his readers to grow in grace and knowledge (3^{1-18}).

(c) THE FIRST EPISTLE OF ST. JOHN

1. **Characteristics of the Epistle.** The treatise called the First Epistle of St. John seems rather to partake of the nature of a homily or ' Pastoral', as Bishop Westcott terms it,† than a formal letter. But it was clearly intended as an ' Encyclical', and we may believe it was addressed, like the Apocalypse, to the Churches in Asia, where St. John during the last thirty years of his life was so prominent an actor.

2. **Its Relation to the Gospel.** Though the most independent of place and time and circumstance of all the writings in the New Testament, it is clearly related to the Gospel, and by the same hand. Indeed, apart from it, it could hardly have been understood. It assumes on the part of its readers an acquaintance with many expressions occurring in it, like ' Light ', ' Life ', ' the Truth ', ' the Word '. In the Gospel we see the original fountain of many

---

* e.g. *The Gospel of Peter ; The Revelation of Peter ; The Preaching of Peter.* Ancient writers saw no harm in attaching one of the great names of the past to their own compositions. Cf. *The Wisdom of Solomon.*

† Bishop Westcott's *Introduction to the Epistles of St. John*, p. xxx.

and various thoughts; in the Epistle they are carried a step further and practically applied. 'The theme of the Epistle', writes Bishop Westcott, 'is "the Christ is Jesus", the theme of the Gospel is 'Jesus is the Christ".'

3. **The Date** is uncertain, nor is there any direct evidence to fix it. Some would place it before the destruction of Jerusalem; others, with far more probability, at some period within the last decade of the first century, between A.D. 90 and A.D. 95. It may have been intended as a 'covering letter' to the fourth Gospel. As the last years of St. John were spent at Ephesus, it is only reasonable to suppose that it was written there. The false teaching with which it deals is that which represented our Lord as having been man in appearance only and not in reality. This was taught, in slightly varying forms, towards the close of the first century and during the early part of the second, by various teachers. One of them, by name Cerinthus, is said to have met St. John personally.

4. **The following Analysis** will present the chief lines of thought: (i) The Apostle sets forth the true nature of fellowship with God, who is Light and Love, and requires purity and holiness in actual life (1). (ii) He then describes the blessings and duties of sonship, contrasts the children of God and the children of the Evil One, and the rival powers of Truth and Error (3–4^6). (iii) He finally enlarges on the essential bond of fellowship and sonship, which is Love, both to the Father and to one another (4^7–5^{21}).

THE SECOND EPISTLE OF ST. JOHN

1. **The Second Epistle** contains only thirteen verses, eight of which are found in substance in the first. It contains no direct intimation as to when or whence it was written. Some have thought that the author's description of himself as *The Elder* is meant to signify that he was not the Apostle and (or) Evangelist. But the evidence for the existence of 'John the Elder' as a separate personage is very slight.

2. **To whom Addressed.** It is addressed to the 'Elect Lady and her children', which is thought by some to refer to 'the Church', or to the 'Lady Eclecta', a person so called for her eminent piety. But neither explanation is quite satisfactory, and the designation must be regarded as enigmatic. Whatever may be the interpretation of the words (vv. 1–3), the greater part of the letter is addressed to more readers than one, and they are exhorted to persevere in love, faith, and godliness, and to beware of false teachers (vv. 4–13).

THE THIRD EPISTLE OF ST. JOHN

1. **The Third Epistle**, written probably much about the same time and from the same place, is marked by a strong individuality. It is addressed to 'Gaius the beloved'. The name Gaius is found in Acts 19[29], 20[4]; Rom. 16[23]; 1 Cor. 1[14] (R.V.); but there is nothing to identify him with any of these. Two other persons are mentioned : the unfaithful Diotrephes, who is sufficiently presumptuous to oppose even an Apostle, and the faithful Demetrius, who receives commendation.

2. **Analysis.** After the salutation (v. 1) the Apostle expresses his joy at the tidings he has received of Gaius (vv. 2–4); commends him for his hospitality and piety (vv. 5–8); and warns him against the ambition and self-assertion of Diotrephes (vv. 9, 10). He testifies his approval of Demetrius, and after expressing a hope of seeing Gaius, concludes with a salutation (vv. 12–14).

(*d*) THE EPISTLE OF ST. JUDE

1. **St. Jude.** The writer of this Epistle describes himself as 'the servant of the Lord Jesus Christ, and the brother of James'. By this James it is thought no other can be intended than 'James, the Lord's brother' (Gal. 1[19]), and first Overseer of the Church at Jerusalem.

2. **Authenticity.** The Epistle, like that of St. James, would seem to have been addressed to the whole body of 'the twelve tribes that were scattered abroad'. It is wanting in the *Pĕshîttâ*, or Syriac Version, and is placed by Eusebius among the 'Disputed Books': but it is distinctly recognized in the Muratorian Fragment, *cir.* A.D. 170. The parallelism between this Epistle and the Second Epistle of St. Peter is very noticeable. Both are probably the work of the same circle. It is remarkable for the quotation from the Book of Enoch (v. 14), and a tradition of a dispute between Michael the Archangel and Satan regarding the body of Moses (v. 9).

3. **Analysis.** The date, place, and occasion are unknown, but (i) the writer states that he has been moved by the dangers of the time to write to those whom he addressed, and urge them to contend for the faith, and not heed the teaching of ungodly men, who were turning the grace of God into lasciviousness (vv. 2–4). (ii) He notices the backsliding of the Israelites after leaving Egypt, the fall of the Angels, the stricken cities of the Plain, as each and all warnings against the doctrine of such teachers, who despised dignities and sinned like Cain and Korah and Balaam (vv. 5–11). (iii) He affirms that they mingled in their love-feasts

for impure purposes, and were no better than rainless clouds, withering trees, wandering stars. Enoch had prophesied that the Lord would come to judge such, and the faithful must be on their guard against them. (iv) In contrast with such teachers he bids his readers build themselves up in faith and prayer and love, and not shrink from rebuking those who needed rebuke (vv. 17–23), and closes with a hearty ascription of praise to God (vv. 24, 25).

III. PROPHETIC.

THE REVELATION OF ST. JOHN

1. The word Revelation is derived from the Latin *revelare* = 'to unveil, to uncover'. It is the equivalent of the Greek word *Apocalypse*, which occurs several times in the New Testament, as Rom. 2⁵; 1 Cor. 14⁶; Gal. 1¹², and other places. As the title of this book, it denotes the 'unveiling' of the future in reference to the Church and the world, and is the only distinctly prophetic book of the New Testament.*

2. Genuineness. The author says that his name was John (1⁴, ⁹, 22⁸). But the difficulty of identifying him with the author of the fourth Gospel was felt by Dionysius of Alexandria as far back as the third century (Euseb. *H. E.* vii. 25). The question will probably never be settled definitely.

3. Date and Place. If the author were John the Apostle, we must admit that after the Council of Jerusalem, A.D. 43 or 44, which is the last occasion on which he is mentioned in the Acts (Acts 15⁴; cp. Gal. 2⁹), his movements are wrapped in obscurity. He seems, however, to have resided for some time at Jerusalem, and thence repaired to Ephesus as a centre from whence he directed the churches of Asia Minor. Subsequently he was exiled to the isle of Patmos, and there remained till he returned to Ephesus, which became henceforth his abode till his death, about A.D. 100. It is generally believed that the book was written at Patmos, but the date is disputed. Some would assign it to the close of the reign of Domitian, A.D. 97; others to an earlier date, between the death of Nero, A.D. 68, and the fall

---

* It is a representative of a class of literature which was produced in considerable abundance in Jewish and Jewish-Christian circles from about 200 B.C. to A.D. 100. It soon became highly conventionalized in form. Daniel 7–12 and Isaiah 24–27 are examples of it in the Old Testament. 2 Esdras (part at least of which is Christian) has found a place in the Apocrypha. Of extra-canonical apocalypses the *Book of Enoch*, which is quoted in Jude 14, is the best known.

of Jerusalem. It is possible that the visions cover a number of years, but were published together. The style defies the principles of Greek grammar, and in this respect differs markedly from that of the Gospel and Epistles. It is conceivable that one who had originally at least thought in Hebrew may have reverted to the idiom of his childhood when in a prophetic trance (1^{10}, 4^2).

4. The Book may be thus divided : *

(A) *The Prologue* (1); (B) *The Messages to the seven Churches* (2, 3); (C) *The Prophetic Visions proper* (4–22).

(A) *The Prologue* commences with (i) the title and description of the book (1^{1-3}); (ii) it then passes on to the vision of the Son of Man commanding St. John to write to the seven Churches (1^{4-20}).

(B) *The Messages to the seven Churches.*

(a) *Ephesus,* reproved for forsaking its first love and first works (2^{1-7}).

(b) *Smyrna,* commended for its works, poverty, endurance of persecution (2^{8-11}).

(c) *Pergamum,* reproved for false doctrine, immoral practices, idolatrous pollutions (2^{12-17}).

(d) *Thyatira,* partly reproved for similar corruptions, and partly commended for its fidelity (2^{18-29}).

(e) *Sardis,* reproved for spiritual deadness combined with merely nominal life (3^{1-6}).

(f) *Philadelphia,* approved for its steadfastness and patience (3^{7-13}).

(g) *Laodicea,* rebuked sternly for lukewarmness (3^{14-22}).†

The predictions relating to the Churches have long been fulfilled. Inasmuch as the rest of the book is a picture of the unending conflict between Good and Evil (Evil in the author's world being represented by the Roman Empire) its predictions have been fulfilled in the past, are being fulfilled from day to day, and are still to be fulfilled in the future. Its certainty that Good will eventually be completely triumphant is not yet, as the late war revealed, the common property of the Christian world. It may be summarized thus:

(C) *The Prophetic Visions.*

(i) The Divine glory, sealed book, and the Lamb (4, 5).

(ii) The vision of the opening of six seals, revealing Victory,

* See further *The Apocalypse of St. John* by R. H. Charles ; also *Studies in the Apocalypse* by the same (T. and T. Clark, 1913).

† For a full discussion of the contents of the letters see *The Letters to the Seven Churches* by Sir W. M. Ramsay (Hodder and Stoughton, 1904).

War, Famine, Death, Delay in vengeance, Catastrophes; the sealing of 144,000 Israelites; and worship by innumerable multitudes of saints, arrayed in white robes (6, 7).

(iii) The opening of the seventh seal; seven angels with seven trumpets; another angel offering incense on the golden altar; followed by the sounding of six trumpets announcing vengeance on the earth for its persecutions, idolatries, and immoralities, viz. on the trees and grass, sea, rivers, sun, moon, and stars, with visions of locusts and warriors (8, 9). The vision of an angel with an open scroll; seven thunders, and the angel's proclamation (10); measuring of the temple and altar; the two witnesses, sounding of the seventh trumpet (10, 11).

(iv) The vision of the woman and the dragon; the conflict between Michael and the dragon; rescue and desolation of the woman; the rising of a beast from the sea, and of the two-horned lamb from the earth (12, 13). The vision of the true Lamb and the 144,000 on Mount Sion; the proclamations of the three angels; the harvest and vintage (14).

(v) The pouring out of the seven bowls containing the last plagues on earth, sea, rivers, sun; thick darkness, Euphrates dried up; the 'three frogs' gather the people to Armageddon; the destruction of Babylon imminent (15, 16). The woman arrayed in purple and scarlet sitting upon the beast; the angel's proclamation of the fall of Babylon, followed by songs of praise and triumph (17–19^{10}).

(vi) The vision of 'The Word of God', attended by the faithful, who destroy the three great enemies, viz. the beast, false prophet, and confederate kings (19$^{11-21}$); the binding of Satan for 1,000 years; the resurrection of the martyrs, the reign of righteousness; general conflict, and final triumph (20$^{1-10}$).

(vii) Visions of the last judgement, the new heaven, new earth, new Jerusalem (20^{11}–22^{5}) with closing words from the angel, Christ, and John, enjoining the universal acceptance and proclamation of these visions, attesting the certainty and speedy accomplishment of the predictions, and concluding with general benediction (22$^{6-21}$).

XXV. CHRONOLOGY AND HARMONY OF THE GOSPELS

(1) CHRONOLOGY.

1. In dealing with the Chronology of the Gospel Period we have to ascertain (i) the starting-point, (ii) the length of our

Lord's life and Ministry, (iii) the arrangement of it as gathered from the Gospels. On all these points there are differences of opinion. The birth of Jesus ought probably to be assigned to a date in or soon after 8 B.C. The modern system of dating by B.C. and A.D. goes no farther back than Dionysius Exiguus, who invented it about the year 525. The evidence for the date of the Nativity provided by Luke 2[1, 2] cannot be interpreted with certainty.[*]

2. **Our Lord's Ministry.** The starting-point of the Ministry is given very clearly in St. Luke 3[1]. Caesar Augustus, under whose reign our Lord was born, had died on 19 August, A.D. 14 and had been succeeded by his step-son Tiberius, who occupied the imperial throne until A.D. 37. The 'fifteenth year of the reign of Tiberius Cæsar' is thus most naturally to be regarded as the year from August A.D. 28 to August A.D. 29, and it was probably during the year A.D. 29 that the ministry of John began. Pilate was now procurator of Judaea ; Caiaphas had been appointed High Priest in A.D. 25, while his father-in-law Annas still probably presided over the Sanhedrin ; Herod Antipas was still carrying on his long rule in Galilee, and Herod Philip in Bashan and the neighbourhood. All these notes of time fit in with the conclusion that A.D. 29 was the beginning of John the Baptist's work. Our Lord's Ministry opened not long afterwards, and thus it is possible to accept the year A.D. 33, which is indicated by various independent considerations, as the date of His Death and Resurrection.[†]

3. **The Duration of His Ministry** is usually reckoned at three and a half years, but some reckon it as two and a half.

4. **Divisions.** The Gospel Narrative may be thus divided:
    Part 1. The Nativity and Early Life of Jesus.
    ,,   2. From the Preaching of John to the First Passover.
    ,,   3. From the First Passover to the Second.
    ,,   4. From the Second Passover to the Third.
    ,,   5. Holy Week.
    ,,   6. The Death and Burial.
    ,,   7. The Resurrection and the Great Forty Days.[‡]

[*] See further Sir W. M. Ramsay in the *Journal of Roman Studies*, vol. vii.
[†] The latter date is that given by Tertullian (*Adversus Iudaeos*, c. 8).
[‡] See A. Huck, *Synopse der drei ersten Evangelien*, 5 Aufl. (Tübingen, 1916) ; Burton and Goodspeed, *A Harmony of the Synoptic Gospels for Historical and Critical Study* (Chicago, 1917) ; W. Sanday, *Outlines of the Life of Christ* (Edinburgh, 2nd edition, 1906) ; Dr. Edersheim's *Life and Times of Jesus the Messiah*.

(2) HARMONY OF THE GOSPELS.

PART I.

The Nativity and Early Life of Jesus.

EVENTS.	LOCALITY.	MATTHEW.	MARK.	LUKE.	JOHN.
The DIVINITY OF CHRIST					1. 1-5
Annunciation of the birth of John the Baptist	Jerusalem			1. 5-25	
Espousal of the Virgin Mary	Nazareth . . .	1. 18		1. 27	
The Annunciation of the birth of Jesus				1. 26-38	
The Visitation of Mary to Elisabeth	Hebron, or Juttah . . .			1. 39-55	
Her return to Nazareth				1. 56	
Joseph's vision	Nazareth . . .	1. 20-25			
Birth and infancy of John the Baptist	Hebron . .			1. 57-80	
BIRTH OF JESUS	Bethlehem . .			2. 1-7	
Adoration by shepherds	,,			2. 8-16	
Circumcision	,,	1. 25		2. 21	
Presentation and purification . .	Jerusalem . .			2. 22-29	
The *Genealogies*		1. 17		3. 23	
Adoration by the wise men . . .	Bethlehem . .	2. 1-12			
Flight into Egypt	Egypt . . .	2. 13-15			
Massacre of the Innocents . . .	Bethlehem . .	2. 16-18			
Return to Nazareth	Nazareth . . .	2. 19-23		2. 39	
Childhood of Jesus	,,			2. 40	
With the doctors in the Temple .	Jerusalem . .			2. 46-50	
Youth of Jesus	Nazareth . . .			2. 51	

PART II.

From the Preaching of John the Baptist to the First Passover.

Ministry of John the Baptist . .	Bethabara* . .	3. 1-4	1. 1-8	3. 1-6	1. 6-15
Baptisms by John	,,	3. 5	1. 5	3. 7	
First testimony of the Baptist to Christ	,,	3. 11, 12	1. 7, 8	3. 15-18	
Baptism of Jesus by John . . .	,,	3. 13-17	1. 9-11	3. 21, 22	
Temptation of Jesus	Wilderness of Judæa . .	4. 1-11	1. 12, 13	4. 1-13	
John the Baptist's second testimony	Bethabara .				1. 19-35
Call of the first disciples	,,				1. 37-51
First miracle, at Cana	Cana				2. 1-11
Visit to Capernaum	Capernaum . .				2. 12
First PASSOVER: first cleansing of Temple	Jerusalem . .				2. 13-23
Discourse with Nicodemus . . .	,,				3. 1-21

PART III.

From the First Passover to the Second.

The Baptist's last testimony . .	Ænon . . .				3. 23-36
Christ's visit to Samaria . . .	Sychar . . .				4. 1-42
Return to Cana	Cana				4. 43-46
Healing of a nobleman's son . .	,,				4. 46-54
Brief visit to Jerusalem; miracle at pool of Bethesda . . .	Jerusalem . .				5. 1-47
Imprisonment of John the Baptist	Machærus . .	4. 12, 17	1. 14, 15		
Christ preaches in Galilee . . .	Galilee . . .			4. 14, 15	
,, ,, at Nazareth . . .	Nazareth . . .		6. 1	4. 15-30	
,, ,, at Capernaum . .	Capernaum . .	4. 13-16		4. 31	
Call of Andrew, Peter, James, and John	,,	4. 18-22	1. 16-20	5. 1-11	
Healing of a demoniac	,,		1. 23-27	4. 33-36	
,, ,, Peter's mother-in-law	,,	8. 14, 15	1. 29-31	4. 38, 39	
,, ,, many sick and diseased	,,	8. 16, 17	1. 32-34	4. 40, 41	
Retirement for solitary prayer . .	,,		1. 35	4. 42	
Circuit through Galilee . . .	Galilee		1. 35-39	4. 42-44	

* Bethabara or Bethany, see R.V. John i. 28.

EVENTS.	LOCALITY.	MATTHEW.	MARK.	LUKE.	JOHN.
Healing of a leper	Galilee	8. 1-4	1. 40-45	5. 12-16	
Retirement for solitary prayer . .	,, ...	. . . .	1. 45	5. 16	
Healing of a paralytic	Capernaum . .	9. 1-8	2. 1-12	5. 18-26	
Call of Matthew (Levi). Discourse at the feast	,, ...	9. 9-17	2. 13-22	5. 27-39	
The disciples pluck the ears of corn	Galilee	12. 1-8	2. 23-28	6. 1-5	
Healing of the man with withered hand	Capernaum . .	12. 9-14	3. 1-6	6. 6-11	
Retirement for solitary prayer . .	,, ...	. . . .	. . . .	6. 12	
Call of the Twelve Apostles . . .	Hill of Hattin (?)	10. 2-4	3. 13-19	6. 13-16	
Sermon on the Mount	,,	5-7. 29	. . . .	6. 17-49	
Healing of the centurion's servant	,,	8. 5-13	. . . .	7. 1-10	
Raising the son of the widow of Nain	Nain	. . . .	. . . .	7. 11-17	
Message from John the Baptist: Christ's testimony respecting him	Capernaum .	11. 2-19	. . . .	7. 18-35	
The woman which was a sinner .	Capernaum (?) .	. . . .	. . . .	7. 36-50	
Tour through Galilee with the twelve	Galilee	. . . .	. . . .	8. 1-3	
Healing of a demoniac	Capernaum . .	12. 22			
Blasphemy against the Holy Ghost	,,	12. 24-37	3. 22-30 .		
The unclean spirit	,,	12. 43-46			
The interruption of His relatives .	,,	12. 46	3. 31		
Parables :—The Sower	Plain of Gennesaret	13. 1-9, 18-23	4. 1, 14-20	8. 4, 11-15	
,, Tares	,,	13. 24			
,, Mustard seed . .	,,	13. 31	4. 30		
,, Leaven	,,	13. 33			
,, Candle	,,	. . . .	4. 21	8. 16	
,, Treasure	,,	13. 44			
,, Pearl	,,	13. 45			
,, Draw-net . . .	,,	13. 47			
Christ calms the storm	Sea of Gennesaret	8. 24-27	4. 37-41	8. 23-25	
The Gergesene demoniacs	Gergesa . . .	8. 28-34	5. 1-15	8. 27-35	
Parables :—Bridegroom	Capernaum . .	9. 15			
New cloth and new wine	,,	9. 16, 17			
Miracles :—Woman with the issue of blood	Gennesaret . .	9. 18	5. 22	8. 41	
Jairus' daughter . .	Capernaum . .	9. 18	5. 22	8. 41	
Two blind men . . .	,,	9. 27-30			
Dumb spirit	,,	9. 32, 33			
Mission of the Twelve Apostles .	,,	10. 1	6. 7-12	9. 1-6	
Death of John the Baptist . . .	Machærus . .	14. 1-12	6. 14-29	9. 7	
Feeding of the five thousand . .	Bethsaida . .	14. 13-21	6. 30-44	9. 12-17	6. 1-13
Walking on the water	Lake of Gennesaret	14. 25	6. 48	. . . .	6. 19
Discourse in Synagogue on the Bread of Life	Capernaum . .	14. 34	. . . . .	. . . . .	6. 26-65

PART IV.

From the Second Passover to the Third.

Opposition of Scribes and Pharisees	Capernaum . .	15. 1			
Discourse on pollution	,,	15. 2-20	7. 1-23		
Healing the daughter of the Syrophœnician woman	Phœnicia . . .	15. 21-29	7. 24-30		
Healing of the deaf and dumb man	Tyre and Sidon		7. 32		
,, of many sick persons . .	Decapolis . . .	15. 30, 31			
Feeding of the four thousand . .	Gennesaret . .	15. 32-39	8. 1-9		
Parable of the leaven	,,	16. 1-12	8. 14-22		
Healing of the blind man . . .	Bethsaida . .		8. 22-27		
St. Peter's confession of Christ . .	CæsareaPhilippi	16. 13-21	8. 27-30		
First Prediction of the Passion . .	,,	16. 21-28	8. 31-38	9. 22-27	
The TRANSFIGURATION	Mount Hermon	17. 1-8	9. 2-8	9. 28-36	
Healing the demoniac child . . .	,,	17. 14-21	9. 14-27	9. 37-42	
Second Prediction of the Passion .	,,	17. 22, 23	9. 31	9. 43, 44	
The stater in the fish's mouth . .	Capernaum . .	17. 27			
Lesson on docility	,,	18. 1-14	9. 33-37	9. 46-48	
,, forgiveness	,,	18. 15	9. 43		
,, self-denial	,,	18. 18			
Parable of the unmerciful servant	,,	18. 23-35			

EVENTS.	LOCALITY.	MATTHEW.	MARK.	LUKE.	JOHN.
Journey to Jerusalem through Samaria	Samaria			9. 51, 52	
Jealousy of the Samaritans	,,			9. 53	
Anger of "the Sons of Thunder"	,,			9. 54–56	
The FEAST OF TABERNACLES	Jerusalem				7. 2–10
Discourses	,,				7. 10–46
Officers sent to arrest Christ	,,				7. 30, 46
The adulteress	,,				8. 3
Discourses	,,				8. 12
Christ threatened with stoning	,,				8. 59
Healing of blind man, and discourses	,,				9. 1
Christ the DOOR	,,				10. 1
,, GOOD SHEPHERD	,,				10. 11
Departure from Jerusalem. Mission of the Seventy	Judæa			10. 1–16	
Return of the Seventy	,,			10. 17–24	
Parable of the Good Samaritan	,,			10. 30–37	
Visit to Martha and Mary	Bethany			10. 38–42	
Jesus teaches His disciples to pray	Judæa		6. 9–13.	11. 1–13	
He heals the mute demoniac, and rebukes the blasphemy of the Pharisees	,,		12. 22–45	11. 14	
Discourses :—The repentant Ninevites	,,		12. 41	11. 29–36	
God's providence to birds and flowers	,,			12. 1–12	
The rich fool	,,			12. 13–21	
The murdered Galilæans	,,			13. 1–5	
The barren fig-tree	,,			13. 6–9	
Healing of the woman with an infirmity	,,			13. 10–17	
Visit to Jerusalem at FEAST OF DEDICATION	Jerusalem				10. 22–30
Attempt to stone Jesus	,,				10. 31
Jesus retires across the Jordan	Peræa				10. 40
Are there few that be saved ?	,,			13. 23–30	
The message to Herod	,,			13. 31–33	
Healing of the man with the dropsy	,,			14. 1–6	
Parable of the Great Supper	,,			14. 15–24	
,, ,, Lost sheep	,,			15. 1–7	
,, ,, Lost coin	,,			15. 8–10	
,, ,, Prodigal son	,,			15. 11–32	
,, ,, Unjust steward	,,			16. 1–13	
,, ,, Dives and Lazarus	,,			16. 19–31	
Sickness of Lazarus	Bethany				11. 1–10
Return of Jesus from Peræa to Bethany	,,				11. 11–16
Resurrection of Lazarus	,,				11. 17–46
The council : advice of Caiaphas	Jerusalem				11. 47–53
Jesus retires to the town of Ephraim	Ephraim				11. 54
Last journey to Jerusalem	Borders of Samaria	19. 1	10. 1	17. 11	
Healing of the ten lepers	,,			17. 12–19	
Parable of the unjust judge	,,			18. 1–8	
,, ,, Pharisee and the publican	,,			18. 9–14	
The question of divorce	,,	19. 3–12	10. 2–12		
Christ blesses little children	,,	19. 13–15	10. 13–16	18. 15–17	
The rich young ruler	,,	19. 16–22	10. 17–22	18. 18–23	
Parable of the labourers in the vineyard	,,	20. 1–16			
Third Prediction of the Passion	,,	20. 17–19	10. 32–34	18. 31–34	
The request of James and John	,,	20. 20–28	10. 35–45		
Healing of blind Bartimæus	Near Jericho	20. 29–34	10. 46–52	18. 35–43	
Jesus at the house of Zacchæus	Jericho			19. 1–10	
Parable of the pounds	,,			19. 11–23	

PART V.
Holy Week.

EVENTS.	LOCALITY.	MATTHEW.	MARK.	LUKE.	JOHN.
The supper in Simon's house . .	Bethany . . .	26. 6-13	14. 3-9	. . . .	12. 1-9
Mary anoints Jesus	,, . . .	26. 7-13	14. 3-8	. . . . .	12. 3-8
Triumphal entry into the city . .	Jerusalem . .	21. 1-11	11. 1-10	19. 29-44	12. 12-19
Survey of the Temple	,,		11. 11		
Retirement to Bethany	Bethany . . .		11. 11		
Withering of the barren fig-tree .	Mount of Olives	21. 18, 19	11. 12-14		
Second cleansing of the Temple .	Jerusalem . .	21. 12-17	11. 15-19	19. 45-48	
Retirement to Bethany	Bethany . . .	21. 17	11. 19		
The lesson of the fig-tree . . .	Mount of Olives	21. 20-22	11. 20-25		
Discourses in the Temple :—					
The rulers' question.	Jerusalem . .	21. 23-27	11. 27-33	20. 1 8	
The parable of the two sons	,, . .	21. 28-32			
The wicked husbandmen . .	,, . .	21. 33-46	12. 1-12	20. 9-19	
The wedding garment . . .	,, . .	22. 1-14			
The subtle questions :—					
(1) of the Pharisees ; *the tri-*					
bute money	,,	22. 15-22	12. 13-17	20. 20-26	
(2) of the Sadducees ; *the*					
resurrection	,,	22. 23-33	12. 18-27	20. 27-39	
(3) of the Lawyer ; *the great*					
commandment	,,	22. 34-40	12. 28-34		
Our Lord's counter-question . . .	,,	22. 41-46	12. 35-37	20. 41-44	
The woes on Scribes and Pharisees	,,	23. 13-33			
The widow's mite	,,		12. 41-44	21. 1-4	
The coming of the Greeks . .	,,				12. 20-3ɔ
The departure to the Mount of					
Olives	Olivet	24. 1, 3	13. 1, 3		
The prediction (1) of the destruction					
of Jerusalem	,, ...	24. 3-28	13. 3-23	21. 5-24	
(2) of the second					
coming . .	,, ...	24. 28-51	13. 23-37	21. 24-36	
Parables :—The Ten virgins . . .	,, ...	25. 1-13			
,, Talents . . .	,, ...	25. 14-30			
,, Sheep and the					
goats .	,, ...	25. 31-46			
The Sanhedrin in council	Jerusalem . .	26. 3-5	14. 1-2	22. 1-2	
Compact of the traitor	,,	26. 14-16	14. 10, 11	22. 3-6	

PART VI.
The Death and Burial.

Preparation of the Passover . .	Jerusalem . .	26. 17-19	14. 12-16	22. 7-13	
Washing the Apostles' feet . . .	,, . .				13. 1-17
The breaking of bread	,, . .	26. 26	14. 22	22. 19	
"One of you shall betray Me" . .	,, . .	26. 21	14. 18	22. 21	13. 21
"Is it I ?"	,, . .	26. 22-25	14. 19		
Giving of the sop. "That thou					
doest, do quickly"	,, . .				13. 26, 27
Departure of Judas	,, . .				13. 30
Peter warned	,, . .	26. 34	14. 30	22. 34	13. 38
Blessing the cup	,, . .	26. 27-28	14. 23-24	22. 17	
The discourses after supper . . .	,, . .				14-16
Christ's prayer for His Apostles .	,, . .				17.
The hymn	,, . .	26. 30	14. 26		
The agony	Gethsemane .	26. 37	14. 33	22. 39	18. 1
The thrice-repeated prayer . . .	,, . .	26. 39-44	14. 36-39	22. 42	
His sweat, and comforting by the					
angel	,, . .			22. 43, 44	
The sleep of the Apostles	,, . .	26. 40-45	14. 37-41	22. 45, 46	
Betrayal by Judas	,, . .	26. 47-50	14. 43, 44	22. 47	18. 2-5
Peter smites Malchus	,, . .	26. 51	14. 47	22. 50	18. 10
Christ heals the ear of Malchus .	,, . .			22. 51	
,, forsaken by His disciples .	,, . .	26. 56	14. 50		
,, led to Annas	Jerusalem . .				18. 12, 13
,, tried by Caiaphas	,, . .	26. 57	14. 53	22. 54	18. 15
Peter follows Christ	,, . .	26. 58	14. 54	22. 55	18. 15
The high priest's adjuration . .	,, . .	26. 63	14. 61		
Christ condemned, buffeted,					
mocked	,, . .	26. 66, 67	14. 64, 65	22. 63-65	

EVENTS.	LOCALITY.	MATTHEW.	MARK.	LUKE.	JOHN.
Peter's denial of Christ	Jerusalem . .	26. 69-75	14. 66-72	22. 54-62	18. 17-27
Christ before Pilate	,,	27. 1, 2	15. 1	23. 1	18. 28
Repentance of Judas	,,	27. 3			
Pilate comes out to the people . .	,,				18. 29
,, speaks to Jesus privately .	,,				18. 33
,, orders Him to be scourged	,,	27. 26	15. 15		19. 1
Jesus crowned with thorns . . .	,,	27. 29	15. 17		19. 2
,, exhibited by Pilate: "Behold the man!"	,,				19. 5
,, accused formally	,,	27. 11	15. 2	23. 2	
,, sent by Pilate to Herod, mocked, arrayed in purple	,,			23. 6-11	
"Behold your King!"	,,				19. 14
Pilate desires to release Him . .	,,	27. 15	15. 6	23. 17	19. 12
,, receives a message from his wife	,,	27. 19			
,, washes his hands . . .	,,	27. 24			
,, releases Barabbas . . .	,,	27. 26			
,, delivers Jesus to be crucified	,,	27. 26	15. 15	23. 25	19. 16
Simon of Cyrene carries the cross	,,	27. 32	15. 21	23. 26	
They give Him vinegar and gall .	Golgotha . . .	27. 34	15. 23	23. 36	
They nail Him to the cross . . .	,,	27. 35	15. 24, 25	23. 33	19. 18
The superscription	,,	27. 37	15. 26	23. 38	19. 19
THE SEVEN WORDS.					
1. *Father, forgive them*	,,			23. 34	
His garments parted, and vesture allotted	,,	27. 35	15. 24	23. 34	19. 23
Passers-by rail, the two thieves revile	,,	27. 39-44	15. 29-32	23. 35	
The penitent thief	,,			23. 40	
2. *To-day shalt thou be with me in Paradise*	,,			23. 43	
3. *Woman, behold thy son, &c.* .	,,				19. 26, 27
Darkness over all the land .	,,	27. 45	15. 33	23. 44, 45	
4. *My God, my God, why hast thou forsaken me?*	,,	27. 46	15. 34		
5. *I thirst*	,,				19. 28
The vinegar	,,	27. 48	15. 36		19. 29
6. *It is finished*	,,				19. 30
7. *Father, into thy hands I commend my spirit*	,,			23. 46	
Rending of the veil	Jerusalem	27. 51	15. 38	23. 45	
Opening of graves, and resurrection of saints	,,	27. 52			
Testimony of centurion	Golgotha . .	27. 54	15. 39	23. 47	
Watching of the women	,,	27. 55	15. 40	23. 49	
The piercing of His side	,,				19. 34
Taking down from the cross, and burial by Joseph of Arimathæa and Nicodemus	,,	27. 57-60	15. 46	23. 53	19. 38-42
A guard placed over the sealed stone	The Garden .	27. 65, 66			

PART VII.

The Resurrection and the Great Forty Days.

Women carry spices to the tomb .	The Garden . .	28. 1	16. 1, 2	24. 1	
An angel had rolled away the stone	,,	28. 2			
Women announce the resurrection	Jerusalem . .	28. 8		24. 9, 10	20. 1, 2
Peter and John run to the tomb .	The Garden . .			24. 12	20. 3
The women return to the tomb . .	,,			24. 1	
The guards report these things to the chief priests	Jerusalem . .	28. 11-15			
APPEARANCES OF CHRIST AFTER HIS RESURRECTION.					
1. To Mary Magdalene . . . . "*All hail! Fear not. Touch me not*"	The Garden . .		16. 9, 10		20. 14
2. To the women returning home "*Go, tell my brethren that they go into Galilee: there shall they see me*"	,,	28. 9 28. 9 28. 10			20. 17
3. To two disciples going to Emmaus	Emmaus . . .		16. 12	24. 13	
(*Exposition of prophecies on the Passion.*)					

EVENTS.	LOCALITY.	MATTHEW.	MARK.	LUKE.	JOHN.
4. To Peter . . . (1 Cor. xv. 5)	Jerusalem			24. 34	
5. To ten Apostles in the upper room	,,			24. 36	20. 19
" *Peace be unto you. As my Father hath sent me, even so send I you* "	,,				20. 21
" *Receive ye the Holy Ghost. Whose soever sins ye remit,* " &c.	,,				20. 22, 23
6. To the eleven Apostles in the upper room	,,		16. 14		20. 26
" *Peace be unto you.*"					
To Thomas :—					
"*Reach hither thy finger,*" &c. .	,,				20. 27
"*Blessed are they that have not seen, and yet have believed* ".	,,				20. 29
7. To the disciples at the Sea of Tiberias	Tiberias				21. 1–24
To Peter :—					
" *Feed my sheep. Feed my lambs*"	,,				21. 15–17
8. To eleven disciples on a mountain in Galilee (1 Cor. xv. 5)	Galilee	28. 16			
" *All power is given unto me in heaven and in earth*" . . .	,,	28. 18			
"*Go ye and teach all nations, baptizing them,*" &c. . . .	,,	28. 19			
"*Lo, I am with you alway, even unto the end of the world. Amen.*"	,,	28. 20			
9. To five hundred brethren at once . . . . (1 Cor. xv. 6)	,,				
10. To St. James . (1 Cor. xv. 7)	,,				
THE ASCENSION (Acts i. 1-2)	Bethany		16. 19	24. 50, 51	

XXVI. OUR LORD'S MIRACLES

MIRACLES.	MATTHEW.	MARK.	LUKE.	JOHN.
I. *Narrated in one Gospel only.*				
Two blind men healed	9. 27–31			
A dumb demoniac healed	9. 32, 33			
Stater in the mouth of the fish	17. 24–27			
The deaf and dumb man healed		7. 31–37		
A blind man healed		8. 22–26		
When Christ passed unseen through the multitude			4. 30	
Draught of fishes			5. 1–11	
Raising the widow's son			7. 11–15	
Healing the crooked woman			13. 11–13	
,, ,, man with the dropsy			14. 1–4	
,, ,, ten lepers			17. 11–19	
,, ,, ear of Malchus, servant of the high priest			22. 50, 51	
Turning water into wine				2. 1–11
Healing the nobleman's son (of fever)				4. 46–54
,, ,, impotent man at Bethesda . . .				5. 1–9
,, ,, man born blind				9. 1–7
Raising of Lazarus				11. 43, 44
Draught of fishes				21. 1–11
II. *Narrated in two Gospels.*				
Demoniac in synagogue cured		1. 23–26	4. 33–35	
Healing centurion's servant (of palsy)	8. 5–13		7. 1–10	
The blind and dumb demoniac	12. 22		11. 14	
Healing the daughter of the Syrophenician . . .	15. 21–28	7. 24–30		
Feeding the four thousand	15. 32–38	8. 1–8		
Cursing the fig-tree	21. 18–22	11. 12–14		
III. *Narrated in three Gospels.*				
Healing the leper	8. 2, 3	1. 40–42	5. 12, 13	
Peter's mother-in-law	8. 14, 15	1. 30, 31	4. 38, 39	
Stilling the storm	8. 26	4. 37–39	8. 22–24	

MIRACLES.	MATTHEW.	MARK.	LUKE.	JOHN.
The legion of devils entering swine	8. 28–34	5. 1–15	8. 27–35	
Healing the man sick of the palsy	9. 2–7	2. 3–12	5. 18–25	
„ woman with issue of blood . . .	9. 20–22	5. 25–29	8. 43–48	
Raising of Jairus' daughter	9. 23–25	5. 38–42	8. 49–56	
Healing the man with a withered hand	12. 10–13	3. 1–5	6. 6–10	
Walking on the sea	14. 25	6. 48–51		6. 19–21
Curing demoniac child	17. 14–18	9. 17–29	9. 38–42	
„ blind Bartimæus (two blind men, Matt. 20)	20. 30–34	10. 46–52	18. 35–43	
IV. Narrated in four Gospels.				
Feeding the five thousand	14. 15, 20	6. 35–44	9. 12–17	6. 5–13

XXVII. OUR LORD'S PARABLES

PARABLES.	MATTHEW.	MARK.	LUKE.	LEADING LESSONS.
I. Recorded in one Gospel only.				
The tares	13. 24–30	. . .	. . .	Good and evil in life and judgment.
The hid treasure	13. 44	. . .	. . .	Value of the Gospel.
The goodly pearl	13. 45, 46	. . .	. . .	The seeker finding salvation.
The draw-net	13. 47, 48	. . .	. . .	Visible Church a mixed body.
The unmerciful servant . . .	18. 23–34	. . .	. . .	Duty of forgiveness.
The labourers in the vineyard	20. 1–16	. . .	. . .	Precedence in service gives no claim to priority in reward. With especial reference to the Jewish Nation.
The two sons	21. 28–30	. . .	. . .	Insincerity and repentance.
The marriage of the king's son	22. 2–14	. . .	. . .	Religion not merely acceptance of benefits.
The ten virgins	25. 1–13	. . .	. . .	Watchful preparation and careless security.
The talents	25. 14–30	. . .	. . .	Use of advantages.
The sheep and goats	25. 31–46	. . .	. . .	Love the test of life.
The seed growing secretly . .	. . .	4. 26–29	. . .	The law of growth in religion.
The householder	. . .	13. 34	. . .	Watchfulness.
The two debtors	. . .	. . .	7. 41, 42	Gratitude for pardon.
The good Samaritan	. . .	. . .	10. 30–35	Active benevolence, going beyond the requirements of convention.
The importunate friend . . .	. . .	. . .	11. 5–8	Perseverance in prayer.
The rich fool	. . .	. . .	12. 16–20	Worldly-mindedness.
Servants watching	. . .	. . .	12. 35–40	The Christian attitude of mind.
The wise steward	. . .	. . .	12. 42–48	Conscientiousness in trust.
The barren fig-tree	. . .	. . .	13. 6–9	Unprofitableness under grace. With especial reference to the Jewish nation.
The great supper	. . .	. . .	14. 16–24	Universality of the Divine call.
Tower; king going to war . .	. . .	. . .	14. 28–33	Prudence and self-denial.
The piece of money	. . .	. . .	15. 8–10	Joy over penitence.
The prodigal son	. . .	. . .	15. 11–32	Fatherly love to returning sinner.
The unjust steward	. . .	. . .	16. 1–8	Making the best of circumstances.
The rich man and Lazarus . .	. . .	. . .	16. 19–31	Reward and punishment in the world to come.
Unprofitable servants	. . .	. . .	17. 7–10	God's claim on all our service.
The unjust judge	. . .	. . .	18. 2–5	Need of persevering prayer.
The Pharisee and publican . .	. . .	. . .	18. 10–14	Self-righteousness and humility.
The pounds	. . .	. . .	19. 12–27	Diligence rewarded, sloth punished.
II. Recorded in two Gospels.				
House on rock, and on the sand	7. 24–27	. . .	6. 47–49	Consistent and false profession.
The leaven	13. 33	. . .	13. 20, 21	Pervading influence of religion.
The lost sheep	18. 12, 13	. . .	15. 4–6	Joy over penitent.
III. Recorded in three Gospels.				
Candle under a bushel . . .	5. 15	4. 21	8. 16; 11. 33	Religion not meant to be concealed.
New cloth on old garment . .	9. 16	2. 21	5. 36	New doctrine on old prejudices.

PARABLES.	MATTHEW.	MARK.	LUKE.	LEADING LESSONS.
New wine in old bottles . . .	9. 17	2. 22	5. 37, 38	New spirit in unregenerate heart.
The sower	13. 3-8	4. 3-8	8. 5-8	Hearers divided into classes.
The mustard-seed	13. 31, 32	4. 30-32	13. 18, 19	Spread of the Gospel.
The wicked husbandmen . .	21. 33-39	12. 1-9	20. 9-32	Rejection of Christ by the Jews.
The fig-tree and all the trees .	24. 32, 33	13. 28, 29	21. 29	Reading the Signs of the Times.

N.B.—*These Miracles and Parables are grouped according to their record by the Evangelists; for their approximate chronological position see "Harmony of the Gospels."*

XXVIII. SPECIAL PRAYERS AND THANKSGIVINGS IN THE NEW TESTAMENT

(See also the Special Songs of Thanksgiving in Luke 1, 2; Rev. 4, 5, 7, 11, 12, 15, 18, 19.)

OF WHOM RECORDED.	REFERENCES.	SUBJECTS.
Apostles	Luke 17. 5	For more faith.
Apostles	Acts 1. 24, 25	On choosing an Apostle.
Blind Bartimæus . .	Mark 10. 47	For sight.
Early Church . . .	Acts 4. 24-30	For support under persecution.
Father of the lunatic boy	Matt. 17. 15	For his only son.
Jairus	— 9. 18	For his little daughter.
Jesus	— 11. 25, 26; Luke 10. 21	Thanksgiving.
Jesus	— 26. 39; Luke 22. 42	Under suffering in Gethsemane.
Jesus	— 27. 46	Under suspension of Divine consolation.
Jesus	Luke 23. 34	For His murderers.
Jesus	— 23. 46	Commending His spirit to God.
Jesus	John 11. 41, 42	Thanksgiving for the Father's acceptance of His prayer.
Jesus	— 12. 27, 28	Imploring His Father's aid.
Jesus	— 17	For His Apostles, and all believers. For unity.
Lord's prayer . . .	Matt. 6. 9; Luke 11. 2 .	The model of supplication for relief of human needs.
Penitent thief . . .	Luke 23. 42	To be remembered by Jesus.
Pharisee's prayer . .	— 18. 11	Thanksgiving for his own righteousness.
Prodigal son	— 15. 18, 19	For forgiveness.
Publican's prayer . .	— 18. 13	For Divine mercy.
St. Paul	Acts 9. 6-11	For instruction and grace.
St. Paul	2 Cor. 12. 8	For relief from personal trial.
St. Paul	Eph. 1. 17-20; 3. 14-21; Phil. 1. 9-11; Col. 1. 9-11; 1 Thess. 3. 10-13; 2 Thess. 1. 11, 12; 2. 16, 17 3. 5; Heb. 13. 20, 21	Intercession for the Churches.
Samaritan woman . .	John 4. 15	For the Living Water.
Stephen	Acts 7. 59, 60	Commendation of his soul; forgiveness of his murderers.
Syrophenician woman .	Matt. 15. 22	For her daughter.
Ten lepers	Luke 17. 13	For cleansing.
The centurion . . .	Matt. 8. 6	For his servant.
The disciples	— 8. 25	To be saved from the storm.
The leper	— 8. 2	For cleansing.
The nobleman . . .	John 4. 49	For his child.
The waiting Church .	Rev. 22. 20	For the coming of Christ.
Two blind men . . .	Matt. 9. 27	For sight.

XXIX. THE NAMES, TITLES, AND OFFICES OF CHRIST

(The R.V. rendering is given in parenthesis.)

Adam, the Second, 1 Cor. 15. 45, 47.
Advocate, an, 1 John 2. 1.
(The) Alpha and (the) Omega, Rev. 1. 8; 22. 13.
Amen, Rev. 3. 14.

Author and Finisher (Perfecter) of our faith, Heb. 12. 2.
Author of eternal salvation, Heb. 5. 9. [(cf. Jn. 8. 25.)
Beginning of the creation of God, Rev. 3. 14.

Blessed and only Potentate, 1 Tim. 6. 15.
Branch, Zech. 3. 8 ; 6. 12.
Bread of God, John 6. 33.
Bread of Life, John 6. 35.

Captain (Author) of Salvation, Heb. 2. 10.
Child (Servant), Holy, Acts 4. 27.
Child, Little, Isa. 11. 6.
Christ, the, Matt. 16. 16 ; Mark 8. 29 ; Luke 9. 20 ; John 6. 69.
Corner-stone, Eph. 2. 20 ; 1 Pet. 2. 6.
Counsellor, Isa. 9. 6.

David, Jer. 30. 9 ; Ezek. 34. 23 ; 37. 24 ; Hos. 3. 5.
David, Son of, Matt. 9. 27 ; 21. 9.
Day-spring, Luke 1. 78.
Day-star, 2 Pet. 1. 19.
Deliverer, Rom. 11. 26.
Desire of all nations, Hag. 2. 7.

Emmanuel, Isa. 7. 14 ; Matt. 1. 23.
Everlasting Father, Isa. 9. 6.

Faithful witness, Rev. 1. 5 ; 3. 14.
Fellow, my, Zech. 13. 7.
First and Last, Rev. 1. 17.
Firstbegotten (Firstborn), Heb. 1. 6 ; Rev. 1. 5.

God, Isa. 40. 9 ; John 20. 28 ; 1 John 5. 20.
God blessed for ever, Rom. 9. 5.
Governor, Matt. 2. 6.

Head over all things, Eph. 1. 22.
Heir of all things, Heb. 1. 2.
High Priest, Heb. 4. 14 ; 5. 10.
Holy, the most, Dan. 9. 24.
Holy One, Luke 4. 34 ; Acts 3. 14 (*and Righteous*) ; Rev. 3. 7 (*he that is holy*).
Horn of Salvation, Luke 1. 69.

Image of God, 2 Cor. 4. 4.

Jesus, Matt. 1. 21 ; 1 Thess. 1. 10.
Just (Righteous) One, Acts 3. 14 ; 7. 52 ; 22. 14.

King of Israel, John 1. 49.
King of the Jews, Matt. 2. 2.
King of kings, 1 Tim. 6. 15 ; Rev. 17. 14 ; 19. 16.

Lamb of God, John 1. 29, 36.
Life, the, John 14. 6.
Life, Bread of, John 6. 35.
Light of the World, John 8. 12 ; 9. 5.
Light, True, John 1. 9 ; 12. 35.
Lion of the tribe of Judah, Rev. 5. 5.
Living stone, 1 Pet. 2. 4.
Lord, Zech. 14. 3 ; Matt. 3. 3 ; Mark 11. 3.
Lord God, Almighty, Rev. 15. 3 ; *of the holy Prophets* (*or the spirits of the Prophets*), 22. 6.

Lord of all, Acts 10. 36.
Lord of Glory, 1 Cor. 2. 8.
Lord of lords, 1 Tim. 6. 15 ; Rev. 17. 14 ; 19. 16.
Lord our Righteousness, Jer. 23. 6.

Maker and Preserver of all things, John 1. 3, 10 ; 1 Cor. 8. 6 ; Col. 1. 16 ; Heb. 1. 2, 10 ; Rev. 4. 11.
Man, the, 1 Tim. 2. 5.
Man, the second, 1 Cor. 15. 47.
Mediator, 1 Tim. 2. 5 ; Heb. 12. 24.
Messiah, Dan. 9. 25 ; John 1. 41.
Mighty God, Isa. 9. 6.
Morning star, Rev. 22. 16.

Nazarene, Matt. 2. 23.

Passover, our, 1 Cor. 5. 7.
Priest for ever, Heb. 5. 6.
Prince, Acts 5. 31.
Prince of Life, Acts 3. 15.
Prince of Peace, Isa. 9. 6.
Prince (Ruler) of the kings of the earth, Rev. 1. 5.
Prophet, Deut. 18. 15 ; Luke 24. 19.
Propitiation, Rom. 3. 25 ; 1 John 2. 2.

Redeemer, Job 19. 25 ; Isa. 59. 20.
Righteous, the, 1 John 2. 1.
Root and offspring of David, Rev. 5. 5 ; 22. 16.
Ruler in Israel, Mic. 5. 2.

Same yesterday, to-day, and for ever, Heb. 13. 8.
Saviour, Luke 2. 11 ; Acts 5. 31.
Servant, my, Isa. 52. 13.
Shepherd and Bishop of souls, 1 Pet. 2. 25.
Shepherd in the land, Zech. 11. 16 ; 13. 7.
Shepherd of the sheep, Great, Heb. 13. 20.
Shepherd, the chief, 1 Pet. 5. 4.
Shepherd, the good, John 10. 11.
Shiloh, Gen. 49. 10.
Son, a, Heb. 3. 6.
Son, the, Ps. 2. 12.
Son, my beloved (chosen), Matt. 3. 17 ; 17. 5 ; Luke 9. 35.
Son, only-begotten, John 1. 14, 18 ; 3. 16, 18.
Son of David, Matt. 9. 27 ; 21. 9.
Son of God, Matt. 8. 29 ; Luke 1. 35.
Son of Man, Matt. 8. 20 ; John 1. 51 ; Acts 7. 56.
Son of the Highest (Most High), Luke 1. 32.
Star, Num. 24. 17.
Star, the bright and (the) morning, Rev. 22. 16.
Sun of Righteousness, Mal. 4. 2.

Truth, the, John 14. 6.

Vine, the, John 15. 1, 5.

Way, John 14. 6.
Witness, faithful and true, Rev. 3. 14.
Wonderful, Isa. 9. 6.
Word, John 1. 1.
Word of God, Rev. 19. 13.

XXX. PROPHECIES RELATING TO CHRIST

1. HIS FIRST ADVENT.
   The fact, Gen. 3. 15 ; Deut. 18. 15 ; Ps. 89. 20 ; Isa. 2. 2 ; 28. 16 ; 32. 1 ; 35. 4 ; 42. 6 ; 49. 1 ; 55. 4 ; Ezek. 34. 24 ; Dan. 2. 44 ; Mic. 4. 1 ; Zech. 3. 8.
   The time, Gen. 49. 10 ; Num. 24. 17 ; Dan. 9. 24 ; Mal. 3. 1.
   His Divinity, Ps. 2. 7, 11 ; 45. 6, 7, 11 ; 72. 8 ; 102. 24–27 ; 89. 26, 27 ; 110. 1 ; Isa. 9. 6 ; 25. 9 ; 40. 10 ; Jer. 23. 6 ; Mic. 5. 2 ; Mal. 3. 1.
   Human Generation, Gen. 12. 3 ; 18. 18 ; 21. 12 ; 22. 18 ; 26. 4 ; 28. 14 ; 49. 10 ; 2 Sam. 7. 14 ; Ps. 18. 4–6, 50 ; 22. 22, 23 ; 89. 4, 29, 36 ; 132. 11 ; Isa. 11. 1 ; Jer. 23. 5 ; 33. 15.
2. HIS FORERUNNER.
   Isa. 40. 3 ; Mal. 3. 1 ; 4. 5.

3. HIS NATIVITY AND EARLY YEARS.
   The fact, Gen. 3. 15 ; Isa. 7. 14 ; Jer. 31. 22.
   The place, Num. 24. 17, 19 ; Mic. 5. 2.
   Adoration by Magi, Ps. 72. 10, 15 ; Isa. 60. 3, 6.
   Descent into Egypt, Hos. 11. 1.
   Massacre of Innocents, Jer. 31. 15.
4. HIS MISSION AND OFFICE.
   Mission, Gen. 12. 3 ; 49. 10 ; Num. 24. 19 ; Deut. 18. 18 ; Ps. 21. 1 ; Isa. 59. 20 ; Jer. 33. 16.
   Priest like Melchizedek, Ps. 110. 4.
   Prophet like Moses, Deut. 18. 15.
   Conversion of Gentiles, Isa. 11. 10 ; Deut. 32. 43 ; Ps. 18. 49 ; 19. 4 ; 117. 1 ; Isa. 42. 1 ; 45. 23 ; 49. 6 ; Hos. 1. 10 ; 2. 23 ; Joel 2. 32.
   Galilee, ministry in, Isa. 9. 1, 2.
   Miracles, Isa. 35. 5, 6 ; 42. 7 ; 53. 4.

Spiritual graces, Ps. 45. 7; Isa. 11. 2; 42. 1; 53. 9; 61. 1, 2.
Preaching, Ps. 2. 7; 78. 2; Isa. 2. 3; 61. 1; Mic. 4. 2.
Purification of Temple, Ps. 69. 9.

5. HIS PASSION.
Rejection by Jews and Gentiles, Ps. 2. 1; 22. 12; 41. 5; 56. 5; 69. 8; 118. 22, 23; Isa. 6. 9, 10; 8. 14; 29. 13; 53. 1; 65. 2.
Persecution, Ps. 22. 6; 35. 7, 12; 56. 5; 71. 10; 109. 2; Isa. 49. 7; 53. 3.
Triumphal entry into Jerusalem, Ps. 8. 2; 118. 25, 26; Zech. 9. 9.
Betrayal by own friend, Ps. 41. 9; 55. 13; Zech. 13. 6.
Betrayal for thirty pieces, Zech. 11. 12.
Betrayer's death, Ps. 55. 15, 23; 109. 8, 9.
Purchase of potter's field, Zech. 11. 13.
Desertion by disciples, Zech. 13. 7.
False accusation, Ps. 27. 12; 35. 11; 109. 2; Ps. 2. 1, 2.
Silence under accusation, Ps. 38. 13; Isa. 53. 7.
Mocking, Ps. 22. 7, 8, 16; 109. 25.
Insult, buffeting, spitting, scourging, Ps. 35. 15, 21; Isa. 50. 6.

Patience under suffering, Isa. 53. 7-9.
Crucifixion, Ps. 22. 14, 17.
Gall and vinegar, offer of, Ps. 69. 21.
Prayer for enemies, Ps. 100. 4.
Cries upon the cross, Ps. 22. 1; 31. 5.
Death in prime of life, Ps. 89. 45; 102. 24.
Death with malefactors, Isa. 53. 9, 12.
Death attested by convulsions of nature, Amos 5. 20; Zech. 14. 4, 6.
Casting lots for vesture, Ps. 22. 18.
Bone not to be broken, Ps. 34. 20.
Piercing, Ps. 22. 16; Zech. 12. 10; 13. 6.
Voluntary death, Ps. 40. 6-8.
Vicarious suffering, Isa. 53. 4-6, 12; Dan. 9. 26.
Burial with the rich, Isa. 53. 9.

6. HIS RESURRECTION.
Ps. 16. 8-10; 30. 3; 41. 10; 118. 17; Hos. 6. 2.

7. HIS ASCENSION.
Ps. 16. 11; 24. 7; 68. 18; 110. 1; 118. 19.
Dominion universal and everlasting, 1 Chron. 17. 11-14; Ps. 2. 6-8; 8. 6; 45. 6, 7; 72. 8; 110. 1-3; Isa. 9. 7; Dan. 7. 14.

8. HIS SECOND ADVENT.
Ps. 50. 3-6; Isa. 9. 6, 7; 66. 18; Dan. 7. 13, 14; Zech. 12. 10; 14. 4-8.

XXXI. PASSAGES FROM O.T. QUOTED IN N.T.*

MATTHEW.

Behold, a virgin shall be with child	1. 23.—Is. 7. 14.
Thou Bethlehem, in the land of Juda	2. 6.—Micah 5. 2.
Out of Egypt have I called my son	2. 15.—Hos. 11. 1.
In Rama was there a voice heard	2. 18.—Jer. 31. 15.
The voice of one crying in the wilderness	3. 3.—Is. 40. 3.
Man shall not live by bread alone	4. 4.—Deut. 8. 3.
He shall give his angels charge	4. 6.—Ps. 91. 11, 12.
Thou shalt not tempt the Lord	4. 7.—Deut. 6. 16.
Thou shalt worship the Lord thy God	4. 10.—Deut. 6. 13.
The land of Zabulon, and the land of Nephthalim	4. 15, 16.—Is. 9. 1, 2; 42. 7.
Thou shalt not kill	5. 21.—Ex. 20. 13.
Thou shalt not commit adultery	5. 27.—Ex. 20. 14.
Whosoever shall put away his wife	5. 31.—Deut. 24. 1
Thou shalt not forswear thyself	5. 33.—Lev. 19. 12
An eye for an eye, and a tooth for a tooth	5. 38.—Ex. 21. 24.
Thou shalt love thy neighbour	5. 43.—Lev. 19. 18.
Be ye therefore perfect	5. 48.—Gen. 17. 1.
Depart... ye that work iniquity	7. 23.—Ps. 6. 8.
Himself took our infirmities	8. 17.—Is. 53. 4.
I will have mercy, and not sacrifice	9. 13; 12. 7.—Hos. 6. 6.
Behold, I send my messenger	11. 10.—Mal. 3. 1.
Behold my servant, whom I have chosen	12. 18-21.—Is. 42. 1-4.
By hearing ye shall hear, and shall not understand	13. 14, 15.—Is. 6. 9, 10.
I will open my mouth in parables	13. 35.—Ps. 78. 2.

MATTHEW (cont.).

Honour thy father and mother	15. 4.—Ex. 20. 12.
He that curseth father or mother	15. 4.—Ex. 21. 17.
This people draweth nigh unto me	15. 8, 9.—Is. 29. 13.
He... made them male and female	19. 4.—Gen. 1. 27.
For this cause shall a man leave father and mother	19. 5.—Gen. 2. 24.
Thou shalt do no murder	19. 18.—Ex. 20. 13.
Honour thy father and thy mother	19. 19.—Ex. 20. 12.
Thou shalt love thy neighbour as thyself	19. 19.—Lev. 19. 18.
Tell ye the daughter of Sion, Behold, thy King cometh	21. 5.—Is. 62. 11; Zech. 9. 9.
Blessed is he that cometh in the name of the Lord	21. 9.—Ps. 118. 26.
My house shall be called the house of prayer	21. 13.—Is. 56. 7.
Ye have made it a den of thieves	21. 13.—Jer. 7. 11.
Out of the mouth of babes	21. 16.—Ps. 8. 2.
The stone which the builders rejected	21. 42.—Ps. 118. 22, 23.
If a man die, having no children	22. 24.—Deut. 25. 5.
I am the God of Abraham	22. 32.—Ex. 3. 6.
Thou shalt love the Lord thy God	22. 37.—Deut. 6. 5.
Thou shalt love thy neighbour as thyself	22. 39.—Lev. 19. 18.
The Lord said... Sit thou on my right hand	22. 44.—Ps. 110. 1.
Blessed is he that cometh in the name of the Lord	23. 39.—Ps. 118. 26.
I will smite the shepherd	26. 31.—Zech. 13. 7.
And they took the thirty pieces of silver	27. 9, 10.—Zech. 11. 12, 13.
They parted my garments	27. 35.—Ps. 22. 18.

** Cf. H. B. Swete, *Introduction to the Old Testament in Greek* (Cambridge, 1900), pp. 381 ff.; W. Dittmar, *Vetus Testamentum in Novo* (Göttingen, 1903). The quotations should be compared not only with the Hebrew, but also with the Greek of the Old Testament. It must also be remembered that accurate quotation is for the most part a modern fashion. The ancients were as a rule satisfied to reproduce the *thought* of an earlier writer.*

MATTHEW (cont.).

My God, my God, why hast thou forsaken me? 27. 46.—Ps. 22. 1.

MARK.

Behold, I send my messenger................. 1. 2.—Mal. 3. 1.
Prepare ye the way of the Lord............. 1. 3.—Is. 40. 3.
Seeing they may see, and not perceive .. 4. 12.—Is. 6. 9, 10.
This people honoureth me with their lips .. 7. 6, 7.—Is. 29. 13.
Honour thy father and thy mother.......... 7. 10.—Ex. 20. 12.
Whoso curseth father or mother............. 7. 10.—Ex. 21. 17.
Where their worm dieth not................. 9. 44.—Is. 66. 24.
God made them male and female.......... 10. 6.—Gen. 1. 27.
They twain shall be one flesh............... 10. 7, 8.—Gen. 2. 24.
Do not commit adultery, Do not kill .... 10. 19.—Ex. 20. 13, 14.
Hosanna; Blessed is he that cometh.......... 11. 9.—Ps. 118. 26.
My house shall be called the house of prayer .. 11. 17.—Is. 56. 7.
Ye have made it a den of thieves........... 11. 17.—Jer. 7. 11.
The stone which the builders rejected .... 12. 10, 11.—Ps. 118. 22, 23.
If a man's brother die, and leave no children 12. 19.—Deut. 25. 5.
I am the God of Abraham................... 12. 26.—Ex. 3. 6.
The Lord our God is one Lord............. 12. 29.—Deut. 6. 4.
Thou shalt love the Lord thy God.............. 12. 30.—Deut. 6. 5.
Thou shalt love thy neighbour............ 12. 31.—Lev. 19. 18.
The Lord said to my Lord, Sit thou on my right hand .... 12. 36.—Ps. 110. 1.
I will smite the shepherd.................. 14. 27.—Zech. 13. 7.
He was numbered with the transgressors .... 15. 28.—Is. 53. 12.
My God, my God, why hast thou forsaken me?.................. 15. 34.—Ps. 22. 1.

LUKE.

To turn the hearts of the fathers .... 1. 17.—Mal. 4. 6.
Every male that openeth the womb........ 2. 23.—Ex. 13. 2, 12.
A pair of turtledoves,&c. 2. 24.—Lev. 12. 8.
The voice of one crying in the wilderness .. 3. 4-6.—Is. 40. 3-5.
Man shall not live by bread alone .... 4. 4.—Deut. 8. 3.
Thou shalt worship the Lord thy God........ 4. 8.—Deut. 6. 13.
He shall give his angels charge over thee .... 4. 10, 11.—Ps. 91. 11, 12.
Thou shalt not tempt the Lord thy God.... 4. 12.—Deut. 6. 16.
The Spirit of the Lord is upon me .... 4. 18, 19.—Is. 61. 1, 2; 58. 6.
Behold, I send my messenger............... 7. 27.—Mal. 3. 1.
That seeing they might not see .... 8. 10.—Is. 6. 9.
Thou shalt love the Lord thy God............ 10. 27.—Deut. 6. 5; Lev. [19. 18.
And thy neighbour as thyself .... 10. 27.—Lev. 19. 18.

LUKE (cont.).

Blessed is he that cometh in the name of the Lord .... 13. 35.—Ps. 118. 26.
Do not commit adultery, Do not kill .... 18. 20.—Ex. 20. 12-16
My house is the house of prayer .... 19. 46.—Is. 56. 7.
Ye have made it a den of thieves .... 19. 46.—Jer. 7. 11.
The stone which the builders rejected .... 20. 17.—Ps. 118. 22, 23.
If a man's brother die, having a wife .... 20. 28.—Deut. 25. 5.
The Lord said unto my Lord, Sit thou on my right hand .... 20. 42, 43.—Ps. 110. 1.
He was reckoned among the transgressors .... 22. 37.—Is. 53. 12.
Say to the mountains, Fall on us............ 23. 30.—Hos. 10. 8.
Into thy hands I commend my spirit ...... 23. 46.—Ps. 31. 5.

JOHN.

The voice of one crying in the wilderness .... 1. 23.—Is. 40. 3.
The zeal of thine house hath eaten me up.... 2. 17.—Ps. 69. 9.
He gave them bread from heaven .... 6. 31.—Is. 78. 24.
They shall be all taught of God .... 6. 45.—Is. 54. 13.
I said, Ye are gods .... 10. 34.—Ps. 82. 6.
Hosanna: Blessed is the King of Israel........ 12. 13.—Ps. 118. 26.
Fear not, daughter of Zion: Behold, thy King 12. 15.—Zech. 9. 9.
Lord, who hath believed our report?......... 12. 38.—Is. 53. 1.
He hath blinded their eyes .... 12. 40.—Is. 6. 9, 10.
He that eateth bread with me .... 13. 18.—Ps. 41. 9.
They hated me without a cause .... 15. 25.—Ps. 35. 19; 69. 4.
They parted my raiment among them .... 19. 24.—Ps. 22. 18.
A bone of him shall not be broken .... 19. 36.—Ex. 12. 46; Ps. 34. [20.
They shall look on him whom they pierced .. 19. 37.—Zech. 12. 10.

ACTS.

Let his habitation be desolate .... 1. 20.—Ps. 69. 25.
His bishoprick let another take .... 1. 20.—Ps. 109. 8.
I will pour out my Spirit upon all flesh ..... 2. 17-21.—Joel 2. 28-32.
I foresaw the Lord always before my face 2. 25-28.—Ps. 16. 8-11.
The Lord said . . . Sit thou on my right hand 2. 34, 35.—Ps. 110. 1.
A prophet shall the Lord . . . raise up . . . like unto me.............. 3. 22, 23.—Deut. 18. 18, 19.
In thy seed shall all the kindreds of the earth 3. 25.—Gen. 22. 18; 12. 3.
This is the stone which was set at nought.... 4. 11.—Ps. 118. 22.
Why did the heathen rage .... 4. 25, 26.—Ps. 2. 1, 2.
* Get thee out of thy country .... 7. 3.—Gen. 12. 1.

* St. Stephen, in this chapter (Acts vii. 2-50), refers to God's dealings with His people, in support of his argument that God's favour has never been limited to one particular place. He glances cursorily at the sacred records, and does not quote literally (see next Table, "Acts," p. 192).

ACTS (cont.).

Who made thee a ruler and a judge over us?	7. 27, 28.—Ex. 2. 14.
I am the God of thy fathers ....,..	7. 32.—Ex. 3. 6.
Put off thy shoes from thy feet	7. 33, 34.—Ex. 3. 5, 7, 8, 10.
A prophet shall the Lord your God raise up ..	7. 37.—Deut. 18. 15.
Make us gods to go before us	7. 40.—Ex. 32. 1.
O ye house of Israel, have ye offered to me slain beasts	7. 42, 43.—Amos 5. 25–27.
Heaven is my throne, and earth is my footstool	7. 49, 50.—Is. 66. 1, 2.
He was led as a sheep to the slaughter......	8. 32, 33.—Is. 53. 7, 8.
I have found David the son of Jesse........	13. 22.—Ps. 89. 20.
Thou art my Son, this day have I begotten thee..................	13. 33.—Ps. 2. 7.
I will give you the sure mercies of David	13. 34.—Is. 55. 3.
Thou shalt not suffer thy Holy One to see corruption	13. 35.—Ps. 16. 10.
Behold, ye despisers, and wonder, and perish	13. 41.—Hab. 1. 5.
I have set thee to be a light of the Gentiles	13. 47.—Is. 49. 6.
After this I will return, and will build . . . the tabernacle	15. 16, 17.—Amos 9. 11, 12.
Thou shalt not speak evil of the ruler of thy people.................	23. 5.—Ex. 22. 28.
Go unto this people, and say, Hearing ye shall hear..................	28. 26, 27.—Is. 6. 9, 10.

ROMANS.

The just shall live by faith	1. 17.—Hab. 2. 4.
The name of God is blasphemed	2. 24.—Is. 52. 5.
Thou mightest be justified in thy sayings ..	3. 4.—Ps. 51. 4.
There is none righteous, no, not one	3. 10.—Ps. 14. 1, 3.
There is none that understandeth	3. 11.—Ps. 14. 2.
They are all gone out of the way	3. 12.—Ps. 14. 3.
Their throat is an open sepulchre	3. 13.—Ps. 5. 9 ; 140. 3.
Whose mouth is full of cursing	3. 14.—Ps. 10. 7.
Their feet are swift to shed blood	3. 15.—Is. 59. 7.
Destruction and misery are in their ways	3. 16, 17.—Is. 59. 7, 8.
There is no fear of God before their eyes	3. 18.—Ps. 36. 1.
Abraham believed God, and it was counted unto him for righteousness	4. 3.—Gen. 15. 6.
Blessed are they whose iniquities are forgiven	4. 7, 8.—Ps. 32. 1, 2.
I have made thee a father of many nations	4. 17.—Gen. 17. 5.
So shall thy seed be ..	4. 18.—Gen. 15. 5.
Thou shalt not covet ..	7. 7.—Ex. 20. 17.
For thy sake we are killed all the day	8. 36.—Ps. 44. 22.

ROMANS (cont.).

In Isaac shall thy seed be called	9. 7.—Gen. 21. 12.
At this time . . . Sarah shall have a son......	9. 9.—Gen. 18. 10.
The elder shall serve the younger	9. 12.—Gen. 25. 23.
Jacob have I loved, but Esau have I hated ...	9. 13.—Mal. 1. 2, 3.
I will have mercy on whom I will have mercy	9. 15.—Ex. 33. 19.
Even for this same purpose have I raised....	9. 17.—Ex. 9. 16.
I will call them my people, which were not my people	9. 25.—Hos. 2. 23.
Ye are not my people..	9. 26.—Hos. 1. 10.
Though the number of the children of Israel	9. 27, 28.—Is. 10. 22, 23.
Except the Lord of Sabaoth had left us a seed	9. 29.—Is. 1. 9.
Behold, I lay in Sion a stumbling-stone	9. 33.—Is. 28. 16.
The man which doeth those things shall live	10. 5.—Lev. 18. 5.
Who shall ascend into heaven	10. 6, 7.—Deut. 30. 12, 13.
The word is nigh thee, even in thy mouth ..	10. 8.—Deut. 30. 14.
Whosoever believeth on him shall not be ashamed	10. 11.—Is. 28. 16.
Whosoever shall call on the name of the Lord	10. 13.—Joel 2. 32.
How beautiful are the feet of them that preach	10. 15.—Is. 52. 7.
Lord, who hath believed our report?	10. 16.—Is. 53. 1.
Their sound went into all the earth	10. 18.—Ps. 19. 4.
I will provoke you to jealousy..............	10. 19.—Deut. 32. 21.
I was found of them that sought me not ..	10. 20.—Is. 65. 1.
All day long I have stretched forth my hands	10. 21.—Is. 65. 2.
Lord, they have killed thy prophets	11. 3.—1 Kin. 19. 10, 14.
I have reserved to myself seven thousand ..	11. 4.—1 Kin. 19. 18.
God hath given them the spirit of slumber	11. 8.—Is. 29. 10.
Let their table be made a snare	11. 9, 10.—Ps. 69. 22, 23.
There shall come out of Sion the Deliverer ..	11. 26, 27.—Is. 59. 20, 21.
Who hath known the mind of the Lord ? ..	11. 34.—Is. 40. 13.
Who hath first given to him	11. 35.—Job 41. 11.
Vengeance is mine ; I will repay	12. 19.—Deut. 32. 35.
If thine enemy hunger, feed him	12. 20.—Prov. 25. 21, 22.
Thou shalt not commit adultery..............	13. 9.—Ex. 20. 13–17; Lev. [19. 18.
Every knee shall bow to me	14. 11.—Is. 45. 23.
The reproaches of them that reproached thee	15. 3.—Ps. 69. 9.
For this cause I will confess to thee among the Gentiles ..	15. 9.—Ps. 18. 49.
Rejoice, ye Gentiles, with his people	15. 10.—Deut. 32. 43.

ROMANS (cont.).

Praise the Lord, all ye
Gentiles.............. 15. 11.—Ps. 117. 1.
There shall be a root of
Jesse .... 15. 12.—Is. 11. 1, 10.
To whom he was not
spoken of, they shall
see .... 15. 21.—Is. 52. 15.

1 CORINTHIANS.

I will destroy the wis-
dom of the wise...... 1. 19.—Is. 29. 14.
He that glorieth, let
him glory in the Lord 1. 31.—Jer. 9. 24.
Who hath known the
mind of the Lord? .. 2. 16.—Is. 40. 13.
He taketh the wise in
their own craftiness.. 3. 19.—Job 5. 13.
The Lord knoweth the
thoughts of the wise 3. 20.—Ps. 94. 11.
Two shall be one flesh.. 6. 16.—Gen. 2. 24.
Thou shalt not muzzle
the mouth of the ox.. 9. 9.—Deut. 25. 4.
The people sat down to
eat and drink .... 10. 7.—Ex. 32. 6.
The earth is the Lord's,
and the fulness there-
of .... 10. 26.—Ps. 24. 1.
With men of other
tongues and other lips 14. 21.—Is. 28. 11, 12.
He must reign, till he
hath put all enemies
under his feet........ 15. 25.—Ps. 110. 1.
All things are put under
him .... 15. 27.—Ps. 8. 6.
Let us eat and drink,
for to-morrow we die 15. 32.—Is. 22. 13.
The first man Adam was
made a living soul .. 15. 45.—Gen. 2. 7.
Death is swallowed up
in victory .... 15. 54.—Is. 25. 8.
O death, where is thy
sting?................. 15. 55.—Hos. 13. 14.

2 CORINTHIANS.

Moses . . . put a veil
over his face .... 3. 13.—Ex. 34. 33.
I believed, and there-
fore have I spoken .. 4. 13.—Ps. 116. 10.
I have heard thee in a
time accepted........ 6. 2.—Is. 49. 8.
I will dwell in them, and
walk in them .... 6. 16.—Lev. 26. 11, 12.
Wherefore come out
from among them.... 6. 17.—Is. 52. 11.
He that had gathered
much had nothing
over.................. 8. 15.—Ex. 16. 18.
He hath dispersed a-
broad .... 9. 9.—Ps. 112. 9.
He that glorieth, let
him glory in the Lord 10. 17.—Jer. 9. 24.
In the mouth of two or
three witnesses ...... 13. 1.—Deut. 19. 15.

GALATIANS.

Abraham believed God,
and it was accounted 3. 6.—Gen. 15. 6.
In thee shall all nations
be blessed .... 3. 8.—Gen. 12. 3.
Cursed is every one that
continueth not ...... 3. 10.—Deut. 27. 26.
The just shall live by
faith .... 3. 11.—Hab. 2. 4.
The man that doeth
them shall live in them 3. 12.—Lev. 18. 5.
Cursed is every one that
hangeth on a tree .... 3. 13.—Deut. 21. 23.

GALATIANS (cont.).

Rejoice, thou barren
that bearest not .... 4. 27.—Is. 54. 1.
Cast out the bond-
woman and her son.. 4. 30.—Gen. 21. 10.
Thou shalt love thy
neighbour as thyself 5. 14.—Lev. 19. 18.

EPHESIANS.

When he ascended up
on high, he led cap-
tivity captive .... 4. 8.—Ps. 68. 18.
Speak every man truth
with his neighbour .. 4. 25.—Zech. 8. 16.
Be ye angry, and sin not 4. 26.—Ps. 4. 4.
For this cause shall a
man leave............ 5. 31.—Gen. 2. 24.
Honour thy father and   [5. 16.
thy mother .... 6. 2, 3.—Ex. 20. 12; Deut.

1 TIMOTHY.

Thou shalt not muzzle
the ox................ 5. 18.—Deut. 25. 4.

2 TIMOTHY.

The Lord knoweth them
that are his .... 2. 19.—Num. 16. 5.

HEBREWS.

Thou art my Son, this
day have I begotten
thee .... 1. 5.—Ps. 2. 7.
I will be to him a Father 1. 5.—2 Sam. 7. 14.
Let all the angels of God
worship him .... 1. 6.—Ps. 97. 7.
Who maketh his angels
spirits .... 1. 7.—Ps. 104. 4.
Thy throne, O God, is
for ever and ever .... 1. 8, 9.—Ps. 45. 6, 7.
Thou, Lord, in the be-
ginning hast laid . . .
the earth .... 1. 10–12.—Ps. 102. 25–27.
Sit on my right hand,
until I make . . . thy
footstool .... 1. 13.—Ps. 110. 1.
What is man, that thou
art mindful of him .. 2. 6–8.—Ps. 8. 4–6.
I will declare thy name
unto my brethren.... 2. 12.—Ps. 22. 22.
I will put my trust in
him .... 2. 13.—Is. 8. 18.
Behold I and the chil-
dren which God hath
given me .... 2. 13.—Is. 8. 18.
To-day if ye will hear
his voice .... 3. 7–11.—Ps. 95. 7–11.
As I have sworn in my
wrath .... 4. 3.—Ps. 95. 11.
And God did rest the
seventh day.......... 4. 4.—Gen. 2. 2.
Thou art my Son, to-day
have I begotten thee 5. 5.—Ps. 2. 7.
Thou art a priest after
the order of Melchi-
sedec .... 5. 6.—Ps. 110. 4.
Blessing I will bless thee 6. 14.—Gen. 22. 17.
See . . . that thou make
all things according to
the pattern .... 8. 5.—Ex. 25. 40.
Behold, the days come,
saith the Lord ...... 8. 8–12.—Jer. 31. 31–34.
This is the blood of the
testament .... 9. 20.—Ex. 24. 8.
Sacrifice and offering
thou wouldest not .. 10. 5–7.—Ps. 40. 6–8.
For ever sat down on
the right hand of God 10. 12, 13.—Ps. 110. 1.
I will put my laws into
their hearts .... 10. 16, 17.—Jer. 31. 33, 34.

190

HEBREWS (cont.).

Vengeance belongeth
unto me............... 10. 30.—Deut. 32. 35, 36.
He that shall come will
come, and will not
tarry .... 10. 37, 38.—Hab. 2. 3, 4.
In Isaac shall thy seed
be called .... 11. 18.—Gen. 21. 12.
My son, despise not
thou the chastening
of the Lord .... 12. 5, 6.—Prov. 3. 11, 12.
Lift up the hands that
hang down .... 12. 12.—Is. 35. 3.
Yet once more I shake
not the earth only .. 12. 26.—Hag. 2. 6.
I will never leave thee,
nor forsake thee .... 13. 5.—Josh. 1. 5.
The Lord is my helper,
I will not fear........ 13. 6.—Ps. 118. 6.

JAMES.

Thou shalt love thy
neighbour .... 2. 8.—Lev. 19. 18.
Do not commit adultery 2. 11.—Ex. 20. 13, 14.
Abraham believed God,
and it was imputed
unto him for right-
eousness............... 2. 23.—Gen. 15. 6.
God resisteth the proud,
but giveth grace unto
the humble .... 4. 6.—Prov. 3. 34.

1 PETER.

Be ye holy; for I am
holy .... 1. 16.—Lev. 11. 44.
All flesh is as grass, and
... glory of man as
... grass .... 1. 24, 25.—Is. 40. 6–8.
Behold, I lay in Sion a   [16.
chief corner-stone.... 2. 6.—Ps. 118. 22; Is. 28.

1 PETER (cont.).

The stone which the
builders disallowed .. 2. 7.—Ps. 118. 22.
Who did no sin, neither
was guile found in his
mouth................ 2. 22.—Is. 53. 9.
Who his own self bare
our sins ... on the
tree .... 2. 24.—Is. 53. 4.
He that will love life,
and see good days.... 3. 10–12.—Ps. 34. 12–16.
God resisteth the proud,
and giveth grace to
the humble .... 5. 5.—Prov. 3. 34.

2 PETER.

The dog is turned to his
own vomit .... 2. 22.—Prov. 26. 11.

REVELATION.

The whole of this book is a reflex of the prophetic visions of the Old Testament. Apocalyptic
writing is an off-shoot of Prophecy proper, and
was extensively practised by the Jews from about
200 B. C.–A. D. 100. The beginnings of it appear in
the Old Testament. In the Revelation of St. John
the time-honoured form is used to convey a
Christian Philosophy of History: viz. the continual conflict between Good and Evil and the
complete eventual triumph of Christ. It is,
therefore, full of references and allusions to the
writings of Moses and the prophets, too numerous
to be tabulated, and often allusive rather than
literal; but the marginal references will better
aid the reader in working out the connexion between this Revelation, which closes Holy Scripture, and the inspirations vouchsafed to the
earlier dispensation, which prepared the way for
the fulness of the glory of Christ.

XXXII. REFERENCES TO THE OLD TESTAMENT, NOT BEING EXACT QUOTATIONS

MATTHEW.

* He shall be called a
Nazarene .... 2. 23.—Is. 11. 1; Zech. 3. 8;
                            6. 12 ; Ps. 22. 6;
                            Is. 53. 3.
The meek shall inherit
the earth .... 5. 5.—Ps. 37. 11.
Shew thyself to the
priest .... 8. 4.—Lev. 14. 3.
The blind receive their
sight .... 11. 5.—Is. 29. 18.
Elias, which was for to
come .... 11. 14 ; 17. 10.—Mal. 4. 5.
David ... did eat the
shewbread .... 12. 3, 4.—1 Sam. 21. 6.
Priests profane the sab-
bath, and are blame-
less .... 12. 5.—Num. 28. 9.
Teaching for doctrines
the commandments of
men .... 15. 9.—Is. 29. 13.
If thy brother trespass
... tell him ... alone 18. 15.—Lev. 19. 17.

MATTHEW (cont.).

In the mouth of two or
three witnesses ...... 18. 16.—Deut. 19. 15.
Moses' command to give
a writing of divorce-
ment .... 19. 7.—Deut. 24. 1.
With God all things are
possible .... 19. 26.—Jer. 32. 17.
The parable of a vine-
yard.................. 21. 33.—Is. 5. 1.
Your house is left unto
you desolate .... 23. 38.—Jer. 22. 5.
The abomination of de-
solation .... 24. 15.—Dan. 12. 11.
Wheresoever the car-
case is, there will the
eagles .... 24. 28.—Job 39. 30.
Immediately after ...
shall the sun be dark-
ened.................. 24. 29.—Is. 13. 10; Ezek.
                            32. 7; Joel 2. 10;
                            3. 15.
Heaven and earth shall
pass away .... 24. 35.—Is. 51. 6.
Depart from me, ye
cursed .... 25. 41.—Ps. 6. 8.
The Son of man goeth,
as it is written ...... 26. 24.—Ps. 22.
At last came two false
witnesses .... 26. 60.—Ps. 35. 11.
They did spit in his face 26. 67.—Is. 50. 6.
He trusted in God .... 27. 43.—Ps. 22. 8.

* This exact term is not found in any prophecy. Chrysostom
and others suppose it to be quoted from some lost book. Jerome
refers it to the Hebrew word *Nezer*, a "sprout," and identifies it
with "the Branch," by which the Messiah is designated by Isaiah
and Zechariah. This view is adopted by most modern expositors.
Others consider it to be equivalent to "a reproach," or "scorn of
men" (Is. liii ; Ps. xxii), and recognise the fulfilment of those
prophecies in the low estimation in which the people of Nazareth
were held by the other Jews (John i. 46).

MATTHEW (*cont.*).

All power is given unto
me .... 28. 18.—Dan. 7. 14.

MARK.

Shew thyself to the
priest .... 1. 44.—Lev. 14. 3.
David did eat the shew-
bread .... 2. 26.—1 Sam. 21. 6
Elias must first come .. 9. 11.—Mal. 4. 5.
Moses suffered . . . bill
of divorcement ...... 10. 4.—Deut. 24. 1.
A certain man planted
a vineyard............ 12. 1.—Is. 5. 1.
More than all whole
burnt-offerings ...... 12. 33.—1 Sam. 15. 22.
Take heed lest any man
deceive you .... 13. 5.—Jer. 29. 8.
The brother shall betray
brother .... 13. 12.—Micah 7. 6.
Abomination of desola-
tion .... 13. 14.—Dan. 12. 2.
The sun shall be dark-
ened.................. 13. 24.—Is. 13. 10.
My words shall not pass
away .... 13. 31.—Is. 40. 8.

LUKE.

Shall give unto him the
throne of . . . David.. 1. 32.—Ps. 132. 11.
Of his kingdom there
shall be no end ...... 1. 33.—Dan. 4. 3.
As he spake to . . . Abra-
ham, and to his seed
for ever .... 1. 55.—Gen. 17. 19.
Oath he sware to . . .
Abraham .... 1. 73.—Gen. 12. 3.
The dayspring from on   [4. 2.
high .... 1. 78.—Num. 24. 17; Mal.
Give light to them that
sit in darkness ...... 1. 79.—Is. 9. 2.
Eight days were accom-
plished for the cir-
cumcising .... 2. 21.—Lev. 12. 3.
The days of her purifi-
cation .... 2. 22.—Lev. 12. 2-4.
For the fall and rising
again .... 2. 34.—Is. 8. 14.
Shew thyself unto the
priest .... 5. 14.—Lev. 14. 3.
David . . . did take and
eat the shewbread .. 6. 4.—1 Sam. 21. 6.
This do, and thou shalt
live .... 10. 28.—Lev. 18. 5.
Depart, ye workers of
iniquity .... 13. 27.—Ps. 6. 8.
Your house is left unto
you desolate.......... 13. 35.—Jer. 22. 25.
If thy brother trespass
against thee .... 17. 3.—Lev. 19. 17.
Parable of the vineyard 20. 9.—Is. 5. 1.
Blessed are the barren 23. 29.—Is. 54. 1.
It behoved Christ to
suffer .... 24. 46.—Is. 53. 5.

JOHN.

One soweth and another
reapeth .... 4. 37.—Micah 6. 15.
If any . . . thirst . .
come unto me........ 7. 37.—Is. 55. 1.
Wells of living water
(illustration of the   [3.
Spirit) .... 7. 38.—Prov. 18. 4; Is. 12.
Of the Spirit . . . they
should receive .... 7. 39.—Is. 44. 3.
Christ's birth at Bethle-
hem, and of David's
house .... 7. 42.—Micah 5. 2.

JOHN (*cont.*).

The testimony of two
men is true .... 7. 17.—Deut. 19. 15. [9.7.
Christ abideth for ever 12. 34.—Ps. 89. 36, 37; Is.
God's command to the
Christ, what he shall
say .... 12. 49.—Deut. 18. 18.
None shall be lost, but
the son of perdition.. 17. 12.—Ps. 109. 8.
They filled a sponge with
vinegar, &c. .... 19. 29.—Ps. 69. 21.
He must rise again from
the dead.............. 20. 9.—Ps. 16. 10.

ACTS.

God promised to give
Canaan for a posses-
sion to Abraham, and
to his seed after him 7. 5.—Gen. 12. 7; 13. 15.
That his seed should
sojourn in a strange
land; and that they
should bring them in-
to bondage, and en-
treat them evil four
hundred years........ 7. 6.—Gen. 15. 13.
After that shall they come
forth, and serve me in
this place .... 7. 7.—Gen. 15. 16.
Abraham begat Isaac .. 7. 8.—Gen. 21. 3.
And circumcised him
the eighth day .... 7. 8.—Gen. 21. 4.
Isaac begat Jacob....... 7. 8.—Gen. 25. 26.
Jacob begat the twelve
patriarchs .... 7. 8.—Gen. 42. 13.
The patriarchs . . . sold
Joseph into Egypt .. 7. 9.—Gen. 37. 4, 11, 28.
But God was with him 7. 9.—Gen. 39. 2, 21.
I have seen the afflic-
tion of my people .... 7. 34.—Ex. 3. 7.
Have ye offered to me
slain beasts .... 7. 42.—Amos 5. 25, 26.
I will carry you away   [20. 4.
beyond Babylon...... 7. 43.—Amos 5. 27; Jer.
God is no respecter of
persons .... 10. 34.—Job 34. 19.

ROMANS.

Who will render to
every man according
to his deeds .... 2. 6.—Ps. 62. 12.
There is no respect of
persons with God .... 2. 11.—Deut. 10. 17.
Shall the thing formed
say to him that
formed it .... 9. 20.—Is. 45. 9.
The potter has power
over the clay .... 9. 21.—Jer. 18. 6.
Eyes that they should
not see .... 11. 8.—Is. 29. 10.

1 CORINTHIANS.

Eye hath not seen .... 2. 9.—Is. 64. 4.

EPHESIANS.

Helmet of salvation .. 6. 17.—Is. 59. 17.

PHILIPPIANS.

Every knee should bow 2. 10.—Is. 45. 23.

2 THESSALONIANS.

Exalteth himself above
all that is called God 2. 4.—Dan. 11. 36.

1 TIMOTHY.

We brought nothing in-
to the world .... 6. 7.—Job 1. 21.

192

HEBREWS.

Abraham's seed . . . as the stars of the sky in multitude, and as the sand by the sea-shore 11. 12.—Gen. 22. 17.

The patriarchs . . . confessed themselves strangers and pilgrims on the earth.......... 11. 13.—Gen. 23. 4 ; 47. 9.

Moses' parents . . . saw he was "a proper child" .... 11. 23.—Ex. 2. 2.

JAMES.

As the flower of the grass he shall pass away .. 1. 10.—Job 14. 2.

1 PETER.

Tasted that the Lord is gracious............ 2. 3.—Ps. 34. 8.

1 PETER (cont.).

A chosen generation .. 2. 9.—Deut. 10. 15.

Which in time past were not a people.......... 2. 10.—Hos. 1. 10.

Fear God. Honour the king .... 2. 17.—Prov. 24. 21.

Charity shall cover the multitude of sins .... 4. 8.—Prov. 10. 12.

2 PETER.

A thousand years as one day .... 3. 8.—Ps. 90. 4.

The heavens shall pass away .... 3. 10.—Ps. 102. 25, 26.

A new heaven and a new earth............. 3. 13.—Is. 65. 17 ; 66. 22.

1 JOHN.

If we say we have no sin .... 1. 8.—Prov. 20. 9.

XXXIII. REFERENCES IN THE NEW TESTAMENT TO INCIDENTS RECORDED IN THE OLD TESTAMENT

David's visit to Ahimelech, at Nob .... Matt. 12. 3, 4.—1 Sam. 21. 1.

Jonah's entombment for three days and nights in the belly of the fish .... — 12. 40. — 16. 4. } Jonah 1. 17.

The Queen of Sheba's visit to Solomon .... — 12. 42.—1 Kings 10. 1.

The death of Abel .... — 23. 35.—Gen. 4. 8.

* Death of Zacharias .. — 23. 35.—2 Chron. 24. 20.

Elijah's visit to the widow of Zarephath Luke 4. 26.—1 Kings 17. 9.

The healing of Naaman's leprosy .... — 4. 27.—2 Kings 5. 14.

Jonah's mission to Nineveh .... — 11. 30.—Jonah 3 ; 4.

The Queen of Sheba's visit to Solomon .... — 11. 31.—1 Kings 10. 1.

The murder of Abel and Zacharias .... — 11. 51.—Gen. 4. 8 ; 2 [Chron. 24. 20, 21.

The deluge in the days of Noah .... — 17. 26.—Gen. 7.

The destruction of Sodom .... — 17. 29.—Gen. 19. 16.

The fate of Lot's wife.. — 17. 32.—Gen. 19. 21.

Moses' vision of the burning bush .... — 20. 37.—Ex. 3.

Moses lifting up the brazen serpent ...... John 3. 14.— Num. 21. 9.

Manna in the wilderness .... — 6. 31.—Ex. 16. 15.

Mosaic enactment of circumcision .... — 7. 22.—Lev. 12. 3.

Mosaic enactment of stoning, as punishment for adultery .. — 8. 5.—Lev. 20. 10.

God appeared unto Abraham, when he was in Mesopotamia, before he dwelt in [Neh. 9. 7. Charran.............. Acts 7. 2.—Gen. 15. 7 ;

Abraham's residence in Charran.............. — 7. 4.—Gen. 11. 31.

Abraham's migration from Charran to Canaan .... — 7. 4.—Gen. 12. 4, 5.

God's promise to give Canaan to Abraham [15. and his seed .... — 7. 5.—Gen. 10. 1-7 ; 13.

Israel's bondage in Egypt .... Acts 7. 6.—Gen. 15. 13.

The birth of Isaac from Abraham .... — 7. 8.—Gen. 21. 3.

His circumcision the eighth day .... — 7. 8.—Gen. 21. 4.

Jacob's birth from Isaac — 7. 8.—Gen. 25. 26.

The birth of the twelve patriarchs from Jacob — 7. 8.—Gen. 42. 13.

Joseph sold into Egypt by his brethren ...... — 7. 9.—Gen. 37. 4, 11, 28.

God's favour to Joseph in Egypt .... — 7. 9.—Gen. 39. 2, 21.

Joseph's deliverances from affliction by God's favour, and his divine gift of wisdom — 7. 10.—Gen. 41. 37-39.

Pharaoh's promotion of Joseph to be ruler over Egypt and over his house .... — 7. 10.—Gen. 41. 40.

The famine over Egypt and Canaan .... — 7. 11.—Gen. 41. 54.

Jacob sending his sons to Egypt to buy corn — 7. 12.—Gen. 42. 2.

Joseph makes himself known to his brethren in Egypt .... — 7. 13.—Gen. 45. 1.

The descent of Jacob and [46. 5, 6. his family into Egypt — 7. 14, 15.—Gen. 46. 9 ;

Jacob's death in Egypt — 7. 15.—Gen. 49. 33.

The burial of the patriarchs at Shechem .. — 7. 16.—Gen. 33. 19 ; [Josh. 24. 32.

The great increase of the Israelites .... — 7. 17.—Ex. 1. 7.

The accession of a king of Egypt hostile to the Israelites .... — 7. 18.—Ex. 1. 8.

Pharaoh dealt subtilly with them .... — 7. 19.—Ex. 1. 10.

The casting of their sons into the river ...... — 7. 19.—Ex. 1. 22.

The concealment of Moses' birth for three months .... — 7. 20.—Ex. 2. 2.

His being cast out, and his adoption by Pharaoh's daughter ...... — 7. 21.—Ex. 2. 3-10.

His murder of an Egyptian, and flight into Midian .... — 7. 24-29.—Ex. 2. 12-15.

The birth of his two sons in Midian ...... — 7. 29.—Ex. 18. 3.

* This Zacharias has likewise been identified with Zechariah the prophet, with Zacharias the father of John the Baptist, and also with Zechariah, the son of Jeberechiah (Isa. viii. 2).

The appearance of an angel to him in a burning bush, in the wilderness of Sinai ...... Acts 7. 30.—Ex. 3. 2.
God's mission to Moses — 7. 35.—Ex. 3. 15-18; 4.
The miracles in Egypt by Moses' mission ... — 7. 36.—Ex. 7-12.
The miracle by Moses in the Red Sea ...... — 7. 36.—Ex. 14. 21, &c.
The exodus .... — 7. 33.—Ex. 12. 41.
Miracles in the wilderness .... — 7. 36.—Ex. 15. 23; 16, &c.
The forty years' wandering in the wilderness .... — 7. 36.—Num. 14. 33; Ps. [95. 10, 11.
The giving of the Law to Moses on Mount Sinai — 7. 38.—Ex. 20—24. 18.
The worship of the golden calf .... — 7. 41.—Ex. 32. 19.
The making of the tabernacle in the wilderness .... — 7. 44.—Ex. 25. 40; 26. 30.
The erection of the tabernacle in Canaan .. — 7. 45.—Josh. 18. 1.
David's desire to build a tabernacle.......... — 7. 46.—2 Sam. 7.
The building of Solomon's Temple ...... — 7. 47.—1 Kings 8.
The exodus .... — 13. 17.—Ex. 12. 41.
The forty years' wandering in the wilderness .... [Ps. 95. 10. — 13. 18.—Num. 14. 33;
God's expulsion of seven nations from Canaan — 13. 19.—Deut. 7. 1.
The division of Canaan among the Israelites by lot .... — 13. 19.—Josh. 14. 2.
The rule of the judges — 13. 20.—Judg. 2. 16.
The judgeship of Samuel the prophet ...... — 13. 20.—1 Sam. 3. 20.
The desire of Israel for a kingdom .... — 13. 21.—1 Sam. 8. 5.
The forty years' reign of Saul, son of Kish, the Benjamite .... — 13. 21.—1 Sam. 10. 21.
God's removal of Saul from the kingdom, and selection of David to succeed him ...... — 13. 22.—1 Chr. 10. 14.
The pillar of a cloud, guiding Israel........ 1 Cor. 10. 1.—Ex. 13. 21.
The passage through the Red Sea .... — 10. 1.—Ex. 14. 22.
The Israelites fed by manna .... — 10. 3.—Ex. 16. 3-35.
Moses bringing water out of the rock ...... — 10. 4.—Ex. 17. 6.
Birth of Ishmael from Abraham and Hagar Gal. 4. 23, 25.—Gen. 16. 15.
The creation of Adam and Eve .... [21, 22. 1 Tim. 2. 13.—Gen. 2. 7,
The priority of Eve's fall — 2. 14.—Gen. 3. 12.
The opposition of the Egyptian magicians to Moses .... 2 Tim. 3. 8.—Ex. 7. 11.
The tabernacle and its furniture .... Heb. 9. 2, 3.—Ex. 25 & 26.
The pot of manna, Aaron's rod, and the two tables, in the Ark of the Covenant .... [16; Num. 17. 10, — 9. 4.—Ex. 16. 33, 34; 25.
The high priest's offering on the Day of Atonement .... — 9. 7.—Ex. 30. 10.
Moses sprinkling the people with the blood of the testament .... — 9. 19, 20.—Ex. 24. 8.
The daily sacrifice .... — 10. 11.—Ex. 29. 38.
The creation of the world .... — 11. 3.—Gen. 1.

God's acceptance of Abel's sacrifice ...... Heb. 11. 4.—Gen. 4. 4.
Enoch's translation .... — 11. 5.—Gen. 5. 24.
Noah's preparation of the ark, and preservation of himself and family................. — 11. 7.—Gen. 6. 15-18.
The call of Abraham .. — 11. 8.—Gen. 12. 1.
His sojourn in Canaan — 11. 9.—Gen. 12. 5, &c.
Isaac and Jacob in Canaan .... — 11. 9.—Gen. 27.
The birth of Isaac from Sarah in her old age .... [14. — 11. 11.—Gen. 18. 11, 12,
Abraham offering up Isaac .... — 11. 17.—Gen. 22.
Isaac blessing Jacob and Esau .... — 11. 20.—Gen. 27.
Jacob blessing Joseph's sons before his death — 11. 21.—Gen. 48. 15.
Joseph's dying command concerning his bones, &c. .... — 11. 22.—Gen. 50. 25.
Moses' return to his own people from Pharaoh's daughter .... — 11. 25.—Ex. 2. 11.
His flight from Egypt.. — 11. 27.—Ex. 2. 15.
The Passover in Egypt, and slaughter of the firstborn .... — 11. 28.—Ex. 12. 21-29.
The passage of the Red Sea, and destruction of the Egyptian army .... — 11. 29.—Ex. 14.
The compassing of Jericho for seven days, and the fall of its walls .... — 11. 30.—Josh. 6. 12-20.
The sparing of Rahab and her household ... — 11. 31.—Josh. 6. 23.
The exploits of the judges, Gideon, Barak, Samson, Jephthah, Samuel .... [Sam. — 11. 32.—Judg. and 1
The exploits of David.. — 11. 32.—2 Sam.
Deliverance of Daniel in the lions' den ..... — 11. 33.—Dan. 6. 22.
Deliverance of the Three Children from the fiery furnace .... — 11. 34.—Dan. 3. 27.
Restoration of children to life by Elijah and Elisha................ [2 Kings 4. 34. — 11. 35.—1 Kings 17. 23;
The visit of angels to Abraham and Lot .. — 13. 2.—Gen. 18. 2; 19. 1.
Rahab's reception and deliverance of the spies .... James 2. 25.—Josh. 2. 1.
The patience of Job .. — 5. 11.—Job 1. 21.
Elijah's prayer for a dearth on Israel .... — 5. 17.—1 Kings 17. 1.
The deluge, the disobedience of the world, and preservation of Noah and his family 1 Pet. 3. 20.—Gen. 6. 3. 2 Pet. 2. 5.—Gen. 7. 1.
Sarah's deference to Abraham, calling him lord .... 1 Pet. 3. 6.—Gen. 18. 12.
The destruction of Sodom and the cities of the plain .... 2 Pet. 2. 6.—Gen. 19.
Balaam rebuked by his ass .... — 2. 15.—Num. 22.
Cain's murder of Abel 1 John 3. 12.—Gen. 4. 8.
The exodus of Israel from Egypt .... Jude 5.—Ex. 12. 41.
The death of unbelievers in the wilderness .... — 5.—Num. 14. 32.
The destruction of Sodom, Gomorrha, &c. — 7.—Gen. 19.

The body of Moses .... Jude 9.—Deut. 34. 5, 6.	The gainsaying of Core
"The way of Cain" .... — 11.—Gen. 4. 8.	(Korah) .... Jude 11.—Num. 16.
The error of Balaam for	Enoch, the seventh from
reward .... — 11. Num. 22.	Adam .... — 14.—Gen. 5. 18.

XXXIV. CHRONOLOGY OF THE ACTS AND PAULINE EPISTLES

A. D.	EVENTS.	EMPERORS OF ROME, AND PROCURATORS OF JUDÆA, ETC.
	The Pentecostal Effusion	TIBERIUS, *Emperor.*
	Spread of the Gospel at Jerusalem.	*Pontius Pilate, Procurator.*
	Preaching of Stephen.	
	Martyrdom of Stephen.	
33	Conversion of Saul of Tarsus.	
34	His retirement to Arabia (Gal. 1. 17).	
35	First visit to Jerusalem after conversion.	
36		Pontius Pilate, accused of maladministration and sent to Rome.
37		Herod Agrippa imprisoned. Death of Tiberius. Accession of GAIUS (Caligula).
38		Release of Herod Agrippa. Riots at Alexandria between Jews and Gentiles who had attempted to put statues of Gaius in synagogues.
39	Herod Antipas exiled to Gaul.	
40	His dominions taken over by Herod Agrippa. Deputation of Jews and Greeks from Alexandria to Gaius, described by Philo in his "Legatio ad Gaium".	
41		CLAUDIUS succeeds Gaius. Herod Agrippa's dominions increased by cession of Judæa, which thus ceases to be a procuratorial province.
42	A flourishing church at Syrian Antioch, where the name "CHRISTIANS" is first used (Acts 11. 26).	
	Persecution by Herod Agrippa.	
43–44	Martyrdom of St. James.	
	Imprisonment of St. Peter.	
	Death of Herod Agrippa (Acts 12. 23).	Judæa again a procuratorial province, *Procurator, C. Cuspius Fadus.*
46	*First Missionary Journey of Saul and Barnabas* begins in spring (Acts 13. 14).	*Tiberius Alexander,* nephew of Philo, *Procurator.*
48	Jerusalem conference.	
49	*Second Missionary Journey begins.*	
49–50	Winter, Paul in Macedonia.	
50–51	Paul in Corinth.	*Ventidius Cumanus, Procurator.*
	Epistle to the Galatians.	
	The Epistles to the Thessalonians.	
51–52	Gallio Proconsul of Achaia.	
	St. Paul leaves Corinth and sails to Ephesus.	
52	At Jerusalem.	*Felix, Procurator.*
	Return to Antioch.	
	St. Paul's Third Missionary Journey.	
53		Claudius dies. Accession of NERO.
54–57	At Ephesus.	
[53–56]	*First Epistle to the Corinthians.*	
	Riot at Ephesus.	
	Leaves for Troas, comes to Macedonia.	
	Second Epistle to the Corinthians.	
	Reaches Corinth and stays three months.	
	Epistle to the Romans.	
[57] 59	Leaves Corinth for Jerusalem.	
	Arrest in the Temple.	
	Sent to Cæsarea (Acts 23. 23).	Nero murders Agrippina.
[57] 59	Interview with Felix (Acts 24).	
[59] 61	St. Paul before Festus and Agrippa.	Recall of Felix. *Porcius Festus Procurator.*
	Appeals to Cæsar (Acts 25. 11)	
	Sails for Rome (Acts 27).	
	Shipwreck at Malta.	

o 2

A. D.	EVENTS.	EMPERORS OF ROME, AND PROCURATORS OF JUDÆA, ETC.
[60] 62	St. Paul reaches Rome, and lives in his own hired house (Acts 28).	Rebellion of Boudicca in Britain.
	Writes his Epistles to *the Philippians, the Colossians, Philemon, and the Ephesians.*	Great earthquake at Pompeii.
[62] 64	St. Paul is heard, and [released or] executed.	*Albinus, Procurator.*
	[Goes to Asia by way of Macedonia.	
[62] 62	Sails with Titus to Crete, and returns to Ephesus.	
	Leaving Timothy there, he goes by Philippi to Corinth.	*Gessius Florus, Procurator.*
	First Epistle to Timothy.	
	Epistle to Titus.	
	Winters at Nicopolis.	
63	Journey to Dalmatia (?), and through Macedonia to Troas.	
	Apprehension. Sent to Rome.	
64	First Trial before the Emperor.	*Great Fire of Rome, ascribed by Nero to the Christians.*
	Second Epistle to Timothy.	
	Martyrdom of St. Paul.]	

The fixed point in Pauline Chronology is given by an inscription which dates the proconsulate of Gallio to July 1, 51—June 30, 52. The events of Acts 18. 12-18 therefore fall within that period. Paul had been in Corinth for 18 months. He had arrived there shortly after the banishment of Jews from Rome (Acts 18. 2). This took place in the 9th year of Claudius, 49-50. He arrived therefore probably early in 50, and was brought before Gallio in autumn 52. He did not depart at once (Acts 18. 18), and when we have allowed for a visit to Ephesus on the way (Acts 18. 19) we cannot suppose that he reached Jerusalem until the tail-end of 52. He then went to Antioch and spent "some time" there (ib. 28). Thus he can hardly have started on his Third Journey until the winter was over. The journey through "the region of Galatia and Phrygia" (where he had numerous churches to visit), and the "upper parts" of Asia Minor in general, must have occupied practically the whole of the travelling season of 53. Thus the 3 years at Ephesus (Acts 20. 31) cannot well have begun before autumn of 53. He left Ephesus not later than Pentecost of the 3rd year (cf. 1 Cor. 16. 8). Thus the earliest probable date for his leaving Ephesus is Whitsuntide 56. This makes "3 years" stand for a period actually not much more than 2¾. Acts then allows for a journey through Macedonia (which 2 Cor. shows to have been no hurried one), 3 months in "Greece", and a visit to Macedonia. After Easter he left Philippi (Acts 20. 6) and hastened to spend Pentecost at Jerusalem (Acts 20. 16). It follows that the earliest date for his arrest at Jerusalem is Whitsuntide 57. But it is very possible that the period covered by this Third Journey was actually longer. The narrative of Acts is in places extremely summary and vague. Thus it may well be that he spent the winter of 53-54 among the churches of Galatia, and did not reach Ephesus till early in 54. He may then have put in a *full* 3 years at Ephesus and not merely the 2 years and a few months allowed for above (indeed the course of events recorded in Acts 19 makes this extremely likely), and he probably left Ephesus in advance of his programme (on account of the riot) and so well before Whitsuntide 57. It is also quite probable that the vague language of Acts 20. 2 covers a much more extended tour than we have allowed for, in Macedonia and the adjacent regions (? Illyricum, cf. Rom. 15. 19), so that the Easter at Philippi would be that of 59, and his arrest at Jerusalem would fall at Whitsuntide 59. From this point on, the chronological reckoning of Acts is complete: 2 years at Caesarea, then the appeal to Rome; the start for Rome in late autumn, a winter in Malta; arrival in Rome next spring, and finally 2 years in Rome. The dates we assign here will depend on the adoption of the shorter or the longer chronology for the Third Journey, thus:

Arrive at Ephesus	. . .	53	or 54
Leave Ephesus	. .	56	or 57
Arrive at Jerusalem	. .	57	or 59
Appeal to Rome	. . .	59	or 61
Arrive at Rome	. . .	60	or 62
End of the 2 years	. .	62	or 64

It is difficult to decide between these alternatives. The arrival of Festus as Procurator (which immediately preceded the appeal) is not precisely dated, but seems rather more likely to have fallen in 61 than in 59. If we accept the longer chronology, then the end of the 2 years imprisonment in Rome coincides with the year in which the Neronian persecution broke out, and according to tradition Paul perished in that persecution (or as a result of it). If on the other hand we accept the shorter chronology, the 2 years imprisonment would end in 62, and there would be time for a release, further ministry, and a second imprisonment before his condemnation and death. But the tradition of this second imprisonment is ill-supported,

For the earlier part of the Apostle's life we must begin reckoning backwards from his arrival at Corinth during the Second Journey. This is securely dated to 50. That journey therefore must have begun in 49. Everything before that depends on the relation of the narrative of Acts to Galatians 1-2, and in particular on the identification of Paul's various visits to Jerusalem. If we take our two sources we have 3 references to such visits (after the first one of all, Acts 9. 26 = Gal. 1. 18): viz. (a) Gal. 2. 1; (b) Acts. 11. 29-30; (c) Acts 15. It is hardly possible that all these three visits are different. All three may be the same, or any two may be identified and distinguished from the third. Practically the possibilities are, *a* = *b* ; *a* = *c* ; and *a* = *b* = .*c*. If *a* = *b*=*c*, then the further question arises, whether the position of *b* or of *c* in Acts represents the true sequence of events. Now Acts 11. 29-30 refers to the great famine in the reign of Claudius. From Tacitus and other sources the maximum intensity of this famine at Rome is dated to 51, or the winter of 50-51. Rome was no doubt the last place to suffer, but its beginning in the eastern provinces is likely to have fallen rather in the years 48-49 than earlier. Now according to Acts 15, Visit *c* fell shortly before

196

the beginning of the Second Journey, which, as we have seen, is pretty securely dated to 49. If then Visit c fell in 48, it coincided with the year which we have seen to be most probable for the famine in Syria and Palestine. This makes it the more likely that the "famine-visit" (b) is in fact identical with the "conference-visit" (c). Observe that the author of Acts has recorded this famine-visit in the context of Agabus' *prediction* of the famine, which may well have preceded the actual outbreak by some considerable time, and the account of the famine itself may be anticipatory. If then we suppose that Acts is giving variant reports of the same visit to which Paul refers in Gal. 2 (which Paul expressly says was his *second* visit), we can utilize Paul's own chronological data in Galatians. According to these, his first visit fell 14 years earlier, i.e. (on the customary inclusive reckoning) in 35, and his conversion 3 years earlier again, i.e. (on the same reckoning) 33. (Ramsay's proposal to regard the 3 and the 14 as running concurrently is unlikely.) This date, some 3 or 4 years after the probable date of the Crucifixion is intrinsically likely enough, but we cannot say more, since the calculation involves several unverifiable assumptions.

XXXV. ST. PAUL'S MISSIONARY JOURNEYS

I.

First Journey with Barnabas and John Mark.

Acts xiii, xiv.

A.D. 43.

PLACES.	REFERENCES.
ANTIOCH,	on the river Orontes, the capital of the Roman province* Syria, is THE STARTING-POINT of the first Missionary Journey (Acts 13. 1). They go to
SELEUCIA,	the port of Antioch, called Seleucia "by the sea". Hence to
CYPRUS,	the native place of Barnabas (Acts 4. 36). At
SALAMIS,	a populous mercantile port on the E. extremity, the Apostles preach in the synagogues, and after traversing the island in a westerly direction reach the capital,
PAPHOS,	(Acts 13. 6–12). After this Saul crosses with his companions to the southern shore of Asia Minor, and lands at
PERGA,	the ancient port of Pamphylia on the river Cestrus. Thence the Apostles make their way across the Taurus range to
(Pisidian) ANTIOCH,	or *Colonia Cæsarea Antiochia*, a flourishing commercial town on the great road from Ephesus into Asia Minor. Its extant coins give prominence to its privileges as a Roman colony † (Acts 13. 14–50). Driven out by the rulers, they follow the great road to
ICONIUM (*Konieh*),	on the table-land of Lycaonia. Acts 14. 1–5. Thence to
LYSTRA,	*Colonia Iulia Felix Gemina Lustra*, a small rural town of simple heathens, S.W. of Iconium (Acts 14. 7–20), and
DERBE,	a small town, S.E. of Lystra. They return by the same route through Lystra, Iconium, and Antioch to
PERGA,	and proceed thence to
ATTALIA (*Adalia*),	about sixteen miles west of Perga, having a fine port, and thence sail to
(Syrian) ANTIOCH,	where they give a report of their work to a full assembly of the Church, and abide there "no little time with the disciples" (Acts 14. 27, 28, R.V.).

II.

St. Paul's Second Missionary Journey with Silas and Timothy.

Acts xv. 36–xviii. 22.

A.D. 49.

PLACES.	REFERENCES.
ANTIOCH.	St. Paul (Acts 15. 36) sets out with Silas or Silvanus (Acts 15. 37–41) by land through
SYRIA AND CILICIA,	confirming the Churches, and delivering the decrees of the Council of Jerusalem. Hence they proceed, probably past Tarsus, to

* Roman provinces were divided into two classes, (i) *Senatorial*, and (ii) *Imperial*. (i) *Senatorial* provinces were governed by a Proconsul (Ἀνθύπατος) who was appointed by lot, held his authority for a year, but had no military power. (ii) *Imperial* provinces were governed by a *legatus pro prætore* (Ἀντιστράτηγος). He was appointed by the Emperor himself, held authority as long as the latter wished, and had all the pomp of a military commander. Syria was an *Imperial* province.

† Roman colonies were essentially distinct from those of ancient Greece or of modern Europe. They were converted virtually into garrison towns, governed by Roman laws, and endowed with Roman rights and privileges.

St. Paul's Second and Third Missionary Journeys

PLACES.	REFERENCES.
DERBE AND LYSTRA. PHRYGO-GALATIC REGION.	(Acts 16. 1; 2 Tim. 1. 5). Then through the This refers to Iconium and Pisidian Antioch. Being forbidden by Divine intimation to preach the word in the province Asia *, they make their way (Acts 16. 7, R.V.) "over against"
MYSIA,	that is Mysia Minor, which belonged to Bithynia. But again "the Spirit of Jesus" (Acts 16. 7, R.V.) forbids their proceeding in the direction of Bithynia, and under Divine guidance they make their way to
ALEXANDRIA TROAS,	a Roman colony, on the N.W. coast of Asia Minor. Here St. Luke joins the Apostle †, and a vision of a Macedonian invites him to Greece, Thereupon they embark, and after touching at SAMOTHRACIA, land at
NEAPOLIS (Kavalla), PHILIPPI,	a seaport of Thrace. Thence they proceed across the Pharsalian plain to a Roman colony of Macedonia (Acts 16. 11), founded by Augustus, on the banks of the river Gangites (Acts 16. 13). After the events of Acts 16. 13-40, leaving Luke at Philippi Paul, Silas, and Timothy pass through AMPHIPOLIS and APOLLONIA to
THESSALONICA,	the metropolis of Macedonia, where they stay three Sabbath-days (Acts 17. 2), and Paul preaches with much success. But his enemies, the Jews, accuse him before the rulers of the city or "politarchs" ‡ (Acts 17. 6), and succeed in driving him thence to
BERŒA,	about sixty miles S.W. of Thessalonica. Thence he is sent by the brethren by sea (probably from Dium) to
ATHENS,	which he reaches alone, Silas and Timothy having been left behind (Acts 17. 14). After a short time here, he repairs to
CORINTH,	the capital of the Roman province of Achaia, and the residence of the proconsul § Gallio. Here he is joined by Silas and Timothy, and for a year and a half the Apostle makes this great mercantile centre his headquarters, writing the *Epistle to the Galatians* and two *Epistles to the Thessalonians*, and working with Aquila and Priscilla at his craft of tent-making (Acts 18. 2, 3). Eventually he sails with Aquila and Priscilla from
CENCHREÆ, EPHESUS, CÆSAREA,	the eastern port of Corinth, to where he leaves his two companions, going on himself to and thence by land to Jerusalem to keep the Feast of Pentecost (Acts 18. 21); hence he returns to
(Syrian) ANTIOCH,	and remains there "some time" (Acts 18. 23).

III.

St. Paul's Third Missionary Journey with Timothy and others.

Acts xviii. 23–xxi. 17.

A.D. 53.

PLACES.	REFERENCES.
(Syrian) ANTIOCH.	After staying some time at Antioch, St. Paul, accompanied by Timothy and probably Titus, commences his third Missionary tour by visiting the Churches of
GALATIA AND PHRYGIA,	of which visit no details are given; but from 1 Cor. 16. 1, 2, we infer that he exhorted the members of these Churches to relieve by weekly offertories their poorer brethren in Judæa. Thence he proceeds to
EPHESUS,	the capital of Roman Asia,‖ and makes the city his centre of activity for upwards of three years (Acts 19). At length, at the instigation of Demetrius, a craftsman engaged in the manufacture of silver shrines of Artemis (Diana), he is assaulted during the great annual Pan-Ionic Festival, and compelled hastily to depart. With Tychicus and Trophimus (Acts 20. 4) he proceeds to

* Including Mysia, Lydia, and Caria.

† Note the change of person in Acts 16. 10. The frequent illnesses of the Apostle would make the services of "the beloved physician" (Col. 4. 14) very acceptable.

‡ Evidence found accidentally on an ancient archway of Thessalonica attests St. Luke's fidelity here to facts. An inscription still legible of the date A.D. 69–79 gives this very title "politarchs" to the magistrates, and names seven such who bore the office. It is now in the British Museum.

§ Achaia was a *senatorial* province under Augustus; then placed on the list of *imperial* provinces; then restored by Claudius to the senate. Thus the title *proconsul* is absolutely accurate (Acts 18. 12, R.V.)

‖ Ephesus, in the accurate description of St. Luke, as a "free city," has its "proconsul" (Acts 19. 38, R.V.), its townclerk or "recorder" (Acts 19. 35), its "Asiarchs" (Acts 19. 31, R.V. marg.), its popular "assembly" (Acts 19. 39); while the city is the Νεωκόρος or "Guardian of the Shrine" of Artemis (Acts 19. 35), of which the silversmiths make models; and mysterious symbols, called "Ephesian letters," copied from inscriptions on various parts of the image (Acts 19. 19), are used as amulets and charms.

PLACES	REFERENCES.
TROAS,	where he is in the greatest anxiety (2 Cor. 2. 12) about the effect of his letter to the Corinthians. At length, the suspense becoming unbearable (2 Cor. 2. 13), he resolves to proceed to Macedonia, and presses on to
PHILIPPI,	where he is at last relieved by the tidings brought by Titus (2 Cor. 7. 6); and he writes in the fulness of a thankful heart his *Second Epistle to the Corinthians.* Then, while Titus, Luke, and Trophimus proceed to Corinth, he continues his labours in the northern regions of Greece, and penetrates into "the parts about Illyricum" on the eastern shore of the Adriatic Sea (Rom. 15. 19), and with the approach of winter, A.D. [57] 59, removes to Achaia, and takes up his abode at
CORINTH.	Here, during a stay of three months, he writes his *Epistle to the Romans.* He proceeds by land through Macedonia to
PHILIPPI,	while Sopater of Beroea, Aristarchus and Secundus of Thessalonica, Gaius of Derbe, Timothy, Tychicus, and Trophimus proceed in advance to Troas. At Philippi the Apostle stays behind with St. Luke, and there keeps the Feast of the Passover (Acts 20. 6). Then they set sail, and in five days reach
TROAS,	and join the other disciples. St. Paul then goes by land to meet his companions, who had gone round by ship, at a seaport of Mysia, opposite Lesbos.
ASSOS.	At Assos they all embark, and touch at
MITYLENE,	the chief town of Lesbos. The next day they anchor off Chios (Acts 20. 15), and the day following put in at
TROGYLLIUM,	a promontory on the mainland opposite the island of Samos. The next day they touch at
MILETUS,	the ancient capital of Ionia. (Acts 20. 17–38.) Launching thence, they sail with a fair wind past Coos and Rhodes to
PATARA,	a seaport of Lycia, where they change vessels, and embark on one sailing direct to Syria. Sighting Cyprus, and leaving it on the left hand, they make straight for the port of
TYRE,	where their vessel is bound to unload her cargo, and the Apostle is able to remain seven days in the society of the Tyrian Christians (Acts 21. 4). At length, he proceeds to
PTOLEMAIS,	the modern *Acre.* Here the sea voyage comes to an end; and after remaining one day the little company set out on foot for
CÆSAREA,	and find a home in the house of Philip the Evangelist (Acts 21. 8). With Mnason of Cyprus, "an early disciple" (Acts 21. 16, R.V.), St. Paul sets out by carriage for
JERUSALEM	(Acts 21. 17 ff.). Claudius Lysias, the Roman commandant, extricates him from the hands of the mob, and eventually sends him to Cæsarea to the governor Felix (Acts 23. 26–35).

XXXVI. ST. PAUL'S VOYAGE TO ROME,

With St. Luke, Aristarchus, and certain prisoners under charge of Julius,

a Centurion of the Augustan Cohort.

Acts xxvii, xxviii.

A.D. [59] 61.

PLACES.	REFERENCES.
	Having appealed from the tribunal of Festus to that of the emperor at Rome (Acts 25. 11), St. Paul sets sail from
CÆSAREA	in a ship of Adramyttium, a seaport of Mysia, in charge of Julius, a centurion of "the Augustan cohort" (Acts 27. 1). They first touch at
SIDON,	probably for purposes of trade, and thence sail "under the lee" (Acts 27. 4, R.V.), i.e. along the north side of
CYPRUS,	and "across the sea which is off" Cilicia and Pamphylia*, to
MYRA,	then a flourishing seaport of Lycia. Here the centurion finds an Alexandrian corn-vessel bound for Italy, and trans-ships his charge into her, and she sets sail, laden with a heavy cargo and upwards of 276 souls on board. Owing to unfavourable winds, it is only after many days (Acts 27. 7) that they come over against
CNIDUS,	a promontory of Caria, at the extreme south-west of the peninsula of Asia Minor. Here the wind stops their direct course (Acts 27. 7), and the vessel is driven southward to

---

* The direct course would have been straight to Patara, keeping to the south of Cyprus.

PLACES.	REFERENCES.
SALMONE,	the eastern promontory of Crete. Rounding it, they work their way with difficulty under the shelter of its southern coast to
FAIR HAVENS,	near which, about five miles to the east, was the city of Lasæa. Here St. Paul advises them to winter, but the harbour being incommodious, they resolve to try and reach
PHŒNIX (R.V.),	*the town of palms,** a harbour looking north-east and south-east.† Weighing anchor, they set sail, but are caught by a violent wind, called Euraquilo (Acts 27. 14, R.V.), "beating" down from the heights of Ida on the Cretan shore ‡, and are driven under the lee of
CAUDA (R.V.),	or *Clauda,* an island § south-west of Crete, and with much difficulty succeed in hoisting on board the boat, which they are towing behind (Acts 27. 16). They then proceed to undergird the vessel, i.e. to pass strong cables round her hull, and being afraid they should drift on the Syrtis, a dangerous sandbank north of Libya, they lower the gear (Acts 27. 17, R.V.), and drive slowly before the wind. On the next day they proceed to lighten the ship by throwing the freight overboard (Acts 27. 18, R.V.), and on the *third* day they cast out the tackling, probably the mainyards, of the ship. At midnight of the *fourteenth* day, as they are drifting to and fro in "the sea of Hadria" (Acts 27. 27, R.V.), they suspect from the noise of the breakers they are nearing land. After sounding they let go four anchors from the stern, and on the next day run the ship aground on a creek, where two seas met, of the island of
MELITA (*Malta*),	at that time much uncultivated, and inhabited by a population of Phœnician origin; and here by swimming or floating on portions of the wreck they effect a landing. The people receive them hospitably. St. Paul miraculously heals the father of Publius, the chief Roman officer ‖ of the island, who is afflicted with fever and dysentery, and after a stay of three months, sails in another Alexandrian corn-ship, called "the Twin Brothers" (Acts 28. 11, R.V.), and reaches
SYRACUSE,	the chief city of Sicily. Here they stay three days, and from thence shape a course northwards towards the straits of Messina. But the wind being against them, they are constrained after "making a circuit" (Acts 28. 13, R.V.) to put into
RHEGIUM,	at the extreme south-west of Italy, where they remain one day. On the following morning they reach
PUTEOLI (*Pozzuoli*),	in the Bay of Naples, at this time the regular harbour for the Alexandrian corn-fleets. Here they rest seven days, with certain of the brethren, and then proceed by land to
FORUM APPI,	about forty miles from Rome, where a welcome company of brethren meets them, and the Apostle "thanks God and takes courage" (Acts 28. 15). Ten miles further on they reach
THE THREE TAVERNS,	where a second company greets them, and thus at length the Apostle reaches the imperial city, A.D. [60] 62, and is handed over by Julius to the prefect of the prætorian guard.

* Several towns of Crete have palm-trees on their coins.

† Literally "down the south-west wind and down the north-west wind," Acts 27. 12, R.V. marg.

‡ "The wind would descend from Mount Ida, which was just above them, *in heavy squalls and eddies,* and drive the now helpless ship far from the shore." Sir C. Penrose in Conybeare and Howson.

§ Cauda or Clauda, now Govdo. See Acts 27. 16, R.V.

‖ The chief officer of Malta, under the governor of Sicily, was called πρῶτος Μελιταίων, *Primus Melitensium.* The title is found on an inscription from the island Gaulus, close to Malta. Böckh, *Corpus Inscr. Grœc.* No. 5,754.

PART V

PALESTINE, ITS INHABITANTS, PHYSICAL GEOGRAPHY, CUSTOMS, ETC.

XXXVII. POLITICAL CONDITION OF JUDAEA IN THE FIRST CENTURY A.D.

1. **The Political Condition of Palestine** during the first century A.D. was singularly complicated and anomalous, and its complications perplexed even the sagacious Tacitus. (i) Towards the end of the previous century it was a single united kingdom under Herod the Great (Matt. 2^1). (ii) On his death (4 B.C.) it was split up into a set of principalities under his sons; his son Archelaus receiving Idumaea, Judaea, and Samaria, with the title not of king (Matt. 2^{22}) but of ethnarch ; Herod Antipas obtaining Galilee and Peraea with the title of tetrarch (Luke 3^1); Herod Philip receiving with the same title the region beyond Jordan, including Batanaea, Trachonitis, and Auranitis (Luke 3^1). The Herodian family thus seemed securely established, but (iii) in A.D. 6 Judaea and Samaria were reduced to the condition of a Roman province, while Galilee, Ituraea, and Trachonitis continued under native princes (Luke 3^1). Then (iv), A.D. 42–4, in the person of Herod Agrippa I the old kingdom of Palestine was restored (Acts 12^1). Finally (v), in 44, the whole country was reduced to the condition of a Roman province, and Roman procurators once more governed it (Acts 23^{26}, 24^{27}). Thus within fifty years the country passed through five distinct phases of government.

2. **Archelaus.** During his reign of ten years Archelaus made many foes, and exercised great cruelty alike towards Jews and Samaritans ; putting to death, according to Josephus, 3,000 Jews in the Temple not long after his accession. In A.D. 6, a complaint was preferred by his brothers and his subjects against him, before the emperor, on the ground of his tyranny. On repairing to Rome he was condemned to forfeit his province, and banished to Vienne in Gaul. And now ' the sceptre indeed departed from Judah ' and the kingdom of David and Solomon sank into the condition of a Roman province.

3. **Coponius** (A.D. 6–9?). On the deposition of Archelaus, A. D. 6, Quirinius, the imperial legate in Syria, who was stationed at Antioch, received orders from the Emperor Augustus to annex Idumaea, Judaea, and Samaria to the empire, and to place them under a procurator of their own, who was to reside at Caesarea on the sea, and hold the country with Roman troops. Coponius, the first procurator under this arrangement, placed a small garrison in the tower of Antonia, on the north-west of the Temple, and came up from Caesarea to Jerusalem at the great festivals, leaving the government during his absence to the High Priest and ecclesiastical authorities. With the Roman governors came the Roman fiscal system, customs and excise, and this was regarded by the Jews as the last and most degrading mark of their subjection to a foreign power. The efforts of the Jewish authorities prevented any actual outbreak against it in Jerusalem itself, but in the North desperate endeavours were again and again made to free the country. The effort, however, was always in vain. Nothing could withstand the terrible Roman legions.

4. **Pontius Pilate** (A.D. 26–37). So long as Augustus occupied the imperial throne, the procurators were rapidly changed, Marcus Ambivius succeeding Coponius in A.D. 9 (?), Annius Rufus following in A.D. 12, and Valerius Gratus in A.D. 15. But in the last year the new Emperor, Tiberius, resolved to check such rapid changes, and Valerius Gratus held his command till A. D. 26, when he was succeeded by Pontius Pilate. The new governor brought with him his wife and a Roman household to Caesarea (Matt. 27[19]). Between the garrison and the Jewish people there was no love lost. His attempts to introduce the Roman standards into the city; to hang up some brazen shields as trophies in Herod's Palace; to use the funds of the Temple for the erection of a public aqueduct, and to crush in blood the insurrection which this caused, increased the general ill-will, while his cruelty to certain Galilaeans, whose blood he mingled with their sacrifices (Luke 13[1]), roused feelings of horror and dread. Before his tribunal our Lord was brought, and after Pilate had covered himself with ignominy for all time by condemning Him to be crucified, he was sent to answer before the Emperor the complaints of certain Samaritans against his rule, A.D. 36, and is said by Eusebius to have died by his own hand.

5. **Herod Agrippa I.** In the years immediately following Pilate's death, A.D. 41–4, Palestine once more came under the Herodian dynasty. Herod Agrippa I, a grandson of Herod the Great, who

in 37 had received from Caligula the tetrarchies of Philip and Lysanias with the title of king and in 40 that of Antipas, received from Claudius in 41 Judaea and Samaria as well—in fact his grandfather's whole kingdom. To ingratiate himself with the Jews, he carefully observed the Pharisaic traditions, offered many sacrifices, and conformed to the Mosaic ritual. Further to conciliate the Jews he became the persecutor of the Christians, put James the Elder to death, and would have slain St. Peter also, had it not been for his miraculous deliverance (Acts 12[1-10]). But Palestine did not long enjoy his rule. After he had reigned little more than three years, he was sitting at Caesarea on the judgement-seat, clad in his royal robes, when the people saluted him as a god, and he was suddenly smitten and died a horrible death A.D. 44 (Acts 12[23]).

6. **Cuspius Fadus.** On the death of Agrippa I, his son Herod Agrippa II being thought too young for the throne, the whole of Palestine was taken possession of as Roman territory, and its administration was given over to a procurator under the direction of the legate of Syria. The Roman procurators, even the best of them, instead of exercising mildness and toleration towards the Jews, only applied themselves with inexorable severity to suppress any movement of the national life. This was especially true in the cases of Cuspius Fadus, A.D. 44, Tiberius Alexander, A.D. 48, Ventidius Cumanus, A.D. 48-52, and Felix, A.D. 52-60. Fadus suppressed the revolt of Theudas (Josephus, *Antiq.* XX. i. 1-2, Acts 5[36] which, however, places the revolt earlier). The rule of Alexander, an apostate Jew, was as stained with blood as that of the Romans themselves. Felix, to use the words of Tacitus, 'exercised royal functions with all manner of cruelty and lust in the spirit of a slave', and his government like that of his predecessor essentially developed the bitter feeling against Rome. One of frequent revolts is referred to in Acts 21[38]. At the same time the strifes and rivalries among the priests themselves, the war to the death between the Zealots and those of moderate political opinions, and other excesses of desperate fanatics increased the miseries of the nation. Paul was a prisoner for the two years of Festus (Acts 23, 24).

7. **Porcius Festus** was sent by Nero to succeed Felix in A.D. 60, and, 'though disposed to act righteously, he found himself totally unable to undo the mischief wrought by his predecessor' (Schürer). For his treatment of Paul see Acts 25-7. After holding office for two years he died in Judaea, and the two

procurators who succeeded him did all in their power to intensify the bitter conflict, and hurry it on to its inevitable conclusion.

8. **Albinus and Gessius Florus.** Of these, Albinus, A. D. 62–4, perpetrated every kind of wickedness, increased the taxes to an unprecedented extent, and while the distracted country groaned under the heaviest burdens, the procurator and the high priest Ananias alone enriched themselves. The last procurator, Gessius Florus, A. D. 64–6, was also the worst, for so unbounded was his tyranny that the people looked back with regret on the administration even of Albinus. He plundered not only individuals, but even communities, and laid deliberate schemes of iniquity for reaping his harvest of plunder. Many towns and villages were entirely deserted, and when the governor of Syria visited Jerusalem a multitude of suppliant Jews entreated his interference, only to see Florus standing by his side and mocking at their complaints. By such outrages the cup of the people's sorrow was filled to the brim, and it needed only a spark to kindle the conflagration, the materials for which had long been gathering.

9. **Repulse of Cestius Gallus.** The fatal flame broke out in A. D. 66 at Caesarea, where the heathen populace had a few years before ousted the Jews after an edict of Nero had condemned them to forfeit the rights of Roman citizens. The consequent rebellion extended in every direction, and at length Cestius Gallus marched from Antioch at the head of 10,000 Roman troops and 13,000 allies (including some under the command of Agrippa II) to quell the disturbance in Judaea. After vainly attempting to storm the Temple Mount, he drew off his forces, but was attacked by the Jews when entangled in the pass of Beth-horon, and suffered a disgraceful defeat. Nero, on receiving news of this disaster, handed over the command of the war with Judaea to Vespasian, who, after reducing the whole country save Jerusalem, Herodium, Mascida, and Machaerus, was himself proclaimed Emperor, A. D. 69, and upon this left for Rome, empowering his son Titus to continue the war.

10. **Titus** at the head of four legions and numerous auxiliary troops arrived before the walls of the Holy City a few days before the Passover, A. D. 70. Vast multitudes were assembled at the time within the walls to keep the Feast, and the rival factions seemed bent on destroying one another instead of making head against the common foe. Famine and pestilence raged fearfully, and hundreds of thousands of dead bodies were thrown over the

walls. After Titus had penetrated the outer walls, and the fortress Antonia, the Jews retired to the fortified courts of the Temple. Extremely anxious to save the Temple, Titus gave strict orders that it should be spared. But a soldier threw a blazing brand into the building, and all efforts to extinguish the fire were in vain.

11. Capture of the City. Titus would at the last moment have checked the fury of his troops. But the legionaries, maddened by the length of the siege, flung torches into the midst of the splendid pile, and hurried to the work of carnage. The slaughter was terrible. The splendid Temple was consumed by flames, and not one stone was left upon another (Matt. 24^2). The upper city was taken some weeks afterwards, and then the whole was levelled with the ground. More than one million of Jews perished in this war, and more than 90,000 prisoners were sold as slaves, or reserved for gladiatorial exhibitions. Among the spoils borne in the triumph of Titus were the table of shewbread, the golden candlestick, and the Book of the Law. The still extant triumphal arch erected in honour of Titus by the Roman Senate bears on one side a representation of the vessels of the Temple ; and many coins were struck bearing on one side the figure of the captive daughter of Judah standing under a palm-tree, with the inscription 'Judaea devicta', and on the other the escutcheon of the Roman legions.*

* See Schürer's *Jewish People in the Time of Jesus Christ,* vol. ii, pp. 145–243, on which the foregoing is largely dependent.

XXXVIII. FAMILY OF THE HERODS

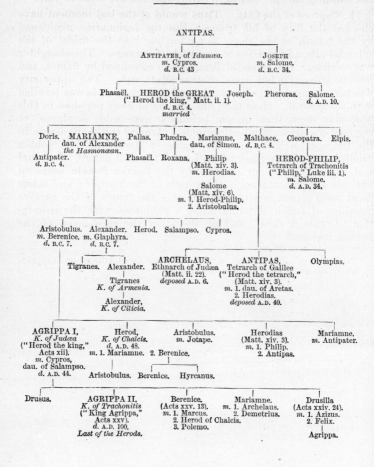

ANTIPAS.

ANTIPATER, of *Idumœa.*
m. Cypros.
d. B.C. 43

JOSEPH
m. Salome.
d. B.C. 34.

Phasaël.   HEROD the GREAT   Joseph.   Pheroras.   Salome.
("Herod the king," Matt. ii. 1).   *d.* A.D. 10.
d. B.C. 4.
married

Doris.   MARIAMNE,   Pallas.   Phædra.   Mariamne,   Malthace.   Cleopatra.   Elpis.
| dau. of Alexander   dau. of Simon.   *d.* B.C. 4.
Antipater.   *the Hasmonæan.*
d. B.C. 4.   Phasaël.   Roxana.   Philip   HEROD-PHILIP,
                                                        (Matt. xiv. 3).   Tetrarch of Trachonitis
                                                        m. Herodias.   ("Philip," Luke iii. 1).
                                                                           m. Salome.
                                                        Salome   *d.* A.D. 34.
                                                        (Matt. xiv. 6).
                                                        m. 1. Herod-Philip.
                                                             2. Aristobulus.

Aristobulus.   Alexander.   Herod.   Salampso.   Cypros.
m. Berenice.   *m.* Glaphyra.
d. B.C. 7.   *d.* B.C. 7.

Tigranes.   Alexander.   ARCHELAUS,   ANTIPAS,   Olympias.
             | Ethnarch of Judæa   Tetrarch of Galilee
             Tigranes   (Matt. ii. 22).   ("Herod the tetrarch,"
             K. of Armenia.   *deposed* A.D. 6.   (Matt. xiv. 3).
             | *m.* 1. dau. of Aretas.
             Alexander,   2. Herodias.
             K. of Cilicia.   *deposed* A.D. 40.

AGRIPPA I,   Herod,   Aristobulus.   Herodias   Mariamne.
K. of Judæa   *K. of Chalcis.*   *m.* Jotape.   (Matt. xiv. 3).   *m.* Antipater.
("Herod the king,"   *d.* A.D. 48.   *m.* 1. Philip.
Acts xii).   *m.* 1. Mariamne.   2. Berenice.   2. Antipas.
m. Cypros,
dau. of Salampso. |
d. A.D. 44.   Aristobulus.   Berenice.   Hyrcanus.

Drusus.   AGRIPPA II,   Berenice,   Mariamne.   Drusilla
             K. of Trachonitis   (Acts xxv. 13).   *m.* 1. Archelaus.   (Acts xxiv. 24).
             ("King Agrippa,"   *m.* 1. Marcus.   2. Demetrius.   *m.* 1. Azizus.
             Acts xxv).   2. Herod of Chalcis.   2. Felix.
             d. A.D. 100.   3. Polemo.
             Last of the Herods.   Agrippa.

XXXIX. JEWISH SECTS, PARTIES, etc.

Introductory.

THE return from the Captivity in Babylon was the beginning for the Jews of long years of struggle for the maintenance of their distinctive national and religious life. The dominant Hellenism threatened to absorb or destroy all that was characteristic of the old Hebraism. Hence there arose among the Jews at various times and under various names a national party, men who, by emphasizing what was distinctive in Judaism, sought to retain the old isolation and resist the Gentile. It is in this struggle between Judaism and Hellenism that the more important Jewish sects and parties find their explanation. The struggle had a twofold aspect, religious and political. The Pharisees, for example, embodied the principle of rigid observance of the Mosaic Law with its overgrowth of Rabbinic tradition ; the Zealots were the extreme party of political independence : while the opposite principle of moderation and concession found expression on the religious side in the Sadducees and on the political in the Herodians. The following is a list of the main distinctions in Biblical times :—

1. Pharisees
2. Sadducees } Distinctions chiefly religious.
3. Essenes

4. Herodians
5. Zealots
6. Galilaeans } Distinctions chiefly political.
7. Assassins

In addition to these the following various terms may here be conveniently explained :—

8. Scribes.
9. Lawyers.
10. Nazarites.
11. Proselytes.
12. Publicans.
13. Samaritans.
14. Sanhedrin.
15. Synagogue.

1. *The Pharisees.*

The Pharisees (Heb. *Pĕrushim*, 'separated ones') arose as the successors of the *Chasidim* ('pious ones'), who were repelled by

207

the introduction into Judaea of Greek fashions and ideas, which followed on the conquests of Alexander, and who ardently supported the Maccabaean revolt against Antiochus Epiphanes. They seem to have become estranged from the Hasmonaean dynasty by the secularization of its spirit; the Pharisees, in whom the *Chasidim* were apparently absorbed, were certainly hostile to almost all the later Hasmonaean princes. The name well implies their distinctive principle, that of religious separation, not from their fellow Jews, but from the outside heathen world. This separation was to be preserved by a scrupulous adherence to the very letter of the traditional law. But this intense legalism, which may originally have been a genuine expression of the national religious sentiment, had become in New Testament days a cloak for all manner of hypocrisy, and our Lord exposes with terrible severity the hollowness of their piety (e. g. Matt. 23).

They formed an association, numbering, as Josephus tells us, 6,000 members. The *practical* obligations of Pharisaism were broadly two: (1) To observe with great strictness all the ordinances concerning ceremonial purity; (2) To be most scrupulous in the payment of tithes and other religious dues. In the interpretation of both these forms of religious duty the oral traditions of the Rabbis were ranked equally with, or even above, the letter of Scripture itself. On both points their insincerity was rebuked by our Lord: as to purity, in Matt. 23^{25}; Luke 11^{39}; and as to tithing, in Luke 11^{42}, 18^{12}; Matt. 23^{23}. In *doctrinal* beliefs the Pharisees were sharply opposed to the Sadducees. They held to the belief in the existence of angels and spirits; expected the resurrection of the dead, and a future of reward or penalty; and carried their emphasis on the Divine pre-ordination to the verge of fatalism. They cherished the old theocratic idea, and were naturally opposed to the Herodian and Roman powers. But they were primarily a religious organization, not a political body. The bad side of the later Pharisaism is sufficiently prominent in the Gospel history: its good side should not be overlooked. The names of Hillel, his grandson Gamaliel (Acts 5^{34}), and St. Paul (Acts 22^{3}, 23^{6}, 26^{5}; Phil. 3^{5}) show that the society had attractions for what was best in the nation, while affording shelter to much that was false and bad. For a defence of the Pharisees see C. G. Montefiore, *The Synoptic Gospels, passim.*

2. *The Sadducees.*

The Sadducees. The derivation of the name has been in dispute. A Jewish legend derives it from one Tsadoq (Zadok), the traditional teaching of whose school that virtue was to be sought for its own sake, and not for future reward, found its embodiment in Sadduceeism. Some have been in favour of a derivation from the Heb. *Tsaddîq*, 'righteous'; and Dr. Edersheim suggests that the name was chosen as a retort upon the more arrogant title of 'pious', adopted by the Pharisees. But the form *Tsaddûq* (not *Tsaddîq*) implies a personal origin and may refer to Zadôq (Tsadôq) the priest of Solomon whose posterity were alone entitled to perform priestly service in the Temple.

In doctrine the Sadducees were in general opposed to the Pharisees. Dr. Edersheim says : ' Perhaps Sadduceeism may best be described as a general reaction against the extremes of Pharisaism, springing from moderate and rationalistic tendencies ; intended to secure a footing within the recognized bounds of Judaism, and seeking to defend its principles by a strict literalism of interpretation and application.' Practically, however, as often happens, this negative reaction ended in a positive extreme of rationalism. They set aside the authority of tradition in favour of the letter of Scripture, and went on to deny all that Scripture does not plainly and literally teach. From the denial of virtue for reward's sake they seem to have advanced to the denial of any future reward and of any resurrection (Matt. 22[23] ; Mark 12[18] ; Luke 20[27] ; Acts 23[8]) ; while in this last passage they are said to have denied the existence of angel or spirit. Another doctrinal characteristic was their assertion of man's free will as against the exaggerated 'fatalism' of the Pharisees. Their fundamental differences of doctrine naturally led to many differences on points of ritual, ceremony, and interpretation of canon law. They were fewer in number than the Pharisees, but their ranks included many of the highest and wealthiest. In Apostolic days the high priest and his party were of this sect (Acts 4[1], 5[17]). They were less prominent than the Pharisees in their opposition to our Lord, though we find the two sects named together as seeking to entrap Him by questions (Matt. 16[1], 22[34]), and linked by Him in His warning to His disciples (Matt. 16[6]) ; while John the Baptist bestows on both the scathing appellation 'generation of vipers' (Matt. 3[7]). When, after our Lord's death, it became clear that the cardinal doctrine of the new Christian sect was His 'resurrection from the dead', the opposition of the Sadducees became more pronounced (Acts 4[1, 2], 5[17], 23[6-10]).

3. *The Essenes.*

The Essenes are not mentioned in Scripture, but are described by Josephus as one of the 'three philosophical sects among the Jews', the other two being of course the Pharisees and the Sadducees. Their chief interest for the Biblical student lies in the alleged connexion between Essenism and Christianity. De Quincey in his well-known essay identifies the two, maintaining that under the name of Essenes (Gk. Ἐσσηνοί and Ἐσσαῖοι) Josephus is really describing the early Christian community. But this view is untenable, if only from the radical differences between Christian doctrine and practice as set forth in the New Testament, and the doctrine and practice of the Essenes as detailed by Philo and Josephus. Thus Dr. Edersheim says with emphasis, ' Neither John the Baptist and his baptism, nor the teaching of Christianity, had any connexion with Essenism ' (*Jesus the Messiah*, vol. i, p. 325). And Bishop Lightfoot, at the close of his exhaustive essay on the Essenes (*Colossians*, p. 413), declares, 'Thus at whatever point we test the teaching and practice of our Lord by the characteristic tenets of Essenism the theory of affinity fails'.

The derivation of the name is very doubtful. Bishop Lightfoot hesitates between the Syriac *chase*, pl. *chasēn*, ' pious' (on the whole the most probable derivation) and the Hebrew *chāshā*, 'to be silent', inclining to the latter, according to which the term would signify ' the silent ones, who meditate on mysteries'. Dr. Edersheim identifies the name with the Hebrew *chitsōnim*, ' outsiders ', and supposes that they were so called by the Pharisees to indicate contemptuously their position with regard to orthodox Judaism. ' While the Pharisees and Sadducees were parties *within* the Synagogue, the Essenes were, although strict Jews, yet separatists, and, alike in doctrine, worship, and practice, *outside* the Jewish body ecclesiastic.'

Their distinctive principles were the striving after *purity* and *community of goods*. In the former and in their rigorous keeping of the Sabbath and reverence for the Law they find contact with the Pharisees : Essenism has even been described as an exaggerated Pharisaism. But the differences are fundamental. Purity to the Pharisee meant freedom from ceremonial defilement ; the way to it lay in the rigid observance of ordinances ; the attainment of it conferred the merit of sanctity. The Essenes sought a purity more absolute, a freedom from the pollution that comes of contact with the material, in order that the spirit might find a freer and larger fellowship with the Divine. To this end they lived a life separate from the world. Their settlements were chiefly in the country districts, where the defilements of the cities were unknown. Their life was of extreme simplicity, and communistic in character.

Under direction of the officers of the order they worked, prayed, and took their meals together ; from a common fund they administered charity to those in need. They offered no animal sacrifices, but only gifts of incense to the temple ; their common meals were sacramental. All members of the order passed through a novitiate of three successive grades, each lasting a year. Admission to full membership involved the taking of a terrible oath binding to separation, a severe asceticism, and the most absolute secrecy.

The exclusiveness and mysticism of their doctrine are in the Epistle to the Colossians strikingly contrasted with the free revelation of God in Jesus Christ. In their punctilious observance of the Sabbath, their abstinence from forbidden food, and the frequency of their lustrations, they resembled and went beyond the Pharisees. But besides this they practised a rigorous discipline. Marriage was repudiated. They abstained from meat and wine. The use of oil for anointing—so necessary in hot climates—was esteemed a luxury, and forbidden. Their food, dress, work, were of the simplest ; their intercourse with the world was limited to a charity freely shown to all. They rejected the Levitical priesthood and sacrifices: their only sacrifice was the common meal, their only priests the baker who prepared the meal and the officer who presided over it. Josephus gives the number of the brotherhood as 4,000, but—mainly no doubt through the practice of celibacy—they would seem to have quickly diminished and died out. Schürer traces foreign influences in the system. Much of their distinctive doctrine reappears in the latter Gnostic heresies.

4. *The Herodians.*

The Herodians were a political party rather than a religious sect. They were the partisans of the Idumaean dynasty, which, springing from heathenism, remained in taste, inclination, barbarity, and licentiousness, heathen still, though from state policy conforming outwardly to the Jewish ritual observances. Their distinctive principle was that of concession to the reigning power. Supported in authority and position solely by Roman might, they endeavoured to repay their benefactors by performing their part of the compact in leavening the Jewish nation with laxity of moral tone, religious indifferentism, and the policy of temporizing under Roman ascendancy. Hence they vied with the Sadducees in scepticism and the Greeks in licentiousness, pandered to the vice and cruelty of the Herods, and truckled to the Romans. Their natural opponents were the Pharisees, who held tenaciously to all that was Jewish, and resisted all Gentile contamination. It is the more significant that Herodian and Pharisee are found joined in deadly hostility to Jesus (Mark 3[6], Matt. 22[16]). 'Their alliance was due to the recognition by both that Jesus was their greatest common foe' (Eaton). On the teaching of both He utters the same condemnation (Mark 8[15]).

5. *The Zealots.*

The Zealots are named by Josephus as a fourth party, supplementary to the Pharisees, Sadducees, and Essenes. They were the party of political resistance to Herod and the Romans, Nationalists politically as the Pharisees were Nationalists religiously. Hence they are the very antithesis of the Herodians. These 'brave free highlanders of Galilee' took up their arms under Eleazar at the beginning of the reign of Herod the Great, and both then and in subsequent risings were repressed with merciless severity. But their spirit of fervid nationalism was never quenched. Their name indicates the intensity of their zeal (Gk. $\zeta\eta\lambda\omega\tau\acute{\eta}s$); according to Josephus, the party under that name did not exist till the last days of Jerusalem, but its tendencies had previously existed under the style 'the fourth philosophy'. One of the apostles, Simon, is surnamed *the Zealot* in Luke 6[15], Acts 1[13], while in Matt. 10[4] (R.V.) he receives the corresponding Hebrew title of *The Cananaean* (Heb. *qanna*, 'zealous',—Gk. $\zeta\eta\lambda\omega\tau\acute{\eta}s$). We must then infer either that in his case the name means simply 'the zealous one', or that the Evangelist thought the name referred to the political party of later days, or that Simon actually joined the Zealots later. (Cf. article by K. Lake in *Harvard Theol. Rev.*, Jan. 1917). They were responsible for much of the bloodshed and internecine strife of the Jewish War.

6. *The Galilaeans.*

The Galilaeans, i. e. natives of Galilee, were looked down upon by the southern Jews as an ignorant and rustic folk. Thus the name became a term of reproach.

Moreover, they were a people of passionate and excitable temperament, a spirit which found expression in the Zealots. In the 'days of the taxing' (Luke 2[2]) we learn from Josephus that a serious rising in resistance to the tax took place under one Judas. And when this was finally crushed and Judas slain, the lawless spirit still survived to be a source of constant anxiety to the Roman authorities. So that the name Galilaean became almost a synonym for lawlessness and violence, and it was with intent to arouse prejudice that at His trial our Lord was said to be of Galilee (Matt. 26[69]; cf. Mark 14[70]).

7. *The Assassins.*

The Assassins (Acts 21[38], R.V.). This is a better rendering of the word σικάριοι—the Greek form of the Latin word *sicarii*, from *sica*, 'a short sword or dagger'—than the 'murderers' of the A.V. They were a secret society, well known at Rome in the last troubled years of the Republic. With dagger concealed beneath the cloak they secretly murdered their own or their patron's enemies, generally escaping detection by the swiftness of the attack and an adroit mingling with the horror-stricken crowd. It would appear that the extreme fanatics among the 'Zealots' formed themselves into a Jewish branch of these *Sicarii*, visiting Jerusalem at feast times, and secretly dispatching those whom they deemed the enemies of their country. The incidental notice in Acts 21[38] receives full and striking confirmation from Josephus.

8. *The Scribes.*

The Scribes (Gk. γραμματεύς, a term which means more than 'writer', and implies learning, the Latin *litteratus*. The Hebrew equivalent is *Sōpherim*). The New Testament order of Scribes apparently had its rise in Ezra, of whom we read that 'he was a ready scribe in the law of Moses', and that he 'had set his heart to seek the law of the Lord, and to do it, and to teach in Israel statutes and judgements' (Ezra 7[6–10]). The work begun by him was committed either by himself or his successors to a formally constituted order of scribes. Their functions were to guard, transcribe, and interpret the sacred oracles. Gradually this function of interpretation became the most important, and from it the later scribe derived his great authority. ' He is the Divine aristocrat among the vulgar herd of rude and profane "country-people" who "know not the Law" and are "cursed". More than that, his order constitutes the ultimate authority on all questions of faith and practice; he is "the Exegete of the Laws", the "teacher of the Law", and along with the chief priests and elders, a judge in the ecclesiastical tribunals, whether of the capital or in the provinces. Although generally appearing in company with the Pharisees, he is not necessarily one of them, for they represent a religious party, while he has a status and holds an office.' *

Their legitimate office of interpretation of the Scriptures is illustrated in Matt. 2[4], 17[10]; Mark 12[35]; while their burdensome additions to the Mosaic Law (afterwards collected into the *Mishnah*, or 'second Law') receive terrible condemnation from our Lord in

* Edersheim, *Jesus the Messiah*, i, p. 93.

Matt. 23. They are frequently joined with the 'priests' and 'elders' as one constituent of the Sanhedrin.

9. *The Lawyers.*

The Lawyers (Gk. νομικός, from νόμος, 'law') are generally regarded as identical with the Scribes. The 'lawyer' of Matt. 22[35] is called a 'scribe' in the parallel passage of Mark 12[28]. The difference may have been one of function; the same man being called 'scribe' as being a 'learned man', or 'lawyer' as skilled in different matters of law, or yet again 'teacher of the law' (Luke 5[17]; Acts 5[34]; 1 Tim. 1[7]), having regard to his function of teaching. But it is quite possible that certain of the scribes received a technical training to fit them to plead in the ecclesiastical courts on questions of Sabbath observance, divorce, and the like. In this case the 'lawyers' would form a class within a class. 'One learned in the Old Testament Scriptures, a scribe, a jurist' (Souter).

10. *The Nazarites.*

The Nazarites, or Nazirites (Heb. *nāzar*, to 'separate or consecrate', whence *nāzīr*, 'a separated one', i. e. to God, Judges 13[5]), were not a brotherhood but individuals under a personal vow. They were of two classes, 'Nazarites for life', those who in infancy were dedicated under this vow to God, and the more usual 'Nazarites of days', who bound themselves for a limited period, generally 30 days, sometimes 60 or 100 or even longer. Of the former class were Samson, Samuel, John the Baptist; while the references in Amos 2[11, 12], Acts 21[23–6], evidently point to 'Nazarites of days'. The vow of St. Paul at Cenchreae was of another kind. The meaning of the Nazarite vow was to symbolize the consecration due to God. Its outward accompaniments were of the simplest kind: abstinence from all wine and strong drink was rigidly enjoined, pollution from dead bodies prohibited, and the hair allowed to grow long. The details of the vow and the ceremonies of release are fully set forth in Numbers 6.

To avoid possible misconception, it may be well to note that the words *Nazarite* and *Nazarene* are wholly unconnected. The form 'Nazirite' (as in R.V.), while etymologically correct, better marks the distinction.

11. *The Proselytes.*

The Proselytes (Gk. προσήλυτος, 'that has come to' (Souter)) were Gentiles converted to Judaism. They are said to have been of two kinds, viz. 'Proselytes of Righteousness', and 'Proselytes of the Gate', but the latter phrase seems to be of very late origin. Yet there seems to have been in ancient times a distinction between those who were circumcised, admitted to the full religious privileges, and charged with the entire obligations of the Mosaic covenant, and who were also baptized, being wholly immersed in the presence of three witnesses who acted, in some measure, as sponsors, and those who were allowed to join in the worship of God, standing in the outer 'court of the Gentiles', but were not bound by the ceremonial laws of Moses, but only by the moral ones, or, as they were called, the Seven Precepts of Noah, directed against idolatry, profanity, murder, uncleanness, theft, rebellion, eating of blood. They were not circumcised, nor is it certain that they were baptized. They are probably those spoken of as 'devout men' in the Acts of the Apostles (Acts 13[50], 16[14], 17[4, 17], &c.). A difference was made between various nations, no heathens being admitted direct into the condition of Proselytes of Righteousness. Edomites and Egyptians had this privilege in the third generation, while Ammonites and Moabites were excluded till the tenth, before which they had none of the civil rights and advantages peculiar to the Jew by descent. This exclusiveness caused the controversy in the Christian Church as to the admission of the Gentile converts without circumcision (Acts 15). One of the seven 'deacons' was a Proselyte from Antioch.

12. *The Publicans.*

The Publicans were the tax-collectors of the civil power. The taxes were farmed by rich Roman citizens of the Equestrian Order, or sometimes by a joint-stock company at Rome, who had agents in the provinces to arrange the actual collection from the people. These agents divided the country into districts, and offered each district to public competition, to be farmed by the highest bidder. The purchaser was usually required to pay the purchase money, either wholly or by instalments, in advance, and he was at liberty to recoup himself. He was always a native of the country, well versed in its resources and the temper of its people; using his knowledge and power to extort as much as possible for his own profit. In this he was backed by the Equestrian Order at Rome, who carried most oppressive decrees in the Senate against defaulters. Strictly speaking, the term *publicani* applies only to the direct farmers of the taxes from the Government; the subordinate agents were called *portitores*; the 'publicans' of the A.V. being taken from the inexact rendering of the Gk. τελῶναι by the Lat. Vulgate. Such were the Jewish 'Publicans'; univer-

sally despised ; branded as 'plunderers', as 'beasts of prey';
classed with 'bears and lions', and coupled with the vilest and
most contemptible characters. As much of the tax was an *ad
valorem* duty on property and produce, which the publican gauged,
there was ample opportunity for unjust exaction. To this general
odium must be added the peculiar sting to 'Abraham's seed, in
bondage to no man', that they were no longer free ; and the
question was ever rife, whether it were 'lawful to pay tribute to
Caesar'; thus the publicans, as unscrupulous agents of a heathen
power, were regarded as traitors to their country and their God.
Even our Lord classes them with 'heathen men' (Matt. 18^{17}); and
the Jews forbade marriage with a family in which there was one
publican, since it had thereby become polluted.

13. *The Samaritans.*

The Samaritans were by origin a mixed heathen people, derived
from the colonists whom the King of Assyria sent to inhabit the
land of Samaria after he had carried the Israelites captive
(2 Kings 17^{24}). These colonists had been drawn from various
eastern nations ; and they continued to practise their different
forms of national idolatry, until the plagues sent among them by
God led them to petition the King of Assyria for a priest of the
God of the country to teach them the old form of worship
(2 Kings 17$^{26-41}$). He was stationed at Beth-el, and they endeavoured to combine a formal reverence for God with the practice
of their own heathen rites. In all probability intermarriages
took place between these heathen settlers and the remnant of the
ten tribes, so that in course of time the Samaritans might justly
claim a partial Israelite descent. After the Captivity of Judah they
sought an alliance with the returned Jews, offering to aid in the
work of restoring the Temple. The alliance was decisively refused,
and the Samaritans became the Jews' bitter enemies (Ezra 4$^{1-6}$).
Some amount of intermarriage however took place, and when
Nehemiah enforced the Mosaic Law as to mixed marriages (according to Josephus, *Antiq.* XI. vii. 2, viii. 2), Manasses, a Jewish
priest, who had married the daughter of Sanballat, chief of the
Samaritans, was expelled from Judah, and headed a secession to
Shechem, where he taught the people the Mosaic ritual, and
erected a rival temple on Mount Gerizim ; and this mixed community began to claim descent from the patriarchs, and a share
in the promises, adopting the Pentateuch and Books of Joshua
and Judges as their sacred books. Having the advantage of occupying a place of peculiar sanctity (Shechem), surrounded by the

tombs and memorials of the patriarchs, dividing the two portions of the Israelite people (Galilaeans and Jews), and with the most natural access to the territory over Jordan, they held a very strong vantage-ground, which they used to annoy their neighbours. They erected false beacons to render nugatory the announcements of the great festivals ; refused a passage through their territory to pilgrims going up to the feasts (Luke 9$^{51-56}$) ; defiled the temple by scattering dead men's bones upon its altar ; and are said to have welcomed the invasion of Alexander the Great, and offered him their temple for a heathen fane—proceedings which resulted in its final destruction by the Jews under John Hyrcanus (130 B.C.).

The old feud between the ten tribes and the house of David was renewed with double hostility by the Samaritans, Shechem and Jerusalem being the centres of animosity, each possessing rival claims to sanctity. Hence the point of the Samaritan woman's questions to our Lord (John 4), and the readiness with which her fellow-citizens accepted the overture of one ' being a Jew ' to receive them into full religious communion. The Samaritans now number not 100 persons, living at Nablous (Shechem), preserving an ancient copy of the Pentateuch, keeping up an annual sacrifice of the Passover on Mount Gerizim, living peaceful and moral lives, and observing, with some peculiar variations, the Mosaic Law.

14. *The Sanhedrin.*

The Sanhedrin (Aramaic form of the Gk. συνέδριον, lit. ' a sitting together ' ; in A.V. and R.V., ' council ') was the great ' Council ' of the Jewish Church and people, which, after Alexander's conquest, if not before,* held chief authority ' in all causes and over all persons, ecclesiastical and civil '. It was suggested by the old institution of seventy-two elders (six from each tribe), appointed by Moses, at Jethro's suggestion, to relieve him in the administration of justice (Ex. 18^{14} ; Num. 11^{16}). There is no trace of such a tribunal in the Book of Joshua, or in the time of the Judges or of the Kings. It consisted of an equal number (twenty-four) of priests, scribes, and elders, all of whom were required to be married, above thirty years of age, well instructed in the Law, and of good report among the people. This constituted the Supreme Court of Judicature and Administrative Council, taking cognizance of false doctrine and teaching, as well as of breaches of the Mosaic Law, and regulating both civil and ecclesiastical observances peculiar to the Jewish nation. The power of life and

* We first meet with the name after Pompey's and Caesar's political rearrangement of Palestine.

of death was taken from it by the Roman government (John 18³¹), which otherwise covenanted to respect its decrees ; though during the interval between the death of Tiberius and the accession of Caligula, and in the absence of Pilate at Rome, the opportunity was seized to stone Stephen and to put others to death.

The Sanhedrin usually met in the hall Gazîth, within the Temple precincts, though special meetings were sometimes held in the house of the high priest (Matt. 26³). He was generally (but not necessarily) the president.* There were also two vice-presidents ; two scribes, or ' heralds ', one registering the votes of acquittal (or noes), and the other of conviction (or ayes) ; and a body of lictors, or attendants (Matt. 26⁵⁸). The assembly sat in the form of a semicircle, the president occupying the centre of the arc, the prisoner that of the centre of the chord, while the two heralds sat a little in advance of the president, on his right hand and his left.

There were also lesser councils or tribunals in the towns; of three members, where the male inhabitants did not exceed 120, and, in other cases, of twenty-three. These were subordinate to the great Sanhedrin. Probably to one of these lesser tribunals reference is made in the ' judgement ' of Matt. 5²².

15. *The Synagogue.*

The Synagogue (Gk. συναγωγή, ' a gathering together '; Heb. *Kěnésĕth*), applied in earlier times to the whole *congregation* of Israel and to a national assembly, was later the term used both for the congregation in a provincial town, and for the room in which it met during the week for mutual instruction, disputation, and administration of justice, and on the sabbath for prayer and praise, not sacrifice. The institution of the Synagogue in this narrower sense dates probably from the Captivity in Babylon. These buildings were the schools of the children, the debating clubs and libraries of the youths ; there were 480 of them in Jerusalem.

The principal officers of the synagogue were :—

1. The Baṭlanîn (*men of leisure*). It was a rule, at least in later times, that no synagogue should be erected in any place unless it contained ten ' men of leisure ' who could devote their time to the administration of the synagogue. These were the ' Rulers of

---

* Some Jewish and Christian scholars accept the tradition of the Talmud that the presidency was vested not in the High Priest but in successive ' Pairs ' of leaders. Others assert the constant or usual presidency of the High Priest ; and there is an intermediate view that the Sanhedrin enjoyed political rights only in theory, but was prevented from practising them through the usurpation of them by the High Priest and others. See further Sir G. A. Smith, *Jerusalem*, i. 414-23.

the Synagogue', also called the 'shepherds', and the 'elders': they had special seats of honour assigned them during divine worship (Acts 13[15]; Matt. 23[6]). They also formed the local tribunal or Sanhedrin or Beth-Dîn; and had a chief (Mark 5[22, 35f, 38], &c.).

2. **The Sheliach** (*Delegate*). He was one of the elders, delegated by the Chief Shepherd or Director (*Parnas*) to recite the most sacred portions of the liturgy. The office was not permanently vested in one person, but one so delegated was the mouthpiece, for the time being, of the congregation. In large towns the qualifications required were considerable and were strictly exacted: they may have been the groundwork of those required for the Christian ministry (1 Tim. 3[1—7]). This was the office held by our Lord on the memorable occasion at Nazareth (Luke 4[16]); cp. the freedom with which Paul took part.

3. **The Chazzan** (literally *Inspector*), the permanent minister or attendant (Luke 4[20]), whose duties were partly ecclesiastical, partly civil. He had charge of the sacred rolls and frequently acted as schoolmaster.

4. **The Methurgeman** (*Interpreter*). As the synagogue came principally into use in later times, when Hebrew was not well known and Greek was more generally used in common life, the Law was expounded to the congregation by an interpreter, selected for his learning and knowledge of languages. To guard against false interpretation, the learned formed a guild of 'interpreters', who drew up a Book of Paraphrases on the hebdomadal lessons, which from them was called the 'Targum'. This word Methurgeman, or Turgeman, has been corrupted into the modern *Dragoman*.*

XL. GEOGRAPHY AND TOPOGRAPHY OF THE BIBLE

THE HOLY LAND

Introduction.

In considering the Geography of the Bible, our thoughts at once centre in the land whose familiar title 'The Promised Land' marks it as the home promised to and occupied by the Israelites,

* For full accounts of the Synagogues and their worship, see Edersheim, *Jesus the Messiah*, Bk. 3, chap. 10; Schürer, *History of the Jewish People in the Time of Christ*, Engl. Transl. Div. II, vol. ii, 52–89; Moore, *Judaism*, vol. i, pp. 281 ff.

and whose yet more sacred name 'THE HOLY LAND' identifies it as the scene of the life and ministry of our Lord. It would seem from Gen. 15[18] that the territory promised to Israel—from the River of Egypt to the Euphrates—was of far greater extent than that actually possessed at any time, excepting for a brief period during the reign of Solomon, and then probably Solomon's influence as far as the Euphrates was commercial and not political. The boundaries of the country as it was permanently held were, on the north the mountains of Lebanon; on the south the valley of the Arnon in Moab with a line from the Salt Sea (Dead Sea) through the wilderness beyond Beer-Sheba to the mouth of the Wady el-Arish, 'The River of Egypt'; on the east the Syrian Desert; on the west the Mediterranean Sea, with Philistia on the south-west and Phoenicia in the north-west.

This land, more extensive than the CANAAN of the Old Testament, which lay to the west of Jordan,* is now known as PALESTINE (i. e. Philistia), a name given in early times to a part of the sea-board only, but applied soon after the Christian era to the whole country of the Jews. Its extreme length is referred to under two formulas: (1) 'From the entering in of Hamath unto the brook of Egypt' (1 Kings 8[65], R.V.); (2) 'From Dan to Beer-sheba' (1 Kings 4[25]). The former phrase is the more accurate, and by it the latter must be interpreted. The 'entering in of Hamath' is in all probability the pass at the northern end of the valley of Lebanon, leading to the valley of the Orontes, i. e. the land of Hamath. The brook of Egypt (*Wady el-Arish*) forms a natural boundary to the south-west, intersecting the principal road from Palestine to Egypt. The length of the territory thus determined is about 270 miles. The phrase 'from Dan to Beer-sheba' literally taken would give a distance far short of this—say 150. But it is probable that both these places, as important centres of local government, lent their names to the surrounding district, so that the two expressions are practically equivalent, and alike are used to designate the whole length of the territory ruled by David and Solomon. The extreme breadth from sea to desert was some 80 miles.

Though of insignificant extent, Palestine was at the centre

---

* The name Canaan, meaning *lowland*, was originally applied to the maritime plain from Gaza to the northern limit of Phoenicia, but later to the whole country west of Jordan, across which the Canaanites (a name given by some Old Testament writers to all the tribes dispossessed by Israel) had spread. Other writers call them Amorites, a name originally applied to the hill-tribes behind Phoenicia, but extended southwards across the whole hill country, 'Mount of the Amorites'.

of the ancient world. To the south-west was Egypt, with her wealth and culture ; across the eastern desert lay BABYLONIA, with the Empires of the MEDES and PERSIANS beyond ; to the north-east stretched the ASSYRIAN EMPIRE ; through Asia Minor the Hittite state and civilization were long dominant; while nearer home, on the north, lay the populous kingdoms of SYRIA ; and over the sea were GREECE and ROME. It was inevitable that the Jews, being so situated, should find their land the meeting-point of many national interests, military, political, and economic. With all the powers mentioned their history was closely linked, until the final destruction of Jerusalem by the Roman armies in A. D. 70.

(i) *Physical Features.*

1. **General View.** The most striking physical feature of Palestine is the deep gorge through which the Jordan flows in an almost direct line from north to south, dividing the land into two unequal parts.

(a) *West of the Jordan Valley.* From the western side of this Jordan Valley there rises an irregular mountain range, extending from the slopes of Lebanon in the north to Beer-sheba in the south, with only one important break—the Plain of Esdraëlon. The ridges and peaks are numerous but of no considerable height, the loftiest summit (*Jebel Jermak*—2½ miles south-west of *el-Jish*) being only 3,934 feet above the Mediterranean level. Throughout its length the range is scored by many ravines and valleys, running chiefly east and west. The eastern and western slopes of this backbone of hills differ considerably in character. On the east the mountains fall away abruptly to the Jordan Valley, terminating as they approach the Dead Sea in precipitous cliffs. On the west the fall is much more gradual ; and opposite the Judaean portion of the range a stretch of low-hills known as the Shephelah (A.V. 'lowlands') intervenes before the plain is reached, which extends to the shores of the Mediterranean. This plain is triangular in shape, narrow in the north, and widening out considerably in the south. It is broken only by the ridge of Carmel, which comes within 200 yards of the coast and joins the southern boundary of the Bay of Acre.

(b) *East of the Jordan Valley and the Dead Sea* the country may fairly be described as a vast tableland, of an average height of over 2,000 feet, very flat throughout Hauran (the ancient Bashan) except towards the Lake of Galilee, but south of the Yarmuk and across Gilead rising into peaks and ridges whose

221

greatest elevation reaches 4,245 feet; but again flat with many knolls across the Plateau of Moab, which is cut by the deep valleys of Nahaliel (Wady Zerka Main) and of the Arnon (Wadies Mojib and Waleh). The western wall of this plateau climbs steeply from the Jordan Valley, sometimes in sheer cliffs. Eastward the high ground gradually sinks into the desert beyond. The whole region, like that on the west of Jordan, is intersected by numerous deep water-cut ravines, but its general character is less rugged, and it is also much more fertile.

2. The Valley of the Jordan. This valley is the central portion of a great crack or fault in the earth's surface, extending from Antioch in the north, to the Gulf of Akaba, the eastern arm of the Red Sea, in the south. Where this cleft separates Lebanon and Anti-Lebanon (or Hermon) the four distinctive perennial sources of Jordan appear. (1) The highest issues from the foot of a buttress of Hermon a little north of Hâsbeyâ and flows south as the Nahr Hâsbanî, which, fed by other springs from Hermon, is joined by (2) the Nahr Bareighit, the smallest contribution of the four and the only one from the side of Lebanon, and then by the combined waters from Hermon; (3) the Nahr el-Leddan, which has issued 12 ft. broad by 3 deep from the Mound or Fell, êl-Kâdi, and of (4) the Nahr Baniasî, that with equal suddenness breaks on a breadth of 30 ft. from the foot of the cliff of Bânias, the ancient Paneas or Caesarea Philippi. The united stream expands into the LAKE OF HULEH (doubtless the Lake Semechonitis of Josephus, but hardly Joshua's 'Waters of Merom', which were probably springs), then collects again, and makes a rapid descent of 689 ft. in the nine miles to the SEA OF GALILEE. Its course through the whole length of this lake—thirteen miles—may sometimes be traced.

At its exit the stream enters a valley stretching for sixty-five miles to the north end of the Dead Sea, with an average breadth of eight miles. But through this the stream has worn a channel which gradually deepens into a great cleft—a 'valley within a valley', which from 200 yds. widens near Jericho to a mile and is 150 ft. deep. Through this the river flows with ceaseless windings; at first with a very rapid current, then more gently as it nears the Dead Sea.

For the most part, the stream itself is hidden beneath the thick growth of willow and tamarisk which lines its terraced sides of marl and overhangs the water. Its width varies from 80 to 150 ft., its depth in summer from 4 to 12 ft., but between January and March it rises so as to feed the thick jungle on its banks which was known as 'the pride' or 'rankness (not *swelling*) of Jordan', a symbol of trouble and danger by the number of wild beasts it sheltered (Jer. 12^5, 49^{19}, 50^{44}).

There are fords at many points, notably from *Beisân* (Beth-shean)—where the western wall of mountains is broken by an arm of the Plain of Esdraëlon (*see* Plains), giving easy access to Galilee and the coast—down to the confluence of the Jabbok, and three or four near Jericho. One of the fords (*'Abarah*), in the neighbourhood of *Beisân*, is supposed by some to be the true site of Bethabara (R.V. Bethany), where our Lord was baptized, but the reading Bethany is the more strongly supported, and a comparison of Matt. 3 and John 10^{40} with John 1^{28} suggests a site farther south, nearer both the wilderness of Judaea and Jerusalem. Others would read Bethanabra and equate it with Bethnimrah (3 miles east of Jordan, opposite Jericho).

3. **Mountains.** The mountain system west of Jordan may be conveniently divided into four separate groups, the division, however, being rather political than strictly physical. From north to south the groups are thus named :—(*a*) Mountains of UPPER GALILEE ; (*b*) Mountains of LOWER GALILEE ; (*c*) Mountains of SAMARIA ; and (*d*) Mountains of JUDAEA. On the northern boundary of Palestine are the notable Syrian Mountains—the ranges of LEBANON—divided by the valley of *El Buka'a* into Lebanon on the west and Anti-Libanus on the east. The general elevation of this range is considerably greater than that of any of the groups more strictly belonging to Palestine. The most important mountain, HERMON, in the Anti-Libanus range, culminates in three peaks, the highest of which is 9,052 feet above sea-level, and forms a landmark for nearly all Palestine.

(*a*) *Mountains of Upper Galilee.* This group extends from the river *Kasimiyeh*, about five miles to the north of Tyre, to three miles south of *Jebel Jermak*, its highest peak, a distance of some twenty-five miles in all. The average elevation of the mass is nearly 2,700 feet. It is much broken by valleys, running in general from east to west. The heights are well wooded, and form a pleasant contrast to the bare and unfertile southern hills. The group terminates in a peak 3,400 feet high, which sinks abruptly into a valley 2,400 feet below. Immediately south of this valley rise the

(*b*) *Mountains of Lower Galilee.* This group, stretching southwards to the great Plain of Esdraëlon, comprises several low but well-marked ranges, running from east to west, and separated by fertile plains. Its average elevation is not more than 1,400 feet. Of the individual summits the most important is *Jebel et-Tor* (MOUNT TABOR), an isolated wooded hill in the Nazareth group, 1,843 feet above the Mediterranean. The Nazareth range stretches westwards towards the beautiful range of Carmel, from which it is separated by the gorge of the *Nahr el-Mukutta* (Kishon).

(*c*) *The Mountains of Samaria* rise south of the Esdraëlon Plain, and continue without a break into the hills of Judaea. A north-west spur pushes up to the sea in a magnificently wooded ridge, never rising to a greater height than 1,810 feet; its natural beauties are well expressed by its name, CARMEL, usually The Carmel = the garden-land.

The northern portion of the Samarian Hills is of an average height of about 2,000 feet, not broken by any prominent peak. Towards the Jordan lie the MOUNTAINS OF GILBOA, a low range about 1,650 feet in height.

The main ridge rises somewhat sharply into MOUNT EBAL (3,077 feet), the highest point of the range, which is separated from the more southerly MOUNT GERIZIM (2,849 feet) by the fertile valley of SHECHEM (now Nablûs). South of Gerizim is the 'hill country of Ephraim' (A.V. 'Mount Ephraim'), including several prominent peaks, while the general elevation of the mass is higher than in the north. But Mount Ephraim appears sometimes to be applied to all the Samarian highlands.

(*d*) *The Mountains of Judaea.* This group, stretching southwards to Beer-sheba, is the highest of the four, the average elevation being about 2,500 feet. North of Jerusalem, the highest point is Neby Samwil (2,935 feet), the site of the ancient watch-tower of MIZPAH. Jerusalem is 340 feet below this, and then the general tendency of the highlands is upward until the neighbour-hood of Hebron is reached, where the heights vary from 3,000 to 3,400 feet. From Hebron the land descends to Beer-sheba, where it sinks into the desert lowlands known in ancient times as the NEGEB (South Country).

East of the main ridge the DESERT or WILDERNESS OF JUDAEA (average elevation 1,400 feet) sinks gradually to the Jordan Valley and Dead Sea, the latter 1,290 feet below sea-level. It is not an absolutely barren tract, but is not fertile enough to repay cultivation. It contains the oasis of ENGEDI.*

4. **Plains.** (1) *Maritime :*—From the northern promontory *Rás en-Nákura* to the base of Carmel stretches the PLAIN OF AKKA

---

* For the mountains east of Jordan, *see* pp. 221, 243.

(*Acre*), a fertile and well-watered tract about twenty miles long and four miles broad.

Immediately south of Carmel the belt of land along the shore is barely 200 yards in width, but it gradually expands into the PLAIN OF SHARON, so celebrated in the Old Testament for its beauty and fertility. This plain has an actual length of forty-four miles, beginning four miles north of Caesarea and terminating nine miles south of Joppa. Its breadth varies from about six miles in the north to twelve in the south, and it gradually slopes upward from the coast to a height of 200 feet above the sea.

South of Sharon is the PLAIN OF PHILISTIA, extending forty miles along the coast, and widening out beyond Gaza to a breadth of fifteen miles.

(2) *Central :*—By far the most important of the inland plains is ESDRAËLON (known also as the VALLEY OF MEGIDDO), the great battle-field of Palestine. Its average height is 250 feet; in shape it is an irregular triangle, bounded on the north by the Galilaean hills, on the east by the mountains of Gilboa and the hill of Moreh, and on the south and west by the hills of Samaria and the range of Carmel.

Eastward the great plain divides into three arms: one to the north-east, between Mount Tabor and Jebel Duhy; another running eastwards, with a fairly steep declivity, into the Jordan Valley, between Jebel Duny and Mount Gilboa; and the third stretching southwards towards En-gannim. The middle arm is, in the strict sense of the term, the ancient VALLEY OF JEZREEL, the town from which it took its name standing at the north-western end of Mount Gilboa, with Naboth's vineyard at its foot. In this valley were fought most of the battles between Israel and the Syrians.

Among the other inland plains and vales may be mentioned (i) the small PLAIN or VALE OF AJALON, so celebrated in the history of Joshua, an offshoot of Sharon about midway between Joppa and Jerusalem; (ii) the fertile Sahil Makhneh east and south of Mount Gerizim; (iii) the wide PLAIN (A.V. Heb. CIRCLE) OF THE JORDAN (Gen. $13^{10, 12}$ &c.).

(3) *East of Jordan* mention need only be made of the PLAINS OF BASHAN, lying away to the eastward of the Sea of Galilee, and so often celebrated in the Old Testament as a region of unparalleled fertility, and the Plateau of Moab.

5. **Water System.** The supply of water in Palestine is fairly abundant, though it is somewhat irregularly distributed. In

Q

addition to the Jordan there are thirteen perennial streams, including the Nahr el-Kasimiyeh or Litany on the northern border, while the mountains, excepting those in the south, are full of excellent SPRINGS, especially at Shechem. Some districts, however, are ill provided ; notably the Judaean Desert, where there is scarcely any water during the long dry season except that which is obtained from very infrequent wells and many rock-hewn cisterns. Various HOT SPRINGS, indicating volcanic action, are to be found in the Jordan Valley and round the shores of the Sea of Galilee and of the Dead Sea, also at *El-Hammeh* (Amatha), on the river *Yarmuk.* The water of these is generally salt or sulphurous.

(1) *Rivers.* Foremost among the rivers is the JORDAN (already described in detail). Rising in the valley of Lebanon it passes through Lake Huleh and the Sea of Galilee into the Dead Sea, from which there is no visible outlet. The direct distance from the most northerly of its three sources (the rise of the *Hasbany*) to its mouth is about 125 miles, but owing to its short and frequent windings the actual length of the stream is nearly 300 miles.

The KISHON (*Nahr el-Mukutta*) drains the Plain of Esdraëlon and falls into the Bay of *Akka.*

The YARMUK (Hebrew name unknown) is an important stream east of Jordan, draining the great plateau of Hauran. It descends through a deep gorge into the Jordan about five miles south of the Sea of Galilee.

The JABBOK (*Zerka*) rises in the eastern plateau, winds down a narrow gorge, and falls into the Jordan twenty-four miles north of the Dead Sea. Excepting during the winter months it is almost dry. This stream was the boundary between the territories of Sihon and Og (Joshua 12); it was also the northern frontier of Ammon, and the scene of Jacob's wrestling with the angel (Gen. 32^{22-4}).

The ARNON (*Mojib*) flows through a rocky chasm on the east of the Dead Sea. It formed the boundary between Moab and the Ammonites, and became the southern frontier of the Israelites east of Jordan.

The BROOK KIDRON, reaching from Jerusalem to the Dead Sea is now generally dry.

In addition may be mentioned several short streams on the Plain of Sharon—among them the Nahr-es-Zerka or Crocodile River, the Nahr el-Mefjir or Dead River of the Crusades, the Nahr Iskanderuneh or Salt River of the Crusades, and the Nahr el-Auja, next to the Jordan the most considerable in Palestine.

2. *Lakes.* These are :—(1) *The Lake of Huleh* in the north, four miles long by four broad, and seven feet above the Mediterranean level ; (2) The SEA OF GALILEE, 682 feet below the Mediterranean, thirteen miles long by seven and a half broad, 'remarkable for its shoals of fish, for the violence of its sudden thunderstorms, and for the hot springs along the shore' ; (3) The DEAD SEA, 1,292 feet below the Mediterranean, forty-seven miles by ten miles in extent. The water of this sea is so exceedingly nauseous that no fish can live in it, except at those points where fresh water flows in. There is no visible outlet, and the sea is kept at the same level only by the rapid evaporation which goes on in this region.

(ii) *Political Divisions.*

1. Old Testament Times. The book of Joshua presents the conquest of Canaan as the result of a single series of campaigns, carried out under a single chief, resulting in a final division of the land among the tribes. (Joshua 1–12, 13^{15}–21^{42}). This representation, it is now agreed, has foreshortened the actual process of conquest, and refers back to Joshua the establishment of conditions which were achieved only at a later date. This section, in fact, is a good source of topographical information, and an excellent authority for our knowledge of the districts occupied and the conditions existing in the time of David and Solomon, when at last Israel succeeded in dominating the entire country. But, for the story of the actual process of occupation,[*] we must go to the more antique account in Judges 1, neglecting, as a harmonistic gloss, the sentence which (in verse 1) professes to place the events of that chapter 'after the death of Joshua', and reading the chapter as, substantially, a more authentic account of the invasion. There we find that the conquest was slow and difficult, that it was carried out by the individual efforts of distinct tribes or groups of tribes, and that in many districts it was quite inconclusive.

In the south, we find, Judah and Simeon occupied the *Negeb* and the hill-country[†] ; but their connexion with the centre was barred by Jerusalem and other Canaanite fortresses, while the Philistines succeeded in keeping them out of the maritime plain.

---

[*] On the reasons for accepting this as the more authentic account, cf. Burney, *Israel's settlement in Canaan* (Schweich Lectures).

[†] Perhaps advancing northward from Kadesh, and acting separately from the Joseph-tribes (cf. Burney, *op. cit.*). This would explain the isolation of Judah from the rest of Israel, which is evidenced by the fact that Judah is not mentioned at all in Deborah's Song (Judges 5), that it is not heard of as part of the Israelite polity till the time of David, and that its relations with the rest of Israel were almost uniformly uneasy even then.

In the centre the Joseph-tribes conquered much of the land ; but a line of Canaanite hill-towns hemmed them in on the north. In the north the remainder of the tribes seem to be more or less subject to the Canaanites.

The book of Judges ascribes this conquest, such as it was, to the work of invasion from a single centre at a single time. Archaeological evidence, however, gives strong reason for believing that any organized unity of the Hebrew tribes was achieved only at a later date, and that the process of Hebrew settlement in Canaan began long before Joshua. Thus among the place-names of conquests made by Thutmosis III of Egypt (1479 B.C.) occur names which are read as *Jacob-el* and (more doubtfully) *Joseph-el*. The Amarna tablets, *c.* 1400, speak of Bedawin *Habiru* as invading southern Palestine ; and most, though not all, scholars agree in identifying these as the Hebrews, or the Hebrews as a branch of these.* Sethos I (1313) and Rameses II (1293) claim to have conquered *'Asaru* in Canaan, in the hinterland of southern Phoenicia—the position assigned in the Bible to the Israelite tribe of Asher. Finally Merneptah (1225) boasts of having desolated *Ysiraal* in Canaan. All this evidence accumulates to place the first settlement of Israelite elements in Canaan at a date considerably anterior to the usually accepted date for the Exodus.

Certain enigmatic passages in the Biblical record suggest the same inference ; e. g. Genesis 34 and 49. In fact, if it be admitted that the patriarchal stories must be read as narratives of early tribal movements and tribal relations, we have every ground for carrying back the beginnings of Hebrew settlement in Canaan to the immigration of Abraham and Lot (i. e. to a date about contemporary with the time of Hammurabi in Mesopotamia, probably the same as Amraphel in Genesis 14), *c.* 2100 B.C.

The story of the process of Hebrew occupation will therefore be somewhat as follows:—From 2000 B.C. or earlier, Aramaean nomads had been pressing in on the land from the north-east. Of these the ancestors of the Israelite tribes formed one section. For centuries they lived as a floating semi-nomadic population, existing on sufferance among the Canaanite settlements, and constantly liable to enforced shifts of position according to circumstances. Some—like Simeon and Levi (cf. Genesis 34, 49$^{5-7}$)—were broken and dispersed. Others—the tribes in the north, perhaps—remained in semi-subjection, such as they are found enduring in Judges 1. Some—the Joseph-tribes—were squeezed down into Egypt and there enslaved ; whilst Judah seems to have been

* For a discussion ending in favour of this identification, cf. Burney, *op. cit.*

formed out of, or recruited by, a miscellaneous collection of clans (cf· Genesis 38[1f.]; 1 Sam. 27[10], 30[26f.]). About 1200,* the movement began, which resulted in the Exodus of the tribes from Egypt and the invasion of Canaan. This invasion took place perhaps in two separate detachments, Judah and Simeon advancing from the south, while the Joseph-tribes under Joshua made a thrust into the centre from the east.

This picture of the process is of course largely hypothetical, and is based on a series of inferences from the Biblical and archaeological evidences ; but it has the merit of a certain verisimilitude, and of embodying all the reliable evidence available. What is less questionable, for the book of Judges makes it plain at every point, is that the Hebrew invasion of Canaan was no act of national conquest. The Hebrew tribes overran parts of the country, and established themselves mainly in village-settlements ; but the Canaanites remained for long independent, and the Hebrews became dominant only gradually, and by peaceful amalgamation rather than warlike force.

At first the Hebrews seem to have possessed no properly-organized unity as a nation. But in time they began to draw together and the tradition of Mosaic Yahwism became common property. The need for national unity of a more formal sort was forced on them by the incessant raids of surrounding tribes and by the long oppression of the Philistines. The Judges were only temporary and local chiefs in emergencies. Unity and liberty came together, with the establishment of the monarchy. Under David and Solomon, in fact, Israel seemed on the way to a dominant position in the Near East. Egypt and Babylon were both quiescent. Israel under David made large annexations, and to Solomon is imputed a kingdom extending from the Brook of Egypt to the

* This is the date, if we accept the usual view that Merneptah was the Pharaoh of the Exodus, and that the period of the Judges lasted about 200 years (1 Kings 6[1] gives 480 years, but that is probably an artificially-computed figure). Another view is that the Exodus is the Hebrew version of the expulsion of the Hyksos from Egypt (*c.* seventeenth century) ; that the nomadic period must have lasted about 200 years, that the invasion of Palestine took place *c.* 1370, and may be referred to in the Amarna letters which speak of the incursions of the *Habiru*, and that the period of the Judges lasted 400 years. The arguments for this view are stated in Hall, *Ancient History of the Near East.* Burney (*op. cit.*) and others disagree with it, arguing that it makes the connexion between Moses and Joshua unhistorical, that the cities which the Hebrews built (Exodus 1[11]) are store-cities of Rameses' reign, and that it is inexplicable that Judges should contain no mention of the aggressions of Sethos I, Rameses II, and Merneptah, which on this hypothesis took place after the Hebrew occupation of Palestine.

Euphrates (1 Kings 4²⁴, 9²⁶). This, however, may represent commercial rather than political influence; for soon after his death his alleged tributaries are described as again independent. Solomon's division of the kingdom into twelve provinces for fiscal purposes (1 Kings 4⁷⁻¹⁹) may have been intended to break up the old tribal feeling. Certainly, from his time, the tribal names seem to have become mainly geographical expressions, implying no political division; and, though in certain cases an interest is shown in the tracing of descent from a particular tribe, for the most part families seem to have determined their tribe from the situation of their home or from similar circumstances. But later, though not till long after the Exile, the habit arose, and became general, of tracing descent to the ancient tribes and their primitive clans.

The unified kingdom had a short life. The old dissension between South and North recurred in the time of Rehoboam (c. 935 B.C.), and led to a revolt which ended in the establishment of two separate kingdoms, JUDAH (comprising the tribes of Judah and Benjamin) and ISRAEL. The northern boundary of Judah was never definitely fixed; it oscillated between Ramah and Bethel. Moreover, the 'Ten Tribes' who formed the kingdom of Israel could not have included the half-tribe of southern Dan, which became absorbed in Judah, nor Simeon, which seems to have been scattered beyond its supposed limits. (Cf. 1 Chron. 4³⁹⁻⁴³, which narrates two Simeonite expeditions in search of new territory, and 2 Chron. 15⁹, 34⁶, where we find Simeonites among the northern tribes. Judith the heroine is said, in the apocryphal book that bears her name, to have been a Simeonite (9²); but Bethulia, her city, was in the territory of Manasseh.)

The provision (in Joshua 21) of forty-eight cities with their pasture for the tribe of Levi can never have been practicable. It embodies the dream of a later priestly writer, envisaging Israel as a theocratic people. So also the CITIES OF REFUGE most probably represent a late attempt to systematize and regulate the antique right of taking 'sanctuary'. at a local altar (Exodus 21¹³.) The origin of the Levitical monopoly of priestly duties is a question of much difficulty. One view is that there never was a secular tribe of Levi, but that all people holding priestly position were called 'Levites', and that to this profession a tribal status was later given. The alternative is to hold that an originally secular tribe acquired gradually a position of priestly privilege. It is certain that no such monopoly belonged to the Levites in the period of the Judges or the early monarchy; it is not till Ezekiel and the later sections of the Hexateuch that the severance of Levi, as the priestly body, from the rest of Israel, became complete.

The capital of Judah was always Jerusalem. The capital of the northern kingdom was at first Shechem, afterwards Tirzah, and finally Samaria. After the Israelites had been carried into captivity by the Assyrians (722 or 721 B.C.), the name Samaria became applied to the whole of the northern kingdom (2 Kings 17²⁴). About 715 it was repopulated by heathen colonists from Assyria, with whom the remnants of the Israelite inhabitants coalesced to form a people of mixed blood. The southern kingdom survived the northern for 135 years. Occasionally independent, but for the most part a vassal, first of Assyria, then of Egypt, then of Babylonia, the Judaean monarchy came to a close in 587/6 B.C., with the capture of Jerusalem by Nebuchadrezzar, and the second great Jewish Exile.

2. **Between the Old and New Testaments.** On the conquest of the Babylonian Empire by the Medes and Persians the whole land of Palestine passed, together with Syria, under the sway of the victors. Within the fifth satrapy of the Persian Empire with its capital at Damascus or more probably Samaria, Jerusalem and its surroundings formed a Medinah or Province under a Jewish governor, Hebron and other southern districts having fallen to the Edomites. The old tribal and political divisions had become practically effaced, but bitter religious rivalry prevailed between Samaria and Jerusalem. After the triumphs of Alexander the Great, and the division of his conquests, the whole country became subject, first to the Egyptian Ptolemies, and after 198 B.C. to the Syrian Seleucids. After the great Maccabaean revolt the ancient boundaries were gradually in great measure restored, especially under Alexander Jannaeus and Queen Alexandra, 103–67 B.C.; and the kingdom of the Hasmonaean priest-princes, as described by Josephus (Ant. iii. 15⁴), extended along the seaboard from the Brook of Egypt to Mount Carmel and the border of Phoenicia, while across the Jordan it included the regions of the ancient Bashan and Gilead, down to Heshbon and Medeba. The Idumaeans, the inveterate enemies of Israel, were effectually held in check; and in the words of Ewald, 'almost the whole of the dominions was reconquered over which Israel had formerly ruled in the best days of its earthly power'.

3. **New Testament Times.** In the time of our Saviour we find the land west of Jordan divided into four provinces: GALILEE in the north; SAMARIA in the centre; and JUDAEA and IDUMAEA

in the south. East of Jordan the ancient Bashan had become the four provinces of GAULONITIS, AURANITIS, BATANAEA, and TRACHONITIS, with the country of the ITURAEI lying to the north. South of these lay PERAEA, the 'beyond Jordan' of the Gospels, covering much the same ground as Gilead of the Old Testament.

The region spoken of three times in the New Testament as DECAPOLIS (*the ten cities*) cannot be geographically defined. It would seem that on the conquest of Syria by the Romans in 65 B. C., ten cities were rebuilt and endowed with certain privileges. Of these, Damascus was the most northerly, and Philadelphia, probably, the most southerly. All, with the single exception of Scythopolis, lay east of Jordan.

The whole of this territory was under the Roman sway and in close connexion with the Roman province Syria. But Herod the Great ruled it as a subject-king. At first appointed governor of Galilee in 47 B. C., he was made king of Judaea 40 B. C., and, aided by the Roman arms, gradually extended his kingdom over the whole country.

The Tetrarchies. On Herod's death, 4 B. C., his kingdom passed by will to his three sons, as already narrated. Archelaus received Judaea, Samaria, and Idumaea, with the title of Ethnarch ; Herod Antipas became Tetrarch of Galilee and Peraea ; while the northeast provinces, 'the Ituraean and Trachonitic region', went to Herod Philip. A fourth Tetrarchy of Abilene in the Lebanon district is assigned by Luke to Lysanias, who cannot be certainly identified.

In A. D. 6, Archelaus was deposed, and Judaea, now formally annexed to the Roman province Syria, was henceforth governed by a Roman Procurator, with Caesarea for his capital. Of these procurators Pontius Pilate was the fifth from Coponius. In A. D. 41, Judaea was added to the kingdom of Herod Agrippa I, who already held the dominions formerly ruled over by the tetrarchs Philip and Antipas.

Thus, for a time, the greatness of the kingdom of Herod the Great was revived under his grandson ; but on the accession of Herod Agrippa II, the newly-acquired territory was again taken over by Rome ; and on the destruction of Jerusalem in A. D. 70 the whole country was finally annexed to the Roman province Syria.

(iii) *Notes on Important Places.*

Accho (R.V. Acco), or *Akka*, north of Mount Carmel, was occupied by Phoenicians, whom the tribe of Asher could not dislodge. It is only once mentioned in the Old Testament (Judges 1³¹), and once in the New, under its later Greek name, *Ptolemais* (Acts 21⁷), but frequently in the Books of

Maccabees. Under the Crusaders it became the seat of the Christian kingdom, and the head-quarters of the Knights Templars, from whom it derived its modern name *Saint Jean d'Acre*, modern Acre, one of the earliest instances of the vulgar addition of *r* to a terminal *a*. The plain of Accho is the most fertile in Palestine.

Achaia. A Roman province including part of the mainland of Greece, Peloponnesus (or Morea), and the adjacent islands. Its capital was the famous city of Corinth. It was the scene of the labours of Paul and of Apollos (Acts 18¹²). For *Achaia*, in Romans 16⁵ (A.V.), read *Asia*, as in the Revised Version.

Alexandria. A city on the north coast of Egypt, founded by Alexander the Great, and peopled largely by Jews. It was the birthplace of Apollos (Acts 18²⁴).

Antioch, the capital of the Seleucidae, is situated sixteen miles from the sea (forty-one from the mouth of the tortuous Orontes); its seaport was Seleucia. It was the third city in the Roman Empire; became the first centre of Christian Missions under Paul and Barnabas (Acts 13¹, ²); and after the destruction of Jerusalem was the head of the Eastern Church, its Patriarchate extending to Babylon, and including the whole of Syria and Palestine. It is to be distinguished from *Antioch in Pisidia*.

Arabah. The name given in many passages in the R.V. to the deep valley extending from Hermon to the eastern arm of the Red Sea. The A.V. uses the word once only (Joshua 18¹⁸); elsewhere rendering it 'plain', &c.

Aram. See below on **Syria**.

Asia, in the New Testament (Acts 2⁹), is the name applied to the western third of Asia Minor only. It was a Roman province, and included, among other important cities, Ephesus, Smyrna, Pergamum, Thyatira, Sardis, Philadelphia, and Laodicea (Rev. 2³).

Babylon, the metropolis of Chaldaea, the ancient land of Shinar, was built by Nimrod on the site of the Tower of Babel (Gen. 10¹⁰). It was a city of considerable size and strength, and for its magnificence, which it chiefly owed to Nebuchadrezzar, could not be surpassed (Dan. 4³⁰). It is not surprising that such a city should have given its name to the whole region round about it. It was the scene of many dark experiences in the history of the Israelites; hence its metaphorical use in the Book of Revelation.

Beer-Sheba— '*well of seven*', but taken in Gen. 21³¹ as '*well of the oath*'—lay on the border of the Southern Desert, twenty-eight miles south-west of Hebron. To it Abraham retired after the destruction of Sodom, and dug a well (Gen. 21³⁰), and Isaac also according to another document (Gen. 26²⁵, ³³), apparently because after the death of Abraham the Philistines had stopped up the well here, as also those in the valley of Gerar, which the servants of Abraham had dug (Gen. 26¹⁵⁻¹⁸). Three wells are now open to view at this place, of which the largest is over 40 ft. deep, lined with masonry to a depth of 28 ft., but some have found remains of others. Here also Abraham built an altar, and planted a sacred grove round it, which became the first fixed sanctuary in Palestine, and here Jacob and his whole family sacrificed, as they went down into Egypt. Here also Abraham received orders to take Isaac and sacrifice him, and here were enacted all the chief events of Isaac's life :—his own birth, and that of Esau and Jacob ; the purchase by Jacob of Esau's birthright, and his reception of his father's blessing. Here Samuel's sons sat as judges (1 Sam. 8²), and Elijah left his servant here when fleeing to Mount Sinai (1 Kings 19³). It was the birthplace of one Queen of Judah, Zibiah, mother of Jehoash (2 Kings 12¹) ; a place of idolatrous worship (2 Kings 23⁸) ;

a sanctuary by which men swore (Amos 5[5]); and the centre of local government for the south of Judah.

Bethany lies on the eastern shoulder of the Mount of Olives, little more than a mile east of Jerusalem. It is celebrated for our Lord's visits to the house of Lazarus on three occasions: once when Mary sat at His feet (Luke 10[38-42]); again when He raised Lazarus (John 11); and again when, in Simon's house, Mary anointed His 'body for the burial' (Matt. 26[6,7]); from which time, till the night of His betrayal, He appears to have slept there every night. It is now called *el-Aziriyeh* (obviously derived from Lazarus), and lies on the ancient road running from the Garden of Gethsemane by the southern end of the Mount of Olives to Jericho. By this road our Lord may have passed on His public entry into Jerusalem (Luke 19); but there is also a more direct, though steeper, road from Gethsemane up to the summit of Olivet and thence down to Bethany.

Beth-el (*Beitin*). Formerly a Canaanitish royal city called *Luz* (Gen. 28[19]), at the head of the pass of Michmash and Ai, about ten miles north of Jerusalem. Its strong position on the high road from Jerusalem to Shechem made it a very desirable possession; hence it was one of Joshua's first conquests, and became the border-fortress of Israel. Here Abraham built his second altar, received the second promise from Jehovah, and returned to sacrifice after going to Egypt. Jacob, fleeing from Esau, slept under the shelter of Abraham's altar, had a vision of angels, and gave to the spot its name, 'house of God'; returning after twenty years to perform his vow there he rebuilt the altar, set up a pillar, and received from God the ratification of his change of name (cf. Gen. 32[28], 35[10]). It was also honoured in the days of the Judges by being chosen as the resting-place of the Ark for a time, and here an altar was set up (Judges 20[18, 26-8], R.V.). Jeroboam I made it the chief sanctuary of his idolatrous worship, setting up a calf and an altar, which Josiah long afterwards destroyed. But in Elijah's last visit to the place before his translation there was a school of the Prophets existing there. Under Jeroboam II it was a royal residence, with a royal chapel and chaplains, when the prophet Amos was sent there to warn Israel (Amos 7[13]). After the Captivity, the priest sent from Assyria to teach the settlers was stationed at Beth-el.

Bethlehem—'*house of bread*'—is about five miles south of Jerusalem. It is also called Ephrath and Ephratah (Mic. 5[2]), to distinguish it from the northern city of the same name. On the road to it was the scene of Rachel's death and burial (Gen. 35[19]); it was the residence of Boaz and Ruth (Ruth 4[11]); and the birthplace of David (1 Sam. 17[12]). It was once captured by the Philistines (2 Sam. 23[14]). It was the last rallying-point of the remnant of Judah after the invasion of Nebuchadrezzar (Jer. 41[17]), and the birthplace of our Lord (Luke 2[11]).

Bethsaida—'*house of fishing*.'—It has been supposed that two towns were so called, situated near the head of the Sea of Galilee, deriving their name from the great shoals of fish attracted thither either by the issuing Jordan or by the hot springs:—

1. *Et-Tell*, a mound with many ruins close to the issue of the Jordan into the lake or less probably at Mas'adiyeh. On the east of Jordan, rebuilt by Philip the Tetrarch, and called *Julias*, after Julia, daughter of the Emperor Augustus. It was near here that Christ fed the five thousand (Luke 9[10-17]). This was certainly east of Jordan.

2. *Et-Tabghah* (?), on the western side of the Sea of Galilee about three miles south-east of Chorazin, as some have supposed on the grounds that to

reach it is described (Mark 6⁴⁵) as *going to the other side*, i. e. from the east of Jordan, and that it is called Bethsaida of Galilee (John 12²¹). But to go to the other side does not necessarily imply a passage from the east to the west of the Lake, and again, when John's Gospel was written, 'Galilee' covered the eastern as well as the western coast of the Lake. It was the residence of Andrew, Peter, James, John, and Philip (probably also of Thomas, John 21²), and the scene of two miraculous draughts of fishes.

Caesarea was only a poor landing-place, thirty-one miles north of Joppa, till Herod the Great built there a city and a harbour worthy of the Roman power, made it the seat of government, and called it Caesarea Sebaste (Augusta), in honour of the emperor (13 B.C.). It was the seat of the procurator and the central depot of Roman troops.

Caesarea Philippi (*Banias*), upon the principal springs of the Jordan. Here Herod the Great erected a temple to Caesar Augustus, which Philip (Luke 3¹) enlarged, calling it by the name of the reigning emperor (Tiberius Caesar), with the addition of his own. It was here that Peter confessed Christ's Deity, six days before He was transfigured.

Calvary. *See* Jerusalem.

Capernaum (*Khan Minyeh*, or *Tell Hum*) was a Roman settlement near the Sea of Galilee, the exact site of which is not definitely settled. On the lake-shore (Matt. 4¹³) near the plain of Gennesaret (compare John 6¹⁷, Matt. 14³⁴), and on a high road from Damascus to the Levant, it was a centre of Roman taxation and government in Galilee, and accordingly possessed a garrison (Matt. 8⁵), with centurions and other officers, as well as civil representatives of the Roman power, together with a large staff of tax-gatherers (Mark 2¹⁵) ; while the Jews possibly were too small and poor a colony to build their own synagogue (Luke 7⁵). Our Lord made it 'His own city' (Matt. 9¹) and 'home' (Mark 2¹) after His expulsion from Nazareth, and often taught in its synagogue. Here Levi sat at receipt of custom, and entertained our Lord and many publicans (tax-gatherers) at a feast. Here Christ healed among others Peter's mother-in-law (Mark 1³¹) ; the palsied man (Matt. 9²⁻⁷) ; a centurion's servant (Matt 8⁵) ; a man with an unclean spirit (Mark 1²³) ; called Peter, Andrew, and Levi (Mark 1¹⁶, 2¹⁴) ; sent Peter for the tribute-money ; raised Jairus's daughter ; most probably converted Mary, a native of the village of Magdala ; preached the sermon on the 'Bread of Life' (John 6⁵⁹), and that 'in the Plain' ; and foretold the overthrow of Capernaum from its proud and elevated position (Matt. 11²³,²⁴), noting the similarity of its site in the 'garden of Princes' to that of Sodom in the 'garden of the Lord' (Gen. 13¹⁰).

Chorazin (*Kerâzeh*), a city near Capernaum. The scene of some of the mighty works of our Lord, and denounced by Him for its unbelief (Matt. 11²¹; Luke 10¹³).

Colossae. An important city of Phrygia, in the Roman province Asia. It was the site of one of those early Christian churches to which Paul addressed his epistles. In the same valley of the river Lycus lay also the cities of Laodicea and Hierapolis.

Corinth. Capital of the province Achaia, and seat of the Governor (Acts 18¹²), with a large population both of Roman freedmen and of Jews, besides Greeks. Scene of the labours of Paul and Apollos. The home of an important church to which Paul addressed two epistles, one from Ephesus and one from Macedonia.

Damascus (now *Dimishk-esh-Shām* = Damascus of Syria, usually shortened to *esh-Sham*) is one of the most ancient cities in the world. It has existed as a city without intermission for about 4,000 years, and is still prosperous, with a population of about 300,000. It owes its continued prosperity to its unique position at the foot of the barren mountains that form the eastern termination of Anti-Libanus, and at the edge of the wide sandy desert that stretches for eight days' journey to the Euphrates. It is a paradise in a wilderness, the 'garden of the Lord' in the middle of wide-spread desolation. Its luxuriance is due to the river Abana, which bursts out from the mountains, forces a passage through the limestone rock, and distributes its waters over the alluvial deposit brought down by its boisterous torrent. It may have been visited by Abraham in his journey to Canaan; from it he obtained his steward (Gen. 15[2]), and to it he pursued the four kings who sacked Sodom. Coming under Aramaean influence by the twelfth century B. C., it was towards the end of the eleventh subjugated by David (2 Sam. 8[6]), after which, under the dynasty of the Hadads, and as chief of a confederacy of Aramaean states, its policy was to encourage internecine war between the rival kingdoms of Israel and Judah, siding sometimes with one, sometimes with the other, and it was alternately conquered and victorious, until the Assyrians triumphed over Aram and Israel (2 Kings 16[9]). It is called by Isaiah 'the head of Aram (or Syria)' (Isa. 7[8]). For a time it became inferior to Antioch; after the battle of Issus it passed into the hands of the Romans; in Paul's time it was held by Aretas the Arabian (2 Cor. 11[32]). It grew in magnificence, and when captured by Mohammedan Arabs (A. D. 634) was 'one of the first cities of the East'.

Decapolis—'*ten cities*' (Matt. 4[25])—a territory in Bashan and Gilead, extending north to Damascus, and south to Philadelphia, covered or affected by the power of a league of ten or more Greek cities, the earliest of which were colonized by veterans from the army of Alexander (whence its Greek name). The most important of the cities were Damascus, Gerasa, Gadara, Hippos, Pella, Philadelphia, and Scythopolis: the last-named the only one west of the Jordan. Each had its own suburban territory, and in some cases these suburban territories must have joined; but Pliny describes the whole as interpenetrated by the Jewish tetrarchies. The gods worshipped were those of Greece along with the Semitic Astarte; and each city had its own *Tuchē* or Civic Fortune.

Ephesus. An important commercial city of Asia Minor, and capital of the Roman province Asia. Celebrated for a splendid temple of Artemis or Diana (Acts 19[24]). It became the Christian centre of Asia through the preaching of Paul and his subsequent sojourn there of nearly three years (Acts 19[10]). To the metropolitan church there Paul addressed the letter known as the Epistle to the Ephesians, which was probably a circular letter to all the Asiatic churches.

Gadara (*Mkes*). The name both of a city, one of those comprised in Decapolis, six miles south-east of the Sea of Galilee on a height south of the Yarmuk, and of the surrounding district. The district was the scene of a notable miracle of our Lord (see **Gergesa**). R.V., Gadarenes, Matt. 8[28]; Gerasenes, Mark 5[1], Luke 8[26, 37].

Galatia. A Roman province in Asia Minor, where Paul laboured during his first, second and third missionary journeys (Acts 16[6] &c.). To the churches there Paul addressed his Epistle to the Galatians.

Gennesaret—'*garden of Princes*' (?). The fertile plain at the north-west corner of the Sea of Galilee, which is also called the Lake of Gennesaret (Luke 5[1]).

Gerasa. *See* **Gergesa**.

Gergesa. Said to have been a city on the east shore of the Sea of Galilee, whose site is attested by the modern ruins of Kersa. Given by Matthew (A.V.) as the site of the 'Gadarene miracle' (Matt. 8²⁸). If so, the city was included in the district of Gadara, as Gadara itself may have been in the larger district of Gerasa, an important city of Gilead, some twenty miles east of Jordan. But that Gerasa can hardly have been the one implied in the story of the miracle; we must look for it at Kersa. The name Gerasa, which is nearer to Kersa than Gergesa is, does not occur in the A.V. or R.V. (English version), but there is great variation in the Greek MSS. between the readings Gadarenes, Gergesenes, and Gerasenes. Probably the true reading is Gadarenes in Matthew; Gerasenes in Mark and Luke.

Gethsemane. *See* **Jerusalem.**

Gibeon (*el-Jib*), situated on an isolated hill about five miles north of Jerusalem, and possessing a fine fountain and fertile plain, was the chief city of the Hivites, and consequently of great strength. Falling into the hands of Joshua, it was allotted to Benjamin, and assigned to the priests. It was the site of the tabernacle under David and Solomon, which still contained the brazen altar of sacrifice, but not the ark, which was still in 'The city of David' (1 Kings 8¹, 1 Chron. 21²⁹, 2 Chron. 1⁴⁻⁶).

Gilead. 1. Mountainous and richly-wooded region east of Jordan, lying between Bashan on the north and Moab and Ammon on the south. It was divided in half by the Jabbok (Deut. 3¹², ¹³). In some passages the name seems used for the whole country east of Jordan occupied by Israel (Num. 32²⁹, 2 Sam. 24⁶, &c.)

2. Mount Gilead (Judges 7³) is evidently a mountain west of Jordan, probably Gilboa. In Gen. 31²¹, ²³, ²⁵ Mount Gilead or The Mountain of Gilead is either the whole range or some conspicuous peak upon it.

3. In the received text of Hosea 6⁸, 12¹¹ ⁽¹²⁾ Gilead appears as if the name of a city. But the reading is uncertain; in 6⁸ some Greek texts read Gilgal.

Gilgal, always with article, The Gilgal = The Circle (of sacred stones). 1. Important as being the first camping-place of the Israelites after crossing the Jordan (Joshua 4¹⁹, 9⁶). The site has recently been identified hardly two miles south-east of Jericho. See also 1 Sam. 10⁸, 11¹⁴, 15¹²ff.

2. The residence of Elisha and site of a School of Prophets (2 Kings 2¹, 4³⁸). Either *Jiljiliyeh*, seven miles north of Bethel, or more probably *Juleijil*, two and a half miles east of Shechem (Deut. 11³⁰).

Golgotha. *See* **Jerusalem.**

Gomorrah. One of the five 'Cities of the Plain', four of which were destroyed by fire and brimstone. There is little doubt that these cities stood in the Jordan Valley, immediately north of the Dead Sea, but, with one exception, all traces of them have disappeared. *See* **Zoar.**

Goshen. 1. Fertile district in Egypt, immediately to the east of the ancient delta of the Nile, and west of the south section of the Suez Canal. At one time it was irrigated by a canal from the Nile to Crocodile Lake. It was here that Jacob and his descendants settled until the Exodus (Gen. 45¹⁰).

2. (Joshua 10⁴¹, 11¹⁶.) District in Southern Palestine, not identified.

3. (Joshua 15⁵¹.) Town in the highlands of Judah.

Hebron. One of the most ancient cities of the world, its foundation being nearly contemporary with that of Damascus. Some have held that its other name, KIRJATH-ARBA (*the city of four*), implies that it consisted of four villages, but the name may record rather a confederation of tribes or chiefs. It is situated on a cluster of heights about nineteen miles south-west of Jerusalem.

Sarah died here, and was buried in the cave of Machpelah, also the burying-place of Abraham, Isaac, Rebekah, Leah, and Jacob. It became the inheritance of Caleb (Joshua 14[13]), and was a Levitical city and a city of Refuge (Joshua 21[13]). David made Hebron his first capital, and here received from the heads of the ten tribes the offer of the kingdom (2 Sam. 2[1]). It is now called *El-Khalil*, i. e. the city of 'the Friend'.

Hinnom, Valley of. *See* **Jerusalem.**

Jericho is distant some fifteen miles from Jerusalem, to the north-east, in the deep valley of the Jordan, but nearly five miles from the river itself. It was the first acquisition of Joshua, miraculously delivered into his hands, and burnt by him at God's command (Joshua 6). The curse imprecated on any one who should rebuild it fell upon Hiel the Beth-elite in the time of Ahab, 500 years later (1 Kings 16[34]).

The Jericho of later times was probably a little south of the site of the old city. Given by Antony to Cleopatra, it was rented of her by Herod the Great, who afterwards built a palace there, in which he died. Jericho was visited by our Lord, and was the scene of the healing of Bartimaeus, and the conversion of Zacchaeus (Mark 10[46-52], Luke 19[1-10]).

Jerusalem (derivation uncertain ; *possession* or *foundation of peace*, or *hearth of peace* = *inviolate hearth*, or *abiding peace*, or *He* (a deity) *casts a perfect lot*).

(*a*) Position. The city stands just over the watershed between the Mediterranean and the Dead Sea, about thirty-two miles from the sea and eighteen and a half from the Jordan, thus facing the desert and the sirocco, but under the influence of the western damp winds and rains. Its natural position is one of great strength. On the west and south is the deep gorge of *Hinnom* ; on the east that of the *Kidron* (or *Valley of Jehoshaphat*) : these unite at the south-east angle of the enclosed ridge, thus isolating the city on three of its sides. The ridge itself is cleft from north to south by the valley of the *Tyropoeon*, rising gradually from the south to the level of the plateau and dividing the site of the city into two hills, of which according to the older opinion Șion was that on the west and *Moriah* on the east ; but recent investigation and argument have proved that Șion, called after David's capture of it 'the city of David' or, more properly ' David's-Burgh', was on the eastern hill between the Kidron and the Tyropoeon valleys (see Sir G. A. Smith, *Jerusalem*, vol. i, ch. vi). Of these the western is the higher, reaching an elevation of 2,550 feet above the sea, and Șion the more precipitous. Further, the former was divided by a shallow lateral depression into two, which may be called the south-west and the north-west hills respectively ; while the eastern hill called also Ophel (or *swelling*) and lying above Gihon, the one fountain of the site, was separated on the north by a depression from the part of the city's later site called Bezetha. The Akra of later times was probably according to Josephus on the east hill, south of the Temple area. On Șion David offered the expiatory sacrifice to stay the destroying angel (2 Sam. 24[25]), and there Solomon built the Temple (2 Chron. 3[1]).

(*b*) History. The identification of Jerusalem with the Salem of which Melchizedek was king (Gen. 14[18]) is uncertain. In the Amarna letters (*c.* 1400 B.C.) the city is mentioned under the name Urusalim, as a distinct principality, the prince of which is called Abdi-hiba. In the Book of Judges the city appears as the stronghold of the Jebusites, resisting all assaults of the Israelites. The citadel of Șion remained unconquered till captured by David (1 Chron. 11[4-9]). Henceforth Jerusalem was the capital and the centre of the Jewish national life, though the small dimensions of the city prevented it from being much more than the seat of government. David built a wall round it 'from *Millo* and inward' (2 Sam. 5⁹), Millo, meaning *filling*, being either the citadel itself or some rampart upon it, and by transferring the Ark to Șion made this the great sanctuary of the nation. Solomon surrounded the city with a fortified wall, and built himself a palace and the Temple on Șion. Part of the wall was broken down by Jehoash, but rebuilt by Uzziah and Jotham, while Hezekiah and Manasseh seem to have added to it. The city and Temple were destroyed by Nebuchadrezzar (586 B.C.), and restored under Ezra and Nehemiah. The subsequent fortunes of Jerusalem cannot here be detailed. Many troubles befell the city, especially during the Maccabaean period. In 63 B.C. it was taken by the Romans, and again by Herod and the Romans 37 B.C. Herod rebuilt the Temple with great magnificence, and enclosed the city by restoring a second and outer wall of uncertain date. A third wall was built by Agrippa subsequently to the times of our Lord, to enclose Bezetha, the northern suburb of the city. In A.D. 70 Jerusalem was finally taken and destroyed by the Romans under Titus.

(c) TOPOGRAPHY. It must be remembered that the modern city is built on the debris of the earlier city, which in some places is 40 to 50 feet deep ; hence some of the sites can only be doubtfully identified, while some are quite unknown. Not a little has been done, however, by recent excavations.

Calvary, see *Golgotha*.

Gethsemane, the scene of our Lord's agony, was across the brook Kidron (John 18¹, R.V.), and probably at the foot of the Mount of Olives.

Golgotha, 'the place where Jesus was crucified', was called 'the place of a skull', apparently on account of its peculiar resemblance to a skull ; it was ' without the gate ', i. e. outside the walls of Jerusalem, 'nigh to the city' (John 19¹⁷⁻²⁰, Heb. 13¹²). There is no evidence that the spot was known in the early centuries of the Christian era, Jerusalem after its destruction by Titus (A.D. 70) remaining for many years desolate and uninhabited by Jew or Christian. In the time of Constantine the place now occupied by the Church of the Holy Sepulchre was suggested, it is said, by his mother, the Empress Helena (or by Macarius, according to Eusebius), as the site of Calvary. Josephus writes (*Wars*, v.4. 2) : 'The second wall took its beginning from that gate which they call "Gennath", which belonged to the first wall ; it only encompassed the northern quarter of the city, and reached as far as the tower Antonia.' In 1885 the south-west portion of this wall was discovered and examined to the extent of 120 feet in length, where the excavations ceased ; it was about 8 feet thick, constructed with stones ' of the same size and character in every way as the largest of the stones in the so-called Tower of David opposite' (Merrill). Until the remainder of this wall is traced its course cannot be shown with certainty, and therefore the site of Golgotha cannot be determined, though the position of the Church of the Holy Sepulchre remains a possible candidate for it.

About 250 yards west of the Damascus Gate there is a remarkable hill of rock, in outline resembling a skull ; this place is regarded by Dr. Chaplin, Major Conder, Professor Hull, and many other authorities as the most fitting site for Calvary ; near it are rock-cut Jewish tombs, one of these constructed for a round stone to be rolled before the opening (Matt. 27⁶⁰) ; but till the course of the second wall is established, we cannot be sure of this suggestion.

Pool of Bethesda has been identified with a twin-pool discovered in 1888, about 160 yards north-west of St. Stephen's Gate, but the balance of the evidence available refers it to the Virgin's Spring, the ancient Gihon.

Pool of Siloam, at the southern extremity of the Tyropoeon Valley. Its waters still issue from a subterranean rock-hewn conduit starting from Gihon, and flow out as in the old description (Isa. 8⁶).

The Valley of Hinnom (Neh. 11³⁰), or, more fully, the Valley of the Sons of Hinnom (Joshua 15⁸). The Hebrew name is *Gê-hinnôm*, Aram. *Gehinnam*; hence Gehenna (Matt. 5²², R.V., &c.).

This valley was the scene of the idolatrous worship of a god named by the Hebrew text Molek, but there are grounds for believing that this was a divine title Melek = King, and applied by the superstition of the time, inspired by a literal interpretation of Exod. 13¹², to the God of Israel. In the religious reforms of Josiah the worship was abolished, and the valley desecrated for ever (2 Kings 23¹⁰). Henceforth the Jews used it as a place into which they cast all manner of refuse and the bodies of animals and criminals. To prevent infection great fires were kept always burning (the Gehenna of fire, R.V.), and the place became the type and symbol of the place of future punishment.

Topheth, corrupted from Tephath = *a fireplace*, was the name of a place in the Valley of Hinnom, used in a similar symbolical sense to Gehenna.

The TEMPLE was built on the crown of Șion, the eastern hill, 'the threshing-floor of Ornan', by Divine appointment (2 Chron. 3¹). The Sanctuary would seem to have stood on the summit of the rock, in which graduated platforms were constructed, forming the courts of the Jews and of the women. The *Naos* was small (60 by 20 cubits), and was divided into the Holy of Holies and Holy Place (i. e. a chancel and nave), the former used once a year, the latter occupied only by the priests performing daily service. In the former was the ark ; in the latter the altar of incense (in the centre of the further end), with the table of shewbread on one side and the golden candlestick on the other. These two parts were separated by a veil, which is generally supposed to have been the one rent at the crucifixion. Surrounding the Sanctuary, but on a lower platform, was the Court of the Gentiles, beyond which strangers were not allowed to pass (Acts 21²⁸). Solomon finished his Temple, about 1000 B.C. ; it was destroyed, 585 B.C. ; rebuilt under Ezra and Nehemiah, 515 B.C. ; polluted by Antiochus, 167 B.C. ; its restoration commenced by Herod, 17 B.C. ; finished A. D. 29 ; again destroyed by Titus A. D. 70.

Joppa (*Jaffa, Yâfa*), the seaport of Judaea, was allotted to Dan (Joshua 19⁴⁶). Here the timber from Lebanon for building Solomon's Temple was landed (2 Chron. 2¹⁶), and again for rebuilding it (Ezra 3⁷), From it Jonah embarked when he fled to Tarshish ; here Peter restored Dorcas to life, saw his vision, and received the messengers of Cornelius.

Kadesh, or Kadesh-barnea, was ' in the wildernesso of Zin ' (Num. 27¹⁴, Deut. 32⁵¹), which ran 'along by the *of sied Edom*' (Num. 34⁸˒⁴, Joshua 15¹⁻³). According to Num. 20¹⁶, and Josephus, *Ant.* 4. 4, 5, it was in the '*border*' of Edom, i. e. of Mount Seir—the rugged mountain range extending from Moab on the north to Elath on the south ; see Deut. 1¹ ; 2⁸, R.V., where the ' Arabah ' (west of Mount Seir) is mentioned.

Dr. Trumbull, in his work ' Kadesh-barnea ', has offered strong reasons for identifying that city with a place now called 'Ain *Kadis*, situate about thirty-five miles west of the Arabah or forty-five miles west of the foot of the range of Mount Seir. Dr. Trumbull's view has been adopted by the majority of Biblical scholars, and may now be accepted as substantiated.

Laodicea. An important city of Asia Minor on the river Lycus. The seat of one of the ' Seven Churches of Asia ' (Rev. 3¹⁴).

Macedonia. A Roman province lying to the north of Achaia, extending from the Aegean to the Adriatic. The first country in Europe which received the Gospel, when visited by Paul and his companions (Acts 16⁹⁻¹², 18⁵˒⁶).

Nazareth. There is a plateau on the cluster of hills which form the northern wall of the Plain of Esdraëlon. Near it there is what appears to be the margin of an extinct volcano, on the sides of whose crater the village of Nazareth still clings with its houses tier above tier. It is now clear that Nazareth was a city of more importance than was formerly supposed, lying as it did near many roads from the Jordan Valley and Eastern Palestine to the coast of the Mediterranean. It was the home of our Lord for eight and twenty years (Luke 2⁴, ³⁹, ⁵¹). His familiar title of 'the Nazoraean' or 'Nazaraean' was probably a term of contempt; its exact meaning is uncertain. Its application to Him derived special force from His early connexion with Nazareth, and the play upon the similarity of the words (cf. Matt. 2²³).

Nineveh. The capital of Assyria. Built (according to Hebrew tradition) on the river Tigris by Nimrod (Gen. 10¹¹). Visited by the prophet Jonah, when the population was so great that the number of children alone was computed to be 120,000 (Jonah 4¹¹).

Philippi. A city of Macedonia, where St. Paul first preached the Gospel in Europe; where Lydia and the jailer were converted (Acts 16¹²⁻⁴⁰); and which became the seat of a Christian church addressed by the Apostle in one of his Epistles.

Ptolemais (Acts 21⁷). Same as Accho.

Rome. The capital of Italy and the Roman Empire, situated on the Tiber, fifteen miles from its mouth. It was the residence of many Jews (Acts 2¹⁰, 18²) and of many Christians, whom St. Paul was anxious to visit (Acts 19²¹), and to whom he wrote an Epistle. It was the scene of his first and second imprisonment, and of his martyrdom.

Samaria, the name of a city and a province. The city was built by Omri, King of Israel, who made it his capital instead of Tirzah (1 Kings 16²⁴). Henceforth the northern kingdom itself was known as Samaria. The city stood on the hill of Shemer, five and a half miles north-west of Shechem. It was occupied by the Syrians (i.e. the Aramaeans, 1 Kings 20³⁴), taken (722 B. C.) by the Assyrians, and rebuilt by Herod the Great.

Selah (or Sela). Probably Petra (2 Kings 14⁷, Isa. 16¹). The ancient capital of Arabia, founded by descendants of Esau. It occupies the sides of a deep valley and its branches, in the heart of Mount Seir. It was captured and destroyed by the followers of Muhammed. The temples, palaces, and tombs are hewn out of the sandstone rock, and are in a remarkable state of preservation. It was formerly the junction from which the incense-carriers' route out of Arabia divided into a branch north to Damascus and another west to Gaza.

Shechem (*Nablûs*), on the side of Gerizim, was the first spot on which Abraham built an altar (Gen. 12⁶, ⁷); hence it is the most ancient sacred place in Hebrew history. This altar Jacob rescued from the Amorites (Gen. 48²²), and rebuilt in the parcel of land he bought of the children of Hamor (Gen. 33¹⁸⁻²⁰), which became the burial place of the Patriarchs (Acts 7¹⁶). It was the scene of the slaughter of the Shechemites by Simeon and Levi (Gen. 34²⁵). At Shechem Joshua assembled the Israelites to offer sacrifice, and to read out the blessings (from Gerizim) and curses (from Ebal) of the Law, immediately on entering the Promised Land; and here again he assembled them to renew the covenant before he died, when he set up a pillar as a witness (Joshua 24²⁶). At this pillar Abimelech was made king, and Rehoboam met the heads of tribes who sought redress. Here the ten tribes revolted, and made Jeroboam their king. Its site is still known as 'The Pillar'. The well of Jacob, where our Lord conversed with the Samaritan woman (John 4), was nearer to *Askar* than to SHECHEM, and is hence called SYCHAR. Shechem was then the chief city of the Samaritan sect, a remnant of whom still reside there. A mile distant to the east is Joseph's tomb, and somewhat further is Juleijil, the ancient Gilgal (q. v.).

Shiloh lies a little off the road, on a knoll rising out of a secluded dell, 'on the north side of Beth-el, on the east side of the highway that goeth up from Beth-el to Shechem, and on the south of Lebonah' (Judges 21¹⁹). Here, according to Jewish tradition, Joshua had set up the tabernacle, made the allotment of Canaan to the tribes, and dismissed them to their possessions with his benediction. This represents the effort of later writers to connect traditional events of early history with a place which had certainly become, after the Hebrew invasion, one of the first great Hebrew sanctuaries. A built temple stood there from early days (1 Sam. 3³), in which the ark was kept; and at this place a tradition of image-less worship persisted, even when Israel had in general accustomed itself to the use of heathen emblems in its worship of Yahweh. Here Eli lived and died, Samuel ministered before the Lord, and an annual festival was held in honour of the ark (Judges 21¹⁹⁻²⁴). After the capture of the ark by the Philistines, Shiloh declined; but Ahijah prophesied there (1 Kings 14¹⁻¹⁷). Its destruction was made a warning to Jerusalem (Jer. 7¹²⁻¹⁴, 26⁶).

Syria. This Greek form is probably derived from the Babylonian *Suri*, the designation of an uncertain extent of territory which included first Mesopotamia, and then also the region south and west of the Euphrates with part of Asia Minor. From the middle of the second millennium B.C. it was chiefly populated by Aramaean peoples. The Greek translators of the Old Testament (followed by our English versions) use the form Syria and Syrians to render the Hebrew *Aram*.

Thessalonica. A large and important city of Macedonia. It was visited by St. Paul on his second missionary journey, and was the seat of a Christian church, to which he addressed two Epistles.

Tiberias (*Tubariya*). A town on the west shore of the Sea of Galilee founded by Herod Antipas about A.D. 22 in honour of the emperor. It gave its name to the sea (John 6¹, 21¹), and still retains traces of its ancient grandeur; on account of its pagan character it seems to have been avoided by Jesus.

Tirzah—'*pleasantness*', the second capital of Israel, lies eleven and a half miles to the north-east of Shechem (the first capital), and is beautifully situated (Song of Sol. 6⁴). It was originally the seat of a Canaanitish king (Joshua 12²⁴). Here Zimri murdered Elah; here also he burnt his own palace over his head when the city was taken by Omri (1 Kings 16¹⁰, ¹⁸).

Tyre (*Tsor*)—'*the rock*'. An ancient Phoenician city. Its marvellous wealth and commerce are described by Ezekiel (27), and its destruction by Nebuchadrezzar foretold (Ezek. 26⁷), which happened after thirteen years' siege. It was rebuilt on an island rock, but again stormed by Alexander, who in order to reach it built a mole that, widened by deposits of sand, still connects it with the mainland. David and Solomon made peace with Hiram, its king (2 Sam. 5¹¹, 1 Kings 5). Our Lord once visited this neighbourhood (Matt. 15²¹), and St. Paul landed at its port (Acts 21³).

Zidon (*Saïda*)—'*fishing*', the mother city of Phoenicia (Isa. 23¹²) (hence *Sidonians* = Phoenicians generally), is said to take its name from a son of Canaan; but was more probably so called from the primary occupation of its Canaanite builders, *Sidon* being the Greek spelling of the Syriac *Saïda*. It is one of the oldest cities in the world, and was already famous in Joshua's time (19²⁸). Its architects were the best in Syria (1 Kings 5). Ahab married

242

the daughter of Ethbaal, its king. It was captured by Shalmaneser, 720 B. C., and again by the Persians, 350 B. C. Paul touched there on his voyage to Rome (Acts 27⁵). Eight miles south-west of Zidon stood Zarephath, where Elijah was received by the widow (1 Kings 17⁹).

Zoar. The only one of the five 'Cities of the Plain' which escaped the visitation that destroyed the others (Gen. 13¹⁰, 19²²). Its site has probably been identified about seven miles to the north-east of the Dead Sea, where ruins have been noted by recent travellers.

LEVITICAL CITIES (Joshua 21¹³⁻³⁹).

Hebron, Libnah, Jattir, Eshtemoa, Holon, Debir, Ain, Juttah, Beth-shemesh (*Judah* and *Simeon*); **Gibeon, Geba, Anathoth, Almon or Allemeth** (*Benjamin*); **Shechem, Gezer, Kibzaim, Beth-horon** (*Ephraim*); **Eltekeh or Elteke, Gibbethon, Aijalon, Gath-rimmon** (*Dan*); **Tanach or Taanach, Gath-rimmon, Golan, Be-eshterah** (*Manasseh*); **Kishon or Kishion, Dabareh or Daberath, Jarmuth, Engannim** (*Issachar*); **Mishal, Abdon, Helkath, Rehob** (*Asher*); **Kedesh, Hammoth-dor, Kartan** (*Naphtali*); **Jokneam, Kartah, Dimnah, Nahalal** (*Zebulun*); **Bezer, Jahazah or Jahaz, Kedemoth, Mephaath** (*Reuben*); **Ramoth-Gilead, Mahanaim, Heshbon, Jazer** (*Gad*).

CITIES OF REFUGE (Joshua 21⁷⁻³⁹).

HEBRON (in *Judah*), SHECHEM (in *Ephraim*), KEDESH (in *Naphtali*), BEZER (in *Reuben*), GOLAN (in *Manasseh*), RAMOTH (in *Gad*).

XLI. MOUNTAINS OF SCRIPTURE

NAME.	REFERENCES.	ASSOCIATIONS.
ABARIM . . .	Num. 33. 47, 48 . .	Balaam's blessing; the name means the *mountains* or *territories* across i. e. Jordan.
ARARAT . . .	Gen. 8. 4	The region where Noah's ark rested.
BASHAN . . .	Deut. 3. 13 . . .	Part of Og's territory; famous for its oaks and wild cattle.
CARMEL . . .	1 Kings 18. 19 . .	Elijah's sacrifice (distinct from the southern town called Carmel), see above, p. 224.
EBAL	Deut. 27. 4 . . . Josh. 8. 32, 33.	Cursing of law-breakers; site of the stones inscribed with the Law.
GERIZIM . . .	John 4. 20 . . .	Blessing of the keepers of the Law; site of Samaritan temple.
GILBOA . . .	1 Sam. 31. 8 . .	Scene of Saul's death.
GILEAD . . .	Gen. 31. 48 . . .	Scene of the covenant between Laban and Jacob.
HERMON . . .	Deut. 4. 48 . . .	The conjectured site of the Transfiguration; also called *Sirion* and *Senir* (Deut. 3. 9).
HOR	Num. 20. 27, 28 . .	Scene of Aaron's death. Now Jebel Haroûn (*Aaron's mount*).
„	Num. 34. 7 . . .	The boundary of the Land of Israel towards the north; possibly Hermon, but the reading is doubtful.
HOREB* . . .	Ex. 3. 1 . . . . Deut. 5. 2. 1 Kings 19. 8.	Scene of burning bush; giving of the Law; Elijah's vision.
LEBANON . . .	2 Chron. 2, 8–10 .	Source of timber for Solomon's Temple.
MORIAH . . .	2 Chron. 3. 1 . . .	Place of Abraham's intended sacrifice (Gen. 22. 2).
NEBO	Deut. 34. 1 . . .	The range from one of whose headlands (PISGAH) Moses saw the Promised Land. Those headlands form the western edge of the Moabite plateau above the Jordan. *The headland* (not top) *of the Pisgah* (Deut. 3. 27, &c.) is probably the promontory south of the Wady Uyûn Mûsa which still bears the name Neba.
OLIVET . . .	2 Sam. 15. 30 . . Matt. 24. 3. Acts 1. 9–12.	Scene of David's flight from Absalom; of Christ's weeping over Jerusalem; and of His Ascension.
SEIR	Gen. 32. 3 ; 36. 8 . Deut. 2. 22.	A mountain range practically coextensive with Edom; taken by Esau from the Horites. But the territory of Edom extended across the Arabah at the foot of the range and the name *Seir* follows it (Deut. 1. 44).
SINAI	Ex. 19. 1–11 . . .	In Arabia; scene of Israelite encampment for nearly a year, and of giving of the Law. See Horeb.
TABOR . . .	Judg. 4. 14 . . . Mark 9. 2.	Scene of Barak's camp, and, possibly, but not probably, of Christ's transfiguration.
ZION (spelt SION in N. T.)	2 Sam. 5. 7 . . .	Stronghold of Jebusites, stormed by Joab; site of David's palace and the Temple; see above on Jerusalem.

* Probably Horeb is the name of the district, Sinai of the mountain, or else the difference is due to the authors of different documents from which the Old Testament has been compiled.

XLII. RIVERS, LAKES, ETC. OF SCRIPTURE

NB.—R. = *River*; L. = *Lake*; B. = *Brook*; S. = *Sea*; W. = *Waters*.

NAME.	SITUATION.	REFERENCES.	ASSOCIATIONS.	MODERN NAME.
ABANA, R. . . (R.V. ABANAH or AMANAH.)	Damascus, *Syria.*	2 Kings 5. 12 .	Commended by Naaman. It is one of the chief channels of the Bărădâ, which rises in the range of Anti-Libanus, flows through fertile plains, and passes through Damascus to the lakes about eighteen miles further east, where it is absorbed.	Bărădâ .
ARNON, R. . .	E. of Salt Sea .	Num. 21. 13–15.	Boundary of Moab and the Amorites; scene of a victory of the Israelites in their passage to the Promised Land; always a political as well as a physical frontier.	El-Mojib.
CHEBAR, R. . .	Chaldaea . . .	Ezek. 1. 1, 3. .	Scene of Ezekiel's visions	Nahr Malcha ?
CHERITH, B. . .	'Before Jordan'; probably the Wady Kell.	1 Kings 17. 5 .	Elijah fed by ravens.	
CHINNERETH, S. or, CHINNEROTH . *Galilee, S.* . . *Gennesaret, L.* *Tiberias, S.*	Jordan Valley.	Num. 34. 11 . Josh. 11. 2. Matt. 15. 29. Luke 5. 1. John 6. 1.	Its name varied at different times, being generally taken from some important city on its shore, or from the likeness of its shape to a harp. It was the scene of most of our Lord's ministerial life in Galilee.	Bahr Tuba-riyeh.
EGYPT, River of. (R.V. Brook.) " Stream of.	. . . .	Num. 34. 5 . 1 Kings 8. 65. Is. 27. 12 . .	SW. boundary of Promised Land.	El-Arish. El-Arish.
EUPHRATES, R. .	Mesopotamia.	Gen. 2. 14..	The river on which Babylon was built; called in R.V. 'the river' (1 Kings 4. 21). NE. boundary of Solomon's alleged dominions. One boundary of Eden.	Eu-phrates.
GIHON, R. . . .	Eden	Gen. 2. 13 . .	A boundary of Eden.	
GREAT SEA . .	. . . . . .	Ezek. 47. 15, 19, 20.	. . . .	Mediter-ranean.
HIDDEKEL, R. .	Eden	Gen. 2. 14 . .	A boundary of Eden	Tigris, or Dijlat.
JABBOK, R. . .	Gilead . . .	Gen. 32. 22 . .	Boundary between the two halves of Gilead ; scene of Jacob's wrestling in prayer.	Zerka.
JORDAN, R. . .	The great river of Palestine .	2 Kings 5. 10 .		Esh-Sheriah el Kebir, 'the great watering-place', which the name Jordan also possibly means.
KANAH, R. . . (R.V. Brook.)	Palestine . .	Josh. 16. 8 . .	Border of inheritance of Ephraim and Manasseh.	
KIDRON, B. . .	Judaea . . .	2 Sam. 15. 23 John 18. 1.	Scene of Adonijah's rebellion. Crossed by Christ and His apostles on the night of betrayal.	Wady en-Nâr.
KISHON, R. . .	Palestine . .	Judg. 4. 7; 5. 21; 1 Kings 18. 40.	Scene of Sisera's defeat, and of the slaughter of the prophets of Baal.	Nahr Mu-kutta.
MEROM, W. . .	Upper Jordan (?)	Josh. 11. 5 . .	Scene of Joshua's victory over several kings.	Huleh is usually, but wrongly, identified with it.
PHARPAR, R. .	Damascus, *Syria.*	2 Kings 5. 12 .	Praised by Naaman	Taura, or Nahr el-Awaj ?
PISON, R. . . .	Eden	Gen. 2. 11. .	A boundary of Eden.	
SALT SEA . .	Palestine, S. of the Jordan.	Gen. 14. 3 . .	Geologists and the surveyors of the P. E. F. (Prof. Hull, Sir Charles Wilson, Major Conder and others) are of opinion that the Cities of the Plain were situated at the north end of the Salt Sea.	Dead Sea, or Bahr Lût.
Sea of the Ara-bah or Plain. *East Sea.* *The Sea.*	. . . .	Deut. 4. 49. Joel 2. 20. Ezek. 47. 8.		
ZARED, B. . .	. . . . . .	Num. 21. 12 . .	Boundary between Edom and Moab.	Probably the Wady es-Sul-tani.

244

XLIII. GEOLOGY AND MINERALOGY OF BIBLE LANDS

1. **The Sinaitic Mountains**, which reach, in the case of Jebel Katharina, an elevation of 8,551 feet,* are formed of granitic, gneissic, and schistose rocks, traversed by numerous ridges and dykes of felstone-porphyry, andesite, diorite, and basalt ; the latter being newer than (and therefore intersecting) the former. Mount Sinai (Jebel Mûsa) reaches an elevation of 7,450 feet, and is formed of granitoid gneiss, coarse below and fine at the top of the mountain. The crystalline rocks of this group are probably amongst the oldest in the world, and referable to the Archaean age.

2. **Towards the North** these are overlain by Carboniferous sandstone and limestone, containing at Wâdy Nasb numerous fossils such as corals, crinoids, and brachiopods of Lower Carboniferous age. Above these come the representatives of the Nubian sandstone succeeded by white limestones and marls with bands of flint referable to the Cretaceous age. These limestones, with others of the Eocene period generally known as 'Nummulite Limestone', form a continuous escarpment overlooking the Isthmus of Suez on the west and ranging eastwards along the southern margin of the plateau of Badiet-et-Tîh into the valley of the Arabah. This plateau, which is 170 miles across between Port Said and Akabah, is remarkably sterile and waterless, but contains several high limestone ridges and deep valleys which doubtless were once river-channels, but are now dry. Towards the north it merges into the rugged tableland of southern Judaea and stretches through western Palestine to the Lebanon, where the Lower Cretaceous beds emerge.

3. **The Maritime Plain** extending from the Isthmus of Suez by Gaza and Jaffa to the base of Mount Carmel, is formed of yellow sandstone and beds of calcareous sand and gravel with species of shells such as *Pectunculus violascens*, *Purpura hemastoma*, now inhabiting the Mediterranean. This formation indicates that the coast has been raised considerably in recent (or Pleistocene) times. Throughout nearly its whole length the coast is bounded by enormous sand-dunes which, impelled by the prevalent westerly winds, are constantly advancing inwards, and are supposed to have entombed ancient Gaza and other towns of Philistia. Further inland the plain is formed of calcareous sandstone, probably of Upper Eocene age ; and from beneath this formation rises the

* Another calculation gives 8,619.

tableland of western Palestine, formed of Eocene and Cretaceous limestones and marls, penetrated by deep valleys, along the sides of which the strata crop out in terraces of naked rock, or only covered by a thin coating of soil. This tableland lies along the line of an anti-clinal axis, ranging northward from the desert of Eṭ-Ṭîh by Hebron, Jerusalem, Shechem and Nazareth, to the valley of the Leontes, the strata dipping west and east on either side of this geological saddle. Towards the edge of the Jordan valley the beds are often much contorted and broken, and have evidently been subjected to great disturbance and lateral thrusting.

4. The Valley of the Jordan and the depression of the Arabah valley, stretching from the Dead Sea along the flanks of the mountains of Moab and Edom to the Gulf of Akabah, is now known to coincide with a great line of fracture and displacement (or a 'fault'), along which the strata have been relatively elevated on the east side and depressed on the west. Hence the strata are very different on each side of the valley; and from the eastern banks of the Dead Sea southwards the older crystalline rocks of the Sinaitic mountains are found again cropping out, surmounted by the Nubian sandstone, and this again by the Cretaceous limestones; but nowhere do the older rocks appear along the western side of the valley till we approach the head of the Gulf of Akabah. The rock-hewn city of Petra (Selah) is hewn out of Nubian sandstone. The bed of the Jordan-Arabah depression is formed of alluvium and ancient lake deposits, as the waters of the Dead Sea (now nearly 1,300 feet below the level of the Mediterranean) formerly rose to about the same level as that of the outer sea. These lake deposits form well-marked terraces on both sides of the valley; the most remarkable being at a level of about 600 feet above the surface of the Dead Sea. The deposits of salt rock overlain by marl which border the Dead Sea on the west at Jebel Usdum, and at El-Lissan (The Tongue), are representatives of the 600-feet terrace.

5. Jerusalem is built on a platform of limestone nearly horizontal in position, and is divided by Oscar Fraas into the following stages:—

1. Craie blanche (*Sénonien* D'Orb). 2. Étage supérieur des Hippurites ('Mizzi'). 3. Étage inférieur des Hippurites ('Meleki'). 4. Zone des *Ammonites rhotamargensis* (Turonien). The beds No. 2 ('Mizzi') afford the principal building stone, and consist of rose-coloured and yellow limestone and marble. No. 3 is of softer consistency, and in it the reservoirs, sepulchres, and caverns under the city have been excavated.

6. **Volcanic Rocks,** chiefly in the form of sheets and dykes of basalt, occur on the tableland of Moab, resting on the lime-stone plateau; but north and east of the Sea of Galilee in Haurân and Jaulân, the whole country is overspread by vast sheets of basaltic lava, while numerous extinct volcanoes rise above the surface. West of the Jordan these are again met with at Jebel Safed and Jebel Jish, an old crater now containing water and called Birket-el-Jish. To the west of the Lake of Tiberias occur several other volcanic masses, one of these, Kurn Hattin, being an old volcano, rising 1,178 feet above the sea, and sending forth a large stream of basaltic lava towards the Sea of Galilee. Volcanic rocks are also found on the plain of Jezreel. It is doubtful whether any of these volcanoes remained active into the human period. There are no extinct volcanoes among the Sinaitic mountains.*

(i) Mineral Substances.

Clay (Isa. 29[16]) ... Heb. (1) *Ḥômer*: Gk. πηλός.

A tenacious earth, like that so called by us, used for making bricks and earthenware, and documents (clay tablets); also in a natural state for the floors and ceilings of houses. It was less cohesive than ours, and accordingly for the former purpose was bound together by an admixture of straw before being baked.

—— (Isa. 41[25]) ... Heb. (2) *Ṭîṭ*: Gk. πηλός.

Ṭîṭ (*lit.* 'dirt') was, and still is, the common building material of the mud-houses of the peasantry of Palestine.

Dust (Gen. 3[14]; Isa. 47[1]) ... Heb. *ʿAphar*: Gk. γῆ.

ʿAphar, dry earth, or dust, also used in building (Lev. 14[41 f.]).

Earth (Gen. 1[22]) ... Heb. (1) *Eretz*: Gk. ἡ γῆ.

Eretz, the earth, or globe generally.

—— (Gen. 9[10]) ... Heb. (2) *Adâmah*: Gk. γῆ.

Adâmah, red earth, abundant in Philistia and South Judaea (about Beersheba).

Nitre (Jer. 2[22]) ... Heb. *Néther*: Gk. νίτρον: R.V. 'lye'.

This word probably indicates the common carbonate of soda, not the nitre of the moderns. *Borith* on the other hand is a vegetable alkali.

Salt (1 Chron. 18[12]) ... Heb. *Melaḥ*: Gk. ἅλς.

Salt is very abundant in the neighbourhood of the Dead Sea, the water

* For further information, consult Tristram's *Land of Israel*; Dawson's *Egypt and Syria*; Hull's *Geology of Arabia Petraea and Palestine* (Mem. Palest. Expl. Soc.); Hull's *Mount Seir*; Fraas' *Aus dem Orient.* M. Blanckenhorn in the *Zeitschrift des deutschen Palästina-Vereins,* xix. 1-64, xxviii. 75 ff., xxxv. 113 ff.; T. G. Bonney, *Geol. Mag.* for 1904, pp. 575-82; G. A. Smith, *Jerusalem,* i, chaps. 3, 4, and *Atlas to The Hist. Geogr. of the Holy Land,* No. 13.

of which is highly charged with it. A ridge of salt-rock runs into that sea, called *El-lisan*; another is found at Kashm Usdum, at the south end of the Dead Sea, and there are deposits at various points round all the coasts. But as Dead Sea salt is much mixed with earth, purer supplies were probably imported from a distance, just as to-day the villagers of Moab bring it from the salt-pans of Wady Sirhân in Arabia. Salt frequently enters into the symbolical acts and language of the Bible. Saltpits are referred to in Zeph. 2⁹; a city of Salt in Josh. 15⁶²; and the valley of Salt also in 2 Sam. 8¹³.

Sand (Prov. 27³; Jer. 5²²) ... Heb. *Ḥôl*: Gk. *ἄμμος*.

Sand abounds along the seaboard of Palestine, and is used to symbolize abundance, insecurity, extensiveness, and weight.

Slime (Gen. 11³) ... Heb. *Ḥêmâr*: Gk. *ἄσφαλτος*: R.V. Marg. 'bitumen'.

A kind of asphalt, whence the Dead Sea was called *Lacus Asphaltites*. The asphalt of the Dead Sea is found in certain valleys, notable *Wady Mahawat* and *Ain Jidi* (Engedi), which enter the Ghôr from the west.

Sulphur (Gen. 19²⁴; Ps. 11⁶) ... Heb. *Gophrith*: Gk. *θεῖον*.

Sulphur, or brimstone, is found in some of the valleys entering the Vale of Siddim, and in the plain of the Ghôr.

(ii) METALS.

Brass (Exod. 38⁸; 2 Kings 25¹³) ... Heb. *Nĕḥôsheth*: Gk. *χαλκός*.

Copper was well known to the Israelites and Egyptians before the Exodus. The latter had, for a long time previous to that event, obtained it from Arabia. It was also largely exported from Cyprus, whence its name; from the Lebanons, where a district at the foot of Hermon was called 'The Land of Nuchashi (2 Sam. 8⁸); and from Edom and North Arabia. In most passages *Nĕḥôsheth* is now thought to be bronze, of which many ancient specimens have been found in Assyria. The Egyptians and Israelites also were familiar with tin (which *see*), and could have made that alloy of the two called bronze possibly from a copper ore containing tin; but the Hebrew term is used indifferently for pure copper and its alloys. Being very hard and easily fusible, it is probable that bronze was the material of the 'brazen sea', the Temple columns, sacrificial 'forks', the brazen serpent, the 'mirrors' of the Hebrew women, and the 250 censers of the followers of Korah. In fact in early English 'brass' means 'bronze'. Gesenius and others, from the etymology, identify it with the 'burnished brass' (*ḳalal*) of Ezek. 1⁷. Others consider it to be an accidentally discovered alloy of copper and zinc, a light-coloured brass. A white alloy of copper and nickel was in use for coins in Septuagint times.

Gold (1 Kings 9²⁸) ... Heb. (1) *Zāhāb*: Gk. *χρυσίον*.

—— (Job 28¹⁷) ... Heb. (2) *Pâz*: Gk. *χρυσίον*: A.V. and R.V. 'fine gold'. *Pâz* is perhaps short for *Zāhāb mûphaz*, 'refined gold'.

—— (Job 22²⁴) ... Heb. (3) *Bétzer*: Gk. *Σωφίρ*: A.V. 'gold'; R.V. 'treasure', probably 'precious ore'.

—— (Ps. 68¹³) ... Heb. (4) *Ḥârûtz*: Gk. *χρυσίον*: A.V. and R.V. 'yellow gold'; archaic and poetical.

Metals

Gold (*contd.*) (Job 28¹⁵) . . . Heb. (5) *Ságúr*, perhaps 'closed' or 'sterling gold'.

—— (Job 28¹⁹) . . . Heb. (6) *Kéthem*: Gk. χρυσίον καθαρόν: A.V. and R.V. 'pure gold'; also poetical.

There are six different words used for 'gold' in the Old Testament, which show its use, and high estimation: (1) *Záháb* is its earliest and most common name, referring to its colour. (2) *Páz* is the native metal, as found. (3) *Bétzer* is gold-dust, and fragments of ore. (4) *Hárútz* is either 'dug out', or has reference to its 'lustre'. (5) *Ságúr* ('treasured'), and (6) *Kéthem* ('concealed'), show its high value. No indication of native gold has been found in Palestine, to which it was imported perhaps from Spain (Tarshish = Tartessus), but chiefly from Arabia, where were Ophir, Sheba, &c. Some modern Egyptologists maintain that gold was found in Egypt in ancient times, and believe that they have found some old worked-out mines of it beyond Assouan. Gold was used as a medium of exchange as early as Abram's time, like money, but was weighed, not counted, in the same manner as silver (*see* Gen. 23¹⁶).

Iron and **Steel** (Gen. 4²²; Deut. 8⁹) . . . Heb. *Barzel*: Gk. σίδηρος.

Recent discoveries show the very ancient existence of iron in Assyria, as also in Egypt under the Pharaohs. Iron ore was found in considerable quantities in Syria, in Canaanite times, and tools were made of iron extracted from the ore, especially goads, mattocks, files, and coulters, as also were spears and swords (1 Sam. 13²¹, ²²). Ancient sources of the ore have been found at Ikzim on Carmel and near Burme north of the Jabbok; Josephus mentions an 'Iron Mountain' running in length as far as Moab. It is doubtful whether the 'chariots of iron' of Jabin and the 'iron bed' of Og are to be taken literally; perhaps a reference to their great strength is intended, but in the latter case we should probably render 'basalt sarcophagus', basalt being still called iron by the peasants east of Jordan. So too in Amos 1³; the present threshing sledges having basalt teeth. 'Steel', in A.V. of Jer. 15¹², is an erroneous rendering for 'brass'; but steel is supposed to be meant by the 'northern iron' of that verse; the most famous makers in old times being the Chalybes, near the Black Sea; and Damascus steel has had a very long celebrity. In Nahum 2³, 'torches', the translation of *peládoth* (rendered as 'steel' both in Arabic and Syriac, and also in R.V.), is conjectured to be an error for 'scythes' on the wheels of war-chariots.

Lead (Exod. 15¹⁰) . . . Heb. *'Ophéreth*: Gk. μόλιβος.

Lead was known to the Hebrews; it was anciently used to purify silver, and in later times as a plummet or weight, and also for soldering metals. Writing tablets were made from it. It was found in the Sinaitic rocks before the time of Moses, and was one of the wares brought to the Tyrian market from Tarshish.

Silver (Gen. 23¹⁵) . . . Heb. *Késeph*: Gk. ἀργύριον.

Abram was 'rich in silver'. After 1600 B.C. it was largely imported into Egypt, and afterwards into Palestine, from Arabia. The Israelites possessed much gold and silver in the wilderness; of the former 'the calf' was made. Silver was used for all kinds of ornaments for the person and house, was stamped by David, and was very abundant in Solomon's time; and in the time of the Maccabees it was coined into money; hence *késeph* is a silver coin.

249

Tin (Num. 31²²) . . . Heb. *Bĕdîl*: Gk. μόλιβος, and κασσίτερος.

Tin was early known to the Hebrews, being one of the imports of Egypt from Spain, through Phoenician merchants, who also obtained it (as Herodotus and Strabo tell us) from Britain. It was a great commodity in the fair at Tyre. It was used for the preparation of bronze, its alloy with copper. The ancients did not always distinguish tin from lead.

XLIV. NOTES ON PRECIOUS STONES OF THE BIBLE

Cf. the three lists in Ex. 28¹⁷⁻²⁰, Ezek. 28¹³, Rev. 21¹⁹, ²⁰.

Adamant. Ezek. 3⁹. Perhaps corundum. Heb. *Shâmir* is also translated 'diamond' in A.V.

Agate. Is. 54¹²; spoken of as material for windows.

Amethyst. Gk. ἀμέθυστος, because thought to be a charm against drunkenness. Heb. *Aḫlâmah*, because the Jews supposed it to bring pleasant *dreams*.

Chalcedony. Perhaps a green stone, found near Chalcedon (Pliny). The use of the word for the modern stone is not found earlier than the fifteenth century.

Chrysolyte. Probably the yellow sapphire or jargoon.

Chrysoprasus. Possibly the plasma.

Diamond. Jer. 17¹. Heb. *Shâmir*, see Adamant, and Yahǎlom, perhaps onyx, alabaster, or jasper. The diamond could not be in the high priest's breast-plate, because the Hebrews knew no means of engraving upon it.

Jacinth. Probably the pale blue sapphire.

Jasper. Probably the plasma.

Ligure. Probably the yellow jargoon.

Onyx. Gen. 2¹². Onyx, turquoise, amazon-stone, or aquamarine.

Sapphire. Ex. 24¹⁰. The lapis lazuli.

Sardius, Sardine. Rev. 4³. The golden sard was the favourite for engraving.

Topaz. The peridot.

XLV. NOTES ON BOTANY OF THE BIBLE

Algum or **Almug.** Timber used in building the Temple (1 Kings 10¹¹, ¹², 2 Chron. 2⁸, 9¹⁰, ¹¹). (1) From Lebanon, (2) From Ophir; the latter was probably red sandal-wood.

Almond. Heb. *Shâḳed* = 'hasten' (see the play on the word in Jer. 1¹¹, ¹²), because the almond blossoms before the leaves come out.

Aloes or **Lign-Aloes.** (1) Ps. 45⁸, a spice. (2) Num. 24⁶, a vigorous native tree.

Anise. = dill. Matt. 23²³.

Apple. Probably apricot. S. of S. 2³, Joel 1¹².

Ash. A tree from which idols were made (Is. 44¹⁴). Probably the Aleppo pine.

Barley. Ruth 1²², Judg. 7¹³. Barley harvest in March or April.

Bay Tree. Ps. 37³⁵. Heb. *Ezraḥ* = 'a native'. Probably no particular species, but a tree in its native soil (so R.V.).

Bdellium. Gen. 2¹². A gum, or a precious stone.

Bramble, Briar, Thistle, Thorn. Various words, used generally.

Bulrush. (1) Ex. 2³, Job 8¹¹. Heb. *Gôme'* = 'papyrus'. (2) Is. 19⁷ *'Arôth* = 'meadows' (R.V.). (3) Job. 8¹¹. Gen. 41² *Aḫû* = 'reed-grass' (R.V.). (4)

Ex. 2³,⁵, Jonah 2⁵. *Sugh* = 'water weeds'. (5) Is. 9¹⁴, 19¹⁵. *Agmôn*, the common reed. (6) Gen. 41⁵,²². *Kâneh*, of any stem or shaft. Cf. Ex. 25³¹, Ezek. 40⁵.

Bush, Burning. Ex. 3²⁻⁴. Heb. *Sĕneh*, the thorny acacia of Arabia.

Camphire. *Henna*, used by the Arabs as a cosmetic. S. of S. 1¹⁴, 4¹³.

Cane, Sweet. Is. 43¹⁴, Jer. 6²⁰. Probably the calamus, a spice.

Caper. = Hyssop.

Cassia. Ex. 30²⁴, Ps. 45⁸. A spice plant.

Cedar. In the Pentateuch an aromatic juniper. Elsewhere the cedar of Lebanon.

Chesnut. Gen. 30³⁷. R.V. 'plane-tree'.

*CITRON. Lev. 23⁴⁰. A.V. 'boughs of goodly trees'. The citron is still used on the feast of Tabernacles.

Cockle. Job. 31⁴⁰. Probably an aroideous plant.

Corn. (1) Heb. *Dâgân*, general. Num. 18²⁷. (2) *Kâmah*, standing corn. Judg. 15⁵. (3) *Bar*, grain. Gen. 41⁴⁹. (4) *Shibbôleth*, an ear of corn. Ruth 2². (5) *Karmel*, early sprouts, Lev. 2¹⁴. (6) *'Abhûr*, corn a year old ; or, earthly produce opposed to heavenly food, i.e. manna. Josh. 5¹¹. (7) *Kâli*, parched corn, Josh. 5¹¹. (8) *Géres*, corn beaten out. Lev. 2¹⁶. (9) *'Omer*, sheaf or handful of corn stalks, Ruth 2⁷. (10) *Bĕlîl*, provender, Job. 24⁶. (11) *Shéber*, the same as (1), Gen. 42¹,²,³.

*COTTON. Esth. 1⁶. 'White and violet-coloured cotton', as R.V. marg.

Cypress. Is. 44¹⁴. R.V. 'holm-tree'.

Desire. Eccles. 12⁵. Perhaps the caper (q.v.), eaten as a stimulant to appetite, and ineffective to decrepit old age.

Elm. Hos. 4¹³, the terebinth. Heb. *elah*, elsewhere translated 'oak' or 'teil-tree'.

Fig. (1) Heb. *T^eénah*, the tree, Gen. 3⁷, Deut. 8⁸. (2) *Pag*, the unripened fig, S. of S. 2¹³. (3) *Bikkûrah*, the early fig, Hos. 9¹⁰. (4) *Dĕbîlah*, a cake of dried figs, 1 Sam. 25¹⁸.

Fir. Probably included pine, cypress, juniper.

Fitches. (1) Is. 28²⁵,²⁷. Heb. *Ketzah*, fennel flower. (3) Ezek. 4⁹. Heb. *Cussemeth*, spelt.

Flax, Heb. *Pishtah, Shêsh, Bad, Bûtz, Sâdîn, Eṭûn, Mikvah* (1 Kings 10²⁸), varieties of linen. But the meaning of *Mikvêh* is very doubtful.

Gall. A very bitter herb. Jer. 2¹⁵, Amos 6¹².

Gopher. Gen. 6¹⁴. Unknown.

Gourd. Jon. 4⁶⁻⁹, a climbing gourd. 2 Kings 4³⁹, the colocynth, as also 'vine of Sodom' in Deut. 32³².

Grass. (1) Heb. *Yérek*, any green herbage. Num. 22⁴. (2) *Déshe*, Gen. 1¹¹, green grass. (3) *Hâtzîr*, Is. 35⁷, fodder. In Palestine down-grass grew on the limestone-hills of Judaea, meadow-grass on the maritime plains, and rank herbage in the Jordan valley.

Grove. (1) Heb. *Ashêrah*, frequent ; supposed to be a wooden image of Astarte. (2) *Eshel* (Gen. 21³³), a tamarisk.

Hazel. Gen. 30³⁷. R.V. 'almond'.

Heath. Jer. 17⁶, 48⁶; dwarf juniper.

Hemlock. (1) A poisonous herb, Deut. 29¹⁸, Hos. 10⁴. (2) Heb. *La'anah* = 'wormwood', Amos 6¹².

Herb. Heb. *'Eseb, Orôth, Yârâk* (cultivated herbs, Prov. 15¹⁷, 2 Kings 4³⁹, 19²⁶), *Mĕrorim* (bitter herbs, Ex. 12⁸).

---

* Names in capital letters, with (*), do not occur in the A V., but the trees, plants, &c., are supposed to be indicated by the original text.

Husks. Luke 15[16].

*LADANUM. Gen. 37[25], 43[11]. A resinous gum. Not 'myrrh', as A.V.

Lily. Sometimes a true lily, sometimes any striking indigenous flower.

Mallow. Job 30[4]. R.V. 'salt-wort'.

Mandrake. Gen. 30[14]. Supposed to be efficacious in love incantations.

Manna. Heb. *Mān hu* = what is it? Not what is now called 'manna'.

Mulberry. The poplar, 2 Sam. 5[23], Luke 17[6]. The 'sycamine' is the black mulberry.

Myrrh. Ex. 30[23], Prov. 7[17]. See Ladanum.

Nettles. (1) Heb. *Ḥārûl*, weeds, Prov. 24[31]. (2) *Ḳimmôsh*, the stinging nettle, twice translated 'thorns' (A.V.).

Nuts. (1) Heb. *Ēgôz*, the walnut, S. of S. 6[11]. (2) *Boṭnîm*, the pistachio, Gen. 43[11].

Oak. (1) Heb. *Allâh, allôn*, the oak, Gen. 35[8], Josh. 24[26]. (2) *Elah*, the teil-tree, Is. 1[29], Gen. 35[4].

Oil tree. Heb. *'Etz shemen.* 1 Kings 6[23], Neh. 8[15], Is. 41[19]; probably the oleaster.

Olive. Gen. 8[11], Deut. 8[8]. In Rom. 11[17] the wild olive.

Palm tree. The date-palm.

Pannag. Ezek. 27[17]. Unknown.

Pine tree. Is. 41[19], 60[13]. The plane.

Rose. A bulbous plant. No true roses are found, except on the Lebanons.

Shittah tree. Is. 41[19]. R.V. 'Acacia'. Hence comes 'Shittim wood', Ex. 26[15].

Sodom, Vine of. See Gourd.

Spicery. Gen. 37[25]. R.V. 'gum tragacanth, or storax'.

Stacte. Ex. 30[34]. A drop of some exuding gum.

Sycamine. See Mulberry. Luke 17[6].

Sycomore. A species of fig. Ps. 78[47], 1 Chron. 27[28].

Teil (Terebinth). Is. 6[13]. The terebinth.

Wheat. Gen. 30[14]. Wheat harvest was from April to June.

With. Judg. 16[7]. 'Supple twigs', or 'new cords'.

XLVI. NOTES ON ANIMALS OF THE BIBLE

Ass (domestic). Judg. 5[10]. The honoured animal for carrying dignitaries. Also used as a beast of burden.

Badger. Ex. 26[14], Ezek. 16[10]. Heb. *Taḥash* seems a generic name for dolphins, seals, &c.

Behemoth. Job 40[15]. The hippopotamus.

Camel. Heb. *Gâmâl*, also *Beker* (the young camel).

Chamois. Deut. 14[5]. Perhaps the wild sheep.

Coney. Lev. 11[5], Ps. 104[18], Prov. 30[26]. The *Hyrax Syriacus*.

Deer. (1) Deut. 12[15]. Heb. *Tsebî*; gazelle. (2) Deut. 14[5], Is. 51[20], *Tô*; perhaps an antelope. (3) Deut. 14[5], *Dîshôn*; another antelope. (4) Deut. 14[5], 1 Kings 4[23]. *Yaḥmûr*, the *Alcephalus bubalis*.

Dog. Never used except in disgust. Never referred to as used in the chase, nor (except Job 30[1]) as tending sheep; but only as guarding the house (Is. 56[10]), warding off wild beasts, or as a predatory animal, even feeding on human bodies, as in the case of Jezebel.

Ferret. Lev. 11[30]. Doubtful. R.V. 'gecko', a lizard.

Fox. Judg. 15[4]. Heb. *Shû'âl* includes fox and jackal. The latter is generally meant.

Goat. (1) Is. 14[9]. Heb. *'Attûd*, translated (R.V. and A.V.) 'chief ones'. (2)
  Tsâphîr, 2 Chron. 29[21]. (3) *Sâ'îr*, Lev. 9[3]. (4) *Tâyish*, Gen. 30[35]. The he-goat
  is used as a symbol of strength and also of impurity.
Goat (wild). Deut. 14[5], Ps. 104[18]. The *Capra ibex*.
Greyhound. Only in Prov. 30[31], where the translation is very doubtful. R.V.
  marg. 'war-horse', LXX 'cock'.
Hart, Hind. Deut. 12[15, 22]. The red deer, or the fallow deer.
Horse. Nah. 3[2, 3], Deut. 17[16]. Only used for chase and war. The kings of
  Israel were forbidden to multiply horses, because connected with the
  worship of the sun.
Hyaena. 1 Sam. 13[18], Is. 13[21], Jer. 12[9]. Probably referred to in these
  passages, though the word is not in A.V. The valley of *Zeboim* is still called
  by Arabs 'the gorge of the hyaena'.
Jackal. See Fox. Perhaps jackals are meant in Is. 13[22] (Heb. *iyyîm*), and also
  when *tannim* is used (A.V. 'dragons').
Lion. Heb. *Arî*, *Kĕphîr*, *Lâyish*, *Lâbî*, *Shâḥal*. All five words occur in Job 4[10, 11].
  The oldest is *Lâyish*, whence the name of the city Laish. Of lion-hunting
  the only mentions are in Job and Ezek. 19[2–9]. A symbol of strength, of the
  tribe of Judah, and of Christ (Rev. 5[5]).
Mole. (1) Heb. *Tinshémeth*. Lev. 11[30]. Perhaps a lizard. (2) *Ḥâphor-pêrôth*.
  Is. 2[20]. Probably the mole-rat.
Mule. Heb. *Péred* = 'mule'. *Rekesh* = 'horse or ass'. *Yĕmim* (Gen. 36[24]) is doubt-
  ful. The mule was not used by the Hebrews till David's time, when with
  the horse it supplanted the ass as a royal beast.
Ox. Heb. *Bâḳâr*, *Abîrim*, *Shôr*. Pastured in the open, but not much used for
  food, since there is little grazing land, but for sacrifices, ploughing, tread-
  ing corn, drawing waggons (Num. 7[3]).
Pygarg. Deut. 14[5], probably a gazelle.
Roe, Roebuck. Deut. 12[15]. The gazelle.
Unicorn. A species of wild ox. 'Unicorn' (from the LXX) is erroneous, as
  the *Rĕêm* has two horns (Deut. 33[17]).
Weasel. Lev. 11[29]. Probably the mole-rat.
Wolf. Frequent.

XLVII. NOTES ON BIRDS OF THE BIBLE

Bittern. Is. 14[23], 34[11], Zeph. 2[14]. R.V. 'hedgehog' or 'porcupine' seems a
  mistake.
Cormorant. (1) Heb. *Shâlâk*, Lev. 11[17], the cormorant. (2) *ḳâath*, Is. 34[11],
  probably the pelican.
Crane. Is. 38[14]. R.V. 'swallow'. Some translate 'stork'.
Cuckoo. Lev. 11[16]. R.V. 'Sea-mew'.
Fowl, Fatted. 1 Kings 4[23]. Probably geese.
Glede. Deut. 14[13]. Probably the buzzard.
Hawk. Job. 39[26], Lev. 11[16]. The nightjar, or an owl.
Lapwing. Lev. 11[19]. The hoopoe.
Ossifrage. Lev. 11[18]. The Lämmer-geier.
Owl. Is. 34[13], perhaps an ostrich. In Is. 34[15], R.V. has 'arrow-snake' (Heb.
  Ḳippôz), and in Is. 34[14] (*Lilith*), 'night-monster'.
Peacock. 1 Kings 10[22]. Imported by Solomon from Malabar or Ceylon.
Pigeon. Ps. 68[13], Matt. 3[16], Gen. 15[9].
Sparrow. Ps. 102[17]; nearly always translated 'bird' or 'fowl' in A.V.

XLVIII. AQUATIC CREATURES OF THE BIBLE

Jonah's Fish. Matt. 12⁴⁰, a 'whale'. But both Heb. and Greek mean a 'sea-monster'. Perhaps a shark.

Onycha. Ex. 30³⁴, Eccles. 24¹⁵. An ingredient from the small shell on the foot of many molluscs.

Purple (fish). The valuable dye was said to come from a small vessel in the throat of a shell-fish, and was one of the peculiar insignia of royalty or official rank.

Tobit's Fish. A crocodile, or one of the *Siluridae*. A sheat-fish? Galen and Dioscorides prescribe the gall of the sheat-fish as an eye-salve.

Whale. Some land-monster in Ex. 7⁹, Deut. 32³³, Ps. 91¹³, Jer. 51³⁴. Some sea-monster (? crocodile) in Job 7¹², Ps. 74¹³, Is. 27¹, Ezek. 29³, 32².

XLIX. NOTES ON REPTILES AND AMPHIBIA OF THE BIBLE

Adder, translated in A.V., Heb. *péthen* (generic) Ps. 58⁴, and *Shĕphíphôn* (Gen. 49¹⁷), '*Aḥshûb* (Ps. 140³), *Tziph'ôni* (Prov. 23³², Job 20¹⁴⁻¹⁶), denoting a venomous serpent.

Chameleon. Lev. 11³⁰, Heb. *Côâḥ*, perhaps the monitor-lizard, *Tinshémeth* (A.V. 'mole'), probably a chameleon.

Dragon. Is. 34¹³, Ezek. 29³. As a symbol of Egypt, the crocodile. Elsewhere thought to be the jackal, or a land-reptile.

Leviathan. Ps. 74¹⁴, Job 41¹. Always the crocodile, except in Ps. 104²⁶; some think in Is. 27¹ it refers to the great python.

Serpent. (1) Heb. *Nâḥâsh*, Ps. 58⁴, Prov. 30¹⁹, generic. (2) *Tannîn*, Ex. 7⁹, ¹⁰, any land or sea monster. (3) *Péthen*, Ps. 58⁴. (4) *Shĕphíphôn*, Gen. 49 ⁷. (5) *Eph'eh*, Job 20¹⁶. (6) '*Aḥshûb*, Ps. 140³. (7) *Tzepha'* (Prov. 23³², Is. 11⁸), of various venomous snakes.

The 'fiery serpents' of Num. 21⁶⁻⁸ (Heb. *Sârâph*) were probably so called from the fever caused by their bites. The 'fiery flying serpent' of Is. 14²⁹ is poetic imagery.

L. NOTES ON INSECTS AND OTHER SMALLER ANIMALS OF THE BIBLE

Bee. Ps. 118¹², 1 Sam. 14²⁵. Mainly the references are to wild bees (Deut. 1⁴⁴).

Beetle. Lev. 11²¹, ²², Heb. *Ḥargôl*, some kind of locust. In Heb. 2¹¹, some render *Ḥâphîs* by 'the scarabaeus' of Egypt, but A.V. and R.V. have 'beam'.

Fly. The flies of the Egyptian plague (Heb. *Arôb*) seem generic. The *Zĕbûb*, mentioned as frequenting the rivers of Egypt (Is. 7¹⁸), was probably the *Tsetse* (so Baal-zebub, the god of Ekron). The *Zĕbûb* of Eccles. 10¹ is the common fly.

Grasshopper. Judg. 6⁵, Lev. 11²². In 2 Chron. 7¹³ translated 'locust'; so also R.V. in Judg. 6⁵.

Hornet. Ex. 23²⁸. Zoreah (Josh. 15³³) = 'the place of hornets'.

Locust. Ex. 10⁴⁻⁶, Lev. 11²². Heb. *Arbeh*, *Sol'âm*, *Ḥargôl*, *Ḥâgâl*, *Gâzâm*, *Yélek*, *Tzĕlâtzal*, *Gêb*, *Ḥâsîl*, translated in A.V. 'beetle', 'cankerworm', 'caterpillar', 'grasshopper', 'locust', 'bald locust', 'palmerworm'.

Snail. Lev. 11³⁰, Heb. *Ḥômet*, perhaps a sand-lizard. In Ps. 58⁸ *Shablûl* is a snail that wastes away; in allusion to the popular error that the slime emitted in its track gradually consumed it, or to the fact of its dying under the influence of salt, or appearing to dry up when subjected to a hot dry atmosphere; so illustrating the wicked blighted by God's curse.

Worm. (1) Heb. *Sâs*, Is. 51⁸, = 'moth'. (2) *Rimmah*, Ex. 16²⁰, Job 25⁶, Is. 14¹¹, = 'maggot' or 'grub'. (3) *Tôlé'ah*, Job 25⁶, Is. 14¹¹, = 'caterpillar'. In Mic. 7¹⁷ serpents are probably meant (R.V. 'crawling things').

LI. MUSIC AND MUSICAL INSTRUMENTS OF THE BIBLE

Vocal Music occupies an important place in Scripture, both in religious worship (1 Chron. 6³²), public rejoicings (1 Sam. 18⁶), and social festivities (Gen. 31²⁷; Isa. 5¹; 24⁹). It is mentioned among the earliest expressions of joy (Exod. 15²¹), and was accompanied by dancing (2 Sam. 6¹⁶), and clapping of hands, especially in the 'chorus' (Ps. 47¹). For worship David chose a body of singers (1 Chron. 16⁴¹); Jehoshaphat appointed a band of singers to praise God in front of his army (2 Chron. 20²¹). After the Captivity we find an equal number of male and female voices (Ezra 2⁶⁵), who sang alternately. They formed a distinguished class, had a separate maintenance (Neh. 11²³), had cities assigned to them (Neh. 7⁷³), and chambers for those in attendance at the Temple (Ezek. 40⁴⁴). From the dedication of some Psalms there would seem to have been a written musical notation, but no certain record of it is extant.

Musical Instruments are among the earliest recorded human inventions (Gen. 4²¹). In Scripture their use seems to be confined to religious worship and social celebrations, except that the sound of the trumpet served as a battle-call. The earliest kinds were a tabret, a stringed instrument (incipient harp), cymbals, and pipe. From these germs all others are developments. As the Hebrew names were obscure, or unintelligible to the translators of our Bible, one general term expressing a well-known instrument often does duty for several kinds of the same type; while the same Hebrew generic word is sometimes translated by different English specific ones, and in other cases the translation is erroneous. The following list will exhibit all the names that occur, either in the English or Hebrew text.

(i) Stringed Instruments.

Harp (Gen. 4²¹; 31²⁷; 1 Sam. 16²³; Job 21¹²; 30³¹; Ps. 137²; Isa. 5¹²) ... Heb. (1) *Kinnôr*: Gk. ψαλτήριον, κιθάρα, and κινύρα.

(1) *Kinnôr*. The most ancient kind, of *Syrian* origin. A lyre, of uncertain shape, probably square or oval, of pieces of wood united by animal

strings, from six to nine (?) in number. It was held under the left (?) arm, and played with the fingers or with a plectrum, or perhaps with both (as on an early Egyptian representation).

Harp (*contd.*) (1 Sam. 10⁵; Neh. 12²⁷; Ps. 33²; 57⁸; 71²²; 81²; 92³; 150 Isa. 5¹²) . . . Heb. (2) *Nébhel, Nēbhel* : Gk. ψαλτήριον, κιθάρα.

(2) *Nébhel.* A later improvement, of *Phoenician* origin (?), having *three* wooden sides (one curved) and *ten* strings. It is usually translated 'psaltery' (as in Ps. 57⁸; 81², A.V. and R.V.); but is rendered 'lute' (*loc. cit.* Prayer-Book), and 'viol' (Isa. 5¹²; Amos 5²³; 6⁵). Some take it to have been a portable harp; the translation *psalterion* suggests the dulcimer : see **Psaltery.** As it is commonly coupled with some other instrument, it is thought to have supplied the bass. But others, founding on 1 Chron. 15²⁰ᶠ·, take *nébhel* to have given the higher, shriller notes, and *kinnôr* the lower.

—— (Ps. 33²; 144⁹) . . . Heb. (3) *'Asôr* : Gk. δεκάχορδον.

(3) *'Asôr.* A smaller instrument, *Assyrian* origin, only mentioned in conjunction with *nébhel*, and accordingly thought to have supplied the treble. Translated 'instrument of ten strings'. But R.V. is correct in rendering it as an epithet of *nébhel*, not as a separate instrument.

—— (Dan. 3⁵,⁷) . . . Aram. (4) written *Ḳîthārōs*, read as *Ḳathrôs* : Gk. κίθαρις.

(4) *Ḳathrôs.* As this name is borrowed from the Greek (*Kithara*), the instrument appears to have been a later introduction, of *Greek* origin (Eng. *cithern, guitar*), imported into the East. It was a lyre, with *four* strings.

Lute. *See* **Harp,** *Nébhel.*

Psaltery (1 Chron. 13⁸; 15¹⁶; 25¹; 2 Chron. 5¹²; 29²⁵; 2 Sam. 6⁵) . . . Heb. (1) *Nébhel* : Gk. νάβλα.

In Psalms, Kings, and Chronicles 'psaltery' is the general translation of *nébhel* (*see* **Harp,** *Nébhel*).

—— (Dan. 3⁵,⁷) . . . Aram. (2) *Psantêrîn* : Gk. ψαλτήριον.

Psantêrîn (Eng. *sawtry*) is erroneously rendered 'psaltery', from a verbal similarity. It should be 'dulcimer', being an instrument formed of strings tightly stretched, by fixed pins and turning screws, over a rectangular sounding-board or box; and was played by hammers struck with the hand against the strings. It is not of the harp genus, but is the germ of the piano. The Arab *santir* is a development of it.

Sackbut (Dan. 3⁵,⁷, &c.) . . . Aram. *Sabbᵉkha* : Gk. σαμβύκη.

A kind of harp, of Oriental origin, known to the Greeks as σάμβυξ (*sambux*); either very small but of high pitch, or very large, with many strings, and of full, rich tone. It is wrongly translated 'sackbut' instead of 'harp'. Cp. Heb. *sᵉbhākah* = network or lattice-work.

Viol (Isa. 14¹¹; Amos 5²³; 6⁵; Isa. 5¹², R.V. 'lute') . . . Heb. *Nébhel* : Gk ψαλτήριον.

See **Harp,** *Nébhel.*

(ii) WIND INSTRUMENTS.

Cornet (Dan. 3⁵,⁷,¹⁰,¹⁵) . . . Aram. (1) *Ḳarna* : Gk. σάλπιγξ.

See **Trumpet,** *Ḳéren.*

Cornet (*contd.*) (1 Chron. 15²⁸ ; 2 Chron. 15¹⁴ ; Ps. 98⁶ ; Hos. 5⁸) ... Heb. (2) *Shôphâr* : Gk. σωφέρ, σάλπιγξ κερατίνη.

See **Trumpet,** *Shôphâr.*

—— (2 Sam. 6⁵) ... Heb. (3) *Meⁿa'an'im* : Gk. κύμβαλα : R.V. 'castanets' ; marg. 'sistra'.

Meⁿa'an'im only occurs in this passage, and though translated 'cornets' in the A.V., is 'cymbals' in the LXX. The Hebrew word is supposed to be derived from a root meaning 'to sway to and fro', or 'vibrate' ; hence it is thought that the Vulgate rendering, *sistra,* is more correct, and that it was a rattle (very common in the East), consisting of an oval hoop with a handle, having cross-bars of metal rods, on which loose rings were threaded, jingling when shaken, like the plates of a timbrel.

Dulcimer (Dan. 3⁵, ¹⁰, ¹⁵) ... Aram. *Sumpônyah* : Gk. συμφωνία : R.V. marg. 'bagpipe'.

It is only mentioned in this chapter, and wrongly rendered 'dulcimer'. From a comparison of its name with almost identical forms in Greek and Italian, it would seem to have been a kind of bagpipe, the use of which was known, from remote antiquity, in Persia, Egypt, and Phoenicia. It would have been better translated 'bagpipe', and the passage read thus : harp (*sabbᵉkha*), dulcimer (*psantêrîn*), bagpipe (*sumpônyah*).

Flute (Dan. 3⁵, ⁷, ¹⁰, ¹⁵) ... Aram. *Mashrôḳîtha* : Gk. σύριγξ.

It occurs only here, and its exact nature is doubtful. It is variously described as a 'double flute', set of 'Pan-pipes', and an 'organ' ; probably 'flute'.

Organ (Gen. 4²¹ ; Job 21¹² ; 30³¹ ; Ps. 150⁴) ... Heb. '*Ugâbh* : Gk. ψαλτήριον, ψαλμός, ὄργανον : R.V. 'pipe'.

The '*ugâbh* of Gen. 4²¹ may or may not be the same instrument as that of Ps. 150⁴. The former was either 'bagpipe' or reeds or 'Pan-pipes', blown obliquely with the mouth ; the latter some take as a set of pipes inserted in a wind-box, and blown from it perpendicularly, either by bellows or by mouth. Such an instrument was known to the Egyptians, as was also the use of bellows.

Pipe (1 Kings 1⁴⁰ ; Isa. 5¹² ; 30²⁹) ... Heb. (1) *Hâlîl* : Gk. αὐλός.

(1) The most ancient form of this genus. 'Flute' or 'oboe', made of reed, and played from a mouthpiece at one end ; used for festival processions (Isa. 30²⁹), national demonstrations (1 Kings 1⁴⁰), holiday dances (Luke 7³²), and funeral dirges (Matt 9²³). Some think the last were played on a 'double pipe'. It is rendered 'instruments of music' in Amos 6⁵.

—— (Exod. 15²⁰ ; Ps. 30¹¹ ; 150⁴ ; Jer. 31⁴, ¹³) ... Heb. (2) *Mâhôl* : Gk. χοροί, χαρά.

(2) 'Pipe' only in A.V. marg. to Ps. 150⁴, but no doubt it means 'dancing' (by which word it is generally translated in the LXX and A.V.).

—— (Pss. 53 and 88, tit.) ... Heb. (3) *Maḥᵃlath* : Gk. μαελέθ.

(3) This title of two Psalms is thought to refer to the instruments accompanying the song, as it seems to have the same root as the two previous words. Gesenius translates it 'lute'. 'Apparently a catchword in a song giving name to tune' (B.D.B.).

Trumpet (Joshua 6⁵) . . . Heb. (1) *Ķéren* : Gk. κέρας, σάλπιγξ.

(1) *Ķéren.* The primitive trumpet, formed of a ram's horn ; though the Hebrew *kéren ha-yōbēl* may mean 'jubilee-trumpet' (see R.V. marg. Joshua 6⁴). The Aramaic is *Ķarna.* In Dan. 3 it is translated 'cornet'; but the word seldom occurs, and only of a *horn.*

—— (Exod. 19¹⁶ ; Joshua 6⁴ ; Judges 3²⁷ ; 7¹⁶ ; 1 Sam. 13³ ; Ps. 47⁵ ; 81³ ; 98⁶ ; Joel 2¹) . . . Heb. (2) *Shôphâr* : Gk. κερατίνη, σάλπιγξ.

(2) *Shôphâr.* A very long horn, *turned up* at the extremity. The national trumpet for rallying the people, and rousing warlike or religious enthusiasm. It was the token that God was on their side ; and it was probably blown only by one divinely commissioned. In 1 Chron. 15²⁸, &c., it is rendered 'cornet', as also in Ps. 98⁶, where in the version of the Book of Common Prayer it is rendered 'shawm'. *See* **Cornet**, *Mᵉna'an'im.*

—— (Num. 10² ; 2 Kings 11¹⁴ ; 1 Chron. 15²⁸ ; 2 Chron. 5¹² ; Ps. 98⁶ ; Hos. 5⁸) . . . Heb. (3) *Ḥᵃṣôṣᵉrah* : Gk. σάλπιγξ.

(3) *Ḥᵃṣôṣᵉrah.* A *straight* trumpet of metal, terminating in a bell-mouth, made by God's directions to Moses, to call an assembly or proclaim the march. It was both a sacred and a martial trumpet ; and was blown to herald the approach of a king. It was used by official heralds, who were often followed by a band of *Shôphârs* (Ps. 98⁶). One hundred and twenty priests blew trumpets from the Temple height, to proclaim the introduction of the ark into the Holy Place (2 Chron. 5¹²) at Solomon's dedication.

—— (Lev. 23²⁴) . . . Heb. (4) *Tᵉru'ah* : Gk. σάλπιγγες : E. vv. 'blowing of trumpets'.

Shawm (Ps. 98⁷, Prayer-book Version).

The A.V. (Ps. 98⁶) has 'cornet'. *See* **Trumpet**, *Shôphâr.*

(iii) Instruments of Percussion.

Bells (Zech. 14²⁰) . . . Heb. *Mᵉṣillóth* : Gk. χαλινός : A.V. marg. bridles'. The LXX translates the Hebrew by a word meaning 'bridle'. The Hebrew word has such an evident affinity to the two following words (translated 'cymbals'), that it would seem to refer to metal cups suspended to bridles, either for ornament or for tinkling purposes.

Cymbals (1 Chron. 15¹⁶, ¹⁹, ²⁸ ; 16⁵, ⁴² ; 25⁶ ; 2 Chron. 5¹³ ; 29²⁵ ; Ezra 3¹⁰ ; Neh. 12²⁷) . . . Heb. (1) *Mᵉṣiltáim* : Gk. κύμβαλα.

—— (2 Sam. 6⁵ ; Ps. 150⁵) . . . Heb. (2) *Ṣelṣᵉlîm* : Gk. κύμβαλα.

These words (1) and (2) do not mark different *species*; but the latter is *generic*, since it is used (Ps. 150⁵) with two differential adjectives, marking two *species*, e.g. (1) 'loud', (2) 'high-sounding' : the former probably shaped like a soup-plate, with wide flat rim, and played by being strapped to the hands and clashed together ; the latter, conical, cup-like, with thin edge, played by bringing down the one sharply on the other while held stationary, eliciting a high-pitched note. Cymbals are mentioned as accessories to music in *sacred* dances. David appointed Asaph chief of the cymbalists.

—— (1 Sam. 18⁶) . . . Heb. (3) *Shᵉlîshîm* : Gk. κύμβαλα : R.V. marg. 'triangles or three-stringed instruments'.

(3) The word occurs only once, and is translated 'instruments of music'

or 'three-stringed instruments'. They were probably 'triangles', 'sistra', or 'rattles' with only three metal rods run through a bow with a handle, a very common Eastern instrument. *See* **Cornet**, $M^e na'an'im$, p. 257.

Tabret (*a*), **Timbrel** (*b*); (*a*) (Gen. 31^{27}; 1 Sam. 10^5; 18^6; Isa. 5^{12}; 24^8; 30^{32}; Jer. 31^4; Ezek. 28^{13}); (*b*) Exod. 15^{20}; Judges 11^{34}; 2 Sam. 6^5; Job 21^{12}; Ps. 81^2; 149^3; 150^4) ... Heb. *Tôph* : Gk. τύμπανον (ψαλτήριον : Job 21^{12}).

The same Hebrew word (*sing.* and *pl.*) represents 'tabret' and 'timbrel'; therefore only one instrument is meant, viz. a simple tambourine, used with the cymbals, as an accompaniment to dancing and singing. There is no proof of cymbals or bells being attached to Jewish tabrets, and so constituting them 'timbrels'.

LII. JEWISH WEIGHTS, MONEY, MEASURES, AND TIME
(i) Weights.

The invention of coining, that is to say of the practice of stamping pieces of gold and silver for purposes of currency, dates from about 700 B.C. This innovation, which to a great extent superseded the use of the balance, originated in Lydia. From Asia Minor it spread into Greece, but it had not penetrated into Syria before the Babylonian conquest of Judah, *c.* 600 B.C. After the return from the Captivity, 536 B.C., there is still no evidence that the Jews possessed any native currency until the time of Simon Maccabaeus, who freed them from foreign rule, 141 B.C. Wherever mention is made of money in the Old Testament before this date, either bullion money or the coinage of the Persians or Syrians is to be understood. The precious metals had, however, always been used from the earliest times in the shape of bars, ingots, or rings, which were weighed in the balance according to a system of weight which the Jews had adopted with modifications from the Phoenicians and Assyrians. The principal weights in use for numerous objects, especially the metals, were the following:

	Grs. Troy.		Equivalent in value (silver being estimated at rather more than 5 shillings an ounce) to				Dols. cents.
			£	s.	d.		
Gêrah ($\frac{1}{20}$ shekel) . . .	11·2	=	0	0	1·6	=	0 3·2
Rébha' ($\frac{1}{4}$ shekel) . . .	56	=	0	0	8	=	0 16
Béka' ($\frac{1}{2}$ shekel)* . . .	112	=	0	1	4	=	0 32
SHÉKEL . . .	224·4	=	0	2	8	=	0 64
Mâneh or Mina (50 shekels?) . (1 lb. 11 oz. 8 dwt. 7 gr.)	11,239	=	6	13	4	=	32 00
Kikkar or Talent (60 manehs?) (117 lb. 19 dwt. 16 gr.)	674,392	=	400	0	0	=	1,920 00

---

* Three *Béka's* have been found in Palestine weighing 90·58, 94·28, and 102·5 grains Troy ; obviously clipped or worn specimens of the *beka'* of the Phoenician standard.

s 2

It must be borne in mind that these equivalents give no idea of the *purchasing power* of money, which must have greatly varied at different times, but was always considerably higher than it is now.

In addition to the above, there was a special Talent and Maneh used only for gold, based upon a gold shekel of 253 gr. The gold shekel was tariffed at 15 silver shekels of 224 gr., and was consequently worth about £2, or 9 *dollars*, 60 *cents*.

Of the above-mentioned denominations the shekel, signifying 'weight', is the principal unit, of which the rest are fractions or multiples. The word Gerah means a grain or bean; Rébha' = 'quarter'; Béka' = 'half'; Maneh (LXX 'mna', Vulgate 'mina', A.V. 'pound') = 'part'; Kikkar = 'circle', 'globe', or 'disk'.

Hebrew names of weights are not found in the New Testament, though the Greek μνᾶ (Luke 19[13]) is doubtless identical with the Hebrew maneh.

(ii) Coins.

The earliest struck coins, as distinguished from the more ancient bullion money, mentioned in the Bible, are the *Adarkon* and *Darkᵉmon*, A.V. 'drams' (1 Chron. 29[7]; Ezra 2[69]; 8[27]; Neh. 7[70–2]), which are, according to R.V., the Persian gold darics first issued in the reign of Darius Hystaspes, 521–485 B.C. Modern authorities incline to return to the 'drams' or 'drachms' of A.V., and, on the basis of Ezra 8[27], to take the terms as measures of weight and not as coins. 1 Chron. 29[7] is of course, in either case, an anachronism so far as David's reign is concerned. The darics were the standard gold currency down to the time of Alexander the Great, and they circulated throughout the East. The obverse of the coin bears a representation of the Persian monarch kneeling, holding a bow in the left hand and a spear in the right.

The daric weighed 130 gr., equivalent to about £1 2s., or 5 *dollars*, 28 *cents*.

After the Macedonian conquest and the subsequent partition of Alexander's empire, the Jews, while tributary to the Ptolemies and Seleucids, made use of the coins of Egypt and the Phoenician ports, tetradrachms, didrachms, and drachms (2 Macc. 4[19]), equivalent to the shekel, ½ shekel, and ¼ shekel.*

The earliest native Jewish coins are half and quarter shekels of bronze, attributed to Simon Maccabaeus, to whom special authority was granted by Antiochus VII (Sidetes), 141 B.C., to coin money with his own stamp: 'I give thee leave to coin money for thy country with thine own stamp' (1 Macc. 15[6]).

---

* For illustrations of these and later coins see G. F. Hill: *British Museum Catalogue of Greek Coins of Palestine*, Plates xx–xxxviii.

The succeeding princes of the Maccabaean or Asmonaean family down to 37 B.C. struck only small bronze coins with Hebrew or bilingual (Hebrew and Greek) inscriptions (Head, *Hist. Num.* p. 682).

The Idumaean or Herodian princes, 37 B.C.–A.D. 100? (Herod the Great and his successors), also coined bronze money bearing their names in the Greek character, e. g. ΒΑΣΙΛΕΩΣ ΗΡΩΔΟΥ, &c. The bronze coin of Herod Agrippa I, A.D. 37–44, has on the obverse the inscription ΒΑCΙΛΕωC ΑΓΡΙΠΑ around an umbrella; and on the reverse the date LS (year 6) and three ears of corn.

The bronze coins of Agrippa II, A.D. 48–100, bear on the obverse the heads of successive Emperors, and on the reverse the standing figure of Fortune holding a cornucopia, &c.

Meantime the Roman Procurators of Judaea, who from 6 B.C. governed the country during the almost nominal reigns of the later Idumaean kings, also struck bronze coins with Greek inscriptions. These do not bear the names of the Procurators, but only those of the Emperors and the years of their reigns. Those of Tiberius with the date 18 were struck in the year of the Crucifixion.

The silver coins current throughout this period were Greek tetradrachms of Antioch, &c., and Roman denarii. The denarius of Tiberius weighed 60 gr., equivalent to $8\frac{1}{4}d.$, or 17 *cents*. The denarius (A.V. *penny*) was the usual day's wages of a field labourer. The thirty pieces of silver, the price of our Lord's betrayal, were probably not denarii but tetradrachms of Antioch, thirty of which would be equivalent to about £3 3s. 9d., or 15 *dollars*, 30 *cents*, the tetradrachm being at that time tariffed at three denarii.

The following are the names and approximate values of the principal coins current in Palestine in New Testament times:

SILVER.

Stater. (A.V. *Piece of Money*, R.V. *Shekel*, Matt. 17[27]) = a tetradrachm of Antioch or Tyre, weight 236–220 gr., equivalent to a Jewish shekel, but officially tariffed at only 3 Roman denarii = 2s. $1\frac{1}{2}d.$, or 51 *cents*.

Argurion. (A.V. *Piece of silver*, Matt. 26[15].) Another name for the same coin.

Didrachmon. (A.V. *Tribute money*, Matt. 17[24]) = two drachms of Antioch, about 112 gr., equivalent to a Jewish half-shekel, about 1s. 4d., or 32 *cents*.

Drachmē. (A.V. *Piece of silver*, Luke 15[8]) = a drachm of Antioch, equivalent to a Roman denarius (*q.v.*).

Denarius or **Denarion.** (A.V. *Penny*, Matt. 18[28], &c.) The Roman Imperial denarius, 60 gr. = $8\frac{1}{4}d.$, or 17 *cents*. American revisers render it by 'shilling'.

BRONZE.

Assarion. (A.V. *Farthing*, Matt. 10[29]) = the Roman As or $\frac{1}{16}$ of the denarius (originally $\frac{1}{10}$), about a halfpenny = 1 *cent*.

Kodrantes (Latin *quadrans*). (A.V. *Farthing*, Matt. 5²⁶) = ¼ As, about half a farthing = ¼ *cent*.

Lepton. (A.V. *Mite*, Mark 12⁴².) The smallest Jewish bronze coin, equivalent to half the kodrantes, or about a quarter-farthing = ⅛ *cent*.

Silver coins, the shekel of the ancient Jewish weight, 224 grs., the half and quarter shekel, were first struck during the First Revolt of the Jews. These have on the obverse a cup or chalice with the inscription שקל ישראל (shekel of Israel) in the old Hebrew characters, and the Hebrew numerals 1–5, corresponding to the years A.D. 66–70. On the reverse is a triple lily, with the legend ירושלם קדשה (Holy Jerusalem).* Bronze was also struck.

On the Conquest of Jerusalem, A.D. 70, the Roman Emperors, Vespasian and Titus, struck coins in Rome and Judaea bearing the inscriptions IVDAEA CAPTA, IVDAEA DEVICTA, and ΙΟΥΔΑΙΑΣ ΕΑΛωΚΥΙΑΣ (Judaea captured).

During the Second Revolt under Simon Barcochba coins were again struck by the Jews, A.D. 132–135. These are shekels and quarter shekels, or rather tetradrachms and denarii and bronze coins bearing Hebrew inscriptions giving the dates in years of the 'deliverance of Israel' or 'of Jerusalem' and bearing the names of 'Simeon' and 'Eleazar the Priest'.

The series of the coins of Jerusalem closes with those of the Roman Colony Ælia Capitolina after the rebuilding of the city by Hadrian, A.D. 136, when the new temple of Jupiter Capitolinus replaced that of Jehovah.

Though there is uncertainty about some of the values given above, yet they throw light on not a few important passages. Thus:

JOSEPH was sold by his brethren for 20 pieces of silver, Heb. *shekels* (Gen. 37²⁸), about £2 10s. of English money, or 12 *dollars*, 80 *cents*. It was two-thirds of the price of an adult slave (Exod. 21³²).

NAAMAN's offering to Elisha (2 Kings 5⁵) of 6,000 pieces (shekels) of gold was equivalent to something over £10,000, or 57,600 *dollars*.

The Temple-tax at Jerusalem was a didrachmon (Matt. 17²⁴) = about 1s. 4d., or 32 *cents*. Our Lord told St. Peter that in the fish's mouth he would find a stater (Matt. 17²⁷) = a Jewish shekel, or 2s. 8d., or 64 *cents*, which would thus pay for the Apostle and his Master.

The DEBTOR, who had been forgiven 10,000 talents (Matt. 18²⁴), i.e. £4,000,000, refused to forgive his fellow servant (Matt. 18²⁸) 100 pence or denarii = £3 10s. 10d., or 17 *dollars*.

In the parable of the householder hiring labourers into his vineyard, he

---

* Numismatists were divided on the question whether these coins belonged to Simon Maccabeus or to the First Revolt against Rome. The attribution has been finally settled on epigraphic grounds by Mr. G. F. Hill in his *British Museum Catalogue of Coins of Palestine*, pp. xcii ff.

is represented as agreeing with them for a penny a day (Matt. 20²)
This at first sight is misleading. But the penny really denotes the
denarius = 8¼*d.*, or 17 *cents*, the ordinary day's wage of a field labourer.
Judas sold our Lord for 30 pieces of silver (Matt. 26¹⁵), i.e. £3 3*s.* 9*d.*, or
15 *dollars*, 30 *cents*, the value of a slave, if killed by a beast

(iii) Measures.

In spite of all that has been written on the scales of measure-
ment used by the Jews, the subject is still involved in much
obscurity. The following tables are those given in Queipo's
Systèmes métriques et monétaires des anciens peuples. Paris, 1859;
but the details differ considerably from more recent estimates.

Long Measure (Primitive).

	Mètres.		
Span (Zéreth)	0·320	=	12·59 inches
2 Spans = 1 Cubit	0·640	=	25·18 ,,

This is supposed to have been the cubit which Jacob brought into
Egypt. The Jews, however, also made use of the Egyptian royal,
and so-called 'Olympic' cubits, which they adopted during their
captivity in Egypt.

At a later period, after their return from Babylon, another cubit
was introduced which perhaps came originally from Asia Minor.
This is known as the common or 'vulgar' cubit, the 'legal' cubit
of the Talmudists.

Long Measure (of the Talmudists).

	Mètres.		
Digit or Finger-breadth	0·023	=	0·91 inches.
4 Digits = 1 Palm	0·092	=	3·64 ,,
3 Palms = 1 Span (Zéreth) . . .	0·277	=	10·92 ,,
2 Spans = 1 Cubit	0·555	=	21·85 ,,
6 Cubits = 1 Reed	3·330	=	10·92 feet

Liquid Measure (earlier).

	Litres.		
Log	0·408	=	0·718 pint
12 Logs = 1 Hīn	4·896	=	1·077 gallons
6 Hīns = 1 Bath	29·376	=	6·465 ,,
10 Baths = 1 Cor or Homer . . .	293·760	=	64·655 ,,

Liquid Measure (later).

	Litres.		
Log	0·297	=	0·523 pint
12 Logs = 1 Hīn	3·570	=	3·142 quarts
6 Hīns = 1 Bath	21·420	=	4·714 gallons
10 Baths = 1 Cor or Homer . . .	214·200	=	47·144 ,,

Dry Measure (earlier).

	Litres.		
Log	0·408	=	0·718 pint
4 Logs = 1 Cab	1·632	=	1·436 quarts
7·2 Logs = 1 'Omer	2·937	=	2·586 ,,
24 Logs or 6 Cabs = 1 Se'ah . . .	9·792	=	2·155 gallons
10 'Omers = 3 Se'ahs = 1 Ephah . .	29·376	=	3·232 pecks
10 Ephahs = 1 Cor or Ḥomer . . .	293·760	=	8·081 bushels

Dry Measure (later).

	Litres.		
Log	0·297	=	0·523 pint
4 Logs = 1 Cab	1·190	=	1·047 quarts
7·2 Logs = 1 'Omer	2·142	=	1·885 ,,
24 Logs or 6 Cabs = 1 Se'ah . . .	7·140	=	1·571 gallons
10 'Omers or 3 Se'ahs = 1 Ephah . .	21·420	=	2·357 pecks
10 Ephahs = 1 Cor or Ḥomer . . .	214·200	=	5·893 bushels

The above equivalents of the Hebrew measures must only be accepted as approximately correct. In the absence of sufficient data we are dependent for the most part upon the doubtful statements of late writers.

N.B.—The foregoing tables will explain many texts in the Bible. Take, for instance, Isaiah 5[10]: 'For ten acres of vineyard shall yield one bath, and a homer of seed shall yield but an ephah' (R.V.). This curse upon the covetous man was, that ten acres of vines should produce only 7 gallons of wine, i. e. one acre should yield less than 3 quarts; and that 32 pecks of seed should only bring forth a crop of 3 pecks, or, in other words, that the harvest should produce a quantity equal to one-tenth only of the seed sown. A *homer* must be carefully distinguished from a *'omer*.

(iv) Time.

The *Natural* Day was from sunrise to sunset.
The *Natural* Night was from sunset to sunrise.
The *Civil* Day was, at least in later times in Israel, from sunset one evening to sunset the next; for, 'the Evening and the Morning were the first day'.

NIGHT (*Ancient*).

First Watch (Lam. 2[19]) till towards midnight.
Middle Watch (Judges 7[19]) including midnight (Exod. 11[4]) till 3 a.m.
Morning Watch (Exod. 14[24]) till 6 a.m.

DAY (*Ancient*).

Morning till about 10 a.m.

Heat of day till about 2 p.m. (?)

Day's decline till about 6 p.m.
Evening or Cool of day.

NIGHT (*New Testament*)
(at equinoxes).

First Watch, *evening* = 6 to 9 p.m.
Second Watch, *midnight* = 9 to 12 p.m.
Third Watch, *cock-crow* = 12 to 3 a.m.
Fourth Watch, *morning* = 3 to 6 a.m.

DAY (*New Testament*)
(according to season).

Third hour = 6 to 9 a.m.
Sixth hour = 9 to 12 midday.
Ninth hour = 12 to 3 p.m.
Twelfth hour = 3 to 6 p.m.

LIII. THE JEWISH CALENDAR

Year.		Month.	English Month (nearly).	Festivals.	Seasons and Productions.
Sacred.	Civil.				
I.	7.	ABIB, or NISAN. (Green ears.) Days 30. Exod. 12².	April.	14. The Passover (Exod. 12¹⁻⁵¹; 13³⁻¹⁰). 16. Firstfruits of Barley harvest presented (Lev. 23¹⁰⁻¹²).	Fall of the latter or spring rains (Deut. 11¹⁴). Floods (Joshua 3¹⁵). Barley ripe at Jericho. Wheat partly in the ear.
II.	8.	ZIV. (Blossom.) Days 29. 1 Kings 6¹.	May.	14. Second Passover, for those who could not keep the first (Num. 9¹⁰, ¹¹).	Barley harvest general (Ruth 1²²). Wheat ripens.
III.	9.	SIVAN. Days 30. Esther 8⁹.	June.	6. Pentecost, or Feast of Weeks. Firstfruits of Wheat harvest (Lev. 23¹⁷, ²⁰), and Firstfruits of all the ground (Exod. 23¹⁹; Deut. 26², ¹⁰).	Wheat harvest. Summer begins. No rain from April to Sept. (1 Sam. 12¹⁷).
IV.	10.	TAMMUZ. Days 29. Zech. 8 ⁹.	July.		Heat increases.
V.	11.	AB. Days 30. Ezra 7⁹.	Aug.		The streams dry up. Heat intense.
VI.	12.	ELUL. Days 29. Neh. 6¹⁵.	Sept.		Vintage (Lev. 26⁵). Heat still intense (2 Kings 4¹⁸⁻²⁰). Grape harvest general (Num. 13²³).

The column between "Festivals" and "Seasons and Productions" contains vertical labels: HARVEST. (rows II–III) and HOT SEASON. (rows V–VI).

The Jewish Calendar

Year.		Month.	English Month (nearly).	Festivals.	Seasons and Productions.
Sacred.	Civil.				
VII.	1.	TISHRI, or ETHANIM. Days 30. 1 Kings 8². 2 Chron. 5³.	Oct.	1. Feast of Trumpets (Num. 29¹). 10. Day of Atonement (Lev. 16). 15. Feast of Tabernacles (Lev. 23³⁴). Firstfruits of Wine and Oil (Deut. 16¹³).	Former or early rains begin (Joel 2²³). Ploughing and sowing begin. Rain continues. Wheat and barley sown. Vintage in North Palestine.
VIII.	2.	BUL. (Rain.) Days 29. 1 Kings 6³⁸.	Nov.		
IX.	3.	KISLEV. Days 30. Neh. 1¹.	Dec.	25. Feast of Dedication (1 Macc. 4⁵²⁻⁹; John 10²², ²³).	Winter begins. Snow on the mountains.
X.	4.	TEBHETH. Days 29. Esther 2¹⁶.	Jan.		Coldest month. Hail, snow (Joshua 10¹¹).
XI.	5.	SHEBAṬ. Days 30. Zech. 1⁷.	Feb.		Weather gradually becomes warmer.
XII.	6.	ADAR. Days 29. Esther 3⁷. Esther 9²⁷.	March.	14, 15. Feast of Purim (Esther 3⁷; 9²¹⁻⁴).	Thunder and hail frequent. Almond tree blossoms.

SEED TIME.

WINTER.

COLD SEASON.

LIV. LIST OF OBSOLETE OR AMBIGUOUS WORDS IN THE ENGLISH AUTHORIZED VERSION

N.B.—Several of these words occur in other passages besides those to which references are given.

WORD.	PASSAGE.	EXPLANATION.
ABIDE	Acts 20. 23	await, wait for.
ABJECTS	Ps. 35. 15.	outcasts, despised persons.
ABOMINATION	Prov. 12. 22	a hateful thing. Hence, an idol, object of worship (Exod. 8. 26).
ABUSE	Judg. 19. 25.	misuse, ill-treat.
ADAMANT, or DIAMOND	Ezek. 3. 9	a stone of impenetrable (*lit.* "indomitable") hardness.
ADDICTED THEMSELVES	1 Cor. 16. 15	devoted, or dedicated themselves.
ADJURE	Matt. 26. 63.	charge solemnly, conjure.
ADMIRATION	Rev. 17. 6	wonder, astonishment.
ADO	Mark 5. 39	stir, tumult, commotion.
ADVENTURE	Deut. 28. 56.	venture; "a. himself"=venture (to go), Acts 19. 31.
ADVERSARY	Matt. 5. 25	an opponent in a law-suit.
ADVERTISE	Num. 24. 14; Ruth 4. 4	to give notice, inform.
ADVISE THYSELF	1 Chr. 21. 12	consider.
ADVISEMENT	1 Chr. 12. 19	consideration.
AFFECT	Gal. 4. 17.	to seek after, pay court to.
AFFECTIONED	Rom. 12. 10.	affected, disposed.
AFFECTIONS	Gal. 5. 24.	desires, passions.
AFORE	Rom. 9. 23	beforehand.
AGONE	1 Sam. 30. 13	ago. (The old form of the word.)
ALBEIT	Ezek. 13. 7	although it be so.
ALL TO BRAKE	Judg. 9. 53	broke all to pieces. *To-brake* is the past tense of the old verb *to-breken*, to break in pieces. (Often treated as if *all-to*=altogether.)
ALLEGE	Acts 17. 3	to show, prove, bring evidence.
ALLOW	Luke 11. 48	to approve of. (Old French; from Lat. *allaudare*.)
ALMS	Acts 3. 3; 10. 2	(of *sing. num.*) a charitable gift.
ALOOF	Ps. 38. 11.	afar off, at a distance.
AMAZEMENT	1 Pet. 3. 6	confusion, fear, bewilderment.
AMBASSAGE	Luke 14. 32	embassy, message.
AMBUSHMENT	2 Chr. 13. 13	ambuscade, men lying in wait.
AMEN	Rom. 16. 27, &c.	so be it; in N. T. translated "verily."
AMERCE	Deut. 22. 19.	to punish by a fine, to fine.
AMIABLE	Ps. 84. 1	lovely.
ANCIENTS	Is. 3. 14, &c.	elders (*sub. plur.*).
AND	Gen. 44. 30; Num. 5. 30	if. (A peculiar use of the word.)
AND IF	Matt. 24. 48.	if. (Literally, if-if; *see* above.)
ANGLE	Is. 19. 8	a fishing-rod, with line and hook.
ANISE	Matt. 23. 23.	a plant cultivated for its aromatic seeds.
ANON	Matt. 13. 20.	i. e. *in one* (instant), immediately.
ANY THING	Acts 25. 8	in any way.
APPARELLED	Luke 7. 25	dressed.
APPARENTLY	Num. 12. 8	plainly, openly.
APPLE OF THE EYE	Deut. 32. 10.	the eye-ball.
APPOINTED	Judg. 18. 11.	armed, equipped, provided.
APPREHEND	Phil. 3. 12	"The passage throughout has reference to the Grecian games ; *apprehend* in the first part of the sentence meaning to lay hold of the goal, and so receive the prize ; in the second part, meaning to take hold of by the hand and introduce to the course, as was customary." (Wright, *Bible Word-Book*.)
APPROVE	(1) Acts 2. 22 ; (2) Rom. 2. 18	(1) to prove, attest; (2) to test, try.
ARK	Gen. 6. 14 ; Ex. 2. 3, 5 ; 37. 1	covered chest, coffer. (Lat. *arca*.) Also used of Noah's vessel, and of the "ark of the covenant," or box in which the tables of the law, &c. were kept.
ARRAY	1 Tim. 2. 9	clothing, dress.
ARRAY, to	Matt. 6. 29	to dress, or clothe.
ARTILLERY	1 Sam. 20. 40	bow and arrows.
ASK AT	Dan. 2. 10	to enquire of.

WORD.	PASSAGE.	EXPLANATION.
ASSAY	Acts 9. 26	to essay, attempt.
ASSURE	1 John 3. 19.	to convince, persuade.
ASSWAGE	Gen. 8. 1.	to subside.
ASTONIED	Job 17. 8	astounded. (Old form of "astonished.")
AT ONE, SET	Acts 7. 26	(would have) reconciled (them). Hence the verb "atone" (to reconcile), and "at-one-ment."
ATTENDANCE	1 Tim. 4. 13	attention.
ATTENT	2 Chr. 6. 40	attentive.
ATTIRED	Lev. 16. 4	covered (as to his head).
AUDIENCE	Acts 13. 16	a hearing.
AVOID	1 Sam. 18. 11	to retire, escape, withdraw.
AVOUCHED	Deut. 26. 17	avowed, declared (to be).
AWAY WITH	Is. 1. 13	"put up with," endure, tolerate.
BACKBITER	Rom. 1. 30	a slanderer.
BACKSIDE	Ex. 3. 1	the back part, rear.
BANK	2 Sam. 20. 15	a mound, for besieging a city.
BANQUET	Esth. 7. 1	in the Hebrew, "to drink;" "banquet" formerly meaning only "dessert."
BARBARIAN	1 Cor. 14. 11.	a foreigner, not a Greek.
BARBAROUS	Acts 28. 2	foreign.
BARBED	Job 41. 7.	furnished with projecting points.
BASE	1 Cor. 1. 28	lowly, humble.
BASER SORT	Acts 17. 5	lower orders (without any idea of wickedness).
BATTLE	1 Chr. 19. 9	a body of troops.
BEAM (*see* MOTE)	Matt. 7. 3	a piece of wood.
BECAUSE	Matt. 20. 31	in order that.
BEEVES	Lev. 22. 21	*plur.* of "beef;" used of oxen.
BEGGARLY	Gal. 4. 9	worthless.
BEHALF	1 Pet. 4. 16	account.
BESOM	Is. 14. 23	a broom.
BESTEAD	Is. 8. 21	beset (with difficulties).
BESTOW	(1) Luke 12. 17 ; (2) 1 Cor. 13. 3	(1) stow away ; (2) give away.
BETIMES	Gen. 26. 31, &c.	early.
BEWRAY	Matt. 26. 73.	to reveal, expose, accuse.
BEWRAYER	2 Macc. 4. 1	an informer.
BID	Matt. 22. 9	to invite ; "bidden "=invited.
BIND	Job 26. 8; Acts 9. 14	to imprison, or confine closely.
BLAINS	Ex. 9. 9	pustules, swellings, boils.
BLASTED	Gen. 41. 6	blighted.
BLASTING	Deut. 28. 22	blight.
BLAZE ABROAD	Mark 1. 45	to blazon, proclaim everywhere.
BOLLED	Ex. 9. 31	bearing pods, or round seed-vessels; "podded for seed."
BONDMAID	Gal. 4. 22.	a female slave.
BONDMAN	Gen. 43. 18	a slave.
BONNET	Ex. 28. 40; 29. 9	a man's head-dress.
BOSSES	Job 15. 26	large studs, projecting ornaments.
BOTCH	Deut. 28. 27	eruption of the skin, a boil.
BOTTOM	Zech. 1. 8	valley.
BOWELS	Phil. 1. 8, &c.	compassionate feelings.
BRASS	Deut. 8. 9	copper, copper money (Matt. 10. 9).
BRAVELY	Judith 10. 4	finely.
BRAVERY	Is. 3. 18	finery, showy dress.
BRAY	Prov. 27. 22	to pound, or bruise.
BREACHES	Judg. 5. 17	creeks, harbours.
BRICKLE	Wisd. 15. 13.	easily broken, brittle.
BRIGANDINE	Jer. 46. 4	a light coat of scale-armour.
BROIDED	1 Tim. 2. 9	braided, plaited.
BROIDERED	Ezek. 16. 10.	embroidered.
BRUIT	Jer. 10. 22	report, rumour. (Fr. *bruit*, noise.)
BUCKLER	Job 15. 26	a small round shield.
BUFFET	Matt. 26. 67	to strike, beat with the hands.
BULWARK	Deut. 20. 20.	a fortification.
BUNCH	Is. 30. 6	a (camel's) hump.
BY	1 Cor. 4. 4	with reference to, against.
BY AND BY	Matt. 13. 21; Luke 21. 9	immediately. Hence, "not by and by "=not at once.
BYWORD	2 Chr. 7. 20	a proverb.
CABIN	Jer. 37. 16	a cell, dark cellar.
CALAMUS	Ex. 30. 23	a (sweet Arabian) reed.
CALKERS	Ezek. 27. 9, 27	men who stop the seams of ships with tow.
CANKER	2 Tim. 2. 17	cancer. (An old spelling.)
CANKERED	James 5. 3	corroded, rusted.
CANKERWORM	Joel 1. 4	a kind of caterpillar.
CAREFUL	Dan. 3. 16	very anxious.
CAREFULNESS	1 Cor. 7. 32	great anxiety.
CARELESS	Judg. 18. 7	free from care.
CARRIAGE	1 Sam. 17. 22; Acts 21. 15	that which is carried ; baggage.

268

List of Obsolete or Ambiguous Words

WORD.	PASSAGE.	EXPLANATION.
CAST	(1) Luke 1. 29; (2) Jer. 38. 11	(1) considered; (2) cast-off.
CAST ABOUT	Jer. 41. 14	turned round, came back again.
CASTAWAY	1 Cor. 9. 27	an outcast.
CAUL	(1) Is. 3. 18; (2) Hos. 13. 8	(1) a net for the hair; (2) the membrane that surrounds the heart.
CHAFED	2 Sam. 17. 8	heated, exasperated, angry.
CHALLENGE	Ex. 22. 9	to claim.
CHAMBERING	Rom. 13. 13	wanton living, sensuality.
CHAMPAIGN	Deut. 11. 30	plain, level country.
CHAPITER	Ex. 36. 38	*capital* of a pillar or column.
CHAPMAN	2 Chr. 9. 14	a merchant, a dealer.
CHAPT	Jer. 14. 4	cracked, through heat and drought.
CHARGED	1 Tim. 5. 16	burdened, put to expense.
CHARGER	Matt. 14. 8; Mark 6. 25	a large dish. (So called from carrying a *charge* or burden.)
CHARGES, BE AT	Acts 21. 24	to discharge the cost, or pay expenses
CHARITY	1 Cor. 13	love in the widest sense.
CHECK	Job 20. 3	reproof, rebuke.
CHEEK TEETH	Joel 1. 6	molar teeth.
CHEER, OF GOOD	Matt. 9. 2	joyful, happy.
CHODE	Gen. 31. 36	did chide, disputed.
CHOLER	Dan. 8. 7; 11. 11	anger.
CIEL	2 Chr. 3. 5; Jer. 22. 14, &c.	to panel, wainscot.
CITHERN	1 Macc. 4. 54	a stringed instrument; the word has now become "guitar." (Lat. *cithara*.)
CLAVE	(1) Gen. 22. 3; (2) Ruth 1. 14	(1) did split; (2) did cling.
CLEAN	Josh. 3. 17	entirely, completely.
CLEAR	Gen. 24. 8	innocent.
CLEAVE	Gen. 2. 24; Rom. 12. 9	adhere, remain faithful (to).
CLOSE	Luke 9. 36	secret, unrevealed.
CLOSET	Matt. 6. 6	a private room, bed-room.
CLOTHED UPON	2 Cor. 5. 2, 4	clothed additionally.
CLOUTED	Josh. 9. 5	patched.
CLOUTS	Jer. 38. 11	rags, pieces of cloth.
COAST	Matt. 8. 34, &c.	a border, region, country.
COCKATRICE	Is. 11. 8	a kind of serpent, the basilisk.
COCKER	Ecclus. 30. 9	to spoil, or pamper, a child.
COCKLE	Job 31. 40	a weed found among corn.
COLLOPS	Job 15. 27	slices, or flakes, of meat or fat.
COLONY	Acts 16. 12	a foreign town, to whose inhabitants were accorded the same privileges as the citizens of Rome itself enjoyed. (Lat. *colonia*.)
COLOUR	Acts 27. 30	pretext, pretence.
COME BY	Acts 27. 16	to get possession of.
COMFORT	Judg. 19. 5	to support, strengthen.
COMMEND	(1) Rom. 3. 5; (2) Acts 14. 23	(1) to bring commendation upon, enhance; (2) to commit to one's charge.
COMMON	(1) Acts 2. 44; (2) Acts 10. 14	(1) shared in by all men alike; (2) profane, unclean to a Jew (because used by all).
COMMUNE WITH	Luke 6. 11	to converse with, consult with.
COMMUNICATE	Gal. 2. 2	to impart.
COMMUNICATION	Luke 24. 17	conversation, talk.
COMMUNION	1 Cor. 10. 16	joint partaking, partaking in common.
COMPACT	Ps. 122. 3	firmly united, strongly built.
COMPASS	Matt. 23. 15	to go all over.
COMPASS, FETCH A	2 Kings 3. 9; Acts 28. 13	to make a circuit.
COMPREHEND	Is. 40. 12; Rom. 13. 9	to comprise, include, contain; also, to overcome (John 1. 5).
CONCEIT	Rom. 12. 16	conceptions, notions, thoughts.
CONCISION	Phil. 3. 2	a meaningless or heathenish cutting; opposed to true circumcision.
CONCLUDE	(1) Acts 21. 25; (2) Rom. 11. 32	(1) to decide; (2) to include, class together.
CONCUPISCENCE	Rom. 7. 8	evil desire, lust.
CONFECTION	Ex. 30. 35	compound of various spices.
CONFOUND	Jer. 1. 17	to put to confusion, destroy.
CONFUSION	Is. 24. 10	ruin, destruction.
CONSCIENCE	1 Cor. 8. 7; Heb. 10. 2	consciousness, knowledge.
CONSIST	Col. 1. 17	subsist, remain unchanged.
CONSORT, to	Acts 17. 4	associate with.
CONSTANTLY	Acts 12. 15	without varying, confidently.
CONTAIN	1 Cor. 7. 9	to remain continent, restrain themselves.
CONTRITE	Ps. 51. 17	ground to powder; hence, humbled, sorrowful. (Lat. *contritus*.)
CONVENIENT	Acts 24. 25; Rom. 1. 28; Eph. 5. 4	becoming, fitting, suitable:
CONVERSATION	(1) Phil. 3. 20; (2) 1 Pet. 1. 15; (3) Heb. 13. 5	(1) citizenship; (2) behaviour; (3) disposition.

269

WORD.	PASSAGE.	EXPLANATION.
CONVERT	Is. 6. 10	to be converted.
CONVINCE	(1) Job 32. 12; (2) John 8. 46	(1) to refute; (2) to convict.
CONY, CONEY	Lev. 11. 5.	a rabbit.
CORN	John 12. 24	a grain.
COTES	2 Chr. 32. 28	huts, sheds (for sheep, &c.).
COUCHETH	Deut. 33. 13	lies, lies flat.
COUNT	Ex. 12. 4	(used as a *sub*.) a reckoning, account.
COUNTERVAIL	Esth. 7. 4	to compensate for.
COURSE, BY	1 Cor. 14. 27.	in due order.
COUSIN	Luke 1. 36, 58	a kinsman or kinswoman.
COVERT	1 Sam. 25. 20	shelter, hiding-place.
CRACKNELS	1 Kings 14. 3	crisp cakes or biscuits.
CRAFT	Acts 18. 3	occupation, trade.
CRAFTSMAN	Acts 19. 24	a skilled workman.
CRAVE	Mark 15. 43	to ask for.
CREATURE	(1) Rom. 1. 25; (2) 8. 19, &c.	(1) created thing; (2) the creation.
CRISPING PINS	Is. 3. 22	irons for crimping or curling hair.
CRUSE	1 Kings 14. 3; 2 Kings 2. 20	small cup or vessel for holding liquids.
CUMBER	Luke 10. 40; 13. 7	encumber, occupy unprofitably.
CUNNING	(1) 1 Kings 7. 14; (2) Gen. 25. 27; (3) Ex. 31. 4	(1) skill, knowledge; (2) knowing, skilful; (3) wrought with peculiar skill.
CURIOUS	(1) Ex. 28. 8; (2) Acts 19. 19 .	(1) carefully or artfully wrought; (2) magical.
CUSTOM	Matt. 9. 9	a tribute, tax, toll.
DAMN	Mark 16. 16	to judge, condemn.
DAMNABLE	2 Pet. 2. 1	destructive.
DAMNATION, or CONDEMNATION	Rom. 3. 8, &c.	These words were used as equivalent terms when the A.V. was issued; sometimes with a graver, sometimes with a lighter meaning. In 1 Cor. 11. 29, the reference is to self-judgment.
DANGER, IN	Matt. 5. 22	liable (to); i.e. liable to be condemned.
DAYSMAN	Job 9. 33	umpire, arbitrator.
DEAL	(1) Gen. 24. 49; (2) Is. 58. 7	(1) to act; (2) to distribute.
DEAL, A	Ex. 29. 40	a part or portion.
DEAR	Acts 20. 24	precious, of value.
DEBATE	Is. 58. 4	strife, contention.
DEBTOR	Rom. 1. 14	one who is under an obligation.
DECENTLY	1 Cor. 14. 40	in a becoming manner.
DECLARE	Gen. 41. 24	to make clear or manifest.
DECLINE	Ex. 23. 2	to turn aside.
DEEM	Acts 27. 27	to conclude, judge, conjecture.
DEFENCED	Is. 36. 1	fenced, defended by fortifications.
DEGREE	1 Tim. 3. 13	rank, station, position.
DEHORT	1 Macc. 9. 9	to dissuade.
DELICATELY	1 Sam. 15. 32	daintily, effeminately (R.V. cheerfully).
DELICIOUSLY	Rev. 18. 7	luxuriously.
DELIGHTSOME	Mal. 3. 12	delightful.
DEPUTY	Acts 13. 7, &c.	proconsul, governor of a province.
DESCRIBE	Josh. 18. 4, 6	to mark out.
DESCRY	Judg. 1. 23	to spy out, reconnoitre.
DESIRED	2 Chr. 21. 20	regretted. (From Lat. *desiderare*.)
DESPITE	Heb. 10. 29	contempt, contumely.
DESPITEFULLY	Matt. 5. 44	spitefully, maliciously.
DETERMINATE	Acts 2. 23	determined upon, fixed.
DISALLOW	1 Pet. 2. 4, 7	to disapprove of, reject.
DISANNUL	Gal. 3. 15, 17	to annul entirely.
DISCOVER	Is. 22. 8	to uncover, lay bare.
DISPOSITION	Acts 7. 53	appointment.
DISSOLVE	Dan. 5. 16	to solve.
DO TO WIT	2 Cor. 8. 1	to make to know.
DOCTOR	Luke 2. 46	a teacher.
DOUBT	Ecclus. 9. 13	to fear, be afraid of.
DRAUGHT	Matt. 15. 17	} a privy.
DRAUGHT HOUSE	2 Kings 10. 27	
DRESS	Gen. 2. 15	to trim, till.
DUKE	Gen. 33. 15	a leader, commander, chief.
DURE	Matt. 13. 21	to last, endure.
EAR, to	Deut. 21. 4; 1 Sam. 8. 12; Is. 30. 24	to plough, till the ground. (Chaucer has "to ere;" from A.S. *erian*, to plough.)
EARING	Gen. 45. 6; Ex. 34. 21	ploughing.
EARNEST	2 Cor. 1. 22; 5. 5; Eph. 1. 14	a pledge, security.
EDIFY	Acts 9. 31	to build; also, to build up.
ELEMENTS	Gal. 4. 9	rudiments, beginnings.
EMERODS	1 Sam. 5. 6	a disease now called the piles.
EMINENT	Ezek. 16. 24	high, lofty.
EMULATIONS	Gal. 5. 20	jealousies.
ENDAMAGE	Ezra 4. 13	to injure, damage.

WORD.	PASSAGE.	EXPLANATION.
ENDUE	Gen. 30. 20	to endow, furnish with.
ENLARGE	Ps. 4. 1	to set at liberty.
ENSAMPLE	1 Cor. 10. 11	example.
ENSIGN	Num. 2. 2	flag, banner.
ENSUE	1 Pet. 3. 11	to pursue diligently.
ENTREAT	Matt. 22. 6	to treat, deal with.
EQUAL	Ezek. 18. 25	just, right.
ESCHEW	1 Pet. 3. 11	to avoid, shun.
ESTATES	Mark 6. 21	states, ranks, men of rank.
EVANGELISTS	Acts 21. 8; Eph. 4. 11; 2 Tim. 4. 5	"Ministers of the Church, who assisted the Apostles in spreading the Gospel, or Evangel, of our Lord Jesus Christ." (Wright.)
EVIDENTLY	Acts 10. 3	clearly, plainly, visibly.
EVILFAVOURED-NESS	Deut. 17. 1	ugliness, deformity.
EXCHANGER	Matt. 25. 27	money-changer, banker.
EXERCISED	2 Pet. 2. 14	made familiar.
EXORCISTS	Acts 19. 13	"The original meaning of the word *exorcise* was to *adjure*, as in Matt. 26. 63. Hence exorcists were those who pretended to cast out devils by commanding them in the Divine Name to come forth." (Wright.)
EXPECT	Heb. 10. 13	to await, wait.
EXPRESS	Heb. 1. 3	exact, very.
EYESERVICE	Eph. 6. 6; Col. 3. 22	service performed only when under supervision.
FAIN	1 Macc. 6. 54	glad; also, gladly (Luke 15. 16).
FAN	Matt. 3. 12	a winnowing-fan.
FANNERS	Jer. 51. 2	winnowers.
FAST	Ruth 2. 8	close, near.
FAT	Joel 2. 24	vessel for liquor; same as "vat."
FAUCHION	Judith 13. 6	a curved sword.
FEAR	Gen. 31. 42	an object of fear.
FEARFUL	Matt. 8. 26	timid, afraid.
FELLOES	1 Kings 7. 33	the pieces making up the rim of a wheel.
FERVENT	2 Pet. 3. 10, 12	burning.
FINE	Job 28. 1	to refine (gold, &c.).
FITCHES	Is. 28. 25, 27	vetches; small kind of pea.
FLAGON	2 Sam. 6. 19	a large bottle or flask.
FLOOR	Matt. 3. 12	threshing-floor.
FLUX	Acts 28. 8	an issue; "bloody f."=dysentery.
FRAME	Judg. 12. 6	to contrive, manage.
FRAY	Deut. 28. 26	to scare, frighten away.
FRET	Lev. 13. 51, 55	to corrode, to eat away, as a moth (or an ulcer) does.
FRONTLETS	Ex. 13. 16	head-bands over the forehead.
FROWARD	Deut. 32. 20	perverse, self-willed.
FULLER	Mal. 3. 2; Mark 9. 3	a bleacher of cloth.
FURNITURE	Gen. 31. 34	equipment, harness.
GAINSAY	Luke 21. 15	to speak against, i.e. contradict.
GALLANT	Is. 33. 21	splendid.
GARDEN HOUSE	2 Kings 9. 27	a summer-house.
GARNER	Matt. 3. 12	a granary, barn.
GENDER	2 Tim. 2. 23	to produce, engender.
GENERATION	Matt. 3. 7	offspring, brood.
GHOST	Matt. 27. 50	spirit; "yield up the ghost"=to die.
GIN	Amos 3. 5	a trap or snare.
GIVE PLACE	Gal. 2. 5	to give way, yield (to).
GLISTER	Luke 9. 29	to shine, sparkle, glitter.
GO ABOUT	John 7. 20	to endeavour, try.
GO BEYOND	1 Thess. 4. 6	to overreach, cheat.
GO TO	Gen. 11. 3	come now!
GOODMAN	Matt. 20. 11	master of the house.
GOVERNOR	James 3. 4	helmsman, steersman.
GREAVES	1 Sam. 17. 6	armour for the legs.
GRISLED	Gen. 31. 10	of a grey colour, or mixed with grey.
GRUDGE	Ps. 59. 15	to grumble, murmur.
GUILTY OF	Matt. 26. 66	worthy of.
HABERGEON	Job 41. 26	a coat of mail for the neck and breast.
HAFT	Judg. 3. 22	handle of a knife, or dagger.
HALE	Luke 12. 58 ; Acts 8. 3	to drag forcibly, as an arrested person ; to *haul.*
HALT (*sub.*)	Luke 14. 21	lame, crippled.
HALT (*v.*)	Ps. 38. 17	to limp, go lamely (hence, hesitate).
HARDLY	Matt. 19. 23	with difficulty.
HARDNESS	2 Tim. 2. 3	hardship.
HARNESS	1 Kings 22. 34	body-armour of a soldier.
HARNESSED	Ex. 13. 18	armed, covered with armour.

271

List of Obsolete or Ambiguous Words

WORD.	PASSAGE.	EXPLANATION.
HEADY	2 Tim. 3. 4	headstrong, wilful.
HEALTH	Ps. 67. 2	"saving health"=salvation.
HEAVY	1 Kings 14. 6	sad.
HELL	{ Hab. 2. 5 { Acts 2. 27 { Matt. 10. 28	the grave. *Hades*, place of departed spirits. *Gehenna*, place of torment.
HELVE	Deut. 19. 5	handle of an axe.
HIS	Acts 12. 10; 1 Cor. 15. 38, &c.	Used for *neut.* "its," which occurs once only in A.V. (*see* Lev. 25. 5), where edit. of 1611 has "it."
HOISE	Acts 27. 40	to hoist; "hoised"=hoisted.
HOLD	Ex. 20. 7	to consider, esteem, account.
HONEST	Rom. 12. 17	honourable, comely.
HONESTY	1 Tim. 2. 2	honourable conduct.
HOSEN	Dan. 3. 21	trousers and stockings in one piece.
HOUGH	Josh. 11. 6, 9; 2 Sam. 8. 4	to cut the hamstrings or "hocks" of animals.
HOWBEIT	Judg. 4. 17	nevertheless.
HUNGRED, AN	Matt. 12. 1	very hungry.
HUSBANDMAN	Gen. 9. 20	a farmer.
ILL FAVOURED	Gen. 41. 3	ill-looking.
ILLUMINATED	Heb. 10. 32	i.e. enlightened (R.V.).
IMPLEAD	Acts 19. 38	to accuse, indict, plead against.
IMPORTABLE	Prayer of Manasses	insufferable, insupportable.
IMPOTENT	Acts 4. 9	powerless, strengthless.
INCONTINENT	2 Tim. 3. 3	intemperate, unrestrained.
INDIFFERENT	Ecclus. 42. 5	fair, impartial.
INDITE	Ps. 45. 1	to dictate for writing, compose.
INFORMED	Dan. 9. 22	instructed, taught.
INJURIOUS	1 Tim. 1. 13	insolent, outrageous.
INQUISITION	Deut. 19. 18	search, examination.
INSTANT	Luke 23. 23, &c.	urgent, importunate.
INSTANTLY	Acts 26. 7	with urgent importunity.
INTEND	Ps. 21. 11	to meditate, plan, plot.
INWARD	Job 19. 19	intimate, closely allied.
JACINTH	Rev. 9. 17	a precious stone, the hyacinth.
JANGLING, VAIN	1 Tim. 1. 6	babbling, vain talking.
JEOPARD, to	Judg. 5. 18	to hazard or risk, jeopardise.
JEWRY	John 7. 1, &c.	"Judæa properly so called; the part of Palestine occupied by the tribes of Judah and Benjamin after the Captivity." (Wright.)
JOT, OR TITTLE	Matt. 5. 18	"Jot" is "jod," the smallest Hebrew letter (*i*, or *iota*, in Gk.); hence, a very small quantity or portion.
JOY	Ps. 21. 1	to rejoice.
JUSTIFY	Deut. 25. 1	to acquit.
KERCHIEF	Ezek. 13. 18, 21	a cloth worn over the head.
KIND	Gen. 1. 11	"after his k."=according to its nature.
KINE	Gen. 41. 2; 1 Sam. 6. 7	the old plural of "cow;" "milch kine"=milking-cows.
KNOP	Ex. 25. 33	the bud of a flower, a carved imitation of one; now spelt "knob."
LACK	Mark 10. 21	to be deficient in; as *sub.*, want.
LATCHET	Mark 1. 7	a thong, lace.
LAUD	Rom. 15. 11	to praise.
LAVER	Ex. 38. 8	a vessel for washing in, cistern.
LAWYER	Matt. 22. 35	an expounder of the Mosaic Law.
LAY AT	Job 41. 26	to strike at.
LEASING	Ps. 4. 2; 5. 6	lying, falsehood.
LEES	Is. 25. 6	dregs, sediment.
LET	2 Thess. 2. 7	to hinder, prevent.
LEWD	(1) Acts 17. 5; (2) Ezek. 16. 27.	(1) ignorant, unlearned; (2) vicious.
LEWDNESS	Acts 18. 14	wickedness.
LIBERTINE	Acts 6. 9	the child of a freed slave.
LIEN	Gen. 26. 10	lain (*pp.* of "lie").
LIGHTEN	Luke 2. 32	to enlighten, illuminate.
LIGHTLY	Mark 9. 39	easily, carelessly.
LIGHTNESS	2 Cor. 1. 17	fickleness, levity.
LIGURE	Ex. 28. 19; 39. 12	an (unknown) precious stone.
LIKE	(1) Deut. 23. 16; (2) 1 Chr. 28. 4	(1) to please; (2) to approve of.
LIKING	Dan. 1. 10	bodily condition; "worse liking"=less plump.
LIST	John 3. 8	to please, choose, like.
LIVELY	Acts 7. 38	full of life, life-giving.
LODGE	Is. 1. 8	a hut.
LOFT	Acts 20. 9	an upper room.
LOOK	Is. 5. 2	to expect.
LOOK IN THE FACE	2 Kings 14. 8, 11	to meet in battle.

WORD	PASSAGE	EXPLANATION.
LUCRE	1 Tim. 3. 3	profit; "filthy lucre"=base gain.
LUST	Ex. 15. 9; 2 Tim. 4. 3 . . .	desire, wish, pleasure.
LUSTY	Judg. 3. 29	vigorous, strong.
MAGNIFICAL . .	1 Chr. 22. 5	magnificent.
MAKEST THOU .	Judg. 18. 3	dost thou.
MAN OF WAR . .	Luke 23. 11	a soldier, warrior.
MANDRAKE . . .	Gen. 30. 14	a plant, supposed to ensure conception; mandra- [gora.
MANNER, WITH THE	Num. 5. 13	"taken with the manner"=caught in the very act.
MANSIONS . . .	John 14. 2	abiding-places.
MARISH	Ezek. 47. 11	marsh, swampy-ground.
MATTER	James 3. 5	fuel for fire.
MAUL	Prov. 25. 18	heavy hammer; (hence, *mall-et*).
MAW	Deut. 18. 3	the stomach of animals.
MEAT	Gen. 1. 29, 30	food of any kind. "It is remarkable that in the '*meat* offering' there was nothing but flour and oil." (Wright.) The R.V. adopts "meal offering" uniformly.
MEET	Matt. 3. 8	suitable, fit.
MERCHANTMAN .	Matt. 13. 45	merchant.
MESS	Gen. 43. 34	a dish of food.
METE	Matt. 7. 2	to measure.
METEYARD . . .	Lev. 19. 35	a measuring-rod.
MILCH	Gen. 32. 15	giving milk (as cows).
MINCING	Is. 3. 16	walking with very short steps.
MIND	(1) Phil. 3. 19; (2) Acts 20. 13	(1) to care for, attend to; (2) to intend.
MINDED	Ruth 1. 18	disposed, determined.
MINISH	Ex. 5. 19	to diminish, lessen.
MINISTER (*sub.*)	Luke 4. 20	servant, attendant.
MINISTER (*v.*) .	2 Cor. 9. 10	to supply.
MITE	Mark 12. 42	a very small coin, half-a-farthing.
MORE PART . . .	Acts 19. 32	greater part, the majority.
MORTIFY	Rom. 8. 13; Col. 3. 5 . . .	to kill (metaphorically), to subdue.
MOTE (*see* BEAM).	Matt. 7. 3	a minute particle, as of dust.
MOTIONS	Rom. 7. 5	emotions, passions, workings.
MUFFLER	Is. 3. 19	a covering for the lower part of the face.
MUNITION . . .	Nah. 2. 1	fortress, fortifications.
MURRAIN	Ex. 9. 3	cattle-plague.
MUSE	Luke 3. 15	to meditate.
NAUGHTY. . . .	Jer. 24. 2	bad, worthless, good for nothing.
NECROMANCER .	Deut. 18. 11	one who pretends to call up the dead for purposes of divination.
NEEDS	Gen. 17. 13	of necessity.
NEESING	Job 41. 18	old form of "sneezing."
NEPHEW	1 Tim. 5. 4	a grandson.
NETHER	Ex. 19. 17	lower. (Compare *be-neath*.)
NETHERMOST . .	1 Kings 6. 6	lowest of all.
NITRE	Prov. 25. 20	natron, carbonate of soda.
NOISE ABROAD .	Luke 1. 65	to spread a report everywhere.
NOISOME	Ps. 91. 3	noxious, hurtful.
NOTHING	James 1. 6	not at all.
NOVICE	1 Tim. 3. 6	one newly admitted into the Christian body.
NURTURE	Eph. 6. 4	education, training, discipline.
OBEISANCE . . .	Gen. 37. 7	an outward act of homage.
OBLATION . . .	Lev. 7. 38	an offering (in sacrifice).
OBSERVE	Mark 6. 20	to treat with respect.
OCCUPIER . . .	Ezek. 27. 27	a trader.
OCCUPY	Luke 19. 13	to trade.
OCCURRENT . . .	1 Kings 5. 4	chance, occurrence.
OF	(1) Mark 1. 9; (2) Acts 13. 29; (3) 1 Cor. 15. 47	used in various senses: (1) instead of "by;" (2) for "concerning;" (3) "out of," or "from."
OFFENCE	Rom. 9. 33	that against which one stumbles.
OFFEND	Matt. 18. 9	to cause to stumble, make to sin.
OPEN	Acts 17. 3	to explain clearly.
ORDAIN	1 Kings 12. 32, 33	to appoint, order, arrange.
OR EVER	Acts 23. 15	before ever, before at all.
OSSIFRAGE . . .	Lev. 11. 13	bearded vulture; *lit.* "bone-breaker."
OUCHES	Ex. 28. 11	settings of gold or silver for precious stones; (*lit.* sockets).
OUTGOINGS . . .	Josh. 17. 9, 18; Ps. 65. 8 . .	utmost limits or boundaries.
OUTLANDISH . .	Neh. 13. 26	foreign.
OVERCHARGED . .	Luke 21. 34	overburdened.
OVERPASS . . .	Jer. 5. 28	pass over, take no notice of.
PAIN	Rev. 12. 2	to strive in pain.
PAINFUL	Ps. 73. 16	laborious, difficult.

T

WORD.	PASSAGE.	EXPLANATION.
PAINFULNESS . .	2 Cor. 11. 27	unsparing toil.
PALMERWORM . .	Joel 1. 4	a caterpillar.
PARCEL	Gen. 33. 19	a piece, portion.
PARTICULARLY . .	Acts 21. 19	in detail, one by one.
PASS	Ezek. 32. 19	to surpass, exceed.
PASSAGE	Judg. 12. 6	a ford; also, a pass (1 Sam. 14. 4).
PASTOR	Jer. 23. 1	a shepherd.
PEELED	Ezek. 29. 18	stripped of the skin.
PEEP	Is. 8. 19	to chirp, utter low sounds.
PERADVENTURE . .	Gen. 31. 31	perhaps.
PERSECUTE . . .	Ps. 7. 1	to pursue.
PHYLACTERIES . .	Matt. 23. 5	charms, or amulets worn on the forehead or arm, and inscribed with certain texts. (*See* "Gloss. of Ant.")
PILL	Gen. 30. 37, 38	to strip off the bark, to peel.
PLAT	2 Kings 9. 26	small patch of ground, plot.
PLATTER	Matt. 23. 36	a dish.
PLAY	2 Sam. 2. 14	to fence, fight with swords.
POLL	2 Sam. 14. 26	to cut the hair of the head.
PORT	Neh. 2. 13	a gate.
POST	2 Chr. 30. 6	a messenger, letter-carrier.
POTSHERD . . .	Ps. 22. 15	a fragment of broken pottery.
POWER	2 Chr. 32. 9	an army, host.
PRESENTLY . . .	Matt. 26. 53	immediately.
PRESSFAT . . .	Hag. 2. 16	the vat of a winepress.
PREVENT	1 Thess. 4. 15	to go before, anticipate, precede.
PRICKS	Acts 9. 5	goads (for driving cattle).
PROFESS	Matt. 7. 23	to declare openly.
PROPER	Heb. 11. 23	comely, fair.
PROPHESY . . .	(1) 1 Cor. 11. 5; (2) Matt. 26. 68	(1) to expound, explain; (2) to speak out, tell aloud.
PROPHET	Acts 13. 1	preacher, or divine. (*See* "Gloss. of Ant.")
PROSELYTE . . .	Matt. 23. 15	a convert; *esp.* to Judaism.
PROVE	John 6. 6	to test, try, put to the proof.
PROVOKE	2 Cor. 9. 2	to stimulate, incite.
PSALTERY	Dan. 3. 5	a stringed instrument to sing to.
PUBLICAN . . .	Matt. 9. 10; Luke 5. 27 . . .	a farmer of public revenue; *esp.* a native collector of the tribute imposed by the Romans.
PULSE	Dan. 1. 12	leguminous plants, beans, peas, &c.
PURCHASE . . .	1 Tim. 3. 13	to gain, win, acquire.
PURGE	Heb. 1. 3	to purify, clear away.
PYGARG	Deut. 14. 5	a kind of antelope.
QUATERNION . .	Acts 12. 4	a party (or guard) of four men.
QUICK	Acts 10. 42	alive. Also, lively (Heb. 4. 12).
QUICKEN	Rom. 8. 11	to revive, make alive.
QUIT	1 Cor. 16. 13	to acquit oneself, behave.
RANGE	Prov. 28. 15	to roam in search of prey.
RANGES	(1) Lev. 11. 35; (2) 2 Kings 11. 8	(1) chimney racks; (2) ranks of soldiers.
RASE	Ps. 137. 7	to lay level with the ground.
RAVENING . . .	Luke 11. 39	greediness, rapacity.
RAVIN (*sub.*) . .	Nah. 2. 12	plunder.
RAVIN (*v.*) . . .	Gen. 49. 27	to seize upon prey.
REASON	Acts 24. 25	to discourse, talk.
RECEIPT OF CUSTOM	Matt. 9. 9; Mark 2. 14; Luke 5. 27	"place of toll" (Revised Version).
RECOMPENSE . .	Heb. 10. 30	to repay, requite.
REFUSE	Ps. 118. 22	to reject.
REINS	Ps. 7. 9; Job 16. 13	the kidneys (spoken of as if the seat of joy, pain, &c).
RELIGIOUS . . .	James 1. 26	making an outward profession of religion.
RENT	Jer. 4. 30	old form of "to rend," to tear.
REPROVE	Job 6. 25	to disprove, prove to be wrong.
REREWARD . . .	Is. 52. 12; 58. 8	rear-guard (*lit.* rear-ward).
RESIDUE	Ex. 10. 5	the rest, the remainder.
REWARD	2 Tim. 4. 14	to requite, repay.
RINGSTRAKED . .	Gen. 30. 35	streaked with rings.
RIOTOUS	Prov. 23. 20	dissolute, wanton.
ROAD	1 Sam. 27. 10	a raid, inroad.
ROOM	Luke 14. 8; 1 Cor. 14. 16 . .	a place; *esp.* at table.
SAVE	1 Kings 3. 18	except.
SAVOUR	Matt. 16. 23	to relish; *met.* to understand.
SCALL	Lev. 13. 30	an eruption on the head or face.
SCANT	Mic. 6. 10	deficient, scanty.
SCARCENESS . .	Deut. 8. 9	scarcity.
SCRABBLE . . .	1 Sam. 21. 13	to scratch, scrawl, make marks.
SCRIP	1 Sam. 17. 40	a small bag or wallet, made of a "scrap" of stuff (Skeat).

WORD.	PASSAGE.	EXPLANATION.
SEAR	1 Tim. 4. 2	to scorch (as with a hot iron).
SEASON	Gen. 40. 4	a time, a while.
SECURE	Judg. 8. 11	without care.
SEETHE	Ex. 16. 23	to boil; *perf.* "sod," *part.* "sodden."
SENTENCE	Acts 15. 19	opinion, decision.
SERVITOR	2 Kings 4. 43	a servant or attendant.
SET	Matt. 5. 1	seated; also, appointed (Acts 12. 21).
SET BY	1 Sam. 18. 30	valued, esteemed.
SET ON	Acts 18. 10	to attack.
SET TO HIS SEAL	John 3. 33	(has) attached his seal to, attested.
SETTLE	Ezek. 43. 14	a bench, seat.
SEVERALLY	1 Cor. 12. 11	separately, individually.
SHAMEFACEDNESS	1 Tim. 2. 9	(better "shamefastness," as in R.V.); modesty.
SHERD	Is. 30. 14	a fragment, shred, broken piece.
SHIPMASTER	Jonah 1. 6	captain of a ship.
SHIPMEN	Acts 27. 27	sailors.
SHOELATCHET	Gen. 14. 23	lace of a shoe, strap, fastening.
SHROUD	Ezek. 31. 3	shelter of a tree (A.S. *scrúd*).
SIGNET	Gen. 38. 18	a seal.
SILLY	2 Tim. 3. 6	innocent, simple.
SILVERLING	Is. 7. 23	a small silver coin.
SIMILITUDE	Hos. 12. 10	a parable.
SIMPLE	Rom. 16. 19	innocent, guileless.
SINCERE	1 Pet. 2. 2	pure.
SITH	Ezek. 35. 6	since, forasmuch as.
SKILL	1 Kings 5. 6	to shew skill in, understand.
SLEIGHT	Eph. 4. 14	artifice, trick, deceitfulness.
SLIME	Gen. 11. 3; 14. 10	bitumen (a kind of mud).
SOD, SODDEN	Gen. 25. 29; Ex. 12. 9	boiled; from the *verb* "to seethe."
SOJOURN	Gen. 12. 10	to dwell for a time.
SOMETIME	1 Pet. 3. 20	} once, formerly.
SOMETIMES	Eph. 2. 13	
SOOTHSAYER	Dan. 2. 27	a diviner, foreteller of future events.
SOOTHSAYING	Acts 16. 16	divination, pretence of predicting.
SORCERER	Ex. 7. 11	a fortune-teller (by casting lots).
SORE	Gen. 19. 9	greatly, severely; as *adj.* severe.
SORT	Acts 17. 5	degree, kind, condition, rank.
SPED	Judg. 5. 30	succeeded.
SPEED	Gen. 24. 12	success, fortune.
SPOKEN FOR	Cant. 8. 8	asked (for) in marriage.
SPORT	2 Pet. 2. 13	to disport or amuse oneself.
SPRING	Judg. 19. 25	to dawn; as *sub.* dawn (1 Sam. 9. 26).
STABLISH	2 Sam. 7. 13	to establish, confirm.
STAGGER	Rom. 4. 20	to stumble, hesitate.
STAND	Eph. 6. 13	to stand firm; to consist (1 Cor. 2. 5).
STAND TO	Deut. 25. 8	to agree to, abide by.
STAY (*sub.*)	Ps. 18. 18	a support.
STAY (*v.*)	(1) Cant. 2. 5; (2) 2 Sam. 24. 16	(1) to support; (2) to stop, hold back.
STEAD	1 Chron. 5. 22	place (A.S. *stede*).
STOMACH	2 Macc. 7. 21	courage.
STOMACHER	Is. 3. 24	part of a woman's dress, a covering for the bosom.
STONE BOW	Wisd. 5. 22	a cross-bow for shooting stones.
STRAIGHTWAY	Luke 5. 39	immediately, at once.
STRAIN AT	Matt. 23. 24	more correctly, "strain out;" i.e. to get rid of by using a strainer.
STRAIT	Matt. 7. 13	narrow; also, strict (Acts 26. 5).
STRAITLY	Gen. 43. 7	strictly, closely.
STRAITNESS	Deut. 28. 53	scarcity of food, severe famine.
STRAKE	Gen. 30. 37	a streak.
"	Acts 27. 17	did strike.
STRANGE	Gen. 42. 7	foreign.
STRAW	Matt. 21. 8	to strew, or scatter.
STRICKEN IN YEARS	Luke 1. 7	advanced in years.
STRIKE	2 Kings 5. 11	to rub gently (cf. Ex. 12. 7).
STUFF	1 Sam. 30. 24	the furniture or baggage of an army, &c.
SUNDER	Job 41. 17	to separate, part asunder.
SUNDRY	Heb. 1. 1	several, various, separate.
SUPPLE	Ezek. 16. 4	to make or render pliant.
SURELY	Prov. 10. 9	securely.
SURFEITING	Luke 21. 34	sickness caused by gluttony.
SWADDLE	Ezek. 16. 4	to swathe, bandage (as infants).
SWEAR	Ex. 13. 19	to make or cause to swear.
SWELLING	2 Pet. 2. 18	haughty, arrogant, proud.
SWINE	Lev. 11. 7	a pig (in the *sing.*); also, pigs.
TABERING	Nah. 2. 7	beating, as on a tabor or drum.
TABERNACLE	Num. 24. 5; Matt. 17. 4	a tent or moveable dwelling. The feast of tabernacles=feast of booths.

WORD.	PASSAGE.	EXPLANATION.
TABLE	Luke 1. 63	a writing-tablet.
TABLET	Ex. 35. 22	an ornament for a necklace.
TABRET	Gen. 31. 27	a small drum or tambourine.
TACHES	Ex. 26. 6	attachments, fastenings.
TAKE	(1) Prov. 6. 2; (2) 1 Cor. 6. 7	(1) to catch; (2) to endure.
TALE	Ex. 5. 8, 18	a (fixed) number, a total.
TARGET	1 Sam. 17. 6	a light shield, buckler.
TAVERNS	Acts 28. 15	shops. "The three taverns," a station on the Appian way.
TEIL TREE	Is. 6. 13	a kind of oak, terebinth.
TELL	Gen. 15. 5	to count, number.
TEMPER	Ex. 29. 2	to mix, compound.
TEMPERANCE	Acts 24. 25	moderation, self-restraint.
TEMPT	Matt. 4. 7	to test, put to the test.
TEMPTATION	Deut. 4. 34	trial.
TENDER	2 Macc. 4. 2	to be careful for, to regard.
TESTAMENT	Heb. 9. 16	a will; also, a covenant, as in the N. T.
TETRARCH	Matt. 14. 1	a ruler over the fourth part of a country.
THOUGHT	Matt. 6. 25	great anxiety, excessive care.
TIMBREL	Ex. 15. 20	a small tambourine.
TIRE (*sub.*)	Is. 3. 18	a head-dress.
TIRE (*v.*)	2 Kings 9. 30	to adorn with a head-dress.
TITTLE	Matt. 5. 18; Luke 16. 17	a small line drawn over an abridged word, or a slight projection in some Hebrew letters; hence, a small particle. See JOT.
TO	Matt. 3. 9	used with the sense of "for."
TO BRAKE	Judg. 9. 53	broke in pieces. *See* ALL TO BRAKE.
TONGUES	Acts 10. 46	various (strange) languages.
TORMENTOR	Matt. 18. 34	a torturer, executioner.
TOUCHING	Matt. 18. 19	concerning; "as touching"=with regard to.
TRANSLATION	Heb. 11. 5	removal; from *translate*, to transfer.
TRAVAIL	Is. 53. 11; Jer. 30. 6	labour, pain; also, trouble.
TRESPASS	1 Kings 8. 31	to transgress, sin.
TROW	Luke 17. 9	to think, imagine, suppose.
TUTOR	Gal. 4. 2	a guardian.
TWAIN	Is. 6. 2	two.
UNDERGIRD	Acts 27. 17	to pass ropes tightly round the hull of a ship, so as to keep the timbers from starting in a gale.
UNDERSETTERS	1 Kings 7. 30, 34	pedestals, supports.
UNDERTAKE	Is. 38. 14	to be surety for.
UNEQUAL	Ezek. 18. 25, 29	unjust.
UNICORN	Num. 23. 22	*lit.* "a *one-horned* animal;" but here, the bison.
UNJUST	Luke 16. 8	dishonest.
UNSAVOURY	2 Sam. 22. 27	without savour (i. e. wisdom); foolish.
UNTOWARD	Acts 2. 40	obstinate, perverse.
UNWITTINGLY	Josh. 20. 3	unconsciously, unintentionally.
UTTER	Ezek. 42. 1	outer. "Uttermost"=last (Matt. 5. 26).
"	Lev. 5. 1	to disclose, make known.
VAGABOND	Acts 19. 13	fugitive, wandering.
VENISON	Gen. 25. 28	flesh of hunted animals.
VERY	John 7. 26	true, real, actual.
VEX	Matt. 15. 22	to harass, torment.
VIRTUE	Mark 5. 30	efficacy, might.
VOID	Gen. 1. 2	empty.
WARD	Gen. 40. 3	prison (*lit.* guard).
WARE	Acts 14. 6	aware.
WATCH	(1) Lam. 2. 19; (2) Judg. 7. 19; (3) Ex. 14. 24; (4) Matt. 14. 25	"Before the Captivity the night was divided into three parts or watches; the *first* watch occurs in (1); the *middle* watch (2); and the *morning* watch (3). These probably varied in length according to the time of year. In (4) a *fourth* watch is mentioned, having been introduced among the Jews by the Romans." (Wright).
WAX	Luke 1. 80	to grow, or become.
WAY	Acts 19. 9, 23	the Christian life and doctrine.
WEALTH	Ps. 112. 3	prosperity, welfare (cf. 1 Cor. 10. 24).
WEENING	2 Macc. 5. 21	imagining.
WHIT	1 Sam. 3. 18; 2 Cor. 11. 5	a bit; atom. "Every whit"=wholly; "not a whit"=not at all.
WILL WORSHIP	Col. 2. 23	a worship of one's own choosing.
WIMPLE	Is. 3. 22	veil or covering for the throat or neck.
WINEBIBBER	Matt. 11. 19	an immoderate wine-drinker, drunkard.
WINEFAT	Mark 12. 1	wine-vat.
WINK AT	Acts 17. 30	to close the eyes to.
WISE	Lev. 19. 17	mode, manner, way (A.S. *wise*).

Word.	Passage.	Explanation.
Wist	Mark 14. 40.	knew (A.S. *wiste*).
Wit, to	2 Cor. 8. 1	to know (A.S. *witan*).
With	Judg. 16. 7	young twig of a willow or osier.
Withal	(1) 1 Kings 19. 1; (2) Job 2. 8.	(1) besides, likewise; (2) with.
Without	2 Cor. 10. 13, 15	beyond.
Wittingly	Gen. 48. 14	intentionally, knowingly.
Witty	Prov. 8. 12	skilful, clever.
Woe worth the day	Ezek. 30. 2	evil be to the day; let the day be accursed.
Wont	Matt. 27. 15	accustomed.
Worship	Luke 14. 10.	honour, reverence.
Wot	Gen. 21. 26	to know. Also, "we wot," Ex. 32. 1; "wot ye not," Rom. 11. 2; "wotteth not," Gen. 39. 8.
Wreathen	Ex. 28. 14	twisted; used in connexion with "work."
Wrest	Ex. 23. 2	to pervert.
Wrought	Matt. 20. 12	worked.
Yearn	Gen. 43. 30; 1 Kings 3. 26	to long for earnestly or anxiously, to be moved with tenderness, grief, or pity.
Yokefellow	Phil. 4. 3.	a fellow-worker, "companion in labour."

LV–LVI. GLOSSARY OF ANTIQUITIES CUSTOMS, ETC.

Altar. An erection usually of stones or of a single stone, but sometimes of metal, on which certain victims or parts of victims were burnt, and their blood sprinkled. The first mentioned was that built by Noah (Gen. 8[20]). God commanded the Hebrew altars to be made of earth or of unhewn stones, and without steps. The worshippers of Baal built their altars on hill-tops, hence 'altars on *high places*' were an abomination to the Lord. In the Temple at Jerusalem the brazen altar of burnt sacrifice was *outside* the Holy Place, in the court in front of it. The golden altar of incense stood inside.

Anathema. 'Anathema' is a Greek word denoting a thing or person devoted to God, and hence, as animals so devoted were put to death, doomed to destruction, accursed. In 1 Cor. 16[22] it is not to be joined in one expression with **Maran-atha** (which see).

Angel is the Greek word (ἄγγελος) for a 'messenger', and is used generally of the 'ministering spirits' sent out as messengers of God; less frequently of men so sent. The 'angels of the churches' in Revelation (2[1], &c.) may be a designation of their bishops, but more probably the phrase points to a heavenly representative of each Church, in some sort the embodiment of its spirit and responsible for its life. The expression 'Angel of the Lord' seems to vary in meaning, sometimes signifying the manifested presence of the Lord Jehovah.

Apostle is from the Greek, meaning 'one who is sent forth, a delegate'. The word is used specially of 'the twelve', also of St. Paul. All the apostles had 'seen the Lord', and this was an essential qualification of apostleship in a strict technical sense (Acts 1[21-26]; 1 Cor. 9[1, 2]). Under this limitation the term was freely applied to prominent teachers in the early Christian Church, notably to Barnabas. In two passages Paul places 'apostles' first among the various orders of the Church's ministry (1 Cor. 12[28]; Eph. 4[11]). The word is once applied to Christ himself (Heb. 3[1]).

Ark. The word means a covered chest or box. Three important arks are mentioned, viz. :—

1. Noah's ark (Heb. *Têbhâh*).

2. That in which the infant Moses was hidden by his mother (Heb. *Tébháh*).

3. The Ark of the Covenant (Heb. *Arôn*). This sacred object was a chest made of acacia wood overlaid with gold, the lid of which constituted the ' mercy-seat ' (Exod. 25[17]), or place of propitiation, over which two cherubim extended their wings. Within it were put the two tables of stone, on which the Decalogue was engraven. It was 2½ cubits long, 1½ broad, and 1½ deep. Around its upper edge was a cornice of gold, and it was carried in front of the people on their march by the Levites, who bore it by means of two poles of shittim wood covered with gold, which were passed through two rings on each side of the ark. In it were also placed, by Divine command, an omer of manna and Aaron's rod which budded. The Egyptians had a sacred ark in connexion with some of their mystic rites. The Egyptian ark or chest which contained the dead body in the funeral procession was treated with the greatest reverence, because the pious dead were identified with the gods Osiris, Seker, and Ptah. The ark was made in the form of a shrine, and was ornamented on the outside with figures of the genii of the dead, and with inscriptions referring to them. Arks were usually mounted on runners.

Atonement, Day of. This fast was observed on the 10th of the month Tisri, as the great day of national humiliation, and expiation of the sins both of the priests and the people. The ritual is prescribed in Lev. 16, 23[26-32] ; Num. 29[7-11]. On this day (i) the High Priest, arrayed, not in his gorgeous robes, but in the white linen garments common to himself and the rest of his order, brought a bullock as a sin-offering and a ram as a burnt-offering for himself and the priests. (ii) He then brought to the door of the tabernacle two he-goats as a sin-offering, and a ram for a burnt-offering for the people. (iii) Having presented them before the Lord, he cast two lots upon them, one inscribed *for Jehovah*, the other *for Azazel* (or *dismissal*, Lev. 16[8], R.V.). (iv) Then he slew the bullock at the brazen altar, and having censed the Mercy Seat of the Ark in the Holy of Holies, sprinkled the blood seven times before it, and made atonement for himself and his own order. (v) He next slew the goat on which the lot *for Jehovah* had fallen, and sprinkled its blood as a sin-offering for the people as he had done that of the bullock, and, as he returned, sprinkled the blood of both victims on the Golden Altar of Incense. (vi) Then coming forth he laid both his hands on the goat upon which the lot *for Azazel* had fallen (A.V. ' the scapegoat '), and having solemnly confessed over it the sins of the people, sent it away ' by the hand of a fit man ' into the wilderness, ' unto a land not inhabited ', to be there let loose, laden with its typical burden of the sins of the people. The key to the expressive imagery of this great day of expiation is given in Heb. 9[10].

Baalism was the worship of the powers of generation practised by the Canaanite race. Their creed was, that out of a self-existent chaotic deep sprang spontaneously the heavenly bodies and the earth ; that, from the procreative power of the sun, acting upon the fertile womb of the earth, all visible matter was produced : hence, the significance of the abandonment of Ahab and his subjects to the sole influence of this worship of Nature, which resulted in the almost entire destruction of animal and vegetable life. The word ' Baal ' means *Master, Owner, Possessor.*

Baptism. A Sacrament or symbolic rite of universal obligation, instituted by our Lord as a means of admission into the Christian Church. Baptism had been practised by John the Baptist as a sign of repentance, and in preparation for the coming of the Messiah. The original mode of Baptism was immersion. Hence the metaphorical use of the word (Mark 10^{38}; Luke 12^{50}) of an overwhelming by sorrow. The rite has its connexion with the purificatory use of water in the Jewish Church. But the word baptism (Gk. βάπτισμα) is not used of the Mosaic washings. These are indeed described by a cognate word (Gk. βαπτισμός), Mark 7^4; Heb. 6^2, 9^{10}; but the very use of the two similar words seems intended to mark off the Christian rite of Baptism as separate and unique.

Bottle. Various words are rendered in the A.V. of the O.T. by 'bottle'. In the New the only one so rendered is ἀσκός (Matt. 9^{17}; Mark 2^{22}) = the Latin *uter*, a skin-bottle. The larger bottles were made of the skin of a he-goat, the smaller of a kid's skin. When the animal was killed, they cut off its feet and its head, and they drew it in this manner out of the skin, without cutting it open. They afterwards dressed the inside of the skin with tannin, and having sewn up the apertures at the legs and tail, filled the skin with a decoction of bark and water until saturated. When used for wine, the skins were hung up in the houses, and so became smoked and shrivelled; hence the Psalmist's simile, 'like a bottle in the smoke' (Ps. 119^{83}). They were mended by stitching on a patch, and covering it over with pitch. They are still extensively manufactured at Hebron, and are used by the vendors of water and wine at Jerusalem, who carry them strapped to their backs, and draw the liquid from a tap fixed in one of the hind legs.

Bracelet. Bracelets for the arms and anklets for the legs were commonly worn by Eastern married women of all ranks, and were regarded as an eligible mode of investing money, as they could not be taken for the debts of the husband. They were usually cable-like rings, with an opening through which the wrist could be slipped; but the higher classes wore bracelets formed like broad bands, richly chased, jointed and closed by a pin passing through sockets. The anklets were similar in form, but frequently adorned with little bells. Both are still common in the East, with scarcely any variation in the patterns; they are of gold, silver, brass, and coloured glass, the last being extensively manufactured at Hebron. Those worn by the Hebrews were never jewelled; but men seem to have used bracelets as well as women (2 Sam. 1^{10}; S. of S. 5^{14}).

Bread was principally in the form of thin cakes, baked upon the hearth or in the oven; those eaten by the poor were made of barley-meal, with oil instead of butter. They were leavened or unleavened, and kneaded in a trough. Wheaten flour was common in Egypt, but a luxury in Palestine, and was one of the offerings in the Sanctuary. The Congregation were bound to offer fine flour for twelve cakes ('shewbread'), to be placed every Sabbath in two rows on the table of shewbread, which was to be eaten by the priests in the sacred precincts (Exod. 25^{30}; Matt. 12^4).

Burial of the dead was practised by the Hebrews from the earliest times, and three of their most ancient cemeteries still remain, viz. Machpelah, Shechem, and the Valley of Jehoshaphat. It is thought that cremation was only used for the bodies of persons who were denied religious burial; 'the burning for the dead' (2 Chron. 16^{14}) was the vaporizing of the sweet perfumes, as a mark of especial honour, at the funeral of kings and other distinguished persons. Burial places were usually outside the city or village, and the dead were carried to the grave on biers, amid the wailing of their friends, especially of women. The days of mourning were in general thirty. Burial was refused to criminals; and the 'burial of an ass' was exposure to birds and beasts of prey. Some ancient tombs had heavy stone superstructures over them, as the Tomb of Hiram. Israelite tombs were usually in caves in the limestone rock, the hard stratum (*missi*) being left as a roof, and the softer (*malaki*), which is below, being cut into. Around Jerusalem are large caves, containing several chambers or vaults for bodies, somewhat resembling the Roman catacombs. It is the custom in hot countries for the burial to take place a few hours after death. The Babylonians and Assyrians are supposed to have burnt their dead. The ancient Egyptians hewed tombs in the mountains and in the rocky ground; they also built Pyramids to hold the bodies of certain of their kings.

Butter. The Hebrews were ignorant of the art of *churning* butter; but they made a kind of clotted cream by subjecting new milk to fermentation, which imparted to it a pleasant acid flavour somewhat resembling that of lemon cream. Even now churned butter is never used by native Syrians, but this clotted cream, called *Leben*, continues to be universally consumed. This was probably the 'butter in a lordly dish' which Jael brought to Sisera, when she had 'opened a bottle of milk' (Judg. 4¹⁹, 5²⁵).

Camel's hair. Raiment of camel's hair (Matt. 3⁴) was not a skin, but a coat of cloth, woven from the hair of the camel. Such is the ordinary outer garment of the Bedawin of to-day. The present common dress of a shepherd on the hills of Judaea is a loose coat of camel's hair, in broad stripes of black and white, girt around the loins with a leathern belt. It has narrow sleeves, does not come below the knee, and seems to be almost his only garment.

Candle. Wherever the word occurs in the A.V. the R.V. more correctly substitutes *lamp* (with the single exception of Jer. 25¹⁰). The Jews and most other ancient nations used earthenware lamps, shaped like a butter-boat partially covered over, in which oil was burnt, the wick protruding through a lip or spout. It was set on a 'candlestick', i. e. a lamp-stand. The woman seeking her lost piece of silver would have this candlestick in one hand and a short hand-broom in the other, as she stooped and swept the house (Luke 15⁸). The Jews frequently light their houses with seven-branched candlesticks in memory of the sacred lamp-stand within the sanctuary.

Corban (Heb. *Ḳorbān*, an offering). The word is used in the O.T. of anything offered or vowed to God. By a perverted tradition the word became a formula by which it was possible to retain in one's own possession what it was inconvenient to part with (Mark 7¹¹).

Corn (treading out). In Syria and Asia Minor, at the present day, grain is trodden out of the ear. The unthreshed wheat is laid upon the ground in a circle, and a yoke of oxen driven round and round over it, dragging after them a heavy log of wood, on the under surface of which are inserted rows of thin flint stones, about two inches apart, and projecting half an inch from the surface. On this the driver stands, or sometimes sits in a chair.

Crown. Two words are so translated in the N.T. The more frequent is the Greek στέφανος, a garland, wreath, chaplet. It formed the prize at the Greek games, and was worn by feasters. Hence it became a symbol of victory or joy. This was the 'crown' of thorns placed in mockery on the Saviour's head. The other word, διάδημα, diadem (so rendered in R.V.), occurs only in Revelation 12³, 13¹, 19¹². It was originally the Persian badge of royalty, a ribbon of blue and white worn round the turban: thus the word means a crown as the sign and symbol of kingship.

Crucifixion was unknown to the Jews, until introduced by the Romans, who used it only for the punishment of slaves and the lowest malefactors.

But persons were hanged on a tree after they were slain as far back as the days of Joshua (8²⁹), whilst in Egypt hanging was a very early penalty.

Dedication, Feast of. This feast was instituted to commemorate the cleansing of the Temple after its defilement by Antiochus Epiphanes (Dan. 11³¹). Its institution is recorded in 1 Macc. 4⁵²⁻⁹. Established by Judas Maccabaeus, it was kept on the 25th of the winter month *Chisleu*, December, and lasted eight days. It was celebrated nearly in the same manner as the Feast of Tabernacles—the offering of many sacrifices, the carrying of branches of trees, and other rejoicings. It is mentioned only once in the Canonical Scriptures, John 10²², under the name of τὰ ἐγκαίνια.

Devil. The word is a contracted form of *Diabolus*, the Greek διάβολος. This word properly means a malicious accuser, and is used in the Greek Testament and LXX as an equivalent of the Hebrew word **Satan**, which means an adversary. The connexion between the ideas of the two words is well shown in Job I. In many passages of the N.T. the Hebrew word Satan is retained, while another designation is ὁ πονηρός, 'the evil one'. Satan's emissaries are spoken of in the N.T. not as devils, but as evil or unclean spirits and demons (Greek δαιμόνια). Layard discovered bowls inscribed with forms of Jewish exorcism among the ruins of Babylon; instances of exorcism are referred to by Josephus and other Jewish writers; they are also noticed in early Christian writings: and forms of exorcism are used in connexion with Baptism in many ancient churches, *see* e.g. the First Prayer Book of Edward VI.

Divination, Magic, Witchcraft, &c. From time immemorial the Eastern nations have used 'curious arts', and have professed to hold communication with the spirit world through the medium of superstitious practices. Large numbers of magical formulae, lists of lucky and unlucky days, incantations and such like have been found inscribed upon Babylonian and Assyrian tablets, and there is evidence to show that to some extent similar practices prevailed in Egypt. Pharaoh had his Magicians, and Nebuchadrezzar had his Astrologers. There are various Hebrew words by which these traffickers in superstitious rites were described. They may be classified thus :—

(*a*) **Diviners** professed to see visions or to obtain information by gazing into a cup (Gen. 44⁵), by means of arrows, by the inspection of livers of victims, and by teraphim, a kind of image (Ezek. 21²¹). Compare the divination amongst the Midianites (Num. 22⁷) and the Philistines (1 Sam. 6²).

(*b*) **Wizards, Witches,** or **Sorcerers,** literally knowing ones, thought-readers (Lev. 19³¹; Deut. 18¹¹).

(*c*) **Necromancers** (Deut. 18¹¹), supposed to be possessed with familiar spirits, e.g. the witch of En-dor, who was professedly a 'medium' between the living and the dead.

(*d*) **Soothsayers, Monthly Prognosticators, and Observers of Times,** were Astrologers, who would draw horoscopes and foretell events by examining the conjunctions and oppositions of the heavenly bodies (Is. 2⁶, 47¹³, &c.).

(*e*) **Magicians** or 'engravers' (Ex. 32⁴) were perhaps originally a literary caste. Compare the case of the magi or wise men who came from the East to worship Christ.

(*f*) **Enchanters** were serpent charmers, and another class were probably conjurers, gifted with sleight of hand.

The Israelites were strictly forbidden to have anything to do with these various classes of superstition. Their practices savoured of heathenism and idolatry, and tended to divert men's minds from the true source of knowledge and power. No witch was to live amongst the people. Men were not to seek to wizards that peeped (R.V. *chirp*) and muttered, but to the Law and the Testimony (Is. 8[19-21]).

What were the secrets of these practices, or indeed of their later representatives in the Greek period (Acts 19[19]), the Middle Ages, or more modern times, none but the initiated could tell. Probably amongst their hidden arts there may be reckoned quickness of wit, the power of a strong will over a weak one, the possession of secret information, the strange gift called *clairvoyance*, the modern hypnotism or 'second sight', the use of drugs and mechanical devices.

Fasts. The only fast appointed by the Law was the Day of Atonement on the 10th of Tisri (Lev. 16), but during the Captivity four annual fasts were observed by the Jews: (i) The fast of the fourth, fifth, seventh, and tenth months (Zech. 7[3, 5], 8[19]). (ii) Fasts were sometimes proclaimed (a) publicly on occasions of national humiliation (1 Sam. 7[6]; 2 Chron. 20[3]; Joel 1[14], 2[15]); (b) by cities and bodies of men on occasions in which they were specially concerned (Judg. 20[26]; 1 Sam. 31[13]; 2 Sam. 1[12]; (c) by individuals in times of difficulty and peril (Ezra 8[21-3]; Esth. 4[16]). (iii) In the New Testament we have reference to (a) 'the fast', i.e. the 'Day of Atonement' (Acts 27[9]); (b) the weekly fasts (Matt. 9[14]; Mark 2[18]; Luke 5[33], 18[12]; Acts 10[30]). They seem to have been introduced some time after the Captivity, and were observed on the second and fifth days of the week. (c) Fasting is specially connected with Ordination (Acts 13[3], 14[23]). The fasts of forty days by Moses (Ex. 24[18], 34[28]) and by Elijah (1 Kings 19[8]) are shadows of the great fast of our Lord (Matt. 4[2]; Mark 1[12, 13]; Luke 4[2]).

Feasts. (i) The *weekly* festival was the sabbath, commemorating God's rest from creation, and deliverance from bondage in Egypt (Exod. 20[8-11]). (ii) The *monthly* festival was the day of the new moon, on which rest was not enjoined, but additional services (Num. 10[10], 28[11]). (iii) The new moon of the seventh month Tisri, or *Feast of Trumpets*, began the civil year, and that of Abib the ecclesiastical year (Num. 29[1]; Exod. 12[2]). (iv) The *great* festivals were (a) *Passover*, on the eve of the 14th of Abib, which lasted to the 21st (Exod. 12); (b) *Pentecost* (the fiftieth day after), or feast of weeks, on completion of the harvest (Exod. 23[16]; Deut. 16[9-11]); (c) *Tabernacles*, from the 15th to 23rd of Tisri, commemorating the ingathering of all fruits (Exod. 34[22]; Levit. 23[34-43]). The people lived for a week in booths, to remind them of their desert wanderings. The last day was 'the great day' (John 7[37]). This feast was preceded by the Day of Atonement (Lev. 16). (v) Every seventh year was *sabbatical*, when the land had rest. Every fiftieth was a *jubilee*, when slaves were freed, land sold reverted to its original owner, and mortgages were cancelled. (vi) To these were added *Purim* ('Lots'), 14th and 15th of Adar, in remembrance of the deliverance by Esther (Esth. 9[24-6]); and (vii) the *Dedication* of the Second Temple, celebrated on the 25th of Chisleu (John 10[22]).

Garments. The garments of Syrian men in the present day differ but little from those worn in the time of Moses. The chief are a coarse linen shirt, linen drawers, loose pantaloons with a girdle to sustain them, an inner vest buttoned to the throat, a long loose robe with a leathern girdle, an embroidered cloth or velvet jacket, a *keffiyeh* or silk handkerchief for the head (secured by a cord), hose and sandals. Besides these, a long loose robe with short sleeves was worn in full dress (instead of the jacket or girded robe), and the *aba*, a coarse cloak of goat's or camel's hair, very large, so as to form a covering by night as well as by day; it was the former our Lord laid aside when He washed the disciples' feet (John 13⁴), and the latter with which Elijah smote the waters of Jordan (2 Kings 2⁸). Women's dress varied according to their estate in life (e.g. maid, wife, or widow). It differed from the men's principally in the veil and cap, fitting close to the head, concealing the hair, and being profusely covered with gold and silver ornaments and with charms. The list of female clothing in Is. 3¹⁸⁻²³ is scarcely intelligible now. The 'hem of the garment' referred to in the New Testament is the fringe which all Jews wore in obedience to the order given in Num. 15³⁸. It is now represented by the *Tallith* or cloth worn by the Jews at prayers.

Gospel. The A.S. equivalent of the Greek εὐαγγέλιον, Lat. *evangelium*, good tidings (see above, p. 140). In the N.T. the word is used, previously to the death of Jesus Christ, of the good tidings concerning the coming establishment of the kingdom of God. Afterwards, and in general, it is the good tidings of salvation through Jesus. Hence the term was applied to a narrative of the facts concerning Jesus Christ (as in Mark 1¹), and subsequently to the written record of these facts as in the titles of the 'Gospels'.

Hell. In the O.T. this is the A.V. translation of the Heb. *Shĕôl*, the dark, mysterious abode of the dead. The R.V. in general renders it *grave* or *pit*, with Sheôl in the margin, or leaves that word in the text. In the Prophetical books, however, the rendering *hell* is retained (see the Revisers' Preface). In the N.T. the word *hell* is a translation of the Greek word Hades, the equivalent of the Hebrew Sheôl, or of Gehenna, the place of torment. The R.V. retains Hades and Gehenna in the text.

Hellenists, or 'Jews of the Grecian speech', denoted those Jews who, by settling in a foreign country, had adopted the Greek civilization, and with it the use of the Greek tongue. Thus in Acts 6¹ we read, 'There arose a murmuring of the Grecian Jews' (R.V. marg. 'Hellenists') 'against the Hebrews'. Again, Acts 9²⁹, we read that St. Paul 'spake and disputed against the Grecian Jews' (R.V. marg. 'Hellenists'), 'but they went about to kill him'. The word is carefully to be distinguished from 'Hellenes' = *Gentiles*. See John 7³⁵, A.V. and R.V.

Inn was originally only a plot of ground, near a spring or well, and sometimes secured by a wall or fence, allotted as a camping-ground for the use of travellers. This was the 'inn' of the O.T. (Gen. 43²¹, &c., R.V. 'lodging place'). In later times, some wealthy benefactor would raise the wall, build a few arches, unite them to the wall by a roof, close them with doors, and separate them by partitions, thus providing a separate room for each party; while the cattle were littered in the central open space, or in sheds abutting on the outside wall, or in natural caves around it. This is the modern Khan or caravansary, and such, it is thought, was 'the inn' at Bethlehem; though the word translated 'inn' may simply mean 'guest-chamber', and is so rendered in Mark 14¹⁴; Luke 22¹¹.

Jewels. Precious stones are nowhere mentioned in the Bible as personal ornaments, except in connexion with religious worship, but 'jewels of gold and silver' were so worn, the chief of which were bracelets, anklets, chains, ear-rings, even nose-rings, brooches, and medallions on the forehead, (Cf. Is. 3¹⁶⁻²³.) All these were worn by women; but men wore bracelets, official gold chains, and signet-rings. The Ishmaelites wore ear-rings; and the Amalekites adorned the necks of their camels with gold chains.

Jot, or *Yod*, the smallest letter of the Hebrew alphabet in its later form. The tittle (Gk. κεραία, a little horn) was the minute projecting line which serves to distinguish certain of the Hebrew letters from others (Matt. 5¹⁸).

Jubilee, year of. At the end of seven times seven years, that is, forty-nine entire years, the fiftieth was observed as the year of *Jubilee*, a word of uncertain meaning. The directions for its observance are given in Lev. 25[8-16, 23-55]. Proclaimed by the sound of trumpets, it was kept on the tenth day of the seventh month Tisri. During this year the soil was to lie fallow, all Hebrew bondmen were to be liberated, and all land that had been alienated was to return to those to whom it had been allotted at the original distribution (Lev. 27[24]).

Landmarks were usually a single block or small pile of stones laid upon the ground, and are still so in Palestine. They might easily be shifted by a dishonest landowner ; hence the severe curse upon their removal (Deut. 27[17]). In Egypt, the land had to be re-measured and allotted after each inundation of the Nile. A fine collection of landmarks or boundary-stones is exhibited in the Assyrian Room, Northern Gallery, British Museum.

Maran-atha (*Mâran ĕthâ*). Two Chaldee words signifying 'our Lord hath come'. It would seem probable that the phrase was used by the early Christians as a kind of watchword of mutual encouragement and hope. So the words in 1 Cor. 16[22] are nearly equivalent to the similar expressions in Phil. 4[5]; Rev. 22[20].

Marriage. This ceremony is performed in the 'upper room' of private houses. The betrothed pair stand under a canopy, the bride being veiled, both wearing crowns, which are several times exchanged during the ceremony. The officiating minister is not a priest, nor necessarily a rabbi, but an elder, who, standing under the canopy, and holding a cup of blessing, invokes a benediction on the assembly. He gives a cup of wine to the betrothed, who pledge one another. The bridegroom then drains the cup, dashes it to the ground, and crushes it with his heel, a symbol, it is said, that their happiness cannot be without alloy while Jerusalem is in the hands of the heathen. The marriage contract is next read, and attested by each person present drinking of a cup of wine. The friends next walk round the canopy, chanting psalms and showering rice upon the couple. The ceremony is concluded by the elder invoking the seven blessings upon them, drinking the benedictory cup, and passing it round to the assembly. After dark, the bridegroom leads the bride homewards, attended by the friends of each, while others join the procession on its way, bearing hymeneal lamps in token of respect. Arrived at the bridegroom's house all are invited to a feast, which by the rich is repeated for seven nights, or even longer (Matt. 25[1-13]).

Mill was not a building, but a pair of millstones of granite or basalt, placed one upon the other, the lower one being larger and stationary, and the upper loose, with a hole through its centre into which the corn was put. This upper stone was turned briskly round by a wooden handle, fixed in its surface near the circumference. The grinding was always done by women, generally by two at a time (Matt. 24[41]), seated on the ground opposite to each other, each holding the handle and alternately pushing and pulling the stone in its revolution. The 'nether millstone' became a proverb for weight and hardness. The Mosaic Law mercifully forbade the seizure of millstones for debt (Deut. 24[6]).

Mite (Gr. *lepton*, Mark 12[42] ; Luke 12[59], 21[2]), from the same root as *minute*, anything very small. 'Sche cast two mynutis, that is, a farthing' (*Wyclif*). Very small coins, known as 'beggars' money', not current in the market (being scarcely of estimable value), may still be seen used as alms in Asia Minor.

Nethinim (1 Chron. 9[2]; Ezra 2[58]) were the descendants of those Gibeonites whom Joshua reduced to slavery, making them hewers of wood and drawers of water for the sanctuary (Josh. 9[27]). They accompanied the Jews to and from captivity, and lived with the other servants of the Temple on Ophel, the southern continuation of Mount Moriah.

Offerings for the Altar were *animal* (1. Burnt-offerings, 2. Peace-offerings, 3. Sin-offerings) and *vegetable* (1. Meal-offerings and drink-offerings for the great altar in the Court, 2. Incense and meal-offerings for the altar in the Holy Place). Every burnt-offering and peace-offering was accompanied by a meal-offering and drink-offering (Num. 15[5, 7, 10], R.V.), in proportion to the victim, thus :—

	Flour.	Oil.	Wine.
With a bullock	$\frac{3}{10}$ ephah.	$\frac{1}{2}$ hīn.	$\frac{1}{2}$ hīn.
With a ram	$\frac{2}{10}$,,	$\frac{1}{3}$,,	$\frac{1}{3}$,,
With a he-lamb or kid . .	$\frac{1}{10}$,,	$\frac{1}{4}$,,	$\frac{1}{4}$,,

These offerings were (1) *Public* sacrifices, at the cost and on behalf of the 'whole congregation' (e.g. daily morning and evening sacrifices, and those on festivals); (2) *Private* sacrifices, enjoined by law on particular occasions, or provided by the voluntary devotion of the worshipper—as *thank-offerings*. Besides these, there were special sacrifices on the Day of Atonement, Passover, &c. A *trespass*-offering was a sin-offering accompanied by a pecuniary fine.

Paradise. Probably a Persian word signifying a park, and used by the LXX as a translation of the Heb. *Eden.* The word occurs three times in the N.T. The later Jewish speculation distinguished in Hades, the common abode of the dead, the two regions of Paradise and Gehenna. It is probably in reference to this belief that our Lord uses the word in His assurance to the dying robber (Luke 23[43]; cf. 16[23]). In the other two passages, both highly symbolical, the word points to some region of heavenly blessedness (2 Cor. 12[3, 4]; Rev. 2[7]).

Passover. The Passover was a great Historical Festival. Year after year it recalled, as in 'a living drama', the great facts of the national deliverance from Egyptian bondage. The directions for its yearly celebration are given in Exod. 23[15]; Lev. 23[5-8]; Num. 28[16-25]. It lasted from the 14th to the 21st of *Nisan* or *Abib.* (i) On the 10th of that month, each paschal company, which might not exceed twenty or be less than ten, was to select a lamb or kid, a male of the first year, and keep it till the 14th day. (ii) On that day, if declared free from blemish, it was to be slain *between the evenings* in the Court of the Tabernacle, and its blood poured round the Altar of Burnt-Offering. (iii) It was then, after being flayed, to be taken to the house where the paschal company intended to assemble, and there eaten, roast with fire, with unleavened bread and bitter herbs, not a bone of it being allowed to be broken. It was the nation's annual Birthday Feast, the Festival of Redemption; its chief features being (1) the offering of a *single victim* for each paschal company; (2) the *Paschal meal*, with which the festival began; (3) the eating of unleavened bread during the whole time it lasted.

Phylacteries (Gk. safeguards). The Hebrews were commanded to bind the enactments of the Law on their hands, and as frontlets between their eyes, and to write them on the door-posts of their houses (Deut. 6[8, 9]). Adopting a strictly literal interpretation of these words, they wrote a summary of the Moral Law (Ex. 13[1-16]; Deut. 6[4-9], 11[13-21]) on three strips of parchment; two of these they rolled up, and placed in two small cylinders in square cases of leather, and bound one on the forehead and the other on the centre of the back of the right hand with leathern straps. These were called Phylacteries, and were worn, and are still worn, by Israelites at their prayers. The Pharisees made them as conspicuous as possible (Matt. 23[5]), and wore them always. The third parchment was placed in a case of wood or metal, called a *Mezuzeh*, and affixed to the posts of their outer door and gates. It had a small aperture in front, through which was seen the word *Shaddai* (The Almighty).

Pools. Jerusalem, being on the top of a mountain, had an insufficient water supply. One never-failing spring, issuing from near Mount Moriah, is collected in the pool of Siloam, and its overflow in the well of Joab. Besides these, there are the two pools of Gihon on the west side of Jerusalem; that of Hezekiah, by the Jaffa Gate; that called *Birket Israel*, near St. Stephen's Gate, fed from a spring or reservoir under Pilate's house and the adjoining barracks. The houses of the wealthy had, and still have, extensive cisterns for storing rain-water. There is some uncertainty as to the position of the ancient pools just named. The Pool of Bethesda has, it is thought, lately been discovered 350 ft. north of the Birket Israel.

Porters were 'the door-keepers' and police of the Temple (2 Chron. 31[14]). They lived on the adjoining Mount Ophel. They were divided into companies, under the command of the 'Captain of the Temple', and one division was always on duty, keeping guard day and night. Josephus says that it took twenty of them to shut the great brazen gates (Acts 21[30]).

Prophet. The literal meaning of the Greek word (προφήτης, from πρόφημι, to speak forth) is a *forth-teller*, i. e. one who speaks forth a message which has been communicated to him through Divine inspiration. In Greek writers it is used specially of the *interpreters* of oracles. In Biblical usage the word retains its specific meaning. The power to foretell is rather incidental to the prophetic gift than characteristic of it. The essential qualities of the prophet are (i) inspiration, insight; (ii) power to speak. This is borne out by the application of the word to (i) the O.T. prophets (Heb. *nābhî*); (ii) John the Baptist; (iii) the Messiah; (iv) any one who speaks in God's name and under His inspiration. In Tit. 1[12] the term prophet is applied to a Greek poet, the poetic gift being a form of inspiration.

Purim. The Feast of Purim, or *Lots*, was instituted to commemorate the preservation of the Jews in Persia from the massacre with which they were threatened by the machinations of Haman (Esther 9[24-6]). It began on the 14th day of the twelfth month Adar, and lasted two days. It derived its name from the fact that Haman had cast lots to ascertain what day would be auspicious for him to carry out the bloody decree which the king had issued at his instance (Esther 9[24]). After a preliminary fast on the 13th of Adar, in memory of the fast of Esther (Esther 4[16]), it was celebrated with great rejoicings. The Book of Esther was publicly read, and the name of Haman was received with execrations by young and old, and noisy demonstration of anger, contempt, and scorn.

Quaternion. A Roman guard of four soldiers, detailed to act as sentries over a prisoner (Acts 12[4]). In the strictest custody (as in the case of Peter) each hand of the prisoner was handcuffed to a separate soldier, inside the cell while the other two kept sentry outside the door. These four were relieved every three hours, day and night, so that there were four quaternions required for one day's service, and four for the night watches. To the quaternion charged with Christ's crucifixion His clothes fell as a perquisite.

Sabbath. This is a Hebrew word signifying *Cessation*, and so *Rest*. The week of seven days is a very ancient institution, and is supposed to have been known in Ur of the Chaldees before the age of Abraham. The seventh day was regarded by the most ancient Babylonians as a *dies non*, a day of prohibition on which it was unlucky to do certain things; it was called *Shabattu*, which is explained on an old inscription as 'a day of rest for the heart' (*yum nuch libbi*). This falls in well with the primeval ordinance given in Gen. 2 and re-stated in the Fourth Commandment. The Sabbath was observed by our Lord and the Apostles, though the minute and burdensome traditions of the Pharisees were rejected and the spirit of the observance was reasserted in the saying 'The Sabbath was made for man'. The transition from the Jewish Sabbath to the Christian Lord's Day cannot be exactly marked. At first in all probability the two days were observed, the festival in commemoration of our Lord's resurrection beginning at sunset on the seventh day. This practice would be furthered through the needs of the Gentile converts on whom the Jewish day of rest was not binding. See especially Acts 20[7]. Gradually the Christian festival superseded the Jewish, adding to the idea of *rest* that of *worship*. The expression Lord's Day occurs in the N.T. only at Rev. 1[10], and even there is of doubtful interpretation.

Shoe. Shoes were only soles strapped under the foot. Frequently they were dispensed with, while on a journey an extra pair was taken (Matt. 10[10]). To unloose their clasp (or latchet), to bring them, or carry them away, was the office of the lowest slave. 'To pluck off the shoe' was and still is connected with certain kinds of contract among the Jews (Ruth 4[7]). To kick, or cast off, one's shoe over a person, was the symbol of his greatest humiliation, like treading on his neck; while to wash the feet of another was an act of abject servility (Pss. 60[8], 108[9]). To shake off the dust from the shoe was an imprecation of a curse upon individuals, a declaration of war against nations.

Tabernacle. An oblong tent, with a wooden framework covered with cloth and skins, made by Divine command as a movable place of worship in the wilderness. It was set up, taken down, and carried by the Levites; when stationary, the Pillar of Cloud rested on it. It consisted of a small inner compartment, the 'Holy of Holies', entered only on the Day of Atonement by the high priest alone, containing nothing but the Ark with its mercy-seat; and a larger compartment, the 'Holy Place, or Sanctuary' (in which were the altar of incense, table of shewbread, and golden candlestick), used for the daily service. These two were separated by a thick veil, and the whole was surrounded by the Court of the Tabernacle. When Joshua entered Canaan he set up the tabernacle at Shiloh, where residences for the priests were added to it, and it assumed so permanent a character that it is even called 'the temple' in 1 Sam. 3[3]. The word is also frequently used in the O.V. in its literal meaning of 'tent'.

Tabernacles, Feast of. The Feast of Tabernacles, or, as it was otherwise called, of Ingathering (Exod. 34[22]), was celebrated on the 15th of the seventh month Tisri, and lasted seven days. It was the most joyous of all the festivals, as being (i) a feast of thanksgiving for the completion of the ingathering of fruits and of the vintage, and (ii) as commemorating the dwelling of the Israelites in tents during their wanderings in the wilderness (Lev. 23[43]). (1) The chief passages relating to it are Exod. 23[16] ; Lev. 23[34] ; Num. 29[12-39] ; Deut. 16[13-15]. (2) During it the Israelites were commanded to live in tents or booths of green boughs of the olive, pine, palm, myrtle, and other trees with thick foliage (Neh. 8[14, 15]). (3) If the festival fell in a Sabbatical year, portions of the Law, chiefly Deuteronomy, were read each day in public (Deut. 31[10-12] ; Neh. 8[18]). (4) The most remarkable celebrations of this feast, were (a) at the dedication of Solomon's Temple (1 Kings 8[2, 65]) ; and (b) after the return from the Captivity (Ezra 3[4]). For other customs connected with this feast alluded to in the New Testament, see John 7[37], 8[12], which latter passage seems to allude to the lighting up of the golden candelabra in the Court of the Women on the evenings of the festival.

Temple was the name given to the whole sacred precincts on Mount Moriah, including the sanctuary and the various 'courts'. The sanctuary was planned according to the general design of the original 'Holy of Holies'. In the 'Holy Place' there were ten tables of shewbread and ten golden candlesticks (five of each on either side). The great brazen 'laver' stood on twelve brazen oxen, with their faces outwards. The altar of burnt-offering was very much larger than the original one. The accounts in Kings and Chronicles should be compared throughout. In Herod's time there was a far greater elaboration of 'courts', and at one stage was a trellised fence, and 'notices' on stone tablets, prohibiting the uncircumcised from passing within the sacred enclosures on pain of death. One of these notices has latterly been brought to light. The parts of the Temple referred to in the New Testament are :—(i) The *Hieron*, or sacred place as a whole, including the courts and precincts, from which our Lord drove the sellers of victims for sacrifice. (ii) The *Naos*, or Holy place, concerning which He said, 'Destroy this temple, and in three days I will raise it up'. (iii) Solomon's Porch, in which He walked in winter time, and where Peter preached to the multitude after healing the lame man ; it was part of the colonnade or cloisters that ran round the outer Court. (iv) The Treasury, where there were alms-boxes with trumpet-shaped openings into which rich and poor cast their offerings (Mark 12[41]) ; these were in the Women's Court. (v) The Beautiful Gate, supposed to have stood facing east, where the Golden Gate stands now. (vi) The doors or gates which were shut when St. Paul was excluded (Acts 21[30]) ; these were the large folding doors at the entrance, and were so heavy that it took twenty men to shut them. (vii) The middle wall of partition beyond which the Gentiles might not go. (viii) The veil which was rent in twain from top to bottom. This is usually thought to be that which separated the Holy from the Most Holy place ; but others think it was the first veil.

Tongues (Gift of). A strange and obscure manifestation in the Apostolic Church, especially at Corinth. It seems to have consisted in an ecstatic out pouring of praise in utterances unintelligible to speaker or hearer. It is referred to in 1 Cor. 12 and 13, and dealt with at length in 1 Cor. 14 : cf. also Mark 16[17] (R.V. marg.), Acts 10[46], 19[6]. The miracle described in Acts 2[4-] apparently differs from this 'speaking with tongues', and goes beyond it in ascribing sudden power to speak in languages previously unknown. Possibly however, the account may indicate the same mysterious kind of utterance which the Apostle Paul afterwards writes.

Tophet was the furnace in the Valley of the Sons of Hinnom in which human sacrifices were offered. The Valley (Ge) of Hinnom was subsequently called in Greek **Gehenna**, and this word was used to indicate the doom of the ungodly.

Tribute was of two kinds : (1) The half-shekel, which every Jew, wherever resident, was expected to contribute for the maintenance of the Temple (Matt. 17²⁴). (2) The tax, custom, dues, &c., exacted from them by their Roman subjugators for the maintenance of the civil authorities (Matt. 22¹⁷). The former was, if possible (but not necessarily), paid in Jewish, the latter in Roman coin.

Urim and Thummim ('Lights and Perfections'). These were the sacred symbols (worn upon the breastplate of the high priest, 'upon his heart'), by which God gave oracular responses for the guidance of His people in temporal matters. What they were is unknown ; they are introduced in Exodus (28³⁰) without explanation, as if familiar to the Israelites of that day. The LXX translates Urim and Thummim by 'manifestation and truth'. Some scholars suppose that they were the twelve stones of the breastplate ; others that they were two additional stones concealed in its fold. Josephus adds to these the two sardonyx buttons, worn on the shoulders, which, he says, emitted luminous rays when the response was favourable ; but the precise mode in which the oracles were given is lost in obscurity.

Vestment. It was and still is customary for every Jew, on entering the Synagogue for religious worship, to put on the *Tallith* or scarf of white lamb's wool with blue stripes and fringes at each end. This was worn over the shoulders, except during prayers, when it covered the head. It marked the worshipper as being a true Israelite. It was perhaps some similar vestment which Jehu ordered 'him that was over the vestry' to supply to each worshipper of Baal (2 Kings 10²²), the acceptance of which was the profession of being a true Baalite.

Vinegar. The Hebrew term *ḥômêts* was applied to a beverage consisting usually of wine or strong drink turned sour. By itself it formed a nauseous draught (Ps. 69²¹), and its acid taste passed into a proverb (Prov. 10²⁶). It was drunk by labourers (Ruth 2¹⁴). Similar to the *ḥômêts* of the Hebrews was the *acetum* of the Romans, which, under the name of *posca*, was the ordinary drink of the Roman soldiers (Matt. 27⁴⁸ ; Mark 15³⁶ ; John 19 ²⁹, ³⁰).

Weeks, Feast of. The Feast of Weeks (Ex. 34²²), or of **Harvest** (Ex. 23¹⁶), or of **Pentecost** (Acts 2¹), from the Greek word for the *fiftieth* day, was kept at the end of seven complete weeks from the 16th of Nisan. The passages bearing on it will be found in Ex. 23¹⁶ ; Lev. 23¹⁵⁻²¹ ; Num. 28²⁶⁻³¹. (i) The festival lasted but one day. (ii) Its chief feature was the offering of *two leavened loaves*, made from the new corn of the now completed harvest, which together with two lambs as a thank-offering were waved before the Lord. (iii) It was pre-eminently an expression of gratitude for the harvest, which began with the first ripe sheaf of barley at the Passover and ended with that of the two loaves of the newly-ripened wheat. (iv) In its festive joy the servants and strangers, the fatherless and the widow, were to share with the freeborn Israelite (Deut. 16¹¹).

Windows in an Oriental house consist mainly of apertures for the admission of light and air. They are sometimes partially closed with lattice-work, or wooden trellis-work, or curtains. The mother of Sisera is described (Judges 5²⁸) as 'looking out at a window, and crying through the lattice' (comp. S. of S. 2⁹ ; Eccl. 12³).

DICTIONARY OF
SCRIPTURE PROPER NAMES,

WITH THEIR PRONUNCIATION AND MEANING:

TOGETHER WITH COMPENDIOUS REFERENCES TO SOME OF THE PRINCIPAL
INCIDENTS CONNECTED WITH THE PERSONS AND PLACES MENTIONED
IN HOLY SCRIPTURE.

NOTE.—*The accent (′) shows where the stress of the voice should fall. (?) denotes meanings which are conjectural. Modern research has caused some of the older interpretations given in this list to be questioned.*

A A R

AARON, a′-ron, light (?). Ex. 4. 14.
BROTHER of MOSES, the FIRST HIGH PRIEST, cometh forth to meet Moses; can speak well; appointed by God to be Moses' spokesman. Ex. 4. 14, 16, 27.
with Moses appeals to Pharaoh; chided by him. Ex. 5. 1.
his rod becomes a serpent. Ex. 7. 10.
changes the waters into blood. Ex. 7. 20.
causes the plagues of frogs, lice, flies. Ex. 8. 5, 17, 24.
with Moses—the plague of boils. Ex. 9. 10.
with Hur holds up Moses' hands. Ex. 17. 12.
set apart for priest's office. Ex. 28.
makes the golden calf. Ex. 32. 4; God's anger thereat. Ex. 32. 7; Deut. 9. 20.
his excuse to Moses. Ex. 32. 22.
consecration. Ex. 29; Lev. 8.
offers sacrifice. Lev. 9.
his sons (Nadab and Abihu) offer strange fire, and die. Lev. 10. 1; Num. 3. 4.
his sons (Eleazar and Ithamar) censured by Moses. Lev. 10. 16.
not to drink wine when going into the tabernacle. Lev. 10. 8.
speaks against Moses. Num. 12.
rebuked by God. Num. 12. 9.
spoken against by Korah. Num. 16. 3.
makes atonement, and the plague is stayed. Num. 16. 46—48.
his rod buds, and is kept in ark for a token. Num. 17. 8.
for unbelief excluded from the promised land. Num. 20. 12.
dies on mount Hor. Num. 20. 28.
chosen by God. Ps. 105. 26; Heb. 5. 4.
his line. 1 Chr. 6. 49.
AARONITES, a′-ron-ites, descendants of Aaron. 1 Chr. 12. 27.
ABADDON, a-bad′-don, destruction.
angel of the bottomless pit. Rev. 9. 11.
ABAGTHA, a-bag′-thah, given by fortune. Esther 1. 10.
ABANA, a-ba′-nah, stony.
river of Damascus. 2 Kin. 5. 12.
ABARIM, a-ba′-rim, regions beyond. Num. 27. 12.
mountains of, including Nebo, Pisgah, Hor. Deut. 32. 49.
ABBA, ab′-bah, father. Mark 14. 36; Rom. 8. 15; Gal. 4. 6.
ABDA, ab′-dah, servant. 1 Kin. 4. 6.
ABDEEL, ab′-de-el, same as ABDIEL. Jer. 36. 26.
ABDI, ab′-di, servant of Jehovah. 1 Chr. 6. 44.
ABDIEL, ab′-di-el, s. of God. 1 Chr. 5. 15.

A B I

ABDON, ab′-don, servile. A judge. Judg. 12. 13.
ABED-NEGO, a-bed′-ne-go, servant or worshipper of Nebo. Dan. 1. 7.
saved in fiery furnace. Dan. 3. See Is. 43. 2.
ABEL, a′-bel, (1) vanity. Gen. 4. 2. (2) A meadow. 2 Sam. 20. 14.
second son of Adam. Gen. 4. 2.
his offering accepted. Gen. 4. 4.
slain by Cain. Gen. 4. 8.
righteous. Matt. 23. 35; 1 John 3. 12.
blood of. Luke 11. 51; Heb. 12. 24.
faith of. Heb. 11. 4.
ABEL-BETH-MAACHAH, a′-bel-beth-ma′-a-kah, meadow of the house of Maachah. 1 Kin. 15. 20.
ABEL-MAIM, a′-bel-ma′-im, m. of the waters. 2 Chr. 16. 4.
ABEL-MEHOLAH, a′-bel-me-ho′-lah, m. of dancing. Judg. 7. 22; 1 Kin. 4. 12; 19. 16.
ABEL-MIZRAIM, a′-bel-miz-ra′-im, m. of Egypt. Mourning of the Egyptians. Gen. 50. 11.
ABEL-SHITTIM, a′-bel-shit′-im, m. of acacias. Num. 33. 49.
ABEZ, a′-bez, whiteness. Josh. 19. 20.
ABI, a′-bi, shortened form of ABIAH. 2 Kin. 18. 2.
ABIA, a-bi′-ah, Greek form of following. Matt. 1. 7.
ABIAH, a-bi′-ah, same as ABIJAH. 2 Kin. 18. 2.
ABI-ALBON, a′-bi-al′-bon, father of strength. 2 Sam. 23. 31.
ABIASAPH, a-bi′-a-saf, f. of gathering. Ex. 6. 24.
ABIATHAR, ab-ia′-thar, f. of plenty. 1 Sam. 22. 20.
ABIB, a′-bib, an ear of corn, or green ear. Ex. 13. 4. the Hebrew passover month, Ex. 23. 15; 34. 18.
ABIDAH, a-bi′-dah, father of knowledge. Gen. 25. 4.
ABIDAN, a-bi′-dan, f. of a judge. Num. 1. 11.
ABIEL, a-bi′-el, f. of strength. 1 Sam. 9. 1.
ABIEZER, a′-bi-e′-zer, f. of help. Josh. 17. 2. ancestor of Gideon. Judg. 6.
ABIEZRITE, a′-bi-ez′-rite, a descendant of ABI-EZER. Judg. 6. 11.
ABIGAIL, a-bi-ga′le, father of exultation. 1 Sam. 25. 14.
wife of Nabal, and afterwards of David. 1 Sam. 25. 39.
mother of Chileab, according to 2 Sam. 3. 3, or Daniel, according to 1 Chr. 3. 1.
ABIHAIL, a-bi-ha′le, f. of strength. Num. 3. 35.
ABIHU, a-bi′-hoo, He (i.e. God) is my f. Ex. 6. 23. brother of Nadab, offers strange fire, and dies. Lev. 10. 2.
ABIHUD, a-bi′-hood, f. of Judah. 1 Chr. 8. 3.
ABIJAH, a-bi′-jah, f. of Jehovah. 1 Kin. 14. 1. king of Judah, walked in the sins of his father. 1 Kin. 15. 3.
makes war against Israel, 2 Chr. 13.

ABIJAH.—*cont.*
—— (son of Jeroboam), his death foretold by Ahijah the prophet. 1 Kin. 14. 12.
ABIJAM, a-bi'-jam, another mode of spelling ABIJAH. 1 Kin. 14. 31.
ABILENE, a'-bi-le'-ne, a grassy place (?). Luke 3. 1.
ABIMAEL, a-bi-ma'-el, father of Mael. Gen. 10. 28.
ABIMELECH, a-bi'-me-lek, *f.* of the king. Gen. 20. 2. (king of Gerar) reproved by God about Abraham's wife. Gen. 20. 3.
rebukes Abraham and restores Sarah. Gen. 20. 9, 14.
healed at Abraham's prayer. Gen. 20. 17.
—— (another), Isaac rebuked by, for denying his wife. Gen. 26. 10.
covenants with Isaac. Gen. 26. 27.
—— (king at Shechem), son of the judge Gideon. Judg. 8. 31.
murders his brethren. Judg. 9. 5.
his death. Judg. 9. 54.
ABINADAB, a-bi'-na-dab, *f.* of nobility. 1 Sam. 7. 1.
receives the ark from Philistines. 2 Sam. 6. 3.
ABINER, ab'-ner, same as ABNER. 1 Sam. 14. 50.
ABINOAM, a-bi-no'-am, *f.* of pleasantness. Judg. 4. 6.
ABIRAM, a-bi'-ram, *f.* of loftiness. Num. 16. 1.
with Korah and Dathan, rebels against Moses. Num. 16.
his punishment. Num. 16. 31; 26. 10.
ABISHAG, a-bi'-shag, *f.* of error (?). 1 Kin. 1. 3.
the Shunammite, ministers to David, cause of breach between Solomon and Adonijah. 1 Kin. 2. 22.
ABISHAI, a-bi'-shai, *f.* of a gift. 1 Sam. 26. 6.
brother of Joab. 1 Chr. 2. 16;
with David carries off Saul's spear. 1 Sam. 26. 6–9.
slays three hundred men. 2 Sam. 23. 18. *See also* 1 Chr. 11. 20; 18. 12.
ABISHALOM, a-bi'-sha-lom', *f.* of peace. 1 Kin. 15. 2.
ABISHUA, a-bi-shu'o-ah, *f.* of welfare. 1 Chr. 6. 4.
ABISHUR, a-bi'-shoor, *f.* of the wall. 1 Chr. 2. 28.
ABITAL, a-bi'-tal, *f.* of dew. 2 Sam. 3. 4.
ABITUB, a-bi'-toob, *f.* of goodness. 1 Chr. 8. 11.
ABIUD, a-bi'-ood, Greek form of ABIHUD. Matt. 1. 13.
ABNER, ab'-ner, *f.* of light. 1 Sam. 14. 50.
cousin of Saul, commander of his army. 1 Sam. 14. 50.
reproved by David. 1 Sam. 26. 5, 14.
makes Ish-bosheth king. 2 Sam. 2. 8.
goes over to David. 2 Sam. 3. 8.
slain by Joab. 2 Sam. 3. 27.
mourned by David. 2 Sam. 3. 31.
ABRAM, ab'-ram, a high *f.* Gen. 11. 26.
ABRAHAM, a'-bra-ham, *f.* of a great multitude. Gen. 17. 5.
—— (Abram) begotten by Terah. Gen. 11. 27.
blessed by God, and sent to Canaan. Gen. 12. 5.
goes down to Egypt. Gen. 12. 10.
causes his wife to pass as his sister. Gen. 12. 13; 20. 2.
strife between him and Lot. Gen. 13. 7.
separates from Lot. Gen. 13. 11.
his seed to be as the dust of the earth. Gen. 13. 16.
delivers Lot from captivity, and refuses the spoil. Gen. 14. 16.
blessed by Melchizedek, king of Salem. Gen. 14. 19; Heb. 7. 4.
his faith counted for righteousness. Gen. 15. 6.
God's covenant with. Gen. 15. 18; Ps. 105. 9.
he and house circumcised. Gen. 17.
entertains angels. Gen. 18.
pleads for Sodom. Gen. 18. 23.
sends away Hagar and Ishmael. Gen. 21. 14.
his faith in offering Isaac. Gen. 22.
buys Machpelah of Ephron the Hittite for a burying-place. Gen. 23.
sends for a wife for his son. Gen. 24.
gives his goods to Isaac. Gen. 25. 5.
dies (in a good old age). Gen. 25. 8.

his faith and works. Is. 41. 8; 51. 2; John 8. 31; Acts 7. 2; Rom. 4; Gal. 3. 6; Heb. 11. 8; James 2. 21.
his posterity. Gen. 25. 1.
ABSALOM, ab'-sa-lom, *f.* of peace. 2 Sam. 3. 3.
David's son. 2 Sam. 3. 3.
slays Amnon. 2 Sam. 13. 28.
conspires against David. 2 Sam. 15.
David flies from. 2 Sam. 15. 17.
caught by head in an oak. 2 Sam. 18. 9.
slain by Joab. 2 Sam. 18. 14.
wept by David. 2 Sam. 18. 33; 19. 1.
ACCAD, ak'-ad, fortress (?). Gen. 10. 10.
ACCHO, ak'-o, sand-heated. Judg. 1. 31.
ACELDAMA, a-kel'-da-mah', field of blood. Matt. 27. 8; Acts 1. 19.
ACHAIA, a-ka'-yah, Greece. Acts 18. 12.
Paul in. Acts 18.
contribution for poor by. Rom. 15. 26; 2 Cor. 9. 2. *See* 1 Cor. 16. 15; 2 Cor. 11. 10.
ACHAICUS, a-ka'-ik-us, belonging to Achaia. 1 Cor. 16. 17.
ACHAN, or ACHAR, a'-kan, a'-kar, troubler. Josh. 7. 18.
takes the accursed thing; is stoned. Josh. 7; 22. 20; 1 Chr. 2. 7.
ACHAZ, a'-kaz, Greek form of AHAZ. Matt. 1. 9.
ACHBOR, ak'-bor, a mouse. Gen. 36. 38.
ACHIM, a'-kim, short form of JACHIN (?). Matt. 1. 14.
ACHISH, a'-kish, angry (?).
king of Gath, succours David. 1 Sam. 21. 10; 27. 2; 28. 1; 29. 6. *See* 1 Kin. 2. 39.
ACHMETHA, ak'-me-thah, fortress (?). Ezra 6. 2.
ACHOR, a'-kor, trouble. Josh. 7. 24.
valley of, Achan slain there. Josh. 7. 26. *See* Hos. 2. 15.
ACHSA, ak'-sah, same as following. 1 Chr. 2. 49.
ACHSAH, ak'-sah, anklet. Josh. 15. 16.
Caleb's daughter, won in marriage by Othniel. Judg. 1. 13.
asks her father's blessing. Judg. 1. 15.
ACHSHAPH, ak'-shaf, enchantment. Josh. 11. 1.
ACHZIB, ak'-zib, deceit. Josh. 15. 44.
ADADAH, a'd-a-dah, festival (?). Josh. 15. 22.
ADAH, a'-dah, ornament. Gen. 4. 19.
ADAIAH, a-da'-yah, whom Jehovah adorns. 2 Kin. 22. 1.
ADALIA, a-da'l-yah, upright (?). Esth. 9. 8.
ADAM, a'-dam, red. Gen. 2. 19.
created. Gen. 1.
called the son of God. Luke 3. 38.
blessed. Gen. 1. 28.
placed in Eden. Gen. 2. 8.
first called Adam. Gen. 2. 19.
creatures named by. Gen. 2. 19.
calls his wife Eve. Gen. 3. 20.
his fall and punishment. Gen. 3.
hides from God. Gen. 3. 8.
ground cursed for his sake. Gen. 3. 17.
his death. Gen. 5. 5.
his transgression. Job 31. 33; Rom. 5. 14.
first Adam. 1 Cor. 15. 45; 1 Tim. 2. 13.
in, all die. 1 Cor. 15. 22.
ADAM, the last. 1 Cor. 15. 45.
ADAMAH, a-dah'-mah, red earth. Josh. 19. 36.
ADAMI, a-da'h-mi, human. Josh. 19. 33.
ADAR, a'-dar, fire (?). Esth. 3. 7.
ADBEEL, ad'-be-el, miracle of God (?). Gen. 25. 13.
ADDAN, a'd-dahn, humble (?).
a city of the captivity. Ezra 2. 59.
ADDAR, a'd-dar, greatness (?). 1 Chr. 8. 3.
ADDI, a'd-di, ornament (?). Luke 3. 28.
ADDON, a'd-don, same as ADDAN. Neh. 7. 61.
ADER, a'-der, flock. 1 Chr. 8. 15.
ADIEL, a'-di-el, ornament of God. 1 Chr. 4. 36.
ADIN, a'-din, slender. Ezra 2. 15.
ADINA, a-di'-nah, same as preceding. 1 Chr. 11. 42.
ADINO, a-di'-no. 2 Sam. 23. 8.
ADITHAIM, a-di-tha'-im, twofold ornament. Josh. 15. 36.

ADLAI, a'd-lai, just (?). 1 Chr. 27. 29.
ADMAH, ad'-mah, same as ADAMAH. Gen. 10. 19.
　city of the plain. *See* SODOM.
ADMATHA, ad'-math-ah. Esth. 1. 14.
ADNA, ad'-nah, pleasure. Ezra 10. 30.
ADNAH, same as preceding. 2 Chr. 17. 14.
ADONI-BEZEK, a-do'-ni-be'-zek, lord of Bezek.
　Judg. 1. 5.
ADONIJAH, a'-do-ni'-jah, Jehovah is my Lord.
　2 Sam. 3. 4.
　fourth son of David, usurps the kingdom. 1 Kin.
　1. 5, 11, 25.
　is pardoned by Solomon. 1 Kin. 1. 53.
　seeking to obtain Abishag, is slain. 1 Kin. 2.
　17—25.
ADONIKAM, a'-do-ni'-kam, lord of enemies. Ezra
　2. 13.
ADONIRAM, a'-do-ni'-ram, lord of height. 1 Kin.
　4. 6.
ADONI-ZEDEC, a-do'-ni-ze'-dek, lord of justice.
　king of Jerusalem, resists Joshua. Josh. 10. 1.
　his death. Josh. 10. 26.
ADORAIM, a-do-ra'-im, two chiefs (?). 2 Chr. 11. 9.
ADORAM, a-do'-ram, contracted from ADONIRAM.
　2 Sam. 20. 24.
ADRAMMELECH, ad-ram'-me-lek, magnificence of
　the king (?), king of fire (?). 2 Kin. 17. 31.
ADRAMYTTIUM, ad'-ra-mit'-ti-um. Acts 27. 2.
ADRIA, a'-dri-ah. Acts 27. 27.
ADRIEL, a'd-ri-el, flock of God. 1 Sam. 18. 19.
ADULLAM, a-dul'-am, justice of the people. Josh.
　12. 15.
　cave of. 1 Sam. 22. 1; 1 Chr. 11. 15.
ADULLAMITE, a-dul'-am-ite, a native of Adullam.
　Gen. 38. 1.
ADUMMIM, a-dum'-im, the red (men?). Josh. 15. 7.
ÆNEAS, e'-ne-as, praiseworthy (?).
　healing of. Acts 9. 33.
ÆNON, e'-non, springs. John baptizes at. John
　3. 23.
AGABUS, ag'-ab-us, probably Greek form of Hagab.
　famine and Paul's sufferings foretold by. Acts
　11. 28; 21. 10.
AGAG, a'-gag, flaming (?). Num. 24. 7.
　king of Amalek, spared by Saul, slain by Samuel.
　1 Sam. 15.
　spoken of by Balaam. Num. 24.
AGAGITE, a'-gag-ite. Esth. 3. 1.
AGAR, a'-gar, same as HAGAR. Gal. 4. 24.
AGEE, a'-gee, fugitive (?). 2 Sam. 23. 11.
AGRIPPA, a-grip'-ah. Acts 25. 13.
　Paul's defence before. Acts 25. 22; 26.
　almost persuaded. Acts 26. 28.
AGUR, a'-goor, an assembler.
　prophecy. Prov. 30.
AHAB, a'-hab, uncle.
　king of Israel. 1 Kin. 16. 29.
　marries Jezebel; his idolatry. 1 Kin. 16. 31.
　meets Elijah. 1 Kin. 18. 17.
　defeats the Syrians. 1 Kin. 20.
　punished for sparing Ben-hadad. 1 Kin. 20. 42.
　takes Naboth's vineyard. 1 Kin. 21. 17.
　his repentance. 1 Kin. 21. 27.
　trusts false prophets, and is mortally wounded at
　Ramoth-gilead. 1 Kin. 22. 6, 34; 2 Chr. 18.
　—— (son of Kolaiah), and Zedekiah, lying pro-
　phets. Jer. 29. 21.
AHARAH, a'-har-ah, after the brother. 1 Chr. 8. 1.
AHARHEL, a-har'-hel, behind the breastwork.
　1 Chr. 4. 8.
AHASAI, a'-ha-zai, probably a corruption of
　JAHZERAH. Neh. 11. 13.
AHASBAI, a-ha's-bai. 2 Sam. 23. 34.
AHASUERUS, a-haz-u-e'-rus, king (?).
　reigns from India to Ethiopia. Esth. 1. 1.
　Vashti's disobedience to, and divorce. Esth. 1. 12;
　2. 4.
　makes Esther queen. Esth. 2. 17.
　advances Haman. Esth. 3. 1.
　his decree to destroy the Jews. Esth. 3. 12.
　rewards Mordecai's loyalty. Esth. 6.

AHASUERUS.—*cont.*
　hangs Haman. Esth. 7. 9; 8. 7.
　advances Mordecai. Esth. 9. 4; 10.
AHAVA, a'-ha-vah. Ezra 8. 15.
AHAZ, a'-haz, possessor. 2 Kin. 15. 38.
　king of Judah. 2 Kin. 16.
　spoils the temple. 2 Kin. 16. 17.
　his idolatry. 2 Chr. 28. 2.
　afflicted by Syrians. 2 Chr. 28. 5.
　comforted by Isaiah. Is. 7.
　will not ask a sign. Is. 7. 12.
AHAZIAH, a'-haz-i'-ah, whom Jehovah upholds.
　1 Kin. 22. 40.
　king of Judah, his wicked reign. 2 Kin. 8. 25.
　goes with Joram to meet Jehu. 2 Kin. 9. 21.
　smitten by Jehu. 2 Kin. 9. 27; 2 Chr. 22. 9.
　—— king of Israel. 1 Kin. 22. 40, 49.
　his sickness and idolatry. 2 Kin. 1.
　his judgment by Elijah. 2 Kin. 1.
AHBAN, ah'-ban, brotherly. 1 Chr. 2. 29.
AHER, a'-her, following. 1 Chr. 7. 12.
AHI, a'-hi, brother. 1 Chr. 5. 15.
AHIAH, a-hi'-ah, brother of Jehovah. 1 Sam. 14. 3.
AHIAM, a-hi'-am, b. of the father (?). 2 Sam. 23.
　33.
AHIAN, a-hi'-an, brotherly. 1 Chr. 7. 19.
AHIEZER, a'-hi-e'-zer, brother of help. Num. 1. 12.
AHIHUD, a-hi'-hood, b. of (?). Num. 34. 27.
AHIJAH, a-hi'-jah, same as AHIAH. 1 Kin. 11. 29.
　prophesies to Jeroboam against Solomon, 1 Kin.
　11. 31; against Jeroboam, and foretells his son's
　death. 1 Kin. 14. 7.
AHIKAM, a-hi'-kam, b. of the enemy. 2 Kin. 22. 12.
　protects Jeremiah. Jer. 26. 24.
AHILUD, a-hi'-lood, b. of one born. 2 Sam. 8. 16.
AHIMAAZ, a-hi-ma'-az, b. of anger.
　son of Zadok, serves David. 2 Sam. 15. 27; 17.
　17; 18. 19.
AHIMAN, a-hi'-man, b. of a gift. Num. 13. 22.
AHIMELECH, a-hi'-me-lek, b. of the king. 1 Sam.
　21. 1.
　slain by Saul's order, for assisting David. 1 Sam.
　22. 18.
AHIMOTH, a-hi'-moth, b. of death. 1 Chr. 6. 25.
AHINADAB, a-hi'-na-dab, b. of a nobleman. 1 Kin.
　4. 14.
AHINOAM, a-hi-no'-am, b. of grace. 1 Sam. 14. 50.
AHIO, a-hi'-o, brotherly. 2 Sam. 6. 3.
AHIRA, a-hi'-rah, b. of a wicked man. Num. 1.
　15.
AHIRAM, a-hi'-ram, b. of a tall man. Num. 26. 38.
AHIRAMITE, a-hi'-ram-ite, a descendant of Ahi-
　ram. Num. 26. 38.
AHISAMACH, a-hi'-sa-mak, b. of aid. Ex. 31. 6.
AHISHAHAR, a-hi'-sha-har, b. of the dawn. 1 Chr.
　7. 10.
AHISHAR, a-hi'-shar, b. of the singer. 1 Kin. 4. 6.
AHITHOPHEL, a-hi'-tho-fel, b. of impiety. 2 Sam.
　15. 12.
　his treachery. 2 Sam. 15. 31; 16. 20.
　disgrace, and suicide. 2 Sam. 17. 1, 23. *See* Ps.
　41. 9; 55. 12; 109.
AHITUB, a-hi'-toob, b. of goodness. 1 Sam. 14. 3.
AHLAB, ah'-lab, fertility. Judg. 1. 31.
AHLAI, ah'-lai, sweet (?). 1 Chr. 2. 31.
AHOAH, a-ho'-ah, same as AHIJAH (?). 1 Chr. 8. 4.
AHOHITE, a-hoh'-ite, a descendant of Ahoah. 2
　Sam. 23. 9.
AHOLAH, a-ho'-lah, (she has) her own tent.
　—— (Samaria), and AHOLIBAH (Jerusalem), their
　adulteries. Ezek. 23. 4.
AHOLIAB, a'-holi-a'b, father's tent. Ex. 31. 6.
　inspired to construct the tabernacle. Ex. 35. 34;
　36, &c.
AHOLIBAH, a'-holi-b'ah, my tent is in her. Ezek.
　23. 4.
AHOLIBAMAH, a'-holi-ba'-mah, tent of the high
　place. Gen. 36. 2.
AHUMAI, a-hoo'-mai, brother of (*i. e.* dweller near)
　water. 1 Chr. 4. 2.
AHUZAM, a-hooz'-am, their possession. 1 Chr. 4. 6.

AHUZZATH, a-hooz'-ath, possession. Gen. 26. 26.
AI, a'i, a heap of ruins. Josh. 7. 2.
men of, contend with Israel. Josh. 7. 5.
AIAH, ai'-ah, hawk. 2 Sam. 3. 7.
AIJA, ai'-jah, same as AI. Neh. 11. 31.
AJAH, a'-jah, same as AIAH. Gen. 36. 24.
AIATH, ai'-ath, ruins. Is. 10. 28.
AIJALON, ai'-ja-lon, place of gazelles. Josh. 21. 24.
AIJELETH SHAHAR, ai-ye'-leth sha'-har, morning hind. Ps. 22 title.
AIN, a'-in, an eye, or fountain. Num. 34. 11.
AJALON, ad'-jal-on, same as AIJALON. Josh. 19. 42.
AKAN, a'-kan. Gen. 36. 27.
AKKUB, a'k-kub, insidious. 1 Chr. 3. 24.
AKRABBIM, ak-rab-bim, scorpions. Num. 34. 4.
ALAMETH, a-la'-meth, covering. 1 Chr. 7. 8.
ALAMMELECH, a-la'm-me-lek, king's oak. Josh. 19. 26.
ALAMOTH, a-la-moth', virgins (?). Ps. 46 title.
ALEMETH, a-le'-meth, same as ALAMETH. 1 Chr. 8. 36.
ALEXANDER, al'-ex-an'-der, defending men. Mark 15. 21.
—— a member of the council. Acts 4. 6.
—— an Ephesian Jew. Acts 19. 33.
—— the coppersmith. 1 Tim. 1. 20; 2 Tim. 4. 14.
ALEXANDRIA, al'-ex-an'-dri-a, the city named after Alexander. Acts 18. 24.
ALIAH, a'l-iah, same as ALVAH. 1 Chr. 1. 51.
ALIAN, a'l-ian, same as ALVAN. 1 Chr. 1. 40.
ALLELUIA, al-el-oo'-ya, praise ye the Lord. Rev. 19. 1.
ALLON, al'-on, an oak. 1 Chr. 4. 37.
ALLON-BACHUTH. al-on-bak'-ooth, oak of weeping. Gen. 35. 8; 1 Kin. 13. 14.
ALMODAD, al-mo'-dad, extension (?). Gen. 10. 26.
ALMON, al'-mon, hidden. Josh. 21. 18.
ALMON-DIBLATHAIM, al'-mon-dib'-lath-a'-im, hiding of the two cakes (?). Num. 33. 46.
ALOTH, a'-loth, yielding milk (?). 1 Kin. 4. 16.
ALPHA, al'-fah, the first letter of the Greek alphabet. Rev. 1. 8; 21. 6; 22. 13.
ALPHÆUS, al-fee'-us, successor. Matt. 10. 3.
AL-TASCHITH, al'-tash-kith', 'do not destroy.' Ps. 57 title.
ALUSH, a'-loosh. Num. 33. 13.
ALVAH, al'-vah. Gen. 36. 40.
ALVAN, a'l-vahn, tall. Gen. 36. 23.
AMAD, a'm-ad, eternal people (?). Josh. 19. 26.
AMAL, a'-mal, labour, sorrow. 1 Chr. 7. 35.
AMALEK, am'-al-ek. Gen. 36. 12.
fights with Israel in Rephidim, and is defeated. Ex. 17. 8, 13.
perpetual war declared against. Ex. 17. 16; Deut. 25. 17.
smitten by Gideon. Judg. 7. 12.
by Saul. 1 Sam. 14. 48; 15. 8.
by David. 1 Sam. 27. 9; 30. 17.
AMALEKITE, am-al'-ek-ite, self-accused of killing Saul, slain by David. 2 Sam. 1. 10, 15.
AMALEKITES, am-al'-ek-ites, descendants of Amalek. Gen. 14. 7.
AMAM, a'-mam, metropolis (?). Josh. 15. 26.
AMANA, a-ma'-nah. fixed (?). Cant. 4. 8.
AMARIAH, a'-mar-i'-ah, Jehovah has said. 1 Chr. 6. 7.
AMASA, a-ma'-sa, burden.
captain of the host of Absalom. 2 Sam. 17. 25.
slain by Joab. 2 Sam. 20. 9, 10; 1 Kin. 2. 5.
AMASAI, a-ma'-sai, burdensome. 1 Chr. 6. 25.
AMASHAI, a-ma'sh-ai. Neh. 11. 13.
AMASIAH, a'-mas-i'-ah, burden of Jehovah. 2 Chr. 17. 16.
AMAZIAH, a'-maz-i'-ah, Jehovah strengthens, king of Judah, his good reign. 2 Kin. 14. 1; 2 Chr. 25. 1.
defeats Edom. 2 Chr. 25. 11.
defeated by Joash king of Israel. 2 Chr. 25. 21.
slain at Lachish. 2 Kin. 14. 19.
—— priest of Beth-el. Amos 7. 10.
AMI, a'-mi, probably same as AMON. Ezra 2. 57.

AMINADAB, a-mi'-na-dab, same as AMMINADAB. Matt. 1. 4.
AMITTAI, a-mi't-tai, true. 2 Kin. 14. 25.
AMMAH, am'-ah. 2 Sam. 2. 24.
AMMI, am'-i, my people. Hos. 2. 1.
AMMIEL, am'-i-el, people of God. Num. 13. 12.
AMMIHUD, am-i'-hood, p. of praise (?). Num. 1. 10.
AMMINADAB, am-i'-na-dab, p. of the prince. Ex. 6. 23.
AMMI-NADIB, am-i'-na-dib, same as preceding. Cant. 6. 12.
AMMISHADDAI, a'm-i-sha'd-ai, p. of the Almighty. Num. 1. 12.
AMMIZABAD, am-i'-za-bad, p. of the giver (i.e. Jehovah). 1 Chr. 27. 6.
AMMON, am'-on, son of my p. (?).
children of. Gen. 19. 38.
not to be meddled with. Deut. 2. 19.
not to enter the congregation. Deut. 23. 3.
make war on Israel, and are conquered by Jephthah. Judg. 11. 4, 33.
slain by Saul. 1 Sam. 11. 11.
outrage David's servants. 2 Sam. 10.
tortured by David. 2 Sam. 12. 26.
prophecies concerning. Jer. 25, 21; 49. 1; Ezek. 21. 28; 25, 2, 3; Amos 1. 13; Zeph. 2. 8.
AMMONITES, am'-on-ites, a tribe descended from Ammon. Deut. 2. 20.
AMMONITESS, am'-on-ite-ess, feminine of preceding. 2 Chr. 12. 13.
AMNON, am'-non, faithful.
son of David. 2 Sam. 3. 2.
outrages Tamar. 2 Sam. 13.
slain by Absalom. 2 Sam. 13. 28.
AMOK, a'-mok, deep. Neh. 12. 7.
AMON, a'-mon. 2 Kin. 21. 18.
king of Judah. 2 Kin. 21. 19; 2 Chr. 33. 20.
his idolatry. 2 Kin. 21. 21; 2 Chr. 33. 23.
killed by his servants. 2 Kin. 21. 23.
AMORITE, am'-or-ite, mountaineer. Gen. 10. 16.
AMORITES, am'-or-ites, their iniquities, Gen. 15. 16; Deut. 20. 17; Josh. 3. 10.
AMOS, a'-mos, burden.
declares God's judgment upon the nations. Amos 1. 1, 2.
and upon Israel. Amos 3. 1, &c.
his call. Amos 7. 14, 15.
foretells Israel's restoration. Amos 9. 11.
AMOZ, a'-moz, strong. Is. 1. 1.
AMPHIPOLIS, am-phi'-pol-is, named from the river Strymon flowing round the city. Acts 17. 1.
AMPLIAS, am'-pli-as, short form of Ampliatus, enlarged. Rom. 16. 8.
AMRAM, am'-ram, people of the Highest (i.e. God). Ex. 6. 18.
AMRAMITES, am'-ram-ites, the descendants of Amram. Num. 3. 27.
AMRAPHEL, am'-ra-fel. Gen. 14. 1.
AMZI, am'-zi, strong. 1 Chr. 6. 46.
ANAB, a'-nab, place fertile in grapes. Josh. 11. 21.
ANAH, a'-nah. Gen. 36. 2.
ANAHARATH, a-na'-har-ath. Josh. 19. 19.
ANAIAH, an-ai'-ah, Jehovah has answered. Neh. 8. 4.
ANAK, a'-nak, long-necked (?). Num. 13. 22.
ANAKIM, a'-nak-im, a tribe called after Anak. Deut. 1. 28.
—— (giants). Num. 13. 33; Deut. 9. 2.
cut off by Joshua. Josh. 11. 21.
ANAMIM, a'-nam-im. Gen. 10. 13.
ANAMMELECH, a-nam'-me-lek, idol of the king (?), or shepherd and flock (?). 2 Kin. 17. 31.
ANAN, a'-nan, a cloud. Neh. 10. 26.
ANANI, an-a'-ni, shortened form of Ananiah. 1 Chr. 3. 24.
ANANIAH, an-an-i'-ah, whom Jehovah covers. Neh. 3. 23.
ANANIAS, an-an-i'-as, Greek form of HANANIAH.
—— (and Sapphira), their lie and death. Acts 5. 1.
—— (disciple), sent to Paul at Damascus. Acts 9. 10; 22. 12

ARTAXERXES, ar'-ta-xerk'-ses, honoured king (?).
Ezra 4. 8.
(king of Persia), oppresses the Jews. Ezra 4.
—— (Longimanus), permits Ezra to restore the
temple, Ezra 7 ; and Nehemiah to rebuild Jeru-
salem. Neh. 2.
ARTEMAS, ar'-te-mas, shortened form of Artemi-
dorus (?). Tit. 3. 12.
ARUBOTH, a-roob'-oth, windows. 1 Kin. 4. 10.
ARUMAH, a-room'-ah, elevated. Judg. 9. 41.
ARVAD, ar'-vad, wandering. Ezek. 27. 8.
ARVADITES, ar'-vad-ites, inhabitants of Arvad.
Gen. 10. 18.
ARZA, ar'-zah, earth. 1 Kin. 16. 9.
ASA, a'-sah, physician.
his good reign. 1 Kin. 15. 8.
wars with Baasha. 1 Kin. 15. 16.
his prayer against the Ethiopians. 2 Chr. 14. 11.
his zeal. 2 Chr. 15.
seeks aid of the Syrians. 2 Chr. 16.
reproved by Hanani the seer. 2 Chr. 16. 7.
reigns forty years, and dies much honoured.
2 Chr. 16. 10.
ASAHEL, a'-sa-hel, whom God made.
his rashness ; slain by Abner in self-defence.
2 Sam. 2. 18 ; 3. 27 ; 23. 24 ; 1 Chr. 11. 26.
ASAHIAH, a'-sah-i'-ah. 2 Kin. 22. 12.
ASAIAH, a-sai'-ah. 1 Chr. 4. 36.
ASAPH, a'-saf, collector. 2 Kin. 18. 18.
a Levite, musical composer, and leader of David's
choir, 1 Chr. 6. 39 ; 2 Chr. 5. 12 ; 29, 30 ; 35. 15 ; Neh.
12, 46 ; Psalms 50 and 73 to 83 ascribed to him.
ASAREEL, a-sa'r-eel, whom God has bound. 1 Chr.
4. 16.
ASARELAH, a-sar-e'l-ah, same as JESHARELAH.
1 Chr. 25. 2.
ASENATH, a'-se-nath, she who is of Neith (i.e. a
goddess of the Egyptians) (?). Gen. 41. 45.
wife of Joseph. Gen. 41. 45 ; 46.
ASER, a'-ser, same as ASHER. Luke 2. 36.
ASHAN, a'-shan, smoke. Josh. 15. 42.
ASHBEA, ash'-be-ah, I conjure. 1 Chr. 4. 21.
ASHBEL, ash'-bel, blame (?). Gen. 46, 21.
ASHBELITES, ash'-bel-ites, the descendants of Ash-
bel. Num. 26. 38.
ASHCHENAZ, ash'-ken-az, same as ASHKENAZ. 1
Chr. 1. 6.
ASHDOD, ash'-dod, a strong place. Josh. 15. 46.
city of Philistines ; the ark carried there ; men
of, smitten. 1 Sam. 5.
reduced by Uzziah. 2 Chr. 26. 6.
predictions concerning. Jer. 25. 20 ; Amos 1. 8 ;
Zeph. 2. 4 ; Zech. 9. 6.
ASHDODITES, ash'-dod-ites, the inhabitants of
Ashdod. Neh. 4. 7.
ASHDOTH-PISGAH, ash'-doth-piz'-gah, springs of
Pisgah. Josh. 12. 3.
ASHDOTHITES, ash'-doth-ites, same as ASHDODITES.
Josh. 13. 3.
ASHER, ash'-er, fortunate, happy.
son of Jacob. Gen. 30. 13.
his descendants. Num. 1. 40 ; 26. 44 ; 1 Chr. 7. 30 ;
their inheritance. Josh. 19. 24 ; Judg. 5. 17. *See*
Ezek. 48. 34 ; Rev. 7. 6.
Anna, prophetess, descended from. Luke 2. 36.
ASHERAH, ash-er'-ah, the goddess Ashtoreth.
2 Kin. 17. 10.
ASHERITES, a'-sher-ites, descendants of Asher.
Judg. 1. 32.
ASHIMA, a-shi'-ma. 2 Kin. 17. 30.
ASHKELON, ash'-kel-on, migration.
—— (Askelon) taken. Judg. 1. 18 ; 14. 19 ; 1 Sam.
6. 17 ; 2 Sam. 1. 20.
prophecies concerning. Jer. 25. 20 ; 47. 5 ; Amos
1. 8 ; Zeph. 2. 4 ; Zech. 9. 5.
ASHKENAZ, ash'-ken-az. Gen. 10. 3.
ASHNAH, ash'-nah, strong. Josh. 15. 33.
ASHPENAZ, ash'-pen-az. Dan. 1. 3.
ASHRIEL, ash'-ri-el, same as ASRIEL. 1 Chr. 7. 14.
ASHTAROTH, ash'-tar-oth, statues of Ashtoreth.
Josh. 9. 10.

ASHTAROTH.—*cont.*
idolatrous worship of, by Israel. Judg. 2. 13 ;
1 Sam. 12. 10 ; by Solomon, 1 Kin. 11. 5, 33.
ASHTERATHITE, ash-ter'-ath-ite, a native of Ash-
teroth. 1 Chr. 11. 44.
ASHTEROTH KARNAIM, ash'-ter-oth kar-na'-im,
Ashteroth of the two horns. Gen. 14. 5.
ASHTORETH, ash-tor'-eth, she who enriches. 1 Kin.
11. 5.
ASHUR, ash'-oor. 1 Chr. 2. 24.
ASHURITES, ash'-oor-ites. 2 Sam. 2. 9.
ASHVATH, ash'-vath. 1 Chr. 7. 33.
ASIA, a'-shah. Acts 2. 9.
ASIEL, a'-si-el, created by God. 1 Chr. 4. 35.
ASKELON, see ASHKELON. Judg. 1. 18.
ASNAH, as'-nah, bramble. Ezra 2. 50.
ASNAPPER, as-nap'-er, same as ASSUR-BANI-PAL,
Assur has formed a son. Ezra 4. 10.
ASPATHA, as-pa'h-thah. Esth. 9. 7.
ASRIEL, as'-ri-el, the prohibition of God. Num.
26. 31.
ASRIELITES, as'-ri-el-ites, the family of Asriel.
Num. 26. 31.
ASSHUR, ash'-oor, the gracious One (?). Gen. 10. 22.
ASSHURIM, ash-oor'-im. Gen. 25. 3.
ASSIR, as'-eer, captive. Ex. 6. 24.
ASSOS, as'-os. Acts 20. 13.
ASSYRIA, as-ir'-ya, the land so named from AS-
SHUR. Gen. 2. 14.
Israel carried captive to. 2 Kin. 15. 29 ; 17.
army of, miraculously destroyed. 2 Kin. 19. 35 ;
Is. 37. 36.
prophecies concerning. Is. 8 ; 10. 5 ; 14. 24 ; 30.
31 ; 31. 8 ; Mic. 5. 6 ; Zeph. 2. 13.
its glory. Ezek. 31. 3.
ASSYRIANS, as-ir'-yans, inhabitants of Assyria.
Is. 10. 5.
ASTAROTH, as'-tar-oth, same as ASHTORETH. Deut.
1. 4.
ASUPPIM, a-soop'-im. 1 Chr. 26. 15.
ASYNCRITUS, a-sin'-krit-us, incomparable, disci-
ple. Rom. 16. 14.
ATAD, a'-tad, buckthorn. Gen. 50. 10.
ATARAH, a-ta'h-rah, a crown. 1 Chr. 2. 26.
ATAROTH, a-ta'h-roth, crowns. Num. 32. 3.
ATER, a'-ter, bound, shut up. Ezra 2. 16.
ATHACH, a'-thak, lodging-place. 1 Sam. 30. 30.
ATHAIAH, a-thai'-ah, whom Jehovah made (?).
Neh. 11. 4.
ATHALIAH, ath'-al-i'-ah, whom Jehovah has af-
flicted.
daughter of Ahab, mother of Ahaziah. 2 Kin. 8. 26.
slays the seed royal, Joash only saved. 2 Kin.
11. 1 ; 2 Chr. 22. 10.
slain by order of Jehoiada. 2 Kin. 11. 16 ; 2 Chr.
23. 15.
ATHLAI, a'th-lai, shortened form of Athaliah.
Ezra 10. 28.
ATHENIANS, ath-e'-ni-ans, natives of Athens. Acts
17. 21.
ATHENS, ath'-ens.
Paul preaches to the philosophers at. Acts 17.
15 ; 1 Thess. 3. 1.
men of, described. Acts 17. 21.
ATROTH, at'-roth, same as ATAROTH. Num. 32. 35.
ATTAI, a't-tai, opportune. 1 Chr. 2. 35.
ATTALIA, at'-ta-li'-a, so called from Attalus, the
royal founder of the city, sea-port. Acts 14. 25.
AUGUSTUS, aw-gust'-us, venerable. Luke 2. 1.
AVA, a'-vah. 2 Kin. 17. 24.
AVEN, a'-ven, nothingness. Ezek. 30. 17.
AVIM, av'-im, ruins. Josh. 18. 23.
AVITH, a'-vith. Gen. 36. 35.
AZAL, a'-zal, root of a mountain. Zech. 14. 5.
AZALIAH, a'-zal-i'-ah, whom Jehovah has re-
served. 2 Kin. 22. 3.
AZANIAH, a'-zan-i'-ah, whom Jehovah hears. Neh.
10. 9.
AZARAEL, a-zar'-eel, whom God helps. Neh. 12. 36.
AZAREEL, a-zar'-eel, same as preceding. 1 Chr.
12. 6.

AZARIAH, a'-zar-i'-ah, whom Jehovah aids. 2 Chr. 22. 6.
—— (Uzziah), king of Judah, his good reign. 2 Kin. 14. 21; 2 Chr. 26.
his wars. 2 Chr. 26.
invades the priest's office. 2 Chr. 26. 16.
struck with leprosy. 2 Kin. 15. 5; 2 Chr. 26, 20.
—— prophet, exhorts Asa. 2 Chr. 15.
AZAZ, a'-zaz, strong. 1 Chr. 5. 8.
AZAZIAH, a'-zaz-i'-ah, whom Jehovah strengthened. 1 Chr. 15. 21.
AZBUK, az'-book. Neh. 3. 16.
AZEKAH, a-ze'-kah, dug over. Josh. 10. 10.
AZEL, a'-zel, noble. 1 Chr. 8. 37.
AZEM, a'-zem, strength, bone. Josh. 15. 29.
AZGAD, az'-gad, strong in fortune. Ezra 2. 12.
AZIEL, az'-i-el, whom God strengthens. 1 Chr. 15. 20.
AZIZA, a-zi'-zah, strong. Ezra 10. 27.
AZMAVETH, az-ma'-veth, strength (?). 2 Sam. 23. 31.
AZMON, az'-mon, robust. Num. 34. 4.
AZNOTH-TABOR, az'-noth-ta'-bor, ears (*i. e.* summits) of Tabor. Josh. 19. 34.
AZOR, a'-zor, helper. Matt. 1. 13.
AZOTUS, a-zo'-tus, the Greek form of ASHDOD. Acts 8. 40.
AZRIEL, az'-ri-el, help of God. 1 Chr. 5. 24.
AZRIKAM, az-ri'-kam, help against an enemy. 1 Chr. 3. 23.
AZUBAH, a-zoob'-ah, forsaken. 1 Kin. 22. 42.
AZUR, a'-zoor, same as AZOR. Jer. 28. 1.
AZZAH, az'-ah, strong, fortified. Deut. 2. 23.
AZZAN, az'-an, strong. Num. 34. 26.
AZZUR, az'-oor, same as AZOR. Neh. 10. 17.

BAAL, ba'-al, lord, master, possessor, owner.
worshipped. Num. 22. 41; Judg. 2. 13; 8. 33; 1 Kin. 16, 32; 18. 26; 2 Kin. 17. 16; 19. 18; 21. 3; Jer. 2. 8; 7. 9; 12. 16; 19. 5; 23. 13; Hos. 2. 8; 13. 1, &c.
his altars and priests destroyed by Gideon. Judg. 6. 25; by Elijah. 1 Kin. 18. 40; by Jehu. 2 Kin. 10. 18; by Jehoiada. 2 Kin. 11. 18; by Josiah. 2 Kin. 23. 4; 2 Chr. 34. 4.
BAALAH, ba'-al-ah, mistress. Josh. 15. 10.
BAALATH, ba'-al-ath, same as preceding. Josh. 19. 44.
BAALATH-BEER, ba'-al-ath-be'-er, having a well. Josh. 19. 8.
BAAL-BERITH, ba'-al-be-ri'th, lord of covenant. Judg. 8. 33.
BAALE, ba'-al-ay, plural of Baal. 2 Sam. 6. 2.
BAAL-GAD, ba'-al-gad', lord of fortune. Josh. 11. 17.
BAAL-HAMON, ba'-al-ha'-mon, place of a multitude. Cant. 8. 11.
BAAL-HANAN, ba'-al-ha'-nan, lord of benignity. Gen. 36. 38.
BAAL-HAZOR, ba'-al-ha'-zor, having a village. 2 Sam. 13. 23.
BAAL-HERMON, ba'-al-her'-mon, place of Hermon. Judg. 3. 3.
BAALI, ba'-al-i, my lord. Hos. 2. 16.
BAALIM, ba'-al-im, lords. Judg. 2. 11; 2 Chr. 28. 2.
BAALIS, ba'-al-is. Jer. 40. 14.
BAAL-MEON, ba'-al-me'-on, place of habitation. Num. 32. 38.
BAAL-PEOR, ba'-al-pe'-or, lord of the opening. Num. 25. 3,
the trespass of Israel concerning. Num. 25; Deut. 4. 3; Ps. 106. 28; Hos. 9. 10.
BAAL-PERAZIM, ba'-al-pe-raz'-im, place of breaches. David's victory over Philistines at. 2 Sam. 5. 20.
BAAL-SHALISHA, ba'-al-sha-lish'-ah, lord (or place) of Shalisha. 2 Kin. 4. 42.
BAAL-TAMAR, ba'-al-ta'-mar, place of palm trees. Judg. 20. 33.
BAAL-ZEBUB, ba'-al-ze-bo'ob, lord of flies.
false god of Ekron, Ahaziah rebuked for sending to enquire of. 2 Kin. 1. 2.

BAAL-ZEPHON, ba'-al-ze-pho'n, place of Zephon, or sacred to Zephon. Ex. 14. 2.
BAANA, ba'-a-nah. 1 Kin. 4. 12.
BAANAH, ba'-a-nah,
and Rechab, for murdering Ish-bosheth, slain by David. 2 Sam. 4. 2.
BAARA, ba'-a-rah, foolish. 1 Chr. 8. 8.
BAASEIAH, ba'-as-i'-ah, work of Jehovah. 1 Chr. 6. 40.
BAASHA, ba'-ash-ah, wicked (?).
king of Israel, destroys the house of Jeroboam, 1 Kin. 15. 16, 27; Jehu's prophecy concerning him. 1 Kin. 16. 1.
BABEL, ba'-bel, confusion.
Nimrod king of. Gen. 10. 10.
confusion of tongues at the building of. Gen. 11. 9.
BABYLON, bab'-il-on, Greek form of Bab-ilu, the gate of God. Gen. 10. 10; 2 Kin. 17. 30; 20. 12.
ambassadors from, to Hezekiah. 2 Kin. 20. 12; 2 Chr. 32. 31; Is. 39.
Jewish captivity there. 2 Kin. 25; 2 Chr. 36; Jer. 39; 52.
return from. Ezra 1; Neh. 2.
greatness of. Dan. 4. 30.
taken by the Medes. Dan. 5. 30.
fall of. Is. 13. 14; 21. 2; 47; 48; Jer. 25. 12; 50; 51.
church in. 1 Pet. 5. 13.
—— the Great. Rev. 14. 8; 17; 18.
BABYLONISH, bab'-il-one-ish, of, or belonging to, Babylon. Josh. 7. 21.
BACA, ba'-kah, weeping.
valley of misery. Ps. 84. 6.
BACHRITES, bak'-rites, the family of Becher. Num. 26. 35.
BAHARUMITE, ba-ha-r'um-ite, an inhabitant of Bahurim. 1 Chr. 11. 33.
BAHURIM, ba-hoor'-im, (town of) young men. 2 Sam. 16. 5.
BAJITH, ba'-yith (same as BETH), house. Is. 15. 2.
BAKBAKKAR, bak-bak'-ar. 1 Chr. 9. 15.
BAKBUK, bak'-book, a bottle. Ezra 2. 51.
BAKBUKIAH, bak'-book-i'-ah, emptying (*i.e.* wasting) of Jehovah. Neh. 11. 17.
BALAAM, ba'-la-am, destruction (?). Num. 22. 5.
requested by Balak to curse Israel, is forbidden. Num. 22. 13.
his anger. Num. 22. 27.
blesses Israel. Num. 23. 19; 24.
his prophecies. Num. 23. 9, 24; 24. 17.
his wicked counsel. Num. 31. 16; Deut. 23. 4. *See* Josh. 24. 9; Judg. 11. 25; Mic. 6. 5; 2 Pet. 2. 15; Jude 11; Rev. 2. 14.
slain. Num. 31. 8; Josh. 13. 22.
BALAC, ba'-lac, same as BALAK. Rev. 2. 14.
BALADAN, ba'-la-dan, He has given a son. 2 Kings 20. 12.
BALAH, ba'-lah. Josh. 19. 3.
BALAK, ba'-lak, to make empty. Num. 22. 2.
BAMAH, ba'-mah, high place. Ezek. 20. 29.
BAMOTH, ba'-moth, high places. Num. 21. 19.
BAMOTH-BAAL, ba'-moth-ba'-al, *h. p.* of Baal. Josh. 13. 17.
BANI, ba'-ni, built. 2 Sam. 23. 36.
BARABBAS, bar-a'b-as, son of Abba or father. Mark 15. 7.
a robber, released instead of Jesus. Matt. 27. 16; Mark 15. 6; Luke 23. 18; John 18. 40.
BARACHEL, ba'-rak-el, whom God blessed. Job 32. 6.
BARACHIAS, ba-rak-i'-as, whom Jehovah blesses. Matt. 23. 35.
BARAK, ba'-rak, thunderbolt, lightning. Judg. 4. 6.
delivers Israel from Sisera. Judg. 4. 5; Heb. 11. 32.
BARHUMITE, bar'-hoom-ite, same as BAHARUMITE. 2 Sam. 23. 31.
BARIAH, ba-ri'-ah, a fugitive. 1 Chr. 3. 22.
BAR-JESUS, bar-je'-sus, son of Jesus.
(Elymas) smitten with blindness by Paul. Acts 13. 6.

BAR-JONA, bar-jo'-nah, son of Jona (Simon). Matt. 16. 17.

BARKOS, bar'-kos, painter (?). Ezra 2. 53.

BARNABAS, bar'-na-bas, son of exhortation.
Levite of Cyprus, sells his lands. Acts 4. 36.
preaches at Antioch. Acts 11. 22.
accompanies Paul. Acts 11. 30; 12. 25; 13; 14; 15; 1 Cor. 9. 6.
his contention. Acts 15. 36.
his error. Gal. 2. 13.

BARSABAS, bar'-sa-bas, s. of Seba. Acts 1. 23.

BARTHOLOMEW, bar-thol'-o-mew, s. of Talmai.
the apostle. Matt. 10. 3; Mark 3. 18; Luke 6. 14; Acts 1. 13.

BARTIMÆUS, bar'-ti-me'-us, s. of Timai.
blindness cured near Jericho. Mark 10. 46.

BARUCH, ba'-rook, blessed. Jer. 32. 12.
receives Jeremiah's evidence. Jer. 32. 13; 36.
discredited by Azariah, and carried into Egypt. Jer. 43. 6.
God's message to. Jer. 45.

BARZILLAI, bar-zil'l-ai, of iron.
loyalty to David. 2 Sam. 17. 27.
David's recognition of. 2 Sam. 19. 31; 1 Kin. 2. 7.

BASHAN, ba'-shan, soft rich soil.
conquered. Num. 21. 33; Deut. 3. 1; Ps. 68. 15, 22; 135. 10; 136. 20.

BASHAN-HAVOTH-JAIR, ba'-shan-hav'-oth-ja'-yir, Bashan of the villages of Jair. Deut. 3. 14.

BASHEMATH, ba'-shem-ath, sweet-smelling. Gen. 26. 34.

BASMATH, same as BASHEMATH. 1 Kin. 4. 15.

BATH-RABBIM, bath-rab'-im, daughter of many. Cant. 7. 4.

BATH-SHEBA, bath'-she-bah, d. of the oath. 2 Sam. 11. 3.
wife of Uriah, taken by David. 2 Sam. 11; 12.
appeals to David for Solomon against Adonijah. 1 Kin. 1. 15.
intercedes with Solomon for Adonijah. 1 Kin. 2. 19.

BATH-SHUA, bath'-shoo-ah. 1 Chr. 3. 5.

BAVAI, ba'-vai. Neh. 3. 18.

BAZLITH, baz'-lith, a making naked (?). Neh. 7. 54.

BAZLUTH, baz'-looth, same as BAZLITH. Ezra 2. 52.

BEALIAH, be'-al-i'-ah, whom Jehovah rules. 1 Chr. 12. 5.

BEALOTH, be-a'h-loth, citizens (?), plural of BAA-LAH. Josh. 15. 24.

BEBAI, be-bai. Ezra 8. 11.

BECHER, be'-ker, a young camel. Gen. 46. 21.

BECHORATH, be-kor'-ath, offspring of the first birth. 1 Sam. 9. 1.

BEDAD, be'-dad, separation, part. Gen. 36. 35.

BEDAN, be'-dan, son of Dan (?). 1 Sam. 12. 11.

BEDEIAH, be-di'-ah. Ezra 10. 35.

BEELIADA, be-el'-ya-dah', whom Baal has known. 1 Chr. 14. 7.

BEELZEBUB, be-el'-ze-bub', same as BAALZEBUB. Matt. 10. 25.
prince of devils. Matt. 12. 24; Mark 3. 22; Luke 11. 15.
Christ's miracles ascribed to. Matt. 12. 24, &c.

BEER, be'-er, a well. Num. 21. 16.

BEERA, be-er'-ah, same as BEER. 1 Chr. 7. 37.

BEERAH, be-er'-ah, same as BEER. 1 Chr. 5. 6.

BEER-ELIM, be'-er-el'-im, well of heroes. Is. 15. 8.

BEERI, be'-er-i, man of the w. Gen. 26. 34.

BEER-LAHAI-ROI, be'-er-la-hai'-ro'-i, w. of vision (of God) to the living. Gen. 16. 14.

BEEROTH, be-er'-oth, wells. Josh. 9. 17.

BEEROTHITE, be-er'-oth-ite, a native of Beeroth. 2 Sam. 23. 37.

BEER-SHEBA, be'-er-she'-bah, well of the oath.
Abraham dwells at. Gen. 21. 31; 22. 19; 28. 10.
Hagar relieved at. Gen. 21. 14.
Jacob comforted at. Gen. 46. 1.
Elijah flees to. 1 Kin. 19. 3.

BEESH-TERAH, be-esh'-te-rah, house or temple of Astarte (?). Josh. 21. 27.

BEHEMOTH, be-he'-moth, the water-ox. Job 40. 15.

BEL, bel, another form of BAAL, an idol. Is. 46. 1; Jer. 50. 2.

BELA, be'-lah, destruction. Gen. 14. 2.

BELAH, be'-lah, same as BELA. Gen. 46. 21.

BELAITES, be'-la-ites, descendants of BELA. Num. 26. 38.

BELIAL, be'-li-al, worthless. [19. 22.
men of, wicked men so called. Deut. 13. 13; Judg. sons of. 1 Sam. 10. 27.

BELSHAZZAR, bel-shaz'-ar, Bel protect the king. Dan. 5. 1.
his profane feast, warning, and death. Dan. 5.

BELTESHAZZAR, bel'-te-shaz'-ar, preserve his life. Daniel so named. Dan. 1. 7; 4. 8, &c.

BEN, ben, son. 1 Chr. 15. 18.

BENAIAH, ben-ai'-ah, whom Jehovah has built. 2 Sam. 8. 18.
valiant acts of. 2 Sam. 23. 20; 1 Chr. 11. 22; 27. 5.
proclaims Solomon king. 1 Kin. 1. 32.
slays Adonijah, Joab, and Shimei. 1 Kin. 2. 25—46.

BEN-AMMI, ben'-am'-i, son of my own kindred. Gen. 19. 38.

BENE-BERAK, be-ne'-be-rak', sons of Barak, or of lightning. Josh. 19. 45.

BENE-JAAKAN, be-ne-ja'-ak-an, s. of Jaakan. Num. 33. 31.

BEN-HADAD, ben-ha'-dad, s. of Hadad.
king of Syria, his league with Asa against Baasha. 1 Kin. 15. 18.
——wars with Ahab. 1 Kin. 20.
baffled by Elisha. 2 Kin. 6. 8.
besieges Samaria. 2 Kin. 6. 24; 7.
slain by Hazael. 2 Kin. 8. 7.
——son of Hazael, wars with Israel. 2 Kin. 13. 3, 25. See Jer. 49. 27; Amos 1. 4.

BEN-HAIL, ben-ha'-yil, son of the host. 2 Chr. 17. 7.

BEN-HANAN, ben-ha'-nan, s. of one who is gracious. 1 Chr. 4. 20.

BENINU, be-ni'-noo, our s. Neh. 10. 13.

BENJAMIN, ben'-ja-min, s. of the right hand, i.e. fortunate. Gen. 35. 18.
(first named Ben-oni, "son of my sorrow"), Patriarch, youngest son of Jacob, his birth at Beth-lehem. Gen. 35. 16.
goes into Egypt. Gen. 43. 15.
Joseph's stratagem to detain. Gen. 44.
Jacob's prophecy concerning. Gen. 49. 27.
HIS DESCENDANTS. Gen. 46. 21; 1 Chr. 7. 6.
twice numbered. Num. 1. 36; 26. 38.
blessed by Moses. Deut. 33. 12.
their inheritance. Josh. 18. 11.
their wickedness chastised. Judg. 20; 21.
the first king chosen from. 1 Sam. 9; 10.
support the house of Saul. 2 Sam. 2.
afterwards adhere to that of David. 1 Kin. 12. 21; 1 Chr. 11.
the tribe of Paul. Phil. 3. 5. See Ps. 68. 27; Ezek. 48. 32; Rev. 7. 8.

BENJAMITE, ben'-jam-ite. a man of the tribe of Benjamin. Judg. 20. 35.

BENO, ben-o', his son. 1 Chr. 24. 26.

BEN-ONI, be'n-o'-ni, s. of my sorrow. Gen. 35. 18.

BEN-ZOHETH, ben-zo'-heth, s. of Zoheth. 1 Chr. 4. 20.

BEON, be'-on, contracted from BAAL-MEON. Num. 32. 3.

BEOR, be'-or. Gen. 36. 32.

BERA, be'-rah. Gen. 14. 2.

BERACHAH, be'-rak-ah, blessing. 1 Chr. 12. 3.
valley of, why so named. 2 Chr. 20. 26.

BERACHIAH, be'-rak-i'-ah, whom Jehovah hath blessed. 1 Chr. 6. 39.

BERAIAH, be-rai'-ah, whom Jehovah created. 1 Chr. 8. 21.

BEREA, be-re'-ah.
city of Macedonia, Paul preaches at. Acts 17. 10.
people "more noble." Acts 17. 11.

BERECHIAH, be'-rek-i'-ah, same as BERACHIAH. 1 Chr. 3. 20.

BERED, be'-red, hail. Gen. 16. 14.

BERI, be'-ri, man of the well. 1 Chr. 7. 36.

BERIAH, be-ri'-ah, in evil (?). Gen. 46. 17.

BERIITES, be-ri'-ites, descendants of Beriah. Num. 26. 44.

BERITES, ber'-ites. 2 Sam. 20. 14.

BERITH, be'-rith, a covenant. Judg. 9. 46.

BERNICE, ber-ni'-see, Victoria. Acts 25. 13.

BERODACH-BALADAN, be'-ro-dak-bal'-a-dan, Berodach (same as MERODACH) has given a son. 2 Kin. 20. 12.

BEROTHAH, be-ro'-thah, wells. Ezek. 47. 16.

BEROTHAI, be-ro'-thai, my wells. 2 Sam. 8. 8.

BEROTHITE, be-ro'-thite, same as BEEROTHITE. 1 Chr. 11. 39.

BESAI, be-sai, sword (?), or victory (?). Ezra 2. 49.

BESODEIAH, be'-sod-i'-ah, in the secret of Jehovah. Neh. 3. 6.

BESOR, be'-sor, cool. 1 Sam. 30. 9.

BETAH, be'-tah, confidence. 2 Sam. 8. 8.

BETEN, be'-ten. Josh. 19. 25.

BETHABARA, beth-ab'-ar-ah, house of passage. place where John baptized. John 1. 28.

BETH-ANATH, beth'-an-ath, echo. Josh. 19. 38.

BETH-ANOTH, beth'-an-oth. Josh. 15. 59.

BETHANY, beth'-an-y, house of dates.
visited by Christ, Matt. 21. 17 ; 26. 6 ; Mark 11. 1 : Luke 19. 29 ; John 12. 1.
raising of Lazarus at, John 11. 18.
ascension of Christ at. Luke 24. 50.

BETH-ARABAH, beth-a-ra'h-bah, h. of the desert. Josh. 15. 6.

BETH-ARAM, beth-a'-ram, h. of the height. Josh. 13. 27.

BETH-ARBEL, beth-arb'-el, h. of the ambush of God. Hos. 10. 14.

BETH-AVEN, beth-a'-ven, h. of vanity (i.e. of idols). Josh. 7. 2.

BETH-AZMAVETH, beth'-az-ma'-veth, h. of strength. Neh. 7. 28.

BETH-BAAL-MEON, beth'-ba'-al-me-on', h. of Baal-meon. Josh. 13. 17.

BETH-BARAH, beth-ba'-rah, same as BETHABARA. Judg. 7. 24.

BETH-BIREI, beth-bir'-i, house of my creation. 1 Chr. 4. 31.

BETH-CAR, beth'-kar, h. of pasture. 1 Sam. 7. 11.

BETH-DAGON, beth-da'-gon, h. of Dagon. Josh. 15. 41.

BETH-DIBLATHAIM, beth'-dib-la-tha'-im, h. of the two cakes. Jer. 48. 22.

BETH-EL, beth'-el, h. of God. Gen. 12. 8.
(Luz), city of Palestine, named Beth-el by Jacob. Gen. 28. 19 ; 31. 13.
altar built by Jacob at. Gen. 35. 1.
occupied by the house of Joseph. Judg. 1. 22.
sons of prophets resident there. 2 Kin. 2. 2, 3 ; 17. 28.
the king's chapel. Amos 7. 13.
idolatry of Jeroboam at. 1 Kin. 12. 28 ; 13. 1.
reformation by Josiah at. 2 Kin. 23. 15.

BETHELITE, beth'-el-ite, a native of Bethel. 1 Kin. 16. 34.

BETH-EMEK, beth-e'-mek, house of the valley. Josh. 19. 27.

BETHER, be'-ther, separation. Cant. 2. 17.

BETHESDA, beth-esd'-ah, house of mercy.
pool of, at Jerusalem, miracles wrought at. John 5. 2.

BETH-EZEL, beth-e'-zel, house of firmness (?). Mic. 1. 11.

BETH-GADER, beth-ga'-der, h. of the wall. 1 Chr. 2. 51.

BETH GAMUL, beth-ga'-mool, h. of the weaned. Jer. 48. 23.

BETH-HACCEREM, beth'-hak-er'-em, h. of the vineyard. Neh. 3. 14.

BETH-HARAN, beth-ha'-ran. Num. 32. 36.

BETH-HOGLAH, beth-hog'-lah, h. of the partridge. Josh. 15. 6.

BETH-HORON, beth-ho'-ron, h. of the hollow. Josh. 10. 10.

BETH-JESIMOTH, beth-je-shim'-oth, h. of the deserts. Num. 33. 49.

BETH-LEBAOTH, beth'-le-ba'-oth, house of lionesses. Josh. 19. 6.

BETH-LEHEM, beth'-le-hem, h. of bread. Gen. 35. 19.

BETH-LEHEM EPHRATAH, beth'-le-hem ef'-ra-tah, B. the fruitful (?).
(originally Ephratah), Naomi and Ruth return to. Ruth 1—4.
David anointed at. 1 Sam. 16. 13 ; 20. 6.
well of. 2 Sam. 23. 15 ; 1 Chr. 11. 17.
Christ's birth at. Matt. 2. 1 ; Luke 2. 4 ; John 7. 42 ; predicted. Mic. 5. 2 (Ps. 132. 5, 6).
babes of, slain. Matt. 2. 16.

BETHLEHEMITE, beth'-le-hem-ite, a man of Bethlehem. 1 Sam. 16. 1.

BETH-LEHEM-JUDAH, beth'-le-hem-joo'-dah, B. of Judah. Judg. 17. 7.

BETH-MAACHAH, beth'-ma'-ak-ah, house of Maachah. 2 Sam. 20. 14.

BETH-MARCABOTH, beth'-mar'-kab-oth, h. of chariots. Josh. 19. 5.

BETH-MEON, be'th-me-o'n, h. of habitation. Jer. 48. 23.

BETH-NIMRAH, beth'-nim'-rah, h. of sweet water. Num. 32. 36.

BETH-PALET, beth'-pa'-let, h. of escape, or of Pelet. Josh. 15. 27.

BETH-PAZZEZ, beth'-paz'-ez, h. of dispersion. Josh. 19. 21.

BETH-PEOR, beth'-pe'-or, temple of Peor. Deut. 3. 29.

BETHPHAGE, be'th-fa gee, house of unripe figs. Matt. 21. 1.

BETH-PHELET, beth'-fe'-let, same as BETH-PALET. Neh. 11. 26.

BETH-RAPHA, beth'-ra'-fah, house of Rapha. 1 Chr. 4. 12.

BETH-REHOB, beth'-re'-hob, h. of Rehob. Judg. 18. 28.

BETHSAIDA, beth'-sai'-dah, h. of fishing.
of Galilee, native place of Philip, Peter, and Andrew. Mark 6. 45; John 1. 44; 12. 21.
blind man cured at. Mark 8. 22.
condemned for unbelief. Matt. 11. 21.
Christ feeds the five thousand at. Luke 9. 10—17.

BETH-SHAN, beth'-shan', h. of rest. 1 Sam. 31. 10.

BETH-SHEAN, beth'-she'-an, same as BETH-SHAN. Josh. 17. 11.

BETH-SHEMESH, beth'-she'-mesh, house of the sun. Josh. 15. 10.
men of, punished for looking into the ark. 1 Sam. 6. 19.
great battle at. 2 Kin. 14. 11.

BETHSHEMITE, beth'-shem'-ite, a native of Bethshemesh. 1 Sam. 6. 14.

BETH-SHITTAH, beth'-shit'-ah, house of acacias. Judg. 7. 22.

BETH-TAPPUAH, beth'-tap-oo'-ah, h. of apples. Josh. 15. 53.

BETHUEL, beth'-oo-el, h. of God. Gen. 22. 22.

BETHUL, beth-ool', same as BETHEL (?). Josh. 19. 4.

BETH ZUR, beth'-zoor', house of the rock. Josh. 15. 58.

BETONIM, be-to'-nim, pistachio nuts. Josh. 13. 26.

BEULAH, be-ool'-ah, married. Is. 62. 4.

BEZAI, be'-zai. Ezra 2. 17.

BEZALEEL, be-zal'-e-el, in the shadow of God (?).
constructs the tabernacle. Ex. 31. 2 ; 35. 30 ; 36—38.

BEZEK, be'-zek, lightning (?). Judg. 1. 4.

BEZER, be'-zer, ore of precious metal. Deut. 4. 43.

BICHRI, bik'-ri, young. 2 Sam. 20. 1.

BIDKAR, bid'-kar, cleaver (?). 2 Kin. 9. 25.

BIGTHA, big'-thah. Esth. 1. 10.

BIGTHAN, big'-than, given by God.
and Teresh, their conspiracy against Ahasuerus. Esth. 2. 21.

BIGTHANA, big-thah'-nah, same as BIGTHAN. Esth. 6. 2.

BIGVAI, big'-vai. Ezra 2. 2.

BILDAD, bil'-dad, son of contention (?). Job 2. 11.
his answers to Job. Job 8 ; 18 ; 25.

BILEAM, bil'-e-am, same as BALAAM (?), or IB-
LEAM (?). 1 Chr. 6. 70.
BILGAH, bil'-gah, cheerfulness. 1 Chr. 24. 14.
BILGAI, bil'-gai, same as BILGAH. Neh. 10. 8.
BILHAH, bil'-hah, modesty. Gen. 29. 29.
Jacob's children by. Gen. 30. 5.
BILHAN, bil'-han, modest. Gen. 36. 27.
BILSHAN, bil'-shan, seeker (?). Ezra 2. 2.
BIMHAL, bim'-hal. 1 Chr. 7. 33.
BINEA, bi'-ne-ah. 1 Chr. 8. 37.
BINNUI, bin'-oo-i, a building. Ezra 8. 33.
BIRSHA, bir'-shah. Gen. 14. 2.
BIRZAVITH, bir'-za-vith, wounds (?). 1 Chr. 7. 31.
BISHLAM, bish'-lam. Ezra 4. 7.
BITHIAH, bith'-yah, daughter (*i.e.* worshipper) of
Jehovah. 1 Chr. 4. 18.
BITHRON, bith'-ron, a broken place. 2 Sam. 2. 29.
BITHYNIA, bi-thin'-yah. Acts 16. 7.
BIZJOTHJAH, biz-joth'-jah, contempt of Jehovah.
Josh. 15. 28.
BIZTHA, biz'-thah. Esth. 1. 10.
BLASTUS, blast'-us, a shoot. Acts 12. 20.
BOANERGES, bo'-an-er'-jes, sons of thunder.
James and John surnamed by Christ. Mark 3. 17.
BOAZ, bo'-az, fleetness. Ruth 2. 1.
his conduct towards Ruth. Ruth 2 ; 3 ; 4.
ancestor of David and Christ. Ruth 4. 17, 22 ;
Matt. 1. 5—16 ; Luke 3. 23, 32.
―――― and Jachin (strength and stability), pillars
of the temple. 2 Chr. 3. 17.
BOCHERU, bo'-ke-roo, firstborn (?). 1 Chr. 8. 38.
BOCHIM, bo'-kim, weepers. Judg. 2. 1.
Israel rebuked by an angel at. Judg. 2. 1—3.
Israel repent at. Judg. 2. 4, 5.
BOHAN, bo'-han, thumb (?). Josh. 15. 6.
BOOZ, bo'-oz, same as BOAZ. Matt. 1. 5.
BOSCATH, bos'-kath, stony, elevated ground. 2
Kin. 22. 1.
BOSOR, bo'-sor, Greek and Aramaic form of BEOR.
2 Pet. 2. 15.
BOZEZ, bo'-zez, shining. 1 Sam. 14. 4.
BOZKATH, boz'-kath, same as BOSCATH. Josh. 15.
39.
BOZRAH, boz'-rah, sheepfold. Gen. 36. 33.
prophecies concerning. Is. 34. 6 ; 63. 1 ; Jer. 48.
24 ; 49. 13 ; Amos 1. 12.
BUKKI, book'-i, wasting. Num. 34. 22.
BUKKIAH, book'-yah, wasting from Jehovah. 1
Chr. 25. 4.
BUL, bool, rain. 1 Kin. 6. 38.
BUNAH, boon'-ah, prudence. 1 Chr. 2. 25.
BUNNI, boon'-i, built. Neh. 9. 4.
BUZ, booz, contempt. Gen. 22. 21.
BUZI, booz'-i, descended from Buz. Ezek. 1. 3.
BUZITE, booz'-ite, a descendant of Buz. Job 32. 2.

CABBON, kab'-on, cake. Josh. 15. 40.
CABUL, cah'-bool, displeasing (?). Josh. 19. 27.
CÆSAR, see'-zar. Matt. 22. 17.
Augustus. Luke 2. 1.
Tiberius. Luke 3. 1.
Claudius, time of dearth. Acts 11. 28.
Paul appeals to. Acts 25. 11.
household of. Phil. 4. 22.
CÆSAREA, see'-zar-e'-a, named after Augustus
Cæsar. Acts 8. 40.
CÆSAREA PHILIPPI, see'-zar-e'-a fil-ip'-i, named
after Philip the tetrarch.
visited by Christ. Matt. 16. 13 ; Mark 8. 27.
―――― (Stratonis), Peter sent there. Acts 10.
Paul visits. Acts 21. 8.
Paul sent to Felix there. Acts 23. 23.
CAIAPHAS, kai'-a-fas, depression (?).
high priest, prophesies concerning Christ. John
11. 49.
his counsel. Matt. 26. 3.
he condemns Him. Matt. 26. 65 ; Mark 14. 63 ;
Luke 22. 71.
CAIN, kane, possession. Gen. 4. 1. Josh. 15. 57.
his anger. Gen. 4. 5.
murders Abel. Gen. 4. 8 ; 1 John 3. 12.

CAIN—*cont.*
his punishment. Gen. 4. 11 ; Jude 11.
CAINAN, kay'-nan, possessor. Gen. 5. 9.
CALAH, ka'-lah. Gen. 10. 11.
CALCOL, kal'-kol. 1 Chr. 2. 6.
CALEB, ka'-leb, a dog.
faith of. Num. 13. 30 ; 14. 6.
permitted to enter Canaan. Num. 26. 65 ; 32. 12 ;
Deut. 1. 36.
his request. Josh. 14. 6.
his possessions. Josh. 15. 13.
gives his daughter to Othniel to wife. Judg.
1. 13.
CALEB-EPHRATAH, ka'-leb-ef'-rat-ah, C. the fruitful. 1 Chr. 2. 24.
CALNEH, kal'-nay. Gen. 10. 10.
CALNO, kal'-no, same as CALNEH. Is. 10. 9.
CALVARY, kal'-va-ry, skull. Luke 23. 33.
CAMON, ka'-mon, abounding in stalks. Judg. 10. 5.
CANA, ka'-nah.
Christ turns water into wine at. John 2.
nobleman visits Christ at. John 4. 47.
CANAAN, ka'-na-an, low region. Gen. 9. 18.
land of. Ex. 23. 31 ; Josh. 1. 4 ; Zeph. 2. 5.
promised to Abraham. Gen. 12. 7 ; 13. 14 ; 17. 8.
inhabitants of. Ex. 15. 15.
their wickedness at Sodom and Gomorrah. Gen.
13. 13 ; 19.
Israelites not to walk in the ways of. Lev. 18.
3, 24, 30 ; 20. 23.
daughters of. Gen. 28. 1, 6, 8.
language of. Is. 19. 18.
kingdoms of. Ps. 135. 11.
king of. Judg. 4. 2, 23, 24 ; 5. 19.
wars of. Judg. 3. 1.
dwelling of Abraham in, Gen. 12. 6. Isaac and
Jacob. Gen. 28. Esau. Gen. 36. Joseph. Gen.
37.
allotted to children of Israel. Josh. 14.
the spies visit, and their report. Num. 13.
Moses sees, from Pisgah. Num. 27. 12 ; Deut. 3.
27 ; 34. 1.
―――― a son of Ham, grandson of Noah, cursed
on account of his father's mockery of Noah.
Gen. 9. 25.
CANAANITE, ka'-na-an-ite, a zealot. Mark 3. 18.
CANAANITES, ka'-na-an-ites, inhabitants of Canaan. Judg. 1. 1.
CANAANITESS, ka'-na-an-ite-ess, feminine of preceding. 1 Chr. 2. 3.
CANDACE, kan'-da-see, Queen of Ethiopia. Acts 8. 27.
CANNEH, kan'-ay, probably same as CALNEH. Ezek.
27. 23.
CAPERNAUM, ka-per'-na-um, city of consolation (?).
Christ dwells at. Matt. 4. 13 ; John 2. 12.
preaches at. Matt. 4. 17 ; Mark 1. 21.
miracles at. Matt. 8. 5 ; 17. 24 ; John 4. 46 ; 6. 17.
parables at. Matt. 13. 18, 24 ; Mark 4.
condemned for impenitence. Matt. 11. 23 ; Luke
10. 15.
CAPHTHORIM, kaf'-thor-im, same as CAPHTORIM.
1 Chr. 1. 12.
CAPHTOR, kaf'-tor. Deut. 2. 23.
CAPHTORIM, kaf'-tor-im, inhabitants of Caphtor.
Gen. 10. 14.
CAPPADOCIA, kap'-ad-o'-sha. Acts 2. 9 ; 1 Pet. 1. 1.
CARCAS, kar'-kas. Esth. 1. 10.
CARCHEMISH, kar'-kem-ish, fortress of Chemosh.
Jer. 46. 2.
CAREAH, ka-re'-ah, bald. 2 Kin. 25. 23.
CARMEL, karm'-el, park. Josh. 12. 22.
Nabal's conduct to David at. 1 Sam. 25.
mount, Elijah and the prophets of Baal. 1 Kin. 18
the Shunammite woman goes to Elisha at. 2 Kin
4. 25.
her child restored to life by Elisha. 2 Kin
4. 34.
CARMELITE, karm'-el-ite, a native of Carmel. 1
Sam. 30. 5.
CARMELITESS, karm'-el-ite-ess, feminine of pre-
ceding. 1 Sam. 27. 3.

CARMI, karm'-i, a vine-dresser. Gen. 46. 9.
CARMITES, karm'-ites, descendants of Carmi. Num. 26. 6.
CARPUS, karp'-us, fruit (?). 2 Tim. 4. 13.
CARSHENA, kar'-shena. Esth. 1. 14.
CASIPHIA, ka-sif'-yah, silver (?). Ezra 8. 17.
CASLUHIM, kas'-loo-him. Gen. 10. 14.
CASTOR, kas'-tor.
  and Pollux, Paul's ship. Acts 28. 11.
CEDRON, keed'-ron, same as KIDRON. John 18. 1.
CENCHREA, ken'-kre-ah, millet, small pulse.
  Paul shaves his head at. Acts 18. 18.
  seaport of Corinth, church there. Rom. 16. 1.
CEPHAS, kee'-fas.
  (Peter), a stone. John 1. 42; 1 Cor. 1. 12; 3. 22;
  9. 5; 15. 5; Gal. 2. 9. *See* PETER.
CHALCOL, kal'-kol, same as CALCOL. 1 Kin. 4. 31.
CHALDEA, kal-de'-ah. Jer. 50. 10.
CHALDEANS, kal-de'-ans, inhabitants of Chaldea.
  afflict Job. Job 1. 17.
  besiege Jerusalem. 2 Kin. 24. 2; 25. 4; Jer. 37–39.
  wise men of, preserved by Daniel. Dan. 2. 24.
  prophecies concerning. Is. 23. 13; 43. 14; 47. 1;
  48. 14; Hab. 1. 5.
CHALDEES, kal-dees', same as preceding. Gen. 11. 28.
CHANAAN, ka'-na-an, another form of Canaan.
  Acts 7. 11.
CHARASHIM, kar'-ash-im, craftsmen. 1 Chr. 4. 14.
CHARCHEMISH, same as CARCHEMISH. 2 Chr. 35. 20.
CHARRAN, kar'-an, same as HARAN. Acts 7. 2.
CHEBAR, ke'-bar, great (?).
  the river, Ezekiel's visions at. Ezek. 1; 3. 15;
  10. 15.
CHEDORLAOMER, ke-dor'-la-o'-mer, glory of Lao-mer (?).
  king of Elam, takes Lot prisoner, but subdued
  by Abram. Gen. 14.
CHELAL, ke'-lal, completion. Ezra 10. 30.
CHELLUH, kel'-oo. Ezra 10. 35.
CHELUB, kel'-oob, bird-trap. 1 Chr. 4. 11.
CHELUBAI, kel-oo'-bai, same as CALEB. 1 Chr. 2. 9.
CHEMARIMS, kem-ah'-rims, persons dressed in
  black attire. Zeph. 1. 4.
CHEMOSH, keem'-osh, subduer.
  god of Moab. Num. 21. 29; Judg. 11. 24; Jer.
  48. 7, 13, 46.
  worshipped by Solomon. 1 Kin. 11. 7.
CHENAANAH, ke-na'-an-ah, probably fem. of Ca-naan. 1 Kin. 22. 11.
CHENANI, ke'-nane'-i, probably same as CHE-NANIAH. Neh. 9. 4.
CHENANIAH, ke'-nan-i'-ah, whom Jehovah sup-ports. 1 Chr. 15. 22.
CHEPHAR-HAAMMONAI, ke-far'-hah-am'-on-ai, vil-lage of the Ammonites. Josh. 18. 24.
CHEPHIRAH, ke-fi'-rah, same as CAPHAR. Josh. 9. 17.
CHERAN, ke'-ran. Gen. 36. 26.
CHERETHIMS, ke'-reth-ims, Cretans (?). Ezek. 25. 16.
CHERETHITES, ke'-reth-ites, probably same as pre-ceding. 2 Sam. 8. 18.
  (and Pelethites), David's guard. 2 Sam. 15. 18.
CHERITH, ke'-rith, gorge (?). 1 Kin. 17. 3.
CHERUB, cher'-ub, blessing (?), strong (?). Ezra 2. 59.
CHERUBIM, cher' oob-im, plural of CHERUB.
  in garden of Eden. Gen. 3. 24.
  for the mercy seat and the temple. Ex. 25.
  18; 37. 7; 1 Kin. 6. 23; 2 Chr. 3. 10; Ps. 80. 1;
  Ezek. 41. 18.
  Ezekiel's visions of. Ezek. 1; 10.
CHESALON, ke-sah'-lon, hope. Josh. 15. 10.
CHESED, ke'-sed, conqueror (?). Gen. 22. 22.
CHESIL, ke'-sil, a fool. Josh. 15. 30.
CHESULLOTH, ke-sool'-oth, confidences. Josh. 19. 18.
CHEZIB, ke'-zib, false. Gen. 38. 5.
CHIDON, ki'-don, javelin. 1 Chr. 13. 9.

CHILEAB, kil'-e-ab, probably another form of CA-LEB. 2 Sam. 3. 3.
CHILION, kil'-yon, wasting away. Ruth 1. 2.
CHILMAD, kil'-mad. Ezek. 27. 23.
CHIMHAM, kim'-ham, longing. 2 Sam. 19. 37.
CHINNERETH, kin'-er-eth, a lyre. Josh. 19. 35.
CHINNEROTH, kin'-er-oth, plural of CHINNERETH.
  Josh. 11. 2.
CHIOS, ki'-os. Acts 20. 15.
CHISLEU, kis'-lew. Neh. 1. 1.
CHISLON, kis'-lon, confidence, hope. Num. 34. 21.
CHISLOTH-TABOR, kis'-loth-ta'-bor, flanks (?) of
  Tabor. Josh. 19. 12.
CHITTIM, kit'-im, probably Cyprus.
  prophecies of. Num. 24. 24; Is. 23. 1, 12; Dan.
  11. 30.
CHIUN, ki'-oon, image. Amos 5. 26.
CHLOE, klo'-ee. 1 Cor. 1. 11.
CHOR-ASHAN, kor-ash'-an, smoking furnace. 1 Sam.
  30. 30.
CHORAZIN, ko-ra'-zin. Matt. 11. 21.
CHOZEBA, ko-ze'-bah, deceiver. 1 Chr. 4. 22.
CHRIST, the anointed. See *Subject-Index*, p. 439.
CHUB, choob. Ezek. 30. 5.
CHUN, choon, establishment. 1 Chr. 18. 8.
CHUSHAN-RISHATHAIM, koosh'-an-rish-a-tha'-im.
  Oppresses Israel. Judg. 3. 8, 9, 10.
CHUZA, koo'-zah. Luke 8. 3.
CILICIA, si-lish'-ya.
  disciples there. Acts 15. 23, 41.
  the country of Paul. Acts 21. 39; Gal. 1. 21.
  Paul born at Tarsus in. Acts 22. 3.
CINNEROTH, kin'-er-oth, same as CHINNEROTH.
  1 Kin. 15. 20.
CIS, kis. Acts 13. 21, same as KISH.
CLAUDA, klawd'-ah. Acts 27. 16.
CLAUDIA, klawd'-yah. 2 Tim. 4. 21.
CLAUDIUS, klawd'-yus. Acts 11. 28.
CLAUDIUS LYSIAS, klawd'-yus lis-yas.
  chief captain, rescues Paul. Acts 21. 31; 22. 24;
  23. 10.
  sends him to Felix. Acts 23. 26.
CLEMENT, klem'-ent.
  fellow labourer of Paul. Phil. 4. 3.
CLEOPAS, kle'-op-as, either a shortened form of
  Cleopatros, or a Greek form of Alphæus.
  a disciple. Luke 24. 18. *See* EMMAUS.
CLEOPHAS, kle'-of-as, probably same as preceding.
  John 19. 25.
CNIDUS, kni'-dus, nettle (?). Acts 27. 7.
COL-HOZEH, kol-ho'-zeh, every one that seeth.
  Neh. 3. 15.
COLOSSE, ko-los'-ee.
  brethren at, encouraged and warned. Col. 1; 2.
  exhorted to holiness. Col. 3; 4.
COLOSSIANS, ko-los'-yans, people of Colosse.
CONANIAH. 2 Chr. 35. 9, same as CONONIAH.
CONIAH, ko-ni'-ah, contracted from JECONIAH.
  Jer. 22. 24.
CONONIAH, kon-on-i'-ah, whom Jehovah has set
  up. 2 Chr. 31. 12.
COOS, ko'-os.
  Paul sails to. Acts 21. 1.
CORE, ko'-re, Greek form of KORAH. Jude 11.
CORINTH, kor'-inth.
  Paul and Apollos at. Acts 18; 19. 1.
CORINTHIANS, kor-inth'-yans, inhabitants of Co-rinth. Acts 18. 8.
  their divisions, &c., censured. 1 Cor. 1; 5; 11. 18.
  their faith and graces. 2 Cor. 3.
  instructed concerning spiritual gifts. 1 Cor. 14;
  and the resurrection. 1 Cor. 15.
  exhorted to charity, &c. 1 Cor. 13; 14. 1; 2 Cor.
  8; 9.
  their false teachers exposed. 2 Cor. 11. 3, 4, 13.
  Paul commends himself to. 2 Cor. 11; 12.
CORNELIUS, kor-neel'-yus. Acts 10. 1.
  devout centurion, his prayer answered. Acts 10.
  3; sends for Peter. 10. 9; baptized, 10. 48.
COSAM, ko'-sam. Luke 3. 28.

Coz, koz, thorn. 1 Chr. 4. 8.

Cozbi, kos'-bi, deceitful, slain by Phineas. Num. 25. 15.

Crescens, kres'-ens, growing.
goes to Dalmatia. 2 Tim. 4. 10.

Crete, kreet.
visited by Paul. Acts 27. 7.

Cretes or Cretians, kreet'-yans, inhabitants of Crete. Acts 2. 11. Tit. 1. 12.

Crispus, krisp'-us, curled.
baptized by Paul. Acts 18. 8; 1 Cor. 1. 14.

Cumi, koom'-i, arise. Mark 5. 41.

Cush, koosh, black. Gen. 10. 6.

Cushan, koosh'-an, same meaning as Cush. Hab. 3. 7.

Cushi, koosh'-i, same meaning as Cush.
announces Absalom's death. 2 Sam. 18. 21.

Cuth, kooth. 2 Kin. 17. 30.

Cuthah, kooth'-ah, same as Cuth. 2 Kin. 17. 24.

Cyprus, si'-prus. Acts 4. 36.
disciples there. Acts 11. 19.
Paul and Barnabas preach there. Acts 13. 4.
Barnabas and Mark go there. Acts 15. 39.

Cyrene, si-re'-nee. Matt. 27. 32.
disciples of. Acts 11. 20; 13. 1.
Simon of. Mark 15. 21.

Cyrenian, si-reen'-yan, a native of Cyrene. Acts 6. 9.

Cyrenius, si-reen'-yus, Greek form of the Roman name Quirinus.
governor of Syria. Luke 2, 2.

Cyrus, si'-rus, the sun. 2 Chr. 36. 22.
king of Persia, prophecies concerning. Is. 44. 28; 45. 1. *See* Dan. 6. 28; 10. 1.
his proclamation for rebuilding the temple. 2 Chr. 36. 22; Ezra 1.

Dabareh, da'-bar-ay, pasture. Josh. 21. 28.

Dabbasheth, dab-ash'-eth, hump of a camel. Josh. 19. 11.

Daberath, da'-ber-ath. Josh. 19. 12, same as Dabareh.

Dagon, da'-gon, fish.
national idol-god of the Philistines, sacrificed to. Judg. 16. 23.
smitten down in temple at Ashdod. 1 Sam. 5. 3, 4.
Saul's head fastened in house of. 1 Chr. 10. 10.

Dalaiah, da-lai'-ah, whom Jehovah hath delivered. 1 Chr. 3. 24.

Dalmanutha, dal'-ma-noo'-thah. Mark 8. 10.

Dalmatia, dal'-ma'-shah. 2 Tim. 4. 10.

Dalphon, dal'-fon, proud (?). Esth. 9. 7.

Damaris, dam'-ar-is, calf (?).
cleaves to Paul. Acts 17. 34.

Damascenes, dam'-as-eens', people of Damascus. 2 Cor. 11. 32.

Damascus, dam-ask'-us, activity (?). Gen. 14. 15.
mentioned. Gen. 15. 2.
subjugated by David. 2 Sam. 8. 6; 1 Chr. 18. 6.
Elisha's prophecy there. 2 Kin. 8. 7.
taken by Tiglath-pileser, king of Assyria. 2 Kin. 16. 9.
restored to Israel by Jeroboam. 2 Kin. 14. 28.
king Ahaz copies an altar there. 2 Kin. 16. 10.
Paul's journey to. Acts 9; 22. 6.
Paul restored to sight, and baptized there. Acts 9. 17, 18.
prophecies concerning. Is. 7. 8; 8. 4; 17. 1; Jer. 49. 23; Amos 1. 3.

Dan, judge,
son of Jacob, by Rachel's handmaid. Gen. 30. 6.
—— Tribe of, numbered. Num. 1. 38; 26. 42.
their inheritance. Josh. 19. 40.
blessed by Jacob. Gen. 49. 16.
blessed by Moses. Deut. 33. 22.
win Laish, and call it Dan. Judg. 18. 29.
set up idolatry. Judg. 18. 30; 1 Kin. 12. 29.

Dan-jaan, dan'-ja'-an, woodland (?). Dan. 2 Sam. 24. 6.

Daniel, dan'-yel, God's judge. Dan. 1. 6.

Daniel—*cont.*
(Belteshazzar), with other captives, taken from Jerusalem to Babylon. Dan. 1. 3.
taught the learning of the Chaldeans. Dan. 1. 4.
will not take the king's meat or drink. Dan. 1. 8.
has understanding in dreams. Dan. 1. 17.
interprets the royal dreams. Dan. 2; 4; and hand-writing on wall. Dan. 5. 17.
made chief president by Darius. Dan. 6. 2.
conspired against by the princes. Dan. 6. 4.
idolatrous decree against, issued. Dan. 6. 9; breach thereof, Dan. 6. 10.
cast into the lions' den. Dan. 6. 16; preservation in, Dan. 6. 22.
his vision of the four beasts. Dan. 7. 12; ram and he-goat, Dan. 8. 3.
his prayer. Dan. 9. 3.
promise of return from captivity. Dan. 9. 20; 10. 10; 12. 13.
name mentioned. Ezek. 14. 14, 20; 28. 3.

Danites, dan'-ites, descendants of Dan. Judg. 13. 2.

Dannah, dan'-ah. Josh. 15. 49.

Dara, da'-rah, probably contracted from the next word. 1 Chr. 2. 6.

Darda, dar'-dah, pearl of wisdom (?). 1 Kin. 4. 31.

Darius, da-ri'-us, governor (?). Ezra 4. 5.
decree concerning the rebuilding of the temple. Ezra 6.
—— (the Median) takes Babylon. Dan. 5. 31; his decree to fear the God of Daniel. Dan. 6. 25.

Darkon, dark'-on, scatterer (?). Ezra 2. 56.

Dathan, da'-than. Num. 16. 1.

David, da'-vid, beloved.
King, son of Jesse. Ruth 4. 22; 1 Chr. 2; Matt. 1.
anointed by Samuel. 1 Sam. 16. 8.
plays the harp before Saul. 1 Sam. 16. 19.
his zeal and faith. 1 Sam. 17. 26, 34.
kills Goliath of Gath. 1 Sam. 17. 49.
at first honoured by Saul. 1 Sam. 18.
Saul jealous of, tries to kill. 1 Sam. 18. 8, 12.
afterwards persecuted by him. 1 Sam. 19; 20.
loved by Jonathan. 1 Sam. 18. 1; 19. 2; 20; 23. 16; and by Michal. 1 Sam. 18. 28; 19. 11.
overcomes the Philistines. 1 Sam. 18. 27; 19. 8.
flees to Naioth. 1 Sam. 19. 18.
eats of the shewbread. 1 Sam. 21; Ps. 52; Matt. 12. 4.
flees to Gath, and feigns madness. 1 Sam. 21. 10, 13; Ps. 34; 56.
dwells in the cave of Adullam. 1 Sam. 22; Ps. 63; 142.
escapes Saul's pursuit. 1 Sam. 23; Ps. 57.
twice spares Saul's life. 1 Sam. 24. 4; 26. 5.
his wrath against Nabal appeased by Abigail. 1 Sam. 25. 23.
dwells at Ziklag. 1 Sam. 27.
dismissed from the army by Achish. 1 Sam. 29. 9.
chastises the Amalekites, and rescues the captives. 1 Sam. 30. 16.
kills messenger who brings news of Saul's death. 2 Sam. 1. 15.
laments the death of Saul and Jonathan. 2 Sam. 1. 17.
becomes king of Judah. 2 Sam. 2. 4.
forms a league with Abner. 2 Sam. 3. 13.
laments Abner's death. 2 Sam. 3. 31.
avenges the murder of Ish-bosheth. 2 Sam. 4. 9.
becomes king of all Israel. 2 Sam. 5. 3; 1 Chr. 11.
his victories. 2 Sam. 2; 5; 8; 10; 12. 29; 21. 15; 1 Chr. 18—20; Ps. 60.
brings the ark to Zion. 2 Sam. 6; 1 Chr. 13; 15.
his psalms of thanksgiving. 2 Sam. 22; 1 Chr. 16. 7; Ps. 18; 103; 105.
Michal despises him for dancing before the ark. 2 Sam. 6. 20.
reproves her. 2 Sam. 6. 21.
desires to build God a house. 2 Sam. 7. 2; and is forbidden by Nathan. 1 Chr. 17. 4.
God's promises to him. 2 Sam. 7. 11; 1 Chr. 17. 10.
his prayer and thanksgiving. 2 Sam. 7. 18; 1 Chr. 17. 16.

EGYPT—*cont.*
children of Israel depart from. Ex. 13. 17.
army of, pursue and perish in the Red sea. Ex. 14.
kings of, harass Judah. 1 Kin. 14. 25; 2 Kin. 23.
29; 2 Chr. 12. 2; 35. 20; 36. 3; Jer. 37. 5.
the "remnant of Judah" go there. Jer. 43. 7.
Jesus taken to. Matt. 2. 13.
prophecies concerning. Gen. 15. 13; Is. 11. 11;
19; 20; 27. 12; 30. 1; Jer. 9. 26; 25. 19; 43. 8; 44.
28; 46; Ezek. 29—32; Dan. 11. 8; Hos. 9. 3; 11;
Joel 3. 19; Zech. 10. 10; 14. 18.
EGYPTIAN, e-jip'-shan, a native of Egypt. 1 Sam.
30. 11.
EHI, e'-hi, shortened from AHIRAM. Gen. 46. 21.
EHUD, e'-hud, joined together (?).
judge, delivers Israel. Judg. 3. 15.
EKER, e'-ker, same as ACHAR. 1 Chr. 2. 27.
EKRON, ek'-ron, eradication. Josh. 13. 3.
taken. Judg. 1. 18.
men of, smitten with emerods. 1 Sam. 5. 12.
their trespass offering for recovery. 1 Sam. 6. 17.
prophecies concerning. Amos 1. 8; Zeph. 2. 4;
Zech. 9. 5.
EKRONITES, ek'-ron-ites, inhabitants of Ekron.
Josh. 13. 3.
ELADAH, el'-a-dah, whom God clothes. 1 Chr. 7. 20.
ELAH, e'-lah, terebinth. Gen. 36. 41.
king of Israel. 1 Kin. 16. 8, 10.
—— valley of, Saul sets the battle in array
against the Philistines. 1 Sam. 17. 2.
David slays Goliath there. 1 Sam. 17. 49.
ELAM, e'-lam.
son of Shem. Gen. 10. 22.
—— Chedorlaomer, king of. Gen. 14.
ELAMITES, e'-lam-ites, inhabitants of Elam. Ezra
4. 9; Acts 2. 9.
ELASAH, el'-a-sah, whom God made. Ezra 10. 22.
ELATH, el'-lath, a grove. Deut. 2. 8.
EL-BETH-EL, el-beth'-el, the house of God. Gen.
35. 7.
ELDAAH, el'-da-ah, whom God called. Gen. 25. 4.
ELDAD, el'-dad, whom God loves. Num. 11. 26.
ELEAD, el'-e-ad, whom God praises. 1 Chr. 7. 21.
ELEALEH, el'-e-a'-lay, whither God ascends. Num.
32. 3.
ELEASAH, e'l-e-a'-sah, same as ELASAH. 1 Chr. 2.
39.
ELEAZAR, el'-e-a'-zar, whom God aids.
son of Aaron, and chief priest. Ex. 6. 23; 28; 29;
Lev. 8; Num. 3. 2; 4. 16; 16. 36; 20. 26, 28; 27.
22; 31. 13; 34. 17; Josh. 17. 4; 24. 33.
—— son of Abinadab, keeps the ark. 1 Sam. 7. 1.
—— one of David's captains. 2 Sam. 23. 9; 1 Chr.
11. 12.
EL-ELOHE-ISRAEL, el'-el-o'-he-iz'-ra-el, God, the
God of Israel.
the altar erected by Jacob at Shalem. Gen. 33. 20.
ELEPH, e'-lef, ox. Josh. 18. 28.
ELHANAN, el'-ha'-nan, whom God gave.
one of David's warriors. 2 Sam. 21. 19; 23. 24;
1 Chr. 11. 26; 20. 5.
ELI, e'-li, my God.
ELI, Eli, lama sabachthani? Matt. 27. 46; Mark
15. 34.
ELI, e'-li, height. 1 Sam. 1. 3.
high priest and judge, blesses Hannah, who bears
Samuel. 1 Sam. 1. 17, 20.
Samuel brought to. 1 Sam. 1. 25.
wickedness of his sons. 1 Sam. 2. 22.
rebuked by God, 1 Sam. 2. 27.
ruin of his house shewed to Samuel by God.
1 Sam. 3. 11.
his sons slain. 1 Sam. 4. 10.
his death. 1 Sam. 4. 18.
ELIAB, el-i'-ab, whose father is God. Num. 1. 9.
ELIADA, ELIADAH, el-i'-ya-dah, whom God cares
for. 2 Sam. 5. 16.
ELIAH, el-i'-ah, same name as ELIJAH. 1 Chr.
8. 27.
ELIAHBA, e'l-i-ah'-bah, whom God hides. 2 Sam.
23. 32.

ELIAKIM, el-i'-a-kim, whom God establishes. 2
Kin. 18. 18.
chief minister of Hezekiah; his conference with
Rabshakeh's ambassadors; mission to Isaiah.
2 Kin. 18; 19.
prefigures kingdom of Christ. Is. 22. 20—25.
—— son of Josiah, made king by Pharaoh, and
named Jehoiakim. 2 Kin. 23. 34; 2 Chr. 36. 4.
ELIAM, el-i'-am, same as AMMIEL. 2 Sam. 11. 3.
ELIAS, el-i'-as, same as ELIJAH. Matt. 27. 47, 49;
Mark 15. 35, 36. John 1. 21. *See* ELIJAH.
ELIASAPH, el-i'-a-saf, whom God added. Num.
1. 14.
ELIASHIB, el-i'-a-shib, whom God restores.
high priest, builds the wall. Neh. 3. 1.
allied unto Tobiah. Neh. 13. 4.
ELIATHAH, el-i'-a-thah, to whom God comes. 1 Chr.
25. 4.
ELIDAD, el-i'-dad, whom God loves. Num. 34. 21.
ELIEL, el-i'-el, to whom God is strength. 1 Chr.
5. 24.
ELIENAI, el-i-e'-nai, unto Jehovah my eyes are
raised (?). 1 Chr. 8. 20.
ELIEZER, el'-i-e'-zer, my God is help.
Abraham's steward. Gen. 15. 2.
—— son of Moses. Ex. 18. 4; 1 Chr. 23. 15.
—— prophet, 2 Chr. 20. 37.
ELIHOENAI, el'-i-ho-e'-nai, same as ELIOENAI.
Ezra 8. 4.
ELIHOREPH, el-i-ho'-ref, to whom God is the reward. 1 Kin. 4. 3.
ELIHU, el-i'-hoo, whose God is He. 1 Sam. 1. 1.
reproves Job's friends, Job 32; and Job's im-
patience, Job 33. 8; and self-righteousness,
Job 34. 5.
declares God's justice, Job 33. 12; 34. 10; 35. 13;
36; power, Job 33—37; and mercy, Job 33. 23;
34. 28.
ELIJAH, el-i'-jah, my God is Jehovah.
the Tishbite, prophet, predicts great drought,
1 Kin. 17. 1; Luke 4. 25; James 5. 17.
hides at the brook Cherith, and is fed by ravens.
1 Kin. 17. 5 (19. 5).
raises the widow's son. 1 Kin. 17. 21.
his sacrifice at Carmel. 1 Kin. 18. 38.
slays the prophets of Baal at the brook Kishon.
1 Kin. 18. 40.
flees from Jezebel into the wilderness of Beer-
sheba. 1 Kin. 19; Rom. 11. 2.
anoints Elisha. 1 Kin. 19. 19.
by God's command denounces Ahab in Naboth's
vineyard. 1 Kin. 21. 17.
his prediction fulfilled. 1 Kin. 22. 38; 2 Kin. 9. 36;
10. 10.
condemns Ahaziah for enquiring of Baal-zebub.
2 Kin. 1. 3, 16.
two companies sent to take him burnt with fire
from heaven. 2 Kin. 1. 10; Luke 9. 54.
divides Jordan. 2 Kin. 2. 8.
taken up by chariot of fire. 2 Kin. 2. 11.
his mantle taken by Elisha. 2 Kin. 2. 13.
appears at Christ's transfiguration. Matt. 17. 3;
Mark 9. 4; Luke 9. 30.
precursor of John the Baptist. Mal. 4. 5; Matt.
11. 14; 16. 14; Luke 1. 17; 9. 8, 19; John 1. 21.
ELIKA, el-i'-kah, whom God purifies (?). 2 Sam.
23. 25.
ELIM, eel'-im, oaks. Ex. 15. 27.
ELIMELECH, el-i'-me-lek, to whom God is king.
Ruth 1. 2.
ELIOENAI, el'-i-o-e'-nai, unto Jehovah my eyes
are turned. 1 Chr. 3. 23.
ELIPHAL, el'-i-fal, whom God judges. 1 Chr. 11. 35.
ELIPHALET, el'-i-fa-let, to whom God is salvation
2 Sam. 5. 16.
ELIPHAZ, el-i'-faz, to whom God is strength. Gen
36. 4.
reproves Job, Job 4; 5; 15; 22.
God's wrath against him. Job 42. 7; he offers
a burnt offering, and Job prays for him. Job
42. 8.

ELIPHELEH, el-i'-fe-lay, whom God distinguishes. 1 Chr. 15. 18.

ELIPHELET, el-i'-fe-let, same as ELIPHALET. 1 Chr. 3. 8.

ELISABETH, el-iz'-a-beth, same as ELISHEBA.
cousin of Virgin Mary, and mother of John the Baptist. Luke 1. 5.
angel promises her a son. Luke 1. 13.
her salutation to Mary. Luke 1. 42.

ELISEUS, el'-i-se'-us, Greek form of ELISHA. Luke 4. 27.

ELISHA, el-i'-shah, to whom God is salvation.
—— (Eliseus), succeeds Elijah. 1 Kin. 19. 16.
receives his mantle, and divides Jordan. 2 Kin. 2. 13.
heals the waters with salt. 2 Kin. 2. 22.
bears destroy the children who mock him. 2 Kin. 2. 24.
his miracles: water. 2 Kin. 3. 16; oil, 4. 4; Shunammite's son, 4. 32; death in the pot, 4. 40; feeds a hundred men with twenty loaves, 4. 44; Naaman's leprosy, 5. 14; iron swims, 6. 5; Syrians struck blind, 6. 18.
prophesies plenty in Samaria when besieged. 2 Kin. 7. 1.
sends to anoint Jehu. 2 Kin. 9. 1.
his death. 2 Kin. 13. 20.
miracle wrought by his bones. 2 Kin. 13. 21.

ELISHAH, el-i'-shah. Gen. 10. 4.

ELISHAMA, el-i'-sha-mah, whom God hears. Num. 1. 10.

ELISHAPHAT, el-i'-sha-fat, whom God judges. 2 Chr. 23. 1.

ELISHEBA, el-i'-she-bah, to whom God is the oath. Ex. 6. 23.

ELISHUA, el-i'-shoo'-ah, same as ELISHA. 2 Sam. 5. 15.

ELIUD, el-i'-ood, God of Judah. Matt. 1. 14.

ELIZAPHAN, el-i'-za-fan, whom God protects. Num. 3. 30.

ELIZUR, el-i'-zoor, God is a Rock. Num. 1. 5.

ELKANAH, el'-ka'-nah, whom God possessed. Ex. 6. 24.
Samuel's father. 1 Sam. 1.

ELKOSHITE, el'-kosh-ite, inhabitant of Elkosh. Nah. 1. 1.

ELLASAR, el-ah'-sar. Gen. 14. 1.

ELMODAM, el-mo'-dam, same as ALMODAD. Luke 3. 28.

ELNAAM, el-na'-am, whose pleasure God is. 1 Chr. 11. 46.

ELNATHAN, el-na'-than, whom God gave. 2 Kin. 24. 8.

ELOI, el-o'-i, my God. Mark 15. 34.

ELON, e'-lon, oak. Gen. 26. 34.
judges Israel. Judg. 12. 11.

ELON-BETH-HANAN, e'-lon-beth'-ha'-nan, oak of the house of grace. 1 Kin. 4. 9.

ELONITES, e'-lon-ites, descendants of Elon. Num. 26. 26.

ELOTH, e'-loth, same as ELATH. 1 Kin. 9. 26.

ELPAAL, el-pa'-al, to whom God is the reward. 1 Chr. 8. 11.

ELPALET, el-pa'-let, same as ELIPHALET. 1 Chr. 14. 5.

EL-PARAN, el-par'-an, oak of Paran. Gen. 14. 6.

ELTEKEH, el'-te-kay, whose fear is God. Josh. 19. 44.

ELTEKON, el'-te-kon, whose foundation is God. Josh. 15. 59.

ELTOLAD, el-to'-lad, whose posterity is from God. Josh. 15. 30.

ELUL, el'-ool. Neh. 6. 15.

ELUZAI, el-oo'-zai, God is my praises. 1 Chr. 12. 5.

ELYMAS, el'-im-as, a wise man. Acts 13. 8.
(Bar-jesus). Acts 13. 8.

ELZABAD, el-za'-bad, whom God gave. 1 Chr. 12. 12.

ELZAPHAN, el-za'-phan, whom God protects. Ex. 6. 22.

EMIMS, eem'-ims, terrible men, giants. Gen. 14. 5; Deut. 2. 10.

EMMANUEL, em-man'-u-el, same as IMMANUEL.
God with us. Is. 7. 14; 8. 8; Matt. 1. 23.

EMMAUS, em-a'-us, hot springs (?). Luke 24. 13.
Christ talks with Cleopas and another on the way to. Luke 24. 15.

EMMOR, em'-or, same as HAMOR. Acts 7. 16.

ENAM, e'-nam, two fountains. Josh. 15. 34.

ENAN, e'-nan, having eyes. Num. 1. 15.

EN-DOR, en'-dor, fountain of Dor. Josh. 17. 11.
witch of. 1 Sam. 28. 7.

ENEAS, e'-ne-as. Acts 9. 33, 34.

EN-EGLAIM, en'-eg-la'-im, f. of two calves. Ezek. 47. 10.

EN-GANNIM, en-gan'-im, f. of gardens. Josh. 15. 34.

EN-GEDI, en'-ged-i, f. of the kid.
city of Judah. Josh. 15. 62.
David dwells there. 1 Sam. 23. 29; 24. 1.

EN-HADDAH, en-had'-ah, f. of sharpness, i.e. swift f. Josh. 19. 21.

EN-HAKKORE, en'-hak-o'-ree, f. of him that calleth. Judg. 15. 19.

EN-HAZOR, en-ha'-zor, f. of the village. Josh. 19. 37.

EN-MISHPAT, en-mish'-pat, f. of judgment. Gen. 14. 7.

ENOCH, e'-nok, experienced (?). Gen. 4. 17.
his faith, Heb. 11. 5; prophecy, Jude 14; translation. Gen. 5. 24.

ÆNON, e'-non, rich in springs. John 3. 23.

ENOS, e'-nos, man. Gen. 4. 26.

ENOSH, e'-nosh, same as ENOS. 1 Chr. 1. 1.

EN-RIMMON, en'-rim'-on, fountain of the pomegranate. Neh. 11. 29.

EN-ROGEL, en'-ro'-gel, f. of the fuller.
fountain. Josh. 15. 7; 18. 16; 2 Sam. 17. 17; 1 Kin. 1. 9.

EN-SHEMESH, en'-she'-mesh, f. of the sun. Josh. 15. 7.

EN-TAPPUAH, en'-tap-oo'-ah, f. of the apple tree. Josh. 17. 7.

EPÆNETUS, e-pe'-net-us, laudable. Rom. 16. 5.

EPAPHRAS, ep'-af-ras, contracted from the next word (?).
commended. Col. 1. 7; 4. 12.

EPAPHRODITUS, ep-af'-ro-di'-tus, handsome.
Paul's joy at his recovery. Phil. 2. 25; his kindness. Phil. 4. 18.

EPENETUS, same as EPÆNETUS. Rom. 16. 5.

EPHAH, ep'-ah. Gen. 25. 4.

EPHAI, e'-phai, languishing. Jer. 40. 8.

EPHER, e'-fer, calf. Gen. 25. 4.

EPHES-DAMMIM, e'-fez-dam'-im, boundary of blood. 1 Sam. 17. 1.

EPHESIANS, e-fe'-zi-ans, inhabitants of Ephesus. Acts 19. 28.
Paul's epistle to. Eph. 1.
election. Eph. 1. 4.
adoption of grace. Eph. 1. 6.
dead in sin quickened. Eph. 2. 1, 5.
Gentiles made nigh. Eph. 2. 13.
unity and kindness enjoined. Eph. 4—6.

EPHESUS, ef'-es-us.
visited by Paul. Acts 18. 19; 19. 1.
miracles there. Acts 19. 11.
tumult there. Acts 19. 24.
Paul's address at Miletus to the elders of. Acts 20. 17.
Paul fights with beasts there. 1 Cor. 15. 32.
tarries there. 1 Cor. 16. 8.

EPHLAL, ef'-lal, judgment. 1 Chr. 2. 37.

EPHPHATHA, ef'-ath-ah, be opened. Mark 7. 34.

EPHOD, e'-fod. Num. 34. 23.

EPHRAIM, ef'-ra-im, fruitful (?).
younger son of Joseph. Gen. 41. 52.
Jacob blesses Ephraim and Manasseh. Gen. 48. 14.
his descendants numbered. Num. 1. 10, 32; 2. 18; 26. 35; 1 Chr. 7. 20.
their possessions. Josh. 16. 5; 17. 14; Judg. 1. 29.
chastise the Midianites. Judg. 7. 24.
quarrel with Gideon. Judg. 8. 1; and Jephthah, Judg. 12.
revolt from the house of David. 1 Kin. 12. 25.

EPHRAIM—*cont.*
chastise Ahaz and Judah. 2 Chr. 28. 6, 7.
release their prisoners. 2 Chr. 28. 12.
carried into captivity. 2 Kin. 17. 5; Ps. 78. 9, 67; Jer. 7. 15.
repenting, called God's son. Jer. 31. 20.
prophecies concerning. Is. 7; 9. 9; 11. 13; 28. 1; Hos. 5—14; Zech. 9. 10; 10. 7.
EPHRAIMITES, ef′-ra-im-ites, inhabitants of Ephraim. Judg. 12. 4.
EPHRAIN, ef-ra′-in, same as EPHRON. 2 Chr. 13. 19.
EPHRATH, or EPHRATAH, ef′-rat-ah, fruitful (?). 1 Chr. 2. 50.
—— (Beth-lehem). Gen. 35. 16; Ps. 132. 6; Micah 5. 2.
EPHRATHITES, ef′-rath-ites, inhabitants of Ephrath. Ruth 1, 2.
EPHRON, ef′-ron, or of belonging to a calf. Gen. 23. 8.
the Hittite, sells Machpelah to Abraham. Gen. 23. 10.
EPICUREANS, ep′-ik-u-re′-ans, followers of Epicurus.
philosophers, encounter Paul at Athens. Acts 17. 18.
ER, watchful. Gen. 38. 3.
ERAN, e′-ran. Num. 26. 36.
ERANITES, e′-ran-ites, posterity of Eran. Num. 26. 36.
ERASTUS, e-rast′-us, beloved.
ministers to Paul. Acts 19. 22; Rom. 16. 23; 2 Tim. 4. 20.
ERECH, e′-rek. Gen. 10. 10.
ERI, e′-ri, same as ER. Gen. 46. 16.
ERITES, er′-ites, descendants of Eri. Num. 26. 16.
ESAIAS, e′-sai-as, same as ISAIAH. Matt. 3. 3.
ESAR-HADDON, e′-sar-had′-on, Assur giveth a brother.
powerful king of Assyria. 2 Kin. 19. 37; Ezra 4. 2; Is. 37. 38.
ESAU, e′-saw, hairy.
son of Isaac. Gen. 25. 25; (Mal. 1. 2; Rom. 9. 13).
sells his birthright. Gen. 25. 29 (Heb. 12. 16).
deprived of the blessing. Gen. 27. 38.
his anger against Jacob. Gen. 27. 41; and reconciliation. Gen. 33.
his riches and descendants. Gen. 36; 1 Chr. 1. 35.
ESEK, e′-sek, strife. Gen. 26. 20.
ESH-BAAL, esh-ba′-al, man of Baal. 1 Chr. 8. 33.
ESHBAN, esh′-ban. Gen. 36. 26.
ESHCOL, esh′-kol, cluster. Gen. 14. 13.
grapes of. Num. 13. 23.
ESHEAN, esh′-e-an, support (?). Josh. 15. 52.
ESHEK, e′-shek, oppression. 1 Chr. 8. 39.
ESHKALONITES, esh′-ka-lon-ites, men of Ashkalon. Josh. 13. 3.
ESHTAOL, esh′-ta-ol. Josh. 15. 33.
ESHTAULITES, esh-ta′-ol-ites, inhabitants of Eshtaol. 1 Chr. 2. 53.
ESHTEMOA, esh′-te-mo′-ah, obedience. Josh. 21. 14.
ESHTEMOH, esh′-te-mo′, same as ESHTEMOA. Josh. 15. 50.
ESHTON, esht′-on, womanly. 1 Chr. 4. 11.
ESLI, es′-li, same as AZALIAH (?). Luke 3. 25.
ESROM, es′-rom, same as HEZRON. Matt. 1. 3.
ESTHER, es′-ter, star. Esth. 2. 7.
(Hadassah), made queen in the place of Vashti. Esth. 2. 17.
pleads for her people. Esth. 7. 3, 4.
ETAM, e′-tam, a place of ravenous creatures. Judg. 15. 8.
ETHAM, e′-tham, boundary of the sea (?). Ex. 13. 20.
ETHAN, e′-than, firmness. 1 Kin. 4. 31.
ETHANIM, e-than′-nim, gifts (?). 1 Kin. 8. 2.
ETHBAAL, eth-ba′-al, living with Baal. 1 Kin. 16. 31.
ETHER, e′-ther, plenty. Josh. 15. 42.
ETHIOPIA, e′-thi-ope′-yah, (region of) burnt faces. Gen. 2. 13.
ETHIOPIAN, e′-thi-ope′-yan, a native of Ethiopia. Jer. 13. 23.

ETHIOPIANS, e′-thi-ope′-yans, invading Judah, subdued by Asa. 2 Chr. 14. 9. *See* Num. 12. 1; 2 Kin. 19. 9; Esth. 1. 1; Job 28. 19.
prophecies concerning. Ps. 68. 31; 87. 4; Is. 18; 20; 43. 3; 45. 14; Jer. 46. 9; Ezek. 30. 4; 38. 5; Nah. 3. 9; Zeph. 3. 10.
ETHNAN, eth′-nan, a gift. 1 Chr. 4. 7.
ETHNI, eth′-ni, bountiful. 1 Chr. 6. 41.
EUBULUS, eu-bew′-lus, good counsellor. 2 Tim. 4. 21.
EUNICE, eu-ni′-see.
commended (Acts 16. 1); 2 Tim. 1. 5.
EUODIAS, eu-ode′-yas, success. Phil. 4. 2.
EUPHRATES, eu-fra′-tes, the fertile river (?).
river. Gen. 2. 14; 15. 18; Deut. 11. 24; Josh. 1. 4; 2 Sam. 8. 3; Jer. 13. 4; 46. 2; 51. 63.
typical. Rev. 9. 14; 16. 12.
EUROCLYDON, eu-rok′-ly-don, storm from the east.
a wind. Acts 27. 14.
EUTYCHUS, eu′-tyk-us, fortunate. Acts 20. 9.
restored. Acts 20. 7.
EVE, eve, life. Gen. 3. 20.
created. Gen. 1. 27; 2. 18.
her fall and fate. Gen. 3. *See* ADAM.
EVI, e′-vi. Num. 31. 8.
EVIL-MERODACH, e′-vil-me′-ro-dak, man of Merodach. 2 Kin. 25. 27.
king of Babylon, restores Jehoiachin. 2 Kin. 25. 27; Jer. 52. 31.
EXODUS, ex′-od-us, departure.
EZAR, e′-zar, treasure. 1 Chr. 1. 38.
EZBAI, ez′-bai. 1 Chr. 11. 37.
EZBON, ez′-bon. Gen. 46. 16.
EZEKIAS, ez′-ekₑi′-as, same as HEZEKIAH. Matt. 1. 9.
EZEKIEL, ez-e′-ki-el, whom God will strengthen. Ezek. 1. 3.
sent to house of Israel. Ezek. 2; 3; 33. 7.
his visions of God's glory. Ezek. 1; 8; 10; 11. 22.
of the Jews' abominations, &c. Ezek. 8. 5.
their punishment. Ezek. 9; 11.
of the resurrection of dry bones. Ezek. 37.
his vision of the measuring of the temple. Ezek. 40.
intercedes for Israel. Ezek. 9. 8; 11. 13.
his dumbness. Ezek. 3. 26; 24. 26; 33. 22.
his parables. Ezek. 15; 16; 17; 19; 23; 24.
exhorts Israel against idols. Ezek. 14. 1; 20. 1; 33. 30.
rehearses Israel's rebellions. Ezek. 20; and the sins of the rulers and people of Jerusalem. 22; 23; 24.
predicts Israel's and the nations' doom. Ezek. 21; 25.
EZEL, e′-zel, departure. 1 Sam. 20. 19.
EZEM, e′-zem, bone. 1 Chr. 4. 29.
EZER, e′-zer, help. 1 Chr. 4. 4.
EZION-GABER, or EZION-GEBER, e′-zi-on-ga′-ber, the backbone of a giant.
on the Red Sea. Num. 33. 35; 1 Kin. 9. 26.
EZNITE, ez′-nite. 2 Sam. 23. 8.
EZRA, ez′-rah, help. Ezra 7. 1.
scribe, goes up from Babylon to Jerusalem. Ezra 7. 1; 8. 1.
his commission from Artaxerxes to rebuild the temple. Ezra 7. 11.
fast ordered by. Ezra 8. 21.
reproves the people. Ezra 10. 9.
reads the book of the law. Neh. 8.
reforms corruptions. Ezra 10; Neh. 13.
EZRAHITE, ez′-rah-ite, a descendant of Zerah. 1 Kin. 4. 31.
EZRI, ez′-ri, the help of Jehovah (?). 1 Chr. 27. 26.

FAIR HAVENS. Acts 27. 8.
FELIX, fe′-lix, happy. Acts 23. 24.
governor of Judæa, Paul sent to. Acts 23. 23.
Paul's defence before him. Acts 24. 10.
trembles at Paul's preaching, but leaves him bound. Acts 24. 25.
FESTUS, fest′-us, joyful. Acts 24. 27.
governor of Judæa. Acts 24. 27.

Festus—*cont.*
Paul brought before him. Acts 25.
Paul's defence before. Acts 25. 8; 26.
acquits Paul. Acts 25. 14; 26. 31.
Fortunatus, for'-tu-na'-tus, prosperous.
succours Paul. 1 Cor. 16. 17.

Gaal, ga'-al, loathing. Judg. 9. 26.
Gaash, ga'-ash, shaking. Josh. 24. 30.
Gaba, ga'-bah, hill. Josh. 18. 24.
Gabbai, gab'-ai, a collector of tribute. Neh. 11. 8.
Gabbatha, gab'-ath-ah, height (pavement). John 19. 13.
Gabriel, ga'-bri-el, man of God.
archangel, appears to Daniel. Dan. 8. 16; 9. 21.
to Zacharias. Luke 1. 19.
to Mary. Luke 1. 26.
Gad, gad, a troop, good fortune.
birth of. Gen. 30. 11.
his descendants. Gen. 46. 16.
blessed by Jacob. Gen. 49. 19.
——tribe of, blessed by Moses. Deut. 33. 20.
numbered. Num. 1. 24; 26. 15.
their possessions. Num. 32; 34. 14.
divers commands to. Deut. 27. 13; Josh. 4. 12.
commended by Joshua. Josh. 22. 1.
charged with idolatry. Josh. 22. 11.
their defence. Josh. 22. 21.
——seer, his message to David. 2 Sam. 24. 11; 1 Chr. 21. 9; 2 Chr. 29. 25.
Gadarenes, gad'-ar-eens', inhabitants of Gadara, or Gergesenes, Christ's miracle in the country of. Matt. 8. 28; Mark 5. 1; Luke 8. 26.
Gaddi, gad'-i, fortunate. Num. 13. 11.
Gaddiel, gad'-i-el, fortune sent from God. Num. 13. 10.
Gadi, ga'-di. 2 Kin. 15. 14.
Gadites, gad'-ites, persons belonging to the tribe of Gad. Deut. 3. 12.
Gaham, ga'-ham, sunburnt (?). Gen. 22. 24.
Gahar, ga'-har, hiding-place. Ezra 2. 47.
Gaius, ga'-yus. The Greek form of Caius. Acts 19. 29.
his piety. 3 John.
Galal, ga'-lal, worthy (?). 1 Chr. 9. 15.
Galatia, ga-la'-shah, a place colonised by Gauls. Acts 16. 6.
Galatians, ga-la'-shans, inhabitants of Galatia. Gal. 3. 1.
Paul visits. Acts 16. 6.
reproved. Gal. 1. 6; 3.
exhorted. Gal. 5. 6.
their love to Paul. Gal. 4. 13.
Galeed, gal'-e-ed, witness-heap. Gen. 31. 47.
Galileans, gal'-il-e'-yans, slaughter of. Luke 13. 1.
disciples so called. Acts 1. 11; 2. 7.
Galilee, gal'-il-ee, circuit. Josh. 20. 7.
Isaiah's prophecy concerning. Is. 9. 1; Matt. 4. 15.
work of Christ there. Matt. 2. 22; 15. 29; 26. 32; 27. 55; 28. 7; Mark 1. 9; Luke 4. 14; 23. 5; 24. 6; Acts 10. 37; 13. 31.
Gallim, gal'-im, heaps. 1 Sam. 25. 44.
Gallio, gal'-yo.
dismisses Paul. Acts 18. 12.
Gamaliel, ga-ma'-li-el, benefit of God. Num. 1. 10.
advises the council. Acts 5. 34.
Paul brought up at feet of. Acts 22. 3.
Gammadims, gam-ah'-dims, warriors (?). Ezek. 27. 11.
Gamul, ga'-mool, weaned. 1 Chr. 24. 17.
Gareb, ga'-reb, scabby. 2 Sam. 23. 38.
Garmite, garm'-ite, bony. 1 Chr. 4. 19.
Gashmu, gash'-moo, same as Geshem. Neh. 6. 6.
Gatam, ga'-tam. Gen. 36. 11.
Gath, gath, wine-press. Josh. 11. 22.
Goliath of. 1 Sam. 17. 4.
men of, smitten with emerods. 1 Sam. 5. 8.
David a refugee there. 1 Sam. 27. 4.
taken by David. 1 Chr. 18. 1.
by Hazael. 2 Kin. 12. 17.
Uzziah breaks down the wall of. 2 Chr. 26. 6.

Gath-hepher, gath-he'-fer, the wine-press of the well. 2 Kin. 14. 25.
Gath-rimmon, gath-rim'-on, wine-press of the pomegranate. Josh. 19. 45.
Gaza, ga'-zah, same as **Azzah**. Gen. 10. 19.
Samson carries away the gates of. Judg. 16.
destruction of, foretold. Jer. 47; Amos 1. 6; Zeph. 2. 4; Zech. 9. 5.
Gazathites, ga'-zath-ites, inhabitants of Gaza. Josh. 13. 3.
Gazer, ga'-zer, place cut off. 2 Sam. 5. 25.
Gazez, ga'-zez, shearer. 1 Chr. 2. 46.
Gazites, ga'-zites, inhabitants of Gaza. Judg. 16. 2.
Gazzam, gaz'-am, eating up. Ezra 2. 48.
Geba, ge'-bah, hill. Josh. 21. 17.
Gebal, ge'-bal, mountain. Ps. 83. 7.
Geber, ge'-ber, man. 1 Kin. 4. 13.
Gebim, ge'-bim, trenches. Is. 10. 31.
Gedaliah, ged-al-i'-ah, whom Jehovah has made great.
governor of the remnant of Judah. 2 Kin. 25. 22 (Jer. 40. 5).
treacherously killed by Ishmael. 2 Kin. 25. 25 (Jer. 41).
Gedeon, ged'-e-on, Greek form of Gideon. Heb. 11. 32.
Geder, ged'-er, wall. Josh. 12. 13.
Gederah, ged-er'-ah, enclosure, sheep-fold. Josh. 15. 36.
Gederathite, ged-er'-ath-ite, an inhabitant of Gederah. 1 Chr. 12. 4.
Gederite, ged'-er-ite, native of Geder. 1 Chr. 27. 28.
Gederoth, ged-er'-oth, sheep-folds. Josh. 15. 41.
Gederothaim, ged-er'-oth-a'-im, two sheep-folds. Josh. 15. 36.
Gedor, ged'-or, wall. Josh. 15. 58.
conquered by Simeonites. 1 Chr. 4. 41.
Gehazi, ge-ha'-zi, valley of vision.
servant of Elisha. 2 Kin. 4. 12.
his covetousness. 2 Kin. 5. 20.
Geliloth, gel-il'-oth, regions. Josh. 18. 17.
Gemalli, ge-mal'-i, possessor of camels. Num. 13. 12.
Gemariah, gem'-ar-i'-ah, whom Jehovah has completed. Jer. 29. 3.
Genesis, jen'-es-is, generation, or beginning.
Gennesaret, gen-es'-a-ret. Matt. 14. 34.
a lake of Palestine, miracles wrought there. Matt. 17. 27; Luke 5. 1; John 21. 6.
Gentiles, jen'-tiles.
origin of. Gen. 10. 5.
their state by nature. Rom. 1. 21; 1 Cor. 12. 2; Eph. 2; 4. 17; 1 Thess. 4. 5.
God's judgments on. Joel 3. 9.
their conversion predicted. Is. 11. 10; 42. 1; 49. 6 (Matt. 12. 18; Luke 2. 32; Acts 13. 47); 62. 2; Jer. 16. 19; Hos. 2. 23; Mal. 1. 11; Matt. 8. 11.
prediction fulfilled. John 10. 16; Acts 8. 37; 10; 14; 15; Eph. 2; 1 Thess. 1. 1.
calling of. Rom. 9. 24. *See* Is. 66. 19.
become fellow-citizens of the saints. Eph. 2. 11.
Christ made known to. Col. 1. 27.
Genubath, ge-noob'-ath. 1 Kin. 11. 20.
Gera, ge'-ra, a grain. Gen. 46. 21.
Gerah, ge'-rah. Ex. 30. 13.
Gerar, ge'-rar, sojourning. Gen. 10. 19.
herdmen of, strive with Isaac's. Gen. 26. 20.
Gergesenes, ger'-ge-seens', inhabitants of Gerasa. Matt. 8. 28.
Gerizim, ge-rize'-im, persons living in a desert.
mount of blessing. Deut. 11. 29; 27. 12; Josh. 8. 33.
Gershom, ger'-shom, expulsion.
son of Moses. Ex. 2. 22; 18. 3.
(Gershon), son of Levi. Gen. 46. 11; Num. 3. 17.
Gershonites, ger'-shon-ites, descendants of Gershon. Num. 3. 21.
their duties in the service of the tabernacle. Num. 4. 7; 10. 17.
Gesham, ge'-sham. 1 Chr. 2. 47.

GESHEM, ge'-shem, stout (?). Neh. 2. 19.
GESHUR, ge'-shoor, bridge. 2 Sam. 3. 3.
　Absalom takes refuge there after killing Amnon.
　　2 Sam. 13. 37; 14. 23 (Josh. 13. 13).
GESHURI, ge-shoor'-i, inhabitants of Geshur. Deut.
　3. 14.
GESHURITES, ge-shoor'-ites, same as preceding.
　Josh. 12. 5.
GETHER, ge'-ther, dregs (?). Gen. 10. 23.
GETHSEMANE, geth-sem'-an-e, oil-press.
　garden of, our Lord's agony there. Matt. 26. 36;
　　Mark 14. 32; Luke 22. 39; John 18. 1.
GEUEL, geu'-el, majesty of God. Num. 13. 15.
GEZER, ge'-zer, precipice. Josh. 10. 33.
GEZRITES, gez'-rites, dwelling in a desert land.
　1 Sam. 27. 8.
GIAH, gi'-ah, gushing forth. 2 Sam. 2. 24.
GIBBAR, gib'-ar, a hero. Ezra 2. 20.
GIBBETHON, gib'-eth-on, a lofty place. Josh. 19. 44.
GIBEA, gib'-e-ah, hill. 1 Chr. 2. 49.
GIBEAH, gib'-e-ah, hill. Josh. 15. 57.
　a city of Benjamin. Judg. 19. 14.
　sin of its inhabitants. Judg. 19. 22.
　their punishment. Judg. 20.
　the city of Saul. 1 Sam. 10. 26; 11. 4; 14. 2; 15.
　　34; 2 Sam. 21. 6.
GIBEATH, gib'-e-ath, hill. Josh. 18. 28.
GIBEON, gib'-e-on, pertaining to a hill. Josh. 9. 3.
　its inhabitants deceive Joshua. Josh. 9.
　delivered by him from the five kings. Josh. 10.
　Saul persecutes them. 2 Sam. 21. 1.
　David makes atonement. 2 Sam. 21. 3—9.
　Solomon's dream at. 1 Kin. 3. 5.
　tabernacle of the Lord kept at. 1 Chr. 16. 39;
　　21. 29.
GIBEONITES, gib'-e-on-ites, inhabitants of Gibeon.
　2 Sam. 21. 1.
GIBLITES, gib'-lites, inhabitants of Gebal. Josh.
　13. 5.
GIDDALTI, gid-al'-ti, I have increased. 1 Chr. 25. 4.
GIDDEL, gid'-el, gigantic. Ezra 2. 47.
GIDEON, gid'-e-on, one who cuts down. Judg. 6. 11.
　God appoints him to deliver Israel from the
　　Midianites. Judg. 6. 14.
　destroys the altar and grove of Baal. Judg. 6.
　　25, 27.
　called Jerubbaal. Judg. 6. 32.
　God gives him two signs. Judg. 6. 36—40.
　his army reduced, and selected by a test of water.
　　Judg. 7. 2—7.
　his stratagem. Judg. 7. 16.
　subdues the Midianites. Judg. 7. 19; 8.
　makes an ephod of the spoil. Judg. 8. 24.
　his death. Judg. 8. 32. *See* Heb. 11. 32.
GIDEONI, gid'-e-on-i, cutting down. Num. 1. 11.
GIDOM, gi'-dom. Judg. 20. 45.
GIHON, gi'-hon, a river. Gen. 2. 13.
GILALAI, gil'-a-lai, dungy (?). Neh. 12. 36.
GILBOA, gil-bo'-ah, bubbling fountain. 1 Sam. 28. 4.
　mount, Saul slain there. 1 Sam. 31: 2 Sam. 1. 21.
GILEAD, gil'-e-ad, hill of witness. Gen. 31. 21.
　land of, granted to the Reubenites, &c. Num. 32.
　invaded by the Ammonites. Judg. 10. 17.
　Jephthah made captain of. Judg. 11.
GILEADITE, gil'-e-ad-ite, inhabitant of Gilead.
　Judg. 10. 3.
GILGAL, gil'-gal, a circle.
　Joshua encamps there. Josh. 4. 19; 9. 6.
　Saul made king there. 1 Sam. 10. 8; 11. 14.
　Saul sacrifices at. 1 Sam. 13. 8; 15. 12.
GILOH, gi'-lo, exile. Josh. 15. 51.
GILONITE, gi'-lon-ite, an inhabitant of Giloh.
　2 Sam. 15. 12.
GIMZO, gim'-zo, a place abounding with sycamores.
　2 Chr. 28. 18.
GINATH, gi'-nath, garden. 1 Kin. 16. 21.
GINNETHO, gin'-eth-o, garden. Neh. 12. 4.
GINNETHON, gin'-eth-on, same as preceding. Neh.
　10. 6.
GIRGASHITE, gir'-gash-ite, dwelling in a clayey
　soil. 1 Chr. 1. 14.

GIRGASHITES, gir'-gash-ites, descendants of Ca-
　naan. Gen. 10. 15; 15. 21.
　communion with, forbidden. Deut. 7. 1.
　driven out. Josh. 3. 10; 24. 11.
GIRGASITE, gir'-gas-ite, same as preceding. Gen.
　10. 16.
GISPA, gis'-pah, flattery. Neh. 11. 21.
GITTAH-HEPHER, git'-tah-he'-fer, wine-press of
　the well. Josh. 19. 13.
GITTAIM, git'-a-im, two wine-presses. 2 Sam. 4. 3.
GITTITES, git'-ites, inhabitants of Gath. Josh.
　13. 3.
GITTITH, git'-ith, after the manner of Gittites.
　Ps. 8, title.
GIZONITE, gi'-zon-ite. 1 Chr. 11. 34.
GOATH, go'-ath, lowing. Jer. 31. 39.
GOB, gobe, pit, cistern. 2 Sam. 21. 18.
GOG. 1 Chr. 5. 4.
GOG and MAGOG. Ezek. 38; 39; Rev. 20. 8.
GOLAN, go'-lan, exile. Deut. 4. 43.
GOLGOTHA, gol'-goth-ah, place of a skull. Matt.
　27. 33; Mark 15. 22; Luke 23. 33; John 19. 17.
GOLIATH, go-li'-ath, exile (?). 1 Sam. 17. 4.
　of Gath. 1 Sam. 17; 21. 9; 22. 10.
GOMER, go'-mer, complete. Gen. 10. 2.
GOMORRAH, go-mor'-ah. Gen. 10. 19.
　(and Sodom). Gen. 18. 20; 19. 24, 28; Is.
　　1. 9; Matt. 10. 15; Mark 6. 11.
GOMORRHA, go-mor'-ah, same as preceding. Matt.
　10. 15.
GOSHEN, go'-shen, land of (Egypt). Israelites placed
　there. Gen. 45. 10; 46. 34; 47. 4.
　no plagues there. Ex. 8. 22; 9. 26.
　—— (Canaan). Josh. 10. 41; 11. 16.
GOZAN, go'-zan. 2 Kin. 17. 6.
GREECE, grees, country of the Greeks. Acts 20. 2.
　prophecies of. Dan. 8. 21; 10. 20; 11. 2; Zech. 9.
　　13.
　Paul preaches in. Acts 16; 20.
GRECIA, greesh'-ah, same as GREECE. Dan. 8. 21.
GRECIAN, greesh'-an, a Jew who speaks Greek.
　Acts 11. 20.
GREEK, the language of Greece. Acts 21. 37.
GREEKS, inhabitants of Greece. Acts 18. 17.
　would see Jesus. John 12. 20.
　believe in Him. Acts 11. 21; 17. 4.
GUDGODAH, gud-go'-dah, thunder (?). Deut. 10. 7.
GUNI, goon'-i, painted with colours. Gen. 46. 24.
GUNITES, goon'-ites, descendants of Guni. Num.
　26. 48.
GUR, goor, a young lion. 2 Kin. 9. 27.
GUR-BAAL, goor-ba'-al, Gur of Baal. 2 Chr. 26. 7.

HAAHASHTARI, ha'-a-hash'-tar-i, the muleteer (?).
　1 Chr. 4. 6.
HABAIAH, hab-ai'-ah, whom Jehovah hides. Ezra
　2. 61.
HABAKKUK, ha-bak'-ook, embrace. Hab. 1. 1.
　prophet, his burden, complaint to God, his
　　answer, and faith. Hab. 1; 2; 3.
HABAZINIAH, hab'-az-in-i'-ah, lamp of Jehovah (?).
　Jer. 35. 3.
HABOR, ha'-bor, joining together. 2 Kin. 17. 6.
HACHALIAH, hak-al-i'-ah, whom Jehovah dis-
　turbs. Neh. 1. 1.
HACHILAH, hak-i'-lah, dark. 1 Sam. 23. 19.
HACHMONI, hak'-mon-i, wise. 1 Chr. 27. 32.
HACHMONITE, hak'-mon-ite, a descendant of
　Hachmoni. 1 Chr. 11. 11.
HADAD, ha'-dad. Gen. 36. 35.
　Edomite. 1 Kin. 11. 14.
HADADEZER, had-ad-e'-zer, whose help is Hadad.
　2 Sam. 8. 3.
　—— (Hadarezer); king of Zobah, David's wars
　　with. 2 Sam. 8; 10. 15; 1 Chr. 18.
HADADRIMMON, had'-ad-rim'-on, named from
　Hadad and Rimmon. Zech. 12. 11.
HADAR, ha'-dar, enclosure. Gen. 25. 15.
HADAREZER, had'-ar-e'-zer, same as HADADEZER.
　1 Chr. 18. 3.
HADASHAH, had-ash'-ah, new. Josh. 15. 37.

HADASSAH, had-as'-ah, myrtle. Esth. 2. 7.
HADATTAH, had-at'-ah, new. Josh. 15. 25.
HADID, ha'-did, sharp. Ezra 2. 33.
HADLAI, had'-lai, rest. 2 Chr. 28. 12.
HADORAM, had-or'-am. Gen. 10. 27.
HADRACH, had'-rak. Zech. 9. 1.
HAGAB, ha'-gab, locust. Ezra 2. 46.
HAGABA, hag-a'-ba, same as HAGAB. Neh. 7. 48.
HAGAR, ha'-gar, flight. Gen. 16. 3.
—— mother of Ishmael. Gen. 16.
—— fleeing from Sarah is comforted by an angel. Gen. 16. 10, 11.
—— sent away with her son, Gen. 21. 14; allegory of, Gal. 4. 24.
HAGARENES, hag'-ar-e'-nes, inhabitants of Hagar. Ps. 83. 6.
HAGARITES, hag'-ar-ites, same as preceding. 1 Chr. 5. 10.
HAGERITE, hag'-er-ite, same as HAGARENE. 1 Chr. 27. 31.
HAGGAI, hag'-ai, festive.
—— prophet. Ezra 5; 6. 14. *See* Hag. 1; 2.
HAGGI, hag'-i, same as preceding. Gen. 46. 16.
HAGGERI, hag'-er-i. 1 Chr. 11. 38.
HAGGIAH, hag-i'-ah, festival of Jehovah. 1 Chr. 6. 30.
HAGGITES, hag'-ites, the posterity of Haggi. Num. 26. 15.
HAGGITH, hag'-ith, festive. 2 Sam. 3. 4.
HAI, hai, same as AI. Gen. 12. 8.
HAKKATAN, hak'-ah-tan, the small. Ezra 8. 12.
HAKKOZ, hak'-oz, the thorn. 1 Chr. 24. 10.
HAKUPHA, ha-koo'-fah. Ezra 2. 51.
HALAH, ha'-lah, same as CALAH (?). 2 Kin. 17. 6.
HALAK, ha'-lak, smooth. Josh. 11. 17.
HALHUL, hal'-hool. Josh. 15. 58.
HALI, ha'-li, necklace. Josh. 19. 25.
HALLELUJAH, hal-el-oo'-ya, praise the Lord. Rev. 19. 1.
HALLELUJAH (Alleluia). Ps. 106; 111; 113; 146; 148; 149; 150; Rev. 19. 1, 3, 4, 6.
HALLOHESH, hal-o'-hesh, same as following. Neh. 10. 24.
HALOHESH, hal-o'-hesh, the enchanter. Neh. 3. 12.
HAM, ham, warm. Gen. 9. 18.
—— son of Noah, cursed. Gen. 9. 22.
—— his descendants. Gen. 10. 6; 1 Chr. 1. 8; Ps. 105. 23; smitten by the Simeonites. 1 Chr. 4. 40.
HAMAN, ha'-man. Esth. 3. 1.
HAMAN'S advancement. Esth. 3.
—— anger against Mordecai. Esth. 3. 8.
—— his fall. Esth. 7.
HAMATH, ha'-math, fortress.
—— (Syria). Num. 34. 8; Josh. 13. 5; 2 Kin. 14. 28; 17. 24.
—— conquered. 2 Kin. 18. 34; Is. 37. 13; Jer. 49. 23.
HAMATHITE, ha'-math-ite, a dweller at Hamath. Gen. 10. 18.
HAMATH-ZOBAH, ha'-math-zo'-bah, fortress of Zobah. 2 Chr. 8. 3.
HAMMATH, ham'-ath, warm springs. Josh. 19. 35.
HAMMEDATHA, ham'-ed-ah'-thah, given by the moon (?). Esth. 3. 1.
HAMMELECH, ham-me'-lek, the king. Jer. 36. 26.
HAMMOLEKETH, ham'-mo-le'-keth, the queen. 1 Chr. 7. 18.
HAMMON, ham'-on, warm. Josh. 19. 28.
HAMMOTH-DOR, ham'-oth-dor', warm springs of Dor. Josh. 21. 32
HAMONAH, ha-mo'-nah, multitude. Ezek. 39 16.
HAMON-GOG, ham'-on-gog', *m.* of Gog. Ezek. 39. 11.
HAMOR, ha'-mor, ass. Gen. 33. 19.
—— father of Shechem. Gen. 34; Acts 7. 16.
HAMUEL, ham'-oo-el, heat (wrath) of God. 1 Chr. 4. 26.
HAMUL, ha'-mool, who has experienced mercy. Gen. 46. 12.
HAMULITES, ha'-mool-ites, the posterity of Hamul. Num. 26. 21.

HAMUTAL, ha-moo'-tal, refreshing like dew. 2 Kin. 23. 31.
HANAMEEL, han'-am-e'-el, probably another form of HANANEEL. Jer. 32. 7.
HANAN, ha'-nan, merciful. 1 Chr. 8. 23.
HANANEEL, han'-an-e'-el, whom God graciously gave. Neh. 3. 1.
HANANI, ha-na'-ni, probably same as HANANIAH. 1 Kin. 16. 1.
—— prophet. 2 Chr. 16. 7.
—— brother of Nehemiah. Neh. 1. 2; 7. 2; 12. 36.
HANANIAH, han'-an-i'-ah, whom Jehovah graciously gave. 1 Chr. 3. 19.
—— false prophet. Jer. 28.
—— his death. Jer. 28. 16.
HANES, ha'-nees. Is. 30. 4.
HANIEL, han'-i-el, favour of God. 1 Chr. 7. 39.
HANNAH, han'-ah, gracious.
—— her song. 1 Sam. 2.
—— vow and prayer. 1 Sam. 1. 11; answered. 1 Sam. 1. 19.
HANNATHON, han-a'-thon, gracious. Josh. 19. 14.
HANNIEL, han'-i-el, same as HANIEL. Num. 34. 23.
HANOCH, ha'-nok, same as ENOCH. Gen. 25. 4.
HANOCHITES, ha'-nok-ites, descendants of Hanoch. Num. 26. 5.
HANUN, ha'-noon, whom (God) pities. 2 Sam. 10. 1.
—— king of the Ammonites, dishonours David's messengers. 2 Sam. 10. 4.
—— chastised. 2 Sam. 12. 30.
HAPHRAIM, haf-ra'-im, two pits. Josh. 19. 19.
HARA, ha'-ra, mountainous. 1 Chr. 5. 26.
HARADAH, har-a'-dah, fear. Num. 33. 24.
HARAN, ha'-ran, mountaineer. Gen. 11. 27.
—— son of Terah. Gen. 11. 26.
—— (city of Nahor), Abram comes to. Gen. 11. 31; departs from. Gen. 12. 4.
—— Jacob flees to Laban at. Gen. 27. 43; 28. 10; 29.
HARARITE, ha'-rar-ite, a mountaineer. 2 Sam. 23. 11.
HARBONAH, har-bo'-nah. Esth. 7. 9.
HAREPH, ha'-ref, plucking. 1 Chr. 2. 51.
HARETH, ha'-reth, thicket. 1 Sam. 22. 5.
HARHAIAH, har-hai'-ah, dried up (?). Neh. 3. 8.
HARHAS, har'-has. 2 Kin. 22. 14.
HARHUR, har'-hoor, inflammation. Ezra 2. 51.
HARIM, ha'-rim, flat-nosed. 1 Chr. 24. 8.
HARIPH, ha'-rif, autumnal showers. Neh. 7. 24.
HARNEPHER, har-ne'-fer. 1 Chr. 7. 36.
HAROD, ha'-rod, terror. Judg. 7. 1.
HARODITE, har'-od-ite, inhabitant of Harod. 2 Sam. 23. 25.
HAROEH, ha-ro'-eh, the seer. 1 Chr. 2. 52.
HARORITE, har'-or-ite, probably another form of HARODITE. 1 Chr. 11. 27.
HAROSHETH, ha-rosh'-eth, carving. Judg. 4. 2.
HARSHA, har'-shah, enchanter, magician. Ezra 2.52.
HARUM, ha'-room, high (?). 1 Chr. 4. 8.
HARUMAPH, ha-roo'-maf, flat-nosed. Neh. 3. 10.
HARUPHITE, ha-roof'-ite. 1 Chr. 12. 5.
HARUZ, ha'-rooz, active. 2 Kin. 21. 19.
HASADIAH, ha'-sad-i'-ah, whom Jehovah loves. 1 Chr. 3. 20.
HASENUAH, ha'-se-noo'-ah, she that is hated. 1 Chr. 9. 7.
HASHABIAH, ha'-shab-i'-ah, whom Jehovah esteems. 1 Chr. 6. 45.
HASHABNAH, ha-shab'-nah, same as preceding (?). Neh. 10. 25.
HASHABNIAH, ha'-shab-ni'-ah, same as HASHABIAH. Neh. 3. 10.
HASHBADANA, hash'-bad-a'-na. Neh. 8. 4.
HASHEM, ha'-shem, fat. 1 Chr. 11. 34.
HASHMONAH, hash-mo'-nah, fatness, fat soil. Num. 33. 29.
HASHUB, hash'-oob, thoughtful. Neh. 3. 11.
HASHUBAH, hash-oob'-ah, same as preceding. 1 Chr. 3. 20.
HASHUM, hash'-oom, rich. Ezra 2. 19.
HASHUPHA, hash-oof'-ah, another form of HASUPHA. Neh. 7. 46.

HASRAH, haz'-rah, probably same as HARHAS. 2 Chr. 34. 22.

HASSENAAH, has'-en-a'-ah, the thorny. Neh. 3. 3.

HASSHUB, hash'-oob, same as HASHUB. 1 Chr. 9. 14.

HASUPHA, has-oof'-ah, one of the Nethinims. Ezra 2. 43.

HATACH, ha'-tak. Esth. 4. 5.

HATHATH, ha'-thath, terror. 1 Chr. 4. 13.

HATIPHA, ha-tee'-fah, seized. Ezra 2. 54.

HATITA, ha-tee'-tah, digging. Ezra 2. 42.

HATTIL, hat'-il, wavering. Ezra 2. 57.

HATTUSH, hat'-oosh, assembled(?). 1 Chr. 3. 22.

HAURAN, how'-ran, hollow land. Ezek. 47. 16.

HAVILAH, ha-vil'-ah. Gen. 10. 7.

HAVOTH-JAIR, hav'-oth-ja'-ir, villages of Jair. Num. 32. 41.

HAZAEL, ha'-za-el, whom God watches over.
king of Syria. 1 Kin. 19. 15.
Elisha's prediction. 2 Kin. 8. 7.
slays Ben-hadad. 2 Kin. 8. 15.
oppresses Israel. 2 Kin. 9. 14; 10. 32; 12. 17; 13. 22.

HAZAIAH, ha-zai'-ah, whom Jehovah watches over. Neh. 11. 5.

HAZAR-ADDAR, ha'-zar-ad'-ar, Addar-town. Num. 34. 4.

HAZAR-ENAN, ha'-zar-e'-nan, fountain-town. Num. 34. 9.

HAZAR-GADDAH, ha'-zar-gad'-ah, luck-town. Josh. 15. 27.

HAZAR-HATTICON, ha'-zar-hat'-ik-on, middle-town. Ezek. 47. 16.

HAZARMAVETH, ha'-zar-ma'-veth, death-town. Gen. 10. 26.

HAZAR-SHUAL, ha'-zar-shoo'-al, jackal-town. Josh. 15. 28.

HAZAR-SUSAH, ha'-zar-soo'-sah, mare-town. Josh. 19. 5.

HAZAR-SUSIM, ha'-zar-soo'-sim, horses-town. 1 Chr. 4. 31.

HAZELELPONI, haz'-lel-po'-ni, the shadow looking on me. 1 Chr. 4. 3.

HAZERIM, haz-e'-rim, villages. Deut. 2. 23.

HAZEROTH, haz-e'-roth, same as HAZERIM. Num. 11. 35.

HAZEZON-TAMAR, ha'-ze-zon-ta'-mar, pruning of the palm. Gen. 14. 7.

HAZIEL, ha'-zi-el, the vision of God. 1 Chr. 23. 9.

HAZO, ha'-zo, vision. Gen. 22. 22.

HAZOR, ha'-zor, castle. Josh. 11. 1.
Canaan, burnt. Josh. 11. 10; 15. 25.

HEBER, he'-ber. Gen. 10. 21; Luke 3. 35.
—— the Kenite. Judg. 4. 11.
(1) same as EBER. 1 Chr. 5. 13; (2) fellowship. Gen. 46. 17.

HEBERITES, he'-ber-ites, descendants of Heber. Num. 26. 45.

HEBREW, he'-broo, the (name of Abraham), Gen. 14. 13; the language spoken by the Jews: John 19. 20. Or a Jew: Jer. 34. 9.

HEBREWESS, he'-broo-ess', a Jewess. Jer. 34. 9.

HEBREWS, he'-broos, descendants of Abraham. Gen. 40. 15; 43. 32; Ex. 2. 6; 2 Cor. 11. 22; Phil. 3. 5.

HEBRON, heb'-ron, alliance.
—— (Mamre), in Canaan, Abraham dwells there. Gen. 13. 18; 23. 2.
the spies come to. Num. 13. 22.
taken. Josh. 10. 36.
given to Caleb. Josh. 14. 13; 15. 13.
David reigns there. 2 Sam. 2. 1; 3. 2; 5. 1; 1 Chr. 11; 12. 38; 29. 27.

HEBRONITES, he-bron-ites, the people of Hebron. Num. 3. 27.

HEGAI, or HEGE, he'-gai. Esth. 2. 3, 8.

HELAH, he'-lah, rust. 1 Chr. 4. 5.

HELAM, he'-lam, stronghold. 2 Sam. 10. 16.

HELBAH, hel'-bah, fatness. Judg. 1. 31.

HELBON, hel'-bon, fertile. Ezek. 27. 18.

HELDAI, hel'-dai, terrestrial. 1 Chr. 27. 15.

HELEB, he'-leb, fat, fatness. 2 Sam. 23. 29.

HELED, he'-led, the world. 1 Chr. 11. 30.

HELEK, he'-lek, portion. Num. 26. 30.

HELEKITES, he'-lek-ites, descendants of Helek. Num. 26. 30.

HELEM, he'-lem, another form of HELDAI. 1 Chr. 7. 35.

HELEPH, he'-lef, exchange. Josh. 19. 33.

HELEZ, he'-lez, liberation. 2 Sam. 23. 26.

HELI, he'-li, the Greek form of ELI. Luke 3. 23.

HELKAI, hel'-kai, another form of HILKIAH. Neh. 12. 15.

HELKATH, hel'-kath, a portion. Josh. 19. 25.

HELKATH-HAZZURIM, hel'-kath-haz'-oor-im, the field of swords (?). 2 Sam. 2. 16.

HELON, he'-lon, strong. Num. 1. 9.

HEMAM, he'-mam, same as HOMAM. Gen. 36. 22.

HEMAN, he'-man, faithful. 1 Kin. 4. 31.

HEMATH, he'-math; (1) fortress, 1 Chr. 2. 55; (2) same as HAMATH, Amos 6. 14.

HEMDAN, hem'-dan, pleasant. Gen. 36. 26.

HEN, hen, favour. Zech. 6. 14.

HENA, he'-nah. 2 Kin. 18. 34.

HENADAD, hen'-a-dad, favour of Hadad (?). Ezra 3. 9.

HENOCH, he'-nok, same as ENOCH. 1 Chr. 1. 3.

HEPHER, he'-fer, pit. Josh. 12. 17.

HEPHERITES, he'-fer-ites, descendants of Hepher. Num. 26. 32.

HEPHZI-BAH, heph'-zi-bah, in whom is my delight.
queen of Hezekiah, and mother of Manasseh. 2 Kin. 21. 1.
the restored Jerusalem. Is. 62. 4.

HERES, he'-res, the sun. Judg. 1. 35.

HERESH, he'-resh, artificer. 1 Chr. 9. 15.

HERMAS and HERMES, her'-mas and her'-mes, of Rome, saluted by Paul. Rom. 16. 14.

HERMOGENES, her-mog'-e-nees. 2 Tim. 1. 15.

HERMON, her'-mon, lofty. Deut. 3. 8.
mount. Deut. 4. 48; Josh. 12. 5; 13. 5; Ps. 89. 12; 133. 3.

HERMONITES, her'-mon-ites, the summits of Hermon. Ps. 42. 6.

HEROD, her'-od (the Great), king of Judæa. Matt. 2. 1.
troubled at Christ's birth. Matt. 2. 3.
slays the babes of Bethlehem. Matt. 2. 16.
—— (Antipas) reproved by John the Baptist, imprisons him, Luke 3. 19; beheads him. Matt. 14; Mark 6. 14.
desires to see Christ. Luke 9. 9.
scourges Him, and is reconciled to Pilate. Luke 23. 7; Acts 4. 27.
—— (Agrippa) persecutes the church. Acts 12. 1.
his pride and miserable death. Acts 12. 23.

HERODIANS, he-ro'-di-ans, partisans of Herod.
a sect, rebuked by Christ. Matt. 22. 16; Mark 12. 13.
plot against him. Mark 3. 6; 8. 15; 12. 13.

HERODIAS, he-ro'-di-as. Matt. 14. 3.
married to Herod Antipas. Mark 6. 17.
plans the death of John the Baptist. Matt. 14; Mark 6. 24.

HERODION, he-ro'-di-on. Rom. 16. 11.
Paul's kinsman. Rom. 16. 11.

HESED, he'-sed, mercy. 1 Kin. 4. 10.

HESHBON, hesh'-bon, counting. Num. 21. 25.
city of Sihon, taken. Num. 21. 26; Deut. 2. 24; Neh. 9. 22; Is. 16. 8.

HESHMON, hesh'-mon, fatness. Josh. 15. 27.

HETH, sons of. Gen. 10. 15.
their kindness to Abraham. Gen. 23. 7; 25. 10.

HETHLON, heth'-lon, hiding-place. Ezek. 47. 15.

HEZEKI, hez'-ek-i, shortened from HIZKIAH. 1 Chr. 8. 17.

HEZEKIAH, hez'-ek-i'-ah, the might of Jehovah. 2 Kin. 18. 1.
king of Judah. 2 Kin. 18. 19 (2 Chr. 28. 27).
abolishes idolatry. 2 Kin. 18.
attacked by the Assyrians, his prayer and deliverance. 2 Kin. 19.
his life lengthened, shadow of dial goes back-

HEZEKIAH.—*cont.*
ward, displays his treasure, Isaiah's prediction.
2 Kin. 20 (Is. 38); his passover. 2 Chr. 30. 13.
his piety, and good reign. 2 Chr. 29.
his death. 2 Kin. 20. 20.
HEZION, hez′-yon, vision. 1 Kin. 15. 18.
HEZIR, he′-zir, swine. 1 Chr. 24. 15.
HEZRAI, hez′-rai, enclosed wall. 2 Sam. 23. 35.
HEZRO, hez′-ro, same as preceding. 1 Chr. 11. 37.
HEZRON, hez′-ron, same as HEZRAI. Gen. 46. 12.
HEZRONITES, hez′-ron-ites, descendants of Hezron. Num. 26. 6.
HIDDAI, hid′-ai, the rejoicing of Jehovah. 2 Sam. 23. 30.
HIDDEKEL, hid-ek′-el. Gen. 2. 14.
HIEL, hi′-el, God liveth. 1 Kin. 16. 34.
——— *See* JERICHO.
HIERAPOLIS, hi′-e-ra′-pol-is, a sacred or holy city. Col. 4. 13.
HIGGAION, hig-a′-yon, meditation. Ps. 9. 16.
HILEN, hi′-len. 1 Chr. 6. 58.
HILKIAH, hilk-i′-ah, portion of Jehovah. 2 Kin. 18. 18.
finds the book of the law. 2 Kin. 22. 8.
HILLEL, hil′-el, praising. Judg. 12. 13.
HINNOM, hin′-ome, valley of, (Josh. 15. 8); 2 Kin. 23. 10; 2 Chr. 28. 3; 33. 6; Jer. 7. 31; 19. 11; 32. 35. *See* TOPHET AND MOLOCH.
HIRAH, hi′-rah, nobility. Gen. 38. 1.
HIRAM, hi′-ram, noble (?) (Huram), king of Tyre, sends aid to David and Solomon. 2 Sam. 5. 11; 1 Kin. 5; 9. 11; 10. 11; 1 Chr. 14. 1; 2 Chr. 2. 11.
——— principal brass-worker to Solomon. 1 Kin. 7. 13.
HITTITES, hit′-ites, descendants of Heth. Gen. 15. 20; Judg. 1. 26; 3. 5.
HIVITES, hive′-ites, villagers. Gen. 10. 17; Ex. 3. 8, 17.
deceive Joshua. Josh. 9.
HIZKIAH, hizk-i′-ah, might of Jehovah. Zeph. 1. 1.
HIZKIJAH, hizk-i′-jah, same as preceding. Neh. 10. 17.
HOBAB, ho′-bab, beloved. Num. 10. 29. *See* JETHRO.
HOBAH, ho′-bah, a hiding-place. Gen. 14. 15.
HOD, hode, splendour. 1 Chr. 7. 37.
HODAIAH, ho-dai′-ah, praise of Jehovah. 1 Chr. 3. 24.
HODAVIAH, ho′-dav-i′-ah, Jehovah is his praise. 1 Chr. 5. 24.
HODESH, ho′-desh, new moon. 1 Chr. 8. 9.
HODEVAH, ho′-de-vah, same as HODAVIAH. Neh. 7. 43.
HODIAH, ho-di′-ah, same as HODAIAH. 1 Chr. 4. 19.
HODIJAH, ho-di′-jah, same as preceding. Neh. 8. 7.
HOGLAH, hog′-lah, partridge. Num. 26. 33.
HOHAM, ho′-ham. Josh. 10. 3.
HOLON, ho′-lon, sandy. Josh. 15. 51.
HOMAM, ho′-mam, destruction. 1 Chr. 1. 39.
HOPHNI, hof′-ni, pugilist; and PHINEHAS, sons of Eli. 1 Sam. 1. 3.
their sin and death. 1 Sam. 2. 12, 22; 4. 11.
HOPHRA, hof′-rah, priest of the sun. Jer. 44. 30.
HOR, mountain. Num. 20. 23.
mount, Aaron dies on. Num. 20. 25.
HORAM, ho′-ram. Josh. 10. 33.
HOREB, ho′-reb, desert, mount (Sinai). Ex. 3. 1; 17. 6; 33. 6; Deut. 1. 6; 4. 10.
law given. Ex. 19; 20; Deut. 4. 10; 5. 2; 18. 16; 1 Kin. 8. 9; Mal. 4. 4.
Moses twice there for forty days. Ex. 24. 18; 34. 28; Deut. 9. 9.
Elijah there for forty days. 1 Kin. 19. 8.
HOREM, ho′-rem. Josh. 19. 38.
HOR-HAGIDGAD,·hor′-hag-gid′-gad, mountain of Gudgodah. Num. 33. 32.
HORI, ho′-ri, cave-dweller. Gen. 36. 22.
HORIMS, hor′-ims, descendants of Hori. Deut. 2. 12.
HORITES, hor′-ites, same as preceding. Gen. 14. 6.
HORMAH, hor′-mah, a devoting, a place laid waste. Num. 14. 45.

HORMAH.—*cont.*
destruction of. Num. 21. 3; Judg. 1. 17.
HORONAIM, hor′-o-na′-im, two caverns. Is. 15. 5.
HORONITE, hor′-on-ite, native of Beth-horon. Neh. 2. 10.
HOSAH, ho′-sah, fleeing to Jehovah for refuge (?). Josh. 19. 29.
HOSANNA, ho-san′-nah, save us we pray, children sing, to Christ, Matt. 21. 9, 15; Mark 11. 9; John 12. 13 (Ps. 118. 25, 26).
HOSEA, ho-ze′-ah, salvation. Hos. 1. 1.
prophet, declares God's judgment against idolatrous Israel, Hos. 1; 2; 4; and his reconciliation. Hos. 2. 14; 11; 13; 14.
HOSHAIAH, ho-shai′-ah, whom Jehovah has set free. Neh. 12. 32.
HOSHAMA, ho′-sha-mah. 1 Chr. 3. 18.
HOSHEA, ho-she′-ah, same as HOSEAH. Deut. 32. 44.
last king of Israel, his wicked reign, defeat by the king of Assyria, and captivity. 2 Kin. 15. 30; 17.
HOTHAM, ho′-tham, signet ring. 1 Chr. 7. 32.
HOTHAN, ho′-than. 1 Chr. 11. 44.
HOTHIR, ho′-thir. 1 Chr. 25. 4.
HUKKOK, hook′-oke, decreed. Josh. 19. 34.
HUKOK, hook′-oke, same as preceding. 1 Chr. 6. 75.
HUL, hool, circle. Gen. 10. 23.
HULDAH, hool′-dah, weasel. 2 Kin. 22. 14.
HUMTAH, hoom′-tah, fortress (?). Josh. 15. 54.
HUPHAM, hoo′-fam, inhabitant of the shore (?). Num. 26. 39.
HUPHAMITES, hoo′-fam-ites, descendants of Hupham. Num. 26. 39.
HUPPAH, hoop′-ah, covering. 1 Chr. 24. 13.
HUPPIM, hoop′-im, same as HUPHAM (?). Gen. 46. 21.
HUR, hoor, cavern. Ex. 17. 10.
HURAI, hoo′-rai, another way of writing Hiddai. 1 Chr. 11. 32.
HURAM, hoo′-ram, the older way of spelling Hiram. 2 Chr. 2. 13.
HURI, hoo′-ri, linen-worker (?). 1 Chr. 5. 14.
HUSHAH, hoo′-shah, haste. 1 Chr. 4. 4.
HUSHAI, hoo′-shai, hasting, loyalty. 2 Sam. 15. 32.
defeats Ahithophel's counsel. 2 Sam. 16. 16; 17. 5.
HUSHAM, hoo′-sham, haste. Gen. 36. 34.
HUSHATHITE, hoo′-shath-ite, inhabitant of Hushah. 2 Sam. 23. 27.
HUSHIM, hoosh′-im, those who make haste. Gen. 46. 23.
HUZ. Gen. 22. 21.
HUZZAB, hooz′-ab, it is decreed. Nah. 2. 7.
HYMENÆUS, hi′-men-æ′-us, belonging to Hymen. 1 Tim. 1. 20; 2 Tim. 2. 17.

IBHAR, ib′-har, whom God chooses. 2 Sam. 5. 15.
IBLEAM, ib′-le-am, He destroys the people. Josh. 17. 11.
IBNEIAH, ib-ni′-ah, whom Jehovah will build up. 1 Chr. 9. 8.
IBNIJAH, ib-ni′-jah, same as preceding. 1 Chr. 9. 8.
IBRI, ib′-ri, Hebrew. 1 Chr. 24. 27.
IBZAN, ib′-zan, active (?). Judg. 12. 8.
I-CHABOD, i′-ka-bod, inglorious. 1 Sam. 4. 21; 14. 3.
ICONIUM, i-kon′-yum, gospel preached at. Acts 13. 51; 14. 1; 16. 2.
Paul persecuted at. 2 Tim. 3. 11.
IDALAH, id′-al-ah, snares (?). Josh. 19. 15.
IDBASH, id′-bash, honeyed. 1 Chr. 4. 3.
IDDO, id′-o, (1) loving, 1 Chr. 27. 21; (2) Ezra 8. 17; (3) seasonable, Zech. 1. 1.
IDUMEA, i′-du-me′-ah, same as EDOM. Is. 34. 5.
IGAL, i′ gal, whom God will avenge. Num. 13. 7.
IGDALIAH, ig′-dal-i′-ah, whom Jehovah shall make great. Jer. 35. 4.
IGEAL, i′-ge-al, same as IGAL. 1 Chr. 3. 22.
IIM, i′-im, ruins. Num. 33. 45.
IJE-ABARIM, i-je-a-bar′-im, ruinous heaps of Abarim. Num. 21. 11.
IJON, i′-jon, a ruin. 1 Kin. 15. 20.
IKKESH, ik′-esh, perverseness of mouth. 2 Sam. 23. 26.

ILAI, ee'-lai, most high. 1 Chr. 11. 29.
ILLYRICUM, il-lir'-ik-um, gospel preached there. Rom. 15. 19.
IMLA, im-lah, same as IMLAH. 2 Chr. 18. 7.
IMLAH, im'-lah, whom (God) will fill up. 1 Kin. 22. 8.
IMMANUEL, im-an'-u-el (*See* EMMANUEL), God with us. Is. 7. 14; Matt. 1. 23.
IMMER, im'-er, talkative. 1 Chr. 9. 12.
IMNA, im'-nah, whom (God) keeps back. 1 Chr. 7. 35.
IMNAH, im'-nah, whom (God) assigns (?). 1 Chr. 7. 30.
IMRAH, im'-rah, stubborn. 1 Chr. 7. 36.
IMRI, im'-ri, eloquent. 1 Chr. 9. 4.
INDIA, ind'-ya. Esth. 1. 1.
IPHEDEIAH, if'-ed-i'-ah, whom Jehovah frees. 1 Chr. 8. 25.
IR, eer, city. 1 Chr. 7. 12.
IRA, i'-rah, watchful. 2 Sam. 20. 26.
IRAD, i'-rad. Gen. 4. 18.
IRAM, i'-ram, belonging to a city. Gen. 36. 43.
IRI, i'-ri, same as IRAM. 1 Chr. 7. 7.
IRIJAH, i-ri'-jah, whom Jehovah looks on. Jer. 37. 13.
IR-NAHASH, ir-na'-hash, snake-town. 1 Chr. 4. 12.
IRON, i'-ron, reverence. Josh. 19. 38.
IRPEEL, ir'-pe-el, which God heals. Josh. 18. 27.
IR-SHEMESH, ir'-she'-mesh, sun-town. Josh. 19. 41.
IRU, i'-roo, same as IRAM. 1 Chr. 4. 15.
ISAAC, i'-zak, laughter. Gen. 17. 19.
  his birth promised. Gen. 15. 4; 17. 16; 18. 10;
    born. Gen. 21. 2.
  offered by Abraham. Gen. 22. 7.
  marries Rebekah. Gen. 24. 67.
  blesses his sons, Gen. 27. 28; dies, Gen. 35. 29.
ISAIAH, i-zai'-ah, salvation of Jehovah (Esaias), prophet. Is. 1. 1; 2. 1.
  sent to Ahaz. Is. 7; and Hezekiah. Is. 37. 6;
    38. 4; 39. 3.
  prophesies concerning various nations. Is. 7;
    8; 10; 13—23; 45—47.
  referred to in Matt. 3. 3; 4. 14; 8. 17; 12. 17; 13.
    14; 15. 7; Mark 1. 3; Luke 3. 4; 4. 17; John 1.
    23; 12. 38; Acts 8. 32; 28. 25; Rom. 9. 27; 10.
    16; 15. 12.
ISCAH, is'-kah. Gen. 11. 29.
ISCARIOT, is-kar'-i-ot, man of Kerioth. Judas, Matt. 10. 4; Mark 3. 19.
  his treachery. Matt. 26. 21; Mark 14. 18; Luke 22. 47; John 18. 3.
  death, Matt. 27. 5; Acts 1. 18.
ISHBAH, ish'-bah, praising. 1 Chr. 4. 17.
ISHBAK, ish'-bak. Gen. 25. 2.
ISHBI-BENOB, ish'-bi-ben-ob'e, one who dwells at Nob. 2 Sam. 21. 16.
ISH-BOSHETH, ish-bo'-sheth, man of shame. 2 Sam. 2. 8; 3. 7; 4. 5, 8.
ISHI, eesh'-i, my husband. Hos. 2. 16.
ISHI, yish'-i, salutary. 1 Chr. 2. 31.
ISHIAH, ish-i'-ah, whom Jehovah lends. 1 Chr. 7. 3.
ISHIJAH, ish-i'-jah, same as ISHIA. Ezra 10. 31.
ISHMA, ish'-mah. 1 Chr. 4. 3.
ISHMAEL, ish'-ma-el, whom God hears, son of Abram. Gen. 16. 15; 17. 20; 21. 17; 25. 17; his descendants. Gen. 25. 12; 1 Chr. 1. 29.
——— son of Nethaniah, slays Gedaliah. 2 Kin. 25. 25; Jer. 40. 14; 41.
ISHMAELITES, ish'-ma-el-ites, descendants of Ishmael. Judg. 8. 24.
ISHMAIAH, ish-mai'-ah, whom Jehovah hears. 1 Chr. 27. 19.
ISHMEELITES, ish'-me-el-ites, same as ISHMAELITES. Gen. 37. 25.
IS'IMERAI, ish'-mer-ai, whom Jehovah keeps. 1 Chr. 8. 18.
ISHOD, ish'-hode, man of glory. 1 Chr. 7. 18.
ISHPAN, ish'-pan, cunning (?). 1 Chr. 8. 22.
ISH-TOB, ish'-tobe, men of Tob. 2 Sam. 10. 6.
ISHUAH, ish'-oo-ah, level. Gen. 46. 17.
ISHUAI, ish'-oo-ai, same as ISUI. 1 Chr. 7. 30.
ISHUI, ish'-oo-i, same as ISHUAH. 1 Sam. 14. 49.

ISMACHIAH, is-mak-i'-ah, whom Jehovah upholds. 2 Chr. 31. 13.
ISMAIAH, is-mai'-ah, same as ISHMAIAH. 1 Chr. 12. 4.
ISPAH, is'-pah, bald. 1 Chr. 8. 16.
ISRAEL, iz'-ra-el, soldier of God, Jacob so called after wrestling with God. Gen. 32. 28; 35. 10; Hos. 12. 3.
ISRAELITES, iz'-ra-el-ites, descendants of Israel. Ex. 9. 7.
  in Egypt. Ex. 1—12.
  the first passover instituted. Ex. 12.
  flight from Egypt. Ex. 12. 31.
  pass through the Red Sea. Ex. 14.
  their journeys. Ex. 14. 1, 19; Num. 9. 15; Ps. 78. 14.
  fed by manna and water in the wilderness. Ex. 16. 4; 17. 1; Num. 11; 20.
  God's covenant at Sinai. Ex. 19; 20; Deut. 29. 10.
  their idolatry. Ex. 32. *See also* 2 Kin. 17; Ezra 9; Neh. 9; Ezek. 20; 22; 23; Acts 7. 39; 1 Cor. 10. 1.
  their rebellious conduct rehearsed by Moses. Deut. 1; 2; 9.
  conquer and divide Canaan under Joshua. Josh. 1; 12; 13.
  governed by judges. Judg. 2; by kings. 1 Sam. 10; 2 Sam.; 1 & 2 Kin.; 1 & 2 Chr.
  their captivity in Assyria, 2 Kin. 17; in Babylon, 2 Kin. 25; 2 Chr. 36; Jer. 39; 52; their return, Ezra; Neh.; Hag.; Zech.
  God's wrath against, Ps. 78; 106; deliverances of. Ps. 105.
  their sufferings our examples. 1 Cor. 10. 6.
ISRAELITISH, iz'-ra-el-ite-ish, after the fashion of an Israelite. Lev. 24. 10.
ISSACHAR, is'-ak-ar, he is hired (?). Gen. 30. 18; 35. 23.
  descendants of. Gen. 46. 13; Judg. 5. 15; 1 Chr. 7. 1. *See* Num. 1. 28; 26. 23; Gen. 49. 14; Deut. 33. 18; Josh. 19. 17; Ezek. 48. 33; Rev. 7. 7.
ISSHIAH, ish-hi'-ah, same as ISHIAH. 1 Chr. 24. 21.
ISUAH, is'-oo-ah, same as ISHUAH. 1 Chr. 7. 30.
ISUI, is'-oo-i, same as ISHUI. Gen. 46. 17.
ITALIAN, it'-al-yan, belonging to Italy. Acts 10. 1.
ITALY, it'-a-ly. Acts 18. 2.
ITHAI, ee'-thai, ploughman. 1 Chr. 11. 31.
ITHAMAR, i'-tha-mar, island of palms. Ex. 6. 23; Lev. 10. 6; his charge. Num. 4.
ITHIEL, ith'-i-el, God is with me. Neh. 11. 7; Prov. 30. 1.
ITHMAH, ith'-mah, bereavedness. 1 Chr. 11. 46.
ITHNAN, ith'-nan. Josh. 15. 23.
ITHRA, ith'-rah, excellence. 2 Sam. 17. 25.
ITHRAN, ith'-ran, same as ITHRA. Gen. 36. 26.
ITHREAM, ith'-re-am, remainder of the people. 2 Sam. 3. 5.
ITHRITE, ith'-rite, descendants of Jether (?). 2 Sam. 23. 38.
ITTAH-KAZIN, it'-ah-ka'-zin, time of the chief. Josh. 19. 13.
ITTAI, it'-tai, same as ITHAI (the Gittite). 2 Sam. 15. 19; 18. 2.
ITURÆA, i'-tu-re'-ah, a province so named from Jetur. Luke 3. 1.
IVAH, i'-vah. 2 Kin. 18. 34.
IZEHAR, iz'-e-har, oil. Num. 3. 19.
IZEHARITES, i'-ze-har'-ites, the descendants of Izehar. Num. 3. 27.
IZHAR, iz'-har, same as IZEHAR. Ex. 6. 18.
IZHARITES, iz'-har-ites, the same as IZEHARITES. 1 Chr. 26. 23.
IZRAHIAH, iz-rah-i'-ah, whom Jehovah brought to light. 1 Chr. 7. 3.
IZRAHITE, iz'-rah-ite, probably same as ZARHITE. 1 Chr. 27. 8.
IZRI, iz'-ri, a descendant of Jezer. 1 Chr. 25. 11.

JAAKAN, ja'-ak-an, one who turns. Deut. 10. 6.
JAAKOBAH, ja'-ak-o'-bah, same as JACOB. 1 Chr. 4. 36.
JAALA, ja'-a-lah, wild she-goat. Neh. 7. 58.

JAALAH, ja'-a-lah, same as JAALA. Ezra 2. 56.

JAALAM, ja'-a-lam, whom God hides. Gen. 36. 5.

JAANAI, ja'-a-nai, whom Jehovah answers. 1 Chr. 5. 12.

JAARE-OREGIM, ja'-ar-e-or'-eg-im, forests of the weavers. 2 Sam. 21. 19.

JAASAU, ja'-a-saw. Ezra 10. 37.

JAASIEL, ja-as'-i-el, whom God created. 1 Chr. 27. 21.

JAAZANIAH, ja'-az-an-i'-ah, whom Jehovah hears. 2 Kin. 25. 23.

JAAZER, ja'-a-zer, whom (God) aids. Num. 21. 32.

JAAZIAH, ja'-az-i'-ah, whom Jehovah strengthens. 1 Chr. 24. 26.

JAAZIEL, ja'-az'-i-el, whom God strengthens. 1 Chr. 15. 18.

JABAL, ja'-bal. Gen. 4. 20.

JABBOK, jab'-ok, pouring out, river. Gen. 32. 22; Num. 21. 24; Deut. 3. 16; Josh. 12. 2.

JABESH, ja'-besh, dry. 2 Kin. 15. 10.

JABESH-GILEAD, ja'-besh-gil'-e-ad, Jabesh of Gilead. Judg. 21. 8.

   inhabitants smitten by Israel. Judg. 21.

   threatened by Ammonites. 1 Sam. 11. 1; delivered by Saul. 1 Sam. 11. 11.

JABEZ, ja'-bez, causing pain, prayer of. 1 Chr. 4. 9.

JABIN, ja'-bin, whom He (God) considered. Judg. 4. 2.

   king of Hazor, conquered by Joshua. Josh. 11.

  —— (another), destroyed by Barak. Judg. 4.

JABNEEL, jab'-ne-el, may God cause to be built. Josh. 15. 11.

JABNEH, jab'-nay, which (God) causes to be built. 2 Chr. 26. 6.

JACHAN, ja'-kan, troubled. 1 Chr. 5. 13.

JACHIN, ja'-kin, whom (God) strengthens one of the pillars of the porch of the temple. 1 Kin. 7. 21; 2 Chr. 3. 17.

JACHINITES, ja'-kin-ites, descendants of Jachin. Num. 26. 12.

JACOB, ja'-kob, supplanter, his birth. Gen. 25. 26; birthright, 25. 33; blessing, 27. 27; sent to Padanaram, 27. 43; 28. 1; his vision of the ladder, and vow, 28. 10; marriages, 29; sons, 29. 31; 30; dealings with Laban, 31; his vision of God's host, 32. 1; his prayer, 32. 9; wrestles with an angel, 32. 24; Hos. 12. 4; reconciled with Esau. Gen. 33; builds an altar at Beth-el, 35. 1; his grief for Joseph and Benjamin, 37; 42. 38; 43; goes down to Egypt, 46; brought before Pharaoh, 47. 7; blesses his sons, 48; 49.

   his death, and burial. Gen. 49. 33; 50. *See* Ps. 105. 23; Mal. 1. 2; Rom. 9. 10; Heb. 11. 21.

JACOB'S WELL. John 4. 5.

JADA, ja'-dah, wise. 1 Chr. 2. 28.

JADAU, ja'-daw. Ezra 10. 43.

JADDUA, jad'-oo-ah, skilled. Neh. 10. 21.

JADON, ja'-don, a judge. Neh. 3. 7.

JAEL, ja'-el, same as JAALA, kills Sisera. Judg. 4. 17; 5. 24.

JAGUR, ja'-goor, a lodging. Josh. 15. 21.

JAH, poetic form of JEHOVAH. Ps. 68. 4.

JAHATH, ja'-hath. 1 Chr. 6. 20.

JAHAZ, ja'-haz, a place trodden down. Num. 21. 23.

JAHAZA, ja'-haz-ah, same as JAHAZ. Josh. 13. 18.

JAHAZAH, same as JAHAZA. Josh. 21. 36.

JAHAZIAH, ja'-haz-i'-ah, whom Jehovah watches over. Ezra 10. 15.

JAHAZIEL, ja-haz'-i-el, whom God watches over. 1 Chr. 16. 6.

   comforts Jehoshaphat. 2 Chr. 19. 14.

   prophecies against Moab and Ammon. 2 Chr. 20. 14.

JAHDAI, jah'-dai, whom Jehovah directs. 1 Chr. 2. 47.

JAHDIEL, jah'-di-el, whom God makes glad. 1 Chr. 5. 24.

JAHDO, jah'-do, union. 1 Chr. 5. 14.

JAHLEEL, jah'-le-el, hoping in God. Num. 26. 26.

JAHLEELITES, jah'-le-el-ites, descendants of Jahleel. Num. 26. 26.

JAHMAI, jah'-mai. 1 Chr. 7. 2.

JAHZAH, ja'-zah, same as JAHAZ. 1 Chr. 6. 78.

JAHZEEL, jah'-ze-el, whom God allots. Gen. 46. 24.

JAHZEELITES, jah'-ze-el-ites, descendants of Jahzeel. Num. 26. 48.

JAHZERAH, jah-ze'-rah, may he bring back. 1 Chr. 9. 12.

JAHZIEL, jah'-zi-el, same as JAHZEEL. 1 Chr. 7. 13.

JAIR, ja'-er, (*i.e.* God) enlightens. Num. 32. 41.

   Gileadite, judge. Judg. 10. 3.

JAIRITE, ja'-er-ite, a descendant of JAIR. 2 Sam. 20. 26.

JAIRUS, ja-i'-rus, Greek form of JAIR, daughter of, raised. Matt. 9. 18; Mark 5. 22; Luke 8. 41.

JAKAN, ja'-kan, same as JAAKAN. 1 Chr. 1. 42.

JAKEH, ja'-kay, pious (?). Prov. 30. 1.

JAKIM, ja'-kim, (God) sets up. 1 Chr. 8. 19.

JALON, ja'-lon, passing the night. 1 Chr. 4. 17.

JAMBRES, jam'-brees. 2 Tim. 3. 8.

JAMES, the English equivalent for Jacob in the New Testament.

  —— (APOSTLE), son of Zebedee, called. Matt. 4. 21; Mark 1. 19; Luke 5. 10.

   ordained one of the twelve. Matt. 10. 2; Mark 3. 14; Luke 6. 13.

   witnessed Christ's transfiguration. Matt. 17. 1; Mark 9. 2; Luke 9. 28.

   present at the passion. Matt. 26. 36; Mark 14. 33.

   slain by Herod. Acts 12. 2.

  —— (APOSTLE), son of Alphæus. Matt. 10. 3; Mark 3. 18; 6. 3; Luke 6. 15; Acts 1. 13; 12. 17.

   his judgment respecting ceremonial. Acts 15. 13—29. *See* 1 Cor. 15. 7; Gal. 1. 19; 2. 9.

   his teaching. James 1—5.

   mentioned. Acts 21. 18; 1 Cor. 15. 7; Gal. 1. 19; 2. 9.

JAMIN, ja'-min, right hand. Gen. 46. 10.

JAMINITES, ja'-min-ites, descendants of Jamin. Num. 26. 12.

JAMLECH, jam'-lek, He makes to reign. 1 Chr. 4. 34.

JANNA, jan'-nah, probably another form of John. Luke 3. 24.

JANNES and JAMBRES, magicians of Egypt. 2 Tim. 3. 8 (Ex. 7. 11).

JANOAH, ja-no'-ah, rest. 2 Kin. 15. 29.

JANOHAH, ja-no'-hah, same as preceding. Josh. 16. 6.

JANUM, ja'-noom, sleep. Josh. 15. 53.

JAPHETH, ja'-feth, extension. Gen. 5. 32.

   son of Noah, blessed. Gen. 9. 27.

   his descendants. Gen. 10. 1; 1 Chr. 1. 4.

JAPHIA, ja-fi'-ah, splendid. Josh. 19. 12.

JAPHLET, jaf'-let, may he deliver. 1 Chr. 7. 32.

JAPHLETI, jaf-le'-ti, the Japhletite, or descendant of Japhlet. Josh. 16. 3.

JAPHO, ja'-fo, beauty. Josh. 19. 46.

JARAH, ja'-rah, forest. 1 Chr. 9. 42.

JAREB, ja'-reb, one who is contentious. Hos. 5. 13.

JARED, ja'-red, descent. Gen. 5. 15; Luke 3. 37.

JARESIAH, ja'-res-i'-ah, whom Jehovah nourishes. 1 Chr. 8. 27.

JARHA, jar'-hah. 1 Chr. 2. 34.

JARIB, ja'-rib, adversary. 1 Chr. 4. 24.

JARMUTH, jar'-mooth, height. Josh. 10. 3.

JAROAH, ja-ro'-ah, moon (?). 1 Chr. 5. 14.

JASHEN, ja'-shen, sleeping. 2 Sam. 23. 32.

JASHER, ja'-sher, upright, book of. Josh. 10. 13; 2 Sam. 1. 18.

JASHOBEAM, ja-shob'-e-am, the people returns, valour of. 1 Chr. 11. 11.

JASHUB, ja'-shoob, he returns. Num. 20. 24.

JASHUBI-LEHEM, ja-shoob'-i-le'-hem, giving bread (?). 1 Chr. 4. 22.

JASHUBITES, ja'-shoob-ites, descendants of Jashub. Num. 26. 24.

JASIEL, ja-si'-el, whom God made. 1 Chr. 11. 47.

JASON, ja'-son, Græco-Judæan equivalent of Joshua, persecuted at Thessalonica. Acts 17. 5; Rom. 16. 21.

JATHNIEL, jath'-ni-el, God gives. 1 Chr. 26. 2.

JATTIR, jat'-yer, excelling. Josh. 15. 48.

JAVAN, ja'-van, wine (?), son of Japheth. Gen. 10. 2.

JAZER, ja'-zer, same as JAAZER. Num. 32. 1.

JAZIZ, ja'-ziz, wanderer (?). 1 Chr. 27. 31.

JEARIM, je-ar'-im, forests. Josh. 15. 10.

JEATERAI, je-at'-er-ai'. 1 Chr. 6. 21.

JEBERECHIAH, je-ber'-ek-i'-ah, whom Jehovah blesses. Is. 8. 2.

JEBUS, je'-bus, a place trodden down (?). Judg. 19. 10.

JEBUSI, je-boo'-si, a Jebusite. Josh. 18. 16.

JEBUSITES, je-boo'-sites, the descendants of Jebus, the son of Canaan. Gen. 15. 21; Num. 13. 29; Josh. 15. 63; Judg. 1. 21; 19. 11; 2 Sam. 5. 6.

JECAMIAH, jek'-am-i'-ah. 1 Chr. 3. 18.

JECHOLIAH, jek'-ol-i'-ah, Jehovah is strong. 2 Kin. 15. 2.

JECHONIAS, jek'-on-i'-as, the Greek way of spelling Jeconiah. Matt. 1. 11, 12; 1 Chr. 3. 17.

JECOLIAH, jek'-ol-i'-ah, same as JECHOLIAH. 2 Chr. 26. 3.

JECONIAH, jek'-on-i'-ah, Jehovah establishes. 1 Chr. 3. 16.

JEDAIAH, jed-ai'-ah, (1) Jehovah—(?). 1 Chr. 4. 37. (2) Jehovah knoweth. 1 Chr. 24. 7.

JEDIAEL, je-di'-a-el, known of God. 1 Chr. 7. 6.

JEDIDAH, jed-i'-dah, beloved. 2 Kin. 22. 1.

JEDIDIAH, jed'-id-i'-ah (beloved of the Lord), a name of Solomon. 2 Sam. 12. 25.

JEDUTHUN, jed-ooth'-oon, friendship (?). 1 Chr. 16. 38; 41; 25. 6.

JEEZER, je-e'-zer, contracted from ABIEZER. Num. 26. 30.

JEEZERITES, je-ez'-er-ites, descendants of Jeezer. Num. 26. 30.

JEGAR-SAHADUTHA, je-gar'-sa-ha-doo'-thah, the heap of testimony. Gen. 31. 47.

JEHALELEEL, je-hal'-el-e'-el, he praises God. 1 Chr. 4. 16.

JEHALELEL, je-hal'-e-lel, same as preceding. 2 Chr. 29. 12.

JEHDEIAH, jed-i'-ah, whom Jehovah makes glad. 1 Chr. 24. 20.

JEHEZEKEL, je-hez'-e-kel, same as EZEKIEL. 1 Chr. 24. 16.

JEHIAH, je-hi'-ah, Jehovah lives. 1 Chr. 15. 24.

JEHIEL, je-hi'-el, God liveth. 1 Chr. 15. 18.

JEHIELI, je-hi'-el-i, a Jehielite. 1 Chr. 26. 21.

JEHIZKIAH, je'-hizk-i'-ah, same as HEZEKIAH. 2 Chr. 28. 12.

JEHOADAH, je-ho'-a-dah, whom Jehovah adorns. 1 Chr. 8. 36.

JEHOADDAN, je-ho'-ad-an, Jehovah is beauteous (?). 2 Kin. 14. 2.

JEHOAHAZ, je-ho'-a-haz, whom Jehovah holds fast, son of Jehu, king of Israel. 2 Kin. 10. 35; 13. 4.

—— (Shallum), king of Judah, his evil reign. 2 Kin. 23. 31; 2 Chr. 36. 1.

JEHOASH, je-ho'-ash, Jehovah supports. 2 Kin. 11. 21.

JEHOHANAN, je-ho'-han-an, Jehovah is gracious. 1 Chr. 26. 3.

JEHOIACHIN, je-ho'-ya-kin, Jehovah has established.

king of Judah, his defeat and captivity. 2 Kin. 24. 6; 2 Chr. 36. 8.

JEHOIADA, je-ho'-ya-dah, Jehovah knoweth. 2 Sam. 8. 18.

high priest, deposes and slays Athaliah, and restores Jehoash. 2 Kin. 11. 4; 2 Chr. 23; repairs the temple. 2 Kin. 12. 7; 2 Chr. 24. 6. abolishes idolatry. 2 Chr. 23. 16.

JEHOIAKIM, je-ho'-ya-kim, Jehovah has set up.

—— (Eliakim), made king of Judah by Pharaoh-nechoh, his evil reign and captivity. 2 Kin. 23; 34; 24. 1; 2 Chr. 36. 4; Dan. 1. 2. *See* Jer. 22. 18.

JEHOIARIB, je-ho'-ya-rib, Jehovah will contend. 1 Chr. 9. 10.

JEHONADAB, je-ho'-na-dab, Jehovah is bounteous. 2 Kin. 10. 15.

JEHONATHAN, je-ho'-na-than, same as JONATHAN. 1 Chr. 27. 25.

JEHORAM, je-ho'-ram, Jehovah is high.

—— (son of Jehoshaphat), king of Judah, 1 Kin. 22. 50; 2 Kin. 8. 16; his cruelty and death, 2 Chr. 21. 4, 18.

—— (Joram), king of Israel, son of Ahab. 2 Kin. 1. 17; 3. 1; his evil reign. 2 Kin. 3. 2; slain by Jehu. 2 Kin. 9. 24.

JEHOSHABEATH, je-ho'-shab'-e-ath, Jehovah is the oath. 2 Chr. 22. 11.

JEHOSHAPHAT, je-hosh'-af-at, whom Jehovah judges.

king of Judah, his good reign. 1 Kin. 15. 24; 2 Chr. 17; his death. 1 Kin. 22. 50; 2 Chr. 21. 1.

—— valley of, Joel 3. 2.

JEHOSHEBA, je-ho'-she-bah, same as JEHOSHABEATH. 2 Kin. 11. 2; 2 Chr. 22. 11.

JEHOSHUA, je-hosh'-oo-ah, same as JOSHUA. Num. 13. 16.

JEHOSHUAH, je-hosh'-oo-ah, same as JOSHUA. 1 Chr. 7. 27.

JEHOVAH, je-ho'-vah, the Eternal One.

JEHOVAH (ELOHIM, I AM THAT I AM). Ex. 6. 3; Ps. 83. 18; Is. 12. 2; 26. 4.

JEHOVAH-JIREH, je-ho'-vah-ji'-ray, Jehovah will provide. Gen. 22. 14.

JEHOVAH-NISSI, je-ho'-vah-nis'-i, Jehovah my banner. Ex. 17. 15.

JEHOVAH-SHALOM, je-ho'-vah-sha'-lom, Jehovah send peace. Judg. 6. 24.

— SHAMMAH, je-ho'-vah-sham'-mah (the LORD is there). Ezek. 48. 35.

— TSIDKENU, je-ho'-vah-tsid-ke'-nu (the LORD is our righteousness). Jer. 23. 6.

JEHOZABAD, je-ho'-za-bad, Jehovah gave. 2 Kin. 12. 21.

JEHOZADAK, je-ho'-za-dak, Jehovah is just. 1 Chr. 6. 14.

JEHU, je'-hu, Jehovah is He (?), son of Hanani, prophesies against Baasha. 1 Kin. 16. 1. rebukes Jehoshaphat. 2 Chr. 19. 2; 20. 34.

—— son of Nimshi, to be anointed king of Israel. 1 Kin. 19. 16; 2 Kin. 9. 1. his reign. 2 Kin. 9. 10.

JEHUBBAH, je-hoob'-ah, hidden. 1 Chr. 7. 34.

JERUCAL, je-hoo'-kal, Jehovah is mighty. Jer. 37. 3.

JEHUD, je'-hood, praise. Josh. 19. 45.

JEHUDI, je-hood'-i, a Jew. Jer. 36. 14.

JEHUDIJAH, je-hood-i'-jah, a Jewess. 1 Chr. 4. 18.

JEHUSH, je'-hoosh, to whom God hastens. 1 Chr. 8. 39.

JEIEL, ji'-el. 1 Chr. 5. 7.

JEKABZEEL, je-kab'-ze-el, God gathers. Neh. 11. 25.

JEKAMEAM, je-kam'-e-am. 1 Chr. 23. 19.

JEKAMIAH, jek'-am-i'-ah, same as JECAMIAH. 1 Chr. 2. 41.

JEKUTHIEL, je-koo'-thi-el, the fear of God. 1 Chr. 4. 18.

JEMIMA, je-mi'-mah, dove. Job 42. 14.

JEMUEL, jem-oo'-el, day of God. Gen. 46. 10.

JEPHTHAE, jef'-thah, Greek way of writing Jephthah. Heb. 11. 32.

JEPHTHAH, jef'-thah, God opens. Judg. 11. 1. judge, his dealings with the Gileadites. Judg. 11. 4.

defeats the Ammonites. Judg. 11. 14. his rash vow. Judg. 11. 30, 34. chastises the Ephraimites. Judg. 12.

JEPHUNNEH, je-foon'-eh, for whom it is prepared. Num. 13. 6.

JERAH, je'-rah, the moon. Gen. 10. 26.

JERAHMEEL, je-rah'-me-el, whom God loves. 1 Chr. 2. 9.

JERAHMEELITES, je-rah'-me-el-ites, descendants of Jerahmeel. 1 Sam. 27. 10.

JERED, je'-red, descent. 1 Chr. 1. 2.

JEREMAI, jer-e'-mai, dwelling in heights. Ezra 10. 33.

JEREMIAH, jer'-em-i'-ah, whom Jehovah has appointed.
(prophet), his call and visions. Jer. 1.
his mission. Jer. 1. 17; 7.
his complaint. Jer. 20. 14.
his message to Zedekiah. Jer. 21. 3; 34. 1.
foretells the seventy years' captivity. Jer. 25. 8.
arraigned, condemned, but delivered. Jer. 26.
denounces the false prophet Hananiah. Jer. 28. 5.
writes to the captives in Babylon. Jer. 29.
his promises of comfort and redemption to Israel. Jer. 31.
writes a roll of a book. Jer. 36. 4; Baruch reads it. Jer. 36. 8.
imprisoned by Zedekiah. Jer. 32; 37; 38.
released. Jer. 38. 7.
predicts slaughter of innocents. Jer. 31. 15; fulfilled. Matt. 2. 17.
with all the remnant of Judah carried into Egypt. Jer. 43. 4.
various predictions. Jer. 46—51; 51. 59.
mentioned. Matt. 16. 14; 27. 9.

JEREMIAS, jer'-em-i'-as, Greek form of Jeremiah. Matt. 16. 14.

JEREMOTH, je-re'-moth, high places. 1 Chr. 8. 14.

JEREMY, jer'-em-y, shortened English form of Jeremiah. Matt. 2. 17.

JERIAH, jer-i'-ah, whom Jehovah regards (?). 1 Chr. 23. 19.

JERIBAI, jer-ee'-bai, contentious. 1 Chr. 11. 46.

JERICHO, jer'-ik-o, a fragrant place. Num. 22. 1.
the spies at. Josh. 2. 1.
capture of. Josh. 6. 20 (Heb. 11. 30).
rebuilt by Hiel. 1 Kin. 16. 34. *See* Josh. 6. 26.

JERIEL, je-ri'-el, founded by God. 1 Chr. 7. 2.

JERIJAH, jer-i'-jah, same as JERIAH. 1 Chr. 26. 31.

JERIMOTH, jer-ee'-moth, same as JEREMOTH. 1Chr. 7. 7.

JERIOTH, je-ri'-oth, curtains. 1 Chr. 2. 18.

JEROBOAM I., jer'-ob-o'-am, whose people are many. 1 Kin. 11. 26.
promoted by Solomon. 1 Kin. 11. 28.
Ahijah's prophecy to. 1 Kin. 11. 29.
made king. 1 Kin. 12. 20 (2 Chr. 10).
his idolatry, withered hand, denunciation. 1 Kin. 12; 13; 14.
death. 1 Kin. 14. 20.
evil example. 1 Kin. 15. 34.

JEROBOAM II. 2 Kin. 13. 13; 14. 23—29.

JEROHAM, je-ro'-ham, who is loved. 1 Sam. 1. 1.

JERUBBAAL, jer-oob-ba'-al, let Baal plead. Judg. 6. 32.

JERUBBESHETH, jer-oob-be'-sheth, let shame plead, another name for JERUBBAAL. 2 Sam. 11. 21.

JERUEL, je-roo'-el, same as JERIEL. 2 Chr. 20. 16.

JERUSALEM, je-roo'-sa-lem, founded in peace (?). Josh. 10. 1.
—— Adoni-zedec, king of, slain by Joshua. Josh. 10.
borders of. Josh. 15. 8.
David reigns there. 2 Sam. 5. 6.
the ark brought there. 2 Sam. 6.
saved from the pestilence. 2 Sam. 24. 16.
temple built at. 1 Kin. 5—8; 2 Chr. 1—7.
sufferings from war. 1 Kin. 14. 25; 2 Kin. 14. 11; 25; 2 Chr. 12; 24; 36; Jer. 39; 52.
capture and destruction by Nebuchadrezzar. Jer. 52. 12—15.
captives return: and rebuilding of the temple begun by Cyrus. Ezra 1—3; continued by Artaxerxes. Neh. 2.
wall rebuilt and dedicated by Nehemiah. Neh. 12. 38.
abominations there. Ezek. 16. 2.
presentation of Christ at. Luke 2. 22.
the child Jesus tarries at. Luke 2. 42.

JERUSALEM.—*cont.*
Christ rides into. Matt. 21. 1; Mark 11. 7; Luke 19. 35; John 12. 14.
laments over it. Matt. 23. 37; Luke 13. 34; 19. 41.
foretells its destruction. Matt. 24; Mark 13; Luke 13. 34; 17. 23; 19. 41; 21.
disciples filled with the Holy Ghost at. Acts 2. 4.
which is above. Gal. 4. 26.
the new. Rev. 21. 2.

JERUSHA, je-roo'-shah, possession. 2 Kin. 15. 33.

JERUSHAH, je-roo'-shah, same as preceding. 2 Chr. 27. 1.

JESAIAH, je-sai'-ah, same as ISAIAH. 1 Chr. 3. 21.

JESHAIAH, je-shai'-ah, same as preceding. 1 Chr. 25. 3.

JESHANAH, je-shan'-ah, old. 2 Chr. 13. 19.

JESHARELAH, jesh'-ar-el'-ah, right before God (?). 1 Chr. 25. 14.

JESHEBEAB, je-sheb'-e-ab, father's seat. 1 Chr. 24. 13.

JESHER, je'-sher, uprightness. 1 Chr. 2. 18.

JESHIMON, je-shim'-on, the waste. Num. 21. 20.

JESHISHAI, je-shee'-shai, like an old man. 1 Chr. 5. 14.

JESHOHAIAH, je-sho-hai'-ah, whom Jehovah humbles. 1 Chr. 4. 36.

JESHUA (Joshua), jesh'-oo-ah, Jehovah is salvation. Ezra 2. 2; Neh. 8. 17. *See* JOSHUA.

JESHUAH, jesh'-oo-ah, help. 1 Chr. 24. 11.

JESHURUN, jesh-oor'-oon, righteous, symbolical name of Israel. Deut. 32. 15; 33. 5, 26; Is. 44. 2.

JESIAH, je-si'-ah. 1 Chr. 12. 6.

JESIMIEL, je-sim'-i-el, whom God founds (?). 1 Chr. 4. 36.

JESSE, jes'-sy, gift (?). Ruth 4. 17.
David's father. Ruth 4. 22.
and his sons sanctified by Samuel. 1 Sam. 16. 5.
his son David anointed to be king. 1 Sam. 16. 13. *See* Is. 11. 1.
his posterity. 1 Chr. 2. 13.

JESUI, je-soo'-i, same as ISHUA. Num. 26. 44.

JESUITES, je'-soo-ites, the posterity of Jesui. Num. 26. 44.

JESURUN, je-soor'-oon, wrongly printed for Jeshurun. Isai. 44. 2.

JESUS, je'-sus, Saviour. Matt. 1. 21. *See* CHRIST, Subject-Index, p. 439.

JETHER, je'-ther, same as ITHRA. Judg. 8. 20.

JETHETH, je'-theth. Gen. 36. 40.

JETHLAH, jeth'-lah, lofty. Josh. 19. 42.

JETHRO, jeth'-ro, same as ITHRA. Ex. 3. 1.
Moses' father-in-law. Ex. 18. 12.

JETUR, je'-toor, an enclosure. Gen. 25. 15.

JEUEL, je-oo'-el, same as JEIEL. 1 Chr. 9. 6.

JEUSH, je'-oosh, same as JEHUSH. Gen. 36. 5.

JEUZ, je'-ooz, counsellor. 1 Chr. 8. 10.

JEW, joo, an Israelite. Esth. 2. 5.

JEWESS, joo'-ess, a female Jew. Acts 16. 1.

JEWISH, joo'-ish, of or belonging to Jews. Tit. 1. 14.

JEWRY, joo'-ry, Old English name for Judea. Dan. 5. 13.

JEWS, jooz, inhabitants of Judea (Israelites first so called). 2 Kin. 16. 6.
Christ's mission to. Matt. 15. 24; 21. 37; Acts 3. 26.
Christ's compassion for. Matt. 23. 37; Luke 19. 41.
Christ rejected by. Matt. 11. 20; 13. 15, 58; John 5. 16, 38, 43; Acts 3. 13; 13. 46; 1 Thess. 2. 15.
gospel first preached to, Matt. 10. 6; Luke 24. 47; Acts 1. 8.
St. Paul's teaching rejected by, Acts 13. 46; 28. 24, 28, &c.

JEZANIAH, jez'-an-i'-ah, Jehovah adorns (?). Jer. 40. 8.

JEZEBEL, jez'-e-bel, unmarried.
wife of Ahab, 1 Kin. 16. 31.
kills the prophets, 1 Kin. 18. 4; 19. 2.
causes Naboth to be put to death. 1 Kin. 21.
her violent death. 2 Kin. 9. 30.

JEZER, je'-zer, anything made. Gen. 46. 24.

JEZERITES, je'-zer-ites, descendants of Jezer. Num. 26, 49.
JEZIAH, jez-i'-ah, whom Jehovah assembles. Ezra 10. 25.
JEZIEL, jez-i'-el, the assembly of God. 1 Chr. 12. 3.
JEZLIAH, jez-li'-ah, deliverance (?). 1 Chr. 8. 18.
JEZOAR, je-zo'-ar, splendid. 1 Chr. 4. 7.
JEZRAHIAH, jez'-rah-i'-ah, Jehovah shines forth. Neh. 12. 42.
JEZREEL, jez'-re-el, God scatters. 1 Chr. 4. 3. *See* AHAB.
JEZREELITE, jez'-re-el-ite, an inhabitant of Jezreel. 1 Kin. 21. 6.
JEZREELITESS, jez'-re-el-ite-ess, feminine of preceding. 1 Sam. 27. 3.
JIBSAM, jib'-sam, fragrant. 1 Chr. 7. 2.
JIDLAPH, jid'-laf, weeping (?). Gen. 22. 22.
JIMNA, jim'-nah, same as IMNA. Num. 26. 44.
JIMNAH, jim'-nah, same as IMNAH. Gen. 46. 17.
JIMNITES, jim'-nites, descendants of Jimnah. Num. 26. 44.
JIPHTAH, jif'-tah, same as JEPHTHAH. Josh. 15. 43.
JIPHTHAH-EL, jif'-thah-el, which God opens. Josh. 19. 14.
JOAB, jo'-ab, Jehovah is father. 2 Sam. 2. 13.
nephew of David, and captain of the host. 2 Sam. 8. 16.
kills Abner. 2 Sam. 3. 23.
intercedes for Absalom, 2 Sam. 14; slays him in an oak, 2 Sam. 18. 14.
reproves David's grief. 2 Sam. 19. 5.
slays Amasa. 2 Sam. 20. 9.
unwillingly numbers the people. 2 Sam. 24. 3 (1 Chr. 21. 3).
joins Adonijah's usurpation. 1 Kin. 1. 7.
slain by Solomon's command. 1 Kin. 2. 5, 28.
JOAH, jo'-ah, Jehovah is brother. 2 Kin. 18. 18; 2 Chr. 34. 8.
JOAHAZ, jo'-a-haz, whom Jehovah holds. 2 Chr. 34. 8.
JOANNA, jo-an'-ah, Greek way of writing Jehonan. Luke 3. 27 ; 8. 2, 3 ; 24. 10.
JOASH, jo'-ash, whom Jehovah supports (?). 2 Kin. 11. 2.
(Jehoash), king of Israel. 2 Kin. 13. 10.
visits Elisha sick. 2 Kin. 13. 14.
defeats the Syrians. 2 Kin. 13. 25.
chastises Amaziah. 2 Kin. 14. 8; 2 Chr. 25. 17.
—— king of Judah. 2 Kin. 11. 4; 2 Chr. 23.
repairs the temple. 2 Kin. 12; 2 Chr. 24.
kills Zechariah. 2 Chr. 24. 17.
slain by his servants. 2 Kin. 12. 20; 2 Chr. 24. 23.
JOATHAM, jo'-ath-am, Greek form of Jotham. Matt. 1. 9.
JOB, jobe, (1) a desert, Gen. 46. 13; (2) one persecuted.
his character, Job 1. 1, 8; 2. 3 (Ezek. 14. 14, 20).
his afflictions and patience. Job 1. 13, 20; 2. 7, 10 (James 5. 11).
complains of his life. Job 3.
reproves his friends. Job 6; 7; 9; 10; 12—14; 16; 17; 19; 21; 23; 24; 26—30.
solemnly protests his integrity. Job 31.
humbles himself. Job 40. 3; 42. 1.
God accepts and doubly blesses. Job 42. 10.
JOBAB, jo'-bab, a desert. Gen. 10. 29.
JOCHEBED, jo'-ke-bed, Jehovah is glorious (?). mother of Moses. Ex. 6. 20; Num. 26. 59.
JOED, jo'-ed, for whom Jehovah is witness. Neh. 11. 7.
JOEL, jo'-el, Jehovah is might.
delivers God's judgments. Joel 1—3.
proclaims a fast, and declares God's mercy. Joel 1. 14; 2. 12; 3.
quoted. Acts 2. 16.
JOELAH, jo'-el-ah, He helps (?). 1 Chr. 12. 7.
JOEZER, jo'-e-zer, Jehovah is help. 1 Chr. 12. 6.
JOGBEHAH, jog'-be-hah, lofty. Num. 32. 35.
JOGLI, jo'-gli, an exile. Num. 34. 22.
JOHA, jo'-hah, Jehovah lives (?). 1 Chr. 8. 16.

JOHANAN, jo-ha'-nan, Jehovah is gracious. 2 Kin. 25. 23; Jer. 40. 8, 15; 41. 11; 42; 43.
JOHN, English way of spelling Johanan. Matt. 3. 1.
the APOSTLE, called, Matt. 4. 21; Mark 1. 19; Luke 5. 10.
ordained. Matt. 10. 2; Mark 3. 17.
enquires of Jesus. Mark 13. 3.
reproved. Matt. 20. 20; Mark 10. 35—40; Luke 9. 50.
sent to prepare the passover. Luke 22. 8.
declares the divinity and humanity of Jesus Christ. John 1; 1 John 1; 4; 5.
Christ's love for. John 13. 23; 19. 26; 21. 7, 20, 24.
his care for Mary the Lord's mother. John 19. 27.
meets for prayer. Acts 1. 13.
accompanies Peter before the council. Acts 3; 4.
exhorts to obedience, and warns against false teachers. 1 John 1—5.
sees Christ's glory in heaven. Rev. 1. 13.
writes the Revelation. Rev. 1. 19.
forbidden to worship the angel. Rev. 19. 10; 22. 8.
—— (MARK). Acts 12. 12, 25. *See* MARK.
—— the BAPTIST, his coming foretold. Is. 40. 3; Mal. 4. 5; Luke 1. 17.
his birth and circumcision. Luke 1. 57.
office, preaching, and baptism. Matt. 3; Mark 1; Luke 3; John 1. 6; 3. 26; Acts 1. 5; 13. 24.
baptizes Christ. Matt. 3; Mark 1; Luke 3; John 1. 32; 3. 23.
imprisoned by Herod, Matt. 4. 12; Mark 1. 14; Luke 3. 20; and beheaded, Matt. 14; Mark 6. 14.
sends his disciples to Christ. Matt. 11. 1; Luke 7. 18.
Christ's testimony to. Matt. 11. 11, 14; 17. 12; Mark 9. 11; Luke 7. 27.
his disciples receive the Holy Ghost. Acts 18. 24; 19. 1.
JOIADA, jo'-ya-dah, Jehovah knows. Neh. 12. 10.
JOIAKIM, jo'-ya-kim, shortened from Jehoiakim. Neh. 12. 10.
JOIARIB, jo'-ya-rib, whom Jehovah defends. Ezra 8. 16.
JOKIM, jo'-kim, shortened from Jehoiakim. 1 Chr. 4. 22.
JOKDEAM, jok'-de-am, burning of the people. Josh. 15. 56.
JOKMEAM, jok'-me-am. 1 Chr. 6. 68.
JOKNEAM, jok'-ne-am, possessed by the people. Josh. 12. 22.
JOKSHAN, jok'-shan, fowler. Gen. 25. 2.
JOKTAN, jok'-tan, small. Gen. 10. 25.
JOKTHEEL, jok'-the-el, subdued by God. Josh. 15. 38.
JONA, jo'-nah, a Greek way of spelling Johanan. John 1. 42.
JONADAB, jo'-na-dab, same as JEHONADAB. 2 Sam. 13. 3.
—— (Jehonadab), son of Rechab. 2 Kin. 10. 15.
JONAH, jo'-nah, dove.
prophet. 2 Kin. 14. 25.
his disobedience, punishment, prayer, and repentance. Jonah 1—4.
a type of Christ. Matt. 12. 39; Luke 11. 29.
JONAN, jo'-nan, contracted from JOHANAN. Luke 3. 30.
JONAS, jo'-nas, (1) same as JONA. John 21. 15. (2) Or JONAH. Matt. 12. 39.
JONATH-ELEM-RECHOKIM, jo'-nath-e'-lem-re-ko-kim', the silent dove afar off. Title of Ps. 56.
JONATHAN, jo'-na-than, whom Jehovah gave.
son of Saul, smites the Philistines. 1 Sam. 13. 2; 14.
his love for David. 1 Sam. 18. 1; 19; 20; 23. 16.
slain by the Philistines. 1 Sam. 31. 2.
David's lamentation for. 2 Sam. 1. 17.
—— son of Abiathar. 2 Sam. 15. 27; 1 Kin. 1. 42.
—— one of David's nephews, his deeds. 2 Sam 21. 21; 1 Chr. 20. 7.
—— a Levite, hired by Micah. Judg. 17. 7; 18.
JOPPA, jop'-ah, beauty (?).
(Jaffa). 2 Chr. 2. 16; Jonah 1. 3.
Tabitha raised at, Acts 9. 36.

JOPPA—*cont.*
Peter dwells at, Acts 10. 5; 11. 5.
JORAH, jo'-rah, watering (?). Ezra 2. 18.
JORAI, jo'-rai, archer (?). 1 Chr. 5. 13.
JORAM, jo'-ram, same as JEHORAM. 2 Sam. 8. 10.
JORDAN, jor'-dan, flowing down. Gen. 13. 10.
river, waters of, divided for the Israelites. Josh. 3; 4; Ps. 114. 3; by Elijah and Elisha, 2 Kin. 2. 8, 13.
Naaman's leprosy cured at. 2 Kin. 5. 10.
John baptizes there. Matt. 3; Mark 1. 5; Luke 3. 3. *See* Job 40. 23; Ps. 42. 6; Jer. 12. 5; 49. 19; Zech. 11. 3.
JORIM, jo'-rim, a form of JORAM (?). Luke 3. 29.
JORKOAM, jor'-ko-am, spreading of the people (?). 1 Chr. 2. 44.
JOSABAD, jo'-sa-bad, same as JEHOZABAD. 1 Chr. 12. 4.
JOSAPHAT, jo'-saf-at, Greek form of Jehoshaphat. Matt. 1. 8.
JOSEDECH, jo'-se-dek, same as JEHOZADAK. Hag. 1. 1.
JOSEPH, jo'-sef, he shall add.
son of Jacob. Gen. 30. 24. *See* Ps. 105. 17; Acts 7. 9; Heb. 11. 22.
his dreams, and the jealousy of his brethren. Gen. 37. 5.
sold to the Ishmeelites. Gen. 37. 28.
slave to Potiphar. Gen. 39.
resists Potiphar's wife. Gen. 39. 7.
interprets the dreams of Pharaoh's servants, Gen. 40; and of Pharaoh, predicting famine, Gen. 41. 25.
made ruler of Egypt. Gen. 41. 39.
prepares for the famine. Gen. 41. 48.
receives his brethren and father. Gen. 42—46.
gives direction concerning his bones. Gen. 50. 25.
his death. Gen. 50. 26.
—— son of Heli, husband of the Virgin. Matt. 1. 19; 2. 13, 19; Luke 1. 27; 2. 4.
—— of Arimathæa. Matt. 27. 57; Mark 15. 42; Luke 23. 50; John 19. 38.
—— (Barsabas), Justus. Acts 1. 23.
JOSES, jo'-ses. Matt. 13. 55.
JOSIAH, jo'-shah, Jehovah presents (?). 1 Chr. 4. 34.
JOSHAPHAT, jo'-sha-fat, shortened from Jehoshaphat. 1 Chr. 11. 43.
JOSHAVIAH, jo'-shav-i'-ah, same as JOSIAH. 1 Chr. 11. 46.
JOSHBEKASHAH, josh'-be-ka'-shah, seat of hardship (?). 1 Chr. 25. 4.
JOSHUA, josh'-you-ah, Jehovah is salvation. Num. 14. 6.
(Hoshea, Oshea, Jehoshua, Jeshua, and Jesus), son of Nun. 1 Chr. 7. 27; Heb. 4. 8.
discomfits Amalek. Ex. 17. 9.
ministers to Moses. Ex. 24. 13; 32. 17; 33. 11.
spies out Canaan. Num. 13. 16.
ordained to succeed Moses. Num. 27. 18; 34. 17; Deut. 1. 38; 3. 28; 34. 9.
reassured by God. Josh. 1.
harangues his officers. Josh. 1. 10.
crosses river Jordan. Josh. 3.
erects memorial pillars. Josh. 4.
re-enacts circumcision. Josh. 5.
assaults and destroys Jericho. Josh. 6.
condemns Achan. Josh. 7.
subdues Ai. Josh. 8.
his victories. Josh. 10—12.
apportions the land. Josh. 14—21; Heb. 4. 8.
his charge to the Reubenites. Josh. 22.
exhortation to the people. Josh. 23.
reminds them of God's mercies. Josh. 24.
renews the covenant. Josh. 24. 14.
his death. Josh. 24. 29; Judg. 2. 8.
his curse, Josh. 6. 26; fulfilled, 1 Kin. 16. 34.
JOSIAH, jo-si'-ah, whom Jehovah heals. 2 Kin. 21. 24.
prophecy concerning, 1 Kin. 13. 2; fulfilled, 2 Kin. 23. 15.
reigns well. 2 Kin. 22.

JOSIAH—*cont.*
repairs the temple. 2 Kin. 22. 3.
hears the words of the book of the law. 2 Kin. 22. 8.
Huldah's message from God to him. 2 Kin. 22. 15.
ordains the reading of the book. 2 Kin. 23.
keeps a signal passover to the Lord. 2 Chr. 35.
slain by Pharaoh-nechoh at Megiddo. 2 Kin. 23. 29.
JOSIAS, jo-si'-as, Greek form of Josiah. Matt. 1. 10.
JOSIBIAH, jos'-ib-i'-ah, to whom God gives a dwelling. 1 Chr. 4. 35.
JOSIPHIAH, jos'-if-i'-ah, whom Jehovah will increase. Ezra 8. 10.
JOTBAH, jot'-bah, pleasantness (?). 2 Kin. 21. 19.
JOTBATH, jot'-bath, same as JOTBAH. Deut. 10. 7.
JOTBATHAH, jot-bah'-thah, same as JOTBAH. Num. 33. 33.
JOTHAM, jo'-tham, Jehovah is upright. Judg. 9. 5.
son of Gideon, his apologue. Judg. 9. 7.
—— king of Judah. 2 Kin. 15. 32; 2 Chr. 27.
JOZABAD, jo'-za-bad, same as JEHOZABAD. 1 Chr. 12. 20.
JOZACHAR, jo'-za-kar, whom Jehovah has remembered. 2 Kin. 12. 21.
JOZADAK, jo'-za-dak, same as JEHOZADAK. Ezra 3. 2.
JUBAL, joo'-bal, music (?).
inventor of harp and organ. Gen. 4. 21.
JUCAL, joo'-kal, same as JEHUCAL. Jer. 38. 1.
JUDA, joo'-dah, same as JUDAH. Luke 3. 30.
JUDAH, joo'-dah, praised.
son of Jacob. Gen. 29. 35.
his descendants. Gen. 38; 46. 12; Num. 1. 26; 26. 19; 1 Chr. 2—4.
pledges himself for Benjamin. Gen. 43. 3.
his interview with Joseph. Gen. 44. 18;—46. 28.
blessed by Jacob. Gen. 49. 8.
—— tribe of, their blessing by Moses. Deut. 33. 7.
their inheritance. Josh. 15.
they make David king, 2 Sam. 2. 4; and adhere to his house, 1 Kin. 12; 2 Chr. 10; 11. *See* JEWS.
JUDAS, joo'-das, Greek form of Judah. Matt. 10. 4.
(JUDE, Lebbæus, Thaddæus), APOSTLE, brother of James. Matt. 10. 3; Mark 3. 18; Luke 6. 16; Acts 1. 13.
his question to our Lord. John 14. 22.
enjoins perseverance. Jude 3, 20.
denounces false disciples. Jude 4.
—— the Lord's brother. Matt. 13. 55; Mark 6. 3.
—— (Barsabas). Acts 15. 22.
—— ISCARIOT. Matt. 10. 4; Mark 3. 19; Luke 6. 16; John 6. 70.
betrays Jesus. Matt. 26. 14, 47; Mark 14. 10, 43; Luke 22. 3, 47; John 13. 26; 18. 2.
hangs himself. Matt. 27. 5 (Acts 1. 18).
JUDE, jood, abbreviated from Judas. Jude 1.
JUDEA, joo-de'-ah (land of Judah). Ezra 5. 8.
JUDITH, joo'-dith (probably from the same). Gen. 26. 34.
JULIA, joo'-li-ah, *feminine* form of Julius. Rom. 16. 15.
JULIUS, joo'-li-us, downy. Acts 27. 1.
JUNIA, joo'-ni-ah.
saluted by Paul. Rom. 16. 7.
JUPITER, joo'-pit-er.
Barnabas addressed as. Acts 14. 12;—19. 35.
JUSHAB-HESED, joo'-shab-he'-sed, whose love is returned. 1 Chr. 3. 20.
JUSTUS, just'-us, upright. Acts 1. 23.
JUTTAH, joot'-ah, extended. Josh. 15. 55.

KABZEEL, kab'-ze-el, God has gathered, Josh. 15. 21.
KADESH, ka'-desh, consecrated. Gen. 20. 1.
KADESH-BARNEA, ka'-desh-bar'-ne-ah. Num. 34. 4.
Israelites murmur against Moses and Aaron, threaten to stone Caleb and Joshua, and provoke God's anger. Num. 13; 14; Deut. 1. 19; Josh. 14. 6.
KADMIEL, kad'-mi-el, eternity of God (?). Ezra 2. 40.
KADMONITES, kad'-mon-ites, Orientals. Gen. 15. 19.

KALLAI, kal'-ai, swift. Neh. 12. 20.
KANAH, ka'-nah, a place of reeds. Josh. 19. 28.
KAREAH, ka-re'-ah, bald. Jer. 40. 8.
KARKAA, kar-ka'-ah, floor. Josh. 15. 3.
KARKOR, kar'-kor, plain (?). Judg. 8. 10.
KARNAIM, kar-na'-im, two horns. Gen. 14. 5.
KARTAH, kar'-tah, city. Josh. 21. 34.
KARTAN, kar'-tan, double city. Josh. 21. 32.
KATTATH, kat'-ath, small (?). Josh. 19. 15.
KEDAR, ke'-dar, black-skinned.
  son of Ishmael. Gen. 25. 13; 1 Chr. 1. 29; Ps. 120. 5; Cant. 1. 5; Jer. 2. 10; Ezek. 27. 21.
  —— tribe of, prophecies concerning. Is. 21. 16; 42. 11; 60. 7; Jer. 49. 28.
KEDEMAH, ke-de'-mah, eastward. Gen. 25. 15.
KEDEMOTH, ke-de'-moth, eastern parts. Josh. 13. 18.
KEDESH, ke'-desh, sanctuary. Josh. 12. 22.
KEDRON (Kidron, Cedron), ke'-dron, brook and ravine, near garden of Gethsemane, frequented by our Lord. John 18. 1.
  crossed by David. 2 Sam. 15. 23.
  idols destroyed there. 1 Kin. 15. 13; 2 Kin. 23. 6; 2 Chr. 29. 16; Jer. 31. 40. *See* KIDRON.
KEHELATHAH, ke-he-lah'-thah, assembly. Num. 33. 22.
KEILAH, ke-ee'-lah, sling (?). Josh. 15. 44.
  David there. 1 Sam. 23. 1, 12.
KELAIAH, ke-lai'-ah, contempt (?). Ezra 10. 23.
KELITA, ke-li'-tah, dwarf. Neh. 8. 7.
KEMUEL, ke-moo'-el, congregation of God. Gen. 22. 21.
KENAN, ke'-nan, smith (?). 1 Chr. 1. 2.
KENATH, ke'-nath, possession. Num. 32. 42.
KENAZ, ke'-naz, hunting. Gen. 36. 11.
KENEZITE, ke'-nez-ite, descendant of Kenaz. Num. 32. 12.
KENITES, keen'-ites, descendants of an unknown man named Kain. Gen. 15. 19.
  their fate foretold. Num. 24. 22.
KENIZZITES, ke'-niz-ites, same as KENEZITE. Gen. 15. 19.
KEREN-HAPPUCH, ke'-ren-hap'-ook, horn of paint, one of Job's daughters. Job 42. 14.
KERIOTH, ke-ri'-oth, cities.
  a city of Judah. Josh. 15. 25; Jer. 48. 24, 41; Amos 2. 2.
KEROS, ke'-ros, crook (?). Ezra 2. 44.
KETURAH, ke-too'-rah, incense.
  Abraham's wife, Gen. 25; her children, 1 Chr. 1. 32.
KEZIA, ke-zi'-ah, cassia. Job 42. 14.
KEZIZ, ke'-ziz, cut off. Josh. 18. 21.
KIBROTH - HATTAAVAH, kib' - roth - hat - ta' - a - vah, graves of lust. Num. 11. 34.
KIBZAIM, kib-za'-im, two heaps. Josh. 21. 22.
KIDRON, kid'-ron, turbid. 2 Sam. 15. 23.
KINAH, ki'-nah, song of mourning, lamentation. Josh. 15. 22.
KIR, kir, town, 2 Kin. 16. 9; Is. 15. 1; 22. 6; Amos 1. 5; 9. 7.
KIR-HARASETH, kir'-ha-ras'-eth, brick-town. 2 Kin. 3. 25; Is. 16. 7, 11.
KIR-HARESETH, kir'-ha-res'-eth, same as preceding. Is. 16. 7.
KIR-HARESH, kir-har'-esh, same as preceding. Is. 16. 11.
KIR-HERES, kir-her'-es, same as preceding. Jer. 48. 31.
KIRIATHAIM, kir'-yath-a'-im, same as KIRJATH-AIM. Ezek. 25. 9.
KIRIOTH, ki-ri'-oth, cities. Amos 2. 2.
KIRJATH, kir'-jath, city (?). Josh. 18. 28.
KIRJATHAIM, kir'-jath-a'-im, double city. Num. 32. 37.
KIRJATH-ARBA, kir'-jath-ar'-bah, city of Arba. Gen. 23. 2.
KIRJATH-ARIM, kir'-jath-ar'-im, contracted from KIRJATH-JEARIM. Ezra 2. 25.
KIRJATH-BAAL, kir'-jath-ba'-al, city of Baal. Josh. 15. 60.
KIRJATH-HUZOTH, kir'-jath-hooz'-oth, c. of streets. Num. 22. 39.

KIRJATH-JEARIM, kir'-jath-je'-ar-im, c. of woods. Josh. 9. 17; 18. 14; 1 Chr. 13. 6.
  the ark brought to. 1 Sam. 7. 1.
  ark fetched from. 1 Chr. 13. 5; 2 Chr. 1. 4.
KIRJATH-SANNAH, kir'-jath-san'-ah, c. of thorns. Josh. 15. 49.
KIRJATH-SEPHER, kir'-jath-se'-fer, book-city. Josh. 15. 15.
KISH, kish, bow.
  Saul's father. 1 Sam. 9. 1.
KISHI, kish'-i, bow of Jehovah. 1 Chr. 6. 44.
KISHION, kish'-i-on, hardness. Josh. 19. 20.
KISHON, ki'-shon, tortuous.
  waters of Megiddo. Judg. 4. 7; 5. 21; 1 Kin. 18. 40.
KISON, ki'-son, same as KISHON. Ps. 83. 9.
KITHLISH, kith'-lish, fortified. Josh. 15. 40.
KITRON, kit'-ron, burning. Judg. 1. 30.
KITTIM, kit'-im, same as CHITTIM. Gen. 10. 4.
KOA, ko'-ah, prince. Ezek. 23. 23.
KOHATH, ko'-hath, assembly.
  son of Levi. Gen. 46. 11.
  his descendants. Ex. 6. 18; 1 Chr. 6. 2.
  their duties. Num. 4. 15; 10. 21; 2 Chr. 29. 12; 34. 12.
KOHATHITES, ko'-hath-ites, descendants of Kohath. Num. 3. 27.
KOLAIAH, kol-ai'-ah, voice of Jehovah (?). Neh. 11. 7.
KORAH, ko'-rah, bald.
  Dathan, &c., their sedition and punishment. Num. 13; 26. 9; 27. 3.
  (Core), Jude 11.
KORAHITES, ko'-rah-ites, descendants of Korah. 1 Chr. 9. 19.
KORATHITES, ko'-rath-ites, same as preceding. Num. 26. 58.
KORE, ko'-re, partridge. 1 Chr. 9. 19.
KORHITE, kor'-ite, same as KORATHITE. 2 Chr. 20. 19.
KOZ, thorn. Ezra 2. 61.
KUSHAIAH, kush-ai'-ah, longer form of Kishi. 1 Chr. 15. 17.

LAADAH, la'-ad-ah, order (?). 1 Chr. 4. 21.
LAADAN, la'-ad-an, put in order (?). 1 Chr. 7. 26.
LABAN, la'-ban, white.
  hospitality of. Gen. 24. 29.
  gives Jacob his two daughters. Gen. 29.
  envies and oppresses him. Gen. 30. 27; 31. 1.
  his dream. Gen. 31. 24.
  his covenant with Jacob. Gen. 31. 43.
LACHISH, la'-kish, impregnable. Josh. 10. 3.
  conquered. Josh. 10. 31; 12. 11.
  Amaziah slain at. 2 Kin. 14. 19.
LAEL, la'-el, (devoted) to God. Num. 3. 24.
LAHAD, la'-had, oppression. 1 Chr. 4. 2.
LAHAI-ROI, la-hai-ro'-i, to the living is sight Gen. 24. 62.
LAHMAM, lah'-mam. Josh. 15. 40.
LAHMI, lah'-mi, warrior. 1 Chr. 20. 5.
LAISH, la'-ish, lion. 1 Sam. 25. 44.
  taken. Judg. 18. 14.
LAKUM, la'-koom, fort (?). Josh. 19. 33.
LAMA, lam'-ah, why? Matt. 27. 46.
LAMECH, la'-mek, destroyer.
  descendant of Cain. Gen. 4. 18.
  —— father of Noah. Gen. 5. 25, 29.
LAODICEA, la'-od-i-se'-ah. Col. 2. 1.
LAODICEANS, la'-od-i-se'-ans, inhabitants of La odicea. Rev. 1. 11; 3. 14.
  Paul's epistle to, Col. 4. 16.
LAPIDOTH, la'-pid-oth, torches. Judg. 4. 4.
LASEA, la-se'-ah. Acts 27. 8.
LASHA, la'-shah, fissure. Gen. 10. 19.
LASHARON, la-sha'-ron, of the plain. Josh. 12. 18.
LATIN, lat'-in, the language spoken by Roman John 19. 20.
LAZARUS, laz'-ar-us, Greek form of Eleazar. Luk 16. 20.
  and the rich man. Luke 16. 19.

LAZARUS, brother of Mary and Martha, raised from the dead. John 11; 12. 1.

LEAH, le'-ah, languid. Gen. 29. 16, 31; 30. 17; 31. 4; 33. 2; 49. 31. *See* Ruth 4. 11.

LEBANAH, le-bah'-nah, white. Ezra 2. 45.

LEBANON, leb'-an-on, the white (mountain). Deut. 1. 7.

—— forest and mountain. Deut. 3. 25; Judg. 3. 3; 1 Kin. 5. 14.

—— its cedars. 2 Kin. 14. 9; 2 Chr. 2. 8; Ps. 92. 12; Cant. 3. 9; Is. 40. 16; Hos. 14. 5.

LEBAOTH, le-ba'-oth, lionesses. Josh. 15. 32.

LEBBÆUS, leb-e'-us. Matt. 10. 3. *See* JUDE.

LEBONAH, leb-o'-nah, frankincense. Judg. 21. 19.

LECAH, le'-kah, journey (?). 1 Chr. 4. 21.

LEHABIM, le-hah'-bim. Gen. 10. 13.

LEHI, le'-hi, jaw-bone. Judg. 15. 9.

LEMUEL, lem'-oo-el, (devoted) to God (?).

—— king, his lesson. Prov. 31. 1.

LESHEM, le'-shem, precious stone. Josh. 19. 47.

LETUSHIM, le-toosh'-im, the hammered. Gen. 25. 3.

LEUMMIM, le-oom'-im, peoples. Gen. 25. 3.

LEVI, le'-vi, associate (?).

—— son of Jacob. Gen. 29. 34.

—— avenges Dinah. Gen. 34. 25; 49. 5.

—— *See* MATTHEW.

LEVIATHAN, le-vi'-a-than, a water monster. Ps. 104. 26.

LEVITES, le'-vites, descendants of Levi, mentioned. Ex. 6. 25; 32. 26.

—— their service. Ex. 38. 21.

—— appointed over the tabernacle. Num. 1. 47.

—— their divisions, Gershonites, Kohathites, Merarites. Num. 3.

—— duties of. Num. 3. 23; 4; 8. 23; 18.

—— their consecration. Num. 8. 5.

—— inheritance of. Num. 35; Deut. 18; Josh. 21.

—— not to be forsaken. Deut. 12. 19; 14. 27.

—— their genealogies. 1 Chr. 6; 9.

—— charged with the temple service. 1 Chr. 23—27.

—— twenty-four courses, instituted by David, 1 Chr. 23. 6; re-divided by Ezra, Ezra 6. 18.

—— their sin censured. Mal. 1. 2; Ezek. 22. 26.

LEVITICUS, le-vit'-ic-us, the book which treats of the affairs of the Levitical law.

LIBERTINES, lib'-ert-ines, freedmen. Acts 6. 9.

LIBNAH, lib'-nah, whiteness. Num. 33. 20.

—— subdued. Josh. 10. 29; 21. 13.

—— rebels. 2 Kin. 8. 22.

—— attacked by Assyrians. 2 Kin. 19. 8; Is. 37. 8.

LIBNI, lib'-ni, white. Ex. 6. 17.

LIBNITES, lib'-nites, descendants of Libni. Num. 3. 21.

LIBYA, lib'-yah. Jer. 46. 9; Ezek. 30. 5; Dan. 11. 43; Acts 2. 10.

LIKHI, lik'-hi, fond of learning (?). 1 Chr. 7. 19.

LINUS, li'-nus, flax. 2 Tim. 4. 21.

LO-AMMI, lo-am'-i, not my people. Hos. 1. 9.

LOD, lode, strife (?). 1 Chr. 8. 12.

LO-DEBAR, lo'-de-bar, without pasture (?). 2 Sam. 9. 4.

LOIS, lo'-is. 2 Tim. 1. 5.

LO-RUHAMAH, lo-ru-hah'-mah, not having obtained mercy. Hos. 1. 6.

LOT, veil. Gen. 11. 27.

—— (Abram's nephew), separates from Abram. Gen. 13. 10.

—— captured by four kings, and rescued by Abram. Gen. 14.

—— entertains angel visitors. Gen. 19. 1.

—— saved from Sodom. Gen. 19. 16; 2 Pet. 2. 7.

—— his wife turned into a pillar of salt. Gen. 19. 26; Luke 17. 28, 32.

LOTAN, lo'-tan, veiling. Gen. 36. 20.

LUBIMS, loob'-ims, same as LEHABIM. 2 Chr. 12. 3.

LUCAS, loo'-kas, same as LUKE. Phil. 24.

LUCIFER, loo'-sif-er, light-bearer. Is. 14. 12.

LUCIUS, loosh'-yus, a noble (?).

—— of Cyrene, a teacher. Acts 13. 1; Rom. 16. 21.

LUD, lood, strife (?). Gen. 10. 22.

LUDIM, lood'-im. Gen. 10. 13.

LUHITH, loo'-hith, abounding in boards. Is. 15. 5.

LUKE, of or belonging to Lucania.

—— the beloved physician, companion of Paul. Col. 4. 14; 2 Tim. 4. 11; Phil. 24 (Acts 16. 12; 20. 5).

LUZ, looz, almond tree. Gen. 28. 19.

LYCAONIA, li'-ka-o'-ni-ah. Acts 14. 6.

LYCIA, lish'-yah. Acts 27. 5.

LYDDA, lid'-dah, Greek form of LOD (?).

—— miracle at. Acts 9. 32.

LYDIA, lid'-yah.

—— of Thyatira, piety of. Acts 16. 14, 40.

LYSANIAS, li-sa'-ni-as, ending sorrow. Luke 3. 1.

LYSIAS, lis'-yas, a person of Lysia. Acts 23. 26.

LYSTRA, lis'-trah. Acts 14. 6.

—— miracle at. Acts 14. 8.

—— Paul and Barnabas taken for gods at. Acts 14. 11.

—— Paul stoned at, by Jews. Acts 14. 19.

MAACAH, ma'-ak-ah (same as MAACHAH). 2 Sam. 3. 3.

MAACHAH, ma'-ak-ah, royal (?). 1 Kin. 2. 39.

—— queen, her idolatry. 1 Kin. 15. 13; 2 Chr. 15. 16.

MAACHATHI, ma'-a-chah'-thi, an inhabitant of Maachah. Deut. 3. 14.

MAACHATHITES, ma-ak'-ath-ites, plural of preceding. Josh. 12. 5.

MAADAI, ma'-a-dai, adorned. Ezra 10. 34.

MAADIAH, ma'-ad-i'-ah, ornament of Jehovah. Neh. 12. 5.

MAAI, ma'-ai, compassionate (?). Neh. 12. 36.

MAALEH-ACRABBIM, ma'-al-eh-ak'-rab-im, ascent of scorpions. Josh. 15. 3.

MAARATH, ma'-ar-ath, a treeless place. Josh. 15. 59.

MAASEIAH, ma'-as-i'-ah, work of Jehovah. Ezra 10. 18.

MAASIAI, ma'-as-i-ai, same as AMASHAI (?). 1 Chr. 9. 12.

MAATH, ma'-ath, small (?). Luke 3. 26.

MAAZ, ma'-az, wrath. 1 Chr. 2. 27.

MAAZIAH, ma'-az-i'-ah. 1 Chr. 24. 18.

MACEDONIA, mas'-ed-o'-ni-ah.

—— Paul's mission there. Acts 16. 9; 17.

—— liberality of. 2 Cor. 8; 9; 11. 9; Phil. 4. 15.

—— its churches. 1 & 2 Thess.

MACHBANAI, mak-ban'-ai, cloak. 1 Chr. 12. 13.

MACHBENAH, mak'-be-nah', clad with a cloak (?). 1 Chr. 2. 49.

MACHI, ma'-ki. Num. 13. 15.

MACHIR, ma'-kir, sold. Gen. 50. 23.

MACHIRITES, ma'-kir-ites, the descendants of Machir. Num. 26. 29.

MACHNADEBAI, mak-nad'-eb-ai. Ezra 10. 40.

MACHPELAH, mak-pe'-lah, a doubling. Gen. 23. 9.

—— field of. Gen. 23.

—— patriarchs buried there. Gen. 23. 19; 25. 9; 35. 29; 49. 30; 50. 12.

MADAI, ma'-dai. Gen. 10. 2.

MADIAN, ma'-di-an, Greek form of MIDIAN. Acts 7. 29.

MADMANNAH, mad-man'-ah, dunghill. Josh. 15. 31.

MADMEN, mad'-men, dungheap. Jer. 48. 2.

MADMENAH, mad-may'-nah, same as MADMEN. Is. 10. 31.

MADON, ma'-don, place of contention. Josh. 11. 1.

MAGBISH, mag'-bish, congregating. Ezra 2. 30.

MAGDALA, mag'-dal-ah, tower. Matt. 15. 39.

MAGDALENE, mag'-dal-e'-ne, inhabitant of Magdala. Matt. 27. 56.

MAGDIEL, mag'-di-el, praise of God. Gen. 36. 43.

MAGOG, ma'-gog. Gen. 10. 2.

MAGOR-MISSABIB, ma'-gor-mis'-a-bib, fear round about. Jer. 20. 3.

MAGPIASH, mag'-pi-ash. Neh. 10. 20.

MAHALAH, mah'-hal-ah, disease. 1 Chr. 7. 18.

MAHALALEEL, ma'-ha-lal'-e-el, praise of God. Gen. 5. 12.

MAHALATH, mah'-al-ath, a musical instrument. Gen. 28. 9.

MAHALATH LEANNOTH, m. le-an-oth'. Ps. 88, title.

MAHALI, ma'-ha-li, weak. Ex. 6. 19.

MAHANAIM, ma'-han-a'-im, two camps. Gen. 32. 2.
Jacob's vision at. Gen. 32.
Ish-bosheth made king at. 2 Sam. 2. 8.
David takes refuge from Absalom at. 2 Sam.
17. 24.
MAHANEH-DAN, ma'-han-e-dan', camp of Dan.
Judg. 18. 12.
MAHARAI, ma'-ha-rai, impetuous. 2 Sam. 23. 28.
MAHATH, ma'-hath, taking hold (?). 1 Chr. 6. 35.
MAHAVITE, ma'-hav-ite. 1 Chr. 11. 46.
MAHAZIOTH, ma-haz'-i-oth, visions. 1 Chr. 25. 4.
MAHER-SHALAL-HASH-BAZ, ma'-her-sha'-lal-hash'-
baz, the spoil hastens, the prey speeds. Is. 8. 1.
MAHLAH, mah'-lah, same as MAHALAH. Num. 26.
33.
MAHLI, mah'-li, same as MAHALI. 1 Chr. 6. 19.
MAHLITES, mah'-lites, the descendants of Mahli.
Num. 3. 33.
MAHLON, mah'-lon, a sick person.
and Chilion die in Moab. Ruth 1. 2.
MAHOL, ma'-hol, a dance. 1 Kin. 4. 31.
MAKAZ, ma'-kaz, end (?). 1 Kin. 4. 9.
MAKHELOTH, mak'-hel-oth, assemblies. Num. 33.25.
MAKKEDAH, mak'-ed-ah, place of shepherds (?).
Josh. 10. 10.
cave of, five kings hide in. Josh. 10. 16.
MAKTESH, mak'-tesh, a mortar. Zeph. 1. 11.
MALACHI, mal'-ak-i, the messenger of Jehovah.
deplores and reproves Israel's ingratitude. Mal.
1; 2.
foretells the Messiah and His messenger. Mal.
3; 4.
MALCHAM, mal'-kam, their king. 1 Chr. 8. 9.
MALCHIAH, malk-i'-ah, Jehovah's king. 1 Chr. 6.
40.
MALCHIEL, malk'-i-el, God's king. Gen. 46. 17.
MALCHIELITES, malk'-i-el-ites, the descendants of
Malchiel. Num. 26. 45.
MALCHIJAH, malk-i'-jah, same as MALCHIAH. 1
Chr. 9. 12.
MALCHIRAM, malk-i'-ram, king of height (?). 1
Chr. 3. 18.
MALCHI-SHUA, malk'-i-shoo'-ah, king of aid. 1
Chr. 8. 33.
MALCHUS, mal'-kus, Greek form of Malluch. John
18. 10.
wounded by Peter. John 18. 10; Matt. 26. 51;
Mark 14. 47.
healed by Jesus. Luke 22. 51.
MALELEEL, ma'-le-le-el', same as MAHALALEEL.
Luke 3. 37.
MALLOTHI, mal-o'-thi. 1 Chr. 25. 4.
MALLUCH, mal'-ook, counsellor. 1 Chr. 6. 44.
MAMMON, mam'-on, fulness.
worship of. Matt. 6. 24; Luke 16. 9.
MAMRE, mam'-re, fatness.
Abram dwells there. Gen. 13. 18; 14; 18; 23.
17; 35. 27.
MANAEN, ma-na'-en, Greek form of Menahem.
Acts 13. 1.
MANAHATH, ma-na'-hath, rest. Gen. 36. 23.
MANAHETHITES, ma-na'-heth-ites, inhabitants of
Manahath (?). 1 Chr. 2. 52.
MANASSEH, ma-nas'-ay, one who causes to forget.
firstborn son of Joseph. Gen. 41. 51.
his blessing. Gen. 48.
his descendants numbered, &c. Num. 1. 34; 26.
29; Josh. 22. 1; 1 Chr. 5. 23; 7. 14.
their inheritance. Num. 32. 33; 34. 14; Josh.
13. 29; 17.
incline to David's cause. 1 Chr. 9. 3; 12. 19; 2
Chr. 15. 9; 30. 11.
—— king of Judah, his reign. 2 Kin. 21; 2
Chr. 33.
MANASSES, ma-nas'-es, Greek form of Manasseh.
Matt. 1. 10.
MANASSITES, ma-nas'-ites, members of the tribe
of Manasseh. Deut. 4. 43.
MANEH, ma'-ne, a weight. Ezek. 45. 12.
MANOAH, ma-no'-ah, rest.
(father of Samson). Judg. 13; 16. 31.

MAOCH, ma'-ok, oppressed (?). 1 Sam. 27. 2.
MAON, ma'-on, habitation. Josh. 15. 55.
MAONITES, ma'-on-ites. Judg. 10. 12.
MARA, ma'-rah, sad. Ruth 1. 20.
MARAH, ma'-rah, bitter.
bitter waters healed there. Ex. 15. 23.
MARALAH, mar'-al-ah, trembling. Josh. 19. 11.
MARANATHA, ma'-ran-ah'-thah, our lord cometh.
1 Cor. 16. 22.
MARCUS, mar'-kus. Col. 4. 10.
MARESHAH, ma-resh'-ah, capital. Josh. 15. 44.
MARK, English form of Marcus.
EVANGELIST. Acts 12. 12.
goes with Paul and Barnabas. Acts 12. 25; 13. 5.
leaves them at Perga. Acts 13. 13.
contention about him. Acts 15. 37.
approved by Paul. 2 Tim. 4. 11.
MAROTH, mar'-oth, bitterness. Mic. 1. 12.
MARS' HILL, English of Areopagus. Acts 17. 22.
MARSENA, mar'-se-nah. Esth. 1. 14.
MARTHA, mar'-thah, lady.
instructed by Christ. John 11. 5, 21.
reproved by Him. Luke 10. 38.
MARY, Greek form of Miriam. Matt. 1. 16.
the VIRGIN, mother of Jesus, visited by the angel
Gabriel. Luke 1. 26.
believes, and magnifies the Lord. Luke 1. 38,
46; John 2. 5.
Christ born of. Matt. 1. 18; Luke 2.
witnesses the miracle at Cana. John 2. 1.
desires to speak with Christ. Matt. 12. 46; Mark
3. 31; Luke 8. 19.
commended to John by Christ at His crucifixion.
Matt. 27. 56; John 19. 25.
MARY MAGDALENE. Luke 8. 2.
at the cross. Matt. 27. 56; Mark 15. 40; John
19. 25.
Christ appears first to. Matt. 28. 1; Mark 16.
1; Luke 24. 10; John 20. 1.
—— sister of Lazarus, commended. Luke 10.
42.
Christ's love for. John 11. 5, 33.
anoints Christ's feet, John 12. 3; (head), Matt.
26. 6; Mark 14. 3.
MARYS, THE THREE, at the cross. John 19. 25.
MASCHIL, mas'-kil, understanding. Ps. 53, title.
MASH. Gen. 10. 23.
MASHAL, ma'-shal, entreaty (?). 1 Chr. 6. 74.
MASREKAH, mas-rek'-ah, vineyard. Gen. 36. 36.
MASSA, mas'-ah, burden. Gen. 25. 14.
MASSAH, mas'-ah, temptation.
the rebellion at. Ex. 17. 7; Deut. 9. 22; 33. 8.
MATHUSALA, ma-thoo'-sa-lah, Greek form of Me-
thuselah. Luke 3. 37.
MATRED, ma'-tred, pushing forward. Gen. 36. 39.
MATRI, ma'-tri, rainy. 1 Sam. 10. 21.
MATTAN, mat'-an, a gift.
slain. 2 Kin. 11. 18; 2 Chr. 23. 17.
MATTANAH, mat'-an-ah, same as preceding. Num.
21. 18.
MATTANIAH, mat'-an-i'-ah, gift of Jehovah. 2 Kin
24. 17.
MATTATHA, mat'-ath-ah, a Greek form of above.
Luke 3. 31.
MATTATHAH, mat'-ath-ah, gift of Jehovah. Ezra
10. 33.
MATTATHIAS, mat'-ath-i'-as, a Greek form of the
preceding. Luke 3. 26.
MATTENAI, mat'-en-ai, liberal. Ezra 10. 33.
MATTHAN, mat'-than, gift. Matt. 1. 15.
MATTHAT, mat'-that, another form of Matthan.
Luke 3. 24.
MATTHEW, English way of spelling Mattathiah.
(Levi). APOSTLE and EVANGELIST, called. Matt
9. 9; Mark 2. 14; Luke 5. 27.
sent out. Matt. 10. 3; Mark 3. 18; Luke 6. 15;—
Acts 1. 13.
MATTHIAS, math-i'-as, another Greek form o
Mattathias, apostle. Acts 1. 23; 26.
MATTITHIAH, mat-ith-i'-ah, another form of Mat
tathias. 1 Chr. 9. 31.

MAZZAROTH, maz'-ar-oth, the signs of the zodiac. Job 38. 32.

MEAH, me'-ah, a hundred. Neh. 3. 1.

MEARAH, me-ar'-ah, cave. Josh. 13. 4.

MEBUNNAI, me-boon'-ai, built (?). 2 Sam. 23. 27.

MECHERATHITE, me-ker'-ath-ite, inhabitant of Mecherah (?). 1 Chr. 11. 36.

MEDAD, me'-dad.
   prophesies. Num. 11. 26.

MEDAN, me'-dan, contention. Gen. 25. 2.

MEDEBA, me'-deb-ah, flowing water (?). Num. 21. 30.

MEDES, inhabitants of Media. 2 Kin. 17. 6.
   capture Babylon (Is. 21. 2). Dan. 5. 28, 31.

MEDIA, me'-di-ah, Greek form of Madai. Esth. 1. 3.
   Israel taken captive to. 2 Kin. 17. 6; 18. 11; Esth. 2. 6.
   Daniel's prophecy of. Dan. 8. 20.

MEGIDDO, me-gid'-o, place of troops. Josh. 12. 21; 17. 11; Judg. 1. 27; 5. 19.
   Ahaziah and Josiah slain there. 2 Kin. 9. 27; 23. 29; Zech. 12. 11.

MEGIDDON, me-gid'-on, same as preceding. Zech. 12. 11.

MEHETABEEL, me-het'-ab-e'-el, lengthened form of the following. Neh. 6. 10.

MEHETABEL, me-het'-ab-el, God makes happy. Gen. 36. 39.

MEHIDA, me-hi'-dah. Ezra 2. 52.

MEHIR, me'-hir, price. 1 Chr. 4. 11.

MEHOLATHITE, me-ho'-lath-ite, native of Meholah. 1 Sam. 18. 19.

MEHUJAEL, me-hoo'-ja-el, struck by God. Gen. 4. 18.

MEHUMAN, me-hoo'-man. Esth. 1. 10.

MEHUNIM, me-hoon'-im. Ezra 2. 50.

MEHUNIMS, me-hoon'-ims, the people of Maon (?). 2 Chr. 26. 7.

ME-JARKON, me'-jar'-kon, waters of yellowness. Josh. 19. 46.

MEKONAH, me-ko'-nah, a base. Neh. 11. 28.

MELATIAH, mel'-at-i'-ah, whom Jehovah freed. Neh. 3. 7.

MELCHI, melk'-i, Greek form of Melchiah. Luke 3. 24.

MELCHIAH, melk-i'-ah, Jehovah's king. Jer. 21. 1.

MELCHISEDEC, melk-is'-ed-ek, Greek form of Melchizedek. Heb. 5. 6.

MELCHI-SHUA, melk'-i-shoo'-ah, same as MALCHI-SHUA. 1 Sam. 14. 49.

MELCHIZEDEK, melk-iz'-ed-ek, king of righteousness.
   king of Salem, blesses Abram. Gen. 14. 18.
   his priesthood and Aaron's. Ps. 110. 4; Heb. 5. 6, 10; 6. 20; 7. 1.

MELEA, mel'-e-ah, fulness (?). Luke 3. 31.

MELECH, mel'-ech, king. 1 Chr. 8. 35.

MELICU, me-lee'-koo, same as MALLUCH. Neh. 12. 14.

MELITA, mel'-it-ah.
   Paul shipwrecked near, and lands at, Acts 28. 1; received kindly by the people, Acts 28. 2; shakes off the viper at, Acts 28. 5; heals Publius' father and others at, Acts 28.

MELZAR, mel'-zar, steward.
   favours Daniel. Dan. 1. 11.

MEMPHIS, mem'-fis, in Egypt. Hos. 9. 6.

MEMUCAN, me-moo'-kan. Esth. 1. 14.

MENAHEM, me-na'-hem, comforter.
   king of Israel, his evil rule. 2 Kin. 15. 14, 18.

MENAN, me'-nan. Luke 3. 31.

MENE, me'-ne, numbered.

MENE, TEKEL, UPHARSIN. Dan. 5. 25—28.

MEONENIM, me-o'-nen-im. Judg. 9. 37.

MEONOTHAI, me-o'-no-thai', my habitations. 1 Chr. 4. 14.

MEPHAATH, me-fa'-ath, beauty. Josh. 13. 18.

MEPHIBOSHETH, mef-ib'-osh-eth, destroying shame.
   son of Jonathan, his lameness. 2 Sam. 4. 4.
   cherished by David. 2 Sam. 9. 1.
   slandered by Ziba. 2 Sam. 16. 1; 19. 24.
   spared by David. 2 Sam. 21. 7.

MERAB, me'-rab, increase.
   Saul's daughter. 1 Sam. 14. 49; 18. 17.
   her five sons hanged by the Gibeonites. 2 Sam. 21. 8.

MERAIAH, me-rai'-ah, contumacy. Neh. 12. 12.

MERAIOTH, me-rai'-oth, rebellions. 1 Chr. 6. 6.

MERARI, me-rah'-ri, bitter. Gen. 46. 11.

MERARITES, descendants of Levi. Ex. 6. 19; 1 Chr. 6. 1; 23. 21; 24. 26.
   their duties and dwellings. Num. 4. 29; 7. 8; 10. 17; Josh. 21. 7; 1 Chr. 6. 63.

MERATHAIM, mer'-ath-a'-im, rebellions. Jer. 50. 21.

MERCURIUS, mer-ku'-ri-us.
   Paul so called. Acts 14. 12.

MERED, me'-red, rebellion. 1 Chr. 4. 17.

MEREMOTH, mer-e'-moth, elevations. Ezra 8. 33.

MERES, me'-res, worthy (?). Esth. 1. 14.

MERIBAH, me-ree'-bah, water of strife.
   Israel rebels there. Ex. 17. 7; Num. 20. 13; 27. 14; Deut. 32. 51; 33. 8; Ps. 81. 7.

MERIB-BAAL, me'-rib-ba'-al, contender (?) against Baal. 1 Chr. 8. 34.

MERODACH, me'-ro-dak. Jer. 50. 2.

MERODACH-BALADAN, me'-ro-dak-bal'-a-dan, Merodach gives a son.
   (or Berodach) BALADAN, sends messengers to Hezekiah. 2 Kin. 20. 12; 2 Chr. 32. 31; Is. 39; —Jer. 50. 2.

MEROM, me'-rom, a high place.
   waters of. Josh. 11. 5.

MERONOTHITE, me-ro'-noth-ite, an inhabitant of Meronoth. 1 Chr. 27. 30.

MEROZ, me'-roz, refuge (?).
   cursed. Judg. 5. 23.

MESECH, me'-sech, same as MESHECH. Ps. 120. 5.

MESHA, me'-shah, deliverance. 2 Kin. 3. 4.

MESHACH, me'-shak. Dan. 1. 7. *See* SHADRACH.

MESHECH, me'-shek, tall (?).
   son of Japheth. Gen. 10. 2.
   traders of, Ezek. 27. 13; 32. 26; 38. 2; 39. 1.

MESHELEMIAH, me-shel'-em-i'-ah, Jehovah repays. 1 Chr. 9. 21.

MESHEZABEEL, me-she'-zab-el, God delivers. Neh. 3. 4.

MESHILLEMITH, me-shil'-em-ith, recompense. 1 Chr. 9. 12.

MESHILLEMOTH, me-shil'-em-oth, retribution. 2 Chr. 28. 12.

MESHOBAB, me-sho'-bab, brought back. 1 Chr. 4. 34.

MESHULLAM, me-shool'-am, friend. 2 Kin. 22. 3.

MESHULLEMETH, me-shool-e'-meth, feminine of preceding. 2 Kin 21. 19.

MESOBAITE, me-so'-ba-ite, inhabitant of Mesoba (?). 1 Chr. 11. 47.

MESOPOTAMIA, mes'-o-pot-a'-mi-ah, amidst the rivers. (Ur), country of the two rivers.
   Abram leaves. Gen. 11. 31; 12. 1; 24. 4, 10. *See* Acts 2. 9; 7. 2.
   king of, slain by Othniel. Judg. 3. 8.

MESSIAH, mes-i'-ah, anointed (anointed CHRIST).
   Prince, prophecy about. Dan. 9. 25.

MESSIAS, mes-i'-as, Greek form of the above. John 1. 41; 4. 25. *See* Is. 9. 6.

METHEG-AMMAH, me'-theg-am'-ah, bridle of Ammah. 2 Sam. 8. 1.

METHUSAEL, me-thoo'-sa-el, man of God. Gen. 4. 18.

METHUSELAH, me-thoo'-se-lah, man of the dart (?). Gen. 5. 21.
   his great age. Gen. 5. 27.

MEUNIM, me-oon'-im, same as MEHUNIM. Neh. 7. 52.

MEZAHAB, me'-za-hab, water of gold. Gen. 36. 39.

MIAMIN, mi'-ya-min, on the right hand. Ezra 10. 25.

MIBHAR, mib'-har, choicest. 1 Chr. 11. 38.

MIBSAM, mib'-sam, sweet odour. Gen. 25. 13.

MIBZAR, mib'-zar, a fortress. Gen. 36. 42.

MICAH, mi'-kah, who (is) like unto Jehovah? Judg. 17. 1.
   makes and worships idols. Judg. 17; 18.

MICAH, prophet (Jer. 26. 18); denounces Israel's sin. Mic. 1—3; 6; 7.
predicts the Messiah. Mic. 4; 5; 7.
MICAIAH, mi-kai'-ah, fuller form of Micah.
foreswarns Ahab. 1 Kin. 22; 2 Chr. 18.
MICHAEL, mi'-ka-el, who (is) like unto God?
Dan. 10. 13, 21; 12. 1.
Archangel. Jude 9; Rev. 12. 7.
MICHAH, mi'-kah, same as MICAH. 1 Chr. 24. 24.
MICHAIAH, mi-kai'-ah, same as MICAIAH. Neh. 12. 35.
MICHAL, mi'-kal, brook. 1 Sam. 14. 49.
David's wife, 1 Sam. 18. 20.
given to another. 1 Sam. 25. 44.
restored to David. 2 Sam. 3. 13.
mocks his religious dancing, and is rebuked. 2 Sam. 6, 16, 20; 1 Chr. 15. 29.
MICHMAS, mik'-mas, later form of Michmash. Ezra 2. 27.
MICHMASH, mik'-mash, treasured. 1 Sam. 13. 2.
MICHMETHAH, mik'-meth-ah, hiding place (?). Josh. 16. 6.
MICHRI, mik'-ri, precious (?). 1 Chr. 9. 8.
MICHTAM, mik'-tam, writing (?). Ps. 16, title.
MIDDIN, mid'-in, extensions. Josh. 15. 61.
MIDIAN, mid'-yan, strife. Gen. 25. 2.
sons of. Gen. 25. 4.
——— land of. Ex. 2. 15. *See* 1 Kin. 11. 18; Is. 60. 6; Hab. 3. 7.
MIDIANITES, mid'-yan-ites, people of Midian. Gen. 37. 28.
their cities destroyed by Moses. Num. 31. 1.
subdued by Gideon. Judg. 6—8. *See* Ps. 83. 9; Is. 9. 4; 10. 26.
MIGDAL-EL, mig'-dal-el, tower of God. Josh. 19. 38.
MIGDAL-GAD, mig'-dal-gad, tower of Gad. Josh. 15. 37.
MIGDOL, mig'-dol. Ex. 14. 2.
MIGRON, mig'-ron, a precipice. Is. 10. 28.
MIJAMIN, mi'-ja-min, same as MIAMIN. 1 Chr. 24. 9.
MIKLOTH, mik'-loth, staves, lots. 1 Chr. 8. 32.
MIKNEIAH, mik-ni'-ah, possession of Jehovah. 1 Chr. 15. 18.
MILALAI, mil'-al-ai, eloquent (?). Neh. 12. 36.
MILCAH, mil'-kah, counsel (?). Gen. 11. 29; 22. 20.
MILCOM, mil'-kom, same as MOLOCH.
false god. 1 Kin. 11. 5, 33; 2 Kin. 23. 13.
MILETUM, mi-le'-tum, improper form of MILETUS. 2 Tim. 4. 20.
MILETUS, mi-le'-tus.
Paul takes leave of elders at, Acts 20. 15.
Trophimus left at, 2 Tim. 4. 20.
MILLO, mil'-o, a mound.
house of, Judg. 9. 6; 1 Sam. 5. 9.
MINIAMIN, min'-ya-min, full form of Miamin. 2 Chr. 31. 15.
MINNI, min'-i, Armenia. Jer. 51. 27.
MINNITH, min'-ith, allotment. Judg. 11. 33.
MIPHKAD, mif'-kad, place of meeting. Neh. 3. 31.
MIRIAM, mir'-yam, rebellion (?).
sister of Moses and Aaron. Ex. 15. 20; Num. 26. 59.
song of. Ex. 15. 20, 21.
murmurs against Moses. Num. 12. 1, 2.
is smitten with leprosy, and shut out of the camp. Num. 12. 10, 15.
her death. Num. 20. 1.
MIRMA, mir'-mah, fraud. 1 Chr. 8. 10.
MISGAB, mis'-gab, height. Jer. 48. 1.
MISHAEL, mish'-a-el, who is what God is? Ex. 6. 22.
MISHAL, mi'-shal, prayer. Josh. 21. 30.
MISHEAL, mi'-she-al, same as MISHAL. Josh. 19. 26.
MISHAM, mi'-sham, cleansing. 1 Chr. 8. 12.
MISHMA, mish'-mah, report. Gen. 25. 14.
MISHMANNAH, mish-man'-ah, fatness. 1 Chr. 12. 10.
MISHRAITES, mish'-ra-ites. 1 Chr. 2. 53.
MISPERETH, mis-per'-eth, number. Neh. 7. 7.
MISREPHOTH-MAIM, mis'-re-foth-ma'-im, burning of waters. Josh. 11. 8.
MITHCAH, mith'-kah, place of sweetness. Num. 33. 28.

MITHNITE, mith'-nite. 1 Chr. 11. 43.
MITHREDATH, mith'-re-dath, given by Mithra. Ezra 1. 8.
MITYLENE, mit'-il-e'-ne. Acts 20. 14.
MIZAR, mi'-zar, smallness. Ps. 42. 6.
MIZPAH, miz'-pah (Gilead), a look out.
Jacob and Laban meet at. Gen. 31. 49.
Jephthah at, Judg. 10. 17; 11. 11; 20. 1.
Samuel at, 1 Sam. 7. 5.
——— (Moab). 1 Sam. 22. 3.
MIZPAR, miz'-par, number. Ezra 2. 2.
MIZPEH, miz'-peh, watch-tower. Josh. 11. 3.
MIZRAIM, miz-ra'-im, fortresses. Gen. 10. 6.
MIZZAH, miz'-ah. Gen. 36. 13.
MNASON, na'-son, an old disciple. Acts 21. 16.
MOAB, mo'-ab, progeny of a father, Gen. 19. 37.
his descendants, and territory, Deut. 2. 9, 18; 34. 5.
MOABITES, mo'-ab-ites, people of Moab. Deut. 2. 9.
excluded from the congregation. Deut. 23. 3.
conquered by Ehud, Judg. 3. 12; by David, 2 Sam. 8. 2; by Jehoshaphat and Jehoram, 2 Kin. 1. 1; 3.
their overthrow. 2 Chr. 20. 23.
prophecies concerning. Ex. 15. 15; Num. 21. 29; 24. 17; Ps. 60. 8; 83. 6; Is. 11. 14; 15; 16; 25. 10; Jer. 9. 26; 25. 21; 48; Ezek. 25. 8; Amos 2. 1; Zeph. 2. 8.
MOABITESS, mo'-ab-ite-ess, a lady of Moab. Ruth 4. 5.
MOADIAH, mo'-ad-i'-ah, festival of Jehovah. Neh. 12. 17.
MOLADAH, mo-la'-dah, birth. Josh. 15. 26.
MOLECH, mo'-lek, English form for Moloch, Lev. 18. 21; 20. 2.
worship of. 1 Kin. 11. 7; 2 Kin. 23. 10; Jer. 32. 35; Amos 5. 26; Acts 7. 43.
MOLOCH, mo'-lok, king. Amos 5. 26.
MOLID, mo'-lid, begetter. 1 Chr. 2. 29.
MORASTHITE, mo'-rasth-ite, native of Moresheth. Jer. 26. 18.
MORDECAI, mor'-dek-ai, worshipper of Merodach (?). Esth. 2. 5.
reveals conspiracy against king Ahasuerus. Esth. 2. 21.
is hated by Haman. Esth. 3. 5.
honoured by the king. Esth. 6.
advanced. Esth. 8—10 (Ezra 2. 2; Neh. 7. 7).
MOREH, mo'-reh, archer. Gen. 12. 6.
MORESHETH-GATH, mo-resh'-eth-gath', the possession of Gath. Mic. 1. 14.
MORIAH, mor-i'-ah, provided by Jehovah. Gen. 22. 2.
mount. Gen. 22.
David's sacrifice there. 2 Sam. 24. 18; 1 Chr. 21. 18; 22. 1.
temple built on. 2 Chr. 3. 1.
MOSERA, mo-se'-rah, bond. Deut. 10. 6.
MOSEROTH, mo-se'-roth, bonds. Num. 33. 30.
MOSES, mo'-zes, saved from the water.
born, and hidden. Ex. 2 (Acts 7. 20; Heb. 11. 23).
escapes to Midian. Ex. 2. 15.
revelation from God. Ex. 3; confirmed by signs, Ex. 4.
returns to Egypt. Ex. 4. 20.
intercedes with Pharaoh for Israel. Ex. 5—12.
leads Israel forth. Ex. 14.
meets God in mount Sinai. Ex. 19. 3 (24. 18).
brings the law to the people. Ex. 19. 25; 20—23; 34. 10; 35. 1; Lev. 1; Num. 5; 6; 15; 27—30; 36; Deut. 12—26.
instructed to build the tabernacle. Ex. 25—31; 35; 40; Num. 4; 8—10; 18; 19.
his grief at Israel's idolatry. Ex. 32. 19.
his intercession. Ex. 32. 11 (33. 12).
again meets God in the mount. Ex. 34. 2.
skin of his face shines. Ex. 34. 29 (2 Cor. 3. 7, 13)
sets apart Aaron. Lev. 8; 9.
numbers the people. Num. 1; 26.
sends out the spies to Canaan. Num. 13.
intercedes for the murmuring people. Num. 14. 13

MOSES—*cont.*
Korah's sedition against. Num. 16.
for his unbelief suffered not to enter Canaan. Num. 20. 12; 27. 12; Deut. 1. 35; 3. 23.
his government of Israel in the wilderness. Num. 20; 21.
makes the brazen serpent. Num. 21. 9 (John 3. 14).
recounts Israel's history, and exhorts to obedience. Deut. 1; 3—12; 27—31.
his charge to Joshua. Deut. 3. 28; 31. 7, 23.
his death, Deut. 34. 5; his body, Jude 9.
seen at Christ's transfiguration. Matt. 17. 3; Mark 9. 4; Luke 9. 30.
his meekness, Num. 12. 3; dignity, Deut. 34. 10; faithfulness, Num. 12. 7; Heb. 3. 2.
MOZA, mo'-zah, fountain. 1 Chr. 2. 46.
MOZAH, mo'-zah, same as MOZA. Josh. 18. 26.
MUPPIM, moop'-im, probably written for Shupham. Gen. 46. 21.
MUSHI, moo'-shi, withdrawn. Ex. 6. 19.
MUTH-LABBEN, mooth'-la-ben', death to the son (?). Ps. 9, title.
MYRA, mi'-rah, balsam. Acts 27. 5.
MYSIA, mish'-yah. Acts 16. 7.

NAAM, na'-am, pleasantness. 1 Chr. 4. 15.
NAAMAH, na'-am-ah, pleasant. Gen. 4. 22.
NAAMAN, na'-am-an, pleasantness. 2 Kin. 5. 1.
the Syrian, his anger. 2 Kin. 5. 11.
his leprosy healed. 2 Kin. 5. 14.
his request. 2 Kin. 5. 17. *See* Luke 4. 27.
NAAMATHITE, na-am'-ath-ite. Job 2. 11.
NAAMITES, na'-am-ites, descendants of Naaman. Num. 26. 40.
NAARAH, na'-ar-ah, a girl. 1 Chr. 4. 5.
NAARAI, na'-ar-ai, youthful. 1 Chr. 11. 37.
NAARAN, na'-ar-an, same as NAARAH. 1 Chr. 7. 28.
NAARATH, na'-ar-ath, to Naarah. Josh. 16. 7.
NAASHON, na'-ash-on, enchanter. Ex. 6. 23.
NAASSON, na-as'-on, Greek form of NAASHON. Matt. 1. 4.
NABAL, na'-bal, foolish. 1 Sam. 25. 3.
conduct to David. 1 Sam. 25. 10.
Abigail intercedes for. 1 Sam. 25. 18.
his death. 1 Sam. 25. 38.
NABOTH, na'-both, fruits (?).
slain by Jezebel. 1 Kin. 21.
his murder avenged. 2 Kin. 9. 21.
NACHON, na'-kon, prepared. 2 Sam. 6. 6.
NACHOR, na'-kor, snorting. Josh. 24. 2.
NADAB, na'-dab, liberal. Ex. 6. 23.
son of Aaron, offers strange fire. Lev. 10. 1, 2.
—— king of Israel, slain by Baasha. 1 Kin. 14. 20; 15. 25, 28.
NAGGE, nag'-e, Greek form of Nogah. Luke 3. 25.
NAHALAL, na'-hal-al, a pasture. Josh. 21. 35.
NAHALIEL, na-hal'-i-el, valley of God. Num. 21. 19.
NAHALLAL, na'-hal-al, same as NAHALAL. Josh. 19. 15.
NAHALOL, na'-hal-ol, same as preceding. Judg. 1. 30.
NAHAM, na'-ham, consolation. 1 Chr. 4. 19.
NAHAMANI, na'-ham-a'-ni, comforter. Neh. 7. 7.
NAHARAI, na'-ha-rai, one who snores. 1 Chr. 11. 39.
NAHARI, na'-har-i, same as preceding. 2 Sam. 23. 37.
NAHASH, na'-hash, serpent.
the Ammonite, invades Jabesh-Gilead. 1 Sam. 11.
NAHATH, na'-hath, descent. Gen. 36. 13.
NAHBI, nah'-bi, hidden. Num. 13. 14.
NAHOR, na'-hor, another way of spelling Nachor. Gen. 11. 22.
Abram's brother. Gen. 11. 26; 22. 20; 24. 10.
NAHSHON, nah'-shon, same as NAASHON. Num. 1. 7.
NAHUM, na'-hoom, comforter.
vision of. Nah. 1. 1—3.
NAIN, na'-in, pasture.
miracle at. Luke 7. 11.
NAIOTH, nai'-oth, habitations. 1 Sam. 19. 18.
school of prophets. 1 Sam. 19. 23 : 20. 1.
NAOMI, na'-om-i, pleasant. Ruth 1. 2.

NAPHISH, na'-fish, cheerful. Gen. 25. 15.
NAPHTALI, naf'-tal-i, my wrestling.
son of Jacob. Gen. 30. 8; 35. 25; 46. 24; 49. 21; Deut. 33. 23.
—— tribe of, numbered. Num. 1. 42; 10. 27; 13. 14; 26. 48; Judg. 1. 33.
subdue the Canaanites. Judg. 4. 10; 5. 18; 6. 35; 7. 23.
carried captive. 2 Kin. 15. 29. *See* Is. 9. 1; Matt. 4. 13.
NAPHTUHIM, naf'-too-him. Gen. 10. 13.
NARCISSUS, nar-sis'-us, benumbing.
household of. Rom. 16. 11.
NATHAN, na'-than, gift.
the prophet. 2 Sam. 7.
shews David his sin. 2 Sam. 12. 1.
anoints Solomon king. 1 Kin. 1. 34; 1 Chr. 29. 22.
—— book of. 2 Chr. 9. 29.
—— son of David. 2 Sam. 5. 14; Zech. 12. 12; Luke 3. 31.
NATHANAEL, na-than'-a-el, gift of God.
"Israelite indeed." John 1. 45; 21. 2.
NATHAN-MELECH, na'-than-me'-lek, gift of the king. 2 Kin. 23. 11.
NAUM, na'-oom, same as NAHUM. Luke 3. 25.
NAZARENE, naz'-ar-een', a native of Nazareth. Acts 24. 5.
NAZARETH, naz'-ar-eth, branch. Luke 1. 26.
Jesus of. Matt. 2. 23; 21. 11; Luke 1. 26; 2. 39, 51; 4. 16; John 1. 45; 18. 5; Acts 2. 22; 3. 6.
NAZARITE, naz'-ar-ite, one separated. Num. 6. 2.
NAZARITES, law of the. Num. 6.
NEAH, ne'-ah, of a slope. Josh. 19. 13.
NEAPOLIS, ne-a'-po-lis, new city. Acts 16. 11.
NEARIAH, ne'-ar-i'-ah, servant of Jehovah. 1 Chr. 3. 22.
NEBAI, ne'-bai, fruitful. Neh. 10. 19.
NEBAIOTH, ne-bai'-oth, high places. 1 Chr. 1. 29.
NEBAJOTH, ne-ba'-joth, same as NEBAIOTH. Gen. 25. 13.
NEBALLAT, ne-bal'-at. Neh. 11. 34.
NEBAT, ne'-bat, aspect. 1 Kin. 11. 26.
NEBO, ne'-bo, a lofty place. Deut. 32. 49.
NEBUCHADNEZZAR, neb'-u-kad-nez'-ar, another way of spelling the following. 2 Kin. 24. 1.
king of Babylon. Jer. 20; 21; 25; 27; 28; 32; 34; Ezek. 26. 7; 29. 19.
captures Jerusalem. 2 Kin. 24; 25; 2 Chr. 36; Jer. 37—39; 52; Dan. 1. 1.
his dreams. Dan. 2; 4.
sets up the golden image. Dan. 3.
his madness. Dan. 4. 33.
his restoration and confession. Dan. 4. 34.
NEBUCHADREZZAR, neb'-u-kad-rez'-ar, Nebo protect the landmark. Jer. 21. 2.
NEBUSHASBAN, neb'-u-shas'-ban, Nebo will save me. Jer. 39. 13.
NEBUZAR-ADAN, neb'-u-zar'-a-dan', Nebo gives posterity. 2 Kin. 25. 8.
his care of Jeremiah. Jer. 39. 11; 40. 1.
NECHO, ne'-ko, conqueror (?). Jer. 46. 2.
NECHOH, same as NECHO. 2 Kin. 23. 29.
NEDABIAH, ned'-ab-i'-ah, Jehovah is bountiful (?) 1 Chr. 3. 18.
NEGINAH, neg-een'-ah, a stringed instrument. Ps. 61, title.
NEGINOTH, neg-een'-oth, stringed instruments. Ps. 4; 54; 55; 76; 77, title.
NEGO, ne'-go, same as NEBO. Dan. 1. 7.
NEHELAMITE, ne-he-lam'-ite. Jer. 29. 24.
NEHEMIAH, ne'-hem-i'-ah, Jehovah comforts.
his grief for Jerusalem. Neh. 1.
his prayer for. Neh. 1. 5.
his visit to. Neh. 2. 3, 9, 17.
his conduct at. Neh. 4—6; 8—10; 13.
NEHILOTH, ne-hil'-oth, flutes. Ps. 5, title.
NEHUM, ne'-hoom, consolation. Neh. 7. 7.
NEHUSHTA, ne-hoosh'-tah, bronze. 2 Kin. 24. 8.
NEHUSHTAN, ne-hoosh'-tan, brazen.
the brazen serpent of Moses, idolatrously used by Israelites, so called by Hezekiah, and destroyed by him. 2 Kin. 18. 4.

NEIEL, ni'-el, moved by God. Josh. 19. 27.
NEKEB, ne'-keb, cavern. Josh. 19. 33.
NEKODA, ne-ko'-dah, a herdman. Ezra 2. 48.
NEMUEL, ne-moo'-el, same as JEMUEL (?). Num. 26. 9.
NEMUELITES, ne-moo'-el-ites, descendants of Ne-muel. Num. 26. 12.
NEPHEG, ne'-feg, sprout. Ex. 6. 21.
NEPHISH, ne'-fish, same as NAPHISH. 1 Chr. 5. 19.
NEPHISHESIM, ne-fish'-es-im, expansions. Neh. 7. 52.
NEPHTHALIM, nef'-tal-im, Greek form of Naphtali. Matt. 4. 13.
NEPHTOAH, nef-to'-ah, opened. Josh. 15. 9.
NEPHUSIM, ne-foos'-im, a better form for Nephi-shesim. Ezra 2. 50.
NER, light. 1 Sam. 14. 50.
NEREUS, ne'-roos, liquid (?). Rom. 16. 15.
NERGAL, ner'-gal, lion. 2 Kin. 17. 30.
NERGAL-SHAREZER, ner'-gal-shar-e'-zer, Nergal protect the king. Jer. 39. 3.
NERI, ne'-ri, Greek form of Neriah. Luke 3. 27.
NERIAH, ner-i'-ah, lamp of Jehovah. Jer. 32. 12.
NETHANEEL, neth-an'-e-el, same as NATHANAEL. Num. 1. 8.
NETHANIAH, neth'-an-i'-ah, whom Jehovah gave. 2 Kin. 25. 23.
NETHINIMS, neth'-in-ims, the appointed. 1 Chr. 9. 2; Ezra 2. 43; 7. 7, 24; 8. 17; Neh. 10. 28.
NETOPHAH, ne-to'-phah, dropping. Ezra 2. 22.
NETOPHATHI, net-of'-ath-i, an inhabitant of Neto-phah. Neh. 12. 28.
NETOPHATHITE, net-of'-ath-ite, same as the pre-ceding. 2 Sam. 23. 28.
NEZIAH, ne-zi'-ah, illustrious. Ezra 2. 54.
NEZIB, ne'-zib, garrison. Josh. 15. 43.
NIBHAZ, nib'-haz. 2 Kin. 17. 31.
NIBSHAN, nib'-shan, level (?). Josh. 15. 62.
NICANOR, ni-ka'-nor, one of the seven deacons. Acts 6. 5.
NICODEMUS, nik'-o-de'-mus, Pharisee and ruler.
goes to Jesus by night. John 3. 1.
takes His part. John 7. 50.
assists at Christ's burial. John 19. 39.
NICOLAITANES, nik'-o-la'-it-ans, named after Nico-las. Rev. 2. 6.
NICOLAS, nik'-o-las. Acts 6. 5.
NICOPOLIS, nik-o'-pol-is, city of victory. Tit. 3. 12.
NIGER, ni'-ger, black. Acts 13. 1.
NIMRAH, nim'-rah, limpid (water). Num. 32. 3.
NIMRIM, nim'-rim, clear waters. Is. 15. 6.
NIMROD, nim'-rod, an inhabitant of Marad (?). Gen. 10. 8.
mighty hunter. Gen. 10. 9.
NIMSHI, nim'-shi, discloser (?). 1 Kin. 19. 16.
NINEVEH, nin'-ev-ay, dwelling (?). Gen. 10. 11.
Jonah's mission to. Jonah 1. 1; 3. 2.
denounced by Jonah. Jonah 3. 4.
repenting, is spared by God. Jonah 3. 5—10 (Matt. 12. 41; Luke 11. 32).
the burden of. Nah. 1. 1; 2; 3.
NINEVITES, nin'-ev-ites, inhabitants of Nineveh. Luke 11. 30.
NISAN, ni'-san, month. Neh. 2. 1; Esth. 3. 7.
NISROCH, nis'-rok, eagle (?). 2 Kin. 19. 37; Is. 37. 38.
NO, abode (?). Nah. 3. 8.
multitude of, threatened. Jer. 46. 25; Ezek. 30. 14.
NO AMON, no a'-mon, abode of Amon. Jer. 46. 25.
NOADIAH, no'-ad-i'-ah, whom Jehovah meets. Neh. 6. 14.
NOAH, no'-ah, (1) rest. Gen. 5. 29. (2) wandering. Num. 26. 33.
son of Lamech. Gen. 5. 29.
finds grace with God. Gen. 6. 8.
ordered to build the ark. Gen. 6. 14.
with his family and living creatures enters into the ark. Gen. 7.
flood assuaging, goes forth. Gen. 8. 18.

NOAH—*cont.*
God blesses and makes a covenant with. Gen. 9, 1, 8.
is drunken, and mocked of Ham. Gen. 9. 22.
his death. Gen. 9. 29.
NOB, nobe, high place.
city of, David comes to, and eats hallowed bread at. 1 Sam. 21. 1.
smitten by Saul. 1 Sam. 22. 19.
NOBAH, no'-bah, a barking. Num. 32. 42.
NOD, node, flight, wandering. Gen. 4. 16.
NODAB, no'-dab, nobility. 1 Chr. 5. 19.
NOE, no'-e, Greek form of Noah. Matt. 24. 37.
NOGAH, no'-gah, brightness. 1 Chr. 3. 7.
NOHAH, no'-hah, rest. 1 Chr. 8. 2.
NON, none, same as NUN. 1 Chr. 7. 27.
NOPH, nofe, same as MEMPHIS.
city, warned, Is. 19. 13; Jer. 2. 16; 46. 14; Ezek. 30. 13.
NOPHAH, no'-fah, windy. Num. 21. 30.
NUN, noon, fish. Ex. 33. 11.
NYMPHAS, nim'-fas, shortened form of Nymphodo-rus. Col. 4. 15.

OBADIAH, ob'-ad-i'-ah, worshipper of Jehovah. Obad. 1.
prophet, his prediction. Obad. 17.
—— Levite, porter in the temple. Neh. 12. 25.
—— sent by Ahab to find water. 1 Kin. 18. 3.
meets Elijah. 1 Kin. 18. 7.
how he hid a hundred prophets. 1 Kin. 18. 4, 13.
OBAL, o'-bal, hill (?). Gen. 10. 28.
OBED, o'-bed, worshipping (God). Ruth 4. 17.
OBED-EDOM, o'-bed-e'-dom, serving Edom.
prospered while taking charge of the ark. 2 Sam. 6. 10; 1 Chr. 13. 14; 15. 18, 24; 16. 5.
his sons, 1 Chr. 26. 4, 5.
OBIL, o'-bil, camel keeper. 1 Chr. 27. 30.
OBOTH, o'-both, bottles (of skin). Num. 21. 10.
OCRAN, ok'-ran, troublesome. Num. 1. 13.
ODED, o'-ded, setting up (?).
prophet. 2 Chr. 15. 1; 28. 9.
OG, circle (?).
king of Bashan. Num. 21. 33; Deut. 3. 1; Ps. 135. 11; 136. 20.
OHAD, o'-had, might. Gen. 46. 10.
OHEL, o'-hel, tent. 1 Chr. 3. 20.
OLIVET, ol'-iv-et, place of olives.
(Olives) mount. 2 Sam. 15. 30; Matt. 21. 1; 24. 3; Mark 11. 1; 13. 3; Luke 21. 37; John 8. 1; Acts 1. 12.
OLYMPAS, o-limp'-as, bright (?). Rom. 16. 15.
OMAR, o'-mar, talkative. Gen. 36. 11.
OMEGA, o'-meg-ah, great O. Rev. 1. 8, 11; 21. 6; 22. 13.
OMRI, om'-ri, like a sheaf (?).
king of Israel. 1 Kin. 16. 16, &c.; Mic. 6. 16.
ON, the sun. Gen. 41. 45.
ONAM, o'-nam, wealthy. Gen. 36. 23.
ONAN, o'-nan, strong. Gen. 38. 4.
ONESIMUS, o-ne'-sim-us, profitable. Col. 4. 9; Philem. 10.
ONESIPHORUS, o'-nes-if'-or-us, bringing profit. 2 Tim. 1. 16.
ONO, o'-no, strong. 1 Chr. 8. 12.
OPHEL, o'-fel, a hill. 2 Chr. 27. 3.
OPHIR, o'-feer.
gold of. Gen. 10. 29; 1 Kin. 9. 28; 10. 11; 22. 48; 1 Chr. 29. 4; 2 Chr. 8. 18; Job 22. 24; Ps. 45. 9; Is. 13. 12.
OPHNI, of'-ni, man of the hill. Josh. 18. 24.
OPHRAH, of'-rah, fawn. 1 Chr. 4. 14.
OREB, o'-reb, raven. Judg. 7. 25.
OREN, o'-ren, pine tree. 1 Chr. 2. 25.
ORION, o-ri'-on. Job 9. 9.
ORNAN, or'-nan (ARAUNAH). 2 Sam. 24. 16; 1 Chr. 21. 15.
ORPAH, orp'-ah, hind (?). Ruth 1. 4.
OSEE, o'-zee, same as HOSEA. Rom. 9. 25.
OSHEA, o-she'-ah, same as JOSHUA. Num. 13. 8.
OTHNI, oth'-ni, powerful (?). 1 Chr. 26. 7.

OTHNIEL, oth'-ni-el, powerful man of God. Josh. 15. 17; Judg. 1. 13; 3. 9.

OZEM, o'-zem, strength. 1 Chr. 2. 15.

OZIAS, o-zi'-as, Greek form of Uzziah. Matt. 1. 8.

OZNI, oz'-ni, hearing. Num. 26. 16.

OZNITES, oz'-nites, descendants of Ozni. Num. 26. 16.

PAARAI, pah'-a-rai, devoted to Peor (?). 2 Sam. 23. 35.

PADAN-ARAM, pa'-dan-a'-ram, the plain of Syria. Gen. 25. 20; 28. 2.

PADON, pa'-don, redemption. Ezra 2. 44.

PAGIEL, pag'-i-el, intervention of God. Num. 1. 13.

PAHATH-MOAB, pa'-hath-mo'-ab, governor of Moab. Ezra 2. 6.

PAI, pa'-i, bleating. 1 Chr. 1. 50.

PALAL, pa'-lal, judge. Neh. 3. 25.

PALESTINA, pal'-es-ti'-nah, land of strangers (?). predictions about. Ex. 15. 14; Is. 14. 29, 31.

PALLU, pal'-oo, distinguished. Ex. 6. 14.

PALLUITES, pal'-oo-ites, descendants of Pallu. Num. 26. 5.

PALTI, pal'-ti, deliverance of Jehovah. Num. 13. 9.

PALTIEL, pal'-ti-el, deliverance of God. Num. 34. 26.

PALTITE, palt'-ite, a descendant of Palti. 2 Sam. 23. 26.

PAMPHYLIA, pam-fil'-yah.
Paul preaches there. Acts 13. 13; 14. 24; 27. 5.

PAPHOS, pa'-fos.
Paul at. Acts 13. 6.
Elymas the sorcerer at. Acts 13. 8.

PARAH, pa'-rah, heifer. Josh. 18. 23.

PARAN, pa'-ran, cavernous.
mount. Gen. 21. 21; Num. 10. 12; 12. 16; 13. 26; Deut. 33. 2; Hab. 3. 3.

PARBAR, par'-bar, open apartment. 1 Chr. 26. 18.

PARMASHTA, par-mash'-tah, superior (?). Esth. 9. 9.

PARMENAS, par'-men-as, standing firm. Acts 6. 5.

PARNACH, par'-nak. Num. 34. 25.

PAROSH, pa'-rosh, flea. Ezra 2. 3.

PARSHANDATHA, par'-shan-da'-thah, given to Persia (?). Esth. 9. 7.

PARTHIANS, parth'-yans. Acts 2. 9.

PARUAH, par-oo'-ah, flourishing. 1 Kin. 4. 17.

PARVAIM, parv-a'-im, oriental regions (?). 2 Chr. 3. 6.

PASACH, pa'-sak, divider. 1 Chr. 7. 33.

PAS-DAMMIM, pas-dam'-im, shortened from Ephes-dammim. 1 Chr. 11. 13.

PASEAH, pa-se'-ah, lame. 1 Chr. 4. 12.

PASHUR, pash'-oor, prosperity round about.
his cruelty to Jeremiah. Jer. 20.

PATARA, pat'-ar-ah. Acts 21. 1.

PATHROS, path'-ros.
in Egypt. Is. 11. 11; Jer. 44. 1, 15; Ezek. 29. 14; 30. 14.

PATHRUSIM, path-roos'-im, people of Pathros. Gen. 10. 14.

PATMOS, pat'-mos.
place of St. John's exile. Rev. 1. 9.

PATROBAS, pat'-ro-bas. Rom. 16. 14.

PAU, pa'-oo, older form of Pai. Gen. 36. 39.

PAUL, or PAULUS, little. Acts 13. 9.
as a persecutor. Acts 7. 58; 8. 1; 9. 1; 22. 4; 26. 9; 1 Cor. 15. 9; Gal. 1. 13; Phil. 3. 6; 1 Tim. 1. 13.
as a convert to the Gospel. Acts 9. 3; 22. 6; 26. 12.
as a preacher. Acts 9. 19, 29; 13. 1, 4, 14; 17. 18 (2 Cor. 11. 32; Gal. 1. 17).
stoned at Lystra. Acts 14. 8, 19.
contends with Barnabas. Acts 15. 36.
is persecuted at Philippi. Acts 16.
the Holy Ghost given by his hands to John's disciples at Ephesus. Acts 19. 6.
restores Eutychus. Acts 20. 10.
his charge to the elders of Ephesus, at Miletus. Acts 20. 17.

PAUL—*cont.*
his return to Jerusalem, and persecution there. Acts 21.
his defence before the people and the council. Acts 22; 23.
before Felix. Acts 24; Festus, Acts 25; and Agrippa, Acts 26.
appeals to Cæsar at Rome. Acts 25.
his voyage and shipwreck. Acts 27.
miracles by, at Melita. Acts 28. 3, 8.
at Rome, reasons with the Jews. Acts 28. 17.
his love to the churches. Rom. 1. 8; 15; 1 Cor. 1. 4; 4. 14; 2 Cor. 1; 2; 6; 7; Phil. 1; Col. 1; 1 & 2 Thess.
his sufferings. 1 Cor. 4. 9; 2 Cor. 11. 23; 12. 7; Phil. 1. 12; 2 Tim. 3. 11.
divine revelations to. 2 Cor. 12. 1.
defends his apostleship. 1 Cor. 9; 2 Cor. 11; 12; 2 Tim. 3. 10.
commends Timothy, &c. 1 Cor. 16. 10; Phil. 2. 19; 1 Thess. 3. 2.
commends Titus. 2 Cor. 7. 13; 8. 23.
blames Peter. Gal. 2. 14.
pleads for Onesimus. Philem.
his epistles mentioned by St. Peter. 2 Pet. 3. 15.

PEDAHEL, pe-dah'-el, God redeemed. Num. 34. 28.

PEDAHZUR, pe-dah'-zoor, the Rock redeemed. Num. 1. 10.

PEDAIAH, pe-dah-i'-ah, whom Jehovah redeemed. 1 Chr. 27. 20.

PEKAH, pe'-kah, open-eyed.
king of Israel. 2 Kin. 15. 25.
his victory over Judah. 2 Chr. 28. 6.
denounced in prophecy. Is. 7. 1.

PEKAHIAH, pe'-kah-i'-ah, whose eyes Jehovah opened.
king of Israel. 2 Kin. 15. 22.

PEKOD, pe'-kod, visitation. Jer. 50. 21.

PELAIAH, pe-la'-yah, whom Jehovah made distinguished. 1 Chr. 3. 24.

PELALIAH, pe-lal-i'-ah, whom Jehovah judged. Neh. 11. 12.

PELATIAH, pe'-lat-i'-ah, whom Jehovah delivered. Ezek. 11. 1.

PELEG, pe'-leg, division. Gen. 10. 25.

PELET, pe'-let, liberation. 1 Chr. 2. 47.

PELETH, pe'-leth, swiftness. Num. 16. 1.

PELETHITES, pel'-eth-ites, runners. 2 Sam. 8. 18.

PELONITE, pel'-on-ite. 1 Chr. 11. 27.

PENIEL, pe-nee'-el, the face of God.
scene of Jacob's wrestling with an angel. Gen. 32. 30.
Gideon's vengeance upon, Judg. 8. 17.

PENINNAH, pe-nin'-ah, coral. 1 Sam. 1. 2. *See* HANNAH.

PENTECOST, pen'-te-kost, fiftieth.
(feast of weeks), how observed. Lev. 23. 15; Deut. 16. 9.
Holy Spirit given at. Acts 2.

PENUEL, pe-noo'-el, old form of Peniel. Gen. 32. 31.

PEOR, pe'-or, point.
(Baal), Num. 23. 28; 25. 3, 18; Josh. 22. 17.

PERAZIM, pe-raz'-im, breaches. Is. 28. 21.

PERES, pe'-res, divided. Dan. 5. 28.

PERESH, pe'-resh, distinction. 1 Chr. 7. 16.

PEREZ, pe'-rez, breach. 1 Chr. 27. 3.

PEREZ-UZZA, pe'-rez-uz'-ah, same as following. 1 Chr. 13. 11.

PEREZ-UZZAH, pe'-rez-uz'-ah, breach of Uzzah. 2 Sam. 6. 8.

PERGA, por' gah
visited by Paul. Acts 13. 13; 14. 25.

PERGAMOS, per'-ga-mos, citadel (?).
epistle to. Rev. 1. 11; 2. 12.

PERIDA, pe-ri'-dah, a recluse. Neh. 7. 57.

PERIZZITES, per'-iz-ites, belonging to a village. Gen. 13. 7; 15. 20; 34. 30; Judg. 1. 4; 2 Chr. 8. 7.

PERSIA, per'-shah.
kingdom of. 2 Chr. 36. 20; Esth. 1. 3; Ezek. 27. 10; 38. 5; Dan. 6.

PERSIA—*cont.*
prophecies concerning. Is. 21. 2; Dan. 5. 28; 8. 20; 10. 13; 11. 2.
PERSIAN, per'-shan, belonging to Persia. Dan. 6. 28.
PERSIS, per'-sis, a Persian woman.
the beloved. Rom. 16. 12.
PERUDA, pe-roo'-dah, same as PERIDA. Ezra 2. 55.
PETER, pe'-ter, a stone. Matt. 16. 18.
APOSTLE, called. Matt. 4. 18; Mark 1. 16; Luke 5; John 1. 35.
sent forth. Matt. 10. 2; Mark 3. 16; Luke 6. 14.
tries to walk to Jesus on the sea. Matt. 14. 29.
confesses Jesus to be the Christ. Matt. 16. 16; Mark 8. 29; Luke 9. 20.
witnesses the transfiguration. Matt. 17; Mark 9; Luke 9. 28; 2 Pet. 1. 16.
his self-confidence reproved. Luke 22. 31; John 13. 36.
thrice denies Christ. Matt. 26. 69; Mark 14. 66; Luke 22. 57; John 18. 17.
his repentance. Matt. 26. 75; Mark 14. 72; Luke 22. 62.
the assembled disciples addressed by. Acts 1. 15.
the Jews preached to by. Acts 2. 14; 3. 12.
brought before the council. Acts 4.
condemns Ananias and Sapphira. Acts 5.
denounces Simon the sorcerer. Acts 8. 18.
restores Æneas and Tabitha. Acts 9. 32, 40.
sent for by Cornelius. Acts 10.
instructed by a vision not to despise the Gentiles. Acts 10. 9.
imprisoned, and liberated by an angel. Acts 12.
his decision about circumcision. Acts 15. 7.
rebuked by Paul. Gal. 2. 14.
bears witness to Paul's teaching. 2 Pet. 3. 15.
comforts the church, and exhorts to holy living by his epistles. 1 & 2 Pet.
his martyrdom foretold by Christ. John 21. 18; 2 Pet. 1. 14.
PETHAHIAH, pe'-thah-i'-ah, whom Jehovah looses. 1 Chr. 24. 16.
PETHOR, pe'-thor. Num. 22. 5.
PETHUEL, pe-thoo'-el, God's opening (?). Joel 1. 1.
PEULTHAI, pe-ool'-thai, deed of Jehovah. 1 Chr. 26. 5.
PHALEC, fa'-lek, Greek form of Peleg. Luke 3. 35.
PHALLU, fal'-oo, an English way of spelling Pallu. Gen. 46. 9.
PHALTI, fal'-ti, deliverance of Jehovah. 1 Sam. 25. 44.
PHALTIEL, fal'-ti-el, deliverance of God. 2 Sam. 3. 15.
PHANUEL, fan-oo'-el, Greek form of Penuel. Luke 2. 36.
PHARAOH, fa'-roh, the sun (title of rulers of Egypt). Gen. 12. 14; Ezek. 29. 3.
Abram's wife taken into house of. Gen. 12. 15.
Pharaoh plagued because of her. Gen. 12. 17.
—— (patron of Joseph), his dreams, &c. Gen. 40.
his hospitality to Joseph's father and brethren. Gen. 47.
—— (oppressor of the Israelites). Ex. 1. 8.
daughter preserves Moses. Ex. 2. 5, 10; Acts 7. 21.
miracles performed before, and plagues sent. Ex. 7—10.
grants Moses' request. Ex. 12. 31.
repenting, pursues Israel, and perishes in the Red sea. Ex. 14 (Neh. 9. 10; Ps. 135. 9; 136. 15; Rom. 9. 17).
—— (father-in-law of Solomon). 1 Kin. 3. 1.
shelters Hadad, Solomon's adversary. 1 Kin. 11. 19.
PHARAOH-HOPHRA, fa'-roh-hof'-rah, Pharaoh the priest of the sun.
his fate predicted. Jer. 44. 30. *See* Ezek. 30—32.
compared to a dragon. Ezek. 29. 3.
PHARAOH-NECHO, fa'-roh-ne'-ko, Pharaoh the lame.
slays Josiah. 2 Kin. 23. 29; 2 Chr. 35. 20.
his wars with Israel. 2 Kin. 23. 33; 2 Chr. 36. 3.
PHARES, fa'-res, Greek form of Pharez. Luke 3. 33.

PHAREZ, fa'-rez, breach. Gen. 38. 29; Ruth 4. 18.
PHARISEES, far'-is-ees, the separated.
celebrated ones: Nicodemus, John 3. 1; Simon, Luke 7; Gamaliel, Acts 5. 34; Saul of Tarsus, Acts 23. 6; 26. 5; Phil. 3. 5.
Christ entertained by. Luke 7. 36; 11. 37; 14. 1.
Christ utters woes against. Matt. 23. 13; Luke 11. 42.
Christ questioned by, about divorce. Matt. 19. 3; eating, Matt. 9. 11; 15. 1; Mark 2. 16; Luke 5. 30; forgiveness of sin, Luke 5. 21; sabbath, Matt. 12. 2, 10; fasting, Mark 2. 18; tribute, Matt. 22. 17.
deride Christ. Luke 16. 14.
murmur against Christ. Matt. 9. 34; Luke 15. 2.
denounced by Christ. Matt. 5. 20; 16. 6; 21. 43; 23. 2; Luke 11. 39.
people cautioned against. Mark 8. 15; Luke 12. 1.
seek a sign from Christ. Matt. 12. 38; 16. 1.
take counsel against Christ. Matt. 12. 14; Mark 3. 6.
Nicodemus remonstrates with. John 7. 51.
cast out the man cured of blindness. John 9. 13.
dissensions about. John 9. 16.
send officers to take Christ. John 7. 32.
contend about circumcision. Acts 15. 5.
their belief in the resurrection, &c. Acts 23. 8.
and publican. Luke 18.
PHAROSH, fa'-rosh, same as PAROSH. Ezra 8. 3.
PHARPAR, far'-par, swift. 2 Kin. 5. 12.
PHARZITES, farz'-ites, descendants of Pharez. Num. 26. 20.
PHASEAH, fa-se'-ah, same as PASEAH. Neh. 7. 51.
PHEBE, fe'-be, moon. Rom. 16. 1.
PHENICE, fe-ni'-see, palm tree. Acts 11. 19; 15. 3; 27. 12.
PHENICIA, fe-nish'-yah, land of palms. Acts 21. 2.
PHICHOL, fi'-kol, attentive (?). Gen. 21. 22.
PHILADELPHIA, fil'-a-delf'-yah, brotherly love.
church of, commended. Rev. 1. 11; 3. 7.
PHILEMON, fil-e'-mon, affectionate.
Paul's letter to, concerning Onesimus. Philem.
PHILETUS, fil-e'-tus, beloved. 2 Tim. 2. 17.
PHILIP, fil'-ip, lover of horses.
APOSTLE, called. John 1. 43.
sent forth. Matt. 10. 3; Mark 3. 18; Luke 6. 14; John 12. 22; Acts 1. 13.
remonstrated with by Christ. John 14. 8.
—— deacon, elected. Acts 6. 5.
preaches in Samaria. Acts 8. 5.
baptizes the eunuch. Acts 8. 27.
his four virgin daughters prophesy. Acts 21. 8.
—— (brother of Herod). Matt. 14. 3; Mark 6. 17; Luke 3. 1, 19.
PHILIPPI, fil-ip'-i, a town so called after Philip of Macedon.
Paul persecuted at. Acts 16. 12.
church at, commended and exhorted. Phil. 1—4.
PHILIPPIANS, fil-ip'-yans, the people of Philippi. Phil. 4. 15.
PHILISTIA, fil-ist'-yah, the land of the Philistines. Gen. 21. 34; Ex. 13. 17; Josh. 13. 2; 2 Kin. 8. 2; Ps. 60. 8.
PHILISTIM, fil'-ist-im, wanderers. Gen. 10. 14.
PHILISTINES, fil'-ist-ines, same as PHILISTIM. Gen. 21. 34.
origin of. Gen. 10. 14; 1 Chr. 1. 12.
fill up Isaac's wells. Gen. 26. 15.
contend with Joshua, Josh. 13; Shamgar, Judg. 3. 31; Samson, Judg. 14—16; Samuel, 1 Sam. 4; 7; Jonathan, 1 Sam. 14; Saul, 1 Sam. 17; David, 1 Sam. 18.
their wars with Israel. 1 Sam. 4. 1; 28; 29; 31; 2 Chr. 21. 16.
mentioned. Ps. 60. 8; 83. 7; 87. 4; 108. 9; Is. 2. 6; 9. 12; 11. 14; Jer. 25. 20.
their destruction predicted. Jer. 47; Ezek. 25. 15; Amos 1. 8; Obad. 19; Zeph. 2. 5; Zech. 9. 6.
PHILOLOGUS, fil-o'-log-us, talkative.
Julia, and all saints with them. Rom. 16. 15.

PHINEHAS, fin′-e-as, serpent's mouth. Ex. 6. 25.
slays Zimri and Cozbi. Num. 25. 7, 11; Ps. 106. 30.
sent against the Midianites, Reubenites, and
Benjamites. Num. 31. 6; Josh. 22. 13; Judg. 20. 28.
—— son of Eli, his sin and death. 1 Sam. 1. 3;
2. 22; 4. 11.

PHLEGON, fleg′-on, zealous, burning. Rom. 16. 14.

PHRYGIA, frij′-yah. Acts 2. 10; 16. 6; 18. 23.

PHURAH, foor′-ah, branch (?). Judg. 7. 10.

PHUT, foot. Gen. 10. 6.

PHUVAH, foo′-vah, mouth. Gen. 46. 13.

PHYGELLUS, fi-gel′-us, little fugitive.
and Hermogenes turned away from Paul. 2 Tim.
1. 15.

PI-BESETH, pi-be′-seth, the city of Bast. Ezek. 30.
17.

PI-HAHIROTH, pi′-ha-hi′-roth, where sedge grows.
Ex. 14. 2.

PILATE, pi′-lat, armed with a javelin (?). Matt.
27. 2.
Pontius, governor of Judæa during our Lord's
ministry, sufferings, and death. Luke 3. 1.
Christ delivered to, admonished by his wife,
examines Jesus, washes his hands, but delivers
Him to be crucified. Matt. 27; Mark 15; Luke
23; John 18; 19.
grants request of Joseph of Arimathæa. Matt.
27. 57; Mark 15. 42; Luke 23. 50; John 19. 38.
See Acts 3. 13; 4. 27; 13. 28; 1 Tim. 6. 13.

PILDASH, pil′-dash, steel (?). Gen. 22. 22.

PILEHA, pi′-le-hah, ploughman (?). Neh. 10. 24.

PILTAI, pil′-tai, whom Jehovah delivers. Neh.
12. 17.

PINON, pi′-non, darkness. Gen. 36. 41.

PIRAM, pi′-ram, like a wild ass. Josh. 10. 3.

PIRATHON, pir-ah′-thon, leader. Judg. 12. 15.

PIRATHONITE, pir-ah′-thon-ite, an inhabitant of
Pirathon. Judg. 12. 13.

PISGAH, piz′-gah, a part, boundary.
mount. Num. 21. 20; 23. 14; Deut. 3. 27; 34. 1.

PISIDIA, pi-sid′-yah. Acts 13. 14; 14. 24.

PISON, pi′-son, flowing stream (?), a river in Eden.
Gen. 2. 11.

PISPAH, pis′-pah, expansion. 1 Chr. 7. 38.

PITHOM, pi′-thom.
(and Raamses), cities built by Israelites in E-
gypt, Ex. 1. 11.

PITHON, pi′-thon, simple (?). 1 Chr. 8. 35.

PLEIADES, pli′-ad-ees, (coming at) the sailing
season (?). Job 9. 9; 38. 31; Amos 5. 8.

POCHERETH of ZEBAIM, po-ke′-reth of Ze-ba′-im,
offspring of gazelles (?). Ezra 2. 57.

POLLUX, pol′-ux. Acts 28. 11.

PONTIUS, pon′-shus, belonging to the sea. Mat.
27. 2. *See* PILATE.

PONTUS, pont′-us, sea. Acts 2. 9.

PORATHA, po-rah′-thah, having many chariots (?).
Esth. 9. 8.

PORCIUS FESTUS, por′-shus fest′-us. Acts 24. 27.

POTIPHAR, pot′-i-far, belonging to the sun. Gen.
37. 36.
Joseph's master. Gen. 39.

POTI-PHERAH, pot′-i-fer′-ah, same as POTIPHAR.
Gen. 41. 45.

PRISCA, pris′-kah, ancient. 2 Tim. 4. 19.

PRISCILLA, pris-il′-ah, diminutive of PRISCA. Acts
18. 2.
(and AQUILA). Acts 18; Rom. 16. 3; 1 Cor. 16. 19.

PROCHORUS, prok′-or-us, he that presides over the
choir. Acts 6. 5.

PTOLEMAIS, tol′-em-a′-is, city of Ptolemy.
Paul at. Acts 21. 7.

PUA, poo′-ah, same as PHUVAH. Num. 26. 23.

PUAH, poo′-ah, splendour. Ex. 1. 15.

PUBLIUS, pub′-li-us.
entertains Paul. Acts 28. 7.

PUDENS, pu′-dens, shamefaced. 2 Tim. 4. 21.

PUHITES, poo′-hites. 1 Chr. 2. 53.

PUL, pool, (1) a short name for Tiglath-Pileser (?).
2 Kin. 15. 19. (2) son (?). Is. 66. 19.
king of Assyria, 1 Chr. 5. 26.

PUNITES, poon′-ites, descendants of Pua. Num.
26. 23.

PUNON, poon′-on, same as PINON. Num. 33. 42.

PUR, poor, a lot. Esth. 3. 7.

PURIM, poor′-im, lots. Esth. 9. 26.
feast of, Esth. 9. 20.

PUT, poot, same as PHUT. 1 Chr. 1. 8.

PUTEOLI, poo-te′-o-li, wells.
(Pozzuoli), seaport of Italy. Acts 28. 13.

PUTIEL, poot′-i-el. Ex. 6. 25.

QUARTUS, kwart′-us, the fourth. Rom. 16. 23.

RAAMAH. ra′-am-ah, trembling. Gen. 10. 7.

RAAMIAH, ra′-am-i′-ah, trembling of Jehovah.
Neh. 7. 7.

RAAMSES, ra-am′-ses, son of the sun. Ex. 1. 11.

RABBAH, rab′-ah, capital city. Josh. 13. 25.
city, 2 Sam. 11: 12. 26; Jer. 49. 2; Ezek. 21. 20;
25. 5; Amos 1. 14.

RABBATH, rab′-ath, same as RABBAH. Deut. 3. 11.

RABBI, rab′-i, master. Matt. 23. 7. 8; John 1. 38; 3. 2.

RABBITH, rab′-ith, populous. Josh. 19. 20.

RABBONI, rab-o′-ni, my master.
title addressed to Christ by Mary. John 20. 16.

RAB-MAG, rab′-mag, most exalted. Jer. 39. 3.

RAB-SARIS, rab′-sar-is, chief eunuch. 2 Kin. 18. 17.

RAB-SHAKEH, rab′-sha-kay, chief of the cupbearers.
2 Kin. 18. 17.
reviles Hezekiah. 2 Kin. 18. 19; 19. 1; Is. 36. 4.

RACHAB, ra′-kab, Greek form of Rahab. Matt. 1. 5.

RACHAL, ra′-kal, traffic. 1 Sam. 30. 29.

RACHEL, ra′-chel, ewe. Gen. 29. 6.
(Rahel) and Jacob. Gen. 29. 10, 28; 30; 31. 4, 19,
34; 35. 16.

RADDAI, rad′-ai, subduing. 1 Chr. 2. 14.

RAGAU, ra′-gaw, Greek form of Reu. Luke 3. 35.

RAGUEL, ra-goo′-el, friend of God. Num. 10. 29.

RAHAB, ra′-hab, (1) broad. Josh. 2. 1. (2) violence.
Ps. 87. 4.
the harlot. Josh. 2; 6. 22. *See* Matt. 1. 5; Heb.
11. 31; James 2. 25.
—— (EGYPT). Ps. 87. 4; 89. 10; Is. 51. 9.

RAHAM, ra′-ham. 1 Chr. 2. 44.

RAHEL, ra′-hel, same as RACHEL. Jer. 31. 15.

RAKEM, ra′-kem, variegated. 1 Chr. 7. 16.

RAKKATH, rak′-ath, shore. Josh. 19. 35.

RAKKON, rak′-on, same as RAKKATH. Josh. 19. 46.

RAM, high. Ruth 4. 19.

RAMA, ra′-mah, Greek form of Ramah. Matt. 2. 18.

RAMAH, ra′-mah, high place. Josh. 18. 25; Judg.
4. 5; 1 Sam. 1. 19; 7. 17; 8. 4; 19. 18; 25. 1; Jer.
31. 15.

RAMATH, ra′-math, same as preceding. Josh. 19. 8.

RAMATHAIM, ra′-math-a′-im, double high place.
1 Sam. 1. 1.

RAMATHITE, ra′-math-ite, a native of Ramah.
1 Chr. 27. 27.

RAMATH-LEHI, ra′-math-le′-hi, height of Lehi.
Judg. 15. 17.

RAMATH-MIZPEH, ra′-math-miz′-peh, height of
Mizpeh. Josh. 13. 26.

RAMESES, ra′-me-sees, same as RAAMSES. Gen.
47. 11.

RAMIAH, ram-i′-ah, Jehovah is high. Ezra 10. 25.

RAMOTH, ra′-moth, plural of Ramah. 1 Chr. 6. 73.

RAMOTH-GILEAD, ra′-moth-gil′-yad. heights of Gilead. Deut. 4. 43; 1 Kin. 4. 13, 22; 2 Kin. 8. 28;
9. 1; 2 Chr. 18; 22. 5.

RAPHA, ra′-fah, giant (?). 1 Chr. 8. 37.

RAPHU, ra′-foo, healed. Num. 13. 9.

REAIA, re-ai′-ah, Jehovah has seen. 1 Chr. 5. 5.

REAIAH, correct form of Reaia. 1 Chr. 4. 2.

REBA, re′-bah, a fourth part. Num. 31. 8.

REBECCA, Greek form of Rebekah. Rom. 9. 10.

REBEKAH, re-bek′-ah, a noose.
history of. Gen. 22; 24. 15, 67; 27. 6, 43; 49. 31;
Rom. 9. 10.

RECHAB, re′-kab, horseman. 2 Kin. 10. 15.

RECHABITES, re′-kab-ites, descendants of Rechab.
Jer. 35. 2.

RECHAH, re'-kah, side (?). 1 Chr. 4. 12.
REELAIAH, re'-el-ai'-ah, trembling caused by Jehovah. Ezra 2. 2.
REGEM, re'-gem, friend. 1 Chr. 2. 47.
REGEM-MELECH, re'-gem-me'-lek, friend of the king. Zech. 7. 2.
REHABIAH, re'-hab-i'-ah, Jehovah enlarges. 1 Chr. 23. 17.
REHOB, re'-hob, street. 2 Sam. 8. 3.
REHOBOAM, re'-hob-o'-am, who enlarges the people. 1 Kin. 11. 43.
    king of Judah, 1 Kin. 11 ; 12 ; 14 ; 2 Chr. 9—12.
REHOBOTH, re-ho'-both, roominess. Gen. 10. 11 ; 26. 22.
REHUM, re'-hoom, merciful. Ezra 4. 8.
REI, re'-i, friendly. 1 Kin. 1. 8.
REKEM, re'-kem, same as RAKEM. Num. 31. 8.
REMALIAH, rem'-al-i'-ah, whom Jehovah adorned. 2 Kin. 15. 25.
REMETH, re'-meth, a high place. Josh. 19. 21.
REMMON, rem'-on, more correctly spelt RIMMON. Josh. 19. 7.
REMMON-METHOAR, rem'-on-me-tho'-ar, R. stretching (to Neah). Josh. 19. 13.
REMPHAN, rem'-fan. Acts 7. 43.
REPHAEL, re'-fa-el, whom God healed. 1 Chr. 26. 7.
REPHAH, re'-fah, riches. 1 Chr. 7. 25.
REPHAIAH, ref-ai'-ah, whom Jehovah healed. 1 Chr. 3. 21.
REPHAIM, re-fa'-im, giants. 2 Sam. 5. 18.
REPHAIMS, re-fa'-ims, same as REPHAIM. Gen. 14. 5.
REPHIDIM, re-fee'-dim, supports.
    Amalek subdued there by Joshua. Ex. 17.
RESEN, re'-sen, bridle. Gen. 10. 12.
RESHEPH, re'-shef, flame. 1 Chr. 7. 25.
REU, re-oo', same as RAGUEL. Gen. 11. 18.
REUBEN, roo'-ben, behold a son (?).
    son of Jacob. Gen. 29 ; 30 ; 35 ; 37 ; 42 ; 49 ; 1 Chr. 5. 1.
REUBENITES, roo'-ben-ites, descendants of Reuben.
    their number and possessions. Num. 1 ; 2 ; 26 ; 32 ; Deut. 3. 12 ; Josh. 13. 15 ; 1 Chr. 5. 18.
    dealings of Moses and Joshua with, Num. 32 ; Deut. 33 ; Josh. 1 ; 22.
    go into captivity, 1 Chr. 5. 26 (Rev. 7. 5).
REUEL, roo'-el, friend of God. 1 Chr. 9. 8.
REUMAH, room'-ah, exalted. Gen. 22. 24.
REZEPH, re'-zef, a stone. 2 Kin. 19. 12.
REZIA, rez'-yah, delight. 1 Chr. 7. 39.
REZIN, re'-zin, firm.
    king of Syria. 2 Kin. 15. 37 ; 16. 5, 9 ; Is. 7. 1.
REZON, re'-zon, lean.
    of Damascus. 1 Kin. 11. 23.
RHEGIUM, re'-ji-um. Acts 28. 13.
RHESA, re'-sah, chieftain (?). Luke 3. 27.
RHODA, ro'-dah, a rose. Acts 12. 13.
RHODES, rodes.
    island of. Acts 21. 1.
RIBAI, rib'-ai, contentious. 2 Sam. 23. 29.
RIBLAH, rib'-lah, fertility. Num. 34. 11.
    in Syria. 2 Kin. 23. 33 ; 25. 6 ; Jer. 39. 5 : 52. 9.
RIMMON, rim'-on, (1) pomegranate, 2 Sam. 4. 2 ; (2) idol, 2 Kin. 5. 18.
RIMMON-PAREZ, rim'-on-pa'-rez, pomegranate of the breach. Num. 33. 19.
RINNAH, rin'-ah, shout. 1 Chr. 4. 20.
RIPHATH, ri'-fath. Gen. 10. 3.
RISSAH, ris'-ah, ruin. Num. 33. 21.
RITHMAH, rith'-mah, broom. Num. 33. 18.
RIZPAH, riz'-pah, hot coal. 2 Sam. 3. 7.
ROBOAM, rob-o'-am, Greek form of Rehoboam. Matt. 1. 7.
ROGELIM, ro'-gel-im, fullers. 2 Sam. 17. 27.
ROHGAH, ro'-gah, outcry. 1 Chr. 7. 34.
ROMAMTI-EZER, ro-mam'-ti-e'-zer, I have exalted help. 1 Chr. 25. 4.
ROMANS, ro'-mans, men of Rome. John 11. 48.
    St. Paul's teaching to. *See* Epistle to Romans, *also* FAITH, WORKS, RIGHTEOUSNESS.

ROME, strength (?).
    strangers of, at Pentecost. Acts 2. 10.
    Jews ordered to depart from. Acts 18. 2.
    Paul preaches there. Acts 28.
ROSH, head. Gen. 46. 21.
RUFUS, roo'-fus, red. Mark 15. 21.
    (chosen in the Lord). Rom. 16. 13.
RUHAMAH, roo-hah'-mah, compassionated. Hos. 2. 1.
RUMAH, roo'-mah, height. 2 Kin. 23. 36.
RUTH, rooth, friendship (?). Ruth 1. 4.
    story of. Ruth 1—4.
    Christ descended from, Matt. 1. 5.

SABACHTHANI, sa-bac-thah'-ni, thou hast forsaken me. Mark 15. 34.
SABAOTH, sab-a'-oth (Hosts), the Lord of. Rom. 9. 29 ; James 5. 4.
SABEANS, sab-e'-ans, people of Seba. Job 1. 15 ; Is. 45. 14.
SABTAH, sab'-tah, rest (?). Gen. 10. 7.
SABTECHA, sab'-te-kah. 1 Chr. 1. 9.
SABTECHAH, sab'-te-kah. Gen. 10. 7.
SACAR, sa'-kar, hire, reward. 1 Chr. 11. 35.
SADDUCEES, sad'-u-sees (named from ZADOK, founder of the sect).
    their controversies with Christ, Matt. 16. 1 ; 22. 23 ; Mark 12. 18 ; Luke 20. 27 ; with the apostles, Acts 4. 1 ; with Paul, Acts 23. 6.
    their doctrines. Matt. 22. 23 ; Mark 12. 18 ; Acts 23. 8.
SADOC, sa'-dok, Greek form of Zadok. Matt. 1. 14.
SALA, sa'-lah, Greek form of Salah. Luke 3, 35.
SALAH, sa'-lah, sprout (?). Gen. 10. 24.
SALAMIS, sal'-am-is. Acts 13. 5.
SALATHIEL, sa-la'-thi-el, Greek form of Shealtiel. 1 Chr. 3. 17.
SALCAH, or SALCHAH, sal'-kah, road. Deut. 3. 10.
SALEM, sa'-lem, perfect. Gen. 14. 18 ; Heb. 7. 1.
SALIM, sa'-lim, Greek form of Salem. John 3. 23.
SALLAI, sal'-ai, exaltation. Neh. 11. 8.
SALLU, sal'-oo, same as SALLAI. 1 Chr. 9. 7.
SALMA, sal'-mah, garment. 1 Chr. 2. 11.
SALMON, sal'-mon, shady. Ps. 68. 14.
SALMONE, sal-mo'-ne. Acts 27. 7.
SALOME, sal-o'-me, perfect. Mark 15. 40 ; 16. 1.
SALU, sa'-loo, same as SALLU. Num. 25. 14.
SAMARIA, sa-ma'-ri-ah, Greek equivalent of Shomron, which means guard.
    (city of). 1 Kin. 16. 24 ; 20. 1 ; 2 Kin. 6. 24.
    —— (region of), visited by Christ. Luke 17. 11 ; John 4.
    gospel preached there. Acts 8.
SAMARITAN, sa-mar'-it-an.
    parable of the good. Luke 10. 33.
    miracle performed on. Luke 17. 16.
SAMARITANS, sa-mar'-it-ans, inhabitants of Samaria. 2 Kin. 17. 29.
SAMGAR-NEBO, sam-gar'-ne-bo, Be gracious, Nebo, Jer. 39. 3.
SAMLAH, sam'-lah, garment. Gen. 36. 36.
SAMOS, sa'-mos, a height (?). Acts 20. 15.
SAMOTHRACIA, sa'-mo-thra'-shah. Acts 16. 11.
SAMSON, sam'-son, like the sun. Judg. 13—16.
    delivered up to Philistines. Judg. 16. 21.
    his death. Judg. 16. 30.
SAMUEL, sam'-u-el, name of God, or, heard of God. 1 Sam. 1. 20.
    born, and presented to the Lord. 1 Sam. 1. 19, 26.
    ministers to the Lord. 1 Sam. 3.
    the Lord speaks to. 1 Sam. 3. 11.
    judges Israel. 1 Sam. 7 ; 8. 1 ; Acts 13. 20.
    anoints Saul king. 1 Sam. 10. 1.
    rebukes Saul for sin. 1 Sam. 13 ; 15. 16.
    anoints David. 1 Sam. 16 ; 19. 18.
    his death. 1 Sam. 25. 1 ; 28. 3.
    his spirit consulted by Saul. 1 Sam. 28. 12.
    as a prophet. Ps. 99. 6 ; Acts 3. 24 ; Heb. 11. 32.
SANBALLAT. san-bal'-at, Sin (the moon) giveth life (?). Neh. 2. 10 ; 4 ; 6. 2 ; 13. 28.
SANSANNAH, san-san'-ah, palm branch. Josh. 15. 31.

SAPH, threshold. 2 Sam. 21. 18.
SAPHIR, saf'-ir, beautiful. Mic. 1. 11.
SAPPHIRA, saf-i'-rah, Greek form of the above (feminine). Acts 5. 1.
SARA, sa'-rah, Greek form of Sarah. Heb. 11. 11.
SARAH, sa'-rah, princess. Gen. 17. 15.
(Sarai). Gen. 11; 12; 20. 2. *See* ABRAHAM.
her death and burial. Gen. 23 (Heb. 11. 11; 1 Pet. 3. 6).
SARAI, sa'-rai, contentious (?). Gen. 11. 29.
SARAPH, sa'-raf, burning. 1 Chr. 4. 22.
SARDIS, sard'-is.
church of. Rev. 1. 11; 3. 1.
SARDITES, sard'-ites, descendants of Sered. Num. 26. 26.
SAREPTA, sa-rep'-tah, Greek form of Zarephath. Luke 4. 26.
SARGON, sar'-gon, [God] appoints the king. Is. 20. 1.
SARID, sa'-rid, survivor. Josh. 19. 10.
SARON, sa'-ron, Greek form of Sharon. Acts 9. 35.
SARSECHIM, sar'-se-kim. Jer. 39. 3.
SARUCH, sa'-rook, Greek form of Serug. Luke 3. 35.
SATAN, sa'-tan, adversary. 1 Chr. 21. 1. *See* DEVIL, *Subject-Index*, p. 445.
SAUL, asked for. 1 Sam. 9. 2.
king of Israel, his parentage, anointing by Samuel, prophesying, and acknowledgment as king, 1 Sam. 9; 10.
his disobedience, and rejection by God. 1 Sam. 14. 31; 15.
possessed by an evil spirit, quieted by David. 1 Sam. 16, 14, 15, 23.
favours David, 1 Sam. 18. 5; seeks to kill him, 1 Sam. 18. 10; pursues him, 1 Sam. 20; 23; 24; 26.
slays priests for succouring David. 1 Sam. 22. 9.
enquires of the witch of En-dor. 1 Sam. 28. 7.
his ruin and suicide. 1 Sam. 28. 15; 31; 1 Chr. 10.
his posterity. 1 Chr. 8. 33.
—— of Tarsus. *See* PAUL.
SCEVA, se'-vah, left-handed. Acts 19. 14.
SCYTHIAN, sith'-yan. Col. 3. 11.
SEBA, se'-bah, man (?). Gen. 10. 7.
SEBAT, se'-bat, rest (?). Zech. 1. 7.
SECACAH, se-kah'-kah, enclosure. Josh. 15. 61.
SECHU, se'-koo, watch-tower. 1 Sam. 19. 22.
SECUNDUS, se-cun'-dus, second. Acts 20. 4.
SEGUB, se'-goob, elevated. 1 Kin. 16. 34.
SEIR, se'-ir, hairy.
mount, Edom, land of Esau. Gen. 14. 6; 32. 3; 36. 8, 20; Deut. 33. 2; Josh. 24. 4; Is. 21. 11; Ezek. 25. 8.
predictions about. Num. 24. 18; Ezek. 35. 2.
SEIRATH, se-ir'-ath, well wooded. Judg. 3. 26.
SELA, se'-lah, rock. Is. 16. 1.
SELA-HAMMAHLEKOTH, se'-lah-ham-ah'-lek-oth, rock of escapes. 1 Sam. 23. 28.
SELAH, se'-lah, forte (?), a musical direction, pause. Ps. 3. 2; 4. 2; 24. 6; 39. 5, 11; 46. 3; 48. 8; 50. 6; Hab. 3. 3, 9, 12, &c.
SELED, se'-led, exultation, or burning. 1 Chr. 2. 30.
SELEUCIA, se-loo'-shah, called after Seleucus.
apostles at. Acts 13. 4.
SEM, Greek form of Shem. Luke 3. 36.
SEMACHIAH, sem'-ak-i'-ah, whom Jehovah sustains. 1 Chr. 26. 7.
SEMEI, sem'-e-i, Greek form of Shimei. Luke 3. 26.
SENAAH, sen-a'-ah, perhaps thorny. Ezra 2. 35.
SENEH, se'-nay, crag, thorn. 1 Sam. 14. 4.
SENIR, se'-nir, coat of mail. 1 Chr. 5. 23.
SENNACHERIB, sen-ak'-er-ib, Sin (the moon) multiplies brethren. 2 Kin. 18. 13; 2 Chr. 32: Is. 36. 37.
SENUAH, se-noo'-ah, bristling (?). Neh. 11. 9.
SEORIM, se-or'-im, barley. 1 Chr. 24. 8.
SEPHAR, se'-far, a numbering. Gen. 10. 30.
SEPHARAD, se-far'-ad. Obad. 20.
SEPHARVAIM, se'-far-va'-im. 2 Kin. 17. 24; 18. 34; 19. 13.
SEPH, se'-rah, abundance. Gen. 46. 17.
SERAIAH, ser-ai'-ah, soldier of Jehovah (?). 2 Sam. 8. 17.
SERAPHIMS, ser'-af-ims, burning ones. Is. 6. 2.

SERED, se'-red, fear. Gen. 46. 14.
SERGIUS, ser'-ji-us. Acts 13. 7.
SERUG, se'-roog, shoot. Gen. 11. 20.
SETH, substitute.
son of Adam. Gen. 4. 25; 5. 3.
SETHUR, se'-thoor, hidden. Num. 13. 13.
SHAALABBIN, sha'-al-ab'-in, earths of foxes. Josh. 19. 42.
SHAALBIM, sha-alb'-im, same as preceding. Judg. 1. 35.
SHAALBONITE, sha-alb'-on-ite, inhabitant of Shaalbim. 2 Sam. 23. 32.
SHAAPH, sha'-af, anger (?). 1 Chr. 2. 47.
SHAARAIM, sha'-ar-a'-im, two gates. 1 Sam. 17. 52.
SHAASHGAZ, sha-ash'-gaz, beauty's servant (?). Esth. 2. 14.
SHABBETHAI, shab'-e-thai, born on the sabbath. Ezra 10. 15.
SHACHIA, sha'-ki-ah, lustful. 1 Chr. 8. 10.
SHADDAI, shad'-ai, Almighty. Num. 1. 6.
SHADRACH, shad'-rak. Dan. 1. 7.
Meshach, and Abed-nego, their faith and sufferings, and deliverance. Dan. 1; 3.
SHAGE, sha'-ge, wanderer. 1 Chr. 11. 34.
SHAHARAIM, sha'-har-a'-im, two dawns. 1 Chr. 8. 8.
SHAHAZIMAH, sha-ha-zee'-mah, lofty places. Josh. 19. 22.
SHALEM, sha'-lem, safe, perfect. Gen. 33. 18.
SHALIM, sha'-lim, foxes. 1 Sam. 9. 4.
SHALISHA, sha-lish'-ah, a third part. 1 Sam. 9. 4.
SHALLECHETH, shal-e'-keth, felling. 1 Chr. 26. 16.
SHALLUM, shal'-oom, retribution. 2 Kin. 15. 10; 22. 14; 2 Chr. 34. 22; Jer. 22. 11.
SHALLUN, shal'-oon, spoliation. Neh. 3. 15.
SHALMAI, shal'-mai, peaceful (?). Ezra 2. 46.
SHALMAN, shal'-man, shortened form of following. Hos. 10. 14.
SHALMANESER, shal'-man-e'-zer, Shalman be propitious. 2 Kin. 17. 3.
carries ten tribes captive. 2 Kin. 17; 18. 9.
SHAMA, sha'-mah, obedient. 1 Chr. 11. 44.
SHAMARIAH, sha'-mar-i'-ah, whom Jehovah guards. 2 Chr. 11. 19.
SHAMED, sha'-med, destroyer. 1 Chr. 8. 12.
SHAMER, sha'-mer, keeper. 1 Chr. 6. 46.
SHAMGAR, sham'-gar, destroyer (?).
judges Israel. Judg. 3. 31; 5. 6.
SHAMHUTH, sham'-hooth, notoriety (?). 1 Chr. 27. 8.
SHAMIR, sha'-mir, a thorn. 1 Chr. 24. 24.
SHAMMA, sham'-ah, desert. 1 Chr. 7. 37.
SHAMMAH, sham'-ah, same as SHAMMA. Gen. 36. 13.
his valour. 2 Sam. 23. 11.
SHAMMAI, sham'-ai, wasted. 1 Chr. 2. 28.
SHAMMOTH, sham'-oth, deserts. 1 Chr. 11. 27.
SHAMMUA, sham'-oo-ah, famous. Num. 13. 4.
SHAMMUAH, same as preceding. 2 Sam. 5. 14.
SHAMSHERAI, sham'-sher-ai. 1 Chr. 8. 26.
SHAPHAM, sha'-fam, bald. 1 Chr. 5. 12.
SHAPHAN, sha'-fan, coney.
repairs the temple. 2 Kin. 22. 3; 2 Chr. 34. 8.
SHAPHAT, sha'-fat, judge. Num. 13. 5.
SHAPHER, sha'-fer, pleasantness. Num. 33. 23.
SHARAI, shar'-ai, free. Ezra 10. 40.
SHARAIM, shar-a'-im, same as SHAARAIM. Josh. 15. 36.
SHARAR, shar'-ar, firm. 2 Sam. 23. 33.
SHAREZER, shar-e'-zer, [God] protect the king. 2 Kin. 19. 37.
SHARON, sha'-ron, plain. 1 Chr. 27. 29.
rose of. Cant. 2. 1.
SHARONITE, sha'-ron-ite, one who lives in Sharon. 1 Chr. 27. 29.
SHARUHEN, sha-roo'-hen. Josh. 19. 6.
SHASHAI, shash'-ai, pale. Ezra 10. 40.
SHASHAK, sha'-shak, activity (?). 1 Chr. 8. 14.
SHAUL, sha-ool, same as SAUL. Gen. 46. 10.
SHAULITES, sha'-ool-ites, the family of Shaul. Num. 26. 13.
SHAVEH, sha'-vay, plain. Gen. 14. 17.
SHAVEH KIRIATHAIM, sha'-vay kir-iath-a'-im, plain of Kiriathaim. Gen. 14. 5.

SHAVSHA, shav'-shah, another name of Seraiah. 1 Chr. 18. 16.

SHEAL, she'-al, prayer. Ezra 10. 29.

SHEALTIEL, she-al'-ti-el, I asked from God. Ezra 3. 2.

SHEARIAH, she'-ar-i'-ah, gate of Jehovah. 1 Chr. 8. 38.

SHEAR-JASHUB, she'-ar-ja'-shoob, the remnant shall return. Is. 7. 3.

SHEBA, she'-bah, an oath. Gen. 25. 3; 2 Sam. 20. 1; Job 6. 19; Ps. 72. 10; Jer. 6. 20; Ezek. 27. 22; 38. 13.

—— queen of. 1 Kin. 10; 2 Chr. 9; Matt. 12. 42.

—— (Benjamite) revolts. 2 Sam. 20.

SHEBAH, seven. Gen. 26. 33.

SHEBAM, she'-bam, fragrance. Num. 32. 3.

SHEBANIAH, she'-ban-i'-ah, whom Jehovah hides. 1 Chr. 15. 24.

SHEBARIM, she-bar'-im, breaches. Josh. 7. 5.

SHEBER, she'-ber, breaking. 1 Chr. 2. 48.

SHEBNA, sheb'-nah, youth (?).

the scribe. 2 Kin. 18. 18; 19. 2; Is. 22. 15; 36. 3; 37. 2.

SHEBUEL, she-boo'-el, captive of God. 1 Chr. 23. 16.

SHECANIAH, she'-kan-i'-ah, same as following. 1 Chr. 24. 11.

SHECHANIAH, she'-kan-i'-ah, Jehovah dwells. 1 Chr. 3. 21.

SHECHEM, she'-kem, back, shoulder. Gen. 34. 2.

the Hivite. Gen. 34.

—— city of. Josh. 17. 7; Ps. 60. 6.

charge of Joshua at. Josh. 24.

its treachery and penalty. Judg. 9. 1, 41.

SHECHEMITES, she'-kem-ites, people of Shechem. Num. 26. 31.

SHEDEUR, she'-de-oor, giving forth of light. Num. 1. 5.

SHEHARIAH, she'-har-i'-ah, Jehovah seeks. 1 Chr. 8. 26.

SHELAH, she'-lah, petition.

son of Judah. Gen. 38. 5.

SHELANITES, she'-lan-ites, descendants of Shelah. Num. 26. 20.

SHELEMIAH, she'-lem-i'-ah, whom Jehovah repays. 1 Chr. 26. 14.

SHELEPH, she'-lef, drawing out. Gen. 10. 26.

SHELESH, she'-lesh, triad. 1 Chr. 7. 35.

SHELOMI, she-lo'-mi, peaceful. Num. 34. 27.

SHELOMITH, she-lo'-mith, peacefulness. Lev. 24. 11.

SHELOMOTH, she-lo'-moth, same as Shelomith. 1 Chr. 24. 22.

SHELUMIEL, she-loom'-i-el, friend of God. Num. 1. 6.

SHEM, name. Gen. 5. 32; 9. 26; 10. 21; 11. 10; 1 Chr. 1. 17.

SHEMA, she'-mah, (1) echo (?), Josh. 15. 26; (2) fame, 1 Chr. 2. 43.

SHEMAAH, she-ma'-ah, fame. 1 Chr. 12. 3.

SHEMAIAH, she-mai'-ah, Jehovah has heard.

prophet. 1 Kin. 12. 22; 2 Chr. 11. 2; 12. 5 (Jer. 29. 24).

SHEMARIAH, she'-mar-i'-ah, Jehovah guards. 1 Chr. 12. 5.

SHEMEBER, shem-e'-ber, soaring on high (?). Gen. 14. 2.

SHEMER, she'-mer, guardian. 1 Kin. 16. 24.

SHEMIDA, shem-i'-dah, fame of wisdom. Num. 26. 32.

SHEMIDAH, shem-i'-dah, same as preceding. 1 Chr. 7. 19.

SHEMIDAITES, shem-id'-a-ites, descendants of Shemida. Num. 26. 32.

SHEMINITH, she-mi'-nith, eighth. 1 Chr. 15. 21.

SHEMIRAMOTH, she-mi'-ram-oth, most high name. 1 Chr. 15. 18.

SHEMUEL, she'-moo-el, same as SAMUEL. Num. 34. 20.

SHEN, tooth. 1 Sam. 7. 12.

SHENAZAR, she-na'-zar. 1 Chr. 3. 18.

SHENIR, she'-nir, same as SENIR. Deut. 3. 9.

SHEPHAM, she'-fam, nakedness. Num. 34. 10.

SHEPHATHIAH, she'-fat-i'-ah, an incorrect way of spelling the next word. 1 Chr. 9. 8.

SHEPHATIAH, she'-fat-i'-ah, whom Jehovah defends. 2 Sam. 3. 4.

SHEPHI, she'-fi, baldness. 1 Chr. 1. 40.

SHEPHO, she'-fo, same as SHEPHI. Gen. 36. 23.

SHEPHUPHAN, she'-foof-an, serpent (?). 1 Chr. 8. 5.

SHERAH, she'-rah, consanguinity. 1 Chr. 7. 24.

SHEREBIAH, she'-reb-i'-ah, heat of Jehovah. Ezra 8. 18.

SHERESH, she'-resh, root. 1 Chr. 7. 16.

SHEREZER, sher-e'-zer, same as SHAREZER (?). Zech. 7. 2.

SHESHACH, she'-shak, a name for Babel. Jer. 25. 26; 51. 41.

SHESHAI, shesh-ai, clothed in white (?). Num. 13. 22.

SHESHAN, she'-shan, lily (?). 1 Chr. 2. 31.

SHESHBAZZAR, shesh-baz'-ar. Ezra 1. 8; 5. 14.

SHETH, shayth, tumult. Num. 24. 17.

SHETHAR, she'-thar, star. Esth. 1. 14.

SHETHAR-BOZNAI, she'-thar-boz'-nai, bright star. Ezra 5. 3.

and Tatnai oppose rebuilding of temple. Ezra 5. 6.

SHEVA, she'-vah, vanity. 2 Sam. 20. 25.

SHIBBOLETH, shib'-ol-eth, an ear of corn, or a flood. Judg. 12. 6.

SHIBMAH, shib'-mah, fragrant. Num. 32. 38.

SHICRON, shik'-ron, drunkenness. Josh. 15. 11.

SHIGGAION, shig-ai'-on, irregular. Ps. 7, title.

SHIGIONOTH, shig'-i-o'-noth. Hab. 3. 1.

SHIHON, shi'-hon, ruin. Josh. 19. 19.

SHIHOR, shi'-hor, black. 1 Chr. 13. 5.

SHIHOR-LIBNATH, shi'-hor-lib'-nath. Josh. 19. 26.

SHILHI, shil'-hi, darter. 1 Kin. 22. 42.

SHILHIM, shil'-him, aqueducts. Josh. 15. 32.

SHILLEM, shil'-em, requital. Gen. 46. 24.

SHILOAH, shi-lo'-ah, outlet of water. Is. 8. 6.

SHILOH, shi'-lo, rest, Messiah. Gen. 49. 10.

—— site of tabernacle. Josh. 18. 1; Judg. 21. 19; 1 Sam. 1. 3; 2. 14; 3. 21; Ps. 78. 60; Jer. 7. 12; 26. 6.

SHILONI, shi'-lo-ni, native of Shiloh. Neh. 11. 5.

SHILONITE, shi'-lo-nite, same as preceding. 1 Kin. 11. 29.

SHILSHAH, shil'-shah, triad. 1 Chr. 7. 37.

SHIMEA, shim'-e-ah, famous. 1 Chr. 3. 5.

SHIMEAH, shim'-e-ah, same as SHEMAAH. 2 Sam. 21. 21.

SHIMEAM, shim'-e-am, same as preceding. 1 Chr. 9. 38.

SHIMEATH, shim'-e-ath, fame. 2 Kin. 12. 21.

SHIMEATHITE, shi'-me-ath-ite. 1 Chr. 2. 55.

SHIMEI, shim'-e-i, my fame. Num. 3. 18.

curses David. 2 Sam. 16. 5.

slain by Solomon. 1 Kin. 2. 36.

SHIMEON, shim'-e-on, a hearkening. Ezra 10. 31.

SHIMHI, shim'-hi, same as SHIMEI. 1 Chr. 8. 21.

SHIMI, shim'-i, same as preceding. Ex. 6. 17.

SHIMITES, shim'-ites, descendants of Shimei. Num. 3. 21.

SHIMMA, shim'-ah, rumour. 1 Chr. 2. 13.

SHIMON, shi'-mon. 1 Chr. 4. 20.

SHIMRATH, shim'-rath, watchfulness. 1 Chr. 8. 21.

SHIMRI, shim'-ri, watchful. 1 Chr. 4. 37.

SHIMRITH, shim'-rith, vigilant. 2 Chr. 24. 26.

SHIMROM, shim'-rome, watch-post. 1 Chr. 7. 1.

SHIMRON, shim'-rone, watchful. Josh. 11. 1.

SHIMRONITES, shim'-ron-ites, descendants of Shimron. Num. 26. 24.

SHIMRON-MERON, shim'-ron-me'-ron. Josh. 12. 20.

SHIMSHAI, shim'-shai, sunny. Ezra 4. 8.

SHINAB, shi'-nab, hostile (?). Gen. 14. 2.

SHINAR, shi'-nar. Gen. 10. 10.

SHIPHI, shi'-fi, abundant. 1 Chr. 4. 37.

SHIPHMITE, shif'-mite, a native of Shephan 1 Chr. 27. 27.

SHIPHRAH, shif'-rah, beauty. Ex. 1. 15.

SHIPHTAN, shif'-tan, judicial. Num. 34. 24.

SHISHA, shi'-shah, brightness. 1 Kin. 4. 3.

SHISHAK, shi'-shak, illustrious. 1 Kin. 11. 40.
invades and spoils Jerusalem. 1 Kin. 14. 25;
2 Chr. 12.
SHITRAI, shit'-rai, official. 1 Chr. 27. 29.
SHITTIM, shit'-im, acacias. Num. 25. 1.
SHIZA, shi'-zah, cheerful(?). 1 Chr. 11. 42.
SHOA, sho'-ah, opulent. Ezek. 23. 23.
SHOBAB, sho'-bab, apostate. 2 Sam. 5. 14.
SHOBACH, sho'-bak, pouring. 2 Sam. 10. 16.
SHOBAI, sho'-bai, bright(?). Ezra 2. 42.
SHOBAL, sho'-bal, stream. Gen. 36. 20.
SHOBEK, sho'-bek, forsaker. Neh. 10. 24.
SHOBI, sho'-bi, taking captive. 2 Sam. 17. 27.
SHOCHO, sho'-ko, same as the next word. 2 Chr.
28. 18.
SHOCHOH, sho'-ko, a hedge. 1 Sam. 17. 1.
SHOCO, sho'-ko, same as the preceding. 2 Chr.
11. 7.
SHOHAM, sho'-ham, onyx. 1 Chr. 24. 27.
SHOMER, sho'-mer, watchman. 2 Kin. 12. 21.
SHOPHACH, sho'-fak, same as SHOBAK. 1 Chr. 19.
16.
SHOPHAN, sho'-fan, baldness. Num. 32. 35.
SHOSHANNIM, sho-shan'-im, lilies. Ps. 45, title.
SHOSHANNIM-EDUTH, sh.-e'-dooth, lilies a testi-
mony. Ps. 80, title.
SHUA, shoo'-ah, wealth. 1 Chr. 2. 3.
SHUAH, shoo'-ah, depression. Gen. 25. 2.
SHUAL, shoo'-al, jackal. 1 Chr. 7. 36.
SHUBAEL, shoo'-ba-el, same as SHEBUEL (?). 1 Chr.
24. 20.
SHUHAM, shoo'-ham, pitman (?). Num. 26. 42.
SHUHAMITES, shoo'-ham-ites, the descendants of
Shuham. Num. 26. 42.
SHUHITE, shoo'-hite, a descendant of Shua. Job
8. 1.
SHULAMITE, shoo'-lam-ite, same as SHELOMITH.
Cant. 6. 13.
SHUMATHITES, shoo'-math-ites, people of Shumah.
1 Chr. 2. 53.
SHUNAMMITE, shoon'-am-ite, an inhabitant of
Shunem. 1 Kin. 1. 3.
SHUNEM, shoon'-em, two resting-places. Josh.
19. 18; 1 Sam. 28. 4; 2 Kin. 4. 8.
SHUNI, shoon'-i, quiet. Gen. 46. 16.
SHUNITES, shoon'-ites, descendants of Shuni.
Num. 26. 15.
SHUPHAM, shoo'-fam, serpent. Num. 26. 39.
SHUPHAMITES, shoo'-fam-ites, the descendants of
Shupham. Num. 26. 39.
SHUPPIM, shoop'-im. 1 Chr. 7. 12.
SHUR, shoor, a fort. Gen. 16. 7.
SHUSHAN, shoo'-shan.
city, Artaxerxes at. Neh. 1. 1; Esth. 2. 8; 3. 15.
SHUSHAN-EDUTH, sh.-e'-dooth, lily of the testi-
mony. Ps. 60, title.
SHUTHALHITES, shoo'-thal-ites, the descendants of
Shuthelah. Num. 26. 35.
SHUTHELAH, shoo-theel'-ah, plantation (?). Num.
26. 35.
SIA, si'-ah, assembly. Neh. 7. 47.
SIAHA, si'-a-hah, council. Ezra 2. 44.
SIBBECAI, sib'-e-kai, entangling. 1 Chr. 11. 29.
SIBBECHAI, same as preceding. 2 Sam. 21. 18.
SIBBOLETH, sib'-o-leth, same as SHIBBOLETH.
Judg. 12. 6.
SIBMAH, sib'-mah, same as SHIBMAH. Josh. 13.
19.
SIBRAIM, sib-ra'-im, two hills (?). Ezek. 47. 16.
SICHEM, si'-kem, the shoulder-blade. Gen. 12. 6.
SIDDIM, sid'-im, the plains. Gen. 14. 3.
SIDON, si'-don, fishing.
son of Canaan. Gen. 10. 15.
—— (Zidon), city of. Josh. 19. 28; 1 Kin. 5. 6;
Acts 27. 3.
SIDONIANS, si-do'-ni-ans, persons living in Sidon.
Deut. 3. 9.
SIHON, si'-hon, brush.
king of the Amorites. Num. 21. 21; Deut. 1. 4; 2.
26; Ps. 135. 11; 136. 19.
SIHOR, si'-hor, same as SHICHOR. Josh. 13. 3.

SILAS, si'-las, shortened form of Silvanus. Acts
15. 22; 16. 19; 17. 4. *See* 2 Cor. 1. 19; 1 Thess. 1.
1; 1 Pet. 5. 12.
SILLA, sil'-ah, way, highway (?). 2 Kin. 12. 20.
SILOAM, si-lo'-am, same as SHILOAH. John 9. 7.
SILVANUS, sil-vane'-us, of the forest. 2 Cor. 1. 19.
SIMEON, sim'-e-on, same as SHIMEON.
son of Jacob. Gen. 29. 33; 34. 7. 25; 42. 24.
his descendants. Gen. 46. 10; Ex. 6. 15; Num. 1.
22; 26. 12; 1 Chr. 4. 24; 12. 25.
prophecy concerning. Gen. 49. 5.
—— blesses Christ. Luke 2. 25.
SIMON, si'-mon, same as preceding.
brother of Christ. Matt. 13. 55; Mark 6. 3.
—— (Zelotes), APOSTLE. Matt. 10. 4; Mark 3. 18;
Luke 6. 15.
—— (Pharisee), reproved. Luke 7. 36.
—— (leper). Matt. 26. 6; Mark 14. 3.
—— (of Cyrene), bears the cross of Jesus. Matt.
27. 32; Mark 15. 21; Luke 23. 26.
—— (a tanner), Peter's vision in his house.
Acts 9. 43; 10. 6.
—— (a sorcerer), baptized, Acts 8. 9; rebuked
by Peter, Acts 8. 18.
—— PETER. *See* PETER.
SIMRI, sim'-ri, same as SHIMRI. 1 Chr. 26. 10.
SIN, clay. Ex. 16. 1.
(Zin), wilderness of. Ex. 16; Num. 13. 21; 20;
27. 14.
SINA, si'-nah, Greek form of Sinai. Acts 7. 30.
SINAI, si'-nai, pointed. Ex. 19. 1.
mount. Deut. 33. 2; Judg. 5. 5; Ps. 68. 8, 17;
Gal. 4. 24.
SINIM, sin'-im, Chinese (?). Is. 49. 12.
SINITE, sin'-ite. Gen. 10. 17.
SION, si'-on, (1) lifted up, Deut. 4. 48; (2) Greek
name for Mount Zion, Matt. 21. 5.
SIPHMOTH, sif'-moth, bare places (?). 1 Sam. 30.
28.
SIPPAI, sip'-ai, belonging to the doorstep (?). 1
Chr. 20. 4.
SIRAH, si'-rah, withdrawing. 2 Sam. 3. 26.
SIRION, sir'-i-on, a coat of mail.
mount. Deut. 3. 9; Ps. 29. 6.
SISAMAI, sis'-a-mai, fragrant (?). 1 Chr. 2. 40.
SISERA, si'-ser-ah, binding in chains (?). Judg. 4.
2, 21; 5. 24; 1 Sam. 12. 9; Ps. 83. 9.
SITNAH, sit'-nah, contention. Gen. 26. 21.
SIVAN, si'-van, bright. Esth. 8. 9.
SMYRNA, smir'-nah, myrrh. Rev. 1. 11.
SO, Hebrew form of Egyptian word Shebek. 2
Kin. 17. 4.
SOCHO, so'-ko, same as SHOCHO. 1 Chr. 4. 18.
SOCHOH, same as SHOCHOH. 1 Kin. 4. 10.
SOCOH, same as SHOCO. Josh. 15. 35.
SODI, so'-di, an acquaintance. Num. 13. 10.
SODOM, sod'-om, burning. Gen. 10. 19.
its iniquity and destruction. Gen. 13. 13; 18. 20;
19. 4–24; Deut. 23. 17; 1 Kin. 14. 24.
Lot's deliverance from. Gen. 19.
a warning. Deut. 29. 23; 32. 32; Is. 1. 9; 13. 19;
Lam. 4. 6; Matt. 10. 15; Luke 17. 29; Jude 7;
Rev. 11. 8.
SODOMA, sod'-om-ah, Greek form of the preceding.
Rom. 9. 29.
SODOMITES, sod'-om-ites, persons who were as
wicked as the men of Sodom. 1 Kin. 15. 12.
SOLOMON, sol'-om-on, peaceable. 2 Sam. 5. 14.
king of Israel. 2 Sam. 12. 24; 1 Kin. 1. 2. 24;
1 Chr. 28. 9; 29.
asks of God wisdom. 1 Kin. 3. 5 (4. 29); 2 Chr.
1. 7.
the wise judgment of. 1 Kin. 3. 16.
his league with Hiram for building the temple.
1 Kin. 5; 2 Chr. 2.
builds the temple (2 Sam. 7. 12; 1 Chr. 17. 11).
1 Kin. 6; 7; 2 Chr. 3—5; the dedication, 1 Kin.
8; 2 Chr. 6.
God's covenant with. 1 Kin. 9; 2 Chr. 7. 12.
the queen of Sheba visits. 1 Kin. 10; 2 Chr. 9;
Matt. 6. 29; 12. 42.

SOLOMON—*cont.*
David's prayer for. Ps. 72.
his idolatry, rebuke, and death. 1 Kin. 11. 1, 9, 14, 31, 41; 2 Chr. 9. 29; Neh. 13. 26.
his Proverbs and Canticles. Prov. 1. 1; Eccles. 1. 1; Cant. 1. 1.
SON OF GOD. *See* CHRIST.
—— of MAN. *See* CHRIST.
SOPATER, so'-pa-ter. Acts 20. 4.
SOPHERETH, so-fer'-eth, scribe. Ezra 2. 55.
SOREK, so'-rek, choice vine. Judg. 16. 4.
SOSIPATER, so-si'-pat-er. Rom. 16. 21.
SOSTHENES, sos'-then-ees. Acts 18. 17.
SOTAI, so'-tai, deviator. Ezra 2. 55.
SPAIN. Rom. 15. 24.
STACHYS, sta'-kis, an ear of corn. Rom. 16. 9.
STEPHANAS, ste'-fan-as, crowned. 1 Cor. 1. 16.
STEPHEN, ste'-ven, English form of Stephanas.
deacon and protomartyr. Acts 6. 5, 8; 7. 58.
STOICKS, sto'-ics, philosophers whose founder taught in a famous porch or Stoa. Acts 17. 18.
SUAH, soo'-ah, sweepings. 1 Chr. 7. 36.
SUCCOTH, sook'-oth, booths.
(Canaan). Gen. 33. 17; Josh. 13. 27; 1 Kin. 7. 46; Ps. 60. 6.
punished by Gideon. Judg. 8. 5, 16.
—— (in Egypt). Ex. 12. 37; 13. 20.
SUCCOTH-BENOTH, suc-coth'-be-noth. 2 Kin. 17. 30.
SUCHATHITES, sook'-ath-ites. 1 Chr. 2. 55.
SUKKIIMS, sook'-i-ims, nomads. 2 Chr. 12. 3.
SUR, soor. 2 Kin. 11. 6.
SUSANCHITES, soo'-sank-ites, inhabitants of Susa or Susinak. Ezra 4. 9.
SUSANNA, su-san'-ah, lily. Luke 8. 3.
SUSI, soo'-si, horseman. Num. 13. 11.
SYCHAR, si'-kar, drunken (?). John 4. 5.
SYCHEM, si'-kem, Greek form of Shechem. Acts 7. 16.
SYENE, si-e'-ne, opening. Ezek. 29. 10.
SYNTYCHE, sin'-ty-kee, fortunate. Phil. 4. 2.
SYRACUSE, si'-ra-kuse. Acts 28. 12.
SYRIA, sir'-yah. Judg. 10. 6.
SYRIAN, sir'-yan, inhabitant of Syria. Gen. 25. 20.
SYRIANS, sir'-yans. Gen. 25. 20; Deut. 26. 5.
subdued by David. 2 Sam. 8; 10.
contend with Israel. 1 Kin. 10. 29; 11. 25; 20; 22; 2 Kin. 6. 24; 7; 8. 13; 13. 7; 16. 6; 2 Chr. 18.
employed to punish Joash. 2 Chr. 24. 23. *See* 2 Chr. 28. 23; Is. 7. 2; Ezek. 27. 16; Hos. 12. 12; Amos 1. 5.
gospel preached to. Matt. 4. 24; Acts 15. 23; 18. 18; Gal. 1. 21.
SYROPHENICIAN, si'-ro-fee-nish'-yan, Phenician living in Syria. Mark 7. 26.

TAANACH, ta'-a-nak, castle (?). Josh. 12. 21.
TAANATH-SHILOH, ta'-a-nath-shi'-lo, fig-tree of Shiloh (?). Josh. 16. 6.
TABBAOTH, tab'-a-oth, rings. Ezra 2. 43.
TABBATH, tab'-ath, pleasantness. Judg. 7. 22.
TABEAL, tab'-e-al, God is good. Is. 7. 6.
TABEEL, tab'-e-el, another way of writing Tabeal. Ezra 4. 7.
TABERAH, tab-er'-ah, burning. Num. 11. 3.
TABITHA, tab'-ith-ah, gazelle. Acts 9. 36.
TABOR, ta'-bor, height. Josh. 19. 22.
(mount). Judg. 4. 14. *See* Judg. 8. 18; 1 Sam. 10. 3; Ps. 89. 12; Jer. 46. 18; Hos. 5. 1.
TABRIMON, tab'-rim-on, Rimmon is good. 1 Kin. 15. 18.
TACHMONITE, tak'-mon-ite, same as HACHMONITE (?). 2 Sam. 23. 8.
TADMOR, tad'-mor, city of palms (?).
(Palmyra), built by Solomon. 1 Kin. 9. 18.
TAHAN, ta'-han, camp. Num. 26. 35.
TAHANITES, ta'-han-ites, descendants of Tahan. Num. 26. 35.
TAHAPANES, ta'-ha-pan'-es, head of the land. Jer. 2. 16.
TAHPANHES, same as preceding. Jer. 43. 7.
TAHPENES, tah'-pen-es. 1 Kin. 11. 19.

TAHATH, ta'-hath, substitute. 1 Chr. 6. 24.
TAHREA, tah-re'-ah, cunning (?). 1 Chr. 9. 41.
TAHTIM-HODSHI, tah'-tim-hod'-shi, nether land newly inhabited (?). 2 Sam. 24. 6.
TALITHA, ta-li'-tha, girl. Mark 5. 41.
TALMAI, tal'-mai, abounding in furrows. Num. 13. 22.
TALMON, tal'-mon, oppressed. 1 Chr. 9. 17.
TAMAH, ta'-mah, joy. Neh. 7. 55.
TAMAR, ta'-mar, a palm tree. Gen. 38. 6.
TAMMUZ, tam'-ooz, son of life (?).
women weeping for. Ezek. 8. 14.
TANACH, ta'-nak, same as TAANACH. Josh. 21. 25.
TANHUMETH, tan-hoom'-eth, consolation. 2 Kin. 25. 23.
TAPHATH, ta'-fath, a drop(?). 1 Kin. 4. 11.
TAPPUAH, tap-oo'-ah, apple. 1 Chr. 2. 43.
TARAH, ta'-rah, station. Num. 33. 27.
TARALAH, ta'-ra-lah, reeling (?). Josh. 18. 27.
TAREA, ta-re'-ah, same as TAHREA. 1 Chr. 8. 35.
TARPELITES, tar'-pel-ites, people of Tarpel. Ezra 4. 9.
TARSHISH, tar'-shish. Gen. 10. 4; 1 Kin. 10. 22; 2 Chr. 9. 21; 20. 36; Jer. 10. 9; Ezek. 27. 12; 38. 13.
Jonah going there. Jonah 1. 3.
prophecies concerning. Ps. 48. 7; 72. 10; Is. 2. 16; 23; 60. 9; 66. 19.
TARSUS, tar'-sus, city of the apostle Paul. Acts 9. 11; 11. 25; 21. 39.
TARTAK, tar'-tak. 2 Kin. 17. 31.
TARTAN, tar'-tan, military chief. 2 Kin. 18. 17.
TATNAI, tat'-nai, gift (?).
and Shethar-boznai hinder the rebuilding of the temple. Ezra 5. 3; 6. 13.
TEBAH, te'-bah, slaughter. Gen. 22. 24.
TEBALIAH, te-bal-i'-ah, whom Jehovah has immersed. 1 Chr. 26. 11.
TEBETH, te'-beth. Esth. 2. 16.
TEHAPHNEHES, te-haph'-ne-hes, same as TAHAPANES. Ezek. 30. 18.
TEHINNAH, te-hin'-ah, cry for mercy. 1 Chr. 4. 12.
TEKEL, te'-kel, weighed. Dan. 5. 25.
TEKOA, te-ko'-ah, sound of trumpet (1 Chr. 2. 24; 4. 5).
widow of. 2 Sam. 14 (Jer. 6. 1).
TEKOAH, te-ko'-ah, same as TEKOA. 2 Sam. 14. 2.
TEKOITE, te-ko'-ite, inhabitant of Tekoah. 2 Sam. 23. 26.
TEL-ABIB, tel-a'-bib, hill of ears of corn. Ezek. 3. 15.
TELAH, te'-lah. 1 Chr. 7. 25.
TELAIM, te-la'-im, lambs. 1 Sam. 15. 4.
TELASSAR, tel'-as'-ar, Assyrian hill. Is. 37. 12.
TELEM, te'-lem, oppression. Ezra 10. 24.
TEL-HARESHA, tel-har'-e-shah, forest-hill. Neh. 7. 61.
TEL-HARSA, tel-har'-sah, same as preceding. Ezra 2. 59.
TEL-MELAH, tel-me'-lah, salt-hill. Ezra 2. 59.
TEMA, te'-mah, a desert. Gen. 25. 15; Job 6. 19; Is. 21. 14; Jer. 25. 23.
TEMAN, te'-man, on the right hand. Gen. 36. 11; Jer. 49. 7, 20; Ezek. 25. 13; Amos 1. 12; Obad. 9; Hab. 3. 3.
TEMANI, te'-man-i, descendants of Teman. Gen. 36. 34.
TEMANITE, te'-man-ite, same as preceding. Job 2. 11.
TEMENI, te'-men-i, same as TEMANI. 1 Chr. 4. 6.
TERAH, te'-rah, a station (?). Gen. 11. 24.
TERAPHIM, ter'-af-im, nourishers.
of Laban. Gen. 31. 34.
of Micah. Judg. 17. 5; 18. 14.
of Michal. 1 Sam. 19. 13.
TERESH, te'-resh, severe (?). Esth. 2. 21.
TERTIUS, ter'-shus, the third. Rom. 16. 22.
TERTULLUS, ter-tul'-us (*dim.* of TERTIUS). Acts 24. 1.
TETRARCH, tet'-rark, ruler of a fourth part of a country. Matt. 14. 1.
THADDÆUS, thad-e'-us, Greek form of Theudas. Matt. 10. 3.

THAHASH, tha'-hash, seal (?). Gen. 22. 24.

THAMAH, tha'-mah, laughter. Ezra 2. 53.

THAMAR, tha'-mar, Greek equivalent of Tamar. Matt. 1. 3.

THARA, tha'-rah, Greek form of Terah. Luke 3. 34.

THARSHISH, thar'-shish, same as TARSHISH. 1 Kin. 10. 22.

THEBEZ, the'-bez, brightness.
Abimelech wounded at. Judg. 9. 50.

THELASAR, thel'-as'-ar, same as TELASSAR. 2 Kin. 19. 12.

THEOPHILUS, the-o'-fil-us, loved of God. Luke 1. 3.

THESSALONICA, thes'-al-on-i'-kah.
Paul at. Acts 17.
church there instructed. 1 & 2 Thess.

THEUDAS, thoo'-das, praise (?). Acts 5. 36.

THIMNATHAH, thim-nah'-thah, portion. Josh. 19. 43.

THOMAS, tom'-as, a twin.
APOSTLE. Matt. 10. 3; Mark 3. 18; Luke 6. 15; Acts 1. 13.
his zeal. John 11. 16.
his unbelief and confession. John 20. 24.

THUMMIM, thoom'-im, truth (?)
on high priest's breastplate. Ex. 28. 30; Lev. 8. 8; Deut. 33. 8; Ezra 2. 63; Neh. 7. 65.

THYATIRA, thi'-at-i'-rah (Acts 16. 14).
angel of. Rev. t. 11; 2. 18.

TIBERIAS, ti-be'-ri-as, a place named after Tiberius. John 6. 1.

TIBERIUS, ti-be'-ri-us. Luke 3. 1.

TIBHATH, tib'-hath, butchery. 1 Chr. 18. 8.

TIBNI, tib'-ni, made of straw (?). 1 Kin. 16. 21.

TIDAL, ti'-dal, dread. Gen. 14. 1.

TIGLATH-PILESER, tig'-lath-pil-e'-zer, the son of the temple of Sarra is a ground of confidence (?). (Tilgath-pilneser, 1 Chr. 5. 6, 26), 2 Kin. 15. 29; 16. 7; 2 Chr. 28. 20.

TIKVAH, tik'-vah, expectation. 2 Kin. 22. 14.

TIKVATH, tik'-vath, same as TIKVAH. 2 Chr. 34. 22.

TILGATH-PILNESER, til'-gath-pil-ne'-ser, same as TIGLATH-PILESER. 1 Chr. 5. 6.

TILON, ti'-lon, gift (?). 1 Chr. 4. 20.

TIMÆUS, ti-me'-us, polluted (?). Mark 10. 46.

TIMNA, tim'-nah, unapproachable. Gen. 36. 12.

TIMNAH, tim'-nah, a portion. Josh. 15. 10.

TIMNATH, tim'-nath, same as TIMNAH. Gen. 38. 12.

TIMNATH-HERES, tim'-nath-he'-res, portion of the sun. Judg. 2. 9.

TIMNATH-SERAH, tim'-nath-se'-rah, portion of the remainder. Josh. 19. 50.
Joshua buried there. Josh. 24. 30.

TIMNITE, tim'-nite, a man of Timna. Judg. 15. 6.

TIMON, ti'-mon. Acts 6. 5.

TIMOTHEUS, ti-mo'-the-us, honouring God. Acts 16. 1.

TIMOTHY, tim'-oth-y, English form of the above.
accompanies Paul. Acts 16. 3; 17. 14, 15; Rom. 16. 21; 2 Cor. 1. 1, 19.
commended. 1 Cor. 16. 10; Phil. 2. 19.
instructed in letters by Paul. 1 & 2 Tim.

TIPHSAH, tif'-sah, passage. 1 Kin. 4. 24.

TIRAS, ti'-ras, crushing (?). Gen. 10. 2.

TIRATHITES, ti'-rath-ites. 1 Chr. 2. 55.

TIRHAKAH, tir-hah'-kah, distance (?).
Sennacherib's war with. 2 Kin. 19. 9.

TIRHANAH, tir'-han-ah, murmuring (?). 1 Chr. 2. 48.

TIRIA, tir'-i-ah, fear. 1 Chr. 4. 16.

TIRSHATHA, tir-sha'-thah, the feared (?). Ezra 2. 63; Neh. 7. 70.

TIRZAH, tir'-zah, pleasantness. Num. 26. 33; 1 Kin. 14. 17; 15. 21; 16. 8, 15; 2 Kin. 15. 16; Cant. 6. 4 (Josh. 12. 24).

TISHBITE, tish'-bite, inhabitant of Tishbe. 1 Kin. 17. 1.

TITUS, ti'-tus, protected. Gal. 2. 3.
Paul's love for. 2 Cor. 2. 13; 7. 6, 13.
instructed by Paul. Tit. 1—3.

TIZITE, ti'-zite. 1 Chr. 11. 45.

TOAH, to'-ah, low. 1 Chr. 6. 34.

TOB, tobe, good. Judg. 11. 3.

TOB-ADONIJAH, tob'-a-do-ni'-jah, good is my lord Jehovah. 2 Chr. 17. 8.

TOBIAH, tob-i'-ah, Jehovah is good. Ezra 2. 60.
the Ammonite, vexes the Jews. Neh. 4. 3; 6. 1, 12, 14; 13. 4.

TOBIJAH, tob-i'-jah, same as TOBIAH. 2 Chr. 17. 8.

TOCHEN, to'-ken, a measure. 1 Chr. 4. 32.

TOGARMAH, to-gar'-mah, rugged. Gen. 10. 3.

TOHU, to'-hoo, same as TOAH. 1 Sam. 1. 1.

TOI, to'-i, wanderer. 2 Sam. 8. 9.

TOLA, to'-lah, worm. Gen. 46. 13.

TOLAD, to'-lad, birth. 1 Chr. 4. 29.

TOLAITES, to'-la-ites, descendants of Tola. Num. 26. 23.

TOPHEL, to'-fel, lime. Deu. 1. 1.

TOPHET, to'-fet, burning. Is. 30. 33.

TOPHETH, to'-feth, same as TOPHET. 2 Kings 23. 10.
See MOLOCH.

TORMAH, torm'-ah, privily. Judg. 9. 31.

TOU, to'-oo, older form of Toi. 1 Chr. 18. 9.

TRACHONITIS, tra-ko-ni'-tis, rugged. Luke 3. 1.

TROAS, tro'-as, so called from Tros.
visited by Paul. Acts 16. 8; 20. 5; 2 Cor. 2. 12; 2 Tim. 4. 13.

TROGYLLIUM, tro-gil'-yum. Acts 20. 15.

TROPHIMUS, trof'-im-us, master of the house (?).
companion of Paul. Acts 20. 4; 21. 29; 2 Tim. 4. 20.

TRYPHENA, tri-fe'-nah, delicate. Rom. 16. 12.

TRYPHOSA, tri-fo'-sah, delicate. Rom. 16. 12.

TUBAL, too'-bal, production (?). Gen. 10. 2; Is. 66. 19; Ezek. 27. 13; 32. 26; 38; 39.

TUBAL-CAIN, too'-bal-kane', producer of weapons (?). Gen. 4. 22.

TYCHICUS, tik'-ik-us, fortuitous.
companion of Paul. Acts 20. 4; 2 Tim. 4. 12; Tit. 3. 12.
commended. Eph. 6. 21; Col. 4. 7.

TYRANNUS, ti-ran'-us, tyrant. Acts 19. 9.

TYRE, tire, rock. Josh. 19. 29.
its wealth. Ezek. 27.
fall. Ezek. 26. 7.
Christ visits coasts of. Matt. 15. 21.
Paul lands at. Acts 21. 3.

TYRUS, ti'-rus, Latin name of Tyre. Jer. 25. 22.

UCAL, oo'-kal, I shall prevail. Prov. 30. 1.

UEL, oo'-el, will of God (?). Ezra 10. 34.

ULAI, oo'-lai. Dan. 8. 2.

ULAM, oo'-lam, foremost. 1 Chr. 7. 16.

ULLA, ool'-ah, yoke. 1 Chr. 7. 39.

UMMAH, oom'-ah, community. Josh. 19. 30.

UNNI, oon'-i, depressed. 1 Chr. 15. 18.

UPHARSIN, oo-far'-sin, and dividers. Dan. 5. 25.

UPHAZ, oo'-faz, gold of. Jer. 10. 9; Dan. 10. 5.

UR, oor, light.
land of. Gen. 11. 28; 15. 7.

URBANE, ur'-ban, pleasant. Rom. 16. 9.

URI, oo'-ri, fiery. Ex. 31. 2.

URIAH, oo-ri'-ah, light of Jehovah.
the Hittite. 2 Sam. 11; 1 Kin. 15. 5; Matt. 1. 6.

URIAS, oo-ri'-as, Greek form of Uriah. Matt. 1. 6.

URIEL, oo'-ri-el, light of God. 1 Chr. 6. 24.

URIJAH, oo'-ri-jah, same as URIAH.
(priest.) 2 Kin. 16. 10, 16.
—— (prophet). Jer. 26. 20.

URIM, oo'-rim, light. Ex. 28. 30. See THUMMIM.

UTHAI, oo'-thai, helpful. 1 Chr. 9. 4.

UZ, fertile. Gen. 10. 23.

UZAI, oo'-zai, hoped for (?). Neh. 3. 25.

UZAL, ooz'-al, wanderer. Gen. 10. 27.

UZZA, ooz'-ah, strength. 2 Kin. 21. 18.

UZZAH, another form of Uzza.
his trespass. 2 Sam. 6. 3.
his death. 1 Chr. 13. 7.

UZZEN-SHERAH, ooz'-en-she'-rah. 1 Chr. 7. 24.

UZZI, ooz'-i, shortened form of Uzziah. 1 Chr. 6. 5.

UZZIA, ooz-i'-ah, another form of Uzziah. 1 Chr. 11. 44.

UZZIAH, ooz-i′-ah, might of Jehovah. 2 Kin. 15. 13. *See* AZARIAH.
UZZIEL, ooz′-i-el, power of God. Ex. 6. 18.
UZZIELITES, ooz′-i-el-ites, descendants of Uzziel. Num. 3. 27.

VAJEZATHA, va′-je-za′-thah, strong as the wind (?). Esth. 9. 9.
VANIAH, va-ni′-ah, distress (?). Ezra 10. 36.
VASHNI, vash′-ni, strong (?); but perhaps not a proper name. 1 Chr. 6. 28.
VASHTI, vash′-ti, beautiful. Esth. 1. 9.
VOPHSI, vof′-si, expansion (?). Num. 13. 14.

ZAANAIM, za′-an-a′-im, wanderings (?). Judg. 4. 11.
ZAANAN, za′-a-nan, place of flocks. Mic. 1. 11.
ZAANANNIM, za′-a-nan′-im, same as ZAANAIM. Josh. 19. 33.
ZAAVAN, za′-av-an, disturbed. Gen. 36. 27.
ZABAD, za′-bad, gift. 1 Chr. 2. 36.
ZABBAI, zab′-ai. Ezra 10. 28.
ZABBUD, zab′-ood, given. Ezra 8. 14.
ZABDI, zab′-di, the gift of Jehovah. Josh. 7. 1.
ZABDIEL, zab′-di-el, the gift of God. 1 Chr. 27. 2.
ZABUD, za′-bood, same as ZABBUD. 1 Kin. 4. 5.
ZABULON, Greek form of Zebulun. Matt. 4. 13.
ZACCAI, zak′-ai, pure. Ezra 2. 9.
ZACCHÆUS, zak-e′-us, Greek form of Zaccai. Luke 19. 2.
ZACCHUR, zak′-oor, mindful. 1 Chr. 4. 26.
ZACCUR, zak′-oor, same as preceding. Num. 13. 4.
ZACHARIAH, zak′-ar-i′-ah, whom Jehovah remembers.
    last king of Israel of Jehu's race, as foretold by the word of the Lord, begins to reign. 2 Kin. 14. 29.
    smitten by Shallum, who succeeds him. 2 Kin. 15. 10.
ZACHARIAS, zak′-ar-i′-as, Greek form of preceding.
    father of John the Baptist, with Elisabeth his wife, accounted righteous before God. Luke 1. 6.
    is promised a son. Luke 1. 13.
    doubting, is stricken with dumbness. Luke 1. 18, 22.
    his recovery and song. Luke 1. 64, 68.
    —— "son of Barachias," slain "between the temple and the altar." Matt. 23. 35; Luke 11. 51. *See* ZECHARIAH.
ZACHER, za′-ker, memorial. 1 Chr. 8. 31.
ZADOK, za′-dok, just.
    priest. 2 Sam. 8. 17; 15. 24; 20. 25.
    anoints Solomon king. 1 Kin. 1. 39.
ZAHAM, za′-ham, loathing. 2 Chr. 11. 19.
ZAIR, za′-ir, small. 2 Kin. 8. 21.
ZALAPH, za′-laf, wound (?). Neh. 3. 30.
ZALMON, zal′-mon, shady. 2 Sam. 23. 28.
ZALMONAH, zal-mo′-nah, same as preceding. Num. 33. 41.
ZALMUNNA, zal-moon′-ah, shelter denied. Judg. 8. 5.
ZAMZUMMIMS, zam-zoom′-ims, giant race, destroyed by the Ammonites. Deut. 2. 20, 21.
ZANOAH, za-no′-ah, marsh. Josh. 15. 34.
ZAPHNATH-PAANEAH, zaf′-nath-pa′-a-ne′-ah, prince of the life of the age. Gen. 41. 45.
ZAPHON, za′-fon, north. Josh. 13. 27.
ZARA, za′-rah, Greek form of Zarah. Matt. 1. 3.
ZARAH, za′-rah, sunrise (?). Gen. 38. 30.
ZAREAH, za′-re-ah, hornet. Neh. 11. 29.
ZAREATHITES, za′-re-ath-ites, inhabitants of Zareah. 1 Chr. 2. 53.
ZARED, za′-red, exuberant growth. Num. 21. 12.
ZAREPHATH, zar′-ef-ath, workshop for refining metals.
    (Sarepta), Elijah there. 1 Kin. 17. 10. *See* ELIJAH.
ZARETAN, za′-ret-an, same as ZARTHAN. Josh. 3. 16.
ZARETH-SHAHAR, za′-reth-sha′-har, the splendour of the morning. Josh. 13. 19.
ZARHITES, zar′-hites, persons descended from Zerah. Num. 26. 13.
ZARTANAH, zar-tah′-nah. 1 Kin. 4. 12.

ZARTHAN, zar′-than, same as ZARETAN. 1 Kin. 7. 46.
ZATTHU, zat′-thoo, same as ZATTU. Neh. 10. 14.
ZATTU, zat′-oo, irascible (?). Ezra 2. 8.
ZAVAN, za′-van, same as ZAAVAN, 1 Chr. 1. 42.
ZAZA, za′-zah. 1 Chr. 2. 33.
ZEBADIAH, zeb′-ad-i′-ah, full form of ZABDI. 1 Chr. 8. 15.
ZEBAH, ze′-bah, sacrifice.
    and Zalmunna. Judg. 8. 5, 21; Ps. 83. 11.
ZEBAIM, ze-ba′-im, same as ZEBOIM. Ezra 2. 57.
ZEBEDEE, zeb′-ed-ee, Greek form of Zebadiah. Matt. 4. 21; Mark 1. 20.
ZEBINA, ze-bi′-nah, bought. Ezra 10. 43.
ZEBOIM, ze-bo′-im, gazelles. Gen. 10. 19; 14. 2; 19. 25; Deut. 29. 23; Hos. 11. 8.
ZEBUDAH, ze-boo′-dah, given. 2 Kin. 23. 36.
ZEBUL, ze′-bool, habitation. Judg. 9. 28.
ZEBULONITE, ze-bool′-on-ite, a member of the tribe of Zebulun. Judg. 12. 11.
ZEBULUN, ze-bool′-on. Gen. 30. 20; 35. 23; 49. 13; Num. 1. 30; 26. 26; Deut. 33. 18; Josh. 19. 10; Judg. 4. 6; 5. 14, 18; 6. 35; 2 Chr. 30. 11, 18; Ps. 68. 27; Ezek. 48. 26; Rev. 7. 8.
    Christ preaches in the land of (Is. 9. 1); Matt. 4. 13.
ZEBULUNITES, ze-bool′-on-ites, a less correct way of spelling Zebulonites. Num. 26. 27.
ZECHARIAH, zek′-ar-i′-ah, a better way of spelling Zachariah.
    son of Jehoiada, stoned in the court of the Lord's house. 2 Chr. 24. 20, 21.
    —— son of Jeberechiah. Is. 8. 2.
    —— the prophet, his exhortations to repentance, his visions and predictions. Zech. 1—14.
ZEDAD, ze′-dad, hunting (?). Num. 34. 8.
ZEDEKIAH, zed′-ek-i′-ah, justice of Jehovah.
    false prophet. 1 Kin. 22. 11; 2 Chr. 18. 10, 23.
    —— another. Jer. 29. 22.
    —— (Mattaniah), king of Judah. 2 Kin. 24. 17; 25; 2 Chr. 36. 10, 11; Jer. 37; 38; 39; 52.
ZEEB, ze′-eb, wolf. Judg. 7. 25.
ZELAH, ze′-lah, side. Josh. 18. 28.
ZELEK, zel′-ek, fissure. 2 Sam. 23. 37.
ZELOPHEHAD, ze-lo′-fe-had, fracture. Num. 26. 33.
ZELOTES, ze-lo′-tees, Greek equivalent of Canaanite, an emulator. Luke 6. 15.
ZELZAH, zel′-zah, shade in the heat. 1 Sam. 10. 2.
ZEMARAIM, zem′-ar-a′-im, two fleeces. Josh. 18. 22.
ZEMARITE, zem′-ar-ite. Gen. 10. 18.
ZEMIRA, ze-mi′-rah. 1 Chr. 7. 8.
ZENAN, ze′-nan, same as ZAANAN. Josh. 15. 37.
ZENAS, ze′-nas, contraction of Zenodorus. Tit. 3. 13.
ZEPHANIAH, zef′-an-i′-ah, whom Jehovah hid. 2 Kin. 25. 18.
    priest. Jer. 29. 25; 37. 3.
    —— prophet. Zeph. 1; 2; 3.
ZEPHATH, ze′-fath, watch-tower (?). Judg. 1. 17.
ZEPHATHAH, ze′-fath-ah. 2 Chr. 14. 10.
ZEPHI, ze′-fi, same as ZEPHATH. 1 Chr. 1. 36.
ZEPHO, ze′-fo, older form of Zephi. Gen. 36. 11.
ZEPHON, ze′-fon, a looking out. Num. 26. 15.
ZEPHONITES, ze′-fon-ites, descendants of Zephon. Num. 26. 15.
ZER, flint (?). Josh. 19. 35.
ZERAH, ze′-rah, dawn. 2 Chr. 14. 9; 16. 8.
ZERAHIAH, ze′-rah-i′-ah, whom Jehovah caused to rise. 1 Chr. 6. 6.
ZERED, ze′-red, same as ZARED. Deut. 2. 13.
ZEREDA, ze-re′-dah, cool. 1 Kin. 11. 26.
ZEREDATHAH, ze-re-dah′-thah, same as preceding. 2 Chr. 4. 17.
ZERERATH, ze-re′-rath. Judg. 7. 22.
ZERESH, ze′-resh, gold. Esth. 5. 10.
ZERETH, ze′-reth, gold (?). 1 Chr. 4. 7.
ZERI, ze′-ri, same as IZRI. 1 Chr. 25. 3.
ZEROR, ze′-ror, bundle. 1 Sam. 9. 1.
ZERUAH, ze-roo′-ah, leprous. 1 Kin. 11. 26.
ZERUBBABEL, ze-roob′-ab-el, scattered in Babylon. (Zorobabel), prince of Judah. Ezra 2. 2.
    restores the worship of God. Ezra 3. 1; Neh. 12. 47; Hag. 1. 1, 14; 2. 1; Zech. 4. 6.

ZERUIAH, ze-roo'-yah. 1 Sam. 26. 6.
ZETHAM, ze'-tham, olive. 1 Chr. 23. 8.
ZETHAN, ze'-than, same as ZETHAM. 1 Chr. 7. 10.
ZETHAR, ze'-thar. Esth. 1. 10.
ZIA, zi'-ah, motion. 1 Chr. 5. 13.
ZIBA, zi'-bah, planter. 2 Sam. 9. 2.
ZIBEON, zib'-e-on, dyed. Gen. 36. 2.
ZIBIA, zib'-i-ah, gazelle (?). 1 Chr. 8. 9.
ZIBIAH, zib'-i-ah, same as ZIBIA. 2 Kin. 12. 1.
ZICHRI, zik'-ri, famous. 2 Chr. 23. 1; 28.
ZIDDIM, zid'-im, sides. Josh. 19. 35.
ZIDKIJAH, zid-ki'-jah, justice of Jehovah. Neh. 10. 1.
ZIDON, zi'-don, fishing. Gen. 49. 13; Josh. 11. 8; Judg. 10. 6; 18. 7; 1 Kin. 11. 1; Ezra 3. 7; Luke 4. 26; Acts 12. 20.
prophecies concerning. Is. 23; Jer. 25. 22; 27. 3; 47. 4; Ezek. 27. 8; 28. 21; 32. 30; Joel 3. 4; Zech. 9. 2.
ZIDONIANS, zi-done'-yans, inhabitants of Zidon. Judg. 10. 12; 18. 7; 1 Kin. 11. 1.
ZIF, blossom. 1 Kin. 6. 1.
ZIHA, zi'-hah, drought. Ezra 2. 43.
ZIKLAG, zik'-lag. Josh. 15. 31; 1 Sam. 27. 6; 30. 1; 2 Sam. 1. 1; 1 Chr. 12. 1.
ZILLAH, zil'-ah, shade. Gen. 4. 19.
ZILPAH, zil'-pah, dropping. Gen. 29. 24.
ZILTHAI, zil'-thai, shady. 1 Chr. 8. 20.
ZIMMAH, zim'-ah, planning. 1 Chr. 6. 20.
ZIMRAN, zim'-ran, celebrated. Gen. 25. 2.
ZIMRI, zim'-ri, same as ZIMRAN. 1 Kin. 16. 9.
ZIN, thorn.
  wilderness of. Num. 13. 21; Josh. 15. 1.
ZINA, zi'-nah, abundance (?). 1 Chr. 23. 10.
ZION, zi'-on, sunny.
  (mount). 2 Sam. 5. 7; 1 Kin. 8. 1; Rom. 11. 26; Heb. 12. 22; Rev. 14. 1.
ZIOR, zi'-or, smallness. Josh. 15. 54.
ZIPH, zif, flowing. 1 Chr. 4. 16.
ZIPHAH, zi'-fah, feminine of ZIPH. 1 Chr. 4. 16.
ZIPHIMS, zif'-ims, inhabitants of Ziph. Ps. 54, title.

ZIPHITES, zif'-ites, same as ZIPHIMS. 1 Sam. 23. 19.
ZIPHION, zif'-yon, same as ZEPHON. Gen. 46. 16.
ZIPHRON, zif'-ron, sweet smell. Num. 34. 9.
ZIPPOR, zip'-or, bird. Num. 22. 2.
ZIPPORAH, zip-or'-ah, *fem.* of ZIPPOR. Ex. 2. 21; 4. 20.
ZITHRI, zith'-ri, protection of Jehovah (?). Ex. 6. 22.
ZIZ, a flower. 2 Chr. 20. 16.
ZIZA, zi'-zah, abundance. 1 Chr. 4. 37.
ZIZAH, fulness. 1 Chr. 23. 11.
ZOAN, zo'-an, low region. Num. 13. 22; Ps. 78. 12.
ZOAR, zo'-ar, smallness. Gen. 13. 10; 14. 2; 19. 22 (Is. 15. 5); Deut. 34. 3; Jer. 48. 34.
ZOBA, zo'-bah, a plantation. 2 Sam. 10. 6.
ZOBAH, same as preceding.
  kings of, subdued. 1 Sam. 14. 47; 2 Sam. 8. 3; 1 Kin. 11. 23.
ZOBEBAH, zo-be'-bah, walking slowly. 1 Chr. 4. 8.
ZOHAR, zo'-har, light. Gen. 23. 8.
ZOHELETH, zo-he'-leth, serpent stone. 1 Kin. 1. 9.
ZOHETH, zo'-heth, strong (?). 1 Chr. 4. 20.
ZOPHAH, zo'-fah, a cruse (?). 1 Chr. 7. 35.
ZOPHAI, zo'-phai, honeycomb. 1 Chr. 6. 26.
ZOPHAR, zo'-far, chatterer. Job 2. 11; 11; 20; 42. 9.
ZOPHIM, zo'-fim, watchers. Num. 23. 14.
ZORAH, zo'-rah, a place of hornets.
  city of Samson. Josh. 19. 41; Judg. 13. 2. 25; 16. 31.
ZORATHITES, zo'-rath-ites, people of Zorah. 1 Chr. 4. 2.
ZOREAH, zo'-re-ah, same as ZORAH. Josh. 15. 33.
ZORITES, zor'-ites, same as ZORATHITES. 1 Chr. 2. 54.
ZOROBABEL, zo-rob'-ab-el, Greek form of Zerubbabel. Mat. 1. 12.
ZUAR, zoo'-ar, same as ZOAR. Num. 1. 8.
ZUPH, zoof, flag, sedge. 1 Sam. 1. 1.
ZUR, zoor, rock. Num. 25. 15.
ZURIEL, zoor'-i-el, God is the Rock. Num. 3. 35.
ZURISHADDAI, zoor'-i-shad'-ai, whose Almighty is the Rock. Num. 1. 6.
ZUZIMS, zooz'-ims, giants. Gen. 14. 5.

OMEGA, the end, Rev. 1. 8, 11; 21. 6; 22. 13.

SUBJECT-INDEX

TO THE HOLY SCRIPTURES.

CHRIST, LORD JESUS—*cont.*

the Lamb of God, John 1. 29, 36; Rev. 5. 6; 6. 1, 16; 12. 11; 13. 8; 15. 3; 19. 7; 22. 1, 3.
the Mediator, Gal. 3. 19; 1 Tim. 2. 5; Heb. 2. 17; 7. 25; 8. 6; 9. 15; 10. 10; 12. 2, 24; 13. 15.
the Lord our Righteousness, Jer. 23. 6; 33. 16; Mal. 4. 2; Acts 17. 31; Rom. 5. 18; Phil. 1. 11; Heb. 7. 2; 2 Pet. 1. 1.
the Lord of all, Acts 10. 3, 6.
the Lord of glory, 1 Cor. 2. 8; James 2. 1.
King of kings, and Lord of lords, Rev. 19. 16.
Prophet, Priest, and King, Deut. 18. 15; Is. 49; 50; 51; 52; Nah. 1. 15; Matt. 2. 2; 23. 36; 24. 4; 25. 34; Luke 4. 1, 15, 16, 18, 24; 5. 3, 17, 32; 19. 41; 21. 10, 25; 22. 34; 23. 2, 27; John 18. 37; 19. 14, 19; Acts 17. 7; 1 Tim. 1. 17; 6. 15; Heb. 1. 8; 2. 17; 3. 1; Rev. 1. 5; 11. 15; 15. 3; 17. 14; 19. 16.
Alpha and Omega, Rev. 21. 6; 22. 13.

CHRIST (the man CHRIST JESUS).

—— LIFE ON EARTH:—

His miraculous conception and birth predicted, Is. 7. 14; 11. 1; Matt. 1. 18; Luke 1. 31.
accomplished at Bethlehem, Matt. 1. 25; Luke 2. 7.
announced to shepherds by angels, Luke 2. 9-14.
wise men of the East do homage to, Matt. 2. 1.
circumcision of, and presentation in temple, Luke 2. 21. 22.
carried into Egypt, Matt. 2. 13.
first public appearance (doctors in temple), Luke 2. 46.
baptism by John, Matt. 3. 13; Mark 1. 9; Luke 3. 21; John 1. 32; 3. 24.
selection of disciples, Matt. 4. 18; Mark 1. 16; Luke 4. 31; 5. 10; John 1. 38.
begins to preach and heal, Matt. 4. 12; Mark 1. 14; Luke 4. 16.
opposition of the Pharisees begins, Matt. 9. 34.
sufferings and death predicted, Matt. 16. 21; 17. 22, 23; Luke 9. 22.
transfiguration, Matt. 17; Mark 9.
institutes the Lord's Supper, Matt. 26; Mark 14; Luke 22 (1 Cor. 11. 23).
betrayed by Judas, Matt. 26; Mark 14; Luke 22; John 18; Acts 1.
deserted by disciples, Matt. 26; John 18.
taken before Annas and Caiaphas, and Pilate and Herod, Matt. 26. 57; 27; Mark 14. 54; 15; Luke 23; John 18. 19.
pronounced faultless by Pilate, yet delivered up to the Jews, Matt. 27; Mark 15; Luke 23; John 18. 19.
crucified, Matt. 27; Mark 15; Luke 23; John 19.
His legs not broken, John 19. 33.
His side pierced by soldier, John 19. 34.
His garments divided amongst soldiers, Matt. 27. 35; Mark 15. 24; Luke 23. 34; John 19. 24.
yields up the ghost, Matt. 27. 50.
buried, Matt. 27; Mark 15; Luke 23; John 19; in a new sepulchre watched by soldiers and sealed, Matt. 27. 66.
His descent into hell, Eph. 4. 9.
rises from the tomb, Matt. 28; Mark 16; Luke 24; John 20. 21 (1 Cor. 15. 4).
appears to Mary Magdalene and disciples, Matt. 28; Mark 16; Luke 24; John 20.
shews Thomas His hands and feet, John 20. 27.
charge to Peter to feed His lambs, John 21. 15.
ascends into heaven, Mark 16; Luke 24; Acts 1. 9, 10.
seen in heaven by Stephen, Acts 7. 55.
appearances after ascension:—
　to Paul, Acts 9. 4; 18. 9; 22. 8.
　to John, Rev. 1. 13.

—— WORK ON EARTH:—

questions the doctors, Luke 2. 46.
is tempted, Matt. 4; Mark 1. 12; Luke 4.
sermon on the mount. Matt. 5. 6, 7.
cleanses the temple, Ps. 69. 9; John 2. 14.
teaches Nicodemus, John 3.

CHRIST (WORK ON EARTH)—*cont.*

converses with woman of Samaria, John 4.
the people attempt to make Him king, John 6. 15.
taunted by His brethren, John 7. 4.
the people's testimony, Matt. 16. 13; Mark 8. 27; Luke 9. 18; John 7. 12.
message to John the Baptist, Luke 7. 22.
anointed at Simon the Pharisee's house, Luke 7. 36.
pays tribute at Capernaum, Matt. 17. 24.
inculcates humility on apostles, Matt. 18; Mark 9. 33; Luke 9. 49; 22, 24.
departs from Galilee into Judæa, Matt. 19. 1.
teaches respecting divorce, Matt. 19. 3; Luke 16. 18.
reproves Herod ("that fox"), and Jerusalem, Luke 13. 32, 34.
pardons woman taken in adultery, John 8.
compares Martha and Mary ("that good part"), Luke 10. 38-42.
suffers children to come to Him, Matt. 19. 13; Mark 10. 13; Luke 18. 15.
Zacchæus the publican called by, Luke 19. 2.
anointed by Mary at Bethany, Matt. 26. 6; Mark 14. 3; John 12. 3.
His triumphant entry into Jerusalem, Matt. 21; Mark 11; Luke 19; John 12.
drives moneychangers out of temple, Matt. 21. 12; Mark 11. 15; Luke 19 45.
curses the fig tree, Matt. 21. 19; Mark 11. 12.
Greeks would see Jesus, John 12. 20.
His answer, John 12. 23.
　to the chief priests, Luke 20. 3.
　to the Pharisees, Matt. 22. 15.
　to the Sadducees, Mark 12. 18.
glorified by the Father, John 12. 28.
chief priests conspire to kill, Matt. 26. 3; Mark 14. 1.
covenant with Judas to betray, Matt. 26. 13; Mark 14. 10; Luke 22. 3; John 13. 18.
gives directions for the passover, Matt. 26. 17; Mark 14. 12; Luke 22. 7.
foretells Peter's denial, Matt. 26. 34; Mark 14. 29; Luke 22. 31; John 13. 26.
love to His own, John 13. 1.
washes His disciples' feet, John 13. 5.
Peter's protest, John 13. 8.
example to His disciples, John 13. 15.
comforts His disciples, John 14. 1.
promise to them, John 14. 14.
leaves His peace with them, John 14. 27.
commands them to love one another, John 15. 12, 17.
promises the Comforter, John 15. 26; 16. 7.
predicts disciples' persecution, John 16. 2.
"a little while," John 16. 16.
encourages prayer in His name, John 16. 23.
prays for disciples, John 17.
goes over the brook Cedron, John 18. 1.
oftentimes resorted to garden, John 18. 2.
His agony, Matt. 26. 36; Luke 22. 44.
betrayed by Judas, Matt. 26. 47; Mark 14. 43; Luke 22. 47; John 18. 3.
seized by the officers, Matt. 26. 50; Mark 14. 46; Luke 22. 54; John 18. 12.
forbids use of sword, Matt. 26. 52; John 18. 11.
taken before the chief priests, Pilate, and Herod. *See* LIFE ON EARTH.
tried, found innocent, delivered to the Jews, crucifixion. *See* LIFE ON EARTH.
commends His mother to the beloved disciple, John 19. 25.
prays for His executioners, Luke 23. 34.
His promise to the penitent thief, Luke 23. 43.
acknowledged by centurion to be Son of God, Matt. 27. 54; Mark 15. 39; to be righteous, Luke 23. 47.

—— HIS TEACHING:—

preaches repentance at Galilee, Matt. 4. 17.
at Nazareth, Luke 4. 16.

CHRIST (HIS TEACHING)—*cont.*
the gospel of the kingdom, Matt. 4. 23; Mark 1. 14.
testimony concerning John the Baptist, Matt. 11. 7; Luke 7. 24; 20. 4.
upbraids Chorazin, Bethsaida, Capernaum, Matt. 11. 20; Luke 10. 13.
speaks to the Jews respecting the Father and the Son, John 5; 8. 18, 42; 10. 15; 12. 23.
  the bread of life, John 6. 26.
  seed of Abraham, John 8. 31.
  traditions of the elders, Matt. 15. 1; Mark 7. 1.
answers Pharisees asking a sign, Matt. 12. 38; 16. 1; Mark 8. 11; Luke 11. 16; 12. 54; John 2. 18.
teaches His disciples on humility, John 13. 14.
teaches scribes and Pharisees, Matt. 23; Mark 12. 38; Luke 11. 37; 20. 45.
prophesies destruction of Jerusalem, and the last times, Matt. 24; Mark 13; Luke 13. 34; 17. 20; 19. 41; 21.
preaches daily in the temple, Luke 19. 47.
His invitation to the weary and heavy laden, Matt. 11. 23.
His discourses on suffering for the Gospel's sake, Luke 14. 26 (Matt. 10. 37).
  on marriage, Matt. 19; Mark 10.
  riches, Matt. 19. 16; Mark 10. 17; Luke 12. 13; 18. 18.
  on paying tribute, Matt. 22. 15; Mark 12. 13; Luke 20. 20.
  the resurrection, Matt. 22. 23; Mark 12. 18.
  the two great commandments, Matt. 22. 35; Mark 12. 28.
  the Son of David, Matt. 22. 41; Mark 12. 35; Luke 20. 41.
  the widow's mite, Mark 12. 41; Luke 21. 1.
  watchfulness, Matt. 24. 42; Mark 13. 33; Luke 21. 34; 12. 35.
  the last judgment, Matt. 25. 31.
SERMON ON THE MOUNT:—who are the blessed, Matt. 5. 1; salt of the earth, 5. 13; light of the world, 5. 14; the righteousness of scribes and Pharisees, 5. 20; anger with a brother (Raca), 5. 22; thou fool, 5. 22; reconciliation, 5. 24; adultery, 5. 27; right hand and right eye, 5. 29, 30; divorce, 5. 32, 33; oaths, 5. 33; eye for an eye, 5. 38; love to neighbour and enemy, 5. 43; be ye perfect, 5. 48; almsgiving, 6. 1; prayer, 6. 5; no vain repetitions, 6. 7; Lord's Prayer, 6. 9; Luke 11. 2; fasting, Matt. 6. 16; treasure upon earth, 6. 19; evil eye, 6. 23; two masters, 6. 24; God and mammon, 6. 24; no thought for life, 6. 25; fowls of the air, 6. 26; taking thought, raiment, lilies of the field, 6. 27; seek kingdom of God, 6. 33; judge not, 7. 1; beam in eye, 7. 3; holy things not to be cast to dogs, 7. 6; ask, seek, find, 7. 7; Luke 11. 9; bread, stone, fish, serpent, Matt. 7. 9, 10; Luke 11. 11; strait gate, Matt. 7. 13; false prophets, 7. 15; grapes, thorns, figs, thistles, 7. 16; the good and corrupt tree, 7. 17; not to be hearers but doers, 7. 23, 24; house on rock, 7. 24; on sand, 7. 27; taught as having authority, 7. 29.
*Sermon to disciples and multitudes on the plain:—the blessed, Luke 6. 20, 21, 22; woe to the rich, 6. 24; to the full, 6. 25; to those men speak well of, 6. 26; love to enemies, 6. 27, 35; submission under injury, 6. 29; giving, 6. 30, 38; doing as we would be done to, 6. 31; be merciful, 6. 36; judge not, 6. 37; hearers and doers, 6. 46.
epistles to the seven churches in Asia, Rev. 1; 2; 3.

* It is the opinion of some eminent commentators that the sermons on the mount and on the plain were one and the same.

CHRIST (HIS TEACHING)—*cont.*
DISCOURSES:—
  on faith, the centurion's, Matt. 8. 8.
  to those who would follow Him, Luke 9. 23, 57.
  on fasting, Matt. 9. 14; Mark 2. 18; Luke 5. 33.
  on blasphemy, Matt. 12. 31; Mark 3. 28; Luke 11. 15.
  who are His brethren, Matt. 12. 46; Mark 3. 31; Luke 8. 19.
——— CHARACTER OF:—
  holy, Luke 1. 35; Acts 4. 27; Rev. 3. 7.
  righteous, Is. 53. 11; Heb. 1. 9.
  good, Matt. 19. 16.
  faithful, Is. 11. 5; 1 Thess. 5. 24.
  true, John 1. 14; 7. 18; 1 John 5. 20.
  just, Zech. 9. 9; John 5. 30; Acts 22. 14.
  guileless, Is. 53. 9; 1 Pet. 2. 22.
  sinless, John 8. 46; 2 Cor. 5. 21.
  spotless, 1 Pet. 1. 19.
  innocent, Matt. 27. 4.
  harmless, Heb. 7. 26.
  resisting temptation, Matt. 4. 1—10.
  obedient to God the Father, Ps. 40. 8; John 4. 34; 15. 10.
  subject to His parents, Luke 2. 51.
  zealous, Luke 2. 49; John 2. 17; 8. 29.
  meek, Is. 53. 7; Zech. 9. 9; Matt. 11. 29.
  lowly in heart, Matt. 11. 29.
  merciful, Heb. 2. 17.
  patient, Is. 53. 7; Matt. 27. 14.
  long-suffering, 1 Tim. 1. 16.
  compassionate, Is. 40. 11; Matt. 15. 32; Luke 7. 13; 19. 41.
  benevolent, Matt. 4. 23, 24; 9. 35; Acts 10. 38.
  loving, John 13. 1; 15. 13.
  self-denying, Matt. 8. 20; 2 Cor. 8. 9.
  humble, Luke 22. 27; Phil. 2. 8.
  resigned, Luke 22. 42.
  forgiving, Luke 23. 34.
  saints to be conformed to, Rom. 8. 29.
——— COMPASSION OF:—
  necessary to His priestly office, Heb. 5. 2, with verse 7.
MANIFESTED FOR THE
  weary and heavy-laden, Matt. 11. 28—30.
  weak in faith, Is. 40. 11; 42. 3, with Matt. 12. 20.
  tempted, Heb. 2. 18.
  afflicted, Luke 7. 13; John 11. 33.
  diseased, Matt. 14. 14; Mark 1. 41.
  poor, Mark 8. 2.
  perishing sinners, Matt. 9. 36; Luke 19. 41; John 3. 16.
  an encouragement to prayer, Heb. 4. 15.
——— GLORY OF:—
  as divine, John 1. 1—5; Phil. 2. 6, 9, 10.
  God the Son, Matt. 3. 17; Heb. 1. 6, 8.
  equal to the Father, John 10. 30, 38.
  the Firstborn, Col. 1. 5, 18.
  the Firstbegotten, Heb. 1. 6.
  Lord of lords, &c., Rev. 17. 14.
  the image of God, Col. 1. 15; Heb. 1. 3.
  Creator, John 1. 3; Col. 1. 16; Heb. 1. 2.
  the Blessed of God, Ps. 45. 2.
  Mediator, 1 Tim. 2. 5; Heb. 8. 6.
  Prophet, Deut. 18. 15, 16, with Acts 3. 22.
  Priest, Ps. 110. 4; Heb. 4. 15.
  King, Is. 6. 1—5, with John 12. 41.
  Judge, Matt. 16. 27; 25. 31, 33.
  Shepherd, Is. 40. 10, 11; Ezek. 34; John 10; 11; 14.
  Head of the Church, Eph. 1. 22.
  the true Light, Luke 1. 78, 79; John 1. 4, 9.
  the foundation of the Church, Is. 28. 16.
  the Way, John 14. 6; Heb. 10. 19, 20.
  the Truth, 1 John 5. 20; Rev. 3. 7.
  the Life, John 11. 25; Col. 3. 4; 1 John 5. 11.
  Incarnate, John 1. 14.
  in His words, Luke 4. 22; John 7. 46.
  His works, Matt. 13. 54; John 2. 11.

CHRIST (TYPES OF)—*cont.*
sin offering, Lev. 4. 2; Heb. 13. 11.
atonement, sacrifices upon day of, Lev. 16. 15;
Heb. 9. 12.
scapegoat, Lev. 16. 20; Is. 53. 6.
brazen serpent, Num. 21. 9; John 3. 14.
cities of refuge, Num. 35. 6; Heb. 6. 18.
temple, 1 Kin. 6. 1, 38; John 2. 21.
tabernacle, Heb. 9. 8, 11.
veil, Heb. 10. 20.

CHRISTS, false, and prophets, warnings against,
Matt. 7. 15; 24. 4, 5, 11, 24; Mark 13. 22; Acts
20. 29; 2 Thess. 2. 8; 1 Tim. 4. 1; 2 Pet. 2. 1;
Rev. 13.

CHURCH of God, Acts 20. 28; 1 Cor. 1. 2; 10. 32;
11. 22; 15. 9; Gal. 1. 13; 1 Tim. 3. 5.
foundation and increase of, Matt. 16. 18; Acts
2. 47; Col. 1. 18.
authority and teaching of, Matt. 18. 17; Acts 11.
26, 27; 1 Cor. 5. 4; 12. 28.
organization of, Acts 14. 23; 1 Cor. 4. 17; 14. 4, 5.
persecuted, Acts 8. 3; 12. 1; 15. 9; Gal. 1. 13;
Phil. 3. 6.
saluted, Acts 18. 22; Rom. 16. 5; 10. 16; 1 Cor.
16. 19.
loved of Christ, Eph. 5. 25, 29.
edification of, 1 Cor. 14. 4, 19, 28, 34.

CHURCHES, the seven, in Asia, Rev. 1. 4, 11, 20;
2. 7, 11, 17, 29; 3. 6, 13, 22.

CIRCUMCISION, the covenant of, Gen. 17. 10, 23,
24, 25.
Shechemites submit to, Gen. 34. 24.
Zipporah resents it, Ex. 4. 25.
incumbent on strangers sojourning, Ex. 12. 48,
renewed by Joshua, Josh. 5. 2.
of John, Luke 1. 59.
of Jesus, Luke 2. 21.
of Timothy, Acts 16. 3.
superseded by the Gospel, Acts 15; Gal. 5. 2.
of heart, Deut. 10. 16; 30. 6.
spiritual, Phil. 3. 3; Col. 2. 11.
when profitable, and how, Rom. 2. 25; 3. 30; 4. 9;
1 Cor. 7. 19; Gal. 5. 6; 6. 15.

CITIES, spared or besieged, Deut. 20. 10.
to be destroyed, Deut. 20. 16.
of refuge, Num. 35. 6; Deut. 19; Josh. 20.

CLOTHING, coats of skins the first, Gen. 3. 21.
rending of, Gen. 37. 29, 34; Num. 14. 6; Judg.
11. 35; Acts 14. 14.
washing of, ordered, Ex. 19. 10; Lev. 11. 25;
Num. 19. 7.

CLOUD, pillar of, children of Israel guided by,
Ex. 13. 21; 14. 19; Neh. 9. 19; Ps. 78. 14; 105.
39; 1 Cor. 10. 1.
appearance of the Lord in, Ex. 24. 15; 34. 5; Lev.
16. 2; Num. 11. 25; 12. 5; 1 Kin. 8. 10; Ezek.
10. 4; Matt. 17. 5; Luke 21. 27; Rev. 14. 14.

COMMAND of God to Adam, Gen. 2. 16.
to Moses, Ex. 3. 14.
to Joshua, Josh. 1. 9.
of Moses to the sons of Levi, Deut. 31. 10.
of Christ to the twelve, Matt. 10. 5; Mark 16. 15.
to Peter, John 21. 15.

COMMANDMENTS (TEN) delivered, Ex. 20; 31.
18; Deut. 5. 6.
two tables of, broken, Ex. 32. 19.
renewed, Ex. 34. 1; Deut. 10. 1.
fulfilled by Christ, Matt. 5. 17; 19. 17; 22. 35;
Mark 10. 17; Luke 10. 25; 18. 18.

COMMUNION of the Body and Blood of Christ,
1 Cor. 10. 16.
Lord's Supper instituted, Matt. 26. 26; Mark 14.
22; Luke 22. 19; 1 Cor. 11. 23.
self-examination for, Acts 2. 42; 20. 7; 1 Cor. 10.
21; 11. 28.
unworthily partaken, 1 Cor. 11. 27.

COMMUNION of Saints. *See* FELLOWSHIP.

COMPANY, evil, to be avoided, Ps. 1. 1; 26. 4;
Prov. 1. 10; 2. 12; 4. 14; 12. 11; 13. 20; 14. 7;
22. 24; 24. 19; 29. 3, 24; Rom. 1. 32; 1 Cor. 5. 9;
15. 33; Eph. 5. 7.

COMPASSION, Job 6. 14; Ps. 35. 13; Zech. 7. 9;
Rom. 12. 15; 2 Cor. 11. 29; Gal. 6. 2; Col. 3. 12;
Heb. 13. 3; James 1. 27; 1 Pet. 3. 8.
Christ's, Matt. 15. 32; 20. 34; Luke 7. 13, 21; Heb.
2. 17; 4. 15; 5. 2.

CONDEMNATION for sin, universal, Ps. 14. 3;
53. 3; Rom. 3. 12, 19; 5. 12; 6. 23.
for unbelief, John 3. 18.
by the law, 2 Cor. 3. 6, 9.
by impenitence and hypocrisy, Matt. 11. 20; 23.
14.
according to our deeds, 2 Cor. 11. 15.
of false teachers, 2 Pet. 2. 1; Jude 4.
deliverance from, by Christ, John 3. 18; 5. 24;
Rom. 8. 1, 33.
final, Matt. 25. 46; Rev. 20. 15.

CONFESSION of Christ unto salvation, Matt. 10.
32; Mark 8. 35; John 12. 42; Rom. 10. 9; 2 Tim.
2. 12; 1 John 2. 23; 4. 2.
of sin, Lev. 5. 5; Josh. 7. 19; Dan. 9. 20; 1 John 1. 9.
examples of, Num. 12. 11; 21. 7; Josh. 7. 20;
1 Sam. 7; 15. 24; Ezra 9. 6; Neh. 1. 6; 9; Ps.
51; Dan. 9. 4; Luke 23. 41.
at the offering of firstfruits, Deut. 26. 1.
"one to another," James 5. 16.

CONGREGATION (of Israel), all to keep the passover, Ex. 12. &c.
sin offering for, Lev. 4. 13; 16. 17.
to stone offenders, Lev. 24. 14; Num. 14. 10; 15. 35.
who not to enter, Deut. 23. 1.

CONSCIENCE convicts of sin, Gen. 3. 10; 4. 13;
42. 21; 1 Sam. 24. 5; Prov. 20. 27; Matt. 27. 3;
Luke 9. 7; John 8. 9; Rom. 2. 15.
purified by faith, 1 Tim. 1. 19; 3. 9; 2 Tim. 1. 3.
purified by blood of Christ, Heb. 9. 14; 10. 2, 22.
a good, Heb. 13. 18; 1 Pet. 3. 16.
effects of a good, Acts 24. 16; Rom. 13. 5; 14. 22;
2 Cor. 1. 12; 1 Pet. 2. 19.
of others to be respected, Rom. 14. 21; 1 Cor. 8;
10. 28.
seared, 1 Tim. 4. 2; defiled, Tit. 1. 15.
ignorant, Acts 26. 9; Rom. 10. 2.

CONSECRATION of priests, Ex. 29; Lev. 8.
of the Levites, Num. 8. 6.
of Christ, Heb. 7; 8; 10. 20.

CONSIDERATION, exhortations to, Deut. 4. 39;
32. 29; Job 23. 15; 37. 14; Ps. 8. 3; 50. 22; Prov.
6. 6; Eccles. 4. 1; 5. 1; 7. 13; Hag. 1. 5; Matt.
6. 28; 2 Tim. 2. 7; Heb. 3. 1; 7. 4; 10. 24; 12. 3.

CONSOLATION under affliction, Deut. 33. 27; Job
19. 25; Ps. 10. 14; 23; 34. 6; 41. 3; 42. 5; 51. 17;
55. 22; 69. 29; 71. 9, 18; 73. 26; 94. 19; 119. 50;
126; Eccles. 7. 3; Is. 1. 18; 12. 1; Lam. 3. 22;
Ezek. 14. 22; Hos. 2. 14; Mic. 7. 18; Zech. 1. 17;
Matt. 11. 28; Luke 4. 18; 15; John 14; 15; 16;
Rom. 15. 4; 16. 20; 1 Cor. 10. 13; 14. 3; 2 Cor. 1.
3; 5. 1; 7. 6; 12. 9; Col. 1. 11; 1 Thess. 4. 14; 5.
11; 2 Thess. 2. 16; Heb. 4. 9; 6. 18; 12; James 1.
12; 4. 7; 2 Pet. 2. 9; Rev. 2. 10; 7. 14; 14. 13.

CONSPIRACY against Christ, Matt. 26. 3; Mark
3. 6; 14. 1; Luke 22. 2; John 11. 55; 13. 18.
against Paul, Acts 23. 12.

CONSTANCY, Rom. 16. 4.
of Ruth, Ruth 1. 14.

CONTENTMENT, godliness with, great gain, Ps.
37. 16; Prov. 30. 8; 1 Tim. 6. 6.
exhortations to, Ps. 37. 1; Luke 3. 14; 1 Cor. 7. 20;
1 Tim. 6. 8; Heb. 13. 5.

CONTRIBUTION for saints, Acts 20. 35; Rom. 15.
26; 2 Cor. 8.

CONVERSATION (conduct), upright, Ps. 37. 14;
50. 23; Phil. 3. 20; 1 Tim. 4. 12; Heb. 13. 5;
James 3. 13; 1 Pet. 2. 12; 2 Pet. 3. 11.
as becometh the gospel, 2 Cor. 1. 12; Gal. 1. 13;
Eph. 4. 1; Phil. 1. 27; 1 Pet. 1. 15; 2. 12.
(speech). Of the Lord with Moses, Ex. 33. 9. Jesus
with Nicodemus, John 3; with the woman of
Samaria, John 4. 7—27. On the walk to Emmaus, Luke 24. 13. Of Peter with Cornelius,
Acts 10. 27. Of Festus and Agrippa, Acts 26. 31.
See Col. 4. 6.

CONVERSION of sinners 'proceeds from God, 1 Kin. 18. 37; Ps. 19. 7; 78. 34; Prov. 1. 23; Jer. 31. 18; John 6. 44; Acts 3. 26; 11. 11. *See* Ps. 51. 13; Is. 1. 16; 6. 10; Ezek. 18. 23; 36. 25; Joel 2. 13; 2 Cor. 5. 17; 1 Thess. 1. 9.
call to, Is. 1. 16; Matt. 3. 2; 4. 17; 10. 7; Acts 2. 38; 17. 30; James 4. 8.
prayer for, Ps. 80. 7; 85. 4; Lam. 5. 21.
instruments of, blessed, Dan. 12. 3; 1 Tim. 4. 16; James 5. 19.
of the Jews, Acts 2. 41; 4. 32; 6. 7.
of Paul, Acts 9; 22; 26.
of the Gentiles, foretold, Is. 2. 2; 11. 10; 60. 5; 66. 12; fulfilled, Acts 8. 26; 10; 15. 3; Rom. 10; 11; 1 Cor. 1; Eph. 2; 3; 1 Thess. 1.
COUNCIL of the Jews, Matt. 26. 3, 59; Mark 15. 1.
the apostles arraigned before, Acts 4; 5. 27.
Paul's discourse before, Acts 23.
COUNSEL, advantage of good, Prov. 12. 15; 13. 10; 20. 18; 27. 9.
OF GOD, asked by Israel, Judg. 20. 18.
by Saul, 1 Sam. 14. 37.
by David, 1 Sam. 23. 2, 10; 30. 8; 1 Chr. 14. 10. *See* Ps. 16. 7; 33. 11; 73. 24; Prov. 8. 14; Rev. 3. 18.
danger of rejecting, 2 Chr. 25. 16; Prov. 1. 25, 26; Jer. 23. 18—22; Luke 7. 30.
of the wicked, condemned, Job 5. 13; 10. 3; 21. 16; Ps. 1. 1; 5. 10; 33. 10; 64. 2—7; 81. 12; 106. 43; Is. 7. 5; Hos. 11. 6; Mic. 6. 16.
COURAGE, exhortations to, Num. 13. 20; Deut. 31. 6; Josh. 1. 6; 10. 25; 2 Sam. 10. 12; 2 Chr. 19. 11; Ezra 10. 4; Ps. 27. 14; 31. 24; Is. 41. 6; 1 Cor. 16. 13; Eph. 6. 10.
through faith: Abraham, Heb. 11. 8, 17. Moses, Heb. 11. 25. Israelites, Heb. 11. 29. Barak, Judg. 4. 16. Gideon, Judg. 7. 1. Jephthah, Judg. 11. 29. Samson, Judg. 16. 28. Jonathan, 1 Sam. 14. 6. Daniel, Dan. 6. 10, 23. Jonah, Jonah 3. 3. *See* BOLDNESS, CONFIDENCE.
COURSES of the Levites established by David, 1 Chr. 23; 24. *See* Luke 1. 5.
of the singers, 1 Chr. 25.
of the porters, 1 Chr. 26.
of the captains, 1 Chr. 27.
COURTESY, exhortation to, Col. 4. 6; James 3. 17; 1 Pet. 3. 8.
examples of, Acts 27. 3; 28. 7.
COVENANT of GOD:—
with Noah, Gen. 6. 18; 9. 8.
with Abraham, Gen. 15. 7, 18; 17. 2 (Luke 1. 72; Acts 3. 25; Gal. 3. 16, 17).
with Isaac, Gen. 17. 19; 26. 3.
with Jacob, Gen. 28. 13 (Ex. 2. 24; 6. 4; 1 Chr. 16. 16).
with the Israelites, Ex. 6. 4; 19. 5; 24; 34. 27; Lev. 26. 9; Deut. 5. 2; 9. 9; 26. 16; 29; Judg. 2. 1; Jer. 11; 31. 33; Acts 3. 25.
with Phinehas, Num. 25. 13.
with David, 2 Sam. 7. 3; Ps. 89. 3, 28, 34. *See* Ps. 25. 14.
God mindful of, Deut. 7. 9; 1 Kin. 8. 23; Ps. 105. 8; 111. 5, &c.
danger of despising, Deut. 28. 15; Jer. 11. 2; Heb. 10. 29.
COVENANT, signs of:—salt, Lev. 2. 13; Num. 18. 19; 2 Chr. 13. 5; the sabbath, Ex. 31. 12.
book of the, Ex. 24. 7; 2 Kin. 23. 2; Heb. 9. 19.
—— between Abraham and Abimelech, Gen. 21. 27.
Joshua and Israelites, Josh. 24. 25.
David and Jonathan, 1 Sam. 18. 3; 20. 16; 23. 18.
NEW COVENANT, Jer. 31. 31; Rom. 11. 27; Heb. 8. 8.
ratified by Christ (Mal. 3. 1), Luke 1. 68—80; Gal. 3. 17; Heb. 8. 6; 9. 15; 12. 24.
a covenant of peace, Is. 54. 10; Ezek. 34. 25; 37. 26.
unchangeable, Ps. 89. 34; Is. 54. 10; 59. 21.
everlasting, Gen. 9. 16; 17. 13; Lev. 24. 8; Is. 55. 3; 61. 8; Ezek. 16. 60, 62; 37. 26; Heb. 13. 20.

COVETOUSNESS described, Ps. 10. 3; Prov. 21. 26; Eccles. 4. 8; 5. 10; Ezek. 33. 31; Hab. 2; Mark 7. 22; Eph. 5. 5; 1 Tim. 6. 10; 2 Pet. 2. 14.
forbidden, Ex. 20. 17; Luke 12. 15; Rom. 13. 9.
its evil consequences, Prov. 1. 18; 15. 27; 28. 20; Ezek. 22. 13; 1 Tim. 6. 9.
its punishment, Job 20. 15; Is. 5. 8; 57. 17; Jer. 6. 12; 22. 17; Mic. 2. 1; Hab. 2. 9; 1 Cor. 5. 10; 6. 10; Eph. 5. 5; Col. 3. 5.
of Laban, Gen. 31. 41.
of Balaam, Num. 22. 21 (2 Pet. 2. 15; Jude 11).
of Achan, Josh. 7. 21.
of Saul, 1 Sam. 15. 9.
of Ahab, 1 Kin. 21.
of Gehazi, 2 Kin. 5. 20.
of Judas, Matt. 26. 14.
of Ananias and Sapphira, Acts 5.
of Felix, Acts 24. 26.
CROSS, Christ dies upon the, Matt. 27. 32; Phil. 2. 8; Heb. 12. 2.
preaching of, 1 Cor. 1. 18.
to be taken up, self-denial, Matt. 10. 38; 16. 24; offence of the, Gal. 5. 11; persecution for, Gal. 6. 12.
CROWN (and mitre), high priest's, Ex. 29. 6; 39. 30; Lev. 8. 9.
of thorns, John 19. 5.
of righteousness, 2 Tim. 4. 8.
of life, James 1. 12; Rev. 2. 10.
of glory, 1 Pet. 5. 4.
incorruptible, 1 Cor. 9. 25. *See* Rev. 4. 4; 9. 7; 12. 3; 13. 1; 19. 12.
CRUELTY condemned, Ex. 23. 5; Ps. 27. 12; Prov. 11. 17; 12. 10: Ezek. 18. 18.
of Simeon and Levi, Gen. 34. 25; 49. 5.
of Pharaoh, Ex. 1. 8.
of Adoni-bezek, Judg. 1. 7.
of Herod, Matt. 2. 16 (Judg. 9. 5; 2 Kin. 3. 27; 10; 15. 16).
CURSE upon the earth in consequence of the fall, Gen. 3. 17.
upon Cain, Gen. 4. 11.
on Canaan, Gen. 9. 25.
by Job on his birth, Job 3. 1; also by Jeremiah, Jer. 20. 14.
upon the breakers of the law, Lev. 26. 14; Deut. 11. 26; 27. 13; 28. 15; 29. 19; Josh. 8. 34; Prov. 3. 33.
Christ redeems from, Rom. 3; Gal. 3. 1.
CURSED, who so called, Deut. 27. 15; Prov. 11. 26; 27. 14; Jer. 11. 3; 17. 5; Lam. 3. 65; Zech. 5. 3; Mal. 1. 14; Matt. 25. 41; Gal. 3. 10; 2 Pet. 2. 14.
of God to be cut off, Ps. 37. 22.
CURSING forbidden, Ex. 21. 17; Ps. 109. 17; Prov. 30. 11; James 3. 10.
to return blessing for, Matt. 5. 44; Rom. 12. 14.
CUTTING the flesh forbidden, Lev. 19. 28; Deut. 14. 1; practised by prophets of Baal, 1 Kin. 18. 28.

DAMNATION, Matt. 23. 14; Mark 16. 16; John 5. 29; Rom. 3. 8; 13. 2; 2 Thess. 2. 12; 1 Tim. 5. 12; 2 Pet. 2. 3.
DANCING as a mark of rejoicing, Ex. 15. 20; 32. 19; Judg. 11. 34; 1 Sam. 21. 11; 2 Sam. 6. 14; Eccles. 3. 4.
of Herodias's daughter pleases Herod, Matt. 14. 6; Mark 6. 22.
DARKNESS divided from light, Gen. 1. 18.
created by God, Is. 45. 7.
supernatural, Gen. 15. 12; Ex. 10. 21; 14. 20; Josh. 24. 7; Rev. 8. 12; 9. 2; 16. 10.
at the crucifixion, Matt. 27. 45; Mark 15. 33; Luke 23. 44.
figurative of punishment, Matt. 8. 12; 22. 13; 2 Pet. 2. 4, 17; Jude 6.
of the mind, Job 37. 19; Prov. 2. 13; Eccles. 2. 14; Is. 9. 2; 42. 7; John 1. 5; 3. 19; 8. 12; 12. 35; Rom. 13. 12; 1 Cor. 4. 5; 2 Cor. 4. 6; 6. 14; Eph. 5. 8; 1 Thess. 5. 4; 1 Pet. 2. 9; 1 John 1. 5; 2. 9.
powers of. Luke 22. 53; Eph. 6. 12; Col. 1. 13.
DAUGHTERS, their inheritance determined, Num. 27. 6; 36.

DEACONS appointed, Acts 6; Phil. 1. 1.
their qualifications, Acts 6. 3; 1 Tim. 3. 8.
DEAD, the, Job 3. 18; 14. 12; Ps. 6. 5; 88. 10; 115.
17; 146. 4; Eccles. 9. 5; 12. 7; Is. 38. 18.
resurrection of, Job 19. 26; Ps. 49. 15; Is. 26. 19;
Dan. 12. 2, 13; John 5. 25; 1 Cor. 15. 12.
raised by Elijah, 1 Kin. 17. 17; by Elisha, 2 Kin.
4. 32; 13. 21; by CHRIST, Matt. 9. 24; Mark 5.
41; Luke 7. 12; 8. 54; John 11; by Peter, Acts
9. 40; by Paul, Acts 20. 10.
sleep in Jesus, 1 Thess. 4. 13.
DEATH the consequence of Adam's sin, Gen. 2.
17; 3. 19; Rom. 5. 12; 6. 23; 1 Cor. 15. 21.
universal, Job 1. 21; 3. 17; 14. 1; 21. 13; Ps. 49.
19; 89. 48; Eccles. 5. 15; 8. 8; 9. 5, 10; 11. 8;
Heb. 9. 27.
threatened, Rom. 1. 32.
characterized, Gen. 3. 19; Deut. 31. 16 (John 11.
11); Job 1. 21; 3. 13; 10. 21; 12. 22; 14. 2; 16. 22;
24. 17; Ps. 16. 10; 23. 4; 104. 29; Eccles. 9. 10;
Hab. 2. 5; Luke 12. 20; 2 Cor. 5. 1, 8; Phil. 1. 23;
1 Tim. 6. 7; 2 Pet. 1. 14.
as a punishment, Gen. 9. 6; Ex. 21. 12; 22. 18;
31. 14; 35. 2; Lev. 20. 2; 21. 9; 1 Kin. 21. 10;
Matt. 15. 4.
vanquished by Christ, Rom. 6. 9; 1 Cor. 15. 26
(Hos. 13. 14); 2 Tim. 1. 10; Heb. 2. 15; Rev. 1. 18.
prayers and exhortations concerning, 2 Kin. 20. 1;
Ps. 39; 90; Eccles. 9. 10; John 9. 4; 1 Pet. 1. 24.
unknown in heaven, Luke 20. 36; Rev. 21. 4.
persons exempted from:—Enoch, Gen. 5. 24;
Heb. 11. 5; Elijah, 2 Kin. 2. 11. *See* 1 Cor. 15.
51; 1 Thess. 4. 17.
SPIRITUAL, Is. 9. 2; Matt. 4. 16; 8. 22; Luke 1. 79;
John 6. 53; Rom. 5. 15; 6. 13; 8. 6; Eph. 2. 1;
4. 18; Col. 2. 13; 1 Tim. 5. 6; Heb. 6. 1; 9. 14;
1 John 3. 14; Rev. 3. 1.
deliverance from, by Christ, John 5. 24; Rom. 6.
11; Eph. 2. 5; 5. 14; 1 John 5. 12.
ETERNAL, Prov. 14. 12; Dan. 12. 2; Matt. 7. 13;
10. 28; 23. 33; 25. 30, 41; Mark 9. 44; John 5.
29; Rom. 1. 32; 2. 8; 6. 23; 9. 22; 2 Thess. 1. 7;
James 4. 12; 2 Pet. 2. 17.
(the second death), Rev. 2. 11; 19. 20; 20. 14;
21. 8.
salvation from, by Christ, John 3. 16; 8. 51.
by conversion from sin, James 5. 20.
of CHRIST, foretold, Is. 53; Dan. 9. 26; Zech. 13. 7.
See Matt. 26. 31 (Deut. 21. 23; Gal. 3. 13); Heb. 2.
9; 12. 2; 1 Pet. 1. 11.
voluntary, Luke 12. 50; John 10. 11, 18; Heb. 10. 7.
its object, Is. 53; Dan. 9. 26; Matt. 20. 28; 1 Cor.
5. 7; 1 Tim. 2. 6; Tit. 2. 14; Heb. 9. 26; 1 Pet.
1. 18; Rev. 1. 5.
of SAINTS, Num. 23. 10; 2 Kin. 22. 20; Ps. 23. 4;
48. 14; 116. 15; Prov. 14. 32; Is. 26. 19; 57. 1;
Dan. 12. 2; Luke 16. 25; John 11. 11; 2 Cor. 5.
8; Phil. 1. 21; 2 Tim. 4. 8; Heb. 11. 13; Rev. 2.
10.
of Abraham, Gen. 25. 8. Isaac, Gen. 35. 29. Jacob,
Gen. 49. Aaron, Num. 20. 23. Moses, Deut. 34. 5.
Joshua, Josh. 24. 29. David, 1 Kin. 2. Elisha,
2 Kin. 13. 14. Stephen, Acts 7. 54. Dorcas, Acts
9. 37.
of THE WICKED, Job 18. 11; 21. 13; 27. 19; Ps.
34. 16; 49. 14; 73. 19; Prov. 10. 7; 11. 7; 14. 32;
29. 1; Is. 14. 9; Ezek. 3. 19; 18. 23; Dan. 12. 2;
Luke 12. 20; 16. 22; John 8. 21; Acts 1. 25.
of Nadab and Abihu, Lev. 10. 1, 2; Num. 3. 4.
Korah, &c., Num. 16. 32. Hophni and Phinehas,
1 Sam. 4. 11. Absalom, 2 Sam. 18. 9. Ahab, 1
Kin. 22. 34. Jezebel, 2 Kin. 9. 33. Athaliah, 2
Chr. 23. 15. Haman, Esth. 7. 10. Judas, Matt. 27.
5; Acts 1. 18. Ananias, &c., Acts 5. 5. Herod,
Acts 12. 23.
DEBT censured, Ps. 37. 21; Prov. 3. 27; Luke
16. 5; Rom. 13. 8.
DECEIT proceeds from the heart, Jer. 17. 9.
by false prophets, 1 Kin. 22.
(and lying), work of the devil, John 8. 44; Acts
5. 3.

DECEIT—*cont.*
SOME MEMORABLE INSTANCES OF:—
the serpent and Eve, Gen. 3.
Abram and his wife, Gen. 12. 14.
Isaac and his wife, Gen. 26. 10.
Jacob and Esau, Gen. 27.
Jael and Sisera, Judg. 4. 20.
the old prophet, 1 Kin. 13. 18.
Rahab and spies at Jericho, Josh. 2. 1, 4, 5.
Gehazi and Naaman, 2 Kin. 5. 20.
Herod and the wise men, Matt. 2. 7, 8.
Ananias and Sapphira, Acts 5. 1. *See* LYING.
DECISION, how manifested, Ex. 32. 26; Num. 14.
24; Deut. 6. 5; Josh. 1. 7; 24. 15; 1 Kin. 18.
21; 2 Chr. 15. 12; Is. 56. 6; Luke 9. 62; 1 Cor.
15. 58; Heb. 3. 6, 14; James 1. 8; 4. 7.
opposed to wavering, Deut. 5. 32; 1 Kin. 18. 21;
Ps. 78. 8; Matt. 6. 24; James 1. 8.
of Moses, Ex. 32. 26.
of Caleb, Num. 13. 30.
of Joshua, Josh. 24. 15.
of Ruth, Ruth 1. 16.
of Paul, Acts 21. 13; Gal. 1. 16.
DEDICATION of tabernacle, Ex. 40; Lev. 8; 9;
Num. 7.
of temple, 1 Kin. 8; 2 Chr. 5. 6.
of wall of Jerusalem, Neh. 12. 27.
DEEDS of the body mortified, Rom. 8. 13; 13. 14;
1 Cor. 9. 27; denounced, 2 Pet. 2. 10.
DELIVERANCES:—Lot, Gen. 14; 19. Moses, Ex.
2. Israel, Ex. 14; Judg. 4; 7; 15; 1 Sam. 7; 14;
17; 2 Kin. 19; 2 Chr. 14; 20. Daniel, Shadrach,
Meshach, and Abed-nego, Dan. 3. 19; 6. 22. The
Apostles, Acts 5. 19; 12. 7; 16. 26; 28. 1; 2 Tim.
4. 17.
DENIAL OF CHRIST deprecated, 2 Tim. 1. 8;
Tit. 1. 16; 2 Pet. 2. 1; Jude 4.
its punishment, Matt. 10. 33; 2 Tim. 2. 12; 2 Pet.
2. 1; Jude 4, 15.
by Peter, Matt. 26. 69.
by the Jews, John 18. 40; 19. 15; Acts 3. 13.
DENIER OF CHRIST, liar and antichrist, 1 John
2. 22; 4. 3.
will be denied by Him, Matt. 10. 33; Mark 8. 38;
2 Tim. 2. 12.
brought to swift destruction, 2 Pet. 2. 1; Jude
4, 15.
DESPAIR deprecated, Deut. 20. 3; Ps. 27. 13; 31. 24;
37. 1; 42. 11; Prov. 24. 10; Is. 40. 30; Luke 18. 1;
2 Cor. 4. 8; Gal. 6. 9; 2 Thess. 3. 13; Heb. 12. 3.
DEVIL (ABADDON, APOLLYON, BEELZEBUB, BE-
LIAL, SATAN), the adversary of God and man,
1 Pet. 5. 8.
prince of the devils, Matt. 12. 24.
of powers of the air, Eph. 2. 2.
of this world, John 14. 30.
sinner from the beginning, 1 John 3. 8.
cast out of heaven, Luke 10. 18.
cast down to hell, 2 Pet. 2. 4; Jude 6.
as serpent, causes the fall of man, Gen. 3. 1.
lies to Eve, Gen. 3. 4.
cursed by God, Gen. 3. 14.
appears before God, Job 1. 6; 2. 1.
called ABADDON and APOLLYON, Rev. 9. 11.
BEELZEBUB, Matt. 12. 24.
BELIAL, 2 Cor. 6. 15.
SATAN, Luke 10. 18.
tempted CHRIST, Matt. 4. 3—10; Mark 1. 13; Luke
4. 2.
Eve, Gen. 3.
David, 1 Chr. 21. 1.
Job, Job 2. 7.
desired to have the apostles, Luke 22. 31.
resists Joshua, Zech. 3.
repulsed by Christ, Matt. 4. 10; Luke 4. 8, 12.
enters into Judas Iscariot, Luke 22. 3; John 13. 2.
into Ananias, Acts 5. 3.
AS PRINCE AND GOD OF THIS WORLD, HE
perverts the scriptures, Matt. 4. 6.
opposes God's work, Zech. 3. 1; 1 Thess. 2. 18.
hinders the gospel, Matt. 13. 19; 2 Cor. 4. 4.

ENEMIES—*cont.*
David and Saul, 1 Sam. 24. 10; 26, 9.
God delivers out of the hand of, 1 Sam. 12. 11 ;
Ezra 8. 31; Ps. 18. 48; 59; 61. 3.
of God, their punishment, Ex. 15. 6; Deut. 32. 41;
Judg. 5. 31; Esth. 7; 8; Ps. 68. 1; 92. 9; Is. 1.
24; 37. 36; 2 Thess. 1. 8; Rev. 21. 8.
ENTICERS to idolatry to be stoned, Deut. 13. 10.
ENVY, Prov. 14. 30; 27. 4; Eccles. 4. 4; Matt. 27.
18; Acts 7. 9; Rom. 1. 29; 1 Cor. 3. 3; 2 Cor. 12.
20; Gal. 5. 21; 1 Tim. 6. 4; Tit. 3. 3; James 4. 5.
forbidden, Ps. 37. 1; Prov. 3. 31; 24. 1, 19 ; Rom.
13. 13; 1 Pet. 2. 1.
its evil consequences, Job 5. 2; Prov. 14. 30; Is.
26. 11; James 3. 16.
Joseph sold for, Acts 7. 9.
EXACTION (usury, &c.), forbidden, Lev. 25. 35;
Deut. 15. 2; Prov. 28. 8; Ezek. 22. 12; 45. 9;
Luke 3. 13; 1 Cor. 5. 10.
disclaimed, Neh. 5. 1; 10. 31.
EXAMPLE of CHRIST, Matt. 11. 29; John 13. 15;
Rom. 15. 3, 5; Phil. 2. 5; 1 Pet. 2. 21.
prophets, Heb. 6. 12; James 5. 10.
apostles, 1 Cor. 4. 16; 11. 1; Phil. 3. 17; 4. 9;
1 Thess. 1. 6.

FACE of GOD hidden from them that do evil,
Ps. 34. 16; Is. 59. 2; Ezek. 39. 23.
to be sought, 2 Chr. 7. 14; Ps. 31. 16; 80. 3; Dan.
9. 17.
seen by Jacob, Gen. 32. 30.
FAITH, Heb. 11; justification by, Rom. 3. 28;
5. 1, 16; Gal. 2. 16; purification by, Acts 15. 9;
sanctification by, Acts 26. 18.
object of, Father, Son, and Holy Ghost, Mark 11.
22; John 6. 29; 14. 1; 20. 31; Acts 20. 21; 2 Cor.
13. 14.
given by the Spirit, 1 Cor. 2. 5; 12. 9.
in Christ, Acts 8. 12; 2 Tim. 3. 15.
unity of, Eph. 4. 5, 13; Jude 3.
leads to salvation, &c., Mark 16. 16; John 1. 12;
3. 16, 36; 6. 40, 47; Acts 16. 31; Gal. 3. 11; Eph.
2. 8; Heb. 11. 6; 1 Pet. 1. 9; 1 John 5. 10.
works by love, 1 Cor. 13; Gal. 5. 6; Col. 1. 4;
1 Thess. 1. 3; 1 Tim. 1. 5; Philem. 5; Heb. 10. 23;
1 Pet 1. 22; 1 John 3. 14, 23.
without works is dead, James 2. 17, 20.
produces peace, joy, hope in believing, Rom. 5.
1; 15. 13; 2 Cor. 4. 13; 1 Pet. 1. 8.
excludes boasting, &c., Rom. 3. 27; 4. 2; 1 Cor. 1.
29; Eph. 2. 9.
blessings received through, Mark 16. 16; John
6. 40; 12. 36; 20. 31; Acts 10. 43; 16. 31; 26. 18;
Rom. 1. 17 (Hab. 2. 4); Rom. 3. 21; 4. 16; 5. 1;
2 Cor. 5. 7; Gal. 2. 16; 3. 14, 26; Eph. 1. 13; 3. 12,
17; 1 Tim. 1. 4; Heb. 4. 3; 6. 12; 10. 38; 1 Pet.
1. 5; Jude 20.
miracles performed through, Matt. 9. 22; Luke
8. 50; Acts 3. 16.
power of, Matt. 17. 20; Mark 9. 23; 11. 23; Luke
17. 6.
trial of, 2 Thess. 1. 4; Heb. 11. 17; James 1. 3, 12;
1 Pet. 1. 7.
overcometh the world, 1 John 5. 4.
shield of the Christian, Eph. 6. 16; 1 Thess. 5. 8.
contend earnestly for the, Jude 3.
exhortations to continue in, 1 Cor. 16. 13; 2 Cor.
13. 5; Eph. 6. 16; Phil. 1. 27; Col. 1. 23; 2. 7;
1 Thess. 5. 8; 1 Tim. 1. 19; 4. 12; 6. 11; 2 Tim.
2. 22; Tit. 1. 13; Heb. 10. 22.
examples of:—Caleb, Num. 13. 30. Shadrach,
Meshach, and Abed-nego, Dan. 3. 17. Daniel,
Dan. 6. 10. Ninevites, Jonah 3. 5. Peter, Matt.
16. 16. Nathanael, John 1. 49. Martha, John 11.
27. Stephen, Acts 6. 5. Ethiopian eunuch, Acts
8. 37. Barnabas, Acts 11. 24.
FAITHFULNESS commended in the service of
God, 2 Kin. 12. 15; 2 Chr. 31. 12; Matt. 24. 45;
2 Cor. 2. 17; 4. 2; 3 John 5.
towards men, Deut. 1. 16; Ps. 141. 5; Prov. 11.
13; 13. 17; 14. 5; 20. 6; 25. 13; 27. 6; 28. 20;

FAITHFULNESS—*cont.*
Luke 16. 10; 1 Cor. 4. 2; 1 Tim. 3. 11; 6. 2; Tit.
2. 10.
of Abraham, Gen. 22; Gal. 3. 9.
of Joseph, Gen. 39. 4, 22.
of Moses, Num. 12. 7; Heb. 3. 5.
of David, 1 Sam. 22. 14.
of Daniel, Dan. 6. 4.
of Paul, Acts 20. 20.
of Timothy, 1 Cor. 4. 17.
of GOD, Ps. 36. 5; 40. 10; 88. 11; 89. 1; 92. 2; 119.
75; Is. 25. 1; Lam. 3. 23.
FALL of Adam and Eve, Gen. 3. *See* ADAM.
sin and death caused by, Gen. 3. 19; Rom. 5. 12;
1 Cor. 15. 21.
FALSE WITNESSES condemned. *See* DECEIT,
WITNESSES.
FAMILIAR SPIRITS, possessors of, to die, Lev.
20. 27.
not to be sought after, Lev. 19. 31; Is. 8. 19.
Saul destroys, 1 Sam. 28. 3; in his distress enquires of one remaining, 1 Sam. 28. 7; his
punishment, 1 Chr. 10. 13, 14.
Manasseh deals with, 2 Kin. 21. 6.
Paul casts out, Acts 16.
FAMINE threatened, Jer. 14. 15; 15. 2; Ezek. 5.
12; 6. 11; Matt. 24. 7; Acts 11. 28.
described, Jer. 14; Lam. 4; Joel 1.
occurs in Canaan, Gen. 12. Egypt, Gen. 41. Israel, Ruth 1. 1; 2 Sam. 21. 1; 1 Kin. 18. 2;
2 Kin. 6. 25; 7; Luke 4. 25.
Shunammite forewarned of, 2 Kin. 8. 1.
king of Egypt warned of, by Joseph, Gen. 40.
(of God's word), Amos 8. 11.
FAST proclaimed, Lev. 23. 27, 29; 2 Chr. 20. 3;
Ezra 8. 21; Neh. 9; Esth. 4. 16; Joel 2. 15; Jonah 3. 5.
season of, referred to, Acts 27. 9.
the true and the false, Is. 58; Zech. 7; Matt. 6.
16.
FASTING turned into gladness, Zech. 8. 19.
Christ excuses His disciples for not, Matt. 9. 14;
Mark 2. 18; Luke 5. 33.
of Moses (twice) for forty days, Ex. 24. 18; 34.
28; Deut. 9. 9, 18.
of David, 2 Sam. 12. 16.
of Elijah, 1 Kin. 19. 8.
of Christ, Matt. 4. 2, &c.
of Barnabas and Paul, Acts 14. 23.
recommended, 1 Cor. 7. 5.
FATHERLESS, GOD the God of, Ps. 146. 9; Jer.
49. 11; Hos. 14. 3.
God the helper of, Deut. 10. 18; Ps. 10. 14; 146. 9;
father of, Ps. 68. 5.
duty towards, Ex. 22. 22; Deut. 14. 29; 24. 17;
Prov. 23. 10; Is. 1. 17; Jer. 7. 6; James 1. 27.
the wicked oppress, Job 6. 27; 22. 9; Ps. 94. 6; Is.
1. 23; 10. 2; Jer. 5. 28; Ezek. 22. 7.
FATHERS, duty of, Deut. 21. 18; Prov. 3. 12;
13. 24; 19. 18; 22. 6, 15; 23. 13; 29. 15, 17; Luke
11. 11; Eph. 6. 4; Col. 3. 21; Heb. 12. 9.
children to obey, Ex. 20. 12; Prov. 6. 20; Eph.
6. 1; Col. 3. 20.
FAVOUR of GOD bestowed on CHRIST, Matt. 3. 16;
17. 5; Luke 2. 52; John 11. 41; 12. 28.
on the righteous, Job 33. 26; Ps. 5. 12; Prov. 3. 4.
on Job, Job 42. 10; Abraham, Gen. 18. 17; the
Israelites, Ps. 44. 3; 85. 1; the Virgin Mary,
Luke 1. 30; David, Acts 7. 46.
FEAR of GOD, Job 28. 28; Ps. 19. 9; Prov. 1. 7; 8.
13; 9. 10; 14. 27; 15. 33.
enjoined, Deut. 10. 12; Josh. 4. 24; Job 13. 11;
Ps. 2. 11; 76. 7; 130. 4; Jer. 10. 7; Matt. 10. 28;
Luke 12. 5; Heb. 12. 28; Rev. 14. 7; 15. 4.
advantages of, Ps. 15. 4; 25. 14; 31. 19; 33. 18;
60. 4; 61. 5; 85. 9; 103. 11; 111. 5; 112. 1; 145. 19;
147. 11; Prov. 10. 27; 14. 26; 15. 33; 19. 23; 22. 4;
Eccles. 8. 12; Mal. 3. 16; 4. 2; Luke 1. 50; 2 Cor.
7. 1; Rev. 11. 18.
commanded, Lev. 19. 14; Deut. 4. 10; 6. 2; 28.
58: Josh. 24. 14; 1 Sam. 12. 14; 2 Kin. 17. 38;
1 Chr. 16. 30; Ps. 2. 11; 33. 8; Prov. 3. 7; 23. 17;

GOD (AS A SPIRIT)—*cont.*
7. 22; Is. 46. 5, 9; Jer. 10. 6; beside Him, Deut.
4. 35; 1s. 44. 6; before Him, Is. 43. 10; none
good but God, Matt. 19. 17.
fills heaven and earth, 1 Kin. 8. 27; Jer. 23. 24.
should be worshipped in spirit and in truth,
John 4. 24.
—— HIS GLORY:—
exhibited in Christ, John 1. 14; 2 Cor. 4. 6; Heb.
1. 3.
exhibited in His power, Ex. 15. 1, 6; Rom. 6. 4;
holiness, Ex. 15. 11; name, Deut. 28. 58; Neh. 9.
5; majesty, Job 37. 22; Ps. 93. 1; 104. 1; 145. 5,
12; Is. 2. 10; works, Ps. 19. 1; 111. 3.
described as highly exalted, Ps. 8. 1; 113. 4.
Eternal, Ps. 104. 31. Great, Ps. 138. 5. Rich,
Eph. 3. 16.
exhibited to Moses, Ex. 34. 5—7, with Ex. 33. 18—
23. His church, Deut. 5. 24; Ps. 102. 16. Enlightens the church, Is. 60. 1, 2; Rev. 21. 11,
23. Stephen, Acts 7. 55.
declare, 1 Chr. 16. 24; Ps. 145. 5, 11.
magnify, Ps. 57. 5.
saints desire to behold, Ps. 63. 2; 90. 16.
pleaded in prayer, Ps. 79. 9.
the earth is full of, Is. 6. 3.
not to be given to others, Is. 42. 8.
to be feared, Is. 59. 19.
the knowledge of, shall fill the earth, Num. 14.
21; Hab. 2. 14.
—— HIS GOODNESS:—
proclaimed, Ps. 25. 8; Nah. 1. 7; Matt. 19. 17.
is abundant, Ex. 34. 6; Ps. 33. 5. Great, Neh.
9. 35; Zech. 9. 17. Enduring, Ps. 23. 6; 52. 1.
Satisfying, Ps. 65. 4; Jer. 31. 12, 14. Rich, Ps.
104. 24; Rom. 2. 4. Universal, Ps. 145. 9; Matt.
5. 45.
MANIFESTED
in forgiving sins, 2 Chr. 30. 18; Ps. 86. 5; to
His church, Ps. 31. 19; Lam. 3. 25; in providing for the poor, Ps. 68. 10; in doing good,
Ps. 119. 68; 145. 9; in supplying temporal
wants, Acts 14. 17.
leads to repentance, Rom. 2. 4.
—— HIS GIFTS:—
are free and abundant, Num. 14. 8; Rom. 8. 32.
are dispensed according to His will, Eccles. 2.
26; Dan. 2. 21; Rom. 12. 6; 1 Cor. 7. 7.
all blessings are, James 1. 17; 2 Pet. 1. 3.
—— HIS SPIRITUAL GIFTS:—
acknowledge, Ps. 4. 7; 21. 2.
peace, Ps. 29. 11.
strength and power, Ps. 68. 35.
are through Christ, Ps. 68. 18, with Eph. 4. 7,
8; John 6. 27.
Christ the chief of, Is. 42. 6; 55. 4; John 3. 16;
4. 10; 6. 32, 33.
a new heart, Ezek. 11. 19.
pray for, Matt. 7. 7, 11; John 16. 23, 24.
rest, Matt. 11. 28; 2 Thess. 1. 7.
the Holy Ghost, Luke 11. 13; Acts 8. 20.
grace, Ps. 84. 11; James 4. 6.
wisdom, Prov. 2. 6; James 1. 5.
glory, Ps. 84. 11; John 17. 22.
repentance, Acts 11. 18.
righteousness, Rom. 5. 16, 17.
eternal life, Rom. 6. 23.
not repented of by Him, Rom. 11. 29.
faith, Eph. 2. 8; Phil. 1. 29.
to be used for mutual profit, 1 Pet. 4. 10.
—— HIS TEMPORAL GIFTS:—
rain and fruitful seasons, Gen. 27. 28; Lev.
26. 4, 5; Is. 30. 23; Acts 14. 17.
peace, Lev. 26. 6; 1 Chr. 22. 2.
should cause us to remember God, Deut. 8. 18.
wisdom, 2 Chr. 1. 42.
all good things, Ps. 34. 10; 1 Tim. 6. 17.
all creatures partake of, Ps. 136. 25; 145. 15, 16.
life, Is. 42. 5.
to be used and enjoyed, Eccles. 3. 13; 5. 19,
20; 1 Tim. 4. 4, 5.

GOD (HIS GIFTS)—*cont.*
—— HIS TEMPORAL GIFTS:—
pray for, Zech. 10. 1; Matt. 6. 11.
food and raiment, Matt. 6. 25—33.
illustrated, Matt. 25. 15—30.
—— HIS JOY OVER HIS PEOPLE:—
greatness of, Zeph. 3. 17.
ON ACCOUNT OF THEIR
uprightness, 1 Chr. 29. 17; Prov. 11. 20.
fear of Him, Ps. 147. 11.
hope in His mercy, Ps. 147. 11.
meekness, Ps. 149. 4.
praying to Him, Prov. 15. 8.
repentance, Luke 15. 7, 10.
faith, Heb. 11. 5, 6.
LEADS HIM TO
give them the inheritance, Num. 14. 8; 1 Pet.
1. 4.
do them good, Deut. 28. 63; Jer. 32. 41; Acts
14. 17.
prosper them, Deut. 30. 9.
deliver them, 2 Sam. 22. 20.
comfort them, Is. 65. 19.
exemplified: *Solomon*, 1 Kin. 10. 9.
illustrated, Is. 62. 5; Luke 15. 23, 24.
—— HIS LAW:—
is absolute and perpetual, Matt. 5. 18.
GIVEN
to Adam, Gen. 2. 16, 17, with Rom. 5. 12—14.
to Noah, Gen. 9. 6.
to the Israelites, Ex. 20. 2; Ps. 78. 5.
through Moses, Ex. 31. 18; John 7. 19.
through the ministration of angels, Acts 7.
53; Gal. 3. 19; Heb. 2. 2.
DESCRIBED AS
perfect, Ps. 19. 7; Rom. 12. 2; pure, Ps. 19. 8;
exceeding broad, Ps. 119. 96; truth, Ps. 119.
142; holy, just, and good, Rom. 7. 12; spiritual,
Rom. 7. 14; not grievous, 1 John 5. 3.
requires perfect obedience, Deut. 27. 26; Gal.
3. 10; James 2. 10.
requires obedience of the heart, Ps. 51. 6; Matt.
5. 28; 22. 37.
man cannot render perfect obedience to, 1 Kin.
8. 46; Eccl. 7. 20; Rom. 3. 10.
it is man's duty to keep, Eccl. 12. 13.
man cannot be justified by, Acts 13. 39; Rom.
3. 20, 28; Gal. 2. 16; 3. 11.
conscience testifies to, Rom. 2. 15.
all men have transgressed, Rom. 3. 9, 19.
gives the knowledge of sin, Rom. 3. 20; 7. 7.
worketh wrath, Rom. 4. 15.
man, by nature not in subjection to, Rom. 7. 5;
8. 7.
love is the fulfilling of, Rom. 13. 8, 10; Gal. 5.
14; James 2. 8.
designed to lead to Christ, Gal. 3. 24.
sin is a transgression of, 1 John 3. 4.
OBEDIENCE TO,
of prime importance, 1 Cor. 7. 19.
a test of love, 1 John 5. 3.
a characteristic of saints, Rev. 12. 17.
blessedness of keeping, Ps. 119. 1; Matt. 5. 19
1 John 3. 22, 24; Rev, 22. 14.
CHRIST magnified, Is. 42. 21.
came to fulfil, Matt. 5. 17.
explained, Matt. 7. 12; 22. 37—40.
the love of, produces peace, Ps. 119. 165.
SAINTS
should make the subject of their conversation
Ex. 13. 9; prepare their hearts to seek, Ezr
7. 10; pledge themselves to walk in, Neh. 1(
29; pray to understand, Ps. 119. 18; pray fo
power to keep, Ps. 119. 34; keep, Ps. 119. 55
delight in, Ps. 119. 77; Rom. 7. 22; love, Ps
119. 97, 113; lament over the violation of, b
others, Ps. 119. 136; have, written on thei
hearts, Jer. 31. 33, with Heb. 8. 10; shoul
remember, Mal. 4. 4; freed from the bondag
of, Rom. 6. 14; 7. 4, 6; Gal. 3. 13; freed fror
the curse of, Gal. 3. 13.

GOD (HIS LAW)—*cont.*

THE WICKED
forsake, 2 Chr. 12. 1; Jer. 9. 13; refuse to walk in, Ps. 78. 10; cast away, Is. 5. 24; refuse to hear, Is. 30. 9; Jer. 6. 19; forget, Hos. 4. 6; despise, Amos 2. 4.

punishment for disobeying, Neh. 9. 26, 27; Is. 65. 11—13; Jer. 9. 13—16.

is the rule of judgment, Rom. 2. 12.

is established by faith, Rom. 3. 31.

is the rule of life to saints, 1 Cor. 9. 21; Gal. 5. 13, 14.

to be used lawfully, 1 Tim. 1. 8.

—— **HIS ATTRIBUTES:**—

ETERNAL, Gen. 21. 33; Ex. 3. 14; Deut. 32. 40; 33. 27; Job 10. 5; 36. 26; Ps. 9. 7; 90. 2; 92. 8; 93. 2; 102. 12; 104. 31; 135. 13; 145. 13; 146. 6, 10; Eccl. 3. 14; Is. 9. 6; 40. 28; 41. 4; 43. 13; 48. 12; 57. 15; 63. 16; Jer. 10. 10; Lam. 5. 19; Dan. 4. 3, 34; 6. 26; Mic. 5. 2; Hab. 1. 12; Rom. 1. 20; 16. 26; Eph. 3. 9; 1 Tim. 1. 17; 6. 16; 2 Pet. 3. 8; Rev. 1. 8; 4. 9; 22. 13.

IMMUTABLE, Num. 23. 19; 1 Sam. 15. 29; Ps. 33. 11; 119. 89; Mal. 3. 6; Acts 4. 28; Eph. 1. 4; Heb. 1. 12; 6. 17; 13. 8; James 1. 17.

OMNISCIENT, Job 26. 6; 34. 21; Ps. 139; Prov. 15. 3; Is. 44. 7; Ezek. 11. 5; Matt. 12. 25; John 2. 24; Rom. 1. 20.

OMNIPRESENT, Job 23. 9; 26; 28; Ps. 139; Prov. 15. 3; Acts 17. 27.

INVISIBLE, Ex. 33. 20; Job 23. 8; John 1. 18; 4. 24; 5. 37; Col. 1. 15; 1 Tim. 1. 17; 6. 16; Heb. 11. 27; 1 John 4. 12.

UNSEARCHABLE, Job 11. 7; 26. 14; 37. 15; Ps. 145. 3; Eccles. 8. 17; Rom. 11. 33.

INCOMPREHENSIBLE, Job 5. 9; 9. 10; 11. 7; 26. 14; 36. 26; 37. 5; Ps. 36. 6; 40. 5; 106. 2; 139. 6; Eccles. 3. 11; 8. 17; 11. 5; Is. 40. 12; 45. 15; Mic. 4. 12; 1 Tim. 6. 16.

HOLINESS, Gen. 35. 2; Ex. 3. 5; 14; 15; 19; 20; 28. 36; 34. 5; 39. 30; Lev. 11. 44; 21. 8; Josh. 5. 15; 1 Sam. 2. 2; 1 Chr. 16. 10; Ps. 22. 3; 30. 4; 60. 6. *See* PSALMS, Is. 6. 3; 43. 15; 49. 7; 57. 15; Jer. 23. 9; Amos 4. 2; Luke 1. 49; Acts 3. 14; Rom. 7. 12; 1 John 2. 20; Rev. 4. 8; 19. 1.

JUSTICE, &c. Gen. 2. 16; 3. 8; 4. 9; 6. 7; 9. 15; 18. 17, 19; Ex. 32. 33; Lev. 4. 7; 20. 18. 4; 26. 21; Num. 11; 14; 16; 17; 20; 25. 26. 64; 27. 12; 35; Deut. 1. 34—45; 4. 24; 5; 6; 9. 4; 10. 17; 25. 17; 28. 15; 31. 16; 32. 35, 41; Josh. 7. 1; Judg. 1. 7; 2. 14; 9. 56; 1 Sam. 2. 30; 3. 11; 6. 19; 15. 17; 2 Sam. 6. 7; 12. 1; 22; 24. 11; 1 Kin. 8. 20; 2 Chr. 6. 17; 19. 7; Ezra 8. 22; Neh. 9. 33; Job 4. 17; 8; 10. 3; 11. 11; 12. 6; 13. 15; 14. 15; 34. 10; 35. 13; 37. 23; 40. 8. *See* PSALMS. Prov. 11. 21; 15. 8; 28. 9; 30. 5; Eccles. 5. 8; 8. 12; 11. 9; Is. 45. 21; Jer. 5. 9; 9. 24; 23. 20; 32. 19; 50. 7; 51. 9; Lam. 1. 18; Ezek. 7. 27; 16. 35; 18. 10; 33. 17; Dan. 4. 37; 9. 14; Hos. 4; 5; Nah. 1. 3; Hab. 1. 13; Zeph. 3. 5; Mal. 2. 17; 4. 1; Matt. 10. 15; 20; 13; 23. 14; Luke 12. 47; 13. 27; John 7. 18; Acts 10. 34; 17. 31; Rom. 2. 2; Gal. 6. 7; Eph. 6. 8; Col. 3. 25; James 1. 13; 1 John 1. 9; Rev. 15. 3; 16. 7.

KNOWLEDGE, WISDOM, AND POWER, Gen. 1; 3; 6—9; 41. 16; Ex. 4. 11; 7. 10; 12. 29; 14. 15; 33. 19; 34. 5; 35. 30; 36; Num. 11. 23; 12; 22. 9; 23. 4; 24. 16; Deut. 3. 4; 32. 5. 24; 6. 22; 7. 10; 26; 28. 58; 29. 29; 32. 4; Josh. 3. 6; 7. 10; 23. 9; 24; Judg. 2; 1 Sam. 2; 4. 5; 12. 18; 14. 6; 16. 7. 17. 37, 46; 18. 10; 23; 2 Sam. 7. 22; 1 Kin. 8. 27; 22. 22; 1 Chr. 16. 24; 17. 4; 22. 18; 28. 9; 29. 11; 2 Chr. 6. 18; 14. 11; 20. 6; Neh. 9. 5; Job 4. 9; 5. 9; 9. 10; 4. 11; 12; 19. 6; 21. 17; 22. 23; 26. 6; 33. 14; 35; 42; 35; 41. *See* PSALMS. Prov. 3. 19; 5. 21; 8. 22; 15. 3; 16. 9; 19. 21; 21. 30; Eccles. 3. 11; 7. 13; Is. 2. 10; 6. 3; 12. 5; 14. 24; 28. 29; 29. 16; 30. 18; 33. 13; 40. 20; 41. 22; 42. 9; 43; 44. 6, 23; 45. 20; 46. 5; 47. 4; 48. 3; 52. 10; 55. 11; 59. 1; 60. 1; 66. 1; Jer. 3. 14; 5. 22; 10. 6; 14. 22; 29. 23; 32. 17; Lam. 3. 37; Ezek.

GOD (HIS ATTRIBUTES)—*cont.*

8. 12; 11. 5; 22. 14; Dan. 2. 20; 3. 17, 29; 4. 34; 6. 26; Joel 2. 11; Amos 5. 12; 8. 7; Hab. 2. 14; Mal. 3. 16; Matt. 5. 48; 6. 13; 9. 38; 10. 29; 12. 25; 19. 26; 22. 29; Mark 5. 30; 12. 15; Luke 1. 48; 12. 5; 18. 27; John 1. 14; 2. 24; 5. 26; 6. 61; 11. 25; 16. 19; 18. 4; 19. 28; 20. 17; Acts 1. 24; 2. 17; 7. 55; 15. 18; Rom. 1. 20; 4. 17; 8. 29; 11. 34; 15. 19; 16. 27; 1 Cor. 2. 9, 16; 2 Cor. 4. 6; 12. 9; 13. 4; Gal. 2. 8; Eph. 1. 19; 3. 7; 6. 10; Phil. 1. 6; 3. 21; Col. 3. 4; 1 Tim. 1. 12, 17; Heb. 1. 3; 2. 10; 4. 12; James 4. 6; 1 Pet. 2. 20; 1 John 1. 5; 3. 20; Jude 1, 24; Rev. 1. 8; 4. 11; 5. 13; 11. 17; 19. 6; 21. 3.

FAITHFULNESS AND TRUTH, Num. 23. 19; Deut. 7. 8; Josh. 21. 45; 2 Sam. 7. 28; 1 Kin. 8. 56; Ps. 19. 9; 89. 34; 105. 8; 111. 7; 117; 119. 89, 160; 146. 6; Is. 25. 1; 31. 2; 46. 11; 65. 16; Jer. 4. 28; Lam. 2. 17; Ezek. 12. 25; Matt. 24. 35; John 7. 28; Rom. 3. 4; 1 Cor. 1. 9; 15. 58; 2 Cor. 1. 18; 1 Thess. 5. 24; 2 Thess. 3. 3; 2 Tim. 2. 13; Tit. 1. 2; Heb. 6. 18; 10. 23; 11. 11; 13. 5; 2 Pet. 3. 9; Rev. 1. 5; 3. 7; 15. 3; 16. 7.

MERCY, GOODNESS, AND LOVE, Gen. 1. 28; 3. 15; 4. 4; 8. 9; 15. 4; 16. 7; 17; 18. 16; 19. 12; 21. 12; 22. 15; 24. 12; 26. 24; 28. 10; 29. 31; 32. 9, 24; 39. 2; 46; Ex. 1. 20; 2. 23; 3. 7; 6; 16; 17; 20. 6; 22. 27; 23. 20; 29. 45; 32. 14; 33; 12; 34. 6; Lev. 4. 35; 26. 3, 40; Num. 14. 18; 21. 7; Deut. 4. 29; 7. 7; 8; 10. 15; 18. 15; 20. 4; 23. 5; 28. 1; 30; 32. 7, 43; 33; Josh. 20; Judg. 2. 16; 6. 36; 10. 15; 13; 15. 18; 1 Sam. 2. 9; 7; 25. 32; 2 Sam. 7. 5; 12. 13; 1 Kin. 8. 56; 2 Chr. 16. 9; 30. 9; Ezra 8. 18; Neh. 2. 18; 9. 17; Job 5. 17; 7. 17; 11. 6; 33. 14; 36. 11; 37. 23; Ps. 34. 8; 36. 5; 69. 16; Prov. 8. 30; 11. 20; 18. 10; 28. 13; Eccles. 2. 26; 8. 11; Is. 25. 4; 27. 3; 30. 18; 38. 17; 40. 29; 43. 1; 48. 9, 17; 49. 15; 54. 7; 55. 3; 63. 7; Jer. 3. 12; 9. 24; 16. 14; 17. 7; 31. 3, 12; 32. 39; 33. 11; 44. 28; Lam. 3. 22, 31; Ezek. 20. 17; 33. 11; Dan. 9. 9; Hos. 2. 19; 11. 4; 13. 14; 14. 3; Joel 2. 13; Mic. 7. 18; Nah. 1. 7; Hab. 3. 18; Zeph. 3. 17; Mal. 3. 6; 4; Matt. 5. 45; 19. 17; 23. 37; Luke 1. 50, 78; 5. 21; 6. 35; 13. 6; John 1. 4, 9; 3. 16; 4. 10; 14; 15. 9; 16. 7; 17; Acts 14. 17; Rom. 2. 4; 3. 25; 5. 5; 8. 32; 9. 22; 11. 2 Cor. 1. 3; 12. 9; 13. 11; Gal. 1. 4; Eph. 2. 4, 17; 4. 6; 1 Tim. 2. 4; 6. 17; 2 Tim. 1. 9; Tit. 3. 4; Heb. 12. 6; James 1. 5, 17; 5. 11; 1 Pet. 1. 3; 3. 20; 2 Pet. 3. 9, 15; 1 John 1; Jude 21; Rev. 2. 3. *See* PSALMS.

JEALOUSY. Ex. 20. 5; 34. 14; Deut. 4. 24; 5. 9; 6. 15; 29. 20; 32. 16; Josh. 24. 19; Ps. 78. 58; 79. 5; Ezek. 16; 23; Hos. 1; 2; Joel 2. 18; Zeph. 1. 18; Zech. 1. 14; 1 Cor. 10. 22.

—— **HIS CHARACTERS:**—

DISPOSER OF EVENTS, Gen. 6—9; 11. 8; 12; 14. 20; 18. 14; 22; 25. 23; 26; Ex. 9. 16; Deut. 7. 7; 1 Sam. 2. 6; 9. 15; 13. 14; 15. 17; 16; 2 Sam. 7. 8; 22. 1; Ps. 10. 16; 22. 28; 24; 33; 74. 12; 75; Is. 40. 23; 43—45; 64. 8; Jer. 8. 19; 10. 10; 18; 19; Dan. 4; 5; Zech. 14. 9; Luke 10. 21; Rom. 9; Eph. 1. 11; 1 Tim. 1. 17; 6. 15; James 4. 12.

JUDGE OF ALL, Gen. 18. 25; Deut. 32. 36; Judg. 11. 27; Ps. 7. 11; 9. 7; 50; 58. 11; 68. 5; 75. 7; 94. 2; Eccl. 3. 17; 11. 9; 12. 14; Is. 2. 4; 3. 13; Jer. 11. 20; Acts 10. 42; Rom. 2. 16; 2 Tim. 4. 8; Heb. 12. 23; Jude 6; Rev. 11. 18; 18. 8; 19. 11.

SEARCHER OF HEARTS, 1 Chr. 28. 9; Ps. 7. 9; 44. 21; 139. 23; Prov. 17. 3; 24. 12; Jer. 17. 10; Acts 1. 24; Rom. 8. 27; Rev. 2. 23.

SANCTUARY AND REFUGE, Deut. 33. 27; 2 Sam. 22. 3; Ps. 9. 9; 46. 1; 57. 1; 50. 16; 62; 71. 7; 91; 94. 22; 142. 5; Is. 8. 14; Ezek. 11. 16; Heb. 6. 18.

SAVIOUR, Ps. 106. 21; Is. 43. 3, 11; 45. 15; 49. 26; 60. 16; 63. 8; Jer. 14. 8; Hos. 13. 4; Luke 1. 47.

—— **HIS NAMES:**—

Father of Lights, James 1. 17.

God of Heaven, Ezra 5. 11; Neh. 1. 4; 2. 4.

God of Hosts, Ps. 80. 7, 14, 19.

GOD THE HOLY GHOST (EMBLEMS OF)—
cont.
A SEAL, Rev. 7. 2.
  authenticating, John 6. 27; 2 Cor. 1. 22.
  securing, Eph. 1. 13, 14; 4. 30.
CLOVEN TONGUES, Acts 2. 3, 6—11.
THE GIFT OF THE HOLY GHOST:—
  by the Father, Neh. 9. 20; Luke 11. 13.
  to Christ without measure, John 3. 34.
  by the Son, John 20. 22.
GIVEN
  for instruction, Neh. 9. 20.
    upon the exaltation of Christ, Ps. 68. 18;
      John 7. 39.
  in answer to prayer, Luke 11. 13; Eph. 1. 16,
    17.
  through the intercession of Christ, John 14.
    16.
  for comfort of saints, John 14. 16.
  to those who repent and believe, Acts 2. 38.
  according to promise, Acts 2. 38, 39.
  to those who obey God, Acts 5. 32.
  to the Gentiles, Acts 10. 44, 45; 11. 17; 15. 8.
is fructifying, Is. 32. 15.
is abundant, Ps. 68. 9; John 7. 38, 39.
is permanent, Is. 59. 21; Hag. 2. 5; 1 Pet. 4. 14.
a pledge of the continued favour of God, Ezek.
  39. 29.
an earnest of the inheritance of the saints, 2 Cor.
  1. 22; 5. 5; Eph. 1. 14.
received through faith, Gal. 3. 14.
an evidence of union with Christ, 1 John 3. 24;
  4. 13.
GODLY CONVERSATION. *See* CONVERSATION.
GODS, judges described as, Ex. 22. 28; Ps. 82. 1;
  138. 1; John 10. 34; 1 Cor. 8. 5.
  false, worship of, forbidden, Ex. 20. 3; 34. 17;
    Deut. 5. 7; 8. 19; 18. 20.
GOLDEN CANDLESTICK, Ex. 25. 31.
GOSPEL of Christ, its teaching and accompaniments, Matt. 4. 23; 24. 14; Mark 1. 14; Luke 2.
  10; 20. 21; Acts 13. 26; 14. 3; 20. 21; Rom. 1. 2,
  9, 16; 2. 16; 10. 8; 16. 25; 1 Cor. 1. 18; 2. 13; 15.
  1; 2 Cor. 4. 4; 5. 19; 6. 7; Eph. 1. 13; 3. 2, 6, 15;
  Phil. 2. 16; Col. 1. 5; 3. 16; 1 Thess. 1. 5; 2. 8;
  3. 2; 1 Tim. 1. 11; 6. 3; Heb. 4. 2; 1 Pet. 1. 12,
  25; 4. 17.
  preached to Abraham, Gal. 3. 8.
  to the poor and others, Matt. 11. 5; Mark 1. 15;
    13. 10; 16. 15; Luke 4. 18; 24. 47; Acts 13. 46;
    14; 1 Cor. 1. 17; 9. 16; Gal. 2. 2; Rev. 14. 6.
  its effects, Mark 1. 15; 8. 35; Luke 2. 10, 14; 19.
    8; Acts 4. 32; Rom. 1. 16; 12; 13. 29; 16.
    26; 2 Cor. 8; 9; Gal. 1. 16; 2. 14; Eph. 4—6;
    Phil. 1. 5, 17, 27; Col. 1. 23; 3; 4; 1 Thess. 1;
    2; Tit. 2; 3; James 1; 1 & 2 Pet.; 1 John 3;
    Jude 3.
  rejected by the Jews, Acts 13. 26; 28. 25; Rom.
    9—11; 1 Thess. 2. 16.
  from whom hid, 1 Cor. 1. 23; 2. 8; 2 Cor. 4. 3.
  RACE of God and Jesus Christ, Ps. 84. 11; Zech.
    4. 7; Luke 2. 40; John 1. 16; Acts 20. 24; Rom.
    11. 5; 1 Cor. 15. 10; 2 Cor. 8, 9; 2 Tim. 1. 9;
    1 Pet. 5. 5.
  salvation through, Acts 15. 11; Rom. 3. 24; 4.
    4; Eph. 2. 5; 2 Thess. 2. 16; Tit. 3. 7; 1 Pet. 1.
    10.
  effects of, 2 Cor. 1. 12; Tit. 2. 11; 1 Pet. 4. 10.
  See GOSPEL.
  prayer for, Rom. 16. 20; 1 Tim. 1. 2; Heb. 4. 16.
  danger of abusing, Rom. 6; Jude 4; and depart-
    ing from, Gal. 5. 4.
  exhortations concerning, 2 Tim. 1. 9; Heb. 12.
    15, 28; 2 Pet. 3. 18.
  RASS brought forth, Gen. 1. 11.
  man compared to, Ps. 37. 2; 90. 5; 103. 15; Is.
    40. 6; James 1. 10; 1 Pet. 1. 24.
  ROVES for worship, Gen. 21. 33.
  idolatrous, forbidden, Deut. 16. 21; Judg. 6. 25;
    1 Kin. 14. 15; 15. 13; 16. 33; 2 Kin. 17. 16; 21. 3;
    23. 4.

HAIL, plague of, Ex. 9. 23; Josh. 10. 11; Ps. 18.
  12; 78. 47; Is. 28. 2; Ezek. 13. 11; Hag. 2. 17;
  Rev. 8. 7; 11. 19; 16. 21.
HALLOWED BREAD. *See* SHEWBREAD.
HAND of GOD, for blessing, 2 Chr. 30. 12; Ezra
  7. 9; 8. 18; Neh. 2. 18.
  for chastisement, Deut. 2. 15; Ruth 1. 13; Job
    2. 10; 19. 21; 1 Pet. 5. 6.
HANDS, laying on of, Num. 8. 10; 27. 18; Acts
  6. 6; 13. 3; 1 Tim. 4. 14; 2 Tim. 1. 6.
  washing, declaratory of innocence, Deut. 21. 6;
    Ps. 26. 6; Matt. 27. 24.
  lifting up, in prayer, Ex. 17. 11; Ps. 28. 2; 63. 4;
    141. 2; 143. 6; 1 Tim. 2. 8.
HANGING, a punishment, Gen. 40. 22; Num. 25.
  4; Esth. 7. 10; 9. 14.
  the hanged accursed, Deut. 21. 22; Gal. 3. 13.
HAPPY, who so called, Deut. 33. 29; Job 5. 17;
  Ps. 127. 5; 144. 15; 146. 5; Prov. 3. 13; 14. 21;
  28. 14; 29. 18; John 13. 17; Rom. 14. 22; James
  5. 11; 1 Pet. 3. 14; 4. 14.
HARDENED heart deprecated, Deut. 15. 7; 1
  Sam. 6. 6; Ps. 95. 8; Heb. 3. 8; results of, Ex.
  7. 13; 8. 15; Prov. 28. 14; Dan. 5. 20; John 12.
  40.
HARLOTS, Gen. 34. 31; Lev. 19. 29; 21. 7; Deut.
  23. 17; Is. 57. 3; Jer. 3. 3; Matt. 21. 32; 1 Cor.
  6. 15.
  Rahab of Jericho, Josh. 2. 1.
  priests forbidden to marry, Lev. 21. 14.
  Solomon's judgment, 1 Kin. 3. 16.
  figurative, Is. 1. 21; Jer. 2. 20; Ezek. 16; 23;
    Hos. 2; Rev. 17; 18.
HARP (and organ), Gen. 4. 21.
  played on by David, 1 Sam. 16. 16, 23; 2 Sam. 6. 5.
  used in public worship, 1 Chr. 25. 3; Ps. 33. 2; 81.
    2; 150. 3.
  in heaven, Rev. 14. 2.
HARVEST, promise concerning, Gen. 8. 22.
  feast of, Ex. 23. 16; 34. 21; Lev. 19. 9; Is. 9. 3;
    16. 9.
  of the world, Jer. 8. 20; Matt. 13. 30, 39; Rev.
    14. 15.
HATRED forbidden, Ex. 23. 5; Lev. 19. 17; Deut.
  19. 11; Prov. 10. 12, 18; 15. 17; 26. 4; Matt. 5. 43;
  Gal. 5. 20; Tit. 3. 3; 1 John 2. 9; 3. 15; 4. 20.
HAUGHTINESS censured, 2 Sam. 22. 28; Prov.
  6. 17; 16. 18; 21. 4, 24; Is. 2. 11; 3. 16; 13. 11;
  16. 6; Jer. 48. 29.
HEAD of the Church, Christ, Eph. 1. 22; 4. 15;
  5. 23; Col. 1. 18; 2. 10.
  not holding the, Col. 2. 19.
HEALTH of body, Gen. 43. 28; 3 John 2.
  spiritual, Ps. 42. 11; Prov. 3. 8; 12. 18; Is. 58. 8;
    Jer. 8. 15; 30. 17; 33. 6.
HEART of Man, Gen. 6. 5; 8. 21; Eccles. 8. 11; 9.
  3; Jer. 17. 9; Matt. 12. 34; 15. 19; Luke 6. 45;
  Rom. 2. 5.
  searched and tried by God, 1 Chr. 28. 9; 29. 17;
    Ps. 44. 21; 139. 23; Prov. 21. 2; 24. 12; Jer. 12. 3;
    17. 10; 20. 12; Rev. 2. 23.
  enlightened, &c., by Him, 2 Cor. 4. 6; Ps. 27. 14;
    Prov. 16. 1; 1 Thess. 3. 13; 2 Pet. 1. 19.
  a new, promised, Jer. 24. 7; 31. 32; 32. 39; Ezek.
    11. 19; 36. 26.
HEATHEN described, Eph. 2. 12; 4. 18; 5. 12;
  1 Cor. 1. 21.
  gospel preached to, Matt. 24. 14; 28. 19; Rom.
    10. 14; 16. 26; Gal. 1. 16.
  conversion of, Acts 10. 35; Rom. 15. 16.
HEAVEN, the firmament, created, Gen. 1. 1, 8;
  Ps. 8; 19; Is. 40. 22; Rev. 10. 6.
  dwelling-place of God, 1 Kin. 8. 30; Ps. 2. 1; 115.
    3; 123. 1; Is. 6. 1; 66. 1; Ezek. 1. 10; Matt. 6. 9;
    Acts 7. 49; Heb. 8. 1; Rev. 4.
  happiness of, Ps. 16. 11; Is. 49. 10; Dan. 12. 3;
    Matt. 5. 12; 13. 43; Luke 12. 37; John 12. 26;
    14. 2; 17. 24; 1 Cor. 2. 9; 13. 12; 1 Pet. 1. 4; Rev.
    7. 16; 14. 13; 21. 4; 22. 3.
  who enter, Matt. 5. 3; 25. 34; Rom. 8. 17; Heb.
    12. 23; 1 Pet. 1. 4; Rev. 7. 9, 14.

HEAVEN—*cont.*
who do not enter, Matt. 7. 21; 25. 41; Luke 13. 27; 1 Cor. 6. 9; Gal. 5. 21; Rev. 21. 8; 22. 15.
the new, Rev. 21. 1.
HEAVE-OFFERING, Ex. 29. 27; Num. 15. 19; 18. 8, 30.
HEIFER for labour, Gen. 15. 9; Num. 19. 2; Deut. 21. 3; Heb. 9. 13.
HELL (Hades), the grave, Acts 2. 31; 1 Cor. 15. 55; Rev. 20. 13.
place of torment, Matt. 11. 23; 13. 42; 25. 41, 46; Luke 16. 23; 2 Pet. 2. 4; Rev. 14. 10; 20. 10, 15; for whom reserved, Ps. 9. 17; Prov. 5. 5; 7. 27; 9. 18; Matt. 5. 22; 23. 15; 25. 41; Luke 16. 23. *See* Is. 5. 14; 14. 9; 33. 14; Matt. 3. 12.
HERESIES deprecated, 1 Cor. 11. 19; Gal. 5. 20; 2 Pet. 2. 1. *See* Rom. 16. 17; 1 Cor. 1. 10; 3. 3; 14. 33; Phil. 2. 3; 4. 2; Tit. 3. 10; Jude 19.
HID TREASURE, parable, Matt. 13. 44.
HIGH PLACES forbidden, Deut. 12. 2; 1 Kin. 3. 2; 12. 31; 13. 2; 14. 23; Jer. 3. 6.
HIGH PRIEST, Ex. 28. 1.
his garments, Lev. 8. 7.
HIN. *See* MEASURES.
HIRE for labour, not to be kept back, Lev. 19. 13; Deut. 24. 14, 15; James 5. 4.
HOLINESS enjoined, Ex. 19. 22; Lev. 11. 44; 20. 7; Num. 15. 40; Deut. 7. 6; 26. 19; 28. 9; Luke 1. 75; Rom. 12. 1; 2 Cor. 7. 1; Eph. 1. 4; 4. 24; Col. 3. 12; 1 Thess. 2. 12; 1 Tim. 2. 15; Heb. 12. 14; 1 Pet. 1. 15; 2 Pet. 3. 11; Rev. 22. 11.
HOLY GIFTS, Ex. 28. 38; Lev. 10. 12.
HOLY PLACE, laws concerning, Ex. 28. 29; Lev. 6. 16; 16. 2; 2 Chr. 29. 5; Heb. 9. 12.
measure of the most, Ezek. 41. 4.
HOLY SPIRIT. *See* GOD THE HOLY GHOST.
HOLY THINGS, laws respecting, Ex. 28. 38; Lev. 5. 15; 22. 2; Num. 4. 19, 20; 1 Chr. 23. 28; Neh. 10. 33; Ezek. 20. 40; 22. 8.
HOMER. *See* MEASURES.
HONESTY, Rom. 12. 17; 13. 13; 2 Cor. 8. 21; 13. 7; Phil. 4. 8; 1 Thess. 4. 12; 1 Tim. 2. 2; Heb. 13. 18.
HONEY, Gen. 43. 11; 1 Sam. 14. 25; Ps. 19. 10; Prov. 24. 13; 25. 16; 27. 7; Is. 7. 15; Cant. 4. 11; Rev. 10. 9.
not to be used in burnt sacrifices, Lev. 2. 11.
HONOUR due to God, Ps. 29. 2; 71. 8; 145. 5; Mal. 1. 6; 1 Tim. 1. 17; Rev. 4. 11; 5. 13.
granted by God, 1 Kin. 3. 13; Esth. 8. 16; Prov. 3. 16; 4. 8; 8. 18; 22. 4; 29. 23; Dan. 5. 18; John 12. 26.
due to parents, Ex. 20. 12; Deut. 5. 16; Matt. 15. 4; Eph. 6. 2.
to the aged, Lev. 19. 32; 1 Tim. 5. 1.
to the king, 1 Pet. 2. 17.
HOPE (a good), Ps. 16. 9; 22. 9; 31. 24; Acts 24. 15; 28. 20; Rom. 15. 13.
of the wicked will perish, Job 8. 13; 11. 20; 27. 8.
comfort of, Job 11. 18; Ps. 146. 5; Prov. 10. 28; 14. 32; Jer. 17. 7; Lam. 3. 21; Acts 24. 15; Rom. 12. 12; 15. 4; 1 Cor. 13. 13; Eph. 1. 18; 4. 4; Col. 1. 5; Heb. 3. 6.
encouragement under, Ps. 31. 24; 42. 5; 130. 7; Lam. 3. 26; Rom. 8. 24; 15. 13; Col. 1. 23; Tit. 2. 13; Heb. 3. 6; 6. 11; 1 Pet. 1. 13.
prisoners of, Zech. 9. 12.
effect of, Rom. 5. 5; 8. 24; 15. 4; 1 Cor. 13. 7; 1 John 3. 3.
gift of God, Gal. 5. 5; 2 Thess. 2. 16; Tit. 1. 2; 1 Pet. 1. 3.
ready to give reason for, 1 Pet. 3. 15.
HORNETS, as God's instruments of punishment, Ex. 23. 28; Deut. 7. 20; Josh. 24. 12.
HORNS figuratively mentioned, 1 Sam. 2. 1; 2 Sam. 22. 3; Ps. 75. 4.
vision of, Dan. 7. 7; 8. 3; Hab. 3. 4; Rev. 5. 6; 12. 3; 13. 1; 17. 3.
——— of the altar, 1 Kin. 1. 50; 2. 28.
——— of iron, Zedekiah makes, 1 Kin. 22.
HORSE described, Job 39. 19; Prov. 21. 31; Jer. 8. 6.
HORSES, kings forbidden to multiply, Deut. 17. 16; Ps. 33. 17; 147. 10.

HORSES—*cont.*
vision of, Zech. 1. 8; 6; Rev. 6.
HOSPITALITY, Rom. 12. 13; Tit. 1. 8; Heb. 13. 2; 1 Pet. 4. 9.
instances of:—Abraham, Gen. 18. Lot, Gen. 19. Laban, Gen. 24. 31. Jethro, Ex. 2. 20. Manoah, Judg. 13. 15. Samuel, 1 Sam. 9. 22. David, 2 Sam. 6. 19. Barzillai, &c., 2 Sam. 17. 27; 19. 32. The Shunammite, 2 Kin. 4. 8. Nehemiah, Neh. 5. 18. Job, Job 31. 17. Matthew, Luke 5. 29. Zacchæus, Luke 19. 6. Lydia, Acts 16. 15. Publius, &c., Acts 28. 2. Gaius, 3 John 5.
HOST, the heavenly, Luke 2. 13. *See* 1 Chr. 12. 22; Ps. 103. 21; 148. 2.
of the Lord, Gen. 32. 2; Josh. 5. 14; 1 Chr. 9. 19.
HOUR, the third, of day, Matt. 20. 3; Mark 15. 25; Acts 2. 15; 23. 23.
the sixth, Matt. 27. 45; Mark 15. 33; Luke 23. 44; John 4. 6; 19. 14; Acts 10. 9.
the ninth, Acts 3. 1; 10. 3, 30.
at hand, cometh, Matt. 26. 45; John 4. 21; 5. 25; 12. 23; 13. 1; 16. 21; 17. 1.
that very same, Matt. 8. 13; 9. 22; 10. 19; 15. 28; 17. 18; Luke 12. 12; John 4. 53; Acts 16. 18; 33; 22. 13; 1 Cor. 4. 11; 8. 7.
knoweth no man, Matt. 24. 36, 42; 25. 13; Mark 13. 32; Rev. 3. 3.
of temptation, Rev. 3. 10; judgment, Rev. 14. 7; 18. 10.
figurative, Rev. 8. 1; 9. 15.
HOUSE OF GOD, Gen. 28. 17; Judg. 20. 18; 2 Chr. 5. 14; Ezra 5. 8, 15; 7. 20, 23; Neh. 6. 10; Ps. 84. 10; Is. 6. 11; 60. 7; 64. 7; Ezek. 41. 5, 13; 43. 5; Mic. 4. 2; Zech. 7. 2; Matt. 12. 4; 1 Tim. 3. 15; Heb. 10. 21; 1 Pet. 4. 17.
(heaven), Acts 7. 49.
(altars). *See* ALTAR.
(for worship). *See* TEMPLE.
HUMILITY, Prov. 15. 33; 18. 12; 22. 4.
enjoined, Mic. 6. 8; Matt. 18. 20; 25; Mark 9. 33 10. 43; Luke 9. 46; 14. 7; 22. 24; Eph. 4. 2; Col. 3. 12; Phil. 2. 3; James 4. 10; 1 Pet. 5. 5.
benefits of, Ps. 34. 2; 69. 32; Prov. 3. 34; Is. 57. 15; Matt. 18. 4; Luke 14. 11; James 4. 6.
profession of, Ps. 131.
HUNGER, Ex. 16. 3; Ps. 34. 10; Jer. 38. 9; Lam. 4. 9; Luke 15. 17; 2 Cor. 11. 27; Rev. 6. 8.
(and thirst), Ps. 107. 5; Is. 49. 10; 55; Matt. 5. 6 John 6. 35; Rev. 7. 16.
HUSBAND, figuratively, Is. 54. 5; Hos. 2. 7.
HUSBANDS, Gen. 2. 24; Matt. 19. 4; 1 Cor. 7. 2, 3 Eph. 5. 23, 25, 33; Col. 3. 19; 1 Pet. 3. 7.
HUSBANDMAN, John 15. 1; 2 Tim. 2. 6; James 5. 7.
HUSBANDMEN, parable of, Matt. 21. 33; Mar 12. 1; Luke 20. 9.
HYPOCRISY, Is. 29. 15; Matt. 23. 28; Mark 12 15; 1 Tim. 4. 2; Rev. 3. 1; penalty of, Job 8 13; 15. 34; 20. 5; 36. 13; Matt. 24. 51; denounced Matt. 6. 2; 7. 5; 1 Pet. 2. 1.
HYSSOP, Ex. 12. 22; Lev. 14. 4; Num. 19. 6; Ps 51. 7; Heb. 9. 19.

I AM, Ex. 3. 14; John 8. 58; Rev. 1. 18.
IDLENESS reproved, Prov. 6. 6; 18. 9; 24. 30 Rom. 12. 11; 1 Thess. 4. 11; 2 Thess. 3. 10; Hel 6. 12.
evil of, Prov. 10. 4; 12. 24; 13. 4; 19. 15; 20. 4, 13 21. 25; Eccles. 10. 18; 1 Tim. 5. 13.
IDOLATERS not to be spared, Deut. 7. 16; 12. 8, 1 IDOLATRY, Ex. 20. 2; 22. 20; 23. 13; Lev. 26. 1 Deut. 4. 15; 5. 7; 11. 16; 17. 2; 18. 9; 27. 15; P 97. 7; Jer. 2. 11; 1 Cor. 10. 7, 14; 1 John 5. 21.
folly of, 1 Kin. 18. 26; Ps. 115. 4; 135. 15; Is. 4 19; 41; 44. 9; 46. 1; Jer. 2. 26; 10.
monuments of, to be destroyed, Ex. 23. 24; 3 13; Deut. 7. 5.
enticers to, Deut. 13. 1.
Israelites guilty of, Ex. 32; Num. 25; Judg. 2. 1 3. 7; 8. 33; 18. 30; 2 Kin. 17. 12; also Mica' Judg. 17; Solomon, 1 Kin. 11. 5; Jeroboam, Kin. 12. 28; Ahab, &c., 1 Kin. 16. 31; 18. 1

MOUTH—*cont.*
of the wicked, Ps. 32. 9; 63. 11; 107. 42; 109. 2;
144. 8; Prov. 4. 24; 5. 3; 6. 12; 19. 28; Rom. 3.
15; Rev. 13. 5.
of the righteous, &c., Ps. 37. 30; Prov. 10. 31;
Eccles. 10. 12.
of fools, Prov. 14. 3; 15. 2; 18. 7; 26. 7.
MULBERRY TREES, 2 Sam. 5. 23.
MURDER, Gen. 9. 6; Ex. 20. 13; Lev. 24. 17; Deut.
5. 17; 21. 9; Matt. 5. 21; 1 John 3. 15.
examples:—Gen. 4; Judg. 9; 2 Sam. 3. 27; 4; 12.
9; 20. 8; 1 Kin. 16. 9; 21; 2 Kin. 15. 10; 21. 23;
2 Chr. 24. 21.
its penalty, Gen. 4. 12; 9. 6; Num. 35. 30; Jer.
19. 4; Ezek. 16. 38; Gal. 5. 21; Rev. 22. 15.
source of, Matt. 15. 19; Gal. 5. 21.
MURMURING rebuked, Lam. 3. 39; 1 Cor. 10. 10;
Phil. 2. 14; Jude 16.
of Israel, instances of, Ex. 15. 23; 16; 17; Num.
11; 16; 20; 21.
MURRAIN, plague of, Ex. 9. 3; Ps. 78. 50.
MUSIC, invention of, Gen. 4. 21.
its effects on Saul, 1 Sam. 16. 14.
used for worship, 2 Sam. 6. 5; 1 Chr. 15. 28; 16.
42; 2 Chr. 7. 6; 29. 25; Ps. 33; 81; 92; 108; 150;
Dan. 3. 5.
at festivities, Is. 5. 12; 14. 11; Amos 6. 5; Luke
15. 25; 1 Cor. 14. 7.
in heaven, Rev. 5. 8; 14. 2.
MUSTARD SEED, parable of, Matt. 13. 31; Mark
4. 30; Luke 13. 18.
MUZZLING the ox that treadeth out the corn
forbidden, Deut. 25. 4; 1 Cor. 9. 9; 1 Tim. 5.
18.
MYRRH, Ex. 30. 23; Esth. 2. 12; Ps. 45. 8; Cant.
1. 13; Matt. 2. 11; Mark 15. 23; John 19. 39.
MYRTLES, Is. 41. 19; 55. 13; vision of, Zech.
1. 8.
MYSTERY of the kingdom of God made known
by Christ, Mark 4. 11; Eph. 1. 9; 3. 3; 1 Tim.
3. 16; by the disciples to the world, 1 Cor. 4. 1;
13. 2; Eph. 6. 19; Col. 2. 2.
of the raising of the dead, 1 Cor. 15. 51.
of iniquity, 2 Thess. 2. 7; Rev. 17. 5.

NAME of GOD, Ex. 34. 5, 14. *See* Ex. 6. 3; 15. 3;
Ps. 83. 18.
honour due to, Ex. 20. 7; Deut. 5. 11; 28. 58; Ps.
34. 3; 72. 17; 111. 9; Mic. 4. 5; 1 Tim. 6. 1.
—— of CHRIST, prayer in, John 14. 13; 16. 23;
Rom. 1. 8; Eph. 5. 20; Col. 3. 17; Heb. 13. 15;
miracles performed in, Acts 3. 6; 4. 10; 19. 13.
responsibilities of bearing, 2 Tim. 2. 19.
NAME given to children at circumcision, Luke
1. 59; 2. 21.
NAME, value of a good, Prov. 22. 1; Eccles. 7. 1.
NAMES changed by God, Gen. 17. 5, 15; 32. 27;
2 Sam. 12. 25; by man, Dan. 1. 7; by Christ,
Mark 3. 16, 17.
NATIONS, origin of, Gen. 10.
NAVY of Solomon, 1 Kin. 9. 26; 2 Chr. 8. 17.
of Jehoshaphat, 1 Kin. 22. 48.
NEIGHBOUR, how to treat our, Ex. 20. 16; 22.
26; Lev. 19. 18; Deut. 15. 2; 27. 17; Prov. 3. 28;
24. 28; 25. 8, 17; Mark 12. 31; Rom. 13. 9; Gal.
5. 14; James 2. 8.
NET, parable of, Matt. 13. 47.
NEW BIRTH (born again), John 3. 3, 6; 1 Pet. 1. 23.
NIGHT, Gen. 1. 5; Ps. 19. 2; figurative, John 9.
4; Rom. 13. 12; 1 Thess. 5. 5; none in heaven,
Rev. 21. 25 (Is. 60. 20).
NORTH and South, conflicts of, Dan. 11.
NUMBERING of the people, by Moses, Num. 1.
18; 26. 4; by David, 2 Sam. 24; 1 Chr. 21.
of the Levites, Num. 3. 15; 4. 34; 26. 57.

OATH, God ratifies his purpose by, Ps. 132. 11;
Luke 1. 73; Acts 2. 30; Heb. 6. 17.
of the forty Jews, Acts 23. 12, 21.
OATHS, directions about, Lev. 5. 4; 6. 3; 19. 12;
Num. 30. 2; Ps. 15. 4; Matt. 5. 33; James 5. 12.

OATHS—*cont.*
examples of, Gen. 14. 22; 21. 31; 24. 2; Josh. 14. 9;
1 Sam. 20. 42; 28. 10; Ps. 132. 2.
demanded, Ex. 22. 11; Num. 5. 21; 1 Kin. 8. 31;
Ezra 10. 5.
rash:—of Esau, Gen. 25. 33.
of Israel to the Gibeonites, Josh. 9. 19.
Jephthah, Judg. 11. 30.
Saul at Beth-aven, 1 Sam. 14. 24.
Herod to Herodias' daughter, Matt. 14. 7.
OBEDIENCE of CHRIST, Rom. 5. 19; Phil. 2. 8;
Heb. 5. 8.
OBEDIENCE to God enjoined, Ex. 19. 5; 23. 21;
Lev. 26. 3; Deut. 4—8; 11; 29; Is. 1. 19; Jer. 7.
23; 26. 13; 38. 20; Acts 5. 29; James 1. 25.
its blessings, Ex. 23. 22; Deut. 28; 30; Prov. 25.
12; Is. 1. 19; Heb. 11. 8; 1 Pet. 1. 22; Rev. 22.
14.
preferred before sacrifice, 1 Sam. 15. 22; Ps. 50.
8; Mic. 6. 6.
to the faith, Rom. 1. 5; 16. 26; 2 Cor. 7. 15;
1 Pet. 1. 2.
of children to parents, Eph. 6. 1; Col. 3. 20.
to masters, Eph. 6. 5; Col. 3. 22; Tit. 2. 9.
of wives to husbands, Tit. 2. 5.
of people to rulers, Tit. 3. 1; Heb. 13. 17.
OBLATIONS, Lev. 2; 3.
of the spoil, Num. 31. 28.
OFFENCE, giving of, deprecated, 1 Cor. 10. 32;
2 Cor. 6. 3; Phil. 1. 10.
OFFENCES, woe because of, Matt. 18. 7.
how to remedy, Eccles. 10. 4; Matt. 5. 29; 18. 8;
Mark 9. 43; Rom. 16. 17.
Christ was delivered for our, Rom. 4. 25.
OFFERING (of Christ), Heb. 9. 14, 28; 10. 10,
12, 14.
OFFERINGS, laws for, Lev. 1; 22. 21; Deut. 15.
21; Mal. 1. 13.
OIL for lamps, Ex. 27. 20; Lev. 24. 1.
for anointing, Ex. 30. 31; 37. 29.
used in meat offerings, Lev. 2. 1.
miracles of, 1 Kin. 17. 12; 2 Kin. 4. 1.
figurative, Ps. 23. 5; 141. 5; Is. 61. 3; Zech. 4. 12;
Matt. 25. 1.
OINTMENT, Christ anointed with, Matt. 26. 7;
Mark 14. 3; Luke 7. 37; John 11. 2; 12. 3.
OLD AGE, Job 30. 2; Ps. 90. 10; Eccles. 12; Tit. 2. 2.
reverence due to, Lev. 19. 32; Prov. 23. 22; 1 Tim.
5. 1.
OLD MAN, to put off, Rom. 6. 6; Eph. 4. 22; Col.
3. 9.
OLD PROPHET, the, 1 Kin. 13. 11.
OLIVE TREES, vision of, Zech. 4. 3; Rev. 11. 4.
See Judg. 9. 9; Ps. 52. 8; Rom. 11. 17.
OPPRESSION forbidden by God, Ex. 22. 21; Lev.
25. 14; Deut. 23. 16; 24. 14; Ps. 12. 5; 62. 10;
Prov. 14. 31; 22. 16; Eccles. 4. 1; 5. 8; Is. 1. 17;
10; 58. 6; Jer. 22. 17; Ezek. 22. 7; Amos 4. 1;
8. 4; Mic. 2. 2; Mal. 3. 5; James 5. 4.
ORACLE of the temple, 1 Kin. 6. 16; 8. 6; 2 Chr.
4. 20; Ps. 28. 2.
ORACLES (the Holy Scriptures), Acts 7. 38; Rom.
3. 2; Heb. 5. 12; 1 Pet. 4. 11. *See* 2 Sam. 16. 23.
ORDINATION. mode and use of, Acts 6. 6; 14. 23;
1 Tim. 2. 7; 3; 4. 14; 5. 22; 2 Tim. 2. 2; Tit. 1.
5.
ORNAMENTS of apparel, &c., Gen. 24. 22; Prov.
1. 9; 4. 9; 25. 12; Is. 3. 18; Jer. 2. 32; 1 Pet. 3.
3.
OSTENTATION condemned, Prov. 25. 14; 27. 2;
Matt 6. 1.
OUTCASTS of Israel, promised restoration, Is. 11.
12; 16. 3; 27. 13; Jer. 30. 17; Rom. 11.
OVERCOMING, glory and reward of, 1 John 2. 13;
Rev. 2. 7, 11, 17, 26; 3. 5, 12, 21; 21. 7.
OVERSEERS in building the temple, 1 Chr. 9. 29;
2 Chr. 2. 18.
OX, treatment of, Ex. 21. 28; 22. 1; 23. 4; Lev.
17. 3; Deut. 5. 14; 22. 1; Luke 13. 15.
that treadeth out the corn, unlawful to muzzle,
Deut. 25. 4; 1 Cor. 9. 9; 1 Tim. 5. 18.

PALACE, the temple so called, 1 Chr. 29. 1; Ps. 48. 3; 71. 69; 122. 7.
PALM tree and branches, Ex. 15. 27; Lev. 23. 40; Deut. 34. 3; Judg. 1. 16; 3. 13; 2 Chr. 28. 15; John 12. 13; Rev. 7. 9.
PALSY cured by Christ, Matt. 4. 24; 8. 6; 9. 2; Mark 2. 3; Luke 5. 18.
by His disciples, Acts 8. 7; 9. 33.
PAPER REEDS of Egypt, Is. 19. 7.
PARABLE taken up, Hab. 2. 6.
PARABLES, remarkable ones in Old Testament, Judg. 9. 8—15; 2 Sam. 12. 1, 4; 14. 5, 7; 1 Kin. 20. 39; 2 Kin. 14. 9; 2 Chr. 25. 18.
as discourses, Num. 23. 7; 24. 5, 16; Ps. 78. 2; Job 27; Prov. 26. 9.
of the prophets, Is. 5. 1; Jer. 13. 1; 18; 24; 27; Ezek. 16; 17; 19; 23; 24; 31; 33; 37.
of Christ, Matt. 13. 3; 34; Mark 3. 23; 4. 13; Luke 8. 10. See CHRIST.
PARADISE, Rev. 2. 7.
promised by Christ to the penitent thief, Luke 23. 43.
Paul caught up into, 2 Cor. 12. 4.
PARDON of sin, 2 Chr. 30. 18; Neh. 9. 17; Job 7. 21; Ps. 25. 11; Is. 55. 7; Jer. 33. 8; 50. 20.
PARENTS, duty of, Prov. 13. 24; 19. 18; 22. 6, 15; 23. 13; 29. 15, 17; Luke 11. 13; Eph. 6. 4; Col. 3. 21; 1 Tim. 5. 8; Tit. 2. 4.
duty to. See OBEDIENCE.
PARTIALITY condemned, Lev. 19. 15; Deut. 1. 17; 16. 19; Prov. 18. 5; 24. 23; Mal. 2. 9; 1 Tim. 5. 21; James 2. 4; 3. 17; Jude 16.
PASSOVER ordained, Ex. 12. 3, 11.
laws relating to, Lev. 23. 4; Num. 9; 28. 16; Deut. 16.
kept under Moses in Egypt, Ex. 12. 12; at Sinai, Num. 9. 5; under Joshua in Canaan, Josh. 5. 10; by Hezekiah after the captivity of Israel, 2 Chr. 30. 13; by Josiah before the captivity of Judah, 2 Kin. 23. 21; 2 Chr. 35; by Ezra on return from the captivity, Ezra 6. 19.
kept by Christ, Matt. 26. 19; Mark 14. 12; Luke 22. 7; John 13.
a type of Christ's death, 1 Cor. 5. 7.
PASTORS transgressing, Jer. 2. 8; 10. 21; 23.
PASTURE, spiritual, Ps. 23. 2; 74. 1; 79. 13; 95. 7; 100; Ezek. 34. 14; John 10. 9.
PATIENCE commended, Ps. 37. 7; Eccles. 7. 8; Is. 30. 15; 40. 31; Luke 21. 19; Rom. 12. 12; 1 Thess. 5. 14; 2 Thess. 3. 5; 1 Tim. 3. 3; 6. 11; Heb. 12. 1; James 1. 3; 5. 7; 1 Pet. 2. 20; 2 Pet. 1. 6.
blessed results of, Rom. 5. 3· 15. 4; Heb. 6. 12; Rev. 2. 2; 3. 10.
PATRIARCHS, their genealogy, Gen. 5.
PATTERN of the tabernacle, &c., Ex. 25. 9, 40 (Ezek. 43. 10); Heb. 8. 5; 9. 23.
PEACE to be sought of God, Ezra 6. 10; Jer. 29. 7; 1 Tim. 2. 2.
bestowed by God, Lev. 26. 6; 1 Kin. 2. 33; 4. 24; 2 Kin. 20. 19; Prov. 16. 7; Is. 45. 7; Jer. 14. 13.
exhortations to maintain, Ps. 34. 14; Matt. 5. 9; Rom. 12. 18; 14. 19; 1 Cor. 7. 15; Eph. 4. 3; 1 Thess. 5. 13; 2 Tim. 2. 22; James 3. 18; 1 Pet. 3. 11.
— spiritual, gift of God (John 14. 27); Acts 10. 36; Rom. 1. 7; 5. 1; 8. 6; 14. 17; Phil. 4. 7; Col. 3. 15; 1 Thess. 5. 23; 2 Thess. 3. 16; Rev. 1. 4.
proclaimed to the Gentiles, Zech. 9. 10; Eph. 2. 14, 17; 3.
produced by the Spirit, Gal. 5. 22.
denied to the wicked, 2 Kin. 9. 31; Is. 48. 22; 59. 8 (Rom. 3. 17); Jer. 12. 12; Ezek. 7. 25.
to whom promised, Ps. 29. 11; 85. 8; 122. 6; 125. 5; 128. 6; 147. 14; John 14. 27; Gal. 6. 16; Eph. 6. 23.
on earth, Luke 2. 14.
in heaven, Luke 19. 38.
— king of (Melchizedec), Heb. 7. 2.
— the prince of (Christ), Is. 9. 6.
PEACE OFFERINGS, laws pertaining to, Ex. 20. 24; 24. 5; Lev. 3; 6; 7. 11; 19. 5.

PEARL, parable of, Matt. 7. 6; 13. 45. See 1 Tim. 2. 9; Rev. 17. 4.
PECULIAR people of God, Deut. 14. 2; Ps. 135. 4. See Tit. 2. 14; 1 Pet. 2. 9.
PEOPLE of God, their blessings and privileges, Deut. 7. 6; 32. 9; 33; 1 Sam. 12. 22; 2 Sam. 7. 23; Ps. 3. 8; 29. 11; 33. 12; 77. 15; 85; 89. 15; 94. 14; 95. 7; 100; 110; 111. 6; 121; 125; 144. 15; 148. 14; 149. 4; Is. 11. 11; 14. 32; 30. 19; 33. 24; 49. 13; 51. 22; 65. 18; Dan. 7. 27; Joel 2. 18; 3. 16; Zeph. 3. 9, 20; Matt. 1. 21; Luke 1. 17; Acts 15. 14; Rom. 11; 2 Cor. 6. 16; Tit. 2. 14; Heb. 4. 9; 8. 10; 1 Pet. 2. 9; Rev. 5. 9; 21. 3.
PERDITION, what results in, Phil. 1. 28; 1 Tim. 6. 9; Heb. 10. 39; 2 Pet. 3. 7; Rev. 17. 8.
the son of, John 17. 12; 2 Thess. 2. 3.
PERFECTION of GOD, Deut. 32. 4; 2 Sam. 22. 31; Job 36. 4; Matt. 5. 48.
of CHRIST, Heb. 2. 10; 5. 9; 7. 28.
of God's law, Ps. 19. 7; 119; James 1. 25.
of saints, 1 Cor. 2. 6; Eph. 4. 12; Col. 1. 28; 3. 14; 2 Tim. 3. 17. See Matt. 5. 48; 2 Cor. 12. 9; Heb. 6. 1; 11. 40.
PERFUME, the most holy, Ex. 30. 34.
PERJURY condemned, Ex. 20. 16; Lev. 6. 3; 19. 12; Deut. 5. 20; Ezek. 17. 16; Zech. 5. 4; 8. 17; 1 Tim. 1. 10.
PERSECUTION, coming of, Matt. 13. 21; 23. 34; Mark 10. 30; Luke 11. 49; John 15. 20; 2 Cor. 4. 9; 2 Tim. 3. 12.
conduct under, Matt. 5. 44; 10. 22; Acts 5. 41; Rom. 12. 14; Phil. 1. 28; Heb. 10. 34; 1 Pet. 4. 13—19.
results of, Matt. 5. 10; Luke 6. 22; 9. 24; James 1. 2; 1 Pet. 4. 14; Rev. 6. 9; 7. 13.
PERSEVERANCE enjoined, Matt. 24. 13; Mark 13. 13; Luke 9. 62; Acts 13. 43; 1 Cor. 15. 58; 16. 13; Eph. 6. 18; Col. 1. 23; 2 Thess. 3. 13; 1 Tim. 6. 14; Heb. 3. 6, 13; 10. 23, 38; 2 Pet. 3. 17; Rev. 2. 10, 25.
PERSONS, God no respecter of, Deut. 10. 17; 2 Chr. 19. 7; Job 34. 19; Acts 10. 34; Rom. 2. 11; Gal. 2. 6; Eph. 6. 9; Col. 3. 25; 1 Pet. 1. 17.
PESTILENCE, the penalty of disobedience, Lev. 26. 25; Num. 14. 12; Deut. 28. 21; Jer. 14. 12; 27. 13; Ezek. 5. 12; 6. 11; 7. 15; Matt. 24. 7; Luke 21. 11.
Israel visited with, Num. 14. 37; 16. 46; 25. 9; 2 Sam. 24. 15.
removed, Num. 16. 47; 2 Sam. 24. 16.
PIECE of silver, parable, Luke 15. 8; 1 Sam. 2. 36.
PIGEONS as offerings, Lev. 1. 14; 12. 6; Num. 6. 10; Luke 2. 24.
PILGRIMAGE, typical, Gen. 47. 9; Ex. 6. 4; Ps. 119. 54; Heb. 11. 13; 1 Pet. 2. 11.
PILLARS erected by Jacob, Gen. 28. 18; 35. 20; and Absalom, 2 Sam. 18. 18.
in porch of the temple, 1 Kin. 7. 21; 2 Chr. 3. 17; Rev. 3. 12.
of cloud and fire in wilderness, Ex. 13. 21; 33. 9; Neh. 9. 12; Ps. 99. 7.
PIT, the grave, death, Job 17. 16; 33. 18; Ps. 28. 1; 30. 9; 88. 4; 143. 7; Is. 14. 15; 38. 17; Ezek. 26. 20; 32. 18.
as a prison, Is. 24. 22; Zech. 9. 11.
PITCH, used for the ark, &c., Gen. 6. 14; Ex. 2. 3; Is. 34. 9.
PLACES, idolatrous, 1 Kin. 11. 7; 12. 31; 13; Ps. 78. 58; Ezek. 16. 24; destruction of, Lev. 26. 30; 2 Kin. 18. 4; 23; 2 Chr. 14. 3; 17. 6; 34. 3; Ezek. 6. 3.
PLAGUES—of Egypt. See EGYPT.
of Israel. See PESTILENCE.
PLANT, used figuratively, Ps. 128. 3; 144. 12; Cant. 4. 13; Is. 5. 7; 53. 2; Jer. 2. 21; Ezek. 34. 29; Matt. 15. 13.
PLEADING of God with Israel, Is. 1; 3. 13; 43. 26; Jer. 2—6; 13; Ezek. 17. 20; 20. 36; 22; Hos. 2, &c.; Joel 3. 2; Mic. 2.
of Job with God, Job 9. 19; 16. 21.

PROPHETS—*cont.*
Daniel, Dan. 10; Matt. 24. 15; David, Matt.
13. 35; Acts 2. 30; Eldad, Num. 11. 26; Elijah,
1 Kin. 18. 36; Elisha, 2 Kin. 6. 12; Ezekiel,
Ezek. 1. 3; Gad, 1 Sam. 22. 5; Habakkuk,
Hab. 1. 1; Haggai, Ezra 5. 1; 6. 14; Hag. 1. 1;
Hananiah, Jer. 28. 17; Hosea, Hos. 1. 1; Rom.
9. 25; Iddo, 2 Chr. 13. 22; Isaiah, 2 Kin. 20. 11;
Is. 1. 1; Matt. 3. 3; Jehu, 1 Kin. 16. 7; Jere-
miah, 2 Chr. 36. 12; Jer. 1. 5; Joel, Joel 1. 1;
Acts 2. 16; John the Baptist, Luke 7. 28; Joshua,
1 Kin. 16. 34; Jonah, 2 Kin. 14. 25; Jonah 1. 1;
Matt. 12. 39; Malachi, Mal. 1. 1; Medad, Num.
11. 26; Micah, Jer. 26. 18; Mic. 1. 1; Moses,
Deut. 34. 10; Nahum, Nah. 1. 1; Nathan, 1 Kin.
1. 32; Obadiah, Obad. 1; Oded, 2 Chr. 15. 8;
Paul, Acts 13. 9; 27. 10; Samuel, 1 Sam. 3. 20;
Shemaiah, 2 Chr. 12. 5; Zacharias, Luke 1. 67;
Zechariah, Zech. 1. 1; Zephaniah, Zeph. 1. 1.
—— false, Zedekiah, 1 Kin. 22. 11; Jer. 29. 21;
Bar-jesus, Acts 13. 6; denounced, Deut. 13; 18.
20; Is. 9. 15; Jer. 6. 13; 14. 13; 23. 9, 34; 28. 15;
29. 20, 31; Ezek. 13. 3; 14. 9; Matt. 7. 15; 24.
11; 2 Pet. 2. 1; 1 John 4. 1.
PROPHETESSES, Anna, Luke 2. 36; Deborah,
Judg. 4. 4; Huldah, 2 Kin. 22. 14; Miriam, Ex.
15. 20; Noadiah, Neh. 6. 14.
PROPITIATION for sin, Rom. 3. 25; 1 John 2. 2;
4. 10.
PROSELYTES, Jewish, Acts 2. 10; 6. 5; 13. 43.
PROSPERITY of the righteous, Ps. 36. 8; 37. 11,
18; 75. 10; 84. 11; 92. 12; Prov. 3. 2; Eccles.
8. 12.
of the wicked, Job 12. 6; 20. 5; 21. 7; Ps. 17. 10;
37; 73. 3; 92. 7; Eccles. 8. 14; 9. 2; Jer. 12.
dangers of, Deut. 6. 10; Prov. 1. 32; 30. 8; Luke
6. 24; 12. 16; 16. 19; James 5. 1.
PROVERBS of Solomon, Book of Proverbs; collected under Hezekiah, Prov. 25—29.
various, 1 Sam. 10. 12; 24. 13; Luke 4. 23; 2 Pet.
2. 22.
PROVIDENCE of God, Gen. 8. 22; Josh. 7. 14;
1 Sam. 6. 7; Ps. 36. 6; 104; 136; 145; 147; Prov.
16; 19; 20; 33; Matt. 6. 26; 10. 29, 30; Luke 21.
18; Acts 1. 26; 17. 26.
PRUDENCE, Prov. 12. 16, 23; 13. 16; 14. 8, 15,
18; 15. 5; 16. 21; 18. 15; 19. 14; 22. 3; Hos. 14. 9;
Amos 5. 13.
PSALMODY, singing, service of song, Jewish, Ex.
15. 1; 1 Chr. 6. 31; 13. 8; 2 Chr. 5. 13; 20. 22;
29. 30; Neh. 12. 27.
Christian, Matt. 26. 30; Mark 14. 26; James 5. 13.
spiritual songs, Eph. 5. 19; Col. 3. 16.

THE PSALMS

May be divided into Five Parts, as follows:—

  I. DAVIDIC (i.—xli.).
 II. DAVIDIC (xlii.—lxxii.).
III. ASAPHIC (lxxiii.—lxxxix.).
 IV. OF THE CAPTIVITY (xc.—cvi.).
  V. OF RESTORATION (cvii.—cl.).

Or may be classified according to their subjects,
thus:—

(I.) PSALMS OF SUPPLICATION.

1. On account of sin, Ps. 6; 25; 32; 38; 51;
102; 130.
2. suffering, Ps. 7; 10; 13; 17; 22; 31; 35; 41—43;
54—57; 59; 64; 69—71; 77; 86; 88; 94; 109;
120; 140—143.
3. persecution, Ps. 44; 60; 74; 79; 80; 83; 89;
94; 102; 125; 137.
4. public worship, Ps. 26; 27; 42; 43; 63; 65; 84;
92; 95—100; 118; 122; 132; 144; 145—150.
5. trust in God, Ps. 3—5; 11; 12; 16; 20; 23; 27;
28; 31; 42; 43; 52; 54; 56; 57; 59; 61—64; 71;
77; 86; 108; 115; 118; 121; 125; 131; 138; 141.
6. the Psalmist's piety, Ps. 7; 17; 26; 35; 101; 119.

(II.) GRATITUDE.

1. The Psalmist personally, Ps. 9; 18; 30; 32; 34;
40; 61—63; 75; 103; 108; 116; 118; 138; 144.

PSALMS—*cont.*
2. relative to the Church, Ps. 33; 46; 47; 65; 66;
68; 75; 76; 81; 85; 87; 95; 98; 105—107; 124;
126; 129; 134—136; 149.

(III.) ADORATION.

1. Of God's goodness and mercy, Ps. 3; 4; 9; 16;
18; 30—34; 36; 40; 46; 65—68; 84; 85; 91; 99;
100; 103; 107; 111; 113; 116; 117; 121; 126;
145; 146.
2. of God's power, majesty, and glory, Ps. 2; 3;
8; 18; 19; 24; 29; 33; 45—48; 50; 65—68; 76;
77; 89; 91—100; 104—108; 110; 111; 113—118;
135; 136; 139; 145—150.

(IV.) DIDACTIC.

1. Shewing the blessings of God's people and the
misery of His enemies, Ps. 1; 3; 4; 5; 7; 9
—15; 17; 24; 25; 32; 34; 36; 37; 41; 50; 52;
53; 58; 62; 73; 75; 82; 84; 91; 92; 94; 101; 112;
119; 121; 125; 127—129; 133; 149.
2. the excellence of God's law, Ps. 19; 119.
3. the vanity of human life, &c., Ps. 14; 39; 49;
53; 73; 90.

(V.) PROPHETICAL, TYPICAL, AND HISTORICAL.

Ps. 2; 16; 22; 24; 31; 35; 40; 41; 45; 50; 55;
68; 69; 72; 78; 87; 88; 102; 105; 106; 109; 110;
118; 132; 135; 136.
PUBLICAN, parable of Pharisee and, Luke 18. 10.
PUBLICANS, Matt. 5. 46; 9. 11; 11. 19; 18. 17;
Luke 3. 12.
become believers in Jesus, Matt. 21. 32; Luke 5.
27; 7. 29; 15. 1; 19. 2.
PUNISHMENTS:—
burning, Gen. 38. 24; Lev. 20. 14; 21. 9.
hanging, Gen. 40. 22; Deut. 21. 23; Ezra 6. 11;
Esth. 2. 23; 7. 10.
scourging, Lev. 19. 20; Deut. 25. 1; Matt. 27. 26;
Acts 22. 25.
stoning, Lev. 20. 2; 24. 14; 1 Kin. 21. 10; John
8. 59; Acts 7. 58; 14. 19.
beheading, 2 Kin. 6. 31; 10. 7; Matt. 14. 10.
See Heb. 11. 36.
crucifying, Matt. 20. 19; 27. 31, &c.
PURCHASES, Gen. 23; Ruth 4; Jer. 32. 6.
PURIFICATION, laws concerning, Lev. 13—16;
Num. 9. 4; 19; 31. 19 (Mal. 3. 3; Acts 21. 24;
Heb. 9. 13).
of women, Lev. 12; Esth. 2. 12; Luke 2. 22.
of the heart by faith, Acts 15. 9; 1 Pet. 1. 22;
1 John 3. 3. *See* Dan. 12. 10.
PURITY, moral, enjoined, Gal. 5. 16; Eph. 5. 3;
Phil. 2. 15; 4. 8; Col. 3. 5; 1 Tim. 5. 22; Tit.
1. 15; 1 Pet. 2. 11; 2 Pet. 3. 1; 1 John 3. 3.
PURITY of God's word and law, Ps. 12. 6; 19. 8;
119. 140; Prov. 30. 5.

QUAILS, Israel fed with, Ex. 16. 12; sent in wrath,
Num. 11. 31; Ps. 78. 27; 105. 40.
QUARRELLING. *See* STRIFE.
QUICKENING, spiritual, Ps. 71. 20; 80. 18; John
5. 21; 6. 63; Rom. 4. 17; 8. 11; 1 Cor. 15. 45; 2
Cor. 3. 6; Eph. 2. 1; 1 Tim. 6. 13; 1 Pet. 3. 18.
QUIET, the faithful shall dwell in, Prov. 1. 33;
Is. 30. 15; 32. 17, 18.
to be, enjoined, 1 Thess. 4. 11; 2 Thess. 3. 12; 1
Tim. 2. 2; 1 Pet. 3. 4.

RACA (vain fellow), 2 Sam. 6. 20; Matt. 5. 22.
RAILING, 1 Sam. 25. 14; 2 Sam. 16. 7; Mark 15.
29; 1 Cor. 5. 11; 1 Tim. 6. 4; 1 Pet. 3. 9; 2 Pet.
2. 11; Jude 9.
RAIN (the deluge), Gen. 7; Ex. 9. 34; 1 Sam. 12.
17; Ps. 105. 32.
the gift of God, Matt. 5. 45; Acts 14. 17.
withheld, 1 Kin. 17; Jer. 14; Zech. 14. 17; James
5. 17.
emblematic, Lev. 26. 4; Deut. 32. 2; 2 Sam. 23.
4; Ps. 68. 9; Hos. 10. 12.
RAINBOW, God's covenant with Noah, Gen. 9.
12; Ezek. 1. 28.
in heaven, Rev. 4. 3; 10. 1.

RICHES—*cont.*
10; Jer. 9. 23; Matt. 6. 19; 19. 21; Luke 16. 9;
1 Tim. 6. 17; James 1. 9; 1 John 3. 17.
evil use of, Job 20. 15; 31. 24; Ps. 39. 6; 49. 6;
73. 12; Prov. 11. 28; 13. 7, 11; 15. 6; Eccles. 2. 26;
5. 10; James 5. 3.
end of the wicked rich, Job 20. 16; 21. 13; 27. 16;
Ps. 52. 7; Prov. 11. 4; 22. 16; Eccles. 5. 14; Jer. 17.
11; Mic. 2. 3; Hab. 2. 6; Luke 6. 24; 12. 16; 16.
19; James 5. 1.
RIGHTEOUS, blessings and privileges of the,
Job 36. 7; Ps. 1; 5. 12; 14. 5; 15; 16. 3, 11; 32.
11; 34. 15; 37; 52. 6; 55. 22; 58. 10; 64. 10; 89; 92.
12; 97. 11; 112; 125. 3; 146. 8; Prov. 2. 7; 3. 32;
10—13; 12. 26; 28. 1; Is. 3. 10; 26. 2; 60. 21; Ezek.
18; Matt. 13. 43; Acts 10. 35; Rom. 2. 10; 1 Pet.
3. 12; 1 John 3. 7; Rev. 22. 11.
RIGHTEOUSNESS by faith, Gen. 15. 6; Ps. 106.
31; Rom. 4. 3; Gal. 3. 6; James 2. 23.
—— of CHRIST, imputed to the Church, Is. 54.
17; Jer. 23. 6; 33. 16; Rom. 2. 19; Mal. 4. 2; Rom.
1. 17; 3. 22; 10. 3; 1 Cor. 1. 30; 2 Cor. 5. 21; Phil.
3. 9; Tit. 2. 14; 2 Pet. 1. 1.
of the law and faith, Rom. 10.
—— of man, Deut. 9. 4; Is. 64. 6; Dan. 9. 18;
Phil. 3. 9.
RINGS, Gen. 41. 42; Ex. 25. 12; 26. 29; Esth. 3. 10;
Ezek. 1. 18; Luke 15. 22.
RIOTING and REVELLING, Prov. 23. 20; 28. 7;
Luke 15. 13; Rom. 13. 13; 1 Pet. 4. 4; 2 Pet. 2. 13.
RIVER of life, Rev. 22. *See* Ps. 36. 8; 46. 4; 65. 9;
Ezek. 47.
—— of Egypt (Nile), Ex. 1. 22; Ezek. 29. 3, 10;
Moses hidden in, Ex. 2. 5; waters of, turned
into blood, Ex. 7. 15.
ROBBERY, Lev. 19. 13; Ps. 62. 10; Prov. 21. 7; 22.
22; 28. 24; Is. 10. 2; 61. 8; Ezek. 22. 29; Amos 3.
10; 1 Cor. 6. 8; 1 Thess. 4. 6.
ROBE, scarlet, gorgeous, purple, Matt. 27. 28;
Luke 23. 11; John 19. 2.
ROCK, water brought out of, by Moses, Ex. 17. 6;
Num. 20. 10. *See* 1 Cor. 10. 4.
figuratively used, Deut. 32. 4, 15; 2 Sam. 22. 2; 23.
3; Ps. 18. 2; 28. 1; 31. 2; 61. 2; Is. 17. 10; 26. 4;
32. 2. *See* Matt. 7. 24.
ROD of Moses, Ex. 4; of Aaron, Num. 17; Heb. 9. 4.
ROLL of prophecy, Is. 8. 1; Jer. 36. 2; Ezek. 2. 9;
3. 1; Zech. 5. 1. *See* BOOK.
RULERS of the Jews (as Nicodemus), John 3. 1;
7. 48; 12. 42, &c.
of the synagogue: Jairus, Luke 8. 41; Crispus,
Acts 18. 8; Sosthenes, Acts 18. 17.
chosen by Moses, Ex. 18. 25.

SABBATH, day of rest, Gen. 2. 2 (Heb. 4. 4).
to be kept holy, Ex. 16. 23; 20. 8; 23. 12; 31. 13;
34. 21; 35. 2; Lev. 25. 3; Num. 15. 32; Deut. 5.
12; Neh. 10. 31; 13. 15; Is. 56; 58. 13; Jer. 17. 21;
Ezek. 20. 12.
offerings, Num. 28. 9.
the seventh year kept as, Ex. 23. 10; Lev. 25. 1.
Christ the Lord of, Mark 2. 27; Luke 6. 5.
first day of the week kept as (*See* Matt. 28. 1;
Mark 16. 2, 9; John 20. 1, 19, 26); Acts 20. 7; 1
Cor. 16. 2; Rev. 1. 10.
SACRIFICES, Lev. 22. 19; Deut. 17. 1.
types of Christ, Heb. 9; 10.
SAINTS of God, Deut. 33. 2; 1 Sam. 2. 9; Ps.
145. 10; 148. 14; 149; Prov. 2. 8; Dan. 7. 18; Zech.
14. 5.
believers, Rom. 8. 27; Eph. 2. 19; Col. 1. 12; Jude
3; Rev. 5. 8.
obligations of, 2 Cor. 6. 41; Ps. 30. 4; 31. 23; 34. 9;
132. 9; Rom. 16. 2, 15; 1 Cor. 6; 2 Cor. 8; 9; Eph. 4;
6. 18; Philem.; Heb. 6. 10; 13. 24.
SALT, Lev. 2. 13; Mark 9. 49.
Lot's wife becomes a pillar of, Gen. 19. 26.
salt of the earth, Matt. 5. 13 (Luke 14. 34; Col.
4. 6).
—— sea (Siddim), Gen. 14. 3; Num. 34. 3, 12;
Deut. 3. 17; Josh. 3. 16; 12. 3; 15. 1, 2.

SALVATION, Ex. 14. 13; 15; 1 Sam. 11. 13; Ps. 3. 8;
37. 39; 62. 1; 68. 19; Is. 33. 2; 46. 13; 59. 1; 63.
5; Lam. 3. 26; Mic. 7. 7; Hab. 3. 18; Luke 1. 69;
Phil. 1. 19, 28; Rev. 7. 10; 12. 10; 19. 1.
to be wrought out with fear and trembling, Phil.
2. 12.
SANCTIFICATION by Christ, John 17. 19; 1 Cor.
1. 2, 30; 6. 11; Eph. 5. 26; Heb. 2. 11; 10. 10;
Jude 1.
by the Spirit, Rom. 15. 16; 2 Thess. 2. 13; 1 Pet. 1. 2.
SANCTIFIED, the seventh day, Gen. 2. 3; the
firstborn to be, Ex. 13. 2; the people, Ex. 19.
10; Num. 11. 18; Josh. 3. 5; the tabernacle, Ex.
29; 30; Lev. 8. 10; the priests, Lev. 8. 30; 9;
2 Chr. 5. 11.
SANCTUARY, God, of His people, Is. 8. 14; Ezek.
11. 16. *See* Ps. 20. 2; 63. 2; 68. 24; 73. 17; 77.
13; 78. 54; 96. 6; 134; 150; Heb. 8; 9. *See* TEM-
PLE.
SAVIOUR, Christ, Luke 2. 11; John 4. 42; Acts
5. 31; 13. 23; Eph. 5. 23; 2 Pet. 1. 1; 3. 2; 1 John
4. 14; Jude 25.
—— God, Is. 43. 3, 11; Jer. 14. 8; Hos. 13. 4;
Luke 1. 47.
SAVOUR, a sweet (Gen. 8. 21; Ex. 29. 18); type
of Christ, 2 Cor. 2. 14, 15; Eph. 5. 2.
SCAPEGOAT, Lev. 16. 20, 21 (Is. 53. 6).
SCRIPTURE, Gen. 49. 10; Num. 24. 17; Esth. 5. 2;
Ps. 45. 6; Heb. 1. 8.
SCHISM condemned, 1 Cor. 1. 3; 11. 18; 12. 25; 2
Cor. 13. 11.
SCOFFERS, their sin, Ps. 1. 2; 123. 4; Prov. 1. 22;
3. 34; 9. 7, 12; 13. 1; 14. 6; 15. 12; 19. 25, 29; 21.
24; 24. 9; Is. 28. 14; 29. 20; 2 Pet. 3. 3.
SCOURGING, Lev. 19. 20; Deut. 25. 3; 2 Cor. 11. 24.
of Christ, Matt. 27. 26; Luke 23. 16.
SCRIBES, 2 Sam. 8. 17; 20. 25; 1 Kin. 4. 3; 2 Kin.
19. 2; 22. 8; 1 Chr. 27. 32; Ezra 7. 6; Jer. 36. 26.
and Pharisees, censured by Christ, Matt. 15. 3;
23. 2; Mark 2. 16; 3. 22; Luke 11. 15, 53; 20. 1.
conspire against Christ, Mark 11. 18; Luke 20. 19;
22. 2; 23. 10.
persecute Stephen, Acts 6. 12.
SCRIPTURES, the Holy, given by inspiration of
God through the Holy Ghost, Acts 1. 16; 2 Tim.
3. 16; Heb. 3. 7; 2 Pet. 1. 21.
Christ confirms and teaches out of, Matt. 4. 4;
Mark 12. 10; Luke 24. 27; John 7. 42.
testify of Christ, John 5. 39; Acts 10. 43; 18. 28;
1 Cor. 15. 3.
profitable for doctrine, instruction, and rule of
life, Ps. 19. 7; 119. 9; John 17. 17; Acts 20. 32;
Rom. 15. 4; 16. 26; 2 Tim. 3. 16, 17.
make wise unto salvation, John 20. 31; Rom. 1.
2; 2 Tim. 3. 15; James 1. 21; 2 Pet. 1. 19.
to be taught diligently, Deut. 6. 9; 17. 19; 1 Pet.
2. 2.
to be kept unaltered, Deut. 4. 2; Prov. 30. 6; 2
Tim. 1. 13 (Jude 3); Rev. 22. 18.
to be searched, John 5. 39; example, Acts 17. 11.
formerly given by God through the prophets,
Luke 16. 31; Rom. 3. 2; 9. 4; Heb. 1. 1; in the
last days through Jesus Christ, Heb. 1. 2; fulfilled by Him, Matt. 5. 17; Luke 24. 27; John 19.
24; Acts 13. 29.
appealed to by the apostles, Acts 2; 3; 8. 32; 17.
2; 18. 24; 28. 23.
rejecters will be judged by, John 12. 48; Heb. 2. 3;
10. 28; 12. 25.
SCROLL, the heavens compared to, Is. 34. 4; Rev.
6. 14.
SEA, God's power over, Ex. 14. 6; 15; Neh. 9. 11;
Job 38. 11; Ps. 65. 7; 66. 6; 89. 9; 93. 4; 107. 23;
114; Prov. 8. 29; Is. 51. 10; 50. 2; Nah. 1. 4.
the molten, 1 Kin. 7. 23; 2 Chr. 4. 2; of glass,
Rev. 4. 6; 15. 2.
no more, Rev. 21. 1.
SEAL of righteousness, Rom. 4. 11.
SEALS, Gen. 38. 18; Ex. 28. 11; 1 Kin. 21. 8; Job
38. 14; Cant. 8. 6; Jer. 32. 10; Dan. 12. 4; Matt.
27. 66.

SIN—*cont.*
26; 1 John 3. 5; His blood alone redeems from, John 1. 29; Eph. 1. 7; 1 John 1. 7; 3. 5.
fountain for, Zech. 13. 1.
repented of, and confessed, Job 33. 27; Ps. 38. 18; 97. 10; Prov. 28. 13; Jer. 3. 21; Rom. 12. 9; 1 John 1. 9.
prayed, striven against, and mortified, Ps. 4. 4; 19. 13; 39. 1; 51. 2; 139. 23, 24; Matt. 6. 13; Rom. 8. 13; Col. 3. 5; Heb. 12. 4.
excludes from heaven, 1 Cor. 6. 9; Gal. 5. 19; Eph. 5. 5; Rev. 21. 27.
wages of, death, Rom. 6. 23.
punishment of, Gen. 2. 17; Ezek. 18. 4; Rom. 5. 13; Heb. 10. 26; James 1. 15.
SINGING. *See* PSALMODY.
SINS, NATIONAL, bring judgments, Matt. 23. 35, 36; 27. 25; denounced, Is. 1. 24; 30. 1; Jer. 5. 9; 6. 27.
SLANDER, Ex. 23. 1; Ps. 15. 3; 31. 13; 34. 13 (1 Pet. 3. 10); 50. 20; 64. 3; 101. 5; Prov. 10. 18; Jer. 6. 28; 9. 4; Eph. 4. 31; 1 Tim. 3. 11; Tit. 3. 2.
effects of, and conduct under, Prov. 16. 28; 17. 9; 18. 8; 26. 20, 22; Jer. 38. 4; Ezek. 22. 9; Matt. 5. 11; 26. 59; Acts 6. 11; 17. 7; 24. 5; 1 Cor. 4. 12.
SLAYING unpremeditatedly, Num. 35. 11; Deut. 4. 42; 19. 3; Josh. 20. 3.
SLEEP, Gen. 2. 21; 15. 12; 1 Sam. 26. 12; Job 4. 13; Prov. 6. 4–11; 19. 15; 20. 13.
figurative, Ps. 13. 3; Dan. 12. 2; Mark 13. 36; Rom. 13. 11; 1 Cor. 11. 30; 15. 20, 51; 1 Thess. 4. 13–15.
SLING, Judg. 20. 16; Goliath slain by, 1 Sam. 17. 49. *See* 2 Kin. 3. 25; 2 Chr. 26. 14.
figurative 1 Sam. 25. 29; Prov. 26. 8.
SLOTHFULNESS, Prov. 12. 24, 27; 15. 19; 18. 9; 19. 15, 24; 21. 25; 22. 13; 24. 30; 26. 13—16; Eccles. 10. 18; Matt. 25. 26; Rom. 11. 8.
condemned, Prov. 6. 4; Rom. 12. 11; 13. 11; 1 Thess. 5. 6; Heb. 6. 12.
SNAIL, unclean, Lev. 11. 30.
SNUFFERS, gold, Ex. 25. 38; 37. 23.
SOBRIETY, Rom. 12. 3; 1 Thess. 5. 6; 1 Tim. 2. 9; 3. 2; Tit. 1. 8; 2. 12; 1 Pet. 1. 13; 4. 7; 5. 8.
SOLDIERS, admonition to, Luke 3. 14.
at the crucifixion, John 19. 2, 23, 32.
as guards, Matt. 27. 66; 28. 4, 12; Acts 12. 4; 23. 10; 27. 42.
SON of GOD. *See* CHRIST.
—— of man, Ezek. 2. 1; Matt. 8. 20; Acts 7. 56.
SONS of God, Job 1. 6; 38. 7; John 1. 12; Rom. 8. 14; 2 Cor. 6. 18; Heb. 2. 10; 12. 5; James 1. 18; 1 John 3. 1.
obligations of, Eph. 5. 1; Phil. 2. 15; 1 Pet. 1. 14; 2. 9.
SONGS:—of Moses, Red sea, Ex. 15; for water, Num. 21. 17; God's mercy, Deut. 32; and of the Lamb, Rev. 15. 3.
of Deborah, Judg. 5; of Hannah, 1 Sam. 2; of David, 2 Sam. 22 (*see* Psalms); of Mary, Luke 1. 46; of Zacharias, Luke 1. 68; of the angels, Luke 2. 13; of Simeon, Luke 2. 29; of the redeemed, Rev. 5. 9; 19.
SORCERY, Is. 47. 9; 57. 3; Acts 8. 9; 13. 6; Rev. 21. 8; 22. 15.
SORROW, godly, 2 Cor. 7. 10; earthly, Gen. 42. 38; Job 17. 7; Ps. 13. 2; 90. 10; Prov. 10. 22; Is. 35. 10; Luke 22. 45; Rom. 9. 2; 1 Thess. 4. 13; consequence of sin, Gen. 3. 16, 17; Ps. 51.
SOUL, man endowed with, Gen. 2. 7.
atonement for, Lev. 17. 11.
redemption of, Ps. 34. 22; 49. 8, 15.
worth of, Matt. 16. 26; Mark 8. 37.
SOUTH, the king of, Dan. 11.
queen of, Matt. 12. 42.
SPENT, night is far, Rom. 13. 12; day, Judg. 19. 11; Mark 6. 35; Luke 24. 29.
SPICES for religious rites, Ex. 25. 6; 30. 23, 34; 37. 29; Esth. 2. 12; Ps. 45. 8.
for funeral, 2 Chr. 16. 14; Mark 16. 1; Luke 23. 56; John 19. 40.

SPIES sent into Canaan, by Moses, Num. 13. 3, 17, 26; 14. 36; Deut. 1. 22; Heb. 3. 17.
sent to Jericho, by Joshua, Josh. 2. 1, 4, 17, 23; 6. 17, 23.
SPIKENARD, Cant. 1. 12; Mary anoints Christ with, Mark 14. 3; Luke 7. 37; John 12. 3.
SPIRIT of GOD (the HOLY SPIRIT, or HOLY GHOST). *See* article GOD.
SPIRIT of CHRIST, Rom. 8. 9; 1 Pet. 1. 11.
of Antichrist, 1 John 4. 3.
of man, Eccles. 3. 21; 12. 7; Zech. 12. 1; 1 Cor. 2. 11.
broken, Ps. 51. 17; Prov. 15. 13; 17. 22.
born of, John 3. 5; Gal. 4. 29.
fruit of, Gal. 5. 22; Eph. 5. 9.
of truth, John 14. 17; 15. 26; 16. 13.
bondage, Rom. 8. 15.
divination, Acts 16. 16.
dumbness, &c., Mark 9. 17.
fear, 2 Tim. 1. 7.
jealousy, Num. 5. 14.
slumber, Rom. 11. 8.
SPIRITUAL body, gifts, &c., Rom. 1. 11; 1 Cor. 12; 14; 15. 44; Phil. 3. 21; 1 John 3. 2 (1 Cor. 2. 13; 1 Pet. 2. 5).
SPITTING, Num. 12. 14; Deut. 25. 9; Job 30. 10. suffered by Christ (Is. 50. 6); Matt. 26. 67; 27. 30; Mark 10. 34; 14. 65; 15. 19.
SPOIL, its division. Num. 31. 27; 1 Sam. 30. 22.
SPRINKLING of blood, the passover, Ex. 12. 22; Heb. 11. 28.
the covenant of, Ex. 24. 8; Heb. 9. 13.
cleansing the leper by, Lev. 14. 7.
of oil, Lev. 14. 16.
of the blood of Christ, Heb. 10. 22; 12. 24; 1 Pet. 1. 2.
STAR at Christ's birth, Matt. 2. 2.
morning star, Christ, Rev. 22. 16; predicted, Num. 24. 17.
great star falls from heaven, Rev. 8. 10; 9. 1.
STARS created, Gen. 1. 16.
mentioned, Gen. 15. 5; 37. 9; Judg. 5. 20; 1 Cor. 15. 41; Heb. 11. 12; Jude 13; Rev. 8. 12; 12. 1.
not to be worshipped, Deut. 4. 19.
morning, Job 38. 7.
STATUTES of the Lord, 1 Chr. 29. 19; Ps. 19. 8; 119. 12, 16.
STAVES for the tabernacle, Ex. 25. 13; 37. 15; 40. 20; Num. 4. 6.
STEADFASTNESS of the disciples, Acts 2. 42; Col. 2. 5.
urged, Deut. 10. 20; Job 11. 15; 1 Cor. 15. 58; 1 Thess. 5. 21; Heb. 3. 14; 4. 14; 10. 23; 1 Pet. 5. 9; 2 Pet. 3. 17.
STEALING, Ex. 20. 15; 21. 16; Lev. 19. 11; Deut. 5. 19; 24. 7; Ps. 50. 18; Zech. 5. 4; Matt. 19. 18; Rom. 13. 9; Eph. 4. 28; 1 Pet. 4. 15.
restoration inculcated, Ex. 22. 1; Lev. 6. 4; Prov. 6. 30, 31.
STEWARD, parable of, Luke 16. 1.
of God, a bishop is, Tit. 1. 7 (1 Cor. 4. 1; 1 Pet. 4. 10).
STOCKS, Job 13. 27; 33. 11; Prov. 7. 22.
Jeremiah in, Jer. 20. 2.
Paul and Silas in, Acts 16. 24.
STONE, corner, Christ is (Ps. 118. 22; Is. 28. 16); Matt. 21. 42; Mark 12. 10; 1 Pet. 2. 6.
STONES, precious, in the high priest's breastplate, Ex. 28. 17; in the temple, 1 Chr. 29. 2; 2 Chr. 3. 6; in the new Jerusalem, Rev. 21. 19.
STONING, Lev. 20. 2; 24. 14; Deut. 13. 10; 17. 5; 22. 21, of Achan, Josh. 7. 25; Naboth, 1 Kin. 21; Stephen, Acts 7. 58; Paul, Acts 14. 19; 2 Cor. 11. 25.
STRANGERS (among the Israelites), how to be treated, Ex. 22. 21; 23. 9; Lev. 19. 33; Deut. 1. 16; 10. 18; 23. 7; 24. 14; Mal. 3. 5.
regulations as to the passover, the priest's office, marriage, and the laws concerning them, Ex. 12. 43; 34. 16; Lev. 17. 10; 22. 10; 24. 16; Num. 1. 51; 18. 7; 19. 10; 35. 15; Deut. 7. 3; 17. 15;

STRANGERS—*cont.*
25. 5; 31. 12; Josh. 8. 33; Ezra 10. 2; Neh. 13.
27; Ezek. 44. 9. *See* HOSPITALITY.
and pilgrims, 1 Pet. 2. 11.
STRENGTH of Israel, the Lord, Ex. 15. 2; 1 Sam.
15. 29; Ps. 27. 1; 28. 8; 29. 11; 46. 1; 81. 1; Is.
26. 4; Joel 3. 16; Zech. 12. 5.
—— of sin, Rom. 7; 1 Cor. 15. 56.
—— made perfect in weakness, 2 Cor. 12. 9;
Heb. 11. 34; Ps. 8. 2.
STRIFE, Prov. 3. 30; 17. 14; 25. 8; 26. 17; Rom.
13. 13; 1 Cor. 3. 3; Gal. 5. 20; Phil. 2. 3, 14;
2 Tim. 2. 23; Tit. 3. 9; James 3. 14.
its origin, Prov. 10. 12; 13. 10; 15. 18; 16. 28;
22. 10; 23. 29; 26. 20; 28. 25; 30. 33; 1 Tim. 6.
4; 2 Tim. 2. 23; James 4. 1.
its results, Lev. 24. 10; Gal. 5. 15; James 3. 16.
deprecated, 1 Cor. 1. 11; 3. 3; 6; 11. 17.
STUBBORNNESS, penalty of, Deut. 21. 18; Prov.
1. 24; 29. 1.
forbidden, 2 Chr. 30. 8; Ps. 32. 9; 75. 4.
of the Jews, 2 Kin. 17. 14; Jer. 5. 3; 7. 28; 32. 33.
STUMBLINGBLOCK, the blind, Lev. 19. 14; Deut.
27. 18.
figurative of offence, Is. 8. 14; Rom. 9. 32; 14.
21; 1 Cor. 1. 23; 8. 9; 1 Pet. 2. 8.
SUBMISSION to God, James 4. 7.
to rulers, Eph. 5. 21; Heb. 13. 17; 1 Pet. 2. 13; 5. 5.
SUFFERING for Christ, Phil. 1. 29.
SUFFERINGS. *See* CHRIST.
of His followers, Acts 5. 40; 12; 13. 50; 14. 19;
16. 23; 20. 23; 21; 22; 1 Cor. 4. 11; 2 Cor. 1. 4;
4. 8; 6. 4; 11. 23; Phil. 1; 1 Tim. 4. 10; 2 Tim. 3.
10; 1 Pet. 2. 19; 3. 14; 4. 12.
SUN created, Gen. 1. 14; Ps. 19. 4; 74. 16; 1 Cor. 15. 41.
not to be worshipped, Deut. 4. 19; Job 31. 26;
Ezek. 8. 16.
stayed by Joshua, Josh. 10. 12; brought backward
for Hezekiah, 2 Kin. 20. 9; darkened at crucifixion, Luke 23. 44.
SUN of righteousness, Mal. 4. 2.
SUPPER, parable of, Luke 14. 16.
marriage supper of the Lamb, Rev. 19. 9.
Lord's Supper. *See* COMMUNION.
SURETISHIP, evils of, Prov. 6. 1; 11. 15; 17. 18;
20. 16; 22. 26; 27. 13.
SWEAR (and curse), Lev. 5. 1, 4.
falsely, Lev. 6. 3, 5; Ex. 22. 28.
SWEARING, Matt. 5. 34; James 5. 12.
SWINE, Lev. 11. 7; Deut. 14. 8; Is. 65. 4.
devils sent into herd of, Matt. 8. 32; Mark 5. 13;
Luke 8. 33.
typical of unbelievers and apostates, Matt. 7. 6;
2 Pet. 2. 22.
SWORD of the LORD, Gen. 3. 24; Deut. 32. 41;
Judg. 7. 18; 1 Chr. 21. 12; Ps. 45. 3; Is. 34. 5;
66. 16; Jer. 12. 12; 47. 6; Ezek. 21. 4; 30. 24; 32.
10; Zeph. 2. 12.
SYCOMORE tree, 1 Kin. 10. 27; Amos 7. 14; Luke 19. 4.
SYNAGOGUES, Christ teaches in, Matt. 12. 9;
Luke 4. 16; John 6. 59; 18. 20; Paul preaches
in, Acts 13. 5; 14. 1; 18. 4.

TABERNACLE OF GOD, its construction, Ex.
25—27; 36—39; 40; Num. 9. 15.
consecrated by Moses, Lev. 8. 10.
directions concerning its custody and removal,
Num. 1. 50, 53; 3; 4; 9. 18; 1 Chr. 6. 48.
set up at Shiloh, Josh. 18. 1; at Gibeon, 1 Chr.
21. 29; 2 Chr. 1. 3.
David's love for, Ps. 27; 42; 43; 84; 132.
—— of witness, Num. 17. 7; 18. 2; 2 Chr. 24. 6;
Acts 7. 44.
—— of testimony, Ex. 38. 21, &c.; in heaven,
Rev. 15. 5.
parallels from its history, Heb. 8. 2; 9. 2.
TABERNACLE, the human body compared to, 2 Cor.
5. 1; 2 Pet. 1. 13.
TABERNACLES, feast of, Lev. 23. 34; Num. 29.
12; Deut. 16. 13; 2 Chr. 8. 13; Ezra 3. 4; Zech.
14. 16; John 7. 2.

TABLE of the Lord (Jewish), Ex. 25. 23; 31. 8;
37. 10; 40. 4; Ezek. 41. 22.
its holiness, Mal. 1. 7, 12; 1 Cor. 10. 21.
—— the LORD'S. *See* COMMUNION.
of shewbread, Ex. 25. 30; Lev. 24. 6; Num. 4. 7.
TABLES of stone, the law, Ex. 24. 12; 31. 18.
broken, Ex. 32. 19; Deut. 9. 15.
renewed, Ex. 34; Deut. 10.
of stone and the heart, 2 Cor. 3. 3.
TALEBEARERS, Lev. 19. 16; Prov. 11. 13; 18.
8; 26. 20; Ezek. 22. 9; 1 Tim. 5. 13; 1 Pet. 4. 15.
TALENT, gold, Ex. 25. 39; silver, 1 Kin. 20. 39;
lead, Zech. 5. 7.
TALENTS, parables of, Matt. 18. 24; 25. 14.
TALKING, vain, censured, 1 Sam. 2. 3; Job 11. 2;
Prov. 13. 3; 24. 2; Eccles. 10. 14; Ezek. 33. 30;
36. 3; Eph. 5. 4; Tit. 1. 10. *See* SLANDER, TALE-
BEARERS, &c.
TARES, parable of the, Matt. 13. 24.
TAXATION of all the world, under Cæsar Au-
gustus, Luke 2. 1.
TEACHERS appointed in Judah, 2 Chr. 17. 7;
Ezra 7. 10.
Christian (Bishops, Deacons, Elders), Acts 13. 1;
Rom. 12. 7; 1 Cor. 12. 28; Eph. 4. 11; Col. 1. 28;
3. 16; 1 Tim. 3; Tit. 1. 5.
worthy of honour and benevolence, 1 Cor. 9. 9;
Gal. 6. 6; 1 Tim. 5. 17.
FALSE, foretold and described, Jer. 5. 13; 6. 13;
Ezek. 14. 9; 22. 25; Hos. 9. 7; Mic. 2. 11; 3. 11;
Zeph. 3. 4; Matt. 24. 4; Acts 13. 6; 20. 29; 2 Cor.
11. 13; 1 Tim. 1. 6; 4. 1; 6. 3; 2 Tim. 3. 8; Tit.
1. 11; 2 Pet. 2; Jude 4; Rev. 2. 14, 20; not to
be hearkened to, Deut. 13. 1; Matt. 24. 5; Col.
2. 8; 1 Tim. 1. 4; 4. 1; Heb. 13. 9; 2 Pet. 2;
1 John 4. 1; 2 John 10; Jude; Rev. 2. 14; how
to be tested and avoided, Is. 8. 20; Rom. 16.
17; Tit. 3. 10; 1 John 4. 2, 3; 2 John 10; their
condemnation, Deut. 13. 1; 18. 20; Is. 8. 20; 9.
15; Jer. 28. 15; Ezek. 13. 8; 14. 10; Mic. 3. 6;
Gal. 1. 8; 2 Tim. 3. 9; 2 Pet. 2. 1; Jude 4, 10, 16.
TEACHING from God, Ps. 71. 17; Is. 54. 13; Jer.
31. 34; John 6. 45; Gal. 1. 12; Eph. 4. 21; 1 Thess.
4. 9; 1 John 2. 27.
—— of CHRIST, Matt. 5; 7. 29.
TEMPERANCE commended, Prov. 23. 1; 1 Cor.
9. 25; Gal. 5. 23; Eph. 5. 18; Tit. 1. 8; 2. 2; 2 Pet.
1. 6.
TEMPLE, house of the Lord, or place for worship. *See* ALTAR and TABERNACLE.
TEMPLE OF JERUSALEM.
In David's heart to build, 2 Sam. 7. 3; 1 Chr.
17. 2; 28. 2.
David forbidden to build, 2 Sam. 7. 5; 1 Chr.
17. 4; 28. 3.
Solomon to build, 2 Sam. 7. 12; 1 Chr. 17. 11;
28. 5.
David's preparations for, 1 Chr. 28. 11.
Solomon builds, 1 Kin. 6; 2 Chr. 3; 4.
no hammer or axe heard in building, 1 Kin. 6. 7.
dimensions and ornaments of, 2 Chr. 3. 4.
its solemn dedication, 1 Kin. 8; 2 Chr. 6; 7.
glory of the Lord fills, 2 Chr. 5. 14.
plundered by Shishak, king of Egypt, 1 Kin. 14.
25; 2 Chr. 12. 9.
restored by Joash, 2 Kin. 12. 5, 12.
cleansed by Hezekiah, 2 Chr. 29. 5.
polluted by Manasseh, 2 Chr. 33. 7.
repaired by Josiah, 2 Chr. 34.
spoiled by the Chaldeans, 2 Kin. 25. 9; 2 Chr. 36.
decrees of Cyrus and Darius for rebuilding, Ezra
6. 3, 12.
commenced, Ezra 3. 8.
suspended by order of Artaxerxes, Ezra 4. 24.
resumed under Darius, Ezra 6. 7.
finished and dedicated, Ezra 6. 15, 16.
purified by Nehemiah, Neh. 13. 30.
made a den of thieves, Matt. 21. 12; Mark 11.
15; Luke 19. 46.
Christ drives out buyers and sellers, Matt. 21.
12; Mark 11. 15; Luke 19. 45; John 2. 14.

WISDOM—*cont.*
to be sought for, Ps. 90. 12; Matt. 10. 16; Rom. 16. 19; Eph. 5. 15; 2 Tim. 3. 15; James 3. 13.
blessings attending it, Prov. 1. 5; 3. 13; 8. 11; 16. 16; 24. 3, 14; Eccles. 7. 11; 9. 13; 12. 11; Matt. 25. 1.
obtained in answer to prayer by Solomon, &c., 1 Kin. 3. 9; 10. 6; Prov. 2. 3; Dan. 2. 21; James 1. 5.
personified, Prov. 1. 20; 8; 9.
danger of despising, Prov. 1. 24; 2. 12; 3. 21; 5. 12; 8. 36; 9. 12; 10. 21; 11. 12.
apparent in the works of God, Ps. 104. 1, 24; 136. 5; Prov. 3. 19; 6. 6; Jer. 10. 12; Rom. 1. 20; 11. 33.
of Joseph, Gen. 41. 39; 47. 13; Solomon, 1 Kin. 4. 29; Daniel, &c., Ezek. 28. 3; Dan. 1. 17; 5. 14.
worldly, vanity of, Job 5. 13; 11. 12; Prov. 3. 7; Eccles. 2; Is. 5. 21; Jer. 8. 9; Zech. 9. 2; Matt. 11. 25; 1 Cor. 1. 17; 2. 4; 3. 19; 2 Cor. 1. 12; James 3. 15. *See* Gen. 3. 6.
WISE men from the east, Matt. 2.
—— woman, David admonished by, 2 Sam. 14.
WITCHCRAFT, forbidden, Ex. 22. 18; Lev. 19. 26, 31; 20. 6, 27; Deut. 18. 10; Mic. 5. 12; Mal. 3. 5; Gal. 5. 20; Rev. 21. 8; 22. 15.
abolished by Josiah, 2 Kin. 23. 24.
practised by Saul, 1 Sam. 28; Manasseh, 2 Kin. 21. 6; 2 Chr. 33. 6; Israelites, 2 Kin. 17. 17; Simon of Samaria, Acts 8. 9; Philippians, Acts 16. 16; Ephesians, Acts 19. 19.
WITHERED hand of Jeroboam healed, 1 Kin. 13. 6.
—— hand healed by Christ, Matt. 12. 10; Mark 3. 1—5; Luke 6. 6.
WITNESS, God invoked as, Gen. 31. 50; Judg. 11. 10; 1 Sam. 12. 5; Jer. 42. 5; Mic. 1. 2; Rom. 1. 9; 1 Thess. 2. 5.
—— borne to CHRIST, by the Father, Matt. 3. 16; Luke 3. 22; John 5. 37; 12. 28; Heb. 2. 4; 1 John 5. 7.
by the Holy Ghost, Matt. 3. 16; Luke 3. 22; John 1. 33; 15. 26; Acts 5. 32; 20. 23; Heb. 10. 15; 1 John 5. 7.
by the apostles, Acts 1. 8; 2. 32; 4. 33; 5. 32; 10. 41; 22. 15; 26. 16; 1 Pet. 5. 1; Rev. 20. 4.
by the prophets, Acts 10. 43; 1 Pet. 1. 10.
—— Christ the faithful and true, Rev. 1. 5; 3. 14.
—— false, Ex. 20. 16; 23. 1; Lev. 19. 11; Deut. 5. 20; 19. 16; Prov. 6. 16, 19; 12. 17; 19. 5, 9, 28; 21. 28; 25. 18; Jer. 7. 9; Zech. 5. 4; Luke 3. 14.
against Christ, Matt. 26. 60; Mark 14. 56.
WITNESSES, two or three required, Num. 35. 30; Deut. 17. 6; 19. 15; Matt. 18. 16; 2 Cor. 13. 1; 1 Tim. 5. 19.
—— the two, Rev. 11.
WIVES, their duties to husbands, Gen. 3. 16; Ex. 20. 14; Rom. 7. 2; 1 Cor. 7. 3; 14. 34; Eph. 5. 22, 33; Tit. 2. 4; 1 Pet. 3. 1.
good, Prov. 12. 4; 18. 22; 19. 14; 31. 10.
Levitical laws concerning, Ex. 21. 3, 22; 22. 16; Num. 5. 12; 30; Deut. 21. 10, 15; 24. 1; Jer. 3. 1; Matt. 19. 3.
the wife a type of the church, Eph. 5. 23; Rev. 19. 7; 21. 9.
WOES against wickedness, &c., Is. 5. 8; 10. 1; 29. 15; 31. 1; 45. 9; Jer. 22. 13; Amos 6. 1; Mic. 2. 1; Hab. 2. 6; Zeph. 3. 1; Zech. 11. 17; Matt. 26. 24; Luke 6. 24; Jude 11; Rev. 8. 13; 9. 12; 11. 14.

WOES—*cont.*
against unbelief, Matt. 11. 21; 23. 13; Luke 10. 13; 11. 42.
WOLVES, figuratively, Zeph. 3. 3; Matt. 7. 15; 10. 16; Luke 10. 3; Acts 20. 29.
WOMAN, creation and fall of, Gen. 2. 22; 3. Christ the seed of (Gen. 3. 15); Gal. 4. 4.
WOMEN, duty of the aged, Tit. 2. 3; of the young, 1 Tim. 2. 9; 5. 14; Tit. 2. 4; 1 Pet. 3. *See* WIVES.
WONDERFUL, prophetic name of Christ, Is. 9. 6. *See* Judg. 13. 18.
WONDERS, God's, Ex. 3. 20; Ps. 77. 11, &c.; Is. 29. 14; Dan. 6. 27; Acts 7. 36.
WORD of God, a name of Christ, John 1. 1, 14; 1 John 1. 1; 5. 7; Rev. 19. 13.
—— the Scriptures, Luke 5. 1; Acts 4. 31; 8. 14; 13. 7; 16. 6.
WORDS will be judged, Eccles. 5. 2; Ezek. 35. 13; Mal. 2. 17; 3. 13; Matt. 12. 37.
WORKS of God, Job 9; 37—41; Ps. 8; 19; 89; 104; 111; 145; 147; 148; Eccles. 8. 17; Jer. 10. 12.
—— of the law, insufficiency of, Rom. 3. 20; 4. 2; Gal. 3.
—— good, the evidence of faith, Acts 26. 20; James 2. 14; necessary, Matt. 5. 16; Acts 9. 36; 2 Cor. 8; 9; Eph. 2. 10; Phil. 2. 12; 1 Thess. 4. 11; 2 Thess. 2. 17; 3. 8; Heb. 10. 24; 1 Pet. 2. 12.
WORLD created, Gen. 1; 2. *See* John 1. 10; Col. 1. 16; Heb. 1. 2.
its corruption, Rom. 5. 12; 8. 22.
conformity to, Rom. 12. 2; Gal. 6. 14; James 1. 27; 4. 4; 1 John 2. 15.
WORMWOOD, figurative, Deut. 29. 18; Prov. 5. 4; Lam. 3. 15 (Rev. 8. 11).
WORSHIP to be given to God alone, Ex. 20. 1; Deut. 5. 7; 6. 13; Matt. 4. 10; Luke 4. 8; Acts 10. 26; 14. 15; Col. 2. 18; Rev. 19. 10; 22. 8.
mode of, Lev. 10. 3; Eccles. 5; Joel 2. 16; John 4. 24; 1 Cor. 11; 14.
enjoined, 2 Kin. 17. 36; 1 Chr. 16. 29; Ps. 29; 95. 6; 99. 5; 100.
WRATH, Job 5. 2; 19. 29; Ps. 37. 8; Prov. 12. 16; 14. 29; 30. 33; Rom. 12. 19; 13. 5; Gal. 5. 20; Eph. 4. 26; 1 Tim. 2. 8; James 1. 19.
of God, 2 Chr. 28. 11; Job 21. 20; Ps. 106. 23, 32; Prov. 29. 8; Luke 4. 28; Rom. 2. 5, 8; 9. 22; Rev. 6. 17; 11. 18; 16. 1; 19. 15.
WRITING of God, Ex. 31. 18; 32. 16; Dan. 5. 5.
on the wall, expounded, Dan. 5.

YEAR, beginning of, changed, Ex. 12. 1; Lev. 23. 5.
YOKE of Christ, easy, Matt. 11. 30; 1 John 5. 3.
YOKES, typical, Jer. 27.
YOUNG, exhortations to, Lev. 19. 32; Prov. 1. 8; Eccles. 12. 1.
Christ's pattern, Luke 2. 46, 51; Tit. 2. 4; 1 Pet. 5. 5.

ZEAL, Rom. 12. 11; 2 Cor. 7. 10, 11; Rev. 3. 19.
of Phinehas, Num. 25. 7, 11; Ps. 106. 30.
of Jehu, 2 Kin. 10. 16.
of the Jews, Acts 21. 20; Rom. 10. 2.
of Paul, Acts 22. 3; Gal. 1. 14; Phil. 3. 6.
Christ an example of, Ps. 69. 9; John 2. 17.
ZEALOUS of good works, Gal. 4. 18; Tit. 2. 14; Rev. 3. 19.

CONCORDANCE

TO THE HOLY SCRIPTURES.

[NOTE.—*This Concordance has been specially prepared for the Delegates of the Clarendon Press. As it is intended to be used conjointly with the Dictionary of Scripture Proper Names and Subject-Index, which precede it in this Volume, all references to Proper Names, &c., included in the Dictionary and Index, have been designedly omitted from the Concordance.*]

ABASE. Ezek. 21. 26, and *a.* him that is high.
Dan. 4. 37, walk in pride, he is able to *a.*
Mat. 23. 12; Lu. 14. 11; 18. 14, whosoever exalt-
eth himself shall be *a.*
Phil. 4. 12, I know how to be *a.*
See Job 40. 11; Is. 31. 4; 2 Cor. 11. 7.

ABATED. Gen. 8. 3; Lev. 27. 18; Deut. 34. 7;
Judg. 8. 3.

ABHOR. Ex. 5. 21, made our savour to be *a.*
Job 19. 19, my inward friends *a.*
Ps. 78. 59, Lord wroth, and *a.* Israel.
89. 38, thou hast cast off and *a.*
107. 18, soul *a.* all manner of meat.
119. 163, I hate and *a.* lying.
Prov. 22. 14, *a.* of the Lord shall fall there.
Isa. 7. 16, land thou *a.* shall be forsaken.
66. 24, they shall be an *a.* unto all flesh.
Ezek. 16. 25, made thy beauty to be *a.*
Amos 6. 8, I *a.* the excellency of Jacob.
See Lev. 26. 11; Job 42. 6; Rom. 12. 9.

ABIDE. Ex. 5. 21, let servant *a.* instead of lad.
Ex. 16. 29, *a.* every man in his place.
Num. 24. 2, he saw Israel *a.* in tents.
31. 19, *a.* without camp seven days.
1 Sam. 5. 7, ark of God not *a.* with us.
Job 24. 13, nor *a.* in the paths thereof.
Ps. 15. 1, Lord who shall *a.* in thy tabernacle.
91. 1, shall *a.* under the shadow.
Prov. 15. 31, reproof *a.* among wise.
Eccl. 1. 4, the earth *a.* for ever.
Jer. 42. 10, if ye will still *a.* in this land.
49. 18, 33; 50. 40, there shall no man *a.*
Hos. 3. 3, thou shalt *a.* many days.
Joel 2. 11, day very terrible, who can *a.* it.
Mat. 10. 11; Mk. 6. 10; Lu. 9. 4, there *a.* till ye go.
Lu. 2. 8, shepherds *a.* in field.
19. 5, to-day I must *a.* at thy house.
24. 29, *a.* with us, it is toward evening.
John 3. 36, wrath of God *a.* on him.
5. 38, not his word *a.* in you.
14. 16, another Comforter that he may *a.*
15. 4, *a.* in me.
5, he that *a.* in me bringeth.
10, *a.* in his love.
Acts 16. 15, come to my house and *a.*
1 Cor. 3. 14, if any man's work *a.*
13. 13, now *a.* faith, hope, charity.
2 Tim. 2. 13, if we believe not he *a.*
See Gen. 29. 19; Num. 35. 25; Eccl. 8. 15.

ABILITY. Ezra 2. 69, they gave after their *a.*
Dan. 1. 4, had *a.* to stand in the palace.
Matt. 25. 15, to each according to *a.*
1 Pet. 4. 11, as of the *a.* God giveth.
See Lev. 27. 8; Neh. 5. 8; Acts 11. 29.

ABJECTS. Ps. 35. 15, the *a.* gathered themselves
together.

ABLE. Deut. 16. 17, every man give as he is *a.*
Josh. 23. 9, no man *a.* to stand before you.
1 Sam. 6. 20, who is *a.* to stand before God.
1 Kings 3. 9, who is *a.* to judge.
2 Chron. 2. 6, who is *a.* to build.
Prov. 27. 4, who is *a.* to stand before envy.
Amos 7. 10, land not *a.* to bear his words.
Mat. 3. 9, God is *a.* of these stones.
9. 28, believe ye that I am *a.*
20. 22, are ye *a.* to drink of cup.

Lu. 12. 26, not *a.* to do least.
Acts 6. 10, not *a.* to resist wisdom.
Rom. 4. 21, what he had promised he was *a.*
8. 39, *a.* to separate us from love of God.
1 Cor. 10. 13, tempted above that ye are *a.*
2 Cor. 3. 6, *a.* ministers of new testament.
Eph. 3. 18, *a.* to comprehend with all saints.
Phil. 3. 21, *a.* to subdue all things.
Heb. 2. 18, *a.* to succour tempted.
Jas. 4. 12, *a.* to save and destroy.
Jude 24, *a.* to keep you from falling.
Rev. 5. 3, no man *a.* to open book.
6. 17, who shall be *a.* to stand.
See Ex. 18. 21.

ABOARD. Acts 21. 2.

ABODE (*n.*). John 14. 23, we will come and make
our *a.*
See 2 Kings 19. 27; Isa. 37. 28.

ABODE (*v.*). Gen. 49. 24, his bow *a.* in strength.
Ex. 24. 16, glory of the Lord *a.* on Sinai.
Judg. 21. 2, the people *a.* there before God.
Lu. 1. 56, Mary *a.* with her three months.
John 1. 32, the Spirit, and it *a.* on him.
39, they came and *a.* with him.
8. 44, a murderer, and *a.* not in truth.
Acts 14. 3, long time *a.*, speaking boldly.
18. 3, Paul *a.* with them and wrought.
See 1 Sam. 7. 2; Ezra 8. 15.

ABOLISH. 2 Cor. 3. 13, the end of that which is *a.*
Eph. 2. 15, *a.* in his flesh the enmity.
2 Tim. 1. 10, Christ, who hath *a.* death.
See Isa. 2. 18; 51. 6; Ezek. 6. 6.

ABOMINABLE. 1 Kings 21. 26, Ahab *a.* in fol-
lowing idols.
Job 15. 16, how much more *a.* is man.
Ps. 14. 1; 53. 1, they have done *a.* works.
Isa. 14. 19, cast out like *a.* branch.
65. 4; Jer. 16. 18, broth of *a.* things.
Jer. 44. 4, this *a.* thing that I hate.
Tit. 1. 16, in works they deny him, being *a.*
1 Pet. 4. 3, walked in *a.* idolatries.
See Lev. 11. 43; Deut. 14. 3; Rev. 21. 8.

ABOMINATION. Gen. 43. 32; 46. 34, *a.* to Egyptians.
Lev. 18. 26, shall not commit any *a.*
Deut. 7. 26, nor bring *a.* into house.
18. 9, after the *a.* of nations.
12, because of the *a.* the Lord doth drive.
25. 16, do unrighteously are *a.* to God.
1 Sam. 13. 4, Israel had in *a.* with Philistines.
Prov. 3. 32; 11. 20, froward *a.* to the Lord.
8. 7, wickedness an *a.* to my lips.
15. 8, 9, 26; 21. 27, sacrifice, etc. of wicked are *a.*
28. 9, even his prayer shall be *a.*
Isa. 44. 19, residue thereof an *a.*
Jer. 4. 1, put away thine *a.* out of sight.
6. 15; 8. 12, ashamed when committed *a.*
Ezek. 5. 9, the like, because of all thine *a.*
33. 29, land desolate because of all *a.*
Dan. 11. 31; Mat. 24. 15; Mk. 13. 14, *a.* of deso-
lation.
Lu. 16. 15, esteemed among men *a.* with God.
Rev. 21. 27, in no wise enter that worketh *a.*
See Lev. 7. 18; 11. 41; Mal. 2. 11; Rev. 17. 4.

ABOUND. Prov. 28. 20, faithful shall *a.* with
blessings.
Rom. 15. 13, that ye may *a.* in hope.

1 Cor. 15. 58, always *a.* in work.
2 Cor. 1. 5, as sufferings *a.* so consolation *a.*
See Rom. 3. 7 ; 5. 15 ; Phil. 4. 12.

ABOVE. Deut. 28. 13, *a.* only and not beneath.
Job 31. 2, portion of God from *a.*
Prov. 15. 24, way of life *a.* to wise.
Mat. 10. 24 ; Lu. 6. 40, disciple not *a.* master.
John 3. 31, cometh from *a.* is *a.* all.
8. 23, I am from *a.*
Rom. 14. 5, one day *a.* another.
1 Cor. 4. 6, *a.* that which is written.
Gal. 4. 26, Jerusalem *a.* is free.
See Gen. 48. 22 ; Ps. 138. 2 ; Jam. 1. 17.

ABSENT. 1 Cor. 5. 3 ; Col. 2. 5, *a.* in body.
2 Cor. 5. 6, *a.* from Lord.
See Gen. 31. 49 ; 2 Cor. 10. 1. [idols.

ABSTAIN. Acts 15. 20, 29, *a.* from pollutions of
1 Thess. 5. 22, *a.* from all appearance of evil.
1 Pet. 2. 11, *a.* from fleshly lusts.
See 1 Thess. 4. 3 ; 1 Tim. 4. 3.

ABSTINENCE. Acts 27. 21, after long *a.* Paul
stood forth. [plaint.

ABUNDANCE. 1 Sam. 1. 16, out of *a.* of my com-
1 Kings 18. 41, sound of *a.* of rain.
1 Chron. 29. 21, offered sacrifices in *a.*
Ps. 52. 7, trusted in *a.* of riches.
72. 7 ; Jer. 33. 6, *a.* of peace.
Eccl. 5. 10, loveth *a.* with increase.
12, *a.* of rich not suffer to sleep.
Mat. 12. 34 ; Lu. 21. 4, out of *a.* of heart.
13. 12 ; 25. 29, he shall have more *a.*
Lu. 12. 15, life consisteth not in *a.*
2 Cor. 8. 2, of affliction the *a.* of their joy.
12. 7, through *a.* of revelations.
See Job 36. 31 ; Rom. 5. 17 ; Rev. 18. 3.

ABUNDANT. Job 36. 28, clouds drop and distil *a.*
Ps. 145. 7, *a.* utter the memory.
Isa. 56. 12, as this day and more *a.* [all.
1 Cor. 15. 10 ; 2 Cor. 11. 23, laboured more *a.* than
1 Tim. 1. 14, grace was exceeding *a.*
Titus 3. 6, shed *a.* through Jesus Christ.
2 Pet. 1. 11, entrance administered *a.*
See Ex. 34. 6 ; Isa. 55. 7 ; 1 Pet. 1. 3.

ABUSE. 1 Cor. 7. 31, use world as not *a.*
9. 18, that I *a.* not my power.
See 1 Sam. 31. 4 ; 1 Chron. 10. 4.

ACCEPT. Gen. 4. 7, shalt thou not be *a.*
Ex. 28. 38 ; Lev. 10. 19, *a.* before the Lord.
Deut. 33. 11, *a.* the work of his hands.
1 Sam. 18. 5, *a.* in sight of all people.
2 Sam. 24. 23, the Lord thy God *a.* thee.
Esth. 10. 3, *a.* of his brethren.
Job 13. 8 ; 32. 21, will ye *a.* his person.
42. 8, 9, him will I *a.*
Prov. 18. 5, not good to *a.* wicked.
Jer. 14. 12 ; Amos 5. 22, I will not *a.* them.
37. 20 ; 42. 2, supplication be *a.*
Ezek. 20. 40 ; 43. 27, I will *a.*
Mal. 1. 13, should I *a.* this.
Lu. 4. 24, no prophet is *a.*
Acts 10. 35, he that worketh righteousness is *a.*
Rom. 15. 31, service *a.* of saints.
2 Cor. 5. 9, present or absent we may be *a.*
See Ps. 119. 108 ; Eccl. 12. 10 ; Mal. 1. 8.

ACCESS. Rom. 5. 2 ; Eph. 2. 18 ; 3. 12.

ACCOMPLISH. Job 14. 6, *a.* as an hireling.
Ps. 64. 6, they *a.* diligent search.
Prov. 13. 19, desire *a.* is sweet.
Isa. 40. 2, her warfare is *a.*
Lu. 12. 50, straitened till it be *a.*
1 Pet. 5. 9, afflictions are *a.* in brethren.
See Isa. 55. 11 ; Lu. 18. 31 ; 22. 37.

ACCORD. Acts 1. 14 ; 4. 24 ; 8. 6 ; Phil. 2. 2.

ACCORDING. Ex. 12. 25, *a.* as he hath promised.
Deut. 16. 10, *a.* as God hath blessed thee.
Job 34. 11 ; Jer. 17. 10 ; 25. 14 ; 32. 19, *a.* to ways.
Mat. 16. 27 ; Rom. 2. 6 ; 2 Tim. 4. 14, *a.* to works.
John 7. 24, *a.* to the appearance.
Rom. 8. 28, called *a.* to his purpose.

Rom. 12. 6, gifts differing *a.* to grace.
2 Cor. 8. 12, *a.* to that a man hath.
See Mat. 9. 29 ; Tit. 3. 5.

ACCOUNT. Mat. 12. 36, give *a.* in day of judgment.
Lu. 16. 2, give *a.* of stewardship.
20. 35, *a.* worthy to obtain.
Rom. 14. 12, every one give *a.* to God.
Gal. 3. 6, *a.* to him for righteousness.
Heb. 13. 17, watch as they that give *a.*
See Job 33. 13 ; Ps. 144. 3 ; 1 Pet. 4. 5.

ACCURSED. Josh. 6. 18 ; 7. 1 ; 22. 20 ; 1 Chron. 2.
7, *a.* thing.
Rom. 9. 3, wish myself *a.* from Christ.
1 Cor. 12. 3, no man calleth Jesus *a.*
Gal. 1. 8, 9, preach other gospel, let him be *a.*
See Deut. 21. 23 ; Josh. 6. 17 ; Isa. 65. 20.

ACCUSATION. Lu. 19. 8, anything by false *a.*
1 Tim. 5. 19, against elder receive not *a.*
2 Pet. 2. 11 ; Jude 9, railing *a.*
See Mat. 27. 37 ; Mk. 15. 26 ; Lu. 6. 7.

ACCUSE. Prov. 30. 10, *a.* not servant to his master.
Mat. 27. 12, when *a.* he answered nothing.
Lu. 16. 1, was *a.* that he had wasted.
John 5. 45, I will *a.* you to the Father.
Tit. 1. 6, not *a.* of riot or unruly.
See Mat. 12. 10 ; Mk. 3. 2 ; Lu. 11. 54 ; Rev. 12. 10.

ACKNOWLEDGE. Ps. 32. 5 ; 51. 3, I *a.* my sin.
Prov. 3. 6, in all thy ways *a.* him.
Isa. 63. 16, though Israel *a.* us not.
1 John 2. 23, he that *a.* the Son.
See Dan. 11. 39 ; Hos. 5. 15. [53. 3.

ACQUAINT. Job 22. 21 ; Ps. 139. 3 ; Eccl. 2. 3 ; Is.

ACQUAINTANCE. Job 19. 13 ; Ps. 31. 11 ; 55. 13.

ACQUIT. Job 10. 14 ; Nah. 1. 3.

ACTIONS. 1 Sam. 2. 3.

ACTIVITY. Gen. 47. 6.

ADDER. Gen. 49. 17 ; Ps. 58. 4 ; 91. 13 ; 140. 3 ;
Prov. 23. 32.

ADDICTED. 1 Cor. 16. 15.

ADDITION. 1 Kings 7. 29, 30, 36.

ADJURE. Josh. 6. 26 ; 1 Sam. 14. 24 ; 1 Kings 22.
16 ; 2 Chron. 18. 15 ; Mat. 26. 63 ; Mk. 5. 7 ;
Acts 19. 13.

ADMINISTER. 1 Cor. 12. 5 ; 2 Cor. 8. 19, 20 ; 9. 12.

ADMIRE. 2 Thess. 1. 10 ; Jude 16 ; Rev. 17. 6.

ADMONISH. Acts 27. 9, Paul *a.* them.
Rom. 15. 14 ; Col. 3. 16, *a.* one another.
1 Thess. 5. 12, over you in Lord and *a.* you.
2 Thess. 3. 15, *a.* him as a brother.
Heb. 8. 5, Moses was *a.* of God.
See Eccl. 4. 13 ; 12. 12 ; Jer. 42. 19.

ADMONITION. 1 Cor. 10. 11 ; Eph. 6. 4 ; Tit. 3. 10.

ADO. Mk. 5. 39.

ADOPTION. Rom. 8. 15, 23 ; 9. 4 ; Gal. 4. 5 ; Eph. 1. 5.

ADORN. Isa. 61. 10 ; Rev. 21. 2, bride *a.* herself.
1 Tim. 2. 9 ; 1 Pet. 3. 3, 5, women *a.*
Tit. 2. 10, *a.* doctrine of God.
See Jer. 31. 4 ; Lu. 21. 5.

ADVANCED. 1 Sam. 12. 6 ; Esth. 3. 1 ; 5. 11 ; 10. 2.

ADVANTAGE. Rom. 3. 1, what is a man *a.*
Rom. 3. 1 ; 1 Cor. 15. 32, what *a.* ?
2 Cor. 2. 11, lest Satan get *a.*
See Job 35. 3 ; Jude 16.

ADVENTURE. Deut. 28. 56 ; Judg. 9. 17 ; Acts 19. 31.

ADVERSARY. Deut. 32. 43 ; Ps. 89. 42 ; Isa. 59.
18 ; Jer. 46. 10 ; Nah. 1. 2 ; Lu. 13. 17, his *a.*
Ex. 23. 22, I will be *a.* to thy *a.*
Num. 22. 22, angel stood for *a.*
1 Kings 5. 4, neither *a.* nor evil.
11. 14, 23, Lord stirred up *a.*
Job 31. 35, that mine *a.* had written.
Ps. 38. 20 ; 69. 19 ; 109. 4, 20, 29 ; Isa. 1. 24, my *a.*
74. 10, how long shall *a.* reproach.
Isa. 50. 8, who is mine *a.*
64. 2 ; Jer. 30. 16 ; Mic. 5. 9, thy *a.*
Amos 3. 11, *a.* shall be round the land.
Mat. 5. 25, agree with thine *a.*

Lu. 12. 58, when thou goest with thine *a*.
1 Cor. 16. 9, there are many *a*.
Phil. 1. 28, terrified by your *a*.
1 Tim. 5. 14, give no occasion to *a*.
Heb. 10. 27, indignation shall devour *a*.
1 Pet. 5. 8, 9, because your *a*. the devil.
See 1 Sam. 2. 10; Isa. 9. 11; 11. 13.
ADVERSITY. 1 Sam. 10. 19; 2 Sam. 4. 9; 2 Chron. 15. 6, all *a*.
Ps. 10. 6, I shall never be in *a*.
94. 13; Prov. 24. 10; Eccl. 7. 14, day of *a*.
Prov. 17. 17, brother is born for *a*.
Isa. 30. 20, bread of *a*.
Heb. 13. 3, remember them which suffer *a*.
See Ps. 31. 7; 35. 15.
ADVERTISE. Num. 24. 14; Ruth 4. 4.
ADVICE. 1 Sam. 25. 33, blessed be thy *a*.
2 Sam. 19. 43, that our *a*. should not be first.
2 Chron. 10. 9, 14, what *a*. give ye.
Prov. 20. 18, with good *a*. make war.
2 Cor. 8. 10, herein I give my *a*.
See Judg. 19. 30; 20. 7; 2 Chron. 25. 17.
ADVISE. Prov. 13. 10, with the well *a*. is wisdom.
Acts 27. 12, the more part *a*. to depart.
See 2 Sam. 24. 13; 1 Kings 12. 6; 1 Chron. 21. 12.
ADVISEMENT. 1 Chron. 12. 19.
ADVOCATE. 1 John 2. 1, an *a*. with the Father.
AFAR OFF. Jer. 23. 23, a God *a*.
30. 10; 46. 27, I will save them from *a*.
Mat. 26. 58; Mk. 14. 54; Lu. 22. 54, followed *a*.
Acts 2. 39, promise to all *a*.
Eph. 2. 17, preached to you *a*.
Heb. 11. 13, seen the promises *a*.
See Gen. 22. 4; Ezra 3. 13.
AFFAIRS. 1 Chron. 26. 32, pertaining to God and *a*. of king.
2 Tim. 2. 4, entangleth himself with *a*.
See Dan. 2. 49; 3. 12; Eph. 6. 21, 22. [thren.
AFFECTED. Acts 14. 2, minds evil *a*. against bre-
Gal. 4. 17, 18, zealously *a*.
See Lam. 3. 51. [God.
AFFECTION. 1 Chr. 29. 3, have set *a*. to house of
Rom. 1. 26, vile *a*.
31; 2 Tim. 3. 3, without natural *a*.
12. 10, be kindly *a*. one to another.
Gal. 5. 24, crucified flesh with *a*.
Col. 3. 2, set your *a*. on things above.
5, inordinate *a*.
See 2 Cor. 7. 15.
AFFINITY. 1 Kin. 3. 1; 2 Chr. 18. 1; Ezra 9. 14.
AFFIRM. Acts 25. 19, Jesus, whom Paul *a*. to be alive.
See Rom. 3. 8; 1 Tim. 1. 7; Tit. 3. 8.
AFFLICT. Lev. 16. 29, 31; Num. 29. 7; Isa. 58. 3, 5, *a*. your souls.
Num. 11. 11, wherefore hast thou *a*.
Ruth 1. 21, Almighty hath *a*. me.
1 Kings 11. 39, I will *a*. seed of David.
2 Chr. 6. 26; 1 Kin. 8. 35, turn when thou dost *a*.
Job 6. 14, to *a*. pity should be shewed.
Ps. 44. 2, how thou didst *a*. people.
55. 19, God shall hear and *a*.
82. 3, do justice to the *a*.
90. 15, the days wherein thou hast *a*.
119. 67, before I was *a*.
140. 12, maintain cause of *a*.
Prov. 15. 15, days of the *a*. evil.
22. 22, neither oppress the *a*.
31. 5, pervert judgment of *a*.
Isa. 51. 21, hear thou *a*. and drunken.
53. 4, 7, smitten of God and *a*.
54. 11, thou *a*. tossed with tempest.
63. 9, in all their *a*. he was *a*.
Lam. 1. 5, 12, the Lord hath *a*.
Nah. 1. 12, I will *a*. no more.
Zeph. 3. 12, I will leave an *a*. people.
2 Cor. 1. 6, *a*. it is for consolation.
1 Tim. 5. 10, if she have relieved the *a*.
Heb. 11. 37, destitute, *a*., tormented.

Jas. 4. 9, be *a*. and mourn and weep.
5. 13, is any *a*., let him pray.
See Ex. 1. 11, 12; 22. 22, 23.
AFFLICTION. Gen. 29. 32; Deut. 26. 7; Ps. 25. 18, looked on *a*.
Ex. 3. 7; Acts 7. 10, 11, 34, have seen *a*. of people.
Deut. 16. 3; 1 Kings 22. 27; 2 Chron. 18. 26, bread of *a*.
2 Chron. 20. 9, cry to thee in *a*.
33. 12, in *a*. besought the Lord.
Job 5. 6, *a*. cometh not forth of the dust.
30. 16, 27, days of *a*.
36. 8, cords of *a*.
Ps. 34. 19, many are *a*. of righteous.
119. 50, this my comfort in *a*.
132. 1, remember David and all his *a*.
Isa. 30. 20, water of *a*.
48. 10, furnace of *a*.
Jer. 16. 19, refuge in day of *a*.
Lam. 3. 1, man that hath seen *a*.
Hos. 5. 15, in their *a*. they will seek.
Mk. 4. 17, *a*. ariseth for the word's sake.
Acts 20. 23, bonds and *a*. abide me.
2 Cor. 2. 4, out of much *a*. I wrote.
4. 17, light *a*. for moment.
8. 2, great trial of *a*.
Phil. 1. 16, add *a*. to bonds.
Heb. 10. 32, great fight of *a*.
11. 25, suffer *a*. with people.
Jas. 1. 27, visit fatherless in *a*.
See 2 Kings 14. 26; Col. 1. 24.
AFFRIGHT. Isa. 21. 4, fearfulness *a*. me.
Mk. 16. 5; Lu. 24. 37, they were *a*.
6, be not *a*. ye seek Jesus.
See Deut. 7. 21; 2 Chron. 32. 18; Jer. 51. 32.
AFOOT. Mk. 6. 33; Acts 20. 13.
AFORETIME. Dan. 6. 10, prayed as *a*.
Rom. 15. 4, things were written *a*.
See Isa. 52. 4; Jer. 30. 20.
AFRAID. Mat. 14. 27; Mk. 5. 36; 6. 50; John 6. 20, be not *a*.
Gen. 20. 8; Ex. 14. 10; Mk. 9. 6; Lu. 2. 9, sore *a*.
Lev. 26. 6; Job 11. 19; Isa. 17. 2; Ezek. 34. 28; Mic. 4. 4; Zeph. 3. 13, none make *a*.
Judg. 7. 3, whosoever is fearful and *a*.
1 Sam. 18. 29, Saul yet the more *a*.
Neh. 6. 9, they all made us *a*.
Job 3. 25, that I was *a*. of is come.
9. 28, I am *a*. of sorrows.
Ps. 27. 1, of whom shall I be *a*.
56. 3, 11, what time I am *a*.
65. 8, *a*. at thy tokens.
91. 5, *a*. for terror by night.
112. 7, *a*. of evil tidings.
Isa. 51. 12, be *a*. of a man that shall die.
Mk. 9. 32; 10. 32, *a*. to ask him.
John 19. 8, Pilate was more *a*.
Gal. 4. 11, I am *a*. of you.
Heb. 11. 23, not *a*. of commandment.
See Deut. 1. 17; Ps. 3. 6.
AFRESH. Heb. 6. 6.
AFTERNOON. Judg. 19. 8.
AFTERWARDS. 1 Sam. 24. 5, *a*. David's heart smote him.
Ps. 73. 24, *a*. receive me to glory.
Prov. 20. 17, deceit sweet, but *a*.
24. 27, prepare work and *a*. build.
29. 11, wise man keepeth till *a*.
John 13. 36, thou shalt follow me *a*.
1 Cor. 15. 23, *a*. they that are Christ's.
See Ex. 11. 1; Mat. 21. 32; Gal. 3. 23.
AGAINST. Lu. 2. 34; Acts 19. 36; 28. 22, spoken *a*.
See Gen. 16. 12; Mat. 12. 30; Lu. 11. 23.
AGATE. Ex. 28. 19; 39. 12, an *a*.
Is. 54. 12, make thy windows of *a*.
Ezek. 27. 16, and *a*.
AGED. 2 Sam. 19. 32; Job 15. 10; Tit. 2. 2, *a*. men.
Philem. 9, Paul the *a*.
See Job 12. 20; 29. 8; 32. 9.

AGES. Eph. 2. 7 ; 3. 5, 21 ; Col. 1. 26.
AGONE. 1 Sam. 30. 13.
AGONY. Lu. 22. 44.
AGREE. Amos 3. 3, except they be *a.*
  Mat. 5. 25, *a.* with adversary.
  18. 19, two of you shall *a.*
  Mk. 14. 56, 59, witness *a.* not.
  Acts 15. 15, to this *a.* words of the prophets.
  1 John 5. 8, these three *a.* in one.
  See Mat. 20. 2 ; Lu. 5. 36 ; Acts 5. 9 ; Rev. 17. 17.
AGREEMENT. Isa. 28. 15 ; 2 Cor. 6. 16.
AGROUND. Acts 27. 41.
AHA. Ps. 35. 21 ; 40. 15 ; 70. 3 ; Isa. 44. 16 ; Ezek.
  25. 3 ; 26. 2 ; 36. 2.
AILETH. Gen. 21. 17 ; Judg. 18. 23 ; 1 Sam. 11. 5 ;
  2 Sam. 14. 5 ; Ps. 114. 5 ; Isa. 22. 1.
AIR. Job 41. 16, no *a.* can come between.
  1 Cor. 9. 26, as one that beateth the *a.*
  14. 9, ye shall speak into *a.*
  1 Thess. 4. 17, meet Lord in *a.*   [9. 2.
  See 2 Sam. 21. 10 ; Eccl. 10. 20 ; Acts 22. 23 ; Rev.
ALARM (how sounded). Num. 10. 5, when ye
  blow an *a.*
  Jer. 4. 19 ; 49. 2, *a.* of war.
  Joel 2. 1, sound *a.* in holy mountain.
  See 2 Chron. 13. 12 ; Zeph. 1. 16.
ALAS. 2 Kings 6. 5, 15, *a.* my master.
  Ezek. 6. 11, stamp and say *a.*
  See Num. 24. 23 ; Jer. 30. 7 ; Rev. 18. 10.
ALBEIT. Ezek. 13. 7 ; Philem. 19.
ALIEN. Deut. 14. 21, sell it to an *a.*
  Ps. 69. 8, an *a.* unto my mother's children.
  Eph. 2. 12, *a.* from commonwealth.
  Heb. 11. 34, armies of the *a.*
  See Ex. 18. 3 ; Job 19. 15 ; Isa. 61. 5 ; Lam. 5. 2.
ALIENATED. Ezek. 23. 17 ; Eph. 4. 18 ; Col. 1. 21.
ALIKE. Job 21. 26, lie down *a.* in dust.
  Ps. 33. 15, fashioneth hearts *a.*
  Eccl. 9. 2, things cometh *a.* to all.
  See Ps. 139. 12 ; Eccl. 11. 6 ; Rom. 14. 5.
ALIVE. Lev. 16. 10, scapegoat presented *a.*
  Num. 16. 33, went down *a.* into pit.
  Deut. 4. 4, are *a.* every one of you.
  32. 39 ; 1 Sam. 2. 6, I kill and I make *a.*
  Ezek. 13. 18 ; 18. 27, save soul *a.*
  Mk. 16. 11, heard that he was *a.*
  Lu. 15. 24, 32, son was dead and is *a.*
  24. 23, angels who said he was *a.*
  Acts 1. 3, showed himself *a.*
  Rom. 6. 11, 13, *a.* to God.
  1 Cor. 15. 22, all be made *a.*
  1 Thess. 4. 15, we who are *a.* and remain.
  Rev. 1. 18, I am *a.* for evermore.
  See 2 Kings 5. 7 ; Dan. 5. 19 ; Rev. 2. 8 ; 19. 20.
ALLEGING. Acts 17. 3.
ALLEGORY. Gal. 4. 24, which things are an *a.*
ALLOW. Lu. 11. 48 ; Acts 24. 25 ; Rom. 7. 15 ; 14. 22.
ALLOWANCE. 2 Kings 25. 30.
ALL THINGS. 1 Cor. 6. 12, *a.* are lawful, but not
  expedient.
ALLURE. Hos. 2. 14 ; 2 Pet. 2. 18.
ALMIGHTY. Ex. 6. 3, by the name of God *A.*
  Job 11. 7, canst thou find out the *A.*
  29. 5, when *A.* was yet with me.
  Ezek. 1. 24 ; 10. 5, I heard as voice of *A.*
  Rev. 1. 8 ; 4. 8 ; 11. 17, *A.* who was, and is.
  See Gen. 17. 1 ; Job 21. 15 ; Ps. 91. 1.
ALMS. Mat. 6. 1 ; Lu. 11. 41 ; 12. 33 ; Acts 10. 2.
ALMOND. Num. 17. 8, and yielded *a.*
  Jer. 1. 11, a rod of an *a.* tree.
  Eccl. 12. 5, *a.* tree shall flower.
ALOES. Ps. 45. 8, smell of . . . . and *a.*
  Cant. 4. 14, *a.* with all the chief spices.
  John 19. 39, a mixture of myrrh and *a.*
ALONE. Num. 11. 14 ; Deut. 1. 9, bear all these
  people *a.*

1 Kings 11. 29, they two *a.* in field.
Job 1. 15, escaped *a.* to tell.
Ps. 136. 4, *a.* doeth great wonders.
Mat. 4. 4 ; Lu. 4. 4, not live by bread *a.*
Lu. 9. 18, 36 ; John 6. 15, Jesus was *a.*
  13. 8, let *a.* this year also.
See Gen. 2. 18 ; Mat. 18. 15 ; Jas. 2. 17.   [3. 16.
ALREADY. Eccl. 1. 10 ; Mal. 2. 2 ; John 3. 18 ; Phil.
ALTAR. Mat. 5. 23, bring gift to *a.*
  23. 18, swear by *a.*
  1 Cor. 9. 13 ; 10. 18, wait at *a.*
  Heb. 13. 10, we have an *a.*
  See 1 Kings 13. 2 ; Isa. 19. 19 ; Acts 17. 23.
ALTER. Ps. 89. 34, nor *a.* thing gone out of my lips.
  Lu. 9. 29, fashion of countenance *a.*
  See Lev. 27. 10 ; Dan. 6. 8.
ALTOGETHER. Ps. 14. 3 ; 53. 3, *a.* become filthy.
  50. 21, *a.* such an one as thyself.
  Cant. 5. 16, he is *a.* lovely.
  See Ps. 19. 9 ; 39. 5 ; 139. 4.
ALWAYS. Job 7. 16, I would not live *a.*
  Ps. 103. 9, not *a.* chide.
  Mat. 28. 20, I am with you *a.*
  Mk. 14. 7 ; John 12. 8, me ye have not *a.*
  Phil. 4. 4, rejoice in Lord *a.*
  See Ps. 16. 8 ; Isa. 57. 16 ; John 11. 42.
AMAZED. Mat. 19. 25, disciples exceedingly *a.*
  Mk. 2. 12 ; Lu. 5. 26, *a.* and glorified God.
  14. 33, he began to be sore *a.*
  Lu. 9. 43, *a.* at mighty power of God.
  See Ezek. 32. 10 ; Acts 3. 10 ; 1 Pet. 3. 6.
AMBASSADORS. 2 Chron. 32. 31, the business of
  the *a.*
  2 Cor. 5. 20, we are *a.* for Christ.
  See Prov. 13. 17 ; Isa. 18. 2 ; 33. 7 ; Jer. 49. 14 ;
  Obad. 1.   Eph. 6. 20.
AMBER. Ezek. 1. 4, 27 ; 8. 2, as the colour of *a.*
AMEN (tantamount to an oath). Num. 5. 22, the
  woman shall say, *A.*
  Deut. 27. 15–26, the people shall say, *A.*
  Ps. 41. 13 ; 72. 19 ; 89. 52, *A.* and *A.*
  106. 48, let all the people say, *A.*
  Mat. 6. 13, and the glory for ever, *A.*
  1 Cor. 14. 16, of the unlearned say, *A.*
  2 Cor. 1. 20, and in him, *A.*
  Rev. 3. 14, These things saith the *A.*
  See Rev. 22. 20.
AMEND. Jer. 7. 3 ; 26. 13 ; 35. 15 ; John 4. 52.
AMIABLE. Ps. 84. 1.   [4. 3.
AMISS. 2 Chr. 6. 37 ; Dan. 3. 29 ; Lu. 23. 41 ; Jas.
ANCHOR. Heb. 6. 19, have as an *a.* of the soul.
ANCIENT OF DAYS. Dan. 7. 22, until the *a.* came.
ANGEL. Gen. 48. 16, the *A.* who redeemed me.
  Ps. 34. 7, *a.* of Lord encampeth.
  78. 25, man did eat *a.* food.
  Eccl. 5. 6, nor say before *a.* it was error.
  Isa. 63. 9, *a.* of his presence saved them.
  Hos. 12. 4, he had power over *a.*
  Mat. 13. 39, reapers are the *a.*
  Mk. 12. 25 ; Lu. 20. 36, are as *a.* in heaven.
  Lu. 22. 43, an *a.* strengthening him.
  John 5. 4, *a.* went down at a certain season.
  Acts 12. 15, it is his *a.*
  1 Cor. 6. 3, we shall judge *a.*
  2 Cor. 11. 14, transformed into *a.* of light.
  Heb. 2. 2, word spoken by *a.*
  16, not nature of *a.*
  13. 2, entertained *a.* unawares.
  1 Pet. 1. 12, *a.* desire to look into.
  See Gen. 19. 1 ; Ps. 8. 5 ; Mat. 25. 41 ; Heb. 2. 7.
ANGER. Gen. 49. 7, cursed be their *a.*
  Neh. 9. 17, slow to *a.*
  Ps. 6. 1 ; Jer. 10. 24, rebuke me not in *a.*
  30. 5, *a.* endureth but a moment.
  Prov. 15. 1, grievous words stir up *a.*
  19. 11, discretion deferreth *a.*
  Eccl. 7. 9, *a.* resteth in bosom of fools.
  Mk. 3. 5, he looked on them with *a.*

Col. 3. 8, put off *a.*, wrath, malice.
See Ps. 37. 8; 85. 3; 90. 7; Prov. 16. 32.

ANGRY. Ps. 7. 11, God is *a.* with the wicked.
Prov. 14. 17, he that is soon *a.*
22. 24, make no friendship with *a.* man.
25. 23, so doth an *a.* countenance.
Jonah 4. 4, doest thou well to be *a.?*
Mat. 5. 22, whosoever is *a.* with brother.
John 7. 23, are ye *a.* at me.
Eph. 4. 26, be *a.* and sin not.
Tit. 1. 7, bishop not soon *a.*
See Gen. 18. 30; Prov. 21. 19; Eccl. 5. 6; 7. 9.

ANGUISH. Ex. 6. 9, hearkened not for *a.*
Job 7. 11, I will speak in *a.* of spirit.
Rom. 2. 9, tribulation and *a.* on every soul.
2 Cor. 2. 4, out of much *a.* of heart.
See Gen. 42. 21; Isa. 8. 22; John 16. 21.

ANOINT. Deut. 28. 40; 2 Sam. 14. 2, *a.* not thyself.
Isa. 21. 5, arise and *a.* shield.
61. 1: Lu. 4. 18, *a.* to preach.
Mk. 14. 8, *a.* my body to burying.
Lu. 7. 46, my head thou didst not *a.*
John 9. 6, *a.* eyes of blind man.
12. 3, Mary *a.* feet of Jesus.
2 Cor. 1. 21, he which *a.* us is God.
1 John 2. 27, the same *a.* teacheth.
Rev. 3. 18, *a.* thine eyes with eyesalve.
See Judg. 9. 8; Ps. 2. 2; 84. 9; Jas. 5. 14.

ANOINTED. 1 Sam. 26. 9.

ANOINTING OIL. Ex. 30. 25, it shall be an holy *a.*
37. 29, he made the holy *a.*

ANON. Mat. 13. 20; Mk. 1. 30.

ANOTHER. Prov. 27. 2, let *a.* praise thee.
2 Cor. 11. 4; Gal. 1. 6, 7, *a.* gospel.
Jas. 5. 16, pray one for *a.*
See 1 Sam. 10. 6; Job 19. 27; Isa. 42. 8; 48. 11.

ANSWER (*n.*). Job 19. 16; 32. 3; Cant. 5. 6; Mic.
3. 7; John 19. 9, no *a.*
Prov. 15. 1, a soft *a.* turneth.
Prov. 16. 1, *a.* of tongue from the Lord.
1 Pet. 3. 15, be ready to give *a.*
21, *a.* of good conscience.
See Job 35. 12; Lu. 2. 47; 2 Tim. 4. 16.

ANSWER (*v.*). Job 11. 2, multitude of words be *a.*
Ps. 65. 5, by terrible things wilt thou *a.*
Prov. 1. 28, I will not *a.*
18. 13, *a.* a matter before he heareth.
26. 4, 5, *a.* not a fool.
Eccl. 10. 19, money *a.* all things.
Lu. 21. 14, meditate not what to *a.*
2 Cor. 5. 12, somewhat to *a.*
Col. 4. 6, how ye ought to *a.*
Tit. 2. 9, not *a.* again.
See 1 Kings 18. 29; Ps. 138. 3; Isa. 65. 12, 24.

ANTIQUITY. Isa. 23. 7.

APART. Mat. 14. 13, desert place *a.*
23; 17. 1; Lu. 9. 28, mountain *a.*
Mk. 6. 31, come ye yourselves *a.*
See Ps. 4. 3; Zech. 12. 12; Jas. 1. 21.

APPARENTLY. Num. 12. 8.

APPEAR. Col. 3. 4; 1 Tim. 6. 14; 2 Tim. 1. 10; 4. 8;
Tit. 2. 13; Heb. 9. 28; 1 Pet. 1. 7, *a.* of Christ.
1 Sam. 16. 7, man looketh on the outward *a.*
Ps. 42. 2, when shall I *a.* before God.
90. 16, let thy work *a.*
Cant. 2. 12, flowers *a.* on earth.
Mat. 6. 16, *a.* to men to fast.
23. 28, outwardly *a.* righteous.
Rom. 7. 13, that it might *a.* sin.
2 Cor. 5. 10, we must all *a.*
12, glory in *a.*
1 Thess. 5. 22, *a.* of evil.
1 Tim. 4. 15, profiting may *a.*
See Ex. 23. 15; Mat. 24. 30; Lu. 19. 11.

APPEASE. Gen. 32. 20; Prov. 15. 18; Acts 19. 35.

APPERTAIN. Num. 16. 30; Jer. 10. 7; Rom. 4. 1.

APPETITE. Job 38. 39; Prov. 23. 2; Eccl. 6. 7;
Isa. 29. 8.

APPLY. Ps. 90. 12; Prov. 2. 2; 22. 17; 23. 12;
Eccl. 7. 25.

APPOINT. Job 7. 3, wearisome nights are *a.*
14. 5, thou hast *a.* bounds.
30. 23, house *a.* for all living.
Ps. 79. 11; 102. 20, preserve those *a.* to die.
Mat. 24. 51; Lu. 12. 46, *a.* him his portion.
Acts 6. 3, seven men whom we may *a.*
1 Thess. 5. 9, not *a.* to wrath.
See Job 14. 13; Ps. 104. 19; Acts 17. 31.

APPREHEND. Acts 12. 4; 2 Cor. 11. 32; Phil. 3. 12.

APPROACH. Isa. 58. 2, take delight in *a.* God.
Lu. 12. 33, where no thief *a.*
1 Tim. 6. 16, light no man can *a.*
Heb. 10. 25, as ye see the day *a.*
See Deut. 31. 14; Job 40. 19; Ps. 65. 4.

APPROVE. Acts 2. 22, a man *a.* of God.
Rom. 16. 10, *a.* in Christ.
Phil. 1. 10, *a.* things that are excellent.
2 Tim. 2. 15, show thyself *a.*
See Ps. 49. 13; 1 Cor. 11. 19; Phil. 1. 10.

APT. 2 Kings 24. 16; 1 Tim. 3. 2; 2 Tim. 2. 24.

ARCHANGEL. 1 Thess. 4. 16, voice of *a.*
Jude 9, Michael the *a.* contending.

ARCHERS. Gen. 21. 20, and became an *a.*
49. 23, the *a.* have sorely grieved him.
1 Sam. 31. 3, and the *a.* hit him.
2 Chron. 35. 23, and the *a.* shot at king Josiah.
Job 16. 13, his *a.* compass me.
See 1 Kin. 22. 34.

ARGUING. Job 6. 25.

ARGUMENTS. Job 23. 4.

ARIGHT. Ps. 50. 23; 78. 8; Prov. 15. 2; 23. 31.

ARISE. 1 Kings 18. 44, there *a.* a little cloud.
Neh. 2. 20, *a.* and build.
Ps. 68. 1, let God *a.*
88. 10, dead *a.* and praise thee.
112. 4, to upright *a.* light.
Mal. 4. 2, Sun of righteousness *a.*
Mk. 2. 11; Lu. 7. 14; 8. 54; Acts 9. 40, I say *a.*
Lu. 15. 18, I will *a.* and go.
Eph. 5. 14, *a.* from the dead.
2 Pet. 1. 19, till daystar *a.*
See Isa. 26. 19; Jer. 2. 27.

ARMOUR (Goliath's), 1 Sam. 17. 54, but he put
his *a.* in his tent.
1 Kin. 22. 38, and they washed his *a.*
Isa. 22. 8, didst look in that day to *a.*
Lu. 11. 22, his *a.* wherein he trusted.
Rom. 13. 12, let us put on *a.* of light.
2 Cor. 6. 7, approving by *a.* of righteousness.
Eph. 6. 11, 13, put on the *a.* of God.
See 2 Cor. 10. 3; 1 Thess. 5. 8.

ARMS. Deut. 33. 27, underneath are the everlasting *a.*
See Gen. 49. 24; Job 22. 9; Ps. 37. 17; Mk. 10. 16.

ARMY. 1 Sam. 17. 10, I defy the *a.* of Israel.
Job 25. 3, is there any number of his *a.*
Lu. 21. 20, Jerusalem compassed with *a.*
Acts 23. 27, then came I with an *a.*
Heb. 11. 34, *a.* of the aliens.
See Cant. 6. 4; Ezek. 37. 10.

ARRAY. Jer. 43. 12, shall *a.* himself with land.
Mat. 6. 29; Lu. 12. 27, *a.* like one of these.
1 Tim. 2. 9, not with costly *a.*
Rev. 7. 13, *a.* in white robes.
See Job 40. 10; Rev. 17. 4; 19. 8.

ARRIVED. Lu. 8. 26; Acts 20. 15.

ARROGANCY. 1 Sam. 2. 3, Prov. 8. 13; Isa. 13.
11; Jer. 48. 29.

ARROW. Num. 24. 8, pierce through with *a.*
Ps. 38. 2, thine *a.* stick fast.
76. 3, brake the *a.* of the bow.
91. 5, *a.* that flieth by day.
Prov. 25. 18, false witness sharp *a.*
26. 18, casteth *a.* and death.
Ezek. 5. 16, evil *a.* of famine.
See Deut. 32. 23; 2 Sam. 22. 15; Job 6. 4; 41. 28.

ARTIFICER. Gen. 4. 22; 1 Chron. 29. 5; 2 Chron. 34. 11; Isa. 3. 3.
ARTILLERY. 1 Sam. 20. 40.   [high.
ASCEND. Ps. 68. 18; Rom. 10. 6; Eph. 4. 8, *a*. ou
John 1. 51, angels of God *a*.
3. 13, no man hath *a*. to heaven.
20. 17, I am not yet *a*.
Rev. 8. 4, smoke of incense *a*.
11. 12, they *a*. up to heaven.
See Ps. 24. 3; 139. 8.
ASCRIBE. Deut. 32. 3; Job 36. 3; Ps. 68. 34.
ASHAMED. Job 11. 3, shall no man make *a*.
Ps. 25. 3, let none that wait be *a*.
31. 1, let me never be *a*.
34. 5, their faces were not *a*.
Isa. 45. 17, not *a*. world without end.
65. 13, ye shall be *a*.
Jer. 2. 26, as a thief is *a*.
6. 15; 8. 12, were they *a*.
12. 13, *a*. of your revenues.
14. 4, plowmen were *a*.
Lu. 16. 3, to beg I am *a*.
Rom. 1. 16, not *a*. of Gospel.
5. 5, hope maketh not *a*.
9. 33; 10. 11, believeth shall not be *a*.
2 Tim. 1. 8, not *a*. of testimony.
2. 15, workman that needeth not to be *a*.
Heb. 2. 11, not *a*. to call them brethren.
11. 16, not *a*. to be called their God.
1 Pet. 4. 16, suffer as Christian, not be *a*.
See Gen. 2. 25; 2 Tim. 1. 12.
ASHES. Gen. 18. 27, which am but dust and *a*.
Job 2. 8, and he sat down among the *a*.
13. 12, remembrances are like unto *a*.
30. 19, and become like dust and *a*.
42. 6, and repent in dust and *a*.
Ps. 102. 9, I have eaten *a*. like bread.
Isa. 44. 20, he feedeth on *a*.
Jonah 3. 6, king sat in *a*.
Heb. 9. 13, if the *a*. of an heifer.
See 2 Sam. 13. 19; Esth. 4. 1; Isa. 58. 5; Mat. 11. 21.
ASIDE. 2 Kings 4. 4; Mk. 7. 33; Heb. 12. 1.
ASK. Ps. 2. 8; Isa. 45. 11, *a*. of me.
Isa. 65. 1, sought of them that *a*. not.
Mat. 7. 7; Lu. 11. 9, *a*. and it shall be given.
21. 22, whatsoever ye *a*.
Mk. 6. 22, *a*. what thou wilt.
John 14. 13; 15. 16, *a*. in my name.
Jas. 1. 5, let him *a*. of God.
1 Pet. 3. 15, *a*. reason of hope.
1 John 3. 22; 5. 14, whatsoever we *a*.
See Deut. 32. 7; John 4. 9, 10; 1 Cor. 14. 35.
ASLEEP. Mat. 8. 24; Mk. 4. 38, but he was *a*.
26. 40; Mk. 14. 40, disciples *a*.
1 Cor. 15. 6, some are fallen *a*.
1 Thess. 4. 13, 15, them that are *a*.
2 Pet. 3. 4, since fathers fell *a*.
See Cant. 7. 9.
ASP. Deut. 32. 33, the cruel venom of *a*.
Job 20. 14, 16, it is the gall of *a*.
Isa. 11. 8, play on the hole of the *a*.
Rom. 3. 13, the poison of *a*.
ASS. Num. 22. 30, am not I thine *a*.
Prov. 26. 3, bridle for *a*.
Isa. 1. 3, *a*. his master's crib.
Jer. 22. 19, burial of an *a*.
Zech. 9. 9; Mat. 21. 5, riding on *a*.
Lu. 14. 5, *a*. fallen into pit.
2 Pet. 2. 16, dumb *a*. speaking.
See Gen. 49. 14; Ex. 23. 4; Deut. 22. 10.
ASSAULT. Esth. 8. 11; Acts 14. 5; 17. 5.
ASSAY. Acts 9. 26, Saul *a*. to join disciples.
Acts 16. 7, they *a*. to go to Bithynia.
Heb. 11. 29, Egyptians *a*. to do.
See Deut. 4. 34; 1 Sam. 17. 39; Job 4. 2.
ASSENT. 2 Chron. 18. 12; Acts 24. 9.
ASSIGNED. Gen. 47. 22; Josh. 20. 8; 2 Sam. 11. 16.

ASSIST. Rom. 16. 2.
ASSOCIATE. Isa. 8. 9.
ASSURANCE. Isa. 32. 17, effect of righteousness *a*.
Col. 2. 2, full *a*. of understanding.
1 Thess. 1. 5, gospel came in much *a*.
Heb. 6. 11; 10. 22, full *a*. of hope.
See Deut. 28. 66; Acts 17. 31.
ASSURE. 2 Tim. 3. 14; 1 John 3. 19.
ASSWAGE. Gen. 8. 1; Job 16. 5.
ASTONIED. Ezra 9. 3; Job 17. 8; Dan. 3. 24; 4. 19.
ASTONISHED. Mat. 7. 28; 22. 33; Mk. 1. 22; 6. 2;
11. 18; Lu. 4. 32, *a*. at his doctrine.
Lu. 2. 47, *a*. at his understanding.
5. 9, *a*. at draught of fishes.
24. 22, women made us *a*.
Acts 9. 6, Saul trembling and *a*.
12. 16, saw Peter, they were *a*.
13. 12, deputy believed, being *a*.
See Job 26. 11; Jer. 2. 12.
ASTONISHMENT. 2 Chron. 29. 8; Jer. 25. 9, *a*. and hissing.
Ps. 60. 3, made us drink wine of *a*.
Jer. 8. 21, *a*. hath taken hold.
See Deut. 28. 28, 37; Ezek. 5. 15.
ASTROLOGERS. Isa. 47. 13, let now the *a*.
Dan. 2. 2; 4. 7; 5. 7, the *a*.
ATHIRST. Mat. 25. 44; Rev. 21. 6; 22. 17.
ATONEMENT. Lev. 23. 28; 25. 9, a day of *a*.
2 Sam. 21. 3, wherewith shall I make *a*.
Rom. 5. 11, by whom we received *a*.
See Lev. 4. 20; 16. 17; Num. 8. 21.
ATTAIN. Ps. 139. 6, I cannot *a*. to it.
2 Sam. 23. 19; 1 Chron. 11. 26, he *a*. not to first three.
Rom. 9. 30, Gentiles *a*. to righteousness.
Phil. 3. 11, 12, 16, that I might *a*.
See Gen. 47. 9; Prov. 1. 5; Ezek. 46. 7; 1 Tim. 4. 6.
ATTEND. Ps. 17. 1; 61. 1; 142. 6, *a*. to my cry.
Prov. 4. 20, my son *a*. to my words.
See Ps. 55. 2; 86. 6.
ATTENDANCE. 1 Tim. 4. 13; Heb. 7. 13.
ATTENT. 2 Chron. 6. 40; 7. 15.
ATTENTIVE. Neh. 1. 6; Job 37. 2; Ps. 130. 2;
Lu. 19. 48.
ATTIRE. Jer. 2. 32; Ezek. 23. 15.
AUDIENCE. 1 Chron. 28. 8, in *a*. of our God.
Lu. 7. 1; 20. 45, in *a*. of people.
Acts 13. 16, ye that fear God give *a*.
See Ex. 24. 7; Acts 15. 12.
AUGMENT. Num. 32. 14.
AUSTERE. Lu. 19. 21.
AUTHOR. 1 Cor. 14. 33; Heb. 5. 9; 12. 2.
AUTHORITY. Mat. 7. 29; Mk. 1. 22, as one having *a*.
8. 9; Lu. 7. 8, I am a man under *a*.
Mat. 21. 23; Lu. 4. 36, by what *a*.
Lu. 9. 1, power and *a*. over devils.
19. 17, have *a*. over ten cities.
John 5. 27, *a*. to execute judgment.
1 Cor. 15. 24, put down all *a*.
1 Tim. 2. 2, kings and all in *a*.
12, suffer not a woman to usurp *a*.
Tit. 2. 15, rebuke with all *a*.
1 Pet. 3. 22, angels and *a*. subject.
See Prov. 29. 2; 2 Cor. 10. 8; Rev. 13. 2.
AVAILETH. Esth. 5. 13; Gal. 5. 6; Jas. 5. 16.
AVENGE. Deut. 32. 43, he will *a*. blood.
Josh. 10. 13, sun stayed till people *a*.
1 Sam. 24. 12, the Lord judge and *a*.
2 Sam. 22. 48; Ps. 18. 47, it is God that *a*. me.
Esth. 8. 13, Jews *a*. themselves.
Isa. 1. 24, I will *a*. me of mine enemies.
Lu. 18. 3, *a*. me of my adversary.
See Gen. 4. 24; Lev. 19. 18; Jer. 5. 9; 9. 9.
AVENGER. Ps. 8. 2; 44. 16, enemy and *a*.
1 Thess. 4. 6, the Lord is the *a*.
See Num. 35. 12; Deut. 19. 6; Josh. 20. 5.
AVERSE. Mic. 2. 8.

AVOID. Prov. 4. 15, *a.* it, pass not by it.
1 Tim. 6. 20 ; 2 Tim. 2. 23 ; Tit. 3. 9, *a.* babblings.
See Rom. 16. 17 ; 2 Cor. 8. 20.
AVOUCHED. Deut. 26. 17, 18.
AWAKE. Ps. 17. 15, when I *a.*, with thy likeness.
73. 20, as a dream when one *a.*
Prov. 23. 35, *a.* I will seek it again.
Isa. 51. 9, *a.*, *a.*, put on strength.
Joel 1. 5, *a.* ye drunkards.
Zech. 13. 7, *a.* O sword.
Lu. 9. 32, when *a.* they saw his glory.
Rom. 13. 11, high time to *a.*
1 Cor. 15. 34, *a.* to righteousness.
Eph. 5. 14, *a.* thou that sleepest.
See Jer. 51. 57 ; John 11. 11.
AWARE. Cant. 6. 12 ; Jer. 50. 24 ; Lu. 11. 44.
AWE. Ps. 4. 4 ; 33. 8 ; 119. 161.
AWL. Ex. 21. 6 ; Deut. 15. 17.
AXE. Ps. 74. 5, famous as he had lifted up *a.*
Isa. 10. 15, shall the *a.* boast.
Mat. 3. 10 ; Lu. 3. 9, the *a.* is laid to root.
See 1 Sam. 13. 20 ; 1 Kings 6. 7 ; 2 Kings 6. 5.

B.

BABBLER. Eccl. 10. 11 ; Acts 17. 18.
BABBLING. Prov. 23. 29 ; 1 Tim. 6. 20 ; 2 Tim. 2. 16.
BABE. Ps. 8. 2 ; Mat. 21. 16, out of mouth of *b.*
17. 14, leave their substance to *b.*
Isa. 3. 4, *b.* shall rule over them.
Mat. 11. 25 ; Lu. 10. 21, revealed to *b.*
Rom. 2. 20, teacher of *b.*
1 Cor. 3. 1, *b.* in Christ.
1 Pet. 2. 2, newborn *b.*
See Ex. 2. 6 ; Lu. 2. 12, 16 ; Heb. 5. 13.
BACK. Josh. 8. 26, drew not his hand *b.*
1 Sam. 10. 9, he turned his *b.*
Neh. 9. 26, cast law behind *b.*
Ps. 129. 3, plowers plow on my *b.*
Prov. 10. 13 ; 19. 29 ; 26. 3, rod for *b.*
Isa. 38. 17, cast sins behind *b.*
50. 6, gave *b.* to smiters.
See Num. 24. 11 ; 2 Sam. 19. 10 ; Job 26. 9.
BACKBITERS. Rom. 1. 30.
BACKBITING. Ps. 15. 3 ; Prov. 25. 23 ; 2 Cor. 12. 20.
BACKSLIDER. Prov. 14. 14, *b.* in heart filled with
his own ways.
Jer. 3. 6, 8, 11, 12, *b.* Israel.
8. 5, perpetual *b.*
14. 7, our *b.* are many.
Hos. 4. 16, as a *b.* heifer.
11. 7, bent to *b.* from me.
14. 4, will heal their *b.*
See Jer. 2. 19 ; 5. 6 ; 31. 22 ; 49. 4.
BACKWARD. 2 Kings 20. 10 ; Isa. 38. 8, let sha-
dow return *b.*
Job 23. 8, *b.*, but I cannot perceive.
Ps. 40. 14 ; 70. 2, driven *b.*
Isa. 59. 14, judgment is turned *b.*
Jer. 7. 24, they went *b.* and not forward.
See Gen. 9. 23 ; 49. 17 ; John 18. 6.
BAD. Gen. 24. 50 ; 31. 24, 29 ; Lev. 27. 12, 14, 33 ;
Num. 13. 19 ; 24. 13 ; 2 Sam. 13. 22 ; 14. 17 ;
1 Kings 3. 9 ; Mat. 22. 10 ; 2 Cor. 5. 10, good or *b.*
See Lev. 27. 10 ; Ezra 4. 12 ; Jer. 24. 2 ; Mat. 13. 48.
BADGERS' SKINS. Ex. 25. 5, and *b.*
26. 14, a covering above of *b.*
BADNESS. Gen. 41. 19.
BAG. Deut. 25. 13 ; Prov. 16. 11 ; Mic. 6. 11, *b.* of
weights.
Job 14. 17, transgression sealed in *b.*
Isa. 46. 6, lavish gold out of *b.*
Hag. 1. 6, *b.* with holes.
Lu. 12. 33, *b.* that wax not old.
John 12. 6 ; 13. 29, a thief, and had the *b.*
See 1 Sam. 17. 40 ; 2 Kings 5. 23 ; Prov. 7. 20.
BAKE. Gen. 19. 3 ; Lev. 26. 26 ; 1 Sam. 28. 24 ;
Isa. 44. 15, *b.* bread.

Ex. 12. 39 ; Lev. 24. 5, *b.* cakes.
See Gen. 40. 17 ; Ex. 16. 23 ; Lev. 2. 4 ; Num. 11. 8.
BAKER. Gen. 40. 1 ; 41. 10 ; 1 Sam. 8. 13 ; Jer. 37. 21 ;
Hos. 7. 4.
BALANCE. Lev. 19. 36 ; Prov. 16. 11 ; Ezek. 45. 10,
just *b.*
Job 37. 16, the *b.* of clouds.
Ps. 62. 9, laid in *b.*, lighter than vanity.
Prov. 11. 1 ; 20. 23 ; Hos. 12. 7 ; Amos 8. 5 ; Mic. 6.
11, false *b.*
Isa. 40. 12, 15, weighed hills in *b.*
46. 6, weigh silver in the *b.*
Rev. 6. 5, a pair of *b.*
See Job 6. 2 ; 31. 6 ; Jer. 32. 10.
BALD. 2 Kings 2. 23, go up, thou *b.* head.
Jer. 48. 37 ; Ezek. 29. 18, every head *b.*
See Lev. 13. 40 ; Jer. 16. 6 ; Ezek. 27. 31.
BALDNESS. Isa. 3. 24, instead of well set hair *b.*
22. 12, call to weeping and *b.*
Mic. 1. 16, enlarge thy *b.* as eagle.
See Lev. 21. 5 ; Deut. 14. 1 ; Ezek. 7. 18 ; Amos 8. 10.
BALL. Isa. 22. 18.
BALM. Jer. 8. 22 ; 46. 11, *b.* in Gilead.
See Gen. 37. 25 ; 43. 11 ; Jer. 51. 8 ; Ezek. 27. 17.
BANDS. Ps. 2. 3 ; 107. 14, break their *b.* asunder.
73. 4, there are no *b.* in their death.
Hos. 11. 4, drew them with *b.* of love.
Zech. 11. 7, two staves, Beauty and *B.*
Mat. 27. 27 ; Mk. 15. 16, gathered to him whole *b.*
See Job 38. 31 ; Eccl. 7. 26 ; Lu. 8. 29 ; Col. 2. 19.
BANISHED. 2 Sam. 14. 13 ; Ezra 7. 26 ; Lam. 2. 14.
BANK. Lu. 19. 23, gavest not money into *b.*
See Gen. 41. 17 ; 2 Sam. 20. 15 ; Ezek. 47. 7.
BANNER. Ps. 20. 5, in name of God set up *b.*
See Ps. 60. 4 ; Cant. 2. 4 ; 6. 4 ; Isa. 13. 2.
BANQUET. Esth. 5. 4 ; Job 41. 6 ; Cant. 2. 4 ;
Dan. 5 ; Amos 6. 7.
BAPTISM. Mat. 20. 22 ; Mk. 10. 38 ; Lu. 12. 50, to
be baptised with *b.*
21. 25 ; Mk. 11. 30 ; Lu. 7. 29 ; 20. 4 ; Acts 1. 22 ;
18. 25 ; 19. 3, *b.* of John.
Mk. 1. 4 ; Lu. 3. 3 ; Acts 13. 24 ; 19. 4, *b.* of repent-
ance.
Rom. 6. 4 ; Col. 2. 12, buried with him by *b.*
Eph. 4. 5, one Lord, one faith, one *b.*
Heb. 6. 2, doctrine of *b.*
See Mat. 3. 7 ; 1 Pet. 3. 21.
BAPTIZE. Mat. 3. 11 ; Mk. 1. 8 ; Lu. 3. 16 ; John
1. 26, *b.* with Holy Ghost.
14, I have need to be *b.*
16, Jesus when *b.* went up.
Mk. 16. 16, he that believeth and is *b.*
Lu. 3. 7, multitude came to be *b.*
12 ; 7. 29, publicans to be *b.*
21, Jesus being *b.*, and praying.
7. 30, Pharisees and lawyers being not *b.*
John 1. 33, he that sent me to *b.*
3. 22, 23, tarried with them and *b.*
4. 1, 2, Jesus made and *b.* more.
Acts 2. 38, repent and be *b.*
41, gladly received word were *b.*
8. 12, *b.* both men and women.
13, *b.* in name of Jesus.
36, what doth hinder to be *b.*
9. 18, Saul arose and was *b.*
10. 47, can any forbid *b.*
16. 15, 33, *b.* and household.
18. 8, many believed and were *b.*
22. 16, be *b.* and wash away thy sins.
Rom. 6. 3 ; Gal. 3. 27, were *b.* into Jesus.
1 Cor. 1. 13, were ye *b.* in name of Paul.
10. 2, were all *b.* in cloud.
12. 13, all *b.* into one body.
1 Cor. 15. 29, *b.* for the dead.
See Mat. 28. 19 ; John 1. 25, 28, 31.
BARBARIANS. Acts 28. 4 ; Rom. 1. 14 ; 1 Cor. 14. 11.
BARBAROUS. Acts 28. 2.
BARBED. Job 41. 7.

BARBER. Ezek. 5. 1.
BARE (*v.*). Ex. 19. 4; Deut. 1. 31; Isa. 53. 12; 63. 9;
  Mat. 8. 17; 1 Pet. 2. 24.
BARE (*ad.*). Isa. 52. 10; 1 Cor. 15. 37.
BARLEY. Ex. 9. 31, *b.* was in the ear.
  Deut. 8. 8, a land of wheat and *b.*
  Ruth. 1. 22, beginning of *b.* harvest.
  John 6. 9, five *b.* loaves.
  Rev. 6. 6, three measures of *b.*
BARKED. Joel 1. 7.
BARN. Job 39. 12, gather thy seed into *b.*
  Mat. 6. 26; Lu. 12. 24, nor gather into *b.*
  13. 30, gather wheat into *b.*
  Lu. 12. 18, pull down my *b.*
  See 2 Kings 6. 27; Joel 1. 17; Hag. 2. 19.
BARREL. 1 Kings 17. 12, 14; 18. 33.
BARREN. 2 Kings 2. 19, water naught and ground *b.*
  Ps. 107. 34, turneth fruitful land into *b.*
  Isa. 54. 1, sing, O *b.*, thou that didst not bear.
  2 Pet. 1. 8, neither *b.* nor unfruitful.
  See Ex. 23. 26; Job 24. 21; Lu. 23. 29.
BARS. Job 17. 16, down to the *b.* of the pit.
  Ezek. 38. 11, having neither *b.* nor gates.
  See 1 Sam. 23. 7; Job 38. 10; Ps. 107. 16; Isa. 45. 2.
BASE. Job 30. 8, children of *b.* men.
  Mal. 2. 9, I have made you *b.*
  Acts 17. 5, fellows of *b.* sort.
  1 Cor. 1. 28, *b.* things of the world.
  2 Cor. 10. 1, in presence am *b.*
  See 2 Sam. 6. 22; Isa. 3. 5; Ezek. 17. 14; Dan. 4. 17.
BASKET. Deut. 28. 5, 17, blessed be thy *b.*
  Amos 8. 1, *b.* of summer fruit.
  Mat. 14. 20; Mk. 6. 43; Lu. 9. 17; John 6. 13,
    twelve *b.*
  15. 37; Mk. 8. 8, seven *b.*
  16. 9; Mk. 8. 19, how many *b.*
  See Gen. 40. 16; Ex. 29. 3; Judg. 6. 19; Jer. 24. 2.
BASON. John 13. 5, poureth water into a *b.*
  See Ex. 12. 22; 24. 6; 1 Chron. 28. 17; Jer. 52. 19.
BASTARD. Deut. 23. 2, a *b.* shall not enter.
  Zech. 9. 6, *b.* shall dwell in Ashdod.
  Heb. 12. 8, *b.* and not sons.
BATH (a measure). 1 Kin. 7. 26, it contained two
    thousand *b.*
  2 Chron. 2. 10, twenty thousand *b.* of wine.
  Ezra 7. 22, an hundred *b.* of wine.
  Is. 5. 10, shall yield one *b.*
BATHE. Lev. 15. 5; 17. 16; Num. 19. 7; Isa. 34. 5.
BATS. Lev. 11. 19; Deut. 14. 18; Isa. 2. 20.
BATTLE. Num. 17. 20, host shouted for *b.*
  47; 2 Chron. 20. 15, the *b.* is the Lord's.
  1 Chron. 5. 20, they cried to God in *b.*
  Ps. 18. 39, strength to *b.*
  55. 18, delivered my soul from *b.*
  Eccl. 9. 11, nor *b.* to strong.
  Jer. 50. 22, sound of *b.* in land.
  See Job 39. 25; 41. 8; Ps. 76. 3; 140. 7.
BATTLEMENTS. Deut. 22. 8; Jer. 5. 10.
BAY TREE. Ps. 37. 35.
BEACON. Isa. 30. 17.
BEAM. Ps. 104. 3, who layeth *b.* in waters.
  Mat. 7. 5; Lu. 6. 42, cast out *b.*
  See Judg. 16. 14; 2 Kings 6. 2; Hab. 2. 11.
BEAR (*v.*). Gen. 4. 13, greater than I can *b.*
  13. 6; 36. 7, land not able to *b.*
  43. 9; 44. 32, let me *b.* blame.
  Ex. 28. 12, Aaron *b.* names before Lord.
  Num. 11. 14; Deut. 1. 9, not able to *b.* people.
  Ps. 91. 12; Mat. 4. 6; Lu. 4. 11, they shall *b.*
    thee up.
  Prov. 18. 14, wounded spirit who can *b.*
  Isa. 52. 11, clean that *b.* vessels.
  Jer. 31. 19, *b.* reproach of youth.
  Lam. 3. 27, good to *b.* yoke in youth.
  Mat. 3. 11, not worthy to *b.*
  27. 32; Mk. 15. 21; Lu. 23. 26, *b.* cross.
  John 16. 12, cannot *b.* them now.

Rom. 13. 4, *b.* not sword in vain.
  15. 1, *b.* infirmities of the weak.
  1 Cor. 13. 7, charity *b.* all things.
  15. 49, *b.* image of the heavenly.
  Gal. 6. 2, 5, *b.* burdens.
  17, *b.* in my body.
  Esth. 1. 22; Jer. 5. 31; Dan. 2. 39, *b.* rule.
  Lev. 24. 15; Ezek. 23. 49; Heb. 9. 28, *b.* sin.
  Ex. 20. 16; 1 Kings 21. 10; Lu. 11. 48; John 1. 7;
    5. 31; 8. 18; 15. 27; Acts 23. 11; Rom. 8. 16;
    1 John 1. 2; 5. 8, *b.* witness.
  See Ex. 28. 38; Deut. 1. 31; Prov. 12. 24.
BEAR (*n.*). Isa. 11. 7, cow and *b.* shall feed.
  59. 11, roar like *b.*
  Hos. 13. 8, as a *b.* bereaved.
  Amos 5. 19; as if a man did flee from *b.*
  See 1 Sam. 17. 34; 2 Sam. 17. 8; Prov. 17. 12.
BEARD. 2 Sam. 10. 5; 1 Chron. 19. 5, till *b.* be
    grown.
  Ps. 133. 2, even Aaron's *b.*
  Ezek. 5. 1, cause razor to pass on *b.*
  See Lev. 13. 29; 1 Sam. 21. 13; 2 Sam. 20. 9.
BEARING. Ps. 126. 6, *b.* precious seed.
  John 19. 17, *b.* cross.
  Rom. 2. 15; 9. 1, conscience *b.* witness.
  2 Cor. 4. 10, *b.* about in body dying of Jesus.
  Heb. 13. 13, *b.* his reproach.
  See Gen. 1. 29; Num. 10. 17; Mk. 14. 13.
BEAST. Job 12. 7, ask *b.*, they shall teach.
  18. 3, counted as *b.*
  Ps. 49. 12, like *b.* that perish.
  73. 22, as *b.* before thee.
  Prov. 12. 10, regardeth life of *b.*
  Eccl. 3. 19, no pre-eminence above *b.*
  1 Cor. 15. 32, fought with *b.*
  Jas. 3. 7, every kind of *b.* is tamed.
  2 Pet. 2. 12; as natural brute *b.*
  See Lev. 11. 47; Ps. 50. 10; 147. 9; Rom. 1. 23.
BEAT. Isa. 2. 4; Joel 3. 10; Mic. 4. 3, *b.* swords.
  Lu. 12. 47, *b.* with many stripes.
  1 Cor. 9. 26, as one that *b.* the air.
  See Prov. 23. 14; Mic. 4. 13; Mk. 12. 5; 13. 9.
BEAUTIFUL. Ps. 48. 2, *b.* for situation is Sion.
  Eccl. 3. 11, every thing *b.* in his time.
  Cant. 6. 4, thou art *b.*, O my love.
  Isa. 4. 2, the branch of the Lord be *b.*
  52. 1, O Zion, put on thy *b.* garments.
  7; Rom. 10. 15, how *b.* are the feet.
  64. 11, *b.* house is burnt up.
  Jer. 13. 20, where is thy *b.* flock?
  Mat. 23. 27, sepulchres which appear *b.*
  Acts 3. 2, 10, at the gate called *b.*
BEAUTY. 1 Chron. 16. 29; 2 Chron. 20. 21; Ps.
    29. 2; 96. 9; 110. 3, *b.* of holiness.
  Ezra 7. 27, to *b.* the Lord's house.
  Ps. 27. 4, behold *b.* of the Lord.
  39. 11, *b.* to consume away.
  50. 2, perfection of *b.*
  Prov. 31. 30, *b.* is vain.
  See 2 Sam. 1. 19; Ps. 90. 17; Zech. 9. 17.
BEAUTY AND BANDS. Zech. 11. 7, two staves, *b.*
BECKON. Lu. 1. 22; John 13. 24; Acts 12. 17;
    21. 40.
BECOMETH. Ps. 93. 5, holiness *b.* thy house.
  Rom. 16. 2; Eph. 5. 3, as *b.* saints.
  Phil. 1. 27; 1 Tim. 2. 10; Tit. 2. 3, as *b.* gospel.
  See Prov. 17. 7; Mat. 3. 15.
BED. Job 7. 13, when I say my *b.* shall comfort.
  33. 15, in slumberings upon *b.*
  Ps. 63. 6, when I remember thee upon my *b.*
  Mat. 9. 66; Mk. 2. 9; John 5. 11, take up *b.*
  See 2 Kings 4. 10; Isa. 28. 20; Mk. 4. 21; Lu.
    8. 16.
BEDSTEAD. Deut. 3. 11, was a *b.* of iron.
BEES. Deut. 1. 44; Judg. 14. 8; Ps. 118. 12; Isa.
    7. 18.
BEEVES. Lev. 22. 19; Num. 31. 28, 38.
BEFALL. Gen. 42. 4; 44. 29, mischief *b.* him.

Gen. 49. 1; Deut. 31. 29; Dan. 10. 14, *b.* in last days.
Judg. 6. 13, why is all this *b.* us?
Ps. 91. 10, no evil *b.* thee.
Eccl. 3. 19, *b.* men, *b.* beasts, one thing *b.*
See Lev. 10. 19; Deut. 31. 17; Acts 20. 19.

BEG. Ps. 37. 25; 109. 10; Prov. 20. 4; Lu. 16. 3.

BEGGARLY. Gal. 4. 9.

BEGIN. Ezek. 9. 6, *b.* at my sanctuary.
1 Pet. 4. 17, judgment *b.* at house of God.
See 1 Sam. 3. 12; 2 Cor. 3. 1.

BEGINNING. Gen. 1. 1, in the *b.* God created heaven.
Job 8. 7, though thy *b.* was small.
Ps. 111. 10; Prov. 1. 7; 9. 10, *b.* of wisdom.
119. 160, word true from *b.*
Eccl. 7. 8, better end than *b.*
Mat. 19. 8, from *b.* not so.
Lu. 24. 47, *b.* at Jerusalem.
John 1. 1, in the *b.* was the Word.
2. 11, this *b.* of miracles.
Heb. 3. 14, hold *b.* of confidence.
Rev. 1. 8; 21. 6; 22. 13, I am the *b.*
See 1 Chron. 17. 9; Prov. 8. 22, 23; Col. 1. 18.

BEGOTTEN. Ps. 2. 7; Acts 13. 33; Heb. 1. 5; 5. 5, this day have I *b.* thee.
1 Pet. 1. 3, *b.* to a lively hope.
See Job 38. 28; 1 Cor. 4. 15; Philem. 10.

BEGUILE. Gen. 29. 25; Josh. 9. 22, wherefore hast thou *b.* me.
2 Pet. 2. 14, *b.* unstable souls.
See Num. 25. 18; 2 Cor. 11. 3.

BEGUN. Gal. 3. 3, having *b.* in Spirit.
Phil. 1. 6, hath *b.* good work.
See Deut. 3. 24; 2 Cor. 8. 6; 1 Tim. 5. 11.

BEHALF. Job 36. 2, speak on God's *b.*
Phil. 1. 29, in *b.* of Christ.
See 2 Chron. 16. 9; 2 Cor. 1. 11; 5. 12.

BEHAVE. 1 Sam. 18. 5, 14, 15, 30, David *b.* wisely.
1 Chron. 19. 13, *b.* ourselves valiantly.
Ps. 101. 2, I will *b.* wisely.
Isa. 3. 5, child shall *b.* proudly.
1 Thess. 2. 10, how unblameably we *b.*
1 Tim. 3. 2, bishop of good *b.*
See Ps. 131. 2; 1 Cor. 13. 5; Tit. 2. 3.

BEHEADED. Mat. 14. 10; Mk. 6. 16; Lu. 9. 9; Rev. 20. 4.

BEHIND. Ex. 10. 26. not hoof be left *b.*
Phil. 3. 13, things which are *b.*
Col. 1. 24, fill up what is *b.*
See 1 Kings 14. 9; Neh. 9. 26; 2 Cor. 11. 5.

BEHOLD. Ps. 37. 37, *b.* the upright.
Mat. 18. 10, their angels always *b.*
John 17. 24, that they may *b.* glory.
2 Cor. 3. 18, *b.* as in a glass.
See Num. 24. 17; Ps. 91. 8; 119. 37.

BEHOVED. Lu. 24. 46; Heb. 2. 17.

BELIEF. 2 Thess. 2. 13.

BELIEVE. Num. 14. 11, how long ere they *b.* me.
2 Chron. 20. 20, *b.* Lord, *b.* prophets.
Ps. 78. 22, they *b.* not in God.
Prov. 14. 15, simple *b.* every word.
Mat. 8. 13, as thou hast *b.* so be it.
9. 28, *b.* ye that I am able.
21. 25; Mk. 11. 31, why then did ye not *b.*
27. 42, come down and we will *b.*
Mk. 5. 36; Lu. 8. 50, only *b.*
9. 23, canst *b.* all things possible.
11. 24, *b.* that ye receive.
16. 13, neither *b.* they them.
Lu. 1. 1, things most surely *b.*
8. 13, which for a while *b.*
24. 25, slow of heart to *b.*
41, *b.* not for joy.
John 1. 7, all through him might *b.*
2. 22, they *b.* the scripture.
3. 12, *b.* heavenly things.
5. 44, how can ye *b.* which receive honour.

John 5. 47, how shall ye *b.* my words.
6. 36, seen me and *b.* not.
7. 5, neither did his brethren *b.*
48, have any of the rulers *b.*?
10. 38, *b.* the works.
11. 15, to intent ye may *b.*
26, never die, *b.* thou this?
48, all men will *b.*
12. 36, *b.* in the light.
17. 21, the world may *b.*
20. 25, I will not *b.*
29, have not seen yet have *b.*
Acts 4. 32, multitude of them that *b.*
13. 39, all that *b.* are justified.
48, ordained to eternal life *b.*
16. 34, *b.* with all his house.
Rom. 4. 11, father of all that *b.*
18, against hope *b.* in hope.
9. 33, *b.* not ashamed.
10. 14, how shall they *b.*
1 Cor. 7. 12, wife that *b.* not.
2 Cor. 4. 13, we *b.* and therefore speak.
Gal. 3. 22, promise to them that *b.*
2 Thess. 1. 10, admired in all that *b.*
Heb. 10. 39, *b.* to saving of soul.
11. 6, must *b.* that he is.
Jas. 2. 19, devils *b.* and tremble.
1 Pet. 2. 6, he that *b.* shall not be confounded.
See Ex. 4. 5; 19. 9; Isa. 43. 10; Mat. 21. 22; John 8. 24; 10. 37; Acts 9. 26.

BELLY. Gen. 3. 14; Job 15. 2; Mat. 15. 17; Mk. 7. 19; John 7. 38; Rom. 16. 18; Phil. 3. 19; Tit. 1. 12.

BELONGETH. Deut. 32. 35; Ps. 94. 1; Heb. 10. 30.

BELOVED. Deut. 33. 12, *b.* dwell in safety.
Ps. 127. 2, giveth his *b.* sleep.
Dan. 9. 23; 10. 11, 19, greatly *b.*
Mat. 3. 17; 17. 5; Mk. 1. 11; 9. 7; Lu. 3. 22; 9. 35; 2 Pet. 1. 17, *b.* son.
Rom. 11. 28, *b.* for fathers' sakes.
Eph. 1. 6, accepted in the *b.*
Col. 4. 9; Philem. 16, *b.* brother.
See Neh. 13. 26; Cant. 2. 16; Rom. 16. 9.

BEMOAN. Job 42. 11; Jer. 15. 5; Nah. 3. 7.

BEND. Ps. 11. 2; Isa. 60. 14; Ezek. 17. 7.

BENEATH. Prov. 15. 24, depart from hell *b.*
Isa. 14. 9, hell from *b.* is moved.
John 8. 23, ye are from *b.*
See Deut. 4. 39; Jer. 31. 37.

BENEFACTORS. Lu. 22. 25.

BENEFIT. Ps. 68. 19, loadeth us with *b.*
1 Tim. 6. 2, partakers of the *b.*
See 2 Chron. 32. 25; Ps. 103. 2; 2 Cor. 1. 15; Philem. 14.

BENEVOLENCE. 1 Cor. 7. 3.

BEREAVE. Gen. 42. 36; 43. 14, *b.* of children.
Eccl. 4. 8, *b.* my soul of good.
Jer. 15. 7; 18. 21, I will *b.* thee.
See Ezek. 5. 17; 36. 12; Hos. 13. 8.

BESEECH. Job 42. 4, hear, I *b.* thee.
Mat. 8. 5; Lu. 7. 3, centurion *b.* him.
Lu. 9. 38, I *b.* thee look on my son.
2 Cor. 5. 20, as though God did *b.* you.
Eph. 4. 1, *b.* you to walk.
Philem. 9, for love's sake *b.* thee.
See Ex. 33. 18; Jonah 1. 14; Rom. 12. 1.

BESET. Ps. 22. 12; 139. 5; Hos. 7. 2; Heb. 12. 1.

BESIDE. Mk. 3. 21; Acts 26. 24; 2 Cor. 5. 13.

BESIEGE. Deut. 28. 52; Eccl. 9. 14; Isa. 1. 8.

BESOUGHT. Ex. 32. 11; Deut. 3. 23; 1 Kings 13. 6; 2 Chron. 33. 12; Jer. 26. 19, *b.* the Lord.
Mat. 8. 31; Mk. 5. 10; Lu. 8. 31, devils *b.* him.
34; Lu. 8. 37, *b.* him to depart.
John 4. 40, *b.* that he would tarry.
2 Cor. 12. 8, I *b.* the Lord thrice.
See Gen. 42. 21; Esth. 8. 3.

BEST. 1 Sam. 15. 9, 15, spared *b.* of sheep.

Ps. 39. 5, at *b.* state vanity.
Lu. 15. 22, *b.* robe.
1 Cor. 12. 31, *b.* gifts.
See Gen. 43. 11 ; Deut. 23. 16 ; 2 Sam. 18. 4.
BESTEAD. Isa. 8. 21.
BESTIR. 2 Sam. 5. 24.
BESTOW. Lu. 12. 17, no room to *b.* my fruits.
1 Cor. 15. 10, grace *b.* on us not in vain.
Gal. 4. 11, lest I have *b.* labour in vain.
1 John 3. 1, manner of love Father *b.*
See 1 Chron. 29. 25 ; Isa. 63. 7 ; John 4. 38.
BETHINK. 1 Kings 8. 47 ; 2 Chron. 6. 37.
BETIMES. Gen. 26. 31 ; 2 Chron. 36. 15 ; Job 8. 5 ;
    Prov. 13. 24.
BETRAY. Mat. 26. 16 ; Mk. 14. 11 ; Lu. 22. 21, 22,
    opportunity to *b.*
    27. 4, I *b.* innocent blood.
1 Cor. 11. 23, same night he was *b.*
See Mat. 24. 10 ; Mk. 14. 18 ; John 6. 64 ; 21. 20.
BETROTH. Hos. 2. 19, 20.
BETTER. 1 Sam. 15. 22, to obey *b.* than sacrifice.
1 Kings 19. 4, I am not *b.* than my fathers.
Ps. 63. 3, lovingkindness *b.* than life.
Eccl. 4. 9, two are *b.* than one.
    7. 10, former days *b.* than these.
Mat. 12. 12, man *b.* than a sheep.
Lu. 5. 39, he saith the old is *b.*
Phil. 2. 3, each esteem other *b.* than himself.
Heb. 1. 4, much *b.* than angels.
    11. 16, a *b.* country.
2 Pet. 2. 21, *b.* not have known the way.
See Eccl. 2. 24 ; Cant. 1. 2 ; Jonah 4. 3.
BEWAIL. Lu. 8. 52, all wept and *b.* her.
Lu. 23. 27, of women which also *b.*
2 Cor. 12. 21, *b.* many who have sinned.
See Deut. 21. 13 ; Judg. 11. 37 ; Rev. 18. 9.
BEWARE. Judg. 13. 4, *b.* and drink not wine.
Job 36. 18, *b.* lest he take thee away.
Mat. 16. 6 ; Mk. 8. 15 ; Lu. 12. 1, *b.* of leaven.
Mk. 12. 38 ; Lu. 20. 46, *b.* of scribes.
Lu. 12. 15, *b.* of covetousness.
Phil. 3. 2, *b.* of dogs, *b.* of evil workers.
See Deut. 6. 12 ; 8. 11 ; 15. 9.
BEWITCHED. Acts 8. 9 ; Gal. 3. 1.
BEWRAY. Isa. 16. 3 ; Prov. 27. 16 ; 29. 24 ; Mat.
    26. 73.
BEYOND. Num. 22. 18 ; 2 Cor. 8. 3 ; Gal. 1. 13 ;
    1 Thess. 4. 6.
BIER. 2 Sam. 3. 31 ; Lu. 7. 14.
BILLOWS. Ps. 42. 7 ; Jonah 2. 3.
BIND. Prov. 6. 21, *b.* them continually upon heart.
Isa. 61. 1, *b.* up brokenhearted.
Mat. 12. 29 ; Mk. 3. 27, *b.* strong man.
    16. 19 ; 18. 18, *b.* on earth.
See Num. 30. 2 ; Job 26. 8 ; 38. 31.
BIRD. 2 Sam. 21. 10, suffered not *b.* to rest.
Cant. 2. 12, time of the singing of *b.*
Jer. 12. 9, heritage like a speckled *b.*
Mat. 8. 20 ; Lu. 9. 58, *b.* of air have nests.
See Ps. 11. 1 ; 124. 7 ; Prov. 1. 17 ; Eccl. 10. 20.
BIRTH. John 9. 1, blind from *b.*
Gal. 4. 19, of whom I travail in *b.*
See Eccl. 7. 1 ; Isa. 66. 9 ; Lu. 1. 14.
BIRTHDAYS. Gen. 40. 20, whic'1 was Pharaoh's *b.*
Mat. 14. 6 ; Mk. 6. 21, when Herod's *b.* was kept.
BIRTHRIGHT. Gen. 25. 31 ; 27. 36 ; Heb. 12. 16.
BISHOP (qualifications of). 1 Tim. 3. 1, if a man
    desire office of *b.*
Tit. 1. 7, *b.* must be blameless.
1 Pet. 2. 25, Shepherd and *B.* of your souls.
See Acts 1. 20 ; Phil. 1. 1.
BIT. Ps. 32. 9 ; Jas. 3. 3.
BITE. Prov. 23. 32, at last it *b.* like serpent.
Mic. 3. 5, prophets that *b.* with teeth.
Gal. 5. 15, if ye *b.* and devour one another.
See Eccl. 10. 8 ; Amos 5. 19 ; 9. 3.

BITTER. Ex. 12. 8 ; Num. 9. 11, with *b.* herbs.
Deut. 32. 24, devoured with *b.* destruction.
Job 13. 26, writest *b.* things.
Isa. 5. 20, that put *b.* for sweet.
    24. 9, drink *b.* to them that drink it.
Jer. 2. 19, an evil thing and *b.*
Mat. 26. 75 ; Lu. 22. 62, Peter wept *b.*
Col. 3. 19, be not *b.* against them.
See Ex. 1. 14 ; 15. 23 ; 2 Kings 14. 26.
BITTERNESS. Job 10. 1 ; 21. 25 ; Isa. 38. 15, in *b.*
    of soul.
Prov. 14. 10, heart knoweth own *b.*
Acts 8. 23, in the gall of *b.*
Eph. 4. 31, let all *b.* be put away.
Heb. 12. 15, lest any root of *b.*
See 1 Sam. 15. 32 ; Prov. 17. 25 ; Rom. 3. 14.
BLACK. Mat. 5. 36 ; Jude 13 ; Rev. 6. 5.
BLADE. Judg. 3. 22 ; Mat. 13. 26 ; Mk. 4. 28.
BLAME. 2 Cor. 6. 3 ; 8. 20 ; Gal. 2. 11 ; Eph. 1. 4.
BLAMELESS. 1 Cor. 1. 8, be *b.* in day of the Lord.
Phil. 2. 15, that ye may be *b.*
See Mat. 12. 5 ; Phil. 3. 6 ; Tit. 1. 6, 7.
BLASPHEME. 2 Sam. 12. 14, occasion to enemies
    to *b.*
Isa. 52. 5, my name continually is *b.*
Mat. 9. 3, scribes said, this man *b.*
Mk. 3. 29, *b.* against Holy Ghost.
Acts 26. 11, I compelled them to *b.*
Rom. 2. 24, name of God is *b.* through you.
Jas. 2. 7, *b.* that worthy name.
See 1 Kings 21. 10 ; Ps. 74. 10, 18 ; 1 Tim. 1. 20.
BLASPHEMY. Mat. 12. 31, all manner of *b.*
    26. 65 ; Mk. 14. 64, he hath spoken *b.*
Lu. 5. 21, who is this which speaketh *b.* ?
See 2 Kings 19. 3 ; Ezek. 35. 12 ; Mat. 15. 19.
BLAST. Gen. 41. 6 ; Deut. 28. 22 ; 1 Kings 8. 37.
BLAZE. Mk. 1. 45.
BLEATING. Judg. 5. 16 ; 1 Sam. 15. 14.
BLEMISH. Dan. 1. 4, children in whom was no *b.*
Eph. 5. 27, holy and without *b.*
1 Pet. 1. 19, a lamb without *b.* and spot.
See Lev. 21. 17 ; Deut. 15. 21 ; 2 Sam. 14. 25.
BLESS. Deut. 28. 3, *b.* in city, *b.* in field.
1 Chron. 4. 10, Oh that thou wouldest *b.* me.
Prov. 10. 7, memory of just is *b.*
Isa. 32. 20, *b.* are ye that sow.
    65. 16, *b.* himself in God of truth.
Mat. 5. 44 ; Lu. 6. 28 ; Rom. 12. 14, *b.* them that
    curse.
Acts 20. 35, more *b.* to give than receive.
2 Cor. 11. 31, *b.* for evermore.
Tit. 2. 13, looking for that *b.* hope.
Rev. 14. 13, *b.* are dead that die in Lord.
See Gen. 22. 17 ; Hag. 2. 19 ; Jas. 3. 9, 10.
BLESSING. Deut. 23. 5 ; Neh. 13. 2, turned curse
    into *b.*
Job 29. 13, *b.* of him that was ready to perish.
Prov. 10. 22, *b.* of Lord maketh rich.
    28. 20, faithful man shall abound with *b.*
Isa. 65. 8, destroy it not, a *b.* is in it.
Mal. 2. 2, I will curse your *b.*
    3. 10, pour you out a *b.*
Rom. 15. 29, fulness of *b.* of Gospel.
1 Cor. 10. 16, cup of *b.* which we bless.
Jas. 3. 10, proceed *b.* and cursing.
Rev. 5. 12, worthy to receive honour and *b.*
See Gen. 27. 35 ; 39. 5 ; Deut. 11. 26, 29.
BLIND (*v.*). Ex. 23. 8, the gift *b.* the wise.
2 Cor. 3. 14 ; 4. 4, their minds were *b.*
1 John 2. 11, darkness hath *b.*
See Deut. 16. 19 ; 1 Sam. 12. 3.
BLINDNESS. Eph. 4. 18, because of *b.* of the
    heart.
See Deut. 28. 28 ; 2 Kings 6. 18 ; Zech. 12. 4.
BLOOD. Gen. 9. 6, whoso sheddeth man's *b.*
Josh. 2. 19 ; 1 Kings 2. 32, *b.* on head.
Ps. 51. 14, deliver me from *b.*-guiltiness.
    72. 14, precious shall *b.* be in his sight.

Prov. 29. 10, the *b.*-thirsty hate upright.
Isa. 9. 5, garments rolled in *b.*
Jer. 2. 34, the *b.* of poor innocents.
Ezek. 9. 9, land is full of *b.*
18. 13; 33. 5, his *b.* be upon him.
Hab. 2. 12, buildeth a town with *b.*
Mat. 9. 20; Mk. 5. 25; Lu. 8. 43, issue of *b.*
16. 17, flesh and *b.* hath not revealed.
27. 4, I have betrayed innocent *b.*
25, his *b.* be on us and our children.
Mk. 14. 24; Lu. 22. 20, my *b.* shed.
Lu. 22. 20; 1 Cor. 11. 25, new testament in my *b.*
44, sweat as drops of *b.* falling.
John 1. 13, born not of *b.*
6. 54, 55, 56, drinketh my *b.*
Acts 15. 20; 21. 25, abstain from *b.*
17. 26, made of one *b.*
20. 28, church purchased with his *b.*
Rom. 3. 25, through faith in his *b.*
5. 9, justified by his *b.*
1 Cor. 10. 16, communion of *b.* of Christ.
11. 27, guilty of body and *b.* of the Lord.
15. 50, flesh and *b.* cannot inherit.
Eph. 1. 7; Col. 1. 14, redemption through his *b.*
Heb. 9. 22, without shedding of *b.*
10. 29; 13. 20, *b.* of the covenant.
1 Pet. 1. 19, with precious *b.* of Christ.
Rev. 7. 14; 12. 11, in the *b.* of the Lamb.
See Gen. 9. 4; Ex. 4. 9; 12. 13; Lev. 3. 17; Ps. 55. 23; Rev. 16. 6; 17. 6.

BLOSSOM. Isa. 35. 1, desert shall *b.* as the rose.
Hab. 3. 17, fig tree shall not *b.*
See Gen. 40. 10; Num. 17. 5; Isa. 27. 6.

BLOT. Ex. 32. 32; Ps. 69. 28; Rev. 3. 5, *b.* out of book.
Isa. 44. 22, *b.* out as thick cloud.
Acts 3. 19, repent that sins may be *b.* out.
Col. 2. 14, *b.* out handwriting.
See Deut. 9. 14; 2 Kings 14. 27; Jer. 18. 23.

BLUSH. Ezra 9. 6; Jer. 6. 15; 8. 12.

BOAST (*n.*). Ps. 34. 2; Rom. 2. 17, 23; 3. 27.

BOAST (*v.*). 1 Kings 20. 11, not *b.* as he that putteth it off.
Ps. 49. 6; 91. 4, *b.* themselves.
Prov. 27. 1, *b.* not of to-morrow.
2 Cor. 11. 16, that I may *b.* myself a little.
Eph. 2. 9, lest any man should *b.*
Jas. 3. 5, tongue *b.* great things.
See 2 Chron. 25. 19; Prov. 20. 14; Jas. 4. 16.

BOATS. John 6. 22; Acts 27. 16, 30.

BODY. Job 19. 26, worms destroy this *b.*
Prov. 5. 11, when thy flesh and *b.* are consumed.
Mat. 5. 29, *b.* cast into hell.
6. 22; Lu. 11. 34, *b.* full of light.
25; Lu. 12. 22, take no thought for *b.*
Mk. 5. 29, felt in *b.* that she was healed.
Lu. 17. 37, wheresoever the *b.* is.
John 2. 21, the temple of his *b.*
Acts 19. 12, from his *b.* were brought.
Rom. 6. 6, *b.* of sin destroyed.
7. 24, *b.* of this death.
12. 1, present your *b.* a living sacrifice.
4; 1 Cor. 12. 14, many members, one *b.*
1 Cor. 9. 27, I keep under my *b.*
13. 3, though I give my *b.* to be burned.
2 Cor. 5. 8, absent from the *b.*
12. 2, whether in *b.* or out of the *b.*
Gal. 6. 17, I bear in *b.* marks.
Phil. 3. 21, like to his glorious *b.*
1 Pet. 2. 24, in his own *b.* on tree.
See Gen. 47. 18; Deut. 28. 4; Rom. 12. 5.

BODILY. Lu. 3. 22; 2 Cor. 10. 10; Col. 2. 9; 1 Tim. 4. 8.

BOLD. Eccl. 8. 1, the *b.* of face changed.
John 7. 26, he speaketh *b.*
2 Cor. 10. 2, I may not be *b.*
Eph. 3. 12, we have *b.* and access.
Heb. 4. 16, let us come *b.* to throne.

1 John 4. 17, have *b.* in day of judgment.
See Prov. 28. 1; Acts 13. 46; Rom. 10. 20.

BOND. Acts 8. 23, in *b.* of iniquity.
Eph. 4. 3, *b.* of peace.
Col. 3. 14, *b.* of perfectness.
See Num. 30. 2; Ezek. 20. 37; Lu. 13. 16.

BONDAGE. John 8. 33, never in *b.* to any man.
See Rom. 8. 15; Gal. 5. 1; Heb. 2. 15.

BONDMAID. Lev. 19. 20, a woman that is a *b.*
25. 44, and thy *b.*

BONDMAN. Deut. 15. 15; 16. 12; 24. 18.

BONDMEN. Lev. 25. 39, both thy *b.*

BONDWOMAN. Gen. 21. 10; Gal. 4. 30.

BONE. Ex. 12. 46; Num. 9. 12, neither shall ye break a *b.* thereof.
Job 20. 11, *b.* full of sin.
40. 18, *b.* as pieces of brass.
Ps. 51. 8, the *b.* broken may rejoice.
Prov. 12. 4, as rottenness in his *b.*
Mat. 23. 27, full of dead men's *b.*
Lu. 24. 39, spirit hath not flesh and *b.*
See Gen. 2. 23; Ezek. 37. 7; John 19. 36.

BOOK. Job 19. 23, printed in a *b.*
31. 35, adversary had written a *b.*
Isa. 34. 16, seek out of the *b.* of the Lord.
Mal. 3. 16, *b.* of remembrance.
John 21. 25, world could not contain *b.*
Phil. 4. 3; Rev. 3. 5; 13. 8; 17. 8; 20. 12; 21. 27; 22. 19, *b.* of life.
Rev. 22. 19, take away from words of *b.*
See Ex. 17. 14; Ezra 4. 15; Acts 19. 19; 2 Tim. 4. 13.

BOOTH. Job 27. 18; Jonah 4. 5.

BOOTHS. Lev. 23. 42, ye shall dwell in *b.*
Neh. 8. 14, Israel shall dwell in *b.*

BOOTY. Num. 31. 32; Jer. 49. 32; Hab. 2. 7; Zeph. 1. 13.

BORN. Job 5. 7, man *b.* to trouble.
14. 1; 15. 14; 25. 4; Mat. 11. 11, *b.* of a woman.
Ps. 87. 4, this man was *b.* there.
Isa. 9. 6, unto us a child is *b.*
66. 8, shall a nation be *b.* at once.
John 3. 3; 1 Pet. 1. 23, *b.* again.
6, 8, *b.* of Spirit.
1 Cor. 15. 8, as one *b.* out of due time.
1 Pet. 2. 2, as new-*b.* babes.
John 1. 13; 1 John 4. 7; 5. 1, 4, 18, *b.* of God.
See Job 3. 3; Prov. 17. 17; Eccl. 3. 2.

BORNE. Ps. 55. 12, an enemy, then I could have *b.* it.
Isa. 53. 4, *b.* our griefs, carried our sorrows.
Mat. 23. 4; Lu. 11. 46, grievous to be *b.*
See Job 34. 31; Lam. 5. 7; Mat. 20. 12.

BORROW. Deut. 15. 6; 28. 12, lend but not *b.*
Ps. 37. 21, wicked *b.* and payeth not.
Prov. 22. 7, the *b.* is servant.
Mat. 5. 42, him that would *b.* of thee.
See Ex. 3. 22; 11. 2; 22. 14; 2 Kings 4. 3.

BOSOM. Ps. 35. 13, prayer returned into own *b.*
Prov. 6. 27, take fire in his *b.*
Isa. 40. 11, carry lambs in *b.*
Lu. 16. 22, carried into Abraham's *b.*
John 1. 18, in the *b.* of the Father.
13. 23, leaning on Jesus' *b.*
See Ex. 4. 6; Deut. 13. 6; Job 31. 33.

BOSSES. Job 15. 26.

BOTCH. Deut. 28. 27, 35.

BOTTLE. Judg. 4. 19, a *b.* of milk
1 Sam. 1. 24; 10. 3; 16. 20; 2 Sam. 16. 1, a *b.* of wine.
Ps. 56. 8, put thou my tears into thy *b.*
119. 83, like a *b.* in the smoke.
See Gen. 21. 14, 15; Hab. 2. 15.

BOTTLES. Josh. 9. 13, these *b.* of wine.
1 Sam. 25. 18, and two *b.* of wine.
Hos. 7. 5, sick with *b.* of wine.

Job 32. 19, ready to burst like new *b.*
Mat. 9. 17 ; Mk. 2. 22 ; Lu. 5. 37, new wine in old *b.*
BOTTOMLESS. Rev. 9. 1 ; 11. 7 ; 17. 8 ; 20. 1, 2, the
　　b. pit.
BOUGH. Gen. 49. 22 ; Judg. 9. 48 ; Deut. 24. 20 ;
　　Job 14. 9 ; Ps. 80. 10 ; Ezek. 31. 30.
BOUGHT. Lu. 14. 18 ; 1 Cor. 6. 20 ; 7. 23 ; 2 Pet. 2. 1.
BOUND. Ps. 107. 10, being *b.* in affliction.
　　Prov. 22. 15, foolishness *b.* in heart of child.
　　Acts 20. 22, *b.* in spirit to Jerusalem.
　　1 Cor. 7. 27, art thou *b.* to a wife.
　　2 Tim. 2. 9, word of God is not *b.*
　　Heb. 13. 3, in bonds as *b.* with them.
　　See Gen. 44. 30 ; Mat. 16. 19 ; Mk. 5. 4.
BOUNTY. 1 Kings 10. 13 ; 2 Cor. 9. 5.
BOUNTIFUL. Prov. 22. 9, a *b.* eye shall be blessed.
　　Isa. 32. 5, nor churl said to be *b.*
　　See Ps. 13. 6 ; 116. 7 ; 119. 17 ; 2 Cor. 9. 6.
BOWELS. Gen. 43. 30, his *b.* did yearn.
　　Isa. 63. 15, where is sounding of thy *b.*
　　2 Cor. 6. 12, straitened in *b.*
　　Col. 3. 12, *b.* of mercies.
　　Phil. 1. 8, after you in *b.* of Christ.
　　2. 1, if there be any *b.*
　　1 John 3. 17, *b.* of compassion.
　　See Acts 1. 18 ; Philem. 12.
BOWLS. Num. 7. 25, one silver *b.*
　　Eccl. 12. 6, golden *b.* be broken.
　　Amos 6. 6, that drink wine in *b.*
　　Zech. 4. 2, with a *b.* upon the top of it.
BRACELET. Gen. 24. 30 ; Ex. 35. 22 ; Isa. 3. 19.
BRAKE. 2 Kings 23. 14 ; 2 Chron. 34. 4, Josiah *b.*
　　images.
　　Mat. 14. 19 ; 15. 36 ; 26. 26 ; Mk. 6. 41 ; 8. 6 ; 14. 22 ;
　　Lu. 9. 16 ; 22. 19 ; 24. 30 ; 1 Cor. 11. 24, blessed
　　and *b.*
　　See Ex. 32. 19 ; 1 Sam. 4. 18 ; Lu. 5. 6 ; John 19. 32.
BRAMBLE. Judg. 9. 14 ; Isa. 34. 13 ; Lu. 6. 44.
BRANCH. Job 14. 7, tender *b.* not cease.
　　Prov. 11. 28, righteous flourish as *b.*
　　Jer. 23. 5, will raise a righteous *b.*
　　Mat. 13. 32 ; Lu. 13. 19, birds lodge in *b.*
　　21. 8 ; Mk. 11. 8 ; John 12. 13, cut down *b.*
　　See Zech. 3. 8 ; 6. 12 ; John 15. 2, 4, 5, 6 ; Rom. 11.
　　16.
BRAND. Judg. 15. 5, set the *b.* on fire.
　　Zech. 3. 2, as a fire *b.* plucked out.
BRASS. Deut. 8. 9 ; 28. 23 ; 1 Cor. 13. 1.
BRAVERY. Isa. 3. 18.
BRAWLER. Prov. 25. 24 ; 1 Tim. 3. 3 ; Tit. 3. 2.
BRAY. Job 6. 5 ; 30. 7 ; Prov. 27. 22.
BREACH. Isa. 58. 12, the repairer of the *b.*
　　Lam. 2. 13, thy *b.* is great like the sea.
　　See Lev. 24. 20 ; Ps. 106. 23 ; Amos 4. 3 ; 6. 11.
BREAD. Deut. 8. 3 ; Mat. 4. 4 ; Lu. 4. 4, not live
　　by *b.* alone.
　　Ruth 1. 6, visited people in giving them *b.*
　　1 Kings 17. 6, ravens brought *b.* and flesh.
　　Job 22. 7, withholden *b.* from hungry.
　　33. 20, soul abhorreth *b.*
　　Ps. 132. 15, satisfy poor with *b.*
　　Prov. 9. 17, *b.* eaten in secret.
　　12. 11 ; 20. 13 ; 28. 19, satisfied with *b.*
　　31. 27, eateth not *b.* of idleness.
　　Eccl. 11. 1, cast *b.* on waters.
　　Isa. 33. 16, *b.* given and waters sure.
　　55. 2, money for that which is not *b.*
　　10, seed to sower, *b.* to eater.
　　Mat. 4. 3 ; Lu. 4. 3, stones made *b.*
　　6. 11 ; Lu. 11. 3, give us daily *b.*
　　15. 26 ; Mk. 7. 27, take children's *b.*
　　Lu. 24. 35, known in breaking *b.*
　　Acts 2. 42 ; 20. 7 ; 27. 35, breaking *b.*
　　2 Thess. 3. 8, eat any man's *b.* for nought.
　　See Ex. 16. 4 ; 23. 25 ; Josh. 9. 5 ; Judg. 7. 13.
BREAK. Cant. 2. 17 ; 4. 6, day *b.* and shadows flee.
　　Isa. 42. 3 ; Mat. 12. 20, bruised reed shall he not *b.*

Jer. 4. 3 ; Hos. 10. 12, *b.* up fallow ground.
Acts 21. 13, to weep and *b.* my heart.
See Ps. 2. 3 ; Mat. 5. 19 ; 9. 17 ; 1 Cor. 10. 16.
BREATH. Gen. 2. 7 ; 6. 17 ; 7. 15, *b.* of life.
　　Isa. 2. 22, cease from man whose *b.*
　　Ezek. 37. 5, 10, I will cause *b.* to enter.
　　Acts 17. 25, he giveth to all life and *b.*
　　See Job 12. 10 ; 33. 4 ; Ps. 146. 4 ; 150. 6.
BREATHE. Ps. 27. 12 ; Ezek. 37. 9 ; John 20. 22.
BREECHES. Ex. 28. 42 ; Lev. 6. 10 ; 16. 4 ; Ezek.
　　44. 18.
BRETHREN. Mat. 23. 8, all ye are *b.*
　　Mk. 10. 29 ; Lu. 18. 29, no man left house or *b.*
　　Col. 1. 2, faithful *b.* in Christ.
　　1 John 3. 14, because we love the *b.*
　　See Gen. 42. 8 ; Prov. 19. 7 ; John 7. 5.
BRIBE. 1 Sam. 12. 3, have I received any *b.*
　　Ps. 26. 10, right hand is full of *b.*
　　See 1 Sam. 8. 3 ; Isa. 33. 15 ; Job 15. 34.
BRICK. Gen. 11. 3 ; Ex. 1. 14 ; 5. 7 ; Isa. 9. 10 ; 65. 3.
BRIDE. Isa. 61. 10 ; Jer. 2. 32 ; Rev. 21. 2 ; 22. 17.
BRIDEGROOM. Mat. 25. 1, to meet the *b.*
　　John 3. 29, because of *b.* voice.
　　See Ps. 19. 5 ; Isa. 62. 5 ; Mat. 9. 15.
BRIDLE. Prov. 26. 3, a *b.* for the ass.
　　Jas. 1. 26, *b.* not his tongue.
　　3. 2, able to *b.* whole body.
　　See 2 Kings 19. 28 ; Ps. 39. 1 ; Isa. 37. 29.
BRIGANDINE. Jer. 46. 4 ; 51. 3.
BRIGHT. Job 37. 21, *b.* light in the clouds.
　　Isa. 60. 3, to *b.* of thy rising.
　　62. 1, righteousness go forth as *b.*
　　Mat. 17. 5, *b.* cloud overshadowed.
　　2 Thess. 2. 8, *b.* of his coming.
　　Heb. 1. 3, the *b.* of his glory.
　　Rev. 22. 16, the *b.* and morning star.
　　See Lev. 13. 2 ; Jer. 51. 11 ; Zech. 10. 1.
BRIMSTONE. Gen. 19. 24, rained upon Sodom
　　and Gomorrah *b.*
　　Isa. 30. 33, like a stream of *b.*
　　Rev. 9. 17, issued fire and *b.*
　　14. 10, tormented with fire and *b.*
　　19. 20, a lake of fire and *b.*
BRINK. Gen. 41. 3 ; Ex. 2. 3 ; 7. 15 ; Josh. 3. 8.
BROAD. Ps. 119. 96 ; Mat. 7. 13 ; 23. 5.
BROIDED. 1 Tim. 2. 9.
BROIDERED. Ezek. 16. 10, 13 ; 27. 7, 16, 24, *b.* work.
　　See Ex. 28. 4.
BROILED. Lu. 24. 42.
BROKEN. Ps. 34. 18 ; 51. 17 ; 69. 20, *b.* heart.
　　John 10. 35, scripture cannot be *b.*
　　19. 36, bone shall not be *b.*
　　Eph. 2. 14, *b.* down middle wall.
　　See Job 17. 11 ; Prov. 25. 19 ; Jer. 2. 13.
BROOD. Lu. 13. 34.
BROOK. 1 Sam. 17. 40 ; Ps. 42. 1 ; 110. 7.
BROTH. Judg. 6. 19 ; Isa. 65. 4.
BROTHER. Prov. 17. 17, *b.* born for adversity.
　　18. 9, slothful *b.* to waster.
　　19, *b.* offended harder to be won.
　　24, friend closer than *b.*
　　Eccl. 4. 8, neither child nor *b.*
　　Mat. 10. 21, *b.* shall deliver up *b.*
　　1 Cor. 6. 6, *b.* goeth to law with *b.*
　　2 Thess. 3. 15, admonish as *b.*
　　See Gen. 4. 9 ; Mat. 5. 23 ; 12. 50 ; Mk. 3. 35.
BROTHERLY. Rom. 12. 10 ; 1 Thess. 4. 9 ; Heb.
　　13. 1, *b.* love.
　　See Amos 1. 9 ; 2 Pet. 1. 7.
BROW. Isa. 48. 4 ; Lu. 4. 29.
BRUISE (*n.*). Isa. 1. 6 ; Jer. 30. 12 ; Nah. 3. 19.
BRUISE (*v.*). Gen. 3. 15, staff of this *b.* reed.
　　Isa. 42. 3 ; Mat. 12. 20, *b.* reed shall he not break.
　　53. 5, *b.* for our iniquities.
　　See Gen. 3. 15 ; Isa. 53. 10 ; Rom. 16. 20.
BRUIT. Jer. 10. 22 ; Nah. 3. 19.

BRUTISH. Ps. 92. 6, a *b.* man knoweth not.
Prov. 30. 2, I am more *b.* than any.
Jer. 10. 21, pastors are become *b.*
See Ps. 49. 10; Jer. 10. 8; Ezek. 21. 31.

BUCKET. Num. 24. 7; Isa. 40. 15.

BUCKLER. 2 Sam. 22. 31; Ps. 18. 2; 91. 4; Prov. 2. 7.

BUD. Num. 17. 8; Isa. 18. 5; 61. 11; Hos. 8. 7.

BUFFET. Mat. 26. 67; 1 Cor. 4. 11; 2 Cor. 12. 7; 1 Pet. 2. 20.

BUILD. Ps. 127. 1, labour in vain that *b.*
Eccl. 3. 3, a time to *b.* up.
Isa. 58. 12, *b.* old waste places.
Mat. 7. 24; Lu. 6. 48, wise man *b.* on rock.
Lu. 14. 30, began to *b.*, not able to finish.
Acts 20. 32, able to *b.* you up.
Rom. 15. 20, lest I *b.* on another.
1 Cor. 3. 12, if any *b.* on this foundation.
Eph. 2. 22, in whom ye are *b.* together.
See 1 Chron. 17. 12; 2 Chron. 6. 9; Eccl. 2. 4.

BUILDER. Ps. 118. 22; Mat. 21. 42; Mk. 12. 10; Lu. 20. 17; Acts 4. 11; 1 Pet. 2. 7, *b.* refused.
1 Cor. 3. 10, as a wise master-*b.*
Heb. 11. 10, whose *b.* and maker is God.
See 1 Kings 5. 18; Ezra 3. 10.

BUILDING. 1 Cor. 3. 9; 2 Cor. 5. 1; Eph. 2. 21; Col. 2. 7.

BULRUSH. Ex. 2. 3; Isa. 18. 2; 58. 5.

BULWARK. Isa. 26. 1, salvation for walls and *b.*
See Deut. 20. 20; Ps. 48. 13; Eccl. 9. 14.

BUNDLE. Gen. 42. 35; 1 Sam. 25. 29; Mat. 13. 30; Acts 28. 3.

BURDEN. Ps. 55. 22, cast thy *b.* on the Lord.
Eccl. 12. 5, grasshopper shall be a *b.*
Mat. 11. 30, my *b.* is light.
20. 12, borne *b.* and heat of day.
23. 4; Lu. 11. 46, bind heavy *b.*
Gal. 6. 2, 5, bear his own *b.*
See Num. 11. 11; Acts 15. 28; 2 Cor. 12. 16.

BURDENSOME. Zech. 12. 3; 2 Cor. 11. 9; 1 Thess. 2. 6.

BURIAL. Eccl. 6. 3; Jer. 22. 19; Mat. 26. 12; Acts 8. 2.

BURN. Ps. 39. 3, musing the fire *b.*
Prov. 26. 23, *b.* lips and wicked heart.
Isa. 9. 18, wickedness *b.* as fire.
33. 14, dwell with everlasting *b.*
Mal. 4. 1, day that shall *b.* as oven.
Mat. 13. 30, bind tares to *b.* them.
Lu. 3. 17, chaff *b.* with fire unquenchable.
12. 35, loins girded and lights *b.*
24. 32, did not our heart *b.*
John 5. 35, he was a *b.* and shining light
1 Cor. 13. 3, give my body to be *b.*
Heb. 6. 8, whose end is to be *b.*
Rev. 4. 5, lamps *b.* before throne.
19. 20, into a lake *b.*
See Gen. 44. 18; Ex. 3. 2; 21. 25.

BURNT-OFFERING. Ps. 40. 6, *b.* thou hast not required.
Isa. 61. 8, I hate robbery for *b.*
Jer. 6. 20, your *b.* not acceptable.
Hos. 6. 6, knowledge more than *b.*
Mk. 12. 33, love neighbour more than *b.*
See Gen. 22. 7; Lev. 1. 4; 6. 9.

BURST. Job 32. 19; Prov. 3. 10; Mk. 2. 22; Lu. 5. 37.

BURY. Mat. 8. 21; Lu. 9. 59, suffer me to *b.* my father.
22; Lu. 9. 60, let dead *b.* dead.
John 19. 40, manner of the Jews is to *b.*
Rom. 6. 4; Col. 2. 12, *b.* with him by baptism.
1 Cor. 15. 4, he was *b.* and rose again.
See Gen. 23. 4; 47. 29; Mat. 14. 12.

BUSHEL. Mat. 5. 15; Mk. 4. 21; Lu. 11. 38.

BUSINESS. 1 Sam. 21. 8, king's *b.* requireth haste.
Ps. 107. 23, do *b.* in great waters.

Prov. 22. 29, diligent in *b.*
Lu. 2. 49, about my Father's *b.*
Rom. 12. 11, not slothful in *b.*
1 Thess. 4. 11, study to do your own *b.*
See Josh. 2. 14; Judg. 18. 7; Neh. 13. 30.

BUSYBODIES. 2 Thess. 3. 11, but are *b.*
1 Tim. 5. 13, tattlers also and *b.*
1 Pet. 4. 15, *b.* in other men's matters.
See Prov. 20. 3; 26. 17; 1 Thess. 4. 11.

BUTLER. Gen. 40. 1; 41. 9.

BUTTER. Isa. 7. 15, 22, *b.* and honey shall he eat.
See Judg. 5. 25; Job 29. 6; Ps. 55. 21; Prov. 30. 33.

BUY. Lev. 22. 11, *b.* any soul with money.
Prov. 23. 23, *b.* the truth.
Isa. 55. 1, *b.* and eat, *b.* wine and milk.
Mat. 25. 9, go to them that sell and *b.*
John 4. 8, disciples were gone to *b.* meat.
Jas. 4. 13, we will *b.* and sell and get gain.
Rev. 3. 18, *b.* of me gold tried.
13. 17, no man *b.* save he that had mark.
18. 11, no man *b.* her merchandise.
See Gen. 42. 2; 47. 19; Ruth 4. 4; Mat. 13. 44.

BUYER. Prov. 20. 14; Isa. 24. 2; Ezek. 7. 12.

BY-AND-BY. Mat. 13. 21; Mk. 6. 25; Lu. 17. 7; 21. 9.

BYWAYS. Judg. 5. 6.

BYWORD. Job 17. 6; 30. 9, a *b.* of the people.
Ps. 44. 14, a *b.* among the heathen.
See Deut. 28. 37; 1 Kings 9. 7; 2 Chron. 7. 20.

C.

CABINS. Jer. 37. 16.

CAGE. Jer. 5. 27; Rev. 18. 2.

CAKE. 2 Sam. 6. 19, to every man a *c.* of bread.
1 Kings 17. 13, to make me a little *c.* first.
See Judg. 7. 13; Jer. 7. 18; 44. 19; Hos. 7. 8.

CALAMITY. Deut. 32. 35; 2 Sam. 22. 19; Ps. 18. 18, day of *c.*
Ps. 57. 1, until *c.* be overpast.
Prov. 1. 26, I will laugh at your *c.*
17. 5, he that is glad at *c.*
19. 13, foolish son *c.* of father.
27. 10, brother's house in day of *c.*
See Job 6. 2; Prov. 24. 22.

CALF. Ex. 32. 4; Isa. 11. 6; Lu. 15. 23.

CALKERS. Ezek. 27. 9, 27.

CALLING. Rom. 11. 29, *c.* of God without repentance.
1 Cor. 7. 20, abide in same *c.*
Eph. 1. 18, the hope of his *c.*
Phil. 3. 14, prize of high *c.*
2 Thess. 1. 11, worthy of this *c.*
2 Tim. 1. 9, called us with holy *c.*
Heb. 3. 1, partakers of heavenly *c.*
2 Pet. 1. 10, make *c.* and election sure.
See Acts 7. 59; 22. 16; 1 Cor. 1. 26.

CALM. Ps. 107. 29; Jonah 1. 11; Mat. 8. 26; Mk. 4. 39; Lu. 8. 24.

CALVES. 1 Kings 12. 28, made two *c.* of gold.
See Hos. 14. 2; Mal. 4. 2.

CAMEL'S HAIR. Mat. 3. 4, raiment of *c.*

CAMELS. Isa. 60. 6, the multitude of *c.* shall cover thee.
Mat. 19. 24, it is easier for a *c.*
23. 24, strain at a gnat, swallow a *c.*
See Gen. 24. 64; Ex. 9. 3; Lev. 11. 4; Deut. 14. 7; 1 Chron. 5. 21; Job 1. 3.

CAMP (*n.*). Ex. 14. 19, angel went before *c.*
16. 13, quails covered the *c.*
Num. 1. 52, every man by his own *c.*
Deut. 23. 14, Lord walketh in midst of *c.*
See 1 Sam. 4. 6, 7; Heb. 13. 13.

CAMP (*v.*). Isa. 29. 3; Jer. 50. 29; Nah. 3. 17.

CANDLE. Job 29. 3, when his *c.* shined upon my head.
Ps. 18. 28, thou wilt light my *c.*

Prov. 20. 27, spirit of man *c.* of the Lord.
Zeph. 1. 12, search Jerusalem with *c.*
Mat. 5. 15 ; Mk. 4. 21 ; Lu. 8. 16; 11. 33, lighted a *c.*
Rev. 18. 23, *c.* shine no more in thee.
22. 5, need no *c.* nor light.
See Job 18. 6 ; 21. 17 ; Prov. 24. 20.
CANDLESTICK. 2 Kings 4. 10, let us set for
  him a *c.*
See Mk. 4. 21; Heb. 9. 2 ; Rev. 2. 5.
CANKERED. 2 Tim. 2. 17 ; Jas. 5. 3.
CAPTIVE. Ex. 12. 29, firstborn of *c.* in dungeon.
Isa. 51. 14, *c.* exile hasteneth.
52. 2, O *c.* daughter of Zion.
2 Tim. 2. 26, taken *c.* at his will.
3. 6, lead *c.* silly women.
See 2 Kings 5. 2 ; Isa. 14. 2 ; 61. 1 ; Lu. 4. 18.
CAPTIVITY. Rom. 7. 23, into *c.* to law of sin.
2 Cor. 10. 5, bringing into *c.* every thought.
See Job 42. 10 ; Ps. 14. 7 ; 85. 1 ; 126. 1.
CARCASE. Isa. 66. 24 ; Mat. 24. 28 ; Heb. 3. 17.
CARE (*n.*). Jer. 49. 31, nation that dwelleth with-
  out *c.*
Mat. 13. 22 ; Mk. 4. 19, *c.* of this world.
Lu. 8. 14 ; 21. 34, choked with *c.*
1 Cor. 9. 9, doth God take *c.* for oxen.
12. 25, have same *c.* one for another.
2 Cor. 11. 28, the *c.* of all the churches.
1 Pet. 5. 7, casting all your *c.* on him.
See 1 Sam. 10. 2 ; 2 Kings 4. 13 ; 2 Cor. 7. 12.
CARE (*v.*). Ps. 142. 4, no man *c.* for my soul.
John 12. 6, not that he *c.* for poor.
Acts 18. 17, Gallio *c.* for none of those things.
Phil. 2. 20, naturally *c.* for your state.
See 2 Sam. 18. 3 ; Lu. 10. 40.
CAREFUL. Jer. 17. 8, not be *c.* in year of drought.
Dan. 3. 16, we are not *c.* to answer.
Lu. 10. 41, thou art *c.* about many things.
Phil. 4. 6, be *c.* for nothing.
Heb. 12. 17, he sought it *c.* with tears.
See 2 Kings 4. 13 ; Phil. 4. 10 ; Tit. 3. 8.
CAREFULNESS. Ezek. 12. 18 ; 1 Cor. 7. 32 ; 2 Cor.
  7. 11.
CARELESS. Judg. 18. 7 ; Isa. 32. 9 ; 47. 8 ; Ezek.
  39. 6.
CARNAL. Rom. 7. 14, *c.*, sold under sin.
8. 7, *c.* mind is enmity.
1 Cor. 3. 1, not speak but as to *c.*
2 Cor. 10. 4, weapons of our warfare not *c.*
See 1 Cor. 9. 11 ; Col. 2. 18 ; Heb. 7. 16 ; 9. 10.
CARPENTER'S SON. Mat. 13. 55 ; Mk. 6. 3, is not
  this the *c.* ?
CARPENTERS. 2 Sam. 5. 11, and cedar trees
  and *c.*
Zech. 1. 20, and the Lord shewed me four *c.*
CARRIAGE. Judg. 18. 21; Isa. 10. 28 ; 46. 1 ; Acts
  21. 15.
CARRY. 1 Kings 18. 12, Spirit of the Lord shall
  c. thee.
Isa. 40. 11, *c.* lambs in his bosom.
53. 4, *c.* our sorrows.
63. 9, *c.* them all days of old.
Ezek. 22. 9, men *c.* tales to shed blood.
Mk. 6. 55, began to *c.* about in beds.
John 5. 10, not lawful to *c.* thy bed.
21. 18, and *c.* thee whither thou wouldest not.
Eph. 4. 14, *c.* about with every wind.
1 Tim. 6. 7, we can *c.* nothing out.
Heb. 13. 9, not *c.* about with divers.
2 Pet. 2. 17, clouds *c.* with a tempest.
Jude 12, clouds *c.* about of winds.
See Ex. 33. 15 ; Num. 11. 12 ; Deut. 14. 24.
CART. Isa. 5. 18, draw sin as with a *c.* rope.
Amos 2. 13, *c.* full of sheaves.
See 1 Sam. 6. 7 ; 2 Sam. 6. 3 ; 1 Chron. 13. 7 ; Isa. 28.
  28.
CASE. Ps. 144. 15, happy people in such a *c.*
Mat. 5. 20, in no *c.* enter heaven.

John 5. 6, long time in that *c.*
See Ex. 5. 19 ; Deut. 19. 4 ; 24. 13.
CASSIA. Ex. 30. 24, of *c.* five hundred shekels.
Ps. 45. 8, thy garments smell of *c.*
CAST. Prov. 16. 33, lot is *c.* into lap.
Mat. 5. 29 ; Mk. 9. 45, whole body *c.* into hell.
Mk. 9. 38 ; Lu. 9. 49, one *c.* out devils.
Lu. 21. 1, *c.* gifts into treasury.
John 8. 7, first *c.* stone at her.
2 Cor. 10. 5, *c.* down imaginations.
1 Pet. 5. 7, *c.* all care upon him.
1 John 4. 18, love *c.* out fear.
See Ps. 76. 6 ; Prov. 26. 18 ; 3 John 10.
CASTAWAY. 1 Cor. 9. 27, lest I be a *c.*
CASTLE. Num. 31. 10 ; Prov. 18. 19 ; Acts 21. 34.
CATCH. Ps. 10. 9, to *c.* the poor.
Mat. 13. 19, devil *c.* away what was sown.
Lu. 5. 10, from henceforth thou shalt *c.* men.
John 10. 12, wolf *c.* and scattereth sheep.
See 2 Kings 7. 12 ; Ezek. 19. 3 ; Mk. 12. 13.
CATTLE. Gen. 46. 32, their trade to feed *c.*
Ex. 10. 26, our *c.* shall go with us.
Deut. 2. 35 ; 3. 7 ; Josh. 8. 2, the *c.* ye shall take
  for prey.
Ps. 50. 10, *c.* upon a thousand hills.
See Gen. 1. 25 ; 30. 43 ; Jonah 4. 11.
CAUGHT. Gen. 22. 13, ram *c.* by horns.
John 21. 3, that night they *c.* nothing.
2 Cor. 12. 2, *c.* up to third heaven.
16, I *c.* you with guile.
1 Thess. 4. 17, be *c.* up together with them.
See 2 Sam. 18. 9 ; Prov. 7. 13 ; Rev. 12. 5.
CAUSE (*n.*). Mat. 19. 5 ; Mk. 10. 7 ; Eph. 5. 31, for
  this *c.* shall a man leave.
1 Cor. 11. 30, for this *c.* many are sickly.
1 Tim. 1. 16, for this *c.* I obtained mercy.
See Prov. 18. 17 ; 2 Cor. 4. 16 ; 5. 13.
CAUSE (*v.*). Ezra 6. 12, God *c.* his name to dwell.
Ps. 67. 1 ; 80. 3, *c.* his face to shine.
Rom. 16. 17, them who *c.* divisions.
See Deut. 1. 38 ; 12. 11 ; Job 6. 24.
CAUSELESS. 1 Sam. 25. 31 ; Prov. 26. 2.
CAVES. 1 Kin. 18. 4, Obadiah hid them by fifty in *c.*
19. 9, and he came thither into a *c.*
Isa. 2. 19, go into a *c.* for fear of the Lord.
See Gen. 19. 30 ; 23. 19 ; 49. 29 ; Josh. 10. 16 ;
  1 Sam. 13. 6 ; 22. 1 ; 24. 10.
CEASE. Deut. 15. 11, poor never *c.* out of land.
Job 3. 17, the wicked *c.* from troubling.
Ps. 46. 9, he maketh wars to *c.*
Prov. 26. 20, strife *c.*
Eccl. 12. 3, grinders *c.* because few.
Acts 20. 31, I *c.* not to warn.
1 Cor. 13. 8, tongues they shall *c.*
1 Thess. 5. 17, pray without *c.*
1 Pet. 4. 1, hath *c.* from sin.
See Gen. 8. 22 ; Isa. 1. 16 ; 2. 22.
CEDAR. 1 Kin. 5. 6, they hew me *c.* trees out
  of Lebanon.
6. 15, with boards of *c.*
Job 40. 17, he moveth his tail like a *c.*
Ps. 92. 12, grow like a *c.* in Lebanon.
CEDARS (of Lebanon). Judg. 9. 15, devour the *c.*
  of Lebanon.
Isa. 2. 13, upon all the *c.* of Lebanon.
See Ps. 104. 16 ; 148. 9 ; Cant. 5. 15 ; Ezek. 17. 3.
CELEBRATE. Lev. 23. 32 ; Isa. 38. 18.
CELESTIAL. 1 Cor. 15. 40.
CENSER. Ezek. 8. 11, every man his *c.*
Heb. 9. 4, holiest had the golden *c.*
Rev. 8. 3, angel having a golden *c.*
8. 5, angel took the *c.* and filled.
See Lev. 10. 1 ; 16. 12 ; Num. 16. 36 ; 1 Kin. 7. 30.
CEREMONIES. Num. 9. 3.
CERTAIN. Ex. 3. 12, *c.* I will be with thee.
1 Cor. 4. 11, no *c.* dwelling-place.
Heb. 10. 27, a *c.* looking for of judgment.
See Deut. 13. 14 ; 1 Kings 2. 37 ; Dan. 2. 45

CERTIFY. 2 Sam. 15. 28; Gal. 1. 11.

CHAFF. Mat. 3. 12; Lu. 3. 17, burn up c. with fire.
See Jer. 23. 28; Hos. 13. 3; Zeph. 2. 2.

CHAIN. Mk. 5. 3, no not with c.
Acts 12. 7, Peter's c. fell off.
2 Tim. 1. 16, not ashamed of my c.
2 Pet. 2. 4, into c. of darkness.
Jude 6, everlasting c. under darkness.
See Ps. 73. 6; Lam. 3. 7; Isa. 40. 19.

CHALCEDONY. Rev. 21. 19, the third, a c.

CHALLENGETH. Ex. 22. 9.

CHAMBER. 2 Kings 4. 10, little c. on wall.
Ps. 19. 5, as bridegroom coming out of c.
Isa. 26. 20, enter into thy c.
Ezek. 8. 12, c. of imagery.
Mat. 24. 26, in secret c.
Acts 9. 37; 20. 8, in upper c.
See Dan. 6. 10; Joel 2. 16; Prov. 7. 27.

CHAMPION. 1 Sam. 17. 4, 51.

CHANCE. 1 Sam. 6. 9; 2 Sam. 1. 6; Eccl. 9. 11; Lu. 10. 31.

CHANGE (n.). Job 14. 14, till my c. come.
Prov. 24. 21, meddle not with him given to c.
See Judg. 14. 12; Zech. 3. 4; Heb. 7. 12.

CHANGE (v.). Ps. 15. 4, sweareth and c. not.
102. 26, as vesture shalt thou c. them.
Lam. 4. 1, fine gold c.
Mal. 3. 6, I the Lord c. not.
Rom. 1. 23, c. glory of uncorruptible God.
1 Cor. 15. 51, we shall all be c.
2 Cor. 3. 18, c. from glory to glory.
See Job 17. 12; Jer. 2. 36; 13. 23.

CHANT. Amos 6. 5.

CHAPEL. Amos 7. 13, for it is the king's c.

CHAPMEN. 2 Chron. 9. 14.

CHAPT. Jer. 14. 4.

CHARGE. Job 1. 22, nor c. God foolishly.
4. 18, angels he c. with folly.
Mat. 9. 30; Mk. 5. 43; Lu. 9. 21, Jesus c. them.
Acts 7. 60; 2 Tim. 4. 16, lay not sin to their c.
Rom. 8. 33, who shall lay any thing to c.
1 Cor. 9. 18, gospel without c.
1 Tim. 1. 3, c. that they teach no other.
5. 21; 2 Tim. 4. 1, I c. thee before God.
6. 17, c. them that are rich.
See Ex. 6. 13; Ps. 35. 11; 91. 11; Mk. 9. 25.

CHARGEABLE. 2 Sam. 13. 25; 2 Cor. 11. 9; 1 Thess. 2. 9.

CHARIOT. 2 Kin. 2. 11, there appeared a c. of fire.

CHARIOTS. Ex. 14. 6, he made ready his c.
1 Sam. 13. 5, Philistines gathered thirty thousand c.
2 Sam. 10. 18, David slew the men of seven hundred c.
Ps. 20. 7, some trust in c.
Nah. 3. 2, and of the jumping c.
See 2 Kin. 6. 14, 17; Ps. 68. 17.

CHARITY. Rom. 14. 15, now walkest not c.
Col. 3. 14, put on c.
2 Thess. 1. 3, c. aboundeth.
1 Tim. 1. 5, end of commandment is c.
2 Tim. 2. 22, follow faith, c., peace.
Tit. 2. 2, sound in faith, in c.
1 Pet. 4. 8, c. cover sins.
2 Pet. 1. 7, to brotherly kindness c.
Jude 12, spots in feasts of c.
See 1 Cor. 8. 1; 13. 1; 14. 1; 16. 14; Rev. 2. 19.

CHARMER. Deut. 18. 11; Ps. 58. 5; Jer. 8. 17.

CHASE. Lev. 26. 8, five c. hundred.
Deut. 32. 30; Josh. 23. 10, one c. thousand.
See Job 18. 18; Ps. 35. 5; Lam. 3. 52.

CHASTE. 2 Cor. 11. 2; Tit. 2. 5; 1 Pet. 3. 2.

CHASTEN. Deut. 8. 5, as a man c. son.
Ps. 6. 1; 38. 1, nor c. me in displeasure.
94. 12, blessed is the man whom thou c.
Prov. 19. 18, c. thy son while there is hope.

2 Cor. 6. 9, as c. and not killed.
Heb. 12. 6; Rev. 3. 19, whom the Lord loveth he c.
11, no c. seemeth to be joyous.
See Ps. 69. 10; 73. 14; 118. 18.

CHASTISEMENT. Deut. 11. 2; Job 34. 31; Isa. 53. 5.

CHATTER. Isa. 38. 14.

CHEEK. Mat. 5. 39; Lu. 6. 29, smiteth on right c.
See Job 16. 10; Isa. 50. 6; Lam. 3. 30.

CHEER. Prov. 15. 13, maketh a c. countenance.
Zech. 9. 17, corn make young men c.
John 16. 33, be of good c., I have overcome.
Acts 23. 11; 27. 22, 25, be of good c.
Rom. 12. 8, he that sheweth mercy with c.
2 Cor. 9. 7, God loveth a c. giver.
See Judg. 9. 13; Mat. 9. 2; 14. 27; Mk. 6. 50.

CHERISHETH. Eph. 5. 29; 1 Thess. 2. 7.

CHICKENS. Mat. 23. 37.

CHIDE. Ex. 17. 2; Judg. 8. 1; Ps. 103. 9.

CHIEFEST. Cant. 5. 10; Mk. 10. 44; 2 Cor. 11. 5.

CHILD. Gen. 42. 22, do not sin against the c.
Ps. 131. 2, quieted myself as a weaned c.
Prov. 20. 11, a c. is known by his doings.
22. 6, train up a c. in way.
15, foolishness in heart of c.
Isa. 9. 6, to us a c. is born.
65. 20, c. shall die an hundred years old.
Lu. 1. 66, what manner of c.
John 4. 49, come ere my c. die.
1 Cor. 13. 11, when I was a c.
2 Tim. 3. 15, from a c. hast known.
See Ex. 2. 2; Eccl. 4. 13; 10. 16; Heb. 11. 23.

CHILDREN. 1 Sam. 16. 11, are here all thy c.
Ps. 34. 11, come ye c. hearken to me.
45. 16, instead of fathers shall be c.
128. 3, thy c. like olive plants.
Isa. 8. 18; Heb. 2. 13, I and c. given me.
30. 9, lying c., c. that will not hear.
63. 8, c. that will not lie.
Jer. 31. 15; Mat. 2. 18, Rachel weeping for her c.
Ezek. 18. 2, c. teeth on edge.
Mat. 15. 26; Mk. 7. 27, not take c. bread.
17. 26, then are the c. free.
19. 14; Mk. 10. 14; Lu. 18. 16, suffer little c.
Lu. 16. 8, c. of this world wiser than c. of light.
20. 36, c. of God and the resurrection.
John 12. 36; Eph. 5. 8; 1 Thess. 5. 5, c. of light.
Rom. 8. 16; Gal. 3. 26; 1 John 3. 10, witness that we are the c. of God.
Eph. 4. 14, be henceforth no more c.
5. 6; Col. 3. 6, c. of disobedience.
6. 1; Col. 3. 20, c. obey your parents.
1 Tim. 3. 4, having his c. in subjection.
See Num. 16. 27; Esth. 3. 13; Mat. 14. 21.

CHODE. Gen. 31. 36; Num. 20. 3.

CHOICE. 1 Sam. 9. 2, Saul a c. young man.
Acts 15. 7, God made c. among us.
See Gen. 23. 6; 2 Sam. 10. 9; Prov. 8. 10.

CHOKE. Mat. 13. 22; Mk. 4. 19; Lu. 8. 14.

CHOLER. Dan. 8. 7; 11. 11.

CHOSE. Ps. 33. 12, people c. for his inheritance.
89. 19, exalted one c. out of people.
Prov. 16. 16; 22. 1, rather to be c.
Jer. 8. 3, death c. rather than life.
Mat. 20. 16; 22. 14, many called, few c.
Lu. 10. 42, hath c. that good part.
14. 7, they c. the chief rooms.
John 15. 16, ye have not c. me.
Acts 9. 15, he is a c. vessel.
Rom. 16. 13, c. in the Lord.
1 Cor. 1. 27, 28, God hath c. foolish things.
Eph. 1. 4, according as he hath c. us.
1 Pet. 2. 4, c. of God and precious.
9, a c. generation.
See Ex. 18. 25; 2 Sam. 6. 21; 1 Chron. 16. 13.

CHRIST. Mat. 16. 16, thou art the C.
24. 5, many shall come, saying, I am C.
John 4. 25, the Messias which is called C.
29, is not this the C.

John 6. 69, we are sure that thou art that *C.*
Phil. 1. 15, 16, some preach *C.* of contention.
1 Pet. 1. 11, the Spirit of *C.* did signify.
1 John 2. 22, denieth that Jesus is the *C.*
5. 1, whoso believeth Jesus is the *C.*
Rev. 20. 4, they reigned with *C.* a thousand years.
6, priests of God and *C.*
See Mat. 1. 16; 2. 4; Lu. 2. 26.
CHRISTIAN. Acts 11. 26; 26. 28; 1 Pet. 4. 16.
CHRYSOLITE. Rev. 21. 20, the seventh *c.*
CHRYSOPRASUS. Rev. 21. 20, the tenth, a *c.*
CHURCH. Mat. 18. 17, tell it to the *c.*
Acts 2. 47, added to *c.* daily.
7. 38, the *c.* in the wilderness.
19. 37, neither robbers of *c.*
20. 28, feed the *c.* of God.
Rom. 16. 5 : 1 Cor. 16. 19; Philem. 2, *c.* in house.
1 Cor. 14. 28, 34, keep silence in the *c.*
Eph. 5. 24, the *c.* is subject to Christ.
25, as Christ loved the *c.*
Col. 1. 18, 24, head of the body the *c.*
Heb. 12. 23, the *c.* of the firstborn.
See Mat. 16. 18; Rev. 1. 4; 2. 1; 22. 16.
CHURLISH. 1 Sam. 25. 3, but the man was *c.*
CIELED. 2 Chron. 3. 5; Jer. 22. 14; Hag. 1. 4.
CIRCLE. Isa. 40. 22.
CIRCUIT. 1 Sam. 7. 16; Job 22. 14; Ps. 19. 6; Eccl. 1. 6.
CIRCUMCISE. Rom. 4. 11, though not *c.*
Gal. 5. 2, if ye be *c.* Christ shall profit nothing.
Phil. 3. 5, *c.* the eighth day.
See Deut. 30. 6; John 7. 22; Acts 15. 1.
CIRCUMCISION. Rom. 3. 1, what profit is there of *c.*
15. 8, Jesus Christ minister of *c.*
Gal. 5. 6; 6. 15, in Christ neither *c.* availeth.
Phil. 3. 3, the *c.* which worship God.
Col. 2. 11, *c.* without hands.
3. 11, neither *c.* nor uncircumcision.
See Ex. 4. 26; John 7. 22; Acts 7. 8.
CIRCUMSPECT. Ex. 23. 13; Eph. 5. 15.
CISTERN. Eccl. 12. 6, the wheel broken at the *c.*
Jer. 2. 13, hewed out *c.*, broken *c.*
See 2 Kings 18. 31; Prov. 5. 15; Isa. 36. 16.
CITIZEN. Lu. 15. 15; 19. 14; Acts 21. 39; Eph. 2. 19.
CITY. Num. 35. 6; Josh. 15. 59, *c.* of refuge.
2 Sam. 19. 37, I may die in mine own *c.*
Ps. 46. 4, make glad the *c.* of God.
107. 4, found no *c.* to dwell in.
Ps. 127. 1, except Lord build *c.*
Prov. 8. 3, wisdom crieth in *c.*
16. 32, than he that taketh a *c.*
Eccl. 9. 14, a little *c.* and few men.
Isa. 33. 20, *c.* of solemnities.
Zech. 8. 3, a *c.* of truth.
Mat. 5. 14, *c.* set on a hill.
21. 10, all the *c.* was moved.
Lu. 24. 49, tarry in the *c.*
Acts 8. 8, great joy in that *c.*
Heb. 11. 10, a *c.* that hath foundations.
12. 22, the *c.* of living God.
13. 14, no continuing *c.*
Rev. 16. 19, the *c.* of the nations fell.
20. 9, compassed the beloved *c.*
See Gen. 4. 17; 11. 4; Jonah 1. 2; Rev. 14. 8; 21. 10.
CLAD. 1 Kings 11. 29; Isa. 59. 17.
CLAMOUR. Prov. 9. 19; Eph. 4. 31.
CLAP. Ps. 47. 1, *c.* your hands all ye people.
98. 8, let the floods *c.* their hands.
Isa. 55. 12, the trees shall *c.* their hands.
Lam. 2. 15, all that pass by *c.* their hands.
See 2 Kings 11. 12; Job 27. 23; 34. 37.
CLAVE. Ruth 1. 14, Ruth *c.* to her mother-in-law.
2 Sam. 23. 10, his hand *c.* to the sword.
Neh. 10. 29, they *c.* to their brethren.
Acts 17. 34, certain men *c.* to Paul.
See Gen. 22. 3; Num. 16. 31; 1 Sam. 6. 14.

CLAWS. Deut. 14. 6; Dan. 4. 33; Zech. 11. 16.
CLAY. Job 10. 9, thou hast made me as *c.*
13. 12, bodies like to bodies of *c.*
33. 6, I also am formed out of *c.*
Ps. 40. 2, out of the miry *c.*
Dan. 2. 33, part of iron, part of *c.*
John 9. 6, made *c.* and anointed.
Rom. 9. 21, power over the *c.*
See Isa. 29. 16; 41. 25; 45. 9; 64. 8; Jer. 18. 4.
CLEAN. 2 Kings 5. 12, may I not wash and be *c.*
Job 14. 4, who can bring *c.* out of unclean.
15. 15, heavens not *c.* in his sight.
Ps. 24. 4, he that hath *c.* hands.
51. 10, create in me *c.* heart.
77. 8, is his mercy *c.* gone for ever.
Prov. 16. 2, *c.* in his own eyes.
Isa. 1. 16, wash you, make you *c.*
52. 11, be *c.* that bear vessels of the Lord.
Ezek. 36. 25, then will I sprinkle *c.* water.
Mat. 8. 2; Mk. 1. 40; Lu. 5. 12, thou canst make me *c.*
23. 25; Lu. 11. 39, make *c.* the outside.
Lu. 11. 41, all things *c.* unto you.
John 13. 11, ye are not all *c.*
15. 3, *c.* through word I have spoken.
Acts 18. 6, I am *c.*
Rev. 19. 8, arrayed in fine linen *c.* and white.
See Lev. 23. 22; Josh. 3. 17; Prov. 14. 4.
CLEANNESS. 2 Sam. 22. 21; Ps. 18. 20; Amos 4. 6.
CLEANSE. Ps. 19. 12, *c.* me from secret faults.
73. 13, I have *c.* my heart in vain.
Prov. 20. 30, blueness of wound *c.* evil.
Mat. 8. 3, immediately his leprosy was *c.*
10. 8; 11. 5; Lu. 7. 22, *c.* lepers.
23. 26, *c.* first that which is within.
Lu. 4. 27, none was *c.* saving Naaman.
17. 17, were not ten *c.*
Acts 10. 15; 11. 9, what God hath *c.*
2 Cor. 7. 1, let us *c.* ourselves.
Jas. 4. 8, *c.* your hands, ye sinners.
1 John 1. 7, 9, *c.* us from all sin.
See Ezek. 36. 25; Mk. 1. 44.
CLEAR. Gen. 44. 16, now shall we *c.* ourselves.
Ex. 34. 7, by no means *c.* the guilty.
2 Sam. 23. 4, *c.* shining after rain.
Job 11. 17, age shall be *c.* than noonday.
Ps. 51. 4, be *c.* when thou judgest.
Mat. 7. 5; Lu. 6. 42, see *c.* to pull out mote.
Mk. 8. 25, saw every man *c.*
Rom. 1. 20, things from creation *c.* seen.
Rev. 21. 11; 22. 1, light *c.* as crystal.
See Gen. 24. 8; Cant. 6. 10; Zech. 14. 6.
CLEAVE. Josh. 23. 8, *c.* to the Lord your God.
2 Kings 5. 27, leprosy shall *c.* to thee.
Job 29. 10; Ps. 137. 6; Ezek. 3. 26, *c.* to roof of mouth.
Ps. 119. 25, my soul *c.* to dust.
Eccl. 10. 9, he that *c.* wood shall be endangered.
Acts 11. 23, with purpose of heart *c.*
Rom. 12. 9, *c.* to that which is good.
See Gen. 2. 24; Mat. 19. 5; Mk. 10. 7.
CLEFTS. Cant. 2. 14; Isa. 2. 21; Jer. 49. 16; Amos 6. 11; Obad. 3.
CLEMENCY. Acts 24. 4.
CLERK. Acts 19. 35.
CLIMB. John 10. 1, but *c.* up some other way.
See 1 Sam. 14. 13; Amos 9. 2; Lu. 19. 4.
CLODS. Job 21. 33, the *c.* of the valley shall be sweet.
See Job 7. 5; Isa. 28. 24; Hos. 10. 11; Joel 1. 17.
CLOKE. Mat. 5. 40; Lu. 6. 29, let him have thy *c.* also.
1 Thess. 2. 5, a *c.* of covetousness.
1 Pet. 2. 16, a *c.* of maliciousness.
CLOSE (*v.*). Gen. 2. 21; Isa. 29. 10; Mat. 13. 15.
CLOSE. Prov. 18. 24, sticketh *c.* than a brother.
Lu. 9. 36, they kept it *c.*
See Num. 5. 13; 1 Chron. 12. 1; Job 28. 21.
CLOSET. Mat. 6. 6; Lu. 12. 3.

CLOTH. 1 Sam. 19. 13 ; 21. 9 ; Mat. 9. 16 ; Mk. 2. 21.
CLOTHE. Ps. 65. 13, pastures *c.* with flocks.
109. 18, *c.* himself with cursing.
132. 9, *c.* with righteousness.
16, *c.* with salvation.
Prov. 23. 21, drowsiness shall *c.* a man.
31. 21, household *c.* with scarlet.
Isa. 50. 3, *c.* heavens with blackness.
61. 10, *c.* with garments of salvation.
Mat. 6. 30 ; Lu. 12. 28, *c.* grass of field.
31, wherewithal shall we be *c.*
11. 8 ; Lu. 7. 25, man *c.* in soft raiment.
25. 36, 43, naked and ye *c.* me.
Mk. 1. 6, *c.* with camel's hair.
5. 15 ; Lu. 8. 35, *c.* and in right mind.
15. 17, *c.* Jesus with purple.
Lu. 16. 19, *c.* in purple and fine linen.
2 Cor. 5. 2, desiring to be *c.* upon.
1 Pet. 5. 5, be *c.* with humility.
Rev. 3. 18, that thou mayest be *c.*
12. 1, woman *c.* with the sun.
19. 13, *c.* with a vesture dipped in blood.
See Gen. 3. 21 ; Ex. 40. 14 ; Esther 4. 4.
CLOTHES. Deut. 29. 5 ; Neh. 9. 21, *c.* not waxen
    old.
Mk. 5. 28, if I touch but his *c.*
Lu. 2. 7, in swaddling *c.*
Lu. 8. 27, a man that ware no *c.*
19. 36, spread *c.* in the way.
24. 12 ; John 20. 5, linen *c.* laid.
John 11. 44, bound with grave-*c.*
Acts 7. 58, laid down *c.* at Saul's feet.
22. 23, cried out and cast off *c.*
See Gen. 49. 11 ; 1 Sam. 19. 24 ; Neh. 4. 23.
CLOTHING. Ps. 45. 13, her *c.* of wrought gold.
Prov. 27. 26, lambs are for thy *c.*
31. 22, her *c.* is silk and purple.
25, strength and honour are her *c.*
Isa. 3. 7, in my house is neither bread nor *c.*
23. 18, merchandise for durable *c.*
59. 17, garments of vengeance for *c.*
Mat. 7. 15, in sheep's *c.*
Mk. 12. 38, love to go in long *c.*
Acts 10. 30, a man in bright *c.*
Jas. 2. 3, to him that weareth gay *c.*
See Job 22. 6 ; 24. 7 ; 31. 19 ; Ps. 35. 13.
CLOUD. Ex. 13. 21 ; 14. 24 ; Neh. 9. 19, a pillar of *c.*
1 Kings 18. 44, 45, a little *c.*
Ps. 36. 5, faithfulness reacheth to *c.*
97. 2, *c.* and darkness round about him.
99. 7, spake in *c.* pillar.
Prov. 3. 20, *c.* dropped down dew.
Eccl. 11. 4, regardeth the *c.* not reap.
12. 2, nor *c.* return after rain.
Isa. 5. 6, command *c.* rain not.
44. 22, blotted out as thick *c.*
60. 8, fly as a *c.*
Dan. 7. 13 ; Lu. 21. 27, Son of man with *c.*
Hosea 6. 4 ; 13. 3, goodness as morning *c.*
Mat. 17. 5 ; Mk. 9. 7 ; Lu. 9. 34, *c.* overshadowed.
24. 30 ; 26. 64 ; Mk. 13. 26 ; 14. 62, in *c.* with power.
1 Cor. 10. 1, fathers under *c.*
1 Thess. 4. 17, caught up in *c.*
2 Pet. 2. 17, *c.* carried with tempest.
Jude 12, *c.* without water.
Rev. 1. 7, he cometh with *c.*
14. 14 ; 15. 16, white *c.*
See Gen. 9. 13 ; Ex. 24. 15 ; 40. 34.
CLOUT. Josh. 9. 5 ; Jer. 38. 11.
CLOVEN. Lev. 11. 3 ; Deut. 14. 7 ; Acts 2. 3.
CLUSTER. Isa. 65. 8, new wine in *c.*
See Num. 13. 23 ; Cant. 1. 14 ; Rev. 14. 18.
COAL. Prov. 6. 28, hot *c.* and not be burned.
25. 22 ; Rom. 12. 20, heap *c.* of fire.
John 18. 18 ; 21. 9, fire of *c.*
See Job 41. 21 ; Ps. 18. 8 ; Isa. 6. 6.
COAST. 1 Chron. 4. 10 ; Mat. 8. 34 ; Mk. 5. 17.
COAT. Mat. 5. 40, take away thy *c.*
10. 10 ; Mk. 6. 9, neither provide two *c.*

Lu. 6. 29, thy *c.* also.
John 19. 23, *c.* without seam.
21. 7, fisher's *c.*
Acts 9. 39, the *c.* which Dorcas made.
See Gen. 3. 21 ; 37. 3 ; 1 Sam. 2. 19.
COCK. Mat. 26. 34 ; Mk. 13. 35 ; 14. 30 ; Lu. 22. 34.
COCKATRICE. Isa. 11. 8 ; 14. 29 ; 59. 5.
COCKLE. Job 31. 40.
COFFER. 1 Sam. 6. 8, 11, 15.
COFFIN. Gen. 50. 26.
COGITATIONS. Dan. 7. 28.
COLD. Prov. 20. 4, by reason of *c.*
25. 13, *c.* of snow in harvest.
20, garment in *c.* weather.
25, *c.* waters to thirsty soul.
Mat. 10. 42, cup of *c.* water.
24. 12, love of many wax *c.*
2 Cor. 11. 27, in *c.* and nakedness.
Rev. 3. 15, neither *c.* nor hot.
See Gen. 8. 22 ; Job 24. 7 ; 37. 9 ; Ps. 147. 17.
COLLECTION. 2 Chron. 24. 6 ; Acts 11. 29 ; Rom.
    15. 26 ; 1 Cor. 16. 1.
COLLEGE. 2 Kings 22. 14 ; 2 Chron. 34. 22.
COLOUR. Prov. 23. 31, *c.* in the cup.
Acts 27. 30, under *c.* as though.
See Gen. 37. 3 ; Ezek. 1. 4 ; Dan. 10. 6.
COMELY. Ps. 33. 1, praise is *c.*
1 Cor. 11. 13, is it *c.* that a woman.
See 1 Sam. 16. 18 ; Prov. 30. 29 ; Isa. 53. 2.
COMFORT (*n.*). Mat. 9. 22 ; Mk. 10. 49 ; Lu. 8. 48 ;
    2 Cor. 13. 11, be of good *c.*
Acts 9. 31, *c.* of Holy Ghost.
Rom. 15. 4, patience and *c.* of scriptures.
2 Cor. 1. 3, God of all *c.*
7. 13, were comforted in your *c.*
Phil. 2. 1, if any *c.* of love.
See Job 10. 20 ; Ps. 94. 19 ; 119. 50 ; Isa. 57. 6.
COMFORT (*v.*). Gen. 37. 35 ; Ps. 77. 2 ; Jer. 31. 15,
    refused to be *c.*
Ps. 23. 4, rod and staff *c.*
Isa. 40. 1, *c.* ye, *c.* ye, my people.
49. 13 ; 52. 9, God hath *c.* his people.
61. 2, *c.* all that mourn.
66. 13, as one whom his mother *c.*
Mat. 5. 4, they shall be *c.*
Lu. 16. 25, he is *c.*, and thou art tormented.
John 11. 19, to *c.* concerning their brother.
2 Cor. 1. 4, able to *c.* them.
1 Thess. 4. 18, *c.* one another with these words.
5. 11, wherefore *c.* yourselves together.
14, *c.* the feeble minded.
See Gen. 5. 29 ; 18. 5 ; 37. 35.
COMFORTABLE. Isa. 40. 2 ; Hos. 2. 14 ; Zech.
    1. 13.
COMFORTER. Job 16. 2, miserable *c.* are ye all.
Ps. 69. 20, looked for *c.* but I found none.
John 14. 16, give you another *C.*
15. 26, when the *C.* is come.
16. 7, *C.* will not come.
See 2 Sam. 10. 3 ; 1 Chron. 19. 3.
COMFORTLESS. John 14. 18.
COMMAND. Ps. 33. 9, he *c.* and it stood fast.
Lu. 8. 25, he *c.* even the winds.
9. 54, *c.* fire from heaven.
John 15. 14, if ye do what I *c.* you.
Acts 17. 30, *c.* all men everywhere.
See Gen. 18. 19 ; Deut. 28. 8.
COMMANDER. Isa. 55. 4.
COMMANDMENT. Ps. 119. 86, *c.* are faithful.
96, exceeding broad.
127, I love thy *c.*
143, thy *c.* are my delight.
Mat. 15. 9 ; Mk. 7. 7 ; Col. 2. 22, the *c.* of men.
Lu. 23. 56, rested according to *c.*
John 13. 34 ; 1 John 2. 7 ; 2 John 5, a new *c.*
Rom. 7. 12, *c.* is holy, just, and good.
1 Cor. 7. 6 ; 2 Cor. 8. 8, by permission not by *c.*

Eph. 6. 2, first *c.* with promise.
1 Tim. 1. 5, end of the *c.* is charity.
See Esther 3. 3.
COMMEND. Lu. 16. 8, *c.* unjust steward.
23. 46, into thy hands I *c.*
Rom. 3. 5, unrighteousness *c.* righteousness of God.
5. 8, God *c.* his love toward us.
1 Cor. 8. 8, meat *c.* us not.
2 Cor. 3. 1 ; 5. 12, *c.* ourselves.
4. 2, *c.* to every man's conscience.
10. 18, not he that *c.* himself is approved.
See Prov. 12. 8 ; Eccl. 8. 15 ; Acts 20. 32.
COMMISSION. Ezra 8. 36 ; Acts 26. 12.
COMMIT. Ps. 37. 5, *c.* thy way to the Lord.
Jer. 2. 13, have *c.* two evils.
John 2. 24, Jesus did not *c.* himself to them.
5. 22, hath *c.* judgment to Son.
Rom. 3. 2, were *c.* oracles of God.
2 Cor. 5. 19, had *c.* to us word of reconciliation.
1 Tim. 6. 20, keep what is *c.* to thee.
2 Tim. 2. 2, *c.* thou to faithful men.
1 Pet. 2. 23, *c.* himself to him that judgeth.
See Job 5. 8 ; Ps. 31. 5 ; 1 Cor. 9. 17.
COMMODIOUS. Acts 27. 12.
COMMON. Eccl. 6. 1, evil, and it is *c.* among men.
Mk. 12. 37, the *c.* people heard him gladly.
Acts 2. 44 ; 4. 32, all things *c.*
10. 14 ; 11. 8, never eaten any thing *c.*
15 ; 11. 9, call not thou *c.*
1 Cor. 10. 13, temptation *c.* to men.
Eph. 2. 12, aliens from *c.*-wealth.
See Lev. 4. 27 ; Num. 16. 29 ; 1 Sam. 21. 4.
COMMOTION. Jer. 10. 22 ; Lu. 21. 9.
COMMUNE. Job 4. 2, if we *c.* with thee.
Ps. 4. 4 ; 77. 6 ; Eccl. 1. 16, *c.* with own heart.
Zech. 1. 14, angel that *c.* with me.
See Ex. 25. 22 ; 1 Sam. 19. 3 ; Lu. 22. 4.
COMMUNICATE. Gal. 6. 6, let him that is taught *c.*
1 Tim. 6. 18, be willing to *c.*
Heb. 13. 16, do good and *c.*
See Gal. 2. 2 ; Phil. 4. 14, 15.
COMMUNICATION. Mat. 5. 37, let your *c.* be yea.
Lu. 24. 17, what manner of *c.*
1 Cor. 15. 33, evil *c.* corrupt good manners.
Eph. 4. 29, let no corrupt *c.* proceed.
See 2 Kings 9. 11 ; Philem. 6.
COMMUNION. 1 Cor. 10. 16 ; 2 Cor. 6. 14 ; 13. 14.
COMPACT. Ps. 122. 3 ; Eph. 4. 16.
COMPANY. 1 Sam. 10. 5 ; 19. 20, a *c.* of prophets.
Ps. 55. 14, walked to house of God in *c.*
68. 11, great was the *c.* of those.
Mk. 6. 39 ; Lu. 9. 14, sit down by *c.*
2 Thess. 3. 14, have no *c.* with him.
Heb. 12. 22, innumerable *c.* of angels.
See Num. 16. 6 ; Judg. 9. 37 ; 18. 23.
COMPANION. Job 30. 29, a *c.* to owls.
Ps. 119. 63, a *c.* to them that fear thee.
Prov. 13. 20, *c.* of fools shall be destroyed.
28. 7, *c.* of riotous men.
24, the *c.* of a destroyer.
Acts 19. 29, Paul's *c.* in travel.
Phil. 2. 25 ; Rev. 1. 9, brother and *c.* in labour.
See Ex. 32. 27 ; Judg. 11. 38 ; 14. 20.
COMPARE. Prov. 3. 15 ; 8. 11, not to be *c.* to wisdom.
Isa. 40. 18, what likeness will ye *c.* to him?
46. 5, to whom will ye *c.* me.
Lam. 4. 2, *c.* to fine gold.
Rom. 8. 18, not worthy to be *c.* with glory.
1 Cor. 2. 13, *c.* spiritual things with spiritual.
See Ps. 89. 6 ; 2 Cor. 10. 12.
COMPARISON. Judg. 8. 2 ; Hag. 2. 3 ; Mk. 4. 30.
COMPASS (*n.*). 2 Sam. 5. 23 ; 2 Kings 3. 9 ; Isa. 44. 13 ; Acts 28. 13.
COMPASS (*v.*). 2 Sam. 22. 5 ; Ps. 18. 4 ; 116. 3, waves of death *c.* me.
22. 6 ; Ps. 18. 5, sorrows of hell *c.* me.

Ps. 5. 12, with favour *c.* as with a shield.
32. 7, *c.* with songs of deliverance.
10, mercy shall *c.* him about.
Isa. 50. 11, *c.* yourselves with sparks.
Mat. 23. 15, *c.* sea and land.
Lu. 21. 20, Jerusalem *c.* with armies.
Heb. 5. 2, he also is *c.* with infirmity.
12. 1, *c.* about with cloud of witnesses.
See Josh. 6. 3 ; Job 16. 13 ; Jer. 31. 22.
COMPASSION. Isa. 49. 15, that she should not have *c.*
Lam. 3. 22, his *c.* fail not.
32 ; Mic. 7. 19, yet will he have *c.*
Mat. 9. 36 ; 14. 14 ; Mk. 1. 41 ; 6. 34, Jesus moved with *c.*
18. 33, *c.* on thy fellowservant.
20. 34, had *c.* on them and touched.
Mk. 5. 19, the Lord hath had *c.*
9. 22, have *c.*, and help us.
Lu. 10. 33, the Samaritan had *c.*
15. 20, father had *c.*, and ran.
Rom. 9. 15, I will have *c.* on whom I will.
Heb. 5. 2, have *c.* on ignorant.
1 Pet. 3. 8, of one mind, having *c.*
1 John 3. 17, shutteth up bowels of *c.*
Jude 22, of some have *c.*, making a difference.
See Ps. 78. 38 ; 86. 15 ; 111. 4 ; 112. 4.
COMPEL. Mat. 5. 41, *c.* thee to go a mile.
27. 32 ; Mk. 15. 21. *c.* to bear cross.
Lu. 14. 23, *c.* to come in.
Acts 26. 11, I *c.* them to blaspheme.
See Lev. 25. 39 ; 2 Cor. 12. 11 ; Gal. 2. 3.
COMPLAIN. Ps. 144. 14, no *c.* in our streets.
Lam. 3. 39, wherefore doth a living man *c.*
Jude 16, these are murmurers, *c.*
See Num. 11. 1 ; Judg. 21. 22 ; Job 7. 11.
COMPLAINT. Job 23. 2, to-day is my *c.* bitter.
Ps. 142. 2, I poured out my *c.* before him.
See 1 Sam. 1. 16 ; Job 7. 13 ; 9. 27 ; 10. 1.
COMPLETE. Lev. 23. 15 ; Col. 2. 10 ; 4. 12.
COMPREHEND. Job 37. 5 ; Isa. 40. 12 ; John 1. 5 ; Eph. 3. 18.
CONCEAL. Prov. 12. 23, prudent man *c.* knowledge.
25. 2, glory of God to *c.* a thing.
Jer. 50. 2, publish and *c.* not.
See Gen. 37. 26 ; Deut. 13. 8.
CONCEIT. Rom. 11. 25 ; 12. 16, wise in your own *c.*
CONCEIT (reproved). Prov. 3. 7 ; 12. 15 ; 18. 11 ; 20. 5 ; 28. 11 ; Isa. 5. 21.
CONCEIVE. Ps. 7. 14, *c.* mischief, brought forth falsehood.
51. 5, in sin did my mother *c.* me.
Acts 5. 4, why hast thou *c.* this thing.
Jas. 1. 15, when lust *c.* it bringeth forth.
See Job 15. 35 ; Isa. 7. 14 ; 59. 4.
CONCERN. Lu. 24. 27, things *c.* himself.
Rom. 9. 5, as *c.* the flesh Christ came.
16. 19, simple *c.* evil.
Phil. 4. 15, *c.* giving and receiving.
1 Tim. 6. 21, have erred *c.* the faith.
1 Pet. 4. 12, *c.* fiery trial.
See Lev. 6. 3 ; Num. 10. 29 ; Ps. 90. 13 ; 135. 14.
CONCISION. Phil. 3. 2.
CONCLUDE. Rom. 3. 28 ; 11. 32 ; Gal. 3. 22.
CONCLUSION. Eccl. 12. 13.
CONCORD. 2 Cor. 6. 15.
CONCUPISCENCE. Col. 3. 5 ; 1 Thess. 4. 5, mortify evil *c.*
CONDEMN. Job 10. 2, I will say to God, do not *c.* me.
Amos 2. 8, drink wine of the *c.*
Mat. 12. 7, ye would not have *c.* the guiltless.
37, by thy words shalt be *c.*
42 ; Lu. 11. 31, rise in judgment and *c.*
20. 18, shall *c.* him to death.
27. 3, Judas when he saw he was *c.*
Mk. 14. 64, all *c.* him to be guilty.
Lu. 6. 37, *c.* not and ye shall not be *c.*

John 3. 17, God sent not his Son to c.
18, believe not is c.
8. 10, hath no man c. thee?
11, neither do I c. thee.
Rom. 2. 1, thou c. thyself.
8. 3, c. sin in the flesh.
34, who is he that c.?
14. 22, that c. not himself.
Tit. 2. 8, sound speech that cannot be c.
Jas. 5. 6, ye c. and killed the just.
9, grudge not lest ye be c.
1 John 3. 21, if our heart c. us not.
See Job 9. 20; 15. 6; Mat. 12. 41.

CONDEMNATION. John 3. 19, this is the c., that light.
2 Cor. 3. 9, the ministration of c.
1 Tim. 3. 6, the c. of the devil.
Jas. 5. 12, lest ye fall into c.
Jude 4, of old ordained to this c.
See Lu. 23. 40; Rom. 5. 16; 8. 1.

CONDESCEND. Rom. 12. 16.
CONDITION. 1 Sam. 11. 2; Lu. 14. 32.
CONDUIT. 2 Kings 18. 17; 20. 20; Isa. 7. 3; 36. 2.
CONEY. Lev. 11. 5; Ps. 104. 18; Prov. 30. 26.
CONFECTION. Ex. 30. 35; 1 Sam. 8. 13.
CONFEDERATE. Gen. 14. 13; Isa. 7. 2; 8. 12; Obad. 7.
CONFERENCE. Gal. 2. 6.
CONFERRED. Gal. 1. 16.
CONFESS. Prov. 28. 13, whoso c. and forsaketh.
Mat. 10. 32; Lu. 12. 8, c. me before men.
John 9. 22, if any man did c.
12. 42, rulers did not c. him.
Acts 23. 8, Pharisees c. both.
Rom. 10. 9, shall c. with thy mouth.
14. 11; Phil. 2. 11, every tongue c.
Heb. 11. 13, c. they were strangers.
Jas. 5. 16, c. your faults one to another.
1 John 1. 9, if we c. our sins.
4. 2, every spirit that c. Christ.
15, whoso shall c. that Jesus is the Christ.
Rev. 3. 5, I will c. his name before my Father.
See Lev. 16. 21; 1 Kings 8. 33; 2 Chron. 6. 24.

CONFESSION. Rom. 10. 10; 1 Tim. 6. 13.
CONFIDENCE. Ps. 65. 5, the c. of all the ends of the earth.
118. 8, 9, than to put c. in man.
Prov. 3. 26, the Lord shall be thy c.
14. 26, in fear of the Lord is strong c.
Isa. 30. 15, in c. shall be your strength.
Jer. 2. 37, hath rejected thy c.
Eph. 3. 12, access with c. by the faith of him.
Phil. 3. 3, 4, no c. in flesh.
Heb. 3. 6, 14, hold fast c.
10. 35, cast not away c.
1 John 2. 28, we may have c.
3. 21, we have c. toward God.
5. 14, this is the c. we have in him.
See Job 4. 6; 18. 14; 31. 24; Prov. 25. 19.

CONFIDENT. Ps. 27. 3; Prov. 14. 16; 2 Cor. 5. 6; Phil. 1. 6.
CONFIRM. Isa. 35. 3, c. the feeble knees.
Mk. 16. 20, c. the word with signs.
Acts 14. 22, c. the souls of the disciples.
15. 32, 41, exhorted brethren, and c. them.
Rom. 15. 8, c. the promises made to fathers.
See 2 Kings 15. 19.

CONFIRMATION. Phil. 1. 7; Heb. 6. 16.
CONFISCATION. Ezra 7. 26.
CONFLICT. Phil. 1. 30; Col. 2. 1.
CONFORM. Rom. 8. 29; 12. 2; Phil. 3. 10.
CONFOUND. Ps. 22. 5, fathers trusted and were not c.
40. 14; 70. 2, ashamed and c.
Acts 2. 6, multitude were c.
9. 22, Saul c. the Jews.
See Gen. 11. 7; Ps. 71. 13; 129. 5.

CONFUSED. Isa. 9. 5; Acts 19. 32.
CONFUSION. Dan. 9. 7, to us belongeth c. of faces.
Acts 19. 29, city was filled with c.
1 Cor. 14. 33, God not author of c.
See Ps. 70. 2; 71. 1; 109. 29; Isa. 24. 10.
CONGEALED. Ex. 15. 8.
CONGRATULATE. 1 Chron. 18. 10.
CONGREGATION. Num. 14. 10, all the c. bade stone them.
Neh. 5. 13, all the c. said Amen.
Ps. 1. 5, nor sinners in the c. of the righteous.
26. 12, in the c. will I bless the Lord.
Prov. 21. 16, in the c. of the dead.
Joel 2. 16, sanctify the c.
Acts 13. 43, when the c. was broken up.
See Ex. 12. 6; 16. 2; 39. 32; Lev. 4. 13.
CONIES. Ps. 104. 18, the rocks for the c.
Prov. 30. 26, the c. are but a feeble folk.
See Lev. 11. 5; Deut. 14. 7.
CONQUERORS. Rom. 8. 37; Rev. 6. 2.
CONSCIENCE. Acts 24. 16, c. void of offence.
Rom. 2. 15; 9. 1; 2 Cor. 1. 12, c. bearing witness.
13. 5; 1 Cor. 10. 25, 27, 28, for c. sake.
1 Cor. 8. 10, 12, weak c.
1 Tim. 1. 5, 19; Heb. 13. 18; 1 Pet. 3. 16, a good c.
3. 9, mystery of faith in pure c.
4. 2, c. seared with hot iron.
Heb. 9. 14, purge c. from dead works.
10. 22, hearts sprinkled from evil c.
See John 8. 9; Acts 23. 1; 2 Cor. 4. 2.
CONSECRATE. 1 Chron. 29. 5, to c. his service to the Lord.
Mic. 4. 13, I will c.
Heb. 7. 28, who is c. for evermore.
10. 20, living way which he hath c.
See Ex. 28. 3; 29. 35; 32. 29; Lev. 7. 37.
CONSENT. Ps. 50. 18, a thief, thou c. with him.
Prov. 1. 10, if sinners entice thee c. not.
Zeph. 3. 9, to serve with one c.
Lu. 14. 18, with one c. began to make excuse.
See Deut. 13. 8; Acts 8. 1; Rom. 7. 16.
CONSIDER. Ps. 8. 3, when I c. the heavens.
41. 1, blessed is he that c. the poor.
48. 13, c. her palaces.
50. 22, c. this, ye that forget God.
Prov. 6. 6, c. her ways and be wise.
23. 1, c. diligently what is before thee.
24. 12, doth not he c. it.
Prov. 28. 22, and c. not that poverty.
Eccl. 5. 1, they c. not that they do evil.
7. 14, in day of adversity c.
Isa. 1. 3, my people doth not c.
Jer. 23. 20; 30. 24, in latter days ye shall c.
Ezek. 12. 3, it may be they will c.
Hag. 1. 5, 7, c. your ways.
Mat. 6. 28; Lu. 12. 27, c. lilies of the field.
7. 3, c. not the beam.
Lu. 12. 24, c. the ravens.
Gal. 6. 1, c. thyself lest thou also be tempted.
Heb. 3. 1, c. the Apostle and High Priest.
7. 4, now c. how great this man was.
10. 21, c. one another to provoke.
12. 3, c. him that endured.
13. 7, c. the end of their conversation.
See Deut. 32. 29; Judg. 18. 14; 1 Sam. 12. 24.
CONSIST. Lu. 12. 15; Col. 1. 17.
CONSOLATION. Job 15. 11, are the c. of God small.
Lu. 6. 24, ye have received your c.
Rom. 15. 5, the God of c.
Phil. 2. 1, if there be any c. in Christ.
2 Thess. 2. 16, everlasting c.
Heb. 6. 18, strong c.
See Jer. 16. 7; Lu. 2. 25; Acts 4. 36.
CONSPIRACY. 2 Sam. 15. 12; Jer. 11. 9; Acts 23. 13.
CONSTANTLY. 1 Chron. 28. 7; Prov. 21. 28; Tit. 3. 8.
CONSTRAIN. Job 32. 18; Lu. 24. 29; 2 Cor. 5. 14; 1 Pet. 5. 2.

CONSULT. Ps. 83. 3 ; Mk. 15. 1 ; Lu. 14. 31 ; John 12. 10.
CONSUME. Ex. 3. 2, bush was not c.
Deut. 4. 24 ; 9. 3 ; Heb. 12. 29, a c. fire.
1 Kings 18. 38 ; 2 Chron. 7. 1, fire fell and c. the sacrifice.
Job 20. 26, fire not blown shall c. him.
Ps. 39. 11, c. away like a moth.
Mal. 3. 6, therefore ye are not c.
Lu. 9. 54, c. them as Elias did.
Gal. 5. 15, take heed that ye be not c.
Jas. 4. 3, that ye may c. it on your lusts.
See Ex. 32. 10 ; 33. 3 ; Deut. 5. 25 ; Josh. 24. 20.
CONSUMMATION. Dan. 9. 27.
CONSUMPTION. Lev. 26. 16 ; Deut. 28. 22 ; Isa. 10. 22.
CONTAIN. 1 Kings 8. 27 ; 2 Chron. 2. 6 ; 6. 18 ; 1 Cor. 7. 9.
CONTEMN. Ps. 10. 13 ; 15. 4 ; 107. 11 ; Ezek. 21. 10.
CONTEMPT. Prov. 18. 3, wicked cometh, then cometh c.
Dan. 12. 2, awake to everlasting c.
See Esther 1. 18 ; Job 31. 34 ; Ps. 119. 22.
CONTEMPTIBLE. Mal. 1. 7, 12 ; 2. 9 ; 2 Cor. 10. 10.
CONTEND. Isa. 49. 25, I will c. with him that c.
50. 8, who will c. with me.
Jer. 12. 5, how canst thou c. with horses.
See Job 10. 2 ; 13. 8 ; Eccl. 6. 10 ; Jude 3, 9.
CONTENT. Mk. 15. 15, willing to c. the people.
Lu. 3. 14, be c. with your wages.
Phil. 4. 11, I have learned to be c.
1 Tim. 6. 6, godliness with c. is great gain.
6. 8, having food let us be c.
Heb. 13. 5, be c. with such things as ye have.
See Gen. 37. 27 ; Josh. 7. 7 ; Job 6. 28 ; Prov. 6. 35.
CONTENTION. Prov. 18. 18, the lot causeth c. to cease.
19. 13 ; 27. 15, c. of a wife.
23. 29, who hath c.
Acts 15. 39, the c. was sharp.
1 Cor. 1. 11, there are c. among you.
Phil. 1. 16, preach Christ of c.
1 Thess. 2. 2, to speak with much c.
Tit. 3. 9, avoid c. and strivings.
See Prov. 13. 10 ; 17. 14 ; 18. 6 ; 22. 10.
CONTENTIOUS. Prov. 21. 19 ; 26. 21 ; 27. 15 ; Rom. 2. 8 ; 1 Cor. 11. 16.
CONTINUAL. Ps. 34. 1 ; 71. 6, praise c. in my mouth.
40. 11, let thy truth c. preserve me.
73. 23, I am c. with thee.
Prov. 6. 21, bind them c. on thine heart.
15. 15, merry heart hath a c. feast.
Isa. 14. 6, smote with a c. stroke.
52. 5, my name is c. blasphemed.
Lu. 18. 5, lest by her c. coming.
24. 53, were c. in the temple.
Acts 6. 4, give ourselves c. to prayer.
Rom. 9. 2, I have c. sorrow in my heart.
Heb. 7. 3, abideth a priest c.
See Ex. 29. 42 ; Num. 4. 7 ; Job 1. 5.
CONTINUANCE. Deut. 28. 59 ; Ps. 139. 16 ; Isa. 64. 5 ; Rom. 2. 7.
CONTINUE. Job 14. 2, as a shadow and c. not.
Ps. 72. 17, name shall c. as long as the sun.
Isa. 5. 11, c. till wine inflame them.
Jer. 32. 14, evidences may c. many days.
Lu. 6. 12, he c. all night in prayer.
22. 28, that c. with me in my temptation.
John 8. 31, if ye c. in my word.
15. 9, c. ye in my love.
Acts 1. 14 ; 2. 46, c. with one accord.
12. 16, Peter c. knocking.
13. 43, to c. in grace of God.
14. 22, exhorting them to c. in faith.
26. 22, I c. unto this day.
Rom. 6. 1, shall we c. in sin.
12. 12 ; Col. 4. 2, c. in prayer.
Gal. 3. 10, that c. not in all things.

Col. 1. 23 ; 1 Tim. 2. 15, if ye c. in the faith.
1 Tim. 4. 16 ; 2 Tim. 3. 14, c. in them.
Heb. 7. 23, not suffered to c. by reason.
24, this man c. ever.
13. 1, let brotherly love c.
14, here have we no c. city.
Jas. 4. 13, and c. there a year.
2 Pet. 3. 4, all things c. as they were.
1 John 2. 19, no doubt have c. with us.
See 1 Sam. 12. 14 ; 13. 14 ; 2 Sam. 7. 29.
CONTRADICTION. Heb. 7. 7 ; 12. 3.
CONTRARIWISE. 2 Cor. 2. 7 ; Gal. 2. 7 ; 1 Pet. 3. 9.
CONTRARY. Acts 18. 13, c. to the law.
26. 9, many things c. to name of Jesus.
Gal. 5. 17, c. the one to the other.
1 Thess. 2. 15, c. to all men.
1 Tim. 1. 10, c. to sound doctrine.
Tit. 2. 8, he of the c. part may be ashamed.
See Lev. 26. 21 ; Esther 9. 1 ; Mat. 14. 24 ; Acts 17. 7.
CONTRIBUTION. Rom. 15. 26.
CONTRITE. Ps. 34. 18 ; 51. 17 ; Isa. 57. 15 ; 66. 2.
CONTROVERSY. Jer. 25. 31, a c. with the nations.
Mic. 6. 2, hath a c. with his people.
1 Tim. 3. 16, without c. great is the mystery.
See Deut. 17. 8 ; 19. 17 ; 21. 5 ; 25. 1.
CONVENIENT. Prov. 30. 8, feed me with food c.
Acts 24. 25, when I have a c. season.
Rom. 1. 28, things which are not c.
Eph. 5. 4, talking, jesting, are not c.
See Jer. 40. 4 ; Mk. 6. 21 ; 1 Cor. 16. 12.
CONVERSANT. Josh. 8. 35 ; 1 Sam. 25. 15.
CONVERSATION. Ps. 37. 14, such as be of upright c.
50. 23, that ordereth his c. aright.
Phil. 1. 27, c. as becometh the gospel.
3. 20, our c. is in heaven.
1 Tim. 4. 12, an example in c.
Heb. 13. 5, c. without covetousness.
7, considering end of their c.
1 Pet. 1. 15 ; 2 Pet. 3. 11, holy c.
18, redeemed from vain c.
2. 12, your c. honest among Gentiles.
3. 1, won by c. of wives.
2 Pet. 2. 7, vexed with filthy c.
See Gal. 1. 13 ; Eph. 2. 3 ; 4. 22 ; Jas. 3. 13.
CONVERSION. Acts 15. 3.
CONVERT. Ps. 19. 7, perfect, c. the soul.
Isa. 6. 10 ; Mat. 13. 15 ; Mk. 4. 12 ; John 12. 40 ; Acts 28. 27, lest they c.
Mat. 18. 3, except ye be c.
Lu. 22. 32, when c. strengthen thy brethren.
Acts 3. 19, repent and be c.
Jas. 5. 19, 20, and one c. him.
See Ps. 51. 13 ; Isa. 1. 27 ; 60. 5.
CONVICTED. John 8. 9.
CONVINCE. John 8. 46, which of you c. me of sin?
Tit. 1. 9, able to c. gainsayers.
See Job 32. 12 ; Acts 18. 28 ; 1 Cor. 14. 24.
CONVOCATION. Ex. 12. 16 ; Lev. 23. 2 ; Num. 28. 26.
COOK. 1 Sam. 8. 13 ; 9. 23, 24.
COOL. Gen. 3. 8 ; Lu. 16. 24.
COPPER. Ezra 8. 27 ; 2 Tim. 4. 14.
COPY. Deut. 17. 18 ; Josh. 8. 32 ; Prov. 25. 1.
CORBAN. Mk. 7. 11, it is c.
CORD. Prov. 5. 22, holden with the c. of sins.
Eccl. 4. 12, a threefold c.
12. 6, silver c. loosed.
Isa. 5. 18, draw iniquity with c.
54. 2, lengthen c.
Hos. 11. 4, the c. of a man.
John 2. 15, scourge of small c.
See Judg. 15. 13 ; Ps. 2. 3 ; 118. 27 ; Jer. 38. 6.
CORN. Gen. 42. 2 ; Acts 7. 12, c. in Egypt.
Deut. 25. 4 ; 1 Cor. 9. 9 ; 1 Tim. 5. 18, ox treadeth c.

Judg. 15. 5, foxes into standing *c.*
Job 5. 26, like as a shock of *c.*
Ps. 4. 9, in time their *c.* increased.
65. 7, prepared them *c.*
13, valleys covered over with *c.*
72. 16, handful of *c.* in the earth.
Prov. 11. 26, he that withholdeth *c.*
Zech. 9. 17, *c.* shall make men cheerful.
Mat. 12. 1; Mk. 2. 23; Lu. 6. 1, pluck *c.*
Mk. 4. 28, full *c.* in the ear.
John 12. 24, a *c.* of wheat fall into ground.
See Gen. 27. 28; 41. 57; Deut. 33. 28; Isa. 36. 17.

CORNER. Ps. 118. 22; Eph. 2. 20, head stone of *c.*
144. 12, daughters as *c.* stones.
Isa. 28. 16; 1 Pet. 2. 6, a precious *c.* stone.
Mat. 6. 5, pray in *c.* of the streets.
Rev. 7. 1, on four *c.* of the earth.
See Job 1. 19; Prov. 7. 8; 21. 9.

CORNET. 2 Sam. 6. 5; 1 Chron. 15. 28; Dan. 3. 5.

CORPSE. 2 Kings 19. 35; Isa. 37. 36; Nah. 3. 3;
Mk. 6. 29.

CORRECT. Prov. 3. 12, whom the Lord loveth
he *c.*
29. 17, *c.* thy son.
19, servant will not be *c.* by words.
Jer. 10. 24, *c.* me, but with judgment.
30. 11; 46. 28, I will *c.* thee in measure.
Heb. 12. 9, we have had fathers which *c.* us.
See Job 5. 17; Ps. 39. 11; 94. 10.

CORRECTION. Prov. 22. 15, rod of *c.* shall drive it.
Jer. 2. 30; 5. 3; 7. 28; Zeph. 3. 2, receive *c.*
2 Tim. 3. 16, scripture profitable for *c.*
See Job 37. 13; Prov. 3. 11; 7. 22; 15. 10.

CORRUPT. Deut. 4. 16, take heed lest ye *c.*
31. 29, after my death ye will *c.*
Mat. 6. 19; Lu. 12. 33, moth *c.*
7. 17; 12. 33; Lu. 6. 43, a *c.* tree.
1 Cor. 15. 33, evil communications *c.*
2 Cor. 2. 17, not as many, which *c.* the word.
7. 2, we have *c.* no man.
11. 2, lest your minds be *c.*
Eph. 4. 22, put off old man which is *c.*
29, let no *c.* communication.
1 Tim. 6. 5; 2 Tim. 3. 8, men of *c.* minds.
Jas. 5. 1, your riches are *c.*
See Gen. 6. 11; Job 17. 1; Prov. 25. 26.

CORRUPTERS. Isa. 1. 4; Jer. 6. 28.

CORRUPTIBLE. Rom. 1. 23; 1 Cor. 9. 25; 15. 53;
1 Pet. 1. 18; 3. 4.

CORRUPTION. Ps. 16. 10; 49. 9; Acts 2. 27; 13. 35,
not see *c.*
Jonah 2. 6, brought up life from *c.*
Rom. 8. 21, from bondage of *c.*
1 Cor. 15. 42, 50, sown in *c.*
Gal. 6. 8, of flesh reap *c.*
2 Pet. 1. 4, the *c.* that is in world.
2. 12, perish in their own *c.*
See Lev. 22. 25; Job 17. 14; Isa. 38. 17.

CORRUPTLY. 2 Chron. 27. 2; Neh. 1. 7.

COST. 2 Sam. 24. 24; 1 Chron. 21. 24, offer of that
which *c.* nothing.
Lu. 14. 28, sitteth down and counteth *c.*
See 2 Sam. 19. 42; 1 Kings 5. 17; John 12. 3;
1 Tim. 2. 9.

COTTAGE. Isa. 1. 8; 24. 20; Zeph. 2. 6.

COUCH. Lu. 5. 19, let him down with *c.*
5. 24, take up thy *c.*
Acts 5. 15, laid sick on *c.*
See Gen. 49. 4; Job 7. 13; 38. 40; Ps. 6. 6; Amos
6. 4.

COULD. Isa. 5. 4; Mk. 6. 19; 9. 18; 14. 8.

COULTER. 1 Sam. 13. 20, 21.

COUNCIL. Mat. 5. 22; 10. 17; Acts 5. 27; 6. 12.

COUNSEL. Neh. 4. 15, brought their *c.* to nought.
Job 38. 2; 42. 3, darkeneth *c.* by words.
Ps. 1. 1, *c.* of the ungodly.
33. 11; Prov. 19. 21, *c.* of Lord standeth.

Ps. 55. 14, took sweet *c.* together.
73. 24, guide me with thy *c.*
Prov. 1. 25, 30, set at nought all my *c.*
11. 14, where no *c.* is, people fall.
15. 22, without *c.* purposes are disappointed.
21. 30, there is no *c.* against the Lord.
Eccl. 8. 2, I *c.* thee keep king's commandment.
Isa. 28. 29, wonderful in *c.*
30. 1, that take *c.*, but not of me.
40. 14, with whom took he *c.*
46. 10, my *c.* shall stand.
Jer. 32. 19, great in *c.*, mighty in working.
Hos. 10. 6, ashamed of his own *c.*
Mk. 3. 6; John 11. 53, took *c.* against Jesus.
Acts 2. 23, determinate *c.* of God.
4. 28, what thy *c.* determined before.
5. 38, if this *c.* be of men.
20. 27, declare all *c.* of God.
1 Cor. 4. 5, make manifest *c.* of the heart.
Eph. 1. 11, after the *c.* of his own will.
Heb. 6. 17, the immutability of his *c.*
Rev. 3. 18, I *c.* thee to buy gold tried in fire.
See Ex. 18. 19; Josh. 9. 14; 2 Sam. 15. 31.

COUNSELLOR. Prov. 11. 14; 15. 22; 24. 6, in mul-
titude of *c.*
12. 20, to *c.* of peace is joy.
Mic. 4. 9, is thy *c.* perished?
Mk. 15. 43; Lu. 23. 50, an honourable *c.*
Rom. 11. 34, who hath been his *c.*
See 2 Chron. 22. 3; Job 3. 14; 12. 17.

COUNT. Gen. 15. 6; Ps. 106. 31; Rom. 4. 3; Gal.
3. 6, *c.* for righteousness.
Ps. 44. 22, *c.* as sheep for the slaughter.
Prov. 17. 28, even a fool is *c.* wise.
Isa. 32. 15, field be *c.* for a forest.
Mat. 14. 5; Mk. 11. 32, they *c.* him as a prophet.
Lu. 21. 36; Acts 5. 41; 2 Thess. 1. 5, 11; 1 Tim.
5. 17, *c.* worthy.
Acts 20. 24, neither *c.* I my life dear.
Phil. 3. 7, 8, I *c.* loss for Christ.
13, I *c.* not myself to have apprehended.
Heb. 10. 29, *c.* blood an unholy thing.
Jas. 1. 2, *c.* it all joy.
2 Pet. 3. 9, as some men *c.* slackness.
See Num. 23. 10; Job 31. 4; Ps. 139. 18, 22.

COUNTENANCE. 1 Sam. 16. 7, look not on his *c.*
or stature.
12; 17. 42, David of beautiful *c.*
Neh. 2. 2, why is thy *c.* sad?
Job 14. 20, thou changest his *c.*
Ps. 4. 6; 44. 3; 89. 15; 90. 8, light of thy *c.*
Prov. 15. 13, merry heart maketh cheerful *c.*
27. 17, sharpeneth *c.* of his friend.
Eccl. 7. 3, by sadness of *c.* heart made better.
Isa. 3. 9, their *c.* doth witness against them.
Mat. 6. 16, hypocrites of a sad *c.*
28. 3; Lu. 9. 29, *c.* like lightning.
Rev. 1. 16, his *c.* as the sun shineth.
See Gen. 4. 5; Num. 6. 26; Judg. 13. 6.

COUNTRY. Prov. 25. 25, good news from a far *c.*
Mat. 13. 57; Mk. 6. 4; Lu. 4. 24; John 4. 44, in his
own *c.*
21. 33; 25. 14; Mk. 12. 1, went to far *c.*
Lu. 4. 23, do also here in thy *c.*
Acts 12. 20, their *c.* nourished by king's *c.*
Heb. 11. 9, sojourned as in strange *c.*
16, desire a better *c.*
See Gen. 12. 1; 24. 4; Josh. 9. 6; Lu. 15. 13.

COUNTRYMEN. 2 Cor. 11. 26; 1 Thess. 2. 14.

COUPLED. 1 Pet. 3. 2.

COURAGE. Deut. 31. 6; 7. 23; Josh. 10. 25; Ps. 27.
14; 31. 24, be of good *c.*
Acts 28. 15, thanked God and took *c.*
See Num. 13. 20; Josh. 1. 7; 2. 11; 2 Sam. 13. 28.

COURSE. Acts 20. 24; 2 Tim. 4. 7, finished my *c.*
2 Thess. 3. 1, may have free *c.*
Jas. 3. 6, setteth on fire the *c.* of nature.
See Judg. 5. 20; Ps. 82. 5; Acts 13. 25.

COURT. Ex. 27. 9, thou shalt make the c. of the tabernacle.
38. 9, and he made the c.
Ps. 65. 4, that he may dwell in thy c.
84. 2, fainteth for the c. of the Lord.
92. 13, flourish in the c. of our God.
100. 4, enter into his c. with praise.
Isa. 1. 12, who required this to tread my c.?
Lu. 7. 25, live delicately are in kings' c.
See Isa. 34. 13 ; Jer. 19. 14 ; Ezek. 9. 7.
COURTEOUS. Acts 27. 3 ; 28. 7 ; 1 Pet. 3. 8.
COUSIN. Lu. 1. 36, 58.
COVENANT. Num. 18. 19 ; 2 Chron. 13. 5, c. of salt.
25. 12, my c. of peace.
Ps. 105. 8 ; 106. 45, he remembereth his c. for ever.
111. 5, ever mindful of his c.
Isa. 28. 18, your c. with death disannulled.
Mat. 26. 15 ; Lu. 22. 5, they c. with him.
Acts 3. 25, children of the c.
Rom. 9. 4, to whom pertaineth the c.
Eph. 2. 12, strangers from c. of promise.
Heb. 8. 6, mediator of a better c.
12. 24, mediator of the new c.
13. 20, blood of the everlasting c.
See Gen. 9. 15 ; Ex. 34. 28 ; Job 31. 1 ; Jer. 50. 5.
COVER. Ex. 15. 5, depths c. them, sank as stone.
33. 22, I will c. them.
1 Sam. 28. 14, an old man c. with a mantle.
Esth. 7. 8, they c. Haman's face.
Ps. 32. 1 ; Rom. 4. 7, blessed whose sin is c.
73. 6, violence c. them as a garment.
91. 4, he shall c. thee with his feathers.
104. 6, thou c. it with the deep.
Prov. 10. 6, 11, violence c. mouth of the wicked.
12, love c. all sins.
12. 16, a prudent man c. shame.
17. 9, he that c. transgression seeketh love.
28. 13, he that c. sins shall not prosper.
Isa. 26. 21, earth no more c. her slain.
Mat. 8. 24, ship c. with waves.
10. 26 ; Lu. 12. 2, there is nothing c.
1 Cor. 11. 4, having his head c.
6, if women be not c.
7, a man ought not to c. his head.
1 Pet. 4. 8. charity shall c. multitude of sins.
See Gen. 7. 19 ; Ex. 8. 6 ; 21. 33 ; Lev. 16. 13.
COVERING. Job 22. 14, thick clouds are a c. to him.
24. 7, naked have no c. in the cold.
26. 6, destruction hath no c.
31. 19, if I have seen any poor without c.
Isa. 28. 20, c. narrower than he can wrap.
See Gen. 8. 13 ; Lev. 13. 45 ; 2 Sam. 17. 19.
COVERT. Ps. 61. 4 ; Isa. 4. 6 ; 16. 4 ; 32. 2.
COVET. Prov. 21. 26, he c. greedily all the day.
Hab. 2. 9, c. an evil covetousness.
Acts 20. 33, I have c. no man's silver.
1 Cor. 12. 31, c. earnestly the best gifts.
1 Tim. 6. 10, while some c. after, they erred.
See Ex. 20. 17 ; Deut. 5. 21 ; Rom. 7. 7 ; 13. 9.
COVETOUS. Prov. 28. 16, he that hateth c. shall prolong.
Ezek. 33. 31, their heart goeth after c.
Mk. 7. 22, out of heart proceedeth c.
Rom. 1. 29, filled with all c.
1 Cor. 6. 10 ; Eph. 5. 5, nor c. inherit kingdom.
Eph. 5. 3, but c., let it not be named.
2 Tim. 3. 2, men shall be c.
Heb. 13. 5, conversation without c.
2 Pet. 2. 3, through c. make merchandise.
14, exercised with c. practices.
See Ps. 10. 3 ; 119. 36 ; 1 Cor. 5. 10.
COW. Lev. 22. 28 ; Job 21. 10 ; Isa. 11. 7.
CRACKLING. Eccl. 7. 6.
CRAFT. Job 5. 13 ; 1 Cor. 3. 19, taketh wise in their c.
Lu. 20. 23, he perceived their c.
Acts 19. 25, by this c. we have our wealth.
27, our c. is in danger.

2 Cor. 4. 2, not walking in c.
12. 16, being c. I caught you.
Eph. 4. 14, carried away with cunning c.
See Dan. 8. 25 ; Acts 18. 3 ; Rev. 18. 22.
CRAG. Job 39. 28.
CRANE. Isa. 38. 14 ; Jer. 8. 7.
CRASHING. Zeph. 1. 10.
CRAVE. Prov. 16. 26 ; Mk. 15. 43.
CREATE. Isa. 40. 26, who hath c. these things?
43. 7, c. him for my glory.
65. 17, I c. new heavens and new earth.
Jer. 31. 22, the Lord hath c. a new thing.
Amos 4. 13, he that c. wind.
Mal. 2. 10, hath not one God c. us?
1 Cor. 11. 9, neither was man c. for woman.
Eph. 2. 10, c. in Christ Jesus.
4. 24, after God is c. in righteousness.
Col. 1. 16, by him were all things c.
1 Tim. 4. 3, which God c. to be received.
See Gen. 1. 1 ; 6. 7 ; Deut. 4. 32 ; Ps. 51. 10.
CREATION. Mk. 10. 6 ; 13. 19 ; Rom. 1. 20 ; 8. 22 ; 2 Pet. 3. 4.
CREATOR. Eccl. 12. 1 ; Isa. 40. 28 ; Rom. 1. 25 ; 1 Pet. 4. 19.
CREATURE. Mk. 16. 15 ; Col. 1. 23, preach to every c.
Rom. 8. 19, expectation of the c.
2 Cor. 5. 17 ; Gal. 6. 15, new c.
Col. 1. 15, firstborn of every c.
1 Tim. 4. 4, every c. of God is good.
See Gen. 1. 20 ; 2. 19 ; Isa. 13. 21 ; Ezek. 1. 20 ; Eph. 2. 10 ; 4. 24.
CREATURES. Ezek. 1. 5, came the likeness of four living c.
CREDITOR. Deut. 15. 2 ; 2 Kings 4. 1 ; Isa. 50. 1 ; Mat. 18. 23 ; Lu. 7. 41.
CREEK. Acts 27. 39.
CREEP. Ps. 104. 20, beasts of the forest c. forth.
25, in sea are c. things.
Ezek. 8. 10, form of c. things portrayed.
Acts 10. 12 ; 11. 6, Peter saw c. things.
2 Tim. 3. 6, they c. into houses.
Jude 4, certain men c. in unawares.
See Gen. 1. 25 ; 7. 8 ; Lev. 11. 41 ; Deut. 4. 18.
CREW. Mat. 26. 74 ; Mk. 14. 68 ; Lu. 22. 60.
CRIB. Job 39. 9 ; Prov. 14. 4 ; Isa. 1. 3.
CRIMSON. 2 Chr. 2. 7 ; Isa. 1. 18 ; Jer. 4. 30.
CRIPPLE. Acts 14. 8.
CROOKED. Eccl. 1. 15 ; 7. 13, c. cannot be made straight.
Isa. 40. 4 ; 42. 16 ; Lu. 3. 5, c. shall be made straight.
45. 2, make the c. places straight.
59. 8 ; Lam. 3. 9, c. paths.
Phil. 2. 15, in midst of a c. nation.
See Lev. 21. 20 ; Deut. 32. 5 ; Job 26. 13.
CROPS. Lev. 1. 16 ; Ezek. 17. 22.
CROSS. Mat. 16. 24 ; Mk. 8. 34 ; 10. 21 ; Lu. 9. 23 take up c.
27. 32 ; Mk. 15. 21 ; Lu. 23. 26, compelled to bear c.
40 ; Mk. 15. 30, come down from c.
John 19. 25, there stood by c.
1 Cor. 1. 17 ; Gal. 6. 12 ; Phil. 3. 18, c. of Christ.
18, preaching of the c.
Gal. 5. 11, offence of the c.
6. 14, glory save in the c.
Eph. 2. 16, reconcile both by the c.
Phil. 2. 8, the death of the c.
Col. 1. 20, peace through blood of the c.
2. 14, nailing it to his c.
Heb. 12. 2, for joy endured the c.
See Obad. 14 ; Mat. 10. 38 ; John 19. 17, 19.
CROUCH. 1 Sam. 2. 36 ; Ps. 10. 10.
CROWN. Job 19. 9, taken the c. from my head.
Ps. 8. 5 ; Heb. 2. 7, 9, c. with glory and honour.
65. 11, thou c. the year.
103. 4, c. thee with lovingkindness.

Prov. 4. 9, a *c.* of glory shall she deliver.
12. 4, virtuous woman is a *c.*
14. 18, prudent *c.* with knowledge.
16. 31, hoary head a *c.* of glory.
17. 6, children's children are the *c.* of old men.
Isa. 28. 1, woe to the *c.* of pride.
Mat. 27. 29 ; Mk. 15. 17 ; John 19. 2, a *c.* of thorns.
1 Cor. 9. 25, to obtain a corruptible *c.*
Phil. 4. 1, my joy and *c.*
1 Thess. 2. 19, a *c.* of rejoicing.
2 Tim. 2. 5, not *c.* except he strive.
4. 8, a *c.* of righteousness.
Jas. 1. 12 ; Rev. 2. 10, *c.* of life.
1 Pet. 5. 4, a *c.* of glory.
Rev. 3. 11, hold fast, that no man take thy *c.*
4. 10, cast *c.* before throne.
19. 12, on head were many *c.*
See Ex. 25. 25 ; 29. 6 ; Job 31. 36.
CRUCIFY. Mat. 27. 22, all said, let him be *c.*
Mk. 15. 13 ; Lu. 23. 21 ; John 19. 6, 15, *c.* him.
Acts 2. 23, by wicked hands ye have *c.*
Rom. 6. 6, old man is *c.* with him.
1 Cor. 1. 13, was Paul *c.* for you.
23, we preach Christ *c.*
2. 2, save Jesus Christ and him *c.*
2 Cor. 13. 4, though he was *c.* through weakness.
Gal. 2. 20, I am *c.* with Christ.
3. 1, Christ set forth *c.*
5. 24, have *c.* the flesh.
6. 14, the world is *c.* unto me.
Heb. 6. 6, *c.* to themselves afresh.
See Mat. 20. 19 ; 23. 34 ; 27. 31 ; Mk. 15. 20.
CRUEL. Ps. 25. 19, with *c.* hatred.
27. 12, breathe out *c.*
74. 20, full of the habitations of the *c.*
Prov. 5. 9, give thy years to the *c.*
11. 17, *c.* troubleth his own flesh.
12. 10, tender mercies of the wicked are *c.*
27. 4, wrath is *c.*
Cant. 8. 6, jealousy is *c.*
Heb. 11. 36, trials of *c.* mockings.
See Gen. 49. 7 ; Ex. 6. 9 ; Deut. 32. 33.
CRUMBS. Mat. 15. 27 ; Mk. 7. 28 ; Lu. 16. 21.
CRUSE. 1 Sam. 26. 11 ; 1 Kings 14. 3 ; 17. 12 ; 19. 6.
CRUSH. Job 5. 4, children are *c.* in the gate.
39. 15, forgetteth that the foot may *c.* them.
See Lev. 22. 24 ; Num. 22. 25 ; Deut. 28. 33.
CRY (*n.*). 1 Sam. 5. 12, *c.* of the city went up to heaven.
Job 34. 28, he heareth the *c.* of the afflicted.
Ps. 9. 12, forgetteth not *c.* of the humble.
34. 15, ears are open to their *c.*
Prov. 21. 13, stoppeth his ears at the *c.* of the poor.
Mat. 25. 6, at midnight there was a *c.* made.
See Gen. 18. 20 ; Ex. 2. 23 ; Num. 16. 34.
CRY (*v.*). Ex. 14. 15, wherefore *c.* thou unto me ?
Lev. 13. 45, cover his lip, and *c.* unclean.
Job 29. 12, I delivered poor that *c.*
Ps. 147. 9, food to young ravens which *c.*
Prov. 8. 1, doth not wisdom *c.*
Isa. 58. 1, *c.* aloud, spare not.
Mat. 12. 19, he shall not strive nor *c.*
20. 31 ; Mk. 10. 48 ; Lu. 18. 39, they *c.* the more.
Lu. 18. 7, elect who *c.* day and night.
John 7. 37, Jesus *c.* if any man thirst.
Acts 19. 32 ; 21. 34, some *c.* one thing and some another.
See Ex. 5. 8 ; 32. 18 ; 2 Kings 8. 3.
CRYING. Prov. 19. 18 ; Isa. 65. 19 ; Heb. 5. 7 ; Rev. 21. 4.
CRYSTAL. Job 28. 17 ; Ezek. 1. 22 ; Rev. 4. 6 ; 21. 11 ; 22. 1.
CUBIT. Mat. 6. 27 ; Lu. 12. 25.
CUCUMBERS. Num. 11. 5 ; Isa. 1. 8.
CUMBER. Deut. 1. 12 ; Lu. 10. 40 ; 13. 7.
CUNNING. Ps. 137. 5, let my hand forget her *c.*
Jer. 9. 17, send for *c.* women.
Eph. 4. 14, carried about by *c.* craftiness.

2 Pet. 1. 16, not follow *c.* devised fables.
See Gen. 25. 27 ; Ex. 38. 23 ; 1 Sam. 16. 16 ; Dan. 1. 4.
CUP. Ps. 116. 13, take *c.* of salvation.
Mat. 10. 42 ; Mk. 9. 41, *c.* of cold water.
20. 22 ; Mk. 10. 39, drink of my *c.*
23. 25, make clean outside of *c.*
26. 27 ; Mk. 14. 23 ; Lu. 22. 17 ; 1 Cor. 11. 25, took *c.*
39 ; Mk. 14. 36 ; Lu. 22. 42, let this *c.* pass.
Lu. 22. 20 ; 1 Cor. 11. 25, this *c.* is new testament.
John 18. 11, *c.* which my father hath given.
1 Cor. 10. 16, *c.* of blessing we bless.
11. 26, as often as ye drink this *c.*
27, drink this *c.* unworthily.
See Gen. 40. 11 ; 44. 2 ; Prov. 23. 31.
CURDLED. Job 10. 10.
CURE. Lu. 7. 21, in that hour he *c.* many.
9. 1, power to *c.* diseases.
13. 32, I do *c.* to-day.
See Jer. 33. 6 ; 46. 11 ; Hos. 5. 13 ; Mat. 17. 16.
CURIOUS. Ex. 28. 8 ; Ps. 139. 15 ; Acts 19. 19.
CURRENT. Gen. 23. 16.
CURSE (*n.*). Deut. 11. 26, I set before you blessing and *c.*
23. 5, turned *c.* into blessing.
Mal. 3. 9, ye are cursed with a *c.*
Gal. 3. 10, are under the *c.*
Rev. 22. 3, no more *c.*
See Gen. 27. 12 ; Num. 5. 18.
CURSE (*v.*). Lev. 19. 14, not *c.* the deaf.
Num. 23. 8, how shall I *c.* whom God hath not.
Judg. 5. 23, *c.* ye Meroz, *c.* ye bitterly.
Job 2. 9, *c.* God, and die.
Ps. 62. 4, they bless, but *c.* inwardly.
Mal. 2. 2, I will *c.* your blessings.
Mat. 5. 44 ; Lu. 6. 28 ; Rom. 12. 14, bless them that *c.* you.
26. 74 ; Mk. 14. 71, he began to *c.*
Mk. 11. 21, fig tree thou *c.*
John 7. 49, knoweth not the law are *c.*
Gal. 3. 10, *c.* is every one that continueth not.
Jas. 3. 9, therewith *c.* we men.
See Gen. 8. 21 ; 12. 3 ; Num. 22. 6.
CURTAIN. Ex. 26. 36, the length of one *c.*
CUSTOM. Mat. 9. 9 ; Mk. 2. 14 ; Lu. 5. 27, receipt of *c.*
Mat. 17. 25, of whom do kings take *c.*
Lu. 4. 16, as his *c.* was, went into synagogue.
John 18. 39, ye have a *c.*
Acts 16. 21, teach *c.* which are not lawful.
Rom. 13. 7, *c.* to whom *c.*
1 Cor. 11. 16, we have no such *c.*
See Gen. 31. 35 ; Judg. 11. 39 ; Jer. 10. 3.
CUTTING. Ex. 31. 5 ; 35. 33 ; Isa. 38. 10 ; Mk. 5. 5.
CYMBAL. 1 Cor. 13. 1.
CYMBALS. 2 Sam. 6. 5, on cornets and on *c.*
1 Chron. 15. 16, harps and *c.*
16. 5, Asaph made a noise with *c.*
Ps. 150. 5, praise him upon the loud *c.*

D.

DAGGER. Judg. 3. 16, 21, 22.
DAILY. Ps. 13. 2, sorrow in my heart *d.*
68. 19, *d.* loadeth us.
Prov. 8. 30, I was *d.* his delight.
Dan. 8. 11 ; 11. 31 ; 12. 11, *d.* sacrifice taken away.
Mat. 6. 11 ; Lu. 11. 3, our *d.* bread.
Lu. 9. 23, take up cross *d.*
Acts 2. 47, added to church *d.*
6. 1, the *d.* ministration.
16. 5, churches increased *d.*
17. 11, searched the scriptures *d.*
1 Cor. 15. 31, I die *d.*
Jas. 2. 15, destitute of *d.* food.
See Num. 4. 16 ; 28. 24 ; Neh. 5. 18 ; Dan. 1. 5.
DAINTY. Ps. 141. 4, let me not eat of their *d.*
Prov. 23. 3, be not desirous of his *d.*
See Gen. 49. 20 ; Job 33. 20 ; Rev. 18. 14.

DALE. Gen. 14. 17 ; 2 Sam. 18. 18.
DAM. Ex. 22. 30 ; Lev. 22. 27 ; Deut. 22. 6.
DAMAGE. Prov. 26. 6, drinketh *d.*
Acts 27. 10, voyage will be with much *d.*
2 Cor. 7. 9, receive *d.* by us in nothing.
See Ezra 4. 22 ; Esth. 7. 4 ; Dan. 6. 2.
DAMNABLE. 2 Pet. 2. 1.
DAMNATION. Mat. 23. 33, can ye escape the
d. of hell.
Mk. 3. 29, in danger of eternal *d.*
John 5. 29, the resurrection of *d.*
Rom. 13. 2, receive to themselves *d.*
1 Cor. 11. 29, eateth and drinketh *d.*
2 Pet. 2. 3, their *d.* slumbereth not.
See Mat. 23. 14 ; Mk. 12. 40 ; Lu. 20. 47 ; Rom. 3. 8.
DAMNED. Mk. 16. 16 ; Rom. 14. 23 ; 2 Thess. 2. 12.
DAMSEL. Ps. 68. 25, among them were the *d.*
playing.
Mat. 14. 11 ; Mk. 6. 28, given to the *d.*
26. 69 ; John 18. 17, *d.* came to Peter.
Mk. 5. 39, the *d.* is not dead.
Acts 12. 13, a *d.* came to hearken.
16. 16, *d.* possessed with a spirit.
See Gen. 24. 55 ; 34. 3 ; Judg. 5. 30 ; Ruth 2. 5.
DANCE. Ex. 32. 19, he saw the calf, and *d.*
1 Sam. 18. 6, came out singing and *d.*
2 Sam. 6. 14, David *d.* before the Lord.
Job 21. 11, their children *d.*
Ps. 30. 11, turned my mourning into *d.*
149. 3 ; 150. 4, praise him in the *d.*
Eccl. 3. 4, a time to *d.*
Mat. 11. 17 ; Lu. 7. 32, piped, and ye have not *d.*
14. 6 ; Mk. 6. 22, daughter of Herodias *d.*
See Judg. 21. 23 ; Jer. 31. 13 ; Lam. 5. 15.
DANDLED. Isa. 66. 12.
DANGER. Mat. 3. 29 ; Mk. 5. 21 ; Acts 19. 27 ; 27. 9.
DARE. Rom. 5. 7, some would even *d.* to die.
See Job 41. 10 ; Rom. 15. 18 ; 1 Cor. 6. 1 ; 2 Cor. 10. 12.
DARK. Job 12. 25, they grope in the *d.*
22. 13, can he judge through *d.* cloud ?
24. 16, in the *d.* they dig.
38. 2, that *d.* counsel by words.
Ps. 49. 4 ; Prov. 1. 6, *d.* sayings.
69. 23 ; Rom. 11. 10, let their eyes be *d.*
88. 12, wonders be known in the *d.*
Eccl. 12. 2, stars be not *d.*
3, look out of windows be *d.*
Zech. 14. 6, shall not be clear nor *d.*
Mat. 24. 29 ; Mk. 13. 24, sun be *d.*
Lu. 23. 45, sun *d.* and vail rent.
John 20. 1, early, when it was yet *d.*
Rom. 1. 21, foolish heart was *d.*
Eph. 4. 18, understanding *d.*
See Gen. 15. 17 ; Ex. 10. 15 ; Num. 12. 8 ; Joel
2. 10.
DARKNESS. Deut. 5. 22, spake out of thick *d.*
28. 29, grope as the blind in *d.*
1 Sam. 2. 9, wicked shall be silent in *d.*
2 Sam. 22. 10 ; Ps. 18. 9, *d.* under his feet.
29 ; Ps. 18. 28, Lord will enlighten my *d.*
1 Kings 8. 12 ; 2 Chron. 6. 1, dwell in thick *d.*
Job 3. 5 ; Ps. 10. 10, *d.* and shadow of death.
10. 22, land where the light is as *d.*
30. 26, waited for light there came *d.*
Ps. 91. 6, pestilence that walketh in *d.*
97. 2, clouds and *d.* are round about him.
112. 4, to upright ariseth light in *d.*
139. 12, *d.* and light alike to thee.
Prov. 20. 20, lamp be put out in *d.*
Eccl. 2. 13, as far as light excelleth *d.*
14, fool walketh in *d.*
Isa. 58. 10, thy *d.* as noon day.
60. 2, *d.* cover the earth, gross *d.*
Joel 2. 2, day of clouds and thick *d.*
Mat. 6. 23 ; Lu. 11. 34, body full of *d.*
8. 12 ; 22. 13 ; 25. 30, outer *d.*
10. 27 ; Lu. 12. 3, what I tell in *d.* speak.
Lu. 1. 79 ; Rom. 2. 19, light to them that sit in *d.*

Lu. 22. 53 ; Col. 1. 13, the power of *d.*
23. 44, *d.* over all the earth.
John 1. 5, *d.* comprehended it not.
3. 19, loved *d.* rather than light.
John 12. 35, walk while ye have light, lest *d.*
Acts 26. 18, turn from *d.* to light.
Rom. 13. 12 ; Eph. 5. 11, works of *d.*
1 Cor. 4. 5, hidden things of *d.*
2 Cor. 4. 6, light to shine out of *d.*
6. 14, what communion hath light with *d.*?
Eph. 6. 12, rulers of the *d.* of this world.
1 Thess. 5. 5, not of the night nor of *d.*
Heb. 12. 18, to blackness and *d.*
1 Pet. 2. 9, out of *d.* into marvellous light.
2 Pet. 2. 4, into chains of *d.*
1 John 1. 5, in him is no *d.* at all.
6, and walk in *d.*, we lie.
1 John 2. 8, the *d.* is past.
9, hateth his brother, is in *d.*
11, *d.* hath blinded his eyes.
Rev. 16. 10, kingdom full of *d.*
See Gen. 1. 2 ; 15. 12 ; Ex. 10. 21 ; 20. 21.
DARLING. Ps. 22. 20 ; 35. 17.
DART. Job 41. 26 ; Prov. 7. 23 ; Eph. 6. 16.
DASH. Ps. 2. 9 ; Isa. 13. 16 ; Hos. 13. 16, *d.* in pieces.
91. 12 ; Mat. 4. 6 ; Lu. 4. 11, *d.* thy foot.
137. 9, that *d.* thy little ones.
See Ex. 15. 6 ; 2 Kings 8. 12 ; Jer. 13. 14.
DAUB. Ex. 2. 3 ; Ezek. 13. 10 ; 22. 28.
DAUGHTER. Gen. 24. 23, 47 ; Judg. 11. 34, whose *d.*
art thou ?
27. 46, weary of life because of *d.* of Heth.
Deut. 28. 53, eat flesh of sons and *d.*
2 Sam. 1. 20, lest *d.* of Philistines rejoice.
12. 3, lamb was unto him as a *d.*
Ps. 45. 9, kings' *d.* among honourable women.
144. 12, our *d.* as corner-stones.
Prov. 30. 15, horseleech hath two *d.*
31. 29, many *d.* have done virtuously.
Eccl. 12. 4, the *d.* of music.
Isa. 22. 4 ; Jer. 9. 1 ; Lam. 2. 11 ; 3. 48, spoiling of
the *d.*
Jer. 6. 14, healed hurt of *d.* of my people.
8. 21, for hurt of *d.* am I hurt.
9. 1, weep for slain of *d.* of my people.
Mic. 7. 6 ; Mat. 10. 35 ; Lu. 12. 53, *d.* riseth against
mother.
Mat. 15. 28, her *d.* was made whole.
Lu. 8. 42, one only *d.*, about twelve years of age.
13. 16, this woman *d.* of Abraham.
Heb. 11. 24, refused to be son of Pharaoh's *d.*
See Gen. 6. 1 ; Ex. 1. 16 ; 21. 7 ; Num. 27. 8.
DAWN. Ps. 119. 147, I prevented the *d.* of the
morning.
2 Pet. 1. 19, till the day *d.*
See Josh. 6. 15 ; Judg. 19. 26 ; Job 3. 9 ; 7. 4.
DAY. Gen. 41. 9, I do remember my faults this *d.*
Deut. 4. 32, ask of the *d.* that are past.
1 Sam. 25. 8, come in a good *d.*
2 Kings 7. 9, this *d.* is a *d.* of good tidings.
1 Chron. 23. 1, 28 ; 2 Chron. 24. 15, full of *d.*
29. 15 ; Job 8. 9, our *d.* as a shadow.
Neh. 4. 2, will they make an end in a *d.*
Job 7. 1, *d.* like the *d.* of an hireling.
14. 6, till he accomplish his *d.*
19. 25, stand at latter *d.* upon the earth.
21. 30, reserved to *d.* of destruction.
32. 7, I said, *d.* should speak.
Ps. 2. 7 ; Acts 13. 33 ; Heb. 1. 5, this *d.* have I begotten thee.
19. 2, *d.* unto *d.* uttereth speech.
Ps. 84. 10, a *d.* in thy courts.
Prov. 3. 2, 16, length of *d.*
4. 18, more and more to perfect *d.*
27. 1, what a *d.* may bring forth.
Eccl. 7. 1, *d.* of death better than *d.* of birth.
12. 1, while the evil *d.* come not.
Isa. 2. 12 ; 13. 6, 9 ; Joel 1. 15 ; 2. 1 ; Zeph. 1. 7 ;
Zech. 14. 1, *d.* of the Lord.

Isa. 10. 3, in the *d.* of visitation.
27. 3, the Lord will keep it night and *d.*
58. 5, acceptable *d.* to the Lord.
65. 20, an infant of *d.*
Joel 2. 11, 31; Zeph. 1. 14; Mal. 4. 5; Acts 2. 20, great *d.* of the Lord.
Zech. 4. 10, despised *d.* of small things.
Mal. 3. 2, who may abide *d.* of his coming.
Mat. 7. 22, many will say in that *d.*
Mat. 24. 36; Mk. 13. 32, that *d.* knoweth no man.
50; Lu. 12. 46, in a *d.* looked not for.
25. 13, ye know not the *d.* nor the hour.
Lu. 21. 34, that *d.* come unawares.
23. 43, to-*d.* shalt thou be with me.
John 6. 39, raise it again at last *d.*
8. 56, Abraham rejoiced to see my *d.*
9. 4, I must work while it is *d.*
Acts 17. 31, he hath appointed a *d.*
Rom. 2. 5, wrath against *d.* of wrath.
14. 5, esteemeth every *d.* alike.
2 Cor. 6. 2, the *d.* of salvation.
Phil. 1. 6, perform it until *d.* of Christ.
1 Thess. 5. 2; 2 Pet. 3. 10, *d.* cometh as a thief.
5, children of the *d.*
Heb. 13. 8, Jesus Christ same to-*d.* and for ever.
2 Pet. 3. 8, one *d.* as a thousand years.
See Gen. 1. 5; 27. 2; Job 1. 4; Ps. 77. 5; 118. 24; John 11. 24; 12. 48; 1 Cor. 3. 13; Rev. 6. 17; 16. 14; 20. 10.

AYS (last). Isa. 2. 2, it shall come to pass in the last *d.*
See Mic. 4. 1; Acts 2. 17; 2 Tim. 3. 1; Heb. 1. 2; James 5. 3; 2 Pet. 3. 3.

AYSMAN. Job 9. 33.

AYSPRING. Job 38. 12, *d.* to know his place.
Lu. 1. 78, *d.* from on high hath visited us.

AYSTAR. 2 Pet. 1. 19, *d.* arise in your hearts.

EAD. Lev. 19. 28, cuttings for the *d.*
Ruth 1. 8, as ye have dealt with *d.*
1 Sam. 24. 14; 2 Sam. 9. 8; 16. 9, *d.* dog.
Ps. 31. 12, forgotten as a *d.* man.
115. 17, *d.* praise not the Lord.
Prov. 9. 18, knoweth not that the *d.* are there.
Eccl. 4. 2, the *d.* which are already *d.*
9. 4, living dog better than *d.* lion.
5, *d.* know not any thing.
10. 1, *d.* flies cause ointment.
Isa. 26. 19, thy *d.* men shall live.
Jer. 22. 10, weep not for the *d.*
Mat. 8. 22, let the *d.* bury their *d.*
9. 24; Mk. 5. 39; Lu. 8. 52, not *d.*, but sleepeth.
11. 5; Lu. 7. 22, deaf hear, *d.* raised.
22. 32, not God of the *d.*
23. 27, full of *d.* men's bones.
Mk. 9. 10, rising from *d.* should mean.
Lu. 15. 24, 32; Rev. 1. 18, *d.* and is alive again.
16. 31, though one rose from the *d.*
John 5. 25, *d.* shall hear.
6. 49, did eat manna, and are *d.*
11. 25, though *d.*, yet shall he live.
44, he that was *d.* came forth.
Acts 10. 42; 2 Tim. 4. 1, judge of quick and *d.*
26. 23, first that should rise from *d.*
Rom. 6. 2, 11; 1 Pet. 2. 24, *d.* to sin.
7. 4; Gal. 2. 19, *d.* to the law.
14. 9, Lord both of *d.* and living.
1 Cor. 15. 15, if the *d.* rise not.
35, how are the *d.* raised.
2 Cor. 1. 9, trust in God who raiseth *d.*
5. 14, then were all *d.*
Eph. 2. 1; Col. 2. 13, *d.* in trespasses and sins.
5. 14, arise from the *d.*
Col. 1. 18, firstborn from the *d.*
2. 20; 2 Tim. 2. 11, *d.* with Christ.
Thess. 4. 16, *d.* in Christ shall rise first.
Tim. 5. 6, *d.* while she liveth.
Heb. 6. 1; 9. 14, from *d.* works.
11. 4, being *d.*, yet speaketh.
13. 20, brought again from the *d.*
as. 2. 17, 20, 26, faith *d.*

1 Pet. 4. 6, preached to them that are *d.*
Jude 12, twice *d.*
Rev. 1. 5, first-begotten of the *d.*
3. 1, a name that thou livest and art *d.*
14. 13, blessed are the *d.*
20. 5, rest of *d.* lived not again.
12, the *d.* small and great.
13, sea gave up *d.*
See Gen. 23. 3; Ex. 12. 30; Mk. 9. 26; Rev. 1. 18.

DEADLY. Mk. 16. 18, drink any *d.* thing.
Jas. 3. 8, tongue full of *d.* poison.
See 1 Sam. 5. 11; Ps. 17. 9; Ezek. 30. 24.

DEAF. Ps. 58. 4, like *d.* adder that stoppeth.
Isa. 29. 18, shall the *d.* hear the words.
Mat. 11. 5; Lu. 7. 22, the *d.* hear.
Mk. 7. 37, he maketh the *d.* to hear.
9. 25, thou *d.* spirit, come out.
See Ex. 4. 11; Lev. 19. 14; Isa. 42. 18; 43. 8.

DEAL (a measure). Ex. 29. 40, with the one lamb, a tenth *d.* of flour.
Lev. 14. 10, three tenth *d.* of fine flour for a meat offering.

DEAL. Lev. 19. 11, nor *d.* falsely.
Job 42. 8, *d.* with you after folly.
Ps. 75. 4, *d.* not foolishly.
Prov. 12. 22, they that *d.* truly his delight.
Isa. 21. 2; 24. 16, treacherous dealer *d.* treacherously.
26. 10, in land of uprightness *d.* unjustly.
Jer. 6. 13; 8. 10, every one *d.* falsely.
Hos. 5. 7, have *d.* treacherously against the Lord.
Zech. 1. 6, as Lord thought, so hath he *d.*
Mk. 7. 36; 10. 48, the more a great *d.*
Lu. 2. 48, why hast thou thus *d.* with us?
Rom. 12. 3, according as God hath *d.*
See Gen. 32. 9; Ex. 1. 10; Deut. 7. 5; 2 Chron. 2. 3.

DEALING. 1 Sam. 2. 23; Ps. 7. 16; John 4. 9.

DEAR. Jer. 31. 20, is Ephraim my *d.* son.
Acts 20. 24, neither count I my life *d.*
Rom. 12. 19; 1 Cor. 10. 14; 2 Cor. 7. 1; 12. 19; Phil. 4. 1; 2 Tim. 1. 2; 1 Pet. 2. 11, *d.* beloved.
Eph. 5. 1, followers of God as *d.* children.
Col. 1. 13, into kingdom of his *d.* Son.
1 Thess. 2. 8, because ye were *d.* unto us.
See Jer. 12. 7; Lu. 7. 2; Philem. 1.

DEARTH. 2 Chr. 6. 28, if there be a *d.* in the land.
Neh. 5. 3, buy corn because of *d.*
Acts 11. 28, Agabus signified a great *d.*
See Gen. 41. 54; 2 Kings 4. 38; Jer. 14. 1; Acts 7. 11.

DEATH. Num. 16. 29, if these men die common *d.*
23. 10, let me die *d.* of righteous.
Judg. 5. 18, jeoparded lives to the *d.*
16. 16, soul was vexed to *d.*
30, which he slew at his *d.* were more.
Ruth 1. 17, if ought but *d.* part thee and me.
1 Sam. 15. 32, the bitterness of *d.* past.
20. 3, but a step between me and *d.*
2 Sam. 1. 23, in *d.* not divided.
22. 5; Ps. 18. 4; 116. 3, waves of *d.* compassed.
Job 3. 21, long for *d.*, but it cometh not.
7. 15, my soul chooseth *d.*
30. 23, thou wilt bring me to *d.*
Ps. 6. 5, in *d.* no remembrance.
13. 3, lest I sleep the sleep of *d.*
23. 4, valley of shadow of *d.*
48. 14, our guide even unto *d.*
68. 20, the issues from *d.*
89. 48, what man shall not see *d.*
102. 20, loose those appointed to *d.*
107. 10, in darkness and shadow of *d.*
116. 15, precious is *d.* of his saints.
Prov. 7. 27, to chambers of *d.*
8. 36, that hate me love *d.*
14. 32, righteous hath hope in his *d.*
24. 11, deliver them drawn to *d.*
Cant. 8. 6, love is strong as *d.*
Isa. 9. 2; Jer. 2. 6, land of the shadow of *d.*
25. 8; 1 Cor. 15. 56, swallow up *d.* in victory.

Isa. 38. 18, for _d._ cannot celebrate thee.
Jer. 8. 3, _d._ chosen rather than life.
9. 21, _d._ come up to our windows.
Ezek. 18. 32 ; 33. 11, no pleasure in _d._
Hos. 13. 14, O _d._ I will be thy plagues.
Mat. 15. 4 ; Mk. 7. 10, let him die the _d._
16. 28 ; Mk. 9. 1 ; Lu. 9. 27, not taste of _d._
26. 38 ; Mk. 14. 34, my soul is sorrowful to _d._
Mk. 5. 23 ; John 4. 47, lieth at point of _d._
Lu. 2. 26, should not see _d._ before.
22. 33, will go to prison and _d._
John 5. 24 ; 1 John 3. 14, passed from _d._ to life.
8. 51, 52, keep my saying, shall never see _d._
11. 4, sickness not unto _d._
12. 33 ; 18. 32 ; 21. 19, signifying what _d._
Acts 2. 24, having loosed pains of _d._
Rom. 1. 32, such things are worthy of _d._
5. 10 ; Col. 1. 22, reconciled by the _d._
12, _d._ by sin and so _d._ passed on all.
14, 17, _d._ reigned from Adam to Moses.
6. 5, planted in likeness of his _d._
21, end of those things is _d._
23, wages of sin is _d._
8. 2, law of sin and _d._
1 Cor. 3. 22, life or _d._ all are yours.
11. 26, show the Lord's _d._ till he come.
15. 21, by man came _d._
55, 56, O _d._ where is thy sting ?
2 Cor. 1. 9, sentence of _d._ in ourselves.
2. 16, savour of _d._ unto _d._
4. 12, _d._ worketh in us.
11. 23, in _d._ oft.
Phil. 2. 8, _d.,_ even _d._ of the cross.
Heb. 2. 9, taste _d._ for every man.
15, through fear of _d._ were.
Jas. 1. 15, sin bringeth forth _d._
1 John 5. 16, a sin unto _d._
Rev. 1. 18, keys of hell and of _d._
2. 10, be faithful unto _d._
11 ; 6. 14, second _d._
6. 8, his name that sat on him was _d._
9. 6, seek _d._ and _d._ shall flee.
20. 6, _d._ and hell delivered up.
21. 4, no more _d._
See Prov. 14. 12 ; 16. 25 ; John 18. 31 ; Jas. 5. 20.
DEBASE. Isa. 57. 9.
DEBATE. Prov. 25. 9 ; Isa. 58. 4 ; Rom. 1. 29 ;
2 Cor. 12. 20.
DEBT. 2 Kings 4. 7, go, pay thy _d._ and live.
Neh. 10. 31, leave the exaction of every _d._
Prov. 22. 26, be not sureties for _d._
Mat. 18. 27, forgave him the _d._
See 1 Sam. 22. 2 ; Mat. 6. 12 ; Rom. 4. 4.
DEBTOR. Mat. 6. 12, as we forgive our _d._
Lu. 7. 41, creditor which had two _d._
Rom. 1. 14, I am _d._ to the Greeks.
8. 12, we are _d.,_ not to the flesh.
15. 27, their _d._ they are.
Gal. 5. 3, _d._ to do the whole law.
See Ezek. 18. 7 ; Mat. 18. 21 ; 23. 16 ; Lu. 16. 5.
DECAY. Lev. 25. 35 ; Neh. 4. 10 ; Heb. 8. 13.
DECEASE. Isa. 26. 14 ; Mat. 22. 25 ; Lu. 9. 31 ;
2 Pet. 1. 15.
DECEIT. Ps. 10. 7, mouth full of _d._ and fraud.
36. 3, words are iniquity and _d._
55. 23, _d._ men shall not live half their days.
Prov. 12. 5, counsels of wicked are _d._
20. 17, bread of _d._ is sweet.
27. 6, kisses of an enemy are _d._
31. 30, favour is _d._ and beauty vain.
Jer. 14. 14 ; 23. 26, prophesy the _d._ of their heart.
17. 9, heart is _d._ above all things.
48. 10, that doeth work of the Lord _d._
Hos. 11. 12, compasseth me with _d._
Amos 8. 5, falsifying balances by _d._
Zeph. 1. 9, fill their masters' houses with _d._
Mat. 13. 22 ; Mk. 4. 19, the _d._ of riches.
Mk. 7. 22, out of heart proceed _d._
Rom. 3. 13, they have used _d._
2 Cor. 4. 2, handling word of God _d._

2 Cor. 11. 13, false apostles, _d._ workers.
Eph. 4. 22, according to _d._ lusts.
Col. 2. 8, vain _d.,_ after tradition.
See Ps. 50. 19 ; Prov. 12. 20 ; Jer. 5. 27 ; Mic. 6. 11.
DECEIVE. Deut. 11. 16, take heed that your hear
be not _d._
2 Kings 19. 10 ; Isa. 37. 10, let not thy God _d._ thee
Job 12. 16, the _d._ and the _d._ are his.
Jer. 20. 7, thou hast _d._ me and I was _d._
37. 9, _d._ not yourselves.
Obad. 3, pride of heart hath _d._ thee.
Mat. 24. 24, if possible _d._ the very elect.
27. 63, remember that _d._ said.
John 7. 12, nay, but he _d._ the people.
47, are ye also _d._ ?
1 Cor. 6. 9 ; 15. 33 ; Gal. 6. 7, be not _d._
2 Cor. 6. 8, as _d.,_ and yet true.
Eph. 4. 14, whereby they lie in wait to _d._
5. 6 ; 2 Thess. 2. 3 ; 1 John 3. 7, let no man _d._ you
1 Tim. 2. 14, Adam was not _d._
2 Tim. 3. 13, worse and worse, _d._ and being _d._
1 John 1. 8, no sin, we _d._ ourselves.
2 John 7, many _d._ entered into world.
See Gen. 31. 7 ; Isa. 44. 20 ; Ezek. 14. 9 ; Rev. 12. 9
19. 20.
DECENTLY. 1 Cor. 14. 40.
DECISION. Joel 3. 14.
DECK. Job 40. 10, _d._ thyself with majesty.
Isa. 61. 10, as a bridegroom _d._ himself.
Jer. 4. 30, though thou _d._ thee with ornaments.
10. 4, they _d._ it with silver.
See Prov. 7. 16 ; Ezek. 16. 11 ; Rev. 17. 4 ; 18. 16.
DECLARATION. Esth. 10. 2 ; Job 13. 17 ; Lu. 1. 1
2 Cor. 8. 19.
DECLARE. 1 Chron. 16. 24 ; Ps. 96. 3, _d._ glory amon
heathen.
Job 21. 31, who shall _d._ his way to his face.
31. 37, I would _d._ number of my steps.
Ps. 2. 7, I will _d._ decree.
9. 11, _d._ among the people his doings.
19. 1, heavens _d._ glory of God.
30. 9, shall dust _d._ thy truth.
40. 10, I have _d._ thy faithfulness.
66. 16, I will _d._ what he hath done.
75. 9, I will _d._ for ever.
118. 17, live and _d._ the works of the Lord.
145. 4, one generation shall _d._ thy mighty acts
Isa. 3. 9, they _d._ their sin as Sodom.
41. 26 ; 45. 21, who hath _d._ from beginning.
45. 19, I _d._ things that are right.
46. 10, _d._ end from the beginning.
53. 8 ; Acts 8. 33, who shall _d._ his generation.
66. 19, _d._ my glory among Gentiles.
John 17. 26, have _d._ thy name and will _d._ it.
Acts 13. 32, we _d._ to you glad tidings.
17. 23, him _d._ I unto you.
20. 27, _d._ the counsel of God.
Rom. 1. 4, _d._ to be Son of God with power.
1 Cor. 3. 13, day shall _d._ it.
See Josh. 20. 4 ; John 1. 18 ; Heb. 11. 14 ; 1 John 1.
DECLINE. Deut. 17. 11, thou shalt not _d._ fro
sentence.
2 Chron. 34. 2, _d._ neither to right nor left.
Ps. 102. 11 ; 109. 23, days like a shadow that _d._
119. 51, 157, not _d._ from thy law.
See Ex. 23. 2 ; Job 23. 11 ; Prov. 4. 5 ; 7. 25.
DECREASE. Gen. 8. 5 ; Ps. 107. 38 ; John 3. 30.
DECREE. Job 22. 28, thou shalt _d._ a thing and
shall be.
28. 26, made a _d._ for the rain.
Ps. 148. 6, a _d._ which shall not pass.
Prov. 8. 15, by me princes _d._ justice.
29, he gave to the sea his _d._
Isa. 10. 1, _d._ that _d._ unrighteous _d._
Acts 16. 4, delivered the _d._ to keep.
See Dan. 2. 9 ; 6. 8 ; Acts 17. 7 ; 1 Cor. 7. 37.
DEDICATE. Deut. 20. 5, lest he die and anoth
_d._ it.

Judg. 17. 3, wholly *d.* silver to the Lord.
1 Chron. 26. 27, of spoil they did *d.*
Ezek. 44. 29, every *d.* thing shall be theirs.
See 1 Kings 7. 51; 8. 63; 15. 15; 1 Chron. 18. 11;
Heb. 9. 18.
DEED. Ex. 9. 16; 1 Sam. 25. 34; 26. 4, in very *d.*
2 Sam. 12. 14, by this *d.* hast given occasion.
Ezra 9. 13, come upon us for our evil *d.*
Neh. 13. 14, wipe not out my good *d.*
Ps. 28. 4; Isa. 59. 18; Jer. 25. 14; Rom. 2. 6, according to their *d.*
Lu. 11. 48, ye allow the *d.* of your fathers.
23. 41, due reward of our *d.*
24. 19, a prophet mighty in *d.*
John 3. 19, because their *d.* were evil.
8. 41, ye do the *d.* of your father.
Acts 7. 22, Moses, mighty in word and *d.*
Rom. 3. 20, by *d.* of law no flesh justified.
28, justified without *d.* of the law.
Col. 3. 9, put off old man with his *d.*
17, whatsoever ye do in word or *d.*
Jas. 1. 25, shall be blessed in his *d.*
1 John 3. 18, not love in word, but in *d.*
See Gen. 44. 15; Lu. 23. 51; Acts 19. 18.
DEEMED. Acts 27. 27.
DEEP. Gen. 7. 11; 8. 2, fountains of *d.*
Deut. 33. 13, the *d.* that coucheth beneath.
Job 38. 30, face of *d.* is frozen.
41. 31, maketh the *d.* boil like a pot.
Ps. 36. 6, thy judgments are a great *d.*
42. 7, *d.* calleth to *d.*
95. 4, in his hand are the *d.* places.
107. 24, see his wonders in the *d.*
Prov. 22. 14; 23. 27, strange women *d.* pit.
Isa. 63. 13, led them through *d.*
Mat. 13. 5, no *d.* of earth.
Lu. 5. 4, launch into *d.*
6. 48, digged *d.* and laid foundations.
8. 31, command to go into the *d.*
John 4. 11, the well is *d.*
1 Cor. 2. 10, searcheth *d.* things of God.
See Job 4. 13; 33. 15; Prov. 19. 15; Rom. 10. 7.
DEER. Deut. 14. 5; 1 Kings 4. 23.
DEFAME. Jer. 20. 10; 1 Cor. 4. 13.
DEFEAT. 2 Sam. 15. 34; 17. 14.
DEFENCE. Job 22. 25, the Almighty shall be thy *d.*
Ps. 7. 10, my *d.* is of God.
59. 9, 17; 62. 2, for God is my *d.*
89. 18; 94. 22, Lord is *d.*
Eccl. 7. 12, wisdom a *d.*, money a *d.*
Isa. 33. 16, place of *d.* munitions of rocks.
Phil. 1. 7, 17, in *d.* of the Gospel.
See Num. 14. 9; Acts 19. 33; 22. 1.
DEFEND. Ps. 5. 11, shout for joy, because thou *d.*
them.
82. 3, *d.* the poor and fatherless.
Zech. 9. 15, Lord of hosts shall *d.* them.
Acts 7. 24, *d.* him and avenged the oppressed.
See Ps. 20. 1; 59. 1; Isa. 31. 5.
DEFILE. Ex. 31. 14, that *d.* sabbath be put to death.
Num. 35. 33, blood *d.* the land.
2 Kings 23. 13, high places did king *d.*
Neh. 13. 29, they have *d.* the priesthood.
Ps. 74. 7; 79. 1, *d.* dwelling-place of thy name.
106. 39, *d.* with their own works.
Isa. 59. 3, your hands are *d.* with blood.
Jer. 2. 7; 16. 18, ye *d.* my land.
Ezek. 4. 13, eat their *d.* bread.
23. 38, they have *d.* my sanctuary.
36. 17, they *d.* it by their own ways.
Dan. 1. 8, would not *d.* himself with meat.
Mat. 15. 11, 18, 20; Mk. 7. 15, 20, 23, *d.* a man.
John 18. 28, lest they should be *d.*
1 Cor. 3. 17, if any man *d.* temple of God.
8. 7, conscience being weak is *d.*
1 Tim. 1. 10, law for them that *d.* themselves.
Tit. 1. 15, to *d.* nothing pure, even conscience *d.*
Heb. 12. 15, thereby many be *d.*
Jude 8, filthy dreamers *d.* flesh.

Rev. 3. 4, few not *d.* their garments.
See Ex. 31. 41; Lev. 21. 4; Jas. 3. 6; Rev. 21. 27.
DEFRAUD. 1 Sam. 12. 3, 4, whom have I *d.*?
Mk. 10. 19; 1 Cor. 7. 5, *d.* not.
1 Cor. 6. 7, rather suffer to be *d.*
8, do wrong and *d.* your brethren.
2 Cor. 7. 2, we have *d.* no man.
See Lev. 19. 13; 1 Thess. 4. 6.
DEGENERATE. Jer. 2. 21.
DEGREE. Ps. 62. 9, men of low *d.*, high *d.*
1 Tim. 3. 13, purchase to themselves good *d.*
Jas. 1. 9, brother of low *d.* rejoice.
See 2 Kings 20. 9; 1 Chron. 17. 17; Isa. 38. 8; Lu. 1. 52.
DELAY. Mat. 24. 48; Lu. 12. 45, my lord *d.* his coming.
Acts 9. 38, that he would not *d.* to come.
See Ex. 22. 29; 32. 1; Acts 25. 17.
DELECTABLE. Isa. 44. 9.
DELICACY. Rev. 18. 3.
DELICATE. 1 Sam. 15. 32, Agag came to him *d.*
Prov. 29. 21, he that *d.* bringeth up servant.
Isa. 47. 1, no more called tender and *d.*
Lam. 4. 5, that did feed *d.* are desolate.
Lu. 7. 25, that live *d.* are in kings' courts.
See Deut. 28. 54, 56; Jer. 6. 2; Mic. 1. 16.
DELICIOUSLY. Rev. 18. 7.
DELIGHT (*n.*). Deut. 10. 15, Lord had a *d.* in thy fathers.
1 Sam. 15. 22, hath Lord as great *d.* in offerings.
2 Sam. 15. 26, I have no *d.* in thee.
Job 22. 26, shalt thou have *d.* in the Almighty.
Ps. 1. 2, his *d.* is in law of Lord.
16. 3, to excellent in whom is my *d.*
119. 24, testimonies my *d.* and counsel.
77, 92, 174, thy law is my *d.*
143, thy commandments are my *d.*
Prov. 8. 30, I was daily his *d.*
31, my *d.* were with sons of men.
18. 2, fool hath no *d.* in understanding.
19. 10, *d.* not seemly for a fool.
Cant. 2. 3, under his shadow with great *d.*
Isa. 58. 13, call sabbath a *d.*
See Prov. 11. 1; 12. 22; 15. 8; 16. 13.
DELIGHT (*v.*). Job 27. 10, will he *d.* himself in the Almighty?
Ps. 37. 4, *d.* also in the Lord.
11, meek shall *d.* in abundance of peace.
51. 16, thou *d.* not in burnt offering.
94. 19, thy comforts *d.* my soul.
Isa. 42. 1, elect in whom my soul *d.*
55. 2, soul *d.* itself in fatness.
62. 4, the Lord *d.* in thee.
Mic. 7. 18, he *d.* in mercy.
Rom. 7. 22, I *d.* after the inward man.
See Num. 14. 8; Prov. 1. 22; 2. 14; Mal. 3. 1.
DELIGHTSOME. Mal. 3. 12.
DELIVER. Ex. 3. 8; Acts 7. 34, I am come down to *d.* them.
Num. 35. 25, congregation shall *d.* slayer.
Deut. 32. 39; Isa. 43. 13, any *d.* out of my hand.
2 Chron. 32. 13, were gods able to *d.* their lands.
Job 5. 19, shall *d.* thee in six troubles.
36. 18, great ransom cannot *d.*
Ps. 33. 17, nor *d.* any by great strength.
56. 13, *d.* my feet from falling.
144. 10, *d.* David from hurtful sword.
Prov. 24. 11, forbear to *d.* them.
Eccl. 9. 15, by wisdom *d.* city.
Isa. 50. 2, have I no power to *d.*?
Jer. 1. 8, I am with thee to *d.* thee.
39. 17, I will *d.* in that day.
Dan. 3. 17, for God is able to *d.*, and will *d.*
6. 14, king set heart on Daniel to *d.*
Amos 2. 14, neither shall mighty *d.*
9. 1, he that escapeth shall not be *d.*
Mal. 3. 15, they that tempt God are *d.*
Mat. 6. 13; Lu. 11. 4, *d.* us from evil.

D d

Mat. 11. 27 ; Lu. 10. 22, all things *d.* to me of
my Father.
26. 15, I will *d.* him to you.
Acts 2. 23, being *d.* by the counsel of God.
Rom. 4. 25, was *d.* for our offences.
7. 6, we are *d.* from the law.
8. 21, creature shall be *d.*
2 Cor. 4. 11, *d.* to death for Jesus' sake.
2 Tim. 4. 18, *d.* me from every evil work.
Jude 3, faith once *d.* to saints.
See Rom. 8. 32 ; 2 Cor. 1. 10 ; Gal. 1. 4 ; 2 Pet. 2. 7.

DELIVERANCE. 2 Kings 5. 1, by him had given
d. to Syria.
1 Chron. 11. 14, saved by great *d.*
Ps. 32. 7, compass me with songs of *d.*
Lu. 4. 18, preach *d.* to the captives.
Heb. 11. 35, not accepting *d.*
See Gen. 45. 7 ; Joel 2. 32 ; Obad. 17.

DELUSION. Isa. 66. 4 ; 2 Thess. 2. 11.

DEMAND. Dan. 4. 17 ; Mat. 2. 4 ; Lu. 3. 14.

DEMONSTRATION. 1 Cor. 2. 4.

DEN. Job 37. 8, then the beasts go into *d.*
Isa. 11. 8, put hand on cockatrice *d.*
Jer. 7. 11, is this house a *d.* of robbers.
Mat. 21. 13 ; Mk. 11. 17, a *d.* of thieves.
Heb. 11. 38, in deserts and in *d.*
See Judg. 6. 2 ; Dan. 6. 7 ; Amos 3. 4.

DENOUNCE. Deut. 30. 18.

DENY. Josh. 24. 27, lest ye *d.* your God.
Prov. 30. 9, lest I be full and *d.* thee.
Lu. 20. 27, which *d.* resurrection.
2 Tim. 2. 13, he cannot *d.* himself.
Tit. 1. 16, in works they *d.* him.
See 1 Tim. 5. 8 ; 2 Tim. 3. 5 ; Tit. 2. 12.

DEPART. Gen. 49. 10, sceptre shall not *d.* from
Judah.
2 Sam. 22. 22 ; Ps. 18. 21, have not *d.* from my
God.
Job 21. 14 ; 22. 17, they say to God, *d.*
28. 28, to *d.* from evil is understanding.
Ps. 6. 8 ; Mat. 7. 23 ; Lu. 13. 27, *d.* ye workers of
iniquity.
34. 14 ; 37. 27, *d.* from evil, and do good.
105. 38, Egypt was glad when they *d.*
Prov. 15. 24, he may *d.* from hell beneath.
22. 6, when old he will not *d.* from it.
27. 22, yet will not foolishness *d.*
Mat. 14. 16, they need not *d.*
25. 41, *d.* from me, ye cursed.
Lu. 2. 29, lettest thou thy servant *d.* in peace.
4. 13, devil *d.* for a season.
21. 21, let them in midst *d.*
John 13. 1, when Jesus knew he should *d.*
2 Cor. 12. 8, besought that it might *d.* from me.
Phil. 1. 23, desire to *d.*
1 Tim. 4. 1, some shall *d.* from the faith.
2 Tim. 2. 19, nameth Christ *d.* from iniquity.
See Isa. 54. 10 ; Mic. 2. 10 ; 2 Tim. 4. 6 ; Heb. 3. 12.

DEPOSED. Dan. 5. 20.

DEPRIVED. Gen. 27. 45 ; Job 39. 17 ; Isa. 38. 10.

DEPTH. Job 28. 14, *d.* saith, it is not in me.
Ps. 33. 7, he layeth up *d.* in storehouses.
77. 16, waters afraid, *d.* troubled.
106. 9, led through *d.* as through wilderness.
107. 26, they go down again to *d.*
Prov. 8. 24, when no *d.* I was brought forth.
25. 3, heaven for height, earth for *d.*
Mat. 18. 6, better drowned in *d.* of sea.
Mk. 4. 5, no *d.* of earth.
Rom. 11. 33, the *d.* of the riches.
See Isa. 7. 11 ; Mic. 7. 19 ; Rom. 8. 39.

DEPUTED. 2 Sam. 15. 3.

DEPUTY. 1 Kings 22. 47 ; Acts 13. 7 ; 18. 12 ;
19. 38.

DERIDE. Hab. 1. 10 ; Lu. 16. 14 ; 23. 35.

DERISION. Job 30. 1, younger than I have me
in *d.*

Ps. 2. 4, the Lord shall have them in *d.*
44. 13 ; 79. 4, a *d.* to them round us.
Jer. 20. 7, 8, in *d.* daily.
Lam. 3. 14, I was a *d.* to my people.
See Ps. 119. 51 ; Ezek. 23. 32 ; 36. 4 ; Hos. 7. 16.

DESCEND. Ezek. 26. 20 ; 31. 16, with them that
d. into pit.
Mat. 7. 25, 27, rain *d.* and floods came.
Mk. 1. 10 ; John 1. 32, 33, Spirit *d.*
15. 32, let Christ now *d.* from cross.
Rom. 10. 7, who shall *d.* into the deep?
Eph. 4. 10, he that *d.* is same that ascended.
Jas. 3. 15, this wisdom *d.* not.
Rev. 21. 10, great city *d.* out of heaven.
See Gen. 28. 12 ; Ps. 49. 17 ; 133. 3 ; Prov. 30. 4.

DESCENT. Lu. 19. 37 ; Heb. 7. 3, 6.

DESCRIBE. Josh. 18. 4 ; Judg. 8. 14 ; Rom. 4. 6
10. 5.

DESCRY. Judg. 1. 23.

DESERT. Ps. 78. 40, oft did they grieve him in *d*
102. 6, like an owl of the *d.*
Isa. 35. 1, the *d.* shall rejoice.
6 ; 43. 19, streams in the *d.*
40. 3, in *d.* a highway for our God.
Jer. 2. 6, led us through land of *d.*
17. 6, like the heath in the *d.*
25. 24, people that dwell in *d.* shall drink.
Mat. 24. 26, say, behold, he is in the *d.*
Lu. 1. 80, John in *d.* till his showing.
9. 10, aside privately into *d.* place.
John 6. 31, did eat manna in *d.*
See Ex. 5. 3 ; 19. 2 ; Isa. 51. 3 ; Mk. 6. 31.

DESERTS. Ps. 28. 4 ; Ezek. 7. 27.

DESERVE. Judg. 9. 16 ; Ezra 9. 13 ; Job 11. 6.

DESIRE (*n.*). 2 Chron. 15. 15, sought him with
their whole *d.*
Job 34. 36, my *d.* is that Job may be tried.
Ps. 10. 3 ; 21. 2 ; Rom. 10. 1, heart's *d.*
37. 4, he shall give thee the *d.* of thine heart.
54. 7 ; 59. 10 ; 92. 11 ; 112. 8, *d.* on enemies.
92. 11 ; 112. 10 ; 140. 8, *d.* of the wicked.
145. 16, the *d.* of every living thing.
Prov. 10. 24 ; 11. 23, the *d.* of righteous.
13. 12, when *d.* cometh, it is a tree of life.
19. 22, the *d.* of a man is his kindness.
21. 25, the *d.* of slothful killeth him.
Eccl. 12. 5, *d.* shall fail.
Ezek. 24. 16, 21, 25, the *d.* of thine eyes.
Mic. 7. 3, great man uttereth mischievous *d.*
Hab. 2. 5, enlargeth *d.* as hell.
Hag. 2. 7, the *d.* of all nations.
Lu. 22. 15, with *d.* I have *d.* to eat.
Eph. 2. 3, fulfilling *d.* of flesh and mind.
Phil. 1. 23, having a *d.* to depart.
See Gen. 3. 16 ; Job 14. 15 ; 31. 16.

DESIRE (*v.*). Deut. 14. 26, bestow for whatsoever
thy soul *d.*
1 Sam. 2. 16, take as much as thy soul *d.*
12. 13, behold the king whom ye *d.*
Neh. 1. 11, servants who *d.* to fear thy name.
Job 13. 3, I *d.* to reason with God.
Ps. 19. 10, more to be *d.* than gold.
27. 4, one thing I *d.* of the Lord.
34. 12, that *d.* life and loveth many days.
40. 6, sacrifice and offering thou didst not *d.*
45. 11, king greatly *d.* thy beauty.
73. 25, none on earth I *d.* beside thee.
107. 30, to their *d.* haven.
Prov. 3. 15 ; 8. 11, all thou canst *d.* not to be
compared.
13. 4, soul of sluggard *d.*, and hath not.
Eccl. 2. 10, what my eyes *d.* I kept not.
Isa. 53. 2, no beauty that we should *d.*
Hos. 6. 6, I *d.* mercy and not sacrifice.
Mic. 7. 1, soul *d.* first-ripe fruit.
Zeph. 2. 1, gather together, O nation not *d.*
Mat. 12. 46 ; Lu. 8. 20, his brethren *d.*
13. 17, have *d.* to see those things.
20. 20, *d.* a certain thing of him.

Mk. 9. 35, if any *d.* to be first.
10. 35, do for us whatsoever we *d.*
11. 24, what things ye *d.* when ye pray.
15. 6 ; Lu. 23. 25, prisoner whom they *d.*
Lu. 9. 9, who is this, and he *d.* to see him.
10. 24, kings have *d.* to see.
16. 21, *d.* to be fed with crumbs.
20. 46, scribes *d.* to walk in long robes.
22. 15, have *d.* to eat this passover.
31, Satan hath *d.* to have you.
Acts 3. 14, *d.* a murderer to be granted.
1 Cor. 14. 1, and *d.* spiritual gifts.
2 Cor. 5. 2, *d.* to be clothed upon.
Gal. 4. 9, ye *d.* again to be in bondage.
21, ye that *d.* to be under the law.
6. 12, many *d.* to make show in the flesh.
Eph. 3. 13, I *d.* that ye faint not.
Phil. 4. 17, not because I *d.* a gift ; I *d.* fruit.
1 Tim. 3. 1, he *d.* a good work.
Heb. 11. 16, they *d.* a better country.
Jas. 4. 2, ye *d.* to have, and cannot obtain.
1 Pet. 1. 12, the angels *d.* to look into.
2. 2, as babes *d.* sincere milk of word.
1 John 5. 15, we have petitions we *d.*
See Gen. 3. 6 ; Job 7. 2 ; Ps. 51. 6 ; Lu. 5. 39.

DESIRABLE. Ezek. 23. 6, 12, 23.

DESIROUS. Prov. 23. 3 ; Lu. 23. 8 ; John 16. 19 ;
Gal. 5. 26.

DESOLATE. Ps. 25. 16, have mercy, for I am *d.*
40. 15, let them be *d.* for reward.
143. 4, my heart within me is *d.*
Isa. 54. 1 ; Gal. 4. 27, more are children of *d.*
62. 4, nor shall thy land any more be termed *d.*
Jer. 2. 12, be ye very *d.*, saith the Lord.
32. 43 ; 33. 12, *d.* without man or beast.
Ezek. 6. 6, your altars may be made *d.*
Dan. 11. 31 ; 12. 11, abomination that maketh *d.*
Mal. 1. 4, return and build the *d.* places.
Mat. 23. 38 ; Lu. 13. 35, house left to you *d.*
Acts 1. 20, let his habitation be *d.*
Rev. 18. 19, in one hour is she made *d.*
See Ps. 34. 22 ; Jer. 12. 10 ; Joel 2. 3 ; Zech. 7. 14.

DESOLATION. 2 Kings 22. 19, they should be-
come a *d.* and a curse.
Ps. 46. 8, what *d.* he hath made in the earth.
74. 3 ; Jer. 25. 9 ; Ezek. 35. 9, perpetual *d.*
Prov. 1. 27, when your fear cometh as *d.*
3. 25, the *d.* of the wicked.
Isa. 61. 4, raise up former *d.*, the *d.* of many
generations.
Dan. 9. 26, to end of war *d.* are determined.
Zeph. 1. 15, a day of wrath, wasting, and *d.*
Mat. 12. 25 ; Lu. 11. 17, house divided brought
to *d.*
Lu. 21. 20, then know *d.* is nigh.
See Lev. 26. 31 ; Josh. 8. 28 ; Job 30. 14.

DESPAIR. 1 Sam. 27. 1 ; Eccl. 2. 20 ; 2 Cor. 4. 8.

DESPERATE. Job 6. 26 ; Isa. 17. 11 ; Jer. 17. 9.

DESPISE. Num. 11. 20, ye have *d.* the Lord.
15. 31 ; Prov. 13. 13 ; Isa. 5. 24 ; 30. 12, *d.* the word.
1 Sam. 2. 30, that *d.* me shall be lightly esteemed.
Neh. 4. 4, hear, O God, for we are *d.*
Esth. 1. 17, so that they *d.* their husbands.
Job 5. 17 ; Prov. 3. 11 ; Heb. 12. 5, *d.* not chastening.
19. 18, young children *d.* me.
36. 5, God is mighty and *d.* not any.
Ps. 51. 17, contrite heart thou wilt not *d.*
53. 5, put to shame, because God *d.* them.
73. 20, thou shalt *d.* their image.
102. 17, he will not *d.* their prayer.
Prov. 1. 7, fools *d.* wisdom.
30 ; 5. 12, *d.* reproof.
6. 30, men do not *d.* a thief.
15. 5, fool *d.* father's instruction.
20, foolish man *d.* his mother.
32, refuseth instruction *d.* own soul.
19. 16, he that *d.* his ways shall die.

Prov. 30. 17, *d.* to obey his mother, ravens shall.
Eccl. 9. 16, poor man's wisdom is *d.*
Isa. 33. 15, he that *d.* gain of oppressions.
49. 7, saith Lord to him whom man *d.*
Jer. 49. 15, I will make thee small and *d.*
Ezek. 20. 13, 16, they *d.* my judgments.
22. 8, thou hast *d.* holy things.
Amos 2. 4, they *d.* the law of the Lord.
Zech. 4. 10, who hath *d.* day of small things.
Mal. 1. 6, wherein have we *d.* thy name ?
Mat. 6. 24 ; Lu. 16. 13, hold to one, *d.* the other.
18. 10, *d.* not one of these little ones.
Lu. 10. 16, *d.* you, *d.* me ; *d.* him that sent me.
18. 9, righteous, and *d.* others.
Rom. 2. 4, *d.* thou the riches of his goodness.
1 Cor. 1. 28, things *d.* God hath chosen.
4. 10, ye are honourable, but we are *d.*
11. 22, *d.* ye the church of God.
16. 11, let no man therefore *d.* him.
1 Thess. 4. 8, *d.* not man, but God.
5. 20, *d.* not prophesyings.
1 Tim. 4. 12, let no man *d.* thy youth.
6. 2, not *d.* because brethren.
Tit. 2. 15, let no man *d.* thee.
Heb. 12. 2, endured cross, *d.* the shame.
Jas. 2. 6, ye have *d.* the poor.
See Gen. 16. 4 ; 25. 34 ; 2 Sam. 6. 16 ; Rom. 14. 3.

DESPISERS. Acts 13. 41 ; 2 Tim. 3. 3.

DESPITE. Ezek. 25. 6, 15 ; 36. 5 ; Rom. 1. 30 ;
Heb. 10. 29.

DESPITEFULLY. Mat. 5. 44 ; Lu. 6. 28 ; Acts 14. 5.

DESTITUTE. Ps. 102. 17, will regard prayer of *d.*
Prov. 15. 21, folly is joy to him that is *d.* of
wisdom.
1 Tim. 6. 5, *d.* of the truth.
Heb. 11. 37, being *d.*, afflicted, tormented.
See Gen. 24. 27 ; Ezek. 32. 15 ; Jas. 2. 15.

DESTROY. Gen. 18. 23, *d.* righteous with the
wicked.
Ex. 22. 20, he shall be utterly *d.*
Deut. 9. 14, let me alone that I may *d.* them.
1 Sam. 15. 6, depart, lest I *d.* you with them.
2 Sam. 1. 14, *d.* Lord's anointed.
Job 2. 3, movedst me to *d.* without cause.
10. 8, made me, yet thou dost *d.* me.
19. 10, he hath *d.* me on every side.
26, though worms *d.* this body.
Ps. 40. 14 ; 63. 9, seek my soul to *d.* it.
145. 20, all the wicked will he *d.*
Prov. 1. 32, prosperity of fools shall *d.* them.
13. 23, is *d.* for want of judgment.
31. 3, that which *d.* kings.
Eccl. 9. 18, one sinner *d.* much good.
Isa. 10. 7, it is in his heart to *d.*
11. 9 ; 65. 25, *d.* in holy mountain.
19. 3, I will *d.* the counsel thereof.
28. 2, as a *d.* storm.
Jer. 13. 14, I will not spare but *d.* them.
17. 18, *d.* them with double destruction.
23. 1, woe to pastors that *d.* the sheep.
Ezek. 9. 1, with *d.* weapon in his hand.
22. 27, *d.* souls to get dishonest gain.
Dan. 8. 24, he shall *d.* wonderfully.
Hos. 13. 9, thou hast *d.* thyself.
Mat. 5. 17, not to *d.* but to fulfil.
10. 28, fear him that is able to *d.*
12. 14 ; Mk. 3. 6 ; 11. 18, they might *d.* him.
21. 41, he will miserably *d.* those.
22. 7, and *d.* those murderers.
27. 20, ask Barabbas and *d.* Jesus.
Mk. 1. 24 ; Lu. 4. 34, art thou come to *d.*
12. 9 ; Lu. 20. 16, *d.* the husbandmen.
14. 58, say, I will *d.* this temple.
15. 29, thou that *d.* the temple.
Lu. 6. 9, is it lawful to save life or *d.*
9. 56, is not come to *d.* men's lives.
17. 27, flood came and *d.* them all.
John 2. 19, Jesus said, *d.* this temple.
Rom. 14. 15, *d.* not him with thy meat.

1 Cor. 6. 13, God shall *d.* both it and them.
Gal. 1. 23, preacheth the faith he once *d.*
2. 18, if I build the things which I *d.*
2 Thess. 2. 8, *d.* with brightness of his coming.
Heb. 2. 14, *d.* him that had the power.
Jas. 4. 12, able to save and to *d.*
1 John 3. 8, *d.* the works of the devil.
See Gen. 6. 17 ; Isa. 65. 8 ; Rom. 6. 6 ; 2 Pet. 2. 12 ;
Jude 5.

DESTROYER. Ex. 12. 23, not suffer *d.* to come.
Judg. 16. 24, delivered the *d.* of our country.
Job 15. 21, in prosperity the *d.* shall come.
Ps. 17. 4, kept from paths of the *d.*
Prov. 28. 24, the companion of a *d.*
See Job 33. 22 ; Isa. 49. 17 ; Jer. 22. 7 ; 50. 11.

DESTRUCTION. 2 Chron. 22. 4, his counsellors
to his *d.*
26. 16, heart lifted up to *d.*
Esth. 8. 6, endure to see *d.* of my kindred.
Job 5. 21, neither be afraid of *d.*
21. 17, how oft cometh *d.*
26. 6, *d.* hath no covering.
31. 3, is not *d.* to the wicked.
Ps. 9. 6, *d.* are come to a perpetual end.
35. 8, into that very *d.* let him fall.
73. 18, thou castest them down to *d.*
90. 3, turnest man to *d.*
91. 6, the *d.* that wasteth at noon day.
103. 4, redeemeth thy life from *d.*
Prov. 1. 27, your *d.* cometh as a whirlwind.
10. 14, mouth of foolish near *d.*
15, *d.* of poor is their poverty.
14. 28, want of people *d.* of the prince.
16. 18, pride goeth before *d.*
17. 19, exalteth gate seeketh *d.*
18. 7, fool's mouth is his *d.*
27. 20, hell and *d.* never full.
31. 8, such as are appointed to *d.*
Isa. 14. 23, the besom of *d.*
19. 18, the city of *d.*
59. 7, wasting and *d.* in their paths.
60. 18, *d.* be no more heard.
Jer. 17. 18, destroy with double *d.*
46. 20, *d.* cometh out of north.
50. 22, sound of great *d.* in the land.
Lam. 2. 11 ; 3. 48 ; 4. 10, *d.* of the daughter of my
people.
Hos. 13. 14, O grave, I will be thy *d.*
Mat. 7. 13, broad way leadeth to *d.*
Rom. 3. 16, *d.* and misery in their ways.
9. 22, vessels fitted to *d.*
Phil. 3. 18, 19, many walk whose end is *d.*
1 Thess. 5. 3, then sudden *d.* cometh.
2 Thess. 1. 9, punished with everlasting *d.*
1 Tim. 6. 9, lusts drown men in *d.*
2 Pet. 2. 1, bring on themselves swift *d.*
3. 16, wrest to their own *d.*
See Job 21. 20 ; 31. 23 ; Prov. 10. 29 ; 21. 15.

DETAIN. Judg. 13. 15, 16 ; 1 Sam. 21. 7.
DETERMINATE. Acts 2. 23.
DETERMINATION. Zeph. 3. 8.
DETERMINE. Ex. 21. 22, pay as the judges *d.*
1 Sam. 20. 7, be sure evil is *d.* by him.
Job 14. 5, seeing his days are *d.*
Dan. 11. 36, that that is *d.* shall be done.
Lu. 22. 22, Son of man goeth as it was *d.*
Acts 3. 13, Pilate was *d.* to let him go.
17. 26, hath *d.* the times appointed.
1 Cor. 2. 2, I *d.* not to know anything.
See 2 Chron. 2. 1 ; 25. 16 ; Isa. 19. 17 ; Dan. 9. 24.

DETEST. Deut. 7. 26.
DETESTABLE. Jer. 16. 18 ; Ezek. 5. 11 ; 7. 20 ;
11. 18 ; 37. 23.

DEVICE. Esth. 9. 25, *d.* return on his own head.
Ps. 10. 2, let them be taken in the *d.*
33. 10, maketh *d.* of the people of none effect.
37. 7, bringeth wicked *d.* to pass.
Prov. 1. 31, be filled with their own *d.*
12. 2, man of wicked *d.* will he condemn.

Prov. 19. 21, many *d.* in a man's heart.
Eccl. 9. 10, no work nor *d.* in grave.
Jer. 18. 12, will walk after our own *d.*
Dan. 11. 24, 25, he shall forecast *d.*
Acts 17. 29, like stone graven by man's *d.*
2 Cor. 2. 11, not ignorant of his *d.*
See 2 Chron. 2. 14 ; Esth. 8. 3 ; Job 5. 12.

DEVILISH. Jas. 3. 15.
DEVILS (sacrifices offered to). Lev. 17. 7, offer
their sacrifices unto *d.*
See Deut. 32. 17 ; 2 Chron. 11. 15 ; Ps. 106. 37 ; 1 Cor.
10. 20 ; Rev. 9. 20.
DEVILS (confess Jesus to be Christ). Mat. 8. 29 ;
Mk. 1. 24 ; 3. 11 ; 5. 7 ; Lu. 4. 34, 41 ; Acts 19. 15.
Jas. 2. 19, the *d.* also believe and tremble.

DEVISE. Ex. 31. 4 ; 35, 32, 35, *d.* works in gold.
Ps. 35. 4, to confusion that *d.* my hurt.
36. 4, he *d.* mischief on his bed.
41. 7, against me do they *d.* my hurt.
Prov. 3. 29, *d.* not evil against thy neighbour.
6. 14, he *d.* mischief continually.
18, a heart that *d.* wicked imaginations.
14. 22, err that *d.* evil, good.
16. 9, man's heart *d.* his way.
Isa. 32. 7, *d.* wicked devices to destroy poor.
8, the liberal *d.* liberal things.
2 Pet. 1. 16, cunningly *d.* fables.
See 2 Sam. 14. 14 ; Jer. 51. 12 ; Lam. 2. 17 ; Mic. 2. 1.

DEVOTE. Ley. 27. 21, 28 ; Num. 18. 14 ; Ps. 119. 38.
DEVOTIONS. Acts 17. 23.
DEVOUR. Gen. 37. 20, some evil beast hath *d.*
him.
41. 7, 24, seven thin *d.* the seven rank.
Ex. 24. 17 ; Isa. 29. 6 ; 30. 27, 30 ; 33. 14, *d.* fire.
Lev. 10. 2, fire from Lord *d.* them.
Deut. 32. 24, *d.* with burning heat.
2 Sam. 11. 25, sword *d.* one as well as another.
18. 8, wood *d.* more than sword *d.*
2 Sam. 22. 9 ; Ps. 18. 8, fire out of his mouth *d.*
Job 18. 13, death shall *d.* his strength.
Ps. 80. 13, beasts of field *d.* it.
Prov. 20. 25, man who *d.* that which is holy.
30. 14, jaw teeth as knives to *d.*
Isa. 1. 7, strangers *d.* it in your presence.
20, if ye rebel, be *d.* with sword.
Jer. 2. 30, your sword hath *d.* prophets.
3. 24, shame *d.* labour of our fathers.
30. 16, that *d.* thee shall be *d.*
Ezek. 15. 7, fire shall *d.* them.
23. 37, pass through fire to *d.* them.
Hos. 8. 14 ; Amos 1. 14 ; 2. 2, it shall *d.* palaces.
Joel 2. 3, a fire *d.* before them.
Amos 4. 9, fig trees, palmer-worm *d.* them.
Hab. 1. 13, wicked *d.* man that is more righteous.
Zeph. 1. 18 ; 3. 8, *d.* by fire of jealousy.
Mal. 3. 11, will rebuke the *d.* for your sakes.
Mat. 13. 4 ; Mk. 4. 4 ; Lu. 8. 5, fowls *d.* them.
23. 14 ; Mk. 12. 40 ; Lu. 20. 47, *d.* widows' houses
Lu. 15. 30, thy son hath *d.* thy living.
2 Cor. 11. 20, if a man *d.* you.
Gal. 5. 15, ye bite and *d.* one another.
Heb. 10. 27, which shall *d.* adversaries.
1 Pet. 5. 8, seeking whom he may *d.*
See Gen. 31. 15 ; 2 Sam. 2. 26 ; Ps. 50. 3 ; 52. 4.

DEVOUT. Lu. 2. 25, Simeon was just and *d.*
Acts 2. 5 ; 8. 2, *d.* men.
See Acts 10. 2 ; 13. 50 ; 17. 4, 17 ; 22. 12.

DEW. Gen. 27. 28, God give thee the *d.* of
heaven.
Deut. 32. 2, my speech shall distil as the *d.*
33. 13, for the *d.*, and for the deep.
Judg. 6. 37, if the *d.* be on the fleece only.
2 Sam. 1. 21, let there be no *d.*
17. 12, we will light on him as *d.* falleth.
1 Kings 17. 1, there shall not be *d.* nor rain.
Job 38. 28, who hath begotten drops of *d.*
Prov. 3. 20, clouds drop down *d.*
Isa. 18. 4, like *d.* in heat of harvest.
Dan. 4. 15, 23, 25, 33, wet with *d.* of heaven.

Hos. 6. 4 ; 13. 3, goodness as early *d.*
Hag. 1. 10, heaven is stayed from *d.*
See Ex. 16. 13 ; Num. 11. 9 ; Job 29. 19 ; Ps. 110. 3 ; 133. 3 ; Prov. 19. 12 ; Is. 26. 19 ; Hos. 14. 5.

DIADEM. Job 29. 14 ; Isa. 28. 5 ; 62. 3 ; Ezek. 21. 26.

DIAL. 2 Kings 20. 11, it had gone down in the *d.* cf Ahaz.
Isa. 38. 8, gone down in the sun *d.* of Ahaz.

DIAMOND (in high priest's breastplate). Ex. 28. 18 ; 39. 11.
See Jer. 17. 1 ; Ezek. 28. 13.

DID. Mat. 13. 58, he *d.* not many mighty works.
John 4. 29, all things that ever I *d.*
9. 26, what *d.* he to thee?
15. 24, works which none other man *d.*
See Gen. 6. 22 ; 1 Sam. 1. 7 ; Job 1. 5 ; 1 Pet. 2. 22.

DIE. Gen. 2. 17 ; 20. 7 ; 1 Sam. 14. 44 ; 22. 16 ; 1 Kings 2. 37, 42 ; Jer. 26. 8 ; Ezek. 3. 18 ; 33. 8, 14, surely *d.*
Gen. 3. 3 ; Lev. 10. 6 ; Num. 18. 32, lest ye *d.*
27. 4 ; 45. 28 ; Prov. 30. 7, before I *d.*
Ex. 21. 12, smiteth a man that he *d.*
Lev. 7. 24 ; 22. 8 ; Deut. 14. 21 ; Ezek. 4. 14, that *d.* of itself.
Num. 16. 29, if these *d.* common death.
23. 10, let me *d.* death of righteous.
Deut. 31. 14, days approach that thou must *d.*
Ruth 1. 17, where thou *d.* will I *d.*
2 Sam. 3. 33, *d.* Abner as a fool *d.*?
2 Kings 20. 1 ; Isa. 38. 1, shalt *d.* and not live.
2 Chron. 25. 4 ; Jer. 31. 30, every man *d.* for own sin.
Job 2. 9, his wife said, Curse God and *d.*
3. 11, why *d.* I not from the womb?
12. 2, wisdom shall *d.* with you.
14. 14, if a man *d.*, shall he live again?
21. 23, one *d.* in full strength.
25, another *d.* in bitterness of soul.
29. 18, I shall *d.* in my nest.
Ps. 41. 5, when shall he *d.* and name perish?
49. 10, wise men *d.*, likewise the fool.
17, when he *d.* carry nothing away.
Prov. 5. 23, he shall *d.* without instruction.
10. 21, fools *d.* for want of wisdom.
11. 7, *d.* his expectation perish.
Eccl. 2. 16, how *d.* the wise man?
7. 17, why shouldest thou *d.* before thy time?
9. 5, living know they shall *d.*
Isa. 66. 24 ; Mk. 9. 44, worm shall not *d.*
Jer. 27. 13 ; Ezek. 18. 31 ; 33. 11, why will ye *d.*?
28. 16, this year thou shalt *d.*
34. 5, thou shalt *d.* in peace.
Ezek. 18. 4, 20, soul that sinneth shall *d.*
32, no pleasure in death of him that *d.*
33. 8, wicked man shall *d.* in iniquity.
Amos 6. 9, if ten men in house they shall *d.*
9. 10, sinners of my people shall *d.*
Jonah 4. 3, 8, it is better to *d.* than live.
Mat. 15. 4 ; Mk. 7. 10, let him *d.* the death.
22. 27 ; Mk. 12. 22 ; Lu. 20. 32, woman *d.* also.
26. 35 ; Mk. 14. 31, though I *d.* with thee.
Lu. 7. 2, servant was ready to *d.*
16. 22, beggar *d.*, rich man also *d.*
20. 36, nor can they *d.* any more.
John 4. 49, come down ere my child *d.*
11. 21, 32, my brother had not *d.*
37, that even this man should not have *d.*
50 ; 18. 14, that one man *d.* for people.
51, that Jesus should *d.* for nation.
12. 24, except a corn of wheat *d.*
19. 7, by our law he ought to *d.*
Acts 9. 37, Dorcas was sick and *d.*
21. 13, ready also to *d.* at Jerusalem.
25. 11, I refuse not to *d.*
Rom. 5. 7, for righteous man will one *d.*
7. 9, sin revived and I *d.*
8. 34, it is Christ that *d.*
14. 7, no man *d.* to himself.
9, Christ both *d.*, rose, and revived.
15 ; 1 Cor. 8. 11, for whom Christ *d.*

1 Cor. 15. 3, Christ *d.* for our sins.
22, as in Adam all *d.*
31, I *d.* daily.
36, not quickened except it *d.*
2 Cor. 5. 14, if one *d.* for all.
Phil. 1. 21, to *d.* is gain.
1 Thess. 4. 14, we believe that Jesus *d.*
5. 10, who *d.* for us that we should live.
Heb. 7. 8, here men that *d.* receive tithes.
9. 27, appointed unto men once to *d.*
11. 13, these all *d.* in faith.
Rev. 3. 2, things that are ready to *d.*
9. 6, men shall desire to *d.*
14. 13, the dead that *d.* in the Lord.
See Job 14. 10 ; Ps. 118. 17 ; Rom. 5. 6 ; 6. 10.

DIET. Jer. 52. 34.

DYED. Ex. 25. 5 ; Isa. 63. 1 ; Ezek. 23. 15.

DYING. 2 Cor. 4. 10, the *d.* of Lord Jesus.
6. 9, as *d.* and behold we live.
See Num. 17. 13 ; Lu. 8. 42 ; Heb. 11. 21.

DIFFER. Rom. 12. 6 ; 1 Cor. 4. 7 ; 15. 41 ; Gal. 4. 1.

DIFFERENCE. Lev. 10. 10 ; Ezek. 44. 23, a *d.* between holy and unholy.
11. 47 ; 20. 25, *d.* between clean and unclean.
Ezek. 22. 26, they have put no *d.* between.
Acts 15. 9, put no *d.* between us.
Rom. 3. 22 ; 10. 12, for there is no *d.*
See Ex. 11. 7 ; 1 Cor. 12. 5 ; Jude 22.

DIG. Ex. 21. 33, *d.* a pit and not cover it.
Deut. 6. 11 ; Neh. 9. 25, wells *d.* which thou *d.* not.
8. 9, out of hills mayest *d.* brass.
Job 6. 27, ye *d.* a pit for your friend.
24. 16, in the dark they *d.*
Ps. 7. 15 ; 57. 6, *d.* a pit and is fallen.
Isa. 51. 1, hole of pit whence ye are *d.*
Mat. 21. 33, and *d.* a winepress.
25. 18, *d.* in the earth and hid.
Lu. 13. 8, till I *d.* about it.
16. 3, I cannot *d.*, to beg I am ashamed.
See Job 3. 21 ; Ezek. 8. 8 ; 12. 5 ; Lu. 6. 48.

DIGNITY. Eccl. 10. 6, folly set in great *d.*
2 Pet. 2. 10 ; Jude 8, speak evil of *d.*
See Gen. 49. 3 ; Esth. 6. 3 ; Hab. 1. 7.

DILIGENCE. Prov. 4. 23 ; 2 Tim. 4. 9 ; Jude 3.

DILIGENT. Josh. 22. 5, take *d.* heed to commandment.
Ps. 64. 6, accomplish a *d.* search.
Lu. 15. 8, seek *d.* till she find it.
Acts 18. 25, taught *d.* the things of the Lord.
2 Tim. 1. 17, in Rome sought me *d.*
Heb. 12. 15, looking *d.* lest any man fail.
See Deut. 19. 18 ; Prov. 11. 27 ; 23. 1 ; Mat. 2. 7.

DIM. Deut. 34. 7, eye not *d.* nor force abated.
Job 17. 7, eye also *d.* by reason of sorrow.
Lam. 4. 1, gold become *d.*
See Gen. 27. 1 ; 48. 10 ; 1 Sam. 3. 2 ; Isa. 8. 22.

DIMINISH. Deut. 4. 2 ; 12. 32, nor *d.* ought from it.
Prov. 13. 11, gotten by vanity shall be *d.*
Rom. 11. 12, *d.* of them be riches of Gentiles.
See Ex. 5. 8 ; Lev. 25. 16 ; Jer. 26. 2 ; Ezek. 16. 27.

DINE. Gen. 43. 16 ; Lu. 11. 37 ; John 21. 12, 15.

DINNER. Prov. 15. 17 ; Mat. 22. 4 ; Lu. 11. 38 ; 14. 12.

DIP. Lev. 4. 6 ; 9. 9 ; 17. 14, priest shall *d.* his finger.
Ruth 2. 14, *d.* morsel in vinegar.
1 Sam. 14. 27, *d.* rod in honeycomb.
2 Kings 5. 14, Naaman *d.* in Jordan.
Mat. 26. 23 ; Mk. 14. 20, *d.* hand in dish.
John 13. 26, when he had *d.* the sop.
Rev. 19. 13, a vesture *d.* in blood.
See Gen. 37. 31 ; Josh. 3. 15 ; Lu. 16. 24.

DIRECT. Job 32. 14, he hath not *d.* his words.
37. 3, he *d.* it under the whole heaven.
Ps. 5. 3, in morning will I *d.* my prayer.
119. 5, O that my ways were *d.* to keep.
Prov. 3. 6, he shall *d.* thy paths.
11. 5, righteousness shall *d.* his way.
16. 9, the Lord *d.* his steps.

Prov. 21. 29, as for upright he *d.* his way.
Eccl. 10. 10, wisdom profitable to *d.*
Isa. 40. 13, who hath *d.* Spirit of the Lord.
Jer. 10. 23, not in man to *d.* his steps.
2 Thess. 3. 5, *d.* your hearts into love of God.
See Gen. 46. 28 ; Isa. 45. 13 ; 61. 8 ; 1 Thess. 3. 11.
DIRECTION. Num. 21. 18.
DIRECTLY. Num. 19. 4 ; Ezek. 42. 12.
DIRT. Judg. 3. 22 ; Ps. 18. 42 ; Isa. 57. 20.
DISALLOWED. Num. 30. 5, 8, 11 ; 1 Pet. 2. 4, 7.
DISANNUL. Isa. 14. 27, Lord purposed, who shall
   d. it?
28. 18, your covenant with death shall be *d.*
Gal. 3. 15, 17, covenant no man *d.*
See Job 40. 8 ; Heb. 7. 18.
DISAPPOINT. Job 5. 12 ; Ps. 17. 13 ; Prov. 15. 22.
DISCERN. 2 Sam. 19. 35, can I *d.* between good
   and evil?
1 Kings 3. 9, that I may *d.* between good and bad.
   11, understanding to *d.* judgment.
Ezra 3. 13, could not *d.* noise of joy.
Job 4. 16, could not *d.* form thereof.
   6. 30, cannot my taste *d.* perverse things.
Prov. 7. 7, I *d.* among the youths.
Eccl. 8. 5, wise man's heart *d.* time.
Jonah 4. 11, cannot *d.* between right and left.
Mal. 3. 18, *d.* between righteous and wicked.
Mat. 16. 3 ; Lu. 12. 56, *d.* face of sky.
1 Cor. 2. 14, they are spiritually *d.*
   11. 29, not *d.* the Lord's body.
   12. 10, to another is given *d.* of spirits.
Heb. 4. 12, the word is a *d.* of the thoughts.
   5. 14, exercised to *d.* good and evil.
See Gen. 27. 23 ; 31. 32 ; 38. 25 ; 2 Sam. 14. 17.
DISCHARGE. 1 Kings 5. 9 ; Eccl. 8. 8.
DISCIPLE. Isa. 8. 16, seal law among my *d.*
Mat. 10. 1 ; Lu. 6. 13, called his twelve *d.*
   24 ; Lu. 6. 40, *d.* not above his master.
   42, give cup of water in the name of a *d.*
   12. 2, thy *d.* do that which is not lawful.
   15. 2, why do *d.* transgress tradition.
   17. 16, brought to thy *d.*, and they could not cure.
   19. 13 ; Mk. 10. 13, the *d.* rebuked them.
   20. 17, Jesus took *d.* apart.
   22. 16, Pharisees sent their *d.*
   26. 18 ; Mk. 14. 14 ; Lu. 22. 11, keep passover with *d.*
   35, likewise also said the *d.*
   56, all the *d.* forsook him and fled.
   28. 7, tell his *d.* he is risen.
   13, say ye, his *d.* came by night.
Mk. 2. 18 ; Lu. 5. 33, why do *d.* of John fast?
   4. 34, he expounded all things to *d.*
   7. 2, *d.* eat with unwashen hands.
   5, why walk not *d.* according to tradition?
Lu. 5. 30, Pharisees murmured against *d.*
   6. 20, lifted up eyes on *d.*
   11. 1, as John taught his *d.*
   14. 26, 27, 33, cannot be my *d.*
   19. 37, *d.* began to rejoice and praise God.
   39, Master, rebuke thy *d.*
John 2. 11, his *d.* believed on him.
   4. 2, Jesus baptized not, but his *d.*
   6. 22, his *d.* were gone away alone.
   66, many of his *d.* went back.
   7. 3, that thy *d.* may see works.
   8. 31 ; 13. 35, then are ye my *d.* indeed.
   9. 27, will ye also be his *d.*?
   28, thou art his *d.*, we are Moses' *d.*
   13. 5, began to wash *d.* feet.
   15. 8, so shall ye be my *d.*
   18. 15, 16, that *d.* was known.
   17, 25, art not thou one of his *d.*?
   19. 26 ; 20. 2 ; 21. 7, 20, *d.* whom Jesus loved.
   38, a *d.* of Jesus, but secretly for fear.
   20. 18, told *d.* she had seen the Lord.
   21. 23, that that *d.* should not die.
   24, this is the *d.* which testifieth.
Acts 9. 1, slaughter against *d.*
   26, essayed to join himself to *d.*

Acts 11. 26, *d.* called Christians first.
   20. 7, *d.* came together to break bread.
   30, to draw away *d.* after them.
   21. 16, an old *d.* with whom we should lodge.
See Mat. 11. 1 ; John 3. 25 ; 18. 1, 2 ; 20. 26.
DISCIPLINE. Job 36. 10.
DISCLOSE. Isa. 26. 21.
DISCOMFITED. Judg. 4. 15, Lord *d.* Sisera.
   8. 12, Gideon *d.* all the host.
2 Sam. 22. 15 ; Ps. 18. 14, lightnings, and *d.* them.
Isa. 31. 8, his young men shall be *d.*
See Ex. 17. 13 ; Num. 14. 45 ; Josh. 10. 10.
DISCOMFITURE. 1 Sam. 14. 20.
DISCONTENTED. 1 Sam. 22. 2.
DISCONTINUE. Jer. 17. 4.
DISCORD. Prov. 6. 14, 19.
DISCOURAGE. Num. 32. 7, wherefore *d.* the heart
   of the children of Israel.
Deut. 1. 21, fear not, nor be *d.*
   28, our brethren have *d.* our heart.
Col. 3. 21, your children, lest they be *d.*
See Num. 21. 4 ; 32. 9 ; Isa. 42. 4.
DISCOVER. 1 Sam. 14. 8, 11, we will *d.* ourselves
   to them.
2 Sam. 22. 6 ; Ps. 18. 15, foundations of the world *d.*
Job 12. 22, he *d.* deep things.
   41. 13, who can *d.* face of his garment?
Prov. 25. 9, *d.* not a secret to another.
Ezek. 21. 24, your transgressions are *d.*
See Ps. 29. 9 ; Hos. 7. 1 ; Hab. 3. 13 ; Acts 21. 3.
DISCREET. Gen. 41. 33, 39 ; Mk. 12. 34 ; Tit. 2. 5.
DISCRETION. Ps. 112. 5 ; Prov. 11. 22 ; Isa. 28. 26
   Jer. 10. 12.
DISDAINED. 1 Sam. 17. 42 ; Job 30. 1.
DISEASE. Ex. 15. 26 ; Deut. 7. 15, none of these
   d. on you.
Deut. 28. 60, bring on thee all *d.* of Egypt.
2 Kings 1. 2 ; 8. 8, 9, recover of *d.*
2 Chron. 16. 12, in *d.* sought not the Lord.
Job 30. 18, by force of my *d.*
Ps. 103. 3, who healeth all thy *d.*
Eccl. 6. 2, vanity, and it is an evil *d.*
Ezek. 34. 4, *d.* have ye not strengthened.
   21, have pushed *d.* with your horns.
See Mat. 4. 23 ; 14. 35 ; Lu. 9. 1 ; Acts 28. 9.
DISFIGURE. Mat. 6. 16.
DISGRACE. Jer. 14. 21.
DISGUISE. 1 Sam. 28. 8 ; 1 Kings 14. 2 ; 20. 38 ; 22
   30 ; 2 Chron. 18. 29 ; 35. 22 ; Job 24. 15.
DISH. Judg. 5. 25 ; 2 Kings 21. 13 ; Mat. 26. 23
   Mk. 14. 20.
DISHONESTY. 2 Cor. 4. 2.
DISHONOUR. Ps. 35. 26 ; 71. 13, clothed wit'
   shame and *d.*
Prov. 6. 33, a wound and *d.* shall he get.
Mic. 7. 6, son *d.* father.
John 8. 49, I honour my Father, ye *d.* me.
Rom. 9. 21, one vessel to honour, another to *d.*
1 Cor. 15. 43, sown in *d.*
2 Cor. 6. 8, by honour and *d.*
2 Tim. 2. 20, some to honour, some to *d.*
See Ezra 4. 14 ; Rom. 1. 24 ; 2. 23 ; 1 Cor. 11. 4, 5.
DISINHERIT. Num. 14. 12.
DISMAYED. Deut. 31. 8 ; Josh. 1. 9 ; 8. 1 ; 10. 25
   1 Chron. 22. 13 ; 28. 20 ; 2 Chron. 20. 15, 17 ; 32. 7
   Isa. 41. 10 ; Jer. 1. 17 ; 10. 2 ; 23. 4 ; 30. 10 ; 46. 27
   Ezek. 2. 6 ; 3. 9, fear not nor be *d.*
Jer. 17. 18, let them be *d.*, let not me be *d.*
See 1 Sam. 17. 11 ; Jer. 8. 9 ; 46. 5 ; Obad. 9.
DISMISSED. 2 Chron. 23. 8 ; Acts 15. 30 ; 19. 41.
DISOBEDIENCE. Rom. 5. 19 ; Eph. 2. 2 ; 5. 6
   Heb. 2. 2.
DISOBEDIENT. Lu. 1. 17, turn *d.* to wisdom *c*
   just.
Acts 26. 19, not *d.* to heavenly vision.
Rom. 1. 30 ; 2 Tim. 3. 2, *d.* to parents.

1 Tim. 1. 9, law for lawless and *d.*
Tit. 3. 3, we ourselves were sometimes *d.*
1 Pet. 2. 7, to them which be *d.*
3. 20, spirits, which sometime were *d.*
See 1 Kings 13. 26; Neh. 9. 26; Rom. 10. 21.

DISORDERLY. 1 Thess. 5. 14; 2 Thess. 3. 6, 7, 11.

DISPENSATION. 1 Cor. 9. 17, a *d.* of the gospel is committed me.
Eph. 1. 10, in the *d.* of the fulness of times.
3. 2, the *d.* of the grace of God.
Col. 1. 25, according to the *d.* of God.

DISPERSE. Prov. 15. 7, lips of wise *d.* knowledge.
See Ps. 112. 9; Jer. 25. 34; Ezek. 12. 15; 20. 23.

DISPERSED. Esth. 3. 8, and *d.* among the people.
Isa. 11. 12, the *d.* of Judah.
John 7. 35, go unto the *d.* among the Gentiles.

DISPERSED (prophecies concerning). Jer. 25. 24; Ezek. 36. 19; Zeph. 3. 10.

DISPLAYED. Ps. 60. 4.

DISPLEASE. Num. 11. 1, it *d.* the Lord.
22. 34, if it *d.* thee, I will get me back.
2 Sam. 11. 27, thing David had done *d.* the Lord.
1 Kings 1. 6, father had not *d.* him at any time.
Ps. 60. 1, thou hast been *d.*
Prov. 24. 18, lest the Lord see it, and it *d.* him.
Isa. 59. 15, it *d.* him there was no judgment.
Jonah 4. 1, it *d.* Jonah exceedingly.
Mat. 21. 15, scribes saw it, they were *d.*
Mk. 10. 14, Jesus was much *d.*
41, much *d.* with James and John.
See Gen. 48. 17; 1 Sam. 8. 6; 18. 8; Zech. 1. 2.

DISPLEASURE. Deut. 9. 19; Judg. 15. 3; Ps. 2. 5; 6. 1; 38. 1.

DISPOSE. Job 34. 13; 37. 15; Prov. 16. 33; 1 Cor. 10. 27.

DISPOSITION. Acts 7. 53.

DISPOSSESS. Num. 33. 53; Deut. 7. 17; Judg. 11. 23.

DISPUTATION. Acts 15. 2; Rom. 14. 1.

DISPUTE. Job 23. 7, the righteous might *d.* with him.
Mk. 9. 33, what was it ye *d.* of by the way?
1 Cor. 1. 20, where is the *d.* of this world?
Phil. 2. 14, do all things without *d.*
1 Tim. 6. 5, perverse *d.*
See Acts 9. 29; 15. 7; 17. 17; Jude 9.

DISQUIET. 1 Sam. 28. 15, why *d.* to bring me up?
Ps. 42. 5, 11; 43. 5, why art thou *d.* within me?
See Ps. 38. 8; 39. 6; Jer. 50. 34.

DISSEMBLE. Josh. 7. 11; Ps. 26. 4; Prov. 26. 24; Jer. 42. 20; Gal. 2. 13.

DISSENSION. Acts 15. 2; 23. 7, 10.

DISSIMULATION. Rom. 12. 9; Gal. 2. 13.

DISSOLVE. Isa. 34. 4, host of heaven shall be *d.*
Dan 5. 16, thou canst *d.* doubts.
2 Cor. 5. 1, house of tabernacle *d.*
2 Pet. 3. 11, all these things shall be *d.*
12, heavens being on fire shall be *d.*
See Job 30. 22; Ps. 75. 3; Isa. 14. 31; 24. 19; Dan. 5. 12; Nah. 2. 6.

DISTAFF. Prov. 31. 19.

DISTIL. Deut. 32. 2; Job 36. 28.

DISTINCTION. 1 Cor. 14. 7.

DISTINCTLY. Neh. 8. 8.

DISTRACT. Ps. 88. 15; 1 Cor. 7. 35.

DISTRESS. Gen. 42. 21, therefore is this *d.* come upon us.
Judg. 11. 7, why are ye come when ye are in *d.?*
1 Sam. 22. 2, every one in *d.* came to David.
2 Sam. 22. 7; Ps. 18. 6; 118. 5; 120. 1, in *d.* I called.
1 Kings 1. 29, redeemed my soul out of all *d.*
2 Chron. 28. 22, in *d.* Ahaz trespassed more.
Neh. 2. 17, ye see the *d.* we are in.
Ps. 25. 17; 107. 6, 13, 19, 28, out of *d.*
Prov. 1. 27, mock when *d.* cometh.
Isa. 25. 4, a strength to needy in *d.*
Obad. 12, 14; Zeph. 1. 15, day of *d.*

Lu. 21. 23, shall be great *d.* in the land.
25, on earth *d.* of nations.
Rom. 8. 35, shall *d.* separate us?
1 Cor. 7. 26, good for present *d.*
2 Cor. 6. 4, approving ourselves in *d.*
12. 10, take pleasure in *d.*
See Gen. 35. 3; Neh. 9. 37; 2 Cor. 4. 8; 1 Thess. 3. 7.

DISTRIBUTE. Neh. 13. 13, office was to *d.* to brethren.
Job 21. 17, God *d.* sorrows in his anger.
Lu. 18. 22, sell and *d.* to poor.
John 6. 11, given thanks, he *d.*
Rom. 12. 13, *d.* to necessity of saints.
1 Cor. 7. 17, as God hath *d.* to every man.
2 Cor. 9. 13, your liberal *d.*
See Josh. 13. 32; Acts 4. 35; 2 Cor. 10. 13; 1 Tim. 6. 18.

DITCH. Ps. 7. 15, fallen into *d.* he made.
Mat. 15. 14; Lu. 6. 39, both fall into *d.*
See 2 Kings 3. 16; Job 9. 31; Prov. 23. 27; Isa. 22. 11.

DIVERS. Deut. 22. 9, sow vineyard with *d.* kinds.
11, garment of *d.* sorts.
25. 13, not have in bag *d.* weights.
14, *d.* measures, great and small.
Prov. 20. 10, 23, *d.* weights and measures abomination.
Mat. 4. 24; Mk. 1. 34; Lu. 4. 40, *d.* diseases.
24. 7; Mk. 13. 8; Lu. 21. 11, in *d.* places.
Mk. 8. 3, for *d.* of them came from far.
1 Cor. 12. 10, to another *d.* kinds of tongues.
2 Tim. 3. 6; Tit. 3. 3, led away with *d.* lusts.
Jas. 1. 2, joy in *d.* temptations.
See Eccl. 5. 7; Heb. 1. 1; 2. 4; 9. 10; 13. 9.

DIVERSE. Esth. 3. 8, laws *d.* from all people.
1 Cor. 12. 6, *d.* of operations, but same God.
See Esth. 1. 7; 1 Cor. 12. 4, 28.

DIVIDE. Lev. 11. 4, 5, 6, 7, 26; Deut. 14. 7, not eat these of them that *d.* the hoof.
Josh. 19. 49, an end of *d.* the land.
1 Kings 3. 25, *d.* living child in two.
Job 27. 17, innocent shall *d.* silver.
Ps. 68. 12; Prov. 16. 19; Isa. 9. 3; 53. 12, *d.* spoil.
Amos 7. 17, thy land shall be *d.* by line.
Mat. 12. 25; Mk. 3. 24; Lu. 11. 17, kingdom or house *d.*
26; Mk. 3. 26; Lu. 11. 18, *d.* against himself.
Lu. 12. 13, that he *d.* inheritance with me.
14, who made me a *d.?*
52, five in one house *d.*
53, father *d.* against son.
15. 12, he *d.* unto them his living.
Acts 14. 4; 23. 7, multitude *d.*
1 Cor. 1. 13, is Christ *d.?*
12. 11, *d.* to every man severally as he will.
2 Tim. 2. 15, rightly *d.* word of truth.
Heb. 4. 12, piercing to *d.* asunder.
See Dan. 7. 25; Hos. 10. 2; Mat. 25. 32; Lu. 22. 17.

DIVINATION. Num. 23. 23, neither is any *d.* against Israel.
Acts 16. 16, damsel with a spirit of *d.*
See Deut. 18. 10; 2 Kings 17. 17; Ezek. 13. 23.

DIVINE (*v.*). Gen. 44. 15, wot ye not that I can *d.?*
1 Sam. 28. 8, *d.* unto me by the familiar spirit.
Ezek. 13. 9, prophets that *d.* lies.
21. 29, they *d.* lies unto thee.
Mic. 3. 11, prophets *d.* for money.
See Gen. 44. 5; Ezek. 22. 28; Mic. 3. 6.

DIVINE (*ad.*). Prov. 16. 10; Heb. 9. 1; 2 Pet. 1. 3, 4.

DIVINER. 1 Sam. 6. 2; Isa. 44. 25; Jer. 27. 9; 29. 8.

DIVISION. Ex. 8. 23, will put a *d.* between my people.
Judg. 5. 15, for *d.* of Reuben great thoughts of heart.
Lu. 12. 51, I tell you nay, but rather *d.*
John 7. 43; 9. 16; 10. 19, *d.* because of him.
Rom. 16. 17, mark them which cause *d.*
See 1 Cor. 1. 10; 3. 3; 11. 18.

DO. Ruth 3. 5, all thou sayest I will *d.*
Eccl. 3. 12, for a man to *d.* good.
Isa. 46. 11, I will also *d.* it.

Hos. 6. 4, what shall I *d.* unto thee?
Mat. 7. 12, men should *d.* to you, *d.* ye even so.
23. 3, they say, and *d.* not.
Lu. 10. 28, this *d.*, and thou shalt live.
22. 19 ; 1 Cor. 11. 24, this *d.* in remembrance.
John 15. 5, without me ye can *d.* nothing.
Rom. 7. 15, what I would, that *d.* I not.
2 Cor. 11. 12, what I *d.*, that I will *d.*
Gal. 5. 17, ye cannot *d.* the things ye would.
Phil. 4. 13, I can *d.* all things through Christ.
Heb. 4. 13, with whom we have to *d.*
Jas. 1. 23, a hearer, not a *d.* of the word.
See John 6. 38 ; 10. 37 ; Rev. 19. 10 ; 22. 9.
DOCTOR. Acts 5. 34, Gamaliel, a *d.* of the law.
Lu. 2. 46, sitting in the midst of the *d.*
5. 17, *d.* of the law sitting by.
DOCTRINE. Prov. 4. 2, I give you good *d.*
Isa. 28. 9, made to understand *d.*
Jer. 10. 8, the stock is a *d.* of vanities.
Mat. 15. 9 ; Mk. 7. 7, teaching for *d.* command-
ments of men.
16. 12, the *d.* of the Pharisees.
Mk. 1. 27 ; Acts 17. 19, what new *d.* is this?
John 7. 17, do his will shall know of the *d.*
Acts 2. 42, continued in apostles' *d.*
5. 28, filled Jerusalem with your *d.*
Rom. 6. 17, obeyed that form of *d.*
16. 17, contrary to the *d.*
1 Cor. 14. 26, every one hath a *d.*
Eph. 4. 14, every wind of *d.*
1 Tim. 1. 10, contrary to sound *d.*
4. 6, nourished in words of good *d.*
13, give attendance to *d.*
16, take heed to thyself and *d.*
2 Tim. 3. 10, hast fully known my *d.*
16, scripture profitable for *d.*
4. 2, exhort with all longsuffering and *d.*
Tit. 1. 9, by sound *d.* to exhort and convince.
2. 1, things which become sound *d.*
7, in *d.* showing uncorruptness.
10, adorn the *d.* of God our Saviour.
Heb. 6. 1, principles of the *d.*
2, the *d.* of baptisms.
13. 9, not carried about with strange *d.*
2 John 9, abideth in *d.* of Christ.
See Deut. 32. 2 ; Job 11. 4 ; John 7. 16 ; 1 Tim. 5. 17.
DOG. Ex. 11. 7, against Israel not a *d.* move.
Deut. 23. 18, not bring price of *d.* into house.
Judg. 7. 5, that lappeth as *d.* lappeth.
1 Sam. 17. 43 ; 24. 14 ; 2 Sam. 3. 8, am I a *d.*?
2 Sam. 9. 8, upon such a dead *d.* as I am.
2 Kings 8. 13, what, is thy servant a *d.*?
Job 30. 1, disdained to set with *d.*
Ps. 22. 20, darling from power of the *d.*
59. 6, they make noise like a *d.*
Prov. 26. 11 ; 2 Pet. 2. 22, as a *d.* returneth.
17, like one that taketh a *d.* by ears.
Eccl. 9. 4, living *d.* better than dead lion.
Isa. 56. 10, they are all dumb *d.*
66. 3, as if he cut off a *d.* neck.
Mat. 7. 6, give not that which is holy to *d.*
15. 27 ; Mk. 7. 28, the *d.* eat of crumbs.
Phil. 3. 2, beware of *d.*
Rev. 22. 15, without are *d.*
See Ex. 22. 31 ; 1 Kings 14. 11 ; 21. 23 ; 22. 28.
DOING. Ex. 15. 11, fearful in praises, *d.* wonders.
Judg. 2. 19, ceased not from their own *d.*
1 Sam. 25. 3, churlish and evil in his *d.*
1 Chron. 22. 16, arise, and be *d.*
Neh. 6. 3, I am *d.* a great work.
Ps. 9. 11 ; Isa. 12. 4, declare his *d.*
66. 5, terrible in *d.* toward children of men.
77. 12, I will talk of thy *d.*
118. 23 ; Mat. 21. 42 ; Mk. 12. 11, the Lord's *d.*
Mic. 2. 7, are these his *d.*?
Mat. 24. 46 ; Lu. 12. 43, shall find so *d.*
Acts 10. 38, went about *d.* good.
Rom. 2. 7, patient continuance in well *d.*
2 Cor. 8. 11, perform the *d.* of it.
Gal. 6. 9 ; 2 Thess. 3. 13, weary in well *d.*

Eph. 6. 6, *d.* will of God from heart.
1 Pet. 2. 15, with well *d.* put to silence.
3. 17, suffer for well *d.*
4. 19, commit souls in well *d.*
See Lev. 18. 3 ; Prov. 20. 11 ; Isa. 1. 16 ; Jer. 4. 4.
DOLEFUL. Isa. 13. 21 ; Mic. 2. 4.
DOMINION. Gen. 27. 40, when thou shalt have *d.*
37. 8, shalt thou have *d.* over us?
Num. 24. 19, come he that shall have *d.*
Job 25. 2, *d.* and fear are with him.
38. 33, canst thou set the *d.* thereof?
Ps. 8. 6, *d.* over works of thy hands.
19. 13 ; 119. 133, let them not have *d.* over me.
72. 8 ; Zech. 9. 10, *d.* from sea to sea.
Isa. 26. 13, other lords have had *d.* over us.
Dan. 4. 34 ; 7. 14, *d.* is an everlasting *d.*
Mat. 20. 25, princes of Gentiles exercise *d.*
Rom. 6. 9, death hath no more *d.*
14, sin shall not have *d.*
7. 1, law hath *d.* over a man.
2 Cor. 1. 24, not *d.* over your faith.
Eph. 1. 21, above all *d.*
Col. 1. 16, whether they be thrones or *d.*
See Dan. 6. 26 ; 1 Pet. 4. 11 ; Jude 25 ; Rev. 1. 6.
DOOR. Gen. 4. 7, sin lieth at the *d.*
Ex. 12. 7, strike blood on *d.* posts.
33. 8 ; Num. 11. 10, every man at tent *d.*
Judg. 16. 3, Samson took *d.* of the gate.
Job 31. 9, laid wait at neighbour's *d.*
32, I opened my *d.* to the travellers.
38. 17, the *d.* of the shadow of death.
41. 14, who can open *d.* of his face?
Ps. 24. 7, ye everlasting *d.*
78. 23, opened the *d.* of heaven.
84. 10, rather be *d.*-keeper.
141. 3, keep the *d.* of my lips.
Prov. 5. 8, come not nigh *d.* of her house.
8. 3, wisdom crieth at *d.*
26. 14, as *d.* turneth on hinges.
Eccl. 12. 4, *d.* shall be shut in the streets.
Isa. 6. 4, posts of the *d.* moved.
26. 20, enter, and shut thy *d.* about thee.
Hos. 2. 15, for a *d.* of hope.
Mal. 1. 10, who would shut the *d.* for nought?
Mat. 6. 6, when thou hast shut thy *d.*
24. 33 ; Mk. 13. 29, near, even at the *d.*
25. 10, and the *d.* was shut.
27. 60 ; 28. 2 ; Mk. 15. 46, *d.* of sepulchre.
Mk. 1. 33, city gathered at the *d.*
2. 2, not so much as about the *d.*
Lu. 13. 25, master hath shut to the *d.*
John 10. 1, 2, entereth not by *d.*
7. 9, I am the *d.*
18. 16, Peter stood at the *d.* without.
17, damsel that kept the *d.*
20. 19, 26, when *d.* were shut, Jesus came.
Acts 5. 9, feet at the *d.* to carry thee out.
14. 27, opened the *d.* of faith.
1 Cor. 16. 9, great *d.* and effectual.
2 Cor. 2. 12, *d.* opened to me of the Lord.
Col. 4. 3, open a *d.* of utterance.
Jas. 5. 9, judge standeth before the *d.*
Rev. 3. 8, set before thee an open *d.*
20, I stand at *d.* and knock.
4. 1, behold, a *d.* opened in heaven.
See Ex. 21. 6 ; Deut. 11. 20 ; Isa. 57. 8 ; Acts 5. 19
16. 26.
DOTE. Jer. 50. 36 ; Ezek. 23. 5 ; 1 Tim. 6. 4.
DOUBLE. Gen. 43. 12. 15, take *d.* money in hand.
Ex. 22. 4, 7, 9, he shall restore *d.*
Deut. 15. 18, worth a *d.* hired servant.
2 Kings 2. 9, a *d.* portion of thy spirit.
1 Chron. 12. 33 ; Ps. 12. 2, a *d.* heart.
Isa. 40. 2, received *d.* for all her sins.
Jer. 16. 18, recompense their sin *d.*
1 Tim. 3. 8, deacons not *d.* tongued.
5. 17, worthy of *d.* honour.
Jas. 1. 8, a *d.* minded man unstable.
4. 8, purify your hearts, ye *d.* minded.
See Gen. 41. 32 ; Isa. 61. 7 ; Ezek. 21. 14 ; Rev. 18.

DOUBT. Deut. 28. 66, thy life shall hang in d.
Job 12. 2, no d. ye are the people.
Ps. 126. 6, shall d. come again, rejoicing.
Dan. 5. 12, 16, dissolving of d.
Mat. 14. 31, wherefore didst thou d.?
21. 21, if ye have faith, and d. not.
Mk. 11. 23, shall not d. in his heart.
Lu. 11. 20, no d. kingdom of God is come.
John 10. 24, how long dost thou make us to d.?
Acts 5. 24, they d. whereunto this would grow.
28. 4, no d. this man is a murderer.
Rom. 14. 23, he that d. is damned if he eat.
Gal. 4. 20, I stand in d. of you.
1 Tim. 2. 8, pray without wrath and d.
1 John 2. 19, would no d. have continued.
See Lu. 12. 29; Acts 2. 12; Phil. 3. 8.

DOUGH. Num. 15. 20, a cake of the first of your d.
Neh. 10. 37, the firstfruits of our d.
Ezek. 44. 30, give unto the priest the first of
your d.

DOVE. Ps. 55. 6, that I had wings like a d.
Isa. 59. 11, mourn sore like d.
60. 8, flee as a d. to their windows.
Mat. 10. 16, be harmless as d.
21. 12; Mk. 11. 15; John 2. 14, them that sold d.
See Jer. 48. 28; Hos. 7. 11; Mat. 3. 16; Mk. 1. 10.

DOWN. 2 Sam. 3. 35, if I taste ought till sun be d.
2 Kings 19. 30; Isa. 37. 31, again take root d.
Ps. 59. 15, let them wander up and d.
109. 23, I am tossed up and d.
Eccl. 3. 21, spirit of the beast that goeth d.
Zech. 10. 12, walk up and d. in his name.
See Josh. 8. 29; Ps. 139. 2; Ezek. 38. 14.

DOWRY. Gen. 30. 20; 34. 12; Ex. 22. 17; 1 Sam.
18. 25.

DRAG. Hab. 1. 15, 16; John 21. 8.

DRAGON. Deut. 32. 33, their wine is the poison
of d.
Neh. 2. 13, before the d. well.
Job 30. 29, I am a brother to d.
Ps. 91. 13, the d. shalt thou trample.
148. 7, praise the Lord, ye d.
Isa. 43. 20, the d. and owls shall honour me.
Jer. 9. 11, will make Jerusalem a den of d.
Rev. 20. 2, the d., that old serpent.
See Rev. 12. 3; 13. 2, 11; 16. 13.

DRANK. 1 Sam. 30. 12, nor d. water three days
and nights.
2 Sam. 12. 3, and d. of his own cup.
1 Kings 17. 6, and he d. of the brook.
Dan. 1. 5, appointed of the wine he d.
5. 4, they d. wine, and praised the gods.
Mk. 14. 23, and they all d. of it.
Lu. 17. 27, 28, they d., they married.
John 4. 12, than our father, who d. thereof.
1 Cor. 10. 4, for they d. of that spiritual Rock.
See Gen. 9. 21; 24. 46; 27. 25; Num. 20. 11.

DRAUGHT. Mat. 15. 17; Mk. 7. 19; Lu. 5. 4, 9;
John 21. 6, 11.

DRAVE. Ex. 14. 25; Josh. 24. 12; Judg. 6. 9.

DRAW. Job 40. 23, trusteth he can d. up Jordan.
41. 1, canst thou d. out leviathan?
Ps. 28. 3, d. me not away with wicked.
37. 14, wicked have d. out sword.
55. 21, yet were they d. swords.
88. 3, my life d. nigh unto the grave.
Eccl. 12. 1, nor years d. nigh.
Cant. 1. 4, d. me, we will run after thee.
Isa. 5. 18, d. iniquity with cords.
12. 3, d. water from wells of salvation.
Jer. 31. 3, with lovingkindness have I d. thee.
Mat. 15. 8, people d. nigh me with their mouth.
Lu. 21. 8, the time d. near.
28, your redemption d. nigh.
John 4. 11, thou hast nothing to d. with.
15, thirst not, neither come hither to d.
6. 44, except the Father d. him.
12. 32, if lifted up, will d. all men.
Heb. 10. 22, d. near with true heart.

Heb. 10. 38, 39, if any d. back.
Jas. 4. 8, d. nigh to God, he will d.
See Acts 11. 10; 20. 30; Heb. 7. 19; Jas. 2. 6.

DRAWER. Deut. 29. 11; Josh. 9. 21.

DREAD. Gen. 28. 17, how d. is this place!
Deut. 2. 25; 11. 25, begin to put d. of thee.
Isa. 8. 13, let him be your d.
Mal. 4. 5, the great and d. day.
See Gen. 9. 2; Ex. 15. 16; Dan. 9. 4.

DREAM. Job 20. 8, shall fly away as a d.
33. 15, 16, in a d. he openeth the ears.
Ps. 73. 20, as a d. when one awaketh.
126. 1, we were like them that d.
Eccl. 5. 3, a d. cometh through much business.
Jer. 23. 28, prophet that hath a d.
Joel 2. 28; Acts 2. 17, old men d. d.
Jude 8, filthy d. defile the flesh.
See Job 7. 14; Isa. 29. 8; Jer. 27. 9.

DREGS. Ps. 75. 8; Isa. 51. 17.

DRESS. Gen. 2. 15, put man in garden to d. it.
Deut. 28. 39, plant vineyards and d. them.
2 Sam. 12. 4, poor man's lamb, and d. it.
See Ex. 30. 7; Lu. 13. 7; Heb. 6. 7.

DREW. Gen. 47. 29, time d. nigh that Israel must
die.
Ex. 2. 10, because I d. him out of the water.
Josh. 8. 26, Joshua d. not his hand back.
1 Kings 22. 34; 2 Chron. 18. 33, man d. a bow.
2 Kings 9. 24, Jehu d. bow with full strength.
Hos. 11. 4, d. them with cords of a man.
Zeph. 3. 2, she d. not near to her God.
Mat. 21. 34, when time of fruit d. near.
Lu. 24. 15, Jesus himself d. near.
Acts 5. 37, and d. away much people.
See Esth. 5. 2; Lam. 3. 57; Acts 7. 17.

DRINK (*n.*). Lev. 10. 9, do not drink strong d.
when ye go.
Num. 6. 3, separate himself from strong d.
Deut. 14. 26, bestow money for strong d.
29. 6, strong d. these forty years.
Prov. 20. 1, strong d. is raging.
31. 4, not for princes to drink strong d.
6, give strong d. to him that is ready to perish.
Isa. 24. 9, strong d. shall be bitter.
28. 7, erred through strong d.
Mic. 2. 11, prophesy of wine and strong d.
Hab. 2. 15, that giveth his neighbour d.
Hag. 1. 6, ye are not filled with d.
Mat. 25. 35, 37, 42, thirsty, and ye gave me d.
John 4. 9, a Jew, askest d. of me.
6. 55, my blood is d. indeed.
Rom. 12. 20, if thine enemy thirst, give him d.
14. 17, the kingdom of God is not meat and d.
1 Cor. 10. 4, same spiritual d.
Col. 2. 16, judge you in meat or in d.
See Gen. 21. 19; Isa. 5. 11, 22; 32. 6; 43. 20; Lu.
1. 15; 1 Tim. 5. 23.

DRINK (*v.*). Ex. 15. 24, what shall we d.?
17. 1, no water for people to d.
2 Sam. 23. 16; 1 Chron. 11. 18, David would not d.
Ps. 36. 8, d. of the river of thy pleasures.
60. 3, d. the wine of astonishment.
80. 5, gavest them tears to d.
110. 7, he shall d. of the brook in the way.
Prov. 5. 15, d. waters of thine own cistern.
31. 5, lest they d., and forget the law.
7, let him d., and forget his poverty.
Eccl. 9. 7, d. wine with merry heart.
Cant. 5. 1, d., yea, d. abundantly.
Isa. 5. 22, mighty to d. wine.
65. 13, my servants shall d., but ye.
Jer. 35. 2, give Rechabites wine to d.
6, we will d. no wine.
14, to this day they d. none.
Ezek. 4. 11, thou shalt d. water by measure.
Amos 2. 8, d. the wine of the condemned.
Zech. 9. 15, they shall d., and make a noise.
Mat. 10. 42, whoso shall give to d.
20. 22; Mk. 10. 38, are ye able to d.?

Mat. 26. 27, saying, *d.* ye all of it.
29 ; Mk. 14. 25 ; Lu. 22. 18, when I *d.* it new.
42, may not pass except I *d.*
Mk. 9. 41, shall give you cup of water to *d.*
16. 18, if they *d.* any deadly thing.
John 4. 10, give me to *d.*
7. 37, let him come to me, and *d.*
18. 11, cup given me, shall I not *d.* it?
Rom. 14. 21, not good to *d.* wine.
1 Cor. 10. 4, did all *d.* same spiritual drink.
11. 25, as oft as ye *d.* it.
12. 13, made to *d.* into one Spirit.
See Mk. 2. 16 ; Lu. 7. 33 ; 10. 7.

DRIVE. Gen. 4. 14, thou hast *d.* me out.
Ex. 23. 28, hornets shall *d.* out Hivite.
Deut. 4. 19, lest thou be *d.* to worship them.
Job 24. 3, they *d.* away ass of the fatherless.
30. 5, they were *d.* forth from among men.
Prov. 14. 32, wicked *d.* away in his wickedness.
22. 15, rod shall *d.* it away.
25. 23, north wind *d.* away rain.
Jer. 46. 15, stood not, because Lord did *d.* them.
Dan. 4. 25 ; 5. 21, they shall *d.* thee from men.
Hos. 13. 3, as chaff *d.* with whirlwind.
Lu. 8. 29, he was *d.* of the devil.
Jas. 1. 6, wave *d.* with the wind.
See 2 Kings 9. 20 ; Jer. 8. 3 ; Ezek. 31. 11.

DROMEDARIES. 1 Kings 4. 28, straw for the
horses and *d.*
Esth. 8. 10, and young *d.*
Isa. 60. 6, the *d.* of Midian and Ephah.
Jer. 2. 23, thou art a swift *d.* traversing her ways.

DROP (*n.*). Job 36. 27, maketh small the *d.* of water.
Isa. 40. 15, as the *d.* of a bucket.
See Job 38. 28 ; Cant. 5. 2 ; Lu. 22. 44.

DROP (*v.*). Deut. 32. 2, doctrine shall *d.* as the rain.
Job 29. 22, my speech *d.* upon them.
Ps. 65. 11, paths *d.* fatness.
68. 8, heavens *d.* at presence of God.
Eccl. 10. 18, through idleness house *d.* through.
Isa. 45. 8, *d.* down, ye heavens.
Ezek. 20. 46, *d.* thy word toward the south.
See 2 Sam. 21. 10 ; Joel 3. 18 ; Amos 9. 13.

DROPSY. Lu. 14. 2, a man which had the *d.*

DROSS. Ps. 119. 119 ; Prov. 25. 4 ; 26. 23 ; Isa. 1. 22,
25 ; Ezek. 22. 18.

DROUGHT. Deut. 28. 24 ; 1 Kings 17 ; Isa. 58. 11 ;
Jer. 17. 8 ; Hos. 13. 5 ; Hag. 1. 11.

DROVE. Gen. 3. 24 ; 15. 11 ; 32. 16 ; 33. 8 ; John 2. 15.

DROWN. Cant. 8. 7, neither can floods *d.* it.
1 Tim. 6. 9, that *d.* men in perdition.
See Ex. 15. 4 ; Mat. 18. 6 ; Heb. 11. 29.

DROWSINESS. Prov 23. 21.

DRUNK. 2 Sam. 11. 13, David made Uriah *d.*
1 Kings 20. 16, was drinking himself *d.*
Job 12. 25 ; Ps. 107. 27, stagger like a *d.* man.
Jer. 23. 9, I am like a *d.* man.
Lam. 5. 4, we have *d.* water for money.
Hab. 2. 15, makest him *d.* also.
Mat. 24. 49 ; Lu. 12. 45, drink with the *d.*
Acts 2. 15, these are not *d.*
1 Cor. 11. 21, one is hungry, and another *d.*
1 Thess. 5. 7, they that be *d.* are *d.* in the night.
See Lu. 5. 39 ; John 2. 10 ; Eph. 5. 18 ; Rev. 17. 6.

DRUNKARD. Deut. 21. 20, our son is a glutton
and a *d.*
Prov. 23. 21, *d.* and glutton come to poverty.
26. 9, as a thorn goeth into hand of *d.*
1 Cor. 6. 10, nor *d.* shall inherit.
See Ps. 69. 12 ; Isa. 24. 20 ; Joel 1. 5 ; Nah. 1. 10.

DRUNKENNESS. Deut. 29. 19, to add *d.* to thirst.
Eccl. 10. 17, eat for strength, not for *d.*
Ezek. 23. 33, shalt be filled with *d.*
See Lu. 21. 34 ; Rom. 13. 13 ; Gal. 5. 21.

DRY. Prov. 17. 22, a broken spirit *d.* the bones.
Isa. 44. 3, pour floods on *d.* ground.
Mat. 12. 43 ; Lu. 11. 24, through *d.* places.

Mk. 5. 29, fountain of blood *d.* up.
See Ps. 107. 33, 35 ; Isa. 53. 2 ; Mk. 11. 20.

DUE. Lev. 10. 13, 14, it is thy *d.*, and thy sons' *d.*
26. 4 ; Deut. 11. 14, rain in *d.* season.
Ps. 104. 27 ; 145. 15 ; Mat. 24. 45 ; Lu. 14. 42, meat
in *d.* season.
Prov. 15. 23, word spoken in *d.* season.
Mat. 18. 34, pay all that was *d.*
Lu. 23. 41, the *d.* reward of our deeds.
Rom. 5. 6, in *d.* time Christ died.
Gal. 6. 9, in *d.* season we shall reap.
See Prov. 3. 27 ; 1 Cor. 15. 8 ; Tit. 1. 3 ; 1 Pet. 5. 6.

DULL. Mat. 13. 15 ; Acts 28. 27 ; Heb. 5. 11.

DUMB. Ex. 4. 11, who maketh the *d.*?
Prov. 31. 8, open thy mouth for the *d.*
Isa. 35. 6, the tongue of the *d.* shall sing.
53. 7 ; Acts 8. 32, as sheep before shearers is *d.*
56. 10, they are all *d.* dogs.
Ezek. 3. 26, be *d.*, and shalt not be a reprover.
Hab. 2. 19, woe to him that saith to *d.* stone.
Mat. 9. 32 ; 12. 22 ; 15. 30 ; Mk. 7. 37 ; 9. 17, *d.* man.
See Ps. 39. 2 ; Dan. 10. 15 ; Lu. 1. 20 ; 11. 14 ; 2 Pet.
2. 16.

DUNG. 1 Sam. 2. 8 ; Ps. 113. 7, lifteth beggar from
d.-hill.
Lu. 13. 8, till I dig about it, and *d.* it.
14. 35, neither fit for land nor *d.*-hill.
Phil. 3. 8, count all things but *d.*
See Neh. 2. 13 ; Lam. 4. 5 ; Mal. 2. 3.

DUNGEON. Gen. 40. 15 ; 41. 14 ; Ex. 12. 29 ; Jer.
38. 6 ; Lam. 3. 53.

DURABLE. Prov. 8. 18 ; Isa. 23. 18.

DURETH. Mat. 13. 21.

DURST. Mat. 22. 46 ; Mk. 12. 34 ; Lu. 20. 40, nor *d.*
ask questions.
John 21. 12, none of disciples *d.* ask.
See Esth. 7. 5 ; Job 32. 6 ; Acts 5. 13 ; Jude 9.

DUST. Gen. 2. 7, Lord God formed man of *d.*
3. 14, *d.* shalt thou eat.
19, *d.* thou art.
18. 27, who am but *d.* and ashes.
Job 10. 9, wilt thou bring me into *d.* again?
22. 24 ; 27. 16, lay up gold as *d.*
34. 15, man shall turn again to *d.*
42. 6, I repent in *d.* and ashes.
Ps. 30. 9, shall the *d.* praise thee?
102. 14, servants favour *d.* thereof.
103. 14, remembereth that we are *d.*
104. 29, they die and return to their *d.*
Eccl. 3. 20, all are of the *d.*, and turn to *d.* again.
12. 7, then shall the *d.* return to the earth.
Isa. 40. 12, comprehended *d.* of the earth.
65. 25, *d.* shall be serpent's meat.
Lam. 3. 29, he putteth his mouth in the *d.*
Dan. 12. 2, many that sleep in *d.* shall awake.
Mic. 7. 17, lick the *d.* like a serpent.
Mat. 10. 14 ; Mk. 6. 11 ; Lu. 9. 5, shake off *d.* from
feet.
Lu. 10. 11, even *d.* of your city.
Acts 22. 23, as they threw *d.* into the air.
See Ex. 8. 16 ; Num. 23. 10 ; Deut. 9. 21 ; Josh. 7.
6 ; Job 2. 12 ; 39. 14 ; Lam. 2. 10.

DUTY. Eccl. 12. 13, the whole *d.* of man.
Lu. 17. 10, that which was our *d.* to do.
Rom. 15. 27, their *d.* is to minister.
See Ex. 21. 10 ; Deut. 25. 5 ; 2 Chron. 8. 14 ; Ezra 3. 4.

DWELL. Deut. 12. 11, cause his name to *d.* there.
1 Sam. 4. 4 ; 2 Sam. 6. 2 ; 1 Chron. 13. 6, *d.* between
the cherubims.
1 Kings 8. 30 ; 2 Chron. 6. 21, heaven thy *d.* place.
Ps. 23. 6, will *d.* in house of the Lord.
37. 3, so shalt thou *d.* in the land.
84. 10, than to *d.* in tents of wickedness.
132. 14, here will I *d.*
133. 1, good for brethren to *d.* together.
Isa. 33. 14, who shall *d.* with devouring fire?
16, he shall *d.* on high.
57. 15, I *d.* in the high and holy place.

John 6. 56, *d.* in me, and I in him.
14. 10, the Father that *d.* in me.
17, for he *d.* with you, and shall be in you.
Rom. 7. 17, sin that *d.* in me.
Col. 2. 9, in him *d.* fulness of Godhead.
3. 16, word of Christ *d.* in you richly.
1 Tim. 6. 16, *d.* in the light.
2 Pet. 3. 13, wherein *d.* righteousness.
1 John 3. 17, how *d.* the love of God in him?
4. 12, God *d.* in us.
See Rom. 8. 9; 2 Cor. 6. 16; Jas. 4. 5.

E.

EACH. Isa. 57. 2, *e.* one walking in his uprightness.
Ezek. 4. 6, *e.* day for a year.
Acts 2. 3, cloven tongues sat on *e.*
Phil. 2. 3, let *e.* esteem other.
See Ex. 18. 7; Ps. 85. 10; 2 Thess. 1. 3.

EAGLE. Ex. 19. 4, how I bare you on *e.* wings.
2 Sam. 1. 23, were swifter than *e.*
Job 9. 26, *e.* that hasteth to prey.
39. 27, doth the *e.* mount up?
Ps. 103. 5, youth renewed like *e.*
Isa. 40. 31, mount up with wings as *e.*
Ezek. 1. 10, they four also had the face of an *e.*
17. 3, a great *e.* with great wings.
Obad. 4, thou shalt exalt thyself as the *e.*
Mat. 24. 28; Lu. 17. 37, *e.* be gathered.
Rev. 4. 7, the fourth beast was like a flying *e.*
See Dan. 4. 33; Rev. 12. 14.

EAR (*n.*). Neh. 1. 6, let thine *e.* be attentive.
Job 12. 11; 34. 3, doth not *e.* try words?
29. 11, when the *e.* heard me, it blessed me.
42. 5, heard of thee by the hearing of the *e.*
Ps. 45. 10, and incline thine *e.*
58. 4, like the deaf adder that stoppeth her *e.*
78. 1, give *e.*, O my people.
94. 9, he that planted the *e.*, shall he not hear?
Prov. 15. 31, the *e.* that heareth the reproof.
17. 4, liar giveth *e.* to naughty tongue.
18. 15, *e.* of wise seeketh knowledge.
20. 12, hearing *e.*, seeing eye, Lord made.
22. 17, bow down thine *e.*
25. 12, wise reprover on obedient *e.*
Eccl. 1. 8, nor the *e.* filled with hearing.
Isa. 48. 8, from that time thine *e.* not opened.
50. 4, he wakeneth my *e.* to hear.
55. 3, incline your *e.*, and come unto me.
59. 1, nor his *e.* heavy, that it cannot.
Jer. 9. 20, let your *e.* receive word of the Lord.
Amos 3. 12, out of mouth of lion piece of an *e.*
Mat. 10. 27, what ye hear in *e.*, preach.
1 Cor. 2. 9, nor *e.* heard.
12. 16, if *e.* say, because I am not the eye.
See Rev. 2. 7.

EAR (*v.*). Ex. 34. 21; Deut. 21. 4; 1 Sam. 8. 12.

EARLY. Ps. 46. 5, and that right *e.*
63. 1, *e.* will I seek thee.
90. 14, satisfy us *e.* with thy mercy.
Prov. 1. 28; 8. 17, seek me *e.* shall find me.
Cant. 7. 12, get up *e.* to vineyards.
Hos. 6. 4; 13. 3, as *e.* dew.
Jas. 5. 7, the *e.* and latter rain.
See Judg. 7. 3; Lu. 24. 22; John 20. 1.

EARNEST. Job 7. 2, as servant *e.* desireth shadow.
Jer. 31. 20, I do *e.* remember him still.
Mic. 7. 3, do evil with both hands *e.*
Lu. 22. 44, in agony he prayed more *e.*
Rom. 8. 19, the *e.* expectation of the creature.
1 Cor. 12. 31, covet *e.* best gifts.
2 Cor. 1. 22; 5. 5, the *e.* of the Spirit.
5. 2, *e.* desiring to be clothed.
Eph. 1. 14, the *e.* of our inheritance.
Phil. 1. 20, to my *e.* expectation and hope.
Jude 3, *e.* contend for the faith.
See Acts 3. 12; Heb. 2. 1; Jas. 5. 17.

EARNETH. Hag. 1. 6.

EARS. Ex. 10. 2, tell it in *e.* of thy son.
1 Sam. 3. 11; 2 Kings 21. 12; Jer. 19. 3, at which *e.* shall tingle.

2 Sam. 7. 22, we have heard with our *e.*
Job 15. 21, dreadful sound is in his *e.*
28. 22, heard fame with our *e.*
Ps. 18. 6, my cry came even into his *e.*
34. 15, his *e.* are open unto their cry.
115. 6; 135. 17, they have *e.*, but hear not.
Prov. 21. 13, stoppeth *e.* at cry of the poor.
23. 9, speak not in *e.* of a fool.
26. 17, one that taketh dog by the *e.*
Isa. 6. 10; Mat. 13. 15; Acts 28. 27, make *e.* heavy.
Mat. 13. 16, blessed are your *e.*
26. 51; Mk. 14. 47, smote off *e.*
Mk. 7. 33, put his fingers into *e.*
8. 18, having *e.*, hear ye not?
Acts 7. 51, uncircumcised in heart and *e.*
17. 20, strange things to our *e.*
2 Tim. 4. 3, having itching *e.*
Jas. 5. 4, entered into *e.* of the Lord.
1 Pet. 3. 12, his *e.* are open to prayer.
See Mat. 11. 15; Mk. 4. 9.

EARS (*of corn*). Deut. 23. 25; Mat. 12. 1.

EARTH. Gen. 8. 22, while *e.* remaineth.
10. 25, in his days was *e.* divided.
18. 25, shall not Judge of all the *e.* do right?
Num. 14. 21, all *e.* filled with glory.
16. 30, if the *e.* open her mouth.
Deut. 32. 1, O *e.*, hear the words of my mouth.
Josh. 3. 11; Zech. 6. 5, Lord of all the *e.*
23. 14, going way of all the *e.*
1 Kings 8. 27; 2 Chron. 6. 18, will God dwell on the *e.*?
2 Kings 5. 17, two mules' burden of *e.*
Job 7. 1, appointed time to man upon *e.*
9. 24, *e.* given into hand of wicked.
19. 25, stand at latter day upon *e.*
26. 7, hangeth *e.* upon nothing.
38. 4, when I laid foundations of the *e.*
41. 33, on *e.* there is not his like.
Ps. 2. 8, uttermost parts of *e.*
8. 1, excellent is thy name in *e.*
16. 3, to saints that are in the *e.*
25. 13, his seed shall inherit the *e.*
33. 5, the *e.* is full of the goodness.
34. 16, cut off remembrance from the *e.*
37. 9, 11, 22, wait on Lord shall inherit *e.*
41. 2, shall be blessed upon the *e.*
46. 2, not fear, though *e.* be removed.
6, uttered voice, the *e.* melted.
8, desolations made in the *e.*
10, will be exalted in the *e.*
47. 9, shields of the *e.* belong to God.
48. 2, joy of the whole *e.*
50. 4, call to *e.*, that he may judge.
57. 5; 108. 5, glory above all the *e.*
58. 11, a God that judgeth in the *e.*
60. 2, made the *e.* to tremble.
63. 9, lower parts of the *e.*
65. 8, dwell in uttermost parts of *e.*
9, visitest *e.*, and waterest it.
67. 6; Ezek. 34. 27, *e.* yield increase.
68. 8, *e.* shook, heavens dropped.
71. 20, bring me up from depths of the *e.*
72. 6, showers that water the *e.*
16, handful of corn in the *e.*
73. 9, tongue walketh through *e.*
25, none on *e.* I desire beside thee.
75. 3; Isa. 24. 19, *e.* dissolved.
83. 18; 97. 9, most high over all *e.*
90. 2, or ever thou hadst formed the *e.*
97. 1, Lord reigneth, let *e.* rejoice.
99. 1, Lord reigneth, let *e.* be moved.
102. 25; 104. 5; Prov. 8. 29; Isa. 48. 13, laid foundation of *e.*
104. 13, the *e.* is satisfied.
24, the *e.* is full of thy riches.
112. 2, seed mighty upon *e.*
115. 16, *e.* given to children of men.
119. 19, stranger in the *e.*
64, the *e.* full of thy mercy.

Ps. 119. 90, established the *e.*, it abideth.
146. 4, he returneth to the *e.*
147. 8, prepareth rain for the *e.*
148. 13, glory above *e.* and heaven.
Prov. 3. 19; Isa. 24. 1, Lord founded the *e.*
8. 23, set up from everlasting, or ever *e.* was.
26, he had not yet made *e.*, nor fields.
11. 31, righteous recompensed in *e.*
25. 3, the *e.* for depth.
30. 14, teeth as knives to devour poor from *e.*
16, the *e.* not filled with water.
21, for three things *e.* is disquieted.
24, four things little upon *e.*
Eccl. 1. 4, the *e.* abideth for ever.
3. 21, spirit of beast goeth to *e.*
5. 9, profit of the *e.* for all.
12. 7, dust return to *e.*
Isa. 4. 2, fruit of *e.* excellent.
11. 9, *e.* full of knowledge of the Lord.
13. 13, *e.* shall remove out of her place.
14. 16, is this the man that made *e.* tremble?
26. 9, when thy judgments are in the *e.*
21, *e.* shall disclose her blood.
34. 1, let the *e.* hear.
40. 22, sitteth on circle of the *e.*
28, Creator of ends of *e.* fainteth not.
44. 24, spreadeth abroad *e.* by myself.
45. 22, be saved, all ends of the *e.*
49. 13, be joyful, O *e.*
51. 6, the *e.* shall wax old.
66. 1, the *e.* is my footstool.
8, shall *e.* bring forth in one day?
Jer. 15. 10, man of contention to whole *e.*
22. 29; Mic. 1. 2, O *e., e., e.,* hear word of Lord.
31. 22, hath created new thing in *e.*
51. 15, made the *e.* by his power.
Ezek. 9. 9, the Lord hath forsaken the *e.*
43. 2, the *e.* shined with his glory.
Hos. 2. 22, the *e.* shall hear the corn.
Amos 3. 5, bird fall in snare on *e.*
8. 9, darken *e.* in the clear day.
9. 9, least grain fall upon the *e.*
Jonah 2. 6, *e.* with bars about me.
Mic. 6. 2, ye strong foundations of the *e.*
7. 2, good man perished out of the *e.*
17, move like worms of the *e.*
Nah. 1. 5, *e.* burnt up at his presence.
Hab. 2. 14, *e.* filled with knowledge.
3. 3, the *e.* full of his praise.
Hag. 1. 10, *e.* stayed from her fruit.
Zech. 4. 10, eyes of Lord run through *e.*
Mal. 4. 6, lest I smite *e.* with a curse.
Mat. 5. 5, meek shall inherit *e.*
35, swear not by the *e.*
6. 19, treasures upon *e.*
9. 6; Mk. 2. 10; Lu. 5. 24, power on *e.* to forgive.
Mat. 10. 34, to send peace on *e.*
13. 5; Mk. 4. 5, not much *e.*
16. 19; 18. 18, shalt bind on *e.*
18. 19, shall agree on *e.*
23. 9, call no man father on *e.*
25. 18, 25, digged in the *e.*
Mk. 4. 28, *e.* bringeth forth fruit of herself.
31, less than all seeds in the *e.*
9. 3, no fuller on *e.* can white them.
Lu. 2. 14, on *e.* peace.
23. 44, darkness over all *e.*
John 3. 12, I have told you *e.* things.
31, of *e.* is *e.,* and speaketh of the *e.*
12. 32, lifted up from the *e.*
17. 4, I have glorified thee on the *e.*
Acts 8. 33, life taken from the *e.*
9. 4, 8; 26. 14, Saul fell to the *e.*
22. 22, away with such a fellow from *e.*
Rom. 10. 18, sound went into all *e.*
1 Cor. 15. 47, first man is of the *e., e.*
48, as is the *e.,* such are they that are *e.*
49, the image of the *e.*
2 Cor. 4. 7, treasure in *e.* vessels.
Col. 3. 2, affection not on things on *e.*
Phil. 3. 19, who mind *e.* things.

Heb. 6. 7, *e.* drinketh in the rain.
8. 4, if he were on *e.*
11. 13, strangers on the *e.*
12. 25, refused him that spake on *e.*
26, voice then shook the *e.*
Jas. 3. 15, this wisdom is *e.*
5. 5, lived in pleasure on *e.*
7, the precious fruit of the *e.*
18, and the *e.* brought forth her fruit.
2 Pet. 3. 10, the *e.* shall be burnt up.
Rev. 5. 10, we shall reign on the *e.*
7. 3, hurt not the *e.*
18. 1, *e.* lightened with his glory.
20. 11, from whose face the *e.* fled.
21. 1, a new *e.*
See Gen. 1. 1, 11; 3. 17; 7. 10; Ex. 9. 29; Job 12.
8; Ps. 24. 1; Isa. 65. 16; Mic. 1. 4; Zeph. 3. 8;
2 Pet. 3. 7, 13; Rev. 20. 9.

EARTHQUAKE. 1 Kings 19. 11; Isa. 29. 6; Amos
1. 1; Zech. 14. 5; Mat. 24. 7; 27. 54; Acts 16. 26;
Rev. 6. 12; 8. 5; 11. 13; 16. 18.

EASE. Ex. 18. 22, so shall it be *e.* for thyself.
Deut. 28. 65, among nations find no *e.*
Job 12. 5, thought of him that is at *e.*
16. 6, though I forbear, what am I *e.*
21. 23, dieth, being wholly at *e.*
Ps. 25. 13, his soul shall dwell at *e.*
Isa. 32. 9, 11, women that are at *e.*
Amos 6. 1, woe to them that are at *e.*
Mat. 9. 5; Mk. 2. 9; Lu. 5. 23, is *e.* to say.
19. 24; Mk. 10. 25; Lu. 18. 25, *e.* for camel.
1 Cor. 13. 5, not *e.* provoked.
Heb. 12. 1, sin which doth so *e.* beset.
See Jer. 46. 27; Zech. 1. 15; Lu. 12. 19.

EAST. Gen. 41. 6; 23. 27, blasted with *e.* wind.
Ex. 10. 13, Lord brought an *e.* wind.
Job 1. 3, greatest of all men of the *e.*
15. 2, fill his belly with *e.* wind.
27. 21, *e.* wind carrieth him away.
38. 24, scattereth *e.* wind on the earth.
Ps. 48. 7, breakest ships with *e.* wind.
75. 6, promotion cometh not from *e.*
103. 12, as far as *e.* from west.
Isa. 27. 8, stayeth rough wind in day of *e.* wind.
Ezek. 19. 12, the *e.* wind drieth up her fruit.
43. 2, glory of God of Israel came from way of *e.*
47. 1, house stood toward the *e.*
Hos. 12. 1, Ephraim followeth *e.* wind.
13. 15, though fruitful, an *e.* wind shall come.
See Jonah 4. 5, 8; Mat. 2. 1; 8. 11; 24. 27.

EASTER. Acts 12. 4, intending after *E.* to bring
him forth.

EASY. Prov. 14. 6; Mat. 11. 30; 1 Cor. 14. 9; Jas.
3. 17.

EAT. Gen. 2. 17, in day thou *e.* thou shalt die.
9. 4; Lev. 19. 26; Deut. 12. 16, blood not *e.*
24. 33, not *e.* till I have told.
43. 32, Egyptians might not *e.* with Hebrews.
Ex. 12. 16, no work, save that which man must *e.*
23. 11, that the poor may *e.*
29. 34, shall not be *e.* because holy.
Lev. 25. 20, what shall we *e.* seventh year?
Num. 13. 32, a land that *e.* up inhabitants.
Josh. 5. 11, 12, *e.* of old corn of the land.
1 Sam. 14. 30, if haply people had *e.* freely.
28. 20, had *e.* no bread all day.
22, *e.,* that thou mayest have strength.
2 Sam. 19. 42, have we *e.* at all of the king's cost?
1 Kings 19. 5; Acts 10. 13; 11. 7, angel said, Arise
and *e.*
2 Kings 4. 43, 44, they shall *e.,* and leave thereof.
6. 28, give thy son. that we may *e.* him.
Neh. 5. 2, corn, that we may *e.* and live.
Job 3. 24, my sighing cometh before I *e.*
5. 5, whose harvest the hungry *e.* up.
6. 6, *e.* without salt.
21. 25, another never *e.* with pleasure.
31. 17, have *e.* my morsel alone.
Ps. 22. 26, meek shall *e.* and be satisfied.

Ps. 69. 9 ; John 2. 17, zeal hath *e.* me up.
102. 9, have *e.* ashes like bread.
Prov. 1. 31 ; Isa. 3. 10, *e.* fruit of their own way.
13. 25, *e.* to satisfying of soul.
18. 21, they that love it shall *e.* the fruit.
23. 1, sittest to *e.* with ruler.
24. 13, *e.* honey, because it is good.
25. 27, not good to *e.* much honey.
Eccl. 2. 25, who can *e.* more than I ?
4. 5, fool *e.* his own flesh.
5. 11, goods increase, they increased that *e.*
12, sleep be sweet, whether he *e.* little or much.
17, all his days also he *e.* in darkness.
19 ; 6. 2, not power to *e.* thereof.
10. 16, thy princes *e.* in the morning.
17, blessed when princes *e.* in due season.
Isa. 4. 1, we will *e.* our own bread.
7. 15, 22, butter and honey shall he *e.*
11. 7 ; 65. 25, lion *e.* straw like ox.
29. 8, he *e.*, awaketh, and is hungry.
51. 8, worm shall *e.* them like wool.
55. 1, come ye, buy and *e.*
2, *e.* ye that which is good.
10, give bread to the *e.*
65. 13, my servants shall *e.*, but ye shall be.
Jer. 5. 17, they shall *e.* up thine harvest.
15. 16, words were found, and I did *e.* them.
24. 2 ; 29. 17, figs could not be *e.*
31. 29 ; Ezek. 18. 2, the fathers have *e.* sour grapes.
Ezek. 3. 1, 2, 3, *e.* this roll.
4. 10, *e.* by weight.
Dan. 4. 33, *e.* grass as oxen.
Hos. 4. 10 ; Mic. 6. 14 ; Hag. 1. 6, *e.*, and not have enough.
10. 13, have *e.* the fruit of lies.
Mic. 7. 1, there is no cluster to *e.*
Mat. 6. 25 ; Lu. 12. 22, what ye shall *e.*
9. 11 ; Mk. 2. 16 ; Lu. 15. 2, why *e.* with publicans ?
12. 1, ears of corn, and *e.*
4, *e.* shewbread, which was not lawful to *e.*
14. 16 ; Mk. 6. 37 ; Lu. 9. 13, give ye them to *e.*
15. 20, to *e.* with unwashen hands.
27 ; Mk. 7. 28, dogs *e.* of crumbs.
32 ; Mk. 8. 1, multitude have nothing to *e.*
24. 49, to *e.* and drink with the drunken.
Mk. 2. 16, when they saw him *e.* with.
6. 31, no leisure so much as to *e.*
11. 14, no man *e.* fruit of thee.
Lu. 5. 33, but thy disciples *e.* and drink.
10. 8, *e.* such things as are set before you.
12. 19, take thine ease, *e.*, drink.
13. 26, we have *e.* and drunk in thy presence.
15. 23, let us *e.* and be merry.
22. 30, that ye may *e.* at my table.
24. 43, he took it, and did *e.* before them.
John 4. 31, Master, *e.*
32, meat to *e.* ye know not of.
6. 26, because ye did *e.* of loaves.
52, can this man give us his flesh to *e.*
53, except ye *e.* the flesh.
Acts 2. 46, did *e.* their meat with gladness.
9. 9, Saul did neither *e.* nor drink.
11. 3, thou didst *e.* with them.
23. 14, will *e.* nothing until we have slain Paul.
Rom. 14. 2, one believeth he may *e.* all things ;
weak *e.* herbs.
6, *e.* to the Lord.
20, who *e.* with offence.
21, neither to *e.* flesh nor drink wine.
1 Cor. 5. 11, with such an one not to *e.*
8. 7, *e.* it as a thing offered to idol.
8, neither if we *e.* are we better.
13, I will *e.* no flesh while world.
9. 4, have we not power to *e.* ?
10. 3, all *e.* same spiritual meat.
27, *e.*, asking no question.
31, whether ye *e.* or drink.
11. 29, he that *e.* unworthily.
2 Thess. 3. 10, work not, neither should he *e.*
Heb. 13. 10, whereof they have no right to *e.*

Rev. 2. 7, *e.* of the tree of life.
17, will give to *e.* of hidden manna.
19. 18, *e.* flesh of kings.
See Judg. 14. 14 ; Prov. 31. 27 ; Isa. 1. 19 ; 65. 4.

EDGE. Prov. 5. 4 ; Heb. 4. 12 ; Eccl. 10. 10.

EDIFY. Rom. 14. 19, wherewith one may *e.*
15. 2, please his neighbour to *e.*
1 Cor. 8. 1, charity *e.*
14. 3, he that prophesieth speaketh to *e.*
4, *e.* himself, *e.* the church.
10. 23, all things lawful, but *e.* not.
Eph. 4. 12, for *e.* of the body of Christ.
See 2 Cor. 10. 8 ; 13. 10 ; 1 Tim. 1. 4.

EFFECT. Num. 30. 8, make vow of none *e.*
2 Chron. 7. 11, Solomon prosperously *e.* all.
Ps. 33. 10, devices of the people of none *e.*
Isa. 32. 17, the *e.* of righteousness quietness.
Mat. 15. 6 ; Mk. 7. 13, commandment of God of none *e.*
1 Cor. 1. 17, lest cross be of none *e.*
Gal. 5. 4, Christ is become of none *e.*
See Rom. 3. 3 ; 4. 14 ; 9. 6 ; Gal. 3. 17.

EFFECTUAL. 1 Cor. 16. 9, a great door and *e.* is opened.
Eph. 3. 7 ; 4. 16, the *e.* working.
Jas. 5. 16, *e.* prayer of righteous man.
See 2 Cor. 1. 6 ; Gal. 2. 8 ; 1 Thess. 2. 13.

EFFEMINATE. 1 Cor. 6. 9.

EGG. Job 6. 6, taste in the white of an *e.*
Job 39. 14, ostrich leaveth *e.* in earth.
Lu. 11. 12, if he ask an *e.*
See Deut. 22. 6 ; Isa. 10. 14 ; 59. 5 ; Jer. 17. 11.

EITHER. Gen. 31. 24, speak not *e.* good or bad.
Eccl. 11. 6, prosper, *e.* this or that.
Mat. 6. 24 ; Lu. 16. 13, *e.* hate the one.
John 19. 18, on *e.* side one.
Rev. 22. 2, on *e.* side the river.
See Deut. 17. 3 ; 28. 51 ; Isa. 7. 11 ; Mat. 12. 33.

ELDER. 1 Sam. 15. 30, honour me before *e.* of people.
Job 15. 10, aged men, much *e.* than thy father.
32. 4, waited, because they were *e.* than he.
Prov. 31. 23, husband known among *e.*
Mat. 15. 2 ; Mk. 7. 3, tradition of the *e.*
1 Tim. 5. 17, let *e.* that rule be worthy.
Tit. 1. 5, ordain *e.* in every city.
Heb. 11. 2, the *e.* obtained good report.
Jas. 5. 14, call for *e.* of the church.
1 Pet. 5. 1, the *e.* I exhort, who am an *e.*
5, younger submit to the *e.*
See John 8. 9 ; 1 Tim. 5. 2 ; 2 John 1 ; 3 John 1.

ELECT. Isa. 42. 1, mine *e.*, in whom my soul delighteth.
45. 4, mine *e.* I have called by name.
65. 9, 22, mine *e.* shall inherit.
Mat. 24. 22 ; Mk. 13. 20, for *e.* sake days shortened.
24 ; Mk. 13. 22, deceive very *e.*
31 ; Mk. 13. 27, gather together his *e.*
Lu. 18. 7, avenge his own *e.*
Rom. 8. 33, to charge of God's *e.*
Col. 3. 12, put on as the *e.* of God.
1 Tim. 5. 21, charge thee before *e.* angels.
1 Pet. 1. 2, *e.* according to foreknowledge.
2. 6, corner stone, *e.*, precious.
See 2 Tim. 2. 10 ; Tit. 1. 1 ; 1 Pet. 5. 13 ; 2 John 1, 13.

ELECTION. Rom. 9. 11 ; 11. 5 ; 1 Thess. 1. 4 ; 2 Pet. 1. 10.

ELEMENTS. Gal. 4. 3, 9 ; 2 Pet. 3. 10.

ELEVEN. Gen. 32. 22, Jacob took his *e.* sons.
37. 9, and *e.* stars made obeisance.
Acts 1. 26, he was numbered with *e.*
See Mat. 28. 16 ; Mk. 16. 14 ; Lu. 24. 9.

ELOQUENT. Ex. 4. 10 ; Isa. 3. 3 ; Acts 18. 24.

EMBALMED. Gen. 50. 2, the days of those which are *e.*
50. 26, and they *e.* him.
See John 19. 39.

EMBOLDEN. Job 16. 3 ; 1 Cor. 8. 10.

EMBRACE.   Job 24. 8, *e.* rock for want of shelter.
Eccl. 3. 5, a time to *e.*
Heb. 11. 13, seen and *e.* promises.
See Prov. 4. 8 ; 5. 20 ; Lam. 4. 5 ; Acts 20. 1.

EMBROIDER.   Ex. 28. 39 ; 35. 35 ; 38. 23.

EMERALDS.   Ex. 28. 18 ; 39. 11 ; Rev. 4. 3 ; 21. 19.

EMERODS.   Deut. 28. 27, and with *e.*
1 Sam. 5. 6, and smote them with *e.*

EMINENT.   Ezek. 16. 24, 31, 39 ; 17. 22.

EMPIRE.   Esth. 1. 20.

EMPLOY.   Deut. 20. 19 ; 1 Chron. 9. 3 ; Ezra 10. 15 ;
Ezek. 39. 14.

EMPTY.   Gen. 31. 42 ; Mk. 12. 3 ; Lu. 1. 53 ; 20. 10,
sent *e.* away.
Ex. 3. 21, ye shall not go *e.*
23. 15 ; 34. 20 ; Deut. 16. 16, appear before me *e.*
Deut. 15. 13, not let him go away *e.*
Job 22. 9, thou hast sent widows away *e.*
Eccl. 11. 3, clouds *e.* themselves on the earth.
Isa. 29. 8, awaketh, and his soul is *e.*
Jer. 48. 11, Moab *e.* from vessel to vessel.
Nah. 2. 2, the emptiers have *e.* them out.
Mat. 12. 44, come, he findeth it *e.*
See 2 Sam. 1. 22 ; 2 Kings 4. 3 ; Hos. 10. 1.

EMULATION.   Rom. 11. 14 ; Gal. 5. 20.

ENABLED.   1 Tim. 1. 12.

ENCAMP.   Ps. 27. 3, though host *e.* against me.
34. 7, angel of Lord *e.* round.
See Num. 10. 31 ; Job 19. 12 ; Ps. 53. 5.

ENCOUNTERED.   Acts 17. 18.

ENCOURAGE.   Deut. 1. 38 ; 3. 28 ; 2 Sam. 11. 25, *e.*
him.
Ps. 64. 5, they *e.* themselves in an evil matter.
See 1 Sam. 30. 6 ; 2 Chron. 31. 4 ; 35. 2 ; Isa. 41. 7.

END.   Gen. 6. 13, the *e.* of all flesh before me.
Ex. 23. 16 ; Deut. 11. 12, in the *e.* of the year.
Num. 23. 10, let my last *e.* be like his.
Deut. 8. 16, do thee good at thy latter *e.*
32. 29, consider their latter *e.*
Job 6. 11, what is mine *e.*, that I should prolong ?
8. 7 ; 42. 12, thy latter *e.* shall increase.
16. 3, shall vain words have an *e.* ?
26. 10, till day and night come to an *e.*
Ps. 7. 9, wickedness of wicked come to an *e.*
9. 6, destructions come to perpetual *e.*
37. 37, the *e.* of that man is peace.
39. 4, make me to know my *e.*
73. 17, then understood I their *e.*
102. 27, the same, thy years have no *e.*
107. 27, are at their wit's *e.*
119. 96, an *e.* of all perfection.
Prov. 14. 12, the *e.* thereof are ways of death.
17. 24, eyes of fool in *e.* of earth.
19. 20, be wise in thy latter *e.*
25. 8, lest thou know not what to do in *e.*
Eccl. 3. 11, find out from beginning to the *e.*
4. 8, no *e.* of all his labour.
16, no *e.* of all the people.
7. 2, that is the *e.* of all men.
8, better the *e.* of a thing.
10. 13, the *e.* of his talk is madness.
12. 12, of making books there is no *e.*
Isa. 9. 7, of his government shall be no *e.*
46. 10, declaring *e.* from beginning.
Jer. 5. 31, what will ye do in *e.* thereof ?
8. 20, harvest past, summer *e.*
17. 11, at his *e.* shall be a fool.
29. 11, to give you an expected *e.*
31. 17, there is hope in thine *e.*
Lam. 1. 9, remembereth not her last *e.*
4. 18 ; Ezek. 7. 2, our *e.* is near, *e.* is come.
Ezek. 21. 25 ; 35. 5, iniquity shall have an *e.*
Dan. 8. 17, 19 ; 11. 27, at the time of *e.*
11. 45, he shall come to his *e.*, and none shall
help him.
12. 8, what shall be the *e.* ?
13, go thy way till the *e.* be.
Hab. 2. 3, at the *e.* it shall speak.

Mat. 10. 22 ; 24. 13 ; Mk. 13. 13, endureth to *e.*
13. 39, harvest is *e.* of the world.
24. 3, what sign of the *e.* of the world ?
6 ; Mk. 13. 7 ; Lu. 21. 9, the *e.* is not yet.
14, then shall the *e.* come.
31, gather from one *e.* of heaven.
26. 58, Peter sat to see the *e.*
28. 20, I am with you, even unto the *e.*
Mk. 3. 26, cannot stand, but hath an *e.*
Lu. 1. 33, of his kingdom there shall be no *e.*
22. 37, things concerning me have an *e.*
John 13. 1, he loved them unto the *e.*
18. 37, to this *e.* was I born.
Rom. 6. 21, the *e.* of those things is death.
22, the *e.* everlasting life.
10. 4, the *e.* of the law for righteousness.
1 Cor. 10. 11, on whom *e.* of world are come.
Phil. 3. 19, whose *e.* is destruction.
1 Tim. 1. 5, the *e.* of the commandment.
Heb. 6. 8, whose *e.* is to be burned.
16, an oath an *e.* of strife.
7. 3, neither beginning nor *e.* of life.
9. 26, once in the *e.* hath he appeared.
13. 7, considering *e.* of their conversation.
Jas. 5. 11, ye have seen *e.* of the Lord.
1 Pet. 1. 9, receiving the *e.* of your faith.
13, be sober, and hope to the *e.*
4. 7, the *e.* of all things is at hand.
17, what shall the *e.* be of them that obey not?
Rev. 2. 26, keepeth my works unto *e.*
21. 6 ; 22. 13, the beginning and the *e.*
See Ps. 19. 6 ; 65. 5 ; Isa. 45. 22 ; 52. 10 ; Jer. 4. 27.

ENDAMAGE.   Ezra 4. 13.

ENDANGER.   Eccl. 10. 9 ; Dan. 1. 10.

ENDEAVOUR.   Ps. 28. 4 ; Eph. 4. 3 ; 2 Pet. 1. 15.

ENDLESS.   1 Tim. 1. 4 ; Heb. 7. 16.

ENDUE.   Gen. 30. 20 ; 2 Chron. 2. 12 ; Lu. 24. 49 ;
Jas. 3. 13.

ENDURE.   Gen. 33. 14, as the children be able to *e.*
Esth. 8. 6, how can I *e.* to see evil ?
Job 8. 15, hold it fast, but it shall *e.*
31. 23, I could not *e.*
Ps. 9. 7 ; 102. 12 ; 104. 31, Lord shall *e.* for ever.
30. 5, anger *e.* a moment, weeping *e.* for a night.
52. 1, goodness of God *e.* continually.
72. 5, as long as sun and moon *e.*
17, his name shall *e.* for ever.
100. 5, his truth *e.* to all generations.
106. 1 ; 107. 1 ; 118. 1 ; 136. 1 ; 138. 8 ; Jer. 33. 11,
his mercy *e.* for ever.
111. 3 ; 112. 3, 9, his righteousness *e.* for ever.
119. 160, every one of thy judgments *e.*
135. 13, thy name, O Lord, *e.* for ever.
145. 13, thy dominion *e.*
Prov. 27. 24, doth *e.* to every generation.
Ezek. 22. 14, can thy heart *e.* ?
Mat. 10. 22 ; 24. 13 ; Mk. 13. 13, *e.* to the end.
Mk. 4. 17, so *e.* but for a time.
John 6. 27, meat that *e.* unto life.
Rom. 9. 22, God *e.* with much longsuffering.
1 Cor. 13. 7, charity *e.* all things.
2 Tim. 2. 3, *e.* hardness as good soldier.
4. 3, they will not *e.* sound doctrine.
5, watch, *e.* afflictions.
Heb. 10. 34, in heaven a better and *e.* substance.
12. 7, if ye *e.* chastening.
Jas. 1. 12, blessed is man that *e.* temptation.
5. 11, we count them happy which *e.*
1 Pet. 1. 25, the word of the Lord *e.* for ever.
2. 19, if a man for conscience *e.* grief.
See Heb. 10. 32 ; 11. 27 ; 12. 2, 3.

ENEMY.   Ex. 23. 22, I will be *e.* to thine *e.*
Deut. 32. 31, our *e.* themselves being judges.
Josh. 7. 12, Israel turned backs before *e.*
Judg. 5. 31, so let all thy *e.* perish.
1 Sam. 24. 19, if man find *e.*, will he let him go ?
1 Kings 21. 20, hast thou found me, O mine *e.* ?
Job 13. 24, wherefore holdest thou me for *e.* ?
Ps. 8. 2, still the *e.* and avenger.

Ps. 23. 5, in presence of mine *e.*
38. 19, mine *e.* are lively.
61. 3, a strong tower from the *e.*
72. 9, his *e.* shall lick the dust.
119. 98, wiser than mine *e.*
127. 5, speak with *e.* in the gate.
139. 22, I count them mine *e.*
Prov. 16. 7, maketh his *e.* at peace.
24. 17, rejoice not when *e.* falleth.
25. 21 ; Rom. 12. 20, if *e.* hunger, give bread.
27. 6, kisses of *e.* deceitful.
Isa. 9. 11, Lord shall join *e.* together.
59. 19, when *e.* shall come in like a flood.
63. 10, he was turned to be their *e.*
Jer. 15. 11, will cause *e.* to entreat thee well.
30. 14, wounded thee with wound of *e.*
Mic. 7. 6, man's *e.* men of his own house.
Mat. 5. 43, said, thou shalt hate thine *e.*
44 ; Lu. 6. 27, 35, I say, love your *e.*
13. 25, 28, 39, his *e.* sowed tares.
Lu. 19. 43, thine *e.* shall cast a trench.
Acts 13. 10, thou *e.* of all righteousness.
Rom. 5. 10, if when *e.* we were reconciled.
11. 28, concerning the gospel they are *e.*
Gal. 4. 16, am I become your *e.* ?
Phil. 3. 18, the *e.* of the cross.
Col. 1. 21, were *e.* in your mind.
2 Thess. 3. 15, count him not as an *e.*
Jas. 4. 4, friend of the world is the *e.* of God.
See Ps. 110. 1 ; Isa. 62. 8 ; Jer. 15. 14 ; Heb. 10. 13.

ENGAGED. Jer. 30. 21.

ENGINES. 2 Chron. 26. 15, and he made in Jerusalem *e.*
Ezek. 26. 9, and he shall set *e.* of war.

ENGRAFTED. Jas. 1. 21.

ENGRAVE. Ex. 28. 11 ; 35. 35 ; 38. 23 ; Zech. 3. 9 ; 2 Cor. 3. 7.

ENJOIN. Job 36. 23 ; Philem. 8 ; Heb. 9. 20.

ENJOY. Lev. 26. 34 ; 2 Chron. 36. 21, land shall *e.* her sabbaths.
Eccl. 2. 1, *e.* pleasure, this also is vanity.
24 ; 3. 13 ; 5. 18, soul *e.* good.
1 Tim. 6. 17, giveth us all things to *e.*
See Num. 36. 8 ; Isa. 65. 22 ; Heb. 11. 25.

ENLARGE. Deut. 12. 20, when the Lord shall *e.* thy border.
Ps. 4. 1, thou hast *e.* me in distress.
25. 17, troubles of heart *e.*
119. 32, when thou shalt *e.* my heart.
Isa. 5. 14, hell hath *e.* herself.
2 Cor. 6. 11, 13 ; 10. 15, our heart is *e.*
See Isa. 54. 2 ; Hab. 2. 5 ; Mat. 23. 5.

ENLIGHTEN. Ps. 19. 8 ; Eph. 1. 18 ; Heb. 6. 4.

ENMITY. Rom. 8. 7, carnal mind is *e.*
Eph. 2. 15, 16, having abolished the *e.*
Jas. 4. 4, friendship of world *e.* with God.
See Gen. 3. 15 ; Num. 35. 21 ; Lu. 23. 12.

ENOUGH. Gen. 33. 9, 11, I have *e.*, my brother.
45. 28, it is *e.*, Joseph is alive.
Ex. 36. 5, people bring more than *e.*
2 Sam. 24. 16 ; 1 Kings 19. 4 ; 1 Chron. 21. 15 ; Mk. 14.
41 ; Lu. 22. 38, it is *e.*, stay thine hand.
Prov. 28. 19, shall have poverty *e.*
30. 15, four things say not, it is *e.*
16, fire saith not, it is *e.*
Isa. 56. 11, dogs which can never have *e.*
Jer. 49. 9, will destroy till they have *e.*
Hos. 4. 10, eat, and not have *e.*
Obad. 5, stolen till they had *e.*
Mal. 3. 10, room *e.* to receive it.
Mat. 10. 25, *e.* for disciple.
25. 9, lest there be not *e.*
See Deut. 1. 6 ; 2 Chron. 31. 10 ; Hag. 1. 6 ; Lu. 15. 17.

ENQUIRE. Ex. 18. 15, people come to me to *e.* of God.
2 Sam. 16. 23, as if a man had *e.* of oracle.
2 Kings 3. 11, is there not a prophet to *e.* ?

Ps. 78. 34, returned and *e.* early after God.
Ezek. 14. 3, should I be *e.* of at all by them ?
20. 3, 31, I will not be *e.*
36. 37, I will yet for this be *e.* of.
Zeph. 1. 6, those that have not *e.* for.
Mat. 10. 11, *e.* who in it is worthy.
1 Pet. 1. 10, of which salvation the prophets *e.*
See Deut. 12. 30 ; Isa. 21. 12 ; John 4. 52.

ENRICH. 1 Sam. 17. 25 ; Ps. 65. 9 ; Ezek. 27. 33 ; 1 Cor. 1. 5 ; 2 Cor. 9. 11.

ENSAMPLE. 1 Cor. 10. 11, happened to them for *e.*
Phil. 3. 17, as ye have us for an *e.*
2 Thess. 3. 9, to make ourselves an *e.*
See 1 Thess. 1. 7 ; 1 Pet. 5. 3 ; 2 Pet. 2. 6.

ENSIGN. Ps. 74. 4 ; Isa. 5. 26 ; 11. 10 ; 18. 3 ; 30. 17.

ENSNARED. Job 34. 30.

ENSUE. 1 Pet. 3. 11.

ENTANGLE. Ex. 14. 3 ; Mat. 22. 15 ; Gal. 5. 1.

ENTER. Ps. 100. 4, *e.* his gates with thanksgiving.
119. 130, the *e.* of thy word giveth light.
Isa. 26. 2, righteous nation may *e.* in.
20, *e.* thou into thy chambers.
Ezek. 44. 5, mark well *e.* in of the house.
Mat. 6. 6, prayest, *e.* into thy closet.
7. 13 ; Lu. 13. 24, *e.* in at strait gate.
10. 11 ; Lu. 10. 8, 10, what city ye *e.*
18. 8 ; Mk. 9. 43, better to *e.* into life.
19. 17, if thou wilt *e.* into life, keep.
25. 21, well done, *e.* into joy.
Mk. 5. 12 ; Lu. 8. 32, we may *e.* into swine.
14. 38 ; Lu. 22. 46, lest ye *e.* into temptation.
Lu. 9. 34, feared as they *e.* cloud.
13. 24, many will seek to *e.*
John 3. 4, can he *e.* ?
4. 38, ye are *e.* into their labours.
10. 1, 2, *e.* not by the door.
Rom. 5. 12, sin *e.* into world.
1 Cor. 2. 9, neither have *e.* into heart of man.
Heb. 3. 11, 18, shall not *e.* into rest.
4. 10, he that is *e.* into rest.
6. 20, forerunner is for us *e.*
2 Pet. 1. 11, so an *e.* shall be ministered.
See Ps. 143. 2 ; Prov. 17. 10 ; Mat. 15. 17.

ENTICE. Judg. 14. 15 ; 16. 5, *e.* husband that he may declare.
2 Chron. 18. 19, Lord said, who shall *e.* Ahab ?
Prov. 1. 10, if sinners *e.* thee.
1 Cor. 2. 4 ; Col. 2. 4, with *e.* words.
See Job 31. 27 ; Prov. 16. 29 ; Jas. 1. 14.

ENTIRE. Jas. 1. 4.

ENTREAT. Mat. 22. 6 ; Lu. 18. 32, *e.* them spitefully.

ENTRY. 1 Chron. 9. 19 ; Prov. 8. 3 ; Ezek. 8. 5 ; 40. 38.

ENVIRON. Josh. 7. 9.

ENVY. Job 5. 2, *e.* slayeth the silly one.
Ps. 73. 3, I was *e.* at the foolish.
Prov. 3. 31, *e.* not the oppressor.
14. 30, *e.* is rottenness of the bones.
23. 17, let not heart *e.* sinners.
24. 1, 19, be not *e.* against evil men.
27. 4, who is able to stand before *e.* ?
Eccl. 4. 4, for this a man is *e.*
9. 6, their love, hatred, and *e.* is perished.
Mat. 27. 18 ; Mk. 15. 10, for *e.* they delivered.
Acts 7. 9, patriarchs moved with *e.*
13. 45 ; 17. 5, Jews filled with *e.*
Rom. 1. 29, full of *e.*, murder.
13. 13, walk honestly, not in *e.*
1 Cor. 3. 3, among you *e.* and strife.
13. 4, charity *e.* not.
2 Cor. 12. 20, I fear lest there be *e.*
Gal. 5. 21, works of flesh are *e.*, murders.
26, *e.* one another.
Phil. 1. 15, preach Christ even of *e.*
1 Tim. 6. 4, whereof cometh *e.*
Tit. 3. 3, living in malice and *e.*
Jas. 4. 5, spirit in us lusteth to *e.*
See Gen. 37. 11 ; Ps. 106. 16 ; Ezek. 31. 9 ; 35. 11.

EPHAH. Ex. 16. 36, now an omer is the tenth part of an *e.*

Lev. 19. 36, a just *e.* shall ye have.
Ez k. 45. 10, ye shall have just balances, and a just *e.*
Zech. 5. 6, this is an *e.* that goeth forth.

EPHOD. Ex. 28. 6, they shall make the *e.* of gold.
39. 2, and he made the *e.* of gold.
Judg. 8. 27, and Gideon made an *e.* thereof.
17. 5, and made an *e.*

EPISTLE. 2 Cor. 3. 1, nor need *e.* of commendation.
2, ye are our *e.*
3, to be the *e.* of Christ.
2 Thess. 2. 15; 3. 14, by word or *e.*
2 Pet. 3. 16, as also in all his *e.*
See Acts 15. 30; 23. 33; 2 Cor. 7. 8; 2 Thess. 3. 17.

EQUAL. Ps. 17. 2, eyes behold things that are *e.*
55. 13, a man mine *e.,* my guide.
Prov. 26. 7, legs of lame not *e.*
Isa. 40. 25; 46. 5, to whom shall I be *e.?*
Ezek. 18. 25, 29; 33. 17, 20, is not my way *e.?*
Mat. 20. 12, hast made them *e.* to us.
Lu. 20. 36, are *e.* to angels.
John 5. 18; Phil. 2. 6, *e.* with God.
Col. 4. 1, give servants what is *e.*
See Ex. 36. 22; 2 Cor. 8. 14; Gal. 1. 14.

EQUITY. Ps. 98. 9, judge the people with *e.*
Prov. 1. 3, receive instruction of *e.*
2. 9, understand judgment and *e.*
17. 26, not good to strike princes for *e.*
Eccl. 2. 21, a man whose labour is in *e.*
See Isa. 11. 4; 59. 14; Mic. 3. 9; Mal. 2. 6.

ERECTED. Gen. 33. 20.

ERR. Ps. 95. 10, people that do *e.* in their heart.
119. 21, do *e.* from thy commandments.
Isa. 3. 12; 9. 16, lead thee cause to *e.*
28. 7, they *e.* in vision.
35. 8, wayfaring men shall not *e.*
Mat. 22. 29; Mk. 12. 24, *e.,* not knowing scriptures.
1 Tim. 6. 10, have *e.* from the faith.
21, have *e.* concerning the faith.
Jas. 1. 16, do not *e.,* beloved brethren.
5. 19, if any do *e.* from truth.
See Isa. 28. 7; 29. 24; Ezek. 45. 20.

ERRAND. Gen. 24. 33; Judg. 3. 19; 2 Kings 9. 5.

ERROR. Ps. 19. 12, who can understand his *e.?*
Eccl. 5. 6, neither say thou, it was an *e.*
10. 5, evil which I have seen as an *e.*
Mat. 27. 64, last *e.* worse than first.
Jas. 5. 20, converteth sinner from *e.*
2 Pet. 3. 17, led away with *e.* of wicked.
1 John 4. 6, the spirit of *e.*
See Job 19. 4; Rom. 1. 27; Heb. 9. 7; Jude 11.

ESCAPE. Gen. 19. 17, *e.* for thy life, *e.* to mountain.
1 Kings 18. 40; 2 Kings 9. 15, let none of them *e.*
Esth. 4. 13, think not thou shalt *e.* in king's house.
Job 11. 20, wicked shall not *e.*
19. 20, *e.* with skin of my teeth.
Ps. 55. 8, I would hasten my *e.*
Prov. 19. 5, speaketh lies shall not *e.*
Eccl. 7. 26, whoso pleaseth God shall *e.*
Isa. 20. 6; Heb. 2. 3, how shall we *e.?*
Ezek. 33. 21, one that had *e.* came to me.
Amos 9. 1, he that *e.* shall not be delivered.
Mat. 23. 33, how can ye *e.* damnation?
Lu. 21. 36, worthy to *e.*
John 10. 39, he *e.* out of their hands.
Acts 27. 44, they *e.* all safe to land.
28. 4, he *e.* sea, yet vengeance.
Heb. 11. 34, through faith *e.* edge of sword.
12. 25, if they *e.* not who refused.
2 Pet. 1. 4, *e.* corruption in the world.
20, after they *e.* pollutions.
See Deut. 23. 15; Ps. 124. 7; 1 Cor. 10. 13.

ESCHEW. Job 1. 1; 2. 3; 1 Pet. 3. 11.

ESPECIALLY. Gal. 6. 10; 1 Tim. 4. 10; 5. 8; Philem. 16.

ESPOUSE. Cant. 3. 11; Jer. 2. 2; 2 Cor. 11. 2.

ESPY. Gen. 42. 27; Josh. 14. 7; Jer. 48. 19; Ezek. 20. 6.

ESTABLISH. Ps. 40. 2, and *e.* my goings.
90. 17, *e.* work of our hands.
Prov. 4. 26, let thy ways be *e.*
12. 19, lip of truth *e.* for ever.
16. 12, throne *e.* by righteousness.
20. 18, every purpose *e.* by counsel.
24. 3, by understanding is house *e.*
29. 4, king by judgment *e.* the land.
Isa. 7. 9, if ye will not believe, ye shall not be *e.*
16. 5, in mercy shall the throne be *e.*
Jer. 10. 12; 51. 15, he *e.* world by wisdom.
Mat. 18. 16, two witnesses every word *e.*
Rom. 3. 31, yea, we *e.* the law.
10. 3, to *e.* their own righteousness.
Heb. 13. 9, the heart be *e.* with grace.
2 Pet. 1. 12, be *e.* in the present truth.
See Amos 5. 15; Hab. 2. 12; Acts 16. 5.

ESTATE. Ps. 136. 23, remembered us in low *e.*
Eccl. 1. 16, lo, I am come to great *e.*
Mk. 6. 21, Herod made supper to chief *e.*
Rom. 12. 16, condescend to men of low *e.*
Jude 6, angels kept not first *e.*
See Ezek. 36. 11; Dan. 11. 7; Lu. 1. 48.

ESTEEM. Deut. 32. 15, lightly *e.* rock of salvation.
1 Sam. 2. 30, despise me shall be lightly *e.*
18. 23, I am a poor man, and lightly *e.*
Job 23. 12, I have *e.* the words of his mouth.
36. 19, will he *e.* thy riches?
41. 27, he *e.* iron as straw.
Ps. 119. 128, I *e.* all thy precepts.
Isa. 53. 4, did *e.* him smitten.
Lam. 4. 2, *e.* as earthen pitchers.
Lu. 16. 15, highly *e.* among men.
Rom. 14. 5, one man *e.* one day above another.
14, that *e.* any thing unclean.
Phil. 2. 3, let each *e.* other better.
1 Thess. 5. 13, *e.* highly for work's sake.
Heb. 11. 26, *e.* reproach greater riches.
See Prov. 17. 28; Isa. 29. 17; 1 Cor. 6. 4.

ESTIMATION. Lev. 27. 2-8, 15-19.

ESTRANGED. Job 19. 13; Ps. 78. 30; Jer. 19. 4; Ezek. 14. 5.

ETERNAL. Deut. 33. 27, the *e.* God is thy refuge.
Isa. 60. 15, will make thee an *e.* excellency.
Mat. 19. 16; Mk. 10. 17; Lu. 10. 25; 18. 18, what shall I do that I may have *e.* life?
25. 46, righteous into life *e.*
Mk. 3. 29, is in danger of *e.* damnation.
10. 30, receive in world to come *e.* life.
John 3. 15, believeth in him have *e.* life.
4. 36, gathereth fruit unto life *e.*
5. 39, scriptures, in them *e.* life.
6. 54, drinketh my blood hath *e.* life.
68, thou hast words of *e.* life.
10. 28, give sheep *e.* life.
12. 25, hateth life, shall keep it to life *e.*
17. 2, give *e.* life to as many.
3, this is life *e.,* that they might know thee.
Acts 13. 48, many as were ordained to *e.* life.
Rom. 2. 7, who seek for glory, *e.* life.
5. 21, grace reign to *e.* life.
6. 23, gift of God is *e.* life.
2 Cor. 4. 17, an *e.* weight of glory.
18, things not seen are *e.*
5. 1, house *e.* in the heavens.
Eph. 3. 11, according to *e.* purpose.
1 Tim. 6. 12, 19, lay hold on *e.* life.
Tit. 1. 2; 3. 7, in hope of *e.* life.
Heb. 5. 9, author of *e.* salvation.
6. 2, doctrine of *e.* judgment.
9. 15, promise of *e.* inheritance.
1 Pet. 5. 10, called to *e.* glory by Christ.
1 John 1. 2, *e.* life, which was with the Father.
2. 25, this is the promise, even *e.* life.
3. 15, no murderer hath *e.* life.
5. 11, record, that God hath given to us *e.* life.
13, know that ye have *e.* life.
20, this is true God, and *e.* life.

Jude 7, vengeance of *e.* fire.
See Rom. 1. 20; 1 Tim. 1. 17; 2 Tim. 2. 10; Jude 21.

ETERNITY. Isa. 57. 15.

EUNUCHS. Isa. 56. 4, for thus saith the Lord to the *e.*
Mat. 19. 12, for there are some *e.*
Acts 8. 27, an *e.* of great authority.
See Isa. 56. 3.

EVANGELIST. Acts 21. 8; Eph. 4. 11; 2 Tim. 4. 5.

EVENING. 1 Sam. 14. 24, cursed that eateth till *e.*
1 Kings 17. 6, brought bread morning and *e.*
Ps. 90. 6, in *e.* cut down and withereth.
104. 23, goeth to his labour until the *e.*
141. 2, prayer as the *e.* sacrifice.
Eccl. 11. 6, in *e.* withhold not thine hand.
Jer. 6. 4, shadows of *e.* stretched out.
Hab. 1. 8; Zeph. 3. 3, *e.* wolves.
Zech. 14. 7, at *e.* time shall be light.
Mat. 14. 23, when *e.* was come, he was there alone.
Lu. 24. 29, abide, for it is toward *e.*
See Gen. 30. 16; Ps. 65. 8; Mat. 16. 2; Mk. 14. 17.

EVENT. Eccl. 2. 14; 9. 2, 3.

EVER. Gen. 3. 22, lest he eat, and live for *e.*
43. 9; 44. 32, let me bear blame for *e.*
Ex. 14. 13, ye shall see them no more for *e.*
Lev. 6. 13, fire *e.* burning on altar.
Deut. 5. 29; 12. 28, be well with them for *e.*
13. 16, a heap for *e.*
32. 40, lift up hand and say, I live for *e.*
Job 4. 7, who *e.* perished?
Ps. 9. 7, Lord shall endure for *e.*
12. 7, thou wilt preserve them for *e.*
22. 26, your heart shall live for *e.*
23. 6, dwell in house of the Lord for *e.*
29. 10, Lord sitteth king for *e.*
33. 11, counsel of Lord standeth for *e.*
37. 26, he is *e.* merciful, and lendeth.
48. 14, our God for *e.* and *e.*
49. 9, that he should still live for *e.*
51. 3, my sin is *e.* before me.
52. 8, trust in mercy of God for *e.* and *e.*
61. 4, will abide in tabernacle for *e.*
73. 26, my strength and portion for *e.*
74. 19, forget not congregation of poor for *e.*
81. 15, their time should have endured for *e.*
92. 7, they shall be destroyed for *e.*
93. 5, holiness becometh thine house for *e.*
102. 12, thou shalt endure for *e.*
103. 9, not keep his anger for *e.*
105. 8, remember his covenant for *e.*
119. 89, for *e.* thy word is settled.
132. 14, this is my rest for *e.*
146. 6, Lord keepeth truth for *e.*
10, Lord shall reign for *e.*
Prov. 27. 24, riches not for *e.*
Eccl. 3. 14, whatsoever God doeth shall be for *e.*
Isa. 26. 4, trust in Lord for *e.*
32. 17, assurance for *e.*
34. 10; Rev. 14. 11; 19. 3, smoke shall go up for *e.*
40. 8, word of God shall stand for *e.*
57. 16, will not contend for *e.*
Lam. 3. 31, Lord will not cast off for *e.*
Mat. 6. 13, thine is the glory for *e.*
21. 19; Mk. 11. 14, no fruit grow on thee for *e.*
John 8. 35, servant abideth not for *e.*
12. 34, heard that Christ abideth for *e.*
14. 16, Comforter abide for *e.*
Rom. 9. 5, God blessed for *e.*
1 Thess. 4. 17, so shall we *e.* be with the Lord.
5. 15, *e.* follow good.
2 Tim. 3. 7, *e.* learning.
Heb. 7. 25, he *e.* liveth to make.
13. 8, same yesterday, to day, and for *e.*
See Mat. 24. 21; Lu. 15. 31; John 10. 8.

EVERLASTING. Ex. 40. 15; Num. 25. 13, an *e.* priesthood.
Ps. 90. 2, from *e.* to *e.* thou art God.
139. 24, lead me in way *e.*

Prov. 8. 23, I was set up from *e.*
10. 25, righteous is an *e.* foundation.
Isa. 9. 6, called the *e.* Father.
26. 4, in the Lord is *e.* strength.
33. 14, with *e.* burnings.
35. 10; 51. 11; 61. 7, *e.* joy.
45. 17, with *e.* salvation.
54. 8, with *e.* kindness.
55. 13, for an *e.* sign.
56. 5; 63. 12, an *e.* name.
60. 19, 20, an *e.* light.
Jer. 31. 3, with an *e.* love.
Hab. 3. 6, the *e.* mountains.
Mat. 18. 8; 25. 41, into *e.* fire.
19. 29, inherit *e.* life.
25. 46, into *e.* punishment.
Lu. 16. 9, into *e.* habitations.
18. 30, in world to come *e.* life.
John 3. 16, 36, believeth shall have *e.* life.
4. 14, water springing up into *e.* life.
5. 24, heareth my word hath *e.* life.
6. 27, meat which endureth to *e.* life.
40, seeth Son may have *e.* life.
12. 50, his commandment is life *e.*
Acts 13. 46, unworthy of *e.* life.
Rom. 6. 22, free from sin, the end *e.* life.
Gal. 6. 8, of Spirit reap life *e.*
2 Thess. 1. 9, punished with *e.* destruction.
2. 16, given us *e.* consolation.
Jude 6, reserved in *e.* chains.
Rev. 14. 6, having the *e.* gospel.
See Dan. 4. 3; 7. 27; 2 Pet. 1. 11.

EVERMORE. Ps. 16. 11, pleasures for *e.*
37. 27, do good and dwell for *e.*
121. 8, preserve thy going out for *e.*
133. 3, the blessing, life for *e.*
John 6. 34, *e.* give us this bread.
1 Thess. 5. 16, rejoice *e.*
Heb. 7. 28, consecrated for *e.*
Rev. 1. 18, I am alive for *e.*
See 2 Kings 17. 37; Ps. 77. 8; 106. 31.

EVERY. Gen. 4. 14, *e.* one that findeth me shall slay me.
6. 5, *e.* imagination of heart evil.
Lev. 19. 10, neither shalt gather *e.* grape.
Deut. 4. 4, alive *e.* one of you this day.
2 Kings 18. 31, eat *e.* one of his fig tree.
2 Chron. 30. 18, pardon *e.* one.
Ps. 29. 9, *e.* one doth speak of glory.
32. 6, for this shall *e.* one that is godly.
68. 30, till *e.* one submit himself.
119. 101, refrained from *e.* evil way.
Prov. 2. 9, *e.* good path.
7. 12, in *e.* corner.
14. 15, simple believeth *e.* word.
20. 3, *e.* fool will be meddling.
30. 5, *e.* word of God is pure.
Eccl. 10. 3, saith to *e.* one he is a fool.
Jer. 51. 29, *e.* purpose of the Lord.
Mat. 4. 4, by *e.* word that proceedeth.
7. 8; Lu. 11. 10, *e.* one that asketh.
Mk. 1. 45, came from *e.* quarter.
Lu. 19. 26, to *e.* one which hath shall be given.
Rom. 14. 11, *e.* knee bow, *e.* tongue confess.
2 Cor. 10. 5, *e.* thought.
Eph. 1. 21; Phil. 2. 9, far above *e.* name.
1 Tim. 4. 4, *e.* creature of God.
2 Tim. 2. 19, *e.* one that nameth.
21, *e.* good work.
Heb. 12. 1, *e.* weight.
Jas. 1. 17, *e.* good and perfect gift.
1 Pet. 2. 13, *e.* ordinance of man.
1 John 4. 1, believe not *e.* spirit.
7, *e.* one that loveth.
Rev. 6. 11, robes given to *e.* one.
See Gen. 27. 29; Acts 2. 38; 17. 27; 20. 31.

EVIDENCE. Jer. 32. 10; Heb. 11. 1.

EVIDENT. Gal. 3. 1, Christ hath been *e.* set forth.
11, that no man is justified is *e.*

E e

Phil. 1. 28, an *e.* token of perdition.
See Job 6. 28 ; Heb. 7. 14, 15.

EVIL. Gen. 6. 5 ; 8. 21, thoughts of heart only *e.*
47. 9, few and *e.* have the days.
Ex. 32. 14 ; 2 Sam. 24. 16 ; 1 Chron. 21. 15, repented of the *e.*
Deut. 28. 54, eye *e.* towards his brother.
56, her eye *e.* towards husband.
Job 2. 10, receive good, and not *e.*
30. 26, looked for good, then *e.* came.
Ps. 34. 14 ; 37. 27 ; Prov. 3. 7, depart from *e.*
35. 12 ; 109. 5, they rewarded me *e.*
40. 12, innumerable *e.* have compassed.
Prov. 14. 19, *e.* bow before the good.
15. 3, beholding the *e.* and good.
17. 13, whoso rewardeth *e.* for good.
Isa. 1. 4, a seed of *e.*-doers.
5. 20, that call *e.* good, and good *e.*
7. 15, 16, refuse the *e.* and choose the good.
Jer. 2. 13, have committed two *e.*
19, know it is an *e.* thing and bitter.
24. 3 ; 29. 17, *e.* figs, very *e.*
42. 6, whether good or *e.*, we will obey.
Mat. 5. 45, rise on *e.* and good.
6. 34, sufficient unto the day is the *e.* thereof.
7. 11 ; Lu. 11. 13, if ye, being *e.*
18, good tree cannot bring forth *e.*
9. 4, wherefore think *e.* in your hearts ?
Mk. 9. 39, lightly speak *e.* of me.
Lu. 6. 22, cast out your name as *e.*
35, he is kind to the *e.*
45, *e.* man bringeth forth *e.*
John 3. 20, doeth *e.* hateth light.
18. 23, if I have spoken *e.*
Acts 23. 5, not speak *e.* of ruler.
Rom. 7. 19, the *e.* I would not.
12. 9, abhor that which is *e.*
17, recompense to no man *e.* for *e.*
21, overcome *e.* with good.
1 Thess. 5. 22, appearance of *e.*
1 Tim. 6. 10, the root of all *e.*
2 Tim. 4. 18 ; Jas. 3. 16, every *e.* work.
Tit. 3. 2, speak *e.* of no man.
Jas. 3. 8, tongue an unruly *e.*
1 Pet. 3. 9, not rendering *e.* for *e.*
See Prov. 13. 21 ; Isa. 45. 7 ; Eccl. 12. 1 ; Eph. 5. 16 ; 6. 13.

EXACT. Deut. 15. 2, shall not *e.* it of neighbour.
Neh. 5. 7, 10, 11, you *e.* usury.
10. 31, leave the *e.* of every debt.
Job 11. 6, God *e.* of thee less.
Lu. 3. 13, *e.* no more than what is.
See Ps. 89. 22 ; Isa. 58. 3 ; 60. 17.

EXALT. 1 Chron. 29. 11, *e.* as head above all.
Ps. 12. 8, when vilest men are *e.*
34. 3, let us *e.* his name together.
92. 10, my horn shalt thou *e.*
97. 9, *e.* far above all gods.
Prov. 4. 8, *e.* her, and she shall promote thee.
11. 11, by blessing of upright the city is *e.*
14. 29, he that is hasty of spirit *e.* folly.
34, righteousness *e.* a nation.
17. 19, he that *e.* his gate.
Isa. 2. 2 ; Mic. 4. 1, mountain of Lord's house *e.*
40. 4, every valley shall be *e.*
Ezek. 21. 26, *e.* him that is low.
Mat. 11. 23 ; Lu. 10. 15, *e.* to heaven.
23. 12 ; Lu. 14. 11 ; 18. 14, *e.* himself shall be abased.
2 Cor. 11. 20, if a man *e.* himself.
12. 7, *e.* above measure.
Phil. 2. 9, God hath highly *e.* him.
2 Thess. 2. 4, *e.* himself above all that is called.
1 Pet. 5. 6, he may *e.* in due time.
See Ex. 15. 2 ; Job 24. 24 ; Lu. 1. 52 ; Jas. 1. 9.

EXAMINE. Ps. 26. 2, *e.* me, O Lord.
Acts 4. 9, if we this day be *e.*
22. 24, 29, *e.* by scourging.
1 Cor. 11. 28, let a man *e.* himself.
2 Cor. 13. 5, *e.* yourselves.
See Ezra 10. 16 ; Acts 24. 8 ; 25. 26 ; 1 Cor. 9. 3.

EXAMPLE. John 13. 15, I have given you an *e.*
1 Tim. 4. 12, be thou an *e.* of believers.
1 Pet. 2. 21, Christ suffered, leaving an *e.*
Jude 7, an *e.*, suffering vengeance.
See Mat. 1. 19 ; 1 Cor. 10. 6 ; Heb. 4. 11 ; 8. 5.

EXCEED. Mat. 5. 20, except righteousness *e.*
2 Cor. 3. 9, ministration doth *e.* in glory.
See 1 Sam. 20. 41 ; 2 Chron. 9. 6 ; Job 36. 9.

EXCEEDING. Gen. 15. 1, thy *e.* great reward.
27. 34, an *e.* bitter cry.
Num. 14. 7, land is *e.* good.
1 Sam. 2. 3, so *e.* proud.
Ps. 21. 6, *e.* glad with thy countenance.
43. 4, God my *e.* joy.
119. 96, commandment *e.* broad.
Prov. 30. 24, four things *e.* wise.
Jonah 1. 16, men feared the Lord *e.*
4. 6, *e.* glad of the gourd.
Mat. 2. 10, with *e.* great joy.
4. 8, an *e.* high mountain.
5. 12, rejoice and be *e.* glad.
8. 28, possessed with devils, *e.* fierce.
17. 23 ; 26. 22, they were *e.* sorry.
19. 25, they were *e.* amazed.
26. 38 ; Mk. 14. 34, my soul is *e.* sorrowful.
Mk. 6. 26, king *e.* sorry.
9. 3, raiment *e.* white.
Lu. 23. 8, Herod was *e.* glad.
Acts 7. 20, Moses was *e.* fair.
26. 11, being *e.* mad against them.
Rom. 7. 13, sin might become *e.* sinful.
2 Cor. 4. 17, *e.* weight of glory.
7. 4, *e.* joyful in our tribulation.
Gal. 1. 14, *e.* zealous of traditions.
Eph. 1. 19, the *e.* greatness of his power.
2. 7, the *e.* riches of his grace.
3. 20, able to do *e.* abundantly.
2 Thess. 1. 3, your faith groweth *e.*
2 Pet. 1. 4, *e.* great and precious promises.
Jude 24, present you faultless with *e.* joy.
See 1 Sam. 26. 21 ; Jonah 3. 3 ; Heb. 12. 21.

EXCEL. Gen. 49. 4, thou shalt not *e.*
Prov. 31. 29, thou *e.* them all.
Eccl. 2. 13, wisdom *e.* folly.
2 Cor. 3. 10, the glory that *e.*
See Ps. 103. 20 ; 1 Cor. 14. 12.

EXCELLENCY. Ex. 15. 7, the greatness of thine *e.*
Job 4. 21, doth not their *e.* go away ?
13. 11, shall not his *e.* make you afraid ?
Isa. 60. 15, will make thee an eternal *e.*
1 Cor. 2. 1, not with *e.* of speech.
2 Cor. 4. 7, that the *e.* of the power.
Phil. 3. 8, loss for the *e.* of Christ.
See Gen. 49. 3 ; Ex. 15. 7 ; Eccl. 7. 12 ; Ezek. 24. 21.

EXCELLENT. Job 37. 23, *e.* in power.
Ps. 8. 1, 9, how *e.* is thy name !
16. 3, to the *e.*, in whom is my delight.
36. 7, how *e.* thy lovingkindness !
Prov. 8. 6 ; 22. 20, I will speak of *e.* things.
12. 26, righteous more *e.* than neighbour.
17. 7, *e.* speech becometh not a fool.
27, of an *e.* spirit.
Isa. 12. 5, he hath done *e.* things.
28. 29, is *e.* in working.
Dan. 5. 12 ; 6. 3, *e.* spirit found in Daniel.
Rom. 2. 18 ; Phil. 1. 10, things more *e.*
1 Cor. 12. 31, a more *e.* way.
2 Pet. 1. 17, voice from the *e.* glory.
See Cant. 5. 15 ; Lu. 1. 3 ; Heb. 1. 4 ; 8. 6 ; 11. 4.

EXCEPT. Gen. 32. 26, *e.* thou bless me.
Deut. 32. 30, *e.* their Rock had sold them.
Ps. 127. 1, *e.* Lord build house.
Amos 3. 3, *e.* they be agreed.
Mat. 5. 20, *e.* your righteousness exceed.
18. 3, *e.* ye be converted.
24. 22 ; Mk. 13. 20, *e.* days be shortened.
Mk. 7. 3, Pharisees *e.* they wash oft.
Lu. 13. 3 ; Rev. 2. 5, 22, *e.* ye repent.
John 3. 2, *e.* God be with him.
3. 5, *e.* a man be born again.

John 4. 48, *e.* ye see signs and wonders.
20. 25, *e.* I see print of nails.
Acts 26. 29, *e.* these bonds.
Rom. 10. 15, how preach, *e.* they be sent?
1 Cor. 15. 36, *e.* it die.
2 Tim. 2. 5, *e.* he strive lawfully.
See Rom. 7. 7 ; 1 Cor. 14. 5 ; 15. 27 ; 2 Thess. 2. 3.

EXCESS. Mat. 23. 25 ; Eph. 5. 18 ; 1 Pet. 4. 3, 4.

EXCHANGE. Mat. 16. 26 ; Mk. 8. 37, in *e.* for his soul.
25. 27, put money to *e.*
See Gen. 47. 17 ; Lev. 27. 10 ; Ezek. 48. 14.

EXCLUDE. Rom. 3. 27 ; Gal. 4. 17.

EXCUSE. Lu. 14. 18 ; Rom. 1. 20 ; 2. 15 ; 2 Cor. 12. 19.

EXECRATION. Jer. 42. 18 ; 44. 12.

EXECUTE. Deut. 33. 21, he *e.* the justice of the Lord.
1 Chron. 6. 10 ; 24. 2 ; Lu. 1. 8, *e.* priest's office.
Ps. 9. 16, Lord known by the judgment he *e.*
103. 6, Lord *e.* righteousness and judgment.
Jer. 5. 1, if any *e.* judgment, I will pardon.
John 5. 27, authority to *e.* judgment.
Rom. 13. 4, minister of God to *e.* wrath.
See Hos. 11. 9 ; Mic. 5. 15 ; Joel 2. 11.

EXERCISE. Ps. 131. 1, *e.* myself in things too high.
Jer. 9. 24, *e.* lovingkindness.
Mat. 20. 25 ; Mk. 10. 42 ; Lu. 22. 25, *e.* dominion.
Acts 24. 16, I *e.* myself, to have a conscience.
1 Tim. 4. 7, *e.* thyself unto godliness.
Heb. 5. 14, *e.* to discern good and evil.
12. 11, to them which are *e.* thereby.
2 Pet. 2. 14, heart *e.* with covetous practices.
See Eccl. 1. 13 ; 3. 10 ; Ezek. 22. 29 ; Rev. 13. 12.

EXHORT. Lu. 3. 18, many things in his *e.*
Acts 13. 15, any words of *e.*
Rom. 12. 8, he that *e.,* on *e.*
1 Tim. 6. 2, these things *e.* and teach.
Tit. 1. 9, may be able to *e.*
2. 15, *e.* and rebuke with authority.
Heb. 3. 13 ; 10. 25, *e.* one another daily.
13. 22, suffer word of *e.*
See Acts 11. 23 ; 2 Cor. 9. 5 ; Tit. 2. 6, 9.

EXILE. 2 Sam. 15. 19 ; Isa. 51. 14.

EXPECTATION. Ps. 9. 18, the *e.* of the poor.
62. 5, my *e.* is from him.
Prov. 10. 28 ; 11. 7, 23, *e.* of the wicked.
Isa. 20. 5, ashamed of their *e.*
6, such is our *e.*
Rom. 8. 19, the *e.* of the creature.
Phil. 1. 20, my earnest *e.* and hope.
See Jer. 29. 11 ; Acts 3. 5 ; Heb. 10. 13.

EXPEL. Josh. 23. 5 ; Judg. 11. 7 ; 2 Sam. 14. 14.

EXPENSES. Ezra 6. 4, 8.

EXPERIENCE. Gen. 30. 27 ; Eccl. 1. 16 ; Rom. 5. 4.

EXPLOITS. Dan. 11. 28, 32.

EXPOUND. Judg. 14. 14, 19, could not *e.* riddle.
Mk. 4. 34, when they were alone, he *e.* all things.
Lu. 24. 27, *e.* the scriptures.
See Acts 11. 4 ; 18. 26 ; 28. 23.

EXPRESS. Heb. 1. 3.

EXPRESSLY. 1 Sam. 20. 21 ; Ezek. 1. 3 ; 1 Tim. 4. 1.

EXTEND. Ps. 16. 2 ; 109. 12 ; Isa. 66. 12.

EXTINCT. Job 17. 1 ; Isa. 43. 17.

EXTOL. Ps. 30. 1 ; 145. 1, I will *e.* thee.
68. 4, *e.* him that rideth.
See Ps. 66. 17 ; Isa. 52. 13 ; Dan. 4. 37.

EXTORTION. Ezek. 22. 12 ; Mat. 23. 25.

EXTORTIONER. Ps. 109. 11, let *e.* catch all he hath.
Isa. 16. 4, the *e.* is at an end.
1 Cor. 5. 11, if any man be an *e.*
See Lu. 18. 11 ; 1 Cor. 5. 10 ; 6. 10.

EXTREME. Deut. 28. 22 ; Job 35. 15.

EYE. Gen. 3. 6, pleasant to the *e.*
7, *e.* of both were opened.
27. 1, his *e.* were dim.
49. 12, his *e.* shall be red with wine.
Num. 10. 31, be to us instead of *e.*
16. 14, wilt thou put out *e.*?
24. 3, 15, man whose *e.* are open said.
Deut. 3. 27, lift up *e.,* behold with thine *e.*
12. 8 ; Judg. 17. 6 ; 21. 25, right in own *e.*
16. 19, gift blind *e.* of wise.
28. 32, *e.* look, and fail with longing.
32. 10, kept him as apple of *e.*
34. 7, his *e.* was not dim.
1 Kings 1. 20, *e.* of all Israel upon thee.
8. 29, 52 ; 2 Chron. 6. 20, 40, *e.* open towards this house.
20. 6, whatsoever is pleasant in thine *e.*
2 Kings 6. 17, Lord opened *e.* of young man.
20, open the *e.* of these men.
2 Chron. 16. 9 ; Zech. 4. 10, *e.* of Lord run to and fro.
34. 28, nor thine *e.* see all the evil.
Job 7. 8 ; 20. 9, *e.* that hath seen me.
11. 20, the *e.* of wicked shall fail.
15. 12, what do thine *e.* wink at?
19. 27, mine *e.* shall behold, and not another.
28. 7, path vulture's *e.* hath not seen.
10, his *e.* seeth every precious thing.
29. 11, when the *e.* saw me.
15, I was *e.* to the blind.
31. 16, caused *e.* of widow to fail.
Ps. 11. 4, his *e.* try children of men.
15. 4, in whose *e.* a vile person.
19. 8, enlightening the *e.*
33. 18, *e.* of Lord on them that fear him.
34. 15 ; 1 Pet. 3. 12, *e.* of Lord on the righteous.
36. 1, no fear of God before his *e.*
69. 3 ; 119. 82, 123 ; Lam. 2. 11, mine *e.* fail.
77. 4, holdest mine *e.* waking.
116. 8, delivered mine *e.* from tears.
119. 18, open mine *e.*
132. 4, not give sleep to mine *e.*
Prov. 10. 26, as smoke to the *e.*
20. 12, the seeing *e.*
22. 9, a bountiful *e.*
23. 29, redness of *e.*
27. 20, the *e.* of man never satisfied.
30. 17, the *e.* that mocketh.
Eccl. 1. 8, *e.* is not satisfied with seeing.
2. 14, wise man's *e.* are in his head.
6. 9, better sight of *e.* than wandering of desire.
11. 7, for the *e.* to behold the sun.
Isa. 1. 16, I will hide mine *e.* from you.
29. 10, the Lord hath closed *e.*
33. 17, thine *e.* shall see the king in his beauty.
40. 26 ; Jer. 13. 20, lift up your *e.* on high.
Jer. 5. 21 ; Ezek. 12. 2, have *e.* and see not.
9. 1, mine *e.* a fountain of tears.
13. 17, mine *e.* shall weep sore.
14. 17, let mine *e.* run down with tears.
24. 6, set mine *e.* upon them for good.
Lam. 2. 18, let not apple of *e.* cease.
Ezek. 24. 16, 25, the desire of thine *e.*
Hab. 1. 13, of purer *e.* than to behold evil.
Mat. 5. 29, if right *e.* offend thee.
13. 16, blessed are your *e.*
18. 9 ; Mk. 9. 47, to enter with one *e.*
Mk. 8. 18, having *e.,* see ye not?
Lu. 1. 2, from beginning were *e.*-witnesses.
24. 16, their *e.* were holden.
John 11. 37, could not this man, which opened *e.*
Gal. 4. 15, have plucked out your *e.*
Eph. 1. 18, the *e.* of your understanding.
2 Pet. 2. 14, having *e.* full of adultery.
1 John 2. 16, the lust of the *e.*
See Deut. 11. 12 ; Ezra 5. 5 ; Ps. 32. 8 ; Prov. 3. 7 ;
12. 15 ; 15. 3 ; 16. 2 ; 21. 2 ; Mat. 20. 33 ; John 10.
21 ; 1 Pet. 3. 12.

EYESERVICE. Eph. 6. 6 ; Col. 3. 22, not with *e.* as menpleasers.

F.

FABLES. 1 Tim. 1. 4; 4. 7; 2 Tim. 4. 4; Tit. 1. 14;
2 Pet. 1. 16.

FACE. Gen. 4. 14, from thy *f.* shall I be hid.
32. 30, I have seen God *f.* to *f.*
Ex. 33. 11, Lord spake to Moses *f.* to *f.*
34. 29, skin of *f.* shone.
33 ; 2 Cor. 3. 13, put vail on *f.*
Lev. 19. 32, shall honour the *f.* of the old man.
Deut. 25. 9, spit in his *f.,* saying.
1 Sam. 5. 3, Dagon was fallen on his *f.*
2 Kings 4. 29, 31, lay staff on *f.* of child.
14. 8, let us look one another in *f.*
Ezra 9. 7 ; Dan. 9. 8, confusion of *f.*
Neh. 8. 6, worshipped with *f.* to ground.
Job 1. 11 ; 2. 5, curse thee to thy *f.*
4. 15, spirit passed before my *f.*
13. 24 ; Ps. 44. 24 ; 88. 14, wherefore hidest thou
  thy *f.?*
Ps. 13. 1, how long wilt thou hide thy *f.?*
27. 9 ; 69. 17 ; 102. 2 ; 143. 7, hide not thy *f.*
34. 5, *f.* not ashamed.
84. 9, look upon *f.* of anointed.
Prov. 27. 19, in water *f.* answereth to *f.*
Eccl. 8. 1, wisdom maketh *f.* to shine.
Isa. 3. 15, ye grind *f.* of the poor.
25. 8, wipe tears from off all *f.*
50. 7, set my *f.* like flint.
59. 2, sins have hid his *f.* from you.
Jer. 2. 27, turned their back, and not *f.*
5. 3, their *f.* harder than a rock.
30. 6, all *f.* turned into paleness.
Dan. 10. 6, *f.* as appearance of lightning.
Hos. 5. 5, testifieth to his *f.*
Mat. 6. 17, wash thy *f.*
11. 10 ; Mk. 1. 2 ; Lu. 7. 27, messenger before *f.*
16. 3 ; Lu. 12. 56, discern *f.* of sky.
17. 2, his *f.* did shine as sun.
18. 10, angels behold *f.* of my Father.
Lu. 2. 31, before *f.* of all people.
9. 51, 53, set his *f.* to Jerusalem.
22. 64, struck him on *f.*
1 Cor. 13. 12, then *f.* to *f.*
2 Cor. 3. 18, all, with open *f.*
Gal. 1. 22, I was unknown by *f.*
2. 11, withstood him to the *f.*
Jas. 1. 23, beholding *f.* in glass.
Rev. 20. 11, from whose *f.* earth fled away.
See 1 Kings 19. 13 ; Dan. 1. 10 ; Acts 6. 15 ; 20. 25.

FADE. Isa. 1. 30, whose leaf *f.*
24. 4, earth mourneth and *f.,* the world *f.*
40. 7, the flower *f.*
64. 6, all *f.* as a leaf.
Jer. 8. 13, and the leaf shall *f.*
Ezek. 47. 12, whose leaf shall not *f.*
1 Pet. 1. 4 ; 5. 4, inheritance that *f.* not away.
Jas. 1. 11, rich man shall *f.* away.
See 2 Sam. 22. 46 ; Ps. 18. 45 ; Isa. 28. 1.

FAIL. Gen. 47. 16, if money *f.*
Deut. 28. 32, thine eyes shall *f.* with longing.
Josh. 21. 45 ; 23. 14 ; 1 Kings 8. 56, there *f.* not any
  good thing.
1 Sam. 17. 32, let no man's heart *f.* him.
1 Kings 2. 4 ; 8. 25, shall not *f.* a man on throne.
17. 14, neither shall cruse of oil *f.*
Ezra 4. 22, take heed that ye *f.* not.
Job 14. 11, as waters *f.* from sea.
19. 14, my kinsfolk have *f.*
Ps. 12. 1, the faithful *f.* among men.
31. 10 ; 38. 10, my strength *f.* me.
77. 8, doth his promise *f.*
89. 33, nor suffer my faithfulness to *f.*
142. 4, refuge *f.* me.
Eccl. 10. 3, his wisdom *f.* him.
12. 5, desire shall *f.*
Isa. 15. 6, the grass *f.*
19. 5, waters shall *f.*
31. 3, they shall all *f.* together.
32. 6, cause drink of thirsty to *f.*

Isa. 32. 10, the vintage shall *f.*
34. 16, no one of these shall *f.*
38. 14, eyes *f.* with looking upward.
41. 17, tongue *f.* for thirst.
59. 15, truth *f.*
Jer. 14. 6, their eyes did *f.*
15. 18, as waters that *f.*
48. 33, I caused wine to *f.*
Lam. 3. 22, his compassions *f.* not.
4. 17, our eyes as yet *f.*
Ezek. 12. 22, every vision *f.*
Amos 8. 4, make poor of land to *f.*
Hab. 3. 17, labour of olive shall *f.*
Lu. 12. 33, treasure that *f.* not.
16. 9, when ye *f.* they may receive you.
17, one tittle of law *f.*
21. 26, hearts *f.* them for fear.
22. 32, that thy faith *f.* not.
1 Cor. 13. 8, charity never *f.*
Heb. 1. 12, thy years shall not *f.*
11. 32, time would *f.* me to tell.
12. 15, lest any man *f.* of grace of God.
See Deut. 31. 6 ; Ps. 40. 12 ; 143. 7 ; Isa. 44. 12.

FAIN. Job 27. 22 ; Lu. 15. 16.

FAINT. Gen. 25. 29, 30, came from field, and he
  was *f.*
45. 26, Jacob's heart *f.*
Judg. 8. 4, *f.* yet pursuing.
Job 4. 5, now it is come, and thou *f.*
Ps. 27. 13, I had *f.,* unless I had believed.
107. 5, their soul *f.* in them.
Prov. 24. 10, if thou *f.* in day of adversity.
Isa. 1. 5, whole heart *f.*
10. 18, as when a standardbearer *f.*
40. 28, Creator of earth *f.* not.
29, giveth power to the *f.*
30 ; Amos 8. 13, even youths shall *f.*
31, walk, and not *f.*
44. 12, he drinketh no water, and is *f.*
Jer. 8. 18 ; Lam. 1. 22 ; 5. 17, my heart is *f.*
Mat. 15. 32 ; Mk. 8. 3, lest they *f.* by the way.
Lu. 18. 1, pray, and not *f.*
2 Cor. 4. 1, 16, as we have received mercy, we *f.* not.
Gal. 6. 9, reap, if we *f.* not.
Heb. 12. 3, wearied and *f.* in your minds.
5, nor *f.* when thou art rebuked.
See Deut. 20. 8 ; Ps. 84. 2 ; 119. 81 ; Mat. 9. 36.

FAIR. Job 37. 22, *f.* weather out of the north.
Ps. 45. 2, *f.* than children of men.
Prov. 11. 22, a *f.* woman without discretion.
26. 25, when he speaketh *f.,* believe not.
Cant. 1. 8 ; 5. 9 ; 6. 1, thou *f.* among women.
6. 10, *f.* as the moon.
Isa. 5. 9, houses great and *f.*
Jer. 4. 30, in vain shalt thou make thyself *f.*
12. 6, though they speak *f.* words.
Dan. 1. 15, their countenances appeared *f.*
Mat. 16. 2, it will be *f.* weather.
Acts 7. 20, Moses was exceeding *f.*
Rom. 16. 18, by *f.* speeches deceive.
See Gen. 6. 2 ; Isa. 54. 11 ; Ezek. 27. 12.

FAITH. Deut. 32. 20, children in whom is no *f.*
Mat. 6. 30 ; 8. 26 ; 14. 31 ; 16. 8 ; Lu. 12. 28, ye of
  little *f.*
8. 10 ; Lu. 7. 9, so great *f.*
9. 2 ; Mk. 2. 5 ; Lu. 5. 20, seeing their *f.*
22 ; Mk. 5. 34 ; 10. 52 ; Lu. 8. 48 ; 17. 19, thy *f.* hath
  made thee whole.
29, according to your *f.*
15. 28, great is thy *f.*
17. 20, *f.* as a grain of mustard seed.
21. 21, if ye have *f.,* ye shall not only do this.
23. 23, omitted judgment, mercy, and *f.*
Mk. 4. 40, how is it ye have no *f.?*
11. 22, have *f.* in God.
Lu. 7. 50, thy *f.* hath saved thee.
8. 25, where is your *f.?*
17. 5, increase our *f.*
18. 8, shall he find *f.* on the earth?
22. 32, that thy *f.* fail not.

Acts 3. 16, the *f.* which is by him.
6. 5 ; 11. 24, a man full of *f.*
14. 9, perceiving he had *f.* to be healed.
27, opened the door of *f.*
15. 9, purifying their hearts by *f.*
16. 5, established in the *f.*
26. 18, sanctified by *f.*
Rom. 1. 5, grace for obedience to *f.*
17, revealed from *f.* to *f.*
3. 27, boasting excluded by *f.*
28 ; 5. 1 ; Gal. 2. 16 ; 3. 24, justified by *f.*
4. 5, *f.* counted for righteousness.
16, it is of *f.,* which is of the *f.* of Abraham.
19. 20, being not weak in *f.*
5. 2, we have access by *f.*
10. 8, the word of *f.,* which we preach.
17. *f.* cometh by hearing.
12. 3, the measure of *f.*
6, prophesy according to proportion of *f.*
14. 1, weak in *f.* receive ye.
22, hast thou *f.*?
23, what is not of *f.* is sin.
1 Cor. 2. 5, your *f.* should not stand in wisdom.
13. 2, though I have all *f.*
13, now abideth *f.*
15. 14, and your *f.* is also vain.
16. 13, stand fast in the *f.*
2 Cor. 1. 24, not have dominion over *f.*
4. 13, same spirit of *f.*
5. 7, we walk by *f.*
13. 5, examine whether ye be in the *f.*
Gal. 2. 20, I live by the *f.* of Son of God.
3. 2, by the hearing of *f.*
12, law is not of *f.*
23, before *f.* came.
5. 6, *f.* which worketh by love.
6. 10, the household of *f.*
Eph. 3. 12, access by *f.* of him.
17, dwell in your hearts by *f.*
4. 5, one Lord, one *f.*
13, in the unity of the *f.*
6. 16, the shield of *f.*
Phil. 1. 27, striving together for the *f.* of the gospel.
Col. 1. 23, if ye continue in the *f.*
2. 5, the stedfastness of your *f.*
1 Thess. 1. 3 ; 2 Thess. 1. 11, your work of *f.*
5. 8, the breastplate of *f.*
2 Thess. 3. 2, all men have not *f.*
1 Tim. 1. 2 ; Tit. 1. 4, my own son in the *f.*
5 ; 2 Tim. 1. 5, *f.* unfeigned.
2. 15, if they continue in *f.*
3. 13, great boldness in the *f.*
4. 1, shall depart from the *f.*
5. 8, he hath denied the *f.*
6. 10, 21, erred from the *f.*
12, fight the good fight of *f.*
2 Tim. 3. 8, reprobate concerning the *f*
4. 7, I have kept the *f.*
Tit. 1. 1, the *f.* of God's elect.
Heb. 4. 2, not being mixed with *f.*
6. 1, not laying again the foundation of *f.*
12, through *f.* inherit the promises.
10. 22, in full assurance of *f.*
11. 1, *f.* is substance of things hoped for.
4, 5, 7, 8, 9, etc., by *f.* Abel, etc.
6, without *f.* is is impossible.
13, these all died in *f.*
33, through *f.* subdued kingdoms.
39, a good report through *f.*
12. 2, author and finisher of our *f.*
13. 7, whose *f.* follow.
Jas. 1. 3 ; 1 Pet. 1. 7, the trying of your *f.*
6, let them ask in *f.*
2. 1, have not *f.* with respect of persons.
5, rich in *f.*
14, man say he hath *f.,* can *f.* save him ?
17, *f.* without works is dead.
18, thou hast *f.,* and I have works.
22, *f.* wrought with his works.
5. 15, the prayer of *f.* shall save.
1 Pet. 1. 9, the end of your *f.*

1 Pet. 5. 9, resist stedfast in the *f.*
2 Pet. 1. 1, like precious *f.*
5, add to your *f.* virtue.
1 John 5. 4, overcometh the world, even our *f.*
Jude 3, earnestly contend for the *f.*
20, your most holy *f.*
Rev. 2. 13, hast not denied my *f.*
19, I know thy works and *f.*
13. 10, patience and *f.* of the saints.
14. 12, they that keep the *f.* of Jesus.
See Hab. 2. 4 ; Rom. 1. 12 ; 1 Tim. 4. 6.
FAITHFUL. 2 Sam. 20. 19, one of them that are *f.* in Israel.
Neh. 7. 2, a *f.* man, and feared God.
9. 8, his heart *f.* before thee.
13. 13, counted *f.* to distribute.
Ps. 12. 1, the *f.* fail among men.
89. 37, a *f.* witness in heaven.
101. 6, the *f.* of the land.
119. 86, commandments *f.*
138, testimonies *f.*
Prov. 11. 13, *f.* spirit concealeth.
13. 17, *f.* ambassador is health.
14. 5 ; Isa. 8. 2 ; Jer. 42. 5, a *f.* witness.
20. 6, a *f.* man who can find?
25. 13, as snow in harvest, so is a *f.* messenger.
27. 6, *f.* are wounds of a friend.
28. 20, *f.* man shall abound.
Isa. 1. 21, 26, *f.* city.
Mat. 24. 45 ; Lu. 12. 42, who is a *f.* and wise servant?
25. 21, good and *f.* servant.
23 ; Lu. 19. 17, *f.* in a few things.
Lu. 16. 10, *f.* in least *f.* in much.
Acts 16. 15, if ye have judged me *f.*
1 Cor. 4. 2, required in stewards that a man be *f.*
17, Timothy *f.* in the Lord.
Gal. 3. 9, blessed with *f.* Abraham.
Eph. 6. 21 ; Col. 1. 7 ; 4. 7, a *f.* minister.
1 Thess. 5. 24, *f.* is he that calleth you.
2 Thess. 3. 3, Lord is *f.,* who shall stablish you.
1 Tim. 1. 15 ; 4. 9 ; 2 Tim. 2. 11 ; Tit. 3. 8, a *f.* saying.
3. 11, wives *f.* in all things.
2 Tim. 2. 2, commit to *f.* men.
13, yet he abideth *f.*
Heb. 2. 17, a *f.* high priest.
3. 2, *f.* to him that appointed him
10. 23 ; 11. 11, he is *f.* that promised.
1 Pet. 4. 19, as unto a *f.* Creator.
1 John 1. 9, he is *f.* and just to forgive.
Rev. 2. 10, be thou *f.* unto death.
13, my *f.* martyr.
17. 14, called, and chosen, and *f.*
21. 5 ; 22. 6, these words are true and *f.*
See Deut. 7. 9 ; Dan. 6. 4 ; Rev. 1. 5 ; 3. 14 ; 19. 11.
FAITHFULLY. 2 Chron. 19. 9 ; 34. 12 ; Jer. 23. 28 ; 3 John 5.
FAITHFULNESS. Ps. 5. 9, no *f.* in their mouths.
36. 5, thy *f.* reacheth unto the clouds.
40. 10 ; 88. 11, declared thy *f.*
89. 33, nor suffer my *f.* to fail.
92. 2, show forth thy *f.* every night.
Isa. 11. 5, *f.* the girdle of his reins.
Lam. 3. 23, great is thy *f.*
See 1 Sam. 26. 23 ; Ps. 119. 75 ; 143. 1.
FAITHLESS. Mat. 17. 17 ; Mk. 9. 19 ; Lu. 9. 41 ; John 20. 27.
FALL (*n.*). Prov. 16. 18, haughty spirit before a *f.*
Mat. 7. 27, great was the *f.* of it.
Lu. 2. 34, set for the rise and *f.* of many.
Rom. 11. 12, if the *f.* of them be the riches.
See Jer. 49. 21 ; Ezek. 26. 15 ; 31. 16 ; 32. 10.
FALL (*v.*). Gen. 45. 24, see ye *f.* not out by the way.
Lev. 25. 35, thy brother be *f.* in decay.
1 Sam. 3. 19, let none of his words *f.*
2 Sam. 1. 19, 25, 27, how are the mighty *f.*!
3. 38, great man *f.* this day.
24. 14 ; 1 Chron. 21. 13, *f.* into hands of God.

2 Kings 14. 10, why meddle that thou shouldest *f.*?
Job 4. 13 ; 33. 15, deep sleep *f.* on men.
Ps. 5. 10, let them *f.* by their own counsels.
7. 15, is *f.* into ditch.
16. 6, lines *f.* in pleasant places.
37. 24, though he *f.,* not utterly cast down.
56. 13 ; 116. 8, deliver my feet from *f.*
72. 11, kings shall *f.* down before him.
91. 7, a thousand shall *f.* at thy side.
Prov. 10. 8, 10, a prating fool shall *f.*
11. 14, where no counsel is, the people *f.*
28. 18, he that trusteth in riches shall *f.*
13. 17 ; 17. 20 ; 24. 16, *f.* into mischief.
24. 16, just man *f.* seven times.
17, rejoice not when thine enemy *f.*
26. 27 ; Eccl. 10. 8, diggeth a pit shall *f.* therein.
Eccl. 4. 10, woe to him that is alone when he *f.*
11. 3, where the tree *f.,* there it shall be.
Isa. 14. 12, how art thou *f.!*
34. 4, as the leaf *f.* from the vine.
40. 30, the young men shall utterly *f.*
Jer. 49. 26 ; 50. 30, young men *f.* in her streets.
Ezek. 24. 6, let no lot *f.* on it.
Dan. 3. 5 ; 11. 26 ; Mat. 4. 9, *f.* down and worship.
Hos. 10. 8 ; Lu. 23. 30 ; Rev. 6. 16, say to hills, *f.* on us.
Mic. 7. 8, when I *f.*
Zech. 11. 2, the cedar is *f.*
Mat. 10. 29, sparrow *f.* on ground.
12. 11, *f.* into pit on sabbath day.
15. 14 ; Lu. 6. 39, both *f.* into the ditch.
21. 44 ; Lu. 20. 18, *f.* on this stone.
24. 29 ; Mk. 13. 25, stars *f.* from heaven.
Lu. 8. 13, in time of temptation *f.* away.
10. 18, Satan as lightning *f.* from heaven.
Rom. 14. 4, to his master he standeth or *f.*
13, occasion to *f.*
1 Cor. 10. 12, take heed lest he *f.*
15. 6, 18, some are *f.* asleep.
Gal. 5. 4, ye are *f.* from grace.
1 Tim. 3. 6, *f.* into the condemnation.
7, lest he *f.* into reproach.
6. 9, rich *f.* into temptation.
Heb. 4. 11, lest any *f.* after same example.
6. 6, if they *f.* away.
10. 31, to *f.* into hands of living God.
Jas. 1. 2, joy when ye *f.* into temptation.
11 ; 1 Pet. 1. 24, flower thereof *f.*
5. 12, lest ye *f.* into condemnation.
2 Pet. 1. 10, ye shall never *f.*
3. 17, lest ye *f.* from stedfastness.
See Isa. 21. 9 ; Lam. 5. 16 ; Rev. 14. 8 ; 18. 2.
FALLING. Job 4. 4 ; 2 Thess. 2. 3 ; Jude 24.
FALLOW. Jer. 4. 3 ; Hos. 10. 12.
FALSE. Ex. 20. 16 ; Deut. 5. 20 ; Mat. 19. 18, shalt not bear *f.* witness.
23. 1, shalt not raise a *f.* report.
2 Kings 9. 12, it is *f.,* tell us now.
Ps. 119. 104, 128, I hate every *f.* way.
120. 3, thou *f.* tongue.
Prov. 6. 19 ; 12. 17 ; 14. 5 ; 19. 5 ; 21. 28 ; 25. 18, a *f.* witness.
11. 1 ; 20. 23, a *f.* balance.
Mat. 15. 19, out of heart proceed *f.* witness.
24. 24 ; Mk. 13. 22, *f.* Christs and *f.* prophets.
26. 59, 60 ; Mk. 14. 56, 57, *f.* witness against Christ.
Mk. 13. 22, *f.* prophets shall rise.
Lu. 19. 8, any thing by *f.* accusation.
1 Cor. 15. 15, found *f.* witnesses of God.
2 Cor. 11. 13, such are *f.* apostles.
11. 26, perils among *f.* brethren.
2 Tim. 3. 3 ; Tit. 2. 3, *f.* accusers.
See Gal. 2. 4 ; 2 Pet. 2. 1 ; 1 John 4. 1.
FALSEHOOD. Job 21. 34, in answers remaineth *f.*
Ps. 7. 14, hath brought forth *f.*
144. 8, 11, right hand of *f.*
Isa. 28. 15, under *f.* have we hid ourselves.
57. 4, a seed of *f.*
59. 13, words of *f.*

Mic. 2. 11, walking in the spirit and *f.*
See 2 Sam. 18. 13 ; Jer. 13. 25 ; Hos. 7. 1.
FALSELY. Lev. 6. 3, 5 ; 19. 12 ; Jer. 5. 2 ; 7. 9 ; Zech. 5. 4, swear *f.*
Jer. 5. 31 ; 29. 9, prophets prophesy *f.*
Mat. 5. 11, evil *f.,* for my sake.
1 Tim. 6. 20, science *f.* so called.
See Jer. 43. 2 ; Lu. 3. 14 ; 1 Pet. 3. 16.
FAME. Josh. 9. 9, we heard the *f.* of God.
1 Kings 10. 1 ; 2 Chron. 9. 1, *f.* of Solomon.
Zeph. 3. 19, get them *f.* in every land.
Mat. 4. 24 ; Mk. 1. 28 ; Lu. 4. 14, 37 ; 5. 15, *f.* of Jesus.
9. 31, spread abroad his *f.*
14. 1, Herod heard of the *f.*
See Gen. 45. 16 ; Num. 14. 15 ; Job 28. 22 ; Isa. 66. 19.
FAMILIAR. Job 19. 14 ; Ps. 41. 9 ; Jer. 20. 10.
FAMILY. Gen. 12. 3 ; 28. 14, in thee all *f.* be blessed.
25. 10, return every man to his *f.*
Deut. 29. 18, lest a *f.* turn away from God.
1 Sam. 9. 21, my *f.* the least.
18. 18, what is my father's *f.*?
1 Chron. 4. 38, princes in their *f.*
Ps. 68. 6, setteth the solitary in *f.*
Jer. 3. 14, one of a city, and two of a *f.*
10. 25, on *f.* that call not.
31. 1, God of all the *f.* of Israel.
Zech. 12. 12, every *f.* apart.
Eph. 3. 15, whole *f.* in heaven and earth.
See Num. 27. 4 ; Judg. 1. 25 ; Amos 3. 2.
FAMINE. 2 Sam. 21. 1, a *f.* in days of David.
1 Kings 8. 37 ; 2 Chron. 20. 9, if there be *f.*
18. 2 ; 2 Kings 6. 25, sore *f.* in Samaria.
2 Kings 8. 1, the Lord hath called for a *f.*
Job 5. 20, in *f.* he shall redeem thee.
22, at *f.* thou shalt laugh.
Ps. 33. 19, to keep them alive in *f.*
37. 19, in the days of *f.* shall be satisfied.
Jer. 24. 10 ; 29. 17, will send *f.* among them.
42. 16, *f.* shall follow close.
Lam. 5. 10, black because of *f.*
Ezek. 5. 16, evil arrows of *f.*
36. 29, I will lay no *f.* upon you.
Amos 8. 11, a *f.* not of bread.
Mat. 24. 7 ; Mk. 13. 8 ; Lu. 21. 11, *f.* in divers places.
See Gen. 12. 10 ; 41. 27 ; 47. 13 ; Lu. 15. 14 ; Rom. 8. 35.
FAMISH. Gen. 41. 55 ; Prov. 10. 3 ; Isa. 5. 13 ; Zeph. 2. 11.
FAMOUS. Ruth 4. 11, 14 ; 1 Chron. 5. 24 ; Ps. 74. 5 ; Ezek. 23. 10.
FAN. Isa. 30. 24 ; Jer. 15. 7 ; 51. 2 ; Mat. 3. 12.
FAR. Gen. 18. 25 ; 1 Sam. 20. 9, that be *f.* from thee.
Deut. 12. 21 ; 14. 24, if place too *f.* from thee.
Judg. 19. 11 ; Mk. 6. 35 ; Lu. 24. 29, day *f.* spent.
1 Sam. 2. 30 ; 22. 15 ; 2 Sam. 20. 20 ; 23. 17, be it *f.* from me.
Job 5. 4, children *f.* from safety.
11. 14 ; 22. 23, put iniquity *f.* away.
19. 13, put my brethren *f.* from me.
34. 10, *f.* be it from God to do wickedness.
Ps. 10. 5, thy judgments are *f.* out of sight.
22. 11 ; 35. 22 ; 38. 21 ; 71. 12, be not *f.* from me.
97. 9, *f.* above all gods.
103. 12, *f.* as east from west.
Prov. 31. 10, *f.* above rubies.
Isa. 43. 6 ; 60. 4, 9, sons from *f.*
46. 12, *f.* from righteousness.
57. 19, peace to him that is *f.* off.
Amos 6. 3, put *f.* away evil day.
Mat. 16. 22, be it *f.* from thee, Lord.
Mk. 12. 34, not *f.* from the kingdom.
13. 34, as a man taking a *f.* journey.
John 21. 8, they were not *f.* from land.
Acts 17. 27, not *f.* from every one of us.
Rom. 13. 12, the night is *f.* spent.
2 Cor. 4. 17, a *f.* more exceeding.
Eph. 1. 21, *f.* above all principality.

Eph. 2. 13, *f.* off made nigh.
4. 10, *f.* above all praying.
Phil. 1. 23, which is *f.* better.
Heb. 7. 15, it is yet *f.* more evident.
See Isa. 33. 17; Mat. 15. 8; Mk. 8. 3.

FARE. 1 Sam. 17. 18; Jonah 1. 3; Lu. 16. 19.

FAREWELL. Lu. 9. 61; Acts 18. 21; 2 Cor. 13. 11.

FARM. Mat. 22. 5.

FARTHING. Mat. 5. 26; 10. 29; Mk. 12. 42; Lu.
12. 6.

FASHION. Job 10. 8; Ps. 119. 73, thine hands have
f. me.
31. 15, did not one *f.* us?
Ps. 33. 15, he *f.* hearts alike.
139. 16, in continuance were *f.*
Isa. 45. 9, say to him that *f.* it.
Mk. 2. 12, never saw it on this *f.*
Lu. 9. 29, the *f.* of his countenance.
1 Cor. 7. 31, the *f.* of this world passeth.
Phil. 2. 8, found in *f.* as a man.
See Gen. 6. 15; Ex. 32. 4; Ezek. 42. 11; Jas. 1. 11.

FAST. 2 Sam. 12. 23, he is dead, wherefore should
I *f.*?
Ps. 33. 9, he commanded, and it stood *f.*
65. 6, setteth *f.* the mountains.
Isa. 58. 3, why have we *f.*, and thou seest not?
4, ye *f.* for strife.
5, wilt thou call this a *f.*?
6, is not this the *f.* that I have chosen?
Joel 1. 14, sanctify a *f.*
Zech. 7. 5, did ye at all *f.* unto me?
Mat. 6. 16, when ye *f.*, be not.
18, appear not to *f.*
Mk. 2. 19, can children of bridechamber *f.*?
Lu. 18. 12, I *f.* twice in the week.
See Jer. 14. 12; Mat. 4. 2; Acts 13. 2.

FASTEN. Eccl. 12. 11, as nails *f.* by the masters.
Isa. 22. 23, 25, I will *f.* him as a nail.
Lu. 4. 20, eyes of all were *f.* on him.
Acts 11. 6, when I had *f.* mine eyes.
See 1 Sam. 31. 10; Job 38. 6; Acts 3. 4; 28. 3.

FASTING. Ps. 35. 13, I humbled myself with *f.*
109. 24, knees weak through *f.*
Jer. 36. 6, upon the *f.* day.
Mk. 8. 3, send them away *f.*
1 Cor. 7. 5, give yourselves to *f.* and prayer.
2 Cor. 6. 5, in stripes, in *f.*
11. 27, in *f.* oft.
See Dan. 6. 18; 9. 3; Mat. 17. 21; Mk. 9. 29.

FAT. Gen. 45. 18, shall eat the *f.* of the land.
Gen. 49. 20, his bread shall be *f.*
Deut. 32. 15, Jeshurun waxed *f.*, and kicked.
Neh. 8. 10, eat the *f.*, and drink the sweet.
9. 25, 35, took a *f.* land, and became *f.*
Ps. 17. 10, inclosed in their own *f.*
92. 14, shall be *f.* and flourishing.
119. 70, heart *f.* as grease.
Prov. 11. 25, liberal soul made *f.*
13. 4, soul of diligent made *f.*
15. 30, good report maketh the bones *f.*
Isa. 10. 16, among his *f.* ones leanness.
25. 6, feast of *f.* things.
Hab. 1. 16, by them their portion is *f.*
See Gen. 41. 2; Ex. 29. 13; Lev. 3. 3, 17; 7. 22;
Num. 13. 20; Judg. 3. 17.

FATHER. Gen. 15. 15, go to thy *f.* in peace.
17. 4; Rom. 4. 17, a *f.* of nations.
Ex. 15. 2, he is my *f.*, God, I will exalt him.
20. 5; Num. 14. 18, iniquity of *f.* upon children.
21. 15, he that smiteth his *f.*
17; Lev. 20. 9, he that curseth his *f.*
Judg. 17. 10; 18. 19, be to me a *f.* and a priest.
1 Sam. 10. 12, who is their *f.*?
2 Sam. 10. 2; 1 Chron. 19. 2, as his *f.* showed kindness.
1 Kings 19. 4, no better than my *f.*
2 Kings 2. 12; 13. 14, Elisha cried, my *f.*, my *f.*
6. 21, my *f.*, shall I smite them?
1 Chron. 28. 9, know thou the God of thy *f.*

2 Chron. 32. 13, what I and my *f.* have done.
Ezra 7. 27, blessed be the Lord God of our *f.*
Job 29. 16, I was a *f.* to the poor.
31. 18, brought up with me as with a *f.*
38. 28, hath the rain a *f.*?
Ps. 27. 10, when my *f.* and mother forsake me.
39. 12, as all my *f.* were.
68. 5, *f.* of fatherless.
95. 9; Heb. 3. 9, your *f.* tempted me.
103. 13, as a *f.* pitieth his children.
Prov. 4. 1, the instruction of a *f.*
3, I was my *f.* son.
10. 1; 15. 20, wise son maketh a glad *f.*
17. 21, the *f.* of a fool hath no joy.
25; 19. 13, foolish son grief to his *f.*
Isa. 9. 6, the everlasting F.
49. 23, kings shall be thy nursing *f.*
63. 16; 64. 8, doubtless thou art our *f.*
Jer. 3. 4, wilt thou not cry, my *f.*?
31. 9, I am a *f.* to Israel.
29; Ezek. 18. 2, *f.* have eaten sour grapes.
Ezek. 18. 4, as the soul of the *f.*
22. 7, set light by *f.* and mother.
Mal. 1. 6, if I be a *f.*, where is mine honour?
2. 10, have we not all one *f.*?
Mat. 5. 16, 45, 48, your F. in heaven.
6. 8, 32; Lu. 12. 30, your F. knoweth.
9; Lu. 11. 2, our F. which art in heaven.
7. 21; 12. 50, the will of my F.
8. 21; Lu. 9. 59, to go and bury my *f.*
10. 21, *f.* deliver up the child.
37, he that loveth *f.* or mother.
18. 10, behold the face of my F.
14, not the will of your F.
23. 9, call no man *f.* on earth.
25. 34, ye blessed of my F.
Mk. 14. 36; Rom. 8. 15; Gal. 4. 6, Abba, F.
Lu. 2. 49, about my F. business.
6. 36, as your F. is merciful.
11. 11, of any that is a *f.*
12. 32, it is your F. good pleasure.
15. 21, *f.*, I have sinned.
16. 27, send him to my *f.* house.
22. 42, F., if thou be willing.
23. 34, F., forgive them.
46, F., into thy hands.
John 1. 14, as of the only begotten of the F.
5. 21, as the F. raiseth up the dead.
22, the F. judgeth no man.
23, even as they honour the F.
37; 8. 16; 12. 49; 14. 24, the F. which hath sent me.
6. 37, all the F. giveth me.
46; 14. 8, 9, hath seen the F.
8. 41, we have one F., even God.
44, devil is a liar, and the *f.* of it.
49, I honour my F.
10. 15, as the F. knoweth me.
29, my F. is greater than all.
12. 27, F., save me from this hour.
28, F., glorify thy name.
13. 1, should depart unto the F.
14. 6, no man cometh to the F., but by me.
16; 16. 26, I will pray the F.
28, I am come from the F.
15. 1, my F. is the husbandman.
16, whatsoever ye ask of the F.
16. 16, because I go to the F.
32, the F. is with me.
17. 1, F., the hour is come.
20. 17, I ascend to my F. and your F.
Acts 24. 14, so worship I the God of my *f.*
Rom. 4. 11, the *f.* of all that believe.
1 Cor. 4. 15, yet have we not many *f.*
2 Cor. 1. 3, F. of mercies, God of all comfort.
Gal. 1. 14, zealous of the traditions of my *f.*
4. 2, the time appointed of the *f.*
Eph. 4. 6, one God and F. of all.
6. 4, *f.* provoke not your children.
Phil. 2. 11, to the glory of the F.
22, as a son with the *f.*
Col. 1. 19, it pleased the F. that in him.

1 Tim. 5. 1, entreat him as a *f.*
Heb. 1. 5, I will be to him a *F.*
7. 3, without *f.*. without mother.
12. 9, the *F.* of spirits.
Jas. 1. 17, the *F.* of lights.
2 Pet. 3. 4, since the *f.* fell asleep.
1 John 1. 3, fellowship with the *F.*
2. 1, an advocate with the *F.*
13, I write unto you, *f.*
15, the love of the *F.* is not in him.
23, hath not the *F.*
3. 1, what manner of love the *F.* hath.
5. 7, the *F.*, the Word, and Holy Ghost.
See 1 Chron. 29. 10; Lu. 11. 2; John 5. 26; 20. 7;
Acts 1. 4; 15. 10; Rom. 4. 16.

FATHERLESS. Ps. 10. 14, the helper of the *f.*
Prov. 23. 10, the fields of the *f.*
Isa. 1. 23, they judge not the *f.*
10. 2, that they may rob the *f.*
Jer. 49. 11, leave thy *f.* children.
Hos. 14. 3, in thee the *f.* findeth mercy.
Mal. 3. 5, against those that oppress *f.*
Jas. 1. 27, to visit the *f.* and widows.
See Ex. 22. 22; Deut. 10. 18; 14. 29; 24. 17; Job 31. 17.

FATNESS. Ps. 36. 8, the *f.* of thine house.
63. 5, as with marrow and *f.*
65. 11, thy paths drop *f.*
73. 7, eyes stand out with *f.*
Isa. 55. 2, soul delight itself in *f.*
See Gen. 27. 28; Judg. 9. 9; Rom. 11. 17.

FAULT. Gen. 41. 9, I remember my *f.* this day.
Ps. 19. 12, cleanse me from secret *f.*
Dan. 6. 4, find none occasion nor *f.* in him.
Mat. 18. 15, tell him his *f.*
Lu. 23. 4; John 18. 38; 19. 4, 6, I find no *f.*
Rom. 9. 19, why doth he yet find *f.*?
Gal. 6. 1, overtaken in a *f.*
Jas. 5. 16, confess your *f.*
Rev. 14. 5, are without *f.* before throne.
See Deut. 25. 2; 1 Sam. 29. 3; 2 Sam. 3. 8.

FAULTLESS. Heb. 8. 7; Jude 24.

FAULTY. 2 Sam. 14. 13; Hos. 10. 2.

FAVOUR. Gen. 39. 21, *f.* in the sight of the keeper.
Ex. 3. 21; 11. 3; 12. 36, *f.* in sight of Egyptians.
Deut. 33. 23, satisfied with *f.*
Ps. 5. 12, with *f.* wilt thou compass him.
30. 5, his *f.* is life.
102. 13, the set time to *f.* her.
14, *f.* the dust thereof.
112. 5, a good man showeth *f.*
Prov. 13. 15, good understanding giveth *f.*
14. 35; 19. 12, the king's *f.*
18. 22, obtaineth *f.* of the Lord.
31. 30, *f.* is deceitful.
Lu. 2. 52, increased in *f.* with God and man.
Acts 2. 47, having *f.* with all people.
See Prov. 8. 35; 12. 2; Eccl. 9. 11; Dan. 1. 9.

FAVOURABLE. Judg. 21. 22; Job 33. 26; Ps. 77.
7; 85. 1.

FEAR (*n.*). Gen. 9. 2, the *f.* of you on every beast.
20. 11, *f.* of God not in this place.
Deut. 2. 25; 11. 25; 1 Chron. 14. 17, *f.* of thee on
nations.
Job 4. 6, is not this thy *f.*?
15. 4, thou castest off *f.*
39. 22, he mocketh at *f.*
Ps. 5. 7, in thy *f.* will I worship.
14. 5, there were they in great *f.*
19. 9, *f.* of the Lord is clean.
34. 11, I will teach you the *f.* of the Lord.
36. 1; Rom. 3. 18, no *f.* of God before his eyes.
53. 5, in *f.*, where no *f.* was.
111. 10; Prov. 1. 7; 9. 10, *f.* beginning of wisdom.
Prov. 1. 26, 27, mock when your *f.* cometh.
3. 25, not afraid of sudden *f.*
10. 27, *f.* of Lord prolongeth days.
14. 26, in *f.* of Lord is strong confidence.
27, *f.* of Lord a fountain of life.
15. 16, better little with *f.* of Lord.

Prov. 19. 23, *f.* of Lord tendeth to life.
23. 17, be thou in *f.* of the Lord all the day long.
29. 25, *f.* of man bringeth a snare.
Eccl. 12. 5, when *f.* shall be in the way.
Isa. 8. 12, neither fear ye their *f.*
14. 3, Lord give thee rest from *f.*
29. 13, *f.* toward me taught by men.
Jer. 30. 5, a voice of *f.*, not of peace.
32. 40, I will put my *f.* in their hearts.
Mal. 1. 6, where is my *f.*?
Mat. 14. 26, disciples cried for *f.*
Lu. 21. 26, hearts failing them for *f.*
John 7. 13; 19. 38; 20. 19, for *f.* of the Jews.
1 Cor. 2. 3, with you in weakness and *f.*
2 Cor. 7. 11, what *f.*, what desire.
Eph. 6. 5; Phil. 2. 12, with *f.* and trembling.
Heb. 2. 15, *f.* of death.
11. 7, Noah moved with *f.*
12. 28, with reverence and godly *f.*
Jude 12, feeding themselves without *f.*
23, others save with *f.*
See Ps. 2. 11; 2 Cor. 7. 5, 15; 1 Pet. 2. 18; 3. 2.

FEAR (*v.*). Gen. 22. 12, I know that thou *f.* God.
42. 18, this do, and live, for I *f.* God.
Ex. 1. 21, because they *f.* God.
14. 13, *f.* not, stand still, and see.
18. 21, able men, such as *f.* God.
20. 20, *f.* not, God is come to prove.
Deut. 4. 10, that they may learn to *f.*
5. 29, O that they would *f.* me.
28. 58, *f.* this glorious name.
66, thou shalt *f.* day and night.
1 Chron. 16. 30; Ps. 96. 9, *f.* before him all earth.
Neh. 7. 2, he *f.* God above many.
Job 1. 9, doth Job *f.* God for nought?
11. 15, put iniquity away, thou shalt not *f.*
Ps. 27. 1, whom shall I *f.*?
3, my heart shall not *f.*
31. 19, laid up for them that *f.* thee.
34. 9, *f.* the Lord, ye his saints.
56. 4; 118. 6, will not *f.* what flesh can do.
66. 16, come, all ye that *f.* God.
76. 7, thou art to be *f.*
86. 11, unite my heart to *f.* thy name.
115. 11, ye that *f.* the Lord, trust.
119. 74, they that *f.* thee will be glad.
Prov. 3. 7; 24. 21, *f.* the Lord, and depart.
28. 14, happy is the man that *f.* always.
31. 30, woman that *f.* the Lord.
Eccl. 3. 14, that men should *f.* before him.
5. 7, but *f.* thou God.
9. 2, as he that *f.* an oath.
12. 13, *f.* God, and keep his commandments.
Isa. 8. 12, neither *f.* ye their fear.
35. 4, to them of fearful heart, *f.* not.
41. 10; 43. 5, *f.* thou not, I am with thee.
14, *f.* not, thou worm Jacob.
Jer. 5. 24, neither say they, let us *f.* the Lord.
10. 7, who would not *f.* thee, King of nations?
33. 9, they shall *f.* and tremble.
Dan. 6. 26, that men *f.* before the God of Daniel.
Zeph. 3. 7, I said, surely thou wilt *f.* me.
Mal. 3. 16, they that *f.* the Lord spake.
4. 2, to you that *f.* my name.
Mat. 1. 20, *f.* not to take to thee.
10. 28; Lu. 12. 5, *f.* him who is able.
14. 5; 21. 46, Herod *f.* the multitude.
21. 26; Mk. 11. 32; Lu. 20. 19, we *f.* the people.
Mk. 4. 41, they *f.* exceedingly.
5. 33, woman *f.* and trembling came.
11. 18, scribes *f.* Jesus.
Lu. 9. 34, *f.* as they entered cloud.
12. 32, *f.* not, little flock.
18. 2, judge which *f.* not God.
19. 21, I *f.* thee, because thou art.
23. 40, dost not thou *f.* God?
John 9. 22, because they *f.* the Jews.
Acts 10. 22, just, and one that *f.* God.
35, he that *f.* is accepted.
13. 26, whosoever among you *f.* God.
Rom. 8. 15, bondage again to *f.*

Rom. 11. 20, not highminded, but *f.*
2 Cor. 11. 3 ; 12. 20, I *f.* lest.
1 Tim. 5. 20, rebuke, that others may *f.*
Heb. 5. 7, heard in that he *f.*
　13. 6, I will not *f.* what man.
1 John 4. 18, that *f.* not perfect in love.
　See 1 Kings 18. 12 ; Col. 3. 22 ; Heb. 4. 1.
FEARFUL. Ex. 15. 11, *f.* in praises.
Ps. 139. 14, *f.* and wonderfully made.
Isa. 35. 4, to them of a *f.* heart.
Mat. 8. 26 ; Mk. 4. 40, why are ye *f.*?
Heb. 10. 27, *f.* looking for of judgment.
　31, *f.* thing to fall into the hands.
　See Deut. 20. 8 ; Judg. 7. 3 ; Lu. 21. 11 ; Rev. 21. 8.
FEARFULNESS. Ps. 55. 5 ; Isa. 21. 4 ; 33. 14.
FEAST. Job 1. 4, his sons went and *f.* in their
　houses.
Ps. 35. 16, hypocritical mockers in *f.*
Prov. 15. 15, merry heart continual *f.*
Eccl. 7. 2 ; Jer. 16. 8, the house of *f.*
　10. 19, *f.* is made for laughter.
Isa. 1. 14, your appointed *f.* my soul hateth.
Amos 5. 21, I despise your *f.* days.
　8. 10, turn your *f.* into mourning.
Mat. 23. 6 ; Mk. 12. 39 ; Lu. 20. 46, uppermost
　rooms at *f.*
　26. 5 ; Mk. 14. 2, not on the *f.* day.
Lu. 2. 42, after the custom of the *f.*
　14. 13, when thou makest a *f.*
John 7. 8, go ye up to this *f.*
　14, about the midst of the *f.*
　37, that great day of the *f.*
　13. 29, buy what we need against the *f.*
Acts 18. 21, I must by all means keep this *f.*
1 Cor. 5. 8, let us keep the *f.*
　10. 27, if any bid you to a *f.*
　See Judg. 14. 10 ; Esth. 9. 17 ; Mal. 2. 3 ; Jude 12.
FEATHERS. Job 39. 13 ; Ps. 91. 4 ; Dan. 4. 33.
FED. Gen. 48. 15, who *f.* me all my life long.
Ps. 37. 3, verily thou shalt be *f.*
Ezek. 34. 8, shepherds *f.* themselves, not flock.
Mat. 25. 37, hungered, and *f.* thee.
1 Cor. 3. 2, I have *f.* you with milk.
　See Deut. 8. 3 ; Ps. 78. 72 ; 81. 16 ; Lu. 16. 21.
FEEBLE. Neh. 4. 2, what do these *f.* Jews ?
Job 4. 4 ; Isa. 35. 3 ; Heb. 12. 12, strengthened the
　f. knees.
Ps. 105. 37, not one *f.* person.
Prov. 30. 26, conies a *f.* folk.
Ezek. 7. 17 ; 21. 7, all hands shall be *f.*
1 Thess. 5. 14, comfort the *f.* minded.
　See Gen. 30. 42 ; Jer. 47. 3 ; 1 Cor. 12. 22.
FEED. Gen. 46. 32, trade hath been to *f.* cattle.
1 Kings 17. 4, commanded ravens to *f.* thee.
　22. 27, *f.* him with bread of affliction.
Ps. 28. 9, *f.* them, and lift them up for ever.
Prov. 15. 14, mouth *f.* on foolishness.
　30. 8, *f.* me with food convenient.
Isa. 5. 17, lambs shall *f.* after their manner.
　11. 7 ; 27. 10, cow and bear shall *f.*
　44. 20, he *f.* on ashes.
　61. 5, strangers shall *f.* your flocks.
　65. 25, the wolf and lamb shall *f.*
Jer. 3. 15, pastors *f.* you with knowledge.
　6. 3, *f.* every one in his place.
Hos. 12. 1, Ephraim *f.* on wind.
Zech. 11. 4, *f.* the flock of the slaughter.
Mat. 6. 26, your heavenly Father *f.* them.
Lu. 12. 24, sow not, yet God *f.* them
John 21. 15, 16, 17, *f.* my lambs.
Rom. 12. 20, if enemy hunger, *f.* him.
1 Pet. 5. 2, *f.* the flock of God.
　See Cant. 1. 7 ; Acts 20. 28 ; Rev. 7. 17.
FEEL. Gen. 27. 12, 21, my father will *f.* me.
Acts 17. 27, if haply they might *f.* after.
　See Judg. 16. 26 ; Job 20. 20 ; Eccl. 8. 5.
FEELING. Eph. 4. 19, being past *f.*
Heb. 4. 15, touched with *f.* of infirmities.
FEET. Gen. 49. 10, lawgiver from between his *f.*

Deut. 2. 28, I will pass through on my *f.*
Josh. 3. 15, *f.* of priests dipped in Jordan.
　14. 9, land whereon *f.* have trodden.
Ruth 3. 14, she lay at his *f.*
1 Sam. 2. 9, keep *f.* of his saints.
2 Sam. 22. 37 ; Ps. 18. 36, my *f.* did not slip.
2 Kings 6. 32, sound of his master's *f.*
　13. 21, dead man stood on his *f.*
Neh. 9. 21, their *f.* swelled not.
Job 29. 15, *f.* was I to the lame.
Ps. 8. 6 ; 1 Cor. 15. 27 ; Eph. 1. 22, all things under
　his *f.*
　22. 16, pierced my hands and my *f.*
　31. 8, set my *f.* in a large room.
　40. 2, my *f.* on a rock.
　56. 13 ; 116. 8, deliver my *f.* from falling.
　66. 9, suffered not our *f.* to be moved.
　73. 2, my *f.* were almost gone.
　115. 7, *f.* have they, but walk not.
　119. 105, a lamp to my *f.*
　122. 2, our *f.* shall stand within thy gates.
Prov. 1. 16 ; 6. 18 ; Isa. 59. 7, *f.* run to evil.
　4. 26, ponder path of thy *f.*
　5. 5, her *f.* go down to death.
　6. 13, speaketh with his *f.*
　28, and his *f.* not be burnt.
　7. 11, her *f.* abide not in house.
　19. 2, he that hasteth with his *f.*
Cant. 5. 3, washed my *f.*, how shall I defile ?
　7. 1 ; Isa. 52. 7, how beautiful are *f.*
Isa. 3. 16, tinkling with *f.*
　6. 2, with twain he covered his *f.*
　23. 7, her own *f.* shall carry her.
　26. 6, the *f.* of the poor.
　49. 23 ; Mat. 10. 14 ; Mk. 6. 11 ; Lu. 9. 5 ; Acts
　13. 51, dust of *f.*
　52. 7 ; Nah. 1. 15, the *f.* of him that bringeth.
　60. 13, place of my *f.* glorious.
Lam. 3. 34, crush under *f.* prisoners.
Ezek. 2. 1, 2 ; 3. 24, stand upon thy *f.*
　24. 17, 23, shoes upon thy *f.*
　25. 6, stamped with thy *f.*
　32. 2, troubled waters with thy *f.*
　34. 18, 19, foul residue with *f.*
Dan. 2. 33, 42, *f.* part iron and part clay.
　10. 6 ; Rev. 1. 15 ; 2. 18, *f.* like polished brass.
Nah. 1. 3, clouds are the dust of his *f.*
Zech. 14. 4, *f.* shall stand upon mount of Olives.
Mat. 7. 6, trample them under *f.*
　18. 8, rather than having two *f.*
　28. 9, they held him by the *f.*
Lu. 1. 79, guide our *f.* into way of peace.
　7. 38, she kissed his *f.*, and anointed them.
　8. 35, sitting at the *f.* of Jesus.
　10. 39, Mary sat at Jesus' *f.*
　24. 39, 40, behold my hands and my *f.*
John 11. 2 ; 12. 3, wiped *f.* with her hair.
　12. 3, anointed the *f.* of Jesus.
　13. 5, began to wash disciples' *f.*
　6, dost thou wash my *f.* ?
　8, thou shalt never wash my *f.*
　10, needeth not save to wash his *f.*
　20. 12, one angel at head, other at *f.*
Acts 3. 7, his *f.* received strength.
　4. 35, 37 ; 5. 2, laid at apostles' *f.*
　5. 9, *f.* of them that buried thy husband.
　14. 8, a man impotent in his *f.*
　21. 11, Agabus bound his own hands and *f.*
　22. 3, at *f.* of Gamaliel.
Rom. 3. 15, *f.* swift to shed blood.
　10. 15, the *f.* of them that preach.
　16. 20, bruise Satan under your *f.*
1 Cor. 12. 21, nor head to the *f.*, I have no need.
Eph. 6. 15, your *f.* shod with preparation.
Rev. 1. 17, I fell at his *f.* as dead.
　13. 2, *f.* as *f.* of a bear.
　19. 10 ; 22. 8, at his *f.* to worship.
　See 2 Sam. 4. 4 ; 2 Kings 9. 35 ; 1 Tim. 5. 10.
FEIGN. 1 Sam. 21. 13, David *f.* himself mad.
Ps. 17. 1, prayer not out of *f.* lips.
Jer. 3. 10, turned to me *f.*

Lu. 20. 20, *f.* themselves just men.
See 2 Sam. 14. 2; 1 Kings 14. 5, 6; Neh. 6. 8
FELL. Gen. 4. 5, his countenance *f.*
Josh. 6. 20, the wall *f.* flat.
1 Kings 18. 38, fire of Lord *f.*, and consumed.
2 Kings 6. 5, as one was *f.* a beam.
Dan. 4. 31, then *f.* a voice from heaven.
Jonah 1. 7, lot *f.* on Jonah.
Mat. 7. 25; Lu. 6. 49, house *f.* not.
Lu. 8. 23, Jesus *f.* asleep.
10. 30, 36, *f.* among thieves.
13. 4, upon whom tower *f.*
Acts 1. 25, from which Judas *f.*
26, lot *f.* on Matthias.
13. 36, *f.* on sleep.
2 Pet. 3. 4, since fathers *f.* asleep.
Rev. 16. 19, cities of the nations *f.*
See Mat. 13. 4; Acts 10. 44; 19. 35; 20. 9.
FELLOW. Ex. 2. 13, wherefore smitest thou thy *f.*?
1 Sam. 21. 15, this *f.* to play the madman.
2 Sam. 6. 20. as one of the vain *f.*
2 Kings 9. 11, wherefore came this mad *f.*?
Ps. 45. 7; Heb. 1. 9, oil of gladness above thy *f.*
Eccl. 4. 10, one shall lift up his *f.*
Zech. 13. 7, the man that is my *f.*
Mat. 11. 16, like children calling to their *f.*
24. 49, begin to smite his *f.*-servants.
26. 61, this *f.* said, I am able to destroy.
71; Lu. 22. 59, this *f.* was also with Jesus.
Lu. 23. 2, found this *f.* perverting.
John 9. 29, as for this *f.*
Acts 17. 5, lewd *f.* of the baser sort.
22. 22, away with such a *f.*
24. 5, this man a pestilent *f.*
Eph. 2. 19, *f.*-citizens with the saints.
3. 6, Gentiles *f.*-heirs.
Phil. 4. 3; 1 Thess. 3. 2; Philem. 24, *f.*-labourers.
3 John 8, *f.*-helpers to the truth.
See Col. 4. 11; Philem. 2; Rev. 19. 10; 22. 9.
FELLOWSHIP. Acts 2. 42, in doctrine and *f.*
1 Cor. 1. 9, called to the *f.* of his Son.
10. 20, not have *f.* with devils.
2 Cor. 6. 14, what *f.* hath righteousness?
Eph. 3. 9, the *f.* of mystery.
5. 11, have no *f.* with.
Phil. 1. 5, your *f.* in the gospel.
2. 1, if any *f.* of the Spirit.
3. 10, the *f.* of his sufferings.
1 John 1. 3, our *f.* is with the Father.
7, we have *f.* one with another.
See Lev. 6. 2; Ps. 94. 20; 2 Cor. 8. 4, 13, 14; Gal. 2. 9.
FELT. Ex. 10. 21; Prov. 23. 35; Mk. 5. 29; Acts 28. 5.
FEMALE. Mat. 19. 4; Mk. 10. 6, made them male and *f.*
Gal. 3. 28, in Christ neither male nor *f.*
See Gen. 7. 16; Lev. 3. 1; 27. 4; Deut. 4. 16.
FENCE. Job 10. 11; 19. 8; Ps. 62. 3; Isa. 5. 2.
FERVENT. Acts 18. 25; Rom. 12. 11, *f.* in spirit.
Jas. 5. 16, *f.* prayer availeth much.
1 Pet. 1. 22, with a pure heart *f.*
2 Pet. 3. 10, 12, melt with *f.* heat.
See 2 Cor. 7. 7; Col. 4. 12; 1 Pet. 4. 8.
FETCH. Num. 20. 10, must we *f.* water?
Job 36. 3, I will *f.* my knowledge from far.
Isa. 56. 12, I will *f.* wine.
Acts 16. 37, come themselves and *f.* us out.
See Deut. 19. 5; 2 Sam. 14. 3; Acts 28. 13.
FETTERS. Judg. 16. 21; Ps. 105. 18; 149. 8; Mk. 5. 4; Lu. 8. 29.
FEVER. Deut. 28. 22, the Lord shall smite thee with a *f.*
Mat. 8. 14; Mk. 1. 30, Simon's wife's mother lay sick of a *f.*
John 4. 52, at the seventh hour the *f.* left him.
FEW. Gen. 29. 20, they seemed but a *f.* days.
47. 9, *f.* and evil have the days of my life.

1 Sam. 14. 6, to save by many or *f.*
17. 28, with whom left those *f.* sheep?
2 Kings 4. 3, borrow not a *f.*
Neh. 7. 4, city large, people *f.*
Job 14. 1, man is of *f.* days.
16. 22, when a *f.* years are come.
Eccl. 5. 2, let thy words be *f.*
Mat. 7. 14, *f.* there be that find it.
9. 37; Lu. 10. 2, the labourers are *f.*
15. 34; Mk. 8. 7, a *f.* little fishes.
20. 16; 22. 14, many called, *f.* chosen.
25. 21, faithful in a *f.* things.
Mk. 6. 5, laid hands on a *f.* sick folk.
Lu. 12. 48, beaten with *f.* stripes.
13. 23, are there *f.* that be saved?
Rev. 3. 4, a *f.* names even in Sardis.
See Deut. 7. 7; Ps. 109. 8; Heb. 12. 10.
FIDELITY. Tit. 2. 10, showing good *f.*
FIELD. Deut. 21. 1, if one be found slain in *f.*
1 Sam. 22. 7, will he give every one of you *f.*?
Prov. 24. 30, the *f.* of the slothful.
Isa. 5. 8, that lay *f.* to *f.*
Mat. 13. 38, the *f.* is the world.
44, treasure hid in a *f.*
John 4. 35, look on the *f.*
Jas. 5. 4, labourers which reaped your *f.*
See Mat. 6. 28; 27. 7; Acts 1. 19.
FIERCE. Gen. 49. 7, anger, for it was *f.*
Deut. 28. 50, a nation of a *f.* countenance.
Mat. 8. 28, exceeding *f.*
Lu. 23. 5, and they were more *f.*
2 Tim. 3. 3, men shall be incontinent, *f.*
Jas. 3. 4, driven of *f.* winds.
See 2 Sam. 19. 43; Isa. 33. 19; Dan. 8. 23.
FIERY. Deut. 33. 2, a *f.* law for them.
Dan. 3. 6, a *f.* furnace.
Eph. 6. 16, the *f.* darts of the wicked.
Heb. 10. 27, judgment and *f.* indignation.
1 Pet. 4. 12, concerning the *f.* trial.
See Num. 21. 6; Deut. 8. 15; Isa. 14. 29.
FIG. 1 Kings 4. 25; Mic. 4. 4, dwelt under his *f.* tree.
2 Kings 18. 31; Isa. 36. 16, eat every one of his *f.* tree.
20. 7, Isaiah said, Take a lump of *f.*
Isa. 38. 21, let them take a lump of *f.*
Jer. 24. 1, two baskets of *f.* were set before the temple.
Hab. 3. 17, although *f.* tree shall not blossom.
Mat. 7. 16; Lu. 6. 44, do men gather *f.* of thistles
Lu. 21. 29, behold the *f.* tree.
Jas. 3. 12, can the *f.* tree bear olive berries?
Rev. 6. 13, casteth untimely *f.*
See Judg. 9. 10; Jer. 8. 13; Lu. 13. 6; John 1. 48.
FIGHT. Ex. 14. 14; Deut. 1. 30; 3. 22; 20. 4, Lord *f.* for you.
Josh. 23. 10, he it is that *f.* for you.
1 Sam. 25. 28, *f.* the battles of the Lord.
2 Kings 10. 3, *f.* for your master's house.
Neh. 4. 14, *f.* for your brethren, sons, and wives.
Ps. 144. 1, teacheth my fingers to *f.*
John 18. 36, then would my servants *f.*
Acts 5. 39; 23. 9, *f.* against God.
1 Cor. 9. 26, so *f.* I.
2 Cor. 7. 5, without were *f.*
1 Tim. 6. 12; 2 Tim. 4. 7, the good *f.*
Heb. 10. 32, great *f.* of afflictions.
11. 34, valiant in *f.*
Jas. 4. 1, wars and *f.* among you.
2, ye *f.* and war.
See Zech. 10. 5; 14. 14; Rev. 2. 16.
FIG-TREE. Mat. 21. 19, presently the *f.* withered away.
Mk. 11. 13, seeing a *f.* afar off.
FIG-TREE (parable of). Mat. 24. 32; Lu. 21. 29.
FIGURE. Deut. 4. 16; Rom. 5. 14; 1 Cor. 4. 6; Heb. 9. 9; 1 Pet. 3. 21.
FILL. Num. 14. 21; Ps. 72. 19; Hab. 2. 14, earth *f.* with glory.

Job 23. 4, *f.* my mouth with arguments.
Ps. 81. 10, open mouth, I will *f.* it.
104. 28, they are *f.* with good.
Prov. 3. 10, barns *f.* with plenty.
14. 14, *f.* with his own ways.
30. 22, a fool when *f.* with meat.
Isa. 65. 20, who hath not *f.* his days.
Mat. 5. 6 ; Lu. 6. 21, they shall be *f.*
Mk. 7. 27, let the children first be *f.*
Lu. 1. 15 ; Acts 4. 8 ; 9. 17 ; 13. 9, *f.* with Holy Ghost.
14. 23, that my house may be *f.*
John 16. 6, sorrow hath *f.* your heart.
Acts 5. 28, ye have *f.* Jerusalem with your doctrine.
14. 17, *f.* our hearts with food and gladness.
Rom. 1. 29, *f.* with all unrighteousness.
15. 14, *f.* with all knowledge.
Eph. 1. 23, him that *f.* all in all.
3. 19, *f.* with fulness of God.
5. 18, be *f.* with the Spirit.
Phil. 1. 11, *f.* with fruits of righteousness.
Col. 1. 24, *f.* up what is behind.
Jas. 2. 16, be ye warmed and *f.*
Rev. 15. 1, in them is *f.* up wrath of God.
See Dan. 2. 35 ; Lu. 2. 40 ; 15. 16 ; John 2. 7.
FILTH. Isa. 4. 4, washed away the *f.* of Zion.
1 Cor. 4. 13, as the *f.* of the world.
FILTHINESS. 2 Cor. 7. 1, cleanse from all *f.* of flesh.
Eph. 5. 4, nor let *f.* be named.
Jas. 1. 21, lay apart all *f.*
See Ezek. 22. 15 ; 36. 25.
¶FILTHY. Job 15. 16, how much more *f.* is man ?
Ps. 14. 3 ; 53. 3, altogether become *f.*
Isa. 64. 6, as *f.* rags.
Zech. 3. 3, clothed with *f.* garments.
Col. 3. 8, put off *f.* communication.
1 Tim. 3. 3 ; Tit. 1. 7 ; 1 Pet. 5. 2, *f.* lucre.
2 Pet. 2. 7, vexed with *f.* conversation.
Jude 8, *f.* dreamers.
Rev. 22. 11, he that is *f.*, let him be *f.*
¶FINALLY. 2 Cor. 13. 11 ; Eph. 6 10 ; Phil. 3. 1 ; 4. 8 ; 2 Thess. 3. 1 ; 1 Pet. 3. 8.
¶FIND. Num. 32. 23, be sure your sin will *f.* you out.
Job 9. 10 ; Rom. 11. 33, things past *f.* out.
23. 3, where I might *f.* him.
Prov. 4. 22, life to those that *f.* them.
8. 17 ; Jer. 29. 13, seek me early shall *f.* me.
Prov. 8. 35, whoso *f.* me, *f.* life.
18. 22, *f.* a wife, *f.* a good thing.
Eccl. 9. 10, thy hand *f.* to do, do it.
11. 1, *f.* it after many days.
Isa. 58. 13, *f.* thine own pleasure.
Jer. 6. 16 ; Mat. 11. 29, *f.* rest to your souls.
Mat. 7. 7 ; Lu. 11. 9, seek, and ye shall *f.*
14, few there be that *f.* it.
10. 39, loseth his life shall *f.* it.
22. 9, as many as ye shall *f.*
Mk. 11. 13, he might *f.* any thing thereon.
13. 36, he *f.* you sleeping.
Lu. 15. 4, 8, till he *f.* it.
18. 8, shall he *f.* faith on earth ?
John 1. 41, first *f.* his brother.
Rom. 7. 21, I *f.* a law that when I would.
Heb. 4. 16, *f.* grace to help.
See John 7. 34 ; 2 Tim. 1. 18 ; Rev. 9. 6.
¶FINE. Ps. 19. 10, more to be desired than *f.* gold.
81. 16 ; 147. 14, the *f.* of the wheat.
Prov. 25. 12, as an ornament of *f.* gold.
Lam. 4. 1, how is the *f.* gold changed !
Mk. 15. 46, Joseph brought *f.* linen.
See Job 28. 1, 17 ; Lu. 16. 19 ; Rev. 18. 12 ; 19. 8.
¶INGER. Ex. 8. 19, this is the *f.* of God.
31. 18 ; Deut. 9. 10, written with the *f.* of God.
1 Kings 12. 10 ; 2 Chron. 10. 10, little *f.* thicker.
Prov. 7. 3, bind them on thy *f.*
Isa. 58. 9, the putting forth of the *f.*

Dan. 5. 5, the *f.* of a man's hand.
Mat. 23. 4 ; Lu. 11. 46, not move with *f.*
Lu. 16. 24, the tip of his *f.*
John 8. 6, with his *f.* wrote on ground.
20. 25, put my *f.* into print of nails.
27, reach hither thy *f.*
See Ps. 8. 3 ; Prov. 6. 13 ; Isa. 2. 8 ; 59. 3 ; Lu. 11. 20.
FINISH. 1 Chron. 28. 20, till thou hast *f.*
Neh. 6. 15, so the wall was *f.*
Lu. 14. 28, 29, 30, whether sufficient to *f.*
John 4. 34, to do his will, and *f.* his work.
5. 36, which the Father hath given me to *f.*
17. 4, I have *f.* the work.
19. 30, it is *f.*
Acts 20. 24 ; 2 Tim. 4. 7, that I might *f.* my course.
2 Cor. 8. 6, *f.* in you the same grace.
Heb. 12. 2, Jesus, author and *f.* of our faith.
Jas. 1. 15, sin, when it is *f.*
See Dan. 9. 24 ; Rev. 10. 7 ; 11. 7 ; 20. 5.
FIRE. Gen. 22. 7, behold the *f.* and the wood.
Ex. 3. 2, bush burned with *f.*
22. 6, he that kindled *f.* shall make restitution.
Lev. 10. 2, *f.* from the Lord.
18. 21 ; Deut. 18. 10 ; 2 Kings 17. 17 ; 23. 10, pass through *f.*
Judg. 15. 5, brands on *f.*, and burnt corn.
1 Kings 18. 24, that answereth by *f.*
19. 12, the Lord was not in the *f.*
1 Chron. 21. 26, Lord answered him by *f.*
Ps. 39. 3, musing, the *f.* burned.
74. 7, they have cast *f.* into thy sanctuary.
Prov. 6. 27, can a man take *f.*?
26. 18, mad man who casteth *f.*-brands.
20, no wood, the *f.* goeth out.
21, as wood to *f.*, so is a contentious man.
Isa. 9. 19, as the fuel of the *f.*
24. 15, glorify the Lord in the *f.*
43. 2, walkest through *f.* not be burned.
44. 16, I have seen the *f.*
64. 2, the melting *f.* burneth.
66. 15, the Lord will come with *f.*
16, by *f.* will the Lord plead.
24 ; Mk. 9. 44, neither their *f.* quenched.
Jer. 20. 9, word as a *f.* in my bones.
Ezek. 36. 5, in the *f.* of my jealousy.
Dan. 3. 27, the *f.* had no power.
Amos 4. 11, as a *f.*-brand plucked out.
Nah. 1. 6, fury poured out like *f.*
Zech. 2. 5, a wall of *f.* round about.
3. 2, a brand plucked out of the *f.*
Mal. 3. 2, like a refiner's *f.*
Mat. 3. 10 ; 7. 19 ; Lu. 3. 9 ; John 15. 6, tree cast into *f.*
Mat. 3. 11 ; Lu. 3. 16, baptize with *f.*
13. 42, cast them into furnace of *f.*
18. 8 ; 25. 41 ; Mk. 9. 43, 46, everlasting *f.*
Lu. 9. 54, wilt thou that we command *f.*?
12. 49, come to send *f.* on earth.
17. 29, same day it rained *f.* and brimstone.
Acts 2. 3, cloven tongues like as of *f.*
1 Cor. 3. 13, revealed by *f.*, and the *f.* shall try.
15, saved, yet so as by *f.*
2 Thess. 1. 8, in flaming *f.* taking vengeance.
Heb. 1. 7, his ministers a flame of *f.*
11. 34, quenched violence of *f.*
Jas. 3. 5, a little *f.* kindleth.
6, the tongue is a *f.*
1 Pet. 1. 7, gold tried with *f.*
2 Pet. 3. 7, reserved unto *f.*
12, heavens being on *f.*
Jude 7, vengeance of eternal *f.*
23, pulling them out of the *f.*
Rev. 3. 18, buy gold tried in the *f.*
20. 9, *f.* came down from God.
10, devil cast into lake of *f.*
14, death and hell cast into *f.*
21. 8, the lake that burneth with *f.*
See Isa. 33. 14 ; Jer. 23. 29 ; Heb. 12. 29.
FIRM. Josh. 3. 17 ; Job 41. 24 ; Ps. 73. 4 ; Heb. 3. 6.
FIRMAMENT. Gen. 1. 6, let there be a *f.*

Ps. 19. 1, the *f.* showeth his handywork.
Ezek. 1. 22, the likeness of the *f.*
Dan. 12. 3, shine as the brightness of the *f.*

FIRST. 1 Kings 17. 13, make a little cake *f.*
Ezra 3. 12; Hag. 2. 3, the glory of the *f.* house.
Job 15. 7, art thou the *f.* man born?
Prov. 3. 9, honour the Lord with *f.*-fruits.
18. 17, *f.* in his own cause.
Isa. 43. 27, thy *f.* father hath sinned.
Mat. 5. 24, *f.* be reconciled.
6. 33, seek ye *f.* the kingdom.
7. 5, *f.* cast out the beam.
12. 29; Mk. 3. 27, except he *f.* bind strong man.
45, last state of that man worse than *f.*
17. 10, 11; Mk. 9. 12, Elias must *f.* come.
20. 10, when the *f.* came, they supposed.
22. 38; Mk. 12. 28, 29, 30, the *f.* commandment.
Mk. 4. 28, *f.* the blade.
9. 35. if any desire to be *f.*, same shall be last.
13. 10, gospel must *f.* be published.
Lu. 14. 28, sitteth not down *f.*
17. 25, but *f.* must he suffer many things.
John 1. 41, *f.* findeth his brother Simon.
5. 4, whosoever *f.* stepped in.
8. 7, let him *f.* cast a stone.
Acts 11. 26, called Christians *f.* at Antioch.
Rom. 2. 9, 10, of the Jew *f.*
8. 23, the *f.*-fruits of the Spirit.
29, *f.*-born among many brethren.
11. 16, if the *f.*-fruit be holy.
1 Cor. 12. 28, *f.* apostles, secondarily prophets.
14. 30, let the *f.* hold peace.
15. 20, 23, Christ the *f.*-fruits.
45, the *f.* man was made a living soul.
46, not *f.* which is spiritual.
47, *f.* man is of the earth.
2 Cor. 8. 5, *f.* gave their own selves.
12, if there be *f.* a willing mind.
Eph. 6. 2, the *f.* commandment with promise.
Col. 1. 15, 18, the *f.*-born of every creature.
1 Thess. 4. 16, dead in Christ shall rise *f.*
2 Thess. 2. 3, a falling away *f.*
1 Tim. 1. 16, that in me *f.*
2. 13, Adam was *f.* formed.
3. 10, let these *f.* be proved.
5. 4, learn *f.* to show piety at home.
12, cast off their *f.* faith.
2 Tim. 4. 16, at my *f.* answer no man.
Tit. 3. 10. after *f.* and second admonition.
Heb. 5. 12, which be the *f.* principles.
7. 27, *f.* for his own sins.
10. 9, taketh away the *f.*
Jas. 3. 17, *f.* pure, then peaceable.
1 Pet. 4. 17, if judgment *f.* begin at us.
1 John 4. 19, because he *f.* loved us.
Jude 6, kept not their *f.* estate.
Rev. 2. 4, left thy *f.* love.
5, do thy *f.* works.
20. 5, this is the *f.* resurrection.
21. 1. *f.* heaven and *f.* earth passed away.
See Ex. 4. 8; Num. 18. 13; John 12. 16.

FIR-TREE. Isa. 41. 19, I will set in the desert
the *f.*
55. 13, instead of the thorn shall come up the *f.*
60. 13, the *f.*
Hos. 14. 8, I am like a green *f.*

FISH. Eccl. 9. 12, *f.* taken in an evil net.
Hab. 1. 14, men as the *f.* of the sea.
Mat. 7. 10, if he ask a *f.*
14. 17; Mk. 6. 38; Lu. 9. 13, five loaves and two *f.*
John 21. 3, Peter saith, I go a *f.*
1 Cor. 15. 39, one flesh of beasts, another of *f.*
See Jer. 16. 16; Mat. 4. 19; Mk. 1. 17; Lu. 24. 42.

FISHERS. Mat. 4. 18; Mk. 1. 16, for they were *f.*
John 21. 7, he girt his *f.* coat unto him.
See Lu. 5. 2.

FIT. Job 34. 18, is it *f.* to say to a king?
Lu. 9. 62, is *f.* for the kingdom.
14. 35, it is not *f.* for the dunghill.

Col. 3. 18, submit, as it is *f.* in the Lord.
See Lev. 16. 21; Prov. 24. 27; Ezek. 15. 5; Rom.
9. 22.

FITLY. Prov. 25. 11; Eph. 2. 21; 4. 16.

FIXED. Ps. 57. 7; 108. 1; 112. 7; Lu. 16. 26.

FLAME. Gen. 3. 24, at garden of Eden a *f.* sword.
Judg. 13. 20, angel ascended in *f.*
Isa. 5. 24, as the *f.* consumeth chaff.
29. 6, a *f.* of devouring fire.
43. 2, neither shall *f.* kindle.
66. 15, rebuke with *f.* of fire.
Ezek. 20. 47, the *f. f.* shall not be quenched.
Lu. 16. 24, tormented in this *f.*
See Ps. 29. 7; Heb. 1. 7; Rev. 1. 14; 2. 18.

FLATTER. Job 17. 5, he speaketh *f.* to his friends.
32. 21, 22, give *f.* titles to man.
Ps. 5. 9, they *f.* with their tongue.
12. 2, *f.* lips and double heart.
Prov. 20. 19, meddle not with him that *f.*
26. 28, a *f.* mouth worketh ruin.
1 Thess. 2. 5, neither used we *f.* words.
See Prov. 28. 23; 29. 5; Dan. 11. 21, 32, 34.

FLATTERY. Ps. 78. 36; Prov. 2. 16; 24. 24.

FLEE. Lev. 26. 17, 36, ye shall *f.* when none pur-
sueth.
Num. 10. 35, them that hate thee *f.* before thee.
Neh. 6. 11, should such a man as I *f.*?
Job 14. 2, he *f.* as a shadow.
Ps. 139. 7, whither shall I *f.*?
Prov. 28. 1, the wicked *f.* when no man pursueth
17, he shall *f.* to the pit.
Cant. 2. 17; 4. 6, till shadows *f.* away.
Isa. 35. 10; 51. 11, sighing shall *f.* away.
Mat. 3. 7; Lu. 3. 7, to *f.* from wrath to come.
10. 23, in one city, *f.* to another.
24. 16; Mk. 13. 14; Lu. 21. 21, *f.* to mountains.
26. 56; Mk. 14. 50, forsook him and *f.*
John 10. 5, not follow, but will *f.* from him.
13, the hireling *f.*
1 Tim. 6. 11, *f.* these things.
2 Tim. 2. 22, *f.* youthful lusts.
Jas. 4. 7, he will *f.* from you.
See 1 Cor. 6. 18; 10. 14; Rev. 12. 6, 14.

FLEECE. Judg. 6. 37, I will put a *f.* of wool in
the floor.

FLESH. Gen. 2. 24; Mat. 19. 5; Mk. 10. 8; 1 Cor
6. 16; Eph. 5. 31, one *f.*
6. 12, all *f.* had corrupted his way.
13, end of all *f.* is come.
7. 21, all *f.* died.
Ex. 16. 3, when we sat by the *f.* pots.
Lev. 17. 14, the life of all *f.* is the blood.
19. 28, cuttings in your *f.*
Num. 11. 33, while *f.* was between their teeth.
16. 22; 27. 16, God of spirits of all *f.*
1 Kin. 17. 6, bread and *f.* in morning and evening
2 Chron. 32. 8, with him is an arm of *f.*
Neh. 5. 5, our *f.* is as the *f.* of our brethren.
Job 19. 26, in my *f.* shall I see God.
33. 21, his *f.* is consumed away.
Ps. 16. 9; Acts 2. 26, my *f.* shall rest in hope.
65. 2, to thee shall all *f.* come.
78. 20, can he provide *f.*?
Prov. 5. 11, mourn, when *f.* consumed.
11. 17, the cruel troubleth his own *f.*
23. 20, among riotous eaters of *f.*
Eccl. 4. 5, the fool eateth his own *f.*
12. 12, weariness of the *f.*
Isa. 40. 5, all *f.* shall see it.
6; 1 Pet. 1. 24, all *f.* is grass.
Ezek. 11. 19; 36. 26, a heart of *f.*
Joel 2. 28; Acts 2. 17, pour Spirit on all *f.*
Mat. 16. 17, *f.* and blood hath not revealed it.
24. 22; Mk. 13. 20, there should no *f.* be saved.
26. 41; Mk. 14. 38, spirit willing, *f.* weak.
Lu. 24. 39, spirit hath not *f.* and bones.
John 1. 14, Word made *f.*, and dwelt.
6. 51, 54, 55, bread I give is my *f.*
52, can this man give us his *f.*?

John 6. 63, the *f.* profiteth nothing.
8. 15, ye judge after the *f.*
17. 2, power over all *f.*
Rom. 6. 19, because of the infirmity of your *f.*
8. 3, condemned sin in the *f.*
8, they that are in *f.* cannot please God.
9, not in the *f.,* but the Spirit.
12, 13, to live after the *f.*
9. 3, kinsmen according to the *f.*
5, of whom as concerning the *f.*
13. 14, make not provision for the *f.*
1 Cor. 1. 29, that no *f.* should glory.
15. 39, all *f.* not the same *f.*
50, *f.* and blood cannot inherit.
2 Cor. 12. 7, a thorn in the *f.*
Gal. 1. 16, I conferred not with *f.* and blood.
2. 20, life I now live in the *f.*
5. 17, *f.* lusteth against the Spirit.
Eph. 2. 3, lusts of *f.,* desires of *f.*
Phil. 3. 3, 4, no confidence in the *f.*
1 Tim. 3. 16, manifest in the *f.*
1 Pet. 3. 18, Christ put to death in *f.*
1 John 4. 2 ; 2 John 7, denieth that Christ is come in *f.*
Jude 8, dreamers defile the *f.*
23, hating garment spotted by *f.*
See John 1. 13 ; 3. 6 ; Gal. 5. 19 ; Heb. **2. 14.**
FLESHLY. 2 Cor. 1. 12 ; 3. 3 ; Col. 2. 18 ; 1 Pet. 2. 11.
FLIES. Ex. 8. 21, 31, I will send swarms of *f.* upon thee.
Ps. 78. 45, he sent divers sorts of *f.* among them.
105. 31, he spake, and there came divers sorts of *f.*
FLIGHT. Isa. 52. 12 ; Amos 2. 14 ; Mat. 24. 20 ; Heb. 11. 34.
FLINT. Num. 20. 11 ; Deut. 8. 15 ; 32. 13 ; Ps. 114. 8 ; Isa. 5. 28 ; 50. 7 ; Ezek. 3. 9 ; 1 Cor. 10. 4.
FLOCK. Jer. 13. 20, where is the *f.,* thy beautiful *f.*?
Ezek. 34. 31, the *f.* of my pasture are men.
Zech. 11. 7, the poor of the *f.*
Lu. 12. 32, fear not, little *f.*
Acts 20. 28, take heed to the *f.*
29, not sparing the *f.*
1 Pet. 5. 2, feed the *f.* of God.
3, being ensamples to the *f.*
See Ezek. 36. 37 ; Mal. 1. 14 ; Mat. 26. 31.
FLOOD. Josh. 24. 2, on other side of the *f.*
Job 28. 11, he bindeth *f.* from overflowing.
Ps. 32. 6, in *f.* of great waters.
Cant. 8. 7, neither can *f.* drown love.
Isa. 44. 3, *f.* upon the dry ground.
59. 19, enemy come in like a *f.*
Mat. 7. 25, the *f.* came, and the winds blew.
24. 38, in days before the *f.*
39 ; Lu. 17. 27, knew not till *f.* came.
See Gen. 6. 17 ; 7. 11 ; 8 ; 9. 11 ; Ps. 90. 5 ; 2 Pet. 2. 5 ; Rev. 12. 15.
FLOOR. 1 Sam. 23. 1, they rob the threshing-*f.*
2 Sam. 24. 21, to buy the threshing-*f.* of thee.
Hos. 9. 1, loved a reward on every corn-*f.*
Mic. 4. 12, gather as sheaves into the *f.*
Mat. 3. 12 ; Lu. 3. 17, purge his *f.*
See Deut. 15. 14 ; Dan. 2. 35 ; Joel 2. 24.
FLOUR. Ex. 29. 2, of wheaten *f.* shalt thou make them.
Lev. 2. 2, take thereout his handful of the *f.*
FLOURISH. Ps. 72. 7, in his days shall the righteous *f.*
90. 6, in the morning it *f.*
92. 12, righteous shall *f.* like a palm tree.
103. 15, as flower so he *f.*
Prov. 11. 28, righteous shall *f.* as branch.
14. 11, tabernacle of upright *f.*
Eccl. 12. 5, when the almond tree shall *f.*
Cant. 6. 11 ; 7. 12, whether the vine *f.*
Ezek. 17. 24, have made dry tree to *f.*
Phil. 4. 10, your care of me hath *f.*
See Ps. 92. 14 ; Dan. 4. 4.
FLOW. Ps. 147. 18, wind to blow, and waters *f.*

Cant. 4. 16, that the spices may *f.* out.
Isa. 2. 2, all nations shall *f.* unto it.
64. 1, 3, mountains *f.* at thy presence.
Jer. 31. 12, shall *f.* to the goodness of the Lord.
John 7. 38, shall *f.* living water.
See Job 20. 28 ; Isa. 60. 5 ; Joel 3. 18 ; Mic. 4. 1.
FLOWER. 1 Sam. 2. 33, shall die in *f.* of age.
Job 14. 2, cometh forth as a *f.*
Cant. 2. 12, the *f.* appear on earth.
Isa. 28. 1, 4, glorious beauty is a fading *f.*
40. 6, as the *f.* of the field.
7 ; Nah. 1. 4 ; Jas. 1. 10 ; 1 Pet. 1. 24, *f.* fadeth.
See Job 15. 33 ; Isa. 18. 5 ; 1 Cor. 7. 36.
FLY. Job 5. 7, as sparks *f.* upward.
Ps. 55. 6, then would I *f.* away.
90. 10, and we *f.* away.
Prov. 23. 5, riches *f.* away.
Isa. 60. 8, that *f.* as a cloud.
See Dan. 9. 21 ; Rev. 14. 6 ; 19. 17.
FOAM. Hos. 10. 7 ; Mk. 9. 18 ; Lu. 9. 39 ; Jude 13.
FOES. Ps. 27. 2 ; 30. 1 ; 89. 23 ; Mat. 10. 36 ; Acts 2. 35.
FOLD. Prov. 6. 10 ; 24. 33, *f.* of the hands to sleep.
Eccl. 4. 5, fool *f.* his hands and eateth.
Hab. 3. 17, flock cut off from the *f.*
John 10. 16, one *f.,* and one shepherd.
See Isa. 13. 20 ; 65. 10 ; Nah. 1. 10.
FOLK. Prov. 30. 26 ; Jer. 51. 58 ; Mk. 6. 5 ; John 5. 3.
FOLLOW. Num. 14. 24, Caleb hath *f.* me fully.
1 Kings 18. 21, God, *f.* him.
Ps. 23. 6, goodness and mercy shall *f.* me.
63. 8, my soul *f.* hard after thee.
68. 25, the players *f.* after.
Prov. 12. 11 ; 28. 19, that *f.* vain persons.
Isa. 5. 11, that they may *f.* strong drink.
Hos. 6. 3, if we *f.* on to know the Lord.
Amos 7. 15, took me as I *f.* the flock.
Mat. 4. 19 ; 8. 22 ; 9. 9 ; 16. 24 ; 19. 21 ; Mk. 2. 14 ; 8. 34 ; 10. 21 ; Lu. 5. 27 ; 9. 23, 59 ; John 1. 43 ; 21. 22, Jesus said, *f.* me.
8. 19 ; Lu. 9. 57. 61, Master, I will *f.* thee.
Mk. 10. 28 ; Lu. 18. 28, we left all, and *f.* thee.
32, as they *f.,* they were afraid.
Lu. 22. 54, Peter *f.* afar off.
John 10. 27, my sheep hear my voice, and *f.* me.
13. 36, thou canst not *f.* me now.
Rom. 14. 19, *f.* things that make for peace.
1 Cor. 10. 4, the rock that *f.* them.
14. 1, *f.* after charity.
Phil. 3. 12, I *f.* after.
1 Thess. 5. 15, ever *f.* that which is good.
1 Tim. 5. 24, some men they *f.* after.
6. 11 ; 2 Tim. 2. 22, *f.* righteousness.
Heb. 12. 14, *f.* peace with all men.
13. 7, whose faith *f.*
1 Pet. 1. 11, the glory that should *f.*
2. 21, that ye should *f.* his steps.
2 Pet. 2. 15, *f.* the way of Balaam.
Rev. 14. 4, they that *f.* the Lamb.
13, their works do *f.* them.
See Mk. 9. 38 ; 1 Pet. 3. 13 ; 2 Pet. 1. 16 ; Rev. 6. 8.
FOLLOWER. Eph. 5. 1, *f.* of God, as dear children.
Heb. 6. 12, *f.* of them who through faith.
FOLLY. 1 Sam. 25. 25, and *f.* is with him.
Job 4. 18, his angels he charged with *f.*
24. 12, yet God layeth not *f.* to them.
42. 8, lest I deal with you after your *f.*
Ps. 49. 13, this their way is their *f.*
85. 8, let them not turn again to *f.*
Prov. 13. 16, a fool layeth open his *f.*
14. 8, the *f.* of fools is deceit.
18, the simple inherit *f.*
16. 22, instruction of fools is *f.*
17. 12, rather than a fool in his *f.*
26. 4, answer not a fool according to his *f.*
5, answer fool according to his *f.*
Eccl. 1. 17, to know wisdom and *f.*
2. 13, wisdom excelleth *f.*

Eccl. 7. 25, the wickedness of *f.*
10. 6, *f.* is set in great dignity.
2 Cor. 11. 1, bear with me a little in my *f.*
2 Tim. 3. 9, their *f.* shall be manifest.
See Josh. 7. 15; Prov. 14. 24; Isa. 9. 17.

FOOD. Gen. 3. 6, tree good for *f.*
Ex. 21. 10, her *f.* shall not be diminished.
Deut. 10. 18, in giving him *f.* and raiment.
Job 23. 12, more than my necessary *f.*
24. 5, wilderness yieldeth *f.*
Ps. 78. 25, did eat angels' *f.*
104. 14, bring forth *f.* out of the earth.
136. 25, giveth *f.* to all flesh.
Prov. 6. 8, gathereth her *f.* in harvest.
13. 23, much *f.* in tillage of poor.
30. 8, with *f.* convenient for me.
31. 14, she bringeth her *f.* from afar.
2 Cor. 9. 10, minister bread for your *f.*
1 Tim. 6. 8, having *f.* and raiment.
Jas. 2. 15, destitute of daily *f.*
See Gen. 1. 29; 2. 9; 6. 21; 9. 3; 41. 35; Lev. 22. 7;
Ps. 145. 16; 147. 9.

FOOL. 2 Sam. 3. 33, died Abner as a *f.* dieth?
Ps. 14. 1; 53. 1, *f.* said in his heart.
75. 4, to *f.*, deal not foolishly.
Prov. 1. 7, *f.* despise wisdom.
3. 35, shame the promotion of *f.*
10. 8, 10, a prating *f.* shall fall.
21, *f.* die for want of wisdom.
23, sport to a *f.* to do mischief.
11. 29, the *f.* shall be servant to the wise.
12. 15, way of *f.* right in own eyes.
16, *f.* wrath presently known.
13. 16, *f.* layeth open his folly.
20, companion of *f.* shall be destroyed.
14. 8, folly of *f.* is deceit.
9, *f.* make a mock at sin.
16, the *f.* rageth, and is confident.
15. 2, mouth of *f.* poureth out foolishness.
5, a *f.* despiseth his father's instruction.
16. 22, the instruction of *f.* is folly.
17. 28, a *f.*, when he holdeth his peace, counted wise.
20. 3, every *f.* will be meddling.
29. 11, a *f.* uttereth all his mind.
Eccl. 2. 14, *f.* walketh in darkness.
16, how dieth wise man? as the *f.*
19, who knoweth whether wise or a *f.?*
5. 3, a *f.* voice is known by multitude of words.
10. 14, a *f.* is full of words.
Isa. 35. 8, wayfaring men, though *f.*
Jer. 17. 11, at his end he shall be a *f.*
Hos. 9. 7, the prophet is a *f.*
Mat. 5. 22, shall say, thou *f.*
23. 17, ye *f.* and blind.
Lu. 12. 20, thou *f.*, this night.
24. 25, O *f.*, and slow of heart.
1 Cor. 3. 18, let him become a *f.*
2 Cor. 11. 16, let no man think me a *f.*
12. 11, I am a *f.* in glorying.
Eph. 5. 15, walk not as *f.*, but as wise.
See Prov. 10. 18; 19. 1; 28. 26; Eccl. 10. 3.

FOOLISH. Deut. 32. 6, O *f.* people.
2 Sa. 24. 10; 1 Chr. 21. 8, I have done very *foolishly.*
Job 2. 10, as one of the *f.* women.
Ps. 73. 3, I was envious at the *f.*
Prov. 9. 6, forsake the *f.*, and live.
13, a *f.* woman is clamorous.
14. 1, the *f.* plucketh it down.
17. 25; 19. 13, a *f.* son is grief.
Eccl. 7. 17, neither be thou *f.*
Jer. 4. 22, my people are *f.*
Mat. 7. 26, unto a *f.* man.
Rom. 1. 21, their *f.* heart was darkened.
1 Cor. 1. 20, hath not God made *f.*
Gal. 3. 1, O *f.* Galatians.
3. 3, are ye so *f.?*
Eph. 5. 4, nor *f.* talking.
1 Tim. 6. 9, rich fall into *f.* lusts.
2 Tim. 2. 23; Tit. 3. 9, *f.* questions avoid.

Tit. 3. 3, we were sometimes *f.*
1 Pet. 2. 15, ignorance of *f.* men.
See Job 5. 3; Lam. 2. 14; Ezek. 13. 3.

FOOLISHNESS. Ps. 69. 5, thou knowest my *f.*
Prov. 22. 15, *f.* is bound in heart of child.
24. 9, thought of *f.* is sin.
1 Cor. 1. 18, to them that perish *f.*
21, by the *f.* of preaching.
23, Christ crucified, to Greeks *f.*
25, the *f.* of God is wiser than men.
2. 14, things of Spirit are *f.* to him.
3. 19, wisdom of world *f.* with God.
See 2 Sam. 15. 31; Prov. 27. 22.

FOOT. Gen. 41. 44, without thee no man lift *f.*
Deut. 2. 5, not so much as *f.* breadth.
11. 10, wateredst it with thy *f.*
Ps. 38. 16, when my *f.* slippeth.
91. 12; Mat. 4. 6; Lu. 4. 11, dash *f.* against stone.
94. 18, my *f.* slippeth, thy mercy.
121. 3, not suffer *f.* to be moved.
Prov. 3. 23, thy *f.* shall not stumble.
25. 17, withdraw *f.* from neighbour's house.
Eccl. 5. 1, keep thy *f.* when thou goest.
Isa. 1. 6, from sole of *f.* to head no soundness.
Mat. 14. 13, people followed on *f.*
18. 8; Mk. 9. 45, if thy *f.* offend thee.
1 Cor. 12. 15, if the *f.* say, because I am not.
Heb. 10. 29, trodden under *f.* the Son of God.
See Jer. 12. 5; Mat. 5. 35; Jas. 2. 3.

FORBADE. Mat. 3. 14; Mk. 9. 38; Lu. 9. 49.

FORBEAR. Ex. 23. 5, wouldest *f.* to help.
2 Chron. 35. 21, *f.* from meddling with God.
Neh. 9. 30, many years didst thou *f.* them.
Ezek. 2. 5; 3. 11, whether hear or *f.*
1 Cor. 9. 6, power to *f.* working.
Eph. 4. 2; Col. 3. 13, *f.* one another in love.
6. 9, *f.* threatening.
See Prov. 24. 11; Ezek. 3. 27; Zech. 11. 12.

FORBID. Num. 11. 28, Joshua said, *f.* them.
Mk. 9. 39; Lu. 9. 50, *f.* him not.
10. 14; Lu. 18. 16, children, *f.* them not.
Lu. 6. 29, *f.* not to take coat.
23. 2, *f.* to give tribute.
Acts 10. 47, can any *f.* water?
1 Cor. 14. 39, *f.* not to speak with tongues.
1 Tim. 4. 3, *f.* to marry.
See Acts 16. 6; 28. 31; 1 Thess. 2. 16.

FORCE. Deut. 34. 7, nor natural *f.* abated.
Ezra 4. 23, made them cease by *f.*
Mat. 11. 12, violent take it by *f.*
John 6. 15, perceived they would take him by *f.*
Heb. 9. 17, a testament is of *f.* after.
See Deut. 20. 19; Prov. 30. 33; Amos 2. 14.

FORCIBLE. Job 6. 25.

FOREFATHERS. Jer. 11. 10; 2 Tim. 1. 3.

FOREHEAD. Ex. 28. 38, it shall always be on his *f.*
1 Sam. 17. 49, smote Philistine in his *f.*
Ezek. 3. 8, made thy *f.* strong.
9. 4, set a mark on *f.* of them that sigh.
Rev. 7. 3; 9. 4, sealed in their *f.*
22. 4, his name shall be in their *f.*
See Rev. 13. 16; 14. 1; 17. 5; 20. 4.

FOREIGNER. Ex. 12. 45; Deut. 15. 3; Eph. 2. 19.

FOREKNOW. Rom. 8. 29; 11. 2; 1 Pet. 1. 2.

FOREKNOWLEDGE. Acts 2. 23, delivered by *f.* of God.

FOREMOST. Gen. 32. 17; 33. 2; 2 Sam. 18. 27.

FOREORDAINED. 1 Pet. 1. 20.

FORERUNNER. Heb. 6. 20.

FORESEE. Prov. 22. 3; 27. 12; Gal. 3. 8.

FOREST. Ps. 50. 10, every beast of *f.* is mine.
Isa. 29. 17; 32. 15, field esteemed as *f.*
Jer. 5. 6, lion out of *f.* shall slay them.
26. 18; Mic. 3. 12, high places of the *f.*
46. 23, they shall cut down her *f.*
Amos 3. 4, will lion roar in the *f.?*
See Ezek. 15. 6; 20. 46; Hos. 2. 12.

FORETELL. Mk. 13. 23; Acts 3. 24; 2 Cor. 13. 2.

FOREWARN. Lu. 12. 5; 1 Thess. 4. 6.

FORGAT. Judg. 3. 7, they *f.* the Lord.
Ps. 78. 11, they *f.* his works.
106. 13, soon *f.* his works.
Lam. 3. 17, I *f.* prosperity.
See Gen. 40. 23; Hos. 2. 13.

FORGAVE. Mat. 18. 27, 32, and *f.* him the debt.
Lu. 7. 42, he frankly *f.* them both.
43, he to whom he *f.* most.
2 Cor. 2. 10, if I *f.* any thing.
Col. 3. 13, even as Christ *f.* you.
See Ps. 32. 5; 78. 38; 99. 8.

FORGE. Job 13. 4; Ps. 119. 69.

FORGET. Deut. 4. 9, lest thou *f.* things thine eyes
have seen.
23, lest ye *f.* the covenant.
6. 12; 8. 11. beware lest thou *f.* the Lord.
Job 8. 13, so are the paths of all that *f.* God.
Ps. 9. 17, all nations that *f.* God.
10. 12, *f.* not the humble.
45. 10, *f.* thine own people.
50. 22, consider, ye that *f.* God.
78. 7, that they might not *f.* works of God.
88. 12, in the land of *f.*
102. 4, I *f.* to eat my bread.
103. 2, *f.* not all his benefits.
119. 16, I will not *f.* thy word.
137. 5, if I *f.* thee, O Jerusalem.
Prov. 2. 17, *f.* the covenant of her God.
3. 1, *f.* not my law.
31. 5, lest they drink and *f.*
7, let him drink, and *f.* his poverty.
Isa. 49. 15, can a woman *f.?*
.51. 13, and *f.* the Lord thy Maker.
65. 11, *f.* my holy mountain.
Jer. 2. 32, maid *f.* her ornaments.
23. 27, cause my people to *f.* my name.
Amos 8. 7, I will never *f.* their works.
Phil. 3. 13, *f.* those things which are behind.
Heb. 6. 10, not unrighteous to *f.*
13. 2, not *f.* to entertain.
16, to communicate *f.* not.
Jas. 1. 24, *f.* what manner of man.
See Gen. 41. 51; Lam. 5. 20; Hos. 4. 6.

FORGIVE. Ex. 32. 32, if thou wilt *f.* their sin.
34. 7; Num. 14. 18, *f.* iniquity, transgression.
1 Kings 8. 30, 39 ; 2 Chron. 6. 21, 30, hearest, *f.*
2 Chron. 7. 14, then will I hear and *f.*
Ps. 32. 1 ; Rom. 4. 7, whose transgression is *f.*
86. 5, good, and ready to *f.*
103. 3, who *f.* all thine iniquities.
Mat. 6. 12; Lu. 11. 4, *f.* us, as we *f.*
14, if ye *f.*
15, if ye *f.* not.
9. 6; Mk. 2. 10; Lu. 5. 24, power to *f.* sin.
18. 21, how oft, and I *f.* him?
35, if ye from your hearts *f.*
Mk. 2. 7, who can *f.* sins?
11. 25, *f.* that your Father may *f.*
26, not *f.*, Father will not *f.*
Lu. 6. 37, *f.*, and ye shall be *f.*
7. 47, her sins, which are many, are *f.*
49, who is this *f.* sins also?
17. 3, 4, if brother repent, *f.* him.
23. 34, Father *f.* them, they know not.
Acts 8. 22, thought of thine heart may be *f.*
2 Cor. 2. 7, ye ought rather to *f.*
10, to whom ye *f.* I *f.* also.
12. 13, *f.* me this wrong.
Eph. 4. 32, as God for Christ's sake hath *f.*
Col. 2. 13, quickened, having *f.*
1 John 1. 9, faithful and just to *f.*
See Mat. 9. 2; 12. 31; Mk. 3. 28; Lu. 12. 10.

FORGIVENESS. Ps. 130. 4, *f.* with thee, that
thou mayest be feared.
Mk. 3. 29, hath never *f.*
Acts 5. 31, exalted to give *f.*
Eph. 1. 7; Col. 1. 14, in whom we have *f.*
See Dan. 9. 9; Acts 13. 38; 26. 18.

FORGOTTEN. Deut. 24. 19, and hast *f.* a sheaf.
32. 18, *f.* God that formed thee.
Ps. 9. 18, needy not always *f.*
10. 11, said, God hath *f.*
31. 12, *f.* as a dead man.
42. 9, why hast thou *f.* me?
44. 20, if we have *f.* name of our God.
77. 9, hath God *f.* to be gracious?
Eccl. 2. 16, in days to come all *f.*
8. 10, wicked were *f.* in city.
9. 5, the memory of them is *f.*
Isa. 17. 10, *f.* the God of thy salvation.
44. 21, thou shalt not be *f.* of me.
49. 14, my Lord hath *f.* me.
65. 16, former troubles are *f.*
Jer. 2. 32 ; 13. 25 ; 18. 15, my people have *f.*
3. 21, *f.* the Lord their God.
44. 9, *f.* the wickedness of your fathers.
50. 6, *f.* their restingplace.
Ezek. 22. 12; 23. 35, thou hast *f.* me.
Mat. 16. 5 ; Mk. 8. 14, *f.* to take bread.
Lu. 12. 6, not one *f.* before God.
2 Pet. 1. 9, *f.* that he was purged.
See Lam. 2. 6; Hos. 4. 6; 8. 14 ; 13. 6.

FORM (*n.*). Gen. 1. 2; Jer. 4. 23, without *f.*, and
void.
Job 4. 16, could not discern the *f.*
Isa. 52. 14, *f.* more than sons of men.
Ezek. 10. 8, the *f.* of a man's hand.
Dan. 3. 19, *f.* of visage changed.
25, *f.* of fourth like Son of God.
Mk. 16. 12, appeared in another *f.*
Rom. 2. 20, hast *f.* of knowledge and truth.
Phil. 2. 6, being in the *f.* of God.
7, the *f.* of a servant.
2 Tim. 1. 13, *f.* of sound words.
3. 5, having *f.* of godliness.
See 1 Sam. 28. 14; Ezek. 43. 11 ; Rom. 6. 17.

FORM (*v.*). Deut. 32. 18, forgotten God that *f.* thee.
2 Kings 19. 25 ; Isa. 37. 26, that I have *f.* it.
Job 26. 5, dead things are *f.*
13, hath *f.* crooked serpent.
33. 6, I also am *f.* of clay.
Ps. 90. 2, or ever thou hadst *f.*
94. 9, he that *f.* the eye.
Prov. 26. 10, great God that *f.* all things.
Isa. 43. 1, he that *f.* thee, O Israel.
7 ; 44. 21, I have *f.* him.
10, before me was no God *f.*
21, people have I *f.* for myself.
44. 10, who hath *f.* a god?
54. 17, no weapon *f.* against thee.
Amos 7. 1, he *f.* grasshoppers.
Rom. 9. 20, shall thing *f.* say.
Gal. 4. 19, till Christ be *f.* in you.
See Gen. 2. 7, 19; Ps. 95. 5; Jer. 1. 5.

FORMER. Ruth 4. 7, manner in *f.* time.
Job 8. 8, enquire of the *f.* age.
Ps. 89. 49, where are thy *f.* lovingkindnesses?
Eccl. 1. 11, no remembrance of *f.* things.
7. 10, *f.* days better than these.
Isa. 43. 18, remember not the *f.* things.
46. 9, remember the *f.* things of old.
48. 3, declared *f.* things from beginning.
65. 7, measure their *f.* work.
16, *f.* troubles are forgotten.
Jer. 5. 24; Hos. 6. 3; Joel 2. 23, *f.* and latter rain.
10. 16; 51. 19, the *f.* of all things.
Hag. 2. 9, glory of *f.* house.
Zech. 1. 4; 7. 7, 12, *f.* prophets have cried.
8. 11, I will not be as in *f.* days.
14. 8, half of them toward *f.* sea.
Mal. 3. 4, pleasant as in *f.* years.
Eph. 4. 22, concerning the *f.* conversation.
Rev. 21. 4, for the *f.* things are passed away.
See Gen. 40. 13; Dan. 11. 13; Acts 1. 1.

FORSAKE. Deut. 4. 31; 31. 6; 1 Chron. 28. 20, he
will not *f.*
12. 19, *f.* not the Levite.
32. 15, he *f.* God which made him.

Josh. 1. 5; Heb. 13. 5, I will not fail nor *f.*
Judg. 9. 11, *f.* my sweetness and fruit.
1 Chron. 28. 9, if thou *f.* him, he will cast thee off.
2 Chron. 15. 2, if ye *f.* him, he will *f.* you.
Neh. 10. 39, we will not *f.* house of our God.
13. 11, why is house of God *f.?*
Job 6. 14, he *f.* the fear of the Almighty.
20. 19, oppressed and *f.* the poor.
Ps. 22. 1; Mat. 27. 46; Mk. 15. 34, why hast thou *f.* me?
37. 25, yet have I not seen the righteous *f.*
28, the Lord *f.* not his saints.
119. 8, *f.* me not utterly.
138. 8, *f.* not work of thine own hands.
Prov. 1. 8; 6. 20, *f.* not law of thy mother.
2. 17, *f.* the guide of her youth.
4. 6, *f.* her not, and she shall preserve thee.
27. 10, thy friend, and father's friend, *f.* not.
Isa. 6. 12, a great *f.* in the land.
17. 9, as a *f.* bough.
32. 14; Jer. 4. 29; Ezek. 36. 4, a *f.* city.
54. 6, as a woman *f.*
7, for a small moment *f.*
62. 4, no more be termed *f.*
12, a city not *f.*
Jer. 2. 13; 17. 13, *f.* fountain of living waters.
Mat. 19. 27; Lu. 5. 11, we have *f.* all.
29, that hath *f.* houses.
26. 56; Mk. 14. 50, disciples *f.* him, and fled.
Mk. 1. 18, they *f.* their nets.
Lu. 14. 33, whosoever *f.* not all.
2 Cor. 4. 9, persecuted, but not *f.*
2 Tim. 4. 10, Demas hath *f.* me.
16, all men *f.* me.
Heb. 10. 25, not *f.* assembling of ourselves.
11. 27, by faith Moses *f.* Egypt.
See Ps. 71. 11; Isa. 49. 14; Jer. 5. 7; 22. 9; Ezek. 8. 12.

FORSWEAR. Mat. 5. 33.

FORTRESS. 2 Sam. 22. 2; Ps. 18. 2; Jer. 16. 19, Lord is my *f.*
FORTY STRIPES. Deut. 25. 3, *f. s.* he may give him.
2 Cor. 11. 24, of the Jews five times received I *f. s.* save one.
FORTY YEARS. Ex. 16. 35, Israel did eat manna *f. y.*
Num. 14. 33, your children shall wander in the wilderness *f. y.*
Ps. 95. 10, *f. y.* long was I grieved.
See Judg. 3. 11; 5. 31; 8. 28.

FORWARD. Jer. 7. 24, backward, and not *f.*
Zech. 1. 15, helped *f.* the affliction.
See 2 Cor. 8. 8; 9. 2; 3 John 6.

FOUL. Job 16. 16; Mat. 16. 3; Mk. 9. 25; Rev. 18. 2.

FOUND. Gen. 27. 20, *f.* it so quickly.
37. 32, this have we *f.*
44. 16, hath *f.* out iniquity.
1 Kings 20. 36, a lion *f.* him.
21. 20, hast thou *f.* me?
2 Kings 22. 8, I *f.* book of the law.
2 Chron. 19. 3, good things *f.* in thee.
Job 28. 12, 13, where shall wisdom be *f.?*
33. 24, I have *f.* a ransom.
Ps. 32. 6, when thou mayest be *f.*
36. 2, iniquity *f.* to be hateful.
84. 3, sparrow hath *f.* an house.
Prov. 25. 16, hast thou *f.* honey?
Eccl. 7. 28, one among a thousand have I *f.*
29, this only have I *f.*
Cant. 3. 4, but I *f.* him whom my soul loveth.
Isa. 65. 1; Rom. 10. 20, *f.* of them that sought me not.
Jer. 2. 26, thief ashamed when he is *f.*
34, in thy skirts is *f.*
41. 8, ten men were *f.*
Ezek. 22. 30, I sought for a man, but *f.* none.
Dan. 5. 27, weighed, and *f.* wanting.
Mal. 2. 6, iniquity not *f.* in his lips.
Mat. 7. 25; Lu. 6. 48, it was *f.* on a rock.

Mat. 8. 10; Lu. 7. 9, have not *f.* so great faith.
13. 46, *f.* one pearl of great price.
20. 6, *f.* others standing idle.
21. 19; Mk. 14. 40; Lu. 22. 45, *f.* nothing thereon.
Mk. 7. 2, they *f.* fault.
30, she *f.* the devil gone out.
Lu. 2. 46, they *f.* him in the temple.
8. 35, they *f.* the man clothed.
15. 5, 6, *f.* the sheep.
9, *f.* the piece of money.
24, 32, was lost, and is *f.*
23. 14, I have *f.* no fault.
24. 2, *f.* the stone rolled away.
3, 23, *f.* not the body.
John 1. 41, 45, we have *f.* the Messias.
Acts 7. 11, our fathers *f.* no sustenance.
9. 2, if he *f.* any of this way.
17. 23, I *f.* an altar.
Rom. 7. 10, I *f.* to be unto death.
Gal. 2. 17, we ourselves also are *f.* sinners.
Phil. 2. 8, *f.* in fashion as a man.
Heb. 11. 5, Enoch was not *f.*
12. 17, he *f.* no place of repentance.
Rev. 3. 2, not *f.* thy works perfect.
12. 8, nor was their place *f.* any more.
16. 20, mountains were not *f.*
See Gen. 6. 8; 2 Chron. 15. 4; 2 Cor. 5. 3; Phil. 3. 9.

FOUNDATION. Josh. 6. 26; 1 Kings 16. 34, lay the *f.* in his firstborn.
Job 4. 19, them whose *f.* is in dust.
Ps. 11. 3, if *f.* be destroyed.
82. 5, all the *f.* of earth out of course.
102. 25, of old laid *f.* of earth.
137. 7, rase it even to the *f.*
Prov. 10. 25, righteous an everlasting *f.*
Isa. 28. 16, I lay in Zion a *f.*
58. 12, the *f.* of many generations.
Lu. 6. 48, laid the *f.* on a rock.
49, without a *f.*
Rom. 15. 20, on another man's *f.*
1 Cor. 3. 10, I laid the *f.*
11, other *f.* can no man lay.
12, if any man build on this *f.*
Eph. 2. 20, on the *f.* of the apostles and prophets.
1 Tim. 6. 19, laying up for themselves a good *f.*
2 Tim. 2. 19, the *f.* of God standeth sure.
Heb. 6. 1, not laying the *f.* of repentance.
11. 10, a city that hath *f.*
Rev. 21. 14, the wall had twelve *f.*
See Mat. 13. 35; John 17. 24; Acts 16. 26.

FOUNTAIN. Gen. 7. 11; 8. 2, *f.* of great deep.
Deut. 8. 7, a land of *f.*
2 Chron. 32. 3, took counsel to stop *f.* of water.
Ps. 36. 9, the *f.* of life.
Prov. 5. 16, let thy *f.* be dispersed.
8. 24, no *f.* abounding with water.
13. 14, law of the wise a *f.* of life.
14. 27, fear of the Lord a *f.* of life.
25. 26, a troubled *f.* and corrupt spring.
Eccl. 12. 6, pitcher broken at the *f.*
Cant. 4. 12, a *f.* sealed.
15, a *f.* of gardens.
Jer. 2. 13; 17. 13, forsaken *f.* of living waters.
9. 1, eyes a *f.* of tears.
Hos. 13. 15, his *f.* shall be dried up.
Zech. 13. 1, in that day shall be a *f.* opened.
Jas. 3. 11, 12, doth a *f.* send forth.
Rev. 7. 17, lead them to living *f.*
14. 7, worship him that made *f.* of waters.
21. 6, of the *f.* of life freely.
See Isa. 12. 3; 44. 3; 55. 1; Jer. 6. 7; Joel 3. 18; Mk. 5. 29; John 4. 10.

FOWLS. Gen. 1. 20, and *f.* that may fly above the earth.
7. 3, of *f.* also of the air by sevens.
Ps. 104. 12, the *f.* of heaven have their habitation.
148. 10, creeping things, and flying *f.*

FOXES. Cant. 2. 15, take us the *f.*, the little *f.*
Lam. 5. 18, the *f.* walk upon it.

Mat. 8. 20, the *f.* have holes.
Lu. 13. 32, go ye, and tell that *f.*
See Judg. 15. 4.

FRAGMENTS. John 6. 12, 13, gather up *f.* that remain.
See Mat. 14. 20; Mk. 6. 43; 8. 19; Lu. 9. 17.

FRAIL. Ps. 39. 4.

FRAME. Judg. 12. 6, he could not *f.* to pronounce.
Ps. 94. 20, *f.* mischief by a law.
103. 14, he knoweth our *f.*
Isa. 29. 16, shall thing *f.* say of him that *f.* it?
Eph. 2. 21, building fitly *f.* together.
See Ezek. 40. 2; Hos. 5. 4; Heb. 11. 3.

FRANKLY. Lu. 7. 42.

FRAUD. Ps. 10. 7; Jas. 5. 4.

FRAY. Deut. 28. 26; Jer. 7. 33; Zech. 1. 21.

FREE. Gen. 2. 16, of every tree thou mayest *f.* eat.
Deut. 24. 5, shall be *f.* at home one year.
Josh. 9. 23, there shall none of you be *f.*
1 Sam. 14. 30, if people had eaten *f.*
2 Chron. 29. 31, of *f.* heart offered.
Ezra 2. 68, chief fathers offered *f.*
7. 15, king and counsellors offered *f.* to God.
Ps. 51. 12, with thy *f.* spirit.
88. 5, *f.* among the dead.
Isa. 58. 6, let the oppressed go *f.*
Hos. 14. 4, I will love them *f.*
Mat. 10. 8, *f.* ye have received, *f.* give.
17. 26, then are the children *f.*
Mk. 7. 11, if a man say Corban, he shall be *f.*
John 8. 32, the truth shall make you *f.*
33, how sayest thou, ye shall be *f.?*
36, Son make you *f.*, ye shall be *f.* indeed.
Acts 22. 28, I was *f.* born.
Rom. 3. 24, justified *f.* by his grace.
5. 15, the *f.* gift.
6. 18, 22, being made *f.* from sin.
20, servants of sin, *f.* from righteousness.
8. 2, *f.* from the law of sin and death.
32, with him *f.* give us all things.
1 Cor. 9. 1, am I not *f.?*
19, though *f.* from all men.
12. 13; Eph. 6. 8, whether bond or *f.*
Gal. 3. 28; Col. 3. 11, there is neither bond nor *f.*
5. 1, wherewith Christ hath made us *f.*
2 Thess. 3. 1, word have *f.* course.
1 Pet. 2. 16, as *f.*, and not using liberty.
Rev. 21. 6, give of fountain of life *f.*
22. 17, let him take water of life *f.*
See Ex. 21. 2; Deut. 15. 13; Jer. 34. 9; Gal. 4. 22.

FREEWILL. Lev. 22. 18, and for all his *f.* offerings.
Num. 15. 3, or in a *f.* offering.
Deut. 16. 10, a tribute of a *f.* offering.
See Ezra 3. 5.

FREEWOMAN. Gal. 4. 22.

FRESH. Num. 11. 8; Job 29. 20; 33. 25; Jas. 3. 12.

FRET. Ps. 37. 1, 7, 8; Prov. 24. 19, *f.* not thyself.
Prov. 19. 3, his heart *f.* against the Lord.
See 1 Sam. 1. 6; Isa. 8. 21; Ezek. 16. 43.

FRIEND. Ex. 33. 11, as a man to his *f.*
2 Sam. 19. 6, lovest thine enemies, and hatest *f.*
2 Chron. 20. 7, Abraham thy *f.* for ever.
Job 6. 27, ye dig a pit for your *f.*
42. 10, when he prayed for his *f.*
Ps. 35. 14, as though he had been my *f.*
41. 9, my familiar *f.* hath lifted.
88. 18, lover and *f.* hast thou put far from me.
Prov. 6. 1, if thou be surety for thy *f.*
3, make sure thy *f.*
14. 20, the rich hath many *f.*
16. 28; 17. 9, whisperer separateth chief *f.*
17. 17, *f.* loveth at all times.
18. 24, a *f.* that sticketh closer than a brother.
19. 4, wealth maketh many *f.*
27. 6, faithful are wounds of a *f.*
10, thine own *f.* and father's *f.* forsake not.
17, man sharpeneth countenance of his *f.*

Cant. 5. 16, this is my *f.*
Isa. 41. 8, seed of Abraham my *f.*
Jer. 20. 4, a terror to thy *f.*
Mic. 7. 5, trust not in a *f.*
Zech. 13. 6, wounded in house of my *f.*
Mat. 11. 19; Lu. 7. 34, a *f.* of publicans.
20. 13, *f.*, I do thee no wrong.
22. 12, *f.*, how camest thou hither?
26. 50, *f.*, wherefore art thou come?
Mk. 5. 19, go home to thy *f.*
Lu. 11. 5, which of you shall have a *f.*
8, though he give not because he is his *f.*
14. 12, call not thy *f.*
15. 6, 9, calleth his *f.* and neighbours.
16. 9, *f.* of the mammon.
John 11. 11, our *f.* Lazarus sleepeth.
15. 13, lay down his life for his *f.*
14, ye are my *f.*, if ye do whatsoever I command.
15, not servants, but *f.*
19. 12, thou art not Cæsar's *f.*
Jas. 2. 23, Abraham was called the *f.* of God.
4. 4, a *f.* of the world.
See Prov. 22. 24; Lu. 14. 10; 3 John 14.

FRINGES. Num. 15. 37, that they make them *f.*
Deut. 22. 12, thou shalt make thee *f.*
See Mat. 23. 5.

FROWARD. Deut. 32. 20, a very *f.* generation.
Prov. 2. 12, man that speaketh *f.* things.
3. 32, the *f.* is abomination.
4. 24, put away *f.* mouth.
11. 20; 17. 20, of a *f.* heart.
16. 28, a *f.* man soweth strife.
21. 8, the way of man is *f.*
22. 5, snares are in way of the *f.*
See Prov. 10. 32; Isa. 57. 17; 1 Pet. 2. 18.

FRUIT. Num. 13. 26, showed them the *f.* of the land.
Deut. 26. 2, take the first of all *f.*
33. 14, precious *f.* brought forth.
Ps. 107. 37, yield *f.* of increase.
127. 3, the *f.* of the womb is his reward.
Prov. 8. 19, my *f.* is better than gold.
11. 30, *f.* of the righteous a tree of life.
12. 14; 18. 20, satisfied by the *f.* of his mouth.
Cant. 2. 3, his *f.* was sweet to my taste.
4. 13, 16, orchard with pleasant *f.*
Isa. 3. 10; Mic. 7. 13, the *f.* of their doings.
27. 6, fill face of the world with *f.*
28. 4, the hasty *f.* before summer.
57. 19, I create the *f.* of the lips.
Jer. 17. 10; 21. 14; 32. 19, according to *f.* of doings.
Hos. 10. 13, eaten the *f.* of lies.
Amos 8. 1, basket of summer *f.*
Mic. 6. 7, *f.* of body for sin of soul.
Hab. 3. 17, neither shall *f.* be in vines.
Hag. 1. 10, earth is stayed from her *f.*
Mat. 3. 8; Lu. 3. 8, *f.* meet for repentance.
7. 16, 20, by their *f.* ye shall know them.
12. 33, make tree good, and his *f.* good.
13. 23, is he who beareth *f.*
21. 19, let no *f.* grow on thee.
34, when time of *f.* drew near.
26. 29; Mk. 14. 25, drink of *f.* of vine.
Mk. 4. 28, earth bringeth forth *f.* of herself.
12. 2, receive the *f.* of the vineyard.
Lu. 13. 6, he sought *f.* thereon.
7, I come seeking *f.* on this fig tree.
9, if it bear *f.*, well.
John 4. 36, *f.* to life eternal.
15. 2, branch that beareth *f.*
4, branch cannot bear *f.* of itself.
8, that ye bear much *f.*
16, ordained that ye should bring forth *f.*
Rom. 1. 13, have some *f.* among you.
6. 21, what *f.* had ye then.
7. 4, bring forth *f.* unto God.
2 Cor. 9. 10; Phil. 1. 11, the *f.* of righteousness.
Gal. 5. 22; Eph. 5. 9, the *f.* of the Spirit.
Phil. 1. 22, this is the *f.* of my labour.
4. 17, I desire *f.* that may abound.

Col. 1. 6, the gospel bringeth forth *f.* in you.
2 Tim. 2. 6, first partaker of the *f.*
Heb. 12. 11, peaceable *f.* of righteousness.
13. 15, the *f.* of our lips.
Jas. 3. 17, wisdom full of good *f.*
5. 7, waiteth for the precious *f.*
Jude 12, trees whose *f.* withereth, without *f.*
Rev. 22. 2, yielded her *f.* every month.
See Gen. 30. 2; Ps. 92. 14; Jer. 12. 2; Col. 1. 10.

FROGS. Ex. 8. 6; Ps. 78. 45; 105. 30; Rev. 16. 3.

FRONTLETS. Ex. 13. 16; Deut. 6. 8, for *f.* between thine eyes.

FRUSTRATE. Ezra 4. 5; Isa. 44. 25; Gal. 2. 21.

FUEL. Isa. 9. 5; Ezek. 15. 4; 21. 32.

FULFIL. Ps. 20. 4, the Lord *f.* all thy counsel.
5, *f.* all thy petitions.
145. 19, he will *f.* the desire of them.
Mat. 3. 15, to *f.* all righteousness.
5. 17, not to destroy, but to *f.*
18; 24. 34, till all be *f.*
Mk. 13. 4, what the sign when these shall be *f.*?
Lu. 1. 20, my words shall be *f.* in season.
21. 24, times of the Gentiles be *f.*
22. 16, till it be *f.* in kingdom of God.
John 3. 29; 17. 13, this my joy is *f.*
Acts 13. 25, and as John *f.* his course.
33, God hath *f.* the same unto us.
Rom. 13. 10, love is the *f.* of the law.
Gal. 5. 14, all the law is *f.* in one word.
6. 2, so *f.* the law of Christ.
Eph. 2. 3, *f.* the desires of the flesh.
Phil. 2. 2, *f.* ye my joy.
Col. 4. 17, take heed thou *f.* the ministry.
2 Thess. 1. 11, *f.* good pleasure of his will.
Jas. 2. 8, if ye *f.* the royal law.
See Ex. 5. 13; 23. 26; Gal. 5. 16; Rev. 17. 17.

FULL. Lev. 19. 29, land became *f.* of wickedness.
Deut. 6. 11, houses *f.* of good things.
34. 9, Joshua was *f.* of spirit of wisdom.
Ruth 1. 21, I went out *f.*
2 Kings 6. 17, mountain was *f.* of horses.
1 Chron. 21. 22, 24, for the *f.* price.
Job 5. 26, come to grave in *f.* age.
11. 2, a man *f.* of talk.
14. 1, *f.* of trouble.
20. 11, *f.* of the sins of youth.
21. 23, dieth in his *f.* strength.
32. 18, I am *f.* of matter.
Ps. 10. 7; Rom. 3. 14, mouth *f.* of cursing.
65. 9, which is *f.* of water.
74. 20, *f.* of habitations of cruelty.
88. 3, soul *f.* of troubles.
119. 64, earth is *f.* of thy mercy.
127. 5, happy the man that hath his quiver *f.*
Prov. 27. 7, the *f.* soul loatheth an honeycomb.
20, hell and destruction are never *f.*
30. 9, lest I be *f.*, and deny thee.
Eccl. 1. 7, yet the sea is not *f.*
Hab. 3. 3, earth *f.* of his praise.
Zech. 8. 5, streets *f.* of boys and girls.
Mat. 6. 22; Lu. 11. 36, *f.* of light.
Lu. 6. 25, woe unto you that are *f.*!
11. 39, *f.* of ravening.
John 1. 14, *f.* of grace and truth.
15. 11; 16. 24, that your joy may be *f.*
Acts 6. 3; 7. 55; 11. 24, men *f.* of the Holy Ghost.
9. 36, *f.* of good works.
Rom. 15. 14, ye also are *f.* of goodness.
1 Cor. 4. 8, now ye are *f.*
Phil. 4. 12, I am instructed to be *f.*
18, I am *f.*
2 Tim. 4. 5, make *f.* proof of thy ministry.
Heb. 5. 14, meat to them of *f.* age.
1 Pet. 1. 8, with joy unspeakable and *f.* of glory.
Rev. 15. 7, *f.* of the wrath of God.
See Lev. 2. 14; 2 Kings 4. 6; 10. 21; Amos 2. 13.

FULLY. Num. 14. 24, Caleb hath followed me *f.*
Eccl. 8. 11, heart is *f.* set to do evil.
Rom. 14. 5, let every man be *f.* persuaded.

Rom. 15. 19, I have *f.* preached the gospel.
Rev. 14. 18, her grapes are *f.* ripe.
See 1 Kings 11. 6; Acts 2. 1; Rom. 4. 21.

FULNESS. Ps. 16. 11, *f.* of joy.
John 1. 16, of his *f.* have we received.
Rom. 11. 25, the *f.* of the Gentiles.
Eph. 1. 23, the *f.* of him that filleth all in all.
3. 19, filled with the *f.* of God.
4. 13, the stature of the *f.* of Christ.
Col. 1. 19, in him should all *f.* dwell.
2. 9, the *f.* of the Godhead bodily.
See Num. 18. 27; Ps. 96. 11; Rom. 11. 12.

FURNACE. Deut. 4. 20, Lord hath taken you out of *f.*
Ps. 12. 6, as silver tried in a *f.*
Isa. 48. 10, in the *f.* of affliction.
Mat. 13. 42, into a *f.* of fire.
See Gen. 15. 17; 19. 28; 1 Kings 8. 51; Dan. 3. 6, 11, 15, etc.; Ezek. 22. 18.

FURNISH. Ps. 78. 19; Mat. 22. 10; 2 Tim. 3. 17.

FURROWS. Ps. 65. 10; 129. 3; Hos. 10. 4; 12. 11.

FURTHER. Ezra 8. 36, they *f.* the people.
Job 38. 11, hitherto shalt thou come, but no *f.*
Lu. 24. 28, as though he would have gone *f.*
Acts 4. 17, that it spread no *f.*
2 Tim. 3. 9, they shall proceed no *f.*
See Mk. 5. 35; Phil. 1. 12, 25.

FURIOUS. Prov. 22. 24, with a *f.* man thou shalt not go.
29. 22, a *f.* man aboundeth in transgression.
Nah. 1. 2, the Lord is *f.*
See 2 Kings 9. 20; Ezek. 5. 15; 23. 25.

FURY. Gen. 27. 44, till thy brother's *f.* turn.
Isa. 27. 4, *f.* is not in me.
63. 5, my *f.* upheld me.
Jer. 21. 5, I will fight against thee in *f.*
25. 15, the wine cup of this *f.*
Ezek. 21. 17, I will cause my *f.* to rest.
See Dan. 3. 13, 19; 8. 6; 9. 16; 11. 44.

G.

GAIN. Job 22. 3, is it *g.* to him that thou makest thy ways perfect?
Prov. 1. 19; 15. 27; Ezek. 22. 12, greedy of *g.*
3. 14, the *g.* thereof better than gold.
28. 8, by usury and unjust *g.*
Ezek. 22. 13, 27, at thy dishonest *g.*
Dan. 11. 39, he shall divide the land for *g.*
Mic. 4. 13, consecrate their *g.* to the Lord.
Mat. 16. 26; Mk. 8. 36; Lu. 9. 25, if he *g.* the world.
18. 15, thou hast *g.* thy brother.
25. 17, 22, had also *g.* other two.
Lu. 19. 15, 16, 18, had *g.* by trading.
Acts 16. 19, hope of their *g.* was gone.
19. 24, no small *g.* to the craftsmen.
1 Cor. 9. 19, that I might *g.* the more.
20, that I might *g.* the Jews.
2 Cor. 12. 17, 18, did I make a *g.* of you?
Phil. 1. 21, to die is *g.*
3. 7, *g.* to me, I counted loss.
1 Tim. 6. 5, supposing that *g.* is godliness.
6, godliness with contentment is great *g.*
See Judg. 5. 19; Job 27. 8; Jas. 4. 13.

GAINSAY. Lu. 21. 15; Tit. 1. 9; Jude 11.

GALL. Ps. 69. 21; Lam. 3. 19; Mat. 27. 34; Acts 8. 23.

GALLOWS. Esth. 7. 10, they hanged Haman on the *g.*

GAP. Ezek. 13. 5; 22. 30.

GARDEN. Gen. 2. 8, God planted a *g.* eastward in Eden.
13. 10, as the *g.* of the Lord.
Deut. 11. 10; 1 Kings 21. 2, as a *g.* of herbs.
Cant. 4. 12, a *g.* enclosed.
16, blow upon my *g.*
5. 1, I am come into my *g.*
6. 2, 11, gone down into his *g.*

Isa. 1. 8, as a lodge in a *g.*
30, as a *g.* that hath no water.
51. 3, her desert like the *g.* of the Lord.
58. 11 ; Jer. 31. 12, like a watered *g.*
61. 11, as the *g.* causeth things sown to spring
  forth.
Jer. 29. 5, plant *g.,* and eat the fruit.
Ezek. 28. 13, in Eden the *g.* of God.
31. 8, 9, cedars in *g.* of God.
36. 35, is become like the *g.* of Eden.
Joel 2. 3, land as the *g.* of Eden before them.
John 18. 1, where was a *g.*
26, did not I see thee in the *g.?*
19. 41, there was a *g.,* and in the *g.*
See Gen. 2. 15; Amos 4. 9; 9. 14 ; John 20. 15.
GARMENT. Gen. 39. 12, he left his *g.,* and fled.
49. 11, washed his *g.* in wine.
Josh. 7. 21, a goodly Babylonish *g.*
9. 5, Gibeonites took old *g.*
2 Kings 5. 26, is it a time to receive *g.?*
7. 15, all the way was full of *g.*
Job 37. 17, how thy *g.* are warm.
Ps. 22. 18, they part my *g.* among them.
102. 26 ; Isa. 50. 9 ; 51. 6 ; Heb. 1. 11, wax old
  as a *g.*
104. 2, with light as with a *g.*
6, coveredst it with the deep as with a *g.*
109. 18, clothed himself with cursing as with his *g.*
Prov. 20. 16, take his *g.* that is surety.
25. 20, a *g.* in cold weather.
30. 4, who hath bound the waters in a *g.?*
Eccl. 9. 8, let thy *g.* be always white.
Isa. 52. 1, put on thy beautiful *g.*
61. 3, *g.* of praise for spirit of heaviness.
10, the *g.* of salvation.
Joel 2. 13, rend your heart and not your *g.*
Zech. 13. 4, a rough *g.* to deceive.
Mat. 9. 16; Mk. 2. 21; Lu. 5. 36, new cloth, old *g.*
20. 14, 36 ; Mk. 5. 27 ; Lu. 8. 44, hem of *g.*
21. 8; Mk. 11. 8, spread *g.* in way.
22. 11, 12, wedding *g.*
23. 5, enlarge borders of *g.*
27. 35 ; Mk. 15. 24, parted *g.,* casting lots.
Mk. 11. 7 ; Lu. 19, 35, cast *g.* on colt.
13. 16, not turn back again to take *g.*
Lu. 22. 36, let him sell his *g.*
24. 4, in shining *g.*
Acts 9. 39, showing the coats and *g.*
Jas. 5. 2, your *g.* are motheaten.
Jude 23. the *g.* spotted by the flesh.
Rev. 3. 4, not defiled their *g.*
16. 15, that watcheth, and keepeth his *g.*
GARNER. Ps. 144. 13; Joel 1. 17 ; Mat. 3. 12.
GARNISH. Job 26. 13 ; Mat. 12. 44 ; 23. 29.
GATE. Gen. 28. 17, the *g.* of heaven.
Deut. 6. 9 ; 11. 20, write them on thy *g.*
Ps. 9. 13, the *g.* of death.
118. 19, the *g.* of righteousness.
Prov. 17. 19, exalteth *g.* seeketh destruction.
31. 23, her husband known in the *g.*
Isa. 26. 2, open the *g.,* that righteous may enter.
38. 10, the *g.* of the grave.
45. 1, open the two-leaved *g.*
60. 11, thy *g.* shall be open continually.
18, walls Salvation, and *g.* Praise.
Mat. 7. 13 ; Lu. 13. 24, strait *g.,* wide *g.*
16. 18, *g.* of hell shall not prevail.
Heb. 13. 12, also suffered without the *g.*
Rev. 21. 25, *g.* not shut at all by day.
See Ps. 24. 7 ; Isa. 28. 6 ; Nah. 2. 6.
GATHER. Gen. 41. 35, let them *g.* all the food.
49. 10, to him shall *g.* of the people be.
Ex. 16. 17, *g.,* some more, some less.
Deut. 28. 38, carry much out, and *g.* little in.
30. 3; Ezek. 36. 24, will *g.* thee from all nations.
2 Sam. 14. 14, spilt, which cannot be *g.* up.
Job 11. 10, if he *g.* together, who can hinder?
Ps. 26. 9, *g.* not my soul with sinners.
39. 6, knoweth not who shall *g.* them.
Prov. 6. 8, the ant *g.* her food.
10. 5, he that *g.* in summer.

Prov. 13. 11, he that *g.* by labour shall increase.
Isa. 27. 12, ye shall be *g.* one by one.
40. 11, he shall *g.* the lambs.
56. 8, yet will I *g.* others.
62. 10, *g.* out the stones.
Mat. 3. 12 ; Lu. 3. 17, *g.* wheat into garner.
6. 26, nor *g.* into barns.
7. 16 ; Lu. 6. 44, do men *g.* grapes of thorns ?
12. 30 ; Lu. 11. 23, he that *g.* not scattereth.
13. 28, wilt thou that we *g.* them up ?
29, lest while ye *g.* up the tares.
41, shall *g.* out of his kingdom.
25. 32, before him shall be *g.* all nations.
John 6. 12, *g.* up fragments.
15. 6, men *g.* them, and cast.
1 Cor. 16. 2, that there be no *g.* when I come.
2 Thess. 2. 1, by our *g.* together unto him.
See Mat. 23. 37 ; John 4. 36 ; 11. 52.
GAVE. Gen. 3. 12, the woman *g.* me.
Josh. 21. 44 ; 2 Chron. 15. 15 ; 20. 30, Lord *g.* them
  rest.
1 Sam. 10. 9, *g.* to Saul another heart.
Neh. 8. 8, they read, and *g.* the sense.
Job 1. 21, the Lord *g.*
Ps. 21. 4, he asked life, and thou *g.* it.
68. 11, the Lord *g.* the word.
Eccl. 12. 7, to God who *g.* it.
Amos 2. 12, ye *g.* the Nazarites wine.
Mat. 21. 23; Mk. 11. 28; Lu. 20. 2, who *g.* thee
  this authority ?
25. 35, 42, ye *g.* me meat.
Lu. 15. 16, no man *g.* unto him.
John 10. 29, my Father, who *g.* them.
Acts 2. 4, as the Spirit *g.* them utterance.
26. 10, I *g.* my voice against them.
Rom. 1. 28, God *g.* them over.
1 Cor. 3. 6, God *g.* the increase.
Eph. 4. 8, *g.* gifts unto men.
11, he *g.* some apostles.
See 2 Cor. 8. 5 ; Gal. 1. 4 ; Tit. 2. 14.
GAY. Jas. 2. 3.
GAZE. Ex. 19. 21; Nah. 3. 6; Acts 1. 11; Heb. 10. 33.
GENERATION. Deut. 1. 35, not one of this evil *g.*
32. 5, 20, a perverse and crooked *g.*
Ps. 14. 5, God is in the *g.* of the righteous.
22. 30, it shall be accounted for a *g.*
102. 18, written for the *g.* to come.
145. 4, one *g.* shall praise thy works.
Prov. 27. 24, crown endure to every *g.*
30. 11, there is a *g.* that curseth.
Eccl. 1. 4, one *g.* passeth away.
Isa. 34. 10, from *g.* to *g.* it shall lie waste.
Joel 1. 3, children tell another *g.*
Mat. 3. 7 ; 12. 34 ; 23. 33 ; Lu. 3. 7, *g.* of vipers.
12. 41, in judgment with this *g.*
17. 17 ; Mk. 9. 19 ; Lu. 9. 41, perverse *g.*
23. 36, shall come on this *g.*
24. 34 ; Mk. 13. 30 ; Lu. 21. 32, this *g.* shall not pass.
Lu. 16. 8, are in their *g.* wiser.
17. 25, rejected of this *g.*
1 Pet. 2. 9, a chosen *g.*
See Isa. 53. 8 ; Dan. 4. 3 ; Mat. 1. 1 ; Lu. 11. 30.
GENTILES. Mat. 10. 5, go not in way of the *G.*
John 7. 35, to the dispersed among *G.*
Acts 9. 15, bear my name before the *G.*
13. 42, *G.* besought that these words.
46, we turn to the *G.*
15. 3, declaring conversion of the *G.*
18. 6, from henceforth I will go to the *G.*
Rom. 3. 29, is he not also of the *G.?*
11. 11, salvation is come to the *G.*
13, as the apostle of the *G.*
1 Cor. 5. 1, not so much as named among *G.*
Eph. 4. 17, walk not as other *G.*
2 Tim. 1. 11, I am ordained a teacher of *G.*
3 John 7, taking nothing of the *G.*
See Rom. 2. 9 ; 1 Pet. 2. 12 ; Rev. 11. 2.
GENTLE. 1 Thess. 2. 7, we were *g.* among you.
2 Tim. 2. 24, servant of Lord be *g.*
Tit. 3. 2, *g.,* showing all meekness.

Jas. 3. 17, wisdom is pure and *g.*
1 Pet. 2. 18, not only to the good and *g.*
See 2 Sam. 18. 5 ; 22. 36 ; Gal. 5. 22.

GETTETH. Prov. 3. 13 ; 4. 7 ; 19. 8 ; Jer. 17. 11.

GIFT. Ex. 23. 8 ; Deut. 16. 19, a *g.* blindeth.
2 Sam. 19. 42, hath he given us any *g.*?
2 Chron. 19. 7, with the Lord no taking of *g.*
Ps. 68. 18 ; Eph. 4. 8, *g.* unto men.
72. 10, kings of Sheba and Seba offer *g.*
Prov. 6. 35, not content, though many *g.*
15. 27, he that hateth *g.* shall live.
17. 8, a *g.* is as a precious stone.
18. 16, man's *g.* maketh room for him.
21. 14, a *g.* in secret pacifieth anger.
Eccl. 3. 13 ; 5. 19, enjoy good, it is God's *g.*
7. 7, a *g.* destroyeth the heart.
Is. 1. 23, every one loveth *g.*
Mat. 5. 23, bring thy *g.* to the altar.
24, leave thy *g.* before the altar.
7. 11 ; Lu. 11. 13, know how to give good *g.*
Lu. 21. 1, casting *g.* into treasury.
John 4. 10, if thou knewest the *g.* of God.
Acts 8. 20, thought the *g.* of God may be purchased.
Rom. 1. 11, some spiritual *g.*
5. 15, free *g.,* a *g.* by grace.
6. 23, the *g.* of God is eternal life.
11. 29, *g.* of God without repentance.
12. 6, *g.* differing according to grace.
1 Cor. 7. 7, his proper *g.* of God.
12. 4, diversities of *g.*
31, covet best *g.*
14. 1, 12, desire spiritual *g.*
2 Cor. 9. 15, unspeakable *g.*
Eph. 2. 8, faith the *g.* of God.
Phil. 4. 17, not because I desire a *g.*
1 Tim. 4. 14, neglect not the *g.*
2 Tim. 1. 6, stir up the *g.*
Jas. 1. 17, good and perfect *g.*
See Num. 18. 29 ; Mat. 15. 5 ; Acts 2. 38 ; 10. 45 ;
1 Cor. 13. 2.

GIRD. 2 Sam. 22. 40 ; Ps. 18. 39, hast *g.* me with
strength.
Isa. 45. 5, I *g.* thee, though thou hast not.
Joel 1. 13, *g.* yourselves, and lament.
Eph. 6. 14, having your loins *g.*
See Prov. 31. 17 ; John 13. 4 ; 21. 18 ; Rev. 15. 6.

GIRDLE. Ex. 28. 4, and a *g.*
Jer. 13. 1, go and get thee a linen *g.*
See Isa. 11. 5 ; Mat. 3. 4 ; Mk. 1. 6.

GIRL. Joel 3. 3 ; Zech. 8. 5.

GIVE. Gen. 28. 22, I will *g.* the tenth.
Ex. 30. 15, rich shall not *g.* more, poor not *g.* less.
Deut. 15. 10, thou shalt *g.* him thine heart.
16. 17 ; Ezek. 46. 5, *g.* as he is able.
1 Chron. 29. 14, of thine own have we *g.* thee.
Ezra 9. 9, to *g.* us a reviving.
Ps. 2. 8, I shall *g.* thee the heathen.
6. 5, in the grave who shall *g.* thanks?
29. 11, Lord will *g.* strength.
37. 4, *g.* thee the desires of thy heart.
21, the righteous showeth mercy, and *g.*
84. 11, Lord will *g.* grace and glory.
109. 4, I *g.* myself unto prayer.
Prov. 23. 26, *g.* me thine heart.
Isa. 55. 10, *g.* seed to the sower.
Mat. 5. 42, *g.* to him that asketh.
6. 11 ; Lu. 11. 3, *g.* daily bread.
7. 9, will he *g.* him a stone?
10. 8, freely *g.*
13. 11 ; Mk. 4. 11, it is *g.* to you to know.
16. 26 ; Mk. 8. 37, *g.* in exchange.
19. 21 ; Mk. 10. 21, go sell, and *g.* to the poor.
20. 23 ; Mk. 10. 40, not mine to *g.*
26. 9 ; Mk. 14. 5, sold, and *g.* to the poor.
Lu. 6. 38, *g.,* and it shall be *g.*
John 4. 7, 10, *g.* me to drink.
6. 37, all that the Father *g.* me.
65, no man can come, except it were *g.* him.
10. 28, I *g.* to them eternal life.

John 13. 29, that he should *g.* something to poor.
14. 27, not as the world *g., g.* I.
Acts 3. 6, such as I have *g.* I thee.
6. 4, we will *g.* ourselves to prayer.
20. 35, more blessed to *g.*
Rom. 12. 8, he that *g.,* let him do it.
19, rather *g.* place unto wrath.
1 Cor. 3. 7, God *g.* the increase.
2 Cor. 9. 7, *g.* not grudgingly, a cheerful *g.*
Phil. 4. 15, concerning *g.* and receiving.
1 Tim. 4. 13, *g.* attendance to reading.
15, *g.* thyself wholly to them.
6. 17, who *g.* us richly.
Jas. 1. 5, that *g.* to all men liberally.
4. 6, *g.* more grace, *g.* grace to humble.
2 Pet. 1. 5, *g.* all diligence.
See Mk. 12. 15 ; Lu. 12. 48 ; John 3. 34.

GLAD. Ex. 4. 14, he will be *g.* in heart.
Job 3. 22, *g.* when they can find the grave.
Ps. 16. 9, therefore my heart is *g.*
34. 2 ; 69. 32, humble shall hear, and be *g.*
46. 4, make *g.* the city of God.
104. 15, maketh *g.* the heart of man.
122. 1, I was *g.* when they said.
126. 3, whereof we are *g.*
Prov. 10. 1 ; 15. 20, wise son maketh a *g.* father.
24. 17, let not thine heart be *g.*
Lam. 1. 21, they are *g.* that thou hast done it.
Lu. 15. 32, make merry, and be *g.*
John 8. 56, saw my day, and was *g.*
11. 15, I am *g.* for your sakes.
Acts 11. 23, when he had seen grace of God, was *g.*
See Mk. 6. 20 ; 12. 37 ; Lu. 1. 19 ; 8. 1.

GLADNESS. Num. 10. 10, in day of your *g.*
Deut. 28. 47, servedst not with *g.* of heart.
Neh. 8. 17, there was very great *g.*
Ps. 4. 7, thou hast put *g.* in my heart.
45. 7 ; Heb. 1. 9, the oil of *g.*
97. 11, *g.* is sown for the upright.
Isa. 35. 10 ; 51. 11, they shall obtain joy, and *g.*
Acts 2. 46, did eat with *g.* of heart.
12. 14, opened not for *g.*
14. 17, filling our hearts with food and *g.*
See Ps. 100. 2 ; Prov. 10. 28 ; Isa. 51. 3.

GLASS. 1 Cor. 13. 12, we see through a *g.* darkly.
2 Cor. 3. 18, beholding as in a *g.* the glory of the
Lord.
Rev. 4. 6 ; 15. 2, a sea of *g.,* like unto crystal.

GLEAN. Lev. 19. 10 ; Jer. 6. 9 ; 49. 9.

GLISTERING. 1 Chron. 29. 2 ; Lu. 9. 29.

GLITTERING. Deut. 32. 41 ; Job 20. 25 ; 39. 23 ;
Nah. 3. 3.

GLOOMINESS. Joel 2. 2 ; Zeph. 1. 15.

GLORIFY. Lev. 10. 3, before all people I will be *g.*
Ps. 50. 23, whoso offereth praise *g.* me.
86. 9, all nations shall *g.* thy name.
12, I will *g.* thy name for evermore.
Isa. 24. 15, *g.* the Lord in the fires.
60. 7, I will *g.* house of my glory.
Ezek. 28. 22, I will be *g.* in midst of thee.
Dan. 5. 23, God hast thou not *g.*
Mat. 5. 16, *g.* your Father in heaven.
15. 31, they *g.* God of Israel.
Lu. 4. 15, being *g.* of all.
John 7. 39, because Jesus was not yet *g.*
11. 4, that the Son of God might be *g.*
12. 16, but when Jesus was *g.,* they remembered
28, Father, *g.* thy name : I have both *g.*
13. 32, God shall also *g.* him.
15. 8, herein is my Father *g.*
17. 1, *g.* thy Son.
4, I have *g.* thee on earth.
21. 19, by what death he should *g.* God.
Rom. 1. 21, they *g.* him not as God.
8. 17, suffer with him, that we may be *g.*
30, them he also *g.*
1 Cor. 6. 20, *g.* God in body and spirit.
Gal. 1. 24, they *g.* God in me.
2 Thess. 1. 10, to be *g.* in his saints.

Heb. 5. 5, so Christ *g.* not himself.
See Isa. 25. 5 ; Mat. 9. 8 ; 15. 31 ; Lu. 7. 16.
GLORIOUS. Ex. 15. 11, *g.* in holiness.
Deut. 28. 58 ; 1 Chron. 29. 13, this *g.* name.
Ps. 45. 13, all *g.* within.
66. 2, make his praise *g.*
72. 19, blessed be his *g.* name.
87. 3, *g.* things are spoken.
Isa. 11. 10, his rest shall be *g.*
28. 1, whose *g.* beauty is a fading flower.
60. 13, place of my feet *g.*
63. 1, *g.* in his apparel.
14, to make thyself a *g.* name.
Jer. 17. 12, a *g.* high throne.
Dan. 11. 16, 41, stand in the *g.* land.
45, in the *g.* holy mountain.
Lu. 13. 17, rejoiced for *g.* things done.
Rom. 8. 21, *g.* liberty of children of God.
2 Cor. 3. 7, 8, ministration *g.*
4. 4, light of *g.* gospel.
Eph. 5. 27, a *g.* church.
Phil. 3. 21, like to his *g.* body.
1 Tim. 1. 11, the *g.* gospel of the blessed God.
Tit. 2. 13, the *g.* appearing of the great God.
See Ex. 15. 1 ; 2 Sam. 6. 20 ; Isa. 24. 23.
GLORY. Ex. 33. 18, show me thy *g.*
Num. 14. 21 ; Ps. 72. 19 ; Isa. 6. 3, earth filled with *g.*
Ps. 8. 1, thy *g.* above the heavens.
16. 9, my *g.* rejoiceth.
24. 7, 10, the King of *g.*
73. 24, afterward receive me to *g.*
84. 11, will give grace and *g.*
108. 1, will give praise with my *g.*
145. 11, the *g.* of thy kingdom.
Prov. 3. 35, the wise shall inherit *g.*
17. 6, the *g.* of children are their fathers.
20. 29, the *g.* of young men is their strength.
25. 2, *g.* of God to conceal.
27, for men to search their own *g.* is not *g.*
Isa. 10. 3, where will ye leave your *g.*?
24. 16, even *g.* to the righteous.
42. 8, my *g.* will I not give to another.
43. 7, have created him for my *g.*
60. 7, will glorify house of my *g.*
Jer. 2. 11, my people have changed their *g.*
Ezek. 20. 6, 15, the *g.* of all lands.
31. 18, to whom art thou thus like in *g.*?
Dan. 2. 37 ; 7. 14, God hath given power and *g.*
Hos. 4. 7, change *g.* into shame.
Hag. 2. 7, I will fill this house with *g.*
Mat. 6. 2, that ye may have *g.* of men.
29 ; Lu. 12. 27, Solomon in all his *g.*
16. 27 ; Mk. 8. 38, in *g.* of his Father.
19. 28 ; Lu. 9. 26, Son of man sit in his *g.*
24. 30 ; Mk. 13. 26 ; Lu. 21. 27, power and great *g.*
Lu. 2. 14 ; 19. 38, *g.* to God in the highest.
9. 31, appeared in *g.*, and spake of his decease.
32, they saw his *g.*
24. 26, to enter into his *g.*
John 1. 14, we beheld his *g.*
2. 11, thus did Jesus, and manifested his *g.*
8. 50, I seek not mine own *g.*
17. 5, the *g.* I had with thee.
24, that they may behold my *g.*
Acts 12. 23, he gave not God the *g.*
Rom. 3. 23, come short of *g.* of God.
8. 18, not worthy to be compared with *g.*
11. 36 ; Gal. 1. 5 ; 2 Tim. 4. 18 ; Heb. 13. 21 ; 1 Pet.
5. 11, to whom be *g.*
1 Cor. 2. 8, crucified the Lord of *g.*
10. 31, do all to *g.* of God.
11. 7, woman is the *g.* of the man.
15, long hair, it is a *g.* to her.
15. 40, *g.* of celestial, *g.* of terrestrial.
43, raised in *g.*
2 Cor. 3. 18, beholding as in a glass the *g.*
4. 17, eternal weight of *g.*
Eph. 1. 17, the Father of *g.*
3. 21, to him be *g.* in the church.
Phil. 3. 19, whose *g.* is in their shame.
4. 19, according to his riches in *g.*

Col. 1. 27, Christ in you, the hope of *g.*
3. 4, appear with him in *g.*
2 Thess. 1. 9, the *g.* of his power.
1 Tim. 3. 16, received up into *g.*
Heb. 1. 3, the brightness of his *g.*
2. 10, in bringing many sons to *g.*
3. 3, this man was counted worthy of more *g.*
1 Pet. 1. 8, joy unspeakable and full of *g.*
11, the *g.* that should follow.
24, the *g.* of man as flower of grass.
4. 14, the spirit of *g.* and of God.
5. 10, called to eternal *g.*
2 Pet. 1. 17, voice from the excellent *g.*
Rev. 4. 11 ; 5. 12, worthy to receive *g.*
7. 12, blessing, and *g.*, and wisdom.
18. 1, earth lightened with his *g.*
21. 23, *g.* of God did lighten it.
See Lu. 17. 18 ; 2 Cor. 3. 18 ; Jas. 2. 1 ; Jude 25.
GLORYING. 1 Cor. 5. 6 ; 9. 15 ; 2 Cor. 7. 4 ; 12. 11.
GNASH. Mat. 8. 12 ; 13. 42 ; 22. 13 ; 24. 51 ; 25. 30 ;
Lu. 13. 28, *g.* of teeth.
Mk. 9. 18, he foameth, and *g.* with his teeth.
See Job 16. 9 ; Ps. 35. 16 ; Acts 7. 54.
GNAT. Mat. 23. 24.
GO. Gen. 32. 26, let me *g.*, for the day breaketh.
Ex. 14. 15 ; Job 23. 8, *g.* forward.
23. 23 ; 32. 34, angel shall *g.* before thee.
33. 15, presence *g.* not with me.
Ruth 1. 16, whither thou *g.*, I will *g.*
Ps. 139. 7, whither shall I *g.*?
Prov. 22. 6, the way he should *g.*
30. 29, three things which *g.* well.
Mat. 5. 41 ; to *g.* a mile, *g.* twain.
21. 30, I *g.* sir, and went not.
Lu. 10. 37, *g.* and do likewise.
John 14. 12, I *g.* to the Father.
See Mat. 8. 9 ; Lu. 7. 8 ; 1 Cor. 9. 7 ; Rev. 14. 4.
GOATS. Job 39. 1, wild *g.* of the rock.
GOD. Gen. 5. 22 ; 6. 9, walked with *G.*
16. 13, thou *G.* seest me.
32. 28, hath power with *G.*
48. 21, I die, but *G.* shall be with you.
Num. 23. 19, *G.* is not a man, that he should lie.
23, what hath *G.* wrought?
Deut. 3. 24, what *G.* is there that can do.
33. 27, the eternal *G.* is thy refuge.
1 Sam. 17. 46, may know there is a *G.* in Israel.
1 Kings 18. 21, if the Lord be *G.*, follow him.
39, he is the *G.*, he is the *G.*
Job 22. 13 ; Ps. 73. 11, how doth *G.* know?
Ps. 14. 1 ; 53. 1, hath said, there is no *G.*
22. 1 ; Mat. 27. 46, my *G.*, my *G.*, why hast.
56. 9, this I know, for *G.* is for me.
86. 10 ; Isa. 37. 16, thou art *G.* alone.
Eccl. 5. 2, *G.* is in heaven.
Isa. 44. 8, is there a *G.* beside me?
45. 22 ; 46. 9, I am *G.*, there is none else.
Hos. 11. 9, I am *G.*, and not man.
Amos 5. 27, whose name is the *G.* of hosts.
Jonah 1. 6, arise, call upon thy *G.*
Mic. 6. 8, walk humbly with thy *G.*
Mat. 1. 23, *G.* with us.
22. 32, *G.* is not *G.* of dead.
Mk. 12. 32, one *G.*, and none other.
John 3. 33, that *G.* is true.
4. 24, *G.* is a spirit.
13. 3, come from *G.*, and went to *G.*
20. 17, ascend to my *G.* and your *G.*
Rom. 3. 4, let *G.* be true.
8. 31, if *G.* be for us.
1 Cor. 1. 9 ; 10. 13, *G.* is faithful.
14. 25, that *G.* is in you.
33, *G.* is not author of confusion.
Gal. 3. 20, but *G.* is one.
6. 7, *G.* is not mocked.
2 Thess. 2. 4, above all that is called *G.*
1 Tim. 3. 16, *G.* manifest in the flesh.
Heb. 8. 10, I will be to them a *G.*
11. 16, not ashamed to be called their *G.*

Heb. 12. 23, but ye are come to G.
1 John 1. 5, G. is light.
4. 8, 16, G. is love.
12, no man hath seen G.
5. 19, we know that we are of G.
Rev. 21. 3, G. himself shall be with them.
4, G. shall wipe away all tears.
7, I will be his G.
See Job 33. 12; 36. 5; Ps. 10. 4; 33. 12.

GOD (*an idol*). Gen. 31. 30, stolen my g.
Ex. 32. 1, make us g., which shall go before us.
4, these be thy g.
Judg. 5. 8, they chose new g.
6. 31, if he be a g., let him plead.
10. 14, go and cry to the g. ye have chosen.
17. 5, Micah had a house of g.
18. 24, ye have taken away my g.
2 Kings 17. 29, every nation made g.
33, they feared the Lord, and served own g.
Isa. 44. 15, maketh a g. and worshippeth it.
45. 20, pray to a g. that cannot save.
Jonah 1. 5, cried every man to his g.
Acts 12. 22, the voice of a g., not a man.
14. 11, the g. are come down.
1 Cor. 8. 5, there be g. many.
See Ex. 12. 12; 20. 23; Jer. 2. 11; Dan. 3. 28.

GODDESS. 1 Kings 11. 5; Acts 19. 27, 35, 37.

GODHEAD. Acts 17. 29; Rom. 1. 20; Col. 2. 9.

GODLINESS. 1 Tim. 3. 16, the mystery of g.
4. 7, exercise thyself to g.
8, g. is profitable.
6. 3, doctrine according to g.
5, supposing that gain is g.
2 Tim. 3. 5, a form of g.
Tit. 1. 1, the truth which is after g.
2 Pet. 1. 3, pertain to life and g.
6, and to patience g.
3. 11, in all holy conversation and g.
See 1 Tim. 2. 2, 10; 6. 6, 11.

GODLY. Ps. 12. 1, the g. man ceaseth.
Mal. 2. 15, seek a g. seed.
2 Cor. 1. 12, in g. sincerity.
7. 9, 10, g. sorrow worketh repentance.
2 Tim. 3. 12, all that will live g. in Christ.
Tit. 2. 12, live g. in this world.
Heb. 12. 28, reverence and g. fear.
2 Pet. 2. 9, how to deliver the g.
3 John 6, bring forward after a g. sort.
See Ps. 4. 3; 32. 6; 2 Cor. 7. 9; 11. 2.

GOD SAVE THE KING. 2 Sam. 16. 16, Hushai
said unto Absalom, G.

GOING. Josh. 23. 14, I am g. the way of all the
earth.
2 Sam. 5. 24; 1 Chron. 14. 15, sound of g. in trees.
Job 33. 24, 28, from g. down to pit.
Ps. 17. 5, hold up my g.
40. 2, established my g.
Prov. 5. 21, pondereth all his g.
20. 24, man's g. are of the Lord.
Dan. 6. 14, laboured till g. down of the sun.
Mic. 5. 2, whose g. forth have been from of old.
Mat. 26. 46, rise, let us be g.
Rom. 10. 3, g. about to establish.
1 Tim. 5. 24, g. before to judgment.
See Prov. 7. 27; 14. 15; Isa. 59. 8; Hos. 6. 3.

GOLD. Num. 31. 22, only g., etc., that may abide fire.
Deut. 8. 13, when thy g. is multiplied.
17. 17, nor shall he greatly multiply g.
1 Kings 20. 3, silver and g. is mine.
Job 22. 24, then shalt thou lay up g. as dust.
28. 1, a vein for silver, a place for g.
19, wisdom not valued with g.
31. 24, if I made g. my hope.
Ps. 19. 10, more to be desired than g.
21. 3, thou settest a crown of pure g. upon his
head.
Prov. 25. 11, like apples of g.
Isa. 46. 6, they lavish g. out of the bag.
60. 17, for brass I will bring g.

Hag. 2. 8, the silver is mine, and the g. is mine.
Zech. 4. 2, behold, a candlestick all of g.
13. 9, try them as g. is tried.
Mat. 10. 9, provide neither g. nor silver.
Acts 3. 6, silver and g. have I none.
17. 29, not think Godhead like to g.
20. 33, coveted no man's g.
2 Tim. 2. 20, in great house not only vessels of g.
Jas. 2. 2, man with a g. ring.
5. 3, your g. is cankered.
1 Pet. 1. 7, trial more precious than of g.
18, not redeemed with g.
Rev. 3. 18, buy of me g. tried in the fire.
21. 18, city was pure g.
See Gen. 2. 11; Eccl. 12. 6; Isa. 13. 12.

GONE. Deut. 23. 23, that which is g. out of thy
lips.
1 Kings 20. 40, busy here and there, he was g.
Ps. 42. 4, I had g. with the multitude.
73. 2, my feet were almost g.
77. 8, mercy clean g. for ever.
103. 16, wind passeth, and it is g.
109. 23, I am g. like the shadow.
119. 176; Isa. 53. 6, g. astray like sheep.
Eccl. 8. 10, come and g. from place of the holy.
Jer. 15. 9, sun g. down while yet day.
Mat. 12. 43; Lu. 11. 24, spirit g. out.
25. 8, lamps are g. out.
Mk. 5. 30; Lu. 8. 46, virtue had g. out of him.
John 12. 19, the world is g. after him.
Acts 16. 19, hope of their gains g.
Rom. 3. 12, they are all g. out of the way.
Jude 11, g. in the way of Cain.
See Ps. 89. 34; Cant. 2. 11; Isa. 45. 23.

GOOD (n.). Gen. 14. 21, take the g. to thyself.
24. 10, the g. of his master in his hand.
50. 20, God meant it unto g.
Neh. 5. 19; 13. 31, think upon me for g.
Job 2. 10, shall we receive g.
22. 21, thereby g. shall come.
Ps. 4. 6, who will show us any g.?
14. 1; 53. 1; Rom. 3. 12, none doeth g.
34. 12, loveth days that he may see g.
39. 2, held my peace even from g.
86. 17, a token for g.
Prov. 3. 27, withhold not g.
Eccl. 3. 12, I know there is no g. in them.
5. 11, when g. increase.
9. 18, destroyeth much g.
Mat. 12. 29; Mk. 3. 27, spoil his g.
24. 47, ruler over all his g.
26. 24, been g. for that man.
Lu. 6. 30, of him that taketh away thy g.
12. 19, much g. laid up.
15. 12, the portion of g.
16. 1, accused that he had wasted his g.
19. 8, half of my g. I give.
Acts 10. 38, went about doing g.
Rom. 8. 28, work together for g.
13. 4, minister of God for g.
1 Cor. 13. 3, bestow all my g. to feed.
Heb. 10. 34, joyfully the spoiling of your g.
1 John 3. 17, this world's g.
Rev. 3. 17, rich, and increased with g.
See Job 5. 27; 7. 7; Prov. 11. 17; 13. 21.

GOOD (adj.). Gen. 1. 4, 10, 12, 18, 21, 25, 31, God
saw it was g.
Gen. 2. 18, not g. that man should be alone.
27. 46, what g. shall my life do me?
Deut. 2. 4; Josh. 23. 11, take g. heed.
1 Sam. 2. 24, no g. report I hear.
12. 23, I will teach you the g. way.
25. 15, men were very g. to us.
Ezra 7. 9; Neh. 2. 8, the g. hand of God on him.
Neh. 9. 20, thy g. spirit to instruct.
Ps. 34. 8, taste and see that the Lord is g.
45. 1, my heart is inditing a g. matter.
112. 5, a g. man showeth favour.
119. 68, thou art g., and doest g.
145. 9, the Lord is g. to all.

Prov. 12. 25, a *g.* word maketh the heart glad.
15. 23, in season, how *g.* is it!
20. 18, with *g.* advice make war.
22. 1, a *g.* name rather to be chosen.
25. 25, *g.* news from a far country.
Eccl. 6. 12, who knoweth what is *g.*?
Isa. 55. 2, eat ye that which is *g.*
Lam. 3. 26, it is *g.* that a man hope.
27, *g.* that a man bear yoke.
Zech. 1. 13, answered with *g.* words.
Mat. 5. 13, it is *g.* for nothing.
7. 11 ; Lu. 11. 13, how to give *g.* gifts.
9. 22 ; Lu. 8. 48, be of *g.* comfort.
19. 16, what *g.* thing shall I do?
17 ; Lu. 18. 19, none *g.*, save one.
20. 15, is thine eye evil because I am *g.?*
25. 21, *g.* and faithful servant.
Mk. 9. 50; Lu. 14. 34, salt is *g.*, but.
Lu. 1. 53, filled the hungry with *g.* things.
6. 38, *g.* measure, pressed down.
10. 42, chosen that *g.* part.
12. 32, your Father's *g.* pleasure.
16. 25, thou in thy lifetime receivedst *g.* things.
23. 50, Joseph was a *g.* man, and a just.
John 1. 46, can any *g.* thing come out of Nazareth?
2. 10, kept *g.* wine until now.
7. 12, some said, he is a *g.* man.
10. 11, I am the *g.* shepherd.
33, for a *g.* work we stone thee not.
Rom. 7. 12, the commandment holy, just, and *g.*
18, in my flesh dwelleth no *g.* thing.
12. 2, that *g.* and perfect will of God.
14. 21, it is *g.* neither to eat.
1 Cor. 7. 26, this is *g.* for the present.
15. 33, corrupt *g.* manners.
2 Cor. 9. 8, abound in every *g.* work.
Gal. 6. 6, communicate in all *g.* things.
Phil. 1. 6, hath begun a *g.* work.
Col. 1. 10, fruitful in every *g.* work.
1 Thess. 5. 15 ; 3 John 11, follow that which is *g.*
21, hold fast that which is *g.*
1 Tim. 1. 8, the law is *g.*
3. 1, desireth a *g.* work.
4. 4, every creature of God is *g.*
2 Tim. 3. 3, despisers of *g.*
Tit. 2. 7, a pattern in *g.* works.
14, zealous of *g.* works.
Heb. 6. 5, tasted the *g.* word of God.
13. 9, *g.* thing that the heart be established.
Jas. 1. 17, every *g.* gift.
See 2 Thess. 2. 17 ; Tit. 1. 16 ; 3. 8.

GOODLINESS. Isa. 40. 6.

GOODLY. Gen. 49. 21, giveth *g.* words.
Ex. 2. 2, a *g.* child.
Deut. 8. 12, when thou hast built *g.* houses.
1 Sam. 9. 2, a choice young man, and a *g.*
16. 12, ruddy, and *g.* to look to.
Ps. 16. 6 ; Jer. 3. 19, a *g.* heritage.
Zech. 11. 13, a *g.* price I was prized at.
Mat. 13. 45, *g.* pearls.
Jas. 2. 2, a man in *g.* apparel.
See 1 Sam. 8. 16 ; 1 Kings 20. 3 ; Lu. 21. 5.

GOODNESS. Ex. 33. 19, make all my *g.* pass.
34. 6, abundant in *g.* and truth.
Ps. 16. 2, my *g.* extendeth not to thee.
23. 6, *g.* and mercy shall follow.
27. 13, believed to see the *g.* of the Lord.
31. 19 ; Zech. 9. 17, how great is thy *g.*
33. 5, earth full of thy *g.*
65. 11, crownest the year with thy *g.*
145. 7, the memory of thy *g.*
Prov. 20. 6, proclaim every one his own *g.*
Hos. 6. 4, your *g.* is as a morning cloud.
Rom. 2. 4, the riches of his *g.*
11. 22, the *g.* and severity of God.
See Neh. 9. 25 ; Isa. 63. 7 ; Gal. 5. 22 ; Eph. 5. 9.

GOSPEL. Rom. 2. 16, according to my *g.*
2 Cor. 4. 3, if our *g.* be hid.
Gal. 1. 8, 9, any other *g.*
2. 7, the *g.* of uncircumcision, *g.* of circumcision.

Col. 1. 23, the hope of the *g.*
1 Tim. 1. 11, *g.* of the blessed God.
Rev. 14. 6, everlasting *g.*
See Mat. 4. 23 ; Mk. 16. 15 ; Acts 20. 24.

GOURD. Jonah 4. 6, and the Lord God prepared a *g.*
See Jonah 4. 7, 9, 10.

GOVERNMENT. Isa. 9. 6 ; 1 Cor. 12. 28 ; 2 Pet. 2. 10.

GRACE. Ps. 45. 2, *g.* is poured into thy lips.
Prov. 1. 9, an ornament of *g.*
3. 22, life to thy soul, and *g.* to thy neck.
34 ; Jas. 4. 6, giveth *g.* to the lowly.
Zech. 4. 7, crying, *g.*, *g.* unto it.
12. 10, spirit of *g.* and supplications.
John 1. 14, full of *g.* and truth.
16, all received, and *g.* for *g.*
17, *g.* and truth came by Jesus Christ.
Acts 4. 33, great *g.* was upon them all.
11. 23, when he had seen the *g.*
14. 3, the word of his *g.*
Rom. 1. 7 ; 1 Cor. 1. 3 ; 2 Cor. 1. 2 ; Gal. 1. 3 ; Eph.
1. 2 ; Phil. 1. 2 ; Col. 1. 2 ; 1 Thess. 1. 1 ; 2 Thess.
1. 2 ; Philem. 3 ; 1 Pet. 1. 2 ; 2 Pet. 1. 2 ; Rev.
1. 4, *g.* and peace.
3. 24, justified freely by his *g.*
4. 4, not reckoned of *g.*, but of debt.
5. 2, access into this *g.*
17, abundance of *g.*
20, where sin abounded, *g.* did much more
abound.
6. 14, 15, under *g.*
11. 5, the election of *g.*
2 Cor. 8. 9, know the *g.* of our Lord.
9. 8, able to make all *g.* abound.
12. 9, my *g.* is sufficient.
Gal. 1. 6, 15, who called you by his *g.*
5. 4, ye are fallen from *g.*
Eph. 2. 5, 8, by *g.* ye are saved.
3. 8, to me is this *g.* given.
4. 29, minister *g.* to hearers.
6. 24, *g.* be with all that love our Lord.
Col. 4. 6, let your speech be alway with *g.*
2 Thess. 2. 16, good hope through *g.*
1 Tim. 1. 2 ; 2 Tim. 1. 2 ; Tit. 1. 4 ; 2 John 3, *g.*,
mercy, and peace.
Heb. 4. 16, the throne of *g.*
10. 29, despite to the Spirit of *g.*
12. 28, *g.* to serve God acceptably.
13. 9, heart established with *g.*
Jas. 1. 11, the *g.* of the fashion of it.
4. 6, he giveth more *g.*
1 Pet. 3. 7, heirs of *g.*
5. 5, giveth *g.* to the humble.
2 Pet. 3. 18, grow in *g.*
Jude 4, turning *g.* of God into lasciviousness.
See Acts 20. 24 ; 2 Cor. 6. 1 ; Gal. 2. 21.

GRACIOUS. Gen. 43. 29, God be *g.* to thee.
Ex. 22. 27, I will hear, for I am *g.*
33. 19, I will be *g.* to whom I will be *g.*
Neh. 9. 17, 31, ready to pardon, *g.*, merciful.
Ps. 77. 9, hath God forgotten to be *g.*?
Prov. 11. 16, a *g.* woman retaineth honour.
Isa. 30. 18, wait, that he may be *g.*
Amos 5. 15, may be the Lord will be *g.*
Jonah 4. 2, I know thou art a *g.* God.
Lu. 4. 22, wondered at the *g.* words.
1 Pet. 2. 3, tasted that the Lord is *g.*
See Ex. 34. 6 ; 2 Chron. 30. 9 ; Hos. 14. 2.

GRAFT. Rom. 11. 17, 19, 23, 24.

GRAIN. Mat. 13. 31 ; 17. 20 ; Mk. 4. 31 ; Lu. 13. 19;
17. 6, *g.* of mustard seed.
See Amos 9. 9 ; 1 Cor. 15. 37.

GRANT. Ruth 1. 9, *g.* that you may find rest.
1 Chron. 4. 10, God *g.* him that which he re-
quested.
Job 6. 8, *g.* the thing I long for.
Mat. 20. 21 ; Mk. 10. 37, *g.* that my two sons.
Rev. 3. 21, will I *g.* to sit with me.
See Ps. 20. 4 ; 85. 7 ; Acts 4. 29.

GRAPE. Gen. 49. 11, washed clothes in the blood of *g*.
Num. 6. 3, nor eat moist *g*., or dried.
Deut. 23. 24, then thou mayest eat *g*. thy fill.
24. 21, when thou gatherest the *g*. of thy vine-yard.
32. 14, drink the blood of the *g*.
Cant. 2. 13, 15, vines with tender *g*.
Isa. 5. 2, looked it should bring forth *g*.
17. 6 ; 24. 13, yet gleaning *g*.
Jer. 8. 13, there shall be no *g*.
31. 29, 30 ; Ezek. 18. 2, have eaten a sour *g*.
Amos 9. 13, treader of *g*. shall overtake.
See Lev. 19. 10 ; 25. 5 ; Lu. 6. 44 ; Rev. 14. 18.

GRASS. Deut. 32. 2, as showers upon the *g*.
2 Kings 19. 26 ; Ps. 129. 6, as *g*. on housetops.
72. 6, like rain upon mown *g*.
90. 5, like *g*. which groweth up.
102. 4, 11, withered like *g*.
103. 15, days are as *g*.
Isa. 40. 6 ; 1 Pet. 1. 24, all flesh is *g*.
Mat. 6. 30 ; Lu. 12. 28, if God so clothe the *g*.
See Prov. 27. 25 ; John 6. 10 ; Rev. 8. 7 ; 9. 4.

GRASSHOPPERS. Amos 7. 1, and, behold, he formed *g*.

GRAVE (*n.*). Gen. 42. 38 ; 44. 31, with sorrow to the *g*.
Ex. 14. 11, no *g*. in Egypt.
Num. 19. 16, or a *g*.
Job 5. 26, come to *g*. in full age.
7. 9, he that goeth to the *g*.
14. 13, hide me in the *g*.
17. 1, the *g*. are ready for me.
13, if I wait, the *g*. is mine house.
33. 22, his soul draweth near to the *g*.
Ps. 6. 5, in the *g*. who shall give thee thanks?
31. 17, let wicked be silent in the *g*.
49. 14, like sheep laid in the *g*.
15 ; Hos. 13. 14, the power of the *g*.
Eccl. 9. 10, no wisdom in the *g*.
Isa. 38. 18, the *g*. cannot praise thee.
53. 9, made his *g*. with the wicked.
Hos. 13. 14, O *g*., I will be thy destruction.
John 5. 28, all in the *g*. shall hear.
11. 31, she goeth to the *g*.
1 Cor. 15. 55, O *g*., where is thy victory ?
See Mat. 27. 52 ; Lu. 11. 44 ; Rev. 11. 9 ; 20. 13.

GRAVE (*v.*). Isa. 49. 16, I have *g*. thee upon the palms.
Hab. 2. 18, that the maker hath *g*. it.
See Ex. 28. 9 ; 2 Chron. 2. 7 ; 3. 7.

GRAVE (*adj.*). 1 Tim. 3. 8 ; Tit. 2. 2.

GRAVEL. Prov. 20. 17 ; Isa. 48. 19 ; Lam. 3. 16.

GRAVITY. 1 Tim. 3. 4 ; Tit. 2. 7.

GRAY. Ps. 71. 18 ; Prov. 20. 29 ; Hos. 7. 9.

GREAT. Gen. 12. 2 ; 18. 18 ; 46. 3, make a *g*. nation.
48. 19, he also shall be *g*.
Deut. 29. 24, the heat of his *g*. anger.
1 Sam. 12. 24, consider how *g*. things.
2 Kings 5. 13, bid thee do some *g*. thing.
2 Chron. 2. 5, the house is *g*., for *g*. is our God.
Neh. 6. 3, I am doing a *g*. work.
Job 32. 9, *g*. men not always wise.
36. 18, a *g*. ransom.
Ps. 14. 5 ; 53. 5, there were they in *g*. fear.
19. 11, there is *g*. reward.
31. 19, how *g*. is thy goodness !
92. 5, how *g*. are thy works !
139. 17, how *g*. is the sum of them !
Prov. 18. 16, gift bringeth before *g*. men.
25. 6, stand not in place of *g*. men.
Mat. 5. 12, *g*. is your reward.
19, called *g*. in kingdom of heaven.
13. 46, pearl of *g*. price.
15. 28, *g*. is thy faith.
20. 26, whosoever will be *g*. among you.
22. 36, 38, the *g*. commandment.
Lu. 10. 2, the harvest is *g*.
16. 26, a *g*. gulf fixed.

Acts 8. 9, giving out he was some *g*. one.
19. 28, 34, *g*. is Diana.
1 Tim. 3. 16, *g*. is the mystery.
Heb. 2. 3, so *g*. salvation.
12. 1, so *g*. a cloud of witnesses.
Jas. 3. 5, how *g*. a matter a little fire kindleth !
See Deut. 9. 2 ; Eccl. 2. 9 ; Rev. 7. 9.

GREATER. Gen. 4. 13, punishment *g*. than I can bear.
1 Chron. 11. 9 ; Esth. 9. 4, waxed *g*. and *g*.
Hag. 2. 9, glory of latter house *g*.
Mat. 11. 11 ; Lu. 7. 28, *g*. than he.
12. 6, one *g*. than the temple.
Mk. 12. 31, no commandment *g*. than these.
John 1. 50 ; 5. 20 ; 14. 12, shalt see *g*. things.
4. 12 ; 8. 53, art thou *g*. than our father ?
10. 29 ; 14. 28, my Father is *g*. than all.
13. 16 ; 15. 20, servant not *g*. than his lord.
15. 13, *g*. love hath no man.
1 Cor. 15. 6, the *g*. part remain.
Heb. 6. 13, he could swear by no *g*.
1 John 3. 20, God is *g*. than our hearts.
4. 4, *g*. is he in you than he in world.
3 John 4, no *g*. joy.
See Gen. 41. 40 ; 48. 19 ; Heb. 9. 11.

GREATEST. Mat. 13. 32, it is *g*. among herbs.
18. 1, 4, who is *g*. in kingdom ?
Mk. 9. 34 ; Lu. 9. 46, disputed who should be *g*.
1 Cor. 13. 13, the *g*. of these is charity.
See Job 1. 3 ; Jer. 31. 34 ; Lu. 22. 24.

GREATLY. 2 Sam. 24. 10 ; 1 Chron. 21. 8, I have sinned *g*.
1 Kings 18. 3, Obadiah feared the Lord *g*.
Ps. 28. 7, my heart *g*. rejoiceth.
47. 9, God is *g*. exalted.
89. 7, *g*. to be feared in the assembly.
116. 10, I was *g*. afflicted.
Dan. 9. 23 ; 10. 11, thou art *g*. beloved.
Obad. 2, thou art *g*. despised.
Mk. 12. 27, ye do *g*. err.
See Ps. 62. 2 ; Mk. 9. 15 ; Acts 3. 11 ; 6. 7.

GREATNESS. 1 Chron. 29. 11, thine is the *g*. power, and glory.
Ps. 145. 3, his *g*. is unsearchable.
Prov. 5. 23, in the *g*. of his folly.
Isa. 63. 1, travelling in *g*. of strength.
Eph. 1. 19, the exceeding *g*. of his power.
See 2 Chron. 9. 6 ; Ps. 66. 3 ; 79. 11 ; 150. 2.

GREEDILY. Prov. 21. 26 ; Ezek. 22. 12.

GREEDINESS. Eph. 4. 19.

GREEDY. Prov. 1. 19 ; 15. 27, *g*. of gain.
Isa. 56. 11, they are *g*. dogs.
See Ps. 17. 12 ; 1 Tim. 3. 3.

GREEN. Lev. 23. 14 ; Judg. 16. 7 ; Lu. 23. 31.

GRIEF. 2 Chron. 6. 29, every one shall know his own *g*.
Job 6. 2, Oh that my *g*. were weighed !
Ps. 31. 10, life spent with *g*.
Eccl. 1. 18, in much wisdom is much *g*.
Isa. 53. 3, acquainted with *g*.
Jer. 10. 19, this is a *g*., and I must bear it.
See Jonah 4. 6 ; Heb. 13. 17 ; 1 Pet. 2. 19.

GRIEVE. Gen. 6. 6, it *g*. him at his heart.
45. 5, be not *g*. that ye sold me.
1 Sam. 2. 33, the man shall be to *g*. thine heart.
Ps. 78. 40, they *g*. him in the desert.
95. 10, forty years was I *g*.
Lam. 3. 33, doth not willingly *g*.
Mk. 3. 5, being *g*. for the hardness.
10. 22, he went away *g*.
John 21. 17, Peter was *g*.
Rom. 14. 15, brother *g*. with meat.
Eph. 4. 30, *g*. not the holy Spirit of God.
See Neh. 2. 10 ; 13. 8 ; Ps. 119. 158 ; 139. 21.

GRIEVOUS. Gen. 21. 11, thing was *g*. in Abraham's sight.
50. 11, a *g*. mourning.
Ps. 10. 5, his ways are always *g*.
Prov. 15. 1, *g*. words stir up anger.

Isa. 15. 4, his life shall be *g.*
Jer. 30. 12 ; Nah. 3. 19, thy wound is *g.*
Mat. 23. 4 ; Lu. 11. 46, burdens *g.* to be borne.
Phil. 3. 1, to me is not *g.*
Heb. 12. 11, chastening *g.*
1 John 5. 3, commandments not *g.*
See Eccl. 2. 17 ; Jer. 16. 4 ; Acts 20. 29.

GRIND. Isa. 3. 15, *g.* faces of the poor.
Lam. 5. 13, took young men to *g.*
Mat. 21. 44 ; Lu. 20. 18, it will *g.* him to powder.
See Eccl. 12. 3 ; Mat. 24. 41 ; Lu. 17. 35.

GROAN. Ex. 2. 24, God heard their *g.*
Job 24. 12, men *g.* from out the city.
Joel 1. 18, how do the beasts *g.*!
Rom. 8. 23, we ourselves *g.*
2 Cor. 5. 2, 4, in this we *g.*
See Job 23. 2 ; Ps. 6. 6 ; John 11. 33, 38.

GROPE. Deut. 28. 29 ; Job 5. 14 ; 12. 25 ; Isa. 59. 10.

GROSS. Isa. 60. 2 ; Jer. 13. 16 ; Mat. 13. 15 ; Acts 28. 27.

GROUND. Ex. 3. 5 ; Acts 7. 33, holy *g.*
Job 5. 6, nor trouble spring out of the *g.*
Isa. 35. 7, parched *g.* become a pool.
Jer. 4. 3 ; Hos. 10. 12, break up fallow *g*
Mat. 13. 8 ; Lu. 8. 8, good *g.*
Mk. 4. 16, stony *g.*
Lu. 13. 7, why cumbereth it the *g.*
14. 18, bought a piece of *g.*
19. 44, lay thee even with the *g.*
John 8. 6, he wrote on the *g.*
See Zech. 8. 12 ; Mal. 3. 11 ; John 12. 24.

GROUNDED. Eph. 3. 17 ; Col. 1. 23.

GROW. Gen. 48. 16, let them *g.* into a multitude.
2 Sam. 23. 5, though he make it not to *g.*
Ps. 92. 12, *g.* like a cedar.
Isa. 53. 2, he shall *g.* up before him.
Hos. 14. 5, he shall *g.* as the lily.
Mal. 4. 2, *g.* up as calves of the stall.
Mat. 13. 30, let both *g.* together.
Mk. 4. 27, seed should *g.* up, he knoweth not.
Acts 5. 24, whereunto this would *g.*
Eph. 2. 21, *g.* unto an holy temple.
4. 15, may *g.* up into him.
2 Thess. 1. 3, your faith *g.* exceedingly.
1 Pet. 2. 2, that ye may *g.* thereby.
2 Pet. 3. 18, *g.* in grace.
See 2 Kings 19. 26 ; Jer. 12. 2 ; Zech. 6. 12.

GRUDGE. Lev. 19. 18 ; 2 Cor. 9. 7 ; Jas. 5. 9 ; 1 Pet. 4. 9.

GUESTS. Zeph. 1. 7 ; Mat. 22. 10 ; Lu. 19. 7.

GUIDE. Ps. 25. 9, meek will he *g.* in judgment.
32. 8, I will *g.* thee with mine eye.
48. 14, our *g.* even unto death.
73. 24, *g.* me with thy counsel.
Prov. 6. 7, having no *g.*, overseer, or ruler.
Isa. 58. 11, the Lord shall *g.* thee.
Jer. 3. 4, the *g.* of my youth.
Mat. 23. 16, 24, ye blind *g.*
Lu. 1. 79, *g.* our feet into the way of peace.
John 16. 13, *g.* you into all truth.
See Gen. 48. 14 ; Prov. 11. 3 ; 23. 19.

GUILE. Ps. 32. 2, in whose spirit is no *g.*
34. 13 ; 1 Pet. 3. 10, keep lips from speaking *g.*
John 1. 47, in whom is no *g.*
2 Cor. 12. 16, I caught you with *g.*
1 Pet. 2. 1, laying aside *g.*
22, nor was *g.* found in his mouth.
3. 10, and his lips that they speak no *g.*
See Ex. 21. 14 ; 1 Thess. 2. 3 ; Rev. 14. 5.

GUILTLESS. Ex. 20. 7 ; Deut. 5. 11, will not hold him *g.*
Josh. 2. 19, we will be *g.*
2 Sam. 3. 28, are *g.* of blood.
Mat. 12. 7, ye would not have condemned the *g.*
See Num. 5. 31 ; 1 Sam. 26. 9 ; 1 Kings 2. 9.

GUILTY. Gen. 42. 21, verily *g.* concerning our brother.
Ex. 34. 7 ; Num. 14. 18, by no means clear the *g.*

Lev. 5. 3, when he knoweth of it, he shall be *g.*
Rom. 3. 19, all the world *g.* before God.
1 Cor. 11. 27, *g.* of the body and blood.
Jas. 2. 11, he is *g.* of all.
See Num. 35. 27 ; Prov. 30. 10 ; Mat. 26. 66.

GULF. Lu. 16. 26.

GUSH. 1 Kings 18. 28 ; Ps. 78. 20 ; 105. 41 ; Jer. 9. 18.

H.

HABITATION. Ex. 15. 13, guided them to thy holy *h.*
2 Chron. 6. 2, have built an house of *h.*
Ps. 26. 8, have loved the *h.*
33. 14, from the place of his *h.*
69. 25, let their *h.* be desolate.
74. 20, full of *h.* of cruelty.
89. 14, justice and judgment the *h.* of thy throne.
107. 7, 36, a city of *h.*
132. 13, the Lord desired it for his *h.*
Prov. 3. 33, he blesseth the *h.* of the just.
Isa. 32. 18, dwell in a peaceable *h.*
Jer. 21. 13, who shall enter into our *h.* ?
25. 37, the peaceable *h.* are cut down.
Lu. 16. 9, into everlasting *h.*
Eph. 2. 22, an *h.* of God through the Spirit.
Jude 6, angels which left their own *h.*
See Prov. 8. 31 ; Acts 1. 20 ; 17. 26 ; Rev. 18. 2.

HAIL. Job 38. 22, the treasures of the *h.*
Isa. 28. 17, *h.* sweep away refuge of lies.
See Ex. 9. 18 ; Josh. 10. 11 ; Rev. 8. 7 ; 11. 19 ; 16. 21.

HAIR. Gen. 42. 38 ; 44. 29, bring down gray *h.* with sorrow.
Judg. 20. 16, sling stones at *h.* breadth.
Job 4. 15, the *h.* of my flesh stood up.
Ps. 40. 12, more than the *h.* of my head.
Mat. 3. 4 ; Mk. 1. 6, raiment of camel's *h.*
5. 36, make one *h.* white or black.
10. 30, *h.* of head numbered.
1 Cor. 11. 14, 15, long *h.*, it is a shame.
1 Tim. 2. 9, broided *h.*
1 Pet. 3. 3, plaiting the *h.*
See 2 Sam. 14. 26 ; Hos. 7. 9 ; John 11. 2 ; Rev. 1. 14.

HALE. Lu. 12. 58 ; Acts 8. 3.

HALL. John 18. 28, then led they Jesus from Caiaphas unto the *h.* of judgment.
33 ; 19. 9, then Pilate entered into the judgment *h.*
See Acts 25. 23.

HALLOW. Lev. 22. 32, I am the Lord which *h.* you.
25. 10, shall *h.* the fiftieth year.
Num. 5. 10, every man's *h.* things.
1 Kings 9. 3, I have *h.* this house.
Jer. 17. 22 ; 24. 27, but *h.* ye the sabbath day.
Ezek. 20. 20 ; 44. 24, and *h.* my sabbaths.
Mat. 6. 9 ; Lu. 11. 2, *h.* be thy name.

HALT. 1 Kings 18. 21, how long *h.* ye ?
Ps. 38. 17, I am ready to *h.*
Jer. 20. 10, my familiars watched for my *h.*
See Gen. 32. 31 ; Mic. 4. 6 ; Zeph. 3. 19.

HAND. Gen. 16. 12, *h.* against every man.
24. 2 ; 47. 29, put thy *h.* under my thigh.
27. 22, the *h.* are the *h.* of Esau.
31. 29, in the power of my *h.* to do you hurt.
Ex. 21. 24 ; Deut. 19. 21, *h.* for *h.*, foot for foot.
33. 22, cover with my *h.* while I pass.
Num. 11. 23 ; Isa. 59. 1, Lord's *h.* waxed short.
22. 29, would there were sword in mine *h.*
Deut. 8. 17, my *h.* hath gotten this wealth.
33. 2, from right *h.* went fiery law.
Judg. 7. 2, saying, my own *h.* hath saved me.
1 Sam. 5. 11, *h.* of God was heavy.
6. 9, not his *h.* that smote us, but a chance.
12. 3, of whose *h.* have I received any bribe ?
19. 5 ; 28. 21, put his life in his *h.*
23. 16, Jonathan strengthened his *h.* in God.
26. 18, what evil is in mine *h.* ?
2 Sam. 14. 19, is not *h.* of Joab in this ?
24. 14 ; 1 Chron. 21. 13, let us fall into *h.* of Lord.

1 Kings 18. 44, cloud like a man's *h.*
2 Kings 5. 11, strike his *h.* over the place.
1 Chron. 12. 2, could use right *h.* and left.
Ezra 7. 9; 8. 18; Neh. 2. 8, good *h.* of God.
10. 19, they gave their *h.* that they would.
Neh. 2. 18, strengthened their *h.* for work.
6. 5, with open letter in his *h.*
Job 12. 10, in whose *h.* is the soul.
19. 21, the *h.* of God hath touched me.
40. 14, that thine own *h.* can save.
Ps. 16. 11, at right *h.* pleasures for evermore.
24. 4, clean *h.* and pure heart.
68. 31, stretch out her *h.* unto God.
90. 17, establish thou the work of our *h.*
137. 5, let my right *h.* forget her cunning.
Prov. 3. 16, in left *h.* riches and honour.
6. 10; 24. 33, folding of *h.* to sleep.
10. 4, that dealeth with slack *h.*
11. 21; 16. 5, though *h.* join *h.*
12. 24, *h.* of diligent shall bear rule.
19. 24; 26. 15, slothful man hideth his *h.*
22. 26, be not of them that strike *h.*
Eccl. 2. 24, this I saw was from *h.* of God.
9. 10, whatsoever thy *h.* findeth.
11. 6, in evening withhold not thine *h.*
Isa. 1. 12, who hath required this at your *h.*?
5. 25; 9. 12; 10. 4; 14. 27, his *h.* stretched out still.
14. 26, this is the *h.* that is stretched out.
40. 12, measured waters in hollow of *h.*
44. 5, subscribe with his *h.* to the Lord.
53. 10, pleasure of Lord shall prosper in his *h.*
56. 2, keepeth his *h.* from evil.
Jer. 23. 14, strengthen *h.* of evil doers.
33. 13, shall pass under *h.* of him that telleth.
Lam. 2. 4, with his right *h.* as adversary.
4. 10, *h.* of pitiful women have sodden.
Ezek. 7. 17; 21. 7, all *h.* shall be feeble.
10. 2, fill *h.* with coals of fire.
17. 18, lo, he had given his *h.*
Dan. 4. 35, none can stay his *h.*
Hos. 7. 5, stretched out *h.* with scorners.
Mic. 7. 3, do evil with both *h.* earnestly.
Zeph. 3. 16, let not thine *h.* be slack.
Zech. 13. 6, what are these wounds in thine *h.*?
Mat. 3. 2; 4. 17; 10. 7, kingdom of heaven at *h.*
12; Lu. 3. 17, whose fan is in his *h.*
6. 3, let not left *h.* know.
18. 8; Mk. 9. 43, if thy *h.* or foot offend.
26. 18, my time is at *h.*
46; Mk. 14. 42, he is at *h.* that doth betray.
Mk. 14. 62, sitting on right *h.* of power.
16. 19, sat on right *h.* of God.
Lu. 9. 44, delivered into *h.* of men.
John 10. 28, nor pluck out of my *h.*
29, my Father's *h.*
20. 27, reach hither thy *h.*
Acts 20. 34, these *h.* have ministered.
2 Cor. 5. 1, house not made with *h.*
Phil. 4. 5, moderation be known, the Lord is at *h.*
1 Thess. 4. 11, work with your own *h.*
2 Thess. 2. 2, the day of Christ is at *h.*
1 Tim. 2. 8, lifting up holy *h.*
Heb. 10. 31, the *h.* of living God.
Jas. 4. 8, cleanse your *h.*
1 Pet. 4. 7, end of all things is at *h.*
1 John 1. 1, our *h.* have handled of the Word.
See Isa. 49. 16; Lu. 9. 62; John 18. 22; Col. 2. 14.

HANDLE. Judg. 5. 14, that *h.* pen of the writer.
Ps. 115. 7, hands, but they *h.* not.
Prov. 16. 20, that *h.* a matter wisely.
Jer. 2. 8, they that *h.* the law.
Mk. 12. 4, sent away shamefully *h.*
Lu. 24. 39, *h.* me, and see.
2 Cor. 4. 2, nor *h.* word deceitfully.
Col. 2. 21, taste not, *h.* not.
1 John 1. 1, have *h.* of Word of life.
See Gen. 4. 21; 1 Chron. 12. 8; Ezek. 27. 29.

HANDMAID. Ps. 86. 16; 116. 16; Prov. 30. 23; Lu. 1. 38.

HANG. Deut. 21. 23; Gal. 3. 13, he that is *h.* is accursed.
Job 26. 7, *h.* the earth on nothing.
Ps. 137. 2, we *h.* our harps upon the willows.
Mat. 18. 6; Mk. 9. 42; Lu. 17. 2, millstone *h.* about neck.
22. 40, on these *h.* the law and the prophets.
27. 5, went and *h.* himself.
Heb. 12. 12, lift up the hands which *h.* down.
See Gen. 40. 22; Esth. 7. 10; Lu. 23. 39.

HAPLY. 1 Sam. 14. 30; Mk. 11. 13; Acts 5. 39; 17. 27.

HAPPEN. 1 Sam. 6. 9, it was a chance that *h.*
Prov. 12. 21, there shall no evil *h.* to the just.
Isa. 41. 22, let them show us what shall *h.*
Jer. 44. 23, therefore this evil is *h.*
Mk. 10. 32, to tell what should *h.*
Lu. 24. 14, talked of things that had *h.*
Rom. 11. 25, blindness is *h.* to Israel.
1 Cor. 10. 11, things *h.* for ensamples.
Phil. 1. 12, things which *h.* to me.
1 Pet. 4. 12, as though some strange thing *h.*
2 Pet. 2. 22, it is *h.* according to proverb.
See Eccl. 2. 14; 8. 14; 9. 11; Acts 3. 10.

HAPPY. Gen. 30. 13, *h.* am I.
Deut. 33. 29, *h.* art thou.
Job 5. 17, *h.* is the man whom God correcteth.
Ps. 127. 5, *h.* is the man that hath quiver full.
128. 2, *h.* shalt thou be.
144. 15, *h.* is that people.
Prov. 3. 13, 18, *h.* that findeth wisdom.
14. 21, he that hath mercy, *h.* is he.
28. 14, *h.* is the man that feareth alway.
Jer. 12. 1, why are they *h.* that deal treacherously?
Mal. 3. 15, now we call proud *h.*
John 13. 17, if ye know, *h.* if ye do them.
Rom. 14. 22, *h.* is he that condemneth not.
Jas. 5. 11, we count them *h.* which endure.
1 Pet. 3. 14; 4. 14, *h.* are ye.
See Ps. 146. 5; Prov. 29. 18; 1 Cor. 7. 40.

HARD. Gen. 18. 14, is any thing too *h.* for the Lord?
Deut. 1. 17; 17. 8, cause that is too *h.*
15. 18, it shall not seem *h.* to thee.
1 Kings 10. 1; 2 Chron. 9. 1, prove with *h.* questions.
Job 41. 24, *h.* as piece of nether millstone.
Prov. 13. 15, the way of transgressors is *h.*
18. 19, brother offended *h.* to be won.
Jer. 32. 17, 27, there is nothing too *h.* for thee.
Ezek. 3. 5, 6, to a people of *h.* language.
Mat. 25. 24, thou art an *h.* man.
John 6. 60, this is an *h.* saying.
Acts 9. 5; 26. 14, *h.* to kick against the pricks.
Heb. 5. 11, many things *h.* to be uttered.
2 Pet. 3. 16, things *h.* to be understood.
See Deut. 15. 18; 2 Kings 2. 10; Mk. 10. 24.

HARDEN. Ex. 4. 21; 7. 3; 14. 4, I will *h.* Pharaoh's heart.
14. 17, *h.* hearts of Egyptians.
Job 6. 10, I would *h.* myself in sorrow.
9. 4, who hath *h.* himself against him?
Prov. 21. 29, a wicked man *h.* his face.
28. 14, he that being often reproved *h.* his neck.
29. 1, he that being often reproved *h.* his neck.
Isa. 63. 17, why hast thou *h.* our heart?
Mk. 6. 52; 8. 17, their heart was *h.*
John 12. 40, he hath *h.* their heart.
Acts 19. 9, when divers were *h.*
Rom. 9. 18, whom he will he *h.*
Heb. 3. 13, lest any of you be *h.*
See Deut. 15. 7; 2 Kings 17. 14; Job 39. 16.

HARDLY. Gen. 16. 6; Mat. 19. 23; Mk. 10. 23; Lu. 18. 24.

HARDNESS. Mk. 3. 5, grieved for *h.* of their hearts.
16. 14, upbraided them for *h.* of heart.
2 Tim. 2. 3, endure *h.*, as good soldier.
See Job 38. 38; Mat. 19. 8; Mk. 10. 5; Rom. 2. 5.

HARM. Lev. 5. 16, make amends for *h.*

Num. 35. 23, nor sought his *h.*
1 Sam. 26. 21, I will no more do thee *h.*
2 Kings 4. 41, no *h.* in the pot.
1 Chron. 16. 22 ; Ps. 105. 15, do prophets no *h.*
Prov. 3. 30, if he have done thee no *h.*
Acts 16. 28, do thyself no *h.*
  28. 5, he felt no *h.*
1 Pet. 3. 13, who will *h.* you?
  See Gen. 31. 52 ; Jer. 39. 12 ; Acts 27. 21.
HARMLESS. Mat. 10. 16 ; Phil. 2. 15 ; Heb. 7. 26.
HARP. 1 Sam. 16. 16, cunning player on an *h.*
Ps. 49. 4, dark sayings on the *h.*
  137. 2, hanged *h.* on the willows.
Isa. 5. 12, *h.* and viol are in their feasts.
  24. 8, joy of the *h.* ceaseth.
1 Cor. 14. 7, what is piped or *h.*, except they give.
Rev. 14. 2, harping with their *h.*
  See Gen. 4. 21 ; Ezek. 26. 13 ; Dan. 3. 5.
HARROW. 2 Sam. 12. 31 ; 1 Chron. 20. 3 ; Job
  39. 10.
HART. Deut. 12. 15, and as of the *h.*
1 Kings 4. 23, besides *h.* and roebucks.
  See Ps. 42. 1 ; Isa. 35. 6.
HARVEST. Gen. 8. 22, *h.* shall not cease.
Ex. 23. 16 ; 34. 22, the feast of *h.*
Lev. 19. 9 ; 23. 10 ; Deut. 24. 19, when ye reap *h.*
1 Sam. 12. 17, is it not wheat *h.* to-day?
Job 5. 5, whose *h.* the hungry eateth up.
Prov. 6. 8, the ant gathereth food in *h.*
  10. 5, he that sleepeth in *h.*
  25. 13, cold of snow in time of *h.*
  26. 1, as rain in *h.*
Isa. 9. 3, according to joy in *h.*
  16. 9, thy *h.* is fallen.
  18. 4, dew in heat of *h.*
Jer. 5. 17, they shall eat up thine *h.*
  24, appointed weeks of *h.*
  8. 20, the *h.* is past, the summer ended.
  51. 33, the time of her *h.* shall come.
Joel 3. 13 ; Rev. 14. 15, the *h.* is ripe.
Mat. 9. 37, the *h.* is plenteous.
  38 ; Lu. 10. 2, the Lord of the *h.*
  13. 30, in the time of *h.* I will say.
Mk. 4. 29, putteth in sickle, because *h.* is come.
Lu. 10. 2, the *h.* truly is great.
John 4. 35, the fields are white to *h.*
  See Josh. 3. 15 ; Isa. 23. 3 ; Mat. 13. 39.
HASTE. Ex. 12. 11, shall eat it in *h.*
1 Sam. 21. 8, king's business required *h.*
Ps. 31. 22 ; 116. 11, I said in my *h.*
Prov. 19. 2, he that *h.* with feet sinneth.
  28. 22, he that *h.* to be rich.
Isa. 51. 14, captive exile *h.*
  60. 22, will I, it in his time.
Jer. 1. 12, I will *h.* my word.
Zeph. 1. 14, day of the Lord *h.* greatly.
  See 2 Kings 7. 15 ; Ps. 16. 4 ; 55. 8 ; Eccl. 1. 5.
HASTILY. Prov. 20. 21 ; 25. 8.
HASTY. Prov. 14. 29 ; 21. 5 ; 29. 20 ; Eccl. 5. 2 ; 7. 9.
HATE. Gen. 37. 4, 5, 8, *h.* Joseph yet the more.
Lev. 19. 17, shall not *h.* thy brother.
1 Kings 22. 8 ; 2 Chron. 18. 7, one man, but I *h.*
  him.
2 Chron. 19. 2, and love them that *h.* the Lord.
Ps. 34. 21, they that *h.* righteous shall be desolate.
  97. 10, ye that love the Lord, *h.* evil.
  139. 21, do not I *h.* them that *h.* thee?
Prov. 1. 22, how long will ye *h.* knowledge?
  13. 24, he that spareth his rod *h.* his son.
  14. 20, the poor is *h.* of his neighbour.
  15. 10, he that *h.* reproof shall die.
  27, he that *h.* gifts shall live.
Eccl. 2. 17, I *h.* life.
  3. 8, a time to *h.*
Isa. 1. 14, your feasts my soul *h.*
  61. 8, I *h.* robbery for burnt offering.
Amos 5. 15, *h.* the evil, and love the good.
Mic. 3. 2, who *h.* the good, and love the evil.
Zech. 8. 17, these are things that I *h.*

Mal. 1. 3 ; Rom. 9. 13, I loved Jacob, and *h.* Esau.
Mat. 5. 44 ; Lu. 6. 27, do good to them that *h.* you.
  6. 24, either he will *h.* the one.
  10. 22 ; Mk. 13. 13 ; Lu. 21. 17, ye shall be *h.*
  24. 10, and shall *h.* one another.
Lu. 6. 22, blessed are ye when men shall *h.* you.
  14. 26, and *h.* not his father.
John 3. 20, *h.* the light.
  7. 7, the world cannot *h.* you.
  12. 25, he that *h.* his life.
  15. 18 ; 1 John 3. 13, marvel not if world *h.* you.
  24, they have both seen and *h.*
Eph. 5. 29, no man ever yet *h.* his own flesh.
1 John 2. 9, 11 ; 3. 15 ; 4. 20, *h.* his brother.
  See Gen. 27. 41 ; Deut. 1. 27 ; Prov. 6. 16 ; Rev. 2. 6.
HATEFUL. Ps. 36. 2 ; Ezek. 23. 29 ; Tit. 3. 3.
HATERS. Ps. 81. 15 ; Rom. 1. 30.
HAUGHTY. 2 Sam. 22. 28, thine eyes are upon
  the *h.*
Ps. 131. 1, my heart is not *h.*
Prov. 16. 18, a *h.* spirit before a fall.
  21. 24, proud and *h.* scorner.
Isa. 10. 33, the *h.* shall be humbled.
Zeph. 3. 11, no more be *h.* because.
  See Isa. 2. 11 ; 13. 11 ; 24. 4 ; Ezek. 16. 50.
HAWK. Lev. 11. 16, and the *h.* after his kind.
Job 39. 26, doth the *h.* fly by wisdom?
HEAD. Gen. 3. 15, it shall bruise thy *h.*
  Josh. 2. 19, blood be on his *h.*
  Judg. 11. 9, shall I be your *h.*?
2 Kings 2. 3, take thy master from thy *h.* to-day.
  4. 19, he said, My *h.*, my *h.*
Ps. 24. 7, 9, lift up your *h.*
  66. 12, caused men to ride over our *h.*
  110. 7, therefore shall he lift up the *h.*
  141. 5, oil, which shall not break my *h.*
Prov. 10. 6, blessings on *h.* of the just.
  11. 26, on *h.* of him that selleth corn.
  25. 22 ; Rom. 12. 20, coals of fire on his *h.*
Eccl. 2. 14, a wise man's eyes are in his *h.*
Isa. 1. 5, the whole *h.* is sick.
  35. 10 ; 51. 11, everlasting joy upon their *h.*
  58. 5, to bow down *h.* as bulrush.
  59. 17 ; Eph. 6. 17, helmet of salvation on *h.*
Jer. 9. 1, Oh that my *h.* were waters.
  14. 3, *h.* ashamed, and covered their *h.*
Dan. 2. 38, thou art this *h.* of gold.
Amos 2. 7, that pant after dust on *h.*
  9. 1, cut them in the *h.*
Zech. 1. 21, no man did lift up his *h.*
  4. 7, the *h.*-stone with shoutings.
Mat. 5. 36, neither swear by *h.*
  27. 39 ; Mk. 15. 29, reviled, wagging their *h.*
Lu. 7. 46, my *h.* thou didst not anoint.
  21. 18, not hair of *h.* perish.
  28, then look up, and lift up your *h.*
John 13. 9, also my hands and my *h.*
1 Cor. 11. 3, the *h.* of every man is Christ.
  4, dishonoureth his *h.*
  10, woman to have power on her *h.*
Eph. 1. 22 ; 4. 15 ; Col. 1. 18, the *h.* of the church.
  5. 23, husband is *h.* of the wife.
Col. 2. 19, not holding the *h.*
  See Num. 6. 5 ; Josh. 7. 6 ; Acts 18. 6 ; Rev. 13. 1.
HEAL. Ex. 15. 26, I am the Lord that *h.* thee.
Deut. 32. 39, I wound, I *h.*
2 Kings 2. 22, waters were *h.*
  20. 5, 8, I will *h.* thee.
Ps. 6. 2, O Lord, *h.* me.
  41. 4, *h.* my soul, for I have sinned.
  103. 3, who *h.* all thy diseases.
  107. 20, sent his word, and *h.* them.
Isa. 6. 10, lest they convert and be *h.*
  53. 5, with his stripes we are *h.*
Jer. 6. 14 ; 8. 11, they have *h.* the hurt slightly.
  15. 18, wound refuseth to be *h.*
  17. 14, *h.* me, and I shall be *h.*
Lam. 2. 13, who can *h.* thee?
Hos. 5. 13, yet could he not *h.* thee.

Hos. 6. 1, he hath torn, and he will *h.* us.
14. 4, I will *h.* their backslidings.
Mat. 8. 7, I will come and *h.* him.
8, speak, and my servant shall be *h.*
10. 1, to *h.* all manner of sickness.
8; Lu. 9. 2; 10.9, *h.* the sick.
12. 10; Lu. 14. 3, is it lawful to *h.* on sabbath?
Mk. 3. 2; Lu. 6. 7, whether he would *h.* on the
    sabbath day.
Lu. 4. 18, to *h.* broken-hearted.
23, physician, *h.* thyself.
5. 17, power of the Lord present to *h.*
John 4. 47, that he would come and *h.*
5. 13, he that was *h.* wist not.
Acts 4. 14, beholding the man which was *h.*
5. 16, they were *h.* every one.
14. 9, he had faith to be *h.*
Heb. 12. 13, let it rather be *h.*
Jas. 5. 16, pray that ye may be *h.*
1 Pet. 2. 24, by whose stripes ye were *h.*
Rev. 13. 3, his deadly wound was *h.*
    See Eccl. 3. 3; Isa. 3. 7; Mat. 4. 24; 14. 14.
HEALING. Jer. 14. 19, there is no *h.* for us.
Nah. 3. 19, no *h.* of thy bruise.
Mal. 4. 2, with *h.* in his wings.
Mat. 4. 23, went about *h.* all.
Lu. 9. 11, that had need of *h.*
1 Cor. 12. 9, 28, 30, the gift of *h.*
Rev. 22. 2, for the *h.* of the nations.
    See Jer. 30. 13; Lu. 9. 6; Acts 4. 22; 10. 38.
HEALTH. 2 Sam. 20. 9, art thou in *h.,* my bro-
    ther?
Ps. 42. 11; 43. 5, the *h.* of my countenance.
67. 2, thy saving *h.*
Prov. 3. 8, *h.* to thy navel.
4. 22, they are *h.* to all their flesh.
16. 24, *h.* to the bones.
Isa. 58. 8, thy *h.* shall spring forth.
Jer. 8. 15, looked for a time of *h.*
22, why is not *h.* recovered?
3 John 2, mayest be in *h.*
    See Gen. 43. 28; Jer. 30. 17; Acts 27. 34.
HEAP. Deut. 32. 23, *h.* mischiefs upon them.
Job 16. 4, I could *h.* up words.
27. 16, though he *h.* up silver.
Ps. 39. 6, he *h.* up riches.
Prov. 25. 22; Rom. 12. 20, *h.* **coals of fire.**
Ezek. 24. 10, *h.* on wood.
Hab. 1. 10, they shall *h.* dust.
Mic. 3. 12, Jerusalem shall become *h.*
2 Tim. 4. 3, *h.* to themselves teachers.
Jas. 5. 3, ye have *h.* treasure for last days.
    See Judg. 15. 16; Neh. 4. 2; Eccl. 2. 26.
HEAR. Ex. 6. 12, how shall Pharaoh *h.* me?
1 Sam. 15. 14, lowing of oxen which I *h.*
1 Kings 8. 42, they shall *h.* of thy great name.
18. 26, O Baal, *h.* us.
2 Kings 18. 28; Isa. 36. 13, *h.* words of the great
    kings.
1 Chron. 14. 15, when thou *h.* a sound of going.
Neh. 8. 2, all that could *h.* with understanding.
Job 31. 35, Oh that one would *h.* me!
Ps. 4. 1; 30. 12; 54. 2; 84. 8; 102. 1; 143. 1; Dan.
    9. 17, *h.* my prayer.
3; 17. 6; Zech. 10. 6, the Lord will *h.*
10. 17, cause thine ear to *h.*
49. 1, *h.* this, all ye people.
59. 7, who, say they, doth *h.*?
66. 18, if I regard iniquity, the Lord will not
    h. me.
85. 8, I will *h.* what God the Lord will speak.
102. 20, *h.* groaning of the prisoner.
Prov. 13. 8, the poor *h.* not rebuke.
18. 13, answereth a matter before he *h.*
22. 17, *h.* the words of the wise.
Eccl. 5. 1, more ready to *h.* than give.
7. 5, better to *h.* rebuke of wise.
12. 13, *h.* conclusion of the whole matter.
Isa. 1. 2, *h.,* O heavens, and give ear.
15; Jer. 7. 16; 11. 14; 14. 12; Ezek. 8. 18, make
    many prayers, I will not *h.*

Isa. 6. 9; Mk. 4. 12, *h.* but understand not.
29. 18, shall deaf *h.* words of the book.
33. 13, *h.,* ye that are afar off.
34. 1, let the earth *h.*
42. 20, opening ears, but he *h.* not.
55. 3; John 5. 25, *h.,* and your soul shall live.
Ezek. 3. 27, he that *h.,* let him *h.*
33. 31, they *h.* words, but will not do them.
Mat. 7. 24; Lu. 6. 47, whoso *h.* these sayings.
11. 4, show things ye do *h.* and see.
5; Mk. 7. 37; Lu. 7. 22, the deaf *h.*
13. 17; Lu. 10. 24, those things which ye *h.*
17. 5; Mk. 9. 7, my beloved Son, *h.* him.
18. 16, if he will not *h.* thee.
Mk. 4. 24; Lu. 8. 18, take heed what ye *h.*
Lu. 9. 9, of whom I *h.* such things.
10. 16, he that *h.* you, *h.* me.
John 5. 25, dead shall *h.* voice of Son of God.
30, as I *h.,* I judge.
6. 60, who can *h.* it?
8. 47, he that is of God *h.* God's words.
9. 31, God *h.* not sinners.
11. 42, I know thou *h.* me always.
12. 47, if any man *h.* my words.
14. 24, the word ye *h.* is not mine.
Acts 2. 8, how *h.* we every man?
13. 44, whole city came to *h.*
Rom. 10. 14, *h.* without a preacher.
1 Cor. 11. 18, I *h.* there be divisions.
1 Tim. 4. 16, save thyself, and them that *h.*
Jas. 1. 19, swift to *h.*
1 John 4. 5, the world *h.* them.
6, he that knoweth God *h.* us.
5. 15, we know that he *h.* us.
Rev. 2. 7; 3. 6, 13, 22, let him *h.*
3. 20, if any man *h.* my voice.
    See Deut. 30. 11; 2 Kings 19. 16; 2 Chron. 6. 21.
HEARD. Gen. 3. 8, they *h.* voice of the Lord.
21. 17, God *h.* voice of the lad.
45. 2, Joseph wept, and the Egyptians *h.*
Ex. 3. 7, I have *h.* their cry.
Num. 11. 1; 12. 2, the Lord *h.* it.
Deut. 4. 12, only ye *h.* a voice.
1 Kings 6. 7, nor any tool of iron *h.*
10. 7; 2 Chron. 9. 6, exceedeth the fame I *h.*
2 Kin. 19. 25; Isa. 37. 26, hast thou not *h.* long ago?
Ezra 3. 13; Neh. 12. 43, the noise was *h.* afar off.
Job 15. 8, hast thou *h.* the secret of God?
16. 2, I have *h.* many such things.
19. 7, but I am not *h.*
26. 14, how little a portion is *h.*?
29. 11, when the ear *h.* it, it blessed me.
Ps. 6. 9, the Lord hath *h.* my supplication.
10. 17, hast *h.* the desire of the humble.
34. 4, I sought the Lord, and he *h.*
38. 13, I was as a deaf man, and *h.* not.
61. 5, thou hast *h.* my vows.
81. 5, I *h.* language I understood not.
116. 1, I love the Lord, because he hath *h.*
Cant. 2. 12, voice of turtle is *h.*
Isa. 40. 21, 28, have ye not *h.*?
64. 4, not *h.* what he hath prepared.
65. 19, weeping no more be *h.*
66. 8, who hath *h.* such a thing?
Jer. 7. 13, rising early, but ye *h.* not.
8. 6, I *h.,* but they spake not aright.
51. 46; Obad. 1, a rumour that shall be *h.*
Dan. 12. 8, I *h.,* but understood not.
Zech. 8. 23, we have *h.* God is with you.
Mal. 3. 16, the Lord hearkened, and *h.* it.
Mat. 6. 7, *h.* for much speaking.
26. 65; Mk. 14. 64, ye have *h.* the blasphemy.
Lu. 12. 3, shall be *h.* in the light.
John 4. 42, we have *h.* him ourselves.
8. 6, as though he *h.* not.
11. 41, I thank thee thou hast *h.* me.
Acts 4. 4, many which *h.* believed.
20, cannot but speak things we have *h.*
16. 25, the prisoners *h.* them.
22. 15, witness of what thou hast seen and *h.*
Rom. 10. 14, of whom they have not *h.*

Rom. 10. 18, have they not *h.*?
1 Cor. 2. 9, eye hath not seen, nor ear *h.*
2 Cor. 12. 4, *h.* unspeakable words.
Eph. 4. 21, if so be ye have *h.* him.
Phil. 4. 9, things ye have *h.* and seen in me.
2 Tim. 2. 2, things thou hast *h.* of me.
Heb. 2. 3, confirmed by them that *h.*
4. 2, with faith in them that *h.*
Heb. 5. 7, was *h.* in that he feared.
1 John 1. 1, 3, that which we have *h.* and seen.
Rev. 3. 3, remember how thou hast *h.*
10. 4 ; 14. 2 ; 18. 4, *h.* a voice from heaven.
See Jer. 31. 18 ; John 5. 37 ; Rev. 19. 6 ; 22. 8.

HEARER. Rom. 2. 13 ; Eph. 4. 29 ; Jas. 1. 23.

HEARING. Deut. 31. 11, read this law in their *h.*
2 Kings 4. 31, neither voice nor *h.*
Job 42. 5, by the *h.* of the ear.
Prov. 20. 12, the *h.* ear.
Eccl. 1. 8, nor ear filled with *h.*
Amos 8. 11, a famine of *h.* the word.
Mat. 13. 13, *h.,* they hear not.
Acts 9. 7, *h.* a voice, but seeing no man.
Rom. 10. 17, faith cometh by *h.*
1 Cor. 12. 17, where were the *h.*?
Heb. 5. 11, ye are dull of *h.*
See Acts 28. 27 ; Gal. 3. 2 ; 2 Pet. 2. 8.

HEARKEN. Deut. 18. 15, unto him ye shall *h.*
Josh. 1. 17, so will we *h.* unto thee.
1 Sam. 15. 22, to *h.* than the fat of rams.
Prov. 29. 12, if a ruler *h.* to lies.
Isa. 55. 2, *h.* diligently unto me.
Dan. 9. 19, O Lord, *h.* and do.
Mk. 7. 14, *h.* to me, every one of you.
See Ps. 103. 20 ; Prov. 1. 33 ; 12. 15 ; Acts 4. 19.

HEART. Ex. 23. 9, ye know the *h.* of a stranger.
Deut. 11. 13 ; Josh. 22. 5 ; 1 Sam. 12. 20, 24, serve him with all your *h.*
13. 3 ; 30. 6 ; Mat. 22. 37 ; Mk. 12. 30, 33 ; Lu. 10. 27, love the Lord with all your *h.*
Judg. 5. 16, great searchings of *h.*
1 Sam. 10. 9, God gave him another *h.*
16. 7, the Lord looketh on the *h.*
1 Kings 3. 9, 12, give an understanding *h.*
4. 29, gave Solomon largeness of *h.*
8. 17 ; 2 Chron. 6. 7, it was in the *h.* of David.
11. 4, not perfect, as was *h.* of David.
14. 8, followed me with all his *h.*
1 Chron. 12. 33, not of double *h.*
29. 17 ; Jer. 11. 20, I know thou triest the *h.*
2 Chron. 31. 21, he did it with all his *h.*
32. 25, his *h.* was lifted up.
Neh. 2. 2, nothing else but sorrow of *h.*
Job 23. 16, maketh my *h.* soft.
29. 13, caused the widow's *h.* to sing.
Ps. 10. 6 ; 11. 13 ; 14. 1 ; 53. 1, said in his *h.*
19. 8, rejoicing the *h.*
27. 3, my *h.* shall not fear.
28. 7, my *h.* trusted in him.
64. 6, the *h.* is deep.
73. 7, more than *h.* could wish.
78. 37, their *h.* was not right.
97. 11, gladness sown for upright in *h.*
119. 11, thy word have I hid in my *h.*
80, let my *h.* be sound.
139. 23, search me and know my *h.*
Prov. 4. 23, keep thy *h.* with all diligence.
14. 10, the *h.* knoweth his own bitterness.
21. 1, king's *h.* is in the hand of the Lord.
23. 7, as he thinketh in his *h.*, so is he.
25. 3, king's *h.* is unsearchable.
20, songs to a heavy *h.*
31. 11, *h.* of her husband doth trust.
Eccl. 8. 5, wise man's *h.* discerneth.
Isa. 35. 4, say to them of fearful *h.*
44. 20, a deceived *h.*
57. 1 ; Jer. 12. 11, no man layeth it to *h.*
15, revive *h.* of contrite.
65. 14, sing for joy of *h.*
Jer. 11. 20 ; 20. 12, thou triest the *h.*
17. 9, the *h.* is deceitful above all things.

Jer. 20. 9, in mine *h.* as a burning fire.
24. 7, I will give them a *h.* to know me.
30. 21, that engaged his *h.* to approach.
49. 16 ; Obad. 3, pride of *h.* deceived thee.
Ezek. 11. 19, take stony *h.*
18. 31, make you a new *h.*
36. 26, will give you a *h.* of flesh.
44. 7 ; Acts 7. 51, uncircumcised in *h.*
Dan. 1. 8, Daniel purposed in his *h.*
Joel 2. 13, rend your *h.*
Zech. 7. 12, made *h.* as adamant.
Mal. 2. 2, if ye will not lay it to *h.*
4. 6, turn *h.* of fathers to children.
Mat. 5. 8, blessed are the pure in *h.*
6. 21 ; Lu. 12. 34, there will your *h.* be also.
11. 29, meek and lowly in *h.*
12. 34 ; Lu. 6. 45, out of abundance of the *h.*
15. 19, out of the *h.* proceed evil thoughts.
18. 35, if ye from your *h.* forgive not.
Mk. 2. 8, why reason ye in your *h.*?
8. 17, have ye your *h.* yet hardened?
10. 5 ; 16. 14, hardness of *h.*
Lu. 2. 19, 51, kept them in her *h.*
21. 14, settle it in your *h.*
24. 25, slow of *h.* to believe.
32, did not our *h.* burn within us?
John 14. 1, 27, let not your *h.* be troubled.
Acts 5. 23 ; 7. 54, were cut to the *h.*
11. 23, with purpose of *h.*
Rom. 10. 10, with the *h.* man believeth.
1 Cor. 2. 9, neither have entered into *h.*
2 Cor. 3. 3, in fleshy tables of the *h.*
5. 12, glory in appearance, not in *h.*
Eph. 3. 17, that Christ dwell in your *h.* by faith.
5. 19, singing and making melody in your *h.*
6. 6, doing will of God from the *h.*
Phil. 4. 7, keep your *h.* and minds.
Col. 3. 22, in singleness of *h.*
2 Thess. 3. 5, direct your *h.* into love of God.
Heb. 4. 12, discerner of intents of the *h.*
10. 22, draw near with true *h.*
13. 9, good that the *h.* be established.
Jas. 3. 14, if ye have strife in your *h.*
4. 8, purify your *h.*
1 Pet. 3. 4, the hidden man of the *h.*
15, sanctify the Lord in your *h.*
See Ps. 57. 7 ; 108. 1 ; Col. 3. 15 ; 2 Pet. 1. 19.

HEARTH. Gen. 18. 6 ; Ps. 102. 3 ; Isa. 30. 14 ; Jer. 36. 22.

HEARTILY. Col. 3. 23.

HEAT. Deut. 29. 24, the *h.* of this great anger.
Ps. 19. 6, nothing hid from *h.* thereof.
Eccl. 4. 11, two together, then they have *h.*
Isa. 4. 6 ; 25. 4, a shadow from the *h.*
18. 4, *h.* upon herbs, dew in *h.* of harvest.
49. 10, neither shall *h.* smite them.
Hos. 7. 4, as oven *h.* by the baker.
Mat. 20. 12, burden and *h.* of the day.
Jas. 1. 11, sun no sooner risen with burning *h.*
2 Pet. 3. 10, melt with fervent *h.*
See Dan. 3. 19 ; Lu. 12. 55 ; Acts 28. 3.

HEATH. Jer. 17. 6 ; 48. 6.

HEATHEN. Ps. 2. 1 ; Acts 4. 25, why do the *h.* rage?
8, give *h.* for inheritance.
102. 15, the *h.* shall fear name of the Lord.
Ezek. 36. 24, I will take you from among *h.*
Zech. 8. 13, ye were a curse among the *h.*
Mat. 6. 7, repetitions, as the *h.*
18. 17, let him be as *h.* man.
See Lev. 25. 44 ; Deut. 4. 27 ; Neh. 5. 8.

HEAVEN. Gen. 28. 17, the gate of *h.*
Ex. 20. 22, have talked with you from *h.*
Lev. 26. 19, make your *h.* as iron.
Deut. 10. 14 ; 1 Kings 8. 27 ; Ps. 115. 16, the *h.* and *h.* of heavens.
33. 13, the precious things of *h.*
2 Kings 7. 2, if the Lord make windows in *h.*
Job 15. 15, the *h.* are not clean in his sight.
22. 12, is not God in the height of *h.*?

Ps. 8. 3, when I consider thy *h.*
14. 2 ; 53. 2, had looked down from *h.*
73. 25, whom have I in *h.* ?
89. 6, who in *h.* can be compared to the Lord ?
119. 89, thy word is settled in *h.*
Prov. 8. 27, when he prepared the *h.* I was there.
25. 3, the *h.* for height.
Eccl. 5. 2, for God is in *h.*
Isa. 13. 13 ; Hag. 2. 6, will shake the *h.*
40. 12, meted out *h.* with the span.
65. 17 ; Rev. 21. 1, new *h.* and new earth.
Jer. 7. 18, make cakes to queen of *h.*
23. 24, do not I fill *h.* and earth ?
31. 37, if *h.* can be measured.
Ezek. 1. 1 ; Mat. 3. 16 ; Mk. 1. 10, the *h.* were
opened.
32. 7, I will cover the *h.*
Dan. 7. 13, with clouds of *h.*
Hag. 1. 10, *h.* over you is stayed from dew.
Mal. 3. 10, if I will not open windows of *h.*
Mat. 5. 18, till *h.* and earth pass.
11. 23, exalted to *h.*
24. 29 ; Mk. 13. 25, the powers of *h.*
Mk. 13. 32, no, not the angels in *h.*
Lu. 15. 18, I have sinned against *h.*
John 1. 51, ye shall see *h.* open.
6. 31, 32, bread from *h.*
Acts 4. 12, none other name under *h.*
Rom. 1. 18, wrath of God revealed from *h.*
2 Cor. 5. 1, eternal in the *h.*
2, our house that is from *h.*
Gal. 1. 8, though an angel from *h.* preach.
Eph. 1. 10, gather in one, things in *h.*
3. 15, whole family in *h.*
6. 9 ; Col. 4. 1, your master is in *h.*
Phil. 3. 20, our conversation is in *h.*
Heb. 12. 23, written in *h.*
1 John 5. 7, three that bear record in *h.*
Rev. 4. 1, door opened in *h.*
2, throne set in *h.*
8. 1, silence in *h.*
12. 1, 3, a great wonder in *h.*
See 2 Cor. 12. 2 ; 1 Thess. 4. 16 ; 2 Thess. 1. 7.

HEAVENLY. Lu. 2. 13, multitude of the *h.* host.
John 3. 12, I tell you of *h.* things.
Acts 26. 19, the *h.* vision.
1 Cor. 15. 48, as is the *h.*, such are they.
Eph. 1. 3 ; 2. 6 ; 3. 10, in *h.* places.
Heb. 3. 1, partakers of the *h.* calling.
8. 5 ; 9. 23, shadow of *h.* things.
11. 16, an *h.* country.
See 2 Tim. 4. 18 ; Heb. 6. 4 ; 12. 22.

HEAVENLY FATHER. Mat. 6. 14, your *h. f.* also
will forgive you.
Lu. 11. 13, how much more shall your *h. f.* give
the Holy Spirit to them that ask him ?

HEAVINESS. Ps. 69. 20, I am full of *h.*
Prov. 12. 25, *h.* in the heart maketh it stoop.
14. 13, the end of that mirth is *h.*
Isa. 61. 3, garment of praise for spirit of *h.*
Jas. 4. 9, let your joy be turned to *h.*
See Ezra 9. 5 ; Prov. 10. 1 ; Rom. 9. 2.

HEAVY. Ex. 17. 12, Moses' hands were *h.*
1 Kings 14. 6, sent with *h.* tidings.
Neh. 5. 18, the bondage was *h.*
Job 33. 7 ; Ps. 32. 4, hand *h.*
Prov. 25. 20, songs to a *h.* heart.
31. 6, wine to those of *h.* hearts.
Isa. 58. 6, to undo the *h.* burdens.
Mat. 11. 28, all ye that are *h.* laden.
23. 4, they bind *h.* burdens.
26. 37, he began to be very *h.*
43 ; Mk. 14. 33, their eyes were *h.*
See Prov. 27. 3 ; Isa. 59. 1 ; Lu. 9. 32.

HEDGE. Job 3. 23, whom God hath *h.* in.
Prov. 15. 19, way of slothful an *h.* of thorns.
Eccl. 10. 8, whoso breaketh an *h.*
Lam. 3. 7, he hath *h.* me about.
Hos. 2. 6, I will *h.* up thy way.
Mk. 12. 1, he set a *h.* about it.

Lu. 14. 23, the highways and *h.*
See Isa. 5. 5 ; Ezek. 13. 5 ; 22. 30 ; Nah. 3. 17.
HEED. 2 Sam. 20. 10, took no *h.* to the sword.
Ps. 119. 9, by taking *h.* thereto.
Eccl. 12. 9, preacher gave good *h.*
Isa. 21. 7, hearkened diligently with much *h.*
Jer. 18. 18, let us not give *h.*
1 Tim. 1. 4 ; Tit. 1. 14, neither give *h.* to fables.
4. 1, giving *h.* to seducing spirits.
Heb. 2. 1, give more earnest *h.*
See Prov. 17. 4 ; Acts 3. 5 ; 8. 6.
HEEL. Gen. 3. 15, thou shalt bruise his *h.*
Ps. 49. 5, when the iniquity of my *h.* shall com-
pass me about.
HEIGHT. Ps. 102. 19, from *h.* of his sanctuary.
Prov. 25. 3, the heaven for *h.*
Isa. 7. 11, ask it either in the depth, or in the *h.*
above.
Eph. 3. 18, 19, the *h.* of the love of Christ.
See Job 22. 12 ; Ps. 148. 1 ; Amos 2. 9.
HEIR. 2 Sam. 14. 7, we will destroy the *h.*
Prov. 30. 23, handmaid that is *h.* to her mistress.
Mat. 21. 38 ; Mk. 12. 7 ; Lu. 20. 14, this is the *h.*
Rom. 8. 17, *h.* of God, joint-*h.* with Christ.
Gal. 3. 29, *h.* according to the promise.
4. 7, an *h.* of God through Christ.
Eph. 3. 6, Gentiles fellow-*h.*
Tit. 3. 7, *h.* according to hope of eternal life.
Heb. 1. 14, who shall be *h.* of salvation.
6. 17, the *h.* of promise.
11. 7, *h.* of the righteousness.
Jas. 2. 5, *h.* of the kingdom.
1 Pet. 3. 7, as *h.* together of the grace.
See Jer. 49. 1 ; Mic. 1. 15 ; Rom. 4. 13.
HELL. Deut. 32. 22, fire shall burn to lowest *h.*
2 Sam. 22. 6 ; Ps. 18. 5, sorrows of *h.* compassed me.
Job 11. 8, deeper than *h.*
26. 6, *h.* is naked before him.
Ps. 9. 17, wicked turned into *h.*
16. 10 ; Acts 2. 27, not leave soul in *h.*
55. 15, let them go down quick into *h.*
139. 8, if I make my bed in *h.*
Prov. 5. 5, her steps take hold on *h.*
7. 27, house is the way to *h.*
9. 18, her guests are in the depths of *h.*
15. 11, *h.* and destruction before the Lord.
24, that he may depart from *h.* beneath.
23. 14, deliver his soul from *h.*
27. 20, *h.* and destruction are never full.
Isa. 14. 9, *h.* from beneath is moved.
28. 15, 18, with *h.* are we at agreement.
Ezek. 31. 16, when I cast him down to *h.*
32. 21, shall speak out of the midst of *h.*
Amos 9. 2, though they dig into *h.*
Jonah 2. 2, out of the belly of *h.*
Hab. 2. 5, enlargeth his desire as *h.*
Mat. 5. 22, in danger of *h.* fire.
29, 30, whole body cast into *h.*
10. 28 ; Lu. 12. 5, destroy soul and body in *h.*
11. 23 ; Lu. 10. 15, brought down to *h.*
16. 18, gates of *h.* shall not prevail.
18. 9 ; Mk. 9. 47, having two eyes to be cast into *h.*
23. 15, more the child of *h.*
33, how can ye escape the damnation of *h.* ?
Lu. 16. 23, in *h.* he lift up.
Acts 2. 31, soul not left in *h.*
Jas. 3. 6, tongue set on fire of *h.*
2 Pet. 2. 4, cast angels down to *h.*
See Isa. 5. 14 ; Rev. 1. 18 ; 6. 8 ; 20. 13.
HELP. Gen. 2. 18, 20, an *h.* meet for him.
Deut. 33. 29, the shield of thy *h.*
2 Chron. 26. 15, he was marvellously *h.*
Job 6. 13, is not my *h.* in me ?
Ps. 22. 11, for there is none to *h.*
33. 20, he is our *h.* and our shield.
42. 5, the *h.* of his countenance.
46. 1, a very present *h.* in trouble.
60. 11 ; 108. 12, vain is the *h.* of man.
89. 19, laid *h.* on one that is mighty.
121. 1, the hills from whence cometh my *h.*
124. 8, our *h.* is in the name of the Lord.

Isa. 10. 3, to whom will ye flee for *h.*?
41. 6, they *h.* every one his neighbour.
Hos. 13. 9, in me is thine *h.*
Mat. 15. 25, Lord, *h.* me.
Mk. 9. 24, *h.* thou mine unbelief.
Acts 21. 28, men of Israel, *h.*
26. 22, having obtained *h.* of God.
Heb. 4. 16, grace to *h.* in time of need.
See Isa. 31. 3 ; Rom. 8. 26 ; 2 Cor. 1. 24.

HELPER. Heb. 13. 6.

HEM. Mat. 9. 20, touched the *h.* of his garment.
14. 36, might only touch the *h.* of his garment.
See Num. 15. 38, 39 ; Mat. 23. 5.

HEMLOCK. Hos. 10. 4, judgment springeth up
as *h.*
Amos 6. 12, the fruit of righteousness into *h.*

HEN. Mat. 23. 37 ; Lu. 13. 34.

HENCEFORTH. 2 Cor. 5. 15 ; Gal. 6. 17 ; 2 Tim.
4. 8.

HERITAGE. Job 20. 29, *h.* appointed by God.
Ps. 16. 6 ; Jer. 3. 19, a goodly *h.*
61. 5, the *h.* of those that fear.
127. 3, children are an *h.* of the Lord.
Isa. 54. 17, this is the *h.* of the servants.
Mic. 7. 14, feed flock of thine *h.*
1 Pet. 5. 3, lords over God's *h.*
See Joel 2. 17 ; 3. 2 ; Mal. 1. 3.

HID. 2 Kings 4. 27, the Lord hath *h.* it from me.
Job 3. 21, more than for *h.* treasures.
Ps. 32. 5, mine iniquity have I not *h.*
69. 5, my sins are not *h.*
119. 11, thy word have I *h.* in mine heart.
Zeph. 2. 3, it may be ye shall be *h.*
Mat. 10. 26 ; Mk. 4. 22, there is nothing *h.*
Lu. 19. 42, now they are *h.* from thine eyes.
1 Cor. 2. 7, even the *h.* wisdom.
2 Cor. 4. 3, if our gospel be *h.*
Col. 3. 3, your life is *h.* with Christ.
1 Pet. 3. 4, the *h.* man of the heart.
Rev. 2. 17, to eat of the *h.* manna.
See Gen. 3. 8 ; Mat. 5. 14 ; Mk. 7. 24.

HIDE. Gen. 18. 17, shall I *h.* from Abraham.
Job 14. 13, *h.* me in the grave.
34. 29, when he *h.* his face.
Ps. 10. 11, he *h.* his face.
17. 8, *h.* me under the shadow of thy wings.
27. 5, *h.* me in pavilion.
31. 20, *h.* them in secret of thy presence.
89. 46, how long wilt thou *h.* thyself ?
139. 12, darkness *h.* not from thee.
Isa. 1. 15, I will *h.* mine eyes from you.
3. 9, they *h.* not their sin.
26. 20, *h.* thyself for a little moment.
32. 2, a man shall be as an *h.* place.
45. 15, thou art a God that *h.* thyself.
Ezek. 28. 3, no secret they can *h.* from thee.
Jas. 5. 20, *h.* a multitude of sins.
Rev. 6. 16, *h.* us from the face of him.
See Job 13. 24 ; Prov. 28. 28 ; Amos 9. 3.

HIGH. Job 11. 8, it is as *h.* as heaven.
22. 12, behold stars, how *h.* they are!
41. 34, he beholdeth all *h.* things.
Ps. 62. 9, men of *h.* degree are a lie.
68. 18, thou hast ascended on *h.*
103. 11, as the heaven is *h.* above the earth.
131. 1, in things too *h.* for me.
138. 6, though the Lord be *h.*
139. 6, it is *h.*, I cannot attain unto it.
Eccl. 12. 5, afraid of that which is *h.*
Isa. 32. 15, spirit poured on us from on *h.*
33. 16, he shall dwell on *h.*
35. 8, an *h.*-way shall be there.
62. 10, cast up the *h.*-way.
Jer. 49. 16, though thou make thy nest *h.*
Mat. 22. 9 ; Lu. 14. 23, go into the *h.*-ways.
Lu. 1. 78, dayspring from on *h.*
24. 49, power from on *h.*
Rom. 12. 16, mind not *h.* things.
13. 11, it is *h.* time.

Phil. 3. 14, for prize of the *h.* calling.
See Isa. 57. 15 ; 2 Cor. 10. 5.

HIGHER. Isa. 55. 9, heavens *h.* than the earth.
Lu. 14. 10, friend, go up *h.*
Heb. 7. 26, made *h.* than the heavens.

HILL. Gen. 49. 26, the everlasting *h.*
Deut. 11. 11, a land of *h.* and valleys.
Ps. 2. 6, set my king on holy *h.*
15. 1, who shall dwell in thy holy *h.* ?
24. 3, who shall ascend the *h.* of the Lord ?
43. 3, bring me to thy holy *h.*
50. 10, cattle on a thousand *h.*
95. 4, strength of the *h.* is his.
121. 1, I will lift up mine eyes to the *h.*
Prov. 8. 25, before the *h.* was I brought forth.
Isa. 40. 12, weighed the *h.* in balance.
Jer. 3. 23, salvation hoped for from the *h.*
Hos. 10. 8 ; Lu. 23. 30, to the *h.*, fall on us.
Mat. 5. 14, city set on an *h.*
See Lu. 4. 29 ; 9. 37 ; Acts 17. 22.

HINDER. Gen. 24. 56, *h.* me not.
Job 9. 12 ; 11. 10, who can *h.* him ?
Lu. 11. 52, them that were entering ye *h.*
Acts 8. 36, what doth *h.* me to be baptized ?
1 Cor. 9. 12, lest we *h.* the gospel.
Gal. 5. 7, who did *h.* you ?
1 Thess. 2. 18, but Satan *h.* us.
1 Pet. 3. 7, that your prayers be not *h.*
See Num. 22. 16 ; Neh. 4. 8 ; Isa. 14. 6.

HIRE. Deut. 24. 15, thou shalt give him his *h.*
Mic. 3. 11, priests teach for *h.*
Mat. 20. 7, no man hath *h.* us.
8, give them their *h.*
Mk. 1. 20, in ship with *h.* servants.
Lu. 10. 7, labourer worthy of his *h.*
15. 17, how many *h.* servants.
Jas. 5. 4, *h.* of labourers which is kept back.
See Ex. 12. 45 ; Lev. 25. 40 ; Deut. 15. 18.

HIRELING. Job 7. 1, like the days of an *h.*
2, as *h.* looketh for reward.
14. 6, accomplish, as an *h.*, his day.
Mal. 3. 5, that oppress the *h.*
See Isa. 16. 14 ; 21. 16 ; John 10. 12.

HITHERTO. Josh. 17. 14, the Lord hath blessed
me *h.*
1 Sam. 7. 12, *h.* hath the Lord helped us.
Job 38. 11, *h.* shalt thou come.
John 5. 17, my Father worketh *h.*
16. 24, *h.* have ye asked nothing in my name.
1 Cor. 3. 2, *h.* ye were not able to bear it.
See Judg. 16. 13 ; 2 Sam. 15. 34 ; Isa. 18. 2.

HOARY. Job 41. 32.

HOLD. Gen. 21. 18, *h.* him in thine hand.
Ex. 20. 7 ; Deut. 5. 11, will not *h.* him guiltless.
2 Kings 7. 9, good tidings, and we *h.* our peace.
Esth. 4. 14, if thou altogether *h.* thy peace.
Job 36. 8, *h.* in cords of affliction.
Ps. 18. 35, thy right hand hath *h.* me up.
71. 6, by thee have I been *h.*
73. 23, thou hast *h.* me by my right hand.
119. 117, *h.* me up, and I shall be safe.
Prov. 11. 12, man of understanding *h.* his peace.
17. 28, a fool, when he *h.* his peace.
Isa. 41. 13, the Lord will *h.* thy hand.
62. 1, for Zion's sake will I not *h.* my peace.
Jer. 4. 19, I cannot *h.* my peace.
Amos 6. 10, *h.* thy tongue.
Mat. 6. 24 ; Lu. 16. 13, he will *h.* to the one.
Mk. 1. 25 ; Lu. 4. 35, *h.* thy peace, come out.
Rom. 1. 18, *h.* the truth in unrighteousness.
1 Cor. 14. 30, let the first *h.* his peace.
Phil. 2. 16, *h.* forth the word of life.
29, *h.* such in reputation.
Col. 2. 19, not *h.* the Head.
1 Thess. 5. 21, *h.* fast that which is good.
1 Tim. 1. 19, *h.* faith and good conscience.
3. 9, *h.* the mystery of faith.
2 Tim. 1. 13, *h.* fast form of sound words.
Tit. 1. 9, *h.* fast the faithful word.

Heb. 3. 14, *h.* beginning of confidence.
4. 14 ; 10. 23, *h.* fast our profession.
Rev. 2. 13, thou *h.* fast my name.
25, *h.* fast till I come.
3. 3, *h.* fast, and repent.
11, *h.* that fast which thou hast.
See Job 2. 3 ; Jer. 2. 13 ; 51. 30 ; Ezek. 19. 9.

HOLE. Isa. 11. 8, child shall play on *h.* of the asp.
51. 1, *h.* of pit whence ye are digged.
Jer. 13. 4, hide in a *h.* of the rock.
Ezek. 8. 7, a *h.* in the wall.
Hag. 1. 6, a bag with *h.*
Mat. 8. 20 ; Lu. 9. 58, foxes have *h.*
See Cant. 5. 4 ; Mic. 7. 17 ; Nah. 2. 12.

HOLIER. Isa. 65. 5.

HOLIEST. Heb. 9. 3 ; 10. 19.

HOLILY. 1 Thess. 2. 10.

HOLINESS. Ex. 15. 11, glorious in *h.*
28. 36 ; 39. 30 ; Zech. 14. 20, *h.* to the Lord.
1 Chron. 16. 29 ; 2 Chron. 20. 21 ; Ps. 29. 2 ; 96. 9 ; 110. 3, beauty of *h.*
Ps. 30. 4 ; 97. 12, at remembrance of his *h.*
47. 8, the throne of his *h.*
60. 6 ; 108. 7, God hath spoken in his *h.*
93. 5, *h.* becometh thine house.
Isa. 35. 8, the way of *h.*
63. 15, habitation of thy *h.*
Jer. 23. 9, the words of his *h.*
Obad. 17, upon mount Zion there shall be *h.*
Lu. 1. 75, might serve him in *h.*
Acts 3. 12, as though by our *h.*
Rom. 1. 4, according to the spirit of *h.*
6. 22, fruit unto *h.*
2 Cor. 7. 1, perfecting *h.* in fear of God.
Eph. 4. 24, created in righteousness and *h.*
1 Thess. 3. 13, unblameable in *h.*
4. 7, not called to uncleanness, but *h.*
1 Tim. 2. 15, continue in faith and *h.*
Tit. 2. 3, in behaviour as becometh *h.*
Heb. 12. 10, partakers of his *h.*
14, *h.,* without which no man.
See Ps. 89. 35 ; Isa. 23. 18 ; Jer. 2. 3.

HOLLOW. Gen. 32. 25 ; Judg. 15. 19 ; Isa. 40. 12.

HOLPEN. Ps. 86. 17 ; Isa. 31. 3 ; Dan. 11. 34 ; Lu. 1. 54.

HOLY. Ex. 3. 5 ; Josh. 5. 15, is *h.* ground.
19. 6 ; 1 Pet. 2. 9, an *h.* nation.
20. 8 ; 31. 14, sabbath day, to keep it *h.*
Lev. 10. 10, difference between *h.* and unholy.
20. 7, be ye *h.*
Num. 16. 5, Lord will show who is *h.*
2 Kings 4. 9, this is an *h.* man of God.
Ezra 9. 2 ; Isa. 6. 13, the *h.* seed.
Ps. 20. 6, hear from his *h.* heaven.
22. 3, thou art *h.* that inhabitest.
86. 2, preserve my soul, for I am *h.*
98. 1, his *h.* arm hath gotten victory.
99. 9, worship at his *h.* hill.
145. 17, the Lord is *h.* in all his works.
Prov. 20. 25, who devoureth that which is *h.*
Isa. 6. 3 ; Rev. 4. 8, *h., h., h.,* is the Lord.
52. 10, make bare his *h.* arm.
64. 10, thy *h.* cities are a wilderness.
11, our *h.* and beautiful house.
Ezek. 22. 26, put no difference between *h.* and profane.
Mat. 1. 18, 20, with child of the *H.* Ghost.
3. 11 ; Mk. 1. 8 ; Lu. 3. 16 ; John 1. 33 ; Acts 1. 5, baptize with *H.* Ghost.
7. 6, give not that which is *h.*
12. 31 ; Mk. 3. 29, blasphemy against *H.* Ghost.
Mk. 13. 11, not ye that speak, but *H.* Ghost.
Lu. 1. 15, shall be filled with the *H.* Ghost.
35, that *h.* thing which shall be born of thee.
3. 22, *H.* Ghost descended in bodily shape.
4. 1, Jesus being full of the *H.* Ghost.
12. 12, *H.* Ghost shall teach you.
John 7. 39, the *H.* Ghost was not yet given.
14. 26, the Comforter, which is the *H.* Ghost.

John 17. 11, *h.* Father, keep those.
20. 22, receive ye the *H.* Ghost.
Acts 1. 8, after the *H.* Ghost is come.
2. 4 ; 4. 31, all filled with *H.* Ghost.
4. 27, 30, against thy *h.* child Jesus.
5. 3, to lie to the *H.* Ghost.
6. 3, look out men full of the *H.* Ghost.
7. 51, ye do always resist the *H.* Ghost.
8. 15, prayed that they might receive *H.* Ghost.
9. 31, in comfort of the *H.* Ghost.
10. 44, *H.* Ghost fell on all which heard.
47, received *H.* Ghost as well as we.
15. 8, giving them *H.* Ghost, as he did unto us.
28, seemed good to the *H.* Ghost.
16. 6, forbidden of the *H.* Ghost.
19. 2, have ye received the *H.* Ghost ?
20. 28, *H.* Ghost hath made you overseers.
Rom. 1. 2, promised in the *h.* scriptures.
7. 12, commandment is *h.,* just, and good.
9. 1, bearing witness in *H.* Ghost.
11. 16, if firstfruit be *h.,* if root be *h.*
12. 1, a living sacrifice, *h.,* acceptable to God.
14. 17, joy in the *H.* Ghost.
16. 16 ; 1 Cor. 16. 20 ; 2 Cor. 13. 12 ; 1 Thess. 5. 26 ; 1 Pet. 5. 14, with a *h.* kiss.
1 Cor. 2. 13, words which the *H.* Ghost teacheth.
3. 17, the temple of God is *h.*
7. 14, now are they *h.*
2 Cor. 13. 14, communion of the *H.* Ghost.
Eph. 1. 4 ; 5. 27, be *h.* and without blame.
2. 21, growth to an *h.* temple in the Lord.
Col. 1. 22, present you *h.* and unblameable.
3. 12, elect of God, *h.* and beloved.
1 Thess. 5. 27, all the *H.* brethren.
1 Tim. 2. 8, lifting up *h.* hands.
2 Tim. 1. 9, called us with an *h.* calling.
Tit. 1. 8, bishop must be *h.*
3. 5, the renewing of the *H.* Ghost.
Heb. 3. 1, *h.* brethren, partakers.
1 Pet. 1. 12, *H.* Ghost sent down from heaven.
15 ; 2 Pet. 3. 11, *h.* in all conversation.
2. 5, an *h.* priesthood.
3. 5, the *h.* women, who trusted.
2 Pet. 1. 18, with him in the *h.* mount.
21, *h.* men moved by *H.* Ghost.
Rev. 3. 7, saith he that is *h.*
6. 10, O Lord, *h.* and true.
20. 6, *h.* is he that hath part.
21. 10, the *h.* Jerusalem.
22. 11, he that is *h.,* let him be *h.*
See 2 Tim. 3. 15 ; 1 Pet. 1. 16 ; 2 Pet. 3. 2 : Jude 20.

HOME. Ex. 9. 19, and shall not be brought *h.*
Lev. 18. 9, whether born at *h.* or abroad.
Deut. 24. 5, free at *h.* one year.
Ruth 1. 21, the Lord hath brought me *h.* empty.
2 Sam. 14. 13, fetch *h.* his banished.
1 Kings 13. 7, come *h.* with me.
2 Kings 14. 10 ; 2 Chron. 25. 19, tarry at *h.*
1 Chron. 13. 12, bring ark of God *h.*
Job 39. 12, he will bring *h.* thy seed.
Ps. 68. 12, she that tarried at *h.*
Eccl. 12. 5, man goeth to his long *h.*
Lam. 1. 20, at *h.* there is as death.
Hag. 1. 9, when ye brought it *h.*
Mk. 5. 19, go *h.* to thy friends.
John 19. 27, took her to his own *h.*
20. 10, went away to their own *h.*
1 Cor. 11. 34, let him eat at *h.*
14. 35, ask their husbands at *h.*
2 Cor. 5. 6, at *h.* in the body.
1 Tim. 5. 4, show piety at *h.*
Tit. 2. 5, keepers at *h.*
See Jer. 2. 14 ; Lu. 9. 61 ; 15. 6.

HONEST. Lu. 8. 15, an *h.* and good heart.
Acts 6. 3, men of *h.* report.
Rom. 12. 17 ; 2 Cor. 8. 21, provide things *h.*
13. 13, let us walk *h.,* as in the day.
Phil. 4. 8, whatsoever things are *h.*
1 Pet. 2. 12, conversation *h.* among Gentiles.
See 1 Thess. 4. 12 ; 1 Tim. 2. 2 ; Heb. 13. 18.

HONOUR (*n.*). Num. 22. 17, I will promote thee
　　to *h.*
24. 11, hath kept thee back from *h.*
2 Sam. 6. 22, of them shall I be had in *h.*
1 Kings 3. 13, also given thee riches and *h.*
1 Chron. 29. 28, died full of riches and *h.*
2 Chron. 1. 11, 12, thou hast not asked *h.*
26. 18, neither shall it be for thy *h.*
Esth. 1. 20, the wives shall give their husbands *h.*
Job 14. 21, his sons come to *h.*
Ps. 7. 5, lay mine *h.* in the dust.
8. 5; Heb. 2. 7, crowned him with *h.*
26. 8, place where thine *h.* dwelleth.
49. 12, man being in *h.* abideth not.
96. 6, *h.* and majesty are before him.
149. 9, this *h.* have all his saints.
Prov. 3. 16, in left hand riches and *h.*
4. 8, she shall bring thee to *h.*
5. 9, lest thou give their *h.* to others.
14. 28, in multitude of people is king's *h.*
20. 3, an *h.* to cease from strife.
25. 2, the *h.* of kings to search out.
26. 1, 8, *h.* is not seemly for a fool.
31. 25, strength and *h.* are her clothing.
Eccl. 6. 2, to whom God hath given *h.*
Mal. 1. 6, where is mine *h.*?
Mat. 13. 57; Mk. 6. 4; John 4. 44, not without *h.*
John 5. 41, I receive not *h.* from men.
44, who receive *h.* one of another.
Rom. 2. 7, in well doing seek for *h.*
10, *h.* to every man that worketh good.
12. 10, in *h.* preferring one another.
13. 7, *h.* to whom *h.*
2 Cor. 6. 8, by *h.* and dishonour.
Col. 2. 23, not in any *h.* to satisfying.
1 Thess. 4. 4, possess his vessel in *h.*
1 Tim. 5. 17, elders worthy of double *h.*
6. 1, count masters worthy of *h.*
16, to whom be *h.* and power everlasting.
2 Tim. 2. 20, 21, some to *h.*, some to dishonour.
Heb. 3. 3, more *h.* than the house.
5. 4, no man taketh this *h.* unto himself.
1 Pet. 3. 7, giving *h.* to the wife.
Rev. 4. 11; 5. 12, thou art worthy to receive *h.*
See Rev. 5. 13; 7. 12; 19. 1; 21. 24.

HONOUR (*v.*). Ex. 14. 4, I will be *h.* upon Pha-
　　raoh.
20. 12; Deut. 5. 16; Mat. 15. 4; 19. 19; Mk. 7. 10;
　　10. 19; Lu. 18. 20; Eph. 6. 2, *h.* thy father and
　　mother.
Lev. 19. 32, thou shalt *h.* the face of the old man.
1 Sam. 2. 30, them that *h.* me I will *h.*
15. 30, *h.* me now before elders.
Esth. 6. 6, the king delighteth to *h.*
Ps. 15. 4, he *h.* them that fear the Lord.
Prov. 3. 9, *h.* the Lord with thy substance.
12. 9, better than he that *h.* himself.
Mal. 1. 6, a son *h.* his father.
Mat. 15. 8; Mk. 7. 6, *h.* me with their lips.
John 5. 23, *h.* the Son as they *h.* the Father.
1 Tim. 5. 3, *h.* widows that are widows indeed.
1 Pet. 2. 17, *h.* all men, *h.* the king.
See Isa. 29. 13; 58. 13; Acts 28. 10.

HONOURABLE. Ps. 45. 9, among thy *h.* women.
Isa. 3. 3, take away the *h.* man.
9. 15, ancient and *h.*, he is the head.
42. 21, magnify the law, and make it *h.*
See Lu. 14. 8; 1 Cor. 4. 10; 12. 23; Heb. 13. 4.

HOPE (*n.*). Job 7. 6, my days are spent with-
　　out *h.*
8. 13, the hypocrite's *h.* shall perish.
17. 15, where is now my *h.*?
19. 10, my *h.* hath he removed.
Ps. 16. 9; Acts 2. 26, my flesh also shall rest in *h.*
39. 7, my *h.* is in thee.
119. 116, let me not be ashamed of my *h.*
Prov. 13. 12, *h.* deferred maketh the heart sick.
14. 32, hath *h.* in his death.
26. 12; 29. 20, more *h.* of a fool.
Eccl. 9. 4, to all the living there is *h.*

Jer. 17. 7, the man whose *h.* the Lord is.
31. 17, there is *h.* in thine end.
Hos. 2. 15, for a door of *h.*
Zech. 9. 12, ye prisoners of *h.*
Acts 28. 20, for the *h.* of Israel I am bound.
Rom. 4. 18, who against *h.* believed in *h.*
8. 24, we are saved by *h.*
12. 12, rejoicing in *h.*
1 Cor. 13. 13, faith, *h.*, charity.
15. 19, if in this life only we have *h.*
Eph. 1. 18, the *h.* of his calling.
2. 12, having no *h.*, and without God.
Col. 1. 27, Christ in you, the *h.* of glory.
1 Thess. 4. 13, even as others who have no *h.*
5. 8, for an helmet, the *h.* of salvation.
2 Thess. 2. 16, good *h.* through grace.
Tit. 3. 7, the *h.* of eternal life.
Heb. 6. 18, lay hold on *h.* set before us.
19, *h.* as an anchor of the soul.
1 Pet. 1. 3, begotten to a lively *h.*
3. 15, a reason of the *h.* that is in you.
See Lam. 3. 18; Col. 1. 5; 1 John 3. 3.

HOPE (*v.*). Ps. 22. 9, thou didst make me *h.*
31. 24, all ye that *h.* in the Lord.
42. 5, 11; 43. 5, *h.* thou in God.
71. 14, I will *h.* continually.
Lam. 3. 26, good that a man both *h.* and wait.
Rom. 8. 25, if we *h.* for that we see not.
1 Pet. 1. 13, *h.* to the end.
See Jer. 3. 23; Acts 24. 26; Heb. 11. 1.

HORRIBLE. Ps. 11. 6; 40. 2; Jer. 2. 12; Ezek.
32. 10.

HOSPITALITY. Rom. 12. 13; 1 Tim. 3. 2; Tit. 1.
8; 1 Pet. 4. 9.

HOT. Ps. 39. 3; Prov. 6. 28; 1 Tim. 4. 2; Rev. 3. 15.

HOUR. Mat. 10. 19; Lu. 12. 12, shall be given
　　you in that same *h.*
20. 12, have wrought but one *h.*
24. 36; Mk. 13. 32, that *h.* knoweth no man.
26. 40; Mk. 14. 37, could ye not watch one *h.*?
Lu. 12. 39, what *h.* the thief would come.
22. 53, but this is your *h.*
John 5. 25; Gal. 28, the *h.* is coming, and now is.
11. 9, are there not twelve *h.* in the day?
12. 27, save me from this *h.*
Acts 3. 1, at the *h.* of prayer.
Gal. 2. 5, give place, no, not for an *h.*
Rev. 3. 10, the *h.* of temptation.
See Acts 2. 15; 1 Cor. 4. 11; 16. 30; Rev. 3. 3.

HOUSE. Gen. 28. 17, none other but the *h.* of God.
Deut. 8. 12, when thou hast built goodly *h.*
2 Kings 20. 1; Isa. 38. 1, set thine *h.* in order.
15, what have they seen in thine *h.*?
Neh. 13. 11, why is the *h.* of God forsaken?
Job 30. 23, *h.* appointed for all living.
Ps. 26. 8, have loved the habitation of thy *h.*
65. 4, satisfied with goodness of thy *h.*
69. 9; John 2. 17, the zeal of thine *h.*
84. 3, the sparrow hath found an *h.*
92. 13, planted in the *h.* of the Lord.
118. 26, blessed you out of the *h.* of the Lord.
Prov. 2. 18, her *h.* inclineth to death.
9. 1, wisdom hath builded her *h.*
12. 7, *h.* of the righteous shall stand.
19. 14, *h.* and riches are inheritance.
Eccl. 7. 2, *h.* of mourning, *h.* of feasting.
12. 3, when keepers of the *h.* shall tremble.
Isa. 3. 14, spoil of poor in your *h.*
5. 8, woe unto them that join *h.* to *h.*
64. 11, our holy and beautiful *h.* is burned.
Hos. 9. 15, I will drive them out of mine *h.*
Hag. 1. 4, and this *h.* lie waste.
9, because of mine *h.* that is waste.
Mal. 3. 10, that there may be meat in mine *h.*
Mat. 7. 25; Lu. 6. 48, beat upon that *h.*
10. 12, when ye come into an *h.*
12. 25; Mk. 3. 25, *h.* divided cannot stand.
23. 38, your *h.* is left desolate.
24. 17; Mk. 13. 15, to take anything out of *h.*
Lu. 10. 7, go not from *h.* to *h.*

Lu. 14. 23, that my *h.* may be filled.
18. 14, went down to his *h.* justified.
John 12. 3, *h.* filling with odour.
14. 2, in my Father's *h.* are many mansions.
Acts 2. 46, breaking bread from *h.* to *h.*
5. 42, in every *h.* ceased not to preach.
10. 2 ; 16. 34 ; 18. 8, with all his *h.*
20. 20, I taught you from *h.* to *h.*
1 Cor. 11. 22, have ye not *h.* to eat in?
2 Cor. 5. 1, *h.* not made with hands.
Col. 4. 15, church in his *h.*
1 Tim. 3. 4, 5, 12, ruleth well his own *h.*
5. 8, especially for those of his own *h.*
2 Tim. 3. 6, which creep into *h.*
Tit. 1. 11, subvert whole *h.*
See Mat. 9. 6 ; Lu. 7. 44 ; 19. 5 ; Acts 4. 34.

HOUSEHOLD. Gen. 18. 19, command his *h.* after him.
1 Sam. 27. 3 ; 2 Sam. 2. 3, every man with his *h.*
2 Sam. 6. 20, returned to bless his *h.*
Prov. 31. 27, looketh well to her *h.*
Mat. 10. 36, a man's foes shall be of his own *h.*
Gal. 6. 10, the *h.* of faith.
Eph. 2. 19, of the *h.* of God.
See Gen. 31. 37 ; 47. 12 ; 2 Sam. 17. 23.

HUMBLE. Deut. 8. 2, to *h.* thee and prove thee.
2 Chron. 33. 12, *h.* himself greatly.
Ps. 9. 12 ; 10. 12, forgetteth not cry of the *h.*
34. 2, the *h.* shall hear thereof.
35. 13, I *h.* my soul with fasting.
113. 6, *h.* himself to behold things in heaven.
Prov. 16. 19, better be of *h.* spirit.
Isa. 57. 15, of contrite and *h.* spirit.
Mat. 18. 4 ; 23. 12 ; Lu. 14. 11 ; 18. 14, *h.* himself.
Phil. 2. 8, he *h.* himself.
Jas. 4. 6 ; 1 Pet. 5. 5, God giveth grace to the *h.*
1Pet. 5. 6, *h.* yourselves under mighty hand of God.
See Isa. 2. 11 ; 5. 15 ; Lam. 3. 20.

HUMBLY. 2 Sam. 16. 4 ; Mic. 6. 8.

HUMILITY. Prov. 15. 33 ; 18. 12, before honour is *h.*
22. 4, by *h.* are riches.
See Acts 20. 19 ; Col. 2. 18, 23 ; 1 Pet. 5. 5.

HUNGER. Deut. 8. 3, he suffered thee to *h.*
Job 18. 12, his strength shall be *h.*-bitten.
Ps. 34. 10, young lions do lack, and suffer *h.*
Prov. 19. 15, an idle soul shall suffer *h.*
Isa. 49. 10, shall not *h.* nor thirst.
Jer. 38. 9, he is like to die for *h.*
Mat. 5. 6 ; Lu. 6. 21, blessed are ye that *h.*
Lu. 6. 25, woe unto ye that are full ! for ye shall *h.*
John 6. 35, he that cometh to me shall never *h.*
Rom. 12. 20, if thine enemy *h.*
1 Cor. 4. 11, we both *h.* and thirst.
11. 34, if any man *h.,* let him eat at home.
Rev. 7. 16, they shall *h.* no more.
See Mat. 4. 2 ; 12. 1 ; 25. 35 ; Lu. 15. 17.

HUNGRY. Job 22. 7, withholden bread from *h.*
24. 10, they take away the sheaf from the *h.*
Ps. 50. 12, if I were *h.,* I would not tell thee.
107. 5, *h.* and thirsty, their soul fainted in them.
9, he filleth the *h.* soul with goodness.
146. 7, which giveth food to the *h.*
Prov. 25. 21, if thine enemy be *h.,* give him bread to eat.
27. 7, to the *h.* every bitter thing is sweet.
Isa. 29. 8, when a *h.* man dreameth.
58. 7, is it not to deal thy bread to the *h.?*
65. 13, my servants eat, but ye shall be *h.*
Ezek. 18. 7, given his bread to the *h.*
Lu. 1. 53, he hath filled the *h.* with good things.
Acts 10. 10, and he became very *h.*
1 Cor. 11. 21, one is *h.,* and another drunken.
Phil. 4. 12, instructed both to be full and to be *h.*
See Prov. 6. 30 ; Isa. 8. 21 ; 9. 20 ; Mk. 11. 12.

HUNT. 1 Sam. 26. 20, as when one doth *h.* a partridge.
Jer. 16. 16, *h.* them from every mountain.
Ezek. 13. 18, *h.* souls of my people.

Mic. 7. 2, they *h.* every man his brother.
See Gen. 10. 9 ; 27. 5 ; 1 Sam. 24. 11.

HUNTING. Prov. 12. 27.

HURL. Num. 35. 20 ; 1 Chron. 12. 2 ; Job 27. 21.

HURT. Ps. 15. 4, that sweareth to his own *h.*
Eccl. 8. 9, ruleth over another to his own *h.*
Isa. 11. 9, shall not *h.* nor destroy.
Jer. 6. 14 ; 8. 11, have healed *h.* slightly.
8. 21, for the *h.* of my people.
25. 6, provoke not, I will do no *h.*
Dan. 3. 25, they have no *h.*
6. 23, no manner of *h.* found upon him.
Mk. 16. 18, deadly thing, it shall not *h.*
Lu. 10. 19, nothing shall by any means *h.* you.
Acts 18. 10, no man set on thee to *h.* thee.
Rev. 6. 6, *h.* not the oil and the wine.
See Rev. 7. 2 ; 9. 4 ; 11. 5.

HURTFUL. Ezra 4. 15 ; Ps. 144. 10 ; 1 Tim. 6. 9.

HUSBAND. Ex. 4. 25, a bloody *h.* art thou.
Prov. 12. 4, virtuous wife a crown to her *h.*
31. 11, 23, 28, her *h.* doth safely trust.
Isa. 54. 5, thy Maker is thy *h.*
John 4. 16, go, call thy *h.*
1 Cor. 7. 16, whether thou shalt save thy *h.*
14. 35, let them ask their *h.* at home.
Eph. 5. 22, submit yourselves to your *h.*
25 ; Col. 3. 19, *h.,* love your wives.
1 Tim. 3. 12, the *h.* of one wife.
Tit. 2. 4, teach young women to love their *h.*
5, obedient to their own *h.*
1 Pet. 3. 1, be in subjection to your *h.*
7, ye *h.,* dwell with them.
See Gen. 3. 6 ; Ruth 1. 11 ; Esth. 1. 17, 20.

HYMN. Mat. 26. 30 ; Mk. 14. 26 ; Eph. 5. 19 ; Col. 3. 16.

HYPOCRISY. Mat. 23. 28, within ye are full of *h.*
Mk. 12. 15, he, knowing their *h.*
Lu. 12. 1, leaven of Pharisees, which is *h.*
Jas. 3. 17, wisdom is pure, and without *h.*
See Mat. 32. 6 ; 1 Tim. 4. 2.

HYPOCRITE. Job 8. 13, the *h.* hope shall perish.
20. 5, the joy of the *h.* but for a moment.
36. 13, the *h.* in heart.
Isa. 9. 17, every one is an *h.*
Mat. 6. 2, 5, 16, as the *h.* do.
7. 5 ; Lu. 6. 42 ; 13. 15, thou *h.*
15. 7 ; 16. 3 ; 22. 18 ; Mk. 7. 6 ; Lu. 12. 56, ye *h.*
23. 13 ; Lu. 11. 44, woe unto you, *h.*
24. 51, appoint his portion with the *h.*
See Job 13. 16 ; 27. 8 ; Prov. 11. 9.

HYPOCRITICAL. Ps. 35. 16 ; Isa. 10. 6.

I.

IDLE. Ex. 5. 8, 17, they be *i.*
Prov. 19. 15, an *i.* soul shall hunger.
31. 27, she eateth not bread of *i.*
Mat. 12. 36, every *i.* word men speak.
20. 3, 6, others standing *i.*
See Eccl. 10. 18 ; Ezek. 16. 49 ; 1 Tim. 5. 13.

IDOL. 1 Chron. 16. 26 ; Ps. 96. 5, all gods of the people are *i.*
Isa. 66. 3, as if he blessed an *i.*
Jer. 50. 38, they are mad upon their *i.*
Hos. 4. 17, Ephraim is joined to *i.*
Acts 15. 20, abstain from pollutions of *i.*
1 Cor. 8. 4, we know an *i.* is nothing.
7, with conscience of the *i.*
1 Thess. 1. 9, ye turned to God from *i.*
1 John 5. 21, keep yourselves from *i.*
See Acts 17. 16 ; Gal. 5. 20 ; Col. 3. 5.

IGNORANCE. Acts 3. 17, through *i.* ye did it.
17. 30, the times of *i.* God winked at.
Eph. 4. 18, alienated through *i.*
1 Pet. 2. 15, put to silence *i.* of foolish men.
See Lev. 4. 2, 13, 22, 27 ; 5. 15 ; Num. 15. 24.

IGNORANT. Ps. 73. 22, so foolish was I, and *i.*
Isa. 63. 16, though Abraham be *i.* of us.
Acts 4. 13, perceived they were *i.* men.

Rom. 10. 3, being *i.* of God's righteousness.
1 Cor. 14. 38, if any man be *i.*, let him be *i.*
2 Cor. 2. 11, not *i.* of his devices.
Heb. 5. 2, can have compassion on the *i.*
2 Pet. 3. 5, they willingly are *i.*
See Num. 15. 28 ; Acts 17. 23 ; 1 Tim. 1. 13.

IMAGINATION. Gen. 6. 5 ; 8. 21, *i.* of heart evil.
Deut. 29. 19 ; Jer. 23. 17, walk in *i.* of heart.
1 Chron. 28. 9, understandeth all the *i.* of thoughts.
Rom. 1. 21, vain in their *i,*
2 Cor. 10. 5, casting down *i.*
See Deut. 31. 21 ; Prov. 6. 18 ; Lam. 3. 60.

IMAGINE. Ps. 62. 3, how long will ye *i.* mischief ?
Nah. 1. 9, what do ye *i.* against the Lord ?
11, there is one that *i.* evil.
Zech. 7. 10 ; 8. 17, let none *i.* evil.
See Job 21. 27 ; Ps. 10. 2 ; 21. 11 ; Acts 4. 25.

IMMORTAL. 1 Tim. 1. 17.

IMMORTALITY. Rom. 2. 7 ; 1 Cor. 15. 53 ; 1 Tim.
6. 16 ; 2 Tim. 1. 10.

IMPART. Job 39. 17 ; Lu. 3. 11 ; Rom. 1. 11 ;
1 Thess. 2. 8.

IMPEDIMENT. Mk. 7. 32.

IMPENITENT. Rom. 2. 5.

IMPLACABLE. Rom. 1. 31.

IMPOSE. Ezra 7. 24 ; Heb. 9. 10.

IMPOSSIBLE. Mat. 19. 26 ; Mk. 10. 27 ; Lu. 18. 27,
with men it is *i.*
Lu. 1. 37 ; 18. 27, with God nothing *i.*
See Mat. 17. 20 ; Lu. 17. 1 ; Heb. 6. 4, 18 ; 11. 6.

IMPOTENT. John 5. 3 ; Acts 4. 9 ; 14. 8.

IMPOVERISH. Judg. 6. 6 ; Isa. 40. 20 ; Jer. 5. 17.

IMPRISONMENT. Ezra 7. 26 ; 2 Cor. 6. 5 ; Heb.
11. 36.

IMPUDENT. Prov. 7. 13 ; Ezek. 2. 4 ; 3. 7.

IMPUTE. Lev. 17. 4, blood shall be *i.* to that man.
Ps. 32. 2 ; Rom. 4. 8, to whom the Lord *i.* not
iniquity.
Hab. 1. 11, *i.* his power to his god.
Rom. 5. 13, sin is not *i.* when there is no law.
See 1 Sam. 22. 15 ; 2 Sam. 19. 19 ; 2 Cor. 5. 19.

INCLINE. Josh. 24. 23, *i.* your hearts to the Lord.
1 Kings 8. 58, that he may *i.* hearts to keep law.
Ps. 40. 1 ; 116. 2, he *i.* unto me, and heard my cry.
119. 36, *i.* my heart to thy testimonies.
Jer. 7. 24 ; 11. 8 ; 17. 23 ; 34. 14, nor *i.* ear.
See Prov. 2. 18 ; Jer. 25. 4 ; 44. 5.

INCLOSED. Ps. 17. 10 ; 22. 16 ; Lu. 5. 6.

INCONTINENT. 1 Cor. 7. 5 ; 2 Tim. 3. 3.

INCORRUPTIBLE. 1 Cor. 9. 25, an *i.* crown.
1 Pet. 1. 4, inheritance *i.*
23, born of *i.* seed.
See Rom. 1. 23 ; 1 Cor. 15. 42, 50, 52, 53, 54.

INCREASE (*n.*). Lev. 25. 36, take no usury or *i.*
26. 4, the land shall yield her *i.*
Deut. 14. 22, 28, tithe all *i.*
Ps. 67. 6 ; Ezek. 34. 27, earth shall yield her *i.*
Prov. 18. 20, with the *i.* of his lips.
Eccl. 5. 10, not satisfied with *i.*
Isa. 9. 7, *i.* of his government.
1 Cor. 3. 6, 7, God gave the *i.*
See Jer. 2. 3 ; Eph. 4. 16 ; Col. 2. 19.

INCREASE (*v.*). Job 8. 7, thy latter end shall
greatly *i.*
Ps. 4. 7, that their corn and wine *i.*
62. 10, if riches *i.*, set not your heart upon them.
115. 14, Lord shall *i.* you more and more.
Prov. 1. 5 ; 9. 9, a wise man will *i.* learning.
11. 24, there is that scattereth, and yet *i.*
Eccl. 1. 18, he that *i.* knowledge *i.* sorrow.
Isa. 9. 3, multiplied the nation, and not *i.* the joy.
40. 29, he *i.* strength.
Ezek. 36. 37, *i.* them with men like a flock.
Dan. 12. 4, knowledge shall be *i.*
Hos. 12. 1, he daily *i.* lies.
Hab. 2. 6, that *i.* that which is not his.
Lu. 2. 52, Jesus *i.* in wisdom.

Acts 6. 7, word of God *i.*
16. 5, churches *i.* daily.
Rev. 3. 17, I am rich, and *i.* with goods.
See Eccl. 2. 9 ; 5. 11 ; Mk. 4. 8 ; Col. 2. 19.

INCREDIBLE. Acts 26. 8.

INCURABLE. 2 Chron. 21. 18 ; Jer. 15. 18 ; Mic.
1. 9.

INDEED. 1 Kings 8. 27 ; 2 Chron. 6. 18, will God *i.*
dwell on the earth ?
1 Chron. 4. 10, bless me *i.*
Mk. 11. 32, a prophet *i.*
Lu. 24. 34, the Lord is risen *i.*
John 1. 47, an Israelite *i.*
6. 55, my flesh is meat *i.*, and my blood is drink *i.*
8. 36, ye shall be free *i.*
1 Tim. 5. 3, that are widows *i.*
See Gen. 37. 8 ; Isa. 6. 9 ; Rom. 8. 7.

INDIGNATION. Ps. 78. 49, wrath, *i.*, and trouble.
Isa. 26. 20, till the *i.* be overpast.
Nah. 1. 6, who can stand before his *i.* ?
Mat. 20. 24, moved with *i.*
26. 8, they had *i.*
2 Cor. 7. 11, yea, what *i.*
Heb. 10. 27, fearful looking for of fiery *i.*
Rev. 14. 10, the cup of his *i.*
See Zech. 1. 12 ; Acts 5. 17 ; Rom. 2. 8.

INDITING. Ps. 45. 1.

INDUSTRIOUS. 1 Kings 11. 28.

INEXCUSABLE. Rom. 2. 1.

INFANT. Job 3. 16 ; Isa. 65. 20 ; Lu. 18. 15.

INFIDEL. 2 Cor. 6. 15 ; 1 Tim. 5. 8.

INFIRMITY. Ps. 77. 10, this is mine *i.*
Prov. 18. 14, spirit of man will sustain his *i.*
Mat. 8. 17, himself took our *i.*
Rom. 6. 19, the *i.* of your flesh.
8. 26, the Spirit helpeth our *i.*
15. 1, bear the *i.* of the weak.
2 Cor. 12. 5, 10, glory in mine *i.*
1 Tim. 5. 23, wine for thine often *i.*
Heb. 4. 15, touched with the feeling of our *i.*
See Lu. 5. 15 ; 7. 21 ; John 5. 5 ; Heb. 5. 2.

INFLAME. Isa. 5. 11 ; 57. 5.

INFLICTED. 2 Cor. 2. 6.

INFLUENCES. Job 38. 31.

INGRAFTED. Jas. 1. 21.

INHABIT. Isa. 57. 15 ; 65. 21 ; Amos 9. 14.

INHABITANT. Num. 13. 32, land eateth up *i.*
Judg. 5. 23, curse bitterly the *i.*
Isa. 6. 11, cities wasted without *i.*
33. 24, *i.* shall not say, I am sick.
40. 22, the *i.* thereof are as grasshoppers.
Jer. 44. 22, land without an *i.*
See Jer. 2. 15 ; 4. 7 ; Zech. 8. 21.

INHERIT. Ex. 32. 13, they shall *i.* it for ever.
Ps. 25. 13, shall *i.* the earth.
37. 11, the meek shall *i.* the earth.
Prov. 14. 18, the simple *i.* folly.
Mat. 19. 29, shall *i.* everlasting life.
25. 34, *i.* kingdom prepared.
Mk. 10. 17 ; Lu. 10. 25 ; 18. 18, *i.* eternal life.
1 Cor. 6. 9 ; 15. 50 ; Gal. 5. 21, not *i.* the kingdom.
Heb. 12. 17, when he would have *i.* the blessing.
See Heb. 6. 12 ; 1 Pet. 3. 9 ; Rev. 21. 7.

INHERITANCE. Ps. 16. 5, Lord is portion of
mine *i.*
47. 4, shall choose our *i.* for us.
Prov. 20. 21, an *i.* may be gotten hastily.
Eccl. 7. 11, wisdom good with an *i.*
Mk. 12. 7 ; Lu. 20. 14, the *i.* shall be ours.
Lu. 12. 13, that he divide the *i.* with me.
Acts 20. 32 ; 26. 18, an *i.* among the sanctified.
Eph. 1. 14, earnest of our *i.*
Heb. 9. 15, promise of eternal *i.*
See Eph. 5. 5 ; Col. 1. 12 ; Heb. 1. 4.

INIQUITY. Ex. 20. 5 ; 34. 7 ; Num. 14. 18 ; Deut.
5. 9, visiting the *i.* of the fathers.
34. 7 ; Num. 14. 18, forgiving *i.* and transgression.

Job 4. 8, they that plow *i.* reap the same.
13. 26, to possess the *i.* of my youth.
34. 32, if I have done *i.*, I will do no more.
Ps. 25. 11, pardon mine *i.*, for it is great.
32. 5, mine *i.* have I not hid.
39. 11, when thou dost correct man for *i.*
51. 5, I was shapen in *i.*
66. 18, if I regard *i.* in my heart.
69. 27, add *i.* to their *i.*
79. 8, remember not former *i.*
90. 8, thou hast set our *i.*
103. 3, who forgiveth all thine *i.*
10, not rewarded according to *i.*
107. 17, fools, because of *i.*, are afflicted.
119. 3, they also do no *i.*
130. 3, if thou shouldest mark *i.*
Prov. 22. 8, he that soweth *i.* shall reap vanity.
Isa. 1. 4, a people laden with *i.*
6. 7, thine *i.* is taken away.
40. 2, her *i.* is pardoned.
53. 5, he was bruised for our *i.*
59. 2, your *i.* separated between you and God.
Jer. 5. 25, your *i.* turned away these things.
Ezek. 18. 30, repent, so *i.* shall not be your ruin.
Hab. 1. 13, canst not look on *i.*
Mat. 24. 12, because *i.* shall abound.
Acts 1. 18, purchased with reward of *i.*
8. 23, in the bond of *i.*
Rom. 6. 19, servants to *i.* unto *i.*
2 Thess. 2. 7, the mystery of *i.*
2 Tim. 2. 19, depart from *i.*
Jas. 3. 6, a world of *i.*
See Ps. 36. 2 ; Jer. 31. 30 ; Ezek. 3. 18 ; 18. 26.
INJURIOUS. 1 Tim. 1. 13.
INK. Jer. 36. 18 ; 2 Cor. 3. 3 ; 2 John 12 ; 3 John 13.
INN. Gen. 42. 27 ; Ex. 4. 24 ; Lu. 2. 7 ; 10. 34.
INNOCENT. Job 4. 7, who ever perished, being *i.*?
9. 23, laugh at trial of *i.*
27. 17, the *i.* shall divide the silver.
Ps. 19. 13, *i.* from the great transgression.
Prov. 28. 20, he that maketh haste to be rich
shall not be *i.*
Jer. 2. 34 ; 19. 4, blood of the *i.*
See Gen. 20. 5 ; Ex. 23. 7 ; Mat. 27. 24.
INNUMERABLE. Job 21. 33 ; Ps. 40. 12 ; Heb. 12.
22.
INORDINATE. Ezek. 23. 11 ; Col. 3. 5.
INQUISITION. Deut. 19. 18 ; Esth. 2. 23 ; Ps. 9. 12.
INSCRIPTION. Acts 17. 23.
INSPIRATION. Job 32. 8 ; 2 Tim. 3. 16.
INSTANT. Rom. 12. 12 ; 2 Tim. 4. 2.
INSTRUCT. Neh. 9. 20, thy good spirit to *i.* them.
Ps. 16. 7, my reins *i.* me in night season.
32. 8, I will *i.* thee and teach thee.
Isa. 40. 14, who *i.* him ?
Mat. 13. 52, every scribe *i.* unto the kingdom.
Phil. 4. 12, in all things I am *i.*
See Prov. 21. 11 ; Acts 18. 25 ; 2 Tim. 2. 25.
INSTRUCTION. Ps. 50. 17, thou hatest *i.*
Prov. 1. 7 ; 15. 5, fools despise *i.*
4. 13, take fast hold of *i.*
8. 33, hear *i.*, and be wise.
12. 1, whoso loveth *i.* loveth knowledge.
16. 22, the *i.* of fools is folly.
24. 32, I looked upon it, and received *i.*
2 Tim. 3. 16, profitable for *i.*
See Jer. 17. 23 ; 35. 15 ; Zeph. 3. 7.
INSTRUMENT. Ps. 7. 13, hath prepared *i.* of death.
Isa. 41. 15, a new sharp threshing *i.*
Ezek. 33. 32, of one that can play on an *i.*
Rom. 6. 13, members *i.* of unrighteousness.
See Num. 35. 16 ; Ps. 68. 25 ; 150. 4.
INTEGRITY. Job 2. 3, he holdeth fast his *i.*
31. 6, that God may know my *i.*
Ps. 25. 21, let *i.* preserve me.
26. 1, I walked in *i.*
Prov. 11. 3, the *i.* of the upright.
19. 1 ; 20. 7, that walketh in his *i.*
See Gen. 20. 5 ; Ps. 7. 8 ; 41. 12 ; 78. 72.

INTENTS. Jer. 30. 24 ; Heb. 4. 12.
INTERCESSION. Isa. 53. 12, make *i.* for trans-
gressors.
Rom. 8. 26, the Spirit itself maketh *i.*
Heb. 7. 25, ever liveth to make *i.*
See Jer. 7. 16 ; 27. 18 ; 1 Tim. 2. 1.
INTERCESSOR. Isa. 59. 16.
INTERMEDDLE. Prov. 14. 10 ; 18. 1.
INTREAT. Ruth 1. 16, *i.* me not to leave thee.
1 Sam. 2. 25, if a man sin, who shall *i.* for him ?
Ps. 119. 58, I *i.* thy favour.
Isa. 19. 22, he shall be *i.* of them.
1 Tim. 5. 1, but *i.* him as a father.
Jas. 3. 17, wisdom is easy to be *i.*
See Prov. 18. 23 ; Lu. 15. 28.
INTRUDING. Col. 2. 18.
INVENTIONS. Ps. 106. 29 ; Prov. 8. 12 ; Eccl. 7. 29.
INVISIBLE. Col. 1. 15 ; 1 Tim. 1. 17 ; Heb. 11. 27.
INWARD. Job 38. 36, wisdom in the *i.* parts.
Ps. 51. 6, truth in the *i.* parts.
64. 6, *i.* thought of every one is deep.
Jer. 31. 33, I will put my law in their *i.* parts.
Rom. 7. 22, delight in law of God after the *i.*
man.
2 Cor. 4. 16, the *i.* man is renewed.
See Ps. 62. 4 ; Mat. 7. 15 ; Rom. 2. 29.
ISSUES. Ps. 68. 20 ; Prov. 4. 23.
ITCHING. 2 Tim. 4. 3.

J.

JACINTH. Rev. 9. 17 ; 21. 20.
JANGLING. 1 Tim. 1. 6.
JASPER. Ex. 28. 20 ; Ezek. 28. 13, and a *j.*
Rev. 4. 3, he that sat was to look upon like a *j.*
21. 11, even like a *j.* stone.
18, the building of the wall of it was of *j.*
19, the first foundation was *j.*
JAVELIN. Num. 25. 7, took a *j.* in his hand.
1 Sam. 18. 10, and there was a *j.* in Saul's hand.
19. 10, even to the wall with a *j.*
JEALOUS. Ex. 20. 5 ; 34. 14 ; Deut. 4. 24 ; 5. 9 ; 6. 15 ;
Josh. 24. 19, I am a *j.* God.
1 Kings 19. 10, 14, I have been *j.* for the Lord.
Ezek. 39. 25, will be *j.* for my holy name.
2 Cor. 11. 2, I am *j.* over you.
See Num. 5. 14 ; Joel 2. 18 ; Zech. 1. 14 ; 8. 2.
JEALOUSY. Deut. 32. 16 ; 1 Kings 14. 22, they
provoked him to *j.*
Prov. 6. 34, *j.* is the rage of a man.
Cant. 8. 6, *j.* is cruel as the grave.
Ezek. 36. 5, in fire of *j.* have I spoken.
1 Cor. 10. 22, do we provoke the Lord to *j.*?
See Ps. 78. 58 ; 79. 5 ; Isa. 42. 13.
JESTING. Eph. 5. 4.
JEWELS. Isa. 61. 10 ; Mal. 3. 17.
JOIN. Prov. 11. 21 ; 16. 5, hand *j.* in hand.
Eccl. 9. 4, to him *j.* to living there is hope.
Isa. 5. 8, that *j.* house to house.
Jer. 50. 5, let us *j.* ourselves to the Lord.
Hos. 4. 17, Ephraim is *j.* to idols.
Mat. 19. 6 ; Mk. 10. 9, what God hath *j.*
Acts 5. 13, durst no man *j.* himself.
1 Cor. 1. 10, perfectly *j.* in same mind.
6. 17, *j.* to the Lord.
Eph. 4. 16, whole body *j.* together.
See Acts 8. 29 ; 9. 26 ; 18. 7 ; Eph. 5. 31.
JOINT. Gen. 32. 25 ; Ps. 22. 14 ; Prov. 25. 19, out
of *j.*
Eph. 4. 16, which every *j.* supplieth.
Heb. 4. 12, dividing asunder of *j.* and marrow.
See 1 Kings 22. 34 ; Rom. 8. 17 ; Col. 2. 19.
JOURNEY (*n.*). 1 Kings 18. 27, or he is in a *j.*
Neh. 2. 6, for how long shall thy *j.* be ?
Mat. 10. 10 ; Mk. 6. 8 ; Lu. 9. 3, nor scrip for your *j.*
John 4. 6, Jesus wearied with his *j.*
JOURNEY (*v.*). Num. 10. 29, we are *j.* to the place.
See Gen. 12. 9 ; 13. 11.

JOURNEYINGS. Num. 10. 28, thus were the *j.*
2 Cor. 11. 26, in *j.* often.
JOY. Ezra 3. 13, not discern noise of *j.*
Neh. 8. 10, *j.* of the Lord is your strength.
Job 20. 5, the *j.* of the hypocrite is but a moment.
29. 13, widow's heart sing for *j.*
33. 26, he will see his face with *j.*
41. 22, sorrow is turned into *j.*
Ps. 16. 11, fulness of *j.*
30. 5, *j.* cometh in the morning.
48. 2, the *j.* of the whole earth.
51. 12, restore the *j.* of thy salvation.
126. 5, they that sow in tears shall reap in *j.*
137. 6, prefer Jerusalem above my chief *j.*
Prov. 14. 10, not intermeddle with his *j.*
21. 15, it is *j.* to the just to do judgment.
Eccl. 2. 10, I withheld not my heart from *j.*
9. 7, eat thy bread with *j.*
Isa. 9. 3, not increased the *j.*
12. 3, with *j.* draw water.
24. 8, *j.* of the harp ceaseth.
29. 19, meek shall increase their *j.*
35. 10 ; 51. 11, and everlasting *j.*
65. 14, my servants sing for *j.* of heart.
Jer. 15. 16, thy word was the *j.* of my heart.
31. 13, will turn their mourning into *j.*
49. 25, the city of my *j.*
Lam. 2. 15, the *j.* of the whole earth.
Mat. 13. 20 ; Lu. 8. 13, with *j.* receiveth it.
44, for *j.* goeth and selleth.
25. 21, 23, the *j.* of thy Lord.
Lu. 15. 7, *j.* in heaven over one sinner.
10, there is *j.* in presence of angels.
24. 41, they believed not for *j.*
John 3. 29, this my *j.* is fulfilled.
15. 11 ; 16. 24, that your *j.* may be full.
Acts 8. 8, great *j.* in that city.
20. 24, finish my course with *j.*
2 Cor. 1. 24, helpers of your *j.*
Phil. 2. 2, fulfil ye my *j.*
Heb. 12. 2, for the *j.* that was set before him.
Jas. 1. 2, count it all *j.* when ye fall.
1 Pet. 1. 8, with *j.* unspeakable.
4. 13, glad also with exceeding *j.*
2 John 12, that our *j.* may be full.
Jude 24, faultless, with exceeding *j.*
See Rom. 14. 17 ; Gal. 5. 22 ; Phil. 1. 4.
JOYFUL. Ps. 35. 9, my soul shall be *j.* in the Lord.
63. 5, praise thee with *j.* lips.
66. 1 ; 81. 1 ; 95. 1 ; 98. 6, make a *j.* noise.
Eccl. 7. 14, in day of prosperity be *j.*
Isa. 56. 7, *j.* in my house of prayer.
See 2 Cor. 7. 4 ; Col. 1. 11 ; Heb. 10. 34.
JUDGE (*n.*). Gen. 18. 25 ; Ps. 94. 2, the *j.* of all the earth.
Ps. 50. 6, God is *j.* himself.
68. 5, a *j.* of the widows.
Mic. 7. 3, the *j.* asketh a reward.
Lu. 12. 14, who made me a *j.* over you?
18. 6, the unjust *j.*
Acts 10. 42, the *J.* of quick and dead.
2 Tim. 4. 8, the Lord, the righteous *j.*
Heb. 12. 23, to God the *J.* of all.
Jas. 5. 9, the *j.* standeth before the door.
See 2 Sam. 15. 4 ; Mat. 5. 25 ; Jas. 4. 11.
JUDGE (*v.*). Gen. 16. 5, Lord *j.* between me and thee.
Deut. 32. 36 ; Ps. 7. 8, Lord *j.* the people.
Ps. 58. 11, he is a God that *j.* in the earth.
Isa. 1. 17, *j.* the fatherless.
Mat. 7. 1, *j.* not, that ye be not *j.*
Lu. 7. 43, thou hast rightly *j.*
John 7. 24, *j.* righteous judgment.
Rom. 14. 4, who art thou that *j.* ?
See John 16. 11 ; Rom. 2. 16 ; 3. 6 ; 2 Tim. 4. 1.
JUDGMENT. Deut. 1. 17, the *j.* is God's.
Ps. 1. 5, shall not stand in the *j.*
101. 1, I will sing of mercy and *j.*
Prov. 29. 26, *j.* cometh from the Lord.

Eccl. 11. 9 ; 12. 14, God will bring into *j.*
Isa. 28. 17, *j.* will I lay to the line.
53. 8, taken from prison and from *j.*
Jer. 5. 1, if there be any that executeth *j.*
10. 24, correct with *j.*, not in anger.
Hos. 12. 6, keep mercy and *j.*
Mat. 5. 21, in danger of the *j.*
John 5. 22, Father committed all *j.* to the Son.
9. 39, for *j.* I am come.
16. 8, reprove the world of *j.*
Acts 24. 25, reasoned of *j.* to come.
Rom. 14. 10, we shall all stand before the *j.* seat.
Heb. 9. 27, after this the *j.*
1 Pet. 4. 17, *j.* must begin at house of God.
See Mat. 12. 41 ; Heb. 10. 27 ; Jas. 2. 13.
JUST. Job 9. 2, how should man be *j.* with God ?
Prov. 3. 33, God blesseth the habitation of the *j.*
4. 18, path of *j.* as shining light.
10. 7, memory of *j.* is blessed.
Isa. 26. 7, way of the *j.* is uprightness.
Hab. 2. 4 ; Rom. 1. 17 ; Gal. 3. 11 ; Heb. 10. 38, the *j.* shall live by faith.
Mat. 5. 45, sendeth rain on *j.* and unjust.
Lu. 14. 14, recompensed at resurrection of *j.*
15. 7, ninety and nine *j.* persons.
Acts 24. 15, resurrection both of *j.* and unjust.
Rom. 3. 26, that he might be *j.*
Phil. 4. 8, whatsoever things are *j.*
Heb. 2. 2, a *j.* recompence of reward.
12. 23, spirits of *j.* men made perfect.
1 Pet. 3. 18, the *j.* for the unjust.
See Job 34. 17 ; Acts 3. 14 ; Col. 4. 1.
JUSTICE. 2 Sam. 15. 4, I would do *j.*
Ps. 89. 14, *j.* and judgment are the habitation.
Prov. 8. 15, by me princes decree *j.*
Isa. 59. 4, none calleth for *j.*
Jer. 23. 5, execute judgment and *j.* in the earth.
50. 7, the habitation of *j.*
See Job 8. 3 ; 36. 17 ; Isa. 9. 7 ; 56. 1.
JUSTIFICATION. Rom. 4. 25 ; 5. 16, 18.
JUSTIFY. Job 11. 2, should a man full of talk be *j.* ?
25. 4, how then can man be *j.* with God ?
Ps. 51. 4, be *j.* when thou speakest.
143. 2, in thy sight shall no man living be *j.*
Isa. 5. 23, which *j.* the wicked for reward.
Mat. 11. 19 ; Lu. 7. 35, wisdom is *j.* of her children.
12. 37, by thy words thou shalt be *j.*
Lu. 10. 29, willing to *j.* himself.
18. 14, *j.* rather than the other.
Acts 13. 39, all that believe are *j.*
Rom. 3. 24 ; Tit. 3. 7, *j.* freely by his grace.
5. 1, being *j.* by faith.
9, being now *j.* by his blood.
Gal. 2. 16, man is not *j.* by works of the law.
1 Tim. 3. 16, *j.* in the Spirit.
See Isa. 50. 8 ; Rom. 4. 5 ; 8. 33.
JUSTLY. Mic. 6. 8 ; Lu. 23. 41 ; 1 Thess. 2. 10.

K.

KEEP. Gen. 18. 19, they shall *k.* the way of the Lord.
Num. 6. 24, the Lord bless thee, and *k.* thee.
1 Sam. 2. 9, he will *k.* the feet of his saints.
25. 34, the Lord God hath *k.* me back from hurting thee.
Ps. 17. 8, *k.* me as the apple of the eye.
34. 13, *k.* thy tongue from evil.
91. 11, angels charge to *k.* thee in all thy ways.
121. 3, he that *k.* thee will not slumber.
127. 1, except the Lord *k.* the city.
141. 3, *k.* the door of my lips.
Prov. 4. 6, love wisdom, she shall *k.* thee.
21, *k.* my sayings in midst of thine heart.
23, *k.* thy heart with all diligence.
6. 20, my son, *k.* thy father's commandment.
Eccl. 3. 6, a time to *k.*
5. 1, *k.* thy foot when thou goest.
12. 13, fear God, and *k.* his commandments.
Isa. 26. 3, thou wilt *k.* him in perfect peace.
27. 3, I the Lord do *k.* it, I will *k.* it.

Jer. 3. 5, 12, will he *k.* his anger?
Hab. 2. 20, let the earth *k.* silence.
Mal. 3. 14, what profit that we have *k.*
Mat. 19. 17, if thou wilt enter life, *k.* the commandments.
Lu. 11. 28, blessed are they that *k.*
19. 43, enemies shall *k.* thee in on every side.
John 8. 51, 52, *k.* my sayings.
12. 25, he that hateth his life shall *k.* it.
14. 23, if a man love me, he will *k.* my words.
17. 11, holy Father, *k.* through thine own name.
15, that thou shouldest *k.* them from the evil.
Acts 16. 4, delivered the decrees to *k.*
21. 25, *k.* from things offered to idols.
1 Cor. 5. 8, let us *k.* the feast.
9. 27, I *k.* under my body.
Eph. 4. 3, *k.* the unity of the Spirit.
Phil. 4. 7, the peace of God shall *k.* your hearts.
1 Tim. 5. 22, *k.* thyself pure.
6. 20, *k.* that which is committed.
Jas. 1. 27, *k.* himself unspotted.
1 John 5. 21, *k.* yourselves from idols.
Jude 21, *k.* yourselves in the love of God.
24, him that is able to *k.* you from falling.
Rev. 3. 10, I will *k.* thee from hour of temptation.
22. 9, which *k.* the sayings of this book.
See 1 Pet. 1. 5 ; 4. 19 ; Jude 6 ; Rev. 3. 8.
KEEPER. Ps. 121. 5, the Lord is thy *k.*
Eccl. 12. 3, when the *k.* of the house shall tremble.
Cant. 1. 6, they made me *k.* of the vineyards.
Tit. 2. 5, chaste, *k.* at home.
See Gen. 4. 2, 9 ; Mat. 28. 4 ; Acts 5. 23 ; 16. 27.
KEY. Mat. 16. 19, the *k.* of kingdom of heaven.
Lu. 11. 52, ye have taken away *k.* of knowledge.
Rev. 1. 18, the *k.* of hell and of death.
See Isa. 22. 22 ; Rev. 3. 7 ; 9. 1.
KICK. Deut. 32. 15 ; 1 Sam. 2. 29 ; Acts 9. 5.
KILL. Num. 16. 13, to *k.* us in the wilderness.
2 Kings 5. 7, am I a God to *k.*?
7. 4, if they *k.* us, we shall but die.
Eccl. 3. 3, a time to *k.*
Mat. 10. 28 ; Lu. 12. 4, fear not them that *k.* the body.
Mk. 3. 4, is it lawful to save life, or to *k.*?
John 5. 18, the Jews sought the more to *k.* him.
7. 19, why go ye about to *k.* me?
8. 22, will he *k.* himself?
Rom. 8. 36, for thy sake we are *k.* all the day.
2 Cor. 3. 6, the letter *k.*
6. 9, chastened, and not *k.*
Jas. 4. 2, ye *k.*, and desire to have.
5. 6, ye condemned and *k.* the just.
See Mat. 23. 37 ; Mk. 12. 5 ; Lu. 22. 2.
KIND. 2 Chron. 10. 7, if thou be *k.* to this people.
Mat. 17. 21 ; Mk. 9. 29, this *k.* goeth not out.
Lu. 6. 35, *k.* to unthankful and evil.
1 Cor. 13. 4, charity suffereth long, and is *k.*
See Mat. 13. 47 ; Eph. 4. 32 ; Jas. 3. 7.
KINDLE. Ps. 2. 12, his wrath is *k.* but a little.
Prov. 26. 21, a contentious man to *k.* strife.
Isa. 50. 11, walk in sparks that ye have *k.*
Hos. 11. 8, my repentings are *k.* together.
Lu. 12. 49, what will I, if it be already *k.*?
Jas. 3. 5, how great a matter a little fire *k.*
See Job 19. 11 ; 32. 2 ; Ezek. 20. 48.
KINDLY. Gen. 24. 49 ; 50. 21 ; Ruth 1. 8 ; Rom. 12. 10.
KINDNESS. Ruth 3. 10, thou hast showed more *k.*
2 Sam. 2. 6, I will requite you this *k.*
9. 1, 7, show him *k.* for Jonathan's sake.
Ps. 17. 7 ; 92. 2, thy marvellous loving-*k.*
36. 7, how excellent is thy loving-*k.* !
63. 3, thy loving-*k.* is better than life.
117. 2 ; 119. 76, his merciful *k.*
141. 5, righteous smite me, it shall be a *k.*
Prov. 31. 26, in her tongue is the law of *k.*
Isa. 54. 8, with everlasting *k.*
Jer. 2. 2, I remember the *k.* of thy youth.
31. 3, with loving-*k.* have I drawn thee.

Col. 3. 12, put on *k.*, meekness.
2 Pet. 1. 7, to godliness, brotherly *k.*
See Josh. 2. 12 ; Neh. 9. 17 ; Joel 2. 13 ; Jonah 4. 2.
KINDRED. Acts 3. 25 ; Rev. 1. 7 ; 5. 9 ; 7. 9.
KING. Num. 23. 21, the shout of a *k.* is among them.
Judg. 9. 8, the trees went forth to anoint a *k.*
17. 6, no *k.* in Israel.
1 Sam. 8. 5, now make us a *k.*
19, we will have a *k.*
10. 24 ; 2 Sam. 16. 16, God save the *k.*
Job 18. 14, bring him to the *k.* of terrors.
34. 18, is it fit to say to a *k.*?
Ps. 5. 2 ; 84. 3, my *K.* and my God.
10. 16, the Lord is *K.* for ever.
20. 9, let the *k.* hear us when we call.
74. 12, God is my *K.* of old.
102. 15, the *k.* of the earth shall fear.
Prov. 8. 15, by me *k.* reign.
22. 29, the diligent shall stand before *k.*
31. 3, that which destroyeth *k.*
4, it is not for *k.* to drink wine.
Eccl. 2. 12, what can the man do that cometh after the *k.*?
10. 16, woe to thee when thy *k.* is a child !
20, curse not the *k.*
Isa. 32. 1, a *k.* shall reign in righteousness.
33. 17, thine eyes shall see the *k.* in his beauty.
49. 23, *k.* shall be thy nursing fathers.
Jer. 10. 10, the Lord is an everlasting *k.*
Mat. 22. 11, when the *k.* came in to see the guests.
Lu. 19. 38, blessed be the *K.* that cometh.
23. 2, saying that he himself is Christ a *k.*
John 6. 15, by force, to make him a *k.*
19. 14, behold your *K.*!
15, we have no *k.* but Cæsar.
1 Tim. 1. 17, now unto the *K.* eternal.
6. 15, the *K.* of *k.* and Lord of lords.
Rev. 1. 6 ; 5. 10, made us *k.* and priests unto God.
15. 3, thou *K.* of saints.
See Lu. 10. 24 ; 1 Tim. 2. 2 ; 1 Pet. 2. 17.
KINGDOM. Ex. 19. 6, a *k.* of priests.
1 Chron. 29. 11 ; Mat. 6. 13, thine is the *k.*
Ps. 22. 28, the *k.* is the Lord's.
103. 19, his *k.* ruleth over all.
145. 12, the glorious majesty of his *k.*
Isa. 14. 16, is this the man that did shake *k.*?
Dan. 4. 3, his *k.* is an everlasting *k.*
Mat. 4. 23 ; 9. 35 ; 24. 14, gospel of the *k.*
8. 12, children of the *k.* cast out.
12. 25 ; Mk. 3. 24 ; Lu. 11. 17, *k.* divided against itself.
13. 38, good seed are children of the *k.*
25. 34, inherit the *k.*
Lu. 12. 32, Father's good pleasure to give you the *k.*
22. 29, I appoint unto you a *k.*
John 18. 36, my *k.* is not of this world.
Acts 1. 6, wilt thou restore the *k.* to Israel ?
1 Cor. 15. 24, when he shall have delivered up the *k.*
Col. 1. 13, into the *k.* of his dear Son.
2 Tim. 4. 18, to his heavenly *k.*
Jas. 2. 5, heirs of the *k.* he hath promised.
2 Pet. 1. 11, entrance into everlasting *k.*
See Rev. 1. 9 ; 11. 15 ; 16. 10 ; 17. 17.
KISS. Ps. 85. 10 ; Prov. 27. 6 ; Lu. 7. 38 ; Rom. 16. 16.
KNEW. Gen. 28. 16, the Lord is in this place, and I *k.* it not.
Jer. 1. 5, before I formed thee I *k.* thee.
Mat. 7. 23, I never *k.* you, depart.
John 4. 10, if thou *k.* the gift of God.
2 Cor. 5. 21, who *k.* no sin.
See Gen. 3. 7 ; Deut. 34. 10 ; John 1. 10 ; Rom. 1. 21.
KNOW. 1 Sam. 3. 7, Samuel did not yet *k.* the Lord.
1 Chron. 28. 9, *k.* thou the God of thy father.
Job 5. 27, it, hear it for thy good.
8. 9, we are but of yesterday, and *k.* nothing.
13. 23, make me to *k.* my transgression.
19. 25, I *k.* that my redeemer liveth.

Job 22. 13 ; Ps. 73. 11, how doth God *k.*?
Ps. 39. 4, make me to *k.* mine end.
46. 10, be still, and *k.* that I am God.
56. 9, this I *k.*, for God is for me.
103. 14, he *k.* our frame.
139. 23, *k.* my heart.
Eccl. 9. 5, the living *k.* they shall die.
11. 9, *k.* that for all these things.
Isa. 1. 3, the ox *k.* his owner.
Jer. 17. 9, the heart is deceitful, who can *k.* it?
31. 34 ; Heb. 8. 11, *k.* the Lord, for all shall *k.* me.
Ezek. 2. 5 ; 33. 33, *k.* there hath been a prophet.
Hos. 2. 20, thou shalt *k.* the Lord.
7. 9, yet he *k.* it not.
Mat. 6. 3, let not thy left hand *k.*
13. 11 ; Mk. 4. 11 ; Lu. 8. 10, given to you to *k.*
25. 12, I *k.* you not.
Mk. 1. 24 ; Lu. 4. 34, I *k.* thee, who thou art.
Lu. 19. 42, if thou hadst *k.*
22. 57, 60, I *k.* him not.
John 7. 17, he shall *k.* of the doctrine.
10. 14, I *k.* my sheep, and am *k.* of mine.
13. 7, *k.* not now, but shalt *k.* hereafter.
17, if ye *k.* these things.
35, by this shall all men *k.* ye are my disciples.
Acts 1. 7, it is not for you to *k.*
Rom. 8. 28, we *k.* that all things work.
1 Cor. 2. 14, neither can he *k.* them.
13. 9, 12, we *k.* in part.
Eph. 3. 19, and to *k.* the love of Christ.
2 Tim. 1. 12, I *k.* whom I have believed.
3. 15, thou hast *k.* the scriptures.
1 John 2. 4, he that saith, I *k.* him.
3. 2, we *k.* that when he shall appear.
Rev. 2. 2, 9, 13, 19 ; 3. 1, 8, I *k.* thy works.
See Mat. 6. 8 ; 2 Tim. 2. 19 ; 2 Pet. 2. 9 ; Rev. 2. 17.

KNOWLEDGE. 2 Chron. 1. 10, 11, 12, give me *k.*
Job 21. 14, we desire not *k.* of thy ways.
Ps. 94. 10, he that teacheth man *k.*
139. 6, such *k.* is too wonderful.
144. 3, that thou takest *k.* of him.
Prov. 10. 14, wise men lay up *k.*
14. 6, *k.* is easy to him that understandeth.
17. 27, he that hath *k.* spareth words.
24. 5, a man of *k.* increaseth strength.
30. 3, nor have the *k.* of the holy.
Eccl. 1. 18, increaseth *k.* increaseth sorrow.
9. 10, nor *k.* in the grave.
Isa. 11. 2, the spirit of *k.*
40. 14, who taught him *k.*?
53. 11, by his *k.* justify many.
Dan. 1. 17, God gave them *k.*
12. 4, *k.* shall be increased.
Hos. 4. 6, destroyed for lack of *k.*
Hab. 2. 14, earth shall be filled with the *k.*
Lu. 11. 52, taken away key of *k.*
Acts 4. 13, took *k.* of them.
24. 22, more perfect *k.* of that way.
Rom. 10. 2, zeal of God, but not according to *k.*
1 Cor. 8. 1, *k.* puffeth up.
13. 8, *k.* shall vanish away.
15. 34, some have not the *k.* of God.
Eph. 3. 19, love of Christ, which passeth *k.*
Phil. 3. 8, but loss for the *k.* of Christ.
Col. 2. 3, treasures of wisdom and *k.*
1 Tim. 2. 4 ; 2 Tim. 3. 7, the *k.* of the truth.
Heb. 10. 26, sin after we have received *k.*
2 Pet. 1. 5, 6, to virtue *k.* and to *k.* temperance.
3. 18, grow in grace and *k.*
See Gen. 2. 9 ; 1 Sam. 2. 3 ; Prov. 19. 2 ; Hos. 4. 1.

L.

LABOUR (*n.*). Ps. 90. 10, yet is their strength *l.* and
sorrow.
104. 23, goeth to his *l.* till evening.
Prov. 13. 11, he that gathereth by *l.* shall increase.
14. 23, in all *l.* there is profit.
Eccl. 1. 8, all things are full of *l.*
2. 22, what hath man of all his *l.*?
6. 7, all the *l.* of man is for his mouth.

John 4. 38, are entered into their *l.*
1 Cor. 15. 58, your *l.* is not in vain.
1 Thess. 1. 3 ; Heb. 6. 10, your *l.* of love
Rev. 2. 2, I know thy *l.* and patience.
14. 13, rest from their *l.*
See Gen. 31. 42 ; Isa. 58. 3 ; 2 Cor. 6. 5 ; 11. 23.
LABOUR (*v.*). Ex. 20. 9 ; Deut. 5. 13, six days shalt
thou *l.*
Neh. 4. 21, so we *l.* in the work.
Ps. 127. 1, they *l.* in vain.
144. 14, our oxen may be strong to *l.*
Prov. 16. 26, he that *l.* *l.* for himself.
23. 4, *l.* not to be rich.
Eccl. 4. 8, for whom do I *l.*?
5. 12, the sleep of a *l.* man is sweet.
Mat. 11. 28, all ye that *l.*
John 6. 27, *l.* not for the meat which perisheth.
1 Cor. 3. 9, we are *l.* together with God.
Eph. 4. 28, but rather *l.*, working with his hands.
1 Thess. 5. 12, which *l.* among you.
1 Tim. 5. 17, they who *l.* in word and doctrine.
See Mat. 9. 37 ; 20. 1 ; Lu. 10. 2.
LACK. Mat. 19. 20 ; Lu. 22. 35 ; Acts 4. 34.
LADEN. Isa. 1. 4 ; Mat. 11. 28 ; 2 Tim. 3. 6.
LAMB. Isa. 5. 17, the *l.* feed after their manner.
11. 6, the wolf shall dwell with the *l.*
53. 7 ; Jer. 11. 19, as *l.* to the slaughter.
John 1. 29, 36, behold the *L.* of God.
1 Pet. 1. 19, as of a *l.* without blemish.
Rev. 5. 6 ; 13. 8, stood a *L.* slain.
12. 11, by the blood of the *L.*
22. 1, the throne of God and of the *L.*
See Isa. 40. 11 ; Lu. 10. 3 ; John 21. 15.
LAME. Job 29. 15 ; Prov. 26. 7 ; Isa. 35. 6 ; Heb.
12. 13.
LAMENT. Mat. 11. 17 ; John 16. 20 ; Acts 8. 2.
LAMP. Ps. 119. 105 ; Prov. 13. 9 ; Isa. 62. 1 ; Mat.
25. 1.
LAP. Judg. 7. 6 ; Prov. 16. 33.
LAST. Num. 23. 10, let my *l.* end be like his.
Prov. 23. 32, at the *l.* it biteth like a serpent.
Mat. 12. 45 ; Lu. 11. 26, *l.* state of that man.
19. 30 ; 20. 16 ; Mk. 10. 31 ; Lu. 13. 30, first shall
be *l.*
John 6. 39 ; 11. 24 ; 12. 48, the *l.* day.
See Lam. 1. 9 ; 2 Tim. 3. 1 ; 1 Pet. 1. 5 ; 1 John 2. 18.
LATTER. Job 19. 25 ; Prov. 19. 20 ; Hag. 2. 9.
LAUGH. Prov. 1. 26 ; Eccl. 3. 4 ; Lu. 6. 21 ; Jas.
4. 9.
LAW. Josh. 8. 34, all the words of the *l.*
Ps. 37. 31, the *l.* of his God is in his heart.
40. 8, thy *l.* is within my heart.
119. 70, 77, 92, 174, I delight in thy *l.*
97, 113, 163, 165, how I love thy *l.*
Prov. 13. 14, the *l.* of the wise is a fountain of life.
Isa. 8. 20, to the *l.* and to the testimony.
Mal. 2. 6, the *l.* of truth was in his mouth.
Mat. 5. 17, not come to destroy the *l.*
23. 23, the weightier matters of the *l.*
John 7. 51, doth our *l.* judge any man.
19. 7, we have a *l.*, and by our *l.*
Rom. 2. 14, are a *l.* unto themselves.
3. 20, by the deeds of the *l.*
7. 12, the *l.* is holy.
14, the *l.* is spiritual.
16 ; 1 Tim. 1. 8, the *l.* is good.
8. 3, what the *l.* could not do.
Gal. 3. 24, the *l.* was our schoolmaster.
5. 14, all the *l.* is fulfilled in one word.
23, against such there is no *l.*
6. 2, so fulfil the *l.* of Christ.
1 Tim. 1. 9, the *l.* is not made for a righteous man.
Heb. 7. 16, the *l.* of a carnal commandment.
Jas. 1. 25 ; 2. 12, perfect *l.* of liberty.
2. 8, the royal *l.*
See Ps. 1. 2 ; 19. 7 ; Mat. 7. 12 ; Rom. 10. 4.
LAWFUL. Mat. 12. 2 ; John 5. 10 ; 1 Cor. 6. 12.
LAWLESS. 1 Tim. 1. 9.

LEAD. Deut. 4. 27 ; 28. 37, whither the Lord shall *l.* you.
Ps. 23. 2, he *l.* me beside still waters.
27. 11, *l.* me in a plain path.
31. 3, *l.* me, and guide me.
61. 2, *l.* me to the rock that is higher than I.
139. 10, there shall thy hand *l.* me.
24, *l.* me in the way everlasting.
Prov. 6. 22, when thou goest, it shall *l.* thee.
Isa. 11. 6, a little child shall *l.* them.
42. 16, I will *l.* them in paths not known.
48. 17, I am the Lord which *l.* thee.
Mat. 6. 13 ; Lu. 11. 4, *l.* us not into temptation.
15. 14 ; Lu. 6. 39, if the blind *l.* the blind.
Acts 13. 11, seeking some to *l.* him.
1 Tim. 2. 2, we may *l.* a quiet life.
See John 10. 3 ; 1 Cor. 9. 5 ; 2 Tim. 3. 6 ; Rev. 7. 17.
LEAF. Lev. 26. 36 ; Ps. 1. 3 ; Isa. 64. 6 ; Mat. 21. 19.
LEAN. Deut. 33. 1, *l.* to fear the Lord.
Prov. 3. 5 ; Amos 5. 19 ; Mic. 3. 11 ; John 13. 23 ; 21. 20.
LEARN. Deut. 31. 13, *l.* to fear the Lord.
Prov. 1. 5 ; 9. 9 ; 16. 21, will increase *l.*
22. 25, lest thou *l.* his ways.
Isa. 1. 17, *l.* to do well.
2. 4 ; Mic. 4. 3, neither shall they *l.* war.
29. 11, 12, deliver to one that is *l.*
John 6. 45, every one that hath *l.* of the Father.
7. 15, having never *l.*
Acts 7. 22, *l.* in all the wisdom of the Egyptians.
26. 24, much *l.* doth make thee mad.
Rom. 15. 4, written for our *l.*
Eph. 4. 20, ye have not so *l.* Christ.
2 Tim. 3. 14, in the things thou hast *l.*
Heb. 5. 8, though a Son, yet *l.* he obedience.
See Mat. 9. 13 ; 11. 29 ; Phil. 4. 11 ; Rev. 14. 3.
LEAST. Mat. 5. 19, one of these *l.* commandments.
11. 11 ; Lu. 7. 28, he that is *l.* in kingdom of heaven.
25. 40, 45, done it to the *l.* of these.
Lu. 12. 26, not able to do that which is *l.*
16. 10, faithful in that which is *l.*
Eph. 3. 8, less than the *l.* of all saints.
See Gen. 32. 10 ; Jer. 31. 34 ; 1 Cor. 6. 4.
LEAVE. Gen. 2. 24 ; Mat. 19. 5 ; Mk. 10. 7 ; Eph. 5. 31, *l.* father and mother, and shall cleave.
Ps. 16. 10 ; Acts 2. 27, not *l.* my soul in hell.
27. 9 ; 119. 121, *l.* me not.
Mat. 23. 23, and not to *l.* the other undone.
John 14. 27, peace I *l.* with you.
Heb. 13. 5, I will never *l.* thee.
See Ruth 1. 16 ; Mat. 5. 24 ; John 16. 28.
LEES. Isa. 25. 6 ; Jer. 48. 11 ; Zeph. 1. 12.
LEND. Deut. 15. 6, thou shalt *l.* to many nations.
Ps. 37. 26 ; 112. 5, ever merciful, and *l.*
Prov. 19. 17, he that hath pity on poor *l.* to the Lord.
22. 7, the borrower is servant to the *l.*
Lu. 6. 34, if ye *l.* to them of whom.
See 1 Sam. 1. 28 ; Isa. 24. 2 ; Lu. 11. 5.
LESS. Ex. 30. 15 ; Job 11. 6 ; Isa. 40. 17.
LIARS. Ps. 116. 11 ; John 8. 44 ; Tit. 1. 12 ; Rev. 2. 2 ; 21. 8.
LIBERAL. Prov. 11. 25 ; Isa. 32. 5, 8 ; Jas. 1. 5.
LIBERTY. Ps. 119. 45, I will walk at *l.*
Isa. 61. 1 ; Jer. 34. 8 ; Lu. 4. 18, to proclaim *l.*
Rom. 8. 21, the glorious *l.* of the children of God.
1 Cor. 8. 9, take heed lest this *l.* of yours.
2 Cor. 3. 17, where the Spirit is, there is *l.*
Gal. 5. 1, stand fast in the *l.*
Jas. 1. 25 ; 2. 12, the law of *l.*
See Lev. 25. 10 ; Gal. 5. 13 ; 1 Pet. 2. 16.
LIFE. Gen. 2. 7 ; 6. 17 ; 7. 22, the breath of *l.*
9 ; 3. 24 ; Rev. 2. 7, the tree of *l.*
Deut. 30. 15 ; Jer. 21. 8, I have set before thee *l.*
Josh. 2. 14, our *l.* for yours.
1 Sam. 25. 29, bound in the bundle of *l.*
Ps. 16. 11, show me the path of *l.*
17. 14 ; Eccl. 9. 9, their portion in this *l.*

Ps. 26. 9, gather not my *l.* with bloody men.
27. 1, the strength of my *l.*
30. 5, in his favour is *l.*
34. 12, what man is he that desireth *l.* ?
36. 9, the fountain of *l.*
91. 16, with long *l.* will I satisfy him.
133. 3, even *l.* for evermore.
Prov. 3. 22, so shall they be *l.* to thy soul.
8. 35, whoso findeth me findeth *l.*
15. 24, the way of *l.* is above to the wise.
Mat. 6. 25 ; Lu. 12. 22, take no thought for your *l.*
18. 8 ; 19. 17 ; Mk. 9. 43, to enter into *l.*
Lu. 12. 15, a man's *l.* consisteth not.
23, the *l.* is more than meat.
John 1. 4, in him was *l.*
5. 24 ; 1 John 3. 14, passed from death to *l.*
26, as the Father hath *l.* in himself.
40 ; 10. 10, will not come that ye might have *l.*
6. 33, 47, 48, 54, the bread of *l.*
10. 15, 17 ; 13. 37, I lay down my *l.*
11. 25 ; 14. 6, the resurrection and the *l.*
Rom. 6. 4, in newness of *l.*
11. 15, *l.* from the dead.
2 Cor. 2. 16, the savour of *l.* unto *l.*
Gal. 2. 20, the *l.* that I now live.
Eph. 4. 18, alienated from the *l.* of God.
Col. 3. 3, your *l.* is hid.
1 Tim. 4. 8 ; 2 Tim. 1. 1, the promise of the *l.*
2 Tim. 1. 10, brought *l.* to light by gospel.
Jas. 4. 14, what is your *l.* ?
1 John 1. 2, the *l.* was manifested.
2. 16, the pride of *l.*
5. 11, this *l.* is in his Son.
Rev. 22. 1, 17, river of water of *l.*
See Mat. 10. 39 ; 20. 28 ; Acts 5. 20.

LIGHT. Ex. 10. 23, Israel had *l.* in their dwellings.
Job 18. 5, the *l.* of the wicked.
37. 21, men see not bright *l.* in clouds.
Ps. 4. 6 ; 90. 8, the *l.* of thy countenance.
27. 1, the Lord is my *l.*
36. 9, in thy *l.* shall we see *l.*
97. 11, *l.* is sown for the righteous.
119. 105, a *l.* to my path.
Eccl. 11. 7, the *l.* is sweet.
Isa. 5. 20, darkness for *l.*, and *l.* for darkness.
30. 26, the *l.* of the moon as *l.* of sun.
59. 9, we wait for *l.*
60. 1, arise, shine, for thy *l.* is come.
Zech. 14. 6, the *l.* shall not be clear.
Mat. 5. 14 ; John 8. 12 ; 9. 5, the *l.* of the world.
16, let your *l.* so shine.
6. 22, the *l.* of the body is the eye.
Lu. 12. 35, your loins girded, and *l.* burning.
16. 8, wiser than children of *l.*
John 1. 9, that was the true *L.*
3. 19, *l.* is come into the world.
20, hateth the *l.*
5. 35, burning and shining *l.*
12. 35, yet a little while is the *l.* with you.
36, while ye have *l.*, believe in the *l.*
Acts 26. 18, turn from darkness to *l.*
1 Cor. 4. 5, bring to *l.* hidden things.
2 Cor. 4. 4, *l.* of the gospel.
6, commanded *l.* to shine out of darkness.
11. 14, an angel of *l.*
Eph. 5. 8, now are ye *l.*, walk as children of *l.*
14, Christ shall give thee *l.*
1 Tim. 6. 16, in *l.* which no man can approach.
2 Pet. 1. 19, a *l.* shining in a dark place.
1 John 1. 5, God is *l.*
7, walk in the *l.*, as he is in the *l.*
Rev. 22. 5, they need no candle, neither *l.* of the sun.
See 2 Tim. 1. 10 ; Rev. 7. 16 ; 18. 23 ; 21. 23.

LIGHTNING. Ex. 19. 16 ; Mat. 24. 27 ; Lu. 10. 18.
LIKENESS. Ps. 17. 15, when I awake, with thy *l.*
Isa. 40. 18, what *l.* will ye compare ?
Acts 14. 11, gods are come down in *l.* of men.
Rom. 6. 5, *l.* of his death, *l.* of his resurrection.

Rom. 8. 3, in the *l.* of sinful flesh.
Phil. 2. 7, was made in the *l.* of men.
See Gen. 1. 26 ; 5. 1 ; Ex. 20. 4 ; Deut. 4. 16.
LIMIT. Ps. 78. 41 ; Ezek. 43. 12 ; Heb. 4. 7.
LINE. Ps. 16. 6 ; Isa. 28. 10, 17 ; 34. 11 ; 2 Cor. 10. 16.
LINGER. Gen. 19. 16 ; 43. 10 ; 2 Pet. 2. 3.
LIP. 1 Sam. 1. 13, only her *l.* moved.
Job 27. 4, my *l.* shall not speak wickedness.
33. 3, my *l.* shall utter knowledge.
Ps. 12. 2, 3, flattering *l.*
4, our *l.* are our own.
17. 1, goeth not out of feigned *l.*
31. 18 ; 120. 2 ; Prov. 10. 18 ; 12. 22 ; 17. 7, lying *l.*
Prov. 15. 7, the *l.* of the wise disperse knowledge.
Eccl. 10. 12, the *l.* of a fool will swallow himself.
Cant. 7. 9, causing *l.* of those asleep to speak.
Isa. 6. 5, a man of unclean *l.*
Mat. 15. 8, ·honoureth me with their *l.*
See Ps. 51. 15 ; 141. 3 ; Dan. 10. 16 ; Hab. 3. 16.
LITTLE. Ezra 9. 8, for a *l.* space, a *l.* reviving.
Job 26. 14, how *l.* a portion is heard ?
Ps. 8. 5 ; Heb. 2. 7, a *l.* lower than angels.
37. 16, a *l.* that a righteous man hath.
Prov. 6. 10 ; 24. 33, a *l.* sleep.
15. 16 ; 16. 8, better is a *l.* with fear of Lord.
30. 24, four things *l.* on earth.
Isa. 28. 10, here a *l.* and there a *l.*
40. 15 ; Ezek. 16. 47, as a very *l.* thing.
Hag. 1. 6, bring in *l.*
Mat. 6. 30 ; 8. 26 ; 14. 31 ; 16. 8 ; Lu. 12. 28, *l.* faith.
10. 42 ; 18. 6 ; Mk. 9. 42 ; Lu. 17. 2, *l.* ones.
Lu. 7. 47, to whom *l.* is forgiven.
19. 3, *l.* of stature.
1 Cor. 5. 6 ; Gal. 5. 9, a *l.* leaven.
1 Tim. 4. 8, bodily exercise profiteth *l.*
5. 23, use a *l.* wine.
See John 7. 33 ; 14. 19 ; 16. 16 ; Rev. 3. 8 ; 6. 11.
LIVE. Gen. 17. 18, O that Ishmael might *l.* before
　thee !
45. 3, doth my father yet *l.* ?
Lev. 18. 5 ; Neh. 9. 29 ; Ezek. 20. 11, if a man do,
　he shall *l.*
Deut. 8. 3 ; Mat. 4. 4 ; Lu. 4. 4, not *l.* by bread alone.
Job 7. 16, I would not *l.* alway.
14. 14, shall he *l.* again ?
Ps. 118. 17, I shall not die, but *l.*
Isa. 38. 16, make me to *l.*
55. 3, hear, and your soul shall *l.*
Ezek. 3. 21 ; 18. 9 ; 33. 13, he shall surely *l.*
16. 6, when thou wast in thy blood, *l.*
Hos. 6. 2, we shall *l.* in his sight.
Hab. 2. 4, the just shall *l.* by faith.
Lu. 10. 28, this do, and thou shalt *l.*
John 11. 25, though he were dead, yet shall he *l.*
14. 19, because I *l.*, ye shall *l.* also.
Acts 17. 28, in him we *l.* and move.
Rom. 8. 12, *l.* after the flesh.
14. 8, whether we *l.*, we *l.* unto the Lord.
1 Cor. 9. 14, should *l.* of the gospel.
2 Cor. 6. 9, as dying, and behold we *l.*
Gal. 2. 19, that I might *l.* unto God.
5. 25, if we *l.* in the Spirit.
Phil. 1. 21, for me to *l.* is Christ.
2 Tim. 3. 12, all that will *l.* godly.
Jas. 4. 15, if the Lord will, we shall *l.*
Rev. 1. 18, I am he that *l.*, and was dead.
3. 1, a name that thou *l.*
See Rom. 6. 10 ; 1 Tim. 5. 6 ; Rev. 20. 4.
LIVELY. Ex. 1. 19 ; Acts 7. 38 ; 1 Pet. 1. 3 ; 2. 5.
LIVING. Gen. 2. 7, a *l.* soul.
Job 28. 13 ; Ps. 27. 13 ; 52. 5 ; 116. 9, the land of
　the *l.*
33. 30 ; Ps. 56. 13, light of *l.*
Ps. 69. 28, the book of the *l.*
Eccl. 7. 2, the *l.* will lay it to heart.
9. 5, the *l.* know they shall die.
Cant. 4. 15 ; Jer. 2. 13 ; 17. 13 ; Zech. 14. 8 ; John
　4. 10, *l.* water.
Isa. 38. 19, the *l.* shall praise thee.

Lam. 3. 39, wherefore doth a *l.* man complain ?
Mk. 12. 44, even all her *l.*
Lu. 8. 43, spent all her *l.*
John 6. 51, I am the *l.* bread.
Heb. 10. 20, a new and *l.* way.
See Mat. 22. 32 ; Mk. 12. 27 ; 1 Cor. 15. 43.
LOADETH. Ps. 68. 19.
LOAN. 1 Sam. 2. 20.
LOATHE. Num. 21. 5 ; Job 7. 16 ; Ezek. 6. 9 ; 20. 43 ;
　36. 31.
LODGE. Ruth 1. 16 ; Isa. 1. 21 ; 1 Tim. 5. 10.
LOFTY. Ps. 131. 1 ; Isa. 2. 11 ; 57. 15.
LONG. Job 3. 21, which *l.* for death.
6. 8, that God would grant the thing I *l.* for !
Ps. 63. 1, my flesh *l.* for thee in a dry land.
84. 2, my soul *l.* for courts of the Lord.
119. 174, I have *l.* for thy salvation.
See Deut. 12. 20 ; 28. 32 ; 2 Sam. 23. 15 ; Phil. 1. 8.
LOOK. Gen. 19. 17, *l.* not behind thee.
Num. 21. 8, when he *l.* on the serpent.
Job 33. 27, he *l.* on men.
Ps. 5. 3, and will *l.* up.
34. 5, they *l.* to him, and were lightened.
84. 9, *l.* upon the face of thine anointed.
Isa. 5. 7 ; 59. 11, he *l.* for judgment.
17. 7, at that day shall a man *l.* to his Maker.
45. 22, *l.* unto me, and be saved.
63. 5, I *l.*, and there was none to help.
66. 2, to this man will I *l.*
Jer. 8. 15 ; 14. 19, we *l.* for peace.
39. 12, *l.* well to him.
40. 4, come with me, and I will *l.* well to thee.
Hag. 1. 9, ye *l.* for much.
Mat. 11. 3 ; Lu. 7. 19, do we *l.* for another ?
24. 50, in a day he *l.* not for.
Lu. 9. 62, no man *l.* back is fit for the kingdom.
10. 32, a Levite came and *l.* on him.
22. 61, the Lord turned, and *l.* on Peter.
John 13. 22, disciples *l.* one on another.
Acts 3. 4, 12, said, *l.* on us.
6. 3, *l.* ye out seven men.
2 Cor. 4. 18, we *l.* not at things seen.
10. 7, *l.* upon things after outward appearance.
Phil. 2. 4, *l.* not every man on his own things.
Tit. 2. 13, *l.* for that blessed hope.
Heb. 11. 10, he *l.* for a city.
12. 2, *l.* unto Jesus.
1 Pet. 1. 12, angels desire to *l.* into.
2 John 8, *l.* to yourselves.
See Prov. 14. 15 ; Mat. 5. 28 ; 2 Pet. 3. 12.
LOOSE. Job 38. 31, canst thou *l.* the bands of
　Orion ?
Ps. 102. 20, *l.* those appointed to death.
116. 16, thou hast *l.* my bonds.
Eccl. 12. 6, or ever the silver cord be *l.*
Mat. 16. 19 ; 18. 18, *l.* on earth, be *l.* in heaven.
John 11. 44, *l.* him, and let him go.
Acts 2. 24, having *l.* the pains of death.
1 Cor. 7. 27, art thou *l.* from a wife ?
See Deut. 25. 9 ; Isa. 45. 1 ; 51. 14 ; Lu. 13. 12.
LORD. Ex. 34. 6, the *L.* the *L.* God, merciful.
Deut. 4. 35 ; 1 Kings 18. 39, the *L.* is God.
6. 4, the *L.* our God is one *L.*
Ruth 2. 4 ; 2 Chron. 20. 17 ; 2 Thess. 3. 16, the *L.*
　be with you.
1 Sam. 3. 18 ; John 21. 7, it is the *L.*
Neh. 9. 6 ; Isa. 37. 20, thou art *L.* alone.
Ps. 33. 12, whose God is the *L.*
100. 3, know that the *L.* he is God.
118. 23, this is the *L.* doing.
Zech. 14. 9, one *L.*, and his name one.
Mat. 7. 21, not every one that saith *L.*, *L.*
26. 22, *L.*, is it I ?
Mk. 2. 28 ; Lu. 6. 5, the *L.* of the sabbath.
Lu. 6. 46, why call ye me *L.*, *L.* ?
John 9. 36, who is he, *L.* ?
20. 25, we have seen the *L.*
Acts 2. 36, both *L.* and Christ.
9. 5 ; 26. 15, who art thou, *L.* ?

Eph. 4. 5, one *L.*
See Rom. 10. 12 ; 1 Cor. 2. 8 ; 15. 47 ; Rev. 11. 15.
LORDSHIP. Mk. 10. 42 ; Lu. 22. 25.
LOSE. Mat. 10. 39 ; 16. 25 ; Mk. 8. 35 ; Lu. 9. 24,
shall *l.* it.
16. 26 ; Mk. 8. 36 ; Lu. 9. 25, *l.* his own soul.
John 6. 39, Father's will I should *l.* nothing.
See Judg. 18. 25 ; Eccl. 3. 6 ; Lu. 15. 4, 8.
LOSS. 1 Cor. 3. 15 ; Phil. 3. 7, 8.
LOST. Ps. 119. 176 ; Jer. 50. 6, like *l.* sheep.
Ezek. 37. 11, our hope is *l.*
Mat. 10. 6 ; 15. 24, go to *l.* sheep of Israel.
18. 11 ; Lu. 19. 10, to save that which was *l.*
John 6. 12, that nothing be *l.*
17. 12, none of them is *l.*
18. 9, have I *l.* none.
See Lev. 6. 3 ; Deut. 22. 3 ; 2 Cor. 4. 3.
LOT. Ps. 16. 5, thou maintainest my *l.*
125. 3, not rest on the *l.* of the righteous.
Prov. 1. 14, cast in thy *l.* among us.
16. 33, *l.* is cast into the lap.
18. 18, *l.* causeth contention to cease.
Dan. 12. 13, stand in thy *l.*
Acts 8. 21, neither part nor *l.* in this matter.
See Num. 26. 55 ; Mat. 27. 35 ; Acts 1. 26.
LOUD. Ezra 3. 13 ; Prov. 7. 11 ; 27. 14 ; Lu. 23. 23.
LOVE (*n.*). 2 Sam. 1. 26, wonderful, passing the *l.*
of women.
Prov. 10. 12, *l.* covereth all sins.
15. 17, better a dinner of herbs where *l.* is.
Cant. 2. 4, his banner over me was *l.*
8. 6, *l.* is strong as death.
Jer. 31. 3, loved thee with everlasting *l.*
Hos. 11. 4, the bands of *l.*
Mat. 24. 12, *l.* of many shall wax cold.
John 5. 42, ye have not the *l.* of God in you.
13. 35, if ye have *l.* one to another.
15. 13, greater *l.* hath no man than this.
Rom. 13. 10, *l.* worketh no ill.
2 Cor. 5. 14, the *l.* of Christ constraineth us.
13. 11, the God of *l.* shall be with you.
Eph. 3. 19, the *l.* of Christ, which passeth.
1 Tim. 6. 10, *l.* of money is the root of all evil.
Heb. 13. 1, let brotherly *l.* continue.
1 John 4. 7, *l.* is of God.
8, 16, God is *l.*
10, herein is *l.*, not that we loved God.
18, no fear in *l.*
Rev. 2. 4, thou hast left thy first *l.*
See Gen. 29. 20 ; Gal. 5. 22 ; 1 Thess. 1. 3.
LOVE (*v.*). Lev. 19. 18 ; Mat. 19. 19 ; 22. 39 ; Mk. 12.
31, thou shalt *l.* thy neighbour.
Deut. 6. 5 ; 10. 12 ; 11. 1 ; 19. 9 ; 30. 6 ; Mat. 22. 37 ;
Mk. 12. 30 ; Lu. 10. 27, *l.* the Lord thy God.
Ps. 18. 1, I will *l.* thee, O Lord, my strength.
26. 8, I have *l.* the habitation of thy house.
34. 12, what man is he that *l.* many days?
69. 36, they that *l.* his name.
97. 10, ye that *l.* the Lord.
109. 17, as he *l.* cursing.
122. 6, they shall prosper that *l.* thee.
Prov. 8. 17, I *l.* them that *l.* me.
17. 17, a friend *l.* at all times.
Eccl. 3. 8, a time to *l.*
Jer. 5. 31, my people *l.* to have it so.
31. 3, I have *l.* thee with an everlasting *l.*
Hos. 14. 4, I will *l.* them freely.
Amos 5. 15, hate the evil, and *l.* the good.
Mic. 6. 8, but to *l.* mercy, and walk humbly.
Mat. 5. 44 ; Lu. 6. 27, I say, *l.* your enemies.
46, if ye *l.* them which *l.* you.
Lu. 7. 42, which will *l.* him most?
John 11. 3, he whom thou *l.* is sick.
15. 12, 17, that ye *l.* one another.
21. 15, 16, 17, *l.* thou me?
Rom. 13. 8, owe no man any thing, but to *l.*
Eph. 6. 24, grace be with all them that *l.* our Lord.
1 Pet. 1. 8, whom having not seen, ye *l.*
2. 17, *l.* the brotherhood.

1 John 4. 19, we *l.* him, because he first *l.* us.
Rev. 3. 19, as many as I *l.* I rebuke.
See Gen. 22. 2 ; John 14. 31 ; 1 John 4. 20, 21.
LOVELY. 2 Sam. 1. 23 ; Cant. 5. 16 ; Ezek. 33. 32 ;
Phil. 4. 8.
LOVER. 1 Kings 5. 1 ; Ps. 88. 18 ; 2 Tim. 3. 4 ; Tit.
1. 8.
LOW. Ps. 136. 23 ; Rom. 12. 16 ; Jas. 1. 9, 10.
LOWER. Ps. 8. 5 ; 63. 9 ; Eph. 4. 9 ; Heb. 2. 7.
LOWEST. Deut. 32. 22 ; Ps. 86. 13 ; Lu. 14. 9.
LOWLINESS. Eph. 4. 2 ; Phil. 2. 3.
LOWLY. Prov. 11. 2, with the *l.* is wisdom.
Mat. 11. 29, I am meek and *l.*
See Ps. 138. 6 ; Prov. 3. 34 ; 16. 19 ; Zech. 9. 9.
LUST. Deut. 12. 15, 20, 21 ; 14. 26, whatsoever thy
soul *l.* after.
Ps. 81. 12, gave them up to their own *l.*
Rom. 7. 7, I had not known *l.*
Gal. 5. 24, Christ's have crucified flesh with *l.*
1 Tim. 6. 9, rich fall into hurtful *l.*
Tit. 2. 12, denying worldly *l.*
Jas. 1. 14, when he is drawn of his own *l.*
1 Pet. 2. 11, abstain from fleshly *l.*
1 John 2. 16, the *l.* of the flesh.
17, the world passeth away, and the *l.* thereof.
Jude 16, 18, walking after *l.*
See Mat. 5. 28 ; 1 Cor. 10. 6 ; Rev. 18. 14.
LYING. Ps. 31. 18, let the *l.* lips be put to silence.
119. 163, I abhor *l.*, but thy law I love.
Prov. 6. 17, the Lord hateth a *l.* tongue.
12. 19, a *l.* tongue is but for a moment.
Jer. 7. 4, trust not in *l.* words.
Eph. 4. 25, putting away *l.*
See 1 Kings 22. 22 ; 2 Chron. 18. 21 ; Dan. 2. 9.

M.

MAD. John 10. 20 ; Acts 26. 11, 24 ; 1 Cor. 14. 23.
MADE. Ex. 2. 14, who *m.* thee a prince over us?
Ps. 118. 24, this is the day the Lord hath *m.*
Prov. 16. 4, the Lord *m.* all things for himself.
Eccl. 3. 11, he hath *m.* every thing beautiful.
7. 29, God hath *m.* man upright.
Isa. 66. 2, all these things hath mine hand *m.*
John 1. 3, all things were *m.* by him.
5. 6, wilt thou be *m.* whole?
2 Cor. 5. 21, he hath *m.* him to be sin for us.
Eph. 2. 13, *m.* nigh by the blood of Christ.
3. 7 ; Col. 1. 23, I was *m.* a minister.
Col. 1. 20, having *m.* peace.
Heb. 2. 17, to be *m.* like his brethren.
See Ps. 95. 5 ; 149. 2 ; John 19. 7 ; Acts 17. 24.
MAGNIFY. Josh. 3. 7, this day will I begin to *m.*
thee.
Job 7. 17, what is man, that thou shouldest *m.*
him?
Ps. 34. 3 ; 40. 16 ; Lu. 1. 46, *m.* the Lord.
35. 26 ; 38. 16, that *m.* themselves.
138. 2, thou hast *m.* thy word above all.
Isa. 42. 21, *m.* the law.
Acts 19. 17, the name of Jesus was *m.*
Rom. 11. 13, I *m.* mine office.
See Dan. 8. 25 ; 11. 36 ; Acts 5. 13 ; Phil. 1. 20.
MAIDSERVANTS. Ex. 20. 10, nor thy *m.*
21. 7, if a man sell his daughter to be a *m.*
Deut. 15. 17, unto thy *m.* thou shalt do likewise.
MAIL. 1 Sam. 17. 5.
MAINTAIN. 1 Kings 8. 45 ; 49. 59 ; 2 Chron. 35. 39,
m. their cause.
Ps. 16. 5, thou *m.* my lot.
Tit. 3. 8, 14, careful to *m.* good works.
See Job 13. 15 ; Ps. 9. 4 ; 140. 12.
MAINTENANCE. Ezra 4. 14 ; Prov. 27. 27.
MAKER. Job 4. 17, shall a man be more pure
than his *m.*?
32. 22, my *m.* would soon take me away.
35. 10, none saith, where is God my *m.*?
36. 3, ascribe righteousness to my *m.*
Ps. 95. 6, kneel before the Lord our *m.*

Prov. 14. 31; 17. 5, reproacheth his *m.*
22. 2, the Lord is *m.* of them all.
Isa. 45. 9, that striveth with his *m.*
51. 13, forgettest the Lord thy *m.*
54. 5, thy *m.* is thine husband.
Heb. 11. 10, whose builder and *m.* is God.
See Isa. 1. 31; 17. 7; 22. 11; Hab. 2. 18.
MALICIOUSNESS. Rom. 1. 29; 1 Pet. 2. 16.
MAN. Gen. 3. 22, the *m.* is become as one of us.
8. 21, for *m.* sake.
Num. 23. 19, God is not a *m.*
Neh. 6. 11, should such a *m.* as I flee?
Job 5. 7, *m.* is born to trouble.
10. 4, seest thou as *m.* seeth?
11. 12, vain *m.* would be wise.
14. 1, *m.* that is born of a woman.
15. 7, art thou the first *m.* that was born?
25. 6, *m.* that is a worm.
33. 12, God is greater than *m.*
Ps. 10. 18, the *m.* of earth.
49. 12, *m.* being in honour abideth not.
89. 48, what *m.* is he that liveth?
90. 3, thou turnest *m.* to destruction.
104. 23, *m.* goeth forth to his labour.
118. 6, I will not fear, what can *m.* do?
Prov. 12. 2, a good *m.* obtaineth favour.
Eccl. 6. 12, who knoweth what is good for *m.*
Isa. 2. 22, cease ye from *m.*
Jer. 10. 23, it is not in *m.* to direct his steps.
Lam. 3. 1, I am the *m.* that hath seen affliction
Hos. 11. 9, I am God, and not *m.*
Mat. 6. 24; Lu. 16. 13, no *m.* can serve.
8. 4; Mk. 8. 26, 30; Lu. 5. 14; 9. 21, tell no *m.*
17. 8, they saw no *m.*
John 1. 18; 1 John 4. 12, no *m.* hath seen God.
19. 5, behold the *m.*!
1 Cor. 2. 11, know the things of a *m.*?
11. 8, *m.* is not of the woman.
2 Cor. 4. 16, though our outward *m.* perish.
Phil. 2. 8, in fashion as a *m.*
1 Tim. 2. 5, the *m.* Christ Jesus.
See John 7. 46; 1 Cor. 15. 47; Eph. 4. 24.
MANDRAKES. Gen. 30. 14, found *m.* in the field.
Cant. 7. 13, the *m.* give a smell.
MANEH. Ezek. 45. 12.
MANGER. Lu. 2. 7.
MANIFEST. Mk. 4. 22, nothing hid that shall
not be *m.*
John 2. 11, and *m.* forth his glory.
14. 22, how is it thou wilt *m.* thyself?
1 Cor. 4. 5, who will make *m.* the counsels of the
hearts.
2 Cor. 2. 14, maketh *m.* savour of knowledge.
Gal. 5. 19, the works of the flesh are *m.*
2 Thess. 1. 5, a *m.* token of righteous judgment.
1 Tim. 3. 16, God was *m.* in the flesh.
5. 25, good works of some are *m.* beforehand.
Heb. 4. 13, no creature that is not *m.*
1 John 1. 2, the life was *m.*
3. 5, he was *m.* to take away our sins.
4. 9, in this was *m.* the love of God.
See Rom. 8. 19; John 17. 6; 1 John 3. 10.
MANIFOLD. Ps. 104. 24, how *m.* are thy works!
Eph. 3. 10, the *m.* wisdom of God.
1 Pet. 1. 6, through *m.* temptations.
4. 10, stewards of the *m.* grace of God.
See Neh. 9. 19, 27; Amos 5. 12; Lu. 18. 30.
MANNER. 2 Sam. 7. 19, is this the *m.* of man?
Ps. 144. 13, all *m.* of store.
Isa. 5. 17, lambs shall feed after their *m.*
Mat. 8. 27; Mk. 4. 41; Lu. 8. 25, what *m.* of man
is this!
12. 31, all *m.* of sin shall be forgiven.
Acts 26. 4, my *m.* of life from my youth.
1 Cor. 15. 33, evil communications corrupt good *m.*
Heb. 10. 25, as the *m.* of some is.
Jas. 1. 24, forgetteth what *m.* of man.
1 Pet. 1. 15, holy in all *m.* of conversation.
2 Pet. 3. 11, what *m.* of persons ought ye to be?
See Mat. 4. 23; 5. 11; Lu. 9. 55; Rev. 22. 2.

MANTLE. 2 Kings 2. 8; Job 1. 20; Ps. 109. 29.
MAR. Lev. 19. 27, nor *m.* the corners of thy beard.
1 Sam. 6. 5, images of your mice that *m.* the land.
Job 30. 13, they *m.* my path.
Isa. 52. 14, visage *m.* more than any man.
Mk. 2. 22, wine spilled, and bottles *m.*
See Ruth 4. 6; 2 Kings 3. 19; Jer. 13. 7; 18. 4.
MARBLE. 1 Chron. 29. 2, and *m.* stones in abun-
dance.
Cant. 5. 15, his legs are as pillars of *m.*
MARK. Gen. 4. 15, the Lord set a *m.* on Cain.
Job 22. 15, hast thou *m.* the old way?
Ps. 37. 37, *m.* the perfect man.
48. 13, *m.* well her bulwarks.
130. 3, if thou shouldest *m.* iniquities.
Jer. 2. 22, thine iniquity is *m.* before me.
23. 18, who hath *m.* his word?
Phil. 3. 14, I press toward the *m.* for the prize.
17, *m.* them which walk so.
See Lu. 14. 7; Rev. 13. 16; 20. 4.
MARROW. Job 21. 24; Ps. 63. 5; Prov. 3. 8; Heb.
4. 12.
MARVEL. Mat. 8. 10; Mk. 6. 6; Lu. 7. 9, Jesus *m.*
Mk. 5. 20, all men did *m.*
John 3. 7; 5. 28; 1 John 3. 13, *m.* not.
See Eccl. 5. 8; John 7. 21; Gal. 1. 6.
MARVELLOUS. Job 5. 9, *m.* things without num-
ber.
Ps. 17. 7, *m.* lovingkindness.
118. 23; Mat. 21. 42; Mk. 12. 11, *m.* in our eyes.
John 9. 30, herein is a *m.* thing.
1 Pet. 2. 9, into his *m.* light.
See Ps. 105. 5; 139. 14; Dan. 11. 36; Mic. 7. 15.
MASTER. 2 Kings 6. 32, sound of his *m.* feet behind him.
Mal. 1. 6, if I be a *m.*, where is my fear?
2. 12, the Lord will cut off the *m.* and the scholar.
Mat. 6. 24; Lu. 16. 13, no man can serve two *m.*
10. 24; Lu. 6. 40, disciple not above his *m.*
25, enough for the disciple that he be as his *m.*
17. 24, doth not your *m.* pay tribute?
23. 8, 10, one is your *M.*, even Christ.
26. 25, *M.*, is it I?
Mk. 5. 35; Lu. 8. 49, why troublest thou the *M.*?
9. 5; Lu. 9. 33, *M.*, it is good for us to be here.
10. 17; Lu. 10. 25, good *M.*, what shall I do?
Lu. 13. 25, when once the *m.* of the house is
risen.
John 3. 10, art thou a *m.* of Israel?
11. 28, the *M.* is come, and calleth.
13. 13, ye call me *M.*, and ye say well.
Rom. 14. 4, to his own *m.* he standeth or falleth.
1 Cor. 3. 10, as a wise *m.*-builder.
Eph. 6. 5; Col. 3. 22; Tit. 2. 9; 1 Pet. 2. 18, be
obedient to *m.*
9; Col. 4. 1, *m.*, do the same things to them.
1 Tim. 6. 1, count their *m.* worthy of honour.
2, that have believing *m.*
Jas. 3. 1, be not many *m.*
See Gen. 24. 12; 39. 8; Prov. 25. 13; Eccl. 12. 11.
MASTERY. Ex. 32. 18; 1 Cor. 9. 25; 2 Tim. 2. 5.
MATTER. Ezra 10. 4, arise, for this *m.* belongeth
to thee.
Job 19. 28, the root of the *m.* is found in me.
32. 18, I am full of *m.*
Ps. 45. 1, my heart is inditing a good *m.*
Prov. 16. 20, handleth a *m.* wisely.
18. 13, answereth a *m.* before he heareth it.
Eccl. 10. 20, that which hath wings shall tell the *m.*
12. 13, conclusion of the whole *m.*
Mat. 23. 23, the weightier *m.*
Acts 18. 14, if it were a *m.* of wrong.
1 Cor. 6. 2, to judge the smallest *m.*
2 Cor. 9. 5, as a *m.* of bounty.
Jas. 3. 5, how great a *m.* a little fire kindleth!
See Gen. 30. 15; Dan. 3. 16; Acts 8. 21; 17. 32.
MAY. Mat. 9. 21; 26. 42; Acts 8. 37.
MEAN. Ex. 12. 26; Josh. 4. 6, what *m.* ye by this
service?

Deut. 6. 20, what *m.* the testimonies?
Prov. 22. 29, not stand before *m.* men.
Isa. 2. 9 ; 5. 15 ; 31. 8, the *m.* man.
Ezek. 17. 12, know ye not what these things *m.*?
Mk. 9. 10, what the rising from the dead should *m.*
Acts 21. 39, citizen of no *m.* city.
See Acts 10. 17 ; 17. 20 ; 21. 13.

MEANS. Ex. 34. 7 ; Num. 14. 18, by no *m.* clear guilty.
Ps. 49. 7, none can by any *m.* redeem.
Mal. 1. 9, this hath been by your *m.*
Mat. 5. 26, shalt by no *m.* come out.
Lu. 10. 19, nothing shall by any *m.* hurt you.
John 9. 21, by what *m.* he now seeth.
1 Cor. 8. 9, lest by any *m.* this liberty.
9. 22, that I might by all *m.* save some.
Phil. 3. 11, by any *m.* attain.
2 Thess. 3. 16, give you peace always by all *m.*
See Jer. 5. 31 ; 1 Cor. 9. 27 ; Gal. 2. 2.

MEASURE (*n.*). Deut. 25. 14 ; Prov. 20. 10, thou shalt not have divers *m.*
Job 11. 9, the *m.* is longer than the earth.
28. 25, he weigheth the waters by *m.*
Ps. 39. 4, the *m.* of my days.
Isa. 40. 12, the dust of the earth in a *m.*
Jer. 30. 11 ; 46. 28, I will correct thee in *m.*
Ezek. 4. 11, thou shalt drink water by *m.*
Mat. 7. 2 ; Mk. 4. 24 ; Lu. 6. 38, with what *m.* ye mete.
13. 33 ; Lu. 13. 21, three *m.* of meal.
23. 32, fill up *m.* of your fathers.
Lu. 6. 38, good *m.*, pressed down.
John 3. 34, giveth not the Spirit by *m.*
Rom. 12. 3, to every man the *m.* of faith.
2 Cor. 12. 7, exalted above *m.*
Eph. 4. 7, the *m.* of the gift of Christ.
13, to the *m.* of the stature.
16, in the *m.* of every part.
Rev. 6. 6, a *m.* of wheat for a penny.
21. 17, according to the *m.* of a man.
See Ps. 80. 5 ; Isa. 5. 14 ; Mic. 6. 10.

MEASURE (*v.*). Isa. 40. 12, who hath *m.* the waters?
65. 7, I will *m.* former work into bosom.
Jer. 31. 37, if heaven can be *m.*
33. 22 ; Hos. 1. 10, as the sand cannot be *m.*
2 Cor. 10. 12, *m.* themselves by themselves.
See Ezek. 40. 3 ; 42. 15 ; Zech. 2. 1.

MEAT. Gen. 27. 4, make me savoury *m.*
1 Kings 19. 8, went in strength of that *m.*
Ps. 59. 15, wander up and down for *m.*
69. 21, they gave me also gall for my *m.*
78. 25, he sent them *m.* to the full.
145. 15, *m.* in due season.
Prov. 23. 3, dainties, for they are deceitful *m.*
30. 22, a fool when filled with *m.*
31. 15, she giveth *m.* to her household.
Isa. 65. 25, dust shall be the serpent's *m.*
Ezek. 4. 10, thy *m.* shall be by weight.
47. 12, fruit for *m.*
Dan. 1. 8, not defile himself with king's *m.*
Hab. 1. 16, because their *m.* is plenteous.
3. 17, fields yield no *m.*
Mal. 3. 10, bring tithes, that there may be *m.*
Mat. 6. 25 ; Lu. 12. 23, life more than *m.*?
10. 10, workman worthy of his *m.*
15. 37 ; Mk. 8. 8, of broken *m.*
25. 35, ye gave me *m.*
Lu. 3. 11, he that hath *m.* let him do likewise.
24. 41 ; John 21. 5, have ye any *m.*?
John 4. 32, I have *m.* to eat.
34, my *m.* is to do the will of him that sent me.
6. 27, labour not for the *m.* that perisheth.
Acts 2. 46, did eat *m.* with gladness.
15. 29, abstain from *m.* offered to idols.
Rom. 14. 15, destroy not him with thy *m.*
17, kingdom of God is not *m.* and drink.
20, for *m.* destroy not the work of God.
1 Cor. 6. 13, *m.* for the belly.
8. 13, if *m.* make my brother to offend.
10. 3, the same spiritual *m.*

1 Tim. 4. 3, to abstain from *m.*
Heb. 5. 12, 14, not of strong *m.*
12. 16, who for one morsel of *m.*
See Gen. 1. 29 ; 9. 3 ; Mat. 3. 4 ; Col. 2. 16.

MEDDLE. 2 Kings 14. 10 ; 2 Chron. 25. 19, why *m.* to thy hurt?
Prov. 20. 3, every fool will be *m.*
19, *m.* not with him that flattereth.
26. 17, that *m.* with strife.
See 2 Chron. 35. 21 ; Prov. 17. 14 ; 24. 21.

MEDITATE. Gen. 24. 63, Isaac went out to *m.*
Josh. 1. 8, thou shalt *m.* therein.
Ps. 1. 2, in his law doth he *m.*
63. 6 ; 119. 148, *m.* in the night watches.
77. 12 ; 143. 5, I will *m.* of thy works.
Isa. 33. 18, thine heart shall *m.* terror.
Lu. 21. 14, not to *m.* before.
1 Tim. 4. 15, *m.* upon these things.
See Ps. 19. 14 ; 104. 34 ; 119. 97, 99.

MEEK. Num. 12. 3, Moses was very *m.*
Ps. 22. 26, the *m.* shall eat and be satisfied.
25. 9, the *m.* will he guide.
37. 11 ; Mat. 5. 5, the *m.* shall inherit the earth.
149. 4, will beautify the *m.*
Isa. 29. 19, the *m.* shall increase their joy.
61. 1, good tidings to the *m.*
Mat. 11. 29, for I am *m.*
1 Pet. 3. 4, a *m.* and quiet spirit.
See Ps. 76. 9 ; 147. 6 ; Isa. 11. 4 ; Mat. 21. 5.

MEEKNESS. 2 Cor. 10. 1, by the *m.* of Christ.
Gal. 6. 1, restore in the spirit of *m.*
1 Tim. 6. 11, follow after *m.*
2 Tim. 2. 25, in *m.* instructing.
Tit. 3. 2, showing *m.* to all men.
1 Pet. 3. 15, give reason of hope in you with *m.*
See Zeph. 2. 3 ; Gal. 5. 23 ; Eph. 4. 2.

MEET. Prov. 11. 24, withholdeth more than is *m.*
Mat. 15. 26, not *m.* to take children's bread.
25. 1, 6, to *m.* the bridegroom.
1 Cor. 15. 9, not *m.* to be called an apostle.
1 Thess. 4. 17, to *m.* the Lord in the air.
See Prov. 22. 2 ; Amos 4. 12 ; Mat. 8. 34.

MELODY. Isa. 23. 16 ; 51. 3 ; Amos 5. 23 ; Eph. 5. 19.

MELT. Ps. 46. 6, the earth *m.*
97. 5, the hills *m.*
107. 26, their soul *m.*
147. 18, he sendeth his word, and *m.* them.
Isa. 13. 7, every man's heart shall *m.*
64. 2, as when the *m.* fire burneth.
See Ex. 15. 15 ; Josh. 14. 8 ; Jer. 9. 7.

MEMBER. Ps. 139. 16, all my *m.* were written.
Rom. 6. 13, 19, neither yield your *m.*
12. 4, as we have many *m.*
1 Cor. 6. 15, bodies *m.* of Christ.
Jas. 3. 5, the tongue is a little *m.*
4. 1, lusts which war in your *m.*
See Job 17. 7 ; Mat. 5. 29 ; Eph. 4. 25 ; 5. 30.

MEMORY. Ps. 109. 15 ; 145. 7 ; Prov. 10. 7 ; Eccl. 9. 5.

MEN. 2 Chron. 6. 18, will God dwell with *m.*?
1 Sam. 4. 9 ; 1 Cor. 16. 13, quit yourselves like *m.*
Ps. 9. 20, know themselves to be but *m.*
82. 7, but ye shall die like *m.*
Eccl. 12. 3, strong *m.* shall bow themselves.
Isa. 31. 3, the Egyptians are *m.*, and not God.
46. 8, show yourselves *m.*
Gal. 1. 10, do I now persuade *m.*?
1 Thess. 2. 4, not as pleasing *m.*, but God.
See Ps. 116. 11 ; 1 Tim. 2. 4 ; 1 Pet. 2. 17.

MEND. 2 Chron. 24. 12 ; 34. 10 ; Mat. 4. 21 ; Mk. 1. 19.

MENTION. Gen. 40. 14, make *m.* of me to Pharaoh.
Ps. 71. 16, I will make *m.* of thy righteousness.
Isa. 12. 4, make *m.* that his name is exalted.
63. 7, I will *m.* the lovingkindnesses of the Lord.
Rom. 1. 9 ; Eph. 1. 16 ; 1 Thess. 1. 2, *m.* of you in my prayers.
See Isa. 62. 6 ; Ezek. 18. 22 ; 33. 16.

MERCHANDISE. Prov. 3. 14, *m.* of it better than *m.* of silver.
Isa. 23. 18, *m.* shall be holiness to the Lord.
Mat. 22. 5, one to his farm, another to his *m.*
John 2. 16, my father's house an house of *m.*
2 Pet. 2. 3, make *m.* of you.
See Deut. 21. 14 ; 24. 7 ; Ezek. 26. 12 ; Rev. 18. 11.
MERCHANT. Gen. 23. 16, current money with the *m.*
Isa. 23. 8, whose *m.* are princes.
47. 15, even thy *m.* shall wander.
Rev. 18. 3, 11, the *m.* of the earth.
23, thy *m.* were great men of the earth.
See Prov. 31. 24 ; Isa. 23. 11 ; Mat. 13. 45.
MERCIFUL. Ps. 37. 26, ever *m.*, and lendeth.
67. 1, God be *m.* to us, and bless us.
Prov. 11. 17, the *m.* doeth good to his own soul.
Isa. 57. 1, *m.* men are taken away.
Jer. 3. 12, return, for I am *m.*
Mat. 5. 7, blessed are the *m.*
Lu. 6. 36, be ye *m.*, as your Father is *m.*
18. 13, God be *m.* to me a sinner.
Heb. 2. 17, a *m.* High Priest.
See Ex. 34. 6 ; 2 Sam. 22. 26 ; 1 Kings 20. 31.
MERCY. Gen. 32. 10, not worthy the least of the *m.*
Ex. 33. 19, will show *m.* on whom I will show *m.*
34. 7 ; Dan. 9. 4, keeping *m.* for thousands.
Num. 14. 18 ; Ps. 103. 11 ; 145. 8, longsuffering and of great *m.*
1 Chron. 16. 34, 41 ; 2 Chron. 5. 13 ; 7. 3, 6 ; Ezra 3. 11 ; Ps. 106. 1 ; 107. 1 ; 118. 1 ; 136. 1 ; Jer. 33. 11, his *m.* endureth for ever.
Ps. 23. 6, surely goodness and *m.* shall follow.
25. 7, according to thy *m.* remember me.
33. 22, let thy *m.* be upon us.
52. 8, I trust in the *m.* of God.
59. 10, the God of my *m.*
66. 20, not turned his *m.* from me.
77. 8, is his *m.* clean gone for ever?
85. 10, *m.* and truth are met together.
89. 2, *m.* shall be built up for ever.
90. 14, satisfy us early with thy *m.*
101. 1, I will sing of *m.*
108. 4, thy *m.* is great above the heavens.
115. 1, for thy *m.*, and for thy truth's sake.
119. 64, the earth is full of thy *m.*
130. 7, with the Lord there is *m.*
Prov. 3. 3, let not *m.* and truth forsake thee.
14. 21, 31, he that hath *m.* on the poor.
16. 6 ; 20. 28, *m.* and truth.
Isa. 54. 7, with great *m.* will I gather thee.
Jer. 6. 23, they are cruel, and have no *m.*
Lam. 3. 22, it is of the Lord's *m.*
Hos. 4. 1, because there is no *m.* in the land.
6. 6 ; Mat. 9. 13, I desired *m.*, and not sacrifice.
10. 12, sow in righteousness, reap in *m.*
14. 3, in thee the fatherless find *m.*
Mic. 6. 8, but to do justly, and love *m.*
7. 18, he delighteth in *m.*
Hab. 3. 2, in wrath remember *m.*
Mat. 5. 7, the merciful shall obtain *m.*
9. 27 ; 15. 22 ; 20. 30 ; Mk. 10. 47, 48 ; Lu. 18. 38, 39, thou son of David have *m.* on me.
Lu. 10. 37, he that showed *m.*
Rom. 9. 15, 18, *m.* on whom I will have *m.*
16, of God that showeth *m.*
12. 1, beseech you by the *m.* of God.
8, he that showeth *m.*, with cheerfulness.
2 Cor. 1. 3, the Father of *m.*
Eph. 2. 4, God, who is rich in *m.*
1 Tim. 1. 13, 16, I obtained *m.*, because.
2 Tim. 1. 18, that he may find *m.* in that day.
Heb. 4. 16, obtain *m.*, and find grace.
Jas. 2. 13, without *m.*, that showed no *m.*
1 Pet. 1. 3, according to his abundant *m.*
See Prov. 12. 10 ; Dan. 4. 27 ; 1 Tim. 1. 2.
MERRY. Gen. 43. 34, were *m.* with him.
Judg. 16. 25, their hearts were *m.*
Prov. 15. 13, *m.* heart maketh cheerful countenance.
15, *m.* heart hath a continual feast.

Prov. 17. 22, *m.* heart doeth good like a medicine.
Eccl. 8. 15, nothing better than to eat and be *m.*
9. 7, drink thy wine with a *m.* heart.
10. 19, wine maketh *m.*
Jas. 5. 13, is any *m.* ?
See Lu. 12. 19 ; 15. 23 ; Rev. 11. 10.
MESSENGER. Job 33. 23 ; Prov. 25. 13 ; Isa. 42. 19.
METE. Isa. 40. 12 ; Mat. 7. 2 ; Mk. 4. 24 ; Lu. 6. 38.
MIDDLE. Ezek. 1. 16 ; Eph. 2. 14.
MIDST. Ps. 102. 24, in the *m.* of my days.
Prov. 23. 34, lieth down in *m.* of the sea.
Dan. 9. 27, in the *m.* of the week.
Mat. 18. 2 ; Mk. 9. 36, a little child in the *m.*
20, there am I in the *m.*
Lu. 24. 36 ; John 20. 19, Jesus himself in the *m.*
Phil. 2. 15, in the *m.* of a crooked nation.
Rev. 2. 7, in the *m.* of the Paradise of God.
4. 6 ; 5. 6 ; 7. 17, in the *m.* of the throne.
See Gen. 2. 9 ; Isa. 12. 6 ; Hos. 11. 9.
MIGHT. Deut. 6. 5, love God with all thy *m.*
8. 17, the *m.* of mine hand hath gotten.
2 Sam. 6. 14, David danced with all his *m.*
Eccl. 9. 10, do it with thy *m.*
Isa. 40. 29, to them that have no *m.*
Jer. 9. 23, mighty man glory in his *m.*
51. 30, their *m.* hath failed.
Zech. 4. 6, not by *m.*, nor by power.
Eph. 3. 16 ; Col. 1. 11, strengthened with *m.*
See Eph. 6. 10 ; 2 Pet. 2. 11 ; Rev. 7. 12.
MIGHTILY. Jonah 3. 8 ; Acts 18. 28 ; 19. 20 ; Col. 1. 29.
MIGHTY. Gen. 10. 9, he was a *m.* hunter.
Judg. 5. 23, to the help of the Lord against the *m.*
2 Sam. 1. 19, 25, how are the *m.* fallen !
23. 8, these be the names of the *m.* men whom David had.
1 Chron. 11. 10. the chief of the *m.* men.
Job 9. 4, wise in heart and *m.* in strength.
Ps. 24. 8, strong and *m.*, *m.* in battle.
89. 13, thou hast a *m.* arm.
19, help upon one that is *m.*
93. 4, the *m.* waves of the sea.
Isa. 1. 24 ; 30. 29 ; 49. 26 ; 60. 16, the *m.* One of Israel.
5. 15, *m.* to drink wine.
63. 1, *m.* to save.
Jer. 32. 19, *m.* in work.
Amos 2. 14, neither shall *m.* deliver himself.
Mat. 11. 20 ; 13. 54 ; 14. 2 ; Mk. 6. 2, *m.* works.
Lu. 9. 43, the *m.* power of God.
24. 19, prophet *m.* in deed and word.
Acts 18. 24, *m.* in the scriptures.
1 Cor. 1. 26, not many *m.*
2 Cor. 10. 4, weapons *m.* through God.
Eph. 1. 19, the working of his *m.* power.
See Num. 14. 12 ; Eccl. 6. 10 ; Mat. 3. 11.
MILK. Gen. 49. 12, teeth white with *m.*
Prov. 30. 33, churning of *m.*
Isa. 55. 1, buy wine and *m.*
Lam. 4. 7, Nazarites were whiter than *m.*
Ezek. 25. 4, shall eat thy fruit and drink thy *m.*
Heb. 5. 12, 13, such as have need of *m.*
1 Pet. 2. 2, the sincere *m.* of the word.
See Judg. 4. 19 ; 5. 25 ; Job 21. 24 ; Joel 3. 18.
MIND (*n.*). Neh. 4. 6, the people had a *m.* to work.
Job 23. 13, he is in one *m.*, who can turn him ?
34. 33, should it be according to thy *m.* ?
Ps. 31. 12, as a dead man out of *m.*
Prov. 29. 11, a fool uttereth all his *m.*
Isa. 26. 3, whose *m.* is stayed on thee.
Mk. 5. 15 ; Lu. 8. 35, sitting, in his right *m.*
Lu. 12. 29, neither be of doubtful *m.*
Rom. 8. 7, the carnal *m.* is enmity against God.
12. 16, be of the same *m.*
14. 5, fully persuaded in his own *m.*
2 Cor. 8. 12, if there be first a willing *m.*
13. 11 ; Phil. 1. 27 ; 2. 2, be of one *m.*
Phil. 2. 3, in lowliness of *m.*
5, let this *m.* be in you.
4. 7, peace of God keep your *m.*

1 Tim. 6. 5 ; 2 Tim. 3. 8, men of corrupt *m.*
2 Tim. 1. 7, spirit of sound *m.*
Tit. 3. 1, put them in *m.* to be subject.
1 Pet. 1. 13, the loins of your *m.*
2 Pet. 3. 1, stir up your pure *m.*
See Rom. 8. 6 ; 11. 20 ; 1 Thess. 5. 14 ; Jas. 1. 8.
MIND (*v.*). Rom. 8. 5 ; 12. 16 ; Phil. 3. 16, 19.
MINDFUL. Ps. 8. 4 ; 111. 5 ; Isa. 17. 10 ; 2 Pet. 3. 2.
MINGLE. Lev. 19. 19 ; Isa. 5. 22 ; Mat. 27. 34 ; Lu. 13. 1.
MINISTER (*n.*). Ps. 103. 21, ye *m.* of his.
104. 4 ; Heb. 1. 7, his *m.* a flame of fire.
Isa. 61. 6, men shall call you the *m.* of God.
Joel 1. 9, the Lord's *m.* mourn.
Mat. 20. 26 ; Mk. 10. 43, let him be your *m.*
Rom. 13. 4, he is the *m.* of God to thee.
2 Cor. 3. 6, able *m.* of new testament.
Gal. 2. 17, is Christ the *m.* of sin?
Eph. 3. 7 ; Col. 1. 23, whereof I was made a *m.*
6. 21 ; Col. 1. 7 ; 4. 7, a faithful *m.*
1 Tim. 4. 6, a good *m.*
See 2 Cor. 6. 4 ; 11. 23 ; 1 Thess. 3. 2.
MINISTER (*v.*). 1 Sam. 2. 11, the child did *m.* unto the Lord.
1 Chron. 15. 2, chosen to *m.* for ever.
Dan. 7. 10, thousand thousands *m.* to him.
Mat. 4. 11 ; Mk. 1. 13, angels *m.* to him.
20. 28 ; Mk. 10. 45, not to be *m.* unto, but to *m.*
Lu. 8. 3, which *m.* of their substance.
Acts 20. 34, these hands have *m.*
See 2 Cor. 9. 10 ; Heb. 1. 14 ; 2 Pet. 1. 11.
MINISTRATION. Lu. 1. 23 ; Acts 6. 1 ; 2 Cor. 3. 7 ; 9. 13.
MINISTRY. Acts 6. 4, give ourselves to the *m.*
2 Cor. 4. 1, seeing we have this *m.*
5. 18, the *m.* of reconciliation.
6. 3, that the *m.* be not blamed.
Eph. 4. 12, for the work of the *m.*
Col. 4. 17, take heed to the *m.*
2 Tim. 4. 5, make full proof of thy *m.*
See Acts 1. 17 ; 12. 25 ; Rom. 12. 7 ; Heb. 8. 6.
MINSTREL. 2 Kings 3. 15 ; Mat. 9. 23.
MIRACLE. Judg. 6. 13, where be all his *m.?*
Mk. 9. 39, no man which shall do a *m.* in my name.
Lu. 23. 8, hoped to have seen some *m.*
John 2. 11, beginning of *m.*
4. 54, this is the second *m.*
10. 41, said, John did no *m.*
Acts 2. 22, approved of God by *m.* and signs.
1 Cor. 12. 10, to another, the working of *m.*
See Gal. 3. 5 ; Heb. 2. 4 ; Rev. 13. 14 ; 16. 14 ; 19. 20.
MIRTH. Ps. 137. 3 ; Prov. 14. 13 ; Eccl. 2. 1 ; 7. 4 ; 8. 15.
MIRY. Ps. 40. 2 ; Ezek. 47. 11 ; Dan. 2. 41.
MISCHIEF. Job 15. 35 ; Ps. 7. 14 ; Isa. 59. 4, they conceive *m.*
Ps. 28. 3, *m.* is in their hearts.
94. 20, frameth *m.* by a law.
Prov. 10. 23, it is as sport to a fool to do *m.*
11. 27, he that seeketh *m.*
24. 2, lips talk of *m.*
Ezek. 7. 26, *m.* shall come upon *m.*
Acts 13. 10, O full of all subtilty and all *m.*
See Prov. 24. 8 ; Eccl. 10. 13 ; Mic. 7. 3.
MISERABLE. Job 16. 2 ; Mat. 21. 41 ; 1 Cor. 15. 19 ; Rev. 3. 17.
MISERY. Prov. 31. 7, drink, and remember his *m.* no more.
Eccl. 8. 6, the *m.* of man is great upon him.
Lam. 1. 7, remembered in days of her *m.*
Jas. 5. 1, howl for your *m.* that shall come.
See Judg. 10. 16 ; Job 3. 20 ; 11. 16 ; Rom. 3. 16.
MIXED. Prov. 23. 30, they seek *m.* wine.
Isa. 1. 22, thy wine *m.* with water.
Heb. 4. 2, not being *m.* with faith.
See Ex. 12. 38 ; Num. 11. 4 ; Neh. 13. 3.
MOCK. Gen. 19. 14, he seemed as one that *m.*

Num. 22. 29 ; Judg. 16. 10, 13, 15, thou hast *m.* me.
1 Kings 18. 27, at noon Elijah *m.* them.
2 Chron. 36. 16, they *m.* the messengers of God.
Prov. 1. 26, I will *m.* when your fear cometh.
17. 5, whoso *m.* the poor.
30. 17, the eye that *m.* at his father.
Gal. 6. 7, God is not *m.*
See 2 Kings 2. 23 ; Mat. 2. 16 ; 27. 29 ; Mk. 15. 20.
MOCKER. Ps. 35. 16 ; Prov. 20. 1 ; Isa. 28. 22 ; Jude 18.
MODERATION. Phil. 4. 5.
MOISTURE. Ps. 32. 4 ; Lu. 8. 6.
MOLLIFIED. Isa. 1. 16.
MOMENT. Num. 16. 21, 45, consume them in a *m.*
Job 7. 18, try him every *m.*
21. 13, and in a *m.* they go down.
Ps. 30. 5, his anger endureth but a *m.*
Isa. 26. 20, hide thyself as it were a *m.*
27. 3, I will water it every *m.*
54. 7, for a small *m.* have I forsaken thee.
1 Cor. 15. 51, 52, we shall all be changed, in a *m.*
2 Cor. 4. 17, affliction, which is but for a *m.*
See Ex. 33. 5 ; Ezek. 26. 16 ; 32. 10 ; Lu. 4. 5.
MONEY. 2 Kings 5. 26, is it a time to receive *m.?*
Eccl. 7. 12, *m.* is a defence.
10. 19, *m.* answereth all things.
Isa. 52. 3, redeemed without *m.*
55. 1, he that hath no *m.*
2, wherefore do ye spend *m.*
Mat. 17. 24 ; 22. 19, the tribute *m.*
25. 18, hid his lord's *m.*
Acts 8. 20, thy *m.* perish with thee.
1 Tim. 6. 10, the love of *m.*
See Gen. 23. 9 ; Mk. 6. 8 ; Lu. 9. 3 ; Acts 4. 37.
MORROW. Prov. 27. 1, boast not thyself of to-*m.*
Isa. 22. 13 ; 1 Cor. 15. 32, for to-*m.* we die.
56. 12, to-*m.* shall be as this day.
Mat. 6. 34, take no thought for the *m.*
Jas. 4. 14, ye know not what shall be on the *m.*
See Josh. 5. 12 ; 2 Kings 7. 1 ; Prov. 3. 28.
MORSEL. Job 31. 17 ; Ps. 147. 17 ; Prov. 17. 1 ; Heb. 12. 16.
MORTAL. Job 4. 17, shall *m.* man be more just?
Rom. 6. 12 ; 8. 11, in your *m.* body.
1 Cor. 15. 53, 54, this *m.* must put on immortality.
See Deut. 19. 11 ; 2 Cor. 4. 11 ; 5. 4.
MORTAR. Prov. 27. 22 ; Ezek. 13. 11, 22, 28.
MORTIFY. Rom. 8. 13 ; Col. 3. 5.
MOTE. Mat. 7. 3 ; Lu. 6. 41.
MOTH. Job 27. 18, he buildeth his house as a *m.*
Ps. 39. 11, consume away like a *m.*
Isa. 50. 9, the *m.* shall eat them up.
Hos. 5. 12, unto Ephraim as a *m.*
Mat. 6. 19, where *m.* and rust doth corrupt.
MOTHER. Judg. 5. 7 ; 2 Sam. 20. 19, a *m.* in Israel.
1 Kings 22. 52, Ahaziah walked in the way of his *m.*
2 Chron. 22. 3, his *m.* was his counsellor.
Job 17. 14, to the worm, thou art my *m.*
Ps. 113. 9, a joyful *m.* of children.
Isa. 66. 13, as one whom his *m.* comforteth.
Ezek. 16. 44, as is the *m.*, so is her daughter.
Mat. 12. 48 ; Mk. 3. 33, who is my *m.?*
John 2. 1 ; Acts 1. 14, the *m.* of Jesus.
See Gen. 3. 20 ; 17. 16 ; Gal. 4. 26 ; 1 Tim. 1. 9 ; 5. 2
MOULDY. Josh. 9. 5, 12.
MOUNT. Ex. 18. 5, the *m.* of God.
Ps. 107. 26, they *m.* up to heaven.
Isa. 40. 31, *m.* with wings, as eagles.
See Job 20. 6 ; 39. 27 ; Isa. 27. 13.
MOURN. Gen. 37. 35, down to the grave *m.*
Prov. 5. 11, and thou *m.* at the last.
Isa. 61. 2, to comfort all that *m.*
Jer. 31. 13, I will turn their *m.* into joy.
Mat. 5. 4, blessed are they that *m.*
24. 30, then shall all the tribes of the earth *m.*

Lu. 6. 25, woe to you that laugh, for ye shall *m.*
See Neh. 8. 9; Zech. 7. 5; Jas. 4. 9.
MOURNER. 2 Sam. 14. 2; Eccl. 12. 5; Hos. 9. 4.
MOURNFULLY. Mal. 3. 14.
MOUTH. Job 9. 20, mine own *m.* shall condemn
me.
40. 4, I will lay my hand on my *m.*
Ps. 8. 2; Mat. 21. 16, out of the *m.* of babes.
39. 1, I will keep my *m.* with a bridle.
49. 3, my *m.* shall speak of wisdom.
55. 21, words of his *m.* smoother than butter.
81. 10, open thy *m.* wide.
Prov. 10. 14; 14. 3; 15. 2, the *m.* of the foolish.
13. 2, good by the fruit of his *m.*
3; 21. 23, he that keepeth his *m.*
Eccl. 6. 7, all the labour of a man is for his *m.*
Isa. 29. 13; Mat. 15. 8, this people draw near with *m.*
Ezek. 33. 31, with their *m.* they show much love.
Mal. 2. 6, the law of truth was in his *m.*
Mat. 12. 34; Lu. 6. 45, the *m.* speaketh.
13. 35, I will open my *m.* in parables.
Lu. 21. 15, I will give you a *m.* and wisdom.
Rom. 10. 10, with the *m.* confession is made.
Tit. 1. 11, whose *m.* must be stopped.
Jas. 3. 10, out of the same *m.* proceedeth.
See Lam. 3. 29; John 19. 29; 1 Pet. 2. 22.
MOVE. Ps. 10. 6; 16. 8; 30. 6; 62. 2, I shall not
be *m.*
Mat. 21. 10; Acts 21. 30, all the city was *m.*
John 5. 3, waiting for the *m.* of the water.
Acts 17. 28, in him we live, and *m.*
20. 24, none of these things *m.* me.
See Prov. 23. 31; Isa. 7. 2; 2 Pet. 1. 21.
MUCH. Ex. 16. 18; 2 Cor. 8. 15, he that gathered *m.*
Num. 16. 3, ye take too *m.* upon you.
Lu. 7. 47, for she loved *m.*
12. 48, to whom *m.* is given.
16. 10, faithful in *m.*
See Prov. 25. 16; Eccl. 5. 12; Jer. 2. 22.
MULTIPLY. Isa. 9. 3, thou hast *m.* the nation,
and not increased the joy.
Jer. 3. 16, when ye be *m.* they shall say.
Dan. 4. 1; 6. 25; 1 Pet. 1. 2; 2 Pet. 1. 2; Jude 2,
peace be *m.*
Nah. 3. 16, thou hast *m.* thy merchants.
See Acts 6. 1; 7. 17; 9. 31; 12. 24.
MULTITUDE. Ex. 23. 2, a *m.* to do evil.
Job 32. 7, *m.* of years should teach wisdom.
Ps. 5. 7; 51. 1; 69. 13; 106. 7, in the *m.* of thy
mercy.
33. 16, no king saved by the *m.* of an host.
94. 19, in the *m.* of my thoughts.
Prov. 10. 19, in *m.* of words there wanteth not sin.
11. 14; 15. 22; 24. 6, in the *m.* of counsellors.
Eccl. 5. 3, through the *m.* of business.
Jas. 5. 20; 1 Pet. 4. 8, hide a *m.* of sins.
See Deut. 1. 10; Josh. 11. 4; Lu. 2. 13.
MURMURINGS. Ex. 16. 7; Num. 14. 27; Phil.
2. 14.
MUSE. Ps. 39. 3; 143. 5; Lu. 3. 15.
MUTTER. Isa. 8. 19; 59. 3.
MUTUAL. Rom. 1. 12.
MYSTERY. Mat. 13. 11; 1 Cor. 2. 7; 15. 51; Eph.
5. 32.

N.

NAIL. Ezra 9. 8, give us a *n.* in his holy place.
Isa. 22. 23, fasten as a *n.* in sure place.
John 20. 25, put finger into print of *n.*
Col. 2. 14, *n.* it to his cross.
See Judg. 4. 21; Eccl. 12. 11; Dan. 4. 33.
NAKED. Ex. 32. 25, made *n.* to their shame.
Job 1. 21, *n.* came I out, and *n.* shall I return.
Mat. 25. 36, *n.*, and ye clothed me.
1 Cor. 4. 11, to this present hour we are *n.*
2 Cor. 5. 3, we shall not be found *n.*
Heb. 4. 13, all things are *n.* to eyes of him.
See John 21. 7; Jas. 2. 15; Rev. 3. 17; 16. 15.

NAKEDNESS. Rom. 8. 35; 2 Cor. 11. 27; Rev. 3. 18.
NAME (*n.*). Gen. 32. 29; Judg. 13. 18, wherefore
dost thou ask after my *n.*?
Ex. 3. 15, this is my *n.* for ever.
23. 21, my *n.* is in him.
Josh. 7. 9, what wilt thou do to thy great *n.*?
2 Chron. 14. 11, in thy *n.* we go.
Neh. 9. 10, so didst thou get thee a *n.*
Job 18. 17, he shall have no *n.* in the street.
Ps. 20. 1, the *n.* of God defend thee.
5, in the *n.* of God set up banners.
22. 22; Heb. 2. 12, I will declare thy *n.*
48. 10, according to thy *n.* so is thy praise.
69. 36, they that love his *n.*
111. 9, holy and reverend is his *n.*
115. 1, unto thy *n.* give glory.
138. 2, thy word above all thy *n.*
Prov. 10. 7, the *n.* of the wicked shall rot.
18. 10, the *n.* of the Lord a strong tower.
22. 1; Eccl. 7. 1, good *n.* rather to be chosen.
Cant. 1. 3, thy *n.* is as ointment poured forth.
Isa. 42. 8, I am the Lord, that is my *n.*
55. 13, it shall be to the Lord for a *n.*
56. 5; 63. 12, an everlasting *n.*
57. 15, whose *n.* is Holy.
62. 2, called by a new *n.*
64. 7, there is none that calleth on thy *n.*
Jer. 10. 6, thou art great, and thy *n.* is great.
14. 14; 23. 25; 27. 15, prophesy lies in my *n.*
44. 26, sworn by my great *n.*
Zech. 10. 12, walk up and down in his *n.*
14. 9, one Lord, and his *n.* one.
Mal. 1. 6, wherein have we despised thy *n.*?
4. 2, to you that fear my *n.*
Mat. 6. 9; Lu. 11. 2, hallowed be thy *n.*
10. 22; 19. 29; Mk. 13. 13; Lu. 21. 12; John 15. 21;
Acts 9. 16, for my *n.* sake.
12. 21, in his *n.* shall the Gentiles trust.
18. 5; Mk. 9. 37; Lu. 9. 48, receive in my *n.*
20, gathered together in my *n.*
24. 5; Mk. 13. 6; Lu. 21. 8, many shall come in
my *n.*
Mk. 5. 9; Lu. 8. 30, what is thy *n.*?
9. 39, do a miracle in my *n.*
Lu. 10. 20, *n.* written in heaven.
John 5. 43, if another shall come in his own *n.*
14. 13; 15. 16; 16. 23, 24, 26, whatsoever ye ask
in my *n.*
Acts 3. 16, his *n.* through faith in his *n.*
4. 12, none other *n.* under heaven.
5. 28, that ye should not teach in this *n.*
41, worthy to suffer for his *n.*
Eph. 1. 21, far above every *n.*
Phil. 2. 9, 10, a *n.* above every *n.*
4. 3, whose *n.* are in the book of life.
Col. 3. 17, do all in the *n.* of the Lord Jesus.
Heb. 1. 4, obtained a more excellent *n.*
Jas. 2. 7, that worthy *n.*
Rev. 2. 13, holdest fast my *n.*
17, a *n.* written, which no man knoweth.
3. 1, thou hast a *n.* that thou livest.
4, a few *n.* in Sardis.
13. 1, the *n.* of blasphemy.
14. 1; 22. 4, Father's *n.* in their foreheads.
See Gen. 2. 20; Ex. 28. 9; Isa. 45. 3; John 10. 3.
NAME (*v.*). Eccl. 6. 10, that which hath been is *n.*
already.
Isa. 61. 6, ye shall be *n.* Priests of the Lord.
Rom. 15. 20, not where Christ was *n.*
2 Tim. 2. 19, every one that *n.* the name of Christ.
See 1 Sam. 16. 3; Isa. 62. 2; Lu. 2. 21; 6. 13.
NARROW. Isa. 28. 20; 49. 19; Mat. 7. 14.
NATION. Gen. 10. 32, by these were the *n.* divided.
20. 4, wilt thou slay a righteous *n.*?
Num. 14. 12; Deut. 9. 14, I will make thee a
greater *n.*
2 Sam. 7. 23; 1 Chron. 17. 21, what *n.* like thy
people?
Ps. 33. 12, blessed is the *n.* whose God is the Lord.
147. 20, he hath not dealt so with any *n.*

Prov. 14. 34, righteousness exalteth a *n.*
Isa. 2. 4 ; Mic. 4. 3, *n.* shall not lift sword against *n.*
18. 2, a *n.* scattered and peeled.
26. 2, that the righteous *n.* may enter in.
34. 1, come near, ye *n.,* to hear.
52. 15, so shall he sprinkle many *n.*
Jer. 10. 7, O King of *n.*
Zech. 2. 11, many *n.* shall be joined to the Lord.
8. 22, strong *n.* shall seek the Lord.
Mat. 24. 7 ; Mk. 13. 8 ; Lu. 21. 10, *n.* against *n.*
Lu. 7. 5, he loveth our *n.*
21. 25, distress of *n.*
John 11. 50, that the whole *n.* perish not.
Acts 2. 5, devout men of every *n.*
10. 35, in every *n.* he that feareth.
Phil. 2. 15, crooked and perverse *n.*
Rev. 5. 9, redeemed out of every *n.*
See Deut. 4. 27 ; 15. 6 ; Jer. 2. 11 ; 4. 2 ; 31. 10.
NATIVITY. Gen. 11. 28 ; Jer. 46. 16 ; Ezek. 21. 30 ;
23. 15.
NATURAL. Deut. 34. 7, nor his *n.* force abated.
Rom. 1. 31 ; 2 Tim. 3. 3, without *n.* affection.
1 Cor. 2. 14, the *n.* man receiveth not.
See 1 Cor. 15. 44 ; Phil. 2. 20 ; Jas. 1. 23.
NATURE. 1 Cor. 11. 14, doth not even *n.* itself
teach ?
Eph. 2. 3, by *n.* children of wrath.
Heb. 2. 16, the *n.* of angels.
2 Pet. 1. 4, partakers of the divine *n.*
See Rom. 1. 26 ; 2. 14, 27 ; Gal. 2. 15 ; 4. 8.
NAUGHT. Prov. 20. 14, it is *n.,* saith the buyer.
Isa. 49. 4, spent strength for *n.*
52. 3, ye have sold yourselves for *n.*
Mal. 1. 10, shut the doors for *n.*
Acts 5. 38, if of men, it will come to *n.*
See Deut. 15. 9 ; Job 1. 9 ; Rom. 14. 10 ; 1 Cor. 1. 28.
NAUGHTINESS. 1 Sam. 17. 28 ; Prov. 11. 6 ; Jas.
1. 21.
NAUGHTY. Prov. 6. 12 ; 17. 4 ; Jer. 24. 2.
NAY. Mat. 5. 37 ; 2 Cor. 1. 17, 18, 19 ; Jas. 5. 12.
NEAR. Judg. 20. 34, knew not evil was *n.*
Ps. 22. 11, trouble is *n.*
148. 14, a people *n.* to him.
Prov. 27. 10, better a neighbour that is *n.*
Isa. 50. 8, he is *n.* that justifieth.
55. 6, call upon the Lord while he is *n.*
Obad. 15 ; Zeph. 1. 14, the day of the Lord is *n.*
Mat. 24. 33, it is *n.,* even at the doors.
Mk. 13. 28, ye know that summer is *n.*
See Ezek. 11. 3 ; 22. 5 ; Rom. 13. 11.
NECESSARY. Job 23. 12 ; Acts 15. 28 ; 28. 10 ; Tit.
3. 14.
NECESSITIES. 2 Cor. 6. 4, as the ministers of God,
in *n.*
NECESSITY. Rom. 12. 13, distributing to the *n.*
of saints.
1 Cor. 9. 16, *n.* is laid upon me.
2 Cor. 9. 7 ; Philem. 14, give, not grudgingly, or of *n.*
See Acts 20. 34 ; 2 Cor. 12. 10 ; Phil. 4. 16.
NECK. Prov. 3. 3 ; 6. 21, bind them about thy *n.*
Mat. 18. 6 ; Mk. 9. 42 ; Lu. 17. 2, millstone about
his *n.*
Lu. 15. 20 ; Acts 20. 37, fell on his *n.*
Acts 15. 10, yoke on the *n.* of disciples.
See Neh. 9. 29 ; Isa. 3. 16 ; Lam. 5. 5 ; Rom. 16. 4.
NEED. 2 Chron. 20. 17, ye shall not *n.* to fight.
Prov. 31. 11, he shall have no *n.* of spoil.
Mat. 6. 8 ; Lu. 12. 30, what things ye have *n.* of.
9. 12 ; Mk. 2. 17 ; Lu. 5. 31, *n.* not a physician.
14. 16, they *n.* not depart.
21. 3 ; Mk. 11. 3 ; Lu. 19. 31, 34, the Lord hath
n. of them.
Lu. 11. 8, as many as he *n.*
Acts 2. 45 ; 4. 35, as every man had *n.*
1 Cor. 12. 21, cannot say, I have no *n.* of thee.
Phil. 4. 12, to abound and to suffer *n.*
19, God shall supply all your *n.*
2 Tim. 2. 15, that *n.* not to be ashamed.

Heb. 4. 16, grace to help in time of *n.*
5. 1, ye have *n.* that one teach you.
1 John 3. 17, seeth his brother have *n.*
Rev. 3. 17, rich, and have *n.* of nothing.
21. 23 ; 22. 5, city had no *n.* of the sun.
See Deut. 15. 8 ; Lu. 9. 11 ; John 2. 25 ; Acts 17. 25.
NEEDFUL. Lu. 10. 42 ; Phil. 1. 24 ; Jas. 2. 16.
NEEDY. Deut. 15. 11, thou shalt open thine hand
to thy *n.*
Job 24. 4, they turn the *n.* out of the way.
Ps. 9. 18, the *n.* shall not alway be forgotten.
40. 17 ; 70. 5 ; 86. 1 ; 109. 22, I am poor and *n.*
74. 21, let the poor and *n.* praise thy name.
Prov. 31. 9, plead the cause of the poor and *n.*
Isa. 41. 17, when the *n.* seek water.
See Ezek. 16. 49 ; 18. 12 ; 22. 29 ; Amos 8. 4, 6.
NEGLECT. Mat. 18. 17 ; Acts 6. 1 ; 1 Tim. 4. 14 ;
Heb. 2. 3.
NEGLIGENT. 2 Chron. 29. 11 ; 2 Pet. 1. 12.
NEIGHBOUR. Prov. 3. 28, say not to thy *n.,* go
and come again.
14. 20, the poor is hated even of his *n.*
21. 10, his *n.* findeth no favour.
Eccl. 4. 4, envied of his *n.*
Jer. 22. 13, that useth his *n.* service without wages.
Hab. 2. 15, that giveth his *n.* drink.
Zech. 8. 16 ; Eph. 4. 25, speak every man truth to
his *n.*
Lu. 10. 29, who is my *n.?*
14. 12, call not thy rich *n.*
See Ex. 20. 16 ; Lev. 19. 13 ; Mat. 5. 43 ; Rom. 13. 10.
NEST. Num. 24. 21, thou puttest thy *n.* in a rock.
Deut. 32. 11, as an eagle stirreth up her *n.*
Job 29. 18, I shall die in my *n.*
Ps. 84. 3, the swallow hath found a *n.*
Mat. 8. 20 ; Lu. 9. 58, birds of the air have *n.*
See Prov. 27. 8 ; Isa. 16. 2 ; Jer. 49. 16 ; Obad. 4 ;
Hab. 2. 9.
NET. Ps. 141. 10, let the wicked fall into their
own *n.*
Prov. 1. 17, in vain the *n.* is spread.
Eccl. 9. 12, as fishes taken in an evil *n.*
Hab. 1. 16, they sacrifice unto their *n.*
Mat. 13. 47, kingdom of heaven like a *n.*
Mk. 1. 18, they forsook their *n.*
Lu. 5. 5, at thy word I will let down the *n.*
See Mat. 4. 21 ; Mk. 1. 16 ; John 21. 6.
NETHER. Deut. 24. 6 ; Job 41. 24.
NEVER. Lev. 6. 13, the fire shall *n.* go out.
Job 3. 16, as infants which *n.* saw light.
Ps. 10. 11, he will *n.* see it.
15. 5 ; 30. 6, shall *n.* be moved.
Prov. 27. 20 ; 30. 15, *n.* satisfied.
Isa. 56. 11, which can *n.* have enough.
Mat. 7. 23, I *n.* knew you.
9. 33, it was *n.* so seen in Israel.
26. 33, yet will I *n.* be offended.
Mk. 2. 12, we *n.* saw it on this fashion.
3. 29, hath *n.* forgiveness.
14. 21, if he had *n.* been born.
John 4. 14 ; 6. 35, shall *n.* thirst.
7. 46, *n.* man spake like this man.
8. 51 ; 10. 28 ; 11. 26, shall *n.* see death.
1 Cor. 13. 8, charity *n.* faileth.
Heb. 13. 5, I will *n.* leave thee.
2 Pet. 1. 10, ye shall *n.* fall.
See Judg. 2. 1 ; Ps. 58. 5 ; Jer. 33. 17 ; Dan. 2. 44.
NEW. Num. 16. 30, if the Lord make a *n.* thing.
Ps. 33. 3 ; 40. 3 ; 96. 1 ; 98. 1 ; 144. 9 ; 149. 1 ; Isa.
42. 10 ; Rev. 5. 9 ; 14. 3, a *n.* song.
Eccl. 1. 9, no *n.* thing under the sun.
Isa. 65. 17 ; 66. 22 ; Rev. 21. 1, *n.* heavens and *n.*
earth.
Lam. 3. 23, *n.* every morning.
Mat. 9. 16 ; Mk. 2. 21 ; Lu. 5. 36, *n.* cloth to old
garment.
13. 52, things *n.* and old.
Mk. 1. 27 ; Acts 17. 19, what *n.* doctrine is this ?
John 13. 34 ; 1 John 2. 7, 8, a *n.* commandment.
Acts 17. 21, to tell or hear some *n.* thing.

2 Cor. 5. 17; Gal. 6. 15, a *n.* creature.
Eph. 2. 15; 4. 24; Col. 3. 10, *n.* man.
Heb. 10. 20, *n.* and living way.
Rev. 2. 17; 3. 12, a *n.* name.
21. 5, I make all things *n.*
See Isa. 24. 7; 43. 19; 65. 8; Acts 2. 13.
NEWLY. Deut. 32. 17; Judg. 7. 19.
NEWNESS. Rom. 6. 4; 7. 6.
NEWS. Prov. 25. 25.
NIGH. Num. 24. 17, but not *n.*
Deut. 30. 14; Rom. 10. 8, the word is *n.* unto thee.
Ps. 34. 18, *n.* to them of broken heart.
145. 18, *n.* to all that call upon him.
Eph. 2. 13, made *n.* by the blood of Christ.
See Joel 2. 1; Lu. 21. 20; Heb. 6. 8.
NIGHT. Ex. 12. 42, a *n.* to be much observed.
Job 7. 4, when shall I arise, and the *n.* be gone?
35. 10; Ps. 77. 6, songs in the *n.*
Ps. 30. 5, weeping may endure for a *n.*
91. 5, the terror by *n.*
136. 9; Jer. 31. 35, moon and stars to rule by *n.*
139. 11, the *n.* shall be light about me.
Isa. 21. 4, the *n.* of my pleasure.
11, watchman, what of the *n.?*
Lu. 6. 12, he continued all *n.* in prayer.
John 9. 4, the *n.* cometh, when no man can work.
11. 10, walk in the *n.,* he stumbleth.
Rom. 13. 12, the *n.* is far spent.
1 Thess. 5. 2; 2 Pet. 3. 10, cometh as a thief in the *n.*
Rev. 21. 25; 22. 5, no *n.* there.
See Job 7. 3; Ps. 121. 6; Mat. 27. 64; John 3. 2.
NOBLE. Neh. 3. 5, the *n.* put not their neck.
Job 29. 10, the *n.* held their peace.
Jer. 2. 21, planted thee a *n.* vine.
14. 3, their *n.* sent their little ones to the waters.
Acts 17. 11, Bereans were more *n.*
1 Cor. 1. 26, not many *n.*
See Num. 21. 18; Ps. 149. 8; Eccl. 10. 17.
NOISE. Ezra 3. 13, not discern *n.* of joy.
Ps. 66. 1; 81. 1; 95. 1; 98. 4; 100. 1, joyful *n.*
Ezek. 1. 24; 43. 2, *n.* of great waters.
2 Pet. 3. 10, pass away with great *n.*
See Josh. 6. 27; Mat. 9. 23; Mk. 2. 1; Acts 2. 6.
NOISOME. Ps. 91. 3; Ezek. 14. 21; Rev. 16. 2.
NOTHING. Deut. 2. 7; Neh. 9. 21, thou hast lacked *n.*
2 Sam. 24. 24, neither offer of that which doth cost *n.*
2 Chron. 14. 11, it is *n.* with thee to help.
Neh. 8. 10, portions to them for whom *n.* is prepared.
Job 8. 9, but of yesterday, and know *n.*
Ps. 49. 17, he shall carry *n.* away.
119. 165, *n.* shall offend them.
Prov. 13. 4, the sluggard desireth, and hath *n.*
7, there is that maketh himself rich, yet hath *n.*
Lam. 1. 12, is it *n.* to you?
Mat. 17. 20; Lu. 1. 37, *n.* shall be impossible.
21. 19; Mk. 11. 13, *n.* but leaves.
Lu. 6. 35, hoping for *n.* again.
7. 42, they had *n.* to pay.
John 15. 5, without me ye can do *n.*
1 Cor. 4. 4, I know *n.* by myself.
2 Cor. 6. 10, as having *n.*
13. 8, we can do *n.* against the truth.
1 Tim. 4. 4, *n.* to be refused.
6. 7, brought *n.* into this world, can carry *n.* out.
See Phil. 4. 6; Jas. 1. 4; 3 John 7.
NOURISH. Isa. 1. 2, I have *n.* and brought up children.
1 Tim. 4. 6, *n.* in words of faith.
Jas. 5. 5, have *n.* your hearts.
See Gen. 45. 11; 50. 21; Acts 12. 20; Col. 2. 19.
NOW. Job 4. 5, *n.* it is come upon thee.
Ps. 119. 67, but *n.* have I kept thy word.
Hos. 2. 7, then was it better than *n.*
Lu. 14. 17, all things are *n.* ready.
John 13. 7, thou knowest not *n.*
16. 12, ye cannot bear them *n.*
1 Cor. 13. 12, *n.* I know in part.

Gal. 2. 20, the life I *n.* live.
1 Tim. 4. 8, the life that *n.* is.
1 Pet. 1. 8, though *n.* ye see him not.
1 John 3. 2, *n.* are we sons of God.
See Rom. 6. 22; Gal. 3. 3; Heb. 2. 8.
NUMBER (*n.*). Job 5. 9; 9. 10, marvellous things without *n.*
25. 3, is there any *n.* of his armies?
Ps. 139. 18, more in *n.* than the sand.
147. 4, he telleth the *n.* of the stars.
Acts 11. 21, a great *n.* believed.
16. 5, the churches increased in *n.* daily.
Rev. 13. 17, 18, the *n.* of his name.
See Deut. 7. 7; Hos. 1. 10; Rom. 9. 27.
NUMBER (*v.*). Gen. 41. 49, gathered corn till he left *n.*
2 Sam. 24. 2; 1 Chron. 21. 2, *n.* the people.
Ps. 90. 12, so teach us to *n.* our days.
Eccl. 1. 15, that which is wanting cannot be *n.*
Isa. 53. 12; Mk. 15. 28, he was *n.* with transgressors.
Mat. 10. 30; Lu. 12. 7, hairs are all *n.*
Rev. 7. 9, multitude which no man could *n.*
See Ex. 30. 12; Job 14. 16; Ps. 40. 5; Acts 1. 17.
NURSE. Gen. 35. 8, Deborah Rebekah's *n.* died.
2 Sam. 4. 4, and his *n.* took him up and fled.
1 Thess. 2. 7, even as a *n.* cherisheth her children.
See Ex. 2. 7, 9; Isa. 60. 4.
NURSING. Isa. 49. 23, kings shall be thy *n.* fathers, and their queens thy *n.* mothers.
NURTURE. Eph. 6. 4.

O.

OBEDIENCE. Rom. 5. 19, by the *o.* of one.
16. 26, the *o.* of faith.
Heb. 5. 8, yet learned he *o.*
See Rom. 16. 19; 2 Cor. 10. 5; 1 Pet. 1. 2.
OBEDIENT. Ex. 24. 7, all will we do, and be *o.*
Prov. 25. 12, wise reprover upon an *o.* ear.
Isa. 1. 19, if *o.* ye shall eat.
2 Cor. 2. 9, *o.* in all things.
Eph. 6. 5; Tit. 2. 9, be *o.* to your masters.
Phil. 2. 8, *o.* unto death.
1 Pet. 1. 14, as *o.* children.
See Num. 27. 20; 2 Sam. 22. 45; Tit. 2. 5.
OBEISANCE. Gen. 37. 7; 43. 28; 2 Sam. 15. 5.
OBEY. Deut. 11. 27, a blessing if ye *o.*
Josh. 24. 24, his voice will we *o.*
1 Sam. 15. 22, to *o.* is better than sacrifice.
Jer. 7. 23, *o.* my voice, and I will be your God.
Acts 5. 29, we ought to *o.* God rather than men.
Rom. 6. 16, his servants ye are to whom ye *o.*
Eph. 6. 1; Col. 3. 20, *o.* your parents in the Lord.
2 Thess. 1. 8; 1 Pet. 4. 17, that *o.* not the gospel.
Heb. 13. 17, *o.* them that have rule over you.
1 Pet. 1. 22, purified your souls in *o.* the truth.
See Ex. 5. 2; 23. 21; Dan. 9. 10; Mat. 8. 27.
OBJECT. Acts 24. 19.
OBSCURE. Prov. 20. 20.
OBSCURITY. Isa. 29. 18; 58. 10; 59. 9.
OBSERVATION. Lu. 17. 20.
OBSERVE. Gen. 37. 11, his father *o.* the saying.
Ps. 107. 43, whoso is wise, and will *o.* these things.
Prov. 23. 26, let thine eyes *o.* my ways.
Eccl. 11. 4, he that *o.* the wind.
Jonah 2. 8, that *o.* lying vanities.
Mat. 28. 20, teaching them to *o.* all things.
Mk. 6. 20, Herod feared John, and *o.* him.
10. 20, all these have I *o.*
See Ex. 12. 42; 31. 16; Ezek. 20. 18; Gal. 4. 10.
OBSERVER. Deut. 18. 10.
OBSTINATE. Deut. 2. 30; Isa. 48. 4.
OBTAIN. Prov. 8. 35, shall *o.* favour of the Lord.
Isa. 35. 10; 51. 11, shall *o.* joy and gladness.
Lu. 20. 35, worthy to *o.* that world.
Acts 26. 22, having *o.* help of God.
1 Cor. 9. 24, so run that ye may *o.*
1 Thess. 5. 9; 2 Tim. 2. 10, to *o.* salvation.

1 Tim. 1. 13, I *o.* mercy.
Heb. 4. 16, *o.* mercy, and find grace to help.
9. 12, having *o.* eternal redemption.
1 Pet. 2. 10, which had not *o.* mercy, but now have *o.*
2 Pet. 1. 1, *o.* like precious faith.
See Dan. 11. 21; Hos. 2. 23; Acts 1. 17; 22. 28.

OCCASION. 2 Sam. 12. 14, great *o.* to enemies to blaspheme.
Dan. 6. 4, sought to find *o.*
Rom. 7. 8, sin, taking *o.* by the commandment.
14. 13, an *o.* to fall in his brother's way.
1 Tim. 5. 14, give none *o.* to the adversary.
See Gen. 43. 18; Ezra 7. 20; Ezek. 18. 3.

OCCUPATION. Gen. 46. 33; Jonah 1. 8; Acts 18. 3; 19. 25.

OCCUPY. Ezek. 27. 9; Lu. 19. 13.

ODOUR. John 12. 3; Phil. 4. 18; Rev. 5. 8.

OFFENCE. Eccl. 10. 4, yielding pacifieth great *o.*
Isa. 8. 14; Rom. 9. 33; 1 Pet. 2. 8, a rock of *o.*
Mat. 16. 23, thou art an *o.* to me.
18. 7; Lu. 17. 1, woe to the world because of *o.*!
Acts 24. 16, conscience void of *o.*
Rom. 14. 20, that man who eateth with *o.*
1 Cor. 10. 32; 2 Cor. 6. 3, give none *o.*
Phil. 1. 10, without *o.* till the day of Christ.
See 1 Sam. 25. 31; Rom. 5. 15; 16. 17; Gal. 5. 11.

OFFEND. Job 34. 31, I will not *o.* any more.
Ps. 119. 165, nothing shall *o.* them.
Prov. 18. 19, brother *o.* is harder to be won.
Mat. 5. 29; 18. 9; Mk. 9. 47, if thine eye *o.* thee.
13. 41, gather all things that *o.*
57; Mk. 6. 3, they were *o.* in him.
26. 33, though all shall be *o.*, yet will I never be.
Rom. 14. 21, whereby thy brother is *o.*
Jas. 2. 10, yet *o.* in one point.
See Gen. 20. 9; Jer. 37. 18; 2 Cor. 11. 29.

OFFENDER. 1 Kings 1. 21; Isa. 29. 21; Acts 25. 11.

OFFER. Judg. 5. 2, people willingly *o.* themselves.
Ps. 50. 23, whoso *o.* praise.
Mat. 5. 24, then come and *o.* thy gift.
Lu. 6. 29, one cheek, *o.* also the other.
1 Cor. 8. 1, 4, 7; 10. 19, things *o.* to idols.
Phil. 2. 17, *o.* in the service of your faith.
2 Tim. 4. 6, now ready to be *o.*
Heb. 9. 28, Christ once *o.* to bear the sins of many.
See 2 Chron. 17. 16; Ezra 1. 6; 2. 68; Mal. 1. 8.

OFFICE. 1 Sam. 2. 36, put me into one of the priests' *o.*
Rom. 11. 13, I magnify mine *o.*
1 Tim. 3. 1, the *o.* of a bishop.
Heb. 7. 5, the *o.* of the priesthood.
See Gen. 41. 13; Ps. 109. 8; Rom. 12. 4.

OFFSCOURING. Lam. 3. 45; 1 Cor. 4. 13.

OFFSPRING. Job 27. 14; Acts 17. 28; Rev. 22. 16.

OFTEN. Prov. 29. 1, being *o.* reproved.
Mal. 3. 16, spake *o.* one to another.
Mat. 23. 37; Lu. 13. 34, how *o.* would I have gathered.
1 Cor. 11. 26, as *o.* as ye eat.
1 Tim. 5. 23, thine *o.* infirmities.
See 2 Cor. 11. 26; Heb. 9. 25; 10. 11.

OIL. Ps. 45. 7; Heb. 1. 9, with *o.* of gladness.
92. 10, be anointed with fresh *o.*
104. 15, *o.* to make his face to shine.
Isa. 61. 3, *o.* of joy for mourning.
Mat. 25. 3, took no *o.* with them.
Lu. 10. 34, pouring in *o.* and wine.
See Ex. 27. 20; Mic. 6. 7; Lu. 7. 46.

OLD. Deut. 8. 4; 29. 5; Neh. 9. 21, waxed not *o.*
Josh. 5. 11, did eat of the *o.* corn.
Ps. 37. 25, I have been young, and now am *o.*
71. 18, when I am *o.* forsake me not.
Prov. 22. 6, when he is *o.* he will not.
Isa. 58. 12, build the *o.* waste places.
Jer. 6. 16, ask for the *o.* paths.
Lu. 5. 39, he saith, the *o.* is better.
2 Cor. 5. 17, *o.* things are passed away.

2 Pet. 2. 5, God spared not the *o.* world.
1 John 2. 7, the *o.* commandment is the word.
Rev. 12. 9; 20. 2, that *o.* serpent.
See Job 22. 15; Ps. 77. 5; Mat. 5. 21; Rom. 7. 6.

OMITTED. Mat. 23. 23.

ONCE. Gen. 18. 32, yet but this *o.*
Num. 13. 30, let us go up at *o.*
Job 33. 14; Ps. 62. 11, speaketh *o.*, yea twice.
Isa. 66. 8, shall a nation be born at *o.*?
Heb. 6. 4, *o.* enlightened.
9. 27, *o.* to die.
See Rom. 6. 10; Heb. 10. 10; 1 Pet. 3. 18.

ONE. Job 9. 3, *o.* of a thousand.
Eccl. 7. 27; Isa. 27. 12, *o.* by *o.*
Mk. 10. 21; Lu. 18. 22, *o.* thing thou lackest.
Lu. 10. 42, *o.* thing is needful.
John 9. 25, *o.* thing I know.
17. 11, 21, 22, that they may be *o.*
Gal. 3. 28, all *o.* in Christ.
Eph. 4. 5, *o.* Lord, *o.* faith, *o.* baptism.
See Deut. 6. 4; Mk. 12. 32; 1 Tim. 2. 5.

ONYX. Ex. 28. 20; 39. 13, and an *o.*

OPEN. Num. 16. 30, if the earth *o.* her mouth.
Ps. 49. 4, I will *o.* my dark saying.
51. 15, *o.* thou my lips.
81. 10, *o.* thy mouth wide.
104. 28; 145. 16, thou *o.* thine hand.
119. 18, *o.* thou mine eyes.
Prov. 31. 8, *o.* thy mouth for the dumb.
Isa. 22. 22, he shall *o.*, and none shall shut.
42. 7, to *o.* the blind eyes.
60. 11, thy gates shall be *o.* continually.
Ezek. 16. 63, never *o.* thy mouth.
Mal. 3. 10, *o.* windows of heaven.
Mat. 25. 11; Lu. 13. 25, Lord *o.* to us.
27. 52, graves were *o.*
Mk. 7. 34, that is, be *o.*
Lu. 24. 32, while he *o.* to us the scriptures.
45, then *o.* he their understanding.
Acts 26. 18, to *o.* their eyes, and turn them.
1 Cor. 16. 9, great door and effectual is *o.*
Col. 4. 3, *o.* to us a door of utterance.
See Acts 16. 14; 2 Cor. 2. 12; Heb. 4. 13; Rev. 5. 2.

OPERATION. Ps. 28. 5; Isa. 5. 12; 1 Cor. 12. 6; Col. 2. 12.

OPINION. 1 Kings 18. 21; Job 32. 6.

OPPORTUNITY. Gal. 6. 10; Phil. 4. 10; Heb. 11. 15.

OPPOSE. Job 30. 21; 2 Thess. 2. 4; 2 Tim. 2. 25.

OPPOSITIONS. 1 Tim. 6. 20.

OPPRESS. Ex. 22. 21; 23. 9, *o.* a stranger.
Lev. 25. 14, 17, ye shall not *o.* one another.
1 Sam. 12. 3, whom have I *o.*?
Ps. 10. 18, that the man of earth may no more *o.*
Prov. 14. 31; 22. 16, he that *o.* the poor.
28. 3, a poor man that *o.* the poor.
Jer. 7. 6, if ye *o.* not the stranger.
Hos. 12. 7, he loveth to *o.*
Zech. 7. 10, *o.* not the widow.
See Mal. 3. 5; Acts 7. 24; 10. 38; Jas. 2. 6.

OPPRESSION. Deut. 26. 7, the Lord looked on our *o.*
Ps. 62. 10, trust not in *o.*
119. 134, deliver me from the *o.* of man.
Eccl. 4. 1, I considered the *o.*
7. 7, *o.* maketh a wise man mad.
Isa. 30. 12, ye trust in *o.*
See Isa. 33. 15; Zech. 9. 8; 10. 4.

ORATOR. Isa. 3. 3; Acts 24. 1.

ORDAIN. 1 Chron. 17. 9, I will *o.* a place for my people.
Ps. 8. 2, hast thou *o.* strength.
81. 5, this he *o.* in Joseph.
132. 17, I have *o.* a lamp for mine anointed.
Isa. 26. 12, thou wilt *o.* peace for us.
30. 33, Tophet is *o.* of old.
Jer. 1. 5, I *o.* thee a prophet.
Mk. 3. 14, Jesus *o.* twelve.

John 15. 16, have *o.* you, that ye should bring forth.
Acts 1. 22, one be *o.* to be a witness.
10. 42, *o.* of God to be the Judge.
13. 48, *o.* to eternal life.
14. 23 ; Tit. 1. 5, *o.* elders.
16. 4, decrees that were *o.*
17. 31, by that man whom he hath *o.*
Rom. 13. 1, the powers that be are *o.* of God.
Gal. 3. 19, the law was *o.* by angels.
Eph. 2. 10, good works which God hath before *o.*
Jude 4, of old *o.* to this condemnation.
See 1 Cor. 2. 7 ; 9. 14 ; 1 Tim. 2. 7 ; Heb. 5. 1.

ORDER. Judg. 13. 12, how shall we *o.* the child?
2 Kings 20. 1 ; Isa. 38. 1, set thine house in *o.*
Job 10. 22, land without any *o.*
23. 4, I would *o.* my cause.
37. 19, we cannot *o.* our speech.
Ps. 40. 5, they cannot be reckoned in *o.*
50. 21, I will set them in *o.*
23, to him that *o.* his conversation aright.
110. 4 ; Heb. 5. 6 ; 6. 20 ; 7. 11, the *o.* of Melchisedec.
1 Cor. 14. 40, decently and in *o.*
Tit. 1. 5, that thou shouldest set in *o.*
See Ps. 37. 23 ; Acts 21. 24 ; 1 Cor. 15. 23.

ORDINANCE. Isa. 58. 2 ; Rom. 13. 2, the *o.* of their God.
Mal. 3. 14, what profit that we have kept *o.?*
Eph. 2. 15, commandments contained in *o.*
Col. 2. 14, handwriting of *o.*
Heb. 9. 10, in carnal *o.*
See Jer. 31. 36 ; Luke 1. 6 ; 1 Pet. 2. 13.

ORPHANS. Lam. 5. 3.

OSTRICH. Job 39. 13, or wings and feathers unto the *o.*
Lam. 4. 3, like the *o.* in the wilderness.

OUGHT. 1 Chr. 12. 32, to know what Israel *o.* to do.
Mat. 23. 23 ; Lu. 11. 42, these *o.* ye to have done.
Lu. 24. 26, *o.* not Christ to have suffered?
John 4. 20, the place where men *o.* to worship.
Acts 5. 29, we *o.* to obey God.
Rom. 8. 26, what we should pray for as we *o.*
Heb. 5. 12, when ye *o.* to be teachers.
Jas. 3. 10, these things *o.* not so to be.
2 Pet. 3. 11, what manner of persons *o.* ye to be?
See Rom. 12. 3 ; 15. 1 ; 1 Tim. 3. 15.

OURS. Mk. 12. 7 ; Lu. 20. 14 ; 1 Cor. 1. 2 ; 2 Cor. 1. 14.

OUT. Num. 32. 23, be sure your sin will find you *o.*
Ps. 82. 5, are *o.* of course.
Prov. 4. 23, *o.* of it are the issues of life.
Mat. 12. 34 ; 15. 19, *o.* of abundance of heart the mouth speaketh.
2 Tim. 3. 11, *o.* of them all the Lord delivered me.
4. 2, instant in season, *o.* of season.
See Gen. 2. 9, 23 ; 3. 19 ; John 15. 19 ; Acts 2. 5.

OUTCAST. Ps. 147. 2 ; Isa. 11. 12 ; 27. 13 ; Jer. 30. 17.

OUTGOINGS. Josh. 17. 18 ; Ps. 65. 8.

OUTRAGEOUS. Prov. 27. 4.

OUTRUN. John 20. 4.

OUTSIDE. Judg. 7. 11 ; Mat. 23. 25 ; Lu. 11. 39.

OUTSTRETCHED. Deut. 26. 8 ; Jer. 21. 5 ; 27. 5.

OUTWARD. 1 Sam. 16. 7, looketh on *o.* appearance.
Mat. 23. 27, appear beautiful *o.*
Rom. 2. 28, not a Jew, which is one *o.*
2 Cor. 4. 16, though our *o.* man perish.
See Mat. 23. 28 ; Rom. 2. 28 ; 1 Pet. 3. 3.

OVERCHARGE. Lu. 21. 34 ; 2 Cor. 2. 5.

OVERCOME. Gen. 49. 19, he shall *o.* at last.
Jer. 23. 9, like a man whom wine hath *o.*
John 16. 33, I have *o.* the world.
Rom. 12. 21, be not *o.* of evil, but *o.* evil.
1 John 5. 4, 5, victory that *o.* the world.
Rev. 2. 7, 17, 26 ; 3. 12, 21, to him that *o.*
See Cant. 6. 5 ; 2 Pet. 2. 19 ; Rev. 12. 11.

OVERMUCH. Eccl. 7. 16 ; 2 Cor. 2. 7.

OVERPAST. Ps. 57. 1 ; Isa. 26. 20.

OVERPLUS. Lev. 25. 27.

OVERSEER. Gen. 41. 34 ; Prov. 6. 7 ; Acts 20. 28.

OVERSHADOW. Mat. 17. 5 ; Mk. 9. 7 ; Lu. 1. 35 ; Acts 5. 15.

OVERSIGHT. Gen. 43. 12 ; Neh. 11. 16 ; 1 Pet. 5. 2.

OVERSPREAD. Gen. 9. 19 ; Dan. 9. 27.

OVERTAKE. Amos 9. 13, plowman shall *o.* the reaper.
Gal. 6. 1, if a man be *o.* in a fault.
1 Thess. 5. 4, day should *o.* you as a thief.
See Deut. 19. 6 ; Isa. 59. 9 ; Jer. 42. 16.

OVERTHROW. Ex. 23. 24, utterly *o.* them.
Job 19. 6, God hath *o.* me.
Ps. 140. 4, purposed to *o.* my goings.
Prov. 13. 6, wickedness *o.* the sinner.
Jonah 3. 4, yet forty days, and Nineveh shall be *o.*
Acts 5. 39, if it be of God, ye cannot *o.* it.
See Gen. 19. 21 ; Prov. 29. 4 ; 2 Tim. 2. 18.

OVERTURN. Job 9. 5 ; 12. 15 ; 28. 9 ; Ezek. 21. 27.

OVERWHELM. Job 6. 27, ye *o.* the fatherless.
Ps. 61. 2, when my heart is *o.*
77. 3 ; 142. 3 ; 143. 4, my spirit was *o.*
See Ps. 55. 5 ; 78. 53 ; 124. 4.

OVERWISE. Eccl. 7. 16.

OWE. Lu. 16. 5, 7, how much *o.* thou?
Rom. 13. 8, *o.* no man any thing.
See Mat. 18. 24, 28 ; Lu. 7. 41 ; Philem. 18.

OWN. Num. 32. 42, called it after his *o.* name.
1 Chron. 29. 14, of thine *o.* have we given thee.
Ps. 12. 4, our lips are our *o.*
67. 6, even our *o.* God shall bless us.
Mat. 20. 15, do what I will with mine *o.*
John 1. 11, to his *o.*, and his *o.* received him not.
13. 1, having loved his *o.*
1 Cor. 6. 19, ye are not your *o.*
See Acts 5. 4 ; Phil. 3. 9 ; 1 Tim. 5. 8 ; Rev. 1. 5.

OWNER. Ex. 21. 28 ; 22. 11 ; Eccl. 5. 13 ; Isa. 1. 3.

P.

PACIFY. Prov. 16. 14 ; 21. 14 ; Eccl. 10. 4 ; Ezek. 16. 63.

PAIN. Ps. 55. 4, my heart is sore *p.*
116. 3, the *p.* of hell gat hold upon me.
Acts 2. 24, having loosed the *p.* of death.
Rom. 8. 22, creation travaileth in *p.*
Rev. 21. 4, neither shall there be any more *p.*
See Ps. 73. 16 ; Jer. 4. 19 ; 2 Cor. 11. 27.

PAINTED. 2 Kings 9. 30 · Jer. 4. 30 ; 22. 14 ; Ezek. 23. 40.

PALACE. Ps. 48. 13, consider her *p.*
122. 7, prosperity within thy *p.*
144. 12, the similitude of a *p.*
Jer. 9. 21, death is entered into our *p.*
Lu. 11. 21, a strong man keepeth his *p.*
Phil. 1. 13, manifest in all the *p.*
See 1 Chron. 29. 1 ; Neh. 1. 1 ; 2. 8 ; Isa. 25. 2.

PALE. Isa. 29. 22 ; Jer. 30. 6 ; Rev. 6. 8.

PALM. Isa. 49. 16 ; Mat. 26. 67 ; Mk. 14. 65 ; Rev. 7. 9.

PANT. Ps. 38. 10 ; 42. 1 ; 119. 131 ; Amos 2. 7.

PARCHMENTS. 2 Tim. 4. 13, but especially the *p.*

PARDON. Ex. 23. 21, he will not *p.*
2 Kings 5. 18, the Lord *p.* thy servant.
2 Chron. 30. 18, the good Lord *p.* every one.
Neh. 9. 17, a God ready to *p.*
Isa. 55. 7, he will abundantly *p.*
See Jer. 33. 8 ; 50. 20 ; Lam. 3. 42 ; Mic. 7. 18.

PARENTS. Mat. 10. 21 ; Mk. 13. 12, children rise up against *p.*
Lu. 18. 29, no man that hath left *p.*
21. 16, ye shall be betrayed by *p.*
John 9. 2, who did sin, this man, or his *p.?*
Rom. 1. 30 ; 2 Tim. 3. 2, disobedient to *p.*
2 Cor. 12. 14, not to lay up for *p.*, but *p.* for children.
Eph. 6. 1 ; Col. 3. 20, children, obey your *p.*
See Lu. 2. 27 ; 8. 56 ; 1 Tim. 5. 4 ; Heb. 11. 23.

PART (*n.*). Josh. 22. 25, 27, ye have no *p.* in the Lord.

Ps. 5. 9, their inward *p.* is very wickedness.
51. 6, in hidden *p.* make me to know.
118. 7, the Lord taketh my *p.*
139. 9, dwell in the uttermost *p.*
Mk. 9. 40, he that is not against us is on our *p.*
Lu. 10. 42, that good *p.*
John 13. 8, thou hast no *p.* with me.
Acts 8. 21, neither *p.* nor lot.
2 Cor. 6. 15, what *p.* hath he that believeth?
See Tit. 2. 8 ; Rev. 20. 6 ; 21. 8 ; 22. 19.

PART (*v.*). Ruth 1. 17, if ought but death *p.* thee
and me.
2 Sam. 14. 6, there was none to *p.* them.
Ps. 22. 18, they *p.* my garments.
Lu. 24. 51, while he blessed them he was *p.*
Acts 2. 45, *p.* them to all men.
See Mat. 27. 35 ; Mk. 15. 24 ; Lu. 23. 34 ; John 19. 24.

PARTAKE. Ps. 50. 18, hast been *p.* with adul-
terers.
Rom. 15. 27, *p.* of their spiritual things.
1 Cor. 9. 10, *p.* of his hope.
13 ; 10. 18, *p.* with the altar.
10. 17, *p.* of that one bread.
21, *p.* of the Lord's table.
1 Tim. 5. 22, neither be *p.* of other men's sins.
Heb. 3. 1, *p.* of the heavenly calling.
1 Pet. 4. 13, *p.* of Christ's sufferings.
5. 1, a *p.* of the glory.
2 Pet. 1. 4, *p.* of the divine nature.
See Eph. 3. 6 ; Phil. 1. 7 ; Col. 1. 12 ; Rev. 18. 4.

PARTIAL. Mal. 2. 9 ; 1 Tim. 5. 21 ; Jas. 2. 4 ; 3. 17.

PARTICULAR. 1 Cor. 12. 27 ; Eph. 5. 33.

PARTITION. 1 Kings 6. 21 ; Eph. 2. 14.

PARTNER. Prov. 29. 24 ; Lu. 5. 7 ; 2 Cor. 8. 23.

PASS. Ex. 12. 13, when I see the blood I will
p. over.
Isa. 43. 2, when thou *p.* through waters.
Mat. 26. 39 ; Mk. 14. 36, let this cup *p.*
Lu. 16. 26, neither can they *p.* to us.
1 Cor. 7. 31 ; 1 John 2. 17, fashion of this world *p.*
Eph. 3. 19, love of Christ, which *p.* knowledge.
Phil. 4. 7, which *p.* all understanding.
See Jer. 2. 6 ; Lu. 18. 37 ; Rom. 5. 12 ; Rev. 21. 1.

PASSION. Acts 1. 3 ; 14. 15 ; Jas. 5. 17.

PAST. Job 29. 2, as in months *p.*
Eccl. 3. 15, God requireth that which is *p.*
Cant. 2. 11, the winter is *p.*
Jer. 8. 20, the harvest is *p.*
Rom. 3. 25, of sins that are *p.*
11. 33, ways *p.* finding out.
2 Cor. 5. 17, old things *p.* away.
Eph. 4. 19, being *p.* feeling.
See Eph. 2. 2 ; 2 Tim. 2. 18 ; 1 Pet. 2. 10.

PASTOR. Jer. 3. 15 ; 17. 16 ; 23. 1 ; Eph. 4. 11.

PASTURE. Ps. 95. 7 ; 100. 3 ; Ezek. 34. 14 ; John
10. 9.

PATE. Ps. 7. 16.

PATH. Job 28. 7, there is a *p.* which no fowl
knoweth.
Ps. 16. 11, show me the *p.* of life.
27. 11, lead me in a plain *p.*
65. 11, thy *p.* drop fatness.
77. 19, thy *p.* is in the great waters.
119. 105, a light to my *p.*
Prov. 4. 18, the *p.* of the just.
Isa. 2. 3 ; Mic. 4. 2, we will walk in his *p.*
42. 16, in *p.* they have not known.
58. 12, restorer of *p.* to dwell in.
Jer. 6. 16, ask for the old *p.*
Mat. 3. 3 ; Mk. 1. 3 ; Lu. 3. 4, make his *p.* straight.
See Ps. 139. 3 ; Prov. 3. 17 ; Lam. 3. 9 ; Heb. 12. 13.

PATIENCE. Mat. 18. 26, 29, have *p.* with me.
Lu. 8. 15, bring forth fruit with *p.*
21. 19, in your *p.* possess ye your souls.
Rom. 5. 3, tribulation worketh *p.*
8. 25, with *p.* wait for it.
15. 4, through *p.* and comfort.
5, the God of *p.*

2 Cor. 6. 4, as ministers of God in much *p.*
Col. 1. 11, strengthened with all might to all *p.*
1 Thess. 1. 3, your *p.* of hope.
2 Thess. 1. 4, glory in you for your *p.*
1 Tim. 6. 11, follow after *p.*
Tit. 2. 2, sound in faith, charity, *p.*
Heb. 10. 36, ye have need of *p.*
12. 1, run with *p.*
Jas. 1. 3, trying of your faith worketh *p.*
4, let *p.* have her perfect work.
5. 7, the husbandman hath long *p.*
10, for an example of *p.*
11, ye have heard of the *p.* of Job.
2 Pet. 1. 6, add to temperance *p.*
Rev. 2. 2, 19, I know thy *p.*
3. 10, thou hast kept word of *p.*
13. 10 ; 14. 12, here is the *p.* of saints.
See Eccl. 7. 8 ; Rom. 12. 12 ; 1 Thess. 5. 14.

•PATIENTLY. Ps. 37. 7 ; 40. 1 ; Heb. 6. 15 ; 1 Pet.
2. 20.

PATTERN. 1 Tim. 1. 16 ; Tit. 2. 7 ; Heb. 8. 5 ; 9. 23.

PAVILION. 2 Sam. 22. 12, and he made darkness *p.*
See Ps. 18. 11 ; 27. 5 ; 31. 20 ; Jer. 43. 10.

PAY. Ex. 22. 7, let him *p.* double.
Num. 20. 19, water, I will *p.* for it.
2 Kings 4. 7, sell the oil, and *p.* thy debt.
Ps. 22. 25 ; 66. 13 ; 116. 14, will *p.* my vows.
Prov. 22. 27, if thou hast nothing to *p.*
Eccl. 5. 4, defer not to *p.* it.
Mat. 18. 26, I will *p.* thee all.
18. 28, *p.* that thou owest.
23. 23, ye *p.* tithe of mint.
See Ex. 21. 19 ; Mat. 17. 24 ; Rom. 13. 6 ; Heb. 7. 9.

PEACE. Gen. 41. 16, an answer of *p.*
Num. 6. 26, the Lord give thee *p.*
25. 12, my covenant of *p.*
Deut. 20. 10, proclaim *p.* to it.
23. 6, thou shalt not seek their *p.*
1 Sam. 25. 6 ; Lu. 10. 5, *p.* be to this house.
2 Kings 9. 19, what hast thou to do with *p.*?
31, had Zimri *p.*, who slew his master?
Job 5. 23, beasts shall be at *p.* with thee.
22. 21, acquaint thyself with him, and be at *p.*
Ps. 4. 8, I will lay me down in *p.*
29. 11, the Lord will bless his people with *p.*
34. 14 ; 1 Pet. 3. 11, seek *p.*, and pursue it.
37. 37, the end of that man is *p.*
85. 8, will speak *p.* to his people.
122. 6, pray for *p.* of Jerusalem.
Eccl. 3. 8, a time of *p.*
Isa. 26. 3, keep him in perfect *p.*
32. 17, work of righteousness shall be *p.*
45. 7, I make *p.*, and create evil.
48. 18, thy *p.* as a river.
22 ; 57. 21, no *p.* to the wicked.
52. 7 ; Nah. 1. 15, that publisheth *p.*
59. 8 ; Rom. 3. 17, the way of *p.* they know not.
Jer. 6. 14 ; 8. 11, saying *p.*, *p.*, when there is no *p.*
8. 15 ; 14. 19, we looked for *p.*
34. 5, thou shalt die in *p.*
Ezek. 7. 25, they shall seek *p.*
Dan. 4. 1 ; 6. 25 ; 1 Pet. 1. 2 ; 2 Pet. 1. 2 ; Jude
2, *p.* be multiplied.
Hag. 2. 9, in this place will I give *p.*
Mat. 10. 13, let your *p.* come upon it.
34 ; Lu. 12. 51, to send *p.* on earth.
Mk. 9. 50, have *p.* one with another.
Lu. 1. 79, to guide our feet into way of *p.*
2. 14, on earth *p.*
19. 42, things which belong to thy *p.*
John 14. 27, *p.* I leave, my *p.* I give you.
16. 33, that in me ye might have *p.*
Rom. 1. 7 ; 1 Cor. 1. 3 ; 2 Cor. 1. 2 ; Gal. 1. 3 ; Eph.
1. 2 ; Phil. 1. 2, *p.* from God our Father.
5. 1, we have *p.* with God.
10. 15 ; Eph. 6. 15, the gospel of *p.*
14. 19, follow after the things which make for *p.*
15. 33 ; 16. 20 ; 2 Cor. 3. 11 ; Phil. 4. 9 ; 1 Thess.
5. 23 ; Heb. 13. 20, the God of *p.*

1 Cor. 14. 33, author of *p.*
2 Cor. 13. 11, live in *p.*
Eph. 2. 14, he is our *p.*
  17, *p.* to you which were afar off.
  4. 3, in the bond of *p.*
Phil. 4. 7, *p.* of God which passeth all understanding.
Col. 1. 2 ; 1 Thess. 1. 1 ; 2 Thess. 1. 2 ; 1 Tim. 1. 2 ;
  2 Tim. 1. 2 ; Tit. 1. 4 ; Philem. 3 ; 2 John 3,
  grace and *p.* from God.
  3. 15, let the *p.* of God rule in your hearts.
1 Thess. 5. 13, be at *p.* among yourselves.
2 Thess. 3. 16, Lord of *p.* give you *p.* always.
2 Tim. 2. 22 ; Heb. 12. 14, follow *p.* with all men.
Heb. 7. 2, king of *p.*
Jas. 2. 16, depart in *p.*
  3. 18, fruit of righteousness is sown in *p.*
2 Pet. 3. 14, found of him in *p.*
  See Mat. 5. 9 ; Lu. 24. 36 ; John 20. 19 ; Gal. 6. 16.
PEACEABLE. Isa. 32. 18 ; 1 Tim. 2. 2 ; Heb. 12. 11 ;
  Jas. 3. 17.
PEACEABLY. Gen. 37. 4 ; 1 Sam. 16. 4 ; Jer. 9. 8 ;
  Rom. 12. 18.
PEACOCKS. 2 Chron. 9. 21, the ships of Tarshish
  bringing *p.*
Job 39. 13, gavest thou the goodly wings unto
  the *p.*
PEELED. Isa. 18. 2 ; Ezek. 29. 18.
PEEP. Isa. 8. 19 ; 10. 14.
PELICAN. Lev. 11. 18, and the swan, and the *p.*
  Deut. 14. 17, the *p.,* and the gier eagle.
  Ps. 102. 6, I am like a *p.* of the wilderness.
PEN. Judg. 5. 14, they that handle the *p.*
  Job 19. 24, graven with an iron *p.*
  Ps. 45. 1, my tongue is the *p.* of a ready writer.
  Isa. 8. 1, write in it with a man's *p.*
  Jer. 8. 8, the *p.* of the scribes is in vain.
  17. 1, is written with a *p.* of iron.
  3 John 13, I will not with ink and *p.* write.
PENCE. Mat. 18. 28 ; Mk. 14. 5 ; Lu. 7. 41 ; 10. 35.
PENNY. Mat. 20. 13, didst not thou agree with
  me for a *p.* ?
  22. 19, they brought him a *p.*
  Mk. 12. 15, bring me a *p.*
  Rev. 6. 6, a measure of wheat for a *p.*
PENURY. Prov. 14. 23 ; Lu. 21. 4.
PEOPLE. Ex. 6. 7 ; Deut. 4. 20 ; 2 Sam. 7. 24 ; Jer.
  13. 11, I will take you to me for a *p.*
  Lev. 20. 24, 26, separated from other *p.*
  Deut. 4. 33, did ever *p.* hear voice of God and live?
  33. 29, O *p.* saved by the Lord.
  2 Sam. 22. 44 ; Ps. 18. 43, a *p.* I knew not.
  Ps. 81. 11, my *p.* would not hearken.
  144. 15, happy is that *p.*
  Prov. 30. 25, the ants are a *p.* not strong.
  Isa. 1. 4, a *p.* laden with iniquity.
  27. 11, a *p.* of no understanding.
  43. 4, I will give *p.* for thy life.
  8, blind *p.* that have eyes.
  Jer. 6. 22 ; 50. 41, a *p.* cometh from the north.
  Jonah 1. 8, of what *p.* art thou?
  Lu. 1. 17, a *p.* prepared for the Lord.
  Tit. 2. 14, purify unto himself a peculiar *p.*
  See Mat. 1. 21 ; Rom. 11. 2 ; Heb. 11. 25.
PERCEIVE. Deut. 29. 4, a heart to *p.*
  Josh. 22. 31, we *p.* the Lord is among us.
  Job 9. 11, I *p.* him not.
  23. 8, I cannot *p.* him.
  Isa. 6. 9, see indeed, but *p.* not.
  33. 19, deeper speech than thou canst *p.*
  64. 4, nor *p.* by the ear what God hath.
  Mat. 22. 18, Jesus *p.* their wickedness.
  Mk. 8. 17, *p.* ye not yet?
  Lu. 8. 46, I *p.* that virtue is gone out.
  John 4. 19, I *p.* thou art a prophet.
  Acts 10. 34, I *p.* God is no respecter of persons.
  1 John 3. 16, hereby *p.* we the love of God.
  See 1 Sam. 3. 8 ; Neh. 6. 12 ; Job 33. 14 ; Mk. 12. 28.
PERFECT. Gen. 6. 9, Noah was *p.*

Gen. 17. 1, walk before me, and be thou *p.*
Deut. 18. 13, thou shalt be *p.* with the Lord.
  32. 4, his work is *p.*
2 Sam. 22. 31 ; Ps. 18. 30, his way is *p.*
Ps. 19. 7, law of the Lord is *p.*
  37. 37, mark the *p.* man.
Prov. 4. 18, more and more to *p.* day.
Ezek. 28. 15, thou wast *p.* in thy ways.
Mat. 5. 48 ; 2 Cor. 13. 11, Ye ye *p.*
  19. 21, if thou wilt be *p.*
John 17. 23, be made *p.* in one.
Rom. 12. 2, that *p.* will of God.
1 Cor. 2. 6, wisdom among them that are *p.*
2 Cor. 12. 9, strength made *p.* in weakness.
Eph. 4. 13, unto a *p.* man.
Phil. 3. 12, not as though I were already *p.*
  15, let us, as many as be *p.*
Col. 1. 28, present every man *p.*
  4. 12, may stand *p.* and complete.
2 Tim. 3. 17, that the man of God may be *p.*
Heb. 2. 10, make *p.* through suffering.
  11. 40, without us should not be made *p.*
  12. 23, spirits of just men made *p.*
  13. 21, make you *p.* in every good work.
Jas. 1. 4, patience have her *p.* work.
  17, every good and *p.* gift.
  25, *p.* law of liberty.
  3. 2, the same is a *p.* man.
1 John 4. 18, *p.* love casteth out fear.
  See 2 Chron. 8. 16 ; Lu. 6. 40 ; 2 Cor. 7. 1 ; Eph.
  4. 12.
PERFECTION. Job 11. 7 ; Ps. 119. 96 ; 2 Cor. 13. 9 ;
  Heb. 6. 1.
PERFECTLY. Jer. 23. 20 ; Acts 18. 26 ; 1 Cor. 1. 10.
PERFECTNESS. Col. 3. 14.
PERFORM. Ex. 18. 18, not able to *p.* it thyself
  alone.
Esth. 5. 6 ; 7. 2, to half of kingdom it shall be *p.*
Job 5. 12, cannot *p.* their enterprise.
Ps. 65. 1, unto thee shall the vow be *p.*
  119. 106, I have sworn, and I will *p.* it.
Isa. 9. 7, zeal of the Lord will *p.* this.
  44. 28, shall *p.* all my pleasure.
Jer. 29. 10 ; 33. 14, I will *p.* my good word.
Rom. 4. 21, able also to *p.*
  7. 18, how to *p.* that which is good I find not.
Phil. 1. 6, *p.* it until day of Christ.
  See Job 23. 14 ; Ps. 57. 2 ; Jer. 35. 14 ; Mat. 5. 33.
PERFORMANCE. Lu. 1. 45 ; 2 Cor. 8. 11.
PERIL. Lam. 5. 9 ; Rom. 8. 35 ; 2 Cor. 11. 26.
PERILOUS. 2 Tim. 3. 1.
PERISH. Num. 17. 12, we die, we *p.,* we all *p.*
Deut. 18. 13, thou shalt be a Syrian ready to *p.*
Job 4. 7, who ever *p.,* being innocent?
  29. 13, blessing of him that was ready to *p.*
  34. 15, all flesh shall *p.* together.
Ps. 1. 6, way of ungodly shall *p.*
  37. 20, the wicked shall *p.*
  49. 12, like the beasts that *p.*
  80. 16, they *p.* at rebuke of thy countenance.
  102. 26, they shall *p.,* but thou shalt endure.
Prov. 11. 10 ; 28. 28, when the wicked *p.*
  29. 18, no vision, the people *p.*
  31. 6, strong drink to him that is ready to *p.*
Isa. 27. 13, they shall come that were ready to *p.*
Jer. 7. 28, truth is *p.*
Jonah 1. 6 ; 3. 9, God will think on us, that we *p.*
  not.
  14, let us not *p.* for this man's life.
Mat. 8. 25 ; Lu. 8. 24, save us, we *p.*
  18. 14, that one of these little ones should *p.*
  26, 52, shall *p.* with the sword.
Mk. 4. 38, carest thou not that we *p.* ?
Lu. 13. 3, 5, ye shall all likewise *p.*
  15. 17, I *p.* with hunger.
  21. 18, there shall not an hair of your head *p.*
John 6. 27, labour not for the meat which *p.*
Acts 8. 20, thy money *p.* with thee.
Col. 2. 22, which are to *p.* with the using.

2 Pet. 3. 9, not willing that any should *p.*
See Ps. 2. 12 ; Jer. 6. 21 ; John 10. 28 ; Rom. 2. 12.
PERMISSION. 1 Cor. 7. 6.
PERMIT. 1 Cor. 14. 34 ; 16. 7 ; Heb. 6. 3.
PERNICIOUS. 2 Pet. 2. 2.
PERPETUAL. Ex. 31. 16, sabbath for a *p.* covenant.
Lev. 25. 34, their *p.* possession.
Ps. 9. 6, destructions are come to a *p.* end.
74. 3 ; Jer. 25. 9 ; Ezek. 35. 9, the *p.* desolations.
Jer. 8. 5, a *p.* backsliding.
15. 18, why is my pain *p.*?
Hab. 3. 6, the *p.* hills.
See Gen. 9. 12 ; Jer. 5. 22 ; 50. 5 ; 51. 39 ; Ezek. 46. 14.
PERPETUALLY. 1 Kings 9. 3 ; 2 Chron. 7. 16 ; Amos 1. 11.
PERPLEXED. Lu. 9. 7 ; 24. 4 ; 2 Cor. 4. 8.
PERPLEXITY. Isa. 22. 5 ; Mic. 7. 4 ; Lu. 21. 25.
PERSECUTE. Job 19. 22, why do ye *p.* me?
Ps. 7. 1, save me from them that *p.* me.
10. 2, the wicked doth *p.* the poor.
71. 11, *p.* and take him, there is none to deliver.
143. 3, the enemy hath *p.* my soul.
Mat. 5. 11, 12, blessed are ye when men *p.* you.
44, pray for them that *p.* you.
John 15. 20, if they have *p.* me.
Acts 9. 4 ; 22. 7 ; 26. 14, why *p.* thou me?
22. 4, I *p.* this way unto death.
26. 11, I *p.* them even to strange cities.
1 Cor. 4. 12, being *p.*, we suffer it.
15. 9 ; Gal. 1. 13, I *p.* the church of God.
2 Cor. 4. 9, *p.* but not forsaken.
Phil. 3. 6, concerning zeal, *p.* the church.
See John 5. 16 ; Acts 7. 52 ; Rom. 12. 14 ; Gal. 1. 23 ; 4. 29.
PERSECUTION. Mat. 13. 21 ; Mk. 4. 17, when *p.* ariseth.
2 Cor. 12. 10, take pleasure in *p.*
2 Tim. 3. 12, all that will live godly shall suffer *p.*
See Lam. 5. 5 ; Acts 8. 1 ; Gal. 6. 12 ; 1 Tim. 1. 13.
PERSEVERANCE. Eph. 6. 18.
PERSON. Deut. 10. 17 ; 2 Sam. 14. 14, God, which regardeth not *p.*
2 Sam. 17. 11, go to battle in thine own *p.*
Ps. 15. 4 ; Isa. 32. 5, 6, vile *p.*
26. 4 ; Prov. 12. 11 ; 28. 19, with vain *p.*
105. 37, not one feeble *p.*
Mat. 22. 16 ; Mk. 12. 14, regardest not *p.* of men.
2 Cor. 2. 10, forgave I it in the *p.* of Christ.
Heb. 1. 3, the express image of his *p.*
2 Pet. 3. 11, what manner of *p.* ought ye to be?
See Mal. 1. 8 ; Lu. 15. 7 ; Heb. 12. 16 ; Jude 16.
PERSUADE. 1 Kings 22. 20, who shall *p.* Ahab?
Prov. 25. 15, by long forbearing is a prince *p.*
Mat. 28. 14, we will *p.* him, and secure you.
Acts 26. 28, almost thou *p.* me.
Rom. 14. 5, let every man be fully *p.*
2 Cor. 5. 11, we *p.* men.
Gal. 1. 10, do I now *p.* men or God?
Heb. 6. 9, we are *p.* better things of you.
See 2 Kings 18. 32 ; 2 Chron. 18. 2 ; 2 Tim. 1. 12.
PERTAIN. Rom. 15. 17 ; 1 Cor. 6. 3 ; 2 Pet. 1. 3.
PERVERSE. Deut. 32. 5, a *p.* and crooked generation.
Job 6. 30, cannot my taste discern *p.* things?
Prov. 4. 24, *p.* lips put far from thee.
12. 8, *p.* heart shall be despised.
17. 20, *p.* tongue falleth into mischief.
23. 33, thine heart shall utter *p.* things.
Phil. 2. 15, in the midst of a *p.* nation.
See Num. 23. 21 ; Isa. 30. 12 ; 1 Tim. 6. 5.
PERVERT. Deut. 16. 19, a gift doth *p.* words.
Job 8. 3, doth God *p.* judgment?
Prov. 10. 9, he that *p.* his ways shall be known.
19. 3, the foolishness of man *p.* his way.
Jer. 3. 21, they have *p.* their way.
23. 36, ye have *p.* the words of God.
Acts 13. 10, wilt thou not cease to *p.* right ways?

Gal. 1. 7, would *p.* the gospel.
See Eccl. 5. 8 ; Mic. 3. 9 ; Lu. 23. 2.
PESTILENCE. Ex. 5. 3 ; 9. 15 ; Jer. 42. 17 ; 44. 13.
PESTILENT. Acts 24. 5.
PETITION. 1 Sam. 1. 17, God of Israel grant thee thy *p.*
1 Kings 2. 20, one small *p.*
Esth. 5. 6 ; 7. 2 ; 9. 12, what is thy *p.*?
Dan. 6. 7, whosoever shall ask a *p.*
13, maketh his *p.* three times a day.
See Esth. 7. 3 ; Ps. 20. 5 ; 1 John 5. 15.
PHILOSOPHERS. Acts 17. 18, then certain *p.* of the Epicureans.
PHILOSOPHY. Col. 2. 8.
PHYLACTERIES. Mat. 23. 5, they make broad their *p.*
See Ex. 13. 9, 16 ; Num. 15. 38.
PHYSICIAN. Mat. 9. 12 ; Mk. 2. 17 ; Lu. 5. 31, they that be whole need not a *p.*
Lu. 4. 23, *p.*, heal thyself.
See Jer. 8. 22.
PICK. Prov. 30. 17.
PICTURES. Num. 33. 52 ; Prov. 25. 11 ; Isa. 2. 16.
PIECE. 1 Sam. 2. 36 ; Prov. 6. 26 ; 28. 21, a *p.* of bread.
15. 33, Samuel hewed Agag in *p.*
Ps. 7. 2, rending in *p.* while none to deliver.
50. 22, consider, lest I tear you in *p.*
Jer. 23. 29, hammer that breaketh rock in *p.*
Amos 4. 7, one *p.* was rained upon.
Zech. 11. 12, weighed for my price thirty *p.*
13 ; Mat. 27. 6, 9, took thirty *p.* of silver.
See Lu. 14. 18 ; Acts 19. 19 ; 23. 10 ; 27. 44.
PIERCE. 2 Kings 18. 21 ; Isa. 36. 6, into his hand and *p.* it.
Zech. 12. 10 ; John 19. 37, they shall look on me whom they have *p.*
1 Tim. 6. 10, *p.* themselves with many sorrows.
See Isa. 27. 1 ; Lu. 2. 35 ; Heb. 4. 12 ; Rev. 1. 7.
PIETY. 1 Tim. 5. 4, let them learn first to show *p.* at home.
PILE. Isa. 30. 33 ; Ezek. 24. 9.
PILLAR. Gen. 19. 26, a *p.* of salt.
Job 9. 6 ; 26. 11, the *p.* thereof tremble.
Prov. 9. 1, she hath hewn out her seven *p.*
Gal. 2. 9, Cephas and John, who seemed to be *p.*
1 Tim. 3. 15, the *p.* and ground of the truth.
Rev. 3. 12, him that overcometh will I make a *p.*
See Isa. 19. 19 ; Jer. 1. 18 ; Joel 2. 30 ; Lu. 17. 32 ; Rev. 10. 1.
PILLOW. Gen. 28. 11 ; 1 Sam. 19. 13 ; Ezek. 13. 18 ; Mk. 4. 38.
PILOTS. Ezek. 27. 8.
PIN. Judg. 16. 14 ; Ezek. 15. 3.
PINE. Lev. 26. 39 ; Lam. 4. 9 ; Isa. 38. 12 ; Ezek. 24. 23.
PINE TREE. Is. 41. 19 ; 60. 13, and the *p. t.*
PIPE. Isa. 5. 12, the harp and *p.* are in their feasts.
Mat. 11. 17 ; Lu. 7. 32, we have *p.* unto you.
1 Cor. 14. 7, how shall it be known what is *p.*?
Rev. 18. 22, voice of *p.* shall be heard no more.
See 1 Sam. 10. 5 ; 1 Kings 1. 40 ; Isa. 30. 29.
PIT. Gen. 37. 20, cast him into some *p.*
Ex. 21. 33, 34, if a man dig a *p.*
Num. 16. 30, 33, go down quick into the *p.*
Job 33. 24, deliver him from going down to the *p.*
Ps. 28. 1 ; 143. 7, like them that go down into the *p.*
40. 2, out of an horrible *p.*
Prov. 22. 14 ; 23. 27, a deep *p.* of corruption.
28. 10, shall fall into his own *p.*
Isa. 38. 17, the *p.* of corruption.
Mat. 12. 11 ; Lu. 14. 5, fall into a *p.* on sabbath.
PITCHER. Gen. 24. 14, let down thy *p.*
Judg. 7. 16, lamps within the *p.*
Eccl. 12. 6, or the *p.* be broken.
Lam. 4. 2, esteemed as earthen *p.*

Mk. 14. 13; Lu. 22. 10, a man bearing a *p.* of water.

PITIFUL. Lam. 4. 10; Jas. 5. 11; 1 Pet. 3. 8.

PITY. Deut. 7. 16; 13. 8; 19. 13, thine eye shall have no *p.*
2 Sam. 12. 6, because he had no *p.*
Job 19. 21, have *p.* on me, my friends.
Ps. 69. 20, I looked for some to take *p.*
Prov. 19. 17, that hath *p.* on the poor lendeth.
28. 8, gather for him that will *p.* the poor.
Isa. 13. 18, they shall have no *p.* on fruit.
63. 9, in his *p.* he redeemed them.
Jer. 13. 14, I will not *p.* nor spare.
Ezek. 16. 5, none eye *p.* thee.
24. 21, I will profane what your soul *r.*
Joel 2. 18, the Lord will *p.* his people.
Zech. 11. 5, their own shepherds *p.* them not.
Mat. 18. 33, as I had *p.* on thee.
See Ps. 103. 13; Jer. 15. 5; Lam. 2. 2; Jonah 4. 10.

PLACE. Ex. 3. 5; Josh. 5. 15, *p.* whereon thou standest is holy.
Judg. 18. 10, a *p.* where there is no want.
2 Kings 5. 11, strike his hand over the *p.*
6. 1; Isa. 49. 20, the *p.* is too strait for us.
Ps. 26. 8, the *p.* where thine honour dwelleth.
32. 7; 119. 114, thou art my hiding *p.*
37. 10, thou shalt diligently consider his *p.*
74. 20, the dark *p.* of the earth.
90. 1, our dwelling *p.*
Prov. 14. 26, his children have a *p.* of refuge.
15. 3, the eyes of the Lord in every *p.*
Eccl. 3. 20, all go to one *p.*
Isa. 5. 8, lay field to field, till there be no *p.*
60. 13, the *p.* of my feet.
66. 1, where is the *p.* of my rest?
Jer. 6. 3, they shall feed every one in his *p.*
Mic. 1. 3, the Lord cometh out of his *p.*
Zech. 10. 10, *p.* shall not be found for them.
Mal. 1. 11, in every *p.* incense shall be offered.
Mat. 28. 6; Mk. 16. 6, see the *p.* where the Lord lay.
Lu. 10. 1, two and two into every *p.*
14. 9, give this man *p.*
John 8. 37, my word hath no *p.* in you.
18. 2, Judas knew the *p.*
Acts 2. 1, with one accord in one *p.*
4. 31, the *p.* was shaken.
Rom. 12. 19, rather give *p.* to wrath.
Eph. 4. 27, neither give *p.* to the devil.
Heb. 12. 17, found no *p.* of repentance.
Rev. 20. 11, there was found no *p.* for them.
See Ps. 16. 6; Isa. 40. 4; Eph. 1. 3; 2. 6; 3. 10.

PLAGUE. Lev. 26. 21, I will bring seven times more *p.*
Deut. 28. 59, will make thy *p.* wonderful.
29. 22, when they see the *p.* of that land.
1 Kings 8. 38, every man the *p.* of his own heart.
Ps. 73. 5, nor are they *p.* like other men.
91. 10, nor any *p.* come nigh thy dwelling.
Hos. 13. 14, O death, I will be thy *p.*
Rev. 18. 4, that ye receive not of her *p.*
22. 18, shall add to him the *p.* written.
See Lev. 14. 35; Num. 8. 19; 16. 46; Mk. 3. 10.

PLAIN. Gen. 25. 27, Jacob was a *p.* man.
Ps. 27. 11, lead me in a *p.* path.
Prov. 8. 9, they are *p.* to him that understandeth.
15. 19, the way of the righteous is made *p.*
Isa. 40. 4, rough places *p.*
Hab. 2. 2, write the vision, make it *p.*
See Gen. 13. 10; 19. 17; Isa. 28. 25; Mk. 7. 35.

PLAINLY. Deut. 27. 8, write the words very *p.*
Isa. 32. 4, stammerers shall speak *p.*
John 10. 24, tell us *p.*
16. 25, I shall show you *p.* of the Father.
29, now speakest thou *p.*
See Ex. 21. 5; Ezra 4. 18; John 11. 14; 2 Cor. 3. 12.

PLAITING. 1 Pet. 3. 3.

PLANES. Isa. 44. 13.

PLANT (*n.*). Job 14. 9, bring forth boughs like a *p.*
Ps. 128. 3, children like olive *p.*

Ps. 144. 12, sons as *p.* grown up.
Isa. 5. 7; 17. 10, his pleasant *p.*
16. 8, broken down principal *p.*
53. 2, as a tender *p.*
Ezek. 34. 29, a *p.* of renown.
Mat. 15. 13, every *p.* my Father hath not planted.
See Gen. 2. 5; 1 Chron. 4. 23; Jer. 48. 32.

PLANT (*v.*). Num. 24. 6, as trees which the Lord hath *p.*
2 Sam. 7. 10; 1 Chron. 17. 9, I will *p.* them.
Ps. 1. 3; Jer. 17. 8, like a tree *p.*
80. 15, the vineyard thy right hand hath *p.*
92. 13, *p.* in the house of the Lord.
94. 9, he that *p.* the ear.
Jer. 2. 21, I had *p.* thee a noble vine.
Ezek. 17. 10, being *p.* shall it prosper?
Lu. 17. 6, be thou *p.* in the sea.
Rom. 6. 5, if we have been *p.* together.
1 Cor. 3. 6, I have *p.*
See Mat. 21. 33; Mk. 12. 1; Lu. 20. 9.

PLATE. Ex. 28. 36; 39. 30; Jer. 10. 9.

PLATTED. Mat. 27. 29; Mk. 15. 17; John 19. 2.

PLATTER. Mat. 23. 25; Lu. 11. 39.

PLAY. Ex. 32. 6; 1 Cor. 10. 7, people rose up to *p.*
1 Sam. 16. 17, a man that can *p.* well.
2 Sam. 6. 21, I will *p.* before the Lord.
10. 12, let us *p.* the men.
Job 41. 5, wilt thou *p.* with him?
Ps. 33. 3, *p.* skilfully with a loud noise.
Isa. 11. 8, the sucking child shall *p.*
Ezek. 33. 32, can *p.* well on an instrument.
See 2 Sam. 2. 14; 1 Chron. 15. 29; Ps. 68. 25; Zech. 8. 5.

PLEA. Deut. 17. 8.

PLEAD. Judg. 6. 31, 32, will ye *p.* for Baal?
Job 9. 19, who shall set me a time to *p.*?
13. 19, who will *p.* with me?
16. 21, that one might *p.* for a man.
23. 6, will he *p.* against me with his great power?
Isa. 1. 17, *p.* for the widow.
3. 13, the Lord standeth up to *p.*
43. 26, let us *p.* together.
59. 4, none *p.* for truth.
Jer. 2. 9, I will yet *p.* with you.
Lam. 3. 58, thou hast *p.* the causes of my soul.
Joel 3. 2, I will *p.* with them for my people.
See 1 Sam. 25. 39; Job 13. 6; Isa. 66. 16; Hos. 2. 2.

PLEASANT. Gen. 3. 6, *p.* to the eyes.
2 Sam. 1. 23, were *p.* in their lives.
26, very *p.* hast thou been to me.
Ps. 16. 6, lines fallen in *p.* places.
106. 24, they despised the *p.* land.
133. 1, how *p.* for brethren to dwell together.
Prov. 2. 10, knowledge is *p.* to thy soul.
15. 26, the words of the pure are *p.* words.
16. 24, *p.* words are as honeycomb.
Eccl. 11. 7, it is *p.* to behold the sun.
Cant. 4. 13, 16; 7. 13, with *p.* fruits.
Isa. 64. 11, our *p.* things are laid waste.
Jer. 31. 20, is Ephraim a *p.* child?
Ezek. 33. 32, of one that hath a *p.* voice.
Dan. 10. 3, I ate no *p.* bread.
See Amos 5. 11; Mic. 2. 9; Nah. 2. 9; Zech. 7. 14.

PLEASANTNESS. Prov. 3. 17.

PLEASE. 1 Kings 3. 10, the speech *p.* the Lord.
Ps. 51. 19, then shalt thou be *p.* with sacrifices.
115. 3; 135. 6; Jonah 1. 14, he hath done whatsoever he *p.*
Prov. 16. 7, when a man's ways *p.* the Lord.
Isa. 2. 6, they *p.* themselves in children of strangers.
53. 10, it *p.* the Lord to bruise him.
55. 11, accomplish that which I *p.*
Mic. 6. 7, will the Lord be *p.* with rams?
Mal. 1. 8, offer it, will he be *p.* with thee?
John 8. 29, I do always those things that *p.* him.
Rom. 8. 8, in the flesh cannot *p.* God.
15. 1, to bear, and not to *p.* ourselves.
3, even Christ *p.* not himself.

1 Cor. 1. 21, it *p.* God by the foolishness of preaching.

10. 33, as I *p.* men in all things.

Gal. 1. 10, do I seek to *p.* men?

Eph. 6. 6 ; Col. 3. 22, as men-*p.*

Heb. 11. 6, without faith it is impossible to *p.* God.

See 1 Cor. 7. 32 ; Col. 1. 19 ; 1 Thess. 2, 4 ; 1 John 3. 22.

PLEASURE. 1 Chron. 29. 17, hast *p.* in uprightness.

Esth. 1. 8, do according to every man's *p.*

Job 21. 21, what *p.* hath he in his house?

25, another never eateth with *p.*

22. 3, is it any *p.* to the Almighty?

Ps. 16. 11, *p.* for evermore.

35. 27, hath *p.* in the prosperity of his servants.

51. 18, do good in thy good *p.*

102. 14, thy servants take *p.* in her stones.

103. 21, ye ministers of his that do his *p.*

111. 2, of all them that have *p.* therein.

147. 11, taketh *p.* in them that fear him.

149. 4, the Lord taketh *p.* in his people.

Prov. 21. 17, he that loveth *p.* shall be poor.

Eccl. 5. 4, he hath no *p.* in fools.

12. 1, I have no *p.* in them.

Isa. 44. 28, Cyrus shall perform all my *p.*

53. 10, the *p.* of the Lord shall prosper.

58. 3, in the day of your fast ye find *p.*

13, doing thy *p.* on my holy day.

Jer. 22. 28 ; 48. 38 ; Hos. 8. 8, a vessel wherein is no *p.*

Ezek. 18. 23 ; 33. 11, have I any *p.*?

Mal. 1. 10, I have no *p.* in you, saith the Lord.

Lu. 8. 14, choked with *p.* of this life.

12. 32, Father's good *p.*

Eph. 1. 5, the good *p.* of his will.

Phil. 2. 13, to will and to do of his good *p.*

1 Tim. 5. 6, she that liveth in *p.*

2 Tim. 3. 4, lovers of *p.*

Heb. 10. 38, my soul shall have no *p.* in him.

11. 25, the *p.* of sin for a season.

12. 10, chastened us after their own *p.*

Jas. 5. 5, ye have lived in *p.* on earth.

Rev. 4. 11, for thy *p.* they were created.

See Gen. 18. 12 ; Ps. 5. 4 ; Eccl. 2. 1 ; Tit. 3. 3 ; 2 Pet. 2. 13.

PLENTEOUS. Ps. 86. 5 ; 103. 8, *p.* in mercy.

130. 7, *p.* redemption.

Hab. 1. 16, portion fat and meat *p.*

Mat. 9. 37, the harvest truly is *p.*

See Gen. 41. 34 ; Deut. 28. 11 ; 30. 9 ; Prov. 21. 5 ; Isa. 30. 23.

PLENTIFUL. Ps. 31. 23 ; 68. 9 ; Jer. 2. 7 ; 48. 33 ; Lu. 12. 16.

PLENTY. Gen. 27. 28, *p.* of corn and wine.

Job 22. 25, *p.* of silver.

37. 23, *p.* of justice.

Prov. 3. 10, barns filled with *p.*

See 2 Chron. 31. 10 ; Prov. 28. 19 ; Jer. 44. 17 ; Joel 2. 26.

PLOW. Job 4. 8, that *p.* iniquity shall reap.

Prov. 20. 4, not *p.* by reason of cold.

21. 4, the *p.* of the wicked is sin.

Isa. 2. 4 ; Mic. 4. 3, beat swords into *p.*-shares.

28. 24, doth plowman *p.* all day to sow?

Joel 3. 10, beat your *p.*-shares into swords.

Amos 9. 13, the *p.*-man overtake the reaper.

See Deut. 22. 10 ; 1 Sam. 14. 14 ; Job 1. 14 ; 1 Cor. 9. 10.

PLUCK. Deut. 23. 25, mayest *p.* the ears with thy hand.

2 Chron. 7. 20, then will I *p.* them up.

Job 24. 9, they *p.* the fatherless from the breast.

Ps. 25. 15, he shall *p.* my feet out of the net.

74. 11, *p.* it out of thy bosom.

Prov. 14. 1, foolish *p.* it down with her hands.

Eccl. 3. 2, a time to *p.* up.

Isa. 50. 6, my cheeks to them that *p.*

Jer. 22. 24, yet I would *p.* thee thence.

Amos 4. 11 ; Zech. 3. 2, a firebrand *p.* out,

Mat. 5. 29 ; 18. 9 ; Mk. 9. 47, offend thee, *p.* it out.

Mat. 12. 1 ; Mk. 2. 23 ; Lu. 6. 1, began to *p.* ears.

John 10. 28, nor shall any *p.* out of my hand.

See Gen. 8. 11 ; Lu. 17. 6 ; Gal. 4. 15 ; Jude 12.

POINT. Jer. 17. 1, written with the *p.* of a diamond.

Heb. 4. 15, in all *p.* tempted.

Jas. 2. 10, yet offend in one *p.*

See Gen. 25. 32 ; Eccl. 5. 16 ; Mk. 5. 23 ; John 4. 47.

POLE. Num. 21. 8.

POLICY. Dan. 8. 25.

POLISHED. Ps. 144. 12 ; Isa. 49. 2 ; Lam. 4. 7 ; Dan. 10. 6.

POLL. 2 Sam. 14. 26 ; Ezek. 44. 20 ; Mic. 1. 16.

POMP. Isa. 5. 14 ; 14. 11 ; Ezek. 7. 24 ; 30. 18 ; Acts 25. 23.

PONDER. Prov. 4. 26, *p.* the path of thy feet.

5. 6, lest thou shouldest *p.*

21, the Lord *p.* all his goings.

See Prov. 21. 2 ; 24. 12 ; Lu. 2. 19.

POOL. Ps. 84. 6 ; Isa. 35. 7 ; 41. 18 ; John 5. 2 ; 9. 7.

POOR. Ex. 30. 15, the *p.* shall not give less.

Deut. 15. 11, the *p.* shall never cease.

2 Kings 24. 14, none remained, save *p.* sort.

Job 24. 4, the *p.* of the earth hide.

29. 16, I was a father to the *p.*

Ps. 10. 14, the *p.* committeth himself to thee.

34. 6, this *p.* man cried.

40. 17 ; 69. 29 ; 70. 5 ; 86. 1 ; 109. 22, I am *p.*

49. 2, rich and *p.* together.

Prov. 10. 4, becometh *p.* that dealeth with slack hand.

13. 23, food in the tillage of the *p.*

18. 23, the *p.* useth entreaties.

22. 2, rich and *p.* meet together.

30. 9, lest I be *p.* and steal.

Isa. 41. 17, when *p.* and needy seek water.

Amos 2. 6, they sold the *p.*

Zech. 11. 7, 11, I will feed even you, O *p.* of the flock.

Mat. 5. 3, blessed are the *p.* in spirit.

2 Cor. 6. 10, as *p.*, yet making many rich.

8. 9, for your sakes he became *p.*

See Lev. 27. 8 ; Jas. 2. 2 ; Rev. 3. 17 ; 13. 16.

POPULOUS. Deut. 26. 5 ; Nah. 3. 8.

PORTION. Gen. 31. 14, is there yet any *p.* for us?

48. 22, one *p.* above thy brethren.

Deut. 32. 9, the Lord's *p.* is his people.

2 Kings 2. 9, a double *p.* of thy spirit.

Neh. 8. 10 ; Esth. 9. 19, send *p.* to them.

Job 20. 29, this is the *p.* of a wicked man.

24. 18, their *p.* is cursed.

26. 14 ; 27. 13, how little a *p.* is heard of him?

31. 2, what *p.* of God is there from above?

Ps. 11. 6, this shall be the *p.* of their cup.

16. 5, Lord is the *p.* of mine inheritance.

17. 14, have their *p.* in this life.

73. 26, God is my *p.*

119. 57 ; 142. 5, thou art my *p.*, O Lord.

Prov. 31. 15, giveth a *p.* to her maidens.

Eccl. 2. 10, this was my *p.* of all my labour.

3. 22 ; 5. 18 ; 9. 9, rejoice, for that is his *p.*

5. 19, God hath given power to take *p.*

9. 6, nor have they any more *p.* for ever.

11. 2, give a *p.* to seven.

Isa. 53. 12, divide a *p.* with the great.

61. 7, they shall rejoice in their *p.*

Jer. 10. 16 ; 51. 19, *p.* of Jacob not like them.

12. 10, my pleasant *p.* a wilderness.

52. 34, every day a *p.*

Dan. 1. 8, with *p.* of king's meat.

Mic. 2. 4, he hath changed the *p.* of my people.

Mat. 24. 51, appoint him *p.* with hypocrites.

Lu. 12. 42, their *p.* in due season.

46, his *p.* with unbelievers.

15. 12, the *p.* of goods that falleth.

See Gen. 47. 22 ; Josh. 17. 14 ; Dan. 4. 15 ; 11. 26.

POSSESS. Gen. 22. 17 ; 24. 60, thy seed shall *p.* the gate.

Job 7. 3, made to *p.* months of vanity.

13. 26, *p.* iniquities of my youth.

Prov. 8. 22, the Lord *p.* me in beginning.
Lu. 18. 12, I give tithes of all I *p.*
21. 19, in patience *p.* your souls.
See Lu. 12. 15 ; Acts 4. 32 ; 1 Cor. 7. 30 ; 2 Cor. 6. 10.

POSSESSION. Gen. 17. 8 ; 48. 4, an everlasting *p.*
Prov. 28. 10, good things in *p.*
Eccl. 2. 7 ; Mat. 19. 22 ; Mk. 10. 22, great *p.*
Acts 2. 45, and sold their *p.*
Eph. 1. 14, redemption of purchased *p.*
See Lev. 25. 10 ; 27. 16 ; 1 Kings 21. 15.

POSSIBLE. Mat. 19. 26 ; Mk. 10. 27, with God all things are *p.*
24. 24 ; Mk. 13. 22, if *p.* deceive elect.
26. 39 ; Mk. 14. 35, 36, if *p.* let this cup.
Mk. 9. 23, all things are *p.* to him that believeth.
14. 36 ; Lu. 18. 27, all things are *p.* to thee.
Rom. 12. 18, if *p.* live peaceably.
See Acts 2. 24 ; 20. 16 ; Gal. 4. 15 ; Heb. 10. 4.

POST. Deut. 6. 9 ; Job 9. 25 ; Jer. 51. 31 ; Amos 9. 1.

POSTERITY. Gen. 45. 7 ; Ps. 49. 13 ; 109. 13 ; Dan. 11. 4.

POT. 2 Kings 4. 2, not anything save a *p.* of oil.
40, there is death in the *p.*
Job 41. 31, maketh the deep boil like a *p.*
Zech. 14. 21, every *p.* shall be holiness.
Mk. 7. 4, the washing of cups and *p.*
John 2. 6, six water-*p.*
See Ex. 16. 33 ; Jer. 1. 13 ; John 4. 28 ; Heb. 9. 4.

POTENTATE. 1 Tim. 6. 15.

POUND. Lu. 19. 13 ; John 12. 3.

POUR. Job 10. 10, hast thou not *p.* me out as milk.
29. 6, rock *p.* out rivers of oil.
30. 16, my soul is *p.* out upon me.
Ps. 45. 2, grace is *p.* into thy lips.
62. 8, *p.* out your heart before him.
Prov. 1. 23 ; Isa. 44. 3 ; Joel 2. 28, 29 ; Acts 2. 17, 18, I will *p.* out my Spirit.
Cant. 1. 3, as ointment *p.* forth.
Isa. 26. 16, *p.* out prayer when chastening.
32. 15, till the spirit be *p.* on us.
44. 3, I will *p.* water on thirsty.
53. 12, *p.* out his soul unto death.
Jer. 7. 20 ; 42. 18, my fury shall be *p.* out.
Lam. 2. 19, *p.* out thine heart like water.
Nah. 1. 6, fury is *p.* out like fire.
Mal. 3. 10, if I will not *p.* out a blessing.
Mat. 26. 7 ; Mk. 14. 3, *p.* ointment on his head.
John 2. 15, he *p.* out the changers' money.
See 2 Sam. 23. 16 ; 2 Kings 3. 11 ; Rev. 14. 10 ; 16. 1.

POURTRAY. Ezek. 4. 1 ; 8. 10 ; 23. 14.

POVERTY. Gen. 45. 11 ; Prov. 20. 13, lest thou come to *p.*
Prov. 6. 11 ; 24. 34, thy *p.* come as one that travelleth.
10. 15, destruction of poor is *p.*
11. 24, it tendeth to *p.*
13. 18, *p.* to him that refuseth instruction.
28. 19, shall have *p.* enough.
30. 8, give me neither *p.* nor riches.
31. 7, drink and forget his *p.*
See Prov. 23. 21 ; 2 Cor. 8. 2 ; Rev. 2. 9.

POWDER. Ex. 32. 20 ; 2 Kings 23. 6 ; Mat. 21. 44.

POWER. Gen. 32. 28 ; Hos. 12. 3, hast thou *p.* with God.
Ex. 15. 6, glorious in *p.*
Lev. 26. 19, the pride of your *p.*
Deut. 8. 18, he giveth thee *p.* to get wealth.
2 Sam. 22. 33, God is my strength and *p.*
1 Chron. 29. 11 ; Mat. 6. 13, thine is the *p.* and glory.
2 Chron. 25. 8, God hath *p.* to help.
Job 26. 2, him that is without *p.*
Ps. 49. 15, from the *p.* of the grave.
65. 6, being girded with *p.*
90. 11, who knoweth *p.* of thine anger.
Prov. 3. 27, when it is in *p.* to do it.
18. 21, in the *p.* of the tongue.
Eccl. 5. 19 ; 6. 2, *p.* to eat thereof.

Eccl. 8. 4, where word of king is, there is *p.*
Isa. 40. 29, he giveth *p.* to the faint.
Mic. 3. 8, full of *p.* by the spirit.
Hab. 3. 4, the hiding of his *p.*
Zech. 4. 6, not by might, nor by *p.*
Mat. 9. 6 ; Mk. 2. 10 ; Lu. 5. 24, *p.* on earth to forgive.
8, who had given such *p.* to men.
24. 30 ; Lu. 21. 27, coming in clouds with *p.*
28. 18, all *p.* is given to me.
Lu. 1. 35, the *p.* of the Highest.
4. 6, all this *p.* will I give thee.
14, Jesus returned in the *p.* of the Spirit.
32, his word was with *p.*
5. 17, the *p.* of the Lord was present.
9. 43, amazed at the mighty *p.* of God.
12. 5, that hath *p.* to cast into hell.
11, bring you unto magistrates and *p.*
22. 53, your hour and the *p.* of darkness.
24. 49, with *p.* from on high.
John 1. 12, *p.* to become sons of God.
10. 18, I have *p.* to lay it down.
17. 2, *p.* over all flesh.
19. 10, I have *p.* to crucify thee.
Acts 1. 8, *p.* after the Holy Ghost is come.
3. 12, as though by our own *p.*
5. 4, was it not in thine own *p.*
8. 10, this man is the great *p.* of God.
19, give me also this *p.*
26. 18, from the *p.* of Satan unto God.
Rom. 1. 20, his eternal *p.* and Godhead.
9. 17, that I might show my *p.* in thee.
13. 2, whosoever resisteth the *p.*
1 Cor. 15. 43, it is raised in *p.*
Eph. 2. 2, prince of the *p.* of the air.
3. 7, the effectual working of his *p.*
Phil. 3. 10, the *p.* of his resurrection.
2 Thess. 1. 9, from the glory of his *p.*
2 Tim. 1. 7, spirit of *p.* and love.
3. 5, form of godliness, but denying the *p.*
Heb. 2. 14, him that had *p.* of death.
6. 5, the *p.* of the world to come.
7. 16, the *p.* of an endless life.
Rev. 2. 26, to him will I give *p.*
4. 11, worthy to receive *p.*
See Mat. 22. 29 ; Lu. 22. 69 ; Rom. 1. 16.

POWERFUL. Ps. 29. 4 ; 2 Cor. 10. 10 ; Heb. 4. 12.

PRAISE (*n.*). Ex. 15. 11, fearful in *p.*
Deut. 10. 21, he is thy *p.* and thy God.
Judg. 5. 3 ; Ps. 7. 17 ; 9. 2 ; 57. 7 ; 61. 8 ; 104. 33, I will sing *p.*
Neh. 9. 5, above all blessing and *p.*
Ps. 22. 3, that inhabitest the *p.* of Israel.
25, my *p.* shall be of thee.
33. 1 ; 147. 1, *p.* is comely for the upright.
34. 1, his *p.* continually be in my mouth.
50. 23, whoso offereth *p.* glorifieth me.
65. 1, *p.* waiteth for thee.
66. 2, make his *p.* glorious.
109. 1, O God of my *p.*
148. 14, the *p.* of all his saints.
Prov. 27. 21, so is a man to his *p.*
Isa. 60. 18, call thy gates *P.*
61. 3, garment of *p.*
62. 7, a *p.* in the earth.
Jer. 13. 11, that they might be to me for a *p.*
49. 25, how is the city of *p.*
Hab. 3. 3, earth was full of his *p.*
Zeph. 3. 20, a *p.* among all people.
John 9. 24, give God the *p.*
12. 43, the *p.* of men.
Rom. 2. 29, whose *p.* is not of men.
13. 3, thou shalt have *p.*
1 Cor. 4. 5, every man have *p.* of God.
2 Cor. 8. 18, whose *p.* is in the gospel.
Eph. 1. 6, 12, *p.* of glory of his grace.
Phil. 4. 8, if there be any *p.*
Heb. 13. 15, offer sacrifice of *p.*
1 Pet. 2. 14, *p.* of them that do well.
4. 11, to whom be *p.* and dominion.
See 2 Chron. 29. 30 ; Acts 16. 25 ; 1 Pet. 2. 9.

PRAISE (*v.*). Gen. 49. 8, whom thy brethren shall *p.*
2 Sam. 14. 25, none to be so much *p.*
Ps. 30. 9, shall the dust *p.* thee?
42. 5, 11 ; 43. 5, I shall yet *p.* him.
45. 17, therefore shall the people *p.* thee.
49. 18, men will *p.* thee when thou doest well.
63. 3, my lips shall *p.* thee.
67. 3, 5, let the people *p.* thee.
71. 14, I will yet *p.* thee more and more.
72. 15, daily shall he be *p.*
76. 10, the wrath of man shall *p.* thee.
88. 10, shall the dead arise and *p.* thee?
107. 32, *p.* him in the assembly.
115. 17, the dead *p.* not.
119. 164, seven times a day do I *p.* thee.
145. 4, one generation shall *p.* thy works.
10, all thy works shall *p.* thee.
Prov. 27. 2, let another *p.* thee.
31. 31, her own works *p.* her in the gates.
Isa. 38. 19, the living shall *p.* thee.
See Lu. 2. 13 ; 24. 53 ; Acts 2. 47 ; 3. 8.
PRANCING. Judg. 5. 22 ; Nah. 3. 2.
PRATING. Prov. 10. 8 ; 3 John 10.
PRAY. Gen. 20. 7, a prophet and shall *p.* for thee.
1 Sam. 7. 5, I will *p.* for you to the Lord.
12. 23, sin in ceasing to *p.* for you.
2 Chron. 7. 14, if my people shall *p.*
Ezra 6. 10, *p.* for the life of the king.
Job 21. 15, what profit if we *p.* to him.
Ps. 5. 2, to thee will I *p.*
55. 17, evening, morning, and at noon will I *p.*
122. 6, *p.* for the peace of Jerusalem.
Isa. 45. 20, *p.* to a god that cannot save.
Jer. 7. 16 ; 11. 14 ; 14. 11, *p.* not for this people.
37. 3 ; 42. 2, 20, *p.* now to the Lord for us.
Zech. 7. 2, they sent men to *p.*
Mat. 5. 44, and *p.* for them which despitefully
use you.
6. 5, they love to *p.* standing.
14. 23 ; Mk. 6. 46 ; Lu. 6. 12 ; 9. 28, apart to *p.*
26. 36 ; Mk. 14. 32, while I *p.* yonder.
Mk. 11. 25, and when ye stand *p.*, forgive.
Lu. 11. 1, Lord, teach us to *p.*
18. 1, men ought always to *p.*
John 14. 16 ; 16. 26, I will *p.* the Father.
17. 9, I *p.* for them, I *p.* not for the world.
20, neither *p.* I for these alone.
Acts 9. 11, behold he *p.*
Rom. 8. 26, know not what we should *p.* for.
1 Cor. 14. 15, I will *p.* with the spirit, and *p.* with
understanding also.
Eph. 6. 18, *p.* always with all prayer.
1 Thess. 5. 17, *p.* without ceasing.
1 Tim. 2. 8, that men *p.* everywhere.
Jas. 5. 13, is any afflicted? let him *p.*
16, *p.* one for another.
1 John 5. 16, I do not say he shall *p.* for it.
See Lu. 9. 29 ; 1 Cor. 11. 4 ; 14. 14 ; 1 Thess. 5. 25.
PRAYER. 2 Chron. 7. 15, ears shall be attent to
the *p.*
Job 15. 4, thou restrainest *p.*
16. 17 ; Ps. 4. 1 ; 5. 3 ; 6. 9 ; 17. 1 ; 35. 13 ; 39. 12 ;
66. 19 ; Lam. 3. 8, my *p.*
Ps. 65. 2, thou that hearest *p.*
72. 15, *p.* shall be made continually.
109. 4, I give myself to *p.*
Prov. 15. 8, the *p.* of the upright.
Isa. 1. 15, when ye make many *p.*
56. 7 ; Mat. 21. 13 ; Mk. 11. 17 ; Lu. 19. 46, house
of *p.*
Mat. 21. 22, whatever ye ask in *p.*, believing.
23. 14 ; Mk. 12. 40 ; Lu. 20. 47, long *p.*
Lu. 6. 12, all night in *p.* to God.
Acts 3. 1, the hour of *p.*
6. 4, give ourselves continually to *p.*
12. 5, *p.* was made without ceasing.
16. 13, where *p.* was wont to be made.
Phil. 4. 6, in everything by *p.*
Jas. 5. 15, *p.* of faith shall save the sick.
16, effectual fervent *p.* of a righteous man.

1 Pet. 4. 7, watch unto *p.*
Rev. 5. 8 ; 8. 3, the *p.* of the saints.
See Ps. 72. 20 ; Dan. 9. 21 ; Rom. 12. 12 ; Col. 4. 2.
PREACH. Neh. 6. 7, appointed prophets to *p.* of
thee.
Isa. 61. 1, to *p.* good tidings.
Jonah 3. 2, *p.* the preaching I bid thee.
Mat. 4. 17 ; 10. 7, Jesus began to *p.*
11. 1, to *p.* in their cities.
5, the poor have the gospel *p.*
Mk. 2. 2, he *p.* the word to them.
16. 20, and *p.* everywhere.
Lu. 9. 60, go thou and *p.* kingdom of God.
Acts 8. 5, and *p.* Christ unto them.
10. 36, *p.* peace by Jesus Christ.
13. 38, through this man is *p.* forgiveness.
17. 18, he *p.* Jesus and the resurrection.
Rom. 2. 21, thou that *p.* a man should not steal.
10. 15, how shall they *p.* except.
1 Cor. 1. 18, the *p.* of the cross is foolishness.
21, by the foolishness of *p.*
23, but we *p.* Christ crucified.
9. 27, lest when I have *p.* to others.
15. 11, so we *p.* and so ye believed.
14, then is our *p.* vain.
2 Cor. 4. 5, we *p.* not ourselves.
Phil. 1. 15, some *p.* Christ of envy and strife.
2 Tim. 4. 2, *p.* the word ; be instant.
Heb. 4. 2, word *p.* did not profit.
1 Pet. 3. 19, *p.* to spirits in prison.
See Ps. 40. 9 ; 2 Cor. 11. 4 ; Gal. 1. 8 ; Eph. 2. 17.
PREACHER. Rom. 10. 14, how shall they hear
without a *p.* ?
1 Tim. 2. 7, whereunto I am ordained a *p.*
2 Pet. 2. 5, Noah, a *p.* of righteousness.
See Eccl. 1. 1 ; 7. 27 ; 12. 8 ; 2 Tim. 1. 11.
PRECEPT. Neh. 9. 14, commandedst them *p.*
Isa. 28, 10, 13, *p.* must be upon *p.*
29. 13, taught by *p.* of men.
Jer. 35. 18, ye have kept Jonadab's *p.*
See Ps. 119. 4, etc. ; Dan. 9. 5 ; Mk. 10. 5 ; Heb.
9. 19.
PRECIOUS. Deut. 33. 13, 14, 15, 16, *p.* things.
1 Sam. 3. 1, the word was *p.* in those days.
26. 21, my soul was *p.* in thine eyes.
2 Kings 1. 13, let my life be *p.*
Ezra 8. 27, fine copper, *p.* as gold.
Ps. 49. 8, the redemption of their soul is *p.*
72. 14, *p.* shall their blood be in his sight.
116. 15, in sight of the Lord is death of saints.
126. 6, bearing *p.* seed.
133. 2, like *p.* ointment upon the head.
139. 17, how *p.* are thy thoughts.
Prov. 3. 15, wisdom more *p.* than rubies.
Eccl. 7. 1, good name better than *p.* ointment.
Isa. 13. 12, I will make a man more *p.*
28. 16 ; 1 Pet. 2. 6, a *p.* corner stone.
43. 4, since thou wast *p.* in my sight.
Jer. 15. 19, take the *p.* from the vile.
Lam. 4. 2, the *p.* sons of Zion.
1 Pet. 1. 7, trial of faith more *p.* than gold.
19, the *p.* blood of Christ.
2. 7, to you which believe he is *p.*
2 Pet. 1. 1, like *p.* faith.
4, great and *p.* promises.
See Mat. 26. 7 ; Mk. 14. 3 ; Jas. 5. 7 ; Rev. 21. 11.
PREEMINENCE. Eccl. 3. 19 ; Col. 1. 18 ; 3 John 9.
PREFER. Ps. 137. 6 ; John 1. 15 ; Rom. 12. 10 ;
1 Tim. 5. 21.
PREMEDITATE. Mk. 13. 11.
PREPARATION. Prov. 16. 1, *p.* of the heart.
Eph. 6. 15, feet shod with *p.* of gospel.
See Mat. 27. 62 ; Mk. 15. 42 ; Lu. 23. 54 ; John 19. 14.
PREPARE. 1 Sam. 7. 3, *p.* your hearts to the
Lord.
2 Chron. 20. 33, as yet the people had not *p.*
Ps. 68. 10, thou hast *p.* of thy goodness.
107. 36, that they may *p.* a city.
Prov. 8. 27, when he *p.* the heavens I was there.

Isa. 40. 3; Mal. 3. 1; Mat. 3. 3; Mk. 1. 2; Lu. 1. 76,
  p. way of the Lord.
62. 10, *p.* the way of the people.
Amos 4. 12, *p.* to meet thy God.
Jonah 1. 17, Lord had *p.* a great fish.
Mat. 20. 23; Mk. 10. 40, to them for whom *p.*
John 14. 2, I go to *p.* a place for you.
Rom. 9. 23, afore *p.* to glory.
1 Cor. 2. 9, things God hath *p.*
Heb. 10. 5, a body hast thou *p.* me.
See 1 Chron. 22. 5; Ps. 23. 5; Rev. 21. 2.

PRESCRIBE. Ezra 7. 22; Isa. 10. 1.

PRESENCE. Gen. 4. 16, Cain went out from the *p.*
  of the Lord.
47. 15, why should we die in thy *p.*
Ex. 33. 15, if thy *p.* go not with me.
Job 23. 15, I am troubled at his *p.*
Ps. 16. 11, in thy *p.* is fulness of joy.
17. 2, my sentence come forth from thy *p.*
31. 20, in the secret of thy *p.*
51. 11, cast me not away from thy *p.*
139. 7, whither shall I flee from thy *p.?*
Prov. 14. 7, go from *p.* of a foolish man.
Isa. 63. 9, angel of his *p.* saved them.
Jer. 23. 39; 52. 3, I will cast you out of my *p.*
Jonah 1. 3, to flee from *p.* of the Lord.
Zeph. 1. 7, hold thy peace at *p.* of the Lord.
Lu. 13. 26, we have eaten and drunk in thy *p.*
Acts 3. 19, times of refreshing from the *p.*
2 Cor. 10. 1, 10, who in *p.* am base.
2 Thess. 1. 9, destruction from the *p.* of the Lord.
See Gen. 16. 12; Ps. 23. 5; Prov. 25. 6; Lu. 15. 10.

PRESENT. 1 Sam. 10. 27, they brought him no *p.*
Ps. 46. 1, a very *p.* help in trouble.
John 14. 25, being yet *p.* with you.
Acts 10. 33, all here in *p.* before God.
Rom. 7. 18, to will is *p.* with me.
21, evil is *p.* with me.
8. 18, sufferings of this *p.* time.
12. 1, *p.* your bodies a living sacrifice
1 Cor. 7. 26, good for the *p.* distress.
2 Cor. 5. 8, to be *p.* with the Lord.
9, whether *p.* or absent.
Gal. 1. 4, deliver us from this *p.* world.
Col. 1. 28, *p.* every man perfect.
2 Tim. 4. 10, having loved this *p.* world.
Tit. 2. 12, live godly in this *p.* world.
Heb. 12. 11, no chastening for *p.* seemeth joyous.
2 Pet. 1. 12, established in the *p.* truth.
Jude 24, able to *p.* you faultless.
See Ps. 72. 10; Mat. 2. 11; Lu. 2. 22.

PRESENTLY. Prov. 12. 16; Mat. 21. 19; 26. 53.

PRESERVE. Gen. 32. 30, I have seen God, and
  my life is *p.*
45. 5, did send me before you to *p.* life.
Job 29. 2, as in days when God *p.* me.
Ps. 36. 6, thou *p.* man and beast.
121. 7, the Lord *p.* thee from evil.
8, *p.* thy going out and coming in.
Prov. 2. 8, he *p.* the way of his saints.
11, discretion shall *p.* thee.
20. 28, mercy and truth *p.* the king.
Jer. 49. 11, I will *p.* them alive.
Lu. 17. 33, lose his life shall *p.* it.
See Neh. 9. 6; Isa. 49. 6; Hos. 12. 13; Jude 1.

PRESS. Prov. 3. 10, *p.* burst with new wine.
Amos 2. 13, I am *p.* under you as a cart is *p.*
Mk. 3. 10, they *p.* on him to touch him.
Lu. 6. 38, good measure, *p.* down.
16. 16, every man *p.* into it.
Phil. 3. 14, I *p.* toward the mark.
See Mk. 2. 4; 5. 27; Lu. 8. 19; 19. 3.

PRESUME. Deut. 18. 20; Esth. 7. 5.

PRESUMPTUOUS. Num. 15. 30; Ps. 19. 13; 2 Pet.
  2. 10.

PRETENCE. Mat. 23. 14; Mk. 12. 40; Phil. 1. 18.

PREVAIL. Gen. 32. 28; Hos. 12. 4, power with
  God, and hast *p.*
Ex. 17. 11, Moses held up hand, Israel *p.*

1 Sam. 2. 9, by strength shall no man *p.*
Ps. 9. 19, let not man *p.*
65. 3, iniquities *p.* against me.
Eccl. 4. 12, if one *p.* against him.
Mat. 16. 18, gates of hell shall not *p.*
Acts 19. 20, grew word of God and *p.*
See Job 14. 20; Jer. 20. 7; Lam. 1. 16; John 12. 19.

PREVENT. 2 Sam. 22. 6; Ps. 18. 5, snares of death
  p. me.
Ps. 88. 13, in the morning shall my prayer *p.*
  thee.
119. 147, I *p.* the dawning of the morning.
See Ps. 21. 3; 79. 8; Isa. 21. 14; 1 Thess. 4. 15.

PREY. Isa. 49. 24, shall the *p.* be taken from the
  mighty?
Jer. 21. 9; 38. 2; 39. 18; 45. 5, his life shall be for
  a *p.*
Ezek. 34. 22, my flock shall no more be a *p.*
See Gen. 49. 9; Num. 14. 3; Neh. 4. 4; Amos 3. 4.

PRICE. Lev. 25. 52, the *p.* of his redemption.
2 Sam. 24. 24; 1 Chron. 21. 22, I will buy it at a *p.*
Acts 5. 2, kept back part of the *p.*
1 Cor. 6. 20; 7. 23, bought with a *p.*
1 Pet. 3. 4, meek spirit of great *p.*
See Deut. 23. 18; Prov. 31. 10; Zech. 11. 12.

PRICKS. Num. 33. 55; Acts 9. 5; 26. 14.

PRIDE. Ps. 31. 20, hide them from *p.* of man.
Prov. 8. 13, *p.* do I hate.
14. 3, in mouth of foolish is rod of *p.*
Isa. 28. 1, woe to the crown of *p.*
Jer. 49. 16, *p.* of thine heart hath deceived thee.
See Mk. 7. 22; 1 Tim. 3. 6; 1 John 2. 16.

PRIEST. Lev. 14. 18; Heb. 7. 1, *p.* of most high
  God.
Ex. 19. 6, a kingdom of *p.*
1 Sam. 2. 35, I will raise up a faithful *p.*
2 Chron. 6. 41; Ps. 132. 16, *p.* clothed with sal-
  vation.
13. 9, *p.* of them that are no gods.
15. 3, without a teaching *p.*
Isa. 24. 2, as with the people, so with the *p.*
28. 7, *p.* and prophet have erred.
61. 6, shall be named the *p.* of the Lord.
Jer. 13. 13, will fill *p.* with drunkenness.
Mic. 3. 11, the *p.* teach for hire.
Mal. 2. 7, the *p.* lips should keep knowledge.
Lu. 17. 14, show yourselves to the *p.*
Acts 6. 7, *p.* were obedient to the faith.
Rev. 1. 6; 5. 10; 20. 6, kings and *p.* to God.
See Heb. 2. 17; 3. 1; 4. 15; 7. 26.

PRIESTHOOD. Ex. 40. 15; Num. 25. 13, an everlasting *p.*
Num. 16. 10, seek ye the *p.* also.
Heb. 7. 24, an unchangeable *p.*
1 Pet. 2. 5, an holy *p.*
9, ye are a royal *p.*
See Num. 18. 1; Josh. 18. 7; Neh. 13. 29.

PRINCE. Gen. 32. 28, as a *p.* hast thou power.
Ex. 2. 14; Num. 16. 13, who made thee a *p.* over
  us?
1 Sam. 2. 8; Ps. 113. 8, to set them among *p.*
2 Sam. 3. 38, a *p.* fallen in Israel.
Job 12. 21; Ps. 107. 40, poureth contempt on *p.*
21. 28, where is the house of the *p.?*
31. 37, as a *p.* would I go near him.
Ps. 45. 16, make *p.* in all the earth.
118. 9, than to put confidence in *p.*
146. 3, put not your trust in *p.*
Prov. 8. 15, by me *p.* decree justice.
31. 4, nor for *p.* strong drink.
Eccl. 10. 7, *p.* walking as servants.
16, when thy *p.* eat in the morning.
17, blessed when *p.* eat in due season.
Isa. 34. 12; 40. 23, all her *p.* shall be nothing.
Hos. 3. 4, abide many days without a *p.*
Mat. 9. 34; 12. 24; Mk. 3. 22, by *p.* of devils.
John 12. 31; 14. 30; 16. 11, the *p.* of this world.
Acts 3. 15, and killed the *P.* of life.
5. 31, exalted to be a *P.* and Saviour.

1 Cor. 2. 6, wisdom of the *p.* of this world.
8, which none of *p.* of this world knew.
Eph. 2. 2, the *p.* of the power of the air.
See Isa. 3. 4; Hos. 7. 5; Mat. 20. 25.
PRINCIPAL. Prov. 4. 7; Isa. 28. 25; Acts 25. 23.
PRINCIPALITY. Eph. 6. 12, we wrestle against *p.* and powers.
Tit. 3. 1, to be subject to *p.*
See Rom. 8. 38; Eph. 1. 21; 3. 10; Col. 1. 16.
PRINCIPLES. Heb. 5. 12; 6. 1.
PRINT. Lev. 19. 28; Job 13. 27; 19. 23; John 20. 25.
PRISON. Ps. 142. 7, bring my soul out of *p.*
Eccl. 4. 14, out of *p.* he cometh to reign.
Isa. 53. 8, taken from *p.* and from judgment.
61. 1, opening of the *p.*
Mat. 5. 25; Lu. 12. 58, thou be cast into *p.*
11. 2, John heard in the *p.*
25. 36, 39, in *p.* and ye came unto me.
Lu. 22. 33, to go with thee to *p.* and to death.
2 Cor. 11. 23, in *p.* more frequent.
1 Pet. 3. 19, spirits in *p.*
See Jer. 32. 2; 39. 14; Lu. 3. 20; Acts 5. 18.
PRISONER. Ps. 79. 11; Zech. 9. 12; Mat. 27. 16; Eph. 3. 1.
PRIVATE. 2 Pet. 1. 20.
PRIVATELY. Mat. 24. 3; Mk. 9. 28; Lu. 10. 23; Gal. 2. 2.
PRIVILY. Mat. 1. 19; 2. 7; Acts 16. 37; Gal. 2. 4; 2 Pet. 2. 1.
PRIZE. 1 Cor. 9. 24; Phil. 3. 14.
PROCEED. Gen. 24. 50, the thing *p.* from the Lord.
Deut. 8. 3; Mat. 4. 4, that *p.* out of mouth of God.
Job 40. 5, I will *p.* no further.
Isa. 29. 14, I will *p.* to do a marvellous work.
51. 4, a law shall *p.* from me.
Jer. 9. 3, they *p.* from evil to evil.
Mat. 15. 18; Mk. 7. 21, *p.* out of the mouth.
John 8. 42, I *p.* forth from God.
Jas. 3. 10, *p.* blessing and cursing.
See Lu. 4. 22; John 15. 26; Eph. 4. 29; Rev. 22. 1.
PROCLAIM. Ex. 33. 19; 34. 5, I will *p.* the name of the Lord.
Isa. 61. 1, to *p.* liberty to captives.
2, to *p.* acceptable year.
62. 11, Lord hath *p.*, thy salvation cometh.
Jer. 34. 15, in *p.* liberty every man to his neighbour.
Lu. 12. 3, *p.* upon the housetops.
See Deut. 20. 10; Prov. 20. 6; Jer. 3. 12; Joel 3. 9.
PROCURE. Prov. 11. 27; Jer. 2. 17; 4. 18; 26. 19; 33. 9.
PRODUCE. Isa. 41. 21.
PROFANE. Lev. 18. 21; 19. 12; 20. 3; 21. 6; 22. 2, *p.* name of God.
Jer. 23. 11, prophet and priest are *p.*
Ezek. 22. 26, no difference between holy and *p.*
Mat. 12. 5, priests in temple *p.* sabbath.
Acts 24. 6, hath gone about to *p.* temple.
1 Tim. 1. 9, law for unholy and *p.*
4. 7, refuse *p.* and old wives' fables.
6. 20; 2 Tim. 2. 16, avoiding *p.* babblings.
Heb. 12. 16, any *p.* person.
See Ps. 89. 39; Jer. 23. 15; Mal. 1. 12; 2. 10.
PROFESS. Rom. 1. 22; 2 Cor. 9. 13; 1 Tim. 2. 10; 6. 12.
PROFIT (*n.*). Gen. 25. 32, what *p.* shall birthright do me?
37. 26, what *p.* if we slay?
Job 21. 15, what *p.* if we pray?
Prov. 14. 23, in all labour there is *p.*
Eccl. 1. 3; 3. 9; 5. 16, what *p.* of labour?
2. 11, there was no *p.* under the sun.
5. 9, *p.* of the earth for all.
7. 11, by wisdom there is *p.*
Jer. 16. 19, things wherein is no *p.*
Mal. 3. 14, what *p.* that we have kept.
1 Cor. 10. 33, not seeking own *p.*, but *p.* of many.

2 Tim. 2. 14, about words to no *p.*
Heb. 12. 10, he chasteneth us for our *p.*
See Esth. 3. 8; Ps. 30. 9; Isa. 30. 5; 1 Tim. 4. 15.
PROFIT (*v.*). 1 Sam. 12. 21, vain things which cannot *p.*
Job 33. 27, I have sinned, and it *p.* not.
34. 9, *p.* nothing to delight in God.
Prov. 10. 2, treasures of wickedness *p.* nothing.
11. 4, riches *p.* not in the day of wrath.
Isa. 30. 5, 6, people that could not *p.*
48. 17, the Lord which teacheth thee to *p.*
Jer. 2. 11, changed for that which doth not *p.*
23. 32, they shall not *p.* this people.
Mat. 16. 26; Mk. 8. 36, what is a man *p.*?
1 Cor. 12. 7, to every man to *p.* withal.
Gal. 5. 2, Christ shall *p.* you nothing.
1 Tim. 4. 8, bodily exercise *p.* little.
Heb. 4. 2, the word preached did not *p.*
See Mat. 15. 5; Rom. 2. 25; 1 Cor. 13. 3; Jas. 2. 14.
PROFITABLE. Job 22. 2, can a man be *p.* to God?
Eccl. 10. 10, wisdom is *p.* to direct.
Acts 20. 20, I kept back nothing *p.*
1 Tim. 4. 8, godliness is *p.* to all things.
2 Tim. 3. 16, scripture is *p.* for doctrine.
See Mat. 5. 29; 2 Tim. 4. 11; Tit. 3. 8; Philem. 11.
PROLONG. Deut. 4. 26; 30. 18, ye shall not *p.* your days.
Job 6. 11, what is mine end that I should *p.* my life?
Prov. 10. 27, fear of the Lord *p.* days.
Eccl. 8. 12, though a sinner's days be *p.*
See Ps. 61. 6; Prov. 28. 2; Isa. 13. 22; 53. 10.
PROMISE (*n.*). Num. 14. 34, ye shall know my breach of *p.*
1 Kings 8. 56, hath not failed one word of *p.*
Ps. 77. 8, doth his *p.* fail?
Lu. 24. 49; Acts 1. 4, *p.* of Father.
Acts 2. 39, the *p.* is to you and your children.
26. 6, for hope of the *p.*
Rom. 4. 14, the *p.* made of none effect.
20, staggered not at the *p.*
9. 4, to whom pertain the *p.*
8; Gal. 4. 28, the children of the *p.*
2 Cor. 1. 20, *p.* are yea and Amen.
Gal. 3. 21, is the law against the *p.* of God?
1 Tim. 4. 8; 2 Tim. 1. 1, *p.* of the life that now is.
Heb. 6. 12, through faith and patience inherit the *p.*
9. 15; 10. 36, the *p.* of eternal inheritance.
11. 13, died, not having received *p.*
2 Pet. 1. 4, great and precious *p.*
3. 4, where is the *p.* of his coming?
9, not slack concerning his *p.*
See Eph. 1. 13; 2. 12; 6. 2; Heb. 4. 1; 11. 9.
PROMISE (*v.*). Ex. 12. 25, will give you as he hath *p.*
Num. 14. 40, will go to place the Lord *p.*
Deut. 1. 11; 15. 6, the Lord bless you as he hath *p.*
9. 28, not able to bring into land *p.*
19. 8; 27. 3, give the land he *p.* to give.
Josh. 23. 15, all good things which the Lord *p.*
2 Kings 8. 19; 2 Chron. 21. 7, he *p.* to give him a light.
Mk. 14. 11, they *p.* to give him money.
Rom. 4. 21, what he *p.* he was able to perform.
Heb. 10. 23; 11. 11, he is faithful that *p.*
1 John 2. 25, he hath *p.* eternal life.
See 1 Kings 8. 24; Neh. 9. 15; Ezek. 13. 22.
PROMOTE. Num. 22. 17; 24. 11; Prov. 4. 8.
PROMOTION. Ps. 75. 6; Prov. 3. 35.
PRONOUNCE. Judg. 12. 6; Jer. 34. 5.
PROOF. 2 Cor. 2. 9; 8. 24; 13. 3; Phil. 2. 22; 2 Tim. 4. 5.
PROPER. 1 Chron. 29. 3; 1 Cor. 7. 7; Heb. 11. 23.
PROPHECY. 1 Cor. 13. 8, whether *p.*, shall fail.
2 Pet. 1. 19, sure word of *p.*
21, *p.* came not in old time.
Rev. 1. 3; 22. 7, the words of this *p.*
See Neh. 6. 12; Prov. 31. 1; 1 Tim. 4. 14.

PROPHESY. Num. 11. 25, they *p.* and did not
 cease.
2 Chron. 18. 7, he never *p.* good to me.
Isa. 30. 10, *p.* not to us right things.
Jer. 5. 31, prophets *p.* falsely.
 14. 14 ; 23. 25, prophets *p.* lies.
 28. 9, the prophet which *p.* of peace.
Ezek. 37. 9, *p.* to the wind.
Joel 2. 28 ; Acts 2. 17, your sons shall *p.*
Amos 3. 8, who can but *p.*
 7. 13, *p.* not again any more.
Mic. 2. 11, I will *p.* of wine.
Mat. 26. 68 ; Mk. 14. 65 ; Lu. 22. 64, *p.*, thou Christ.
Rom. 12. 6, let us *p.* according to the proportion.
1 Cor. 13. 9, we *p.* in part.
 14. 39, covet to *p.*
1 Thess. 5. 20, despise not *p.*
 See Amos 2. 12 ; 1 Cor. 11. 5 ; Rev. 10. 11 ; 11. 3.

PROPHET. Ex. 7. 1, Aaron shall be thy *p.*
Num. 11. 29, would all Lord's people were *p.*
 12. 6, if there be a *p.* among you.
Deut. 13. 1, if there arise a *p.* or dreamer.
 18. 15 ; Acts 3. 22 ; 7. 37, the Lord will raise
  up a *P.*
 34. 10, there arose not a *p.* like Moses.
1 Sam. 10. 12 ; 19. 24, is Saul among *p.*?
1 Kings 13. 11, there dwelt an old *p.* in Beth-el.
 18. 22, I only remain a *p.*
 22. 7 ; 2 Kings 3. 11, is there not a *p.* besides?
2 Kings 5. 8, he shall know there is a *p.*
1 Chron. 16. 22 ; Ps. 105. 15, do my *p.* no harm.
2 Chron. 20. 20, believe his *p.*, so shall ye prosper.
Ps. 74. 9, there is no more any *p.*
Isa. 3. 2, the Lord taketh away the *p.*
Jer. 29. 26, mad, and maketh himself a *p.*
 37. 19, where are now your *p.*?
Ezek. 2. 5 ; 33. 33, there hath been a *p.* among
  them.
Hos. 9. 7, the *p.* is a fool.
Amos 7. 14, I was no *p.*, nor *p.* son.
Zech. 1. 5, the *p.*, do they live for ever?
Mat. 7. 15, beware of false *p.*
 10. 41, that receiveth a *p.* in name of a *p.*
 13. 57 ; Mk. 6. 4 ; Lu. 4. 24 ; John 4. 44, a *p.* not
  without honour.
 23. 29 ; Lu. 11. 47, ye build the tombs of the *p.*
Lu. 1. 76, be called the *p.* of the Highest.
 7. 16, a great *p.* is risen.
 28, not a greater *p.* than John.
 39, if he were a *p.* would have known.
 13. 33, it cannot be that a *p.* perish out of.
 24. 19, Jesus, who was a *p.* mighty.
John 4. 19, I perceive thou art a *p.*
 7. 40, of a truth this is the *P.*
 52, out of Galilee ariseth no *p.*
Acts 26. 27, believest thou the *p.*?
1 Cor. 12. 29, are all *p.*?
 14. 37, if any man think himself a *p.*
Eph. 2. 20, built on foundation of *p.*
 4. 11, he gave some *p.*
1 Pet. 1. 10, of which salvation the *p.* enquired.
Rev. 22. 9, I am of thy brethren the *p.*
 See 1 Kings 20. 35 ; Neh. 6. 14 ; 1 Cor. 14. 32.

PROPORTION. 1 Kings 7. 36 ; Job 41. 12 ; Rom.
 12. 6.

PROSPER. Gen. 24. 56, the Lord hath *p.* my way.
 39. 3, the Lord made all Joseph did to *p.*
Num. 14. 41, transgress, but it shall not *p.*
Deut. 28. 29, thou shalt not *p.* in thy ways.
1 Chron. 22. 11, *p.* thou, and build.
2 Chron. 20. 20, believe, so shall ye *p.*
 26. 5, God made him to *p.*
Ezra 5. 8, this work *p.* in their hands.
Neh. 2. 20, the God of heaven will *p.* us.
Job 9. 4, who hardened himself and *p.*
Ps. 1. 3, whatsoever he doeth shall *p.*
 37. 7, fret not because of him who *p.*
 73. 12, the ungodly who *p.* in the world.
 122. 6, they shall *p.* that love thee.
Prov. 28. 13, he that covereth sins shall not *p.*

Eccl. 11. 6, knowest not whether shall *p.*
Isa. 53. 10, pleasure of the Lord shall *p.*
 54. 17, no weapon against thee shall *p.*
 55. 11, it shall *p.* in the thing.
Jer. 2. 37, thou shalt not *p.* in them.
 12. 1, wherefore doth way of wicked *p.*?
 22. 30, no man of his seed shall *p.*
Ezek. 17. 9, 10, shall it *p.*?
 15, shall he *p.*, shall he escape?
1 Cor. 16. 2, lay by as God hath *p.* him.
3 John 2, in health, even as thy soul *p.*
 See Prov. 17. 8 ; Dan. 6. 28 ; 8. 12.

PROSPERITY. Deut. 23. 6, thou shalt not seek
  their *p.*
1 Sam. 25. 6, say to him that liveth in *p.*
Job 15. 21, in *p.* the destroyer shall come.
Ps. 30. 6, in my *p.* I said, I shall never.
 73. 3, when I saw the *p.* of the wicked.
Prov. 1. 32, *p.* of fools shall destroy them.
Eccl. 7. 14, in day of *p.* be joyful.
Jer. 22. 21, I spake to thee in thy *p.*
 See 1 Kings 10. 7 ; Job 36. 11 ; Ps. 35. 27 ; 122. 7.

PROSPEROUS. Gen. 39. 2, he was a *p.* man.
Josh. 1. 8, then thou shalt make thy way *p.*
Job 8. 6, make habitation of thy righteousness *p.*
Zech. 8. 12, the seed shall be *p.*
 See Gen. 24. 21 ; Judg. 18. 5 ; 2 Chr. 7. 11 ; Rom. 1. 10.

PROTECTION. Deut. 32. 38.

PROTEST. Gen. 43. 3 ; Jer. 11. 7 ; Zech. 3. 6 ; 1 Cor.
 15. 31.

PROUD. Job 38. 11, here shall thy *p.* waves be
  stayed.
 40. 11, every one that is *p.*, and abase him.
Ps. 31. 23, rewardeth the *p.* doer.
 40. 4, man that respecteth not the *p.*
 94. 2, render a reward to the *p.*
 101. 5, him that hath a *p.* heart will not I suffer.
 123. 4, soul filled with contempt of the *p.*
 138. 6, the *p.* he knoweth afar off.
Prov. 6. 17, the Lord hateth a *p.* look.
 15. 25, the Lord will destroy house of the *p.*
 16. 5, *p.* in heart is abomination.
 21. 4, a *p.* heart is sin.
Eccl. 7. 8, patient better than *p.* in spirit.
Hab. 2. 5, he is a *p.* man.
Mal. 3. 15, we call the *p.* happy.
Lu. 1. 51, scattered the *p.*
1 Tim. 6. 4, he is *p.*, knowing nothing.
Jas. 4. 6 ; 1 Pet. 5. 5. God resisteth the *p.*
 See Job 9. 13 ; 26. 12 ; Rom. 1. 30 ; 2 Tim. 3. 2.

PROUDLY. Ex. 18. 11 ; 1 Sam. 2. 3 ; Neh. 9. 10 ;
 Isa. 3. 5 ; Obad. 12.

PROVE. Ex. 15. 25, there he *p.* them.
Judg. 6. 39, let me *p.* thee but this once.
1 Sam. 17. 39, I have not *p.* them.
1 Kings 10. 1 ; 2 Chron. 9. 1, she came to *p.* Solomon.
Ps. 17. 3, thou hast *p.* mine heart.
 81. 7, I *p.* thee at the waters.
 95. 9 ; Heb. 3. 9, when your fathers *p.* me.
Mal. 3. 10, *p.* me now herewith.
Lu. 14. 19, I go to *p.* them.
2 Cor. 8. 22, whom we have often *p.* diligent.
 13. 5, *p.* your own selves.
1 Thess. 5. 21, *p.* all things.
 See Eccl. 2. 1 ; 7. 23 ; Dan. 1. 14 ; John 6. 6.

PROVERB. Deut. 28. 37, a *p.* and a byword.
Ps. 69. 11, I became a *p.* to them.
Eccl. 12. 9, set in order many *p.*
Ezek. 16. 44, every one that useth *p.*
Lu. 4. 23, will surely say this *p.*
John 16. 29, speakest plainly, and no *p.*
 See Num. 21. 27 ; 1 Sam. 10. 12 ; Prov. 1. 6.

PROVIDE. Gen. 22. 8, God will *p.* himself a lamb.
 30. 30, when shall I *p.* for mine own house?
Ps. 78. 20, can he *p.* flesh?
Mat. 10. 9, *p.* neither gold nor silver.
Lu. 12. 20, whose shall those things be thou
  hast *p.*?

Lu. 12. 33, *p.* bags that wax not old.
Rom. 12. 17 ; 2 Cor. 8. 21, *p.* things honest.
1 Tim. 5. 8, if any *p.* not for his own.
Heb. 11. 40, having *p.* better thing for us.
See Job 38. 41; Prov. 6. 8 ; Acts 23. 24.

PROVIDENCE. Acts 24. 2.
PROVISION. Gen. 42. 25 ; 45. 21, *p.* for the way.
Ps. 132. 15, I will abundantly bless her *p.*
Rom. 13. 14, make not *p.* for the flesh.
See Josh. 9. 5 ; 1 Kings 4. 7 ; 2 Kings 6. 23.

PROVOCATION. Job 17. 2 ; Ps. 95. 8 ; Ezek. 20. 28.
PROVOKE. Ex. 23. 21, obey his voice and *p.* him not.
Num. 14. 11, how long will this people *p.* me ?
Deut. 31. 20, *p.* me and break my covenant.
Job 12. 6, they that *p.* God are secure.
Ps. 106. 7, they *p.* him at the sea.
29, they *p.* him with their inventions.
Lu. 11. 53, began to urge and *p.* him to speak.
Rom. 10. 19 ; 11. 11, I will *p.* to jealousy.
1 Cor. 13. 5, is not easily *p.*
Gal. 5. 26, *p.* one another.
Eph. 6. 4, *p.* not your children to wrath.
Heb. 10. 24, to *p.* to love and good works.
See Prov. 20. 2 ; Isa. 65. 3 ; Jer. 7. 19 ; 44. 8.

PRUDENCE. 2 Chron. 2. 12 ; Prov. 8. 12 ; Eph. 1. 8.
PRUDENT. Prov. 12. 16, a *p.* man covereth shame.
23, a *p.* man concealeth knowledge.
14. 15, the *p.* looketh well to his going.
16. 21, wise in heart called *p.*
19. 14, *p.* wife is from the Lord.
22. 3 ; 27. 12, *p.* man foreseeth evil.
Isa. 5. 21, woe unto them that are *p.* in their own sight.
Jer. 49. 7, counsel perished from *p.*
Hos. 14. 9, who is *p.* ?
Mat. 11. 25 ; Lu. 10. 21, hast hid things from *p.*
See Isa. 52. 13 ; Amos 5. 13 ; Acts 13. 7.

PRUNE. Lev. 25. 3 ; Isa. 2. 4 ; Joel 3. 10 ; Mic. 4. 3.
PSALTERY. Dan. 3. 5, the sound of the cornet, flute, *p.*, etc.
See 2 Sam. 6. 5 ; 2 Chron. 9. 11.

PUBLIC. Mat. 1. 19 ; Acts 18. 28 ; 20. 20.
PUBLISH. Deut. 32. 3, I will *p.* the name of the Lord.
2 Sam. 1. 20, *p.* it not in Askelon.
Ps. 68. 11, great was the company that *p.* it.
Isa. 52. 7 ; Nah. 1. 15, that *p.* peace.
Mk. 1. 45 ; 5. 20, he began to *p.* it much.
Lu. 8. 39, *p.* throughout the whole city.
See Esth. 1. 20 ; 3. 14 ; Jonah 3. 7 ; Mk. 13. 10.

PUFFED. 1 Cor. 4. 6 ; 5. 2 ; 13. 4 ; Col. 2. 18.
PUFFETH. Ps. 10. 5 ; 12. 5 ; 1 Cor. 8. 1.
PULL. Lam. 3. 11, *p.* me in pieces.
Amos 9. 15, shall no more be *p.* up.
Zech. 7. 11, they *p.* away the shoulder.
Mat. 7. 4 ; Lu. 6. 42, *p.* mote out of thine eye.
Lu. 12. 18, will *p.* down barns.
14. 5, will not *p.* him out on sabbath.
2 Cor. 10. 4, to the *p.* down of strong holds.
Jude 23, *p.* them out of the fire.
See Gen. 8. 9 ; Ezra 6. 11 ; Ps. 31. 4 ; Isa. 22. 19.

PULPIT. Neh. 8. 4.
PULSE. 2 Sam. 17. 28 ; Dan. 1. 12.
PUNISH. Ezra 9. 13, *p.* less than iniquities deserve.
Prov. 17. 26, to *p.* the just is not good.
Isa. 13. 11, I will *p.* the world for their evil.
26. 21, Lord cometh to *p.* inhabitants.
Jer. 13. 21, what wilt thou say when he *p.*
Acts 26. 11, I *p.* them in every synagogue.
2 Thess. 1. 9, with everlasting destruction.
2 Pet. 2. 9, to day of judgment to be *p.*
See Lev. 26. 18 ; Prov. 21. 11 ; 22. 3 ; 27. 12.

PUNISHMENT. Gen. 4. 13, my *p.* is greater than I can bear.
Lev. 26. 41, accept the *p.* of their iniquity.

1 Sam. 28. 10, no *p.* shall happen to thee.
Lam. 3. 39, a man for the *p.* of his sins.
4. 6, *p.* greater than *p.* of Sodom.
22, the *p.* is accomplished.
Ezek. 14. 10, shall bear *p.* of their iniquity.
Mat. 25. 46, everlasting *p.*
Heb. 10. 29, of how much sorer *p.*
1 Pet. 2. 14, the *p.* of evildoers.
See Prov. 19. 19 ; Amos 1. 3 ; 2. 1 ; 2 Cor. 2. 6.

PURCHASE. Ruth 4. 10, have I *p.* to be my wife.
Ps. 74. 2, congregation thou hast *p.*
Acts 1. 18, *p.* a field with reward of iniquity.
8. 20, gift of God *p.* by money.
20. 28, he hath *p.* with his own blood.
Eph. 1. 14, redemption of *p.* possession.
1 Tim. 3. 13, *p.* to themselves a good degree.
See Gen. 49. 32 ; Ex. 15. 16 ; Lev. 25. 33 ; Jer. 32. 11.

PURE. Deut. 32. 14, the *p.* blood of the grape.
2 Sam. 22. 27 ; Ps. 18. 26, with *p.* show thyself *p.*
Job 4. 17, shall man be more *p.* ?
8. 6, if thou wert *p.* and upright.
11. 4, my doctrine is *p.*
16. 17, my prayer is *p.*
25. 5, stars are not *p.* in his sight.
Ps. 12. 6, the words of the Lord are *p.*
19. 8, commandment of the Lord is *p.*
119. 140, thy word is very *p.*
Prov. 15. 26, words of the *p.* are pleasant.
20. 9, who can say, I am *p.* ?
Mic. 6. 11, shall I count them *p.* ?
Zeph. 3. 9, turn to the people a *p.* language.
Acts 20. 26, *p.* from blood of all men.
Rom. 14. 20, all things indeed are *p.*
Phil. 4. 8, whatsoever things are *p.*
1 Tim. 3. 9 ; 2 Tim. 1. 3, in a *p.* conscience.
5. 22, keep thyself *p.*
Tit. 1. 15, to the *p.* all things are *p.*
Jas. 1. 27, *p.* religion.
3. 17, first *p.*, then peaceable.
2 Pet. 3. 1, stir up your *p.* minds.
1 John 3. 3, even as he is *p.*
Rev. 22. 1, a *p.* river of water of life.
See Ex. 27. 20; Ezra 6. 20; Mal. 1. 11.

PURELY. Isa. 1. 25.
PURENESS. Job 22. 30 ; Prov. 22. 11 ; 2 Cor. 6. 6.
PURER. Lam. 4. 7 ; Hab. 1. 13.
PURGE. 2 Chron. 34. 8, when he had *p.* the land.
Ps. 51. 7, *p.* me with hyssop.
65. 3, transgressions, thou shalt *p.* them.
Isa. 1. 25, and purely *p.* away thy dross.
6. 7, thy sin is *p.*
22. 14, this iniquity shall not be *p.*
Ezek. 24. 13, I have *p.* thee and thou wast not *p.*
Mal. 3. 3, *p.* them as gold.
Mat. 3. 12 ; Lu. 3. 17, *p.* his floor.
John 15. 2, he *p.* it, that it may bring forth.
1 Cor. 5. 7, *p.* out the old leaven.
2 Tim. 2. 21, if a man *p.* himself from these.
Heb. 9. 14, *p.* your conscience.
22, all things are *p.* with blood.
See Prov. 16. 6 ; Heb. 1. 3 ; 10. 2 ; 2 Pet. 1. 9.

PURIFY. Tit. 2. 14 ; Jas. 4. 8 ; 1 Pet. 1. 22.
PURITY. 1 Tim. 4. 12 ; 5. 2.
PURLOINING. Tit. 2. 10.
PURPOSE. Job 17. 11, my *p.* are broken off.
Prov. 20. 18, every *p.* established by counsel.
Isa. 14. 27, the Lord hath *p.*, who shall disannul ?
46. 11, I have *p.*, I will also do it.
Mat. 26. 8, to what *p.* is this waste ?
Acts 11. 23, with *p.* of heart.
Rom. 8. 28, called according to his *p.*
9. 11, that the *p.* of God might stand.
Eph. 1. 11, according to the *p.*
3. 11, eternal *p.* in Christ.
See 2 Cor. 1. 17 ; 2 Tim. 1. 9 ; 1 John 3. 8.

PURSE. Prov. 1. 14; Mat. 10. 9 ; Mk. 6. 8 ; Lu. 10. 4
PURSUE. Lev. 26. 17 ; Prov. 28. 1, shall flee when none *p.*
Deut. 19. 6 ; Josh. 20. 5, lest avenger *p.*

Job 13. 25, wilt thou *p.* the stubble?
30. 15, terrors *p.* my soul.
Ps. 34. 14, seek peace and *p.* it.
Prov. 11. 19, he that *p.* evil *p.* it to death.
13. 21, evil *p.* sinners.
Jer. 48. 2, the sword shall *p.* thee.
See Ex. 15. 9 ; 2 Sam. 24. 13 ; 1 Kings 18. 27.
PUSH. Ex. 21. 29 ; 1 Kings 22. 11 ; Job 30. 12.
PUT. Ex. 23. 1, *p.* not thine hand with the wicked.
Lev. 26. 8 ; Deut. 32. 30, *p.* ten thousand to flight.
Judg. 12. 3 ; 1 Sam. 28. 21, I *p.* my life in my hands.
1 Sam. 2. 36, *p.* me into one of priests' offices.
1 Kings 9. 3 ; 14. 21, to *p.* my name there.
Eccl. 10. 10, must he *p.* to more strength.
Isa. 43. 26, *p.* me in remembrance.
Mat. 19. 6 ; Mk. 10. 9, let not man *p.* asunder.
Mk. 10. 16, *p.* his hands on them and blessed.
Philem. 18, *p.* that on mine account.
2 Pet. 1. 14, I must *p.* off this tabernacle.
See Lu. 9. 62 ; John 13. 2 ; 1 Thess. 5. 8.
PUTRIFYING. Isa. 1. 6.

Q.

QUAKE. Joel 2. 10 ; Nah. 1. 5 ; Mat. 27. 51 ; Heb. 12. 21.
QUANTITY. Isa. 22. 24.
QUARREL. Lev. 26. 25 ; 2 Kings 5. 7 ; Mk. 6. 19 ; Col. 3. 13.
QUARTER. Ex. 13. 7 ; Mk. 1. 45 ; Rev. 20. 8.
QUATERNIONS. Acts 12. 4, delivered him to four *q.*
QUEEN. Jer. 44. 17, 25, burn incense unto the *q.*
QUENCH. Num. 11. 2, the fire was *q.*
2 Sam. 21. 17, *q.* not light of Israel.
Cant. 8. 7, many waters cannot *q.* love.
Isa. 34. 10, shall not be *q.* night nor day.
42. 3 ; Mat. 12. 20, smoking flax not *q.*
66. 24, neither shall their fire be *q.*
Mk. 9. 43, 48, fire that never shall be *q.*
Eph. 6. 16, able to *q.* fiery darts.
1 Thess. 5. 19, *q.* not the Spirit.
Heb. 11. 34, *q.* violence of fire.
See Ps. 104. 11 ; 118. 12 ; Ezek. 20. 47 ; Amos 5. 6.
QUESTION. 1 Kings 10. 1 ; 2 Chron. 9. 1, to prove him with *q.*
Mat. 22. 46, neither durst ask him *q.*
Mk. 9. 16, what *q.* ye with them ?
11. 29, I will ask you one *q.*
1 Cor. 10. 25, asking no *q.* for conscience.
1 Tim. 1. 4, which minister *q.* rather.
6. 4, doting about *q.*
2 Tim. 2. 23 ; Tit. 3. 9, unlearned *q.* avoid.
See Mk. 1. 27 ; 9. 10 ; Acts 18. 15 ; 19. 40.
QUICK. Num. 16. 30 ; Ps. 55. 15, go down *q.*
Isa. 11. 3, of *q.* understanding.
Acts 10. 42 ; 2 Tim. 4. 1 ; 1 Pet. 4. 5, Judge of *q.* and dead.
Heb. 4. 12, the word is *q.* and powerful.
See Lev. 13. 10, 24 ; Ps. 124. 3.
QUICKEN. Ps. 71. 20, thou shalt *q.* me again.
80. 18, *q.* us and we will call.
119. 25, *q.* me according to thy word.
37, *q.* me in thy way.
50, thy word hath *q.* me.
Rom. 8. 11, shall also *q.* your bodies.
1 Cor. 15. 36, that thou sowest is not *q.*
Eph. 2. 1, you hath he *q.*
5 ; Col. 2. 13, *q.* us together with Christ.
1 Pet. 3. 18, to death in flesh, *q.* by Spirit.
See John 5. 21 ; 6. 63 ; Rom. 4. 17 ; 1 Tim. 6. 13.
QUICKLY. Ex. 32. 8 ; Deut. 9. 12, have turned aside *q.*
Num. 16. 46, go *q.* to congregation.
Josh. 10. 6, come *q.* and save us.
Eccl. 4. 12, threefold cord not *q.* broken.
Mat. 5. 25, agree with adversary *q.*
Lu. 14. 21, go *q.* into streets and lanes.
John 13. 27, that thou doest, do *q.*

Rev. 2. 5, 16, repent, else I will come *q.*
3. 11 ; 22. 7. 12, I come *q.*
22. 20, surely I come *q.*
See Gen. 18. 6 ; 27. 20 ; Lu. 16. 6 ; Acts 22. 18.
QUICKSANDS. Acts 27. 17, fearing lest they should fall into the *q.*
QUIET. Ps. 107. 30, then are they glad because *q.*
131. 2, I have *q.* myself as a child.
Eccl. 9. 17, words of wise are heard in *q.*
Isa. 7. 4, be *q.*, fear not.
14. 7, earth is at rest and *q.*
32. 18, in *q.* resting places.
33. 20, a *q.* habitation.
Jer. 49. 23, sorrow on the sea, it cannot be *q.*
Ezek. 16. 42, I will be *q.*
Acts 19. 36, ye ought to be *q.*
1 Thess. 4. 11, study to be *q.*
1 Tim. 2. 2, a *q.* and peaceable life.
1 Pet. 3. 4, ornament of a meek and *q.* spirit.
See 2 Kings 11. 20 ; 2 Chron. 14. 1 ; Job 3. 13 ; 21. 23.
QUIETLY. 2 Sam. 3. 27 ; Lam. 3. 26.
QUIETNESS. Job 34. 29, when he giveth *q.*
Prov. 17. 1, better a dry morsel and *q.*
Eccl. 4. 6, better handful with *q.* than both.
Isa. 30. 15, in *q.* and confidence strength.
32. 17, effect of righteousness *q.*
See Judg. 8. 28 ; 1 Chron. 22. 9 ; 2 Thess. 3. 12.
QUIT. Ex. 21. 19 ; Josh. 2. 20 ; 1 Sam. 4. 9 ; 1 Cor. 16. 13.
QUITE. Gen. 31. 15 ; Job 6. 13 ; Hab. 3. 9.
QUIVER. Ps. 127. 5 ; Jer. 5. 16 ; Lam. 3. 13.

R.

RACE. Ps. 19. 5 ; Eccl. 9. 11 ; 1 Cor. 9. 24 ; Heb. 12. 1.
RAGE. 2 Kings 5. 12, turned away in a *r.*
Ps. 2. 1 ; Acts 4. 25, why do the heathen *r.*
Prov. 14. 16, the fool *r.* and is confident.
See Prov. 6. 34 ; 20. 9 ; Dan. 3. 13 ; Hos. 7. 16.
RAGGED. Isa. 2. 21.
RAGING. Ps. 89. 9 ; Prov. 20. 1 ; Lu. 8. 24 ; Jude 13.
RAGS. Prov. 23. 21 ; Isa. 64. 6 ; Jer. 38. 11.
RAIMENT. Gen. 28. 20, if the Lord will give me *r.*
Deut. 8. 4, thy *r.* waxed not old.
24. 13, that he may sleep in his *r.*
17, nor take a widow's *r.* to pledge.
Job 27. 16, though he prepare *r.* as the clay.
Isa. 63. 3, I will stain all my *r.*
Zech. 3. 4, I will clothe thee with *r.*
Mat. 6. 25 ; Lu. 12. 23, the body more than *r.*
28, why take thought for *r.*
11. 8 ; Lu. 7. 25, man clothed in soft *r.*
17. 2 ; Mk. 9. 3 ; Lu. 9. 29, his *r.* was white as light.
1 Tim. 6. 8, having food and *r.*, be content.
Jas. 2. 2, poor man in vile *r.*
Rev. 3. 18, buy white *r.*
See Mat. 3. 4 ; Lu. 10. 30 ; 23. 34 ; Acts 22. 20.
RAIN (*n.*). Lev. 26. 4 ; Deut. 11. 14 ; 28. 12, *r.* in due season.
Deut. 11. 11, drinketh water of the *r.* of heaven.
32. 2, my doctrine shall drop as the *r.*
2 Sam. 23. 4, clear shining after *r.*
1 Kings 18. 41, sound of abundance of *r.*
Ezra 10. 13, a time of much *r.*
Job 5. 10, who giveth *r.* on earth.
37. 6, to small *r.* and to great *r.*
38. 28, hath the *r.* a father.
Ps. 72. 6, like *r.* on mown grass.
Prov. 25. 14, like clouds and wind without *r.*
23, north wind driveth away *r.*
26. 1, as *r.* in harvest.
28. 3, that oppresseth poor is like sweeping *r.*
Eccl. 11. 3, if clouds be full of *r.*
12. 2, nor clouds return after *r.*
Cant. 2. 11, the *r.* is over and gone.
Isa. 4. 6, covert from storm and *r.*
55. 10, as the *r.* cometh down.

Ezek. 38. 22, I will r. an overflowing r.
Hos. 6. 3, he shall come unto us as the r
Mat. 5. 45, r. on just and unjust.
7. 25, the r. descended and floods came.
See Jer. 5. 24; Acts 14. 17; 28. 2; Heb. 6. 7.
RAIN (v.). Ex. 16. 4, I will r. bread from heaven.
Job 20. 23, God shall r. his fury on him.
Ps. 11. 6, on wicked he shall r. snares.
78. 24, 27, and r. down manna.
Ezek. 22. 24, thou art the land not r. upon.
Hos. 10. 12, till he come and r. righteousness.
See Gen. 2. 5; 7. 4; Amos 4. 7; Rev. 11. 6.
RAINY. Prov. 27. 15.
RAISE. Deut. 18. 15; Acts 3. 22, will r. up a Prophet.
Judg. 2. 16, 18, the Lord r. up judges.
1 Sam. 2. 8; Ps. 113. 7, he r. poor out of dust.
Job 41. 25, when he r. himself, mighty are.
Ps. 145. 14; 146. 8, he r. those that be bowed down.
Isa. 45. 13, I have r. him in righteousness.
Hos. 6. 2, in third day he will r. us up.
Mat. 10. 8; 11. 5; Lu. 7. 22, r. the dead.
16. 21; 17. 23; Lu. 9. 22, be r. the third day.
John 2. 19, in three days I will r. it up.
6. 39, 40, 44, 54, I will r. him up at last day.
Acts 2. 24, 32; 3. 15; 4. 10; 5. 30; 10. 40; 13. 30, 33, 34; 17. 31; Rom. 10. 9; 1 Cor. 6. 14; 2 Cor. 4. 14; Gal. 1. 1; Eph. 1. 20, whom God hath r. up.
26. 8, why incredible that God should r. the dead.
Rom. 4. 25, r. again for our justification.
6. 4, like as Christ was r. from the dead.
8. 11, Spirit of him that r. up Jesus.
1 Cor. 6. 14, and will also r. up us by his power.
15. 15, r. up Christ, whom he r. not up.
16, then is not Christ r.
17, if Christ be not r.
35, how are the dead r.
43, it is r. in glory, it is r. in power.
2 Cor. 1. 9, trust in God which r. the dead.
4. 14, he shall r. up us also.
Eph. 2. 6, and hath r. us up together.
Heb. 11. 19, accounting God was able to r. him.
35, women received dead r. to life.
Jas. 5. 15, and the Lord shall r. him up.
See Lu. 20. 37; John 5. 21; 2 Tim. 2. 8.
RAN. Ex. 9. 23; Num. 16. 47; Jer. 23. 21.
RANG. 1 Sam. 4. 5; 1 Kings 1. 45.
RANKS. 1 Kings 7. 4; Joel 2. 7; Mk. 6. 40.
RANSOM. Ex. 21. 30, give for the r. of his life.
30. 12, every man a r. for his soul.
Job 33. 24, I have found a r.
36. 18, a great r. cannot deliver.
Ps. 49. 7, nor give a r. for him.
Prov. 13. 8, the r. of a man's life are his riches.
Isa. 35. 10, the r. of the Lord shall return.
43. 3, I gave Egypt for thy r.
Hos. 13. 14, I will r. them from the grave.
Mat. 20. 28; Mk. 10. 45, to give his life a r.
1 Tim. 2. 6, gave himself a r. for all.
See Prov. 6. 35; Isa. 51. 10; Jer. 31. 11.
RARE. Dan. 2. 11.
RASE. Ps. 137. 7.
RASH. Eccl. 5. 2; Acts 19. 36.
RATHER. Job 7. 15; Jer. 8. 3, death r. than life.
Ps. 84. 10, r. be a doorkeeper.
Mat. 10. 6, go r. to lost sheep.
28, r. fear him that is able.
25. 9, go r. to them that sell.
Mk. 5. 26, but r. grew worse.
Lu. 18. 14, justified r. than the other.
John 3. 19, loved darkness r. than light.
Acts 5. 29, obey God r. than men.
Rom. 8. 34, that died, yea r., that is risen.
12. 19, r. give place to wrath.
1 Cor. 6. 7, why do ye not r. take wrong.
Heb. 11. 25, choosing r. to suffer.
12. 13, let it r. be healed.
See Josh. 22. 24; 2 Kings 5. 13; Phil. 1. 12.

RAVENING. Ps. 22. 13; Ezek. 22. 25; Mat. 7. 15.
RAVENOUS. Isa. 35. 9; 46. 11; Ezek. 39. 4.
REACH. Gen. 11. 4; John 20. 27; 2 Cor. 10. 13.
READ. Deut. 17. 19, king shall r. all his life.
Isa. 34. 16, seek out of book of Lord and r.
Mat. 12. 3; 19. 4; 21. 16; 22. 31; Mk. 2. 25; 12. 10; Lu. 6. 3, have ye not r.
Lu. 4. 16, Jesus stood up to r.
2 Cor. 3. 2, epistle known and r. of all men.
1 Tim. 4. 13, give attendance to r.
See Hab. 2. 2; 2 Cor. 3. 14; Rev. 1. 3; 5. 4.
READINESS. Acts 17. 11; 2 Cor. 8. 11; 10. 6.
READY. Num. 32. 17, we will go r. armed.
Deut. 26. 5, a Syrian r. to perish.
2 Sam. 18. 22, wherefore run, no tidings r.
Neh. 9. 17, thou art a God r. to pardon.
Job 12. 5, r. to slip with his feet.
17. 1, the graves are r. for me.
29. 13, blessing of him r. to perish.
Ps. 38. 17, I am r. to halt.
45. 1, pen of a r. writer.
86. 5, good and r. to forgive.
88. 15, r. to die from my youth.
Prov. 24. 11, deliver those r. to be slain.
31. 6, give strong drink to r. to perish.
Eccl. 5. 1, be more r. to hear.
Isa. 27. 13, shall come that were r. to perish.
32. 4, stammerers r. to speak plainly.
38. 20, the Lord was r. to save me.
Dan. 3. 15, if ye be r. to fall down.
Mat. 22. 4; Lu. 14. 17, all things are r.
8, the wedding is r.
24. 44; Lu. 12. 40, be ye also r.
25. 10, they that were r. went in.
Mk. 14. 38, the spirit is r.
Lu. 22. 33, I am r. to go with thee.
John 7. 6, your time is alway r.
Acts 21. 13, r. not to be bound only, but.
Rom. 1. 15, I am r. to preach at Rome.
2 Cor. 8. 19, declaration of your r. mind.
9. 2, Achaia was r. a year ago.
1 Tim. 6. 18, r. to distribute.
2 Tim. 4. 6, r. to be offered.
Tit. 3. 1, r. to every good work.
1 Pet. 1. 5, r. to be revealed.
3. 15, r. always to give an answer.
5. 2, but of a r. mind.
Rev. 3. 2, things that are r. to die.
See Ex. 17. 4; 19. 11; Ezra 7. 6; Job 15. 23.
REAP. Lev. 25. 11, in jubilee neither sow nor r.
Eccl. 11. 4, regardeth clouds shall not r.
Jer. 12. 13, sown wheat, but shall r. thorns.
Hos. 8. 7, shall r. the whirlwind.
10. 12, sow in righteousness, r. in mercy.
Mic. 6. 15, shalt sow, but not r.
Mat. 6. 26; Lu. 12. 24, sow not, neither r.
25. 26; Lu. 19. 21, r. where I sowed not.
John 4. 38, r. whereon ye bestowed no labour.
1 Cor. 9. 11, if we shall r. your carnal things.
2 Cor. 9. 6, shall r. sparingly.
Gal. 6. 7, that shall he also r.
Jas. 5. 4, cries of them which r.
See Isa. 17. 5; John 4. 36, 37; Rev. 14. 15.
REASON (n.). Job 32. 11, I gave ear to your r.
Prov. 26. 16, seven men that can render a r.
Eccl. 7. 25, to search out the r. of things.
Isa. 41. 21, bring forth your strong r.
1 Pet. 3. 15, a r. of the hope in you.
See 1 Kings 9. 15; Dan. 4. 36; Acts 6. 2.
REASON (v.). Job 9. 14, choose words to r. with you.
13. 3, I desire to r. with God.
15. 3, should he r. with unprofitable talk.
Isa. 1. 18, let us r. together.
Mat. 16. 7; 21. 25; Mk. 8. 16; 11. 31; Lu. 20. 5, the r. among themselves.
Lu. 5. 22, what r. ye in your hearts.
24. 15, while they r. Jesus drew near.
Acts 24. 25, as he r. of righteousness.
See 1 Sam. 12. 7; Mk. 2. 6; 12. 28; Acts 28. 29.

REASONABLE. Rom. 12. 1.
REBEL. Num. 14. 9, only r. not against the Lord.
Josh. 1. 18, whosoever doth r. he shall die.
Neh. 2. 19, will ye r. against the king.
Job 24. 13, that r. against the light.
Ps. 105. 28, they r. not against his word.
Isa. 1. 2, have nourished children and they r.
63. 10, they r. and vexed his holy Spirit.
Lam. 3. 42, we have r., thou hast not pardoned.
Dan. 9. 9, though we have r. against him.
See 1 Sam. 12. 14; Ezek. 2. 3; Hos. 7. 14; 13. 16.
REBELLION. 1 Sam. 15. 23, r. is as the sin of witchcraft.
Job 34. 37, he addeth r. to his sin.
Prov. 17. 11, an evil man seeketh r.
Jer. 28. 16, thou hast taught r.
See Deut. 31. 27; Ezra 4. 19; Neh. 9. 17.
REBELLIOUS. Deut. 21. 18, 20, a stubborn and r. son.
1 Sam. 20. 30, son of perverse r. woman.
Ps. 66. 7, let not the r. exalt themselves.
68. 6, the r. dwell in a dry land.
Isa. 1. 23, r., companions of thieves.
Jer. 5. 23, this people hath a r. heart.
See Ezek. 2. 3; 3. 9; 12. 2; 17. 12; 24. 3.
REBELS. Num. 17. 10; 20. 10; Ezek. 20. 38.
REBUKE (n.). 2 Kings 19. 3; Isa. 37. 3, this is a day of r.
Ps. 39. 11, when thou with r. dost correct.
80. 16, perish at r. of thy countenance.
104. 7, at thy r. they fled.
Prov. 13. 8, the poor heareth not r.
27. 5, open r. is better than secret love.
Eccl. 7. 5, better to hear r. of wise.
Isa. 30. 17, thousand flee at r. of one.
Jer. 15. 15, for thy sake I suffered r.
Phil. 2. 15, without r.
See Deut. 28. 20; Isa. 25. 8; 50. 2.
REBUKE (v.). Ps. 6. 1; 38. 1, r. me not in anger.
Prov. 9. 7, he that r. a wicked man getteth a blot.
8, r. a wise man, and he will love thee.
28. 23, he that r. a man shall find favour.
Isa. 2. 4; Mic. 4. 3, he shall r. many nations.
Zech. 3. 2; Jude 9, the Lord r. thee.
Mal. 3. 11, I will r. the devourer for your sakes.
Mat. 8. 26; Mk. 4. 39; Lu. 8. 24, he r. wind.
16. 22; Mk. 8. 32, Peter began to r. him.
Lu. 4. 39, he r. the fever.
17. 3, if thy brother trespass, r. him.
19. 39, Master, r. thy disciples.
1 Tim. 5. 1, r. not an elder.
20, them that sin, r. before all.
2 Tim. 4. 2, r., exhort, with longsuffering.
Tit. 1. 13; 2. 15, r. them sharply.
Heb. 12. 5, nor faint when thou art r.
See Ruth 2. 16; Neh. 5. 7; Amos 5. 10.
RECALL. Lam. 3. 21.
RECEIPT. Mat. 9. 9; Mk. 2. 14; Lu. 5. 27.
RECEIVE. 2 Kings 5. 26, is it a time to r. money.
Job 4. 12, mine ear r. a little.
22. 22, r. law from his mouth.
Ps. 6. 9, the Lord will r. my prayer.
49. 15, he shall r. me.
68. 18, hast r. gifts for men.
73. 24, afterwards r. me to glory.
Prov. 2. 1, if thou wilt r. my words.
Isa. 40. 2, she hath r. double.
Jer. 2. 30, your children r. no correction.
Hos. 10. 6, Ephraim shall r. shame.
14. 2, r. us graciously.
Mat. 11. 5, the blind r. their sight.
14, if ye will r. it, this is Elias.
18. 5, whoso shall r. one such little child.
19. 12, he that is able let him r. it.
21. 22, ask, believing ye shall r.
Mk. 15. 23, but he r. it not.
16. 19; Acts 1. 9, was r. up into heaven.
Lu. 16. 9, r. you into everlasting habitations.
18. 42; Acts 22. 13, r. thy sight.

John 1. 11, his own r. him not.
12, to as many as r. him.
3. 27, can r. nothing, except.
5. 43, in his own name, him ye will r.
44, which r. honour one of another.
16. 24, ask, and ye shall r.
20. 22, r. ye the Holy Ghost.
Acts 7. 59, r. my spirit.
8. 17, they r. the Holy Ghost.
Acts 10. 43, shall r. remission of sins.
19. 2, have ye r. the Holy Ghost.
20. 24, which I have r. of the Lord.
Rom. 5. 11, by whom we r. atonement.
14. 3, for God hath r. him.
15. 7, r. ye one another.
1 Cor. 3. 8, every man shall r. his own reward.
11. 23, I r. of the Lord that which also I delivered.
2 Cor. 4. 1, as we have r. mercy we faint not.
5. 10, every one may r. things done.
7. 2, r. us; we have wronged no man.
Phil. 2. 29, r. him in the Lord.
4. 15, as concerning giving and r.
Col. 2. 6, as ye have r. Christ.
1 Tim. 3. 16, r. up into glory.
4. 4, if it be r. with thanksgiving.
1 John 3. 22, whatsoever we ask we r.
See Ezek. 3. 10; Acts 20. 35; Jas. 4. 3.
RECKON. Lev. 25. 50, he shall r. with him that bought him.
Ps. 40. 5, thy thoughts cannot be r. up.
Mat. 18. 24, when he had begun to r.
25. 19, lord of servants r. with them.
Rom. 4. 4, reward is not r. of grace.
6. 11, r. yourselves dead to sin.
8. 18, I r. the sufferings of this present time.
See 2 Kings 22. 7; Isa. 38. 13; Lu. 22. 37.
RECOMMENDED. Acts 14. 26; 15. 40.
RECOMPENCE. Deut. 32. 35, to me belongeth r.
Job 15. 31, vanity shall be his r.
Isa. 35. 4, God will come with a r.
Hos. 9. 7, days of r. are come.
Joel 3. 4, will ye render me a r.?
Lu. 14. 12, and a r. be made thee.
2 Cor. 6. 13, for a r., be ye also enlarged.
Heb. 2. 2; 10. 35; 11. 26, just r. of reward.
See Prov. 12. 14; Isa. 34. 8; Jer. 51. 56.
RECOMPENSE. Num. 5. 7, he shall r. his trespass.
Ruth 2. 12, the Lord r. thy work.
2 Sam. 19. 36, why should the king r. me?
Job 34. 33, he will r. it, whether.
Prov. 20. 22, say not, I will r. evil.
Isa. 65. 6, but will r., even r. into their bosom.
Jer. 25. 14; Hos. 12. 2, will r. according to deeds.
Lu. 14. 14, for they cannot r. thee.
Rom. 12. 17, r. to no man evil for evil.
11. 35, it shall be r. to him again.
See 2 Chron. 6. 23; Jer. 32. 18; Heb. 10. 30.
RECONCILE. 1 Sam. 29. 4, wherewith should he r. himself.
Ezek. 45. 20, so shall ye r. the house.
Mat. 5. 24, first be r. to thy brother.
Rom. 5. 10, if when enemies we were r.
Eph. 2. 16, that he might r. both.
See Lev. 16. 20; Rom. 11. 15; 2 Cor. 5. 19.
RECORD. Ex. 20. 24, in places where I r. my name.
Deut. 30. 19; 31. 28, I call heaven to r.
Job 16. 19, my r. is on high.
John 8. 13, thou bearest r. of thyself.
Rom. 10. 2, I bare them r.
Phil. 1. 8, God is my r. how greatly I long.
1 John 5. 7, three that bare r.
10, he believeth not the r.
11, this is the r., that God hath given.
3 John 12, we bare r., and our r. is true.
See Acts 20. 26; John 1. 19; Rev. 1. 2.
RECOUNT. Nah. 2. 5, r. his worthies.

RECOVER. 2 Kings 5. 3, the prophet would *r.* him.
Ps. 39. 13, that I may *r.* strength.
Isa. 11. 11, to *r.* remnant of his people.
Hos. 2. 9, and I will *r.* my wool and flax.
Mk. 16. 18, lay hands on sick, and they shall *r.*
Lu. 4. 18, preach *r.* of sight to blind.
See Isa. 38. 16; Jer. 8. 22; 41. 16; 2 Tim. 2. 16.

RED. Gen. 25. 30, *r.* pottage.
49. 12, eyes *r.* with wine.
2 Kings 3. 22, water *r.* as blood.
Ps. 75. 8, wine is *r.,* full of mixture.
Prov. 23. 31, look not on wine when *r.*
Isa. 1. 18, though your sins be *r.* like crimson.
27. 2, a vineyard of *r.* wine.
63. 2, *r.* in thine apparel.
Mat. 16. 2, fair weather, for the sky is *r.*
See Lev. 13. 19; Num. 19. 2; Nah. 2. 3; Rev. 6. 4.

REDEEM. Gen. 48. 16, angel which *r.* me.
Ex. 6. 6, I will *r.* you.
15. 13, people whom thou hast *r.*
Lev. 27. 28, no devoted thing, shall be *r.*
2 Sam. 4. 9, the Lord hath *r.* my soul.
Neh. 5. 5, nor is it in our power to *r.* them.
8, after our ability have *r.* Jews.
Job 5. 20, in famine he shall *r.* thee.
6. 23, to *r.* me from hand of mighty.
Ps. 25. 22, *r.* Israel out of all his troubles.
34. 22, the Lord *r.* the soul of his servants.
44. 26, *r.* us for thy mercies' sake.
49. 7, none can *r.* his brother.
15, God will *r.* my soul from the grave.
72. 14, he shall *r.* their soul from deceit.
107. 2, let the *r.* of the Lord say so.
130. 8, he shall *r.* Israel.
Isa. 1. 27, Zion shall be *r.* with judgment.
35. 9, the *r.* shall walk there.
44. 22, return, for I have *r.* thee.
50. 2, is my hand shortened that it cannot *r.*
51. 11, the *r.* of the Lord shall return.
52. 3, *r.* without money.
63. 4, the year of my *r.* is come.
Hos. 7. 13, though I *r.* them, they have spoken
    lies.
13. 14, I will *r.* them from death.
Lu. 1. 68, hath visited, and *r.* his people.
24. 21, he who should have *r.* Israel.
Gal. 3. 13, *r.* us from curse of the law.
4. 5, *r.* them that were under the law.
Tit. 2. 14, that he might *r.* us from iniquity.
1 Pet. 1. 18, not *r.* with corruptible things.
Rev. 5. 9, thou hast *r.* us by thy blood.
See Num. 18. 15; 2 Sam. 7. 23; Eph. 5. 16; Col.
    4. 5.

REDEEMER. Job 19. 25, I know that my *r.* liveth.
Ps. 19. 14, O Lord, my strength and my *r.*
78. 35, God was their *r.*
Prov. 23. 11, their *r.* is mighty.
Isa. 47. 4, as for our *r.,* the Lord of hosts is his
    name.
49. 26; 60. 16, know that I am thy *R.*
59. 20, the *R.* shall come to Zion.
63. 16, thou art our *r.*
See Isa. 41. 14; 44. 6; 48. 17; 54. 5; Jer. 50. 34.

REDEMPTION. Lev. 25. 24, grant a *r.* for the land.
Ps. 49. 8, the *r.* of their soul is precious.
111. 9, he sent *r.* to his people.
130. 7, plenteous *r.*
Jer. 32. 7, the right of *r.* is thine.
Lu. 2. 38, that looked for *r.* in Jerusalem.
21. 28, your *r.* draweth nigh.
Rom. 8. 23, the *r.* of our body.
Eph. 4. 30, sealed unto the day of *r.*
See Num. 3. 49; Rom. 3. 24; 1 Cor. 1. 30; Heb. 9. 12.

REDOUND. 2 Cor. 4. 15, grace might *r.*

REFORMATION. Heb. 9. 10, time of *r.*

REFORMED. Lev. 26. 23, if ye will not be *r.*

REFRAIN. Gen. 45. 1, Joseph could not *r.* himself.
Job 7. 11, I will not *r.* my mouth.
29. 9, princes *r.* talking.

Ps. 40. 9, I have not *r.* my lips.
119. 101, *r.* my feet from every evil way.
Prov. 1. 15, *r.* thy foot from their path.
10. 19, he that *r.* his lips is wise.
Acts 5. 38, *r.* from these men.
See Gen. 43. 31; Isa. 64. 12; Jer. 31. 16; 1 Pet. 3. 10.

REFRESH. Ex. 31. 17, he rested and was *r.*
Job 32. 20, I will speak that I may be *r.*
Prov. 25. 13, he *r.* the soul of his masters.
Acts 3. 19, times of *r.* shall come.
1 Cor. 16. 18, they *r.* my spirit.
See 1 Kings 13. 7; Isa. 28. 12; Rom. 15. 32; 2 Cor.
    7. 13.

REFUSE (*n.*). 1 Sam. 15. 9; Lam. 3. 45; Amos 8. 6.

REFUSE (*v.*). Gen. 37. 35, Jacob *r.* to be comforted.
Num. 22. 13, the Lord *r.* to give me leave.
1 Sam. 16. 7, look not on him, for I have *r.* him.
Job 6. 7, things my soul *r.* to touch.
Ps. 77. 2, my soul *r.* to be comforted.
78. 10, they *r.* to walk in his law.
118. 22, stone the builders *r.*
Prov. 1. 24, I have called and ye *r.*
8. 33, be wise and *r.* it not.
10. 17, he that *r.* reproof.
13. 18, shame to him that *r.* instruction.
15. 32, he that *r.* instruction despiseth his soul.
21. 25, his hands *r.* to labour.
Isa. 7. 15, 16, may know to *r.* the evil.
Jer. 8. 5, they *r.* to return.
9. 6, they *r.* to know me.
15. 18, my wound *r.* to be healed.
25. 28, if they *r.* to take the cup.
38. 21, if thou *r.* to go forth.
Zech. 7. 11, they *r.* to hearken.
Acts 7. 35, this Moses whom they *r.*
1 Tim. 4. 4, nothing to be *r.*
7, *r.* profane and old wives' fables.
5. 11, the younger widows *r.*
Heb. 11. 24, Moses *r.* to be called.
12. 25, *r.* not him that speaketh.
See Ex. 4. 23; 10. 3; 1 Kings 20. 35; 2 Kings 5. 16.

REGARD. Gen. 45. 20, *r.* not your stuff.
Ex. 5. 9, let them not *r.* vain words.
Deut. 10. 17, that *r.* not persons.
1 Kings 18. 29, neither voice, nor any that *r.*
Job 4. 20, they perish without any *r.* it.
34. 19, nor *r.* rich more than poor.
39. 7, neither *r.* crying of the driver.
Ps. 28. 5; Isa. 5. 12, they *r.* not works of the Lord.
66. 18, if I *r.* iniquity in my heart.
102. 17, he will *r.* prayer of the destitute.
106. 44, he *r.* their affliction.
Prov. 1. 24, and no man *r.*
5. 2, that thou mayest *r.* discretion.
6. 35, he will not *r.* any ransom.
12. 10, *r.* the life of his beast.
13. 18; 15. 5, he that *r.* reproof.
Eccl. 11. 4, he that *r.* the clouds.
Lam. 4. 16, the Lord will no more *r.* them.
Dan. 11. 37, *r.* God of his fathers, nor *r.* any god.
Mal. 1. 9, will he *r.* your persons.
Mat. 22. 16; Mk. 12. 14, *r.* not the person of men.
Lu. 18. 2, neither *r.* man.
Rom. 14. 6, he that *r.* the day, *r.* it to the Lord.
See Deut. 28. 50; 2 Kings 3. 14; Amos 5. 22; Phil.
    2. 30.

REGENERATION. Mat. 19. 28, in the *r.*
Tit. 3. 5, by the washing of *r.*
See John 1. 13; 3. 3.

REGISTER. Ezra 2. 62; Neh. 7. 5, 64.

REHEARSE. Judg. 5. 11, *r.* the righteous acts.
Acts 14. 27, they *r.* all God had done.
See Ex. 17. 14; 1 Sam. 8. 21; 17. 31; Acts 11. 4.

REIGN. Gen. 37. 8, shalt thou *r.* over us.
Ex. 15. 18; Ps. 146. 10, Lord shall *r.* for ever.
Lev. 26. 17, that hate you shall *r.* over you.
Deut. 15. 6, thou shalt *r.* over many nations.
Judg. 9. 8, the trees said, *r.* thou over us.
1 Sam. 11. 12, shall Saul *r.* over us.
12. 12, nay, but a king shall *r.* over us.

2 Sam. 16. 8, in whose stead thou hast *r*.
Job 34. 30, that the hypocrite *r*. not.
Ps. 47. 8, God *r*. over the heathen.
 93. 1; 96. 10; 97. 1; 99. 1, the Lord *r*.
Prov. 8. 15, by me kings *r*.
 30. 22, for a servant when he *r*.
Eccl. 4. 14, out of prison he cometh to *r*.
Isa. 32. 1, a king shall *r*. in righteousness.
 52. 7, that saith unto Zion, thy God *r*.
Jer. 22. 15, shalt thou *r*. because thou closest?
 23. 5, a king shall *r*. and prosper.
Mic. 4. 7, the Lord shall *r*. over them.
Lu. 19. 14, not have this man to *r*. over us.
 27, that would not I should *r*.
Rom. 5. 14, death *r*. from Adam to Moses.
 17, death *r*. by one.
 21, as sin hath *r*., so might grace *r*.
 6. 12, let not sin *r*. in your bodies.
1 Cor. 4. 8, ye have *r*. as kings without us.
 15. 25, for he must *r*.
2 Tim. 2. 12, if we suffer we shall also *r*. with him.
Rev. 5. 10, we also shall *r*. on the earth.
 11. 15, he shall *r*. for ever and ever.
Rev. 19. 6, the Lord God omnipotent *r*.
 See Isa. 24. 23 ; Luke 1. 33 ; Rev. 20. 4 ; 22. 5.
REINS. Job 16. 13, he cleaveth my *r*. asunder.
 19. 27, though my *r*. be consumed.
Ps. 7. 9, God trieth the *r*.
 16. 7, my *r*. instruct me.
 26. 2, examine me, try my *r*.
 73. 21, thus I was pricked in my *r*.
 139. 13, thou hast possessed my *r*.
Prov. 23. 16, my *r*. shall rejoice.
Isa. 11. 5, faithfulness the girdle of his *r*.
Rev. 2. 23, I am he who searcheth the *r*.
 See Jer. 11. 20 ; 12. 2 ; 17. 10 ; 20. 12 ; Lam. 3. 13.
REJECT. 1 Sam. 8. 7, they have not *r*. thee, but
 they have *r*. me.
 10. 19, ye have *r*. God who saved you.
 15. 23, because thou hast *r*. the word of the Lord.
 16. 1, I have *r*. him from being king.
Isa. 53. 3, despised and *r*. of men.
Jer. 2. 37, the Lord hath *r*. thy confidence.
 7. 29, the Lord hath *r*. the generation.
 8. 9, they have *r*. the word of the Lord.
 14. 19, thou hast utterly *r*. Judah.
Lam. 5. 22, thou hast utterly *r*. us.
Hos. 4. 6, because thou hast *r*. knowledge, I will
 r. thee.
Mat. 21. 42 ; Mk. 12. 10 ; Lu. 20. 17, the stone which
 builders *r*.
Mk. 7. 9, full well ye *r*. the commandment.
Lu. 7. 30, lawyers *r*. the counsel of God.
 17. 25, must first be *r*. of this generation.
Tit. 3. 10, after admonition *r*.
Heb. 12. 17, when he would have inherited was *r*.
 See Jer. 6. 19 ; Mk. 6. 26 ; 8. 31 ; Lu. 9. 22 ; John
 12. 48.
REJOICE. Deut. 12. 7, shall *r*. in all ye put your
 hand to.
 16. 14, thou shalt *r*. in thy feast.
 26. 11, thou shalt *r*. in every good thing.
 28. 63 ; 30. 9, the Lord will *r*. over you.
 30. 9, *r*. for good as he *r*. over thy fathers.
1 Sam. 2. 1, because I *r*. in thy salvation.
1 Chron. 16. 10, let the heart of them *r*. that seek
 the Lord.
2 Chron. 6. 41, let thy saints *r*. in goodness.
Job 21. 12, they *r*. at sound of the organ.
 31. 25, if I *r*. because my wealth was great.
 29, if I *r*. at destruction of him that.
 39. 21, the horse *r*. in his strength.
Ps. 2. 11, *r*. with trembling.
 5. 11, let all that trust in thee *r*.
 9. 14, I will *r*. in thy salvation.
 19. 5, *r*. as a strong man to run a race.
 33. 21, our heart shall *r*. in him.
 35. 15, in mine adversity they *r*.
 26, let them be ashamed that *r*. at my hurt.
 38. 16, hear me, lest they should *r*. over me.

Ps. 51. 8, bones thou hast broken may *r*.
 58. 10, righteous shall *r*. when he seeth.
 63. 7, in shadow of thy wings will I *r*.
 68. 3, let righteous *r*., yea, exceedingly *r*.
 85. 6, that thy people may *r*. in thee.
 89. 16, in thy name shall they *r*. all the day.
 96. 11, let the heavens *r*.
 97. 11, the Lord reigneth, let the earth *r*.
 104. 31, the Lord shall *r*. in his works.
 107. 42, the righteous shall see it and *r*.
 109. 28, let thy servant *r*.
 149. 2, let Israel *r*. in him that made him.
Prov. 2. 14, who *r*. to do evil.
 5. 18, *r*. with the wife of thy youth.
 23. 15, if thine heart be wise, mine shall *r*.
 24, father of the righteous shall greatly *r*.
 25, she that bare thee shall *r*.
 24. 17, *r*. not when thine enemy falleth.
 29. 2, when righteous are in authority people *r*.
 31. 25, she shall *r*. in time to come.
Eccl. 2. 10, my heart *r*. in all my labour.
 3. 12, for a man to *r*. and do good.
 22 ; 5. 19, that a man should *r*. in his works.
 11. 9, *r*. O young man in thy youth.
Isa. 9. 3, as men *r*. when they divide the spoil.
 24. 8, noise of them that *r*. endeth.
 29. 19, poor among men shall *r*.
 35. 1, the desert shall *r*.
 62. 5, as the bridegroom *r*. over the bride.
 64. 5, him that *r*. and worketh righteousness.
 65. 13, my servants shall *r*., but ye.
 66. 14, when ye see this, your heart shall *r*.
Jer. 11. 15, when thou doest evil, then thou *r*.
 32. 41, I will *r*. over them to do them good.
 51. 39, that they may *r*. and sleep.
Ezek. 7. 12, let not buyer *r*.
Amos 6. 13, which *r*. in a thing of nought.
Mic. 7. 8, *r*. not against me.
Hab. 3. 18, yet I will *r*. in the Lord.
Mat. 18. 13, he *r*. more of that sheep.
Lu. 1. 14, many shall *r*. at his birth.
 6. 23, *r*. ye in that day, and leap for joy.
 10. 20, in this *r*. not, but rather *r*. because.
 21, in that hour Jesus *r*. in spirit.
 15. 6, 9, *r*. with me.
John 5. 35, willing for a season to *r*. in his light.
 8. 56, Abraham *r*. to see my day.
 14. 28, if ye loved me, ye would *r*.
 16. 20, ye shall weep, but the world shall *r*.
 22, I will see you again, and your heart shall *r*.
Rom. 5. 2, and *r*. in hope.
 12. 15, *r*. with them that do *r*.
1 Cor. 7. 30, they that *r*. as though they *r*. not.
 13. 6, *r*. not in iniquity, but *r*. in the truth.
Phil. 1. 18, I therein do *r*. and will *r*.
 2. 16, that I may *r*. in the day of Christ.
 3. 1, finally, *r*. in the Lord.
 4. 4, *r*. in the Lord alway, and again I say *r*.
1 Thess. 5. 16, *r*. evermore.
Jas. 1. 9, let the brother of low degree *r*.
 2. 13, mercy *r*. against judgment.
1 Pet. 1. 8, *r*. with joy unspeakable.
 See 1 Kings 1. 40 ; 5. 7 ; 2 Kings 11. 14 ; 1 Chron. 29. 9.
REJOICING. Job 8. 21, till he fill thy lips with *r*.
Ps. 107. 22, declare his works with *r*.
 118. 15, voice of *r*. is in tabernacles of the
 righteous.
 119. 111, they are the *r*. of my heart.
 126. 6, shall doubtless come again *r*.
Prov. 8. 31, *r*. in the habitable part of his earth.
Isa. 65. 18, I create Jerusalem a *r*.
Jer. 15. 16, thy word was to me the *r*. of my heart.
Zeph. 2. 15, this is the *r*. city.
Acts 5. 41, *r*. that they were counted worthy.
Rom. 12. 12, *r*. in hope.
2 Cor. 6. 10, as sorrowful, yet alway *r*.
1 Thess. 2. 19, what is our crown of *r*.
 See Hab. 3. 14 ; Acts 8. 39 ; Gal. 6. 4 ; Jas. 4. 16.
RELEASE. Esth. 2. 18 ; Mat. 27. 17 ; Mk. 15. 11 ;
 John 19. 10.

RELIEVE. Lev. 25. 35, then thou shalt *r.* him.
Ps. 146. 9, he *r.* the fatherless and widow.
Isa. 1. 17, *r.* the oppressed.
Lam. 1. 16, comforter that should *r.* my soul is far
    from me.
See Acts 11. 29 ; 1 Tim. 5. 10, 16.
RELIGION. Acts 26. 5 ; Gal. 1. 13 ; Jas. 1. 26, 27.
RELIGIOUS. Acts 13. 43 ; Jas. 1. 26.
RELY. 2 Chron. 13. 18 ; 16. 7, 8.
REMAIN. Gen. 8. 22, while earth *r.*
  14. 10, they that *r.* fled to the mountain.
Ex. 12. 10, let nothing of it *r.* until morning.
Josh. 13. 1, there *r.* yet much land to be pos-
    sessed.
1 Kings 18. 22, I only *r.* a prophet.
Job 21. 32, yet shall he *r.* in the tomb.
Prov. 2. 21, the perfect shall *r.* in the land.
Eccl. 2. 9, my wisdom *r.* with me.
Jer. 17. 25, this city shall *r.* for ever.
  37. 10, there *r.* but wounded men.
Lam. 2. 22, in day of anger none *r.*
Mat. 11. 23, would have *r.* until this day.
John 6. 12, gather up the fragments that *r.*
  9. 41, ye say, we see, therefore your sin *r.*
Acts 5. 4, whiles it *r.*, was it not thine own ?
1 Cor. 15. 6, the greater part *r.* to this present.
1 Thess. 4. 15, we which are alive and *r.* unto
    coming of the Lord.
Heb. 4. 9, there *r.* a rest to the people of God.
  10. 26, there *r.* no more sacrifice for sins.
Rev. 3. 2, things which *r.* ready to die.
See Ps. 76. 10 ; Lam. 5. 19 ; John 1. 33 ; 1 John 3. 9.
REMEDY. 2 Chron. 36. 16 ; Prov. 6. 15 ; 29. 1.
REMEMBER. Gen. 40. 23, yet did not the butler *r.*
  41. 9, I do *r.* my faults this day.
Ex. 13. 3, *r.* this day ye came out of Egypt.
  20. 8, *r.* the sabbath day.
Num. 15. 33, *r.* all the commandments.
Deut. 5. 15 ; 15. 15 ; 16. 12 ; 24. 18, 22, *r.* thou wast
    a servant.
  8. 2, *r.* all the way the Lord led thee.
  32. 7, *r.* the days of old.
1 Chron. 16. 12, *r.* his marvellous works.
Neh. 13. 14, *r.* me, O God, concerning this.
Job 7. 7, O *r.* my life is wind.
  11. 16, *r.* it as waters that pass away.
  14. 13, appoint me a set time and *r.* me.
  24. 20, the sinner shall be no more *r.*
Ps. 9. 12, when he maketh inquisition he *r.*
  20. 7, we will *r.* the name of the Lord.
  25. 6, *r.* thy mercies, they have been ever of old.
  7, *r.* not sins of my youth, by mercy *r.* me.
  63. 6, when I *r.* thee upon my bed.
  77. 3, I *r.* God and was troubled.
  78. 39, he *r.* that they were but flesh.
  79. 8, *r.* not against us former iniquities.
  89. 47, *r.* how short my time is.
  105. 8, he hath *r.* his covenant for ever.
  119. 55, I have *r.* thy name in the night.
  136. 23, who *r.* us in our low estate.
  137. 1, we wept when we *r.* Zion.
Prov. 31. 7, drink and *r.* his misery no more.
Eccl. 5. 20, not much *r.* the days of his life.
  11. 8, let him *r.* the days of darkness.
  12. 1, *r.* now thy Creator.
Cant. 1. 4, we will *r.* thy love.
Isa. 23. 16, sing songs that thou mayest be *r.*
  43. 18 ; 46. 9, *r.* ye not the former things.
  57. 11, thou hast not *r.* me.
  65. 17, the former heavens shall not be *r.*
Jer. 31. 20, I do earnestly *r.* him still.
  51. 50, ye that have escaped *r.* the Lord.
Lam. 1. 9, she *r.* not her last end.
Ezek. 16. 61 ; 20. 43 ; 36. 31, then shalt thou *r.* thy
    ways.
Amos 1. 9, and *r.* not the brotherly covenant.
Hab. 3. 2, in wrath *r.* mercy.
Zech. 10. 9, they shall *r.* me in far countries.
Mat. 26. 75, Peter *r.* the word of Jesus.
Lu. 16. 25, son, *r.* that thou in thy lifetime.

Lu. 17. 32, *r.* Lot's wife.
  23. 42, Lord *r.* me when thou comest.
  24. 8, and they *r.* his words.
John 2. 22, when he was risen, they *r.*
  15. 20, *r.* the word I said unto you.
Acts 11. 16, then *r.* I the word of the Lord.
  20. 35, *r.* the words of the Lord Jesus.
Gal. 2. 10, that we should *r.* the poor.
Col. 4. 18, *r.* my bonds.
1 Thess. 1. 3, *r.* your work of faith.
Heb. 13. 3, *r.* them that are in bonds.
  7, *r.* them that have the rule over you.
Rev. 2. 5, *r.* from whence thou art fallen.
  3. 3, *r.* how thou hast received.
See Ps. 88. 5 ; 103. 14 ; Mat. 5. 23 ; John 16. 21.
REMEMBRANCE. Num. 5. 15, bringing iniquity
    to *r.*
2 Sam. 18. 18, no son to keep my name in *r.*
1 Kings 17. 18, art thou come to call my sin to *r.*
Job 18. 17, his *r.* shall perish.
Ps. 6. 5, in death there is no *r.* of thee.
  30. 4 ; 97. 12, give thanks at *r.* of his holiness.
  77. 6, I call to *r.* my song in the night.
  112. 6, righteous shall be in everlasting *r.*
Eccl. 1. 11, there is no *r.* of former things.
  2. 16, no *r.* of wise more than the fool.
Isa. 43. 26, put me in *r.*
  57. 8, behind doors hast thou set up thy *r.*
Lam. 3. 20, my soul hath them still in *r.*
Ezek. 23. 19, calling to *r.* days of youth.
Mal. 3. 16, a book of *r.*
Lu. 22. 19 ; 1 Cor. 11. 24, this do in *r.* of me.
John 14. 26, bring all things to your *r.*
Acts 10. 31, thine alms are had in *r.*
2 Tim. 1. 3, I have *r.* of thee in my prayers.
  2. 14, of these things put them in *r.*
See Heb. 10. 3 ; 2 Pet. 1. 12 ; 3. 1 ; Jude 5 ; Rev.
  16. 19.
REMIT. John 20. 23, whose soever sins ye *r.*, are *r.*
REMNANT. Lev. 5. 13, the *r.* shall be the priest's.
2 Kings 19. 4 ; Isa. 37. 4, lift up prayer for the *r.*
Ezra 9. 8, grace shewed to leave us a *r.*
Isa. 1. 9, unless the Lord had left a *r.*
  11. 11, to recover the *r.* of his people.
  16. 14, the *r.* shall be very small and feeble.
Jer. 44. 28, *r.* shall know whose words shall stand.
Ezek. 6. 8, yet will I leave a *r.*
Joel 2. 32, the *r.* whom the Lord shall call.
See Mic. 2. 12 ; Hag. 1. 12 ; Rom. 11. 5 ; Rev. 11. 13.
REMOVE. Deut. 19. 14, shall not *r.* landmark.
Job 9. 5, *r.* the mountains and they know not.
  14. 18, the rock is *r.* out of his place.
Ps. 36. 11, let not hand of wicked *r.* me.
  39. 10, *r.* thy stroke away from me.
  46. 2, not fear though the earth be *r.*
  81. 6, I *r.* his shoulder from burden.
  103. 12, so far hath he *r.* our transgressions.
  119. 22, *r.* from me reproach.
  125. 1, as mount Zion, which cannot be *r.*
Prov. 4. 27, *r.* thy foot from evil.
  10. 30, the righteous shall never be *r.*
Eccl. 11. 10, *r.* sorrow from thy heart.
Isa. 13. 13, earth shall *r.* out of her place.
  24. 20, earth shall be *r.* like a cottage.
  29. 13, have *r.* their heart far from me.
  54. 10, the hills shall be *r.*
Jer. 4. 1, return unto me, then shalt thou not *r.*
Lam. 3. 17, thou hast *r.* my soul from peace.
Mat. 17. 20, ye shall say, *r.* hence, and it shall *r.*
Lu. 22. 42, *r.* this cup from me.
Gal. 1. 6, I marvel ye are so soon *r.*
Rev. 2. 5, or else I will *r.* thy candlestick.
See Job 19. 10 ; Eccl. 10. 9 ; Ezek. 12. 3 ; Heb. 12. 27.
REND. 1 Kings 11. 11, I will *r.* the kingdom.
Isa. 64. 1, that thou wouldest *r.* the heavens.
Hos. 13. 8, I will *r.* the caul of their heart.
Joel 2. 13, *r.* your heart.
Mat. 7. 6, lest they turn again and *r.* you.
See Ps. 7. 2 ; Eccl. 3. 7 ; Jer. 4. 30 ; John 19. 24.
RENDER. Deut. 32. 41, *r.* vengeance.

1 Sam. 26. 23, *r*. to every man his faithfulness.
Job 33. 26, he will *r*. to man his righteousness.
34. 11, the work of a man shall be *r*. to him.
Ps. 28. 4, *r*. to them their desert.
38. 20, they that *r*. evil for good.
79. 12, and *r*. to our neighbour sevenfold.
94. 2, *r*. a reward to the proud.
116. 12, what shall I *r*. to the Lord.
Prov. 24. 12; Rom. 2. 6, *r*. to every man according.
26. 16, wiser than seven men who can *r*. a reason.
Hos. 14. 2, so will we *r*. the calves of our lips.
Joel 3. 4, will ye *r*. me a recompence.
Zech. 9. 12, I will *r*. double.
Mat. 21. 41, *r*. fruits in their seasons.
22. 21; Mk. 12. 17; Lu. 20. 25, *r*. unto Cæsar.
Rom. 13. 7, *r*. to all their dues.
1 Thess. 3. 9, what thanks can we *r*.
5. 15, see that none *r*. evil for evil.
1 Pet. 3. 9, not *r*. evil for evil, or railing.
See Num. 18. 9; Judg. 9. 56; Ps. 62. 12; Isa. 66. 6.
RENEW. Job 10. 17, thou *r*. thy witnesses.
29. 20, my bow was *r*. in my hand.
Ps. 51. 10, and *r*. a right spirit within me.
103. 5, thy youth is *r*. like the eagle's.
104. 30, thou *r*. the face of the earth.
Isa. 40. 31, wait on Lord shall *r*. strength.
41. 1, let the people *r*. their strength.
Lam. 5. 21, *r*. our days as of old.
2 Cor. 4. 16, the inward man is *r*. day by day.
Eph. 4. 23, be *r*. in spirit of your mind.
Col. 3. 10, new man which is *r*. in knowledge.
Heb. 6. 6, if they fall away, to *r*. them again.
See 2 Chron. 15. 8; Rom. 12. 2; Tit. 3. 5.
RENOUNCED. 2 Cor. 4. 2, have *r*. hidden things.
RENOWN. Gen. 6. 4; Num. 16. 2, men of *r*.
Num. 1. 16, the *r*. of the congregation.
Isa. 14. 20, evil doers shall never be *r*.
Ezek. 16. 14, thy *r*. went forth among the heathen.
34. 29, a plant of *r*.
See Ezek. 23. 23; 26. 17; 39. 13; Dan. 9. 15.
RENT. Gen. 37. 33, Joseph is *r*. in pieces.
Josh. 9. 4, bottles old and *r*.
Judg. 14. 5, 6, *r*. lion as he would have *r*. a kid.
1 Kings 13. 3, the altar shall be *r*.
Job 26. 8, the cloud is not *r*. under them.
Mat. 9. 16; Mk. 2. 21, the *r*. is made worse.
27. 51; Mk. 15. 38; Lu. 23. 45, vail was *r*. in twain.
See 1 Sam. 15. 27; Job 1. 20; 2. 12; Jer. 36. 24.
REPAID. Prov. 13. 21, to righteous good shall be *r*.
REPAIR. 2 Chron. 24. 5, gather money to *r*. the house.
Isa. 61. 4, they shall *r*. the waste cities.
See 2 Kings 12. 5; Ezra 9. 9; Neh. 3. 4; Isa. 58. 12.
REPAY. Deut. 7. 10, he will *r*. to his face.
Lu. 10. 35, when I come I will *r*. thee.
Rom. 12. 19, vengeance is mine, I will *r*.
Philem. 19, I have written it, I will *r*. it.
See Job 21. 31; 41. 11; Isa. 59. 18.
REPEATETH. Prov. 17. 9, he that *r*. a matter.
REPENT. Gen. 6. 6, it *r*. the Lord.
Ex. 13. 17, lest the people *r*.
32. 14; 2 Sam. 24. 16; 1 Chron. 21. 15; Jer. 26. 19, Lord *r*. of evil he thought to do.
Num. 23. 19, neither son of man that he should *r*.
Deut. 32. 36, Lord shall *r*. for his servants.
1 Sam. 15. 29, will not *r*., for he is not a man that he should *r*.
Job 42. 6, I *r*. in dust and ashes.
Ps. 90. 13, let it *r*. thee concerning thy servants.
106. 45, Lord *r*. according to his mercies.
110. 4; Heb. 7. 21, Lord hath sworn and will not *r*.
Jer. 8. 6, no man *r*. of his wickedness.
18. 8; 26. 13, if that nation turn I will *r*.
31. 19, after that I was turned I *r*.
Joel 2. 13, he is slow to anger and *r*. him.
Mat. 12. 41; Lu. 11. 32, they *r*. at the preaching.
21. 29, afterward he *r*. and went.
27. 3, Judas *r*. himself.

Lu. 13. 3, except ye *r*.
15. 7, joy over one sinner that *r*.
17. 3, if thy brother *r*., forgive him.
Acts 8. 22, *r*. of this thy wickedness.
Rev. 2. 21, space to *r*., and she *r*. not.
See Acts 2. 38; 17. 30; Rev. 2. 5; 3. 3; 16. 9.
REPENTANCE. Hos. 13. 14, *r*. shall be hid.
Mat. 3. 8; Lu. 3. 8; Acts 26. 2), fruits meet for *r*.
Rom. 2. 4, goodness of God leadeth thee to *r*.
11. 29, gifts of God are without *r*.
2 Cor. 7. 10, *r*. not to be repented of.
Heb. 6. 1, not laying again the foundation of *r*.
6, to renew them again to *r*.
12. 17, no place of *r*., though he sought it.
See Lu. 15. 7; Acts 20. 21; 2 Tim. 2. 25; 2 Pet. 3. 9.
REPLENISH. Gen. 1. 28; 9. 1; Jer. 31. 25; Ezek. 26. 2.
REPLIEST. Rom. 9. 20, that *r*. against God.
REPORT (*n*.). Gen. 37. 2, their evil *r*.
Ex. 23. 1, thou shalt not *r*. a false *r*.
Num. 13. 32, an evil *r*. of the land.
1 Sam. 2. 24, it is no good *r*. I hear.
1 Kings 10. 6; 2 Chron. 9. 5, it was a true *r*. I heard.
Prov. 15. 30, a good *r*. maketh the bones fat.
Isa. 28. 19, a vexation only to understand *r*.
53. 1, who hath believed our *r*.
Acts 6. 3, men of honest *r*.
10. 22, of good *r*. among the Jews.
2 Cor. 6. 8, by evil *r*. and good *r*.
Phil. 4. 8, whatsoever things are of good *r*.
1 Tim. 3. 7, a bishop must have a good *r*.
See Deut. 2. 25; Heb. 11. 2, 39; 3 John 12.
REPORT (*v*.). Neh. 6. 6, it is *r*. among heathen.
Jer. 20. 10, *r*., say they, and we will *r*. it.
Mat. 28. 15, saying is commonly *r*.
Acts 16. 2, well *r*. of by the brethren.
1 Cor. 14. 25, he will *r*. that God is in you.
See Ezek. 9. 11; Rom. 3. 8; 1 Tim. 5. 10; 1 Pet. 1. 12.
REPROACH (*n*.). Gen. 30. 23, hath taken away my *r*.
34. 14, that were a *r*. to us.
1 Sam. 11. 2, lay it for a *r*. upon all Israel.
Neh. 2. 17, build that we be no more a *r*.
Ps. 15. 3, that taketh not up a *r*.
22. 6, a *r*. of men.
31. 11, I was a *r*. among mine enemies.
44. 13; 79. 4; 89. 41, a *r*. to our neighbours.
69. 9; Rom. 15. 3, the *r*. of them that reproach-ed thee.
78. 66, put them to a perpetual *r*.
Prov. 6. 33, his *r*. shall not be wiped away.
14. 34, sin is a *r*. to any people.
18. 3, with ignominy cometh *r*.
Isa. 43. 28, I have given Israel to *r*.
51. 7, fear not the *r*. of men.
Jer. 23. 40, I will bring an everlasting *r*.
31. 19, I did bear the *r*. of my youth.
Lam. 3. 30, he is filled full with *r*.
Ezek. 5. 14, I will make thee a *r*. among nations.
15, Jerusalem shall be a *r*. and a taunt.
Mic. 6. 16, ye shall bear the *r*. of my people.
2 Cor. 11. 21, I speak as concerning *r*.
12. 10, pleasure in *r*. for Christ's sake.
1 Tim. 3. 7, good report lest he fall into *r*.
4. 10, we labour and suffer *r*.
Heb. 11. 26, the *r*. of Christ greater riches.
13. 13, without the camp bearing his *r*.
See Ps. 69. 10; 119. 39; Jer. 6. 10; 20. 8; 24. 9.
REPROACH (*v*.). Num. 15. 30, *r*. the Lord.
Ruth 2. 15, *r*. her not.
2 Kings 19. 22; Isa. 37. 23, whom hast thou *r*.
Job 19. 3, these ten times have ye *r*. me.
27. 6, my heart shall not *r*. me.
Ps. 42. 10, as with a sword mine enemies *r*. me.
44. 16, the voice of him that *r*.
74. 22, how the foolish man *r*. thee.
119. 42; Prov. 27. 11, to answer him that *r*. me.

Prov. 14. 31 ; 17. 5, oppresseth poor *r.* his Maker.
Lu. 6. 22, men shall *r.* you for my sake.
1 Pet. 4. 14, if ye be *r.* for Christ's sake.
See Ps. 55. 12 ; 74. 18 ; 79. 12 ; 89. 51 ; Zeph. 2. 8.
REPROACHFULLY. Job 16. 10 ; 1 Tim. 5. 14.
REPROVE. 1 Chron. 16. 21, *r.* kings for their sakes.
Job 6. 25, what doth your arguing *r.*
13. 10, he will *r.* you if ye accept.
22. 4, will he *r.* thee for fear.
40. 2, he that *r.* God let him answer it.
Ps. 50. 8, I will not *r.* thee for burnt offerings.
141. 5, let him *r.* me, it shall be excellent oil.
Prov. 9. 8, *r.* not a scorner lest he hate thee.
15. 12, a scorner loveth not one that *r.*
19. 25, *r.* one that hath understanding.
29. 1, he that being often *r.*
30. 6, lest he *r.* thee and thou be found.
Isa. 11. 4, *r.* with equity for the meek.
Jer. 2. 19, thy backslidings shall *r.* thee.
John 3. 20, lest his deeds should be *r.*
16. 8, he will *r.* the world of sin.
See Lu. 3. 19 ; Eph. 5. 11, 13 ; 2 Tim. 4. 2.
REPROVER. Prov. 25. 12 ; Ezek. 3. 26.
REPUTATION. Eccl. 10. 1, him that is in *r.* for wisdom.
Acts 5. 34, had in *r.* among the people.
Phil. 2. 7, made himself of no *r.*
29, hold such in *r.*
See Job 18. 3 ; Dan. 4. 35 ; Gal. 2. 2.
REQUEST. Judg. 8. 24, I would desire a *r.* of thee.
Ezra 7. 6, the king granted all his *r.*
Job 6. 8, Oh that I might have my *r.*
Ps. 21. 2, hast not withholden *r.* of his lips.
106. 15, he gave them their *r.*
Phil. 1. 4, in every prayer making *r.* with joy.
4. 6, let your *r.* be made known.
See 2 Sam. 14. 15 ; Neh. 2. 4 ; Esth. 4. 8 ; 5. 3.
REQUESTED. 1 Kings 19. 4, Elijah *r.* that he might die.
REQUIRE. Gen. 9. 5, blood of your lives will I *r.*
31. 39, of my hand didst thou *r.* it.
Deut. 10. 12 ; Mic. 6. 8, what doth the Lord *r.*
Josh. 22. 23 ; 1 Sam. 20. 16, let the Lord himself *r.* it.
Ruth 3. 11, I will do all thou *r.*
1 Sam. 21. 8, the king's business *r.* haste.
2 Sam. 3. 13, one thing I *r.* of thee.
19. 38, whatsoever thou shalt *r.* I will do.
2 Chron. 24. 22, the Lord look on it and *r.* it.
Neh. 5. 12, we will restore and *r.* nothing of them.
Ps. 10. 13, he hath said thou wilt not *r.* it.
40. 6, sin offering hast thou not *r.*
137. 3, they that wasted us *r.* of us mirth.
Prov. 30. 7, two things have I *r.* of thee.
Eccl. 3. 15, God *r.* that which is past.
Isa. 1. 12, who hath *r.* this at your hand ?
Ezek. 3. 18 ; 33. 6, his blood will I *r.* at thine hand.
34. 10, I will *r.* my flock at their hand.
Lu. 11. 50, may be *r.* of this generation.
12. 20, this night thy soul shall be *r.*
48, of him shall much be *r.*
19. 23, I might have *r.* mine own with usury.
1 Cor. 1. 22, the Jews *r.* a sign.
4. 2, it is *r.* in stewards.
See 2 Chron. 8. 14 ; Ezra 3. 4 ; Neh. 5. 18 ; Esth. 2. 15.
REQUITE. Gen. 50. 15, Joseph will certainly *r.* us.
Deut. 32. 6, do ye thus *r.* the Lord.
Judg. 1. 7, as I have done so God hath *r.* me.
2 Sam. 2. 6, I also will *r.* you this kindness.
16. 12, it may be the Lord will *r.* good for this.
1 Tim. 5. 4, learn to *r.* their parents.
See Ps. 10. 14 ; 41. 10 ; Jer. 51. 56.
REREWARD. Josh. 6. 9 ; Isa. 52. 12 ; 58. 8.
RESCUE. Ps. 35. 17, *r.* my soul.
Hos. 5. 14, none shall *r.* him.
See Deut. 28. 31 ; 1 Sam. 14. 45 ; Dan. 6. 27 ; Acts 23. 27.

RESEMBLANCE. Zech. 5. 6, this is their *r.*
RESEMBLE. Judg. 8. 18 ; Lu. 13. 18.
RESERVE. Gen. 27. 36, hast thou not *r.* a blessing.
Ruth 2. 18, gave her mother in law that she had *r.*
Job 21. 30, the wicked is *r.* to day of destruction.
38. 23, which I have *r.* against time of trouble.
Jer. 3. 5, will he *r.* anger for ever.
5. 24, he *r.* the weeks of harvest.
50. 20, I will pardon them whom I *r.*
Nah. 1. 2, the Lord *r.* wrath for his enemies.
1 Pet. 1. 4, an inheritance *r.* in heaven.
2 Pet. 2. 4, to be *r.* to judgment.
3. 7, the heavens and earth are *r.* unto fire.
See Num. 18. 9 ; Rom. 11. 4 ; 2 Pet. 2. 9 ; Jude 6, 13.
RESIDUE. Ex. 10. 5, locusts shall eat the *r.*
Isa. 38. 10, I am deprived of the *r.* of my years.
Jer. 15. 9, *r.* of them will I deliver to the sword.
Ezek. 9. 8, wilt thou destroy all the *r.*
Zech. 8. 11, I will not be to the *r.* as in former days.
Mal. 2. 15, yet had he the *r.* of the Spirit.
Acts 15. 17, that the *r.* might seek the Lord.
See Neh. 11. 20 ; Jer. 8. 3 ; 29. 1 ; 39. 3.
RESIST. Zech. 3. 1, at his right hand to *r.*
Mat. 5. 39, *r.* not evil.
Lu. 21. 15, adversaries shall not be able to *r.*
Rom. 9. 19, who hath *r.* his will.
13. 2, whoso *r.* power, *r.* ordinance of God.
Jas. 4. 6 ; 1 Pet. 5. 5, God *r.* the proud.
7, *r.* the devil, and he will flee.
1 Pet. 5. 9, whom *r.* stedfast in the faith.
See Acts 6. 10 ; 7. 51 ; 2 Tim. 3. 8 ; Heb. 12. 4.
RESORT. Neh. 4. 20, *r.* hither to us.
Ps. 71. 3, whereunto I may continually *r.*
John 18. 2, Jesus ofttimes *r.* thither.
See Mk. 2. 13 ; 10. 1 ; John 18. 20 ; Acts 16. 13.
RESPECT (*n.*). Gen. 4. 4, Lord had *r.* to Abel.
Ex. 2. 25, God had *r.* unto them.
1 Kings 8. 28 ; 2 Chron. 6. 19, have *r.* unto their prayer.
2 Chron. 19. 7 ; Rom. 2. 11 ; Eph. 6. 9 ; Col. 3. 25, there is no *r.* of persons with God.
Ps. 74. 20, have *r.* unto thy covenant.
119. 15, I will have *r.* unto thy ways.
138. 6, yet hath he *r.* to the lowly.
Prov. 24. 23 ; 28. 21, not good to have *r.* of persons.
Isa. 17. 7, his eyes shall have *r.* to Holy One.
22. 11, nor had *r.* to him that fashioned it.
Phil. 4. 11, not that I speak in *r.* of want.
See Heb. 11. 26 ; Jas. 2. 1, 3, 9 ; 1 Pet. 1. 17.
RESPECT (*v.*). Lev. 19. 15, shalt not *r.* person of poor.
Deut. 1. 17, ye shall not *r.* persons in judgment.
Job 37. 24, he *r.* not any that are wise of heart.
See Num. 16. 15 ; 2 Sam. 14. 14 ; Ps. 40. 4 ; Lam. 4. 16.
RESPITE. Ex. 8. 15 ; 1 Sam. 11. 3.
REST (*n.*). Gen. 49. 15, Issachar saw that *r.* was good.
Ex. 31. 15 ; 35. 2 ; Lev. 16. 31 ; 23. 3, 32 ; 25. 4, the sabbath of *r.*
33. 14, my presence shall go with thee, and I will give thee *r.*
Lev. 25. 5, a year of *r.* to the land.
Deut. 12. 10, when he giveth you *r.* from your enemies.
Judg. 3. 30, the land had *r.* fourscore years.
Ruth 3. 1, shall not I seek *r.* for thee.
1 Chron. 22. 9, a man of *r.*, and I will give him *r.*
18, hath he not given you *r.* on every side.
28. 2, to build a house of *r.*
Neh. 9. 28, after they had *r.* they did evil.
Esth. 9. 16, the Jews had *r.* from their enemies.
Job 3. 17, there the weary be at *r.*
11. 18, thou shalt take thy *r.* in safety.
17. 16, when our *r.* together is in the dust.
Ps. 55. 6, then would I fly away and be at *r.*
95. 11 ; Heb. 3. 11, not enter into my *r.*
116. 7, return to thy *r.*, O my soul.
132. 8, arise into thy *r.*

Ps. 132. 14, this is my *r.* for ever.
Eccl. 2. 23, his heart taketh not *r.* in the night.
Isa. 11. 10, his *r.* shall be glorious.
14. 7 ; Zech. 1. 11, earth is at *r.* and quiet.
18. 4, I will take my *r.*
30. 15, in returning and *r.* shall ye be saved.
66. 1, where is the place of my *r.?*
Jer. 6. 16, ye shall find *r.* for your souls.
Ezek. 38. 11, I will go to them that are at *r.*
Mic. 2. 10, depart, this is not your *r.*
Mat. 11. 28, I will give you *r.*
29, ye shall find *r.* to your souls.
12. 43 ; Lu. 11. 24, seeking *r.* and finding none.
26. 45 ; Mk. 14. 41, sleep on and take your *r.*
John 11. 13, of taking *r.* in sleep.
Acts 9. 31, then had the churches *r.*
See Prov. 29. 17 ; Eccl. 6. 5 ; Dan. 4. 4 ; 2 Thess. 1. 7.
REST (*v.*).   Gen. 2. 2, he *r.* on seventh day.
Num. 11. 25, when the Spirit *r.* upon them.
2 Chron. 32. 8, people *r.* on the words.
Job 3. 18, there the prisoners *r.* together.
Ps. 16. 9 ; Acts 2. 26, my flesh shall *r.* in hope.
37. 7, *r.* in the Lord.
Eccl. 7. 9, anger *r.* in bosom of fools.
Isa. 11. 2, the spirit of the Lord shall *r.* upon him.
28. 12, ye may cause the weary to *r.*
57. 20, like the sea when it cannot *r.*
62. 1, for Jerusalem's sake I will not *r.*
63. 14, Spirit of the Lord caused him to *r.*
Jer. 47. 6, *r.* and be still.
Dan. 12. 13, thou shalt *r.* and stand in thy lot.
Mk. 6. 31, come and *r.* awhile.
2 Cor. 12. 9, power of Christ may *r.* on me.
Rev. 4. 8, they *r.* not day and night.
6. 11, *r.* yet for a little season.
14. 13, that they may *r.* from their labours.
See Prov. 14. 33 ; Cant. 1. 7 ; Isa. 32. 18 ; Lu. 10. 6.
RESTORE.   Ex. 22. 4, he shall *r.* double.
Lev. 6. 4, he shall *r.* that he took away.
Deut. 22. 2, things strayed thou shalt *r.* again.
Ps. 23. 3, he *r.* my soul.
51. 12, *r.* to me the joy of thy salvation.
69. 4, I *r.* that which I took not away.
Isa. 1. 26, I will *r.* thy judges as at the first.
Jer. 27. 22, I will *r.* them to this place.
30. 17, I will *r.* health to thee.
Ezek. 33. 15, if wicked *r.* pledge.
Mat. 17. 11 ; Mk. 9. 12, Elias shall *r.* all things.
Lu. 19. 8, I *r.* him fourfold.
Acts 1. 6, wilt thou at this time *r.* the kingdom.
Gal. 6. 1, *r.* such an one in meekness.
See Ruth 4. 15 ; Isa. 58. 12 ; Joel 2. 25 ; Mk. 8. 25.
RESTRAIN.   Gen. 11. 6, nothing will be *r.*
Ex. 36. 6, people were *r.* from bringing.
1 Sam. 3. 13, his sons made themselves vile, and he *r.* them not.
Job 15. 4, thou *r.* prayer before God.
8, dost thou *r.* wisdom to thyself.
Ps. 76. 10, remainder of wrath shalt thou *r.*
See Gen. 8. 2 ; Isa. 63. 15 ; Ezek. 31. 15 ; Acts 14. 18.
RETAIN.   Job 2. 9, dost thou still *r.* integrity.
Prov. 3. 18, happy is every one that *r.* her.
4. 4, let thine heart *r.* my words.
11. 16, a gracious woman *r.* honour.
Eccl. 8. 8, no man hath power to *r.* the spirit.
John 20. 23, whose soever sins ye *r.* they are *r.*
See Mic. 7. 18 ; Rom. 1. 28 ; Philem. 13.
RETIRE.   Judg. 20. 39 ; 2 Sam. 11. 15 ; Jer. 4. 6.
RETURN.   Gen. 3. 19, to dust shalt thou *r.*
Ex. 14. 27, the sea *r.* to his strength.
Judg. 7. 3, whosoever is fearful, let him *r.*
Ruth 1. 16, entreat me not to leave thee or *r.*
2 Sam. 12. 23, he shall not *r.* to me.
2 Kings 20. 10, let the shadow *r.* backward.
Job 1. 21, naked shall I *r.* thither.
7. 10, he shall *r.* no more.
10. 21 ; 16. 22, I go whence I shall not *r.*
15. 22, he believeth not he shall *r.* out of darkness.

Job 33. 25, he shall *r.* to the days of his youth.
Ps. 35. 13, my prayer *r.* into mine own bosom.
73. 10, his people *r.* hither.
90. 3, thou sayest, *r.*, ye children of men.
104. 29, they die and *r.* to their dust.
116. 7, *r.* to thy rest, O my soul.
Prov. 2. 19, none that go to her *r.* again.
26. 11, as a dog *r.* to his vomit.
27, he that rolleth a stone, it will *r.*
Eccl. 1. 7, whence rivers come, thither they *r.* again.
5. 15, naked shall he *r.* to go as he came.
12. 2, nor the clouds *r.* after the rain.
7, dust *r.* to earth and spirit *r.* to God.
Isa. 21. 12, if ye will enquire, enquire ye ; *r.*, come.
35. 10 ; 51. 11, the ransomed of the Lord shall *r.*
44. 22, *r.* unto me, for I have redeemed thee.
45. 23, word is gone out and shall not *r.*
55. 11, it shall not *r.* to me void.
Jer. 4. 1, if thou wilt *r.*, saith the Lord, *r.* unto me.
15. 19, let them *r.* unto thee, but *r.* not thou.
24. 7, they shall *r.* with whole heart.
31. 8, a great company shall *r.* thither.
36. 3, *r.* every man from his evil way.
Ezek. 46. 9, he shall not *r.* by the way he came.
Hos. 2. 7, I will *r.* to my first husband.
5. 15, I will *r.* to my place.
7. 16, they *r.*, but not to the most High.
14. 7, they that dwell under his shadow shall *r.*
Amos 4. 6, yet have ye not *r.* to me.
Joel 2. 14, who knoweth if he will *r.* and repent.
Zech. 1. 16, I am *r.* to Jerusalem with mercies.
8. 3, I am *r.* to Zion and will dwell.
Mal. 3. 7, *r.* to me and I will *r.* to you.
18, then shall ye *r.* and discern.
Mat. 12. 44 ; Lu. 11. 24, I will *r.* into my house.
24. 18, neither let him in the field *r.* back.
Lu. 9. 10, apostles *r.* and told him all.
10. 17, the seventy *r.* with joy.
12. 36, when he will *r.* from wedding.
17. 18, not found that *r.* to give glory.
Acts 13. 34, now no more to *r.* to corruption.
Heb. 11. 15, might have had opportunity to *r.*
1 Pet. 2. 25, now *r.* to the Shepherd of your souls.
See Gen. 31. 3 ; Ex. 4. 18 ; Lev. 25. 10 ; Isa. 55. 7.

REVEAL.   Deut. 29. 29, things *r.* belong unto us and to our children.
1 Sam. 3. 7, nor was word of Lord *r.* to him.
Job 20. 27, the heaven shall *r.* his iniquity.
Prov. 11. 13 ; 20. 19, a talebearer *r.* secrets.
Isa. 22. 14, it was *r.* in mine ears.
40. 5, glory of the Lord shall be *r.*
53. 1 ; John 12. 38, to whom is arm of Lord *r.*
56. 1, my righteousness is near to be *r.*
Jer. 11. 20, unto thee have I *r.* my cause.
33. 6, I will *r.* abundance of peace.
Dan. 2. 22, he *r.* deep and secret things.
28, there is a God that *r.* secrets.
Amos 3. 7, he *r.* his secrets to the prophets.
Mat. 10. 26 ; Lu. 12. 2, nothing covered that shall not be *r.*
11. 25, hast *r.* them unto babes.
16. 17, flesh and blood hath not *r.* it.
Lu. 2. 35, that thoughts of many hearts may be *r.*
17. 30, in day when Son of man is *r.*
Rom. 1. 17, righteousness of God *r.*
18, wrath of God is *r.* from heaven.
8. 18, glory which shall be *r.* in us.
1 Cor. 2. 10, God hath *r.* them by his Spirit.
3. 13, it shall be *r.* by fire.
14. 30, if anything be *r.* to another.
Gal. 1. 16, to *r.* his Son in me.
2 Thess. 1. 7, when Lord Jesus shall be *r.*
2. 3, man of sin be *r.*
8, that wicked one be *r.*
1 Pet. 1. 5, ready to be *r.* in last time.
4. 13, when his glory shall be *r.*
5. 1, partaker of glory that shall be *r.*
See Eph. 3. 5 ; Phil. 3. 15 ; 2 Thess. 2. 6.

REVELATION. Rom. 2. 5, *r.* of righteous judgment.
16. 25, *r.* of the mystery.
1 Cor. 14. 26, every one hath a *r.*
2 Cor. 12. 1, to visions and *r.*
See Gal. 2. 2 ; Eph. 1. 17 ; 3. 3 ; 1 Pet. 1. 13 ; Rev. 1. 1.

REVELLINGS. Gal. 5. 21 ; 1 Pet. 4. 3.

REVENGE. Jer. 15. 15, O Lord, *r.* me.
20. 10, we shall take our *r.* on him.
Nah. 1. 2, the Lord *r.* and is furious.
2 Cor. 7. 11, what *r.* it wrought in you.
10. 6, in readiness to *r.*
See Ps. 79. 10 ; Ezek. 25. 12 ; Rom. 13. 4.

REVENUE. Prov. 8. 19, my *r.* better than silver.
16. 8, better than great *r.* without right.
Jer. 12. 13, ashamed of your *r.*
See Ezra 4. 13 ; Prov. 15. 6 ; Isa. 23. 3 ; Jer. 12. 13.

REVERENCE. Ps. 89. 7 ; Mat. 21. 37 ; Mk. 12. 6 ;
Heb. 12. 9.

REVEREND. Ps. 111. 9, holy and *r.* is his name.

REVERSE. Num. 23. 20 ; Esth. 8. 5, 8.

REVILE. Isa. 51. 7, neither be afraid of *r.*
Mat. 27. 39, they that passed by *r.* him.
Mk. 15. 32, they that were crucified *r.* him.
1 Cor. 4. 12, being *r.* we bless.
1 Pet. 2. 23, when he was *r.*, *r.* not again.
See Ex. 22. 28 ; Mat. 5. 11 ; John 9. 28 ; Acts 23. 4.

REVIVE. Neh. 4. 2, will they *r.* the stones.
Ps. 85. 6, wilt thou not *r.* us.
138. 7, thou wilt *r.* me.
Isa. 57. 15, to *r.* spirit of the humble.
Hos. 6. 2, after two days will he *r.* us.
14. 7 ; they shall *r.* as corn.
Hab. 3. 2, *r.* thy work in midst of years.
Rom. 7. 9, when commandment came sin *r.*
14. 9, Christ both died, rose, and *r.*
See Gen. 45. 27 ; 2 Kings 13. 21 ; Ezra 9. 8.

REVOLT. Isa. 1. 5 ; 31. 6 ; 59. 13 ; Jer. 5. 23.

REWARD (*n.*). Gen. 15. 1, thy exceeding great *r.*
Num. 22. 7, *r.* of divination in their hand.
Deut. 10. 17, God who taketh not *r.*
Ruth 2. 12, full *r.* be given thee of the Lord.
2 Sam. 4. 10, thought I would have given *r.*
Job 6. 22, did I say, give a *r.*
7. 2, as an hireling looketh for *r.*
Ps. 19. 11, in keeping them there is great *r.*
58. 11, there is a *r.* for the righteous.
91. 8, thou shalt see the *r.* of the wicked.
127. 3, fruit of womb is his *r.*
Prov. 11. 18, soweth righteousness a sure *r.*
21. 14, a *r.* in the bosom.
24. 20, no *r.* to the evil man.
Eccl. 4. 9, they have a good *r.* for labour
9. 5, neither have they any more a *r.*
Isa. 1. 23, every one followeth after *r.*
5. 23, justify wicked for *r.*
40. 10 ; 62. 11, his *r.* is with him.
Ezek. 16. 34, thou givest *r.*, and no *r.* is given thee.
Dan. 5. 17, give thy *r.* to another.
Hos. 9. 1, thou hast loved a *r.*
Mic. 3. 11, the heads thereof judge for *r.*
7. 3, judge asketh for a *r.*
Mat. 5. 12 ; Lu. 6. 23, great is your *r.* in heaven.
46, what *r.* have ye.
6. 1, ye have no *r.* of your father.
2, 5, 16, they have their *r.*
10. 41, a prophet's *r.*, a righteous man's *r.*
42 ; Mk. 9. 41, in no wise lose *r.*
Lu. 6. 35, do good and your *r.* shall be great.
23. 41, we receive due *r.* of our deeds.
Acts 1. 18, purchased with *r.* of iniquity.
Rom. 4. 4, *r.* is not reckoned.
1 Cor. 3. 8, every man shall receive his own *r.*
9. 18, what is my *r.* then.
Col. 2. 18, let no man beguile you of your *r.*
3. 24, the *r.* of the inheritance.
1 Tim. 5. 18, labourer worthy of his *r.*
Heb. 2. 2 ; 10. 35 ; 11. 26, recompence of *r.*

2 Pet. 2. 13, the *r.* of unrighteousness.
See 2 John 8 ; Jude 11 ; Rev. 11. 18 ; 22. 12.

REWARD (*v.*). Gen. 44. 4, wherefore have ye *r.*
Deut. 32. 41, I will *r.* them that hate me.
1 Sam. 24. 17, thou hast *r.* me good.
2 Chron. 15. 7, be strong, and your work shall be *r.*
20. 11, behold how they *r.* us.
Job 21. 19, he *r.* him and he shall know it.
Ps. 31. 23, plentifully *r.* the proud doer.
35. 12 ; 109. 5, they *r.* me evil for good.
103. 10, nor *r.* us according to our iniquities.
137. 8, happy is he that *r.* thee.
Prov. 17. 13, whoso *r.* evil, evil shall not depart.
25. 22, heap coals, and the Lord shall *r.* thee.
26. 10, both *r.* the fool and *r.* transgressors.
Jer. 31. 16, thy work shall be *r.*
See 2 Sam. 22. 21 ; Mat. 6. 4 ; 16. 27 ; 2 Tim. 4. 14.

RICH. Gen. 13. 2, Abram was very *r.*
14. 23, lest thou shouldest say, I have made Abram *r.*
Ex. 30. 15, the *r.* shall not give more.
Josh. 22. 8, return with much *r.* to your tents.
Ruth 3. 10, followedst not poor or *r.*
1 Sam. 2. 7, the Lord maketh poor and *r.*
1 Kings 3. 11 ; 2 Chron. 1. 11, neither hast asked *r.*
13, I have given thee both *r.* and honour.
10. 23 ; 2 Chron. 9. 22, Solomon exceeded all for *r.*
1 Chron. 29. 12, both *r.* and honour come of thee.
Job 15. 29, he shall not be *r.*
20. 15, he swallowed down *r.*
27. 19, *r.* man shall lie down, but shall not be gathered.
36. 19, will he esteem thy *r.*
Ps. 37. 16, better than *r.* of many wicked.
39. 6, he heapeth up *r.*
45. 12, the *r.* shall entreat thy favour.
49. 16, be not afraid when one is made *r.*
52. 7, trusted in abundance of *r.*
62. 10, if *r.* increase set not your heart.
73. 12, the ungodly increase in *r.*
104. 24, the earth is full of thy *r.*
112. 3, wealth and *r.* shall be in his house.
Prov. 3. 16, in left hand *r.* and honour.
8. 18, *r.* and honour are with me.
10. 4, hand of diligent maketh *r.*
22, blessing of the Lord maketh *r.*
11. 4, *r.* profit not in day of wrath.
13. 7, poor yet hath great *r.*
18. 23, the *r.* answereth roughly.
21. 17, he that loveth wine shall not be *r.*
23. 5, *r.* make themselves wings.
28. 11, *r.* man is wise in his own conceit.
30. 8, give me neither poverty nor *r.*
Eccl. 5. 13, *r.* kept for owners to their hurt.
10. 20, curse not *r.* in thy bedchamber.
Isa. 45. 3, I will give thee hidden *r.*
53. 9, with the *r.* in his death.
Jer. 9. 23, let not *r.* man glory in his *r.*
17. 11, getteth *r.* and not by right.
Ezek. 28. 5, heart lifted up because of *r.*
Hos. 12. 8, Ephraim said, I am become *r.*
Zech. 11. 5, blessed be the Lord, for I am *r.*
Mat. 13. 22 ; Mk. 4. 19 ; Lu. 8. 14, deceitfulness of *r.*
Mk. 10. 23, hardly shall they that have *r.*
12. 41, *r.* cast in much.
Lu. 1. 53, *r.* he hath sent empty away.
6. 24, woe to you *r.* for ye have received.
12. 21, not *r.* toward God.
14. 12, call not thy *r.* neighbours.
18. 23, sorrowful, for he was very *r.*
Rom. 2. 4, the *r.* of his goodness.
9. 23, make known the *r.* of his glory.
10. 12, the Lord is *r.* to all that call.
11. 12, fall of them the *r.* of the world.
33, the depth of the *r.* of the wisdom.
1 Cor. 4. 8, now ye are full, now ye are *r.*
2 Cor. 6. 10, poor, yet making many *r.*
8. 9, *r.*, yet for your sakes.
Eph. 1. 7, redemption according to the *r.* of grace.
2. 4, God, who is *r.* in mercy.
7, that he might show the exceeding *r.* of grace.

Eph. 3. 8, unsearchable *r.* of Christ.
Phil. 4. 19, according to his *r.* in glory by Christ.
Col. 1. 27, *r.* of the glory of this mystery.
  2. 2, the *r.* of the full assurance.
1 Tim. 6. 9, they that will be *r.* fall into temptation.
  17, nor trust in uncertain *r.*
  18, do good and be *r.* in good works.
Heb. 11. 26, reproach of Christ greater *r.*
Jas. 1. 10, let *r.* rejoice that he is made low.
  2. 5, hath not God chosen the poor, *r.* in faith.
  5. 2, your *r.* are corrupted.
Rev. 2. 9, but thou art *r.*
  3. 17, because thou sayest, I am *r.*
  18, buy of me gold that thou mayest be *r.*
  5. 12, worthy is the Lamb to receive *r.*
  See Lev. 25. 47; Jas. 1. 11; 2. 6; 5. 1; Rev. 6. 15.

RICHLY. Col. 3. 16; 1 Tim. 6. 17.

RIDDANCE. Lev. 23. 22; Zeph. 1. 18.

RIDDLE. Judg. 14. 12; Ezek. 17. 2.

RIDE. Deut. 32. 13, *r.* on high places of the earth.
  33. 26, who *r.* upon the heaven.
Judg. 5. 10, ye that *r.* on white asses.
2 Kings 4. 24, slack not thy *r.* for me.
Job 30. 22, causest me to *r.* upon the wind.
Ps. 45. 4, in thy majesty *r.* prosperously.
  66. 12, hast caused men to *r.* over our heads.
  68. 4, 33, extol him that *r.* on the heavens.
Isa. 19. 1, the Lord *r.* on a swift cloud.
  See Hos. 14. 3; Amos 2. 15; Hab. 3. 8; Hag. 2. 22.

RIDER. Gen. 49. 17; Ex. 15. 1; Job 39. 18; Zech.
  10. 5.

RIDGES. Ps. 65. 10, waterest the *r.* thereof.

RIGHT (*n.*). Gen. 18. 25, shall not Judge of all do *r.*?
Deut. 6. 18; 12. 25; 21. 9, shalt do that is *r.*
  21. 17, the *r.* of the firstborn is his.
2 Sam. 19. 28, what *r.* have I to cry to the king.
Neh. 2. 20, ye have no *r.* in Jerusalem.
Job 34. 6, should I lie against my *r.*
  36. 6, he giveth *r.* to the poor.
Ps. 9. 4, thou maintainest my *r.*
  17. 1, hear the *r.*, O Lord.
  140. 12, Lord will maintain *r.* of the poor.
Prov. 16. 8, great revenues without *r.*
Jer. 17. 11, that getteth riches and not by *r.*
Ezek. 21. 27, till he come whose *r.* it is.
  See Amos 5. 12; Mal. 3. 5; Heb. 13. 10.

RIGHT (*adj.*). Gen. 24. 48, the Lord led me in *r.*
  way.
Deut. 32. 4, God of truth, just and *r.* is he.
1 Sam. 12. 23, I will teach you the good and *r.* way.
2 Sam. 15. 3, thy matters are good and *r.*
Neh. 9. 13, thou gavest them *r.* judgments.
Job 6. 25, how forcible are *r.* words.
  34. 23, he will not lay on man more than *r.*
Ps. 19. 8, the statutes of the Lord are *r.*
  45. 6, sceptre is a *r.* sceptre.
  51. 10, renew a *r.* spirit within me.
  107. 7, he led them forth by the *r.* way.
  119. 75, thy judgments are *r.*
Prov. 4. 11, I have led thee in *r.* paths.
  8. 6, opening of my lips shall be *r.* things.
  12. 5, thoughts of the righteous are *r.*
  15, way of a fool is *r.* in his own eyes.
  14. 12; 16. 25, there is a way that seemeth *r.*
  21. 2, every way of man is *r.* in his own eyes.
  24. 26, kiss his lips that giveth a *r.* answer.
Isa. 30. 10, prophesy not *r.* things.
Jer. 2. 21, planted wholly a *r.* seed.
Ezek. 18. 5, if a man do that which is *r.*
  19; 21. 27; 33. 14, that which is lawful and *r.*
Hos. 14. 9, the ways of the Lord are *r.*
Amos 3. 10, they know not how to do *r.*
Mat. 20. 4, whatsoever is *r.* I will give you.
Mk. 5. 15; Lu. 8. 35, in his *r.* mind.
Lu. 10. 28, thou hast answered *r.*
Eph. 6. 1, obey your parents, this is *r.*
  See Judg. 17. 6; Lu. 12. 57; Acts 8. 21; 2 Pet. 2. 15.

RIGHTEOUS. Gen. 7. 1, thee have I seen *r.* before me.

Gen. 18. 23, wilt thou destroy *r.* with wicked.
  20. 4, wilt thou slay also a *r.* nation?
  38. 26, she hath been more *r.* than I.
Ex. 23. 8, gift perverteth words of the *r.*
Num. 23. 10, let me die the death of the *r.*
Deut. 25. 1; 2 Chron. 6. 23, they shall justify the *r.*
1 Sam. 24. 17, thou art more *r.* than I.
1 Kings 2. 32, two men more *r.* than he.
Job 4. 7, where were the *r.* cut off.
  9. 15, though I were *r.* yet would I not answer.
  15. 14, what is man that he should be *r.*
  17. 9, *r.* shall hold on his way.
  22. 3, is it any pleasure that thou art *r.*
  23. 7, there the *r.* might dispute with him.
  34. 5, Job hath said, I am *r.*
Ps. 1. 5, the congregation of the *r.*
  6, the Lord knoweth the way of the *r.*
  7. 9, the *r.* God trieth the hearts.
  11. 3, what can the *r.* do.
  34. 17, the *r.* cry, and the Lord heareth them.
  19, many are the afflictions of the *r.*
  37. 16, a little that a *r.* man hath.
  21, the *r.* sheweth mercy and giveth.
  25, have not seen the *r.* forsaken.
  29, the *r.* shall inherit the land.
  30, mouth of *r.* speaketh wisdom.
  39, salvation of *r.* is of the Lord.
  55. 22, never suffer the *r.* to be moved.
  58. 11, there is a reward for the *r.*
  69. 28, let them not be written with the *r.*
  92. 12, the *r.* shall flourish like palm tree.
  97. 11, light is sown for the *r.*
  112. 6, *r.* shall be in everlasting remembrance.
  125. 3, rod shall not rest on lot of *r.*
  140. 13, the *r.* shall give thanks.
  141. 5, let the *r.* smite me.
  146. 8, the Lord loveth the *r.*
Prov. 2. 7, he layeth up wisdom for *r.*
  3. 32, his secret is with the *r.*
  10. 3, the Lord will not suffer *r.* to famish.
  11, the mouth of *r.* is a well of life.
  16, labour of *r.* tendeth to life.
  21, lips of *r.* feed many.
  24, desire of the *r.* shall be granted.
  25, the *r.* is an everlasting foundation.
  28, hope of the *r.* shall be gladness.
  30, the *r.* shall never be removed.
  11. 8, the *r.* is delivered out of trouble.
  10, when it goeth well with the *r.*
  21, seed of the *r.* shall be delivered.
  12. 3, the root of the *r.* shall not be moved.
  5, thoughts of the *r.* are right.
  7, house of the *r.* shall stand.
  10, *r.* man regardeth the life of his beast.
  26, the *r.* is more excellent than his neighbour.
  13. 9, the light of the *r.* rejoiceth.
  21, to the *r.* good shall be repaid.
  25, *r.* eateth to the satisfying of his soul.
  14. 9, among the *r.* there is favour.
  32, the *r.* hath hope in his death.
  15. 6, in the house of the *r.* is much treasure.
  19, the way of the *r.* is made plain.
  28, the heart of the *r.* studieth to answer.
  29, he heareth the prayer of the *r.*
  16. 13, *r.* lips are delight of kings.
  18. 10, *r.* runneth into it and is safe.
  28. 1, the *r.* are bold as a lion.
  29. 2, when the *r.* are in authority, people rejoice.
Eccl. 7. 16, be not *r.* overmuch.
  9. 1, the *r.* and the wise are in the hand of God.
  2, one event to *r.* and wicked.
Isa. 3. 10, say to *r.* it shall be well.
  24. 16, songs, even glory to the *r.*
  26. 2, that the *r.* nation may enter.
  41. 2, raised up a *r.* man from the east.
  53. 11, shall my *r.* servant justify.
  57. 1, *r.* perisheth, and no man layeth it.
  60. 21, thy people shall be all *r.*
Jer. 23. 5, raise to David a *r.* branch.
Ezek. 13. 22, with lies ye have made *r.* sad.
  16. 52, thy sisters are more *r.* than thou.

Ezek. 33. 12, the righteousness of the *r.* shall not.
Amos 2. 6, they sold the *r.* for silver.
Mal. 3. 18, discern between the *r.* and wicked.
Mat. 9. 13; Mk. 2. 17; Lu. 5. 32, not come to call *r.*
13. 17, many *r.* men have desired.
43, then shall the *r.* shine forth.
23. 28, outwardly appear *r.* to men.
29, garnish sepulchres of the *r.*
25. 46, the *r.* unto life eternal.
Lu. 1. 6, they were both *r.* before God.
18. 9, trusted they were *r.* and despised others.
23. 47, certainly this was a *r.* man.
John 7. 24, judge *r.* judgment.
Rom. 3. 10, there is none *r.,* no not one.
5. 7, scarcely for a *r.* man will one die.
19, many be made *r.*
2 Thess. 1. 6, it is a *r.* thing with God.
2 Tim. 4. 8, the Lord, the *r.* Judge.
Heb. 11. 4, obtained witness that he was *r.*
1 Pet. 3. 12, eyes of the Lord are over the *r.*
4. 18, if the *r.* scarcely be saved.
2 Pet. 2. 8, Lot vexed his *r.* soul.
1 John 2. 1, Jesus Christ the *r.*
3. 7, *r.* as he is *r.*
Rev. 22. 11, he that is *r.* let him be *r.* still.
See Ezek. 3. 20; Mat. 10. 41; 1 Tim. 1. 9; Jas. 5. 16.

RIGHTEOUSLY. Deut. 1. 16; Prov. 31. 9, judge *r.*
Ps. 67. 4; 96. 10, thou shalt judge the people *r.*
Isa. 33. 15, he that walketh *r.* shall dwell on high.
See Jer. 11. 20; Tit. 2. 12; 1 Pet. 2. 23.

RIGHTEOUSNESS. Gen. 30. 33, so shall my *r.* answer for me.
Deut. 33. 19, offer sacrifices of *r.*
1 Sa. 26. 23; Job 33. 26, render to every man his *r.*
Job 6. 29, return again, my *r.* is in it.
27. 6, my *r.* I hold fast.
29. 14, I put on *r.* and it clothed me.
35. 2, thou saidst, My *r.* is more than God's?
36. 3, I will ascribe *r.* to my Maker.
Ps. 4. 1, hear me, O God of my *r.*
5, offer the sacrifices of *r.*
9. 8, he shall judge the world in *r.*
15. 2, he that worketh *r.* shall never be moved.
17. 15, as for me, I will behold thy face in *r.*
23. 3, leadeth me in paths of *r.*
24. 5, and *r.* from the God of his salvation.
40. 9, I have preached *r.*
45. 7; Heb. 1. 9, thou lovest *r.*
50. 6; 97. 6, heavens shall declare his *r.*
72. 2, he shall judge thy people with *r.*
85. 10, *r.* and peace have kissed each other.
94. 15, judgment shall return unto *r.*
97. 2, *r.* is the habitation of his throne.
111. 3; 112. 3, 9, his *r.* endureth for ever.
118. 19, open to me the gates of *r.*
132. 9, let thy priests be clothed with *r.*
Prov. 8. 18, durable riches and *r.* are with me.
10. 2; 11. 4, but *r.* delivereth from death.
11. 5, *r.* of the perfect shall direct his way.
6, *r.* of the upright shall deliver.
19, *r.* tendeth to life.
12. 28, in the way of *r.* is life.
14. 34, *r.* exalteth a nation.
16. 8, better is a little with *r.*
12, the throne is established by *r.*
31, crown of glory if found in way of *r.*
Eccl. 7. 15, a just man that perisheth in his *r.*
Isa. 11. 5, *r.* the girdle of his loins.
26. 10, yet will he not learn *r.*
32. 1, a king shall reign in *r.*
17, the work of *r.* peace, and the effect of *r.*
41. 10, uphold thee with right hand of my *r.*
46. 12, ye that are far from *r.*
58. 8, thy *r.* shall go before thee.
59. 16, his *r.* sustained him.
62. 2, the Gentiles shall see thy *r.*
64. 6, our *r.* are as filthy rags.
Jer. 23. 6; 33. 16, this is his name, The Lord our *r.*
33. 15, cause the branch of *r.* to grow.
51. 10, the Lord hath brought forth our *r.*

Ezek. 3. 20; 18. 24, righteous man turn from *r.*
14. 14, deliver but their own souls by *r.*
18. 20, the *r.* of the righteous shall be upon him.
33. 13, if he trust to his own *r.*
Dan. 4. 27, break off thy sins by *r.*
9. 7, *r.* belongeth to thee.
24, to bring in everlasting *r.*
12. 3, they that turn many to *r.*
Hos. 10. 12, till he rain *r.* upon you.
Amos 5. 24, let *r.* run down as a stream.
6. 12, turned fruit of *r.* into hemlock.
Zeph. 2. 3, ye meek of the earth, seek *r.*
Mal. 4. 2, shall the Sun of *r.* arise.
Mat. 3. 15, to fulfil all *r.*
5. 6, hunger and thirst after *r.*
10, persecuted for *r.* sake.
20, except your *r.* exceed the *r.*
21. 32, John came to you in the way of *r.*
Lu. 1. 75, in *r.* before him.
John 16. 8, reprove the world of *r.*
Acts 10. 35, he that worketh *r.*
13. 10, thou enemy of all *r.*
24. 25, as he reasoned of *r.*
Rom. 1. 17; 3. 5; 10. 3, the *r.* of God.
4. 6, to whom God imputeth *r.*
11, seal of the *r.* of faith.
5. 17, which receive the gift of *r.*
18, by the *r.* of one.
21, so might grace reign through *r.*
6. 13, yield your members as instruments of *r.*
20, ye were free from *r.*
8. 10, the body is life, because of *r.*
9. 30, the *r.* which is of faith.
10. 3, going about to establish their own *r.*
4, Christ is the end of the law for *r.*
10, with the heart man believeth unto *r.*
14. 17, kingdom of God not meat and drink, but *r.*
1 Cor. 1. 30, Christ is made unto us *r.*
15. 34, awake to *r.*
2 Cor. 5. 21, that we might be made the *r.*
6. 7, the armour of *r.*
14, what fellowship hath *r.*
Gal. 2. 21, if *r.* come by the law.
5. 5, we wait for the hope of *r.*
Eph. 6. 14, the breastplate of *r.*
Phil. 1. 11, filled with the fruits of *r.*
3. 6, touching the *r.* in the law, blameless.
9, not having mine own *r.,* but the *r.* of God.
1 Tim. 6. 11, follow after *r.*
2 Tim. 3. 16, for instruction in *r.*
4. 8, laid up for me a crown of *r.*
Tit. 3. 5, not by works of *r.*
Heb. 1. 8, a sceptre of *r.*
5. 13, unskilful in the word of *r.*
7. 2, by interpretation, King of *r.*
11. 7, heir of the *r.* which is by faith.
33, through faith wrought *r.*
12. 11, the peaceable fruit of *r.*
Jas. 1. 20, wrath of man worketh not *r.* of God.
3. 18, the fruit of *r.* is sown in peace.
1 Pet. 2. 24, dead to sins should live unto *r.*
2 Pet. 2. 5, a preacher of *r.*
21, better not to have known way of *r.*
3. 13, new earth, wherein dwelleth *r.*
1 John 2. 29, every one that doeth *r.*
See Isa. 54. 14; 63. 1; Zech. 8. 8; Rev. 19. 8.

RIGHTLY. Gen. 27. 36; Lu. 7. 43; 20. 21; 2 Tim. 2. 15.

RIGOUR. Ex. 1. 13, 14; Lev. 25. 43, 46, 53.

RINGLEADER. Acts 24. 5, a *r.* of the sect of the Nazarenes.

RIOT. Rom. 13. 13; Tit. 1. 6; 1 Pet. 4. 4; 2 Pet. 2. 13.

RIPE. Gen. 40. 10, brought forth *r.* grapes.
Ex. 22. 29, offer the first of thy *r.* fruits.
Num. 18. 13, whatsoever is first *r.* be thine.
Joel 3. 13, put in sickle, for the harvest is *r.*
Mic. 7. 1, my soul desired the first-*r.* fruit.
Rev. 14. 5, time to reap, for harvest of earth is *r.*
See Num. 13. 20; Jer. 24. 2; Hos. 9. 10; Nah. 3. 12.

RISE. Gen. 19. 2, ye shall *r.* up early.

Gen. 19. 23, the sun was r. when Lot entered Zoar.
Num. 24. 17, a sceptre shall r. out of Israel.
32. 14, ye are r. up in your fathers' stead.
Job 9. 7, commandeth the sun and it r. not.
14. 12, man lieth down and r. not.
24. 22, he r. up, and no man is sure of life.
31. 14, what shall I do when God r. up.
Ps. 27. 3, though war should r. against me.
119. 62, at midnight I will r. to give thanks.
127. 2, it is vain to r. up early.
Prov. 31. 15, she r. up while it is yet night.
28, her children r. up and call her blessed.
Eccl. 12. 4, he shall r. at the voice of the bird.
Isa. 33. 10, now will I r., saith the Lord.
58. 10, then shall thy light r. in obscurity.
60. 1, the glory of the Lord is r. upon thee.
Jer. 7. 13 ; 25. 3 ; 35. 14, I spake unto you, r. up early.
25 ; 25. 4 ; 26. 5 ; 29. 19 ; 35. 15 ; 44. 4, I sent my servants, r. early.
11. 7, r. early and protesting.
25. 27, fall and r. no more.
Lam. 3. 63, maketh down and r. up, I am their music.
Mat. 5. 45, maketh sun to r. on evil and good.
17. 9 ; Mk. 9. 9, until Son of man be r.
20. 19 ; Mk. 9. 31 ; 10. 34 ; Lu. 18. 33 ; 24. 7, the third day he shall r. again.
26. 32 ; Mk. 14. 28, after I am r. I will go before you.
46, r., let us be going.
Mk. 4. 27, should sleep, and r. night and day.
9. 10, what the r. from dead should mean.
10. 49, r., he calleth thee.
Lu. 2. 34, this child is set for the fall and r.
11.-7, I cannot r. and give thee.
22. 46, why sleep ye, r. and pray.
24. 34, the Lord is r. indeed.
John 11. 23, thy brother shall r. again.
Acts 10. 13, r., Peter, kill and eat.
26. 16, r., and stand upon thy feet.
23, the first that should r. from the dead.
Rom. 8. 34, that died, yea rather that is r.
1 Cor. 15. 15, if so be the dead r. not.
20, but now is Christ r.
Col. 3. 1, if ye then be r. with Christ.
1 Thess. 4. 16, the dead in Christ shall r. first.
See Prov. 30. 31 ; Isa. 60. 3 ; Mk. 16. 2 ; Col. 2. 12.

RITES. Num. 9. 3, according to all the r. of it.

RIVER. Ex. 7. 19 ; 8. 5, stretch out hand on r.
2 Sam. 17. 13, that city, and we will draw it into the r.
2 Kings 5. 12, are the r. of Damascus better.
Job 20. 17, ye shall not see the r. of honey.
28. 10, he cutteth out r. among the rocks.
29. 6, the rock poured out r. of oil.
40. 23, he drinketh up a r.. and hasteth not.
Ps. 1. 3, tree planted by the r.
36. 8, the r. of thy pleasures.
46. 4, r., the streams whereof make glad.
65. 9, enrichest it with r. of God.
107. 33, turneth r. into a wilderness.
119. 136, r. of waters run down mine eyes.
137. 1, by the r. of Babylon we sat.
Eccl. 1. 7, all the r. run into the sea.
Isa. 32. 2, shall be as r. of water in a dry place.
43. 2, through the r., they shall not overflow.
19, I will make r. in the desert.
48. 18, then had thy peace been as a r.
66. 12, I will extend peace like a r.
Lam. 2. 18, let tears run down like r.
Mic. 6. 7, be pleased with r. of oil.
John 7. 38, shall flow r. of living water.
Rev. 22. 1, a pure r. of water of life.
See Gen. 41. 1 ; Ex. 1. 22 ; Ezek. 47. 9 ; Mk. 1. 5.

ROAD. 1 Sam. 27. 10, whither have ye made a r.

ROAR. 1 Chron. 16. 32 ; Ps. 96. 11 ; 98. 7, let the sea r.
Job 3. 24, my r. are poured out.
Ps. 46. 3, will not fear, though waters r.
104. 21, young lions r. after their prey.

Prov. 19. 12 ; 20. 2, king's wrath as the r. of a lion.
Isa. 59. 11, we r. like bears.
Jer. 6. 23, their voice r. like the sea.
25. 30, the Lord shall r. from on high.
Hos. 11. 10, he shall r. like a lion.
Joel 3. 16 ; Amos 1. 2, the Lord shall r. out of Zion.
Amos 3. 4, will a lion r. when he hath no prey ?
See Ps. 22. 1 ; 32. 3 ; Zech. 11. 3 ; Rev. 10. 3.

ROARING. Prov. 28. 15, as a r. lion, is a wicked ruler.
Lu. 21. 25, distress, the sea and waves r.
1 Pet. 5. 8, the devil as a r. lion.
See Ps. 22. 13 ; Isa. 31. 4 ; Ezek. 22. 25 ; Zeph. 3. 3.

ROAST. Ex. 12. 9, not raw, but r. with fire.
Prov. 12. 27, slothful man r. not that he took.
Isa. 44. 16, he r. r., and is satisfied.
See Deut. 16. 7 ; 1 Sam. 2. 15 ; 2 Chron. 35. 13.

ROB. Prov. 22. 22, r. not the poor.
Isa. 10. 2, that they may r. the fatherless.
13, I have r. their treasures.
42. 22, this is a people r. and spoiled.
Ezek. 33. 15, if he give again that he had r.
Mal. 3. 8, ye have r. me.
2 Cor. 11. 8, I r. other churches.
See Judg. 9. 25 ; 2 Sam. 17. 8 ; Ps. 119. 61 ; Prov. 17. 12.

ROBBER. Job 12. 6, tabernacles of r. prosper.
Isa. 42. 24, who gave Israel to the r.
Jer. 7. 11, is this house become a den of r.
John 10. 1, the same is a thief and a r.
8, all that came before me are r.
Acts 19. 37, these men are not r. of churches.
2 Cor. 11. 26, in perils of r.
See Ezek. 7. 22 ; 18. 10 ; Dan. 11. 14 ; Hos. 6. 9.

ROBBERY. Phil. 2. 6, thought it not r. to be equal.

ROBE. 1 Sam. 24. 4, cut off skirt of Saul's r.
Job 29. 14, my judgment was as a r.
Isa. 61. 10, covered me with r. of righteousness.
Lu. 15. 22, bring forth the best r.
20. 46, desire to walk in long r.
See Ex. 28. 4 ; Mic. 2. 8 ; Mat. 27. 28 ; Rev. 6. 11.

ROCK. Ex. 33. 22, I will put thee in a clift of r.
Num. 20. 8, speak to the r. before their eyes.
10, must we fetch you water out of this r.
23. 9, from the top of the r. I see him.
24. 21, thou puttest thy nest in a r.
Deut. 8. 15, who brought thee water out of the r.
32. 4, he is the R.
15, lightly esteemed the R. of his salvation.
18, of the R. that begat thee.
30, except their R. had sold them.
31, their r. is not as our R.
37, where is their r. in whom they trusted ?
1 Sam. 2. 2, neither is there any r. like our God.
2 Sam. 22. 2 ; Ps. 18. 2 ; 92. 15, the Lord is my r.
3, the God of my r.
32 ; Ps. 18. 31, who is a r., save our God ?
23. 3, the R. of Israel spake.
1 Kings 19. 11, strong wind brake in pieces the r.
Job 14. 18, the r. is removed out of his place.
19. 24, graven in the r. for ever.
24. 8, embrace the r. for want of shelter.
Ps. 27. 5 ; 40. 2, shall set me up upon a r.
31. 3 ; 71. 3, thou art my r. and my fortress.
61. 2, lead me to the r. that is higher than I.
81. 16, with honey out of the r.
Prov. 30. 26, yet make their houses in the r.
Cant. 2. 14, that art in the clefts of the r.
Isa. 8. 14, for a r. of offence.
17. 10, not mindful of the r. of thy strength.
32. 2, as the shadow of a great r.
33. 16, defence shall be munitions of r.
Jer. 5. 3, they made their faces harder than r.
23. 29, hammer that breaketh the r. in pieces.
Nah. 1. 6, the r. are thrown down by him.
Mat. 7. 25 ; Lu. 6. 48, it was founded upon a r.
16. 18, upon this r. I will build my church.
27. 51, and the r. rent.
Lu. 8. 6, some fell upon a r.

Rom. 9. 33 ; 1 Pet. 2. 8, I lay a *r.* of offence.
1 Cor. 10. 4, spiritual *R.*, and that *R.* was Christ.
Rev. 6. 16, said to the *r.*, fall on us.
See Judg. 6. 20 ; 13. 19 ; 1 Sam. 14. 4 ; Prov. 30. 19.

ROD. Job 9. 34, let him take his *r.* from me.
21. 9, neither is the *r.* of God upon them.
Ps. 2. 9, break them with a *r.* of iron.
23. 4, thy *r.* and thy staff comfort me.
Prov. 10. 13 ; 26. 3, *r.* for the back of fools.
13. 24, he that spareth his *r.*
22. 8, the *r.* of his anger shall fail.
23. 14, thou shalt beat him with the *r.*
29. 15, the *r.* and reproof give wisdom.
Isa. 10. 15, as if the *r.* should shake itself.
11. 1, shall come forth a *r.*
Jer. 48. 17, how is the beautiful *r.* broken.
Ezek. 20. 37, cause you to pass under the *r.*
Mic. 6. 9, hear ye the *r.*, and who hath appointed it.
2 Cor. 11. 25, thrice was I beaten with *r.*
See Gen. 30. 37 ; 1 Sam. 14. 27 ; Rev. 2. 27 ; 11. 1.

RODE. 2 Sam. 18. 9 ; 2 Kings 9. 25 ; Neh. 2. 12 ;
Ps. 18. 10.

ROLL. Josh. 5. 9, I have *r.* away reproach.
Job 30. 14, they *r.* themselves on me.
Isa. 9. 5, with garments *r.* in blood.
34. 4 ; Rev. 6. 14, the heavens shall be *r.* together.
Mk. 16. 3, who shall *r.* us away the stone ?
Lu. 24. 2, they found the stone *r.* away.
See Gen. 29. 8 ; Prov. 26. 27 ; Isa. 17. 13 ; Mat. 27. 60.

ROOF. Gen. 19. 8, under the shadow of my *r.*
Deut. 22. 8, make a battlement for thine *r.*
Job 29. 10 ; Ps. 137. 6 ; Lam. 4. 4 ; Ezek. 3. 26,
tongue cleaveth to *r.* of mouth.
Mat. 8. 8 ; Lu. 7. 6, I am not worthy that thou
shouldest come under my *r.*
Mk. 2. 4, they uncovered the *r.*
See Josh. 2. 6 ; Judg. 16. 27 ; 2 Sam. 11. 2 ; Jer.
19. 13.

ROOM. Gen. 24. 23, is there *r.* for us.
26. 22, the Lord hath made *r.* for us.
Ps. 31. 8, set my feet in a large *r.*
80. 9, thou preparedst *r.* before it.
Prov. 18. 16, a man's gift maketh *r.* for him.
Mal. 3. 10, there shall not be *r.* enough.
Mat. 3. 16 ; Mk. 12. 39 ; Lu. 20. 46, love uppermost *r.*
Mk. 2. 2, there was no *r.* to receive them.
Lu. 2. 7, no *r.* for them in the inn.
12. 17, no *r.* to bestow my goods.
14. 7, how they chose out the chief *r.*
9, begin with shame to take the lowest *r.*
22, it is done, and yet there is *r.*
See Gen. 6. 14 ; 1 Kings 8. 20 ; 19. 16 ; Mk. 14. 15.

ROOT (*n.*). Deut. 29. 18, a *r.* that beareth gall.
2 Kings 19. 30, shall again take *r.* downward.
Job 5. 3, I have seen the foolish taking *r.*
8. 17, his *r.* are wrapped about the heap.
14. 8, the *r.* thereof wax old in the earth.
18. 16, his *r.* shall be dried up.
19. 28, the *r.* of the matter.
29. 19, my *r.* was spread out by the waters.
Prov. 12. 3, *r.* of righteous shall not be moved.
12, *r.* of righteous yieldeth fruit.
Isa. 5. 24, their *r.* shall be rottenness.
11. 1, a Branch shall grow out of his *r.*
10 ; Rom. 15. 12, there shall be a *r.* of Jesse.
27. 6 ; 37. 31, them that come of Jacob to take *r.*
53. 2, as a *r.* out of a dry ground.
Ezek. 31. 7, his *r.* was by great waters.
Hos. 14. 5, cast forth his *r.* as Lebanon.
Mal. 4. 1, leave them neither *r.* nor branch.
Mat. 3. 10 ; Lu. 3. 9, axe laid to *r.* of trees.
13. 6 ; Mk. 4. 6 ; Lu. 8. 13, because they had no *r.*
Mk. 11. 20, fig tree dried up from the *r.*
Rom. 11. 16, if the *r.* be holy.
1 Tim. 6. 10, love of money the *r.* of all evil.
Heb. 12. 15, lest any *r.* of bitterness.
Jude 12, twice dead, plucked up by the *r.*
Rev. 22. 16, *r.* and offspring of David.
See 2 Chron. 7. 20 ; Dan. 4. 15 ; 7. 8 ; 11. 7.

ROOT (*v.*). Deut. 29. 28, Lord *r.* them out.

1 Kings 14. 15, he shall *r.* up Israel.
Job 18. 14, confidence shall be *r.* out.
31. 8, let my offspring be *r.* out.
12, *r.* out all mine increase.
Ps. 52. 5, *r.* thee out of land of the living.
Mat. 13. 29, lest ye *r.* up also the wheat.
15. 13, hath not planted shall be *r.* up.
Eph. 3. 17, being *r.* and grounded in love.
Col. 2. 7, *r.* and built up in him.
See Prov. 2. 22 ; Jer. 1. 10 ; Zeph. 2. 4.

ROSE (*n.*). Cant. 2. 1 ; Isa. 35. 1.

ROSE (*v.*). Gen. 32. 31, the sun *r.* upon him as he
passed.
Josh. 3. 16, waters *r.* up on an heap.
Lu. 16. 31, though one *r.* from the dead.
Rom. 14. 9, to this end Christ both died and *r.*
1 Cor. 15. 4, buried, and *r.* the third day.
2 Cor. 5. 15, live to him who died and *r.*
See Lu. 24. 33 ; Acts 10. 41 ; 1 Thess. 4. 14 ; Rev.
19. 3.

ROT. Num. 5. 21 ; Prov. 10. 7 ; Isa. 40. 20.

ROTTEN. Job 41. 27 ; Jer. 38. 11 ; Joel 1. 17.

ROTTENNESS. Prov. 12. 4 ; 14. 30 ; Isa. 5. 24.

ROUGH. Isa. 27. 8, stayeth his *r.* wind.
40. 4 ; Lu. 3. 5, *r.* places made plain.
Zech. 13. 4, wear a *r.* garment to deceive.
See Deut. 21. 4 ; Jer. 51. 27 ; Dan. 8. 21.

ROUGHLY. Gen. 42. 7, Joseph spake *r.*
Prov. 18. 23, the rich answereth *r.*
See 1 Sam. 20. 10 ; 1 Kings 12. 13 ; 2 Chron. 10. 13.

ROUND. Ex. 16. 14 ; Isa. 3. 18 ; Lu. 19. 43.

ROWED. Jonah 1. 13 ; Mk. 6. 48 ; John 6. 19.

ROYAL. Gen. 49. 20, yield *r.* dainties.
Esth. 1. 7, *r.* wine in abundance.
5. 1 ; 6. 8 ; 8. 15 ; Acts 12. 21, *r.* apparel.
Jas. 2. 8, fulfil the *r.* law.
1 Pet. 2. 9, a *r.* priesthood.
See 1 Chron. 29. 25 ; Isa. 62. 3 ; Jer. 43. 10.

RUBIES. Job 28. 18 ; Prov. 8. 11 ; 31. 10.

RUDDY. 1 Sam. 16. 12 ; Cant. 5. 10 ; Lam. 4. 7.

RUDE. 2 Cor. 11. 6, *r.* in speech.

RUDIMENTS. Col. 2. 8, 20, *r.* of the world.

RUIN. 2 Chron. 28. 23, they were the *r.* of him.
Ps. 89. 40, hast brought his strong holds to *r.*
Prov. 24. 22, who knoweth the *r.* of both.
26. 28, a flattering mouth worketh *r.*
Ezek. 18. 30, so iniquity shall not be your *r.*
21. 15, that their *r.* may be multiplied.
Lu. 6. 49, the *r.* of that house was great.
See Isa. 3. 8 ; Ezek. 36. 35 ; Amos 9. 11 ; Acts 15. 16.

RULE (*n.*). Esth. 9. 1, Jews had *r.* over them.
Prov. 17. 2, a wise servant shall have *r.*
19. 10, servant to have *r.* over princes.
25. 28, no *r.* over his own spirit.
Isa. 63. 19, thou never barest *r.* over them.
1 Cor. 15. 24, when he shall put down all *r.*
Gal. 6. 16, as many as walk according to this *r.*
Heb. 13. 7, 17, them that have the *r.* over you.
See Eccl. 2. 19 ; Isa. 44. 13 ; 2 Cor. 10. 13.

RULE (*v.*). Gen. 1. 16, to *r.* the day.
3. 16, thy husband shall *r.* over thee.
Judg. 8. 23, I will not *r.* over you.
2 Sam. 23. 3, that *r.* over men must be just.
Ps. 66. 7, he *r.* by his power for ever.
89. 9, thou *r.* the raging of the sea.
103. 19, his kingdom *r.* over all.
Prov. 16. 32, that *r.* his spirit.
22. 7, rich *r.* over the poor.
Eccl. 9. 17, him that *r.* among fools.
Isa. 3. 4, babes *r.* over them.
32. 1, princes shall *r.* in judgment.
40. 10, his arm shall *r.* for him.
Ezek. 29. 15, shall no more *r.* over nations.
Rom. 12. 8, he that *r.* with diligence.
Col. 3. 15, peace of God *r.* in your hearts.
1 Tim. 3. 4, one that *r.* well his own house.
5. 17, elders that *r.* well.
See Dan. 5. 21 ; Zech. 6. 13 ; Rev. 2. 27 ; 12. 5.

RULER. Num. 13. 2, every one a *r.* among them.
Prov. 6. 7, ant having no guide, overseer, or *r.*
23. 1, when thou sittest to eat with a *r.*
28. 15, a wicked *r.* over the poor.
Isa. 3. 6, be thou our *r.*
Mic. 5. 2, out of thee shall come *r.*
Mat. 25. 21, I will make thee *r.*
John 7. 26, do the *r.* know that this is Christ?
48, have any of the *r.* believed.
Rom. 13. 3, *r.* not a terror to good works.
See Gen. 41. 43; Neh. 5. 7; Ps. 2. 2; Isa. 1. 10.
RUMOUR. Jer. 49. 14, I have heard a *r.*
Ezek. 7. 26, *r.* shall be upon *r.*
Mat. 24. 6; Mk. 13. 7, wars and *r.* of wars.
See 2 Kings 19. 7; Obad. 1; Lu. 7. 17.
RUN. 2 Sam. 18. 27, the *r.* of the foremost is like.
2 Chron. 16. 9, eyes of Lord *r.* to and fro.
Ps. 19. 5, as a strong man to *r.* a race.
23. 5, my cup *r.* over.
147. 15, his word *r.* very swiftly.
Cant. 1. 4, draw me, we will *r.* after thee.
Isa. 40. 31, they shall *r.* and not be weary.
55. 5, nations shall *r.* to thee.
Jer. 12. 5, if thou hast *r.* with the footmen.
51. 31, one post shall *r.* to meet another.
Dan. 12. 4, many shall *r.* to and fro.
Hab. 2. 2, that he may *r.* that readeth.
Zech. 2. 4, *r.,* speak to this young man.
Lu. 6. 38, good measure *r.* over.
Rom. 9. 16, nor of him that *r.*
1 Cor. 9. 24, they which *r.* in a race *r.* all.
26, I therefore so *r.*
Gal. 2. 2, lest I should *r.* or had *r.* in vain.
5. 7, ye did *r.* well.
Heb. 12. 1, let us *r.* with patience.
1 Pet. 4. 4, that ye *r.* not to same excess.
See Prov. 4. 12; Jer. 5. 1; Lam. 2. 18; Amos 8. 12.
RUSH (*n.*). Job 8. 11; Isa. 9. 14; 19. 15; 35. 7.
RUSH (*v.*). Isa. 17. 13; Jer. 8. 6; Ezek. 3. 12; Acts
2. 2.
RUST. Mat. 6. 19, 20; Jas. 5. 3.

S.

SABBATH. Lev. 25. 8, number seven *s.* of years.
2 Kings 4. 23, it is neither new moon nor *s.*
2 Chron. 36. 21, as long as desolate she kept *s.*
Ezek. 46. 1, on the *s.* it shall be opened.
Amos 8. 5, when will the *s.* be gone.
Mk. 2. 27, the *s.* was made for man.
28; Lu. 6. 5, the Son of man is Lord of the *s.*
Lu. 13. 15, doth not each on *s.* loose.
See Isa. 1. 13; Lam. 1. 7; 2. 6; Mat. 28. 1; John
5. 18.
SACK. Gen. 42. 25; 43. 21; 44. 1, 11, 12; Josh. 9. 4.
SACKCLOTH. 2 Sam. 3. 31, gird you with *s.*
1 Kings 20. 32, they girded *s.* on their loins.
Neh. 9. 1, assembled with fasting and *s.*
Esth. 4. 1, put on *s.* with ashes.
Ps. 30. 11, thou hast put off my *s.*
35. 13, my clothing was *s.*
Jonah 3. 5, and put on *s.*
SACRIFICE (*n.*). Gen. 31. 54, Jacob offered *s.*
Ex. 5. 17, let us go and do *s.* to the Lord.
Num. 25. 2, called people to the *s.* of their gods.
1 Sam. 2. 29, wherefore kick ye at my *s.*
9. 13, he doth bless the *s.*
15. 22, to obey is better than *s.*
Ps. 4. 5, offer the *s.* of righteousness.
27. 6, will I offer *s.* of joy.
40. 6; 51. 16, *s.* thou didst not desire.
51. 17, the *s.* of God are a broken spirit.
118. 27, bind the *s.* with cords.
Prov. 15. 8, *s.* of wicked an abomination.
17. 1, than a house full of *s.* with strife.
21. 3, to do justice is more acceptable than *s.*
Eccl. 5. 1, the *s.* of fools.
Isa. 1. 11, to what purpose is multitude of *s.*
Jer. 6. 20, nor are your *s.* sweet unto me.
33. 18, nor want a man to do *s.*

Dan. 8. 11; 9. 27; 11. 31, daily *s.* taken away.
Hos. 3. 4, many days without a *s.*
6. 6; Mat. 9. 13; 12. 7, I desired mercy and not *s.*
Amos 4. 4, bring your *s.* every morning.
Zeph. 1. 7, the Lord hath prepared a *s.*
Mal. 1. 8, ye offer the blind for *s.*
Mk. 9. 49, every *s.* shall be salted.
12. 33, to love the Lord is more than *s.*
Lu. 13. 1, blood Pilate mingled with *s.*
Acts 7. 42, have ye offered *s.* forty years.
14. 13, and would have done *s.*
Rom. 12. 1, present your bodies a living *s.*
1 Cor. 8. 4; 10. 19, 28, offered in *s.* to idols.
Eph. 5. 2, a *s.* to God for sweet-smelling savour.
Phil. 2. 17, upon the *s.* of your faith.
4. 18, a *s.* acceptable, well pleasing.
Heb. 9. 26, put away sin by *s.* of himself.
10. 12, offered one *s.* for sins.
26, there remaineth no more *s.* for sin.
11. 4, a more excellent *s.*
13. 15, let us offer the *s.* of praise.
16, with such *s.* God is well pleased.
1 Pet. 2. 5, to offer up spiritual *s.*
See 2 Chron. 7. 1; Ezra 6. 10; Neh. 12. 43; Jonah
1. 16.
SACRIFICE (*v.*). Ex. 22. 20, he that *s.* to any god.
Ezra 4. 2, we seek your God, and do *s.* to him.
Neh. 4. 2, will they *s.*
Ps. 54. 6, I will freely *s.* to thee.
106. 37, they *s.* their sons to devils.
107. 22, let them *s.* sacrifices of thanksgiving.
Eccl. 9. 2, to him that *s.* and that *s.* not.
Isa. 65. 3, people that *s.* in gardens.
Hos. 8. 13, they *s.,* but the Lord accepteth not.
Hab. 1. 16, they *s.* unto their net.
1 Cor. 5. 7, Christ our passover is *s.* for us.
10. 20, things Gentiles *s.,* they *s.* to devils.
See Ex. 8. 26; Deut. 15. 21; 1 Sam. 1. 3; 15. 15.
SACRILEGE. Rom. 2. 22, dost thou commit *s.*
SAD. 1 Kings 21. 5, why is thy spirit so *s.*
Eccl. 7. 3, by *s.* of countenance the heart is made
better.
Mat. 6. 16, be not of a *s.* countenance.
Mk. 10. 22, he was *s.* at that saying.
Lu. 24. 17, as ye walk and are *s.*
See Gen. 40. 6; 1 Sam. 1. 18; Neh. 2. 1; Ezek. 13.
22.
SADDLE. 2 Sam. 19. 26; 1 Kings 13. 13.
SAFE. 2 Sam. 18. 29, is the young man *s.*
Job 21. 9, their houses are *s.* from fear.
Ps. 119. 117, hold me up and I shall be *s.*
Prov. 18. 10, righteous run and are *s.*
29. 25, whoso trusteth in the Lord shall be *s.*
Ezek. 34. 27, they shall be *s.* in their land.
Acts 27. 44, so they escaped all *s.*
See 1 Sam. 12. 11; Isa. 5. 29; Lu. 15. 27; Phil.
3. 1.
SAFEGUARD. 1 Sam. 22. 23, with me thou shalt
be in *s.*
SAFELY. Ps. 78. 53, he led them on *s.*
Prov. 1. 33, shall dwell *s.*
3. 23, shalt thou walk *s.*
31. 11, doth *s.* trust in her.
Hos. 2. 18, I will make them to lie down *s.*
See Isa. 41. 3; Zech. 14. 11; Mk. 14. 44; Acts 16. 23.
SAFETY. Job 3. 26, I was not in *s.*
5. 4, his children are far from *s.*
11. 18, thou shalt take thy rest in *s.*
Prov. 11. 14; 24. 6, in the multitude of counsellors
is *s.*
21. 31, *s.* is of the Lord.
1 Thess. 5. 3, when they say peace and *s.*
See Job 24. 23; Ps. 12. 5; 33. 17; Isa. 14. 30.
SAIL. Isa. 33. 23; Ezek. 27. 7; Lu. 8. 23; Acts
27. 9.
SAINTS. 1 Sam. 2. 9, he will keep feet of *s.*
Job 5. 1, to which of the *s.* wilt thou turn.
15. 15, he putteth no trust in his *s.*
Ps. 16. 3, but to the *s.* that are in the earth.

Ps. 30. 4, sing to the Lord, O ye *s.* of his.
37. 28, the Lord forsaketh not his *s.*
50. 5, gather my *s.* together.
89. 5, the congregation of the *s.*
7, to be feared in assembly of *s.*
97. 10, preserveth the souls of his *s.*
116. 15, precious is the death of his *s.*
132. 9, let thy *s.* shout for joy.
149. 9, this honour have all his *s.*
Dan. 7. 18, but the *s.* shall take the kingdom.
8. 13, then I heard one *s.* speaking.
Mat. 27. 52, many bodies of *s.* arose.
Acts 9. 13, evil he hath done to thy *s.*
Rom. 1. 7; 1 Cor. 1. 2, called to be *s.*
8. 27, he maketh intercession for the *s.*
12. 13, distributing to the necessity of *s.*
16. 2, receive her as becometh *s.*
1 Cor. 6. 1, dare any go to law, and not before *s.*
2, the *s.* shall judge the world.
16. 1, concerning collection for *s.*
15, the ministry of *s.*
Eph. 1. 18, his inheritance in the *s.*
2. 19, fellowcitizens with the *s.*
3. 8, less than least of all *s.*
4. 12, perfecting of the *s.*
5. 3, not named among you, as becometh *s.*
Col. 1. 12, the *s.* in light.
1 Thess. 3. 13, at coming of our Lord with *s.*
2 Thess. 1. 10, to be glorified in his *s.*
1 Tim. 5. 10, if she have washed the *s.* feet.
Jude 3, faith once delivered to *s.*
Rev. 5. 8; 8. 3, 4, the prayers of *s.*
See Phil. 4. 21; Rev. 11. 18; 13. 7; 14. 12; 15. 3.

SAKE. Gen. 3. 17, cursed for thy *s.*
8. 21, not curse ground for man's *s.*
12. 13, be well with me for thy *s.*
18. 26, I will spare for their *s.*
30. 27, the Lord hath blessed me for thy *s.*
Num. 11. 29, enviest thou for my *s.*
Deut. 1. 37; 3. 26; 4. 21, angry with me for your *s.*
2 Sam. 9. 1, shew kindness for Jonathan's *s.*
18. 5, deal gently for my *s.*
Neh. 9. 31, for thy great mercies' *s.*
Ps. 6. 4; 31. 16, save me for thy mercies' *s.*
23. 3, he leadeth me for his name's *s.*
44. 22, for thy *s.* are we killed.
106. 8, he saved them for his name's *s.*
Mat. 5. 10, persecuted for righteousness' *s.*
10. 18; Mk. 13. 9; Lu. 21. 12, for my *s.*
24. 22; Mk. 13. 20, for the elect's *s.*
John 11. 15, I am glad for your *s.*
13. 38, wilt thou lay down thy life for my *s.*
Rom. 13. 5; 1 Cor. 10. 25, for conscience *s.*
Col. 1. 24, for his body's *s.* which is the church.
1 Thess. 5. 13, for their work's *s.*
1 Tim. 5. 23, for thy stomach's *s.*
Tit. 1. 11, for lucre's *s.*
2 John 2, for the truth's *s.*
See Rom. 11. 28; 2 Cor. 8. 9; 1 Thess. 3. 9.

SALUTATION. Mk. 12. 38; Lu. 1. 29; Col. 4. 18;
2 Thess. 3. 17.

SALUTE. 1 Sam. 10. 4; 2 Kings 4. 29; Mk. 15. 18.

SALVATION. Gen. 49. 18, I have waited for thy *s.*
Ex. 14. 13; 2 Chron. 20. 17, see the *s.* of the Lord.
15. 2, he is become my *s.*
Deut. 32. 15, lightly esteemed the rock of his *s.*
1 Sam. 11. 13; 19. 5, the Lord wrought *s.* in Israel.
14. 45, Jonathan, who hath wrought this *s.*
2 Sam. 22. 51, he is the tower of *s.* for his king.
1 Chron. 16. 23, shew forth from day to day his *s.*
2 Chron. 6. 41, let thy priests be clothed with *s.*
Ps. 3. 8, *s.* belongeth to the Lord.
9. 14, I will rejoice in thy *s.*
14. 7, O that the *s.* of Israel were come.
25. 5, thou art the God of my *s.*
27. 1; 62. 6; Isa. 12. 2, my light and my *s.*
35. 3, say unto my soul, I am thy *s.*
37. 39, the *s.* of the righteous is of the Lord.
40. 10, I have declared thy faithfulness and *s.*
50. 23, to him will I shew the *s.* of God.

Ps. 51. 12; 70. 4, restore the joy of thy *s.*
68. 20, he that is our God, is the God of *s.*
69. 13, hear me in the truth of thy *s.*
29, let thy *s.* set me up on high.
71. 15, my mouth shall shew forth thy *s.*
74. 12, working *s.* in the midst of the earth.
78. 22, they trusted not in his *s.*
85. 9, his *s.* is nigh them that fear him.
91. 16, will satisfy him and shew him my *s.*
96. 2, shew forth his *s.* from day to day.
98. 3, ends of the earth have seen the *s.*
116. 13, the cup of *s.*
118. 14; Isa. 12. 2, the Lord is become my *s.*
119. 41, let thy *s.* come.
81, my soul fainteth for thy *s.*
123, mine eyes fail for thy *s.*
155, *s.* is far from the wicked.
174, I have longed for thy *s.*
132. 16, I will clothe her priests with *s.*
144. 10, that giveth *s.* unto kings.
149. 4, beautify the meek with *s.*
Isa. 12. 3, the wells of *s.*
26. 1, *s.* will God appoint for walls.
33. 2, be thou our *s.* in time of trouble.
45. 8, earth open and let them bring forth *s.*
17, saved with an everlasting *s.*
49. 8, in a day of *s.* have I helped thee.
51. 5, my *s.* is gone forth.
52. 7, feet of him that publisheth *s.*
10, ends of the earth shall see *s.*
56. 1, my *s.* is near to come.
59. 11, we look for *s.*, but it is far off.
16, his arm brought *s.*
17, an helmet of *s.* on his head.
60. 18, call thy walls *S.*
61. 10, the garments of *s.*
62. 1, the *s.* thereof as a lamp.
63. 5, mine own arm brought *s.*
Jer. 3. 23, in vain is *s.* hoped for.
Lam. 3. 26, wait for the *s.* of the Lord.
Jonah 2. 9, *s.* is of the Lord.
Hab. 3. 8, ride on thy chariots of *s.*
18, I will joy in the God of my *s.*
Zech. 9. 9, thy King, just, and having *s.*
Lu. 1. 69, an horn of *s.* for us.
77, give knowledge of *s.* to his people.
2. 30, mine eyes have seen thy *s.*
3. 6, all flesh shall see the *s.* of God.
19. 9, this day is *s.* come to this house.
John 4. 22, *s.* is of the Jews.
Acts 4. 12, neither is there *s.* in any other.
13. 26, to you is the word of *s.* sent.
16. 17, these men shew to us the way of *s.*
Rom. 1. 16, the power of God to *s.*
10. 10, confession is made to *s.*
13. 11, now is our *s.* nearer.
2 Cor. 1. 6, comforted, it is for your *s.*
6. 2, the day of *s.*
7. 10, sorrow worketh repentance to *s.*
Eph. 1. 13, the Gospel of your *s.*
6. 17; 1 Thess. 5. 8, the helmet of *s.* and sword.
Phil. 1. 19, this shall turn to my *s.*
28, an evident token of *s.*
2. 12, work out your own *s.*
1 Thess. 5. 9, hath appointed us to obtain *s.*
2 Thess. 2. 13, God hath chosen you to *s.*
2 Tim. 3. 15, wise unto *s.*
Tit. 2. 11, grace of God that bringeth *s.*
Heb. 1. 14, for them who shall be heirs of *s.*
2. 3, if we neglect so great *s.*
10, the captain of their *s.*
5. 9, author of eternal *s.*
6. 9, things that accompany *s.*
9. 28, without sin unto *s.*
1 Pet. 1. 5, kept through faith unto *s.*
9, end of faith, *s.* of your souls.
10, of which *s.* the prophets enquired.
2 Pet. 3. 15, longsuffering of the Lord is *s.*
Jude 3, of the common *s.*
Rev. 7. 10, saying, *s.* to our God.
See Job 13. 16; 1 Sam. 2. 1; 2 Sam. 22. 36.

SAME. Job 4. 8, sow wickedness, reap the *s.*
Ps. 102. 27 ; Heb. 1. 12, thou art the *s.*
Mat. 5. 46, do not the publicans the *s.*
Acts 1. 11, this *s.* Jesus shall come.
Rom. 10. 12, the *s.* Lord over all.
12. 16 ; 1 Cor. 1. 10 ; Phil. 4. 2, be of *s.* mind.
Heb. 13. 8, *s.* yesterday, to-day, and for ever.
See 1 Cor. 10. 3 ; 12. 4 ; 15. 39 ; Eph. 4. 10.

SANCTIFY. Lev. 11. 44 ; 20. 7 ; Num. 11. 18 ; Josh.
3. 5 ; 7. 13 ; 1 Sam. 16. 5, *s.* yourselves.
Isa. 5. 16, God shall be *s.* in righteousness.
13. 3, I have commanded my *s.* ones.
29. 23, they shall *s.* the Holy One.
66. 17, *s.* themselves in gardens.
Jer. 1. 5, I *s.* and ordained thee a prophet.
Ezek. 20. 41 ; 36. 23, I will be *s.* in you.
28. 25 ; 39. 27, *s.* in them in sight of heathen.
Joel 1. 14 ; 2. 15, *s.* ye a fast.
John 10. 36, him whom the Father *s.*
17. 17, *s.* them through thy truth.
19, for their sakes I *s.* myself.
Acts 20. 32 ; 26. 18, inheritance among them that
are *s.*
Rom. 15. 16, being *s.* by the Holy Ghost.
1 Cor. 1. 2, to them that are *s.*
6. 11, but now ye are *s.*
7. 14, husband is *s.* by the wife, and the wife is *s.*
Eph. 5. 26, *s.* and cleanse the church.
1 Thess. 5. 23, the very God of peace *s.* you.
1 Tim. 4. 5, it is *s.* by the word of God.
2 Tim. 2. 21, a vessel *s.* for the Master's use.
Heb. 2. 11, he that *s.* and they who are *s.*
10. 10, by the which will we are *s.*
14, perfected for ever them that are *s.*
13. 12, that he might *s.* the people.
1 Pet. 3. 15, *s.* the Lord God in your hearts.
Jude 1, to them that are *s.* by God the Father.
See Gen. 2. 3 ; Ex. 13. 2 ; Job 1. 5 ; Mat. 23. 17.

SANCTUARY. Ex. 15. 17, plant them in the *s.*
25. 8, let them make me a *s.*
36. 1 ; 3. 4, work for the *s.*
Num. 7. 9, service of *s.* belongeth to them.
Neh. 10. 39, where are the vessels of the *s.*
Ps. 74. 7, they have cast fire into thy *s.*
Isa. 60. 13, beautify the place of my *s.*
Lam. 2. 7, the Lord hath abhorred his *s.*
See Dan. 8. 11 ; 9. 17 ; Heb. 8. 2 ; 9. 1.

SAND. Gen. 22. 17, as the *s.* which is upon the sea
shore.
Hos. 1. 10 ; Rev. 20. 8, as the *s.* of the sea.
Heb. 11. 12, the *s.* which is by the sea.
See Job 6. 3 ; Prov. 27. 3 ; Mat. 7. 26.

SANDALS. Mk. 6. 9, be shod with *s.*
Acts 12. 8, bind on thy *s.*

SANG. Ex. 15. 1 ; Neh. 12. 42 ; Job 38. 7.

SANK. Ex. 15. 5, they *s.* into the bottom.

SAP. Ps. 104. 16, trees full of *s.*

SAPPHIRE. Ex. 24. 10, a paved work of a *s.* stone.
28. 18 ; Ezek. 28. 13 ; Rev. 21. 19, and a *s.*
Ezek. 1. 26, as the appearance of a *s.* stone.
10. 1, as it were a *s.* stone.

SARDINE. Rev. 4. 3, like a jasper and *s.* stone.

SARDIUS. Ex. 28. 17, the first row shall be a *s.*
Ezek. 28. 13 ; Rev. 21. 20, *s.* etc.

SARDONYX. Rev. 21. 20, the fifth *s.*

SAT. Judg. 20. 26, they *s.* before the Lord.
Job 29. 25, I *s.* chief.
Ps. 26. 4, have not *s.* with vain persons.
Jer. 15. 17, I *s.* alone because of thy hand.
Ezek. 3. 15, I *s.* where they *s.*
Mat. 4. 16, the people who *s.* in darkness.
Mk. 16. 19, he *s.* on the right hand of God.
Lu. 7. 15, he that was dead *s.* up.
10. 39, Mary *s.* at Jesus' feet.
John 4. 6, *s.* thus on the well.
Acts 2. 3, cloven tongues *s.* upon each.
See Ezra 10. 16 ; Neh. 1. 4 ; Ps. 137. 1 ; Rev. 4. 3.

SATAN. 1 Chron. 21. 1, *S.* provoked David.

Ps. 109. 6, let *S.* stand at his right hand.
Mat. 12. 26 ; Mk. 3. 23 ; Lu. 11. 18, if *S.* cast out *S.*
16. 23 ; Mk. 8. 33 ; Lu. 4. 8, get behind me, *S.*
Lu. 10. 18, I beheld *S.* as lightning fall.
Acts 5. 3, why hath *S.* filled thine heart.
26. 18, turn them from power of *S.*
2 Cor. 12. 7, messenger of *S.* to buffet me.
2 Thess. 2. 9, after the working of *S.*
1 Tim. 1. 20, whom I have delivered unto *S.*
5. 15, already turned aside after *S.*
See Rom. 16. 20 ; 1 Cor. 5. 5 ; 2 Cor. 2. 11 ; 11. 14.

SATIATE. Jer. 31. 14, 25 ; 46. 10.

SATISFY. Job 38. 27, to *s.* the desolate.
Ps. 17. 15, I shall be *s.* when I awake.
22. 26, the meek shall eat and be *s.*
36. 8, they shall be *s.* with fatness.
37. 19, in days of famine be *s.*
59. 15, and grudge if they be not *s.*
63. 5, my soul shall be *s.*
81. 16, with honey should I have *s.* thee.
90. 14, *s.* us early with thy mercy.
91. 16, with long life will I *s.* him.
103. 5, who *s.* thy mouth with good.
104. 13, the earth is *s.*
105. 40, he *s.* them with bread from heaven.
107. 9, he *s.* the longing soul.
132. 15, I will *s.* her poor with bread.
Prov. 6. 30, if he steal to *s.* his soul.
12. 11, he that tilleth his land shall be *s.*
14. 14, a good man shall be *s.* from himself.
19. 23, he that hath it shall abide *s.*
20. 13, open thine eyes and thou shalt be *s.*
30. 15, three things never *s.*
Eccl. 1. 8, the eye is not *s.* with seeing.
4. 8, neither is his eye *s.* with riches.
5. 10, shall not be *s.* with silver.
Isa. 9. 20 ; Mic. 6. 14, shall eat and not be *s.*
53. 11, travail of his soul and be *s.*
58. 10, if thou *s.* the afflicted soul.
11, the Lord shall *s.* thy soul in drought.
Jer. 31. 14, shall be *s.* with my goodness.
Ezek. 16. 28, yet thou couldest not be *s.*
Amos 4. 8, wandered to drink, but were not *s.*
Hab. 2. 5, as death and cannot be *s.*
See Ex. 15. 9 ; Deut. 14. 29 ; Job 19. 22 ; 27. 14.

SAVE. Gen. 45. 7, to *s.* your lives.
47. 25, thou hast *s.* our lives.
Deut. 28. 29, spoiled and no man shall *s.* thee.
33. 29, O people, *s.* by the Lord.
Josh. 10. 6, come up quickly and *s.* us.
Judg. 6. 15, wherewith shall I *s.* Israel ?
1 Sam. 4. 3, the ark may *s.* us.
10. 27, how shall this man *s.* us ?
11. 3, if there be no man to *s.* us we will come.
14. 6, no restraint to *s.* by many or by few.
2 Sam. 19. 9, the king *s.* us, and now he is fled.
2 Kings 6. 10, *s.* himself there, not once nor twice.
Job 2. 6, in thine hand, but *s.* his life.
22. 29, he shall *s.* the humble.
26. 2, how *s.* thou.
Ps. 7. 10, God who *s.* the upright.
20. 6, the Lord *s.* his anointed.
34. 18, he *s.* such as be of a contrite spirit.
44. 3, neither did their own arm *s.* them.
60. 5, *s.* with thy right hand.
72. 4, he shall *s.* the children of the needy.
80. 3 ; Prov. 28. 18 ; Jer. 17. 14 ; Mat. 10. 22 ; 24. 13 ;
Mk. 13. 13 ; 16. 16 ; John 10. 9 ; Acts 2. 21 ; 16. 31 ;
Rom. 5. 9 ; 9. 27 ; 10. 9 ; 11. 26, shall be *s.*
86. 2, *s.* thy servant that trusteth.
109. 31, *s.* him from those that condemn.
118. 25, *s.*, I beseech thee, send prosperity.
119. 94, *s.* me, for I have sought.
146, *s.* me, and I shall keep thy testimonies.
138. 7, thy right hand shall *s.*
Prov. 20. 22, wait on Lord and he shall *s.* thee.
Isa. 35. 4, your God will come and *s.* you.
43. 12, I have declared and have *s.*
45. 20, pray to a god that cannot *s.*
22, look unto me and be ye *s.*

Isa. 47. 15, they shall wander, none shall *s*.
49. 25, I will *s*. thy children.
59. 1, Lord's hand not shortened, that it cannot *s*.
63. 1, mighty to *s*.
Jer. 2. 28, let them arise if they can *s*.
8. 20, summer is ended, and we are not *s*.
11. 12, but they shall not *s*.
14. 9, as a mighty man that cannot *s*.
15. 20; 30. 11; 42. 11; 46. 27, I am with thee to *s*. thee.
17. 14, *s*. me and I shall be *s*.
30. 10, I will *s*. thee from afar.
48. 6, flee, *s*. your lives.
Lam. 4. 17, a nation that could not *s*. us.
Ezek. 3. 18, to warn wicked, to *s*. his life.
34. 22, therefore will I *s*. my flock.
Hos. 1. 7, I will *s*. them by the Lord.
13. 10, is there any other that may *s*. thee.
Hab. 1. 2, cry to thee and thou wilt not *s*.
Zeph. 3. 17, he will *s*.
Mat. 1. 21, *s*. his people from their sins.
16. 25; Mk. 8. 35; Lu. 9. 24, will *s*. his life.
18. 11; Lu. 19. 10, to seek and to *s*. that which was lost.
19. 25; Mk. 10. 26; Lu. 18. 26, who then can be *s*.?
27. 40; Mk. 15. 30, *s*. thyself.
42; Mk. 15. 31, he *s*. others, himself he cannot *s*.
Mk. 3. 4; Lu. 6. 9, is it lawful to *s*.
Lu. 7. 50; 18. 42, thy faith hath *s*. thee.
8. 12, lest they should believe and be *s*.
9. 56, not to destroy but to *s*.
13. 23, are there few that be *s*.?
23. 35, let him *s*. himself.
39, if thou be Christ, *s*. thyself and us.
John 3. 17, that the world might be *s*.
5. 34, these things I say that ye might be *s*.
12. 47, not to judge but to *s*.
Acts 2. 47, such as should be *s*.
4. 12, no other name whereby we must be *s*.
15. 1, except ye be circumcised ye cannot be *s*.
16. 30, what must I do to be *s*.?
27. 43, the centurion willing to *s*. Paul.
Rom. 8. 24, we are *s*. by hope.
10. 1, my prayer is that they might be *s*.
11. 14; 1 Cor. 9. 22, if I might *s*. some.
1 Cor. 1. 18, to us who are *s*.
21, by foolishness of preaching to *s*. some.
3. 15, *s*. yet so as by fire.
5. 5, that the spirit may be *s*.
7. 16, shalt *s*. thy husband.
2 Cor. 2. 15, savour in them that are *s*.
Eph. 2. 5, 8, by grace ye are *s*.
1 Tim. 1. 15, came to *s*. sinners.
2. 4, who will have all men to be *s*.
4. 16, thou shalt *s*. thyself and them.
Heb. 5. 7, able to *s*. him from death.
7. 25, able to *s*. to the uttermost.
10. 39, believe to *s*. of soul.
11. 7, an ark to the *s*. of his house.
Jas. 1. 21, word which is able to *s*. your souls.
2. 14, can faith *s*. him?
4. 12, able to *s*. and destroy.
5. 15, prayer of faith shall *s*. sick.
20, shall *s*. a soul from death.
1 Pet. 3. 20, souls were *s*. by water.
4. 18, righteous scarcely be *s*.
Jude 23, others *s*. with fear.
See Mat. 14. 30 ; John 12. 27 ; 1 Pet. 3. 21.

SAVE (*except*). 2 Sam. 22. 32, who is God, *s*. the Lord?
Mat. 11. 27, nor knoweth any *s*. the Son.
13. 57, *s*. in his own country.
17. 8; Mk. 9. 8, *s*. Jesus only.
Lu. 17. 18, *s*. this stranger.
18. 19, none good *s*. one.
2 Cor. 11. 24, forty stripes *s*. one.
Gal. 6. 14, glory *s*. in the cross.
See Mk. 5. 37 ; Lu. 4. 26 ; Rev. 2. 17 ; 13. 17.

SAVIOUR. 2 Sam. 22. 3, my refuge, my *s*.
2 Kings 13. 5, the Lord gave Israel a *s*.

Ps. 106. 21, they forgat God their *s*.
Isa. 19. 20, he shall send them a *s*.
45. 21, a just God and a *S*.
49. 26, all shall know I am thy *S*.
63. 8, so he was their *S*.
Eph. 5. 23, Christ is the *s*. of the body.
1 Tim. 4. 10, who is the *S*. of all men.
Tit. 2. 10, adorn doctrine of God our *S*.
13, glorious appearing of our *S*.
Jude 25, the only wise God our *S*.
See Neh. 9. 27 ; Obad. 21 ; John 4. 42 ; Acts 5. 31.

SAVOUR. Gen. 8. 21, Lord smelled a sweet *s*.
Ex. 5. 21, have made our *s*. to be abhorred.
Cant. 1. 3, *s*. of thy good ointment.
Joel 2. 20, his ill *s*. shall come up.
Mat. 5. 13 ; Lu. 14. 34, if salt have lost his *s*.
See Eccl. 10. 1 ; Ezek. 6. 13 ; 20. 41 ; Eph. 5. 2.

SAVOUREST. Mat. 16. 23 ; Mk. 8. 33.

SAVOURY. Gen. 27. 4, 7, 14, 31.

SAW. Gen. 22. 4, Abraham *s*. the place.
26. 28, we *s*. the Lord was with thee.
Ex. 10. 23, they *s*. not one another.
24. 10, they *s*. the God of Israel.
2 Chron. 25. 21, they *s*. one another in the face.
Job 29. 11, when the eye *s*. me.
Ps. 77. 16, the waters *s*. thee.
Eccl. 2. 24, this I *s*., it was from hand of God.
Cant. 3. 3, *s*. ye him whom my soul loveth.
Mat. 12. 22, both spake and *s*.
17. 8, they *s*. no man.
Mk. 8. 23, if he *s*. ought.
John 1. 48, under the fig-tree I *s*. thee.
8. 56, Abraham *s*. my day.
20. 20, glad when they *s*. the Lord.
See 1 Sam. 19. 5 ; Ps. 50. 18 ; Isa. 59. 16.

SAY. Ex. 3. 13, what shall I *s*. to them.
4. 12, teach thee what thou shalt *s*.
Num. 22. 19, know what the Lord will *s*.
Judg. 18. 24, what is this ye *s*. to me?
Ezra 9. 10, what shall we *s*. after this?
Mat. 3. 9, think not to *s*. within yourselves.
7. 22, many will *s*. in that day.
16. 13 ; Mk. 8. 27, whom do men *s*. that I am?
23. 3, they *s*. and do not.
Lu. 7. 40, I have somewhat to *s*. to thee.
1 Cor. 12. 3, no man can *s*. that Jesus.
See Lu. 7. 7 ; John 4. 20 ; 8. 26 ; 16. 12.

SAYING. Deut. 1. 23, the *s*. pleased me well.
1 Kings 2. 38, the *s*. is good.
Ps. 49. 4, my dark *s*. upon the harp.
78. 2, utter dark *s*. of old.
Prov. 1. 6, the dark *s*. of the wise.
Mat. 28. 15, this *s*. is commonly reported.
Lu. 2. 51, kept all these *s*. in her heart.
John 4. 37, herein is that *s*. true.
6. 60, an hard *s*., who can hear it?
See John 21. 23 ; Rom. 13. 9 ; 1 Tim. 1. 15.

SCAB. Lev. 13. 2, a *s*. or bright spot.
Deut. 28. 27, and with the *s*.
Isa. 3. 17, the Lord will smite with a *s*.

SCANT. Mic. 6. 10, *s*. measure.

SCARCE. Gen. 27. 30 ; Acts 14. 18.

SCARCELY. Rom. 5. 7 ; 1 Pet. 4. 18.

SCARCENESS. Deut. 8. 9, bread without *s*.

SCAREST. Job 7. 14, thou *s*. me with dreams.

SCATTER. Gen. 11. 4, lest we be *s*. abroad.
Lev. 26. 33, I will *s*. you among the heathen.
Num. 10. 35 ; Ps. 68. 1, let thine enemies be *s*.
Job 18. 15, brimstone shall be *s*. on his habitation.
37. 11, he *s*. his bright cloud.
38. 24, which *s*. the east wind.
Ps. 68. 30, *s*. thou the people that delight in war.
92. 9, the workers of iniquity shall be *s*.
147. 16, he *s*. the hoar frost.
Prov. 11. 24, there is that *s*. and yet increaseth.
20. 8, a king *s*. evil with his eyes.
26, a wise king *s*. the wicked.
Jer. 10. 21, all their flocks shall be *s*.

Jer. 23. 1, woe to pastors that *s.* the sheep.
50. 17, Israel is a *s.* sheep.
Zech. 13. 7; Mat. 26. 31; Mk. 14. 27, sheep shall be *s.*
Mat. 9. 36, *s.* as sheep having no shepherd.
12. 30; Lu. 11. 23, he that gathereth not with me *s.*
See John 11. 52; 16. 32; Acts 8. 1; Jas. 1. 1.
SCENT. Job 14. 9; Jer. 48. 11; Hos. 14. 7.
SCHOLAR. 1 Chron. 25. 8; Mal. 2. 12.
SCHOOLMASTER. Gal. 3. 24, the law was our *s.*
SCIENCE. Dan. 1. 4; 1 Tim. 6. 20.
SCOFF. Hab. 1. 10; 2 Pet. 3. 3.
SCORCH. Mat. 13. 6; Mk. 4. 6; Rev. 16. 8.
SCORN. Esth. 3. 6; Job 16. 20; Ps. 44. 13; 79. 4.
SCORNER. Prov. 9. 8, reprove not a *s.*
13. 1, a *s.* heareth not rebuke.
19. 25, smite a *s.*
28, an ungodly witness *s.* judgment.
29, judgments are prepared for *s.*
21. 11, when a *s.* is punished simple is made wise.
24. 9. the *s.* is an abomination.
Isa. 29. 20, the *s.* is consumed.
Hos. 7. 5, stretched out hands with *s.*
See Ps. 1. 1; Prov. 1. 22; 3. 34; 9. 12.
SCORPIONS. Deut. 8. 15, fiery serpents and *s.*
Lu. 10. 19, power to tread on *s.*
Rev. 9. 3, as the *s.* of the earth.
SCOURGE. Job 5. 21, the *s.* of the tongue.
9. 23, if the *s.* slay suddenly.
Isa. 28. 15, the overflowing *s.*
Mat. 10. 17; 23. 34, they will *s.* you.
John 2. 15, a *s.* of small cords.
Acts 22. 25, is it lawful to *s.* a Roman.
Heb. 12. 6, the Lord *s.* every son.
See Josh. 23. 13; Isa. 10. 26; Mat. 27. 26; John 19. 1.
SCRAPE. Lev. 14. 41; Job 2. 8; Ezek. 26. 4.
SCRIBE. 1 Chron. 27. 32, a wise man and a *s.*
Isa. 33. 18, where is the *s.*?
Jer. 8. 8, the pen of the *s.* is in vain.
Mat. 5. 20, exceed righteousness of the *s.*
7. 29, authority, and not as the *s.*
13. 52, every *s.* instructed unto kingdom.
Mk. 12. 38; Lu. 20. 46, beware of the *s.*
See Ezra 4. 8; 7. 6; Neh. 8. 4; Mat. 8. 19.
SCRIP. 1 Sam. 17. 40; Mat. 10. 10; Lu. 10. 4; 22. 35.
SEARCH (*n.*). Ps. 64. 6; 77. 6; Jer. 2. 34.
SEARCH (*v.*). Num. 13. 2, that they may *s.* the land.
1 Chron. 28. 9, the Lord *s.* all hearts.
Job 11. 7, canst thou by *s.* find out God?
13. 9, is it good that he should *s.* you out?
28. 27, he prepared it and *s.* it out.
29. 16, the cause I knew not I *s.* out.
32. 11, I waited whilst ye *s.* out what to say.
36. 26, can number of his years be *s.* out.
Ps. 44. 21, shall not God *s.* this out?
139. 1, thou hast *s.* me and known me.
23, *s.* me and know my heart.
Prov. 25. 2, honour of kings to *s.* out a matter.
27, for men to *s.* out their own glory.
Eccl. 1. 13; 7. 25, I gave my heart to *s.* wisdom.
Isa. 40. 28, no *s.* of his understanding.
Jer. 17. 10, I the Lord *s.* the heart.
29. 13, when ye shall *s.* for me with all.
31. 37, foundations of the earth *s.* out.
Lam. 3. 40, let us *s.* our ways, and turn.
Ezek. 34. 6, none did *s.* or seek after them.
8, neither did my shepherds *s.* for my flock.
11, I will *s.* my sheep.
Amos 9. 3, I will *s.* and take them out thence.
Zeph. 1. 12, I will *s.* Jerusalem with candles.
John 5. 39; Acts 17. 11, *s.* the scriptures.
Rom. 8. 27, that *s.* hearts knoweth mind.
1 Cor. 2. 10, the Spirit *s.* all things.
1 Pet. 1. 10, which salvation prophets *s.* diligently.
See Job 10. 6; 28. 3; Prov. 2. 4; 1 Pet. 1. 11.

SEARED. 1 Tim. 4. 2, conscience *s.*
SEASON. Gen. 1. 14, for signs, and *s.*, and days.
Deut. 28. 12, give rain in his *s.*
2 Chron. 15. 3, for long *s.* without true God.
Job 5. 26, as a shock of corn in his *s.*
Ps. 1. 3, that bringeth forth fruit in his *s.*
22. 2, I cry in the night *s.*
104. 19, appointed the moon for *s.*
Prov. 15. 23, word spoken in due *s.*
Eccl. 3. 1, to everything there is a *s.* and a time.
Isa. 50. 4, know how to speak a word in *s.*
Jer. 5. 24, former and latter rain in his *s.*
33. 20, day and night in their *s.*
Ezek. 34. 26, cause shower to come down in *s.*
Dan. 2. 21, changeth the times and *s.*
7. 12, lives prolonged for a *s.*
Hos. 2. 9, take away my wine in *s.*
Mat. 21. 41, render the fruits in their *s.*
Lu. 1. 20, my words shall be fulfilled in *s.*
20. 10, at the *s.* he sent servant.
23. 8, desirous to see him of a long *s.*
John 5. 4, angel went down at certain *s.*
35, willing for a *s.* to rejoice.
Acts 1. 7, not for you to know times and *s.*
13. 11, not seeing the sun for a *s.*
24. 25, a convenient *s.*
2 Tim. 4. 2, be instant in *s.*
Heb. 11. 25, pleasures of sin for a *s.*
See 1 Thess. 5. 1; 1 Pet. 1. 6; Rev. 6. 11; 20. 3.
SEAT. 1 Sam. 20. 18, thy *s.* will be empty.
Job 23. 3, that I might come even to his *s.*
29. 7, when I prepared my *s.* in the street.
Ps. 1. 1, the *s.* of the scornful.
Amos 6. 3, cause *s.* of violence to come near.
Mat. 21. 12, *s.* of them that sold doves.
23. 2, scribes sit in Moses' *s.*
6; Mk. 12. 39, chief *s.* in synagogues.
See Ezek. 8. 3; 28. 2; Lu. 1. 52; Rev. 2. 13; 4. 4.
SECRET (*n.*). Gen. 49. 6, come not into their *s.*
Job 11. 6, the *s.* of wisdom.
15. 8, hast thou heard the *s.* of God?
29. 4, the *s.* of God was upon my tabernacle.
Ps. 25. 14, *s.* of Lord is with them that fear.
27. 5, in *s.* of his tabernacle will he hide.
139. 15, when I was made in *s.*
Prov. 3. 32, his *s.* is with the righteous.
9. 17, bread eaten in *s.*
21. 14, a gift in *s.* pacifieth anger.
Isa. 45. 19; 48. 16, I have not spoken in *s.*
Mat. 6. 4, thy Father who seeth in *s.*
6, pray to thy Father which is in *s.*
24. 26, he is in the *s.* chambers.
John 18. 20, in *s.* have I said nothing.
See Prov. 11. 13; 20. 19; Dan. 2. 18; 4. 9.
SECRET (*adj.*). Deut. 29. 29, *s.* things belong to God.
Judg. 3. 19, I have a *s.* errand.
13. 18, my name, seeing it is *s.*
Ps. 19. 12, cleanse thou me from *s.* faults.
90. 8, our *s.* sins.
Prov. 27. 5, open rebuke better than *s.* love.
See Cant. 2. 14; Isa. 45. 3; Jer. 13. 17.
SECRETLY. Gen. 31. 27, flee away *s.*
Deut. 13. 6, entice thee *s.*, saying.
1 Sam. 18. 22, commune with David *s.*
23. 9, Saul *s.* practised mischief.
2 Sam. 12. 12, for thou didst it *s.*
Job 4. 12, a thing was *s.* brought to me.
13. 10, if you *s.* accept persons.
31. 27, my heart hath been *s.* enticed.
Ps. 10. 9, he lieth in wait *s.*
31. 20, keep them *s.* from the strife.
John 11. 28, she called her sister *s.*
19. 38, *s.* for fear of the Jews.
See Deut. 27. 24; Lev. 28. 57; 2 Kings 17. 9.
SECT. Acts 5. 17; 15. 5; 24. 5; 26. 5; 28. 22.
SECURE. Job 11. 18; 12. 6; Mat. 28. 14.
SECURELY. Prov. 3. 29; Mic. 2. 8.
SEDUCE. Mk. 13. 22, show signs to *s.*
1 John 2. 26, concerning them that *s.* you.

Rev. 2. 20, to *s.* my servants.
See Prov. 12. 26 ; 1 Tim. 4. 1 ; 2 Tim. 3. 13.

SEE. Gen. 11. 5, came down to *s.* the city.
44. 23, you shall *s.* my face no more.
45. 28, I will go and *s.* him before I die.
Ex. 12. 13, when I *s.* the blood.
14. 13, *s.* the salvation of the Lord.
33. 20, there shall no man *s.* me and live.
Deut. 3. 25, let me *s.* the good land.
34. 4, I have caused thee to *s.* it.
2 Kings 6. 17, open his eyes, that he may *s.*
10. 16, *s.* my zeal for the Lord.
Job 7. 7, mine eye shall no more *s.* good.
19. 26, yet in my flesh shall I *s.* God.
Ps. 27. 13, believed to *s.* the goodness.
66. 5, come and *s.* the works of God.
94. 9, shall he not *s.*
Isa. 6. 10, lest they *s.* with their eyes.
32. 3, eyes of them that *s.* shall not be dim.
33. 17, shall *s.* the king in his beauty.
40. 5, all flesh shall *s.* it together.
52. 8, they shall *s.* eye to eye.
Jer. 5. 21; Ezek. 12. 12, eyes and *s.* not.
Mat. 5. 8, they shall *s.* God.
12. 38, we would *s.* a sign.
13. 14; Mk. 4. 12; Acts 28. 26, *s.* ye shall *s.*
27. 4, *s.* thou to that.
28. 6, *s.* the place where the Lord lay.
Mk. 8. 18, having eyes *s.* ye not.
Lu. 17. 23, *s.* here or *s.* there.
John 1. 39; 11. 34; Rev. 6. 1, come and *s.*
50, thou shalt *s.* greater things.
9. 25, I was blind, now I *s.*
39, that they who *s.* not might *s.*
Heb. 2. 9, but we *s.* Jesus.
1 Pet. 1. 8, though now we *s.* him not.
1 John 3. 2, we shall *s.* him as he is.
See Mat. 27. 24 ; John 1. 51.

SEED. Gen. 3. 15, enmity between thy *s.*
47. 19, give us *s.*
Ex. 16. 31, manna like coriander *s.*
Lev. 19. 19, thou shalt not sow mingled *s.*
26. 16, ye shall sow your *s.* in vain.
Num. 20. 5, it is no place of *s.*
Deut. 1. 8, to give it to their *s.* after them.
11. 10, not as Egypt where thou sowedst *s.*
14. 22, tithe all the increase of your *s.*
28. 38, thou shalt carry much *s.* into field.
Ps. 126. 6, bearing precious *s.*
Eccl. 11. 6, in the morning sow thy *s.*
Isa. 5. 10, the *s.* of an homer shall yield.
17. 11, in morning make thy *s.* to flourish.
55. 10, give *s.* to the sower.
61. 9, the *s.* which the Lord hath blessed.
Jer. 2. 21, I had planted thee wholly a right *s.*
Joel 1. 17, the *s.* is rotten.
Amos 9. 13, overtake him that soweth *s.*
Hag. 2. 19, is the *s.* yet in the barn ?
Zech. 8. 12, the *s.* shall be prosperous.
Mal. 2. 15, that he might seek a godly *s.*
See Mat. 13. 19 ; Lu. 8. 5 ; 1 Cor. 15. 38 ; 1 Pet. 1. 23.

SEEK. Gen. 37. 15, what *s.* thou ?
Num. 15. 39, that ye *s.* not after your own heart.
16. 10, *s.* ye the priesthood also.
Deut. 4. 29, if thou *s.* him with all thy heart.
12. 5, even to his habitation shall ye *s.* and come.
23. 6 ; Ezra 9. 12, thou shalt not *s.* their peace.
Ruth 3. 1, shall I not *s.* rest for thee.
1 Chron. 28. 9 ; 2 Chron. 15. 2, if thou *s.* him, he will be found.
2 Chron. 19. 3, hast prepared thine heart to *s.* God.
34. 3, Josiah began to *s.* after God.
Ezra 4. 2, we *s.* your God as ye do.
Neh. 2. 10, to *s.* the welfare of Israel.
Job 5. 8, I would *s.* unto God.
8. 5, *s.* unto God betimes.
20. 10, children shall *s.* to please the poor.
39. 29, from thence she *s.* the prey.
Ps. 9. 10, hast not forsaken them that *s.* thee.
10. 4, the wicked will not *s.* after God.

Ps. 10. 15, *s.* out his wickedness till thou find none.
14. 2 ; 53. 2, if there were any that did *s.* God.
24. 6, generation of them that *s.* him.
27. 4, desired, that will I *s.* after.
8, *s.* ye my face, thy face will I *s.*
34. 14 ; 1 Pet. 3. 11, *s.* peace and pursue it.
63. 1, early will I *s.* thee.
69. 32, your heart shall live that *s.* God.
83. 16, that they may *s.* thy name.
122. 9, I will *s.* thy good.
Prov. 1. 28, they shall *s.* me, but not find.
8. 17, those that *s.* me early shall find me.
11. 27, that diligently *s.* good.
21. 6, of them that *s.* death.
23. 30, they that go to *s.* mixed wine.
35, I will *s.* it yet again.
Eccl. 1. 13 ; 7. 25, gave my heart to *s.* wisdom.
Cant. 3. 2, I will *s.* him whom my soul loveth.
Isa. 1. 17, learn to do well, *s.* judgment.
8. 19, should not a people *s.* unto their God.
19. 3, they shall *s.* to charmers.
34. 16, *s.* ye out of the book of the Lord.
41. 17, when the needy *s.* water.
45. 19, I said not, *s.* ye my face in vain.
Jer. 5. 1, any that *s.* the truth.
29. 13, ye shall *s.* me and find when ye search.
30. 17, Zion whom no man *s.* after.
38. 4, this man *s.* not welfare of people.
Lam. 3. 25, the Lord is good to the soul that *s.* him
Ezek. 7. 25, they shall *s.* peace.
34. 16, I will *s.* that which was lost.
Dan. 9. 3, I set my face to *s.* by prayer.
Amos 5. 4, *s.* me and ye shall live.
Zeph. 2. 3, *s.* ye the Lord, all ye meek.
Mal. 2. 7, they should *s.* the law at his mouth.
Mat. 6. 32, after these things do Gentiles *s.*
33 ; Lu. 12. 31, *s.* first the kingdom of God.
7. 7 ; Lu. 11. 9, *s.* and ye shall find.
12. 39 ; 16. 4, adulterous generation *s.* a sign.
28. 5 ; Mk. 16. 6, I know that ye *s.* Jesus.
Mk. 1. 37, all men *s.* for thee.
8. 11, *s.* of him a sign from heaven.
Lu. 13. 7, I come *s.* fruit.
24, many will *s.* to enter in.
15. 8, doth she not *s.* diligently.
19. 10, is come to *s.* and to save.
24. 5, why *s.* ye the living among the dead?
John 1. 38, what *s.* ye?
4. 23, the Father *s.* such to worship him.
7. 25, is not this he whom they *s.* to kill?
34, ye shall *s.* me and shall not find me.
18. 8, if ye *s.* me, let these go their way.
20. 15, woman, whom *s.* thou?
Rom. 3. 11, there is none that *s.* after God.
1 Cor. 1. 22, the Greeks *s.* after wisdom.
10. 24, let no man *s.* his own.
13. 5, charity *s.* not her own.
2 Cor. 12. 14, I *s.* not yours, but you.
Phil. 2. 21, all *s.* their own things.
Col. 3. 1, *s.* those things which are above.
Heb. 11. 6, a rewarder of them that *s.* him.
14, declare plainly that they *s.* a country.
13. 14, but we *s.* one to come.
1 Pet. 5. 8, *s.* whom he may devour.
Rev. 9. 6, in those days shall men *s.* death.
See Jer. 45. 5 ; Mat. 13. 45 ; John 6. 24 ; 1 Cor. 10. 33

SEEM. Gen. 19. 14, he *s.* as one that mocked.
29. 20, they *s.* to him but a few days.
Num. 16. 9, *s.* it but a small thing.
Prov. 14. 12, there is a way that *s.* right.
Lu. 8. 18, taken away that he *s.* to have.
24. 11, words *s.* as idle tales.
1 Cor. 3. 18, if any *s.* to be wise.
11. 16, if any man *s.* to be contentious.
Heb. 4. 1, lest any *s.* to come short.
12. 11, now no chastening *s.* to be joyous.
See Gen. 27. 12; Eccl. 9. 13 ; Acts 17. 18; Gal. 2. 6.

SEEMLY. Prov. 19. 10 ; 26. 1.

SEEN. Gen. 32. 30, I have *s.* God face to face.

Ex. 14. 13, Egyptians whom ye have *s.* to-day.
Judg. 6. 22, because I have *s.* an angel.
2 Kings 20. 15, what have they *s.*
Job 13. 1, mine eye hath *s.* all this.
28. 7, a path the vulture's eye hath not *s.*
Ps. 37. 25, have I not *s.* righteous forsaken
90. 15, years wherein we have *s.* evil.
Eccl. 6. 5, he hath not *s.* the sun.
Isa. 9. 2, have *s.* a great light.
64. 4 ; 1 Cor. 2. 9, neither hath eye *s*
66. 8, who hath *s.* such things.
Mat. 6. 1 ; 23. 5, to be *s.* of men.
9. 33, never so *s.* in Israel.
Mk. 9. 1, till they have *s.* the kingdom of God.
Lu. 5. 26, we have *s.* strange things to-day.
John 1. 18, no man hath *s.* God.
8. 57, hast thou *s.* Abraham?
John 14. 9, he that hath *s.* me hath *s.* the Father.
Acts 11. 23, when he had *s.* the grace of God.
1 Cor. 9. 1, have I not *s.* Jesus Christ.
1 Tim. 6. 16, whom no man hath *s.*, nor can see.
Heb. 11. 1, evidence of things not *s.*
1 Pet. 1. 8, whom having not *s.*, ye love.
See John 5. 37 ; 9. 37 ; 15. 24 ; 20. 29 ; Rom. 1. 20.
SEER. 1 Sam. 9. 9, a prophet was *l*eforetime
　　called a *s.*
2 Sam. 24. 11, the prophet Gad, David's *s.*
SEETHE. Ex. 23. 19 ; 2 Kings 4. 38 ; Ezek. 24. 5.
SEIZE. Job 3. 6 ; Ps. 55. 15 ; Jer. 49. 24 ; Mat. 21. 38.
SELF. Tit. 1. 7 ; 2 Pet. 2. 10.
SELL. Gen. 25. 31, *s.* me thy birthright.
37. 27, come, let us *s.* him.
1 Kings 21. 25, Ahab did *s.* himself to work.
Neh. 5. 8, will ye even *s.* your brethren.
Prov. 23. 23, buy the truth, and *s.* it not.
Joel 3. 8, I will *s.* your sons and daughters.
Amos 8. 5, that we may *s.* corn.
6, and *s.* the refuse of the wheat.
Mat. 19. 21 ; Mk. 10. 21 ; Lu. 12. 33 ; 18. 22, *s.* that
　　thou hast.
Lu. 22. 36, let him *s.* his garment.
Jas. 4. 13, we will buy and *s.*, and get gain.
See Ps. 44. 12 ; Prov. 11. 26 ; 31. 24 ; Mat. 13. 44.
SELLER. Isa. 24. 2 ; Ezek. 7. 12, 13 ; Acts 16. 14.
SEND. Gen. 24. 7, God shall *s.* his angel.
12, *s.* me good speed this day.
Ex. 4. 13, *s.* by hand of him whom thou wilt *s.*
2 Chron. 7. 13 ; Ezek. 14. 9, if I *s.* pestilence.
Ps. 20. 2, *s.* thee help from the sanctuary.
43. 3, *s.* out thy light and truth.
118. 25, *s.* now prosperity.
Isa. 6. 8, whom shall I *s.*? *s.* me.
Mat. 9. 38 ; Lu. 10. 2, *s.* labourers.
12. 20, till he *s.* forth judgment.
15. 23, *s.* her away, for she crieth after us.
Mk. 3. 14, that he might *s.* them to preach.
John 14. 26, whom the Father will *s.* in my name.
17. 8, believed that thou didst *s.* me.
Rom. 8. 3, God *s.* his Son in likeness.
See Lu. 10. 3 ; 24. 49 ; John 20. 21 ; 2 Thess. 2. 11.
SENSUAL. Jas. 3. 15 ; Jude 19.
SENT. Gen. 45. 5, God *s.* me.
Judg. 6. 14, have not I *s.* thee.
Ps. 77. 17, the skies *s.* out a sound.
106. 15, he *s.* leanness into their soul.
107. 20, he *s.* his word and healed them.
Jer. 23. 21, I have not *s.* these prophets.
Mat. 15. 24, I am not *s.* but to lost sheep.
John 4. 34, the will of him that *s.* me.
9. 4, work the works of him that *s.* me.
17. 3, life eternal to know him whom thou hast *s.*
Acts 10. 29, as soon as I was *s.* for.
Rom. 10. 15, preach, except they be *s.*
See Isa. 61. 1 ; John 1. 6 ; 3. 28 ; 1 Pet. 1. 12.
SENTENCE. Ps. 17. 2, let my *s.* come forth.
Prov. 16. 10, a divine *s.* in the lips of the king.
Eccl. 8. 11, because *s.* is not executed speedily.
2 Cor. 1. 9, *s.* of death in ourselves.
See Deut. 17. 9 ; Jer. 4. 12 ; Dan. 5. 12 ; 8. 23.

SEPARATE. Gen. 13. 9, *s.* thyself from me.
Deut. 19. 2, thou shalt *s.* three cities.
Prov. 16. 28 ; 17. 9, whisperer *s.* chief friends.
19. 4, the poor is *s.* from his neighbour.
Mat. 25. 32, he shall *s.* them.
Rom. 8. 35, who shall *s.* us from love of God?
2 Cor. 6. 17, be ye *s.*
Heb. 7. 26, *s.* from sinners.
See Num. 6. 2 ; Ezra 10. 11 ; Isa. 56. 3 ; 59. 2.
SEPARATION. Num. 6. 8 ; 19. 9 ; 31. 23 ; Ezek.
　　42. 20.
SERPENT. Gen. 3. 1, the *s.* was more subtil.
49. 17, Dan shall be *s.* by the way.
Job 26. 13, his hand formed the crooked *s.*
Ps. 58. 4, like the poison of a *s.*
140. 3, sharpened their tongues like a *s.*
Prov. 23. 32, at last it biteth like a *s.*
Eccl. 10. 8, breaketh a hedge, a *s.* shall bite him.
11, *s.* will bite without enchantment.
Isa. 27. 1, the Lord shall punish the *s.*
65. 25, dust shall be the *s.* meat.
Jer. 8. 17, I will send *s.* among you.
Amos 9. 3, I will command the *s.*
Mic. 7. 17, they shall lick dust like a *s.*
Mat. 7. 10 ; Lu. 11. 11, will he give him a *s.*?
10. 16, be ye wise as *s.*
23. 33, ye *s.*, how can ye escape.
Mk. 16. 18, they shall take up *s.*
John 3. 14, as Moses lifted up the *s.*
Rev. 12. 9 ; 20. 2, that old *s.* called the Devil.
See Ex. 4. 3 ; Num. 21. 8 ; 2 Kings 18. 4 ; Jas. 3. 7.
SERVANT. Gen. 9. 25, a *s.* of *s.* shall he be.
Job 3. 19, the *s.* is free.
7. 2, as a *s.* desireth the shadow.
Ps. 116. 16 ; 119. 125 ; 143. 12, I am thy *s.*
Prov. 22. 7, the borrower is *s.* to the lender.
29. 19, a *s.* will not be corrected with words.
Isa. 24. 2, as with *s.* so with master.
Mat. 10. 25, enough for *s.* to be as his lord.
25. 21, good and faithful *s.*
Lu. 12. 47, that *s.* which knew his lord's will.
17. 10, unprofitable *s.*
John 8. 35, *s.* abideth not in house for ever.
15. 15, *s.* knoweth not what his lord doeth.
1 Cor. 7. 21, art thou called, being a *s.*
23, be not ye the *s.* of men.
Eph. 6. 5 ; Col. 3. 22 ; Tit. 2. 9 ; 1 Pet. 2. 18, *s.* be
　　obedient.
See Rom. 6. 16 ; Col. 4. 1 ; 1 Tim. 6. 1 ; Rev. 22. 3.
SERVE. Gen. 25. 23, elder shall *s.* the younger.
Deut. 6. 13 ; 10. 12, 20 ; 11. 13 ; 13. 4 ; Josh. 22. 5 ;
　　24. 14 ; 1 Sam. 7. 3 ; 12. 14, thou shalt fear the
　　Lord and *s.* him.
Josh. 24. 15, choose ye whom ye will *s.*
1 Chron. 28. 9, *s.* him with a perfect heart.
Job 21. 15, what is the Almighty, that we should
　　s. him?
Ps. 22. 30, a seed shall *s.* him.
72. 11, all nations shall *s.* him.
Isa. 43. 23, I have not caused thee to *s.*
24, thou hast made me to *s.* with thy sins.
Jer. 5. 19, so shall ye *s.* strangers.
Dan. 6. 16, thy God whom thou *s.* will deliver.
Zeph. 3. 9, to *s.* him with one consent.
Mal. 3. 17, spareth his son that *s.* him.
18, between him that *s.* God and him that.
Mat. 6. 24 ; Lu. 16. 13, no man can *s.* two masters.
Lu. 10. 40, hath left me to *s.* alone.
15. 29, these many years do I *s.* thee.
John 12. 26, if any man *s.* me, let him.
Acts 6. 2, leave word of God and *s.* tables.
Rom. 6. 6, henceforth we should not *s.* sin.
Gal. 5. 13, by love *s.* one another.
Col. 3. 24, for ye *s.* the Lord Christ.
1 Thess. 1. 9, from idols to *s.* living God.
Rev. 7. 15, they *s.* him day and night.
See Lu. 22. 27 ; Acts 13. 36 ; Heb. 9. 14 ; 12. 28.
SERVICE. Ex. 12. 26, what mean ye by this *s.*?
1 Chron. 29. 5, who is willing to consecrate his *s.*
John 16. 2, will think he doeth God *s.*

Rom. 12. 1, your reasonable s.
Eph. 6. 7, doing s. as to the Lord.
Phil. 2. 30, to supply your lack of s.
See Ezra 6. 18 ; Ps. 104. 14 ; Jer. 22. 13.

SET. Gen. 4. 15, the Lord s. a mark on Cain.
9. 13, I do s. my bow in the cloud.
Deut. 1. 8, I have s. the land before thee.
Job 33. 5, s. thy words in order.
Ps. 16. 8, I have s. the Lord before me.
20. 5, we will s. up our banners.
91. 14, he hath s. his love upon me.
Eccl. 7. 14, hath s. the one against the other.
Cant. 8. 6, s. me as a seal upon thine heart.
Mat. 5. 14, a city s. on a hill.
Acts 18. 10, no man shall s. on thee.
Heb. 6. 18, the hope s. before us.
See Ps. 75. 7 ; 107. 41 ; Eph. 1. 20 ; Col. 3. 2.

SETTLE. Zeph. 1. 12 ; Lu. 21. 14 ; Col. 1. 23.

SEVER. Lev. 20. 26 ; Ezek. 39. 14 ; Mat. 13. 49.

SEW. Gen. 3. 7 ; Job 14. 17 ; Eccl. 3. 7 ; Mk. 2. 21.

SHADE. Ps. 121. 5, the Lord is thy s.

SHADOW. Gen. 19. 8, the s. of my roof.
Job 7. 2, as servant earnestly desireth the s.
14. 2, he fleeth as a s. and continueth not.
17. 7, all my members are as a s.
Ps. 91. 1, under the s. of the Almighty.
102. 11, my days are like a s.
144. 4 ; Eccl. 8. 13, his days are as a s.
Eccl. 6. 12, life which he spendeth as a s.
Cant. 2. 3, under his s. with great delight.
17 ; 4. 6, till the s. flee away.
Isa. 4. 6, for a s. in the daytime.
25. 4, a s. from the heat.
32. 2, as the s. of a great rock.
49. 2 ; 51. 16, in the s. of his hand.
Jer. 6. 4, the s. of evening are stretched out.
Lam. 4. 20, under his s. we shall live.
Hos. 14. 7, they that dwell under his s. shall return.
Acts 5. 15, the s. of Peter might overshadow.
Jas. 1. 17, with whom is no s. of turning.
See Judg. 9. 15, 36 ; Isa. 38. 8 ; Jonah 4. 5.

SHAFT. Ex. 25. 31 ; 37. 17 ; Isa. 49. 2.

SHAKE. Judg. 16. 20, I will s. myself.
Ps. 29. 8, voice of Lord s. wilderness.
72. 16, fruit thereof shall s. like Lebanon.
Isa. 2. 19, when he ariseth to s. the earth.
13. 13 ; Joel 3. 16 ; Hag. 2. 6, 21, I will s. the heavens.
52. 2, s. thyself from the dust.
Hag. 2. 7, I will s. all nations.
Mat. 11. 7 ; Lu. 7. 24, a reed s. with the wind.
Lu. 6. 38, good measure, s. together.
2 Thess. 2. 2, be not soon s. in mind.
Heb. 12. 26, I s. not earth only.
27, things which cannot be s.
See Job 9. 6 ; Ezek. 37. 7 ; Mat. 24. 29.

SHAME. Ps. 4. 2, turn my glory into s.
40. 14 ; 83. 17, let them be put to s.
Prov. 10. 5 ; 17. 2, a son that causeth s.
Isa. 61. 7, for your s. ye shall have double.
Jer. 51. 51, s. hath covered our faces.
Ezek. 16. 52, bear thine own s.
Dan. 12. 2, awake, some to s.
Zeph. 3. 5, the unjust knoweth no s.
Lu. 14. 9, with s. to take lowest room.
Acts 5. 41, worthy to suffer s.
1 Cor. 6. 5 ; 15. 34, I speak this to your s.
Eph. 5. 12, a s. to speak of those things.
Phil. 3. 19, whose glory is in their s.
Heb. 6. 6, put him to an open s.
12. 2, despising the s.
See 1 Cor. 11. 6 ; 14. 35 ; 1 Thess. 2. 2 ; 1 Tim. 2. 9.

SHAPE. Lu. 3. 22 ; John 5. 37 ; Rev. 9. 7.

SHARP. 1 Sam. 13. 20, to s. every man his share.
21, a file to s. the goads.
Ps. 52. 2, tongue like a s. razor.
140. 3, they s. their tongues like a serpent.
Prov. 25. 18, false witness is s. arrow.

Prov. 27. 17, iron s. iron, so a man s. his friend.
Isa. 41. 15, a s. threshing instrument.
Acts 15. 39, the contention was so s.
Heb. 4. 12, s. than any two-edged sword.
See Mic. 7. 4 ; 2 Cor. 13. 10 ; Rev. 1. 16 ; 14. 14.

SHEAF. Deut. 24. 19 ; Ruth 2. 7 ; Ps. 126. 6 ; 129. 7.

SHEARERS. Gen. 38. 12 ; 1 Sam. 25. 7 ; Isa. 53. 7.

SHEATH. 1 Sam. 17. 51 ; 1 Chron. 21. 27 ; Ezek. 21. 3.

SHED. Gen. 9. 6, shall his blood be s.
Mat. 26. 28, s. for many for remission of sins.
Rom. 5. 5, love of God s. in our hearts.
Tit. 3. 6, which he s. on us abundantly.
Heb. 9. 22, without s. of blood is no remission.
See Ezek. 18. 10 ; 22. 3 ; Acts 2. 33.

SHEEP. Gen. 4. 2, Abel was a keeper of s.
Num. 27. 17 ; 1 Kings 22. 17 ; 2 Chron. 18. 16 ; Mat. 9. 36 ; Mk. 6. 34, as s. which have no shepherd.
1 Sam. 15. 14, what meaneth this bleating of s.
Ps. 49. 14, like s. are laid in the grave.
95. 7 ; 100. 3, we are the s. of his hand.
Isa. 53. 6, all we like s. have gone astray.
Jer. 12. 3, pull them out like s. for slaughter.
Ezek. 34. 6, my s. wandered.
Mat. 7. 15, false prophets in s. clothing.
10. 6, go rather to lost s.
12. 12, how much is a man better than a s.
John 10. 2, that entereth by door is shepherd of s.
11, good shepherd giveth his life for the s.
21. 16, feed my s.
See Mat. 10. 16 ; 12. 11 ; 18. 12 ; 25. 32 ; Heb. 13. 20.

SHEET. Judg. 14. 12 ; Acts 10. 11 ; 11. 5.

SHELTER. Job 24. 8 ; Ps. 61. 3.

SHEPHERD. Gen. 46. 34, s. abomination to Egyptians.
Ps. 23. 1, the Lord is my s.
Isa. 13. 20, nor shall s. make their fold there.
40. 11, he shall feed his flock like a s.
56. 11, they are s. that cannot understand.
Jer. 23. 4, I will set s. over them who shall feed.
50. 6, their s. have caused them to go astray.
Amos 3. 12, as the s. taketh out of the mouth.
Zech. 11. 17, woe to the idol s.
John 10. 14, I am the good s.
See Zech. 11. 3 ; Lu. 2. 8 ; 1 Pet. 2. 25 ; 5. 4.

SHIELD. Judg. 5. 8, was there a s. seen.
Ps. 5. 12, compass him as with a s.
33. 20 ; 59. 11 ; 84. 9, the Lord is our s.
84. 11, a sun and s.
91. 4, truth shall be thy s.
Isa. 21. 5, anoint the s.
Eph. 6. 16, taking the s. of faith.
See Prov. 30. 5 ; Jer. 51. 11 ; Ezek. 23. 24 ; 39. 9.

SHINE. Job 22. 28, the light shall s. upon thy ways.
29. 3, when his candle s. upon my head.
Ps. 104. 15, oil to make his face s.
139. 12, the night s. as the day.
Prov. 4. 18, light that s. more and more.
Isa. 9. 2, upon them hath the light s.
60. 1, arise, s., for thy light is come.
Dan. 12. 3, wise shall s. as the brightness.
Mat. 5. 16, let your light so s.
13. 43, the righteous s. as the sun.
2 Cor. 4. 6, God who commanded the light to s.
See John 1. 5 ; 2 Pet. 1. 19 ; 1 John 2. 8 ; Rev. 1. 16.

SHOCK. Judg. 15. 5 ; Job 5. 26.

SHOD. Mk. 6. 9 ; Eph. 6. 15.

SHOOT. Ps. 22. 7, they s. out the lip.
64. 3, to s. their arrows, even bitter words.
144. 6, s. out thine arrows and destroy them.
See 1 Chron. 12. 2 ; Mk. 4. 32 ; Lu. 21. 30.

SHORT. Job 17. 12, the light is s.
20. 5, triumphing of wicked is s.
Ps. 89. 47, remember how s. my time is.
Rom. 3. 23, come s. of the glory of God.
1 Cor. 7. 29, the time is s.
See Num. 11. 23 ; Isa. 50. 2 ; 59. 1 ; Mat. 24. 22.

SHORTER. Isa. 28. 20, the bed is s.

SHORTLY. Gen. 41. 32 ; Ezek. 7. 8 ; Rom. 16. 20.

SHOUT. Ps. 47. 5, God is gone up with a *s.*
  Lam. 3. 8, when I *s.* he shutteth out my prayer.
  1 Thess. 4. 16, shall descend with a *s.*
  See Num. 23. 21; 1 Sam. 4. 5; Isa. 12. 6.

SHOWER. Ps. 65. 10, makest it soft with *s.*
  72. 6, like *s.* that water the earth.
  Ezek. 34. 26, will cause *s.* to come in season.
  See Deut. 32. 2; Job 24. 8; Jer. 3. 3; 14. 22.

SHUN. Acts 20. 27; 2 Tim. 2. 16.

SHUT. Gen. 7. 16, the Lord *s.* him in.
  Isa. 22. 22, he shall open and none shall *s.*
  60. 11, gates shall not be *s.* day nor night.
  Jer. 36. 5, I am *s.* up, I cannot go to the house of
    the Lord.
  Lam. 3. 8, he *s.* out my prayer.
  See Gal. 3. 23; 1 John 3. 17; Rev. 3. 7; 20. 3.

SICK. Prov. 13. 12, maketh the heart *s.*
  23. 35, stricken me and I was not *s.*
  Cant. 2. 5, I am *s.* of love.
  Isa. 1. 5, the whole head is *s.*
  Hos. 7. 5, made him *s.* with bottles of wine.
  Mat. 8. 14, wife's mother *s.*
  Jas. 5. 14, is any *s.?* call elders of the church.
  15, prayer of faith shall save the *s.*

SICKNESS. Ps. 41. 3; Eccl. 5. 17; Mat. 8. 17.

SIFT. Isa. 30. 28; Amos 9. 9; Lu. 22. 31.

SIGHT. Ex. 3. 3, this great *s.*
  Deut. 28. 34, for *s.* of thine eyes.
  Eccl. 6. 9, better is *s.* of eyes.
  Mat. 11. 5; 20. 34; Lu. 7. 21, blind receive *s.*
  26; Lu. 10. 21, it seemed good in thy *s.*
  Lu. 18. 42; Acts 22. 13, receive thy *s.*
  21. 11, fearful *s.* and signs from heaven.
  Rom. 12. 17, things honest in *s.* of all men.
  2 Cor. 5. 7, walk by faith, not by *s.*
  See Eccl. 11. 9; Isa. 43. 4; Dan. 4. 11; Heb. 4. 13.

SIGN. Isa. 7. 11, ask thee a *s.* of the Lord.
  55. 13, for an everlasting *s.*
  Ezek. 12. 6, I have set thee for a *s.*
  Dan. 4. 3, how great are his *s.*
  Mat. 16. 3, *s.* of the times.
  Mk. 16. 20, with *s.* following.
  Lu. 2. 34, for a *s.* which shall be spoken against.
  John 4. 48, except ye see *s.*
  Acts 2. 22, man approved of God by *s.*
  4. 30, that *s.* may be done by the name.
  See Rom. 4. 11; 15. 19; 1 Cor. 1. 22; Rev. 15. 1.

SIGNIFY. John 12. 33; Heb. 9. 8; 1 Pet. 1. 11.

SILENCE. Mat. 22. 34; 1 Tim. 2. 11; 1 Pet. 2. 15.

SILENT. 1 Sam. 2. 9, *s.* in darkness.
  Ps. 28. 1, be not *s.* to me.
  31. 17, let the wicked be *s.* in the grave.
  Zech. 2. 13, be *s.*, all flesh, before the Lord.
  See Ps. 22. 2; 30. 12; Isa. 47. 5; Jer. 8. 14.

SILK. Prov. 31. 22, her clothing is *s.* and purple.
  Ezek. 16. 10, I covered thee with *s.*

SILLY. Job 5. 2; Hos. 7. 11; 2 Tim. 3. 6.

SILVER. 1 Kings 10. 27, king made *s.* as stones.
  Job 22. 25, thou shalt have plenty of *s.*
  Ps. 12. 6; 66. 10, as *s.* is tried.
  Prov. 8. 10, receive instruction and not *s.*
  Eccl. 5. 10, he that loveth *s.* shall not be satisfied.
  Isa. 1. 22, thy *s.* is become dross.
  Jer. 6. 30, reprobate *s.* shall men call them.
  Mal. 3. 3, sit as a refiner and purifier of *s.*
  See Gen. 44. 2; Eccl. 12. 6; Mat. 27. 6; Acts 19. 24.

SIMILITUDE. Num. 12. 8, the *s.* of the Lord.
  Deut. 4. 12, saw no *s.*
  Ps. 144. 12, after the *s.* of a palace.
  Rom. 5. 14, after the *s.* of Adam's transgression.
  Jas. 3. 9, made after the *s.* of God.
  See Hos. 12. 10; Dan. 10. 16; Heb. 7. 15.

SIMPLE (foolish). Ps. 19. 7, making wise the *s.*
  116. 6, the Lord preserveth the *s.*
  119. 130, it giveth understanding to the *s.*
  Prov. 1. 22, how long, ye *s.* ones?
  32, the turning away of the *s.*
  7. 7, and beheld among the *s.*

Prov. 8. 5, O ye *s.* understand wisdom.
  9. 4, whoso is *s.*
  14. 15, the *s.* believeth every word.
  19. 25, and the *s.* will beware.
  22. 3; 27. 12, the *s.* pass on, and are punished.
  Rom. 16. 18, deceive the hearts of the *s.*

SIMPLICITY. 2 Cor. 1. 12, that in *s.* and godly
    sincerity.
  11. 3, from the *s.* that is in Christ.

SIN (*n.*). Gen. 4. 7, *s.* lieth at the door.
  Num. 27. 3, died in his own *s.*
  Deut. 24. 16; 2 Kings 14. 6; 2 Chron. 25. 4, put to
    death for his own *s.*
  Job 10. 6, thou searchest after my *s.*
  Ps. 19. 13, from presumptuous *s.*
  25. 7, remember not *s.* of my youth.
  32. 1, blessed is he whose *s.* is covered.
  38. 18, I will be sorry for my *s.*
  51. 3, my *s.* is ever before me.
  90. 8, our secret *s.*
  103. 10, hath not dealt with us according to our *s.*
  Prov. 5. 22, holden with cords of *s.*
  10. 19, in multitude of words wanteth not *s.*
  14. 9, fools make a mock at *s.*
  34, *s.* is a reproach to any people.
  Isa. 30. 1, to add *s.* to *s.*
  43. 25; 44. 22, not remember *s.*
  53. 10, offering for *s.*
  12, bare the *s.* of many.
  Jer. 51. 5, land filled with *s.*
  Ezek. 33. 16, none of his *s.* shall be mentioned.
  Hos. 4. 8, they eat up *s.* of my people.
  Mic. 6. 7, fruit of my body for *s.* of my soul.
  Mat. 12. 31, all manner of *s.* shall be forgiven.
  John 1. 29, the *s.* of the world.
  8. 7, he that is without *s.*
  16. 8, will reprove the world of *s.*
  19. 11, hath the greater *s.*
  Acts 7. 60, lay not this *s.* to their charge.
  22. 16, wash away thy *s.*
  Rom. 5. 20, where *s.* abounded.
  6. 1, shall we continue in *s.*
  7. 7, I had not known *s.*
  14. 23, whatsoever is not of faith is *s.*
  2 Cor. 5. 21, made him to be *s.* for us.
  2 Thess. 2. 3, that man of *s.*
  1 Pet. 2. 24, his own self bare our *s.*
  See 1 John 1. 8; 3. 4; 4. 10; 5. 16; Rev. 1. 5.

SIN (*v.*). Gen. 42. 22, do not *s.* against the child.
  Ex. 9. 27; 10. 16; Num. 22. 34; Josh. 7. 20; 1 Sam.
    15. 24; 26. 21; 2 Sam. 12. 13; Job 7. 20; Ps. 41. 4;
    Mat. 27. 4; Lu. 15. 18, I have *s.*
  Job 10. 14, if I *s.*, thou markest me.
  Ps. 4. 4, stand in awe and *s.* not.
  39. 1, that I *s.* not with my tongue.
  Prov. 8. 36, he that *s.* against me.
  Isa. 43. 27, thy first father hath *s.*
  Ezek. 18. 4, the soul that *s.* it shall die.
  Hos. 13. 2, now they *s.* more and more.
  Mat. 18. 21, how oft shall my brother *s.*
  John 5. 14; 8. 11, *s.* no more.
  Rom. 6. 15, shall we *s.* because.
  1 Cor. 15. 34, awake to righteousness and *s.* not.
  Eph. 4. 26, be ye angry, and *s.* not.
  1 John 3. 9, he cannot *s.* because born of God.
  See Num. 15. 28; Job 1. 5, 22; Rom. 3. 23.

SINCERE. Phil. 1. 10; 1 Pet. 2. 2.

SINCERITY. Josh. 24. 14; 1 Cor. 5. 8; Eph. 6. 24.

SINFUL. Lu. 5. 8; 24. 7; Rom. 7. 13; 8. 3.

SINGING. Ps. 100. 2; 126. 2; Cant. 2. 12; Eph. 5. 19.

SINGLE. Mat. 6. 22; Lu. 11. 34.

SINGLENESS. Acts 2. 46; Eph. 6. 5; Col. 3. 22.

SINNER. Gen. 13. 13, men of Sodom *s.* exceedingly.
  Ps. 1. 1, standeth not in way of *s.*
  25. 8, teach *s.* in the way.
  26. 9, gather not my soul with *s.*
  51. 13, *s.* shall be converted.
  Prov. 1. 10, if *s.* entice thee.
  13. 21, evil pursueth *s.*

Eccl. 9. 18, one s. destroyeth much good.
Isa. 33. 14, the s. in Zion are afraid.
Mat. 9. 11; Mk. 2. 16; Lu. 5. 30; 15. 2, eat with s.
13; Mk. 2. 17; Lu. 5. 32, call s. to repentance.
11. 19; Lu. 7. 34, a friend of s.
Lu. 7. 37, woman who was a s.
13. 2, suppose ye these were s. above all?
15. 7, 10, joy over one s.
18. 13, be merciful to me a s.
John 9. 16, how can a man that is a s. do such miracles?
25, whether he be a s. I know not.
Rom. 5. 8, while we were yet s.
19, many were made s.
Heb. 7. 26, separate from s.
See Jas. 4. 8; 5. 20; 1 Pet. 4. 18; Jude 15.

SISTER. Job 17. 14; Prov. 7. 4; Mat. 12. 50; 1 Tim. 5. 2.

SIT. 2 Kings 7. 3, why s. we here until we die?
Ps. 69. 12, they that s. in the gate.
107. 10, such as s. in darkness.
Isa. 30. 7, their strength is to s. still.
Jer. 8. 14, why do we s. still?
Ezek. 33. 31, they s. before thee as thy people.
Mic. 4. 4, they s. every man under his vine.
Mal. 3. 3, he shall s. as a refiner.
Mat. 20. 23; Mk. 10. 37, to s. on my right hand.
See Prov. 23. 1; Lam. 3. 63; Acts 2. 2.

SITUATION. 2 Kings 2. 19; Ps. 48. 2.

SKILFUL. 1 Chron. 28. 21; Ps. 33. 3; Ezek. 21. 31; Dan. 1. 4.

SKILL. 2 Chron. 2. 7; Eccl. 9. 11; Dan. 1. 17; 9. 22.

SKIN. Ex. 34. 29, wist not that s. of his face shone.
Job 2. 4, s. for s.
10. 11, thou hast clothed me with s. and flesh.
19. 26, though after my s. worms destroy.
Jer. 13. 23, can the Ethiopian change his s.
Ezek. 37. 6, I will cover you with s.
Heb. 11. 37, wandered in sheep-s.
See Gen. 3. 21; 27. 16; Ps. 102. 5; Mic. 3. 2; Mk. 1. 6.

SKIP. Ps. 29. 6; 114. 4; Jer. 48. 27.

SKIRT. Ps. 133. 2; Jer. 2. 34; Zech. 8. 23.

SLACK. Deut. 7. 10; Prov. 10. 4; Zeph. 3. 16; 2 Pet. 3. 9.

SLAIN. Gen. 4. 23, I have s. a man.
Prov. 7. 26, strong men have been s. by her.
22. 13, the slothful man saith, I shall be s.
24. 11, deliver those ready to be s.
Isa. 22. 2, thy s. men are not s. with the sword.
26. 21, earth shall no more cover her s.
66. 16, the s. of the Lord shall be many.
Jer. 9. 1, weep for the s. of my people.
Lam. 4. 9, s. with sword better than s. with hunger.
Ezek. 37. 9, breathe upon these s.
Eph. 2. 16, having s. the enmity.
Rev. 5. 6, a Lamb as it had been s.
See 1 Sam. 18. 7; 22. 21; Lu. 9. 22; Heb. 11. 37.

SLANDEROUSLY. Rom. 3. 8, as we be s. reported.

SLAUGHTER. Ps. 44. 22, as sheep for the s.
Isa. 53. 7; Jer. 11. 19, brought as a lamb to the s.
Jer. 7. 32; 19. 6, valley of s.
Ezek. 9. 2, every man a s. weapon.
See Hos. 5. 2; Zech. 11. 4; Acts 9. 1; Jas. 5. 5.

SLAVE. Jer. 2. 14; Rev. 18. 13.

SLAY. Gen. 18. : 5, far from thee to s. the righteous.
Job 9. 23, if scourge s. suddenly.
13. 15, though he s. me.
See Gen. 4. 15; Ex. 21. 14; Neh. 4. 11; Lu. 11. 49; 19. 27.

SLEEP (n.). 1 Sam. 26. 12, deep s. from God.
Job 4. 13; 33. 15, when deep s. falleth.
Ps. 13. 3, lest I sleep the s. of death.
127. 2, giveth his beloved s.
Prov. 3. 24, thy s. shall be sweet.
6. 10; 24. 33, yet a little s.
20. 13, love not s. lest.
Eccl. 5. 12, the s. of a labouring man.

Jer. 51. 39, sleep a perpetual s.
Lu. 9. 32, heavy with s.
John 11. 13, of taking rest in s.
Rom. 13. 11, high time to awake out of s.
See Dan. 2. 1; 6. 18; 8. 18; Acts 16. 27; 20. 9.

SLEEP (v.). Ex. 22. 27, raiment, wherein shall he s.
Job 7. 21, now shall I s. in the dust.
Ps. 4. 8, I will lay me down and s.
121. 4, shall neither slumber nor s.
Prov. 4. 16, they s. not, except they have done.
6. 22, when thou s. it shall keep thee.
10. 5, he that s. in harvest is a son that causeth shame.
Cant. 5. 2, I s., but my heart waketh.
Dan. 12. 2, many that s. in the dust.
Mat. 9. 24; Mk. 5. 39; Lu. 8. 52, not dead but s.
13. 25, while men s. the enemy sowed.
26. 45; Mk. 14. 41, s. on now.
Mk. 13. 36, coming suddenly he find you s.
Lu. 22. 46, why s. ye? rise and pray.
John 11. 11, our friend Lazarus s.
1 Cor. 11. 30, for this cause many s.
15. 51, we shall not all s.
Eph. 5. 14, awake thou that s.
1 Thess. 4. 14, them which s. in Jesus.
5. 6, let us not s. as do others.
7, they that s. s. in the night.
10, that whether we wake or s.
See Gen. 28. 11; 1 Kings 18. 27; Acts 12. 6; 1 Cor. 15. 20.

SLEIGHT. Eph. 4. 14, the s. of men.

SLEW. Judg. 9. 54, a woman s. him.
1 Sam. 17. 36, s. both the lion and the bear.
29. 5, Saul s. his thousands.
2 Kings 10. 9, who s. all these?
Ps. 78. 34, when he s. them, then they sought him.
Isa. 66. 3, killeth an ox is as if he s. a man.
Dan. 5. 19, whom he would he s.
Mat. 23. 35, whom ye s. between temple and altar.
Acts 5. 30; 10. 39, whom ye s. and hanged on a tree.
22. 20, kept raiment of them that s. him.
Rom. 7. 11, sin by the commandment s. me.
See Gen. 4. 8; Ex. 2. 12; 13. 15; Neh. 9. 26; Lam. 2. 4.

SLIDE. Deut. 32. 35; Ps. 26. 1; 37. 31; Hos. 4. 16.

SLIGHTLY. Jer. 6. 14; 8. 11, healed hurt s.

SLIME. Gen. 11. 3; 14. 10; Ex. 2. 3.

SLIP. 2 Sam. 22. 37; Ps. 18. 36, feet did not s.
Job 12. 5, he that is ready to s.
Ps. 17. 5, that my footsteps s. not.
38. 16, when my foot s. they magnify.
73. 2, my steps had well nigh s.
Heb. 2. 1, lest we should let them s.
See Deut. 19. 5; 1 Sam. 19. 10; Ps. 94. 18.

SLIPPERY. Ps. 35. 6; 73. 18; Jer. 23. 12.

SLOTHFUL. Judg. 18. 9, be not s. to possess.
Mat. 25. 26, thou s. servant.
Rom. 12. 11, not s. in business.
Heb. 6. 12, that ye be not s.
See Prov. 18. 9; 19. 24; 24. 30; Eccl. 10. 18.

SLOW. Ex. 4. 10, I am s. of speech.
Neh. 9. 17, a God s. to anger.
Prov. 14. 29, s. to wrath is of great understanding.
Lu. 24. 25, s. of heart.
See Acts 27. 7; Tit. 1. 12; Jas. 1. 19.

SLUGGARD. Prov. 6. 6, go to the ant, thou s.
10. 26, so is the s. to them that send him.
13. 4, the soul of the s. desireth.
20. 4, the s. will not plow.
26. 16, the s. is wiser in his own conceit.

SLUMBER. Ps. 121. 3, that keepeth thee will not s.
Prov. 6. 4, give not s. to thine eyelids.
10; 24. 33, a little more s.
Isa. 5. 27, none shall s. among them.
56. 10, loving to s.
Nah. 3. 18, thy shepherds s.
Rom. 11. 8, hath given them the spirit of s.
See Job 33. 15; Mat. 25. 5; 2 Pet. 2. 3.

SMALL. Ex. 16. 14, *s.* round thing, *s.* as hoar frost.
18. 22, every *s.* matter they shall judge.
Num. 16. 9, a *s.* thing that God hath separated.
13, a *s.* thing that thou hast brought us.
Deut. 9. 21, I ground the calf *s.,* even as *s.* as dust.
32. 2, doctrine distil as *s.* rain.
2 Sam. 7. 19; 1 Chron. 17. 17, yet a *s.* thing in thy sight.
1 Kings 2. 20, one *s.* petition of thee.
2 Kings 19. 26, inhabitants of *s.* power.
Job 8. 7, thy beginning was *s.*
15. 11, are consolations of God *s.?*
36. 27, he maketh *s.* the drops of water.
Ps. 119. 141, I am *s.*
Prov. 24. 10, thy strength is *s.*
Isa. 7. 13, is it a *s.* thing to weary men?
16. 14, remnant very *s.* and feeble.
40. 15, nations as the *s.* dust.
54. 7, for a *s.* moment.
60. 22, a *s.* one shall become a strong nation.
Jer. 49. 15, I will make thee *s.* among heathen.
Dan. 11. 23, strong with a *s.* people.
Amos 7. 2, by whom shall Jacob arise? for he is *s.*
Zech. 4. 10, the day of *s.* things.
Mk. 8. 7; John 6. 9, a few *s.* fishes.
Acts 12. 18; 19. 23, no *s.* stir.
15. 2, had no *s.* dissension.
Jas. 3. 4, turned with very *s.* helm.
See Jer. 44. 28; Ezek. 34. 18; 1 Cor. 6. 2.

SMART. Prov. 11. 15, shall *s.* for it.

SMELL. Gen. 27. 27, as *s.* of field which the Lord hath blessed.
Deut. 4. 28, gods that neither see nor *s.*
Job 39. 25, he *s.* the battle.
Ps. 45. 8, thy garments *s.* of myrrh.
115. 6, noses have they, but they *s.* not.
Isa. 3. 24, instead of sweet *s.*
Dan. 3. 27, nor the *s.* of fire.
1 Cor. 12. 17, hearing, where were the *s.?*
Eph. 5. 2, sacrifice for sweet-*s.* savour.
Phil. 4. 18, an odour of a sweet *s.*
See Cant. 1. 12; 2. 13; 4. 10; 7. 8; Amos 5. 21.

SMITE. Gen. 2. 13, wherefore *s.* thou
21. 12, he that *s.* a man.
1 Sam. 26. 8, I will not *s.* him the second time.
2 Kings 6. 18, *s.* this people with blindness.
21, shall I *s.* them?
Ps. 121. 6, the sun shall not *s.* thee by day
141. 5, let the righteous *s.* me.
Prov. 19. 25, *s.* a scorner.
Isa. 10. 24, he shall *s.* thee with a rod.
49. 10, neither shall heat *s.* thee.
50. 6, gave my back to the *s.*
58. 4, to *s.* with the fist of wickedness.
Jer. 18. 18, let us *s.* him with the tongue.
Lam. 3. 30, giveth his cheek to him that *s.*
Ezek. 7. 9, know that I am the Lord that *s.*
21. 14, prophesy, and *s.* thine hands together.
Nah. 2. 10, the knees *s.* together.
Zech. 13. 7, awake, O sword, and *s.* the shepherd.
Mal. 4. 6, lest I *s.* the earth with a curse.
Mat. 5. 39, *s.* thee on the right cheek.
24. 49, shall begin to *s.* his fellow servants.
Lu. 22. 49, shall we *s.* with sword?
John 18. 23, why *s.* thou me?
See Lu. 6. 29; Acts 23. 2; 2 Cor. 11. 20; Rev. 11. 6.

SMITH. 1 Sam. 13. 19; Isa. 44. 12; Jer. 24. 1.

SMITTEN. Num. 22. 28, that thou hast *s.*
Deut. 28. 25, cause thee to be *s.*
1 Sam. 4. 3, wherefore hath the Lord *s.* us?
2 Kings 13. 19, thou shouldest have *s.* five or six times.
Ps. 3. 7, thou hast *s.* all mine enemies.
102. 4, my heart is *s.*
Isa. 24. 12, the gate is *s.* with destruction.
53. 4, *s.* of God.
Jer. 2. 30, in vain have I *s.* your children.
Hos. 6. 1, he hath *s.* and he will bind.
Amos 4. 9, I have *s.* you.
See Job 16. 10; Ezek. 22. 13; Acts 23. 3.

SMOKE. Gen. 19. 28, as the *s.* of a furnace.
Deut. 29. 20, the anger of the Lord shall *s.*
Ps. 37. 20, wicked consume into *s.*
68. 2, as *s.* is driven away.
74. 1, why doth thy anger *s.?*
102. 3, my days are consumed like *s.*
104. 32; 144. 5, he toucheth the hills, and they *s.*
119. 83, like a bottle in the *s.*
Prov. 10. 26, as *s.* to the eyes.
Isa. 6. 4, the house was filled with *s.*
34. 10, the *s.* thereof shall go up for ever.
51. 6, the heavens shall vanish like *s.*
65. 5, these are a *s.* in my nose.
Hos. 13. 3, as the *s.* out of a chimney.
See Rev. 9. 2; 14. 11; 15. 8; 18. 9; 19. 3.

SMOKING. Gen. 15. 17; Ex. 20. 18; Isa. 42. 3; Mat. 12. 20.

SMOOTH. Gen. 27. 11, I am a *s.* man.
1 Sam. 17. 40; Isa. 57. 6, five *s.* stones.
Isa. 30. 10, speak unto us *s.* things.
Lu. 3. 5, rough ways shall be made *s.*
See Ps. 55. 21; Prov. 5. 3; Isa. 41. 7.

SMOTE. Num. 20. 11, Moses *s.* the rock twice.
Judg. 15. 8, Samson *s.* them hip and thigh.
1 Sam. 24. 5, David's heart *s.* him.
Isa. 60. 10, in my wrath I *s.* thee.
Jer. 31. 19, I *s.* upon my thigh.
Hag. 2. 17, I *s.* you with blasting and mildew.
Mat. 26. 68; Lu. 22. 64, who is he that *s.* thee?
Lu. 18. 13, *s.* upon his breast.
Acts 12. 23, immediately angel *s.* him.
See 2 Sam. 14. 7; Dan. 2. 34; Mat. 27. 30.

SNARE. Ex. 10. 7, this man be a *s.* unto us.
Deut. 7. 25, nor take silver of idols, lest thou be *s.*
12. 30, take heed that thou be not *s.* by them.
Josh. 23. 13, they shall be *s.* unto you.
Judg. 8. 27, which thing became a *s.* to Gideon.
1 Sam. 18. 21, that she may be a *s.*
28. 9, wherefore layest thou a *s.* for my life?
2 Sam. 22. 6; Ps. 18. 5, *s.* of death prevented me.
Job 18. 8, he walketh on a *s.*
22. 10, *s.* are round about thee.
Ps. 11. 6, upon the wicked he shall rain *s.*
38. 12, they lay *s.* for me.
64. 5, commune of laying *s.* privily.
69. 22, let their table become a *s.*
91. 3, deliver thee from *s.* of fowler.
124. 7, the *s.* is broken.
Prov. 6. 2; 12. 13, *s.* with words of thy mouth.
7. 23, as a bird hasteth to the *s.*
13. 14; 14. 27, the *s.* of death.
18. 7, a fool's lips are the *s.* of his soul.
22. 25, learn his ways, and get a *s.* to thy soul.
29. 8, bring city into *s.*
25, fear of man bringeth a *s.*
Eccl. 9. 12, *s.* in an evil time.
Isa. 24. 17; Jer. 48. 43, the *s.* are upon thee.
Lam. 3. 47, fear and a *s.* is come upon us.
Ezek. 12. 13, he shall be taken in my *s.*
Hos. 9. 8, the prophet is a *s.*
Amos 3. 5, can a bird fall in a *s.?*
Lu. 21. 35, as a *s.* shall it come.
1 Tim. 3. 7, lest he fall into the *s.*
6. 9, they that will be rich fall into a *s.*
2 Tim. 2. 26, recover out of the *s.* of the devil.
See Ex. 23. 33; Deut. 7. 16; Judg. 2. 3; Eccl. 7. 26.

SNATCH. Isa. 9. 20, shall *s.* and be hungry.

SNOW. Ex. 4. 6; Num. 12. 10; 2 Kings 5. 27, leprous as *s.*
2 Sam. 23. 20, slew lion in time of *s.*
Job 6. 16, wherein the *s.* is hid.
9. 30, wash myself in *s.* water.
24. 19, drought and heat consume *s.* waters.
37. 6, saith to *s.*, be thou on the earth.
38. 22, the treasures of the *s.*
Ps. 51. 7, I shall be whiter than *s.*
147. 16, he giveth *s.* like wood.
Prov. 25. 13, cold of *s.* in harvest.
26. 1, as *s.* in summer.
31. 21, she is not afraid of the *s.*

Isa. 1. 18, your sins shall be white as *s.*
55. 10, as the *s.* from heaven returneth not.
Jer. 18. 14, will a man leave the *s.* of Lebanon?
Lam. 4. 7, Nazarites purer than *s.*
Dan. 7. 9; Mat. 28. 3; Mk. 9. 3, garment white as *s.*
See Ps. 68. 14; 148. 8; Rev. 1. 14.

SNUFFED. Jer. 14. 6; Mal. 1. 13.

SOAKED. Isa. 34. 7, land *s.* with blood.

SOAP. Jer. 2. 22; Mal. 3. 2.

SOBER. 2 Cor. 5. 13, *s.* for your cause.
1 Thess. 5. 6, let us watch and be *s.*
1 Tim. 3. 2; Tit. 1. 8, a bishop must be *s.*
Tit. 2. 2, aged men be *s.*
4, teach young women to be *s.*
1 Pet. 4. 7, be ye therefore *s.*, and watch.
See Acts 26. 25; Rom. 12. 3; Tit. 2. 6.

SODDEN. Ex. 12. 9; 1 Sam. 2. 15; Lam. 4. 10.

SOFT. Job 23. 16, God maketh my heart *s.*
41. 3, will he speak *s.* words?
Ps. 65. 10, thou makest it *s.* with showers.
Prov. 15. 1, a *s.* answer turneth away wrath.
25. 15, a *s.* tongue breaketh the bone.
See Ps. 55. 21; Mat. 11. 8; Lu. 7. 25.

SOFTLY. Gen. 33. 14; Judg. 4. 21; 1 Kings 21. 27; Isa. 38. 15.

SOIL. Ezek. 17. 8, planted in a good *s.*

SOJOURN. Gen. 19. 9, this fellow came in to *s.*
26. 3, *s.* in this land, and I will be with thee.
47. 4, to *s.* in the land are we come.
Deut. 26. 5, *s.* with a few, and became a nation.
Judg. 17. 9, I go to *s.* where I may find place.
2 Kings 8. 1, *s.* wheresoever thou canst *s.*
Ps. 120. 5, woe is me, that I *s.*
Isa. 23. 7, feet carry her afar off to *s.*
Jer. 42. 22, die in place whither we desire to *s.*
Lam. 4. 15, they shall no more *s.* there.
Heb. 11. 9, by faith he *s.* in land of promise.
1 Pet. 1. 17, pass time of your *s.* here in fear.

SOJOURNER. Gen. 23. 4; Ps. 39. 12.

SOLD. Gen. 31. 15, our father hath *s.* us.
45. 4, whom ye *s.* into Egypt.
Lev. 25. 23, the land shall not be *s.* for ever.
42, shall not be *s.* as bondmen.
27. 28, no devoted thing shall be *s.*
Deut. 15. 12, if thy brother be *s.* unto thee.
32. 30, except their Rock had *s.* them.
1 Kings 21. 20, thou hast *s.* thyself to work evil.
Neh. 5. 8, or shall they be *s.* unto us?
Esth. 7. 4, for we are *s.* to be slain.
Isa. 50. 1, have ye *s.* yourselves?
52. 3, ye have *s.* yourselves for nought.
Lam. 5. 4, our wood is *s.* unto us.
Joel 3. 3, they have *s.* a girl for wine.
Amos 2. 6, they *s.* the righteous for silver.
Mat. 10. 29, are not two sparrows *s.* for a farthing?
13. 46, went and *s.* all that he had.
18. 25, his lord commanded him to be *s.*
21. 12; Mk. 11. 15, cast out them that *s.*
26. 9; Mk. 14. 5, might have been *s.* for much.
Lu. 17. 28, they bought, they *s.*, they planted.
Acts 2. 45, and *s.* their possessions.
Rom. 7. 14, *s.* under sin.
1 Cor. 10. 25, whatsoever is *s.* in the shambles.
See Lu. 19. 45; John 12. 5; Acts 5. 1; Heb. 12. 16.

SOLDIER. Ezra 8. 22, ashamed to require *s.*
Mat. 8. 9; Lu. 7. 8, having *s.* under me.
Lu. 3. 14, *s.* demanded, what shall we do?
Acts 10. 7, a devout *s.*
2 Tim. 2. 3, as a good *s.* of Jesus Christ.
See 2 Chron. 25. 13; Isa. 15. 4; Acts 27. 31.

SOLE. Gen. 8. 9, dove found no rest for *s.* of her foot.
2 Sam. 14. 25; Isa. 1. 6, from *s.* of foot to crown.
See Deut. 28. 35, 56, 65; Josh. 1. 3; Job 2. 7.

SOLEMN. Ps. 92. 3, sing praise with a *s.* sound.
See Num. 10. 10; Isa. 1. 13; Lam. 2. 22; Hos. 9. 5.

SOLEMNITY. Isa. 30. 29, when a holy *s.* is kept.
See Deut. 31. 10; Isa. 33. 20; Ezek. 45. 17; 46. 11.

SOLEMNLY. Gen. 43. 3; 1 Sam. 8. 9.

SOLITARY. Ps. 68. 6, God setteth the *s.* in families.
107. 4, wandered in a *s.* way.
Isa. 35. 1, the wilderness and *s.* place shall be glad.
See Job 3. 7; 30. 3; Lam. 1. 1; Mic. 7. 14; Mk. 1. 35.

SOME. Gen. 37. 20, *s.* evil beast.
Ex. 16. 17, and gathered, *s.* more, *s.* less.
1 Kings 14. 13, found *s.* good thing.
Ps. 20. 7, *s.* trust in chariots.
69. 20, I looked for *s.* to take pity.
Dan. 12. 2, *s.* to life, and *s.* to shame.
Mat. 16. 14; Mk. 8. 28; Lu. 9. 19, *s.* say thou art John the Baptist.
28. 17, *s.* doubted.
John 6. 64, *s.* of you that believe not.
Acts 19. 32; 21. 34, *s.* cried one thing, *s.* another.
Rom. 3. 3, what if *s.* did not believe?
5. 7, *s.* would even dare to die.
1 Cor. 6. 11, such were *s.* of you.
15. 34, *s.* have not knowledge.
Eph. 4. 11, *s.* prophets, *s.* evangelists.
1 Tim. 5. 24, *s.* men's sins are open.
Heb. 10. 25, as the manner of *s.* is.
2 Pet. 3. 9, as *s.* men count slackness.
See 1 Tim. 1. 19; 2 Tim. 2. 18; Jude 22.

SOMEBODY. Lu. 8. 46; Acts 5. 36.

SOMETIMES. Eph. 2. 13, *s.* far off.
5. 8, ye were *s.* darkness.
Col. 1. 21, *s.* alienated.
See Col. 3. 7; Tit. 3. 3; 1 Pet. 3. 20.

SOMEWHAT. 1 Kings 2. 14; Gal. 2. 6; Rev. 2. 4.

SON. Gen. 6. 2; Job 1. 6; 2. 1; 38. 7; John 1. 12; Phil. 2. 15; 1 John 3. 1, *s.* of God.
Job 14. 21, his *s.* come to honour.
Ps. 2. 12, kiss the *S.*, lest he be angry.
86. 16, save *s.* of thine handmaid.
116. 16, I am the *s.* of thine handmaid.
Prov. 10. 1; 13. 1; 15. 20; 17. 2; 19. 26, a wise *s.*
17. 25; 19. 13, a foolish *s.*
31. 2, *s.* of my womb, *s.* of my vows.
Isa. 9. 6, unto us a *s.* is given.
14. 12, *s.* of the morning.
Jer. 35. 5, *s.* of the Rechabites.
Ezek. 20. 31; 23. 37, *s.* pass through fire.
Hos. 1. 10, the *s.* of the living God.
Mal. 3. 17, as a man spareth his *s.*
Mat. 11. 27, no man knoweth the *S.*
13. 55; Mk. 6. 3; Lu. 4. 22, the carpenter's *s.*
17. 5, this is my beloved *S.*
22. 42, Christ, whose *s.* is he?
Lu. 7. 12, only *s.* of his mother.
10. 6, if the *s.* of peace.
19. 9, he also is a *s.* of Abraham.
John 1. 18; 3. 18, only begotten *S.*
5. 21; the *S.* quickeneth whom he will.
8. 35, the *S.* abideth ever.
36, if the *S.* make you free.
17. 12; 2 Thess. 2. 3, the *s.* of perdition.
Acts 4. 36, *s.* of consolation.
Rom. 1. 9, serve in the gospel of his *S.*
8. 3, God sending his own *S.*
29, conformed to the image of his *S.*
32, spared not his own *S.*
1 Cor. 4. 14, as my beloved *s.* I warn you.
Gal. 4. 5, the adoption of *s.*
7, if a *s.*, then an heir.
Col. 1. 13, the kingdom of his dear *S.*
Heb. 2. 10, bringing many *s.* to glory.
5. 8, though a *S.*, yet learned he obedience.
11. 24, refused to be called *s.*
12. 6, scourgeth every *s.*
1 John 2. 22, antichrist denieth the *S.*
5. 12, he that hath the *S.* hath life.
See 1 John 1. 7; 4. 9; 5. 10, 11; Rev. 21. 7.

SONGS. Job 30. 9, now am I their *s.*
35. 10; Ps. 77. 6, who giveth *s.* in the night.
Ps. 32. 7, with *s.* of deliverance.
33. 3; Isa. 42. 10, sing unto him a new *s.*
40. 3, he hath put a new *s.* in my mouth.
69. 12, I was the *s.* of drunkards.

Ps. 119. 54, my *s.* in house of my pilgrimage.
137. 4, the Lord's *s.* in a strange land.
Prov. 25. 20, that singeth *s.* to an heavy heart.
Isa. 23. 16, sing many *s.*
35. 10, the ransomed shall come with *s.*
Ezek. 33. 32, as a very lovely *s.*
Amos 8. 3, *s.* of the temple.
Eph. 5. 19 ; Col. 3. 16, in psalms and spiritual *s.*
See Cant. 1. 1 ; Rev. 5. 9 ; 14. 3 ; 15. 3.

SOON. Ex. 2. 18, how is it ye are come so *s.*?
Job 32. 22, my Maker would *s.* take me away.
Ps. 37. 2, shall *s.* be cut down.
58. 3, go astray as *s.* as born.
68. 31, Ethiopia shall *s.* stretch out her hands.
90. 10, it is *s.* cut off.
106. 13, they *s.* forgat his works.
Prov. 14. 17, he that is *s.* angry.
See Mat. 21. 20 ; Gal. 1. 6 ; 2 Thess. 2. 2 ; Tit. 1. 7.

SORE. 2 Chron. 6. 29 ; Isa. 1. 6 ; Lu. 16. 20.

SORROW. Gen. 3. 16, multiply thy *s.*
42. 28, with *s.* to the grave.
Job 6. 10, I would harden myself in *s.*
21. 17, God distributeth *s.* in his anger.
41. 22, *s.* is turned into joy.
Ps. 13. 2, having *s.* in my heart daily.
90. 10, yet is their strength labour and *s.*
116. 3, I found trouble and *s.*
127. 2, to eat the bread of *s.*
Prov. 10. 22, maketh rich, addeth no *s.*
23. 29, who hath *s.*?
Eccl. 2. 23, all his days are *s.*
7. 3, *s.* is better than laughter.
11. 10, remove *s.* from thy heart.
Isa. 17. 11, day of desperate *s.*
35. 10 ; 51. 11, *s.* and sighing shall flee away.
53. 3, a man of *s.*
Jer. 30. 15, thy *s.* is incurable.
49. 23, there is *s.* on the sea.
Lam. 1. 12, any *s.* like unto my *s.*
Mat. 24. 8 ; Mk. 13. 8, beginning of *s.*
Lu. 22. 45, sleeping for *s.*
John 16. 6, *s.* hath filled your heart.
2 Cor. 2. 7, with overmuch *s.*
7. 10, godly *s.* worketh repentance.
1 Thess. 4. 13, *s.* not as others.
1 Tim. 6. 10, pierced with many *s.*
See Prov. 15. 13 ; Hos. 8. 10 ; Rev. 21. 4.

SORROWFUL. 1 Sam. 1. 15, woman of a *s.* spirit.
Ps. 69. 29, I am poor and *s.*
Prov. 14. 13, even in laughter the heart is *s.*
Jer. 31. 25, replenished every *s.* soul.
Zeph. 3. 18, I will gather them that are *s.*
Mat. 19. 22 ; Lu. 18. 23, went away *s.*
26. 37, he began to be *s.*
38 ; Mk. 14. 34, my soul is exceeding *s.*
John 16. 20, ye shall be *s.*
See Job 6. 7 ; 2 Cor. 6. 10 ; Phil. 2. 28.

SORRY. Ps. 38. 18, I will be *s.* for my sin.
Isa. 51. 19, who shall be *s.* for thee ?
See 1 Sam. 22. 8 ; Neh. 8. 10 ; Mat. 14. 9.

SORT. Gen. 6. 19, two of every *s.*
1 Chron. 29. 14, to offer after this *s.*
Dan. 3. 29, deliver after this *s.*
Acts 17. 5, fellows of the baser *s.*
2 Cor. 7. 11 ; 3 John 6, after a godly *s.*
2 Tim. 3. 6, of this *s.* are they.
See Deut. 22. 11 ; Eccl. 2. 8 ; Ezek. 27. 24 ; 38. 4.

SOTTISH. Jer. 4. 22, they are *s.* children.

SOUGHT. Gen. 43. 30, he *s.* where to weep.
Ex. 4. 24, the Lord *s.* to kill him.
1 Sam. 13. 14, the Lord hath *s.* him a man.
1 Chron. 15. 13, we *s.* him not after due order.
2 Chron. 15. 4, when they *s.* him he was found.
15, they *s.* him with their whole desire.
16. 12, in his disease he *s.* not the Lord.
26. 5, as long as he *s.* the Lord.
Ps. 34. 4 ; 77. 2, I *s.* the Lord, and he heard me.
111. 2, *s.* out of all that have pleasure.
Eccl. 7. 29, *s.* out many inventions.
12. 10, the preacher *s.* to find acceptable words.

Isa. 62. 12, shalt be called, *S.* out.
65. 1, *s.* of them that asked not.
Jer. 10. 21, pastors have not *s.* the Lord.
Lam. 1. 19, they *s.* meat to relieve their souls.
Ezek. 22. 30, I *s.* for a man among them.
34. 4, neither have ye *s.* that which was lost.
Lu. 11. 16, *s.* of him a sign.
13. 6, he *s.* fruit thereon.
19. 3, *s.* to see Jesus.
Rom. 9. 32, *s.* it not by faith.
Heb. 12. 17, though he *s.* it carefully with tears.
See Cant. 3. 1 ; Lu. 2. 44 ; 1 Thess. 2. 6.

SOUL. Gen. 2. 7, a living *s.*
Ex. 30. 12, a ransom for his *s.*
Deut. 11. 13, serve him with all your *s.*
13. 6, thy friend, which is as thine own *s.*
30. 2 ; Mat. 22. 37, obey with all thy *s.*
Judg. 10. 16, his *s.* was grieved.
1 Sam. 18. 1 ; 20. 17, loved him as his own *s.*
1 Kings 8. 48, return with all their *s.*
1 Chron. 22. 19, set your *s.* to seek the Lord.
Job 3. 20, life unto the bitter in *s.*
12. 10, in whose hand is the *s.*
16. 4, if your *s.* were in my *s.* stead.
23. 13, what his *s.* desireth, even that he doeth.
31. 30, wishing a curse to his *s.*
33. 22, his *s.* draweth near to the grave.
Ps. 33. 19, to deliver their *s.* from death.
34. 22, redeemeth the *s.* of his servants.
49. 8, the redemption of their *s.* is precious.
62. 1, my *s.* waiteth upon God.
63. 1, my *s.* thirsteth for thee.
74. 19, the *s.* of thy turtledove.
103. 1 ; 104. 1, bless the Lord, O my *s.*
116. 7, return to thy rest, O my *s.*
8, thou hast delivered my *s.* from death.
119. 175, let my *s.* live.
142. 4, no man cared for my *s.*
Prov. 11. 25, the liberal *s.* shall be made fat.
19. 2, *s.* without knowledge.
25. 25, cold waters to thirsty *s.*
Isa. 55. 3, hear, and your *s.* shall live.
58. 10, if thou wilt satisfy the afflicted *s.*
Jer. 20. 13, hath delivered the *s.* of the poor.
31. 12, their *s.* shall be as a watered garden.
Ezek. 18. 4, all *s.* are mine.
22. 25, they have devoured *s.*
Hab. 2. 10, thou hast sinned against thy *s.*
Mat. 10. 28, to destroy both *s.* and body.
16. 26 ; Mk. 8. 36, lose his own *s.*
26. 38 ; Mk. 14. 34, my *s.* is exceeding sorrowful.
Lu. 21. 19, in your patience possess ye your *s.*
Acts 4. 32, of one heart and *s.*
Rom. 13. 1, let every *s.* be subject.
1 Thess. 5. 23, that your *s.* and body be preserved.
Heb. 6. 19, an anchor of the *s.*
13. 17, they watch for your *s.*
Jas. 5. 20, shall save a *s.* from death.
1 Pet. 2. 11, which war against the *s.*
4. 19, commit keeping of *s.* to him.
2 Pet. 2. 14, beguiling unstable *s.*
3 John 2, even as thy *s.* prospereth.
See Prov. 3. 22 ; Ezek. 3. 19 ; Acts 15. 24.

SOUND (*n.*). Lev. 26. 36, the *s.* of a shaken leaf.
1 Kings 18. 41, *s.* of abundance of rain.
Job 15. 21, a dreadful *s.* is in his ears.
Ps. 89. 15, that know the joyful *s.*
92. 3, harp with a solemn *s.*
Eccl. 12. 4, *s.* of grinding is low.
Jer. 50. 22, *s.* of battle in the land.
51. 54, *s.* of a cry cometh.
Ezek. 33. 5, he heard *s.*, and took not warning.
John 3. 8, thou hearest the *s.*, but canst not tell.
Acts 2. 2, suddenly a *s.* from heaven.
Rom. 10. 18, *s.* went into all the earth.
1 Cor. 14. 8, an uncertain *s.*
See 2 Kings 6. 32 ; Rev. 1. 15 ; 9. 9 ; 18. 22.

SOUND (*adj.*). Prov. 2. 7 ; 3. 21 ; 8. 14, *s.* wisdom.
Prov. 14. 30, a *s.* heart is life of the flesh.

1 Tim. 1. 10 ; 2 Tim. 4. 3 ; Tit. 1. 9 ; 2. 1, *s.* doctrine.
2 Tim. 1. 7, spirit of a *s.* mind.
13, form of *s.* words.
See Ps. 119. 80 ; Lu. 15. 27 ; Tit. 2. 2, 8.

SOUND (*v.*). Ex. 19. 19, the trumpet *s.* long.
Joel 2. 1, *s.* an alarm in holy mountain.
Mat. 6. 2, do not *s.* a trumpet before thee.
1 Thess. 1. 8, from you *s.* out word of the Lord.
See Neh. 4. 18 ; 1 Cor. 13. 1 ; 15. 52 ; Rev. 8. 7.

SOUR. Isa. 18. 5 ; Jer. 31. 29 ; Ezek. 18. 2 ; Hos. 4.
18.

SOW. Job 4. 8, they that *s.* wickedness.
Ps. 97. 11, light is *s.* for the righteous.
126. 5, *s.* in tears.
Prov. 6. 16, he that *s.* discord.
Eccl. 11. 4, he that observeth the wind shall not *s.*
6, in morning *s.* thy seed.
Isa. 32. 20, that *s.* beside all waters.
Jer. 4. 3, *s.* not among thorns.
12. 13, they have *s.* wheat, but shall reap thorns.
Hos. 10. 12, *s.* in righteousness, reap in mercy.
Nah. 1. 14, that no more of thy name be *s.*
Hag. 1. 6, ye have *s.* much, and bring in little.
Mat. 6. 26, they *s.* not.
37, he that *s.* good seed.
John 4. 36, both he that *s.* and he that reapeth.
1 Cor. 15. 36, that which thou *s.* is not quickened.
2 Cor. 9. 6, he which *s.* sparingly.
Gal. 6. 7, whatsoever a man *s.*, that shall he reap.
See Lev. 26. 5 ; Deut. 11. 10 ; Jer. 2. 2 ; Jas. 3. 18.

SOWER. Isa. 55. 10 ; Jer. 50. 16 ; Mat. 13. 3 ; Mk.
4. 3 ; Lu. 8. 5 ; 2 Cor. 9. 10.

SPAKE. Ps. 39. 3, then *s.* I with my tongue.
106. 33, he *s.* unadvisedly with his lips.
Mal. 3. 16, *s.* often one to another.
John 7. 46, never man *s.* like this man.
1 Cor. 13. 11, I *s.* as a child.
Heb. 12. 25, refused him that *s.* on earth.
2 Pet. 1. 21, holy men *s.* as they were moved.
See Gen. 35. 15 ; John 9. 29 ; Heb. 1. 1.

SPAN. Ex. 28. 16 ; Isa. 40. 12 ; 48. 13 ; Lam. 2. 20.

SPARE. Gen. 18. 26, I will *s.* for their sakes.
Neh. 13. 22, *s.* me according to thy mercy.
Ps. 39. 13, *s.* me, that I may recover strength.
Prov. 13. 24, he that *s.* the rod.
19. 18, let not thy soul *s.* for his crying.
Joel 2. 17, *s.* thy people.
Mal. 3. 17, I will *s.* them as a man *s.*
Lu. 15. 17, bread enough and to *s.*
Rom. 8. 32, *s.* not his own Son.
11. 21, if God *s.* not the natural branches.
2 Pet. 2. 4, if God *s.* not the angels.
See Prov. 17. 27 ; 21. 26 ; Isa. 54. 2 ; 58. 1.

SPARK. Job 5. 7 ; 18. 5 ; Isa. 1. 31 ; 50. 11.

SPEAK. Gen. 18. 37, to *s.* to God.
Ex. 4. 14, I know he can *s.* well.
33. 11, spake to Moses as a man *s.* to his friend.
Num. 20. 8, *s.* to the rock.
1 Sam. 25. 17, a man cannot *s.* to him.
Job 11. 5, oh that God would *s.* against thee.
13. 7, will ye *s.* wickedly for God ?
32. 7, days should *s.*
33. 14, God *s.* once, yea, twice.
37. 20, if a man *s.* he shall be swallowed up.
Ps. 85. 8, I will hear what the Lord will *s.*
Prov. 23. 9, *s.* not in the ears of a fool.
Cant. 7. 9, causing lips of those asleep to *s.*
Isa. 19. 18, shall *s.* language of Canaan.
63. 1, I that *s.* in righteousness.
65. 24, while they are yet *s.*, I will hear.
Jer. 20. 9, I will not *s.* any more in his name.
Hab. 2. 3, at the end it shall *s.*
Zech. 8. 16 ; Eph 4. 25, *s.* every man the truth.
Mat. 8. 8, *s.* the word only, and my servant.
10. 19 ; Mk. 13. 11, how or what ye shall *s.*
12. 34 ; Lu. 6. 45, of abundance of heart mouth *s.*
36, every idle word that men shall *s.*
Mk. 9. 39, can lightly *s.* evil of me.

Lu. 6. 26, when all men *s.* well of you.
John 3. 11, we *s.* that we do know.
Acts 4. 17, that they *s.* to no man in this name.
20, we cannot but *s.*
26. 25, I *s.* words of truth and soberness.
1 Cor. 1. 10, that ye all *s.* the same thing.
14. 28, let him *s.* to himself and to God.
2 Cor. 4. 13, we believe and therefore *s.*
Eph. 4. 15, *s.* the truth in love.
Heb. 11. 4, he being dead yet *s.*
12. 24, that *s.* better things than that of Abel.
Jas. 1. 19, slow to *s.*
See 1 Cor. 14. 2 ; 1 Pet. 2. 1 ; 2 Pet. 2. 12.

SPEAR. Josh. 8. 18, stretch out the *s.*
Judg. 5. 8, was there a shield or *s.* seen ?
1 Sam. 13. 22, nor *s.* with any but Saul.
17. 7, the staff of his *s.*
45, thou comest to me with a *s.*
Ps. 46. 9, he cutteth the *s.* in sunder.
Isa. 2. 4 ; Mic. 4. 3, beat *s.* into pruninghooks.
See Job 41. 29 ; Jer. 6. 23 ; Hab. 3. 11 ; John 19. 34.

SPECIAL. Deut. 7. 6 ; Acts 19. 11.

SPECTACLE. 1 Cor. 4. 9, made a *s.* to the world.

SPEECH. Gen. 11. 1, earth was of one *s.*
Ex. 4. 10, I am slow of *s.*
Num. 12. 8, not in dark *s.*
Deut. 32. 2, my *s.* shall distil as dew.
1 Kings 3. 10, Solomon's *s.* pleased the Lord.
Job 6. 26, the *s.* of one that is desperate.
15. 3, or with *s.* wherewith he can do no good.
Ps. 19. 2, day unto day uttereth *s.*
3, there is no *s.* where their voice is not heard.
Prov. 17. 7, excellent *s.* becometh not a fool.
Cant. 4. 3, thy *s.* is comely.
Isa. 33. 19, of deeper *s.* than thou canst perceive.
Mat. 26. 73, thy *s.* bewrayeth thee.
1 Cor. 2. 1, not with excellency of *s.*
4. 19, not the *s.*, but the power.
2 Cor. 3. 12, we use great plainness of *s.*
10. 10, his *s.* is contemptible.
Col. 4. 6, let your *s.* be alway with grace.
Tit. 2. 8, sound *s.*, that cannot be condemned.
See Ezek. 3. 5 ; Rom. 16. 18 ; 2 Cor. 11. 6.

SPEECHLESS. Mat. 22. 12 ; Lu. 1. 22 ; Acts 9. 7.

SPEED. Gen. 24. 12, send me good *s.*
2 John 10, receive him not, neither bid him
God *s.*
See Ezra 6. 12 ; Isa. 5. 26 ; Acts 17. 15.

SPEEDILY. Ps. 31. 2, deliver me *s.*
69. 17 ; 143. 7, hear me *s.*
79. 8, let thy mercies *s.* prevent us.
102. 2, when I call, answer me *s.*
Eccl. 8. 11, because sentence is not executed *s.*
Isa. 58. 8, thy health shall spring forth *s.*
Zech. 8. 21, let us go *s.* to pray.
Lu. 18. 8, he will avenge them *s.*
See 1 Sam. 27. 1 ; Ezra 6. 13 ; 7. 17 ; Joel 3. 4.

SPEND. Job 21. 13, they *s.* their days in wealth.
36. 11, they *s.* their days in prosperity.
Ps. 90. 9, we *s.* our years as a tale that is told.
Isa. 55. 2, why *s.* money for that which is not
bread ?
2 Cor. 12. 15, very gladly *s.* and be spent for you.
See Prov. 21. 20 ; Eccl. 6. 12 ; Lu. 10. 35.

SPENT. Gen. 21. 15, water was *s.* in the bottle.
Job 7. 6, days *s.* without hope.
Ps. 31. 10, my life is *s.* with grief.
Isa. 49. 4, I have *s.* my strength for nought.
Acts 17. 21, *s.* their time to tell some new thing.
See Mk. 6. 35 ; Lu. 15. 14 ; 24. 29 ; Rom. 13. 12.

SPILT. 2 Sam. 14. 14, as water *s.*

SPIN. Ex. 35. 25 ; Mat. 6. 28 ; Lu. 12. 27.

SPIRIT. Gen. 6. 3, my *s.* shall not always strive.
Ex. 35. 21, every one whom his *s.* made willing.
Num. 11. 17, take of the *s.* that is on thee.
14. 24, he had another *s.* with him.
16. 22 ; 27. 16, the God of the *s.* of all flesh.
27. 18, a man in whom is the *s.*

Josh. 5. 1, nor was there any more *s.* in them.
1 Kings 22. 21 ; 2 Chron. 18. 20, there came
forth a *s.*
2 Kings 2. 9, let a double portion of thy *s.*
Neh. 9. 20, thou gavest thy good *s.* to instruct.
Job 4. 15, a *s.* passed before my face.
15. 13, thou turnest thy *s.* against God.
26. 4, whose *s.* came from thee ?
32. 8, there is a *s.* in man.
Ps. 31. 5 ; Lu. 23. 46, into thine hand I commit
my *s.*
32. 2, in whose *s.* there is no guile.
51. 10, renew a right *s.* within me.
78. 8, whose *s.* was not stedfast.
104. 4 ; Heb. 1. 7, who maketh his angels *s.*
106. 33, they provoked his *s.*
139. 7, whither shall I go from thy *s.* ?
Prov. 16. 2, the Lord weigheth the *s.*
18, an haughty *s.* goeth before a fall.
19 ; 29. 23 ; Isa. 57. 15, an humble *s.*
32, he that ruleth his *s.* better than he.
Eccl. 3. 21, who knoweth *s.* of man, and *s.* of
beast ?
7. 8, the patient in *s.* better than the proud.
8. 8, no man hath power over *s.* to retain *s.*
11. 5, the way of the *s.*
12. 7, the *s.* shall return to God.
Isa. 4. 4 ; 28. 6, *s.* of judgment.
11. 2 ; Eph. 1. 17, the *s.* of wisdom.
34. 16, his *s.* it hath gathered them.
42. 1, I have put my *s.* upon him.
57. 16, the *s.* should fail before me.
61. 1 ; Lu. 4. 18, the *S.* of the Lord is upon me.
Ezek. 3. 14 ; 8. 3 ; 11. 1, I went in the heat of my *s.*
11. 19 ; 18. 31 ; 36. 26, a new *s.*
Mic. 2. 11, a man walking in the *s.* and falsehood.
Mat. 14. 26 ; Mk. 6. 49, it is a *s.*
26. 41 ; Mk. 14. 38, the *s.* is willing.
Mk. 1. 10 ; John 1. 32, the *S.* descending on him.
8. 12, sighed deeply in his *s.*
Lu. 1. 17, go before him in *s.* and power of Elias.
2. 27, came by the *S.* into the temple.
8. 55, her *s.* came again.
9. 55, ye know not what manner of *s.*
10. 21, Jesus rejoiced in *s.*
24. 39, a *s.* hath not flesh and bones.
John 3. 34, God giveth not the *S.* by measure.
4. 24, God is a *S.,* worship him in *s.* and in truth.
6. 63, it is the *s.* that quickeneth.
14. 17 ; 15. 26 ; 16. 13 ; 1 John 4. 6, *S.* of truth.
Acts 2. 4, began to speak as the *S.* gave utterance.
6. 10, not able to resist the wisdom and *s.*
17. 16, his *s.* was stirred within him.
23. 8, say that there is neither angel nor *s.*
Rom. 8. 1, walk not after the flesh, but after the *S.*
2, the law of the *S.* of life.
11, the *S.* of him that raised up Jesus.
16, the *S.* itself beareth witness.
26, the *S.* maketh intercession.
12. 11, fervent in *s.*
1 Cor. 2. 4, in demonstration of the *S.*
10, the *S.* searcheth all things.
4. 21 ; Gal. 6. 1, in the *s.* of meekness.
6. 17, he that is joined to the Lord is one *s.*
20, glorify God in body and *s.*
12. 4, diversities of gifts, but the same *S.*
10, to another discerning of *s.*
14. 2, in the *s.* he speaketh mysteries.
15. 45, the last Adam made a quickening *s.*
2 Cor. 3. 6, the letter killeth, but the *s.* giveth life.
17, where the *S.* of the Lord is, there is liberty.
Gal. 3. 3, having begun in the *S.*
5. 16, walk in the *S.*
22 ; Eph. 5. 9, the fruit of the *S.*
25, if we live in the *S.,* let us walk in the *S.*
6. 8, he that soweth to the *S.* shall of the *S.* reap.
Eph. 2. 2, the *s.* that worketh in children of disobedience.
18, access by one *S.*
22, habitation of God through the *S.*
3. 16, strengthened by his *S.* in inner man.

Eph. 4. 3, the unity of the *S.*
4, one body and one *S.*
23, renewed in *s.* of your mind.
30, grieve not the holy *S.* of God.
5. 18, be filled with the *S.*
6. 17, take sword of the *S.*
Phil. 1. 27, stand fast in one *s.*
2. 1, if any fellowship of the *S.*
Col. 1. 8, your love in the *s.*
2. 5, absent in flesh, yet with you in the *s.*
1 Thess. 5. 19, quench not the *S.*
2 Thess. 2. 13, chosen through sanctification of
the *S.*
1 Tim. 3. 16, justified in the *S.*
4. 1, giving heed to seducing *s.*
12, be thou an example in *s.*
2 Tim. 4. 22, the Lord Jesus be with thy *s.*
Heb. 1. 14, ministering *s.*
4. 12, dividing asunder of soul and *s.*
9. 14, who through the eternal *S.*
12. 9, in subjection to the Father of *s.*
23, to *s.* of just men made perfect.
Jas. 2. 26, the body without the *s.* is dead.
4. 5, the *s.* lusteth to envy.
1 Pet. 1. 2, through sanctification of the *S.*
3. 4, ornament of a meek and quiet *s.*
18, but quickened by the *S.*
19, preached to *s.* in prison.
4. 6, live according to God in the *s.*
1 John 3. 24, by the *S.* he hath given us.
4. 1, believe not every *s.,* but try the *s.*
2, hereby know ye the *S.* of God.
3, every *s.* that confesseth not.
5. 6, it is the *S.* that beareth witness.
8, the *s.,* the water, and the blood.
Jude 19, sensual, having not the *S.*
Rev. 1. 10, I was in the *S.* on the Lord's day.
2. 7, 11, 17, 29 ; 3. 6, 13, 22, hear what the *S.* saith.
4. 2, I was in the *s.,* and, behold.
11. 11, the *S.* of life from God entered.
14. 13, blessed are the dead : Yea, saith the *S.*
22. 17, the *S.* and the bride say, Come.
See Mat. 8. 16 ; John 3. 5 ; Acts 7. 59 ; Rom. 7. 6.

SPIRITUAL. Hos. 9. 7, the *s.* man is mad.
Rom. 1. 11, impart some *s.* gift.
7. 14, the law is *s.*
15. 27, partakers of their *s.* things.
1 Cor. 2. 13, comparing *s.* things with *s.*
15, he that is *s.* judgeth all things.
3. 1, not speak unto you as unto *s.*
10. 3, all eat the same *s.* meat.
12. 1 ; 14. 1, concerning *s.* gifts.
15. 44, it is raised a *s.* body.
46, that was not first which is *s.*
Gal. 6. 1, ye which are *s.,* restore such an one.
Eph. 5. 19, in psalms and hymns and *s.* songs.
6. 12, *s.* wickedness in high places.
1 Pet. 2. 5, a *s.* house, to offer up *s.* sacrifices.
See 1 Cor. 9. 11 ; Col. 1. 9 ; 3. 16.

SPIRITUALLY. Rom. 8. 6 ; 1 Cor. 2. 14 ; Rev. 11. 8.

SPITE. Ps. 10. 14, thou beholdest mischief and *s.*

SPOIL (*n.*). Judg. 5. 30, necks of them that take *s.*
1 Sam. 14. 32, people flew upon the *s.*
2 Chron. 15. 11, offered to the Lord of the *s.*
20. 25, three days gathering the *s.*
28. 15, with the *s.* they clothed the naked.
Esth. 3. 13 ; 8. 11, take the *s.* of them for a prey.
9. 10, on the *s.* laid they not their hand.
Job 29. 17, I plucked the *s.* out of his teeth.
Ps. 119. 162, rejoice as one that findeth great *s.*
Prov. 16. 19, than to divide *s.* with the proud.
31. 11, he shall have no need of *s.*
Isa. 3. 14, the *s.* of the poor is in your houses.
42. 24, who gave Jacob for a *s.?*
53. 12, divide the *s.* with the strong.
See Is. 9. 3 ; Ezek. 7. 21 ; 38. 13 ; Nah. 2. 9 ; Zech. 14. 1.

SPOIL (*v.*). Ex. 3. 22, ye shall *s.* the Egyptians.
Ps. 76. 5, the stouthearted are *s.*
Cant. 2. 15, the little foxes that *s.* the vines.

Isa. 33. 1, woe to thee that *s.*, and thou wast not *s.*!
42. 22, this is a people robbed and *s.*
Jer. 4. 30, when *s.*, what wilt thou do?
Hab. 2. 8, thou hast *s.* many nations.
Zech. 11. 2, howl because the mighty are *s.*
Col. 2. 15, having *s.* principalities.
See Ps. 35. 10; Isa. 22. 4; Col. 2. 8; Heb. 10. 34.

SPOKEN. Num. 23. 19, hath he *s.*, and shall he not make it good?
1 Sam. 1. 16, out of my grief have I *s.*
1 Kings 18. 24, the people said, it is well *s.*
2 Kings 4. 13, wouldest thou be *s.* for to the king?
Ps. 62. 11, God hath *s.* once.
66. 14, my mouth hath *s.* when in trouble.
87. 3, glorious things are *s.* of thee.
Prov. 15. 23, a word *s.* in due season.
25. 11, a word fitly *s.* is like.
Eccl. 7. 21, take no heed to all words *s.*
Isa. 48. 15, I, even I, have *s.*
Mal. 3. 13, what have we *s.* so much against?
Mk. 14. 9, shall be *s.* of for a memorial.
Lu. 2. 34, for a sign which shall be *s.* against.
Acts 19. 36, these things cannot be *s.* against.
Rom. 1. 8, your faith is *s.* of.
14. 16, let not your good be evil *s.* of.
Heb. 2. 2, the word *s.* by angels.
See Heb. 13. 7; 1 Pet. 4. 14; 2 Pet. 3. 2.

SPOKESMAN. Ex. 4. 16, he shall be thy *s.*

SPORT. Gen. 26. 8; Isa. 57. 4; 2 Pet. 2. 13.

SPOT. Num. 28. 3; 9. 11; 29. 17, lambs without *s.*
Deut. 32. 5, their *s.* is not the *s.* of his children.
Job 11. 15, lift up thy face without *s.*
Jer. 13. 23, or the leopard his *s.*
Eph. 5. 27, glorious church, not having *s.*
1 Tim. 6. 14, commandment without *s.*
Heb. 9. 14, offered himself without *s.*
1 Pet. 1. 19, lamb without blemish and *s.*
2 Pet. 3. 14, that ye may be found without *s.*
Jude 12, these are *s.* in your feasts.
See Cant. 4. 7; 2 Pet. 2. 13; Jude 23.

SPOUSE. Cant. 4. 8; 5. 1; Hos. 4. 13.

SPRANG. Mk. 4. 8; Acts 16. 29; Heb. 7. 14; 11. 12.

SPREAD. Deut. 32. 11, eagle *s.* abroad her wings.
2 Kings 19. 14; Isa. 37. 14, *s.* letter before the Lord.
Job 9. 8, God who alone *s.* out the heavens.
26. 9, he *s.* his cloud upon it.
29. 19, my root was *s.* out by waters.
36. 30, he *s.* his light upon it.
37. 18, hast thou with him *s.* out the sky?
Ps. 105. 39, he *s.* a cloud for a covering.
140. 5, they have *s.* a net by the wayside.
Isa. 1. 15, when ye *s.* forth your hands I will hide.
33. 23, they could not *s.* the sail.
65. 2, *s.* out hands to a rebellious people.
Jer. 8. 2, they shall *s.* them before the sun.
Ezek. 26. 14, a place to *s.* nets upon.
Mat. 21. 8; Mk. 11. 8; Lu. 19. 36, *s.* garments.
Acts 4. 17, but that it *s.* no further.
See Judg. 8. 25; 1 Kings 8. 54; Ezra 9. 5.

SPRIGS. Isa. 18. 5; Ezek. 17. 6.

SPRING. Num. 21. 17, *s.* up, O well.
1 Sam. 9. 26, about the *s.* of the day.
Job 5. 6, neither doth trouble *s.* out of the ground.
38. 16, hast thou entered into the *s.* of the sea?
Ps. 87. 7, all my *s.* are in thee.
104. 10, he sendeth the *s.* into valleys.
107. 33, he turneth water-*s.* into dry ground.
35, turneth dry ground into water-*s.*
Prov. 25. 26, a troubled fountain, and a corrupt *s.*
Isa. 42. 9, before they *s.* forth I tell you.
43. 19, a new thing, now it shall *s.* forth.
45. 8, let righteousness *s.* up together.
58. 8, thine health shall *s.* forth.
11, shall be like a *s.* of water.
Mk. 4. 27, seed should *s.* he knoweth not how.
See Joel 2. 22; John 4. 14; Heb. 12. 15.

SPRINKLE. Job 2. 12; Isa. 52. 15; Ezek. 36. 25.

SPROUT. Job 14. 7, a tree will *s.* again.

SPUNGE. Mat. 27. 48; Mk. 15. 36; John 19. 29.

SPY. Num. 13. 16; Josh. 2. 1; Gal. 2. 4.

STABILITY. Isa. 33. 6, the *s.* of thy times.

STABLE. 1 Chron. 16. 30; Ezek. 25. 5.

STAFF. Gen. 32. 10, with my *s.* I passed over.
Ex. 12. 11, eat it with *s.* in hand.
Num. 13. 23, bare grapes between two on a *s.*
Judg. 6. 21, the angel put forth end of his *s.*
2 Sam. 3. 29, not fail one that leaneth on a *s.*
2 Kings 4. 29, lay my *s.* on face of the child.
18. 21; Isa. 36. 6, thou trustest on *s.*
Ps. 23. 4, thy rod and *s.* comfort me.
Isa. 3. 1, the stay and *s.*, the whole stay of bread.
9. 4, thou hast broken the *s.* of his shoulder.
10. 5, the *s.* in their hand is mine indignation.
15, as if the *s.* should lift up itself.
14. 5, the Lord hath broken the *s.* of the wicked.
Jer. 48. 17, how is the strong *s.* broken?
Zech. 11. 10, took my *s.*, even Beauty.
Mk. 6. 8, take nothing, save *s.* only.
Heb. 11. 21, leaning on the top of his *s.*
See Ex. 21. 19; Num. 22. 27; Isa. 28. 27.

STAGGER. Job 12. 25; Ps. 107. 27, *s.* like a drunken man.
Isa. 29. 9, they *s.*, but not with strong drink.
See Isa. 19. 14; Rom. 4. 20.

STAIN. Job 3. 5; Isa. 23. 9; 63. 3.

STAIRS. 1 Kings 6. 8; Neh. 9. 4; Cant. 2. 14.

STAKES. Isa. 33. 20; 54. 2.

STALK. Gen. 41. 5; Josh. 2. 6; Hos. 8. 7.

STALL. Prov. 15. 17; Hab. 3. 17; Mal. 4. 2.

STAMMERING. Isa. 28. 11; 32. 4; 33. 19.

STAMP. Deut. 9. 21; 2 Sam. 22. 43; Jer. 47. 3.

STAND. Ex. 14. 13; 2 Chron. 20. 17, *s.* still, and see.
Deut. 29. 10, ye *s.* this day all of you before the Lord.
1 Sam. 9. 27, *s.* thou still a while.
1 Kings 8. 11; 2 Chron. 5. 14, priests could not *s.* to minister.
17. 1; 18. 15; 2 Kings 3. 14; 5. 16, the Lord before whom I *s.*
2 Kings 10. 4, two kings stood not, how shall we *s.*?
2 Chron. 34. 32, caused all present to *s.* to it.
Esth. 8. 11, to *s.* for their life.
Job 8. 15, shall lean on his house, but it shall not *s.*
19. 25, he shall *s.* at the latter day.
Ps. 1. 1, nor *s.* in the way of sinners.
5, the ungodly shall not *s.* in judgment.
4. 4, *s.* in awe, and sin not.
10. 1, why *s.* thou afar off?
24. 3, who shall *s.* in his holy place?
33. 11, the counsel of the Lord *s.* for ever.
35. 2, *s.* up for my help.
76. 7, who may *s.* in thy sight?
94. 16, who will *s.* up for me?
109. 31, shall *s.* at right hand of the poor.
122. 2, our feet shall *s.* within thy gates.
130. 3, if thou, Lord, mark iniquities, who shall *s.*?
147. 17, who can *s.* before his cold?
Prov. 22. 29, shall *s.* before kings.
27. 4, who is able to *s.* before envy?
Eccl. 8. 3, *s.* not in an evil thing.
Isa. 7. 7; 8. 10, thus saith the Lord, it shall not *s.*
21. 8, 1 *s.* continually on watchtower.
28. 18, your agreement with hell shall not *s.*
40. 8, the word of God shall *s.* for ever.
65. 5, *s.* by thyself, I am holier than thou.
Jer. 6. 16, *s.* ye in the ways, ask for the old paths.
35. 19, shall not want a man to *s.* before me.
Dan. 11. 16, he shall *s.* in the glorious land.
12. 13, and shall *s.* in thy lot.
Mic. 5. 4, he shall *s.* and feed in strength.
Nah. 2. 8, *s.*, *s.*, shall they cry.
Zech. 3. 1, Satan *s.* at his right hand.
Mal. 3. 2, who shall *s.* when he appeareth?
Mat. 12. 25; Mk. 3. 24, 25; Lu. 11. 18, house divided shall not *s.*
16. 28; Lu. 9. 27, there be some *s.* here.
20. 3, others *s.* idle in the marketplace.

Rom. 5. 2, this grace wherein we *s.*
14. 4, God is able to make him *s.*
1 Cor. 2. 5, faith should not *s.* in wisdom.
16. 13, *s.* fast in the faith.
Gal. 4. 20, I *s.* in doubt of you.
5. 1, *s.* fast in the liberty.
Eph. 6. 13, having done all, to *s.*
Phil. 1. 27, *s.* fast in one spirit.
4. 1; 1 Thess. 3. 8, *s.* fast in the Lord.
1 Thess. 3. 8, we live, if ye *s.* fast.
2 Tim. 2. 19, the foundation of God *s.* sure.
Jas. 5. 9, the judge *s.* before the door.
Rev. 3. 20, I *s.* at the door, and knock.
6. 17, is come, and who shall be able to *s.?*
20. 12, the dead, small and great, *s.* before God.
See Rom. 14. 4; 1 Cor. 10. 12; Rev. 15. 2.

STANDARD. Isa. 10. 18, as when *s.*-bearer fainteth.
49. 22, I will set up my *s.* to the people.
59. 19, Spirit of the Lord shall lift up *s.* against.
62. 10, go through, lift up a *s.*
Jer. 4. 6; 50. 2; 51. 12, set up a *s.*
See Num. 1. 52; 2. 3; 10. 14.

STATE. Ps. 39. 5; Mat. 12. 45; Lu. 11. 26.

STATURE. Num. 13. 32, men of great *s.*
1 Sam. 16. 7, look not on height of his *s.*
Isa. 10. 33, high ones of *s.* hewn down.
45. 14, men of *s.* shall come.
Mat. 6. 27; Lu. 12. 25, not add to *s.*
Lu. 2. 52, Jesus increased in *s.*
19. 3, little of *s.*
Eph. 4. 13, *s.* of the fulness of Christ.
See 2 Sam. 21. 20; Cant. 7. 7; Ezek. 17. 6; 31. 3.

STATUTE. Ex. 18. 16, the *s.* of God.
Lev. 3. 17; 16. 34; 24. 9, a perpetual *s.*
2 Kings 17. 8, *s.* of the heathen.
Neh. 9. 14, *s.* and laws.
Ps. 19. 8, the *s.* of the Lord are right.
50. 16, to declare my *s.*
Ezek. 5. 6, hath changed my *s.*
20. 25, *s.* that were not good.
33. 15, walk in the *s.* of life.
Zech. 1. 6, my *s.*, did they not take hold?
See Ps. 18. 22; 105. 45; 119. 12, etc.; Ezek. 18. 19.

STAVES. Num. 21. 18, nobles digged with *s.*
1 Sam. 17. 43, am I a dog, that thou comest with *s.?*
Hab. 3. 14, strike through with his *s.*
Zech. 11. 7, took unto me two *s.*
Mat. 10. 10; Lu. 9. 3, neither two coats, nor *s.*
See Mat. 26. 47; Mk. 14. 43; Lu. 22. 52.

STAY (*n.*). 2 Sam. 22. 19; Ps. 18. 18, the Lord was my *s.*
Isa. 3. 1, take away the *s.* and staff.
See Lev. 13. 5; 1 Kings 10. 19; Isa. 19. 13.

STAY (*v.*). Gen. 19. 17, neither *s.* in plain.
Ex. 9. 28, ye shall *s.* no longer.
Num. 16. 48; 25. 8; 2 Sam. 24. 35; 1 Chron. 21. 22;
Ps. 106. 30, the plague was *s.*
2 Sam. 24. 16; 1 Chron. 21. 15, *s.* now thine hand.
Job 37. 4, he will not *s.* them.
38. 11, here shall thy proud waves be *s.*
37, who can *s.* the bottles of heaven?
Prov. 28. 17, let no man *s.* him.
Isa. 26. 3, whose mind is *s.* on thee.
27. 8, he *s.* his rough wind.
29. 9, *s.* yourselves, and wonder.
30. 12, ye trust in oppression, and *s.* thereon.
50. 10, trust in name of the Lord, and *s.* on his God.
Dan. 4. 35, none can *s.* his hand.
Hag. 1. 10, heaven is *s.*, earth is *s.*
See Josh. 10. 13; 1 Sam. 24. 7; Jer. 4. 6; 20. 9.

STEAD. Ex. 4. 16, be to him in *s.* of God.
Num. 10. 31, be to us in *s.* of eyes.
32. 14, risen in your fathers' *s.*
Job 16. 4, if your soul were in my soul's *s.*
31. 40, thistles grow in *s.* of wheat.
34. 24, he shall set others in their *s.*
Ps. 45. 16, in *s.* of fathers shall be children.
Prov. 11. 8, the wicked cometh in his *s.*

Isa. 3. 24, in *s.* of girdle a rent.
55. 13, in *s.* of the thorn shall come up the fir tree.
2 Cor. 5. 20, we pray you in Christ's *s.*
See Gen. 30. 2; 2 Kings 17. 24; 1 Chron. 5. 22.

STEADY. Ex. 17. 12, Moses' hands were *s.*

STEAL. Gen. 31. 27, wherefore didst thou *s.* away?
44. 8, how then should we *s.* silver or gold?
Prov. 6. 30, if he *s.* to satisfy his soul.
30. 9, lest I be poor, and *s.*
Jer. 23. 30, prophets that *s.* my words.
Mat. 6. 19, thieves break through and *s.*
John 10. 10, thief cometh not, but to *s.*
See Hos. 4. 2; Mat. 27. 64; Rom. 2. 21.

STEALTH. 2 Sam. 19. 3, by *s.* into city.

STEDFAST. Ps. 78. 8, not *s.* with God.
Dan. 6. 26, living God, and *s.* for ever.
Heb. 2. 2, word spoken by angels was *s.*
3. 14, hold our confidence *s.* to end.
6. 19, hope as anchor, sure and *s.*
1 Pet. 5. 9, resist *s.* in the faith.
See Acts 2. 42; Col. 2. 5; 2 Pet. 3. 17.

STEEL. 2 Sam. 22. 35; Job 20. 24; Jer. 15. 12.

STEEP. Ezek. 38. 20; Mic. 1. 4; Mat. 8. 32.

STEP. 1 Sam. 20. 3, but a *s.* between me and death.
Job 14. 16, thou numberest my *s.*
23. 11, my foot hath held his *s.*
29. 6, I washed my *s.* with butter.
31. 4, doth not he count my *s.?*
7, if my *s.* hath turned out of the way.
Ps. 37. 23, the *s.* of a good man are ordered.
31, none of his *s.* shall slide.
44. 18, nor have our *s.* declined.
56. 6, they mark my *s.*
73. 2, my *s.* had well nigh slipped.
85. 13, set us in the way of his *s.*
119. 133, order my *s.* in thy word.
Prov. 4. 12, thy *s.* shall not be straitened.
5. 5, her *s.* take hold on hell.
16. 9, the Lord directeth his *s.*
Isa. 26. 6, the *s.* of the needy shall tread it down.
Jer. 10. 23, not in man to direct his *s.*
Rom. 4. 12, walk in *s.* of that faith.
2 Cor. 12. 18, walked we not in same *s.?*
1 Pet. 2. 21, that ye should follow his *s.*
See Ex. 20. 26; 2 Sam. 22. 37; Lam. 4. 18; Ezek. 40. 22.

STEWARD. 1 Kings 16. 9, drunk in house of his *s.*
Lu. 12. 42, that faithful and wise *s.*
See Gen. 15. 2; Lu. 8. 3; 1 Cor. 4. 1; 1 Pet. 4. 10.

STICK. Num. 15. 32, gathered *s.* on sabbath.
1 Kings 17. 12, I am gathering two *s.*
Job 33. 21, his bones *s.* out.
Ps. 38. 2, thine arrows *s.* fast in me.
Prov. 18. 24, a friend that *s.* closer than a brother.
Ezek. 37. 16, take *s.*, and write on it.
See 2 Kings 6. 6; Lam. 4. 8; Ezek. 29. 4.

STIFF. Ex. 32. 9; 33. 3; 34. 9; Deut. 9. 6, 13; 10. 16, *s.*-necked people.
Ps. 75. 5, speak not with *s.* neck.
Jer. 17. 23, obeyed not, but made their neck *s.*
Ezek. 2. 4, impudent and *s.*-hearted.
Acts 7. 51, ye *s.*-necked, ye do always resist.
See Deut. 31. 27; 2 Chron. 30. 8; 36. 13.

STILL. Ex. 15. 16, as *s.* as a stone.
Num. 14. 38, Joshua and Caleb lived *s.*
Josh. 24. 10, Balaam blessed you *s.*
Judg. 18. 9, the land is good, and are ye *s.?*
2 Sam. 14. 32, good to have been there *s.*
2 Kings 7. 4, if we sit *s.* here, we die also.
2 Chron. 22. 9, no power to keep *s.* the kingdom.
Job 2. 9, dost thou *s.* retain thine integrity?
Ps. 4. 4, commune with thine heart, and be *s.*
8. 2, *s.* the enemy and avenger.
23. 2, beside the *s.* waters.
46. 10, be *s.*, and know that I am God.
76. 8, earth feared, and was *s.*
83. 1, hold not thy peace, and be not *s.*, O God.
84. 4, they will be *s.* praising thee.
107. 29, so that the waves thereof are *s.*

Ps. 139. 18, when I awake, I am *s.* with thee.
Eccl. 12. 9, he *s.* taught knowledge.
Isa. 5. 25; 9. 12; 10. 4, his hand is stretched out *s.*
30. 7, their strength is to sit *s.*
42. 14, I have been *s.*, and refrained.
Jer. 8. 14, why do we sit *s.*?
31. 20, I do earnestly remember him *s.*
Zech. 11. 16, nor feed that that standeth *s.*
Mk. 4. 39, arose, and said, peace, be *s.*
Rev. 22. 11, unjust *s.*, filthy *s.*, holy *s.*
See Num. 13. 30; Ps. 65. 7; 89. 9; 92. 14.

STING. Prov. 23. 32; 1 Cor. 15. 55; Rev. 9. 10.

STIR. Num. 24. 9, who shall *s.* him up?
Deut. 32. 11, as an eagle *s.* up her nest.
1 Sam. 22. 8, my son hath *s.* up my servant.
26. 19, if the Lord have *s.* thee up.
1 Kings 11. 14, the Lord *s.* up an adversary.
1 Chron. 5. 26; 2 Chron. 36. 22; Hag. 1. 14, God *s.*
up the spirit.
Job 17. 8, the innocent shall *s.* up himself.
41. 10, none dare *s.* him up.
Ps. 35. 23, *s.* up thyself.
39. 2, my sorrow was *s.*
Prov. 10. 12, hatred *s.* up strifes.
15. 18; 29. 22, a wrathful man *s.* up strife.
Isa. 10. 26, the Lord shall *s.* up a scourge.
14. 9, hell from beneath *s.* up the dead.
64. 7, none *s.* up himself to take hold.
Lu. 23. 5, he *s.* up the people.
Acts 17. 16, his spirit was *s.* in him.
19. 23, no small *s.* about this way.
2 Tim. 1. 6, *s.* up gift of God in thee.
2 Pet. 1. 13, I think it meet to *s.* you up.
See Cant. 2. 7; 3. 5; 8. 4; Isa. 22. 2; Acts 12. 18.

STOCK. Job 14. 8, though the *s.* thereof die.
Isa. 40. 24, their *s.* shall not take root.
44. 19, shall I fall down to the *s.* of a tree?
Hos. 4. 12, my people ask counsel at their *s.*
Nah. 3. 6; Heb. 10. 33, a gazing-*s.*
Acts 13. 26, children of the *s.* of Abraham.
See Jer. 2. 27; 10. 8; 20. 2; Phil. 3. 5.

STOLE. 2 Sam. 15. 6, Absalom *s.* the hearts.
Eph. 4. 28, let him that *s.* steal no more.
See 2 Kings 11. 2; 2 Chron. 22. 11;
Mat. 28. 13.

STOLEN. Josh. 7. 11, they have *s.*, and dissembled.
2 Sam. 21. 12, men had *s.* the bones of Saul.
Prov. 9. 17, *s.* waters are sweet.
Obad. 5, *s.* till they had enough.
See Gen. 30. 33; 31. 19; Ex. 22. 7; 2 Sam. 19. 41.

STOMACH. 1 Tim. 5. 23, for thy *s.* sake.

STONE. Gen. 11. 3, they had brick for *s.*
28. 18, 22; 31. 45; 35. 14, set up a *s.* for a pillar.
Deut. 8. 9, a land whose *s.* are iron.
Josh. 24. 27, this *s.* shall be a witness.
2 Sam. 17. 13, till there be not one small *s.* found
there.
2 Kings 3. 25, cast every man his *s.*
Job 5. 23, in league with *s.* of the field.
6. 12, is my strength the strength of *s.*?
14. 19, the waters wear the *s.*
28. 3, he searcheth out the *s.* of darkness.
41. 24, his heart is as firm as a *s.*
Ps. 91. 12; Mat. 4. 6; Lu. 4. 11, lest thou dash thy
foot against a *s.*
118. 22; Mat. 21. 42; Mk. 12. 10, the *s.* which the
builders refused is become the head *s.*
Prov. 27. 3, a *s.* is heavy, a fool's wrath heavier.
Isa. 54. 11, I will lay thy *s.* with fair colours.
60. 17, bring for *s.* iron.
62. 10, gather out the *s.*
Jer. 2. 27, and to a *s.*, thou hast brought me forth.
Dan. 2. 34, a *s.* was cut out of the mountain.
Hab. 2. 11, the *s.* shall cry out of the wall.
19, that saith to the dumb *s.*, arise.
Hag. 2. 15, before *s.* was laid upon *s.*
Zech. 3. 9, upon one *s.* shall be seven eyes.
4. 7, bring forth the head-*s.* thereof.
7. 12, they made their hearts as *s.*

Mat. 7. 9; Lu. 11. 11, will he give him a *s.*?
21. 44; Lu. 20. 18, whosoever shall fall on this *s.*
24. 2; Mk. 13. 2; Lu. 19. 44; 21. 6, not one *s.* upon
another.
Mk. 13. 1, see what manner of *s.* are here!
16. 4; Lu. 24. 2, found *s.* rolled away.
Lu. 4. 3, command this *s.* that it be made bread.
John 1. 42, Cephas, by interpretation a *s.*
8. 7, first cast a *s.*
11. 39, take ye away the *s.*
Acts 17. 29, that the Godhead is like to *s.*
1 Pet. 2. 5, as lively *s.*, are built up.
See 1Sam. 30. 6; 1 Cor. 3. 12; 2 Cor. 3. 3; Rev. 2. 17.

STONY. Ps. 141. 6; Ezek. 11. 19; 36. 26; Mat. 13. 5.

STOOD. Gen. 18. 22, *s.* yet before the Lord.
Num. 14. 19, *s.* behind them.
Josh. 3. 16, waters *s.* upon an heap.
2 Kings 23. 3, all the people *s.* to the covenant.
Esth. 9. 16, Jews *s.* for their lives.
Ps. 33. 9, he commanded, and it *s.* fast.
Lu. 24. 36, Jesus himself *s.* in the midst.
2 Tim. 4. 16, no man *s.* with me.
See Gen. 23. 3; Job 29. 8; Ezek. 37. 10; Rev. 7. 11.

STOOP. Gen. 49. 9, Judah *s.* down.
Prov. 12. 25, heaviness maketh the heart *s.*
John 8. 6, *s.* down, and wrote on the ground.
See 2 Chron. 36. 17; Job 9. 13; Mk. 1. 7; John 20. 11.

STOP. Gen. 8. 2, windows of heaven were *s.*
1 Kings 18. 44, that the rain *s.* thee not.
Ps. 107. 42, iniquity shall *s.* her mouth.
Zech. 7. 11, refused, and *s.* their ears.
Acts 7. 57, *s.* their ears, and ran upon him.
Rom. 3. 19, that every mouth may be *s.*
Tit. 1. 11, whose mouths must be *s.*
Heb. 11. 33, through faith *s.* mouths of lions.
See Gen. 26. 15; Job 5. 16; Ps. 58. 4; Prov. 21. 13.

STORE. Lev. 25. 22; 26. 10, eat of the old *s.*
Deut. 28. 5, blessed be thy basket and *s.*
2 Kings 20. 17, thy fathers have laid up in *s.*
Ps. 144. 13, affording all manner of *s.*
Nah. 2. 9, none end of the *s.* and glory.
Mal. 3. 10, bring tithes into *s.*-house.
Lu. 12. 24, neither have *s.*-house nor barn.
1 Cor. 16. 2, every one lay by him in *s.*
1 Tim. 6. 19, laying up in *s.* a good foundation.
2 Pet. 3. 7, by same word are kept in *s.*
See 1 Kings 10. 10; 1 Chron. 29. 16; Ps. 33. 7.

STORK. Ps. 104. 17, as for the *s.*, the fir trees are
her house.
Jer. 8. 7, yea, the *s.* in the heaven.
Zech. 5. 9, like the wings of a *s.*

STORM. Ps. 55. 8, escape from windy *s.*
83. 15, make them afraid with thy *s.*
107. 29, he maketh the *s.* a calm.
Isa. 4. 6; 25. 4, a covert from *s.*
28. 2, as a destroying *s.*
Ezek. 38. 9, shalt ascend and come like a *s.*
Nah. 1. 3, the Lord hath his way in the *s.*
See Job 21. 18; 27. 21; Mk. 4. 37; Lu. 8. 23.

STORMY. Ps. 107. 25; 148. 8; Ezek. 13. 11.

STORY. 2 Chron. 13. 22; 24. 27.

STOUT. Dan. 7. 20, whose look was more *s.*
Mal. 3. 13, words have been *s.* against me.
See Ps. 76. 5; Isa. 9. 9; 10. 12; 46. 12.

STRAIGHT. Ps. 5. 8, make thy way *s.*
Prov. 4. 25, let eyelids look *s.* before thee.
Eccl. 1. 15; 7. 13, crooked cannot be made *s.*
Isa. 40. 3, make *s.* a highway.
4; 42. 16; 45. 2; Lu. 3. 5, crooked shall be made *s.*
Jer. 31. 9, cause them to walk in a *s.* way.
Mat. 3. 3; Mk. 1. 3; Lu. 3. 4; John 1. 23, make
his paths *s.*
Lu. 13. 13, she was made *s.*
Acts 9. 11, street which is called S.
Heb. 12. 13, make *s.* paths for your feet.
See Josh. 6. 5; 1 Sam. 6. 12; Ezek. 1. 7; 10. 22.

STRAIGHTWAY. Prov. 7. 22, he goeth after her *s.*
Mat. 4. 20; Mk. 1. 18, they *s.* left their nets.

Jas. 1. 24, *s.* forgetteth what manner of man.
See Lu. 14. 5 ; John 13. 32 ; Acts 9. 20 ; 16. 33.
STRAIN. Mat. 23. 24, *s.* at a gnat.
STRAIT. 2 Sam. 24. 14, I am in a great *s.*
Job 20. 22, he shall be in *s.*
Isa. 49. 20, the place is too *s.* for me, give place.
Mic. 2. 7, is spirit of the Lord *s.* ?
Mat. 7. 13 ; Lu. 13. 24, enter in at the *s.* gate.
Lu. 12. 50, how am I *s.* till it be accomplished !
2 Cor. 6. 12, ye are not *s.* in us.
Phil. 1. 23, I am in a *s.* betwixt two.
See 2 Kings 6. 1 ; Job 18. 7 ; 37. 10 ; Jer. 19. 9.
STRAITLY. Gen. 43. 7 ; Josh. 6. 1 ; Acts 4. 17.
STRAITNESS. Deut. 28. 53 ; Job 36. 16.
STRANGE. Gen. 42. 7, Joseph made himself *s.*
Ex. 2. 22 ; 18. 3 ; Ps. 137. 4, in a *s.* land.
Lev. 10. 1 ; Num. 3. 4 ; 26. 61, offered *s.* fire.
1 Kings 11. 1, Solomon loved many *s.* women.
Job 19. 17, my breath is *s.* to my wife.
31. 3, a *s.* punishment to workers.
Prov. 2. 16, to deliver thee from the *s.* woman.
5. 3, 20, for the lips of a *s.* woman.
21. 8, the way of man is froward and *s.*
23. 27, a *s.* woman is a narrow pit.
Isa. 28. 21, his *s.* work, his *s.* act.
Ezek. 3. 5, not sent to people of a *s.* speech.
Zeph. 1. 8, clothed with *s.* apparel.
Lu. 5. 26, we have seen *s.* things to-day.
Acts 17. 20, thou bringest *s.* things to our ears.
26. 11, persecuted them even to *s.* cities.
Heb. 13. 9, carried about with *s.* doctrines.
1 Pet. 4. 4, they think it *s.* ye run not.
12, not *s.* concerning the fiery trial.
See Judg. 11. 2 ; Ezra 10. 2 ; Prov. 2. 16 ; Jer. 8. 19.
STRANGER. Gen. 23. 4 ; Ps. 39. 12, I am a *s.* with you.
Ex. 23. 9, ye know the heart of a *s.*
1 Chron. 29. 15, we are *s.*, as were all our fathers.
Job 15. 19, no *s.* passed among them.
31. 32, the *s.* did not lodge in the street.
Ps. 54. 3, for *s.* are risen up against me.
109. 11, let the *s.* spoil his labour.
146. 9, the Lord preserveth the *s.*
Prov. 2. 16, to deliver thee even from the *s.*
5. 10, lest *s.* be filled with thy wealth.
17, let them be thine own, not *s.* with thee.
6. 1, stricken thy hand with a *s.*
7. 5, from the *s.* which flattereth.
11. 15, he that is surety for a *s.* shall smart.
14. 10, a *s.* doth not intermeddle.
20. 16 ; 27. 13, garment that is surety for a *s.*
27. 2, let a *s.* praise thee.
Isa. 1. 7, your land, *s.* devour it.
2. 6, please themselves in children of *s.*
14. 1, the *s.* shall be joined with them.
56. 3, neither let the son of the *s.* speak.
Jer. 14. 8, why be as a *s.* in the land ?
Ezek. 28. 10, thou shalt die by the hand of *s.*
Hos. 7. 9, *s.* have devoured his strength.
Mat. 25. 35, I was a *s.*, and ye took me in.
Lu. 17. 18, that returned, save this *s.*
Eph. 2. 12, *s.* from the covenant.
19, no more *s.*, but fellowcitizens.
Heb. 11. 13, confessed they were *s.*
13. 2, be not forgetful to entertain *s.*
See Mat. 17. 25 ; John 10. 5 ; 1 Pet. 2. 11.
STRANGLED. Nah. 2. 12 ; Acts 15. 20 ; 21. 25.
STREAM. Ps. 124. 4 ; Isa. 35. 6 ; 66. 12 ; Amos 5. 24.
STREET. Prov. 1. 20 ; Lu. 14. 21 ; Rev. 21. 21 ; 22. 2.
STRENGTH. Ex. 15. 2 ; 2 Sam. 22. 33 ; Ps. 18. 2 ;
28. 7 ; 118. 14 ; Isa. 12. 2, the Lord is my *s.*
Judg. 5. 21, thou hast trodden down *s.*
1 Sam. 2. 9, by *s.* shall no man prevail.
15. 29, the *S.* of Israel will not lie.
Job 9. 19, if I speak of *s.*, lo, he is strong.
12. 13, with him is wisdom and *s.*
Ps. 18. 32, girded me with *s.*
27. 1, the Lord is the *s.* of my life.
29. 11, the Lord will give *s.* to his people.
33. 16, mighty not delivered by much *s.*

Ps. 39. 13, spare me, that I may recover *s.*
46. 1 ; 81. 1, God is our refuge and *s.*
68. 34, ascribe *s.* to God, his *s.* is in the clouds.
35, God giveth *s.* and power.
73. 26, God is the *s.* of my heart.
84. 5, the man whose *s.* is in thee.
7, they go from *s.* to *s.*
96. 6, *s.* and beauty are in his sanctuary.
138. 3, strengthenedst me with *s.* in my soul.
Prov. 10. 29, the way of the Lord is *s.*
Eccl. 9. 16, wisdom is better than *s.*
10. 17, princes eat for *s.*
Isa. 25. 4, a *s.* to the poor, a *s.* to the needy.
40. 29, he increaseth *s.*
51. 9, awake, put on *s.*
Hag. 2. 22, I will destroy the *s.* of the kingdoms.
Lu. 1. 51, he hath showed *s.* with his arm.
Rom. 5. 6, when ye were without *s.*
1 Cor. 15. 56, the *s.* of sin is the law.
Rev. 3. 8, thou hast a little *s.*
See Job 21. 23 ; Prov. 20. 29 ; 2 Cor. 12. 9.
STRENGTHEN. Job 15. 25, he *s.* himself against.
Ps. 20. 2, *s.* thee out of Zion.
104. 15, bread which *s.* man's heart.
Eccl. 7. 19, wisdom *s.* the wise.
Isa. 35. 3, *s.* ye the weak hands.
Lu. 22. 32, when converted, *s.* thy brethren.
Eph. 3. 16 ; Col. 1. 11, to be *s.* with might.
Phil. 4. 13, all things through Christ who *s.* me.
See Lu. 22. 43 ; 1 Pet. 5. 10 ; Rev. 3. 2.
STRETCH. Ps. 68. 31, *s.* out her hands to God.
Isa. 28. 20, shorter than a man can *s.* himself.
Jer. 10. 12 ; 51. 15, he *s.* out the heavens.
Ezek. 16. 27, I have *s.* out my hand over thee.
Mat. 12. 13, *s.* forth thine hand.
See Ps. 104. 2 ; Prov. 1. 24 ; Rom. 10. 21 ; 2 Cor. 10. 14.
STRIKE. Job 17. 3 ; Prov. 22. 26, *s.* hands.
Ps. 110. 5, shall *s.* through kings.
Prov. 7. 23, till a dart *s.* through his liver.
See Prov. 23. 35 ; Isa. 1. 5 ; 1 Tim. 3. 3 ; Tit. 1. 7.
STRIPES. Deut. 25. 3, forty *s.* he may give.
2 Cor. 11. 24, five times received I forty *s.*
STRIVE. Gen. 6. 3, shall not always *s.*
Prov. 3. 30, *s.* not without cause.
Lu. 13. 24, *s.* to enter in at strait gate.
2 Tim. 2. 5, if a man *s.* for mastery.
24, the servant of the Lord must not *s.*
See Isa. 45. 9 ; Jer. 50. 24 ; Mat. 12. 19 ; Heb. 12. 4.
STRONG. 1 Sam. 4. 9 ; 1 Kings 2. 2 ; 2 Chron. 15. 7 ;
Isa. 35. 4 ; Dan. 10. 19, be *s.*
Job 9. 19, if I speak of strength, lo, he is *s.*
Ps. 19. 5, as a *s.* man to run a race.
24. 8, the Lord is *s.*
31. 2, be thou my *s.* rock.
71. 7, thou art my *s.* refuge.
Prov. 10. 15, the rich man's wealth is his *s.* city.
18. 10, the name of the Lord is a *s.* tower.
Eccl. 9. 11, the battle is not to the *s.*
Isa. 40. 26, for that he is *s.* in power.
Mat. 12. 29, first bind the *s.* man.
Rom. 4. 20, *s.* in faith.
1 Cor. 4. 10, we are weak, ye are *s.*
2 Thess. 2. 11, *s.* delusion.
Heb. 5. 12, of milk, and not of *s.* meat.
6. 18, we have a *s.* consolation.
See Prov. 14. 26 ; Joel 3. 10 ; Rom. 15. 1 ; Rev. 5. 2.
STUBBLE. Ps. 83. 13, make them as *s.*
Isa. 33. 11, conceive chaff, bring forth *s.*
41. 2, as driven *s.*
Jer. 13. 24, I will scatter them as *s.*
See Joel 2. 5 ; Nah. 1. 10 ; Mal. 4. 1 ; 1 Cor. 3. 12.
STUDY. Eccl. 12. 12, much *s.* is a weariness of
the flesh.
See 1 Thess. 4. 11 ; 2 Tim. 2. 15.
STUMBLE. Prov. 4. 19, know not at what they *s.*
Isa. 28. 7, they *s.* in judgment.
59. 10, we *s.* at noonday.
Jer. 46. 6 ; Dan. 11. 19, *s.* and fall.
Mal. 2. 8, have caused many to *s.*

1 Pet. 2. 8, that *s.* at the word.
See John 11. 9 ; Rom. 9. 32 ; 11. 11 ; 14. 21.
SUBDUE. Ps. 47. 3, he shall *s.* the people.
Mic. 7. 19, he will *s.* our iniquities.
Phil. 3. 21, able to *s.* all things.
Heb. 11. 33, through faith *s.* kingdoms.
See Dan. 2. 40 ; Zech. 9. 15 ; 1 Cor. 15. 28.
SUBJECT. Lu. 10. 17, devils are *s.* unto us.
Rom. 8. 7, not *s.* to law of God.
20, creature *s.* to vanity.
13. 1, *s.* to the higher powers.
1 Cor. 14. 32, spirits of prophets *s.* to prophets.
15. 28, then shall the Son also be *s.* to him.
Eph. 5. 24, as the church is *s.* to Christ.
Heb. 2. 15, all their lifetime *s.* to bondage.
Jas. 5. 17, a man *s.* to like passions.
1 Pet. 2. 18, servants, be *s.* to your masters.
3. 22, angels and powers *s.* to him.
5. 5, all of you be *s.* one to another.
See Lu. 2. 51 ; Col. 2. 20 ; Tit. 3. 1.
SUBMIT. 2 Sam. 22. 45, *s.* themselves.
Ps. 68. 30, till every one *s.* himself.
Eph. 5. 22, wives *s.* yourselves.
Jas. 4. 7, *s.* yourselves to God.
1 Pet. 2. 13, *s.* yourselves to every ordinance of
man.
See Rom. 10. 3 ; Eph. 5. 21 ; Heb. 13. 17.
SUBSCRIBE. Isa. 44. 5 ; Jer. 32. 44.
SUBSTANCE. Gen. 13. 6, their *s.* was great.
Deut. 33. 11, bless *s.*
Job 30. 22, thou dissolvest my *s.*
Ps. 17. 14, they leave their *s.* to babes.
139. 15, my *s.* was not hid from thee.
Prov. 3. 9, honour the Lord with thy *s.*
28. 8, he that by usury increaseth his *s.*
Cant. 8. 7, give all his *s.* for love.
Jer. 15. 13 ; 17. 3, thy *s.* will I give to spoil.
Hos. 12. 8, I have found me out *s.*
Mic. 4. 13, I will consecrate their *s.*
Lu. 8. 3, ministered to him of their *s.*
15. 13, wasted his *s.*
Heb. 10. 34, a better *s.*
11. 1, the *s.* of things hoped for.
See Prov. 1. 13 ; 6. 31 ; 8. 21 ; 12. 27 ; 29. 3.
SUBTIL. Gen. 3. 1 ; 2 Sam. 13. 3 ; Prov. 7. 10.
SUBTILTY. Gen. 27. 35 ; Mat. 26. 4 ; Acts 13. 10.
SUBVERT. Lam. 3. 36 ; 2 Tim. 2. 14 ; Tit. 1. 11 ; 3. 11.
SUCCESS. Josh. 1. 8, have good *s.*
SUCK. Deut. 32. 13, *s.* honey out of rock.
33. 19, *s.* abundance of the seas.
Job 20. 16, *s.* poison of asps.
Isa. 60. 16, *s.* the milk of the Gentiles.
See Mat. 24. 19 ; Mk. 13. 17 ; Lu. 21. 23 ; 23. 29.
SUDDEN. Job 22. 10 ; Prov. 3. 25 ; 1 Thess. 5. 3.
SUDDENLY. Prov. 29. 1, be *s.* destroyed.
Eccl. 9. 12, when it falleth *s.*
Mal. 3. 1, shall *s.* come to his temple.
Mk. 13. 36, lest coming *s.* he find you sleeping.
1 Tim. 5. 22, lay hands *s.* on no man.
SUFFER. Job 21. 3, *s.* me that I may speak.
Ps. 55. 22, never *s.* righteous to be moved.
89. 33, nor *s.* my faithfulness to fail.
Prov. 19. 15, the idle soul shall *s.* hunger.
Eccl. 5. 12, not *s.* him to sleep.
Mat. 3. 15, *s.* it to be so now.
8. 21 ; Lu. 9. 59, *s.* me first to bury my father.
16. 21 ; 17. 12 ; Mk. 8. 31 ; Lu. 9. 22, *s.* many things.
19. 14 ; Mk. 10. 14 ; Lu. 18. 16, *s.* little children.
23. 13, neither *s.* ye them that are entering to
go in.
Lu. 24. 46 ; Acts 3. 18, behoved Christ to *s.*
Rom. 8. 17, if we *s.* with him.
1 Cor. 3. 15, he shall *s.* loss.
10. 13, will not *s.* you to be tempted.
12. 26, whether one member *s.*, all *s.* with it.
Gal. 6. 12, lest they should *s.* persecution.
2 Tim. 2. 12, if we *s.*, we shall also reign.
3. 12, shall *s.* persecution.
Heb. 13. 3, remember them who *s.*
1 Pet. 2. 21, *s.* for us, leaving an example.

1 Pet. 4. 1, he that hath *s.* in the flesh.
See Gal. 3. 4 ; Phil. 3. 8 ; Heb. 2. 18 ; 5. 8.
SUFFICIENCY. Job 20. 22 ; 2 Cor. 3. 5 ; 9. 8.
SUFFICIENT. Isa. 40. 16, not *s.* to burn.
Mat. 6. 34, *s.* for the day is the evil.
2 Cor. 2. 16, who is *s.* for these things ?
See Deut. 15. 8 ; John 6. 7 ; 2 Cor. 3. 5 ; 12. 9.
SUM. Ps. 139. 17 ; Acts 22. 28 ; Heb. 8. 1.
SUMMER. Gen. 8. 22 ; Ps. 74. 17, *s.* and winter.
Prov. 6. 8 ; 30. 25, provideth meat in *s.*
10. 5, he that gathereth in *s.* is a wise son.
26. 1, as snow in *s.*
Jer. 8. 20, the *s.* is ended.
Mat. 24. 32 ; Mk. 13. 28, ye know *s.* is nigh.
See Dan. 2. 35 ; Zech. 14. 8 ; Lu. 21. 30.
SUMPTUOUSLY. Lu. 16. 19, fared *s.* every day.
SUN. Josh. 10. 12, *s.*, stand thou still.
Judg. 5. 31, as the *s.* in his might.
Job 8. 16, hypocrite is green before the *s.*
Ps. 58. 8, that they may not see the *s.*
84. 11, a *s.* and shield.
121. 6, the *s.* shall not smite thee.
Eccl. 1. 9, no new thing under the *s.*
11. 7, a pleasant thing it is to behold the *s.*
12. 2, while the *s.* or stars be not darkened.
Cant. 1. 6, because the *s.* hath looked upon me.
6. 10, clear as the *s.*
Jer. 15. 9, her *s.* is gone down while yet day.
Joel 2. 10 ; 3. 15, the *s.* be darkened.
Mal. 4. 2, the *S.* of righteousness.
Mat. 5. 45, maketh his *s.* to rise on evil.
13. 43, then shall righteous shine as *s.*
Eph. 4. 26, let not *s.* go down on your wrath.
See 1 Cor. 15. 41 ; Jas. 1. 11 ; Rev. 7. 16 ; 21. 23.
SUPERFLUITY. Jas. 1. 21, *s.* of naughtiness.
SUPPLICATION. 1 Kings 9. 3, I have heard thy *s.*
Job 9. 15, I would make *s.* to my judge.
Ps. 6. 9, the Lord hath heard my *s.*
Dan. 9. 3, to seek by prayer and *s.*
Zech. 12. 10, spirit of grace and *s.*
Eph. 6. 18, with all prayer and *s.*
1 Tim. 2. 1, that *s.* be made for all men.
See Ps. 28. 6 ; 31. 22 ; Phil. 4. 6 ; Heb. 5. 7.
SUPPLY. Phil. 1. 19 ; 2. 30 ; 4. 19.
SUPPORT. Acts 20. 35 ; 1 Thess. 5. 14.
SUPREME. 1 Pet. 2. 13, to the king as *s.*
SURE. Num. 32. 23, be *s.* your sin will find you out.
Job 24. 22, no man is *s.* of life.
Prov. 6. 3, make *s.* thy friend.
Isa. 55. 3 ; Acts 13. 34, the *s.* mercies of David.
2 Tim. 2. 19, the foundation of God standeth *s.*
See Isa. 33. 16 ; Heb. 6. 19 ; 2 Pet. 1. 10, 19.
SURFEITING. Lu. 21. 34, overcharged with *s.*
SURPRISED. Isa. 33. 14 ; Jer. 48. 41 ; 51. 41.
SUSTAIN. Ps. 3. 5 ; 55. 22 ; Prov. 18. 14 ; Isa. 59. 16.
SWALLOW. Ps. 84. 3, the *s.* a nest for her young.
Prov. 26. 2, as the *s.* by flying.
Isa. 38. 14, like a crane or a *s.*
Jer. 8. 7, the *s.* observe the time.
SWAN. Lev. 11. 8 ; Deut. 14. 16, and the *s.*
SWEAR. Ps. 15. 4, that *s.* to his hurt.
Eccl. 9. 2, he that *s.*, as he that feareth an oath.
Isa. 45. 23, to me every tongue shall *s.*
65. 16, shall *s.* by the God of truth.
Jer. 4. 2, *s.*, the Lord liveth, in truth.
23. 10, because of *s.* the land mourneth.
Hos. 4. 2, by *s.*, and lying, they break out.
10. 4, *s.* falsely in making a covenant.
Zech. 5. 3, every one that *s.* shall be cut off.
Mal. 3. 5, a witness against false *s.*
See Zeph. 1. 5 ; Mat. 26. 74 ; Heb. 6. 13.
SWEAT. Gen. 3. 19 ; Ezek. 44. 18 ; Lu. 22. 44.
SWEET. Job 20. 12, though wickedness be *s.*
Ps. 55. 14, we took *s.* counsel together.
104. 34, my meditation shall be *s.*
Prov. 3. 24, thy sleep shall be *s.*
9. 17, stolen waters are *s.*
13. 19, desire accomplished is *s.*

Prov. 16. 24, pleasant words are *s.*
27. 7, to the hungry every bitter thing is *s.*
Eccl. 5. 12, sleep of labouring man is *s.*
11. 7, truly the light is *s.*
Cant. 2. 3, his fruit was *s.* to my taste.
Isa. 5. 20, put bitter for *s.*, and *s.* for bitter.
23. 16, make *s.* melody.
Jas. 3. 11, at same place *s.* water and bitter.
See Judg. 14. 18; Mic. 6. 15; Mk. 16. 1.

SWELLING. Jer. 12. 5; 2 Pet. 2. 18; Jude 16.

SWIFT. Eccl. 9. 11, the race is not to the *s.*
Amos 2. 15, the *s.* of foot shall not deliver.
Rom. 3. 15, feet *s.* to shed blood.
See Job 7. 6; 9. 25; Jer. 46. 6; Mal. 3. 5.

SWIM. 2 Kings 6. 6, iron did *s.*
Ezek. 47. 5, waters to *s.* in.
See Ps. 6. 6; Isa. 25. 11; Ezek. 32. 6; Acts 27. 42.

SWOLLEN. Acts 28. 6, when he should have *s.*

SWOON. Lam. 2. 11, children *s.* in the streets.

SWORD. Ps. 57. 4, their tongue a sharp *s.*
Isa. 2. 4, nation shall not lift up *s.*
Ezek. 7. 15, the *s.* is without, pestilence within.
Mat. 10. 34, not to send peace, but a *s.*
Lu. 2. 35, a *s.* shall pierce thy own soul.
Rom. 13. 4, he beareth not the *s.* in vain.
Eph. 6. 17, the *s.* of the Spirit.
Heb. 4. 12, sharper than twoedged *s.*
Rev. 1. 16; 19. 15, out of his mouth a sharp *s.*
13. 10, that killeth with *s.* must be killed with *s.*
See Isa. 2. 4; Joel 3. 10; Mic. 4. 3; Lu. 22. 38.

T.

TABERNACLE. Ps. 15. 1, abide in thy *t.*
27. 5, in secret of his *t.* shall he hide me.
84. 1, how amiable are thy *t.*!
Isa. 33. 20, a *t.* that shall not be taken down.
See Job 5. 24; Prov. 14. 11; 2 Cor. 5. 1.

TABLE. Ps. 23. 5, thou preparest a *t.*
69. 22, let their *t.* become a snare.
78. 19, can God furnish a *t.* in the wilderness?
128. 3, like olive plants about thy *t.*
Prov. 9. 2, wisdom hath furnished her *t.*
Mat. 15. 27; Mk. 7. 28, from their masters' *t.*
Acts 6. 2, leave word of God, and serve *t.*
2 Cor. 3. 3, fleshy *t.* of the heart.
See Prov. 3. 3; Jer. 17. 1; Mal. 1. 7; 1 Cor. 10. 21.

TABRET. Gen. 31. 27; 1 Sam. 18. 6; Isa. 5. 12, the *t.*

TAKE. Ex. 6. 7, I will *t.* you to me for a people.
34. 9, *t.* us for thine inheritance.
Judg. 19. 30, *t.* advice, and speak your minds.
2 Kings 19. 30; Isa. 37. 31, shall yet *t.* root.
Job 23. 10, he knoweth the way that I *t.*
Ps. 51. 11, *t.* not thy holy spirit from me.
116. 13, I will *t.* the cup of salvation.
Cant. 2. 15, *t.* us the foxes, the little foxes.
Isa. 33. 23, the lame *t.* the prey.
Hos. 14. 2, *t.* with you words.
Amos 9. 2, thence shall mine hand *t.* them.
Mat. 6. 25, 28, 31, 34; 10. 19; Mk. 13. 11; Lu. 12. 11,
22, 26, *t.* no thought.
11. 29, *t.* my yoke.
16. 5; Mk. 8. 14, forgotten to *t.* bread.
18. 16, then *t.* with thee one or two more.
20. 14, *t.* that thine is, and go thy way.
26. 26; Mk. 14. 22; 1 Cor. 11. 24, *t.,* eat; this is my
body.
Lu. 6. 29, forbid him not to *t.* thy coat also.
12. 19, soul, *t.* thine ease.
John 16. 15, he shall *t.* of mine.
1 Cor. 6. 7, why do ye not rather *t.* wrong?
1 Tim. 3. 5, how shall he *t.* care of the church?
1 Pet. 2. 20, if ye *t.* it patiently.
Rev. 3. 11, that no man *t.* thy crown.
See John 1. 29; 10. 18; 1 Cor. 10. 13; Rev. 22. 19.

TALE. Ps. 90. 9; Lu. 24. 11.

TALK. Deut. 5. 24, God doth *t.* with man.
6. 7, *t.* of them when thou sittest.

Job 11. 2, a man full of *t.*
13. 7, will ye *t.* deceitfully for him?
15. 3, reason with unprofitable *t.*
Ps. 71. 24, *t.* of thy righteousness.
145. 11, *t.* of thy power.
Prov. 6. 22, it shall *t.* with thee.
Jer. 12. 1, let me *t.* with thee of thy judgments.
Ezek. 3. 22, arise, and I will *t.* with thee there.
Mat. 22. 15, they might entangle him in his *t.*
Lu. 24. 32, while he *t.* with us by the way.
John 9. 37, it is he that *t.* with thee.
See Prov. 14. 23; John 14. 30; Eph. 5. 4.

TALL. Deut. 1. 28; 2. 10; 2 Kings 19. 23.

TAME. Mk. 5. 4; Jas. 3. 7, 8.

TARE. 2 Sam. 13. 31; 2 Kings 2. 24; Mk. 9. 20.

TARRY. Gen. 27. 44, and *t.* a few days.
Ex. 12. 39, were thrust out, and could not *t.*
2 Kings 7. 9, if we *t.* till morning light.
9. 3, flee, and *t.* not.
Ps. 68. 12, she that *t.* at home divided the spoil.
101. 7, he that telleth lies shall not *t.* in my sight.
Prov. 23. 30, they that *t.* long at the wine.
Isa. 46. 13, my salvation shall not *t.*
Jer. 14. 8, that turneth aside to *t.* for a night.
Hab. 2. 3, though it *t.*, wait for it.
Mat. 25. 5, while the bridegroom *t.*
26. 38; Mk. 14. 34, *t.* here and watch.
Lu. 24. 29, he went in to *t.* with them.
49, *t.* ye in city of Jerusalem until endued.
John 21. 22, if I will that he *t.*
Acts 22. 16, why *t.* thou, arise, and be baptized.
1 Cor. 11. 33, *t.* one for another.
Heb. 10. 37, will come, and will not *t.*
See 1 Sam. 30. 24; Mic. 5. 7; John 3. 22.

TASKMASTERS. Ex. 1. 11, they did set over
them *t.*
5. 6, the *t.* of the people.

TASTE. Num. 11. 8, the *t.* of it as *t.* of fresh oil.
Job 6. 6, is any *t.* in white of egg?
12. 11, doth not the mouth *t.* his meat?
34. 3, trieth words as mouth *t.* meat.
Ps. 34. 8, *t.* and see that the Lord is good.
119. 103, how sweet are thy words to my *t.*!
Jer. 48. 11, his *t.* remained in him.
Mat. 16. 28; Mk. 9. 1; Lu. 9. 27, some, which shall
not *t.* death.
Lu. 14. 24, none bidden shall *t.* of my supper.
John 8. 52, keep my saying, shall never *t.* of death.
Col. 2. 21, touch not, *t.* not.
Heb. 2. 9, *t.* death for every man.
6. 4, and have *t.* of the heavenly gift.
1 Pet. 2. 3, have *t.* that the Lord is gracious.
See 1 Sam. 14. 43; 2 Sam. 19. 35; Mat. 27. 34.

TATTLERS. 1 Tim. 5. 13, *t.* and busybodies.

TAUGHT. Judg. 8. 16, he *t.* the men of Succoth.
2 Chron. 6. 27, thou hast *t.* them the good way.
23. 13, such as *t.* to sing praise.
Ps. 71. 17; 119. 102, thou hast *t.* me.
Prov. 4. 4, he *t.* me also, and said.
11, I have *t.* thee in way of wisdom.
Eccl. 12. 9, he still *t.* the people knowledge.
Isa. 29. 13, their fear is *t.* by precept of men.
54. 13, all thy children shall be *t.* of God.
Jer. 12. 16, as they *t.* my people to swear by Baal.
32. 33, *t.* them, rising up early.
Zech. 13. 5, *t.* me to keep cattle.
Mat. 7. 29; Mk. 1. 22, *t.* as one having authority.
28. 15, and did as they were *t.*
Lu. 13. 26, thou hast *t.* in our streets.
John 6. 45, they shall be all *t.* of God.
8. 28, as my Father hath *t.* me.
Gal. 1. 12, nor was I *t.* it, except by revelation.
6. 6, let him that is *t.* in the word.
Eph. 4. 21, if so be ye have been *t.* by him.
2 Thess. 2. 15, the traditions ye have been *t.*
See Col. 2. 7; 1 Thess. 4. 9; Tit. 1. 9; 1 John 2. 27.

TAUNT. Jer. 24. 9; Ezek. 5. 15; Hab. 2. 6.

TEACH. Ex. 4. 15, I will *t.* you.

Deut. 4. 10, that they may *t.* their children.
6. 7 ; 11. 19, *t.* them diligently.
Judg. 13. 8, *t.* us what we shall do to the child.
1 Sam. 12. 23, I will *t.* you the good way.
2 Sam. 1. 18, bade them *t.* the use of the bow.
2 Chron. 15. 3, without a *t.* priest.
Job 6. 24, *t.* me, and I will hold my tongue.
8. 10, thy fathers, shall not they *t.* thee ?
12. 7, ask the beasts, and they shall *t.* thee.
34. 32, that which I see not *t.* thou me.
36. 22, God exalteth, who *t.* like him ?
Ps. 25. 4, *t.* me thy paths.
8, he will *t.* sinners in the way.
27. 11 ; 86. 11, *t.* me thy way, and lead me.
34. 11, I will *t.* you the fear of the Lord.
51. 13, then will I *t.* transgressors.
90. 12, so *t.* us to number our days.
94. 12, blessed is the man whom thou *t.*
Prov. 6. 13, the wicked man *t.* with his fingers.
Isa. 2. 3 ; Mic. 4. 2, he will *t.* us of his ways.
28. 9, whom shall he *t.* knowledge ?
26, God doth *t.* him discretion.
48. 17, I am thy God which *t.* thee to profit.
Jer. 9. 20, and *t.* your daughters wailing.
Ezek. 44. 23, *t.* my people the difference.
Mic. 3. 11, priests *t.* for hire.
Mat. 28. 19, *t.* all nations.
Lu. 11. 1, *t.* us to pray.
12. 12, the Holy Ghost shall *t.* you.
John 9. 34, dost thou *t.* us?
14. 26, shall *t.* you all things.
Acts 5. 42, they ceased not to *t.* and preach.
Rom. 12. 7, he that *t.*, on *t.*
1 Cor. 4. 17, as I *t.* every where.
11. 14, doth not even nature *t.* you ?
14. 19, that by my voice I might *t.* others.
Col. 1. 28, *t.* every man in all wisdom.
3. 16, *t.* and admonishing one another.
1 Tim. 1. 3, charge some that they *t.* no other.
2. 12, I suffer not a woman to *t.*
3. 2 ; 2 Tim. 2. 24, apt to *t.*
4. 11, these things command and *t.*
6. 2, these things *t.* and exhort.
2 Tim. 2. 2, faithful men, able to *t.*
Tit. 1. 11, *t.* things they ought not.
2. 4, *t.* young women to be sober.
12, *t.* us, that denying ungodliness.
Heb. 5. 12, ye have need that one *t.* you again.
See Mat. 22. 16 ; Mk. 6. 34 ; 12. 14 ; Rev. 2. 20.

TEACHER. 1 Chron. 25. 8, as well *t.* as scholar.
Ps. 119. 99, more understanding than all my *t.*
Prov. 5. 13, have not obeyed the voice of my *t.*
Isa. 30. 20, thine eyes shall see thy *t.*
Hab. 2. 18, a *t.* of lies.
John 3. 2, a *t.* come from God.
Rom. 2. 20, thou art a *t.* of babes.
1 Cor. 12. 29, are all *t.* ?
Eph. 4. 11, evangelists, pastors, and *t.*
1 Tim. 1. 7, desiring to be *t.* of the law.
Tit. 2. 3, aged women, *t.* of good things.
See 1 Tim. 2. 7 ; 2 Tim. 1. 11 ; Heb. 5. 12 ; 2 Pet. 2. 1.

TEAR. Job 16. 9, he *t.* me in his wrath.
18. 4, he *t.* himself in his anger.
Ps. 7. 2, lest he *t.* my soul.
35. 15, they did *t.* me, and ceased not.
50. 22, lest I *t.* you in pieces.
Hos. 5. 14, I will *t.* and go away.
See Mic. 5. 8 ; Zech. 11. 16 ; Mk. 9. 18 ; Lu. 9. 39.

TEARS. 2 Kings 20. 5 ; Isa. 38. 5, I have seen thy *t.*
Job 16. 20, mine eye poureth out *t.*
Ps. 6. 6, I water my couch with *t.*
39. 12, hold not thy peace at my *t.*
42. 3, *t.* have been my meat.
56. 8, put thou my *t.* into thy bottle.
80. 5, the bread of *t.*, and *t.* to drink.
116. 8, thou hast delivered mine eyes from *t.*
126. 5, they that sow in *t.*
Isa. 16. 9, I will water thee with my *t.*
25. 8, will wipe away *t.*
Jer. 9. 1, oh that mine eyes were a fountain of *t.*!

Jer. 13. 17 ; 14. 17, mine eyes run down with *t.*
31. 16, refrain thine eyes from *t.*
Lam. 1. 2, her *t.* are on her cheeks.
2. 11, mine eyes do fail with *t.*
Ezek. 24. 16, neither shall thy *t.* run down.
Mal. 2. 13, covering the altar with *t.*
Lu. 7. 38, to wash his feet with her *t.*
Acts 20. 19, serving the Lord with many *t.*
31, ceased not to warn with *t.*
2 Tim. 1. 4, being mindful of thy *t.*
See 2 Cor. 2. 4 ; Heb. 5. 7 ; 12. 17 ; Rev. 7. 17.

TEDIOUS. Acts 24. 4, that I be not further *t.*

TEETH. Gen. 49. 12, *t.* white with milk.
Num. 11. 33, flesh yet between their *t.*
Job 19. 20, escaped with the skin of my *t.*
Prov. 10. 26, as vinegar to the *t.*
Isa. 41. 15, an instrument having *t.*
Jer. 31. 29 ; Ezek. 18. 2, *t.* set on edge.
Amos 4. 6, cleanness of *t.*
See Mic. 3. 5 ; Zech. 9. 7 ; Mat. 27. 44 ; Rev. 9. 8.

TELL. Gen. 15. 5, *t.* the stars.
32. 29, *t.* me thy name.
2 Sam. 1. 20, *t.* it not in Gath.
Ps. 48. 12, *t.* the towers thereof.
50. 12, if I were hungry, I would not *t.* thee.
Eccl. 6. 12 ; 10. 14, who can *t.* what shall be after?
10. 20, that which hath wings shall *t.*
Jonah 3. 9, who can *t.* if God will turn?
Mat. 18. 15, *t.* him his fault.
17, *t.* it unto the church.
21. 27 ; Mk. 11. 33 ; Lu. 20. 8, neither *t.* I you.
Mk. 5. 19, *t.* how great things.
11. 33 ; Lu. 20. 7, we cannot *t.*
Lu. 13. 32, *t.* that fox.
John 3. 8, canst not *t.* whence.
12, if I *t.* you of heavenly things.
4. 25, he will *t.* us all things.
18. 34, did others *t.* it thee of me?
Acts 17. 21, either to *t.* or hear some new thing.
See Ps. 56. 8 ; Isa. 19. 12 ; Mat. 28. 7 ; 2 Cor. 12. 2.

TEMPER. Ex. 29. 2 ; 30. 35 ; Ezek. 46. 14 ; 1 Cor. 12. 24.

TEMPEST. Job 9. 17, breaketh me with a *t.*
Ps. 11. 6, on wicked he shall rain a *t.*
55. 8, hasten from windy storm and *t.*
Isa. 32. 2, a covert from the *t.*
Heb. 12. 18, not come to darkness and *t.*
2 Pet. 2. 17, clouds carried with a *t.*

TEMPESTUOUS. Ps. 50. 3 ; Jonah 1. 11 ; Acts 27. 14.

TEMPLE. 2 Sam. 22. 7, hear my voice out of his *t.*
Neh. 6. 10, hid ourselves in the *t.*
Ps. 27. 4, to enquire in his *t.*
29. 9, in his *t.* doth every one speak of his glory.
Isa. 6. 1, his train filled the *t.*
Amos 8. 3, songs of the *t.* shall be howlings.
Mal. 3. 1, the Lord shall suddenly come to his *t.*
Mat. 12. 6, one greater than the *t.*
John 2. 19, destroy this *t.*
1 Cor. 3. 16 ; 6. 19 ; 2 Cor. 6. 16, ye are the *t.* of God.
See Hos. 8. 14 ; Rev. 7. 15 ; 11. 19 ; 21. 22.

TEMPORAL. 2 Cor. 4. 18, things seen are *t.*

TEMPT. Gen. 22. 1, God did *t.* Abraham.
Ex. 17. 2, wherefore do ye *t.* the Lord?
Num. 14. 22, have *t.* me these ten times.
Deut. 6. 16 ; Mat. 4. 7 ; Lu. 4. 12, ye shall not *t.* the Lord your God.
Ps. 78. 18, they *t.* God in their heart.
Isa. 7. 12, I will not ask, neither *t.* the Lord.
Mal. 3. 15, they that *t.* God are delivered.
Mat. 22. 18 ; Mk. 12. 15 ; Lu. 20. 23, why *t.* ye me?
Lu. 10. 25, a lawyer, *t.* him.
Acts 5. 9, agreed together to *t.* the Spirit.
15. 10, why *t.* ye God to put a yoke?
1 Cor. 10. 13, will not suffer you to be *t.*
Gal. 6. 1, considering thyself, lest thou be *t.*
Heb. 2. 18, hath suffered, being *t.*
4. 15, in all points *t.* like as we are.
Jas. 1. 13, cannot be *t.*, neither *t.* he any man.
See Mat. 4. 1 ; Mk. 1. 13 ; Lu. 4. 2 ; John 8. 6.

TEMPTATION. Mat. 6. 13, lead us not into *t.*
26. 41; Mk. 14. 38; Lu. 22. 46, lest ye enter into *t.*
Lu. 8. 13, in time of *t.* fall away.
1 Cor. 10. 13, there hath no *t.* taken you.
Gal. 4. 14, my *t.* in flesh ye despised not.
1 Tim. 6. 9, they that will be rich fall into *t.*
Jas. 1. 2, when ye fall into divers *t.*
2 Pet. 2. 9, how to deliver out of *t.*
See Lu. 11. 4; Acts 20. 19; 1 Pet. 1. 6; Rev. 3. 10.
TEMPTER. Mat. 4. 3, and when the *t.* came to
him.
1 Thess. 3. 5, the *t.* have 'empted you.
TEND. Prov. 11. 19; 14. 23; 19. 23; 21. 5.
TENDER. Deut. 28. 54, man that is *t.*
32. 2, distil as small rain on *t.* herb.
2 Kings 22. 19; 2 Chron. 34. 27, thy heart was *t.*
Job 14. 7, the *t.* branch will not cease.
Prov. 4. 3, *t.* in sight of my mother.
Cant. 2. 13, 15; 7. 12, vines with *t.* grapes.
Isa. 47. 1, no more be called *t.*
53. 2, grow up before him as a *t.* plant.
Dan. 1. 9, God brought Daniel into *t.* love.
Lu. 1. 78, through the *t.* mercy of our God.
Eph. 4. 32, be kind and *t.*-hearted.
Jas. 5. 11, the Lord is pitiful, and of *t.* mercy.
See 1 Chron. 22. 5; Ezek. 17. 22; Mk. 13. 28.
TENOR. Gen. 43. 7; Ex. 34. 27.
TENT. Gen. 9. 21, was uncovered within his *t.*
27, he shall dwell in the *t.* of Shem.
12. 8, and pitched his *t.*
25. 27, a plain man, dwelling in *t.*
Num. 24. 5, how goodly are thy *t.*!
1 Sam. 4. 10; 2 Sam. 18. 17, fled every man to his *t.*
1 Kings 12. 16, to your *t.*, O Israel.
Ps. 84. 10, than to dwell in *t.* of wickedness.
Isa. 38. 12, removed as a shepherd's *t.*
54. 2, enlarge the place of thy *t.*
Jer. 10. 20, there is none to stretch forth my *t.*
Acts 18. 3, by occupation they were *t.*-makers.
See Isa. 40. 22; Jer. 4. 20; 35. 7; Zech. 12. 7; Heb.
11. 9.
TENTH. Gen. 28. 22; Lev. 27. 32; Isa. 6. 13.
TERRIBLE. Ex. 34. 10, a *t.* thing I will do.
Deut. 1. 19; 8. 15, that *t.* wilderness.
7. 21; 10. 17; Neh. 1. 5; 4. 14; 9. 32, a mighty
God and *t.*
10. 21, hath done for thee *t.* things.
Judg. 13. 6, like an angel of God, very *t.*
Job 37. 22, with God is *t.* majesty.
39. 20, the glory of his nostrils is *t.*
Ps. 45. 4, thy right hand shall teach thee *t.* things.
65. 5, by *t.* things in righteousness.
66. 3, say unto God, how *t.* art thou !
5, *t.* in his doing.
68. 35, *t.* out of thy holy places.
76. 12, he is *t.* to the kings of the earth.
99. 3, thy great and *t.* name.
145. 6, the might of thy *t.* acts.
Cant. 6. 4, *t.* as an army with banners.
Isa. 25. 4, blast of the *t.* ones.
64. 3, when thou didst *t.* things.
Jer. 15. 21, redeem thee out of hand of the *t.*
Joel 2. 11, the day of the Lord is very *t.*
Heb. 12. 21, so *t.* was the sight.
See Lam. 5. 10; Ezek. 1. 22; 28. 7; Dan. 7. 7.
TERRIBLENESS. Deut. 26. 8; 1 Chron. 17. 21; Jer.
49. 16.
TERRIBLY. Isa. 2. 19, 21; Nah. 2. 3.
TERRIFY. Job 9. 34, let not his fear *t.*
Lu. 21. 9, when ye hear of wars, be not *t.*
24. 37, they were *t.* and affrighted.
Phil. 1. 28, in nothing *t.* by adversaries.
See Job 7. 14; 2 Cor. 10. 9.
TERROR. Gen. 35. 5; Job 6. 4, the *t.* of God.
Deut. 32. 25, the sword without and *t.* within.
Josh. 2. 9, your *t.* is fallen upon us.
Job 18. 11, *t.* shall make him afraid.
24. 17, in the *t.* of the shadow of death.
31. 23, destruction was a *t.* to me.
33. 7, my *t.* shall not make thee afraid.

Ps. 55. 4, the *t.* of death are fallen upon me.
73. 19, utterly consumed with *t.*
91. 5, afraid for the *t.* by night.
Jer. 17. 17, be not a *t.* to me.
20. 4, a *t.* to thyself.
Ezek. 26. 21; 27. 36; 28. 19, I will make thee a *t.*
Rom. 13. 3, rulers are not *t.* to good works.
2 Cor. 5. 11, knowing the *t.* of the Lord.
See Jer. 15. 8; Lam. 2. 22; Ezek. 21. 12; 1 Pet. 3.
14.
TESTIFY. Num. 35. 30, one witness shall not *t.*
Deut. 31. 21, this song shall *t.* against them.
Ruth 1. 21, seeing the Lord hath *t.* against me.
2 Sam. 1. 16, thy mouth hath *t.* against thee.
Neh. 9. 30, *t.* against them by thy spirit.
Job 15. 6, thine own lips *t.* against thee.
Isa. 59. 12, our sins *t.* against us.
Hos. 5. 5; 7. 10, the pride of Israel doth *t.*
Mic. 6. 3, what have I done? *t.* against me.
Lu. 16. 28, send Lazarus, that he may *t.*
John 2. 25, needed not that any should *t.*
3, 32, seen and heard, that he *t.*
5. 39, they *t.* of me.
7. 7, because I *t.* of it.
15. 26, he shall *t.* of me.
21. 24, the disciple which *t.* of these things.
Acts 23. 11, as thou hast *t.* in Jerusalem.
1 Tim. 2. 6, gave himself to be *t.* in due time.
1 Pet. 1. 11, it *t.* beforehand the sufferings.
1 John 4. 14, we have seen and do *t.*
See 1 Cor. 15. 15; 1 Thess. 4. 6; Rev. 22. 16.
TESTIMONY. 2 Kings 17. 15, rejected his *t.*
Ps. 93. 5, thy *t.* are sure.
119. 22, I have kept thy *t.*
24, thy *t.* are my delight.
46, I will speak of thy *t.*
59, I turned my feet to thy *t.*
119, I love thy *t.*
129, thy *t.* are wonderful.
Isa. 8. 16, bind up the *t.*
20, to the law and to the *t.*
Mat. 10. 18; Mk. 13. 9, for a *t.* against them.
Lu. 21. 13, it shall turn to you for a *t.*
John 3. 32, no man receiveth his *t.*
21. 24, we know that his *t.* is true.
Acts 14. 3, *t.* to the word of his grace.
1 Cor. 2. 1, declaring the *t.* of God.
2 Cor. 1. 12, the *t.* of our conscience.
2 Tim. 1. 8, be not ashamed of the *t.*
Heb. 11. 5, Enoch had this *t.*
See Rev. 1. 2; 6. 9; 11. 7; 12. 11; 19. 10.
THANK. Mat. 11. 25; Lu. 10. 21; 18. 11; John 11. 41,
I *t.* thee.
Acts 28. 15, *t.* God, and took courage.
1 Cor. 1. 4, I *t.* God on your behalf.
2 Thess. 1. 3, we are bound to *t.* God.
1 Tim. 1. 12, I *t.* Jesus Christ.
See 1 Chron. 23. 30; Dan. 2. 23; Rom. 6. 17.
THANKS. Neh. 12. 31, companies that gave *t.*
Mat. 26. 27; Lu. 22. 17, took the cup, and gave *t.*
Lu. 2. 38, Anna gave *t.* to the Lord.
Rom. 14. 6, eateth to the Lord, for he giveth *t.*
1 Cor. 15. 57, *t.* be to God, who giveth us the victory.
Eph. 5. 20, giving *t.* always for all things.
1 Thess. 3. 9, what *t.* can we render ?
Rev. 4. 9, give *t.* to him that sat on the throne.
See 2 Cor. 1. 11; 2. 14; 8. 16; 9. 15; Heb. 13. 15.
THANKSGIVING. Ps. 26. 7, the voice of *t.*
95. 2, come before his face with *t.*
Isa. 51. 3, *t.* and melody shall be found therein.
Amos 4. 5, offer a sacrifice of *t.*
Phil. 4. 6, with *t.* let your requests be made.
Col. 4. 2, watch in the same with *t.*
1 Tim. 4. 3, to be received with *t.*
See Neh. 11. 17; 12. 8; 2 Cor. 4. 15; 9. 11.
THAT. Gen. 18. 25, *t.* be far from thee.
Num. 24. 13; 1 Kings 22. 14, *t.* will I speak.
Job 23. 13, even *t.* he doeth.
Ps. 27. 4, *t.* will I seek after.
Zech. 11. 9, *t. t.* dieth, let it die.

THEN. Mat. 10. 15; Mk. 6. 11, than for *t.* city.
13. 12; 25. 29; Mk. 4. 25, *t.* he hath.
John 1. 8, he was not *t.* light.
5. 12, what man is *t.* which said?
13. 27, *t.* thou doest, do quickly.
21. 22, what is *t.* to thee?
Rom. 7. 19, the evil which I would not, *t.* I do.
Jas. 4. 15, we shall live, and do this or *t.*
See Mk. 13. 11; 1 Cor. 11. 23; 2 Cor. 8. 12; Philem. 18.

THEN. Ex. 4. 26, *t.* began men to call.
Josh. 14. 12, if the Lord be with me, *t.* I shall
be able.
Ps. 27. 10, *t.* the Lord will take me up.
55. 12, *t.* I could have borne it.
Isa. 58. 8, *t.* shall thy light break forth.
Ezek. 39. 28, *t.* shall they know.
Mat. 5. 24, *t.* come and offer thy gift.
19. 25; Mk. 10. 26, who *t.* can be saved?
24. 14, *t.* shall the end come.
2 Cor. 12. 10, *t.* am I strong.
See 1 Cor. 4. 5; 13. 12; 1 Thess. 5. 3; 2 Thess. 2. 8.

THESE. Ex. 32. 4, *t.* be thy gods, O Israel.
Eccl. 7. 10, former days better than *t.*
Isa. 60. 8, who are *t.* that fly?
Mat. 5. 37, whatsoever is more than *t.*
23. 23, *t.* ought ye to have done.
25. 40, one of the least of *t.*
John 17. 20, neither pray I for *t.* alone.
21. 15, lovest thou me more than *t.*?
See Job 26. 14; Ps. 73. 12; Jer. 7. 4.

THICK. Deut. 32. 15, thou art grown *t.*
2 Sam. 18. 9, the mule went under the *t.* boughs.
Ps. 74. 5, lifted up axes on the *t.* trees.
Ezek. 31. 3, top was among *t.* boughs.
Hab. 2. 6, ladeth himself with *t.* clay.
See 1 Kings 12. 10; 2 Chron. 10. 10; Neh. 8. 15;
Job 15. 26.

THICKET. Gen. 22. 13; Isa. 9. 18; Jer. 4. 7, 29.

THIEF. Ps. 50. 18, when thou sawest a *t.*
Jer. 2. 26, as the *t.* is ashamed.
Joel 2. 9, enter at windows like a *t.*
Lu. 12. 33, where no *t.* approacheth.
John 10. 1, the same is a *t.* and a robber.
1 Pet. 4. 15, let none suffer as a *t.*
See Prov. 6. 30; 29. 24; Mat. 24. 43.

THIEVES. Isa. 1. 23; Lu. 10. 30; John 10. 8; 1 Cor.
6. 10.

THIGH. Gen. 24. 2; 47. 29, put hand under *t.*
32. 25, touched hollow of Jacob's *t.*
Judg. 15. 8, smote them hip and *t.*
Cant. 3. 8, every man hath sword on his *t.*
See Ps. 45. 3; Jer. 31. 19; Ezek. 21. 12; Rev. 19. 16.

THINE. Gen. 31. 32, discern what is *t.*
1 Sam. 15. 28, to a neighbour of *t.*
1 Kings 20. 4, I am *t.,* and all I have.
1 Chron. 29. 11, *t.* is the greatness.
Ps. 74. 16, the day is *t.,* the night also is *t.*
119. 94, I am *t.,* save me.
Isa. 63. 19, we are *t.*
Mat. 20. 14, take that is *t.*
Lu. 4. 7, worship me, all shall be *t.*
22. 42, not my will, but *t.* be done.
John 17. 6, *t.* they were, and thou gavest them me.
10, all mine are *t.,* and *t.* are mine.
See Gen. 14. 23; Josh. 17. 18; 1 Chron. 12. 18; Lu.
15. 31.

THING. Gen. 21. 11, the *t.* was very grievous.
Ex. 18. 17, the *t.* thou doest is not good.
2 Sam. 13. 33, let not my lord take the *t.* to heart.
2 Kings 2. 10, thou hast asked a hard *t.*
Eccl. 1. 9, the *t.* that hath been.
Isa. 7. 13, is it a small *t.* to weary?
41. 12, as a *t.* of nought.
43. 19; Jer. 31. 22, a new *t.*
Mk. 1. 27, what *t.* is this?
John 5. 14, lest a worse *t.* come unto thee.
Phil. 3. 16, let us mind the same *t.*
See Heb. 10. 29; 1 Pet. 4. 12; 1 John 2. 8.

THINK. Gen. 40. 14, but *t.* on me when it shall
be well.
Neh. 5. 19, *t.* on me, O my God, for good.
Ps. 40. 17, I am poor, yet the Lord *t.* on me.
Prov. 23. 7, as he *t.* in his heart, so is he.
Isa. 10. 7, nor doth his heart *t.* so.
Jonah 1. 6, if God will *t.* upon us.
Mat. 3. 9, *t.* not to say within yourselves.
6. 7, *t.* they shall be heard.
9. 4, why *t.* ye evil in your hearts?
17. 25; 22. 17, what *t.* thou?
22. 42; 26. 66; Mk. 14. 64, what *t.* ye of Christ?
Rom. 12. 3, more highly than he ought to *t.*
1 Cor. 10. 12, that *t.* he standeth.
2 Cor. 3. 5, to *t.* any thing as of ourselves.
Gal. 6. 3, if a man *t.* himself to be something.
Eph. 3. 20, able to do above all we ask or *t.*
Phil. 4. 8, *t.* on these things.
Jas. 1. 7, let not that man *t.* he shall receive.
1 Pet. 4. 12, *t.* it not strange.
See Job 35. 2; Jer. 29. 11; Ezek. 38. 10; Lu. 10. 36.

THIRST (*n.*). Ex. 17. 3, to kill us with *t.*
Deut. 29. 19, to add drunkenness to *t.*
Judg. 15. 18, now I shall die for *t.*
2 Chron. 32. 11, doth persuade you to die by *t.*
Ps. 69. 21, in my *t.* they gave me vinegar.
Isa. 41. 17, when their tongue faileth for *t.*
Amos 8. 11, not a *t.* for water, but of hearing.
2 Cor. 11. 27, in hunger and *t.* often.
See Deut. 28. 48; Job 24. 11; Ps. 104. 11.

THIRST (*v.*). Ps. 42. 2; 63. 1; 143. 6, my soul *t.* for
God.
Isa. 49. 10; Rev. 7. 16, shall not hunger nor *t.*
55. 1, every one that *t.*
Mat. 5. 6, *t.* after righteousness.
John 4. 14; 6. 35, shall never *t.*
7. 37, if any man *t.,* let him come unto me.
19. 28, I *t.*
See Ex. 17. 3; Isa. 48. 21; Rom. 12. 20; 1 Cor. 4. 11.

THIRSTY. Ps. 63. 1; 143. 6, in a *t.* land.
107. 5, hungry and *t.,* their soul fainted.
Prov. 25. 25, as cold waters to a *t.* soul.
Isa. 21. 14, brought water to him that was *t.*
29. 8, as when a *t.* man dreameth.
44. 3, pour water on him that is *t.*
65. 13, but ye shall be *t.*
See Judg. 4. 19; Isa. 32. 6; Ezek. 19. 13; Mat. 25. 35.

THISTLE. Gen. 3. 18, thorns and *t.* shall it bring
forth.
Job 31. 40, let *t.* grow instead of wheat.
Mat. 7. 16, do men gather figs of *t.?*
See 2 Kings 14. 9; 2 Chron. 25. 18; Hos. 10. 8.

THORN. Num. 33. 55; Judg. 2. 3, *t.* in your sides.
Ps. 118. 12, quenched as the fire of *t.*
Prov. 15. 19, way of slothful man is as an hedge
of *t.*
24. 31, it was all grown over with *t.*
26. 9, as a *t.* goeth into hand of drunkard.
Eccl. 7. 6, crackling of *t.* under a pot.
Cant. 2. 2, as the lily among *t.*
Isa. 33. 12, as *t.* cut up shall they be burned.
34. 13, and *t.* shall come up in her palaces.
55. 13, instead of the *t.* shall come up the fir tree.
Jer. 4. 3, sow not among *t.*
12. 13, but shall reap *t.*
Hos. 2. 6, I will hedge up thy way with *t.*
9. 6, *t.* shall be in their tabernacles.
10. 8, the *t.* shall come up on their altars.
Mic. 7. 4, most upright is sharper than *t.* hedge.
2 Cor. 12. 7, a *t.* in the flesh.
See Mat. 13. 7; 27. 29; Mk. 15. 17; John 19. 2.

THOUGHT (*n.*). 1 Chron. 28. 9, the Lord understandeth the *t.*
Job 4. 13, in *t.* from the visions of the night.
12. 5, despised in *t.* of him that is at ease.
42. 2, no *t.* can be withholden from thee.
Ps. 10. 4, God is not in all his *t.*
40. 5, thy *t.* cannot be reckoned.
92. 5, thy *t.* are very deep.
94. 11, the Lord knoweth the *t.* of man.

Ps. 94. 19, in the multitude of my *t.*
139. 2, thou understandest my *t.* afar off.
17, how precious are thy *t.* to me!
23, try me, and know my *t.*
Prov. 12. 5, the *t.* of the righteous are right.
16. 3, thy *t.* shall be established.
24. 9, the *t.* of foolishness is sin.
Isa. 55. 7, and the unrighteous man his *t.*
8, my *t.* are not your *t.*
9, so are my *t.* higher than your *t.*
Mic. 4. 12, they know not the *t.* of the Lord.
Mat. 6. 25, 31, 34; 10. 19; Mk. 13. 11; Lu. 12. 11, 22, take no *t.*
9. 4; 12. 25; Lu. 5. 22; 6. 8; 9. 47; 11. 17, Jesus knowing their *t.*
15. 19; Mk. 7. 21, out of the heart proceed evil *t.*
Lu. 2. 35, the *t.* of many hearts may be revealed.
24. 38, why do *t.* arise in your hearts?
Acts 8. 22, if the *t.* of thine heart may be forgiven.
1 Cor. 3. 20, the Lord knoweth the *t.* of the wise.
2 Cor. 10. 5, bringing into captivity every *t.*
Heb. 4. 12, the word of God is a discerner of the *t.*
Jas. 2. 4, ye are become judges of evil *t.*
See Gen. 6. 5; Jer. 4. 14; 23. 20; Amos 4. 13.
THOUGHT (*v.*). Gen. 48. 11, I had not *t.* to see thy face.
Num. 24. 11, I *t.* to promote thee.
Deut. 19. 19, do to him as he *t.* to have done.
2 Kings 5. 11, I *t.*, he will surely come out.
Neh. 6. 2, they *t.* to do me mischief.
Ps. 48. 9, we have *t.* of thy lovingkindness.
50. 21, thou *t.* I was such an one as thyself.
73. 16, when I *t.* to know this.
119. 59, I *t.* on my ways.
Prov. 30. 32, if thou hast *t.* evil.
Isa. 14. 24, as I have *t.*, so shall it come.
Jer. 18. 8, I will repent of the evil I *t.* to do.
Zech. 8. 14, as I *t.* to punish you.
15, I *t.* to do well.
Mal. 3. 16, for them that *t.* on his name.
Mat. 1. 20, but while he *t.* on these things.
Mk. 14. 72, when he *t.* thereon, he wept.
Lu. 12. 17, he *t.* within himself, what shall I do?
19. 11, *t.* the kingdom of God should appear.
John 11. 13, they *t.* he had spoken of taking of rest.
Acts 10. 19, while Peter *t.* on the vision.
26. 8, why should it be *t.* a thing incredible?
1 Cor. 13. 11, I *t.* as a child.
Phil. 2. 6, *t.* it not robbery to be equal with God.
See Gen. 20. 11; 50. 20; 1 Sam. 1. 13; Heb. 10. 29.
THREAD. Gen. 14. 23; Josh. 2. 18; Judg. 16. 9.
THREATEN. Acts 4. 17; 9. 1; Eph. 6. 9; 1 Pet. 2. 23.
THREEFOLD. Eccl. 4. 12, a *t.* cord.
THRESH. Isa. 41. 15, thou shalt *t.* the mountains.
Jer. 51. 33, it is time to *t.* her.
Mic. 4. 13, arise and *t.*
Hab. 3. 12, thou didst *t.* the heathen.
1 Cor. 9. 10, *t.* in hope.
See Lev. 26. 5; 1 Chron. 21. 20; Isa. 21. 10; 28. 28.
THREW. 2 Kings 9. 33; Mk. 12. 42; Lu. 9. 42; Acts 22. 23.
THROAT. Ps. 5. 9; 115. 7; Prov. 23. 2; Mat. 18. 28.
THRONE. Ps. 11. 4, the Lord's *t.* is in heaven.
94. 20, shall *t.* of iniquity have fellowship with thee?
122. 5, there are set *t.* of judgment.
Prov. 20. 28, his *t.* is upholden by mercy.
Isa. 66. 1; Acts 7. 49, heaven is my *t.*
Jer. 17. 12, a glorious high *t.* from the beginning.
Dan. 7. 9, his *t.* was like the fiery flame.
Mat. 19. 28; 25. 31, the Son of man shall sit in the *t.*
Col. 1. 16, whether they be *t.*
Heb. 4. 16, the *t.* of grace.
Rev. 3. 21, to him will I grant to sit on my *t.*
4. 2, a *t.* was set in heaven.
See Rev. 6. 16; 7. 9; 14. 3; 19. 4; 20. 11; 22. 1.
THRONG. Mk. 3. 9; 5. 31; Lu. 8. 42, 45.

THROW. Mic. 5. 11; Mal. 1. 4; Mat. 24. 2.
THRUST. Job 32. 13, God *t.* him down, not man.
Joel 2. 8, neither shall one *t.* another.
Lu. 10. 15, shall be *t.* down to hell.
13. 28, and you yourselves *t.* out.
John 20. 25, and *t.* my hand into his side.
Rev. 14. 15, *t.* in thy sickle.
See Ex. 11. 1; 1 Sam. 31. 4; Ezek. 34. 21.
TIDINGS. Ps. 112. 7, afraid of evil *t.*
Jer. 20. 15, cursed be the man who brought *t.*
Dan. 11. 44, *t.* out of the east.
Lu. 1. 19; 2. 10; 8. 1; Acts 13. 32; Rom. 10. 15, glad *t.*
See Ex. 33. 4; 1 Kings 14. 6; Jer. 49. 23.
TILL. Gen. 2. 5; Prov. 12. 11; 28. 19; Ezek. 36. 9.
TILLAGE. 1 Chron. 27. 26; Neh. 10. 37; Prov. 13. 23.
TIME. Gen. 47. 29, the *t.* drew nigh.
Job 22. 16, cut down out of *t.*
38. 23, reserved against the *t.* of trouble.
Ps. 32. 6, in a *t.* when thou mayest be found.
37. 19, not ashamed in the evil *t.*
41. 1, deliver him in *t.* of trouble.
56. 3, what *t.* I am afraid.
69. 13; Isa. 49. 8; 2 Cor. 6. 2, acceptable *t.*
89. 47, remember how short my *t.* is.
Eccl. 3. 1, there is a *t.* to every purpose.
9. 11, *t.* and chance happeneth to all.
Isa. 60. 22, I will hasten it in his *t.*
Jer. 46. 21, the *t.* of their visitation.
Ezek. 16. 8, thy *t.* was the *t.* of love.
Dan. 7. 25, a *t.* and *t.* and the dividing of *t.*
Hos. 10. 12, it is *t.* to seek the Lord.
Mal. 3. 11, neither shall vine cast fruit before the *t.*
Mat. 16. 3, the signs of the *t.*
Lu. 19. 44, the *t.* of thy visitation.
Acts 3. 19, the *t.* of refreshing.
21, the *t.* of restitution.
Rom. 13. 11, it is high *t.* to awake.
1 Cor. 7. 29, the *t.* is short.
Eph. 5. 16; Col. 4. 5, redeeming the *t.*
Heb. 4. 16, help in *t.* of need.
1 Pet. 1. 11, what manner of *t.*
Rev. 1. 3, the *t.* is at hand.
10. 6, *t.* no longer.
See Prov. 17. 17; Eph. 1. 10; 1 Tim. 4. 1.
TINGLE. 1 Sam. 3. 11; 2 Kings 21. 12; Jer. 19. 3.
TINKLING. Isa. 3. 16, 18; 1 Cor. 13. 1.
TOGETHER. Prov. 22. 2, meet *t.*
Amos 3. 3, can two walk *t.*?
Mat. 18. 20, where two or three are gathered *t.*
Rom. 8. 28, work *t.* for good.
1 Thess. 4. 17, caught up *t.*
See Mat. 19. 6; Eph. 2. 21; 2 Thess. 2. 1.
TOIL. Gen. 5. 29; 41. 51; Mat. 6. 28; Lu. 12. 27.
TOLERABLE. Mat. 10. 15; 11. 24; Mk. 6. 11; Lu. 10. 12.
TONGUE. Job 5. 21, hid from scourge of the *t.*
20. 12, hide wickedness under his *t.*
Ps. 34. 13; 1 Pet. 3. 10, keep thy *t.* from evil.
Prov. 10. 20, *t.* of the just as choice silver.
12. 18; 31. 26, *t.* of the wise is health.
19, the lying *t.* is but for a moment.
15. 4, a wholesome *t.* is a tree of life.
18. 21, death and life are in the power of the *t.*
21. 23, whoso keepeth his *t.* keepeth his soul.
25. 15, a soft *t.* breaketh the bone.
Isa. 30. 27, his *t.* as a devouring fire.
50. 4, hath given me the *t.* of the learned.
Jer. 9. 5, taught their *t.* to speak lies.
18. 18, let us smite him with the *t.*
Mk. 7. 35, his *t.* was loosed.
Jas. 1. 26, and bridleth not his *t.*
3. 5, the *t.* is a little member.
6, the *t.* is a fire.
8, the *t.* can no man tame.
1 John 3. 18, not love in word, neither in *t.*
See Ps. 45. 1; Lu. 16. 24; Rom. 14. 11; Phil. 2. 11.
TOOL. Ex. 20. 25; 32. 4; Deut. 27. 5; 1 Kings 6. 7.

TOOTH. Ex. 21. 24 ; Prov. 25. 19 ; Mat. 5. 38.

TOPAZ. Ex. 28. 17 ; Rev. 21. 20.

TORCHES. Nah. 2. 3 ; Zech. 12. 6 ; John 18. 3.

TORMENT. Mat. 8. 28, to *t.* before the time.
Lu. 16. 23, being in *t.*
Heb. 11. 37, destitute, afflicted, *t.*
1 John 4. 18, fear hath *t.*
Rev. 9. 5, *t.* as *t.* of a scorpion.
14. 11, the smoke of their *t.*
See Mat. 4. 24 ; Mk. 5. 7 ; Lu. 8. 28.

TORN. Gen. 44. 28, surely he is *t.* in pieces.
Ezek. 4. 14, have not eaten of that which is *t.*
Hos. 6. 1, he hath *t.*, and he will heal us.
See Isa. 5. 25 ; Mal. 1. 13 ; Mk. 1. 26.

TORTOISE. Lev. 11. 29, and the *t.* after his kind.

TOSS. Ps. 109. 23, I am *t.* up and down.
Isa. 22. 18, he will *t.* thee like a ball.
54. 11, afflicted, *t.* with tempest.
Eph. 4. 14, no more children, *t.* to and fro.
See Mat. 14. 24 ; Acts 27. 18 ; Jas. 1. 6.

TOUCH. Gen. 3. 3, nor *t.* it, lest ye die.
1 Sam. 10. 26, a band whose hearts God had *t.*
1 Chron. 16. 22 ; Ps. 105. 15, *t.* not mine anointed.
Job 5. 19, there shall no evil *t.* thee.
6. 7, things my soul refused to *t.*
Isa. 6. 7, lo, this hath *t.* thy lips.
Jer. 1. 9, the Lord *t.* my mouth.
Zech. 2. 8, he that *t.* you, *t.* the apple of his eye.
Mat. 9. 21 ; Mk. 5. 28, if I may but *t.* his garment.
Mk. 10. 13 ; Lu. 18. 15, children, that he should *t.* them.
John 20. 17, *t.* me not.
2 Cor. 6. 17, *t.* not the unclean thing.
Col. 2. 21, *t.* not, taste not.
See Job 19. 21 ; Lu. 7. 14 ; 11. 46 ; 1 Cor. 7. 1.

TOWER. 2 Sam. 22. 3 ; Ps. 18. 2 ; 144. 2, my high *t.*
Ps. 61. 3, a strong *t.* from the enemy.
Prov. 18. 10, the name of the Lord is a strong *t.*
Isa. 33. 18, where is he that counted the *t.?*
See Isa. 2. 15 ; 5. 2 ; Mic. 4. 8 ; Mat. 21. 33.

TRADITION. Mat. 15. 2 ; Mk. 7. 3, thy disciples transgress the *t.*
Gal. 1. 14, zealous of the *t.* of my fathers.
Col. 2. 8, after the *t.* of men.
1 Pet. 1. 18, received by *t.* from your fathers.

TRAFFICK. Gen. 42. 34 ; 1 Kings 10. 15 ; Ezek. 17. 4.

TRAIN. 1 Kings 10. 2 ; Prov. 22. 6 ; Isa. 6. 1.

TRAITOR. Lu. 6. 16 ; 2 Tim. 3. 4.

TRAMPLE. Ps. 91. 13 ; Isa. 63. 3 ; Mat. 7. 6.

TRANQUILLITY. Dan. 4. 27, lengthening of thy *t.*

TRANSFORM. Rom. 12. 2 ; 2 Cor. 11. 13, 14, 15.

TRANSGRESS. Num. 14. 41, wherefore do ye *t.?*
1 Sam. 2. 24, make the Lord's people to *t.*
Neh. 1. 8, if ye *t.*, I will scatter you abroad.
Ps. 17. 3, my mouth shall not *t.*
Prov. 28. 21, for a piece of bread that man will *t.*
Jer. 2. 8, the pastors *t.*
3. 13, only acknowledge that thou hast *t.*
Hab. 2. 5, he *t.* by wine.
See Mat. 15. 2 ; Rom. 2. 27 ; 1 John 3. 4 ; 2 John 9.

TRANSGRESSION. Ex. 34. 7 ; Num. 14. 18, forgiving *t.*
1 Chron. 10. 13, Saul died for his *t.*
Ezra 10. 6, he mourned because of their *t.*
Job 7. 21, why dost thou not pardon my *t.?*
13. 23, make me to know my *t.*
14. 17, my *t.* is sealed up.
31. 33, if I covered my *t.*
Ps. 19. 13, innocent from the great *t.*
25. 7, remember not my *t.*
32. 1, blessed is he whose *t.* is forgiven.
51. 1, blot out all my *t.*
65. 3, as for our *t.*, thou shalt purge them.
107. 17, fools because of their *t.* are afflicted.
Prov. 17. 9, he that covereth a *t.*
Isa. 43. 25 ; 44. 22, blotteth out thy *t.*
53. 5, he was wounded for our *t.*

Isa. 53. 8, for the *t.* of my people was he smitten.
58. 1, show my people their *t.*
Ezek. 18. 22, his *t.* shall not be mentioned.
Mic. 1. 5, what is the *t.* of Jacob?
See Rom. 4. 15 ; 5. 14 ; 1 Tim. 2. 14 ; Heb. 2. 2.

TRANSGRESSOR. Ps. 51. 13, teach *t.* thy ways.
59. 5, be not merciful to any wicked *t.*
Prov. 13. 15, the way of *t.* is hard.
21. 18, the *t.* shall be ransom for the upright.
Isa. 48. 8, thou wast called a *t.* from the womb.
53. 12 ; Mk. 15. 28 ; Lu. 22. 37, numbered with the *t.*
See Dan. 8. 23 ; Hos. 14. 9 ; Gal. 2. 18.

TRANSLATE. 2 Sam. 3. 10 ; Col. 1. 13 ; Heb. 11. 5.

TRAP. Job 18. 10 ; Ps. 69. 22 ; Jer. 5. 26 ; Rom. 11. 9.

TRAVAIL. Ps. 7. 14, he *t.* with iniquity.
Isa. 23. 4, I *t.* not.
53. 11, the *t.* of his soul.
Rom. 8. 22, the whole creation *t.* in pain.
Gal. 4. 19, my children, of whom I *t.*
See Job 15. 20 ; Isa. 13. 8 ; Mic. 5. 3 ; Rev. 12. 2.

TRAVEL. Eccl. 1. 13 ; 2. 23 ; 1 Thess. 2. 9 ; 2 Thess. 3. 8.

TRAVELLER. Judg. 5. 6 ; 2 Sam. 12. 4 ; Job 31. 32.

TREACHEROUS. Isa. 21. 2 ; Jer. 9. 2 ; Zeph. 3. 4.

TREACHEROUSLY. Isa. 33. 1, thou dealest *t.*
Jer. 12. 1, why are they happy that deal *t.?*
Lam. 1. 2, her friends have dealt *t.* with her.
See Hos. 5. 7 ; 6. 7 ; Mal. 2. 10, 15.

TREAD. Deut. 11. 24, whereon soles of feet *t.*
25. 4 ; 1 Cor. 9. 9 ; 1 Tim. 5. 18, not muzzle the ox when he *t.*
Ps. 7. 5, let him *t.* down my life.
44. 5, through thy name will we *t.* them under.
60. 12 ; 108. 13, shall *t.* down our enemies.
91. 13, thou shalt *t.* upon lion and adder.
Isa. 10. 6, to *t.* them down like mire.
16. 10, shall *t.* out no wine.
63. 3, I will *t.* them in mine anger.
Jer. 48. 33, none shall *t.* with shouting.
Ezek. 34. 18, but ye must *t.* the residue.
Hos. 10. 11, loveth to *t.* out corn.
Mal. 4. 3, ye shall *t.* down the wicked.
See Job 9. 8 ; Isa. 41. 25 ; 63. 2 ; Rev. 19. 15.

TREASURE. Gen. 43. 23, God hath given you *t.*
Ex. 19. 5 ; Ps. 135. 4, a peculiar *t.* to me.
Deut. 28. 12, open to thee his good *t.*
Job 3. 21 ; Ps. 17. 14 ; Prov. 2. 4, for hid *t.*
38. 22, the *t.* of the snow.
Prov. 8. 21, I will fill *t.* of those that love me.
10. 2, *t.* of wickedness profiteth nothing.
15. 16, than great *t.* and trouble therewith.
21. 20, there is a *t.* to be desired.
Eccl. 2. 8, I gathered the peculiar *t.* of kings.
Isa. 2. 7, neither is there any end of their *t.*
45. 3, I will give thee the *t.* of darkness.
Jer. 41. 8, slay us not, for we have *t.*
51. 13, waters abundant in *t.*
Dan. 11. 43, power over the *t.* of gold.
Mic. 6. 10, the *t.* of wickedness.
Mat. 6. 21 ; Lu. 12. 34, where your *t.* is.
12. 35, out of the good *t.* of the heart.
13. 44, like unto *t.* hid in a field.
52, out of his *t.* things new and old.
19. 21 ; Mk. 10. 21 ; Lu. 18. 22, thou shalt have *t.* in heaven.
Lu. 12. 21, that layeth up *t.* for himself.
Col. 2. 3, in whom are hid *t.* of wisdom.
2 Cor. 4. 7, we have this *t.* in earthen vessels.
Heb. 11. 26, greater riches than the *t.* in Egypt.
Jas. 5. 3, ye have heaped *t.*
See Deut. 32. 34 ; 33. 19 ; Isa. 33. 6 ; Mat. 2. 11.

TREASURER. Neh. 13. 13 ; Isa. 22. 15 ; Dan. 3. 2.

TREASURY. Mk. 12. 41, the people cast money into the *t.*
Lu. 21. 1, rich men casting their gifts into the *t.*
See Josh. 6. 19 ; Jer. 38. 11 ; Mat. 27. 6.

TREE. Deut. 20. 19, the *t.* is man's life.
Job 14. 7, there is hope of a *t.*

Job 24. 20, wickedness shall be broken as a *t.*
Ps. 1. 3 ; Jer. 17. 8, like a *t.* planted.
104. 16, the *t.* of the Lord are full of sap.
Eccl. 11. 3, where the *t.* falleth.
Isa. 56. 3, I am a dry *t.*
61. 3, called *t.* of righteousness.
Ezek. 15. 2, what is the vine *t.* more than any *t.?*
31. 9, all the *t.* of Eden envied him.
See Mk. 8. 24 ; Lu. 21. 29 ; Jude 12 ; Rev. 7. 3.
TREMBLE. Deut. 2. 25, the nations shall *t.*
Judg. 5. 4 ; 2 Sam. 22. 8 ; Ps. 18. 7 ; 77. 18 ; 97. 4, the earth *t.*
Ezra 9. 4, then assembled to me every one that *t.*
Job 9. 6, the pillars thereof *t.*
26. 11, the pillars of heaven *t.*
Ps. 2. 11, rejoice with *t.*
60. 2, thou hast made earth to *t.*
99. 1, the Lord reigneth, let the people *t.*
104. 32, he looketh on the earth, and it *t.*
Eccl. 12. 3, the keepers of the house shall *t.*
Isa. 14. 16, is this the man that made earth *t.?*
64. 2, that the nations may *t.* at thy presence.
66. 5, ye that *t.* at his word.
Jer. 5. 22, will ye not *t.* at my presence ?
33. 9, they shall *t.* for all the goodness.
Amos 8. 8, shall not the land *t.* for this ?
Acts 24. 25, Felix *t.*
Jas. 2. 19, devils also believe, and *t.*
See Acts 9. 6 ; 16. 29 ; 1 Cor. 2. 3 ; Eph. 6. 5 ; Phil. 2. 12.
TRENCH. 1 Sam. 17. 20 ; 26. 5 ; 1 Kings 18. 32 ; Lu. 19. 43.
TRESPASS. Gen. 31. 36, what is my *t.?*
50. 17, we pray thee forgive the *t.*
Ezra 9. 2, rulers have been chief in this *t.*
Ps. 68. 21, goeth on still in his *t.*
Mat. 6. 14, if ye forgive men their *t.*
18. 15, if thy brother *t.*, tell him his fault.
Lu. 17. 3, if thy brother *t.* against thee.
2 Cor. 5. 19, not imputing their *t.*
Eph. 2. 1, dead in *t.* and sins.
Col. 2. 13, having forgiven you all *t.*
See Num. 5. 6 ; 1 Kings 8. 31 ; Ezek. 17. 20 : 18. 24.
TRIAL. Job 9. 23, the *t.* of the innocent.
2 Cor. 8. 2, a great *t.* of affliction.
See Ezek. 21. 13 ; Heb. 11. 36 ; 1 Pet. 1. 7 ; 4. 12.
TRIBES. Ps. 105. 37, not one feeble person among their *t.*
122. 4, whither the *t.* go up.
Isa. 19. 13, they that are the stay of the *t.*
49. 6, my servant to raise up the *t.*
Hab. 3. 9, according to oaths of the *t.*
Mat. 24. 30, then shall all *t.* of the earth mourn.
See Num. 24. 2 ; Deut. 1. 13 ; 12. 5 ; 18. 5.
TRIBULATION. Deut. 4. 30, when thou art in *t.*
Judg. 10. 14, let them deliver you in *t.*
Mat. 13. 21, when *t.* ariseth.
24. 21, then shall be great *t.*
John 16. 33, in the world ye shall have *t.*
Acts 14. 22, through much *t.*
Rom. 5. 3, we glory in *t.* also.
12. 12, patient in *t.*
See 2 Cor. 1. 4 ; 7. 4 ; Eph. 3. 13 ; Rev. 7. 14.
TRIBUTARY. Deut. 20. 11 ; Judg. 1. 30 ; Lam. 1. 1.
TRIBUTE. Gen. 49. 15, a servant to *t.*
Num. 31. 37, the Lord's *t.*
Deut. 16. 10, *t.* of freewill offering.
Ezra 7. 24, not lawful to impose *t.*
Neh. 5. 4, borrowed money for king's *t.*
Prov. 12. 24, the slothful shall be under *t.*
See Mat. 17. 24 ; 22. 17 ; Lu. 23. 2.
TRIM. 2 Sam. 19. 24 ; Jer. 2. 33 ; Mat. 25. 7.
TRIUMPH. Ex. 15. 1, he hath *t.* gloriously.
Ps. 25. 2, let not mine enemies *t.*
92. 4, I will *t.* in the works of thy hands.
2 Cor. 2. 14, which always causeth us to *t.*
Col. 2. 15, a show of them openly, *t.* over them.
See 2 Sam. 1. 20 ; Job 20. 5 ; Ps. 47. 1.
TRODDEN. Job 22. 15, the old way which wicked men have *t.*

Ps. 119. 118, thou hast *t.* down all that err.
Isa. 5. 5, the vineyard shall be *t.* down.
63. 3, I have *t.* the winepress alone.
Mic. 7. 10, now shall she be *t.* as mire.
Mat. 5. 13, salt to be *t.* under foot.
Lu. 21. 24, Jerusalem shall be *t.* down.
Heb. 10. 29, hath *t.* under foot the Son of God.
See Deut. 1. 36 ; Judg. 5. 21 ; Isa. 18. 2.
TRODE. 2 Kings 14. 9 ; 2 Chron. 25. 18 ; Lu. 12. 1.
TROOP. 2 Sam. 22. 30 ; Ps. 18. 29 ; Hos. 7. 1.
TROUBLE (*n.*). Deut. 31. 17, many *t.* shall befall.
1 Chron. 22. 14, in my *t.* I prepared for the house.
Neh. 9. 32, let not the *t.* seem little.
Job 3. 26, yet *t.* came.
5. 6, neither doth *t.* spring out of the ground.
7, man is born to *t.*
19, shall deliver thee in six *t.*
14. 1, of few days, and full of *t.*
30. 25, weep for him that was in *t.*
34. 29, he giveth quietness, who can make *t.?*
38. 23, I have reserved against the time of *t.*
Ps. 9. 9, a refuge in time of *t.*
22. 11, for *t.* is near.
25. 17, the *t.* of mine heart are enlarged.
22, redeem Israel out of all his *t.*
27. 5, in time of *t.* he shall hide me.
46. 1, a very present help in *t.*
73. 5, they are not in *t.* as other men.
88. 3, my soul is full of *t.*
119. 143, *t.* and anguish have taken hold on me.
138. 7, though I walk in the midst of *t.*
Isa. 17. 14, at eveningtide *t.*
30. 6, into the land of *t.* they will carry riches.
65. 16, because former *t.* are forgotten.
23, they shall not bring forth for *t.*
Jer. 2. 27, in time of *t.* they will say, save us.
8. 15, we looked for health, and behold *t.*
1 Cor. 7. 28, such shall have *t.* in the flesh.
2 Cor. 1. 4, able to comfort them in *t.*
See Prov. 15. 6 ; 25. 19 ; Jer. 11. 12 ; 30. 7 ; Lam. 1. 21.
TROUBLE (*v.*). Josh. 7. 25, why hast thou *t.* us ?
1 Kings 18. 17, art thou he that *t.* Israel ?
18, I have not *t.* Israel, but thou.
Job 4. 5, now it toucheth thee, and thou art *t.*
Ps. 3. 1, how are they increased that *t.* me !
77. 4, I am so *t.* that I cannot speak.
Prov. 25. 26, is as a *t.* fountain.
Isa. 57. 20, the wicked are like the *t.* sea.
Dan. 5. 10, let not thy thoughts *t.* thee.
11. 44, tidings out of the north shall *t.* him.
Mat. 24. 6, see that ye be not *t.*
26. 10 ; Mk. 14. 6, why *t.* ye the woman ?
John 5. 4, an angel *t.* the water.
11. 33 ; 12. 27 ; 13. 21, Jesus groaned, and was *t.*
2 Cor. 4. 8 ; 7. 5, we are *t.* on every side.
Gal. 1. 7, there be some that *t.* you.
6. 17, let no man *t.* me.
See 2 Thess. 1. 7 ; 2. 2 ; Heb. 12. 15 ; 1 Pet. 3. 14.
TROUBLING. Job 3. 17 ; John 5. 4.
TRUCE. 2 Tim. 3. 3, men shall be *t.*-breakers.
TRUE. Gen. 42. 11, we are *t.* men.
1 Kings 22. 16, tell me nothing but that which is *t.*
2 Chron. 15. 3, Israel hath been without the *t.* God.
Neh. 9. 13, thou gavest them *t.* laws.
Ps. 119. 160, thy word is *t.* from the beginning.
Prov. 14. 25, a *t.* witness delivereth souls.
Jer. 10. 10, the Lord is the *t.* God.
Mat. 22. 16 ; Mk. 12. 14, we know that thou art *t.*
Lu. 16. 11, the *t.* riches.
John 1. 9, that was the *t.* light.
4. 23, when the *t.* worshippers.
5. 31, if I bear witness of myself, my witness is not *t.*
6. 32, the *t.* bread.
10. 41, all things that John spake were *t.*
15. 1, I am the *t.* vine.
17. 3 ; 1 John 5. 20, to know thee the only *t.* God.
2 Cor. 6. 8, as deceivers, and yet *t.*
Eph. 4. 24, created in *t.* holiness.

Phil. 4. 8, whatsoever things are *t.*
Heb. 10. 22, draw near with a *t.* heart.
See Rev. 3. 7 ; 6. 10 ; 15. 3 ; 16. 7 ; 19. 9, 11 ; 21. 5.
TRUST.   Job 13. 15, though he slay me, yet will
   I *t.*
   39. 11, wilt thou *t.* him, because his strength is
    great ?
Ps. 25. 2 ; 31. 6 ; 55. 23 ; 56. 3 ; 143. 8,   I *t.* in thee.
   37. 3 ; 40. 3 ; 62. 8 ; 115. 9 ; Prov. 3. 5 ; Isa. 26. 4, *t.*
    in the Lord.
   118. 8, better to *t.* in the Lord.
   144. 2, he in whom I *t.*
Prov. 28. 26, he that *t.* in his own heart is a fool.
Isa. 50. 10, let him *t.* in the name of the Lord.
Jer. 49. 11, let thy widows *t.* in me.
Mic. 7. 5, *t.* ye not in a friend.
Nah. 1. 7, the Lord knoweth them that *t.* in him.
Mat. 27. 43, he *t.* in God, let him deliver him.
Lu. 18. 9, certain which *t.* in themselves.
See Jer. 17. 5 ; 2 Cor. 1. 9 ; 1 Tim. 4. 10.
TRUTH.   Deut. 32. 4, a God of *t.*
Ps. 15. 2, speaketh the *t.* in his heart.
   51. 6, desirest *t.* in inward parts.
   91. 4, his *t.* shall be thy shield.
   117. 2, his *t.* endureth for ever.
   119. 30, I have chosen the way of *t.*
Prov. 23. 23, buy the *t.*
Isa. 59. 14, *t.* is fallen in the streets.
Jer. 9. 3, they are not valiant for the *t.*
Zech. 8. 16, speak every man *t.* to his neighbour.
Mal. 2. 6, the law of *t.* was in his mouth.
John 1. 14, full of grace and *t.*
   8. 32, know the *t.*, and the *t.* shall make you free.
   14. 6, I am the way, the *t.*, and the life.
   16. 13, Spirit of *t.* will guide you into all *t.*
   18. 38, what is *t.?*
Rom. 1. 18, who hold the *t.* in unrighteousness.
1 Cor. 5. 8, unleavened bread of sincerity and *t.*
2 Cor. 13. 8, can do nothing against *t.*, but for the *t.*
Eph. 4. 15, speaking the *t.* in love.
1 Tim. 3. 15, the pillar and ground of *t.*
2 Tim. 2. 15, rightly dividing the word of *t.*
Jas. 5. 19, if any err from the *t.*
See 1 Cor. 13. 6 ; 2 Tim. 3. 7 ; 1 John 3. 19 ; 5. 6.
TRY.   2 Chron. 32. 31, God left him, to *t.* him.
Job 23. 10, when he hath *t.* me.
Ps. 26. 2, *t.* my reins and my heart.
Jer. 9. 7 ; Zech. 13. 9, I will melt them and *t.* them.
1 Cor. 3. 13, shall *t.* every man's work.
Jas. 1. 12, when *t.* he shall receive the crown.
1 John 4. 1, *t.* the spirits.
See Prov. 17. 3 ; Isa. 28. 16 ; 1 Pet. 4. 12 ; Rev. 3. 18.
TURN.   Job 23. 13, who can *t.* him.
Ps. 7. 12, if he *t.* not, he will whet his sword.
Prov. 1. 23, *t.* at my reproof.
Jer. 31. 18 ; Lam. 5. 21, *t.* thou me, and I shall be *t.*
Ezek. 14. 6 ; 18. 30 ; 33. 9 ; Hos. 12. 6 ; Joel 2. 12, re-
    pent, and *t.*
Zech. 9. 12, *t.* you to the strong hold, ye prisoners.
Mat. 5. 39, *t.* the other also.
Acts 26. 18, to *t.* them from darkness to light.
2 Tim. 3. 5, from such *t.* away.
   See Prov. 21. 1 ; 26. 14 ; Hos 7. 8 ; Lu. 22. 61 ; Jas. 1. 17.
TWAIN.   Isa. 6. 2 ; Mat. 5. 41 ; 19. 5 ; Eph. 2. 15.
TWICE.   Job 33. 14 ; Mk. 14. 30 ; Lu. 18. 12 ; Jude 12.
TWINKLING.   1 Cor. 15. 52, in the *t.* of an eye.

U.

UNADVISEDLY.   Ps. 106. 33, he spake *u.*
UNAWARES.   Lu. 21. 34 ; Gal. 2. 4 ; Heb. 13. 2 ;
   Jude 4.
UNBELIEF.   Mk. 9. 24, help thou mine *u.*
Rom. 3. 3, shall *u.* make faith without effect ?
   11. 32, concluded all in *u.*
Heb. 3. 12, evil heart of *u.*
   See Mat. 13. 58 ; Mk. 6. 6 ; 1 Tim. 1. 13 ; Heb. 4. 11.
UNBLAMEABLE.   Col. 1. 22 ; 1 Thess. 3. 13.
UNCERTAIN.   1 Cor. 9. 26 ; 14. 8 ; 1 Tim. 6. 17.
UNCLEAN.   Acts 10. 28 ; Rom. 14. 14 ; 2 Cor. 6. 17.

UNCLOTHED.   2 Cor. 5. 4, not that we would be *u.*
UNCORRUPTNESS.   Tit. 2. 7, in doctrine show-
   ing *u.*
UNCTION.   1 John 2. 20, an *u.* from the Holy One.
UNDEFILED.   Ps. 119. 1, blessed are the *u.*
Jas. 1. 27, pure religion and *u.*
1 Pet. 1. 4, an inheritance *u.*
   See Cant. 5. 2 ; 6. 9 ; Heb. 7. 26 ; 13. 4.
UNDER.   Rom. 3. 9 ; 1 Cor. 9. 27 ; Gal. 3. 10.
UNDERSTAND.   Ps. 14. 2, who can *u.* his errors ?
   73. 17, then *u.* I their end.
   119. 100, I *u.* more than the ancients.
   139. 2, thou *u.* my thought afar off.
Prov. 8. 9, all plain to him that *u.*
   20. 24, how can a man *u.* his own way ?
   29. 19, though he *u.* he will not answer.
Isa. 6. 9, hear ye indeed, but *u.* not.
   28. 19, a vexation only to *u.* the report.
Jer. 9. 24, let him glory in this, that he *u.* me.
Dan. 10. 12, thou didst set thine heart to *u.*
   12. 10, wicked shall not *u.*, the wise shall *u.*
Hos. 14. 9, who is wise, and he shall *u.* these
    things ?
Mat. 13. 51, have ye *u.* all these things ?
   24. 15, whoso readeth, let him *u.*
Lu. 24. 45, that they might *u.* the scriptures.
John 8. 43, why do ye not *u.* my speech ?
Rom. 3. 11, there is none that *u.*
   15. 21, they that have not heard shall *u.*
1 Cor. 13. 2, though I *u.* all mysteries.
   11, I *u.* as a child.
   See 1 Cor. 14. 2 ; Heb. 11. 3 ; 2 Pet. 2. 12 ; 3. 16.
UNDERSTANDING.   Ex. 31. 3 ; Deut. 4. 6, wisdom and *u.*
1 Kings 3. 11, hast asked for thyself *u.*
   4. 29, gave Solomon wisdom and *u.*
   7. 14, filled with wisdom and *u.*
1 Chron. 12. 32, men that had *u.* of the times.
2 Chron. 26. 5, had *u.* in visions.
Job 12. 13, he hath counsel and *u.*
   20, he taketh away the *u.* of the aged.
   17. 4, thou hast hid their heart from *u.*
   28. 12, where is the place of *u.?*
   32. 8, the Almighty giveth them *u.*
   38. 36, who hath given *u.* to the heart ?
   39. 17, neither imparted to her *u.*
Ps. 47. 7, sing ye praises with *u.*
   49. 3, the meditation of my heart shall be of *u.*
   119. 34, 73, 125, 144, 169, give me *u.*
   99, I have more *u.* than my teachers.
   104, through thy precepts I get *u.*
   147. 5, his *u.* is infinite.
Prov. 2. 2, apply thine heart to *u.*
   11, *u.* shall keep thee.
   3. 5, lean not to thine own *u.*
   19, by *u.* hath he established the heavens.
   4. 5, 7, get wisdom, get *u.*
   8. 1, doth not *u.* put forth her voice ?
   9. 6, go in the way of *u.*
   10, the knowledge of the holy is *u.*
   14. 29, he that is slow to wrath is of great *u.*
   16. 22, *u.* is a wellspring of life.
   17. 24, wisdom is before him that hath *u.*
   19. 8, he that keepeth *u.* shall find good.
   21. 30, there is no *u.* against the Lord.
   24. 3, by *u.* an house is established.
   30. 2, have not the *u.* of a man.
Eccl. 9. 11, nor yet riches to men of *u.*
Isa. 11. 2, the spirit of *u.* shall rest on him.
   27. 11, it is a people of no *u.*
   29. 14, the *u.* of prudent men shall be hid.
   40. 14, who showed him the way of *u.?*
   28, there is no searching of his *u.*
Jer. 3. 15, pastors shall feed you with *u.*
Ezek. 28. 4, with thy *u.* thou hast gotten riches.
Dan. 4. 34, mine *u.* returned.
Mat. 15. 16 ; Mk. 7. 18, are ye also without *u.?*
Mk. 12. 33, to love him with all the *u.*
Lu. 2. 47, astonished at his *u.*
   24. 45, then opened he their *u.*

1 Cor. 1. 19, bring to nothing *u.* of prudent.
14. 15, I will pray with the *u.* also.
20, be not children in *u.*
Eph. 4. 18, having the *u.* darkened.
Phil. 4. 7, peace of God, which passeth all *u.*
See Col. 1. 9 ; 2. 2 ; 2 Tim. 2. 7 ; 1 John 5. 20.

UNDERTAKE. Isa. 38. 14, *u.* for me.

UNDONE. Josh. 11. 15 ; Isa. 6. 5 ; Mat. 23. 23 ; Lu. 11. 42.

UNEQUAL. Ezek. 18. 25, 29 ; 2 Cor. 6. 14.

UNFAITHFUL. Ps. 78. 57 ; Prov. 25. 19.

UNFEIGNED. 2 Cor. 6. 6 ; 1 Tim. 1. 5 ; 2 Tim. 1. 5 ; 1 Pet. 1. 22.

UNFRUITFUL. Mat. 13. 22 ; Eph. 5. 11 ; Tit. 3. 14 ; 2 Pet. 1. 8.

UNGODLINESS. Rom. 1. 18 ; 11. 26 ; 2 Tim. 2. 16 ; Tit. 2. 12.

UNGODLY. 2 Chr. 19. 2, shouldest thou help the *u.*?
Job 16. 11, God hath delivered me to the *u.*
Ps. 1. 1, counsel of *u.*
6, the way of the *u.* shall perish.
43. 1, plead my cause against an *u.* nation.
Prov. 16. 27, an *u.* man diggeth up evil.
Rom. 5. 6, Christ died for the *u.*
1 Pet. 4. 18, where shall the *u.* appear?
2 Pet. 3. 7, perdition of *u.* men.
See Rom. 4. 5 ; 1 Tim. 1. 9 ; 2 Pet. 2. 5 ; Jude 15.

UNHOLY. Lev. 10. 10 ; 1 Tim. 1. 9 ; 2 Tim. 3. 2 ; Heb. 10. 29.

UNICORN. Num. 23. 22, he hath as it were the strength of an *u.*
Deut. 33. 17, his horns are like the horns of an *u.*
Job 39. 9, will the *u.* be willing to serve thee?
Isa. 34. 7, the *u.* shall come down with them.

UNITE. Gen. 49. 6 ; Ps. 86. 11.

UNITY. Ps. 133. 1 ; Eph. 4. 3, 13.

UNJUST. Ps. 43. 1 ; Prov. 11. 7 ; 29. 27, *u.* man.
Prov. 28. 8, by that by *u.* gain.
Zeph. 3. 5, the *u.* knoweth no shame.
Mat. 5. 45, he sendeth rain on the just and *u.*
Lu. 18. 6, hear what the *u.* judge saith.
11, not as other men, *u.*
Acts 24. 15, a resurrection both of the just and *u.*
1 Cor. 6. 1, go to law before the *u.*
1 Pet. 3. 18, suffered, the just for the *u.*
Rev. 22. 11, he that is *u.*, let him be *u.* still.
See Ps. 82. 2 ; Isa. 26. 10 ; Lu. 16. 8 ; 2 Pet. 2. 9.

UNKNOWN. Acts 17. 23 ; 1 Cor. 14. 2 ; 2 Cor. 6. 9 ; Gal. 1. 22.

UNLAWFUL. Acts 10. 28 ; 2 Pet. 2. 8.

UNLEARNED. Acts 4. 13 ; 1 Cor. 14. 16 ; 2 Tim. 2. 23 ; 2 Pet. 3. 16.

UNMINDFUL. Deut. 32. 18, thou art *u.*

UNMOVEABLE. Acts 27. 41 ; 1 Cor. 15. 58.

UNPERFECT. Ps. 139. 16, yet being *u.*

UNPREPARED. 2 Cor. 9. 4, find you *u.*

UNPROFITABLE. Job 15. 3, *u.* talk.
Mat. 25. 30 ; Lu. 17. 10, *u.* servant.
See Rom. 3. 12 ; Tit. 3. 9 ; Philem. 11 ; Heb. 7. 18 ; 13. 17.

UNPUNISHED. Prov. 11. 21 ; 16. 5 ; 17. 5 ; 19. 5 ; Jer. 25. 29 ; 49. 12, shall not be *u.*
See Jer. 30. 11 ; 46. 28.

UNQUENCHABLE. Mat. 3. 12 ; Lu. 3. 17.

UNREASONABLE. Acts 25. 27 ; 2 Thess. 3. 2.

UNREPROVEABLE. Col. 1. 22, *u.* in his sight.

UNRIGHTEOUS. Ex. 23. 1, an *u.* witness.
Isa. 10. 1, decree *u.* decrees.
55. 7, let the *u.* man forsake his thoughts.
Rom. 3. 5, is God *u.*?
Heb. 6. 10, God is not *u.* to forget your work.
See Deut. 25. 16 ; Ps. 71. 4 ; Lu. 16. 11 ; 1 Cor. 6. 9.

UNRIGHTEOUSNESS. Lu. 16. 9, mammon of *u.*
Rom. 1. 18, hold the truth in *u.*
2. 8, to them that obey *u.*
3. 5, if our *u.* commend righteousness.

Rom. 6. 13, instruments of *u.*
9. 14, is there *u.* with God?
2 Cor. 6. 14, what fellowship with *u.*?
2 Thess. 2. 12, had pleasure in *u.*
2 Pet. 2. 13, receive the reward of *u.*
1 John 1. 9, cleanse us from all *u.*
5. 17, all *u.* is sin.
See Lev. 19. 15 ; Ps. 92. 15 ; Jer. 22. 13 ; John 7. 18.

UNRULY. 1 Thess. 5. 14 ; Tit. 1. 6 ; Jas. 3. 8.

UNSAVOURY. Job 6. 6, can that which is *u.* be eaten?

UNSEARCHABLE. Job 5. 9 ; Ps. 145. 3 ; Rom. 11. 33 ; Eph. 3. 8.

UNSEEMLY. Rom. 1. 27 ; 1 Cor. 13. 5.

UNSKILFUL. Heb. 5. 13, is *u.* in the word.

UNSPEAKABLE. 2 Cor. 9. 15 ; 12. 4 ; 1 Pet. 1. 8.

UNSPOTTED. Jas. 1. 27, *u.* from the world.

UNSTABLE. Gen. 49. 4 ; Jas. 1. 8 ; 2 Pet. 2. 14.

UNTHANKFUL. Lu. 6. 35 ; 2 Tim. 3. 2.

UNWASHEN. Mat. 15. 20 ; Mk. 7. 2, 5.

UNWISE. Deut. 32. 6 ; Hos. 13. 13 ; Rom. 1. 14 ; Eph. 5. 17.

UNWORTHY. Acts 13. 46 ; 1 Cor. 6. 2 ; 11. 27.

UPBRAID. Mat. 11. 20 ; Mk. 16. 14 ; Jas. 1. 5.

UPHOLD. Ps. 51. 12, *u.* me with thy free spirit.
54. 4, with them that *u.* my soul.
119. 116, *u.* me according to thy word.
145. 14, the Lord *u.* all that fall.
Isa. 41. 10, I will *u.* thee with right hand.
42. 1, my servant, whom I *u.*
63. 5, wondered there was none to *u.*
Heb. 1. 3, *u.* all things by the word of his power.
See Ps. 37. 17 ; 41. 12 ; 63. 8 ; Prov. 20. 28.

UPPERMOST. Mat. 23. 6 ; Mk. 12. 39 ; Lu. 11. 43.

UPRIGHT. Job 12. 4, the *u.* man is laughed to scorn.
17. 8, *u.* men shall be astonied.
Ps. 19. 13, then shall I be *u.*
25. 8 ; 92. 15, good and *u.* is the Lord.
37. 14, such as be of *u.* conversation.
49. 14, the *u.* shall have dominion.
111. 1, the assembly of the *u.*
112. 4, to the *u.* ariseth light.
125. 4, that are *u.* in their hearts.
Prov. 2. 21, the *u.* shall dwell in the land.
11. 3, the integrity of the *u.*
20, such as are *u.* in their way.
14. 11, the tabernacle of the *u.*
15. 8, the prayer of the *u.* is his delight.
28. 10, the *u.* shall have good things.
Eccl. 7. 29, God hath made man *u.*
Cant. 1. 4, the *u.* love thee.
See Isa. 26. 7 ; Jer. 10. 5 ; Mic. 7. 2 ; Hab. 2. 4.

UPRIGHTLY. Ps. 58. 1 ; 75. 2, do ye judge *u.*?
84. 11, withhold no good from them that walk *u.*
Prov. 10. 9 ; 15. 21 ; 28. 18, he that walketh *u.*
Isa. 33. 15, he that speaketh *u.*
See Ps. 15. 2 ; Amos 5. 10 ; Mic. 2. 7 ; Gal. 2. 14.

UPRIGHTNESS. 1 Kings 3. 6, in *u.* of heart.
1 Chron. 29. 17, thou hast pleasure in *u.*
Job 4. 6, the *u.* of thy ways.
33. 23, to show unto man his *u.*
Ps. 25. 21, let *u.* preserve me.
143. 10, lead me into the land of *u.*
Prov. 2. 13, who leave the paths of *u.*
See Ps. 111. 8 ; Prov. 14. 2 ; 28. 6 ; Isa. 26. 7, 10.

UPROAR. Mat. 26. 5 ; Mk. 14. 2 ; Acts 17. 5 ; 21. 31.

UPWARD. Job 5. 7 ; Eccl. 3. 21 ; Isa. 38. 14.

URGE. Gen. 33. 11 ; 2 Kings 2. 17 ; Lu. 11. 53.

URGENT. Ex. 12. 33 ; Dan. 3. 22.

USE. Mat. 6. 7, *u.* not vain repetitions.
1 Cor. 7. 31, they that *u.* this world.
Gal. 5. 13, *u.* not liberty for an occasion.
1 Tim. 1. 8, if a man *u.* it lawfully.
See Ps. 119. 132 ; 1 Cor. 9. 12 ; 1 Tim. 5. 23.

USURP. 1 Tim. 2. 12, I suffer not a woman to *u.*

USURY. Ex. 22. 25, neither shalt thou lay upon him *u.*
Lev. 25. 36, take thou no *u.* of him.
Deut. 23. 20, thou mayest lend upon *u.*
Neh. 5. 7, ye exact *u.*
Ezek. 18. 8, not given forth upon *u.*
13, hath given forth upon *u.*
17, that hath not received *u.*
22. 12, thou hast taken *u.*
UTTER. Ps. 78. 2, I will *u.* dark sayings.
106. 2, who can *u.* the mighty acts?
119. 171, my lips shall *u.* praise.
Prov. 1. 20, wisdom *u.* her voice.
23. 33, thine heart shall *u.* perverse things.
29. 11, a fool *u.* all his mind.
Eccl. 5. 2, let not thine heart be hasty to *u.*
Rom. 8. 26, which cannot be *u.*
2 Cor. 12. 4, not lawful for a man to *u.*
Heb. 5. 11, many things hard to be *u.*
See Job 33. 3 ; Isa. 48. 20 ; Joel 2. 11 ; Mat. 13. 35.
UTTERANCE. Acts 2. 4, as the Spirit gave *u.*
See 1 Cor. 1. 5 ; 2 Cor. 8. 7 ; Eph. 6. 19 ; Col. 4. 3.
UTTERLY. Ps. 119. 8, forsake me not *u.*
Jer. 23. 39, I will *u.* forget you.
Zeph. 1. 2, I will *u.* consume all things.
2 Pet. 2. 12, these shall *u.* perish.
See Deut. 7. 2 ; Neh. 9. 31 ; Isa. 40. 30 ; Rev. 18. 8.
UTTERMOST. Mat. 5. 26 ; 1 Thess. 2. 16 ; Heb. 7. 25.

V.

VAGABOND. Gen. 4. 12, a *v.* shalt thou be in the earth.
See Ps. 109. 10 ; Acts 19. 13.
VAIL. Mat. 27. 51 ; 2 Cor. 3. 14 ; Heb. 6. 19.
VAIN. Ex. 5. 9, not regard *v.* words.
20. 7 ; Deut. 5. 11, shalt not take name of the Lord in *v.*
Deut. 32. 47, it is not a *v.* thing for you.
2 Sam. 6. 20, as one of the *v.* fellows.
2 Kings 18. 20 ; Isa. 36. 5, they are but *v.* words.
Job 11. 12, *v.* man would be wise.
16. 3, shall *v.* words have an end?
21. 34, how then comfort ye me in *v.*?
Ps. 2. 1 ; Acts 4. 25, the people imagine a *v.* thing.
26. 4, I have not sat with *v.* persons.
33. 17, an horse is a *v.* thing for safety.
39. 6, every man walketh in a *v.* show.
60. 11 ; 108. 12, *v.* is the help of man.
89. 47, wherefore hast thou made men in *v.*?
127. 1, labour in *v.*, the watchmen waketh in *v.*
Prov. 12. 11 ; 28. 19, followeth *v.* persons.
31. 30, beauty is *v.*
Eccl. 6. 12, all the days of his *v.* life.
Isa. 1. 13, bring no more *v.* oblations.
45. 18, he created it not in *v.*
19, I said not, seek ye me in *v.*
49. 4 ; 65. 23, laboured in *v.*
Jer. 3. 23, in *v.* is salvation hoped for.
10. 3, the customs of the people are *v.*
46. 11, in *v.* shalt thou use medicines.
Mal. 3. 14, ye have said, it is *v.* to serve God.
Mat. 6. 7, use not *v.* repetitions.
15. 9 ; Mk. 7. 7, in *v.* do they worship me.
Rom. 13. 4, he beareth not the sword in *v.*
1 Cor. 15. 2, unless ye have believed in *v.*
2 Cor. 6. 1, receive not the grace of God in *v.*
Gal. 2. 2, lest I should run in *v.*
Tit. 1. 10, unruly and *v.* talkers.
Jas. 1. 26, this man's religion is *v.*
1 Pet. 1. 18, redeemed from *v.* conversation.
See Prov. 1. 17 ; Rom. 1. 21 ; Gal. 5. 26 ; Phil. 2. 3.
VALIANT. 1 Sam. 18. 17, be *v.* for me.
1 Kings 1. 42, for thou art a *v.* man.
Isa. 10. 13, put down inhabitants like a *v.* man.
Jer. 9. 3, they are not *v.* for truth.
Heb. 11. 34, waxed *v.* in fight.
See Ps. 60. 12 ; 118. 15 ; Isa. 33. 7 ; Nah. 2. 3.
VALUE. Job 13. 4, physicians of no *v.*

Mat. 10. 31 ; Lu. 12. 7, of more *v.*
See Lev. 27. 16 ; Job 28. 16 ; Mat. 27. 9.
VANISH. Isa. 51. 6 ; 1 Cor. 13. 8 ; Heb. 8. 13.
VANITY. Job 7. 3, to possess months of *v.*
15. 31, *v.* shall be his recompence.
35. 13, God will not hear *v.*
Ps. 12. 2, speak *v.* every one with his neighbour.
39. 5, every man at his best state is *v.*
62. 9, are *v.*, lighter than *v.*
144. 4, man is like to *v.*
Prov. 13. 11, wealth gotten by *v.*
30. 8, remove from me *v.*
Eccl. 6. 11, many things increase *v.*
11. 10, childhood and youth are *v.*
Isa. 30. 28, with the sieve of *v.*
Jer. 18. 15, they have burned incense to *v.*
Hab. 2. 13, people shall weary themselves for *v.*
Rom. 8. 20, the creature was made subject to *v.*
Eph. 4. 17, walk in *v.* of mind.
2 Pet. 2. 18, great swelling words of *v.*
See Eccl. 1. 2 ; Jer. 10. 8 ; 14. 22 ; Acts 14. 15.
VAPOURS. Job 36. 27, according to the *v.* thereof.
Ps. 135. 7 ; Jer. 10. 13, he causeth the *v.* to ascend.
148. 8, snow and *v.*
VARIABLENESS. Jas. 1. 17, with whom is no *v.*
VARIANCE. Mat. 10. 35 ; Gal. 5. 20.
VAUNT. Judg. 7. 2 ; 1 Cor. 13. 4.
VEHEMENT. Cant. 8. 6 ; Mk. 14. 31 ; 2 Cor. 7. 11.
VENGEANCE. Deut. 32. 35, to me belongeth *v.*
Prov. 6. 34 ; Isa. 34. 8 ; 61. 2 ; Jer. 51. 6, the day of *v.*
Isa. 59. 17, garments of *v.* for clothing.
Acts 28. 4, whom *v.* suffereth not to live.
Jude 7, the *v.* of eternal fire.
See Mic. 5. 15 ; Nah. 1. 2 ; Lu. 21. 22 ; Rom. 12. 19.
VENISON. Gen. 25. 28, he did eat of his *v.*
27. 3, take me some *v.*
VERILY. Gen. 42. 21 ; Ps. 58. 11 ; 73. 13 ; Mk. 9. 12.
VERITY. Ps. 111. 7 ; 1 Tim. 2. 7.
VESSEL. 2 Kings 4. 6, there is not a *v.* more.
Ps. 31. 12, I am like a potter's *v.*
Isa. 66. 20, bring an offering in a clean *v.*
Jer. 22. 28, a *v.* wherein is no pleasure.
25. 34, fall like a pleasant *v.*
Mat. 13. 48, gathered the good into *v.*
25. 4, the wise took oil in their *v.*
Acts 9. 15, he is a chosen *v.* unto me.
Rom. 9. 22, the *v.* of wrath.
23. the *v.* of mercy.
1 Thess. 4. 4, to possess his *v.* in sanctification.
2 Tim. 2. 21, he shall be a *v.* to honour.
1 Pet. 3. 7, giving honour to the wife as to weaker *v.*
See Isa. 52. 11 ; 65. 4 ; Jer. 14. 3 ; Mk. 11. 16.
VESTRY. 2 Kings 10. 22, him that was over the *v.*
VESTURE. Gen. 41. 42 ; Ps. 22. 18 ; 102. 26 ; Mat. 27. 35 ; Heb. 1. 12 ; Rev. 19. 13.
VEX. Ex. 22. 21 ; Lev. 19. 33, not *v.* a stranger.
Num. 33. 55, those ye let remain shall *v.* you.
2 Sam. 12. 18, how will he *v.* himself?
Job 19. 2, how long will ye *v.* my soul?
Isa. 11. 13, Judah shall not *v.* Ephraim.
Ezek. 32. 9, I will *v.* the hearts of many.
Mat. 15. 22, my daughter is grievously *v.*
2 Pet. 2. 8, *v.* his righteous soul.
See Lev. 18. 18 ; Judg. 16. 16 ; Isa. 63. 10 ; Hab. 2. 7.
VEXATION. Eccl. 1. 14 ; 2. 22 ; Isa. 9. 1 ; 28. 19 ; 65. 14.
VICTORY. 2 Sam. 19. 2, *v.* was turned to mourning.
1 Chron. 29. 11, thine is the *v.*
Ps. 98. 1, hath gotten him the *v.*
Mat. 12. 20, send forth judgment unto *v.*
1 John 5. 4, this is the *v.*, even our faith.
See Isa. 25. 8 ; 1 Cor. 15. 54, 55, 57.
VICTUALS. Ex. 12. 39, neither had they prepared *v.*
Josh. 9. 14, the men took of their *v.*

Neh. 10. 31, bring *v.* on the sabbath.
13. 15, in the day wherein they sold *v.*
Mat. 14. 15 ; Lu. 9. 12, into villages to buy *v.*
See Gen. 14. 11 ; Judg. 17. 10 ; 1 Sam. 22. 10.

VIEW. Josh. 2. 7 ; 7. 2 ; 2 Kings 2. 7 ; Neh. 2. 13.

VIGILANT. 1 Tim. 3. 2 ; 1 Pet. 5. 8.

VILE. 1 Sam. 3. 13, made themselves *v.*
Job 18. 3, wherefore are we reputed *v.?*
40. 4, I am *v.*, what shall I answer thee ?
Ps. 15. 4 ; Isa. 32. 5 ; Dan. 11. 21, a *v.* person.
Jer. 15. 19, take the precious from the *v.*
Lam. 1. 11, see, O Lord, for I am become *v.*
Nah. 3. 6, I will make thee *v.*
Rom. 1. 26, gave them up to *v.* affections.
Phil. 3. 21, shall change our *v.* body.
Jas. 2. 2, a poor man in *v.* raiment.
See 2 Sam. 1. 21 ; Job 30. 8 ; Ps. 12. 8 ; Nah. 1. 14.

VILLANY. Isa. 32. 6 ; Jer. 29. 23.

VINE. Deut. 32. 32, their *v.* is of the *v.* of Sodom.
Judg. 13. 14, may not eat any thing that cometh
  of the *v.*
1 Kings 4. 25, dwelt every man under his *v.*
2 Kings 18. 31 ; Isa. 36. 16, eat every man of his
  own *v.*
Ps. 80. 8, a *v.* out of Egypt.
128. 3, thy wife as a fruitful *v.*
Isa. 24. 7, the new wine mourneth, the *v.* lan-
  guisheth.
Hos. 10. 1, Israel is an empty *v.*
Mic. 4. 4, they shall sit every man under his *v.*
Mat. 26. 29 ; Mk. 14. 25 ; Lu. 22. 18, this fruit of
  the *v.*
John 15. 1, I am the true *v.*
See Deut. 8. 8 ; Cant. 2. 15 ; Joel 1. 7 ; Hab. 3. 17.

VINTAGE. Job 24. 6 ; Isa. 16. 10 ; 32. 10 ; Mic. 7. 1.

VIOL. Isa. 5. 12 ; 14. 11 ; Amos 5. 23 ; 6. 5.

VIOLENCE. Gen. 6. 11, earth was filled with *v.*
Ps. 11. 5, him that loveth *v.*
55. 9, I have seen *v.* in the city.
58. 2, weigh the *v.* of your hands.
72. 14, redeem their soul from *v.*
73. 6, *v.* covereth them as a garment.
Prov. 4. 17, they drink the wine of *v.*
10. 6, *v.* covereth the mouth of the wicked.
Isa. 53. 9, because he had done no *v.*
60. 18, *v.* shall no more be heard.
Ezek. 8. 17 ; 28. 16, they have filled the land with *v.*
Amos 3. 10, store up *v.* in their palaces.
Hab. 1. 3, *v.* is before me.
Mal. 2. 16, one covereth *v.* with his garment.
Mat. 11. 12, kingdom of heaven suffereth *v.*
Lu. 3. 14, do *v.* to no man.
See Mic. 2. 2 ; 6. 12 ; Zeph. 1. 9 ; Heb. 11. 34.

VIOLENT. Ps. 7. 16, his *v.* dealing.
18. 48 ; 140. 1 ; Prov. 16. 29, the *v.* man.
See 2 Sam. 22. 49 ; Eccl. 5. 8 ; Mat. 11. 12.

VIOLENTLY. Isa. 22. 18 ; Mat. 8. 32 ; Mk. 5. 13.

VIRGIN. Isa. 23. 12 ; 47. 1 ; 62. 5 ; Jer. 14. 17.

VIRTUE. Mk. 5. 30 ; Lu. 6. 19 ; 8. 46 ; Phil. 4. 8 ;
  2 Pet. 1. 5.

VIRTUOUS. Ruth 3. 11 ; Prov. 12. 4 ; 31. 10, 29.

VISAGE. Isa. 52. 14 ; Lam. 4. 8 ; Dan. 3. 19.

VISION. Job 20. 8, as a *v.* of the night.
Prov. 29. 18, where there is no *v.*, people perish.
Isa. 22. 1, the valley of *v.*
28. 7, they err in *v.*
Lam. 2. 9, prophets find no *v.* from the Lord.
Hos. 12. 10, I have multiplied *v.*
Joel 2. 28 ; Acts 2. 17, young men shall see *v.*
Zech. 13. 4, ashamed every one of his *v.*
Mat. 17. 9, tell the *v.* to no man.
Lu. 24. 23, had seen a *v.* of angels.
Acts 26. 19, not disobedient to heavenly *v.*
See Job 4. 13 ; Ezek. 1. 1 ; 8. 3 ; Mic. 3. 6.

VISIT. Gen. 50. 24 ; Ex. 13. 19, God will *v.* you.
Ex. 20. 5 ; 34. 7 ; Num. 14. 18 ; Deut. 5. 9, *v.* the
  iniquity of the fathers.
32. 34, when I *v.*, I will *v.* their sin upon them.

Ruth 1. 6, how the Lord had *v.* his people.
Job 5. 24, thou shalt *v.* thy habitation.
7. 18, shouldest *v.* him every morning.
Ps. 8. 4 ; Heb. 2. 6, the son of man, that thou *v.*
  him.
106. 4, *v.* me with thy salvation.
Jer. 5. 9 ; 19. 9, shall I not *v.* for these things ?
29. 10, I will *v.*, and perform my good word.
Ezek. 38. 8, after many days thou shalt be *v.*
Mat. 25. 36, I was sick, and ye *v.* me.
Acts 15. 14, how God did *v.* the Gentiles.
Jas. 1. 27, to *v.* the fatherless and widows.
See Job 31. 14 ; Lu. 1. 68, 78 ; 7. 16.

VISITATION. Job 10. 12, thy *v.* hath preserved.
Isa. 10. 3 ; 1 Pet. 2. 12, in the day of *v.*
Jer. 8. 12 ; 10. 15 ; 46. 21 ; 50. 27 ; Lu. 19. 44, in the
  time of *v.*
See Num. 16. 29 ; Jer. 11. 23 ; Hos. 9. 7.

VOCATION. Eph. 4. 1, worthy of the *v.*

VOICE. Gen. 4. 10, *v.* of thy brother's blood.
27. 22, the *v.* is Jacob's *v.*
Ex. 23. 21, obey his *v.*, provoke him not.
24. 3, all the people answered with one *v.*
32. 18, it is not the *v.* of them that shout.
Deut. 4. 33, did ever people hear *v.* of God and live ?
Josh. 6. 10, nor make any noise with thy *v.*
1 Sam. 24. 16 ; 26. 17, is this thy *v.?*
1 Kings 19. 12, after the fire, a still small *v.*
2 Kings 4. 31, there was neither *v.* nor hearing.
Job 3. 7, let no joyful *v.* come therein.
30. 31, my organ into the *v.* of them that weep.
37. 4, a *v.* roareth.
40. 9, canst thou thunder with a *v.* like him ?
Ps. 5. 3, my *v.* shalt thou hear in the morning.
31. 22 ; 86. 6, the *v.* of my supplications.
42. 4, with the *v.* of joy.
95. 7, to day, if ye will hear his *v.*
103. 20, the *v.* of his word.
Prov. 1. 20, wisdom uttereth her *v.* in the streets.
5. 13, not obeyed the *v.* of my teachers.
8. 1, doth not understanding put forth her *v.?*
4, my *v.* is to the sons of man.
Eccl. 5. 3, a fool's *v.* is known.
12. 4, rise up at the *v.* of the bird.
Cant. 2. 8 ; 5. 2, the *v.* of my beloved.
12, the *v.* of the turtle is heard.
14, sweet is thy *v.*
Isa. 13. 2, exalt the *v.* unto them.
40. 3 ; Mat. 3. 3 ; Mk. 1. 3 ; Lu. 3. 4, *v.* of him that
  crieth.
6, the *v.* said, cry.
48. 20, with a *v.* of singing.
52. 8, with the *v.* together shall they sing.
65. 19, the *v.* of weeping shall be no more heard.
66. 6, a *v.* of noise, a *v.* from the temple.
Jer. 7. 34, the *v.* of mirth, and the *v.* of gladness.
30. 19, the *v.* of them that make merry.
48. 3, a *v.* of crying shall be.
Ezek. 23. 42, a *v.* of a multitude at ease.
33. 32, one that hath a pleasant *v.*
43. 2, *v.* like a noise of many waters.
Nah. 2. 7, lead her as with the *v.* of doves.
Mat. 12. 19, neither shall any man hear his *v.*
Lu. 23. 23, the *v.* of them and of the chief priests
  prevailed.
John 5. 25, the dead shall hear the *v.* of Son of God.
10. 4, the sheep follow, for they know his *v.*
5, they know not the *v.* of strangers.
12. 30, this *v.* came not because of me.
18. 37, every one that is of the truth heareth my *v.*
Acts 12. 14, and when she knew Peter's *v.*
26. 10, I gave my *v.* against them.
1 Cor. 14. 10, there are so many *v.* in the world.
19, that by my *v.* I might teach others.
Gal. 4. 20, I desire now to change my *v.*
1 Thess. 4. 16, descend with *v.* of archangel.
2 Pet. 2. 16, the dumb ass speaking with man's *v.*
Rev. 3. 20, if any man hear my *v.*
4. 5, out of the throne proceeded *v.*
See Gen. 3. 17 ; Ps. 58. 5 ; John 3. 29 ; Acts 12. 22.

VOID. Gen. 1. 2; Jer. 4. 23, without form, and v.
Deut. 32. 28, a people v. of counsel.
Ps. 89. 39, made v. the covenant.
119. 126, they have made v. thy law.
Prov. 11. 12, v. of wisdom.
Isa. 55. 11, my word shall not return to me v.
Jer. 19. 7, make v. the counsel of Judah.
Nah. 2. 10, empty, v., and waste.
Acts 24. 16, a conscience v. of offence.
See Num. 30. 12; Rom. 3. 31; 4. 14.
VOLUME. Ps. 40. 7; Heb. 10. 7.
VOLUNTARY. Lev. 1. 3; 7. 16; Ezek. 46. 12; Col. 2. 18.
VOMIT. Job 20. 15; Prov. 26. 11; 2 Pet. 2. 22.
VOW (n.). Gen. 28. 20; 31. 13, Jacob vowed a v.
Num. 29. 39, these ye shall do beside your v.
Deut. 12. 6, thither bring your v.
Judg. 11. 30, Jephthah vowed a v., and said.
39, her father did with her according to his v.
1 Sam. 1. 21, Elkanah went up to offer his v.
Job 22. 27, thou shalt pay thy v.
Ps. 22. 25; 66. 13; 116. 14, I will pay my v.
50. 14, pay thy v. unto the most High.
56. 12, thy v. are upon me, O God.
61. 5, for thou hast heard my v.
8, that I may daily perform my v.
65. 1, to thee shall the v. be performed.
Prov. 7. 14, this day have I paid my v.
20. 25, after v. to make enquiry.
31. 2, the son of my v.
Eccl. 5. 4, when thou vowest a v., defer not to pay.
Isa. 19. 21, they shall vow a v. unto the Lord.
Jonah 1. 16, feared the Lord, and made v.
Acts 18. 18, shorn his head, for he had a v.
21. 23, four men which have a v. on them.
See 2 Sam. 15. 7; Jer. 44. 25; Nah. 1. 15.
VOW (v.). Deut. 23. 22, if forbear to v., no sin.
Ps. 76. 11, v., and pay to the Lord your God.
132. 2, and v. to the mighty God.
See Num. 21. 2; Eccl. 5. 5; Jonah 2. 9.
VULTURE. Lev. 11. 14; Deut. 14. 13, and the v. after his kind.
Job 28. 7, which the v. eye hath not seen.
Isa. 34. 15, there shall the v. be.

W.

WAG. Jer. 18. 16; Lam. 2. 15; Zeph. 2. 15.
WAGES. Gen. 29. 15, what shall thy w. be?
30. 28, appoint me thy w.
31. 7, changed my w. ten times.
Ex. 2. 9, nurse this child, I will give w.
Jer. 22. 13, useth neighbour's service without w.
Hag. 1. 6, earneth w. to put in bag with holes.
Lu. 3. 14, be content with your w.
John 4. 36, he that reapeth receiveth w.
Rom. 6. 23, the w. of sin is death.
2 Pet. 2. 15, the w. of unrighteousness.
See Ezek. 29. 18; Mal. 3. 5; 2 Cor. 11. 8.
WAGONS. Gen. 45. 19; Num. 7. 7; Ezek. 23. 24.
WALL. Ezek. 22. 18, w. for the multitude.
Amos 5. 16, w. shall be in all streets.
Mic. 1. 8, therefore I will w. and howl.
Mat. 13. 42, there shall be w. and gnashing.
Mk. 5. 38, he seeth them that w. greatly.
Rev. 1. 7, all kindreds of the earth shall w.
18. 15, the merchants shall stand afar off w.
See Esth. 4. 3; Jer. 9. 10, 19, 20; Ezek. 7. 11.
WAIT. Gen. 49. 18, I have w. for thy salvation.
Num. 35. 20; Jer. 9. 8, by laying of w.
2 Kings 6. 33, should I w. for the Lord any longer?
Job 14. 14, I will w. till my change come.
15. 22, he is w. for of the sword.
17. 13, if I w., the grave is my house.
29. 21, to me men w., and kept silence.
23, they w. for me as for rain.
30. 26, when I w. for light, darkness came.
Ps. 25. 3; 69. 6, let none that w. be ashamed.
27. 14; 37. 34; Prov. 20. 22, w. on the Lord.
33. 20, our soul w. for the Lord.
37. 7, w. patiently.

Ps. 52. 9, I will w. on thy name.
62. 1; 130. 6, my soul w. upon God.
5, w. only on God.
65. 1, praise w. for thee in Zion.
69. 3, mine eyes fail while I w. for God.
104. 27, these all w. upon thee.
106. 13, they w. not for counsel.
123. 2, so our eyes w. on the Lord.
Prov. 27. 18, he that w. on his master.
Isa. 30. 18, the Lord w. to be gracious.
40. 31, they that w. on the Lord shall renew.
42. 4, the isles shall w. for his law.
59. 9, we w. for light.
64. 4, prepared for him that w. for him.
Lam. 3. 26, good that a man hope and quietly w.
Dan. 12. 12, blessed is he that w., and cometh to the days.
Hab. 2. 3, though the vision tarry, w. for it.
Zech. 11. 11, poor of the flock that w. upon me.
Mk. 15. 43, who also w. for the kingdom of God.
Lu. 2. 25, w. for the consolation of Israel.
12. 36, like unto men that w. for their lord.
Acts 1. 4, but w. for promise of the Father.
Rom. 8. 23, groan, w. for the adoption.
25, then do we with patience w. for it.
12. 7, let us w. on our ministering.
1 Cor. 9. 13, they which w. at the altar are partakers.
Gal. 5. 5, we w. for the hope.
1 Thess. 1. 10, to w. for his Son from heaven.
See Num. 3. 10; Neh. 12. 44; Isa. 8. 17.
WAKE. Ps. 139. 18, when I w. I am still with thee.
Jer. 51. 39, sleep a perpetual sleep, and not w.
Joel 3. 9, prepare war, w. up the mighty men.
Zech. 4. 1, the angel came again, and w. me.
1 Thess. 5. 10, whether we w. or sleep.
See Ps. 77. 4; 127. 1; Cant. 5. 2; Isa. 50. 4.
WALK. Gen. 17. 1, w. before me, and be perfect.
24. 40, the Lord before whom I w.
48. 15, before whom my fathers did w.
Ex. 16. 4, whether they will w. in my law.
18. 20, the way wherein they must w.
Lev. 26. 12, I will w. among you.
Deut. 23. 14, God w. in midst of the camp.
Judg. 5. 10, speak, ye that w. by the way.
2 Sam. 2. 29, Abner and his men w. all that night.
Job 18. 8, he w. on a snare.
22. 14, he w. in the circuit of heaven.
29. 3, when by his light I w. through darkness.
Ps. 23. 4, though I w. through the valley of the shadow of death.
26. 11, as for me, I will w. in mine integrity.
48. 12, w. about Zion, and go round about her.
55. 14, we w. to house of God in company.
56. 13, that I may w. before God in the light of the living.
84. 11, from them that w. uprightly.
91. 6, the pestilence that w. in darkness.
104. 3, who w. upon wings of the wind.
116. 9, I will w. before the Lord.
119. 45, I will w. at liberty.
138. 7, though I w. in the midst of trouble.
Prov. 10. 9; 28. 18, he that w. uprightly w. surely.
13. 20, he that w. with wise men shall be wise.
19. 1; 28. 6, better is the poor that w. in integrity.
28. 26, whoso w. wisely shall be delivered.
Eccl. 2. 14, the fool w. in darkness.
Isa. 2. 5, let us w. in the light of the Lord.
9. 2, the people that w. in darkness.
20. 3, as my servant hath w. naked and barefoot.
30. 21, a voice saying, this is the way, w. in it.
35. 9, the redeemed shall w. there.
50. 10, that w. in darkness, and hath no light.
11, w. in the light of your fire.
Jer. 6. 16, ask where is the good way, and w. therein.
10. 23, it is not in man that w. to direct his steps.
Ezek. 28. 14, hast w. in midst of stones of fire.
Dan. 4. 37, those that w. in pride.
Hos. 14. 9, the just shall w. in them.
Amos 3. 3, can two w. together?

Mic. 6. 8, to *w.* humbly with thy God.
Nah. 2. 11, where the lion *w.*
Zech. 1. 11, we have *w.* to and fro through the earth.
Mal. 3. 14, what profit that we have *w.* mournfully?
Mat. 9. 5; Mk. 2. 9; Lu. 5. 23; John 5. 8, 11, 12; Acts 3. 6, arise, and *w.*
12. 43; Lu. 11. 24, *w.* through dry places.
14. 29, he *w.* on the water.
Mk. 16. 12, he appeared to two of them, as they *w.*
Lu. 13. 33, I must *w.* to day and to morrow.
John 8. 12, shall not *w.* in darkness.
11. 9, if any man *w.* in the day.
Rom. 4. 12, who *w.* in steps of that faith.
6. 4, *w.* in newness of life.
8. 1, who *w.* not after the flesh, but after the Spirit.
2 Cor. 5. 7, we *w.* by faith.
Gal. 6. 16, as many as *w.* according to this rule.
Eph. 2. 2; Col. 3. 7, in time past ye *w.*
10, ordained that we should *w.* in them.
4. 1, *w.* worthy of the vocation.
17, that ye *w.* not as other Gentiles.
5. 15, *w.* circumspectly.
Phil. 3. 17, mark them which *w.*
18, many *w.,* of whom I told you.
Col. 1. 10; 1 Thess. 2. 12, that ye might *w.* worthy of the Lord.
1 Thess. 4. 1, how ye ought to *w.*
12, ye may *w.* honestly.
2 Thess. 3. 6, from every brother that *w.* disorderly.
1 Pet. 4. 3, when we *w.* in lasciviousness.
5. 8, *w.* about, seeking whom he may devour.
1 John 1. 7, if we *w.* in the light.
2. 6, to *w.,* even as he *w.*
See Gal. 5. 16; Eph. 5. 2; Phil. 3. 16.

WALKING. Deut. 2. 7, the Lord knoweth thy *w.*
Job 31. 26, the moon *w.* in brightness.
Dan. 3. 25, four men loose, *w.* in the fire.
Mat. 14. 25, Jesus went to them, *w.* on the sea.
Mk. 8. 24, I see men as trees, *w.*
Acts 9. 31, *w.* in the fear of the Lord.
See Isa. 3. 16; 2 Cor. 4. 2; 2 Pet. 3. 3; Jude 16.

WALL. Gen. 49. 22, branches run over the *w.*
Ex. 14. 22, the waters were a *w.* to them.
Num. 22. 24, a *w.* being on this side, a *w.* on that.
2 Sam. 22. 30; Ps. 18. 29, have I leaped over a *w.*
2 Kings 20. 2; Isa. 38. 11, turned his face to the *w.*
Ezra 5. 3, who commanded you to make this *w.?*
Neh. 4. 6, so built we the *w.*
Ps. 62. 3, a bowing *w.* shall ye be.
122. 7, peace be within thy *w.*
Prov. 24. 31, the *w.* thereof was broken down.
25. 28, like a city without *w.*
Isa. 26. 1, salvation will God appoint for *w.*
59. 10, we grope for the *w.*
60. 18, thou shalt call thy *w.* Salvation.
Ezek. 8. 7, a hole in the *w.*
Dan. 5. 5, fingers wrote on the *w.*
Amos 5. 19, leaned hand on *w.,* and serpent bit him.
Hab. 2. 11, the stone shall cry out of the *w.*
Acts 23. 3, thou whited *w.*
Eph. 2. 14, the middle *w.* of partition.
See Ezek. 38. 11; Zech. 2. 4; Acts 9. 15; Rev. 21. 14.

WALLOW. Jer. 6. 26; 25. 34, *w.* in ashes.
2 Pet. 2. 22, washed, to her *w.* in the mire.
See 2 Sam. 20. 12; Ezek. 27. 30.

WANDER. Num. 14. 33, your children shall *w.*
Deut. 27. 18, cursed be he that maketh blind to *w.*
Job 12. 24, he causeth them to *w.*
15. 23, he *w.* abroad for bread.
38. 41, young ravens *w.* for lack of meat.
Ps. 55. 7, then would I *w.* far off.
59. 15, let them *w.* up and down.
119. 10, let me not *w.* from thy commandments.
Prov. 27. 8, as a bird that *w.* from nest.
Isa. 16. 3, bewray not him that *w.*
47. 15, *w.* every one to his quarter.
Jer. 14. 10, thus have they loved to *w.*

Lam. 4. 14, they have *w.* as blind men.
Ezek. 34. 6, my sheep *w.* through mountains.
Amos 4. 8, two cities *w.* to one city to drink.
See Hos. 9. 17; 1 Tim. 5. 13; Heb. 11. 37; Jude 13.

WANT (*n.*). Deut. 28. 48, thou shalt serve in *w.*
Judg. 18. 10, a place where there is no *w.*
19. 20, let all thy *w.* lie on me.
Job 24. 8, they embrace the rock for *w.*
31. 19, if I have seen any perish for *w.*
Ps. 34. 9, there is no *w.* to them that fear him.
Amos 4. 6, I have given you *w.* of bread.
Mk. 12. 44, she of her *w.* cast in all.
Lu. 15. 14, he began to be in *w.*
Phil. 2. 25, that ministered to my *w.*
See Prov. 6. 11; Lam. 4. 9; 2 Cor. 8. 14; Phil. 4. 11.

WANT (*v.*). Ps. 23. 1, I shall not *w.*
34. 10, shall not *w.* any good thing.
Prov. 9. 4, for him that *w.* understanding.
10. 19, in multitude of words there *w.* not sin.
13. 25, the belly of the wicked shall *w.*
Eccl. 6. 2, he *w.* nothing for his soul.
Isa. 34. 16, none shall *w.* her mate.
Jer. 44. 18, we have *w.* all things.
Ezek. 4. 17, that they may *w.* bread and water.
John 2. 3, when they *w.* wine.
2 Cor. 11. 9, when I *w.,* I was chargeable to no man.
See Eccl. 1. 15; Dan. 5. 27; Tit. 1. 5; Jas. 1. 4.

WANTON. Isa. 3. 16; Rom. 13. 13; 1 Tim. 5. 11; Jas. 5. 5.

WAR (*n.*). Ex. 32. 17, there is a noise of *w.*
Num. 32. 6, shall your brethren go to *w.,* and shall ye sit here?
Deut. 24. 5, taken a wife, he shall not go out to *w.*
Judg. 5. 8, then was *w.* in the gates.
1 Chron. 5. 22, many slain, because the *w.* was of God.
Job 10. 17, changes and *w.* are against me.
38. 23, reserved against the day of *w.*
Ps. 27. 3, though *w.* should rise against me.
46. 9, he maketh *w.* to cease.
55. 21, *w.* was in his heart.
68. 30, scatter the people that delight in *w.*
Prov. 20. 18, with good advice make *w.*
Eccl. 3. 8, a time of *w.*
8. 8, no discharge in that *w.*
Isa. 2. 4; Mic. 4. 3, nor learn *w.* any more.
Jer. 42. 14, to Egypt, where we shall see no *w.*
Mic. 2. 8, as men averse from *w.*
Mat. 24. 6; Mk. 13. 7; Lu. 21. 9, *w.* and rumours of *w.*
Lu. 14. 31, what king, going to make *w.?*
Jas. 4. 1, from whence come *w.?*
Rev. 12. 7, there was *w.* in heaven.
See Eccl. 9. 18; Ezek. 32. 27; Dan. 7. 21; 9. 26.

WAR (*v.*). 2 Sam. 22. 35; Ps. 18. 34; 144. 1, teacheth my hands to *w.*
2 Chron. 6. 34, if thy people go to *w.*
Isa. 41. 12, they that *w.* against thee.
2 Cor. 10. 3, we do not *w.* after the flesh.
1 Tim. 1. 18, *w.* a good warfare.
2 Tim. 2. 4, no man that *w.* entangleth himself.
Jas. 4. 1, lusts that *w.* in your members.
2, ye fight and *w.,* yet ye have not.
1 Pet. 2. 11, from lusts which *w.* against the soul.
See 1 Kings 14. 19; Isa. 37. 8; Rom. 7. 23.

WARDROBE. 2 Kings 22. 14; 2 Chron. 34. 22.

WARE. Mat. 24. 50; Lu. 8. 27; 2 Tim. 4. 15.

WARFARE. Isa. 40. 2, that her *w.* is accomplished.
2 Cor. 10. 4, weapons of our *w.* are not carnal.
See 1 Sam. 28. 1; 1 Cor. 9. 7; 1 Tim. 1. 18.

WARM. Eccl. 4. 11, how can one be *w.* alone?
Isa. 47. 14, there shall not be a coal to *w.* at.
Hag. 1. 6, ye clothe you, but there is none *w.*
Mk. 14. 54; John 18. 18, Peter *w.* himself.
Jas. 2. 16, be ye *w.* and filled.
See 2 Kings 4. 34; Job 37. 17; 39. 14; Isa. 44. 15.

WARN. Ezek. 3. 18; Acts 20. 31; 1 Thess. 5. 14.

WASH. 2 Kings 5. 10, go, *w.* in Jordan.
12, may I not *w.* in them, and be clean?

Job 9. 30, if I *w.* myself with snow water.
14. 19, thou *w.* away things which grow.
29. 6, when I *w.* my steps with butter.
Ps. 26. 6 ; 73. 13, I will *w.* my hands in innocency.
51. 2, *w.* me throughly from mine iniquity.
7, *w.* me, and I shall be whiter than snow.
Prov. 30. 12, a generation not *w.*
Cant. 5. 12, his eyes are *w.* with milk.
Isa. 1. 16, *w.* you, make you clean.
Jer. 2. 22, though thou *w.* thee with nitre.
4. 14, *w.* thy heart.
Ezek. 16. 4, nor wast *w.* in water to supple thee.
Mat. 6. 17, when thou fastest, *w.* thy face.
27. 24, took water, and *w.* his hands.
Mk. 7. 3, except they *w.* oft, eat not.
Lu. 7. 38, began to *w.* his feet with tears.
44, she hath *w.* my feet with her tears.
John 9. 7, go, *w.* in the pool of Siloam.
Acts 16. 33, he *w.* their stripes.
22. 16, *w.* away thy sins.
1 Cor. 6. 11, but ye are *w.*
Heb. 10. 22, having our bodies *w.* with pure water.
2 Pet. 2. 22, the sow that was *w.*
Rev. 1. 5, that *w.* us from our sins.
7. 14, have *w.* their robes.
See Neh. 4. 23 ; Eph. 5. 26 ; Tit. 3. 5 ; Heb. 9. 10.
WASTE. Deut. 32. 10 ; Job 30. 3, in *w.* wilderness.
1 Kings 17. 14, the barrel of meal shall not *w.*
Ps. 80. 13, the boar out of the wood doth *w.* it.
91. 6, nor for the destruction that *w.* at noonday.
Isa. 24. 1, the Lord maketh the earth *w.*
61. 4, they shall build the old *w.*
Joel 1. 10, the field is *w.*, the corn is *w.*
See Prov. 18. 9 ; Isa. 59. 7 ; Mat. 26. 8 ; Mk. 14. 4.
WATCH (*n.*). Ps. 90. 4, as a *w.* in the night.
119. 148, mine eyes prevent the night *w.*
Jer. 51. 12, make the *w.* strong.
Hab. 2. 1, I will stand upon my *w.*
See Mat. 14. 25 ; 24. 43 ; 27. 65 ; Lu. 2. 8.
WATCH (*v.*). Gen. 31. 49, the Lord *w.* between
me and thee.
Job 14. 16, dost thou not *w.* over my sin ?
Ps. 37. 32, the wicked *w.* the righteous.
102. 7, I *w.*, and am as a sparrow.
130. 6, more than they that *w.* for morning.
Isa. 29. 20, all that *w.* for iniquity are cut off.
Jer. 20. 10, my familiars *w.* for my halting.
31. 28, so will I *w.* over them, to build.
44. 27, I will *w.* over them for evil.
Ezek. 7. 6, the end is come, it *w.* for thee.
Hab. 2. 1, I will *w.* to see what he will say.
Mat. 24. 42 ; 25. 13 ; Mk. 13. 35 ; Lu. 21. 36 ; Acts
20. 31, *w.* therefore.
26. 41 ; Mk. 13. 33 ; 14. 38, *w.* and pray.
1 Thess. 5. 6 ; 1 Pet. 4. 7, let us *w.* and be sober.
Heb. 13. 17, for they *w.* for your souls.
See 1 Cor. 16. 13 ; 2 Tim. 4. 5 ; Rev. 3. 2 ; 16. 15.
WATCH TOWER. 2 Chron 20. 24, Judah came toward the *w.*
Isa. 21. 5, watch in the *w.*
WATER (*n.*). Gen. 26. 20, the *w.* is ours.
49. 4, unstable as *w.*
Deut. 8. 7, a land of brooks of *w.*
11. 11, the land drinketh *w.* of rain of heaven.
Josh. 7. 5, their hearts melted, and became as *w.*
2 Sam. 14. 14, as *w.* spilt on the ground.
1 Kings 13. 22, eat no bread, and drink no *w.*
22, 27 ; 2 Chron. 18. 26, *w.* of affliction.
2 Kings 3. 11, who poured *w.* on Elijah's hands.
20. 20, brought *w.* into the city.
Neh. 9. 11, threwest, as a stone into mighty *w.*
Job 8. 11, can the flag grow without *w.* ?
14. 9, through the scent of *w.* it will bud.
19, the *w.* wear the stones.
15. 16, who drinketh iniquity like *w.*
22. 7, thou hast not given *w.* to weary to drink.
26. 8, he bindeth up the *w.* in his thick clouds.
38. 30, the *w.* are hid as with a stone.
Ps. 22. 14, I am poured out like *w.*
23. 2, beside the still *w.*

Ps. 33. 7, he gathereth the *w.* of the sea.
46. 3, though the *w.* roar and be troubled.
63. 1, a dry and thirsty land, where no *w.* is.
73. 10, *w.* of a full cup are wrung out to them.
77. 16, the *w.* saw thee.
79. 3, their blood have they shed like *w.*
124. 4, then the *w.* had overwhelmed us.
148. 4, praise him, ye *w.* above the heavens.
Prov. 5. 15, drink *w.* out of thine own cistern.
9. 17, stolen *w.* are sweet.
20. 5, counsel is like deep *w.*
25. 25, as cold *w.* to a thirsty soul.
27. 19, as in *w.* face answereth to face.
30. 4, who hath bound the *w.* in a garment ?
Eccl. 11. 1, cast thy bread upon the *w.*
Cant. 4. 15 ; John 7. 38, well of living *w.*
8. 7, many *w.* cannot quench love.
Isa. 1. 22, thy wine is mixed with *w.*
3. 1, take away the whole stay of *w.*
11. 9 ; Hab. 2. 14, as the *w.* cover the seas.
19. 5, the *w.* shall fail from the sea.
28. 17, *w.* shall overflow the hiding place.
32. 20, blessed are ye that sow beside all *w.*
33. 16, his *w.* shall be sure.
35. 6, in the wilderness shall *w.* break out.
41. 17, when the poor seek *w.*
43. 2, when thou passest through the *w.*
16, a path in the mighty *w.*
20, I give *w.* in the wilderness.
44. 3, I will pour *w.* on him that is thirsty.
55. 1, come ye to the *w.*
57. 20, whose *w.* cast up mire and dirt.
Jer. 2. 13 ; 17. 13, the fountain of living *w.*
9. 1, Oh that my head were *w.* !
14. 3, their nobles sent little ones to the *w.*
47. 2, behold, *w.* rise up out of the north.
Ezek. 4. 17, that they may want bread and *w.*
7. 17 ; 21. 7, be weak as *w.*
31. 4, the *w.* made him great.
36. 25, then will I sprinkle clean *w.* upon you.
Amos 8. 11, not famine of bread nor thirst for *w.*
Mat. 3. 11 ; Mk. 1. 8 ; Lu. 3. 16 ; John 1. 26 ; Acts
1. 5 ; 11. 16, baptize you with *w.*
10. 42 ; Mk. 9. 41, whoso giveth a cup of cold *w.*
14. 28, bid me come to thee on the *w.*
27. 24, Pilate took *w.*, and washed.
Lu. 8. 23, ship filled with *w.*
24, and rebuked the raging of the *w.*
16. 24, dip the tip of his finger in *w.*
John 3. 5, except a man be born of *w.*
23, there was much *w.* there.
4. 15, give me this *w.*
5. 3, waiting for moving of the *w.*
19. 34, forthwith came out blood and *w.*
Acts 10. 47, can any forbid *w.* ?
2 Cor. 11. 26, in perils of *w.*
Eph. 5. 26, cleanse it with washing of *w.*
1 Pet. 3. 20, eight souls were saved by *w.*
2 Pet. 2. 17, wells without *w.*
1 John 5. 6, this is he that came by *w.*
Rev. 22. 17, let him take the *w.* of life freely.
See Ps. 29. 3 ; Jer. 51. 13 ; Ezek. 32. 2 ; 47. 1.
WATER (*v.*). Gen. 2. 6, mist that *w.* face of
ground.
13. 10, the plain was well *w.*
Deut. 11. 10, *w.* it with thy foot, as a garden.
Ps. 6. 6, I *w.* my couch with tears.
72. 6, as showers that *w.* the earth.
104. 13, he *w.* the hills from his chambers.
Prov. 11. 25, he that *w.*, shall be *w.*
Isa. 16. 9, I will *w.* thee with my tears.
27. 3, I will *w.* it every moment.
55. 10, returneth not, but *w.* the earth.
58. 11 ; Jer. 31. 12. thou shalt be like a *w.* garden.
Ezek. 32. 6, I will also *w.* with thy blood.
1 Cor. 3. 6, Apollos *w.*, but God gave the increase.
See Ps. 65. 9 ; Ezek. 17. 7 ; Joel 3. 18.
WAVERING. Heb. 10. 23, the profession of our
faith without *w.*
Jas. 1. 5, ask in faith, nothing *w.*

WAVES. Ps. 42. 7, all thy *w.* are gone over me.
65. 7 ; 89. 9 ; 107. 29, stilleth noise of *w.*
93. 4, the Lord is mightier than mighty *w.*
Isa. 48. 18, thy righteousness as the *w.* of the sea.
Jer. 5. 22, though the *w.* toss.
Zech. 10. 11, shall smite the *w.* in the sea.
Jude 13, raging *w.* of the sea.
See Mat. 8. 24 ; 14. 24 ; Mk. 4. 37 ; Acts 27. 41.

WAX (*n.*). Ps. 22. 14 ; 68. 2 ; 97. 5 ; Mic. 1. 4.

WAX (*v.*). Ex. 22. 24 ; 32. 10, my wrath shall *w.* hot.
Num. 11. 23, is the Lord's hand *w.* short?
Deut. 8. 4 ; 29. 5 ; Neh. 9. 21, raiment *w.* not old.
32. 15, Jeshurun *w.* fat, and kicked.
Ps. 102. 26 ; Isa. 50. 9 ; 51. 6 ; Heb. 1. 11, shall *w.*
  old as doth a garment.
Mat. 24. 12, the love of many shall *w.* cold.
Lu. 12. 33, bags which *w.* not old.
See Mat. 13. 15 ; 1 Tim. 5. 11 ; 2 Tim. 3. 13.

WAY. Gen. 6. 12, all flesh had corrupted his *w.*
24. 20, if God will keep me in this *w.*
56, seeing the Lord hath prospered my *w.*
Num. 22. 32, thy *w.* is perverse.
Deut. 8. 6 ; 26. 17 ; 28. 9 ; 30. 16 ; 1 Kings 2. 3 ; Ps.
  119. 3 ; 128. 1 ; Isa. 42. 24, walk in his *w.*
Josh. 23. 14 ; 1 Kings 2. 2, the *w.* of all the earth.
1 Sam. 12. 23, teach you the good and right *w.*
2 Sam. 22. 31 ; Ps. 18. 30, as for God, his *w.* is
  perfect.
2 Kings 7. 15, all the *w.* was full of garments.
2 Chron. 6. 27, when thou hast taught them the
  good *w.*
Ezra 8. 21, to seek of him a right *w.*
Job 3. 23, to a man whose *w.* is hid.
12. 24 ; Ps. 107. 40, to wander where there is no *w.*
16. 22, I go the *w.* whence I shall not return.
19. 8, fenced up my *w.*
22. 15, hast thou marked the old *w.*?
23. 10, he knoweth the *w.* that I take.
24. 13, they know not the *w.* of the light.
31. 4, doth not he see my *w.*?
38. 19, where is the *w.* where light dwelleth?
Ps. 1. 6, the Lord knoweth the *w.* of the righteous.
2. 12, lest ye perish from the *w.*
25. 9, the meek will he teach his *w.*
27. 11 ; 86. 11, teach me thy *w.*
36. 4, in a *w.* that is not good.
37. 5, commit thy *w.* unto the Lord.
39. 1, I will take heed to my *w.*
49. 13, this their *w.* is their folly.
67. 2, that thy *w.* may be known.
78. 50, he made a *w.* to his anger.
95. 10 ; Heb. 3. 10, they have not known my *w.*
101. 2, behave wisely in a perfect *w.*
119. 5, O that my *w.* were directed.
30, I have chosen the *w.* of truth.
59, I thought on my *w.*
168, all my *w.* are before thee.
139. 24, lead me in the *w.* everlasting.
Prov. 2. 8, he preserveth the *w.* of his saints.
3. 6, in all thy *w.* acknowledge him.
17, her *w.* are *w.* of pleasantness.
5. 21, the *w.* of man are before the Lord.
6. 6, consider her *w.*, and be wise.
23 ; 15. 24 ; Jer. 21. 8, the *w.* of life.
12. 15, the *w.* of a fool is right in his own eyes.
15. 19, the *w.* of the slothful man.
16. 7, when a man's *w.* please the Lord.
22. 6, train up a child in the *w.*
23. 19, guide thy heart in the *w.*
26, let thine eyes observe my *w.*
26. 13, there is a lion in the *w.*
Eccl. 11. 5, the *w.* of the spirit.
12. 5, fears shall be in the *w.*
Isa. 2. 3 ; Mic. 4. 2, he will teach us of his *w.*
30. 21, this is the *w.*, walk ye in it.
35. 8, and a *w.*, called the *w.* of holiness.
40. 27, my *w.* is hid from the Lord.
42. 16, the blind by a *w.* they knew not.
24, they would not walk in his *w.*
45. 13, I will direct all his *w.*

Isa. 55. 8, neither are your *w.* my *w.*
58. 2, they delight to know my *w.*
Jer. 6. 16, where is the good *w.*?
17. 10 ; 32. 19, every man according to his *w.*
18. 11, make your *w.* and doings good.
32. 39, I will give them one heart and one *w.*
50. 5, they shall ask the *w.* to Zion.
Ezek. 3. 18, to warn the wicked from his *w.*
18. 29, are not my *w.* equal? are not your *w.*
  unequal?
Joel 2. 7, march every one on his *w.*
Nah. 1. 3, the Lord hath his *w.* in the whirlwind.
Hag. 1. 5, consider your *w.*
Mal. 3. 1, he shall prepare the *w.* before me.
Mat. 7. 13, broad is the *w.* that leadeth.
10. 5, go not into *w.* of Gentiles.
22. 16 ; Mk. 12. 14 ; Lu. 20. 21, teachest the *w.* of
  God.
Mk. 8. 3, they will faint by the *w.*
11. 8 ; Mat. 21. 8 ; Lu. 19. 36, spread garments in
  the *w.*
Lu. 15. 20, when he was yet a great *w.* off.
19. 4, he was to pass that *w.*
John 10. 1, but climbeth up some other *w.*
14. 4, and the *w.* ye know.
6, I am the *w.*, the truth, and the life.
Acts 9. 2, if he found any of this *w.*
27, how he had seen the Lord in the *w.*
16. 17, which show unto us the *w.* of salvation.
18. 26, expounded the *w.* of God more perfectly.
19. 23, no small stir about that *w.*
24. 14, after the *w.* which they call heresy.
Rom. 3. 12, they are all gone out of the *w.*
11. 33, his *w.* are past finding out.
1 Cor. 10. 13, will make a *w.* to escape.
12. 31, a more excellent *w.*
Col. 2. 14, took handwriting of ordinances out of
  the *w.*
Heb. 5. 2, compassion on them out of the *w.*
9. 8, the *w.* into the holiest.
10. 20, by a new and living *w.*
Jas. 1. 8, unstable in all his *w.*
5. 20, the sinner from error of his *w.*
2 Pet. 2. 2, many shall follow their pernicious *w.*
15, which have forsaken the right *w.*
21, better not to have known *w.* of righteousness.
Jude 11, they have gone in the *w.* of Cain.
See Hos. 2. 6 ; Lu. 10. 31 ; Rev. 15. 3.

WEAK. Judg. 16. 7, *w.* as other men.
2 Sam. 3. 1, Saul's house waxed *w.* and *w.*
2 Chron. 15. 7, let not your hands be *w.*
Job 4. 3, thou hast strengthened the *w.* hands.
Ps. 6. 2, I am *w.*
Isa. 14. 10, art thou also become *w.* as we?
35. 3, strengthen ye the *w.* hands.
Ezek. 7. 17 ; 21. 7, shall be *w.* as water.
16. 30, how *w.* is thy heart!
Joel 3. 10, let the *w.* say, I am strong.
Mat. 26. 41 ; Mk. 14. 38, but the flesh is *w.*
Acts 20. 35, ye ought to support the *w.*
Rom. 4. 19, being not *w.* in faith.
8. 3, for the law was *w.*
1 Cor. 1. 27, *w.* things to confound the mighty.
11. 30, for this cause many are *w.*
2 Cor. 10. 10, his bodily presence is *w.*
11. 29, who is *w.*, and I am not *w.*?
12. 10, when I am *w.*, then am I strong.
Gal. 4. 9, turn again to *w.* elements.
1 Pet. 3. 7, giving honour to the wife, as *w.* vessel.
See Job 12. 21 ; Jer. 38. 4 ; Rom. 15. 1 ; 1 Thess. 5. 14.

WEAKNESS. 1 Cor. 1. 25, the *w.* of God.
2. 3, I was with you in *w.*
15. 43, it is sown in *w.*, raised in power.
See 2 Cor. 12. 9 ; 13. 4 ; Heb. 7. 18 ; 11. 34.

WEALTH. Deut. 8. 18, Lord giveth power to get *w.*
1 Sam. 2. 32, thou shalt see an enemy in all the *w.*
2 Chron. 1. 11, thou hast not asked *w.*
Esth. 10. 3, seeking the *w.* of his people.
Job 21. 13, they spend their days in *w.*
31. 25, if I rejoiced because my *w.* was great.

Ps. 44. 12, dost not increase *w.* by price.
49. 6, they that trust in *w.*
10, wise men die, and leave *w.* to others.
112. 3, *w.* and riches shall be in his house.
Prov. 5. 10, lest strangers be filled with thy *w.*
10. 15 ; 18. 11, the rich man's *w.* is his strong city.
13. 11, *w.* gotten by vanity.
19. 4, *w.* maketh many friends.
Acts 19. 25, by this craft we have our *w.*
1 Cor. 10. 24, seek every man another's *w.*
See Deut. 8. 17 ; Ruth 2. 1 ; Ezra 9. 12 ; Zech. 14. 14.
WEALTHY. Ps. 66. 12 ; Jer. 49. 31.
WEANED. 1 Sam. 1. 22 ; Ps. 131. 2 ; Isa. 11. 8 ; 28. 9.
WEAPON. Neh. 4. 17, with the other hand held a *w.*
Isa. 13. 5 ; Jer. 50. 25, the *w.* of his indignation.
54. 17, no *w.* formed against thee shall prosper.
Jer. 22. 7, every one with his *w.*
Ezek. 9. 1, with destroying *w.* in his hand.
2 Cor. 10. 4, the *w.* of our warfare.
See Job 20. 24 ; Ezek. 39. 9 ; John 18. 3.
WEAR. Job 14. 19, the waters *w.* the stones.
Isa. 4. 1, we will *w.* our own apparel.
Zech. 13. 4, nor shall they *w.* a rough garment.
Mat. 11. 8, that *w.* soft clothing.
See Deut. 22. 5 ; Esth. 6. 8 ; Lu. 9. 12 ; 1 Pet. 3. 3.
WEARINESS. Eccl. 12. 12 ; Mal. 1. 13 ; 2 Cor. 11. 27.
WEARY. Gen. 27. 46, I am *w.* of my life.
2 Sam. 23. 10, he smote till his hand was *w.*
Job 3. 17, and the *w.* be at rest.
10. 1, my soul is *w.*
16. 7, now he hath made me *w.*
22. 7, thou hast not given water to the *w.*
Ps. 6. 6, I am *w.* with groaning.
Prov. 3. 11, be not *w.* of the Lord's correction.
25. 17, lest he be *w* of thee.
Isa. 5. 27, none shall be *w.* among them.
7. 13, will ye *w.* my God also ?
28. 12, cause the *w.* to rest.
32. 2, as the shadow of a great rock in *w.* land.
40. 28, God fainteth not, neither is *w.*
31, they shall run, and not be *w.*
43. 22, thou hast been *w.* of me.
46. 1, a burden to the *w.* beast.
50. 4, a word in season to him that is *w.*
Jer. 6. 11, I am *w.* with holding in.
15. 6, I am *w.* with repenting.
20. 9, I was *w.* with forbearing.
31. 25, I have satiated the *w.* soul.
Lu. 18. 5, lest she *w.* me.
Gal. 6. 9 ; 2 Thess. 3. 13, be not *w.* in well doing.
See Judg. 4. 21 ; Ps. 68. 9 ; 69. 3 ; Hab. 2. 13.
WEARY (*v.*). Isa. 43. 24, thou hast *w.* me.
47. 13, *w.* in the multitude of counsels.
57. 10, *w.* in the greatness of thy way.
Jer. 12. 5, with footmen, and they *w.* thee.
Ezek. 24. 12, she hath *w.* herself with lies.
Mic. 6. 3, wherein have I *w.* thee ?
John 4. 6, being *w.,* sat thus on the well.
Heb. 12. 3, lest ye be *w.* and faint.
See Eccl. 10. 15 ; Jer. 4. 31 ; Mal. 2. 17.
WEASEL. Lev. 11. 29.
WEATHER. Job 37. 22 ; Prov. 25. 20 ; Mat. 16. 2.
WEB. Judg. 16. 13 ; Job 8. 14 ; Isa. 59. 5.
WEDGE. Josh. 7. 21 ; Isa. 13. 12.
WEEK. Gen. 29. 27, fulfil her *w.*
Jer. 5. 24, the appointed *w.* of harvest.
Dan. 9. 27, in the midst of the *w.*
Mat. 28. 1 ; Mk. 16. 2, 9 ; Lu. 24. 1 ; John 20. 1, 19 ;
Acts 20. 7 ; 1 Cor. 16. 2, the first day of the *w.*
See Num. 28. 26 ; Dan. 10. 2 ; Lu. 18. 12.
WEEP. Gen. 43. 30, he sought where to *w.*
1 Sam. 1. 8 ; John 20. 13, why *w.* thou ?
11. 5, what aileth the people that they *w.* ?
30. 4, no more power to *w.*
Neh. 8. 9, mourn not, nor *w.*
Job 27. 15, his widows shall not *w.*
30. 25, did not I *w.* for him that was in trouble ?
Eccl. 3. 4, a time to *w.*
Isa. 15. 2, he is gone up to *w.*
22. 4, I will *w.* bitterly.

Isa. 30. 19, thou shalt *w.* no more.
Jer. 9. 1, that I might *w.* day and night.
22. 10, *w.* ye not for the dead.
Joel 1. 5, awake, ye drunkards, and *w.*
Mk. 5. 39, why make ye this ado, and *w.* ?
Lu. 6. 21, blessed are ye that *w.* now.
7. 13 ; 8. 52 ; Rev. 5. 5, *w.* not.
23. 28, *w.* not for me, but *w.* for yourselves.
John 11. 31, she goeth to the grave to *w.* there.
Acts 21. 13, what mean ye to *w.* ?
Rom. 12. 15, and *w.* with them that *w.*
See John 16. 20 ; 1 Cor. 7. 30 ; Jas. 4. 9 ; 5. 1.
WEEPING. 2 Sam. 15. 30, *w.* as they went.
Ezra 3. 13, could not discern noise of joy from *w.*
Job 16. 16, my face is foul with *w.*
Ps. 6. 8, the Lord hath heard the voice of my *w.*
30. 5, *w.* may endure for a night.
102. 9, I have mingled my drink with *w.*
Isa. 65. 19, the voice of *w.* be no more heard.
Jer. 31. 16, restrain thy voice from *w.*
48. 5, continual *w.* shall go up.
Joel 2. 12, turn to me with fasting and *w.*
Mat. 8. 12 ; 22. 13 ; 24. 51 ; 25. 30 ; Lu. 13. 28, *w.*
and gnashing of teeth.
Lu. 7. 38, stood at his feet behind him *w.*
John 11. 33, when Jesus saw her *w.*
20. 11, Mary stood without at sepulchre *w.*
Phil. 3. 18, now tell you even *w.*
See Num. 25. 6 ; Jer. 31. 15 ; Mal. 2. 13 ; Mat. 2. 18 ;
Acts 9. 39.
WEIGH. 2 Sam. 14. 26, *w.* the hair of his head.
Job 6. 2, oh that my grief were *w.* !
31. 6, let me be *w.* in an even balance.
Isa. 26. 7, thou dost *w.* the path of the just.
40. 12, who hath *w.* the mountains ?
Dan. 5. 27, thou art *w.* in the balances.
See Job 28. 25 ; Prov. 16. 2 ; Zech. 11. 12.
WEIGHT. Lev. 26. 26, deliver your bread by *w.*
Job 28. 25, to make the *w.* for the winds.
Ezek. 4. 10, thy meat shall be by *w.*
16, they shall eat bread by *w.*
2 Cor. 4. 17, a more exceeding *w.* of glory.
Heb. 12. 1, lay aside every *w.*
See Deut. 25. 13 ; Prov. 16. 11 ; Mic. 6. 11.
WEIGHTY. Prov. 27. 3 ; Mat. 23. 23 ; 2 Cor. 10. 10.
WELFARE. Neh. 2. 10, to seek *w.* of Israel.
Job 30. 15, my *w.* passeth away.
Ps. 69. 22, which should have been for their *w.*
Jer. 38. 4, seeketh not the *w.* of this people.
See Gen. 43. 27 ; Ex. 18. 7 ; 1 Chron. 18. 10.
WELL (*n.*). Num. 21. 17, spring up, O *w.*
Deut. 6. 11, and *w.* which thou diggedst not.
2 Sam. 23. 15 ; 1 Chron. 11. 17, water of the *w.* of
Bethlehem.
Ps. 84. 6, through valley of Baca make it a *w.*
Prov. 5. 15, waters out of thine own *w.*
10. 11, a *w.* of life.
Cant. 4. 15 ; John 4. 14, *w.* of living waters.
Isa. 12. 3, the *w.* of salvation.
John 4. 6, sat thus on the *w.*
2 Pet. 2. 17, *w.* without water.
See Gen. 21. 19 ; 49. 22 ; 2 Sam. 17. 18.
WELL (*adv.*). Gen. 4. 7, if thou doest *w.*
12. 13, *w.* with me for thy sake.
29. 6, is he *w.* ? and they said, he is *w.*
40. 14, think on me when it shall be *w.* with thee.
Ex. 4. 14, I know he can speak *w.*
Num. 11. 18, it was *w.* with us in Egypt.
Deut. 4. 40 ; 5. 16 ; 6. 3 ; 12. 25 ; 19. 13 ; 22. 7 ; Ruth 3. 1 ;
Eph. 6. 3, that it may go *w.* with thee.
1 Sam. 20. 7, if he say thus, it is *w.*
2 Kings 4. 26, is it *w.* with thee, is it *w.* ?
2 Chron. 12. 12, in Judah things went *w.*
Ps. 49. 18, when thou doest *w.* to thyself.
Prov. 11. 10, when it goeth *w.* with the righteous.
14. 15, looketh *w.* to his going.
30. 29, three things which go *w.*
Eccl. 8. 12, it shall be *w.* with them that fear God.
Isa. 3. 10, say to the righteous, it shall be *w.*
Ezek. 33. 32, one that can play *w.*

Jonah 4. 4, doest thou *w.* to be angry?
Mat. 25. 21; Lu. 19. 17, *w.* done.
Mk. 7. 37, he hath done all things *w.*
Lu. 6. 26, when all men speak *w.* of you.
Gal. 5. 7, ye did run *w.*
See Phil. 4. 14; 1 Tim. 3. 5; 5. 17; Tit. 2. 9.

WENT. Gen. 4. 16, Cain *w.* out from the presence.
Deut. 1. 31, in all the way ye *w.*
2 Kings 5. 26, *w.* not my heart with thee?
Ps. 42. 4, I *w.* with them to the house of God.
106. 32, it *w.* ill with Moses.
Mat. 21. 30, I go, sir, and *w.* not.
Lu. 17. 14, as they *w.* they were cleansed.
18. 10, two men *w.* up into the temple to pray.
See Mat. 11. 7; 20. 1; Lu. 6. 19; John 8. 9.

WEPT. 2 Kings 8. 11, the man of God *w.*
Ezra 10. 1; Neh. 8. 9, the people *w.* very sore.
Neh. 1. 4, I *w.* before God.
Lu. 7. 32, we mourned, and ye have not *w.*
19. 41, beheld the city, and *w.* over it.
John 11. 35, Jesus *w.*
1 Cor. 7. 30, that weep as though they *w.* not.
See 2 Sam. 12. 22; Ps. 69. 10; 137. 1; Rev. 5. 4.

WET. Job 24. 8; Dan. 4. 15; 5. 21.

WHAT. Ex. 16. 15, they wist not *w.* it was.
2 Sam. 16. 10, *w.* have I to do with you?
Ezra 9. 10, *w.* shall we say after this?
Job 7. 17; 15. 14; Ps. 8. 4; 144. 3, *w.* is man?
Isa. 38. 15; John 12. 27, *w.* shall I say?
Hos. 6. 4, *w.* shall I do unto thee?
Mat. 5. 47, *w.* do ye more than others?
Mk. 14. 36, not *w.* I will, but *w.* thou wilt.
John 21. 22, *w.* is that to thee?
See Acts 9. 6; 10. 4; 16. 30; 1 Pet. 1. 11.

WHATSOEVER. Ps. 1. 3, *w.* he doeth shall prosper.
Eccl. 3. 14, *w.* God doeth shall be for ever.
Mat. 5. 37, *w.* is more than these cometh of evil.
7. 12, *w.* ye would that men should do to you.
20. 4, *w.* is right I will give you.
Phil. 4. 8, *w.* things are true.
See John 15. 16; Rom. 14. 23; 1 Cor. 10. 31.

WHEAT. 1 Sam. 12. 17, is it not *w.* harvest to-day?
Job 31. 40, let thistles grow instead of *w.*
Ps. 81. 16; 147. 14, the finest of the *w.*
Jer. 12. 13, they have sown *w.*, but reap thorns.
23. 28, what is the chaff to the *w.*?
Mat. 3. 12, gather his *w.* into the garner.
Lu. 22. 31, that he may sift you as *w.*
See John 12. 24; Acts 27. 38; 1 Cor. 15. 37.

WHEEL. Ex. 14. 25, took off their chariot *w.*
Judg. 5. 28, why tarry the *w.*?
Ps. 83. 13, make them like a *w.*
Prov. 20. 26, a wise king bringeth the *w.* over them.
Eccl. 12. 6, or the *w.* broken at the cistern.
Isa. 28. 28, nor break it with the *w.* of his cart.
Nah. 3. 2, the noise of the rattling of the *w.*
See Isa. 5. 28; Jer. 18. 3; 47. 3; Ezek. 1. 16.

WHELP. 2 Sam. 17. 8; Prov. 17. 12; Hos. 13. 8.

WHEN. 1 Sam. 3. 12, *w.* I begin, I will also.
1 Kings 8. 30, *w.* thou hearest, forgive.
Ps. 94. 8, *w.* will ye be wise?
Eccl. 8. 7, who can tell him *w.* it shall be?
Mat. 24. 3; Mk. 13. 4; Lu. 21. 7, *w.* shall these things be?
See Deut. 6. 7; John 4. 25; 16. 8; 1 John 2. 28.

WHENCE. Gen. 42. 7; Josh. 9. 8, *w.* come ye?
Job 10. 21, *w.* I shall not return.
Isa. 51. 1, the rock *w.* ye are hewn.
Jas. 4. 1, from *w.* come wars?
Rev. 7. 13, *w.* came they?
See Mat. 13. 54; John 1. 48; 7. 28; 9. 29.

WHERE. Gen. 3. 9, *w.* art thou?
Ex. 2. 20; 2 Sam. 9. 4; Job 14. 10, *w.* is he?
Job 9. 24, if not, *w.*, and who is he?
Ps. 42. 3, *w.* is thy God?
Jer. 2. 6, *w.* is the Lord?
Zech. 1. 5, your fathers, *w.* are they?
See Isa. 49. 21; Nah. 1. 10; Lu. 17. 37.

WHEREBY. Lu. 1. 18, *w.* shall I know this?
Acts 4. 12, none other name *w.* we must be saved.
Rom. 8. 15, the spirit of adoption, *w.* we cry.
See Jer. 33. 8; Ezek. 18. 31; 39. 26; Eph. 4. 30.

WHEREFORE. 2 Sam. 12. 23, *w.* should I fast?
Mat. 14. 31, *w.* didst thou doubt?
26. 50, *w.* art thou come?
See 2 Sam. 16. 10; Mal. 2. 15; Acts 10. 21.

WHERETO. Isa. 55. 11; Phil. 3. 16.

WHEREWITH. Judg. 6. 5, *w.* shall I save Israel?
Ps. 119. 42, so shall I have *w.* to answer.
Mic. 6. 6, *w.* shall I come before the Lord?
See Mat. 5. 13; Mk. 9. 5; John 17. 26; Eph. 2. 4.

WHET. Deut. 32. 41; Ps. 7. 12; 64. 3; Eccl. 10. 10.

WHETHER. Mat. 21. 31, *w.* of them did the will.
23. 17, *w.* is greater, the gold or the temple?
Rom. 14. 8, *w.* we live or die.
2 Cor. 12. 2, *w.* in the body, or out of the body.
See 1 Kings 20. 18; Ezek. 2. 5; 3. 11; 1 John 4. 1.

WHILE. 2 Chron. 15. 2, with you, *w.* ye be with him.
Ps. 49. 18, *w.* he lived he blessed his soul.
Isa. 55. 6, *w.* he may be found.
Jer. 15. 9, her sun is gone down *w.* it was yet day.
Lu. 18. 4, he would not for a *w.*
24. 44, *w.* I was yet with you.
John 9. 4, work *w.* it is day.
1 Tim. 5. 6, she is dead *w.* she liveth.
See 1 Sam. 9. 27; 2 Sam. 7. 19; Acts 20. 11.

WHIP. 1 Kings 12. 11; Prov. 26. 3; Nah. 3. 2.

WHIT. 1 Sam. 3. 18; John 7. 23; 13. 10; 2 Cor. 11. 5.

WHITE. Gen. 49. 12, his teeth shall be *w.* with milk.
Num. 12. 10, leprous, *w.* as snow.
Job 6. 6, is any taste in the *w.* of an egg?
Eccl. 9. 8, let thy garments be always *w.*
Cant. 5. 10, my beloved is *w.* and ruddy.
Isa. 1. 18, they shall be *w.* as snow.
Mat. 5. 36, thou canst not make one hair *w.* or black.
John 4. 35, *w.* already to harvest.
Rev. 2. 17, a *w.* stone.
3. 4, walk with me in *w.*
See Dan. 11. 35; 12. 10; Mat. 17. 2; 28. 3.

WHITED. Mat. 23. 27; Acts 23. 3.

WHITER. Ps. 51. 7; Lam. 4. 7.

WHITHER. 2 Kings 5. 25; Cant. 6. 1; Heb. 11. 8.

WHOLE. 2 Sam. 1. 9, my life is yet *w.* in me.
Eccl. 12. 13, this is the *w.* duty of man.
Jer. 19. 11, a vessel that cannot be made *w.*
Ezek. 15. 5, when *w.* it was meet for no work.
Mat. 5. 29, not that thy *w.* body be cast into hell.
9. 12; Mk. 2. 17, the *w.* need not a physician.
13. 33; Lu. 13. 21, till the *w.* was leavened.
16. 26; Mk. 8. 36; Lu. 9. 25, gain the *w.* world.
John 11. 50, expedient that the *w.* nation perish not.
1 Cor. 12. 17, if the *w.* body were an eye.
1 Thess. 5. 23, I pray God your *w.* spirit.
Jas. 2. 10, keep the *w.* law.
1 John 2. 2, for the sins of the *w.* world.
5. 19, the *w.* world lieth in wickedness.
See Mat. 15. 31; John 5. 6; 7. 23; Acts 9. 34.

WHOLESOME. Prov. 15. 4; 1 Tim. 6. 3.

WHOLLY. Job 21. 23, dieth, being *w.* at ease.
Jer. 2. 21, planted thee *w.* a right seed.
46. 28, not *w.* unpunished.
Acts 17. 16, the city *w.* given to idolatry.
1 Thess. 5. 23, sanctify you *w.*
1 Tim. 4. 15, give thyself *w.* to them.
See Lev. 19. 9; Deut. 1. 36; Josh. 14. 8.

WHOMSOEVER. Dan. 4. 17, 25, 32, to *w.* he will.
Mat. 11. 27, to *w.* the Son will reveal him.
21. 44; Lu. 20. 18, on *w.* it shall fall.
Lu. 4. 6, to *w.* I will, I give it.
12. 48, to *w.* much is given.
See Gen. 31. 32; Judg. 11. 24; Acts 8. 19.

WHOSE. Gen. 32. 17, *w.* art thou, *w.* are these?
Jer. 44. 28, shall know *w.* words shall stand.

M m

Mat. 22. 20; Mk. 12. 16; Lu. 20. 24, *w.* is this
image?
Lu. 12. 20, then *w.* shall these things be?
Acts 27. 23, *w.* I am, and whom I serve.
See 1 Sam. 12. 3; Dan. 5. 23; John 20. 23.

WHOSOEVER. 1 Cor. 11. 27, *w.* shall eat this bread.
Gal. 5. 10, bear his judgment, *w.* he be.
Rev. 22. 17, *w.* will, let him take.
See Mat. 11. 6; 13. 12; Lu. 8. 18; Rom. 2. 1.

WHY. 1 Sam. 2. 23, *w.* do ye such things?
Jer. 8. 14, *w.* do we sit still?
27. 13; Ezek. 18. 31; 33. 11, *w.* will ye die?
Mat. 21. 25; Mk. 11. 31; Lu. 20. 5, *w.* did ye not
believe?
Mk. 5. 39, *w.* make ye this ado?
Acts 9. 4; 22. 7; 26. 14, *w.* persecutest thou me?
Rom. 9. 19, *w.* doth he yet find fault?
20, *w.* hast thou made me thus?
See 2 Chron. 25. 16; Lu. 2. 48; John 7. 45; 10. 20.

WICKED. Gen. 18. 23, destroy righteous with *w.*
Deut. 15. 9, a thought in thy *w.* heart.
1 Sam. 2. 9, the *w.* shall be silent.
Job 3. 17, there the *w.* cease from troubling.
8. 22, dwelling place of the *w.* shall come to
nought.
9. 29; 10. 15, if I be *w.,* why labour I in vain?
21. 7, wherefore do the *w.* live?
30, the *w.* is reserved to destruction.
Ps. 7. 9, let the wickedness of the *w.* come to an
end.
11, God is angry with the *w.*
9. 17, the *w.* shall be turned into hell.
10. 4, the *w.* will not seek God.
11. 2, the *w.* bend their bow.
6, upon the *w.* he shall rain snares.
12. 8, the *w.* walk on every side.
26. 5, I will not sit with the *w.*
34. 21, evil shall slay the *w.*
37. 21, the *w.* borroweth, and payeth not.
32, the *w.* watcheth the righteous.
35, I have seen the *w.* in great power.
58. 3, the *w.* are estranged from the womb
68. 2, so let the *w.* perish.
94. 3, how long shall the *w.* triumph?
139. 24, see if there be any *w.* way in me.
145. 20, all the *w.* will he destroy.
Prov. 11. 5, the *w.* shall fall by his own wickedness.
14. 32, the *w.* is driven away.
28. 1, the *w.* flee when no man pursueth.
Eccl. 7. 17, be not overmuch *w.*
8. 10, I saw the *w.* buried.
Isa. 13. 11, I will punish the *w.*
53. 9, he made his grave with the *w.*
55. 7, let the *w.* forsake his way.
57. 20, the *w.* are like the troubled sea.
Jer. 17. 9, the heart is desperately *w.*
Ezek. 3. 18; 33. 8, to warn the *w.*
11. 2, these men give *w.* counsel.
18. 23, have I any pleasure that the *w.* should die?
33. 15, if the *w.* restore the pledge.
Dan. 12. 10, the *w.* shall do wickedly.
Mic. 6. 11, with *w.* balances.
Nah. 1. 3, the Lord will not at all acquit the *w.*
Mat. 12. 45; Lu. 11. 26, more *w.* than himself.
13. 49, sever the *w.* from the just.
18. 32; 25. 26; Lu. 19. 22, thou *w.* servant.
Acts 2. 23, and by *w.* hands have crucified and
slain.
1 Cor. 5. 13, put away that *w.* person.
Eph. 6. 16, the fiery darts of the *w.*
Col. 1. 21, enemies in your mind by *w.* works.
2 Thess. 2. 8, then shall that *W.* be revealed.
See Eccl. 9. 2; Isa. 48. 22; 2 Pet. 2. 7; 3. 17.

WICKEDLY. Job 13. 7, will you speak *w.* for God?
34. 12, God will not do *w.*
Ps. 73. 8; 139. 20, they speak *w.*
Dan. 12. 10, the wicked shall do *w.*
Mal. 4. 1, all that do *w.*
See 2 Chron. 6. 37; 22. 3; Neh. 9. 33; Ps. 106. 6.

WICKEDNESS. Gen. 39. 9, this great *w.*
Judg. 20. 3, how was this *w.*?
1 Sam. 24. 13, *w.* proceedeth from the wicked.
1 Kings 21. 25, sold himself to work *w.*
Job 4. 8, they that sow *w.,* reap the same.
22. 5, is not thy *w.* great?
35. 8, thy *w.* may hurt a man.
Ps. 7. 9, let the *w.* of the wicked come to an end.
55. 11, *w.* is in the midst thereof.
15, *w.* is in their dwellings.
58. 2, in heart ye work *w.*
84. 10, the tents of *w.*
Prov. 4. 17, they eat the bread of *w.*
8. 7, *w.* is an abomination to my lips.
11. 5, the wicked shall fall by his own *w.*
13. 6, *w.* overthroweth the sinner.
26. 26, his *w.* shall be shewed.
Eccl. 7. 25, the *w.* of folly.
Isa. 9. 18, *w.* burneth as the fire.
47. 10, thou hast trusted in thy *w.*
Jer. 2. 19, thine own *w.* shall correct thee.
6. 7, she casteth out her *w.*
8. 6, no man repented of his *w.*
44. 9, have you forgot the *w.* of your kings?
Ezek. 3. 19, if he turn not from his *w.*
7. 11, violence is risen up into a rod of *w.*
31. 11, I have driven him out for his *w.*
33. 12, in the day he turneth from his *w.*
Hos. 9. 15, for the *w.* of their doings.
10. 13, ye have ploughed *w.*
Mic. 6. 10, are treasures of *w.* in house.
Zech. 5. 8, he said, this is *w.*
Mal. 1. 4, the border of *w.*
3. 15, they that work *w.* are set up.
Mk. 7. 21, out of the heart proceed *w.*
Lu. 11. 39, your inward part is full of *w.*
Rom. 1. 29, being filled with all *w.*
1 Cor. 5. 8, nor with the leaven of *w.*
Eph. 6. 12, spiritual *w.* in high places.
1 John 5. 19, the whole world lieth in *w.*
See Gen. 6. 5; Ps. 94. 23; Prov. 21. 12; Jer. 23. 11.

WIDE. Ps. 35. 21, they opened their mouth *w.*
104. 25, this great and *w.* sea.
Prov. 21. 9; 25. 24; Jer. 22. 14, a *w.* house.
Mat. 7. 13, *w.* is the gate that leadeth to destruction.
See Deut. 15. 8; Ps. 81. 10; Nah. 3. 13.

WIFE. Prov. 5. 18; Eccl. 9. 9, the *w.* of thy youth.
18. 22, whoso findeth a *w.* findeth a good thing.
19. 14, a prudent *w.* is from the Lord.
Lu. 14. 20, I have married a *w.*
17. 32, remember Lot's *w.*
1 Cor. 7. 14, the unbelieving *w.* is sanctified.
Eph. 5. 23, the husband is the head of the *w.*
Rev. 21. 9, the bride, the Lamb's *w.*
See 1 Tim. 3. 2; 5. 9; Tit. 1. 6; 1 Pet. 3. 7.

WILES. Num. 25. 18; Eph. 6. 11.

WILFULLY. Heb. 10. 26, if we sin *w.*

WILL. Mat. 8. 3; Mk. 1. 41; Lu. 5. 13, I *w.,* be
thou clean.
18. 14, not the *w.* of your Father.
26. 39, not as I *w.,* but as thou wilt.
Mk. 3. 35, whosoever shall do the *w.* of God.
John 1. 13, born not of the *w.* of the flesh.
4. 34, to do the *w.* of him that sent me.
Acts 21. 14, the *w.* of the Lord be done.
Rom. 7. 18, to *w.* is present with me.
Phil. 2. 13, both to *w.* and to do.
1 Tim. 2. 8, I *w.* that men pray every where.
Rev. 22. 17, whosoever *w.,* let him take.
See Rom. 9. 16; Eph. 1. 11; Heb. 2. 4; Jas. 1. 18.

WILLING. Ex. 35. 5, a *w.* heart.
1 Chron. 28. 9, serve God with a *w.* mind.
29. 5, who is *w.* to consecrate his service?
Ps. 110. 3, *w.* in the day of thy power.
Mat. 26. 41, the spirit is *w.*
2 Cor. 5. 8, *w.* rather to be absent.
8. 12, if there be first a *w.* mind.
1 Tim. 6. 18, *w.* to communicate.
2 Pet. 3. 9, not *w.* that any should perish.
See Lu. 22. 42; John 5. 35; Philem. 14; 1 Pet. 5. 2.

WIN. 2 Chron. 32. 1; Prov. 11. 30; Phil. 3. 8.

WIND. Job 6. 26, reprove speeches which are as *w.*
7. 7, remember that my life is *w.*
Prov. 11. 29, he shall inherit *w.*
25. 23, the north *w.* driveth away rain.
30. 4, gathereth the *w.* in his fists.
Eccl. 11. 4, he that observeth the *w.*
Isa. 26. 18, we have brought forth *w.*
27. 8, he stayeth his rough *w.*
Ezek. 37. 9, prophesy to the *w.*
Hos. 8. 7, they have sown *w.*
Amos 4. 13, he that createth the *w.*
Mat. 11. 7, a reed shaken with the *w.*
John 3. 8, the *w.* bloweth where it listeth.
Eph. 4. 14, carried about with every *w.* of doctrine.
See Acts 2. 2 ; Jas. 1. 6 ; Jude 12.

WINDOWS. Gen. 7. 11 ; Eccl. 12. 3 ; Jer. 9. 21 ;
Mal. 3. 10.

WINGS. Ps. 17. 8 ; 36. 7 ; 57. 1 ; 61. 4 ; 68. 13 ; 91. 4,
the shadow of thy *w.*
18. 10 ; 104. 3, on the *w.* of the wind.
55. 6, Oh that I had *w.* like a dove !
139. 9, the *w.* of the morning.
Prov. 23. 5, riches make themselves *w.*
Mal. 4. 2, with healing in his *w.*
See Ezek. 1. 6 ; Zech. 5. 9 ; Mat. 23. 37 ; Lu. 13. 34.

WINK. Job 15. 12 ; Ps. 35. 19 ; Prov. 6. 13 ; 10. 10 ;
Acts 17. 30.

WINTER. Gen. 8. 22 ; Cant. 2. 11 ; Mat. 24. 20 ; Mk.
13. 18.

WIPE. 2 Kings 21. 13 ; Isa. 25. 8 ; Lu. 7. 38 ; John
13. 5.

WISDOM. Job 4. 21, they die without *w.*
12. 2, *w.* shall die with you.
Prov. 4. 7, *w.* is the principal thing.
16. 16, better to get *w.* than gold.
19. 8, he that getteth *w.* loveth his own soul.
23. 4, cease from thine own *w.*
Eccl. 1. 18, in much *w.* is much grief.
Isa. 10. 13, by my *w.* I have done it.
29. 14, the *w.* of their wise men shall perish.
Jer. 8. 9, they have rejected the word of the Lord ;
and what *w.* is in them ?
Mic. 6. 9, the man of *w.* shall see thy name.
Mat. 11. 19, *w.* is justified of her children.
1 Cor. 1. 17, not with *w.* of words.
24, Christ the *w.* of God.
30, who of God is made unto us *w.*
2. 6, we speak *w.* among them that are perfect.
3. 19, the *w.* of this world is foolishness with God.
2 Cor. 1. 12, not with fleshly *w.*
Col. 1. 9, that ye might be filled with all *w.*
4. 5, walk in *w.* toward them.
Jas. 1. 5, if any lack *w.*
3. 17, the *w.* from above is pure.
Rev. 5. 12, worthy is the Lamb to receive *w.*
13. 18, here is *w.*
See Eccl. 1. 16 ; Rom. 11. 33 ; Col. 2. 3 ; 3. 16.

WISE. Gen. 3. 6, to make one *w.*
Ex. 23. 8, the gift blindeth the *w.*
Deut. 4. 6, this nation is a *w.* people.
32. 29, O that they were *w.* !
1 Kings 3. 12, I have given thee a *w.* heart.
Job 9. 4, he is *w.* in heart.
11. 12, vain man would be *w.*
22. 2, he that is *w.* may be profitable.
32. 9, great men are not always *w.*
Ps. 2. 10, be *w.* now, O ye kings.
19. 7, making *w.* the simple.
36. 3, he hath left off to be *w.*
94. 8, when will ye be *w.* ?
107. 43, whoso is *w.*, and will observe.
Prov. 1. 5, a *w.* man shall attain *w.* counsels.
3. 7, be not *w.* in thine own eyes.
6. 6 ; 8. 33 ; 23. 19 ; 27. 11, be *w.*
9. 12, thou shalt be *w.* for thyself.
11. 30, he that winneth souls is *w.*
16. 21, the *w.* in heart shall be called prudent.
20. 26, a *w.* king scattereth the wicked.

Eccl. 7. 23, I said, I will be *w.*
9. 1, the *w.* are in the hands of God.
12. 11, the words of the *w.* are as goads.
Isa. 19. 11, I am the son of the *w.*
Dan. 12. 3, they that be *w.* shall shine.
Mat. 10. 16, be *w.* as serpents.
11. 25, hid these things from the *w.*
Rom. 1. 14, I am debtor to the *w.*
12. 16, be not *w.* in your own conceits.
1 Cor. 1. 20, where is the *w.* ?
4. 10, ye are *w.* in Christ.
2 Tim. 3. 15, *w.* unto salvation.
See Isa. 5. 21 ; Jer. 4. 22 ; Mat. 25. 2.

WISELY. Ps. 58. 5, charmers, charming never so *w.*
101. 2, I will behave myself *w.*
Prov. 16. 20, that handleth a matter *w.*
See Prov. 21. 12 ; 28. 26 ; Eccl. 7. 10 ; Lu. 16. 8.

WISER. 1 Kings 4. 31 ; Lu. 16. 8 ; 1 Cor. 1. 25.

WISH. Ps. 73. 7, more than heart could *w.*
Rom. 9. 3, I could *w.* myself accursed.
3 John 2, I *w.* above all things.
See Job 33. 6 ; Jonah 4. 8 ; 2 Cor. 13. 9.

WITCH. Ex. 22. 18, thou shalt not suffer a *w.* to
live.
Deut. 18. 10, or a *w.*

WITHDRAW. Job 9. 13 ; Prov. 25. 17 ; 2 Thess.
3. 6.

WITHER. Ps. 1. 3, his leaf shall not *w.*
37. 2, they shall *w.* as the green herb.
129. 6 ; Isa. 40. 7 ; 1 Pet. 1. 24, the grass *w.*
Mat. 21. 19 ; Mk. 11. 21, the fig tree *w.* away.
Jude 12, trees whose fruit *w.*
See Joel 1. 12 ; John 15. 6 ; Jas. 1. 11.

WITHHOLD. Ps. 40. 11, *w.* not thy mercies.
84. 11, no good thing will he *w.*
Prov. 3. 27, *w.* not good from them to whom it is due.
23. 13, *w.* not correction.
Eccl. 11. 6, *w.* not thy hand.
Jer. 5. 25, your sins have *w.* good things.
See Job 22. 7 ; 42. 2 ; Ezek. 18. 16 ; Joel 1. 13.

WITHIN. Mat. 23. 26, cleanse first what is *w.*
Mk. 7. 21, from *w.* proceed evil thoughts.
2 Cor. 7. 5, *w.* were fears.
See Ps. 45. 13 ; Mat. 3. 9 ; Lu. 12. 17 ; 16. 3.

WITHOUT. Gen. 24. 31, wherefore standest thou
w. ?
2 Chr. 15. 3, for a long season *w.* the true God.
Prov. 1. 20, wisdom crieth *w.*
Isa. 52. 3 ; 55. 1, *w.* money.
Jer. 33. 10, *w.* man, *w.* beast, *w.* inhabitant.
Hos. 3. 4, Israel *w.* king, *w.* prince, *w.* sacrifice.
Eph. 2. 12, *w.* God in the world.
Col. 4. 5 ; 1 Thess. 4. 12 ; 1 Tim. 3. 7, them that
are *w.*
Heb. 13. 12, Jesus suffered *w.* the gate.
Rev. 22. 15, for *w.* are dogs.
See Prov. 22. 13 ; Mat. 10. 29 ; Lu. 11. 40.

WITHSTAND. Eccl. 4. 12, two shall *w.* him.
Acts 11. 17, what was I that I could *w.* God ?
Eph. 6. 13, able to *w.* in evil day.
See Num. 22. 32 ; 2 Chron. 20. 6 ; Esth. 9. 2.

WITNESS (*n.*). Gen. 31. 50, God is *w.* betwixt.
Josh. 24. 27, this stone shall be a *w.*
Job 16. 19, my *w.* is in heaven.
Ps. 89. 37, as a faithful *w.* in heaven.
Prov. 14. 5, a faithful *w.* will not lie.
Isa. 55. 4, I have given him for a *w.* to the people.
Jer. 42. 5, the Lord be a true and faithful *w.*
Mat. 24. 14, for a *w.* unto all nations.
John 1. 7, the same came for a *w.*
3. 11, ye receive not our *w.*
5. 36, I have greater *w.* than that of John.
Acts 14. 17, he left not himself without *w.*
Rom. 2. 15, conscience also bearing them *w.*
1 John 5. 9, the *w.* of God is greater.
10, hath the *w.* in himself.
See Isa. 43. 10 ; Lu. 24. 48 ; Acts 1. 8 ; 13. 31.

WITNESS (*v.*). Deut. 4. 26, heaven and earth to *w*.
Isa. 3. 9, countenance doth *w*. against them.
Acts 20. 23, the Holy Ghost *w*. in every city.
Rom. 3. 21, being *w*. by the law and prophets.
1 Tim. 6. 13, before Pilate *w*. a good confession.
See 1 Sam. 12. 3 ; Mat. 26. 62 ; 27. 13 ; Mk. 14. 60.
WITS. Ps. 107. 27, at their *w*. end.
WITTY. Prov. 8. 12, knowledge of *w*. inventions.
WIZARD. Lev. 20. 27, cr that is a *w*.
WOEFUL. Jer. 17. 16, the *w*. day.
WOMAN. Judg. 9. 54, a *w*. slew him.
Ps. 48. 6 ; Isa. 13. 8 ; 21. 3 ; 26. 17 ; Jer. 4. 31 ; 6. 24 ; 13.
    21, 22, 23 ; 30. 6 ; 31. 8 ; 48. 41 ; 49. 22, 24 ; 50. 43,
    pain as of a *w*. in travail.
Prov. 6. 24, to keep thee from the evil *w*.
9. 13, a foolish *w*. is clamorous.
12. 4 ; 31. 10, a virtuous *w*.
14. 1, every wise *w*. buildeth her house.
21. 9, with a brawling *w*. in wide house.
Eccl. 7. 28, a *w*. among all those have I not found.
Isa. 54. 6, as a *w*. forsaken.
Jer. 31. 22, a *w*. shall compass a man.
Mat. 5. 28, whoso looketh on a *w*.
15. 28, O *w*., great is thy faith.
22. 27 ; Mk. 12. 22 ; Lu. 20. 32, the *w*. died also.
26. 10, why trouble ye the *w*.?
13, shall this, that this *w*. hath done, be told.
John 2. 4, *w*., what have I to do with thee?
8. 3, a *w*. taken in adultery.
19. 26, *w*., behold thy son.
Acts 9. 36, this *w*. was full of good works.
Rom. 1. 27, the natural use of the *w*.
1 Cor. 7. 1, it is good for a man not to touch a *w*.
11. 7, the *w*. is the glory of the man.
Gal. 4. 4, God sent forth his Son, made of a *w*.
1 Tim. 2. 12, I suffer not a *w*. to teach.
14, the *w*. being deceived.
See Isa. 49. 15 ; Lu. 7. 39 ; 13. 16 ; Rev. 12. 1.
WOMB. Gen. 49. 25, blessings of the *w*.
1 Sam. 1. 5, the Lord had shut up her *w*.
Ps. 22. 9, took me out of the *w*.
10, cast upon thee from the *w*.
127. 3, the fruit of the *w*. is his reward.
139. 13, thou hast covered me in my mother's *w*.
Eccl. 11. 5, how bones grow in the *w*.
Isa. 44. 2 ; 49. 5, the Lord formed thee from the *w*.
48. 8, a transgressor from the *w*.
49. 15, compassion on son of her *w*.
Hos. 9. 14, give them miscarrying *w*.
Lu. 1. 42, blessed is the fruit of thy *w*.
11. 27, blessed is the *w*. that bare thee.
23. 29, blessed are the *w*. that never bare.
See Job 3. 11 ; 24. 20 ; 31. 15 ; Prov. 30. 16.
WOMEN. Judg. 5. 24, blessed above *w*.
1 Sam. 18. 7, the *w*. answered one another.
2 Sam. 1. 26, passing the love of *w*.
Ps. 45. 9, among thy honourable *w*.
Prov. 31. 3, give not thy strength to *w*.
Lam. 4. 10, the pitiful *w*. have sodden their chil-
    dren.
Mat. 11. 11 ; Lu. 7. 28, among them that are born
    of *w*.
24. 41 ; Lu. 17. 35, two *w*. grinding at the mill.
Lu. 1. 28, blessed art thou among *w*.
1 Cor. 14. 34, let your *w*. keep silence.
1 Tim. 2. 9, *w*. adorn themselves.
11, let the *w*. learn in silence.
5. 14, that the younger *w*. marry.
2 Tim. 3. 6, lead captive silly *w*.
Tit. 2. 3, the aged *w*. in behaviour as becometh
    holiness.
Heb. 11. 35, *w*. received their dead.
See Acts 16. 13 ; 17. 4 ; Phil. 4. 3 ; 1 Pet. 3. 5.
WONDER (*n.*). Ps. 71. 7, as a *w*. unto many.
77. 14, thou art the God that doest *w*.
88. 12, shall thy *w*. be known in the dark?
96. 3, declare his *w*. among all people.
107. 24, his *w*. in the deep.
Isa. 20. 3, walked barefoot for a sign and a *w*.
29. 14, I will do a marvellous work and a *w*.
Joel 2. 30 ; Acts 2. 19, I will show *w*. in heaven.

John 4. 48, except ye see signs and *w*.
Acts 4. 30, that *w*. may be done by the name.
See Rom. 15. 19 ; 2 Cor. 12. 12 ; 2 Thess. 2. 9.
WONDER (*v.*). Isa. 29. 9, stay yourselves, and *w*.
59. 16, he *w*. there was no intercessor.
63. 5, I *w*. there was none to uphold.
Hab. 1. 5, regard, and *w*. marvellously.
Zech. 3. 8, they are men *w*. at.
Lu. 4. 22, all *w*. at the gracious words.
See Acts 3. 11 ; 8. 13 ; 13. 41 ; Rev. 13. 3 ; 17. 6.
WONDERFUL. 2 Sam. 1. 26, thy love was *w*.
Job 42. 3, things too *w*. for me.
Ps. 139. 6, such knowledge is too *w*. for me.
Isa. 9. 6, his name shall be called *W*.
28. 29, who is *w*. in counsel.
See Deut. 28. 59 ; Jer. 5. 30 ; Mat. 21. 15.
WONDERFULLY. Ps. 139. 14 ; Lam. 1. 9 ; Dan.
    8. 24.
WONDROUS. 1 Chron. 16. 9 ; Job 37. 14 ; Ps. 26. 7 ;
    75. 1 ; 78. 32 ; 105. 2 ; 106. 22 ; 119. 27 ; 145. 5 ; Jer.
    21. 2, *w*. works.
Ps. 72. 18 ; 86. 10 ; 119. 18, *w*. things.
WONT. Ex. 21. 29, if the ox were *w*. to push.
Mat. 27. 15, the governor was *w*. to release.
Mk. 10. 1, as he was *w*., he taught them.
Lu. 22. 39, he went, as he was *w*.
Acts 16. 13, where prayer was *w*. to be made.
See Num. 22. 30 ; 2 Sam. 20. 18 ; Dan. 3. 19.
WOOD. Gen. 22. 7, behold the fire and the *w*.
Deut. 29. 11 ; Josh. 9. 21 ; Jer. 46. 22, hewer of *w*.
2 Sam. 18. 8, the *w*. devoured more people.
Ps. 141. 7, as one cleaveth *w*.
Prov. 26. 20, where no *w*. is, the fire goeth out.
See Jer. 7. 18 ; Hag. 1. 8 ; 1 Cor. 3. 12.
WOOL. Ps. 147. 16, he giveth snow like *w*.
Isa. 1. 18, your sins shall be as *w*.
Dan. 7. 9 ; Rev. 1. 14, hair like *w*.
See Prov. 31. 13 ; Ezek. 34. 3 ; 44. 17 ; Hos. 9. 1.
WORD. Deut. 8. 3 ; Mat. 4. 4, every *w*. of God.
30. 14 ; Rom. 10. 8, the *w*. is very nigh.
Job 12. 11, doth not the ear try *w*.?
35. 16, he multiplieth *w*.
38. 2, by *w*. without knowledge.
Ps. 19. 14, let the *w*. of my mouth be acceptable.
68. 11, the Lord gave the *w*.
119. 43 ; 2 Cor. 6. 7 ; Eph. 1. 13 ; Col. 1. 5 ; 2 Tim.
    2. 15 ; Jas. 1. 18, the *w*. of truth.
Prov. 15. 23, a *w*. spoken in due season.
25. 11, a *w*. fitly spoken.
Isa. 29. 21, an offender for a *w*.
30. 21, thine ears shall hear a *w*. behind thee.
50. 4, how to speak a *w*. in season.
Jer. 5. 13, the *w*. is not in them.
18. 18, nor shall the *w*. perish.
44. 28, know whose *w*. shall stand.
Hos. 14. 2, take with you *w*.
Mat. 8. 8, speak the *w*. only.
12. 36, every idle *w*. that men shall speak.
18. 16, that every *w*. may be established.
24. 35, my *w*. shall not pass away.
Mk. 4. 14, the sower soweth the *w*.
8. 38 ; Lu. 9. 26, ashamed of my *w*.
Lu. 4. 22, gracious *w*. which proceeded.
36, amazed, saying, what a *w*. is this!
24. 19, a prophet mighty in deed and *w*.
John 6. 63, the *w*. I speak are life.
68, thou hast the *w*. of eternal life.
12. 48, the *w*. I have spoken shall judge him.
14. 24, the *w*. ye hear is not mine.
17. 8, I have given them the *w*. thou gavest me.
Acts 13. 15, any *w*. of exhortation.
20. 35, remember the *w*. of the Lord Jesus.
26. 25, the *w*. of truth and soberness.
1 Cor. 1. 17, not with wisdom of *w*.
4. 20, not in *w*., but in power.
14. 9, except ye utter *w*. easy to be understood.
2 Cor. 1. 18, our *w*. was not yea and nay.
5. 19, the *w*. of reconciliation.
Gal. 5. 14, all the law is fulfilled in one *w*.
6. 6, him that is taught in the *w*.

Eph. 5. 6, deceive you with vain *w.*
Phil. 2. 16, holding forth the *w.* of life.
Col. 3. 16, let the *w.* of Christ dwell in you.
1 Thess. 1. 5, the gospel came not in *w.* only.
    4. 18, comfort one another with these *w.*
1 Tim. 4. 6, nourished in the *w.* of faith.
    5. 17, labour in the *w.* and doctrine.
2 Tim. 2. 14, strive not about *w.*
    4. 2, preach the *w.*
Tit. 1. 3, in due times manifested his *w.*
    9, holding fast the faithful *w.*
Heb. 1. 3, by the *w.* of his power.
    2. 2, if the *w.* spoken by angels was stedfast.
    4. 2, the *w.* preached did not profit.
    12, the *w.* of God is quick and powerful.
    5. 13, is unskilful in the *w.*
    6. 5, and have tasted the good *w.* of God.
    7. 28, the *w.* of the oath.
    11. 3, the worlds were framed by the *w* of God.
    13. 7, who have spoken to you the *w.*
Jas. 1. 21, the engrafted *w.*
    22, be ye doers of the *w.*
    23, if any be a hearer of the *w.*
    3. 2, if any man offend not in *w.*
1 Pet. 1. 23, being born again by the *w.*
    25, this is the *w.* which is preached.
    2. 2, the sincere milk of the *w.*
    8, them that stumble at the *w.*
    3. 1, if any obey not the *w.*, they may without the *w.*
2 Pet. 1. 19, a more sure *w.* of prophecy.
    3. 2, the *w.* spoken by the prophets.
    5, by the *w.* of God the heavens were of old.
    7, the heavens by the same *w.* are kept in store.
1 John 1. 1, hands have handled, of *W.* of life.
    2. 5, whoso keepeth his *w.*, in him is the love.
    3. 18, let us not love in *w.*
Rev. 3. 8, thou hast kept my *w.*
    10, the *w.* of my patience.
    6. 9, that were slain for the *w.*
    22. 19, take away from the *w.* of this prophecy.
See Isa. 8. 20 ; Jer. 20. 9 ; Mic. 2. 7 ; Rev. 21. 5.
WORK (*n.*). Gen. 2. 2, God ended his *w.*
    5. 29, shall comfort us concerning our *w.*
Ex. 20. 9 ; 23. 12 ; Deut. 5. 13, six days thou shalt do all thy *w.*
    35. 2, six days shall *w.* be done.
Deut. 3. 24, what God can do according to thy *w.*?
    4. 28 ; 27. 15 ; 2 Kings 19. 18 ; 2 Chron. 32. 19 ; Ps. 115. 4 ; 135. 15, the *w.* of men's hands.
1 Chron. 16. 37, as every day's *w.* required.
2 Chron. 31. 21, in every *w.* he began he did it.
    34. 12, the men did the *w.* faithfully.
Ezra 5. 8, this *w.* goeth fast on.
    6. 7, let the *w.* alone.
Neh. 3. 5, their nobles put not their necks to the *w.*
    6. 3, why should the *w.* cease?
    16, they perceived this *w.* was of God.
Job 1. 10, thou hast blessed the *w.* of his hands.
    10. 3 ; 14. 15 ; Ps. 143. 5, the *w.* of thine hands.
    34. 11, the *w.* of a man shall he render unto him.
Ps. 8. 3, the *w.* of thy fingers.
    19. 1, his handy-*w.*
    33. 4, all his *w.* are done in truth.
    40. 5 ; 78. 4 ; 107. 8 ; 111. 4 ; Mat. 7. 22 ; Acts 2. 11, wonderful *w.*
    90. 17, establish thou the *w.* of our hands.
    101. 3, I hate the *w.* of them that turn aside.
    104. 23, man goeth forth to his *w.*
    111. 2, the *w.* of the Lord are great.
    141. 4, to practise wicked *w.*
Prov. 16. 3, commit thy *w.* unto the Lord.
    20. 11, whether his *w.* be pure.
    24. 12 ; Mat. 16. 27 ; 2 Tim. 4. 14, to every man according to his *w.*
    31. 31, let her own *w.* praise her.
Eccl. 1. 14, I have seen all the *w.* that are done.
    3. 17, there is a time for every *w.*
    5. 6, wherefore should God destroy the *w.*?
    8. 9, I applied my heart to every *w.*
    9. 1, their *w.* are in the hand of God.

Eccl. 9. 7, God now accepteth thy *w.*
    10, there is no *w.* in the grave.
    12. 14, God shall bring every *w.* into judgment.
Isa. 2. 8 ; 37. 19 ; Jer. 1. 16 ; 10. 3, 9, 15 ; 51. 18, they worship the *w.* of their own hands.
    5. 19, let him hasten his *w.*
    10. 12, when the Lord hath performed his whole *w.*
    26. 12, thou hast wrought all our *w.* in us.
    28. 21, do his *w.*, his strange *w.*
    29. 15, their *w.* are in the dark.
    49. 4, my *w.* is with my God.
    66. 18, I know their *w.* and their thoughts.
Jer. 32. 19, great in counsel, and mighty in *w.*
    48. 7, thou hast trusted in thy *w.*
Amos 8. 7, I will never forget any of their *w.*
Hab. 1. 5, I will work a *w.* in your days.
Mat. 23. 3, do not ye after their *w.*
    5, all their *w.* they do to be seen of men.
Mk. 6. 5, he could there do no mighty *w.*
John 5. 20, greater *w.* than these.
    6. 28, that we might work the *w.* of God.
    29, this is the *w.* of God, that ye believe.
    7. 21, I have done one *w.*, and ye all marvel.
    9. 3, that the *w.* of God should be made manifest.
    10. 25, the *w.* I do in my Father's name.
    32, for which of those *w.* do ye stone me?
    14. 12, the *w.* I do shall he do, and greater *w.*
    17. 4, I have finished the *w.*
Acts 5. 38, if this *w.* be of men, it will come to nought.
    15. 38, who went not with them to the *w.*
Rom. 3. 27, by what law? of *w.*?
    4. 6, imputeth righteousness without *w.*
    9. 11, not of *w.*, but of him that calleth.
    11. 6, grace, otherwise *w.* is no more *w.*
    13. 12, let us therefore cast off the *w.* of darkness.
    14. 20, for meat destroy not the *w.* of God.
1 Cor. 3. 13, every man's *w.* shall be made manifest.
    9. 1, are not ye my *w.* in the Lord?
Gal. 2. 16, by *w.* of law shall no flesh be justified.
    6. 4, let every man prove his own *w.*
Eph. 2. 9, not of *w.*, lest any man should boast.
    4. 12, the *w.* of the ministry.
    5. 11, the unfruitful *w.* of darkness.
Col. 1. 21, enemies in your mind by wicked *w.*
1 Thess. 5. 13, esteem them in love for their *w.* sake.
2 Thess. 2. 17, in every good word and *w.*
2 Tim. 1. 9 ; Tit. 3. 5, saved us, not according to our *w.*
    4. 5, do the *w.* of an evangelist.
Tit. 1. 16, in *w.* they deny him.
Heb. 6. 1 ; 9. 14, from dead *w.*
Jas. 1. 4, let patience have her perfect *w.*
    2. 14, if he have not *w.*, can faith save him?
    17, faith, if it hath not *w.*, is dead, being alone.
    18, shew me thy faith without thy *w.*
    21, was not Abraham justified by *w.*?
    22, by *w.* was faith made perfect.
2 Pet. 3. 10, earth and *w.* therein shall be burnt up.
1 John 3. 8, destroy the *w.* of the devil.
Rev. 2. 2, 9, 13, 19 ; 3. 1, 8, 15, I know thy *w.*
    26, he that keepeth my *w.* to the end.
    3. 2, I have not found thy *w.* perfect.
    14. 13, and their *w.* do follow them.
See Gal. 5. 19 ; 2 Thess. 1. 11 ; Rev. 18. 6 ; 20. 12.
WORK (*v.*). 1 Sam. 14. 6, the Lord will *w.* for us,
1 Kings 21. 20, sold thyself to *w.* evil.
Neh. 4. 6, the people had a mind to the *w.*
Job 23. 9, on the left hand, where he doth *w.*
    33. 29, all these things *w.* God with man.
Ps. 58. 2, in heart ye *w.* wickedness.
    101. 7, he that *w.* deceit.
    119. 126, it is time for thee to *w.*
Isa. 43. 13, I will *w.*, and who shall let it?
Mic. 2. 1, woe to them that *w.* evil.
Hag. 2. 4, *w.*, for I am with you.
Mal. 3. 15, they that *w.* wickedness are set up.
Mat. 21. 28, son, go *w.* to day in my vineyard.
Mk. 16. 20, the Lord *w.* with them.
John 5. 17, my Father *w.* hitherto, and I *w.*
    6. 28, that we might *w.* the works of God.

John 6. 30, what dost thou *w.?*
9. 4, the night cometh, when no man can *w.*
Acts 10. 35, he that *w.* righteousness is accepted.
Rom. 4. 15, the law *w.* wrath.
5. 3, tribulation *w.* patience.
8. 28, all things *w.* together for good.
1 Cor. 4. 12, and labour, *w.* with our own hands.
12. 6, it is the same God which *w.* all in all.
2 Cor. 4. 12, death *w.* in us.
17, *w.* for us a far more exceeding weight of glory.
Gal. 5. 6, faith which *w.* by love.
Eph. 1. 11, who *w.* all things after the counsel.
2. 2, the spirit that now *w.*
3. 20, the power that *w.* in us.
4. 28, *w.* with his hands the thing that is good.
Phil. 2. 12, *w.* out your own salvation.
1 Thess. 4. 11, *w.* with your own hands.
2 Thess. 2. 7, the mystery of iniquity doth *w.*
3. 10, if any would not *w.,* neither should he eat.
Jas. 1. 3, the trying of your faith *w.* patience.
See Ezek. 46. 1; Prov. 11. 18; 31. 13; Eccl. 3. 9.

WORKMAN. Hos. 8. 6; Eph. 2. 10; 2 Tim. 2. 15.

WORLD. Job 18. 18, chased out of the *w.*
34. 13, who hath disposed the whole *w.?*
37. 12, on the face of the *w.*
Ps. 17. 14, from men of the *w.*
50. 12, the *w.* is mine.
73. 12, the ungodly, who prosper in the *w.*
77. 18; 97. 4, lightnings lightened the *w.*
93. 1, the *w.* also is stablished.
Eccl. 3. 11, he hath set the *w.* in their heart.
Isa. 14. 21, nor fill the face of the *w.* with cities.
24. 4, the *w.* languisheth.
34. 1, let the *w.* hear.
Mat. 4. 8; Lu. 4. 5, all the kingdoms of the *w.*
5. 14, the light of the *w.*
13. 22; Mk. 4. 19, the cares of this *w.* choke,
38, the field is the *w.*
40, in the end of the *w.*
16. 26; Mk. 8. 36; Lu. 9. 25, gain the whole *w.*
18. 7, woe to the *w.* because of offences.
Mk. 10. 30; Lu. 18. 30; Heb. 2. 5; 6. 5, in the *w.* to come.
Lu. 1. 70; Acts 3. 21, since the *w.* began.
2. 1, all the *w.* should be taxed.
16. 8; 20. 34, children of this *w.*
20. 35, worthy to obtain that *w.*
John 1. 10, he was in the *w.*
29, which taketh away the sin of the *w.*
3. 16, God so loved the *w.*
4. 42; 1 John 4. 14, the Saviour of the *w.*
6. 33, he that giveth life unto the *w.*
7. 4, shew thyself to the *w.*
7, the *w.* cannot hate you.
8. 12; 9. 5, I am the light of the *w.*
12. 19, the whole *w.* is gone after him.
31, now is the judgment of this *w.*
47, not to judge the *w.,* but to save the *w.*
13. 1, depart out of this *w.*
14. 17, whom the *w.* cannot receive.
22, manifest thyself unto us, and not unto the *w.*
27, not as the *w.* giveth, give I unto you.
30, the prince of this *w.* cometh.
15. 18; 1 John 3. 13, if the *w.* hate you,
19, the *w.* would love his own.
16. 33, in the *w.* ye shall have tribulation.
17. 9, I pray not for the *w.*
16, they are not of the *w.*
21, that the *w.* may believe.
21. 25, the *w.* could not contain the books.
Acts 17. 6, turned the *w.* upside down.
Rom. 3. 19, that all the *w.* may become guilty.
12. 2, be not conformed to this *w.*
1 Cor. 1. 20, where is the disputer of this *w.?*
2. 6, the wisdom of this *w.*
7. 31, they that use this *w.* as not abusing it.
2 Cor. 4. 4, the god of this *w.* hath blinded.
Gal. 1. 4, this present evil *w.*
6. 14, the *w.* is crucified unto me.
Eph. 2. 2, according to the course of this *w.*

Eph. 2. 12, without God in the *w.*
1 Tim. 6. 7, we brought nothing into this *w.*
17, them that are rich in this *w.*
2 Tim. 4. 10, having loved this present *w.*
Heb. 11. 38, of whom the *w.* was not worthy.
Jas. 1. 27, unspotted from the *w.*
3. 6, the tongue is a *w.* of iniquity.
4. 4, the friendship of the *w.*
2 Pet. 2. 5, God spared not the old *w.*
3. 6, the *w.* that then was.
1 John 2. 15, love not the *w.*
3. 1, the *w.* knoweth us not.
5. 19, the whole *w.* lieth in wickedness.
See 2 Sam. 22. 16; 1 Chron. 16. 30; Prov. 8. 26.

WORLDLY. Tit. 2. 12; Heb. 9. 1.

WORM. Job 7. 5, my flesh is clothed with *w.*
17. 14, I said to the *w.,* thou art my mother.
19. 26, though *w.* destroy this body.
21. 26, shall lie down, and *w.* shall cover them.
24. 20, the *w.* shall feed sweetly on him.
25. 6, man, that is a *w.,* etc.
Ps. 22. 6, I am a *w.,* and no man.
Isa. 14. 11, the *w.* is spread under thee.
41. 14, fear not, thou *w.* Jacob.
66. 24; Mk. 9. 44, 46, 48, their *w.* shall not die.
Mic. 7. 17, like *w.* of the earth.
See Jonah 4. 7; Acts 12. 23.

WORMWOOD. Jer. 9. 15; 23. 15; Amos 5. 7.

WORSE. Mat. 9. 16; Mk. 2. 21, the rent is made *w.*
12. 45; 27. 64; Lu. 11. 26, last state *w.* than the first.
Mk. 5. 26, nothing bettered, but grew *w.*
John 5. 14, lest a *w.* thing come unto thee.
1 Cor. 11. 17, not for the better, but for the *w.*
1 Tim. 5. 8, he is *w.* than an infidel.
2 Tim. 3. 13, shall wax *w.* and *w.*
2 Pet. 2. 20, the latter end is *w.* with them.
See Jer. 7. 26; 16. 12; Dan. 1. 10; John 2. 10.

WORSHIP. Ps. 95. 6, let us *w.* and bow down.
97. 7, *w.* him, all ye gods.
99. 5, *w.* at his footstool.
Isa. 27. 13, shall *w.* the Lord in the holy mount.
Jer. 44. 19, did we *w.* her without our men?
Zeph. 1. 5, them that *w.* the host of heaven.
Mat. 4. 9; Lu. 4. 7, fall down and *w.* me.
15. 9, in vain they do *w.* me.
John 4. 20, our fathers *w.* in this mountain.
22, ye *w.* ye know not what.
12. 20, Greeks came to *w.*
Acts 17. 23, whom ye ignorantly *w.*
24. 14, so *w.* I the God of my fathers.
Rom. 1. 25, *w.* the creature more than the Creator.
1 Cor. 14. 25, so falling down he will *w.* God.
See Col. 2. 18; Heb. 1. 6; Rev. 4. 10; 9. 20.

WORTH. Job 24. 25; Prov. 10. 20; Ezek. 30. 2.

WORTHY. Gen. 32. 10, I am not *w.* of the least.
1 Sam. 26. 16, ye are *w.* to die.
1 Kings 1. 52, if he shew himself a *w.* man.
Mat. 3. 11, whose shoes I am not *w.* to bear.
8. 8; Lu. 7. 6, I am not *w.* that thou shouldest come.
10. 10, the workman is *w.* of his meat.
37, loveth father or mother more than me is not *w.* of me.
22. 8, they which were bidden were not *w.*
Mk. 1. 7; Lu. 3. 16; John 1. 27, not *w.* to unloose.
Lu. 3. 8, fruits *w.* of repentance.
7. 4, that he was *w.* for whom he should do this.
10. 7; 1 Tim. 5. 18, the labourer is *w.* of his hire.
12. 48, things *w.* of stripes.
15. 19, no more *w.* to be called thy son.
20. 35, *w.* to obtain that world.
Acts 24. 2, very *w.* deeds are done.
Rom. 8. 18, not *w.* to be compared with the glory.
Eph. 4. 1; Col. 1. 10; 1 Thess. 2. 12, walk *w.*
Heb. 11. 38, of whom the world was not *w.*
Jas. 2. 7, that *w.* name.
Rev. 3. 4, for they are *w.*
See Nah. 2. 5; Rev. 4. 11; 5. 2; 16. 6.

WOULD. Num. 22. 29, I *w.* there were a sword.
Ps. 81. 11, Israel *w.* none of me.
Prov. 1. 25, ye *w.* none of my reproof.
30, they *w.* none of my counsel.
Dan. 5. 19, whom he *w.* he slew.
Mat. 7. 12 ; Lu. 6. 31, whatsoever ye *w.* that men.
Mk. 3. 13, and calleth unto him whom he *w.*
Rom. 7. 15, what I *w.,* that do I not.
1 Cor. 7. 7, I *w.* that all men were even as I.
Rev. 3. 15, I *w.* thou wert cold or hot.
See Num. 11. 29 ; Acts 26. 29 ; Gal. 5. 17.

WOUND (*n.*). Ex. 21. 25, give *w.* for *w.*
Job 34. 6, my *w.* is incurable.
Ps. 147. 3, he bindeth up their *w.*
Prov. 23. 29, who hath *w.* without cause?
27. 6, faithful are the *w.* of a friend.
Isa. 1. 6, but *w.* and bruises.
Jer. 15. 18, why is my *w.* incurable?
30. 17, I will heal thee of thy *w.*
Zech. 13. 6, what are these *w.* in thy hands?
Lu. 10. 34, bound up his *w.*
See Prov. 6. 33 ; 20. 30 ; Hos. 5. 13 ; Rev. 13. 3.

WOUND (*v.*). Deut. 32. 39, I *w.,* and I heal.
1 Kings 22. 34 ; 2 Chron. 18. 33, carry me out,
for I am *w.*
Job 5. 18, he *w.,* and his hands make whole.
Ps. 64. 7, suddenly shall they be *w.*
109. 22, my heart is *w.* within me.
Prov. 7. 26, she hath cast down many *w.*
18. 14, a *w.* spirit who can bear?
Isa. 53. 5, he was *w.* for our transgressions.
Jer. 37. 10, there remained but *w.* men.
See Gen. 4. 23 ; Mk. 12. 4 ; Lu. 10. 30 ; Acts 19. 16.

WRAP. Isa. 28. 20 ; Mic. 7. 3 ; John 20. 7.

WRATH. Gen. 49. 7, cursed be their *w.*
Deut. 32. 27, were it not I feared the *w.* of the
enemy.
Job 21. 30 ; Prov. 11. 4 ; Zeph. 1. 15 ; Rom. 2. 5 ; Rev.
6. 17, the day of *w.*
36. 18, because there is *w.,* beware.
Ps. 76. 10, the *w.* of man shall praise thee.
90. 7, by thy *w.* are we troubled.
Prov. 16. 14, *w.* of a king is as messengers of death.
19. 19, a man of great *w.* shall suffer.
27. 3, a fool's *w.* is heavier.
4, *w.* is cruel, and anger outrageous.
Eccl. 5. 17, much *w.* with his sickness.
Isa. 13. 9, the day of the Lord cometh with *w.*
54. 8, in a little *w.* I hid my face.
Nah. 1. 2, he reserveth *w.* for his enemies.
Hab. 3. 2, in *w.* remember mercy.
Mat. 3. 7 ; Lu. 3. 7, from the *w.* to come.
Rom. 2. 5, *w.* against the day of *w.*
Eph. 6. 4, provoke not your children to *w.*
1 Thess. 5. 9, God hath not appointed us to *w.*
1 Tim. 2. 8, lifting up holy hands, without *w.*
See Jas. 1. 19 ; Rev. 6. 16 ; 12. 12 ; 14. 8.

WRATHFUL. Ps. 69. 24 ; Prov. 15. 18.

WREST. Ex. 23. 2 ; Deut. 16. 19 ; Ps. 56. 5 ; 2 Pet.
3. 16.

WRESTLE. Gen. 32. 24 ; Eph. 6. 12.

WRETCHED. Num. 11. 15 ; Rom. 7. 24 ; Rev. 3. 17.

WRING. Judg. 6. 38 ; Ps. 75. 8 ; Prov. 30. 33.

WRINKLE. Job 16. 8 ; Eph. 5. 27.

WRITE. Prov. 3. 3 ; 7. 3, *w.* on table of thy heart.
Isa. 10. 1, *w.* grievousness which they have pre-
scribed.
19, few, that a child may *w.* them.
Jer. 22. 30, *w.* ye this man childless.
31. 33 ; Heb. 8. 10, I will *w.* it in their hearts.
Hab. 2. 2, *w.* the vision, make it plain.
See Job 13. 26 ; Ps. 87. 6 ; Rev. 3. 12.

WRITING. Ex. 32. 16 ; John 5. 47 ; Col. 2. 14.

WRITTEN. Job 19. 23, Oh that my words were *w.*
Ps. 69. 28, let them not be *w.* with the righteous.
Ezek. 2. 10, roll was *w.* within and without.
Lu. 10. 20, because your names are *w.* in heaven.
John 19. 22, what I have *w.* I have *w.*

1 Cor. 10. 11, *w.* for our admonition.
2 Cor. 3. 2, ye are our epistle *w.* in our hearts.
See Isa. 4. 3 ; Jer. 17. 1 ; Rev. 2. 17 ; 13. 8.

WRONG. Ex. 2. 13, to him that did the *w.*
1 Chron. 12. 17, there is no *w.* in mine hands.
Job 19. 7, I cry out of *w.,* but am not heard.
Jer. 22. 3, do no *w.*
Mat. 20. 13, friend, I do thee no *w.*
1 Cor. 6. 7, why do ye not rather take *w.?*
2 Cor. 12. 13, forgive me this *w.*
Col. 3. 25, he that doeth *w.* shall receive.
Philem. 18, if he hath *w.* thee.
See Prov. 8. 36 ; Acts 25. 10 ; 2 Cor. 7. 2.

WRONGFULLY. Job 21. 27 ; Ezek. 22. 29 ; 1 Pet.
2. 19.

WROTE. Dan. 5. 5 ; John 8. 6 ; 19. 19 ; 2 John 5.

WROTH. Gen. 4. 6, why art thou *w.?*
Deut. 1. 34 ; 3. 26 ; 9. 19 ; 2 Sam. 22. 8 ; 2 Chron. 28.
9 ; Ps. 18. 7 ; 78. 21, heard your words, and was *w.*
2 Kings 5. 11, but Naaman was *w.,* and went away.
Ps. 89. 38, thou hast been *w.* with thine anointed.
Isa. 47. 6, I was *w.* with my people.
54. 9, I have sworn I would not be *w.*
57. 16, neither will I be always *w.*
64. 9, be not *w.* very sore.
Mat. 18. 34, his lord was *w.,* and delivered.
See Num. 16. 22 ; Isa. 28. 21 ; Mat. 2. 16.

WROUGHT. Num. 23. 23, what hath God *w.!*
1 Sam. 6. 6, when God had *w.* wonderfully.
14. 45, Jonathan hath *w.* with God this day.
Neh. 4. 17, with one of his hands *w.* in the work.
6. 16, this work was *w.* of our God.
Job 12. 9, the hand of the Lord hath *w.* this.
36. 23, who can say, thou hast *w.* iniquity ?
Ps. 31. 19, hast *w.* for them that trust in thee.
68. 28, strengthen that which thou hast *w.* for us.
139. 15, curiously *w.* in lowest parts of the earth.
Eccl. 2. 11, I looked on all my hands had *w.*
Isa. 26. 12, thou also hast *w.* all our works in us.
41. 4, who hath *w.* and done it?
Jer. 18. 3, he *w.* a work on the wheels.
Ezek. 20. 9, I *w.* for my name's sake.
Dan. 4. 2, the wonders God hath *w.* toward me.
Mat. 20. 12, these last have *w.* but one hour.
26. 10 ; Mk. 14. 6, she hath *w.* a good work on me.
John 3. 21, manifest that they are *w.* in God.
Acts 15. 12, what wonders God had *w.*
18. 3, he abode with them, and *w.*
19. 11, *w.* special miracles by hands of Paul.
Rom. 7. 8, *w.* in me all manner of concupiscence.
15. 18, things which Christ hath not *w.*
2 Cor. 5. 5, he that hath *w.* us for the selfsame
thing.
7. 11, what carefulness it *w.* in you.
12. 12, the signs of an apostle were *w.*
Gal. 2. 8, he that *w.* effectually in Peter.
Eph. 1. 20, which he *w.* in Christ.
2 Thess. 3. 8, but we *w.* with labour.
Heb. 11. 33, through faith *w.* righteousness.
Jas. 2. 22, faith *w.* with his works.
1 Pet. 4. 3, to have *w.* the will of the Gentiles.
2 John 8, lose not those things we have *w.*
Rev. 19. 20, the false prophet that *w.* miracles.
See Ex. 36. 4 ; 2 Sam. 18. 13 ; 1 Kings 16. 25.

WRUNG. Lev. 1. 15 ; Ps. 73. 10 ; Isa. 51. 17.

Y.

YARN. 1 Kings 10. 28 ; 2 Chron. 1. 16.

YE. 1 Cor. 6. 11 ; 2 Cor. 3. 2 ; Gal. 6. 1.

YEA. Mat. 5. 37 ; Jas. 5. 12, let your communication be *y., y.*
2 Cor. 1. 17, there should be *y., y.,* and nay, nay.
See 2 Cor. 1. 18 ; Phil. 3. 8 ; 2 Tim. 3. 12.

YEAR. Gen. 1. 14, for seasons, days, and *y.*
47. 9, few and evil have the *y.* of my life been.
Ex. 13. 10, keep this ordinance from *y.* to *y.*
23. 29, I will not drive them out in one *y.*
Lev. 16. 34, make atonement once a *y.*
25. 5, it is a *y.* of rest.

Num. 14. 34, each day for a *y.* shall ye bear.
Deut. 14. 22, thou shalt tithe the increase *y.* by *y.*
15. 9, the *y.* of release is at hand.
26. 12, the third *y.*, which is the *y.* of tithing.
32. 7, consider the *y.* of many generations.
Judg. 11. 40, to lament four days in a *y.*
1 Sam. 2. 19, brought a coat from *y.* to *y.*
7. 16, went from *y.* to *y.* in circuit.
2 Sam. 14. 26, every *y.* he polled it.
1 Kings 17. 1, there shall be dew nor rain these *y.*
2 Chron. 14. 6, the land had rest, no war in those *y.*
Job 10. 5, are thy *y.* as man's days?
15. 20, the number of *y.* is hidden.
16. 22, when a few *y.* are come.
32. 7, multitude of *y.* should teach wisdom.
36. 11, they shall spend their *y.* in pleasures.
26, nor can the number of his *y.* be searched out.
Ps. 31. 10, my *y.* are spent with sighing.
61. 6, prolong his *y.* as many generations.
65. 11, thou crownest the *y.* with thy goodness.
77. 5, the *y.* of ancient times.
10, I will remember the *y.* of the right hand.
78. 33, their *y.* did he consume in trouble.
90. 4, a thousand *y.* in thy sight.
9, we spend our *y.* as a tale that is told.
10, the days of our *y.* are threescore and ten.
102. 24, thy *y.* are throughout all generations.
27, thy *y.* shall have no end.
Prov. 4. 10, the *y.* of thy life shall be many.
5. 9, lest thou give thy *y.* to the cruel.
10. 27, the *y.* of the wicked shall be shortened.
Eccl. 12. 1, nor the *y.* draw nigh.
Isa. 21. 16, according to the *y.* of an hireling.
29. 1, add ye *y.* to *y.*
38. 15, go softly all my *y.*
61. 2 ; Lu. 4. 19, the acceptable *y.* of the Lord.
63. 4, the *y.* of my redeemed is come.
Jer. 11. 23 ; 23. 12 ; 48. 44, the *y.* of their visitation.
17. 8, shall not be careful in *y.* of drought.
28. 16, this *y.* thou shalt die.
51. 46, a rumour shall come in one *y.*
Ezek. 4. 5, I have laid on thee the *y.* of their iniquity.
22. 4, thou art come even unto thy *y.*
38. 8, in latter *y.* thou shalt come.
46. 17, it shall be his to the *y.* of liberty.
Dan. 11. 6, in the end of *y.* they shall join.
Joel 2. 2, to the *y.* of many generations.
Mic. 6. 6, shall I come with calves of a *y.* old ?
Hab. 3. 2, revive thy work in the midst of the *y.*
Mal. 3. 4, the offering be pleasant, as in former *y.*
Lu. 13. 8, let it alone this *y.* also.
Gal. 4. 10, ye observe days and *y.*
Rev. 20. 2, Satan bound for a thousand *y.*
See Zech. 1. 14. 16 ; Jas. 4. 13 ; Rev. 9. 15.

YEARLY. 1 Sam. 1. 3 ; 20. 6 ; Esth. 9. 21.

YEARN. Gen. 43. 30 ; 1 Kings 3. 26.

YELL. Jer. 2. 15 ; 51. 38.

YESTERDAY. Job 8. 9 ; Ps. 90. 4 ; Heb. 13. 8.

YET. Gen. 40. 23, *y.* did not the butler remember.
Ex. 10. 7, knowest thou not *y.*?
Deut. 9. 29, *y.* they are thy people.
12. 9, ye are not as *y.* come.
Judg. 7. 4, the people are *y.* too many.
1 Kings 19. 18, *y.* I have left me.
2 Kings 13. 23, nor cast them from his presence as *y.*
Ezra 3. 6, the foundation was not *y.* laid.
Job 1. 16, while he was *y.* speaking.
13. 15, though he slay me, *y.* will I trust in him.
29. 5, when the Almighty was *y.* with me.
Ps. 2. 6, *y.* have I set my king.
Eccl. 4. 3, he which hath not *y.* been.
Isa. 28. 4, while it is *y.* in his hand.
49. 15, *y.* will I not forget.
Jer. 2. 9, I will *y.* plead with you.
23. 21, *y.* they ran.
Ezek. 11. 16, *y.* will I be to them.

Ezek. 36. 37, I will *y.* for this be enquired of.
Dan. 11. 35, it is *y.* for a time appointed.
Hos. 7. 9, *y.* he knoweth not.
Amos 6. 10, is there *y.* any with thee ?
Jonah 3. 4, *y.* forty days.
Hab. 3. 18, *y.* I will rejoice.
Mat. 15. 17, do not ye *y.* understand ?
19. 20, what lack I *y.* ?
24. 6 ; Mk. 13. 7, the end is not *y.*
Mk. 11. 13, the time of figs was not *y.*
Lu. 24. 44, while I was *y.* with you.
John 2. 4 ; 7. 6 ; 8. 20, hour is not *y.* come.
11. 25, though dead, *y.* shall he live.
Rom. 5. 6, *y.* without strength.
8. 24, why doth he *y.* hope for ?
1 Cor. 3. 15, *y.* so as by fire.
15. 17, ye are *y.* in your sins.
Gal. 2. 20, *y.* not I, but Christ.
Heb. 4. 15, *y.* without sin.
1 John 3. 2, it doth not *y.* appear.
See Acts 8. 16 ; Rom. 9. 19 ; 1 Cor. 3. 3.

YIELD. Gen. 4. 12, not henceforth *y.* strength.
Lev. 19. 25, that it may *y.* the increase.
26. 4, the land shall *y.* her increase.
Num. 17. 8, the rod *y.* almonds.
2 Chron. 30. 8, *y.* yourselves to the Lord.
Neh. 9. 37, it *y.* much increase to the kings.
Ps. 67. 6, the earth *y.* her increase.
107. 37, plant vineyards, which may *y.* fruits.
Prov. 7. 21, she caused him to *y.*
Eccl. 10. 4, *y.* pacifieth great offences.
Hos. 8. 7, if it *y.*, the strangers shall swallow it up.
Joel 2. 22, the fig tree and vine do *y.* their strength.
Hab. 3. 17, though fields shall *y.* no meat.
Mat. 27. 50, cried again, and *y.* up the ghost.
Acts 23. 21, do not thou *y.* to them.
Rom. 6. 13, neither *y.* ye your members, but *y.* yourselves to God.
16, to whom ye *y.* yourselves servants.
Heb. 12. 11, *y.* the peaceable fruits of righteousness.
See Gen. 1. 29 ; Isa. 5. 10 ; Dan. 3. 28.

YOKE. Gen. 27. 40, thou shalt break his *y.*
Lev. 26. 13, I have broken the bands of your *y.*
Num. 19. 2 ; 1 Sam. 6. 7, on which never came *y.*
Deut. 28. 48, he shall put a *y.* on thy neck.
1 Kings 12. 4, thy father made our *y.* grievous.
Isa. 9. 4 ; 10. 27 ; 14. 25, thou hast broken the *y.* of his burden.
58. 6, that ye break every *y.*
Jer. 2. 20, of old time I have broken thy *y.*
27. 2 ; 28. 13, make thee bonds and *y.*
31. 18, as a bullock unaccustomed to the *y.*
Lam. 3. 27, it is good to bear the *y.* in youth.
Mat. 11. 29, take my *y.* upon you.
30, for my *y.* is easy.
Acts 15. 10, to put a *y.* upon the neck of the disciples.
2 Cor. 6. 14, not unequally *y.* with unbelievers.
Gal. 5. 1, entangled with the *y.* of bondage.
Phil. 4. 3, I entreat thee also, true *y.*-fellow.
1 Tim. 6. 1, as many servants as are under the *y.*
See Job 1. 3 ; 42. 12 ; Lam. 1. 14 ; Lu. 14. 19.

YONDER. Gen. 22. 5 ; Num. 23. 15 ; Mat. 17. 20.

YOU. Gen. 48. 21, God shall be with *y.*
Ruth 2. 4, the Lord be with *y.*
1 Chron. 22. 18, is not the Lord with *y.* ?
2 Chron. 15. 2, the Lord is with *y.*, while ye be with him.
Jer. 18. 6, cannot I do with *y.*
42. 11 ; Hag. 1. 13 ; 2. 4, for I am with *y.*
Zech. 8. 23, we will go with *y.*, God is with *y.*
Mat. 7. 12 ; Lu. 6. 21, that men should do to *y.*
28. 20, I am with *y.* alway.
Lu. 10. 16, he that heareth *y.* heareth me.
13. 28, and *y.* yourselves thrust out.
Acts 13. 46, seeing ye put it from *y.*
Rom. 16. 20 ; 1 Cor. 16. 23 ; Phil. 4. 23 ; Col. 4. 18 ;

1 Thess. 5. 28; 2 Thess. 3. 18; 2 Tim. 4. 15; Tit. 3. 15; Heb. 13. 25; 2 John 3; Rev. 22. 21, grace be with *y.*
1 Cor. 6. 11, such were some of *y.*
2 Cor. 12. 14, I seek not yours, but *y.*
Eph. 2. 1; Col. 2. 13, *y.* hath he quickened.
Col. 1. 27, Christ in *y.*
4. 9, a brother, who is one of *y.*
1 Thess. 5. 12, know them that are over *y.*
1 John 4. 4, greater is he that is in *y.*
See Hag. 1. 4; Mal. 2. 1; 2 Cor. 8. 13; Phil. 3. 1; 1 Pet. 2. 7.

YOUNG. Ex. 23. 26, there shall nothing cast their *y.*
Lev. 22. 28, ye shall not kill it and her *y.* in one day.
Deut. 22. 6, thou shalt not take the dam with the *y.*
28. 50, which will not show favour to the *y.*
57, her eyes shall be evil toward her *y.* one.
32. 11, as an eagle fluttereth over her *y.*
1 Chron. 22. 5; 29. 1, Solomon my son is *y.*
2 Chron. 13. 7, when Rehoboam was *y.* and tender.
34. 3, while he was yet *y.*, he began to seek God.
Job 38. 41, when his *y.* ones cry to God, they wander.
39. 16, the ostrich is hardened against her *y.*
Ps. 37. 25, I have been *y.*, and now am old.
78. 71, from following ewes great with *y.*
84. 3, a nest where she may lay her *y.*
147. 9, he giveth food to the *y.* ravens which cry.
Prov. 30. 17, the *y.* eagles shall eat it.
Cant. 2. 9; 8. 14, my beloved is like a *y.* hart.
Isa. 11. 7, their *y.* shall lie down together.
40. 11, and gently lead those that are with *y.*
Jer. 31. 12, flow together for *y.* of the flock.
Ezek. 17. 4, cropped off his *y.* twigs.
John 21. 18, when *y.* thou girdedst thyself.
Tit. 2. 4, teach the *y.* women to be sober.
See Gen. 33. 13; Isa. 30. 6; Mk. 7. 25; John 12. 14.

YOUNGER. Gen. 25. 23, the elder shall serve the *y.*
Job 30. 1, they that are *y.* have me in derision.
Lu. 22. 26, he that is greatest, let him be as the *y.*
1 Tim. 5. 1, intreat the *y.* men as brethren.
1 Pet. 5. 5, ye *y.*, submit yourselves to the elder.
See Gen. 29. 18; Lu. 15. 12; 1 Tim. 5. 2, 11.

YOUNGEST. Gen. 42. 13; Josh. 6. 26; 1 Kings 16. 34.

YOURS. 2 Chron. 20. 15; Lu. 6. 20; 1 Cor. 3. 21.

YOUTH. Gen. 8. 21, imagination is evil from *y.*
46. 34, about cattle from our *y.* till now.
1 Sam. 17. 33, he a man of war from his *y.*
55, whose son is this *y.?*
2 Sam. 19. 7, evil that befell thee from thy *y.*
1 Kings 18. 12, I fear the Lord from my *y.*
Job 13. 26, to possess the iniquities of my *y.*
20. 11, his bones are full of the sin of his *y.*
29. 4, as in days of my *y.*
30. 12, on my right hand rise the *y.*
33. 25, he shall return to the days of his *y.*
36. 14, hypocrites die in *y.*

Ps. 25. 7, remember not the sins of my *y.*
71. 5, thou art my trust from my *y.*
17, thou hast taught me from my *y.*
88. 15, ready to die from my *y.* up.
89. 45, the days of his *y.* hast thou shortened.
103. 5, thy *y.* is renewed like the eagle's.
110. 3, the dew of thy *y.*
127. 4, the children of thy *y.*
129. 1, they have afflicted me from my *y.*
144. 12, as plants grown up in *y.*
Prov. 2. 17, forsaketh the guide of her *y.*
5. 18, rejoice with the wife of thy *y.*
Eccl. 11. 9, rejoice, young man, in thy *y.*
10, childhood and *y.* are vanity.
12. 1, remember now thy Creator in days of *y.*
Isa. 47. 12, wherein thou hast laboured from thy *y.*
54. 4, forget the shame of thy *y.*
Jer. 2. 2, the kindness of thy *y.*
3. 4, thou art the guide of my *y.*
22. 21, this hath been thy manner from thy *y.*
31. 19, bear the reproach of my *y.*
32. 30, have done evil before me from their *y.*
48. 11, hath been at ease from his *y.*
Lam. 3. 27, it is good that he bear the yoke in his *y.*
Ezek. 4. 14, soul not polluted from *y.*
16. 22, thou hast not remembered the days of thy *y.*
Hos. 2. 15, she shall sing as in the days of her *y.*
Joel 1. 8, lament for husband of her *y.*
Zech. 13. 5, man taught me to keep cattle from my *y.*
Mat. 19. 20; Mk. 10. 20; Lu. 18. 21, have kept from my *y.*
Acts 26. 4, my manner of life from my *y.*
1 Tim. 4. 12, let no man despise thy *y.*
See Prov. 7. 7; Isa. 40. 30; Jer. 3. 24, 25.

YOUTHFUL. 2 Tim. 2. 22, flee *y.* lusts.

Z.

ZEAL. 2 Sam. 21. 2, sought to slay them in his *z.*
2 Kings 10. 16, come and see my *z.* for the Lord.
Ps. 69. 9; John 2. 17, the *z.* of thine house.
119. 139, my *z.* hath consumed me.
Isa. 9. 7, the *z.* of the Lord will perform this.
59. 17, clad with *z.* as a cloak.
63. 15, where is thy *z.?*
Ezek. 5. 13, I have spoken it in my *z.*
Rom. 10. 2, they have a *z.* of God.
2 Cor. 9. 2, your *z.* hath provoked many.
Phil. 3. 6, concerning *z.*, persecuting the church.
Col. 4. 13, he hath a great *z.* for you.
See 2 Kings 19. 31; Isa. 37. 32; 2 Cor. 7. 11.

ZEALOUS. Num. 25. 11, he was *z.* for my sake.
Acts 21. 20, they are all *z.* of the law.
1 Cor. 14. 12, as ye are *z.* of spiritual gifts.
Tit. 2. 14, *z.* of good works.
Rev. 3. 19, be *z.* therefore, and repent.
See Num. 25. 13; Acts 22. 3; Gal. 1. 14.

ZEALOUSLY. Gal. 4. 18, *z.* affected.

BIBLE ILLUSTRATIONS

A SERIES OF PLATES
ILLUSTRATING BIBLICAL VERSIONS AND
ANTIQUITIES

SELECTED AND DESCRIBED

BY

H. R. H. HALL, M.B.E., D.Litt., F.B.A., F.S.A.
Late Keeper of Egyptian and Assyrian Antiquities
British Museum

SIDNEY SMITH
Keeper of Egyptian and Assyrian Antiquities
British Museum

S. R. K. GLANVILLE
Department of Egyptian and Assyrian Antiquities
British Museum

OXFORD UNIVERSITY PRESS
London : HUMPHREY MILFORD

1931

LIST OF PLATES

I. ILLUSTRATIONS OF THE LANGUAGES, WRITINGS, AND VERSIONS OF THE OLD AND NEW TESTAMENTS.

II. ILLUSTRATIONS OF OLD TESTAMENT HISTORY AND RELIGION.

(a) EGYPT.

List of Plates

(b) ASSYRIA AND BABYLONIA.

List of Plates

III. ILLUSTRATIONS OF NEW TESTAMENT HISTORY.

BIBLE ILLUSTRATIONS.

THIS series of Bible Illustrations is arranged in three groups, viz.: I. Illustrations of the Languages, Writings, and Ancient Versions of the Scriptures; II. Illustrations of Old Testament History and Religion; and III. Illustrations of New Testament History.

At the head of Group I are tables of the Phoenician and Hebrew and Greek and Latin Alphabets, all possibly descended from the ancient writings of Egypt. Then follow various specimens of Egyptian, Phoenician, Early Semitic, Hebrew, Samaritan, Syriac, Coptic, Greek, and Latin Inscriptions and Biblical sources.

Group II consists of illustrations of the history, religion, and customs (1) of ancient Egypt, and (2) of Babylonia and Assyria. The section which deals with Egypt commences with the religion of the people and their hope of immortality (Plates XIV–XXVII); and then passes to history, chiefly with a view to illustrate the story of the stay of the children of Israel in Egypt, the historical rule of the Egyptian Pharaohs over Palestine, its fall and the invasions of the Hittites and Philistines (Plates XXVIII–XLIII); the civilization of the great people of 'Kaphtor' or Minoan Crete (the prehistoric or 'heroic' Greeks) is also illustrated (Plates XLIV–XLVII) from Egyptian and Cretan monuments and relics. We return to the later history of Egypt on Plates XLVIII, XLIX, which illustrate the period of Egyptian struggle with Assyria described in the Books of Kings. We then pass to representations of typically Egyptian matters often referred to in the Bible (Plates L–LIV). Plate LV, which must be included in this section, forms a link between the two sections, for it represents a document written by a vassal of the king of Egypt, but in the characters and language of Western Asia. The section of Babylonian and Assyrian plates falls into two divisions, the first illustrating the history of the two empires (Plates LVI–LXXXIII), the second dealing with their religion and myths, and customs (Plates LXXXIV–XC).

The plates selected to form Group III are historical and topographical in character, and are comparatively few in number. They include portraits of the Roman emperors from Augustus to Domitian, illustrations of Roman public life with particular reference to the scenes of New Testament History, views of Palestine and of such typical Graeco-Roman remains as those of Ephesus and Ostia, and representations of coins referred to in the New Testament narrative (Plates XCI–CIV).

I. Illustrations of the Languages, Writings, and Versions of the Old and New Testaments.

Plates I, II. Alphabets. The principal languages in which the Holy Scriptures were written down are Hebrew and Greek. Both are written in different alphabetic characters, which derive from a common source. That the Greek alphabet must derive from a Semitic language was always known, from the names of the characters, and from the order, which corresponds to that known from the Hebrew acrostic psalms. And the square Hebrew characters can now be traced back through the forms offered by various inscriptions to the earliest known Semitic alphabet, used throughout Phoenicia, Syria, and Palestine, which may be called 'the North Semitic' alphabet. The oldest inscriptions known as yet in this character are that on the coffin of Ahiram, king of Byblus, in the Phoenician language, and others found with it. The excavator, M. Montet, believes that the finds in the tomb conclusively prove that these inscriptions were written about 1250 B.C., and most scholars consider that this is confirmed by other evidence; but some maintain that the inscriptions need not be prior to the tenth century B.C. The South Semitic inscriptions show a similar alphabet, but the forms of the letters, highly stylized, differ considerably from the northern alphabet, and there are additional letters. It is generally admitted as probable that both alphabets derive from a common original.

Various theories have been formed as to the derivation of the North Semitic alphabet. During the nineteenth century some maintained that it was derived directly from the Egyptian hieroglyphs, a theory of some plausibility since the hieroglyphic system included signs of a true alphabetic character; this view has been recently revived. But the actual forms of the Semitic letters can only be traced to the hieroglyphs by an imaginative process which is not convincing. The discovery of some inscriptions by Sir W. Flinders Petrie in the Sinai peninsula in a new script, which is clearly derived from hieratic signs and may reasonably be interpreted, as Dr. A. H. Gardiner has suggested, as alphabetic, for the expression of a Semitic language, has led to an ingenious explanation of many letters of the North Semitic alphabet as derivations from these characters, but few can accept this view. It is more probable that the Sinai inscriptions, the date of which must lie between 2000 and 1500 B.C., and the Semitic alphabet are parallel phenomena than that the one is derived from the other. Quite a different origin for the alphabet is assumed by those who point out that many of the signs which occur on clay tablets found at Knossos closely resemble early forms of the North Semitic alphabet. The nature of the Cretan script, known as early as 2000 B.C. in a cursive form, is not yet known, but it seems probable that it resembles the Cyprian script derived from it, which was syllabic. The third view of importance is that about 1500 B.C. several systems of writing were invented by individual effort. Of one such script, derived in conception from cuneiform characters, but consisting of alphabetic signs used for expressing a Semitic (probably Phoenician) dialect, excavations at Ras Shamra in Northern Syria have produced evidence. The alphabet which finally prevailed, the 'Northern Semitic', was, it may be, just such an invention, independent in fact, but doubtless inspired by the alphabetic use of signs in Egyptian writing.

The earliest monument showing the use of the alphabet to express the Phoenician language is the inscription of Ahiram, king of Byblos, about 1250 B.C. The earliest document in Aramaic is the account of the victories of Mesha', king of Moab, over the Israelites, on the 'Moabite Stone' (Plate VIII), about 890 B.C. The 'Siloam Inscription', which dates from the end of the eighth century B.C., is the earliest example of written Hebrew. The forms of letters as found in the two latter inscriptions are set out in Plate I.

Phoenician letters appear on Jewish coins to a comparatively late date (see Plate C, no. 2). The Samaritans, too, kept to the same character. But Hebrew writing, as it is known to us in MSS., is in square letters, the lineal descent of which from the old Phoenician alphabet is not so obvious. It has been customary to trace the change in the style of Hebrew writing to the period of the Captivity, and to attribute it mainly to the influence of the Aramaic character of Syriac, the use of which had spread to Babylonia. But, without denying that such an influence may have been at work, it may also be held that the development of the square character was perfectly regular, although, unfortunately, the destruction of early manuscripts has deprived us of the means of following it in its several stages. The elaborate and precise regulations which the Talmud laid down to ensure perfect accuracy in the transcription of the Scriptures would largely tend to create an artificially exact type of writing such as the square Hebrew.

The alphabet probably came to the Greeks, not through the Phoenicians, but directly from the Aramaic inhabitants of Northern Syria. The reason for this assumption is the fact that the names of the letters have Aramaic, not Phoenician, forms. Whether the early forms of Greek alphabets known all derive from one original, directly dependent on borrowing from the Northern Semitic system, or whether the various Greek forms represent independent borrowings, can hardly be proved, owing to insufficient evidence. That the alphabet in any case came to Greece in a form evolved in Asia Minor is not to be doubted. The essential feature of the evolution lay in the use of certain signs which were consonantal in the Semitic languages for the vowel sounds of Greek.

At least as early as the ninth century B.C., the Greeks re-learned the art of writing from the Phoenicians, the great traders and manufacturers of the ancient world, a few of whose stations and colonies were established not earlier than the twelfth century B.C. and probably considerably later in the islands and here and there on the mainlands of Greece and Asia Minor, after the fall of the great civilized Minoan and Mycenaean powers owing to the invasion of the barbarian Aryan Greeks (Achaians and Dorians) from the north. It is not, however, to be supposed that the Greeks received the alphabet from the Phoenicians at one single place, whence it was passed on throughout Hellas ; but rather at several points of contact, whence it was locally diffused among neighbouring cities and their colonies. Hence, while the Greek alphabet is essentially one and the same in all parts of Hellas, it exhibits certain local peculiarities, partly no doubt inherent from its very first adoption at different centres, partly derived from local influences or from local or other causes.

As with Semitic writing, the Greeks at first wrote from right to left. Next came the method of writing called *boustrophēdon*, in which the lines run alternately from right to left and from left to right, or vice versa, as the ox at the plough forms the furrows. This method was commonly followed in the sixth century B.C. Lastly, writing from left to right became universal.

To the two-and-twenty letters of the Phoenicians the early Greeks eventually added five more, to meet the requirements of their language ; but these were not universally employed. Many are the local varieties of forms in the alphabet of ancient Greece ; but they can be conveniently arranged in two geographical groups, Eastern and Western. The Eastern or Ionian group was in use in the Greek cities of Asia Minor, and in certain islands and states of Greece ; the Western, in other islands and states, and generally in the Greek colonies in Italy and Sicily. The two groups chiefly differed in the values to be attached to the letters X and Ψ. In the Eastern group the letters Ξ, X, Ψ have the sounds of *x, kh* (originally *k + h*, not like German *ch*, a guttural, till later), and *ps* ; in the Western group Ξ is wanting, and X, Ψ are sounded as *x* and *kh*. In a word, the special test-letters are :—

Eastern : X = *kh* . Ψ = *ps*,   Western : X = *x* . Ψ = *kh*.

The Romans derived their alphabet from the Greek alphabet of the Western type, not improbably as early as the eighth, if not the ninth, century B.C., through Cumae, an ancient colony of the Euboean city Chalcis. The primitive alphabet thus introduced has been called Pelasgian. The Latin alphabet has twenty letters of the Greek alphabet, and, in addition, three adopted signs. Ψ (X) was not adopted, the sound being represented phonetically by C + H (C = K). Likewise Θ was represented by TH, the sound being T + H, not a dental like our *th* (þ or ð) or the modern Greek *θ*. In Latin these two combinations, like PS for *psi*, were only used for Greek words and names, but their Latin spelling shows us what their Greek pronunciation was. The sound *z* being non-existent in Latin, the letter Z (*zeta*) was not used. When, at a later period, being required for the transliteration of Greek words, it was added to the Latin alphabet, it had to take a place at the end, as its

Greek position had in the adopted alphabet been occupied by the new letter **G**. Till the middle of the third century B. C., the letter **C** (= **K**) was employed to represent both the hard *c* and the *g* sounds ; but gradually **G**, developed from **C**, was employed for the latter sound, and took the place vacated by *zeta*. The third adopted sign, **Y**, is a curious instance of repetition. The primitive sign for *upsilon* had become the Latin **V** ; but, in the time of Cicero, the Greek letter was required for literary purposes, and was thus again incorporated in the Latin alphabet. The position of **Y** shows that it was admitted before **Z**.

Plate III. Ceremonial Palette of slate made for Na'rmerza (Menes), the first historical king of Egypt. It was used for the ceremonial mixing of the paint intended to decorate either the royal image or the king's own face, and is carved with what are among the oldest memorials of the Egyptian hieroglyphic writing. The king is seen attended by his sandal-bearer coming out to inspect the bodies of slain Northern enemies. The royal falcon holds the head of a Northerner by the nose. Below, prisoners escape from (on the other side) the royal bull, emblematic of the king, which butts down the rampart of a rebel fortress. Date about 3300 B.C. Cairo Museum.

Plate IV. Tomb at Gizeh. The doorway of the tomb of a high official called Sethu, with inscriptions cut in the picture-characters or hieroglyphics as used in Egypt during the period of the Early Empire, about 2800 B.C. In the upper compartment the deceased is seated with a table of offerings before him, and the text enumerates a number of the funeral offerings brought to the tomb, such as wine, dates, beer, cakes, fowls, haunches of beef, linen garments, eye-paint, &c. On the right is a figure of the ' royal relative', the princess Nub-hetept, who was probably his wife ; and on the left are his son, Sethu, and daughter, Heptek. The central inscription is a prayer to the god Anubis to grant the deceased funeral offerings and an honourable and happy burial ; and in the panel below are his principal titles. On the right of the door is Nub-hetept, ' the royal relative, the priestess of Hathor, the priestess of Nit (Neith) ', and ' the son of his body Sethu' ; on the left is a figure of the deceased holding the *kherp* sceptre in his right hand and a staff in his left hand. In many early tombs the hieroglyphics are filled with colours, which greatly help the reader to identify them. Objects connected with the sky are painted blue : men, reddish brown; to birds and metals are given their natural colours, &c. Several signs, however, which even at that early period had assumed a conventional form, cannot be interpreted.

Plate V. The Rosetta Stone. From time immemorial the ancient Egyptians employed as characters for their hieroglyphic writing pictures of men and animals, and natural and artificial objects ; they continued to do so, with certain modifications, for some centuries after the birth of Christ. From the fifth or sixth century of our era until the beginning of the present century the key to the decipherment of their inscriptions and writings was lost, and the only available information regarding them was to be gleaned from the works of classical and other early authors. In the sixteenth century a German scholar, Kircher, attempted to decipher certain texts without success, and the same ill result attended the labours of Jablonski in the following century. Towards the end of the eighteenth century some attention was paid to the subject by Zoega, who, observing the occurrence of groups of hieroglyphic characters enclosed within ovals or *cartouches*, rightly conjectured that they must form royal names. But in 1799 the Rosetta Stone was discovered by M. Boussard, an officer employed in the great expedition of Napoleon I. This stone, found at Rosetta, a city near the mouth of the Nile, to which it gives its name, is of black basalt and measures 3 ft. 9 in. by 2 ft. 4½ in. by 11 in. When complete it was inscribed with about fifteen lines of hieroglyphics, thirty-two lines of the demotic, or conventional form of writing common among the laity of Egypt, and fifty-four lines of Greek. Here, then, was a bilingual inscription in Egyptian and Greek, the Greek evidently a translation of the Egyptian. The Greek text proved to be a decree promulgated in the year 195 B. C. by the priesthood assembled at Memphis in honour of Ptolemy V Epiphanes, king of Egypt. In recognition of his benefactions to the country, honours were to be paid to the king's statue, a yearly festival was appointed, and a copy of the decree in hieroglyphics or ' the writing of the priests ', and in demotic, and in Greek, was to be engraved on stone and set up in every temple of the first, second, and third orders. The stone which had now come to light had been placed in the temple near Rosetta. The extreme importance of its discovery was at once recognized ; and, as soon as it was brought to England, copies of the inscriptions were circulated among the scholars and learned societies of Europe. The first to publish any important work in its decipherment was Åkerblad, the Swede, who succeeded in ascertaining the true values of fourteen demotic characters ; he was followed by Young, who in 1814 rightly interpreted six hieroglyphic alphabetic characters. At length, in 1822, the French scholar, Champollion, formulated a demotic and hiero-glyphic alphabet, which has successfully withstood all attacks upon it, and is practically the alphabet in use among Egyptologists to this day. Champollion was better equipped for his work than either Åkerblad or Young, and to him belongs the greater honour of completing the decipherment of Egyptian hieroglyphics ; but the credit of discovering the alphabetic element in the demotic and hieroglyphic characters belongs to Åkerblad and Young. The first clue for the reconstruction of the Egyptian alphabet was found in the names of Ptolemy and Cleopatra, which occur on the Rosetta Stone and also in a bilingual inscription on an obelisk at Philae. With the alphabetic characters thus obtained Champollion was able to spell out the names and the titles of the Greek and Roman rulers of Egypt, and thus eventually to complete the alphabet.

Plate VI. Cretan Writing. Two examples of clay tablets found at Knossos in Crete, and now in the British Museum, on which are incised characters of the Minoan Cretan linear script, which cannot yet be read. Their date is about 1600 B. C. Sir Arthur Evans claims this script as the real origin of the alphabet, in opposition to the view that it was derived from Egyptian hieratic.

Plate VII. Early Semitic and alphabetic writing. 1. A small sphinx of red sandstone, discovered by Sir F. Petrie in Sinai, on which are cut Egyptian hieroglyphs and a peculiar semi-hieroglyphic non-Egyptian script that is claimed by Dr. A. H. Gardiner and others to be the probable origin of the alphabet. Its date is about 2000 B. C. British Museum. 2. The inscription of Ahiram, king of Byblos. The date is probably about 1250 B. C. The opinion that the archaeological evidence does not prove this, is held by some authorities, but there seems to be other evidence of this form of writing at this date.

Plate VIII. The Moabite Stone, bearing an inscription of Mesha', king of Moab, who reigned about the middle of the ninth century B. C. He here records his wars with Israel, and other deeds. The Moabite Stone was discovered by the Rev. F. Klein at Dibhân, in the land of Moab, on August 19, 1868. It measures 3 ft. 10 in. by 2 ft. by 1 ft. 2 in., and is inscribed with thirty-four lines of text, each word of which is separated by a dot. About a year after its discovery the Arabs, hearing of its contemplated removal, broke it into a number of fragments ; but a paper squeeze of the inscription had already been made, and thus, fortunately, almost the whole of the text has been

preserved. A copy of the inscription in Hebrew letters, as transcribed by
Prim and Socin, and a translation are here given :—

אנך . מישע . בן . כמשמלך . מלך . מאב . הד

יבני ו אבי . מלך . על . מאב . שלשן . שת . ואנך . מלכ

תי . אחר . אבי ו ואעש . הבמת . זאת . לכמש . בקרחה ו במשע . מ

שע . כי . השעני . מכל . המלכן . וכי . הראני . בכל . שנאי ו עמר

י . מלך . ישראל . ויענו . את . מאב . ימן . רבן . כי . יאנף . כמש . באר

צה ו ויחלפה . בנה . ויאמר . גם . הא . אענו . את . מאב ו בימי . אמר . כדבר

וארא . בה . ובבתה ו וישראל . אבד . אבד . עלם . וירש . עמרי . את כל [אר]

ץ . מהדבא ו וישב . בה . ימה . וחצי . ימי . בנה . ארבען . שת . ו[יש]

בה . כמש . בימי ו ואבן . את . בעלמען . ואעש . בה . האשוח . ואבן

את . קריתן ו ואש . גד . ישב . בארץ . עטרת . מעלם . ויבן . לה . מלך . י

שראל . את עטרת ו ואלתחם . בקר . ואחזה ו ואהרג . את . כל . העם . מ

הקר . רית . לכמש . ולמאב ו ואשב . משם . את . אראל . דודה . ואס

חבה . לפני . כמש . בקרית ו ואשב . בה . את . איש . שרן . ואת . א[נ]שי

מחרת] . ויאמר . לי . כמש . לך . אחז . את . נבה . על . ישראל ו ו[א]

הלך . בללה . ואלתחם . בה . מבקע . השחרת . עד . הצהרם ו וא[ח]

זה . ואהרג . כלם . שבעת . אלף . מגברן . ומבנ[ז] ו וגברת . ובנ

ת . ורחמת ו וכי . לעשתר . כמש . החרמתה ו ואקח . משם . אר[א]

לי . יהוה . ואסחביהם . לפני . כמש ו ומלך . ישראל . בנה [את]

יהץ . וישב . בה . בהלתחמה . בי ו ויגרשה . כמש . מפני [ו]

אקח . ממאב . מאתן . איש . כל . רשה ו ואשאה . ביהץ . ואחזה .

לספת . על . דיבן ו אנך . בנתי . קרחה . חמת . היערן . וחמת

העפל ו ואנך . בנתי . שעריה . ואנך . בנתי . מגדלתה ו וא

נך . בנתי . בת . מלך . ואנך . עשתי . כלאי . האשו[ח]ן . למ[י]ן . בקרב

הקר ו ובר . אן . בקרב . הקר . בקרחה . ואמר . לכל . העם . עשו ו [ל]

כם . איש . בר . בביתה ו ואנך . כרתי . המכרתת . לקרחה . באסר

[י] . מישראל ו אנך . בנתי . ערער . ואנך . עשתי . חמסלת . בארנן [ו]

אנך . בנתי . בת . במת . כי . הרס . הא ו אנך . בנתי . בצר . כי . עין .

ש . דיבן . חמשן . כי . כל . דיבן . משמעת ו ואנך . מל[כ]

ת[י] . מאת . בקרן . אשר . יספתי . על . הארץ ו ואנך . בנתי . בנת

י . [את . מה]ד[ב]א . ובת . דבלתן ו ובת . בעלמען . ואשא . שם . את . נ[קד]

צאן . הארץ . וחורנן . ישב . בה . ב[ז] . ד[ר]ן . ו[ר]דן . א[מר]

אמר . לי . כמש . רד . הלתחם . בחורנן ו וארד . ו[אלת]

[יש]בה . כמש . בימי . ועל[א]דה . משם . עש[ר]

[ש]ת . שדק ו ואנ

' I am Mesha', the son of Chemosh-melek, the king of Moab, the man of Dibhon ; my father reigned over Moab for thirty years, and I sat on the throne after my father. I built a high place for Chemosh in Korha, a place of salvation for Mesha', for he hath delivered me from all monarchs, and he hath let me look with scorn upon all mine enemies. Now Omri was king over Israel, and he oppressed Moab for many days, for that Chemosh was wroth with the land. His son reigned in his stead, and he said, " Now will I oppress Moab ". Thus spake he even in my days ; but I have gained the victory over him and over his house, and Israel is laid waste for ever. Omri took possession of the land of Medeba and he dwelt therein in his own days and somewhile in the days of his son, even forty years. But in my time Chemosh gave back the land unto me. Then did I build Baal-Meon, and I made..., and I built Kiryathayim. The people of Gad had dwelt in the land of Ataroth from days of old ; and the king of Israel built the city of Ataroth. I assaulted the city and I took it, and I slew all the people thereof in the sight of Chemosh and Moab ; and I carried away the *Ariel* * of David, and I dragged it on the ground before the face of Chemosh at Kerioth. And I carried away the people of Saron and the people of .... And Chemosh said unto me, " Go, carry Nebo over Israel ". And I went up by night, and I fought against the city from dawn even until noon, and I took it, and I slew every man, even seven thousand men, and children, and women, and maidens, and slaves, and I dedicated them unto Ishtar-Chemosh. And I carried away from thence the *Ariels* of Jehovah, and I dragged them on the ground before the face of Chemosh. And the king of Israel built Yahas and dwelt therein after that he had fought against me ; but Chemosh drove him forth before me. I led forth two hundred of the men of Moab, I led them up to Yahas, and I took it that I might join it unto Dibhon. I built Korha, and the forest wall, and the ... wall, I built the doors and the towers thereof. I built the royal palace, and I digged the sluices for the water cisterns in the city. There was no well in the city of Korha ; therefore I said unto all the people, " Let every man dig him a well in his own house " ; and I digged the water courses even unto Korha by the hands of the captives (?) of Israel. I built Aroer, I made the road unto Arnon, I built again Beth-Bamoth, which was ruined. I built Bosor... I added one hundred cities unto the land of Moab. I built Medeba and Beth-Baal-Meon... And Chemosh said unto me : " Go down and fight against Horonayim ", and I went down and I fought against it.... '

Plate IX. Hebrew Pentateuch. The MS. from which this plate is taken is the oldest known MS. of any part of the Hebrew Bible. It was probably written in the latter part of the ninth century, the writing being of a rather earlier style than that of the manuscript of the Prophets at St. Petersburg which is dated in the year 916. There are other MSS. which bear earlier dates, but they are untrustworthy. The MS. before us is a large folio of 186 leaves, measuring 16½ by 13 inches ; but only 130 of them represent the original vellum MS., the rest being of paper supplied at the beginning and end of the volume in the year 1540. The text is written in triple columns, with vowel-points below the letters, according to the Western or Palestinian practice. Along the upper and lower margins the Greater Massorah is written, and the Lesser Massorah is placed in the side margins. The MS. was purchased by the Trustees of the British Museum in 1891.

Plate X. Samaritan Pentateuch. The MS. from which this plate is taken is in the University Library of Cambridge. It is a large volume of

* The *Ariel* was probably a sacred emblem.

312 vellum leaves, measuring 13¼ by 10¾ inches, and contains the old Hebrew text of the Pentateuch with an Arabic version, both in Samaritan characters, arranged in double columns, the Hebrew on the right and the Arabic on the left, written in the year 1219. The Samaritan Pentateuch is of value, as it traditionally represents the Hebrew text dating from the days of Nehemiah. It is also interesting on account of the character in which it is written, the Samaritans having kept to the old form of writing which was in use among the Hebrews before their adoption of the square character, and which is more nearly connected with the original Phoenician. Unfortunately, no Samaritan MS. of the Pentateuch is known of an earlier date than the tenth century.

Plate XI. Syriac Books of the Pentateuch, viz., Genesis, Exodus, Numbers, and Deuteronomy in the Pĕshîttâ or ' simple ' version, which was probably made in the second or third century. The MS. is a quarto volume of 230 leaves of vellum, measuring 10¾ by 8½ inches, and is written in double columns. The first two books were written at Amid in the year of the Greeks 775, that is, A.D. 464. The other books, though undated, undoubtedly form part of the original volume. The MS. is thus the oldest copy of any part of the Bible in any language which bears an actual date. It was obtained for the British Museum, in 1842, from the monastery of St. Mary Deipara in the Nitrian desert in Egypt and is written in the character called Estrangela. Syriac was a language spoken in Syria and Mesopotamia. Aramaic, the vernacular of Palestine in the time of our Lord, was a dialect of Syriac.

Plate XII. Codex Vaticanus (B). This is the oldest of the three great Uncial MSS. of the Bible in Greek, and there can be little hesitation in assigning it to the fourth century. It appears to have already belonged to the Vatican Library as early as the middle of the fifteenth century ; but its previous history is not known. It is a quarto volume, composed of 759 leaves of extremely fine vellum, measuring 10½ by 10 inches. It originally contained the text of the whole Bible ; but it now wants, in the Old Testament, portions of Genesis and the Psalms, and also the books of Maccabees. The New Testament is complete, except in the latter part of Hebrews and in the Apocalypse, which has been supplied by a hand of the fifteenth century. The text is written in three columns to a page, except in the poetical books of the Old Testament, which are in double columns. The original writing was in the purest form of uncials : there is no separation of words ; enlarged letters are not employed ; nor were stops or accents used by the first hand. The division into chapters and sections which is found at a later date does not appear in this MS., which has a system of its own.

Unfortunately a scribe of the tenth or eleventh century, for some unknown reason, but perhaps because he thought the original ink was fading, has retraced the whole of the text, leaving untouched only such letters and words as he considered superfluous or incorrect. Breathings and accents were also added by him. From the facsimile, representing a single column, a sufficient idea may be gathered of the injury done to the MS. by this treatment.

An example of the oldest method of punctuating texts occurs in this column. Their object being to leave no space unoccupied, the early scribes did not necessarily begin a new paragraph with a new line, but went on with the text as though there were no pause, and inserted a short interlinear stroke above the first full line of the paragraph. Thus, between the first letters of lines 2 and 3 we see the stroke marking the paragraph which commences in the second line.

Plate XIII. Old Latin Gospels. This plate is a facsimile page from the uncial gospel MS. of the Old Latin Version of the Bible. This version, which is considered to have had its origin in the Roman province of Africa in the second century, is found in three forms. There appear to have been two independent translations from the Greek Septuagint and the New Testament, which are known as the 'African' and the 'European'; at the same time it is possible that the European may be a revision of the African text. The third form is the 'Italian', which was a revision of the rougher 'European', and was in use in Italy towards the end of the fourth century. There are thirty-eight known MSS. of the Old Latin Version of the New Testament, twenty-eight of them being copies of the Gospels. There exists no MS. containing the whole of the New Testament.

II. Illustrations of Old Testament History and Religion.

a. EGYPT.

The ancient land of Egypt was the long narrow strip of territory through which flows the lower Nile. It was originally divided into two kingdoms: the northern kingdom, or Lower Egypt, which comprised the Delta and the district of Memphis; and the southern kingdom, or Upper Egypt, extending to the First Cataract. The two kingdoms were often united, and as often fell apart. Its full length was about 500 miles. The natives called the country 'Kamit', 'the black', in reference to the dark colour of the soil, or 'To-meri'. The Hebrew name for it was 'Misraim', the modern Arabic 'Misr'. The word 'Egypt' comes from the Latin rendering, 'Aegyptus', of the Greek 'Aiguptos', the derivation of which is uncertain. Upper Egypt was called Patoris, 'the South-land', the Pathros or Pathrusim of the Bible. Lower Egypt was Patomeh, 'the North-land'.

The history of Egypt has been traced back to more than three thousand years before Christ; and her kings have been arranged in thirty dynasties or ruling families, divided into four groups, viz. (1) Dynasties i–x (3300–2400 B.C.), or the Old Kingdom; (2) Dynasties xi–xvii (2400–1580 B.C.), or the Middle Kingdom; (3) Dynasties xviii–xxiii (1580–725 B.C.), or the New Kingdom; and (4) Dynasties xxiv–xxx (725–340 B.C.), or the Later Kingdom.

The chief authority for this arrangement by dynasties is Manetho, an Egyptian priest of the third century B. C., who compiled a history in Greek of the ancient dynasties from the annals preserved in the temples and other sources which have now perished. Manetho's work itself has not survived, and is only known to us through extracts and quotations of later writers; but monuments and inscriptions which have been excavated and deciphered correct and supplement the statements transmitted from him. The adoption of the Greek language by Manetho has had the result of making some of the Egyptian Pharaohs better known by their Greek, than by their native, names. There were kings in Egypt before the Manethonian dynasties began, about 3300 B.C., and we know the names of some of these prehistoric monarchs, especially those of Lower Egypt. The early centre of rule in the Delta was the city of Buto, and in Upper Egypt that of Hierakonpolis. Civilization seems to have radiated from the Delta southwards, but the Hierakonpolite kings eventually conquered the North, and Na'rmerza Meni was the founder of the First Dynasty.

Before the days of the two pre-dynastic kingdoms we can trace Egyptian civilization back almost to its earliest beginnings, in neolithic days, and the flint weapons and pottery of the neolithic Nilotes are well known in our museums. Before the time of the First Dynasty the use of copper had become known and hard stone was fashioned into vases. The rude beginnings of Egyptian civilization must probably be dated well before 4000 B.C.

Of the earliest dynasties we know very little beyond the names of their kings. The first king was said to have been Menes, the traditional founder of Memphis. He was a traditional figure, composed of two, if not three, real Southern conquerors of the North, 'the Scorpion', Na'rmerza, and 'Aḥai. 'Menes' then is a 'conflate' personage of tradition. His name seems to belong really to Na'rmerza; his deeds to the three monarchs named, ' of whom the Scorpion ' and 'Aḥai ('the Fighter') were respectively the predecessor and successor of Na'rmerza Meni. Certain later kings of the first three dynasties have, however, left their mark upon the face of the land in the monuments which they raised or in the engineering works which they carried on, proofs of the high state of civilization of the country in remote ages. The kings of the Fourth Dynasty (about 2800 B.C.) were the great pyramid-builders, the three chief pyramids of Gizeh being the work of the three monarchs Khufu (Kheops), Kha'frā' (Khephren), and Menkaura' (Mykerinos), whose power is to this day attested by these gigantic tombs which they raised to receive their bodies. The Great Sphinx has been assigned to the same period. The Fifth Dynasty (c. 2750-2600 B.C.) also built pyramids and fine funerary Temples, at Abūsīr ; and under the Sixth (c. 2600-2400 B.C.) commercial relations existed with the modern Abyssinia and Kordofan in the south and with the island of Crete and probably Greece itself in the north ; while Phoenicia had been since the time of the Third Dynasty closely connected with Egypt, the ancient city of Kapur or Gebal (the Greek Byblos and modern Jebail) being an Egyptian colony with Egyptian temples as early as the time of Sneferu (2900 B.C.). At the close of the Sixth Dynasty, after the reign of Pepi II (c. 2400 B.C.), the longest recorded reign in history (94 years), Egypt fell a prey to internal dissensions and was probably conquered both by invading negroes from the South (who now seem for the first time to have advanced northwards from the region of the Great Lakes into Nubia), and by Semitic Northerners from Syria. Civilization was restored by a dynasty (the Ninth) that ruled at Herakleopolis, the modern Ahnasiya (the Hanes of the Hebrews) ; and under the Eleventh (c. 2300-2200 B.C.), the first Theban dynasty, the ancient unity of the kingdom was restored. The kings of this dynasty sent mercantile expeditions to the land of Puanet or Punt, the modern Somaliland. The powerful line of kings who formed the Twelfth Dynasty (c. 2200-2000 B.C.), the second dynasty of the Middle Kingdom, consolidated their power, and conferred lasting benefits upon the country by great works. The construction of a large artificial lake on the west of the Nile, to receive the surplus waters of the river and to control its inundations, was accomplished in the reign of Amenemhet III (c. 2000 B.C.). This was the Lake Moeris of the Greeks, who thus rendered the native name ' Mu-uēr ', 'great water', the site of which is now called by the Arabs al-Fayyūm, perpetuating its Coptic name, ' Ph-iom ', 'the sea'. Culture and art flourished under this dynasty, which has left to us some of the most beautiful products of the Egyptian artists. Commercial and artistic relations with the great Minoan civilization of Crete, with its centres at Knossos and Phaistos, were now regular ; and the two arts began to influence one another. In spite of her dominion in Phoenicia, Egypt does not seem to have cultivated close relations with Syria, still less with Babylonia, although in predynastic days connexion with Babylonia undoubtedly existed. In the south the kings of this dynasty were faced by the new problem of the newly-arrived negroes, and found it difficult to keep them south of the frontier fixed by king Senuasret or Senusret (Sesostris) III at the Second Cataract (south of Wadi Halfa).

Under the Old Kingdom the centre of government was Memphis ; under the Middle Kingdom, when the power of Egypt was at its height, it moved up the stream to Thebes, the city which before all others in Egypt became famous for its wealth and for the magnificence of its buildings. In such a country as Egypt, whose length was so disproportionately greater than its breadth, and in which the permanent water-way of the Nile afforded such an easy means of transit from one end of the kingdom to the other, this shifting of the chief centre of administration could, without much difficulty, be managed to suit the exigencies of the moment. The same facility for movement was, however, also a source of weakness. An enemy moving from the north or from the south, after a first success, might sweep up or down the stream with overpowering force and rapidity.

After the energetic rule of the Twelfth Dynasty, there appears to have been a period of reaction or weakness, resulting first in internal troubles, and finally in a great disaster by foreign conquest. From time immemorial the nomad tribes of Edom and Southern Syria had been accustomed to lead down their herds into the fertile plains of the Eastern Delta, and in course of time they had fixed themselves in the land, and had become a large proportion of the inhabitants of that district. This Semitic element in Lower Egypt was no doubt also increased by the trading Phoenicians, who settled in the towns as merchants or artisans. From the Bible we learn how, at a later date, the sons of Jacob came down with their father, and dwelt ' in the best of the land—in the land of Goshen ', and how ' the children of Israel were fruitful, and increased abundantly, and multiplied, and waxed exceeding mighty; and the land was filled with them ' (Exod. 1^7). As in these later days, so no doubt in the earlier period, the Semitic population of Lower Egypt ' increased abundantly ', and prepared the way for the invasion which now overwhelmed the kingdom. Forced on, probably, by a wave of migration of the peoples of Western Asia, the Syrian tribes made a sudden irruption into Egypt, and, carrying all before them and meeting apparently with little opposition, they succeeded in establishing themselves in power at Memphis and in making a complete conquest, at least of Lower Egypt. The dynasties which they founded, namely, the Fifteenth and Sixteenth Dynasties, are known as those of the Hyksos or Shepherd-kings. It has been conjectured that the name has been derived from the Egyptian ' Hik-Shasu ', king of the ' Shasu ' or thieving nomad tribes. The period of the Hyksos domination lies within the five hundred years which separate the Twelfth from the Eighteenth Dynasty. The greatest Hyksos kings were Khayan and Apopi. The Seventeenth Dynasty, which was Theban Egyptian, was a period of revolt. Sekenen-Ra', the Theban under-king, refused tribute, and began the war of liberation, which, after a struggle of one hundred years, ended in the expulsion of the foreign race.

It was probably during the Hyksos rule that the first arrival of the Hebrews in Egypt took place, when ' the patriarch Joseph was sold into Egypt '. The Pharaoh who ' raised Joseph to power and welcomed Jacob and his family into Egypt ' must have been a Hyksos, and, according to one view of the probabilities, the expulsion of the Hyksos (1580 B.C.) is identical with the Exodus of the Hebrews ; that is to say, it is the same event, the unfriendly departure of a great host of Semitic colonists, looked at from the Egyptian rather than the Hebrew angle of vision. This was the view of the great Jewish historian Josephus.

The history of Egypt after the Expulsion of the Hyksos enters on a new phase. Hitherto she had kept within her natural boundaries, and the foreign tyranny to which she had recently been subjected had checked the expansion to which the powerful government of the Twelfth Dynasty might have led the way. Now that the hand of the oppressor was removed, the country revived, and the stimulus given to the national spirit by the late war of liberation no doubt urged on the kings of the Eighteenth and Nineteenth Dynasties (1580-1200 B. C.) in the policy of foreign aggression which marked their reigns and eventually overtaxed the strength of the country and led to its final subjection. The reigns of the early kings of the Eighteenth Dynasty were occupied in organizing the kingdom and in strengthening its borders. Nubia was invaded and placed under tribute, and the Libyans on the west were subdued and punished ; and Egypt was then free to turn her arms to the north-east, from whence her late conquerors had emerged. The first king to enter on a war of Asiatic conquest was Thutimase, Thutmose, or Tuthmosis (Tethmosis, Thothmes) I (1539-1514 B. C.) ; and his son, the famous Tuthmosis III, brought the Syrian and neighbouring nations into subjection. His long reign of more than fifty years (1501-1447 B. C.) was a period of almost ceaseless wars in Asia ; and even the distant kingdom of Assyria paid him tribute. Succeeding kings continued the same policy with more or less success, Amanhatpe or Amenhotep (Amenophis) III (1412-1376 B. C.), in particular, being renowned for his wars in Syria, as well as in Nubia. He was the son of a Mitannian princess, and the ruling classes of Mitanni, a land of Northern Mesopotamia, were Indo-Europeans of Indo-Iranian stock. But in the days of his son, Amenophis IV, who had estranged the powerful priesthood by setting up a heretical monotheistic form of worship, the strength of Egypt waned (see Plate LV). Probably converted by the opinions of the priests of the Sun at On (Heliopolis) and possibly by influences from Western Asia (his father was half a Mitannian), this monarch substituted the monotheistic cult of the Sun-disk for that of the old gods, and even changed his own name to Akh-en-aten, signifying 'Blessed of the Sun-disk'. This religious revolution was one of the most important and most interesting in history, despite the fact that it did not endure. The Atenist cult was that of the actual Sun as the giver of life, and no other deity was to be worshipped. The hymns addressed to the Aten by the king and the believers in 'his Majesty's doctrine' were of a most lofty phraseology, which often reminds us of the Psalms, especially the civth, and at other times of the Rig-Veda. But the sentiments expressed in them, though very charming, are quite materialistic in character : they merely express pleasure at the fact of being alive, and there is no mention whatever of moral responsibility, no conception of sin and atonement for wrongdoing. Thus there does not seem to be much that is of Semitic religious origin in them, in spite of the resemblance to Semitic psalms in their phraseology.

Akh-en-aten's religious revolt was accompanied by a 'modernist' movement in art, which sought to express the king's love of realism in a realistic style which is often hideous. Because the king was personally ugly, ugliness became the fashion, if not a virtue. The royal passion for the truth was in itself estimable, but it was exercised in the usual dogmatic and intolerant manner of such reformers. Akh-en-aten was a fanatic, and his reform was marred by bigotry, with the result that at his death his whole edifice was immediately swept away, and the nation returned to the polytheistic religion of its forefathers.

The heretic king was a heretic also in political matters, and abandoned the conquests of his fathers in Syria to local rebels, aided more or less directly by the Hittite king Suppiluliu or Shubbiluliuma. He did so on deliberately pacificist grounds. The result was chaos in Asia.

But under the kings of the Nineteenth Dynasty, Seti I and his successors, the Asiatic wars were revived with greater vigour than ever, the central figure of the period being the unduly famous monarch Rī'masesu (Rameses) II (1300-1234 B. C.), whose name is perhaps, though unjustly, more widely known than that of any other Pharaoh. He advertised himself well in his numberless monuments (many of which are appropriations from older kings) and his blatant inscriptions and relief-pictures on temple walls. His best-advertised campaign is the one which he undertook against the Khatti or Kheta, the powerful nation of Anatolia and Northern Syria, who are known in the Bible as the Hittites. They had dominated North Syria for two centuries, and the intrigues of their great king Suppiluliu had largely contributed to the revolt of Syria under Akh-en-aten. Rameses now with difficulty defeated them in a great battle under the walls of Kadesh (see Plate XXXIV). But this Pyrrhic victory had little result and in the end Rameses was compelled to make peace with Khattusil, the Hittite king, and about 1279 B. C. a treaty of peace and alliance was concluded between them which is of great interest on account of its remarkable resemblance to modern treaties of the same kind. It even contains extradition clauses. The conquests of Tuthmosis I and III were finally lost now, in spite of the reassertion of Egyptian authority in Palestine and Syria by Seti I, who had created a great Egyptian fortress at Bethshan and had set up his border-stelae in the land of Moab, near Mzērib, south of Damascus, and even as far north as Homs. His son was compelled now, in spite of his boasting, to leave Syria to the Hittites, and content himself with Palestine. Egypt never again conquered north of Galilee and Mount Carmel till Pharaoh Necho for a moment again took the Egyptian arms to the Euphrates at Carchemish, six centuries later. The offensive power of the nation had been exhausted by the protracted struggle under Rameses II.

While the strength of the nation was thus put forth beyond its borders, there is also evidence of its flourishing condition internally. The monuments that remain of the great building operations of the kings of the Eighteenth and Nineteenth Dynasties are innumerable, and many of them are of the first rank. At Thebes, in particular, and in its neighbourhood, were built great temples and other works, the ruins of which bear witness to the energy and resources of the Pharaohs of those dynasties. A queen of the family of Thothmes, Queen Hatshepsut, ruled the kingdom with all the vigour of her race. Her reign is famous for the voyage of discovery to the land of Punt, the land of spices, which lay, as it is thought, on the two shores at the entrance of the Red Sea; and on the walls of the temple of Dair al-Baḥri may be seen the sculptured history of the event. Nubia was finally subjected, and the negro tribes reduced to vassalage and forced to seek for the gold which contributed much of the enormous wealth of Egypt, now the wealthiest nation in the world : ' gold is as water in thy land, my brother', writes a Babylonian king to a pharaoh at this time. Commercial and artistic relations existed with Crete, the Keftiu or Kaphtor of the Egyptians and Hebrews, and Minoan ambassadors brought rich and beautiful gifts from Knossos and the Aegean isles to the court of Thothmes III. Much of the conquered land of Asia was assigned to the god Amon of Thebes, whose priests derived great wealth from it.

The better to carry on their wars with Asia, the kings of this period resided much in the cities of Lower Egypt. Rameses II occupied, for this purpose, the city of San or Tanis. He has been identified as the Pharaoh who oppressed the children of Israel, and compelled them to build ' the treasure-cities, Pithom and Raamses ', and there is little doubt Hebrew prisoners (Aperiu, as the Egyptians called them) were employed in the building of

Per-Ramses (Pelusium), which the Biblical writer called 'Raamses'. They are mentioned at the time. But they were Hebrews taken long after the conquest of the Promised Land, if the Exodus (as some think) was identical with the departure of the Hyksos. In favour of this view is the fact that in the reign of Meneptah, the successor of Rameses, Israel is actually mentioned in an Egyptian inscription as a settled people of Palestine, which had been conquered and ravaged by Meneptah. That is to say, the Israelites must have entered Palestine before the time of Meneptah, at any rate. And it is probable that we have an actual record of their entry in the Amarna letters (p. 572), discovered in the heretic Akh-en-aten's city, in which the tribes of the Khabiru or Khabiri are mentioned as taking advantage of the confusion caused by the king's pacificist policy to enter Canaan. These Khabiru are, it is very probable, the Hebrews, who were known to the Egyptians as Aperiu. The names of the Hebrew leaders, Joshua and others, are not found in the contemporary letters, so that the matter is not certain ; but the identification is highly probable, as there was no other period in the history of the time when a tribe such as the Hebrews could possibly have invaded and over-ridden Palestine. This would place the conquest about 1370 B.C. Meneptah's date is about 1225 B.C. So that Israel had already been a century in Palestine when Rameses II took Hebrew prisoners to build his name-city Raamses. Some scholars, however, have supposed that the Exodus was not identical with the expulsion of the Hyksos, but took place as late as Meneptah's reign. This view rests largely upon the literal acceptance of the tradition that the Hebrew captive labourers of Rameses II were recruited during the stay in the land of Goshen, while those who believe in the earlier date for the Exodus consider that there is here some confusion in the Hebrew record. In any case, the date required for the Exodus if it took place in Meneptah's time (c. 1220 B.C.) seems almost impossibly late. It seems therefore best to suppose that the Exodus took place about 1580 B.C., and the Conquest of Palestine about 1370 B.C., while the episode of the oppression belongs to about 1270 B.C. and has been attached to the account of the Exodus. But this of course is merely a supposition like all other theories on the subject. It is merely more credible and probable than the Meneptah-theory.

No doubt the Syrian wars had tended to increase the Semitic population of the Delta; in addition to ordinary immigration, captives of war would swell the numbers ; and the danger which might arise from this large foreign element was obvious. Libyans, too, from the west had overrun the Delta ; and Meneptah repelled a great Libyan invasion in the fifth year of his reign. In the time of Rameses III (about 1200 B.C.) a second invasion was defeated, as also was an attack upon the Delta by the wandering people of the Philistines, who came by sea and land from their original seats in Kaphtor (Crete and south-west Asia Minor), and with their allies overthrew the Hittite kingdom and occupied Syria. After their defeat the Philistines settled down in the Shephelah, which afterwards bore the name of Philistia or Palestine.

The glory of Egypt now departs from her. The later history of the New Kingdom is the history of decadence, of occasional revivals, and spasmodic triumphs, of internal troubles, of defeats, and of subjection to the foreign yoke. Egypt's enemies began to close in upon her. Now and again an energetic king managed to make head against the enemy. Shashank, the founder of the Twenty-Second Dynasty, himself a man of Libyan blood, carried war beyond the borders. He appears in the Bible as Shishak, the friend and protector of Jeroboam, who, after the secession of the Ten Tribes, made war upon Judah (930 B.C.), and 'came up against Jerusalem ; and he took away the treasures of the house of the Lord, and the treasures of the king's house' (1 Kings 14²⁵, ²⁶). Two hundred years later we find Egypt subject to Nubia, and a Nubian dynasty upon the throne. The first kings of this race were Kashta, Piankhi, and Shabaka, the 'So, King of Egypt' (2 Kings 17⁴) who suffered defeat (720 B. C.) at Raphia on the frontier at the hands of Sargon of Assyria. The attacks of the Assyrians now became sustained. In the year 700 B. C. their warlike king Sennacherib inflicted a severe defeat upon the Egyptian army at Eltekeh in the south of Palestine. The assignment to his reign of the sudden calamity that broke up the Assyrian host (2 Kings 19³⁵) is probably a mistake, as it seems really to have happened to his son Esar-haddon. It is recorded by the Greek historian Herodotus as well as in the Bible. A respite of thirty years left the Nubian Pharaoh, Taharka or Tirhakah, who then occupied the throne of Egypt, leisure to prepare for the final struggle. In the year 671 B. C. the blow fell ; the Assyrians totally defeated the Egyptian forces and occupied the Delta ; Memphis was captured, Thebes fell before the conqueror, and Taharka was driven from his kingdom. A later attempt by Taharka to drive out the Assyrian garrisons was vigorously repulsed, and ended in the destruction of Thebes in 663 B. C. by Ashurbanipal.

Egypt remained subject to Assyria till that power began to wane before the attacks of neighbouring powers. Then Psamatik, the Psammetichus of the Greeks, the vassal king of Saïs, with the aid of Ionian and Carian mercenaries, threw off the yoke and made himself master of the country, thus becoming the founder of the Twenty-Sixth Dynasty, under which Egypt maintained her independence and rose again to some degree of prosperity for the next hundred years. Psammetichus, however, still regarded himself as the ally of Assyria, and when that power was attacked about the year 616 B. C. by a confederation of the Babylonians under Nabopolassar, the Medes under Kyaxares, and the *Umman-Mandu*, or Northern tribes, he came to Assyria's help. His help was vain, however, for in 612 Nineveh was destroyed. The successor of Psammetichus, the warlike Necho (609-593 B. C.), advanced to the reconquest of Syria, now that Assyrian hegemony there was no more, and defeated and slew Josiah, King of Judah, at Megiddo, deposed his son Jehoahaz, and set on the throne Jehoiakim, who paid him tribute (2 Kings 23²⁹⁻³⁵). Necho's campaign, however, ended disastrously in a defeat inflicted on him by Nebuchadrezzar of Babylon, in a great battle at Carchemish ; 'and the king of Egypt came not again any more out of his land : for the king of Babylon had taken from the river of Egypt unto the river Euphrates all that pertained to the king of Egypt' (2 Kings 24⁷). Again, one of his successors, Uahibrē', the Hophra of the Bible, made some attempt at Syrian conquest, and succeeded in capturing Sidon ; but his successor, Amasis II, followed a wiser policy in refraining from foreign campaigns, and during his long and successful reign (569-526 B.C.) restored the internal prosperity of the country. But the end was now approaching. In 539 B.C. the Persians had captured Babylon, and now rapidly marched westward for futher conquests. In 525 B.C. the Persian king Cambyses defeated the Egyptian army with great slaughter before the frontier fortress of Pelusium, and, after capturing Memphis, easily conquered the whole kingdom.

Here practically ends the history of Egypt as an independent power. It is true that for a brief period of sixty years, in the fourth century B. C., she managed to shake herself free of the Persian yoke, but she was again subdued in 340 B. C. From the Persians she passed to Alexander the Great ; for three hundred years she was ruled by the Macedonian house of the Ptolemies ; and on the death of Cleopatra, the last of that race, Egypt became a Roman province (B.C. 30).

Plates XIV and XV. The Gods of Egypt. The Egyptians believed in many gods, to whom they gave the collective title of *netēru*. Some have supposed that the more enlightened priests may have believed in the existence of a hidden unknown deity behind the many *netēru*, but it is difficult to find any warrant for this supposition other than a vague recognition of 'the divine' when 'the god' is generally referred to, as is often the case. And this may be mere henotheism. The gods were numerous and were the subject of the threats and denunciations of the Prophets of Israel from Moses (Exod. 12^{12}) to Jeremiah (Jer. 43^{13}). Their temples and statues were to be seen everywhere, and few indeed are the buildings of Egypt, whether temples, palaces, or tombs, which are not profusely ornamented with representations of them. They are depicted as men and women, animals and birds, or in other forms ; and each one has his or her characteristic emblem. The greater number typified the forces of nature. Each nome, each city, had its local god, or its groups of gods, in triads, or in triads of triads, or in other combinations. But above all there were certain deities who, on account of their antiquity and universal worship, were regarded as the great 'gods of Egypt'.

Ptah, the Creator, identified by the Greeks with Hephaistos, is represented as a mummy. He is sometimes called Ptah-Tanen. In his hands he holds the sceptre⸢, emblem of sovereignty ; on the back of the neck he has the *menat* , or counterweight of his necklace. He was worshipped at Memphis from the earliest times, and was the chief member of the triad of that city. Originally he was regarded as a smith.

Khnumu or **Khnûm,** another creator, worshipped at Elephantine, in the south, was regarded as a potter. He was represented as ram-headed.

Amon (in earlier times Amāna, in later Amōn or Amūn, the Zeus Ammōn of the Greeks), or 'the hidden one', was the chief member of the great triad of Thebes : Amen, Mut 'the mother', and Khonsu, a moon god. After the expulsion of the Hyksos, or 'Princes of the Shasu tribes', about 1580 B.C., by his worshippers the Theban kings, he became the chief god of Egypt. He was identified with Rē', all of whose attributes were bestowed upon him, and was generally called Amon-Rē'. He had neither equal, nor second, nor like, and he was called 'king of the gods', *insu-netēru*, Amonrasonthēr. In the period of the Twentieth Dynasty his priests enjoyed almost absolute power. On his head he wears two plumes, and in his right hand he holds the *'ankh*, the symbol of life, and in his left the sceptre. Related to him was **Minu** or **Min,** the god of fertility, worshipped at Koptos, who also wears plumes.

Ra', Rī' or **Rē'** was the sun-god, and his worship was most ancient. He was the actual representative of God. He has the head of a hawk, on which is borne the sun-disk encircled with a snake. In his right hand he holds the symbol of life. He sails over heaven in the 'boat of millions of years', the course of which cannot be impeded by any of the powers of darkness. The chief seat of his worship was Anu, the On of the Bible and Heliopolis of the Greeks.

Also hawk-headed was **Hure** (Har, Hōr, or Horus), the Upper Egyptian sky-god (see below), and he is often difficult to distinguish from Rē' ; but he does not bear the solar disk on his head. He was usually called Harakhti or Horakhuti (Haremakhti, in Greek Harmachis), 'Horus of the Two Horizons', and his holy cities were Edfu (Behudet) and Hierakonpolis (el Kab) in Upper Egypt. To distinguish him from the other Horus, son of Isis (Harsiēsis or Harpokrátes), he was often called 'the elder Horus', Haroēris.

Djeḥuti, Ṭḥuti, or Thōth, the 'scribe of the gods', was the divine intelligence, and uttered the words which created the heavens and the earth. He invented the arts and sciences, writing and letters, and he measured time. He was the god, also, of right and truth. He has the head of an ibis, and carries a palette and writing reed or the Eye of Horus ; on his head he wears the feather, the symbol of right and truth, and the crescent moon as computer of time. (Both lost in the example illustrated.) Sometimes he is represented as a dog-headed ape. The Greeks identified him with Hermes.

Neith, identified by the Greeks with Athene, was one of the most ancient goddesses of Egypt and was probably of Libyan origin. She appears as a woman wearing the crown of Lower Egypt, and, as goddess of weaving and of the chase, she bears the shuttle and bow and arrows. She carries the symbol of life. **Uŏdjet, Uto** or **Buto** ('the green one'), was another very ancient goddess of the Delta.

Asari or Osiris, the king and judge of the dead and lord of the underworld, was the chief of all the gods of the dead. On his head he wears the *atef* crown, with feathers emblematic of right and truth, and horns, and in his right hand he carries the $\bigwedge$, in his left the $\lceil$. He suffered a cruel death on earth at the hands of his brother Suti or Set, the god of darkness, and his body was mutilated and its members were scattered throughout the land of Egypt. By his divine power he rose again in a glorified body and became the god of the dead. The Egyptians based their hope of resurrection on the resurrection of Osiris. **Isis** was his wife, **Nephthys** his sister, and **Harpokrates** or Harsiēsis, son of Osiris and Isis, represented as a child in the arms of his mother, was later identified with **Hur or Horus**, the sky-god of Upper Egypt, a most ancient deity, who was represented as hawk-headed, like Rē'. He was often called Haroēris, 'Horus the elder ', to distinguish him from ' Horus the child ' (Harpokrates, the Greek form of the Egyptian **Har-p-khrad**). Osiris, Isis, and Horus formed the most popular divine triad in Egypt. Closely connected with them were **Anubis** the jackal, and **Upuot** (**Opho·is**) the wolf, both deities of the necropoles (an instance of propitiation and fear, for both animals lived on the desert border and constantly desecrated the cemeteries in search of carrion). **Ḥa'pi** (**Apis**), the bull of Memphis, was a form of Osiris confused or identified with Ptah, and the composite deity Ptah-Socharis-Osiris was represented as a dwarf. Sokari or Socharis was a Memphite god of the dead. Sarapis was the Greek form of Asar-Hapi, Osiris-Apis. Mnēvis was the bull of Ra'.

Sekhmet was a member of the triad of Memphis : Ptah, Sekhmet, and **Imhotep** (**Imouthes**), a deified sage who in life had been the minister of king Zoser of the Third Dynasty and was connected historically therefore with Memphis. Sekhmet typified the fierce heat of the sun. She appears with the head of a lioness, her solar character being indicated by the sun-disk, encircled with a snake, on her head. She carries the symbol of life. Imouthes is represented as a man seated, reading a scroll of papyrus.

Ḥa'pi, the god of the Nile, is represented as a man with water streaming from his breast. In his left hand is a frog, the emblem of fertility, from whose mouth also flows water. His head is crowned with lotus flowers.

Nepri was the god of harvest, and **Ernutet** (Thermouthis) a goddess of fertility. She was represented as a snake, as also was **Meritseger** (' She who loveth silence '), the local deity of the Theban necropolis, who was a form of the great goddess **Hathor**, whom the Greeks identified with Aphrodite. She resembled both Aphrodite and Ishtar in many respects, but also had a maternal aspect typified by her identification with the cow, and she is sometimes represented as cow-headed, and often identified with Isis, the mother of Horus. Closely connected with her too was **Ubastet** or **Bast**, the cat-goddess, who also corresponded to Aphrodite in some ways, Hathor representing Aphrodite Urania. Bast is to be distinguished from Sekhmet by her pointed ears, whereas the lioness-ears of Sekhmet are round. Closely associated with Hathor as a deity of beauty, fashion, and feminine luxury was **Bes**, a god of Oriental origin depicted as a bearded dwarf with feathers in his head. Semitic deities such as Anaitis, Resheph (Reshpu), and Baal were also worshipped in later times, and Baal was often identified with Bes. **Maahes** was a lion god of Nubian origin. **Didūn** (Tithōnos) was also a Nubian god.

Plate XVI. ' **The Golden Calf.** ' This illustration shows an image of the cow-goddess Hathor, found in the temple of Queen Hatshepsut at Dair al-Baḥri, opposite Thebes in Upper Egypt, by M. Naville and Mr. Currelly in 1906, and now in the Cairo Museum. The cow-image of the goddess was referred to in contemporary inscriptions as 'the cow of gold ', and there is little doubt that it was an image of this kind of the goddess, but made of gold, that the Israelites sought to set up to worship in the Wilderness, more especially because Hathor was the express patroness of the desert and specifically of Sinai.

Plate XVII. Procession of an Ark. Nibma'rī' (Nimmurīya) Amen-hetep III, king of Egypt, offering incense before an ark of Amen-Rē'. The images of the gods were carried in procession by the priests, and incense was burnt before them as they moved along. It was customary to place the image in an ark or shrine, which was set up in a boat resting on a sledge. It was thus either carried on the shoulders of men or drawn on the ground. Here the ark and boat of Amen-Rē' on a sledge are being borne in procession by thirty-two priests with shaven heads, two fan-bearers bringing up the rear. The ark is overshadowed by the winged disk, emblematic of the sun ; and on it is drawn a picture in which are seen the two goddesses of Right and Law, covering with their outstretched wings the beetle, emblematic of the sun-god, which holds aloft the disk of the sun. The legend above the boat reads : ' Amen-Ra', lord of Karnak. May he give all life, and all health, in making millions of festival-cycles of thirty years like unto the Sun for ever.' On the right, overshadowed by a vulture, the emblem of the goddess Mut, the universal mother, is the king, ' Amen-hetep, the prince of Thebes, the lord of diadems, Nibma'rī', the lord of the North and South, the good god, the performer of ceremonies, offering incense unto Amen-Ra' '. In his left hand is the thurible, and with the right hand he drops incense into the flame. The inscription before him reads : ' May he (i. e. Amen) give him life and health like unto the Sun for ever.' Behind the boat is another figure of the king, who ' followeth the god in his course '.

Plate XVIII. Egyptian Magicians and Serpent-charming. 1. A wooden figure of a dancer, wearing a lioness-mask, and holding two serpents, much in the style of the well-known Minoan figures of snake goddesses or priestesses found at Knossos. Twelfth Dynasty ; *c.* 2000 B. C. Manchester Museum. 2. A portrait statue of Kha'muese, son of king Rameses II (*c.* 1250 B. C.), high priest of Ptah at Memphis, and famous in later days as a potent necromancer and magician. British Museum.

Plates XIX–XXIII. Egyptian Burial. The Hebrews, although they adopted several other Egyptian customs, never took over that of embalming the dead as a regular practice, though in earlier times when under considerable Egyptian influence it would appear to have been used for the burial of great persons. Though there can be no doubt that, in common with other oriental nations, they made use of spices in preparing their dead for burial (see 2 Chron. 16[14]), yet the only recorded examples of Hebrews being embalmed or mummified after the Egyptian fashion are the patriarchs Jacob (Gen. 50[2, 3]) and his son Joseph (Gen. 50[26]). The embalmed body of Jacob was taken to Canaan by his sons, and buried in the cave of the field of Machpelah (Gen. 50[13]). Joseph, we are told, was not only embalmed, but was put into a coffin in Egypt (Gen. 50[26]), and it is not impossible that his bones lay in the same coffin when the Israelites buried them in Shechem (Joshua 24[32]). The Bible gives no details of the embalming in either instance, although in the case of Jacob we may assume, from the statement that 'forty days were fulfilled for him', that the process was elaborate.

The practice of embalming among the Egyptians was most ancient. The preservation of the bodies of the dead was one of the first religious duties. The reason for mummification was the natural desire to escape from death. 'O ye who love life and hate death!' begins the ancient supplication for the prayers of the passers-by. So a sham appearance of life was given to the dead, beginning with the king and gradually becoming the fashion among the lower orders of society. The process was naturally surrounded by the protection of an armoury of spells and magical *grimoires* which we now know as 'The Book of the Dead', so that the artificially preserved from death might live again in the Underworld, which it was pathetically hoped would be a mere replica of this world of life and light.

In the oldest method of mummifying, the intestines and other easily corruptible portions were removed, and the body, salted and swathed, was buried in the sand or in a rock-hewn tomb. At a later time, spices and aromatic and astringent substances were used to sweeten the body and arrest decay; and the intestines were mummified separately. Mummies of as early a date as 2000 B.C. are found to consist of nothing but skin and bone. Our word 'mummy' is derived from the Arabic *mûmiâ*, 'bitumen', which substance, however, was not used till Ptolemaic times, if then, for embalming. The process, in its more elaborate forms, was both lengthy and costly; the time required might be as long as seventy days, and the cost might be as much as £250 in modern money. A still larger sum might be spent on decoration; and the cost of the coffins and amulets and of the rock-hewn sepulchre must have been very great :—

Plate XIX. A great coffin or chest of painted cedar wood, adorned inside and out with funerary texts and a sort of guide (with maps) of the Underworld for the use of the dead. This type of rectangular coffin is characteristic of the period from the Sixth to the Twelfth Dynasty (*c.* 2600–2000 B.C.), and is probably of the kind in which the bodies of Jacob and Joseph are said to have been placed after embalmment. British Museum.

Plate XX. Anthropoid coffins of the Fourteenth Dynasty (*c.* 1750 B.C.) and the Nineteenth Dynasty (*c.* 1300 B.C.). The first is that of a king, Antef or Iniatef, and the second that of a private lady. They are both splendidly adorned with gilding.

Plate XXI. Embalmers at work. In the upper scene two embalmers are represented bandaging a mummy. After the body had gone through the process of embalming it was swathed in bandages, never more than a few inches in width, but sometimes of very great length. There are instances of as many as 600 yards of bandaging having been used. As the bandaging proceeded, unguents and spices were used freely, and amulets and other symbols of the Egyptian creed were laid between the folds; at times some object which the deceased had valued in life was thus bound up with his body.

The lower scene represents the process of decorating a mummy. Here the body has evidently been encased in the plaster coating or 'cartonnage', which was very commonly employed for many centuries by the undertakers of Egypt. This cartonnage was usually painted in brilliant colours and was in later times decorated with mythological scenes, and inscribed with prayers and other extracts from the 'Book of the Dead'.

Plate XXII. A Royal Mummy. This body was found at Dair al-Baḥri. On the outer covering is drawn the winged beetle, with a ram's head surmounted by the sun-disk, emblem of the god Khepera, the self-created god, and with a feather in each claw. The four lines of hieratic writing record the 'establishment' of the mummy in a new tomb during the rule of the priest-king Pinodjem, the son of Pai'ankh. On the band round the head of the mummy are drawn figures of the gods, to serve as amulets and protect the body from harm.

Plate XXIII. Egyptian Funeral Scene. As the principal cemeteries of Thebes lay on the west bank of the Nile, the ceremony of removing the dead across the river was an important detail in the funeral. The barge here represented is a typical river-boat, with decorated cabin, on the roof of which is a company of professional mourning women with hair dishevelled and breasts bare. The barge is propelled by rowers and steered with an oar of great length. Once across the river and disembarked, the body was accompanied by a long procession of priests, and mourners, and servants with the possessions of the deceased and furniture for the tomb, and with animals for sacrifice and provisions for the funeral feast. At the entrance to the tomb religious ceremonies were performed, and, sacrifices having been offered, the body was borne to the mummy-chamber, which was straightway walled up.

Plates XXIV–XXVII contain scenes in the life beyond the grave, according to the Egyptian belief. They are taken from two papyri inscribed with the 'Book of the Dead' for two officials, Hunefer and Nekht, respectively, who lived at the end of the fourteenth century B.C. The former held important posts under the king; the latter was a War Office official. The 'Book of the Dead' is the name which we give to the collection of chapters or compositions consisting of prayers, hymns, confessions, &c., whereby the dead might overcome his foes in the underworld, and arrive at the abode of the blessed or 'Fields of Peace'. The Egyptians generally knew it as 'The Chapters of Coming Forth by Day', as the general tendency of its spells was to secure the free movement of the ghost in the underworld of the tomb and to enable him to revisit the glimpses of the sun if possible; in fact, to guarantee some kind of continued life to the dead. It was customary to bury with the dead a papyrus roll containing this text or some selections from it, the extent and quality of the roll being regulated by the price paid for it. Whether the Judgement of the Dead was supposed to take place immediately after death or after burial we are not told; but we may presume that it was more probably after burial. It should be noted that the dead, after passing the trial of his heart, becomes identified with Osiris and is addressed and spoken of by the god's name:

Plates XXIV, XXV. Judgement of the Dead. The two scenes form one picture in the papyrus of Hunefer. The first scene is the weighing of the heart, or conscience, of the dead man Hunefer, in the Hall of the Two Laws, in the presence of Osiris, the judge of the dead. Hunefer, on the left, is led forward by Anubis, the God of the Dead, jackal-headed. In the centre is the 'Great Balance' upon the standard of which is set the head and shoulders of Ma'at, Goddess of Truth. On the left of the Balance Anubis is again shown scrutinizing the tongue, to see that the beam of the Balance is exactly even, for the gods only require that the heart shall counterbalance, not outweigh, the feather, the symbol of 'Right and Law'. On the right of the Balance is a monster called the 'Devourer', part crocodile, part lion, and part hippopotamus, ready to eat up the heart if found too heavy. Beyond, Thoth, the scribe of the gods, holding a reed and palette, stands ready to record the result of the trial. In the upper part of the picture are seated twelve great gods and goddesses, presiding over the trial. The short lines of text above the Balance are the prayers of Hunefer : that the divine powers may in no way obstruct the weighing of his heart, that no false witness may be borne against him in the presence of the god Osiris, that his heart may not be separated from him, but may accompany him to the place whither he is going. The result of the trial is favourable, Thoth thus addressing the gods : 'Hear ye this judgement. The heart of Osiris hath, in very truth, been weighed and his soul hath stood as witness for him ; it hath been found true by trial in the Great Balance. There hath not been found any wickedness in him.' The hieroglyphs over the monster 'Amamit describe its composition : 'its forepart (is that of) a crocodile, its hind-quarters (that of) a hippopotamus, its middle (that of) a lion.'

In the second scene (Plate XXV) Hunefer, now justified, is led into the presence of Osiris by his son Horus. Osiris, the everlasting lord, is enthroned within a shrine, holding the emblems of sovereignty and power, and supported by the goddesses Isis and Nephthys. Before him, on a lotus flower, stand the four gods of the cardinal points, who presided over the intestines of the dead. Their names, Mesti, Hapi, Duamutef and Qebehsnûf, are written over them. To Osiris Horus, called 'the avenger of his father and efficient successor of Un-nefer*', says : 'Behold, I have brought the Osiris Hunefer unto thee. He has been acquitted by the scales whose tongue lies in its proper place.'

Plates XXVI and XXVII are from the papyrus of Nekht.

Plate XXVI. The Soul revisiting the Body. The mummy of Nekht lies on the bier ; his soul in the form of a human-headed bird is alighting on the mummy. The object jutting out from the head of the mummy, or rather the painted mask of the mummy case, represents the festal lump of nard worn at banquets, and ceremonial occasions, and which, as it melted, ran down and scented the clothes of the wearer, 'like the precious ointment upon the head that ran down unto the beard, even unto Aaron's beard, and went down to the skirts of his clothing.' (Ps. 133 ².)

Plate XXVII. The Fields of Satisfaction. In the Sekhet-hetepu or 'Fields of Peace' were, according to one view, the habitations of the blessed in their new life. The scene is divided into four compartments, in the three of which here shown Nekht is represented as occupied at various tasks. He reaps flax, pulling it up with his hands, and barley with the sickle and drives a plough drawn by two oxen for the new sowing. In the top left-hand corner Nekht is seated before a table loaded with first-fruits which he is offering to the *bennu*-bird (a heron).

Plate XXVIII. Names of Egyptian kings mentioned in the Bible. The names of the kings here given are composed of two parts, the *prenomen* and *nomen* ; and the titles *Insibya*, 'King of the North and South', and *Si-Ra'*, 'son of the Sun', were commonly added. Both prenomen and nomen are

---

* A name of Osiris.

enclosed in an oval ring or cartouche. The earliest kings did not employ the cartouche, which first appears in carefully-cut inscriptions as a rope, but with exactly what signification is not known, in the time of the Third Dynasty. The practice of using prenomen as well as nomen is as ancient as the period of the Fifth Dynasty. The six names in the plate may be translated thus : (1) *Usi(r)-ma‘(t)-Rā‘* 'Strong is the Right of Ra‘', *Satepu-n-Rā‘* the chosen one of Ra‘, Ra‘masesu (i. e., child of Ra‘), beloved of Amen'; (2) 'The creator of the double crown is Ra‘ [for] the chosen one of Ra‘, Shashanq, beloved of Amen'; (3) 'Beautiful is the double of Ra‘, Shabaka'; (4) 'Taharqa, the glorious one of Ra‘ and Nefer-Tum'; (5) 'The renewer of the heart is Ra‘, Nekau'; (6) 'The rejoicer of the heart is Ra‘, Ra‘ maketh the heart to be stablished'.

The title of 'King of the North and South', implying sovereignty of Upper Egypt as well as of the Delta, was first adopted by Semti or Ousaphais, a king of the First Dynasty ; and in the Fifth Dynasty the kings began regularly to style themselves 'son of the Sun', because that dynasty was of Heliopolitan origin. In the Bible the kings of Egypt are always referred to by their *nomina*, viz., Rameses (Gen. 47²); Shishak (1 Kings 14²⁵; 2 Chron. 12 ², ⁵, ⁷, ⁹); So or Sabaco (2 Kings 17⁴); Tirhakah (2 Kings 19⁹); Necho (2 Kings 23²⁹; Jer. 46²); Hophra (Jer. 44³⁰). The title 'Pharaoh' is the Egyptian ⟨ ⟩ *per-‘o* 'Great House'. With this title we may compare the Ottoman 'Sublime Porte'.

Plates XXIX–XXXIV illustrate Egyptian history with special reference to the Biblical accounts from the period of the Hyksos (= probably the rule of Joseph in Egypt) to the reign of Rameses II, possibly the traditional Pharaoh of the Oppression.

Plate XXIX. 1. **A portrait of a Hyksos king** (?). This small ivory sphinx probably has the features of one of the Semitic kings of Egypt. the 'Hyksos' or 'Shepherds', of whose rule the story of the stay of the Israelites in Egypt and the prosperity of Joseph is undoubtedly a reminiscence. It is perhaps significant that the king is shown shaking an Egyptian by the ears. The object is of course of Egyptian workmanship, and shows the foreign king wearing the insignia of Egyptian royalty. The date of it is the Middle Kingdom, between the Twelfth and Eighteenth Dynasties, by its style, and this is the period required by this theory of its origin and significance. It was found at Abydos by Prof. Garstang. 2. The head of the mummy of King Ia‘hmase (Aa‘hmes, 1580–1559 B. C.), the Amosis of Manetho, who is possibly, on one theory, the king who expelled the Israelites from Egypt. He certainly was the expeller of the Hyksos, and if we are to regard the Exodus-story as a Jewish version of the expulsion of the Hyksos, as has been suggested, it will have been in the reign of this man that the Israelites, under the leadership of Moses and Aaron, went forth out of Egypt. He reigned for many years after the expulsion, and was buried at Thebes.

Plate XXX. A young portrait of Thutmase (Thothmes or Tuthmosis) III (1501–1447 B. C.), the great Egyptian conqueror of Asia. Cairo Museum. This is a very fine example of Egyptian portraiture.

Plate XXXI. **King Akhenaten and Queen Nefretiti** (1376–1362 B.C.). These two beautiful portraits of the heretical young king and his wife are among the greatest treasures of the Berlin Museum. They were found at al-Amarna, the site of the Laputa-like city or 'Abbey of Théléme', that the heretic founded and where he lived. His new doctrine of the monotheistic worship of the sun, which was founded on the 'Wisdom of the Egyptians' taught by the priests of the sun at On, was maintained by him for several years, but after his death, in the reign of his son-in-law Tutankhamen (whose tomb, with its marvellous treasures, has lately been discovered), polytheism was officially restored and the monotheistic doctrine disappeared. In his time, Syria and Palestine revolted under pressure from the Hittites under their King Supiluliu, and owing to the pacificism and anti-militarism of the king the Asiatic dominion was lost. During the Anarchy the Khabiri (the Hebrews ?) entered the Promised Land of Canaan, according to the theory now generally accepted.

Plate XXXII. The mummied heads of the kings Seti I and his son Rī'-masesu (Rameses) II (1300–1234 B. C.), who reconquered Palestine, and held it down. In the reign of the son of Rameses, Meneptah, Israel is first mentioned, as a settled people that had been ravaged by the Egyptians. It was formerly thought that the Exodus took place in the reign of Meneptah, but there are now recognized serious objections to this view, which would bring the date of that event and *ipso facto* that of the Invasion of Canaan far too late. Rameses, however, may still have been the Pharaoh of the Oppression, if we suppose that the Oppression referred to is that of Israelites taken captive in the wars of Seti and Rameses and transported into the Delta to labour in the ' store-cities' of Pithom and Raamses. These two royal mummies are extremely fine, that of Seti especially so. Both were found, with many other mummies of kings and royal persons, concealed in rock-hewn chambers at Dair al-Baḥrī, on the western bank of the Nile at Thebes, in the year 1871. When the bandages had been removed it was seen how well the embalmers had done their work. The features were still perfect, and even the thin white hairs, though discoloured by the embalming substances, had not been destroyed. From the condition of the fragile bones and atrophied muscles, it is thought that Rameses must have been nearly one hundred years of age at his death.

Plate XXXIII. 1. **Rameses II** : a young portrait : from a statue in the British Museum. 2. A Ramesside king (*c.* 1250 B. C.) : possibly intended for Rameses II or Meneptah. Found in Phoenicia and now in the British Museum. This figure, which is uninscribed, is an example of an official image of the Pharaoh set up in a Phoenician dependency of Egypt.

Plate XXXIV. Rameses in Battle. This scene represents the king routing the nations of Northern Syria, under the walls of a besieged city. The battle is no doubt the one in which Rameses says that he defeated the Hittites and their allies, before the city of Kadesh, on the Orontes. As a matter of fact, it was a Pyrrhic victory, if one at all. Rameses, drawn on a heroic scale as the great warrior, drives the enemy before him, and crushes them under the wheels of his chariot. Above his head is the sun-disk with uraei, the emblem of the visible protecting presence of Ra', the Sun-god. An assault on the walls of the city is being repelled with vigour. The four warriors in the foreground on the right are sons of Rameses. The hiero-glyphic text describes the prowess of Rameses and the submission of the enemy from the walls of the Ramesseum or Memnonium, built in honour of the god Amen-Ra' by Rameses II, at Thebes. They form part of a series of scenes illustrating the war carried on by Rameses II against the nations in Northern Syria in the fifth year of his reign.

Plates XXXV–XXXVII illustrate the story of the Oppression. From time immemorial Semitic immigrants had made a practice of pasturing their flocks and often of settling on the eastern borders of Egypt, and the Israelite settlement under the Hyksos was but a larger movement, probably, of the same kind. And from all time Egyptian pharaohs had brought back from their razzias and wars in Sinai and Southern Palestine troops of Semitic prisoners to labour on their palace or temple buildings or works of public utility such as granaries and dykes.

Plate XXXV. Strangers coming into Egypt. This scene occurs in a series of wall-paintings in the tomb of an Egyptian noble at Beni-hasan in Upper Egypt, of the period of the Twelfth Dynasty, about 2000 B.C. The noble was Khnumu-hotep, administrator of the Eastern desert and prince of the city of Men'at-Khufu, one of whose duties was to receive the tribute of foreigners. The scene represents the arrival of a company of the tribe of the 'Amu from the desert. Commencing with the upper division of the picture, Khnumu-hotep stands on the right facing the royal scribe Nefer-hotep, who holds up an inscription stating that in the sixth year of the king Senusret II a company of thirty-seven of the 'Amu brought an offering of stibium or eye-paint. Behind the scribe is the superintendent of the huntsmen ; and then come the foreigners, headed by their chief Abesha presenting an oryx. The men of the party have beards, and the greater number, both men and women, wear garments embroidered or woven in patterns, contrasting with the simple dress of the Egyptians. Among their weapons will be noticed the throwing-stick. This scene recalls the visit of Jacob's sons to Egypt with their gift of 'a little balm, and a little honey, spices, and myrrh, nuts, and almonds' (Gen. 43²), for Joseph, 'the lord of the land'.

Plate XXXVI. Semites from Palestine or Egypt bringing tribute to the Egyptian court. A fine wall-painting from a tomb of the Eighteenth Dynasty, about 1400 B.C. The facial type of the Semites is admirably rendered. British Museum.

Plate XXXVII. 1. Egyptian Granaries. An ancient wooden model of a granary, enclosed with walls, into which entrance is gained by the door way on the left. The grain is poured into the granaries through openings in the top. The process of loading, carrying, and counting the loads is here seen in action. The model is one of a kind commonly found in tombs of the Eleventh and Twelfth Dynasties, about 2000 B.C. The hieroglyphic inscriptions contain many references to famines caused by the failure of the waters of the Nile. A text records a seven years' famine in the reign of Zoser or Djeser, a king of the Third Dynasty, about 3000 B.C., who speaks thus : 'I upon the throne of my majesty am in grievous trouble for my household, and my heart suffereth by reason of an exceeding great affliction that hath come upon me. In mine own time, for seven years the Nile hath not risen. Grain is scarce, the herb of the field hath come to an end, and all that man eateth hath failed. Every man stealeth from his neighbour. Though they would run, yet can they not move. The babe waileth, and the child hardly draggeth himself along. The hearts of the aged are stricken down ; their legs tremble and they lie prone upon the earth, and their hands are upon their bellies. The counsellors can give no counsel. The storehouses have been broken open, and instead of victuals there cometh forth wind. Every being that liveth is in misery.' Again, an inscription of the Twelfth Dynasty in a tomb at Beni-hasan tells us how a wise governor would act in time of famine : 'When years of hunger came, I arose. I ploughed all the fields of the nome from north to south ; and I made the inhabitants to live, and I provided food for it. No man went hungry therein. I gave to the widow as to the wife, to the younger as to the elder. And when the high waters came, bringing forth wheat and barley and everything in abundance, I sought not again what I had spent on the land.' 2. The second illustration on this Plate shows the process of brickmaking in modern Egypt. Cf. Plates XXXVIII, XXXIX, below.

Plates XXXVIII, XXXIX. Egyptian Forced Labour. The process of brickmaking in Egypt, as represented in the first of these plates, needs no comment. As with all other simple manufactures of a domestic character, when once a practical method of work had been settled, there was nothing to be gained by altering it. The English brickmaker of our own time mixes his material, and moulds and lays out his bricks on the drying ground, just as the Egyptian brickmaker did thousands of years ago. The presence of the taskmasters in this scene is nothing unusual, since no gang-labour in the East is carried out without its taskmasters or *ra*ï*ses*, and in ancient Egypt at any rate certainly never without the assistance of the stick. Such labour as was exacted from the children of Israel (Exod. 1¹⁴) was then nothing unusual. It is interesting that while two at least of the slaves in the brickfield are clearly shown as Semites, all those engaged in hauling stone are Egyptians. Egyptian bricks were usually sun-dried, not fired, and the mud of which they were generally made required the admixture of such a substance as straw or stubble to ensure cohesion. They are of a larger size than our modern bricks; the one represented in Plate XXXIX measures 15 by 7½ inches, and is 5 inches thick. This specimen is of the reign of Rameses II; and, according to the Egyptian custom, it is stamped with his name. The second illustration on Plate XXXVII above shows a scene of brickmaking in Egypt of the present day.

Plates XL–XLVII. The Northern Foreigners: Hittites, Philistines, and Minoans (Mycenaeans). These plates illustrate the non-Semitic foreigners, Anatolians, and Europeans, with whom both Egyptians and Semites came into contact during the latter half of the second millennium B.C.

Plate XL. Hittite relief monuments at Boghâz Kyöi and Yassili Kayâ, in Asia Minor. They represent a king or god guarding the entrance of a palace, a rock relief showing a priest-king (?) under the protection of a god, and a procession of warriors. All date probably from the earlier period of Hittite history contemporary with the Eighteenth Dynasty of Egypt or earlier. Boghâz Kyöi was the site of the Hittite capital, Hattushash. (For Hittite hieroglyphic inscriptions see Plate LXXV.)

Plate XLI. Types of Hittites and Philistines, from the Temple of Rameses III at Medinet Habu, Thebes. The curious physical type of the Hittites, with their glabrous faces, prominent noses, and long pigtails, is well shown; also the European-looking type of the Philistines and their characteristic crests of feathers. Though they differed outwardly, both peoples were Anatolians, the Hittites of the centre and east, the Philistines of the west, the later Caria and Lycia, whence they moved out on their great trek and coasting voyage to Palestine, overthrowing the Hittites on the way, till they were brought to a stand on the borders of Egypt by Rameses III and then settled in Philistia. Of the language of the Philistines we know nothing, but among the Hittites several tongues were spoken, the chief of which were the Hittite proper, or 'Protohattic', an Asianic tongue of no Aryan or Semitic affinities, and the court Hittite, which was an Indo-European language akin to both Greek and Latin. The Philistine culture was apparently a poor reflection of the degenerate Mycenaean civilization (see p. 32); the Hittite was an independent system owing a good deal in art and in other respects on the one hand to the Mycenaean-Minoan centre and on the other to that of Babylonia.

Plates XLII, XLIII. Philistines from Medinet Habu : well showing the European type of face.

Plate XLIV. Minoan Cretan Ambassadors. From wall-paintings in the tombs of Sennemut and Rekhmira' at Thebes (*c.* 1500–1450 B. C.). These are Egyptian representations of Greeks of the Bronze Age from Crete and the Aegean, described by them as 'Great Men of Keftiu and the Isles'. The word Keftiu is undoubtedly identical with the biblical Kaphtor, which in later days was identified with Crete. It is more than probable that this identification is correct, and that from the first the term Keftiu meant Crete ; but with the extension of the Minoan power the term was extended to cover the southern coasts of Asia Minor as far as Cilicia, which may have been included in it, so that the term Ai-Kaphtor, 'Coasts' or 'Isles' of Kaphtor, meant to the Hebrews, as it did to the Egyptians, the northern shores of the Mediterranean from Crete to Cilicia. The two pictures from the tombs of Sennemut and Rekhmira', however, undoubtedly represent Cretans, as we can see from the carefully copied details of their dress and the vases they bear, especially in the tomb of Sennemut (see also Plate XLVII). Tuthmosis III regarded Crete as 'tributary' to him, but there is no proof of any such political subjection to Egypt, though relations between the two countries had existed from the earliest times, even from Neolithic days, and are as apparent under the Sixth and Twelfth Dynasties as under the Eighteenth. Keftiu is first mentioned by the Egyptians about the time of the Eleventh Dynasty (*c.* 2300 B. C.). The biblical term 'Casluhim' associated with 'Caphtorim' is as yet unexplained.

Plates XLV, XLVI. Minoan Cretans (Keftians or men of Kaphtor), as depicted by themselves; the famous 'Cupbearer' fresco discovered by Sir Arthur Evans at Knossos in 1901, which presents so remarkable an analogy in attitude and costume to the Egyptian representations in Plate XLIV ; and the almost equally famous relief group of a chief bidding farewell to or receiving a warrior, from a stone cup found by the Italian excavators at Hagia Triada. Both date about 1600 B. C., and the characteristics of Minoan art at that time, just before the beginning of the Eighteenth Dynasty, are well shown by them, especially the physical characteristics of the race, the narrow waists (probably artificially produced), and the long hair, also the European-Greek type of face.

Plate XLVII. The Art of 'the Isles': a gold cup with *repoussé* scene of a bull escaping from a net and tossing two men in the air, found at Vaphio in the Peloponnese, of the same type as those represented in the tomb of Sennemut (Plate XLIV) ; and a gold mask from the burial of a prince at Mycenae.

Plates XLVIII, XLIX. The Later Phase of Egypt. Plate XLVIII shows a fine portrait-head of a Theban noble of the eighth-seventh centuries B. C., the period of Ethiopian rule and war with Assyria ; and a portrait-head of Tirhakah : Plate XLIX gives portraits of Apries (Pharaoh Hophra) and Psammetichus : no good portrait of Necho, the conqueror of Josiah, is available. Psammetichus has lately come into closer connexion with the Bible narrative owing to the newly discovered fact that he was called upon apparently by the terms of his old subject-alliance with Assyria to come to the help of his erstwhile superior when she was attacked by Kyaxares (Huvakhshatra) and Nabopolassar. This he did, towards the end of his reign (616 B. C.), and drove back Nabopolassar to Babylon. But later on his succours were either non-existent or vain, and, two years before his death, Nineveh fell (612 B.C.) : see p. 21.

Plate L. Egyptian Fishing Scene. This scene was painted on the walls of an Eighteenth-Dynasty tomb at Thebes and is now in the British Museum. The owner is seen canoeing in the papyrus-beds, the pools of wild-fowl, the marshes and the streams, and slaying wild birds with a throwstick. In his frail boat of papyrus-stems are his wife and daughter, and a pet cat hunts on his own among the reeds. In the stream are fish and lilies: in the air flying birds and carefully painted butterflies. The inscription reads: 'Taking recreation and finding pleasure in the Abode of Eternity' ; thus expressing the hope of a blissful after-life.

The papyrus plant was widely cultivated in the Delta of Egypt, and afforded a most useful material for many domestic and other purposes. It grew to the height of six feet, throwing up from its large horizontal root a tapering shaft, triangular in form, which bore a tufted head. Its most important use was in the manufacture of the writing material to which it gave its name, papyrus. The stem was cut longitudinally into thin strips, which were laid side by side to the required width, and across them another layer of strips was laid at right angles. The two layers glued and pressed together formed a sheet of material as flexible and smooth as modern paper. By joining together the sheets rolls of any length could be formed.

We may also see in the papyrus the material of which the 'ark of bulrushes' (Exod. 2³) was constructed. Small boats were in Egypt usually made of papyrus-stalks bound together. In the legend of the death of Osiris we are told that the boat in which Isis sailed about, in order to gather the god's scattered limbs, was made of papyrus because the plant was abhorred by the crocodile. Compare the 'vessels of bulrushes upon the waters', spoken of by Isaiah (18²).

Plate LI. Document on Papyrus. The use of papyrus as a writing material was widespread in the ancient world. From Egypt it was carried to other countries round the Mediterranean ; it was used in Greece and at Rome ; and long after the general establishment of vellum as the ordinary writing material it continued in favour for special purposes in Italy and France through the early Middle Ages. From the earliest times to the first centuries of the Christian era the roll was the usual form of the book (*volumen*, volume), and papyrus was almost invariably the material ; and even when the roll was superseded by the book composed of leaves, still papyrus continued to some extent to be employed.

Plates LII–LIV. With regard to the different objects represented in these plates only a few remarks are necessary.

The scene in Plate LII illustrates an Egyptian custom mentioned in Gen. 41⁴² , where we are told that Pharaoh put a collar (A.V. chain) of gold about Joseph's neck. Here a noble, Parennefer, is being decorated with ' the gold ', the highest order in the gift of the Pharaoh, by his servants in the presence of the king (not shown in the illustration). While other collars worn by nobles and men of rank were usually very elaborate, and were frequently inlaid with precious stones, ' the gold ' consisted of chains of plain gold rings.

Among the musical instruments (Plate LIV) is the *sistrum* (rattle), which was carried by priestesses and used in religious ceremonies, the three loose wires producing a strident rattling noise when shaken. The harp (Plate LIII) was a characteristic Egyptian instrument : harpers were often blind.

Plate LV. Tablet from Tell el-Amarna. The Tell el-Amarna tablets were discovered in 1887 on the site of the ancient city of Akhetaten. More than three hundred are now in the museums of London, Berlin, Paris, and Cairo; a few still remain in private possession. They are of the greatest value for the history of the relations between Egypt and Western Asia in the fourteenth century B. C.; and they prove that the cuneiform writing was in use in the districts now called Palestine and Syria, as well as in Mesopotamia. The script and format of the tablets have certain peculiarities; and the language employed is in some important particulars closely related to the Hebrew of the Old Testament.

The greater number of the Tell el-Amarna tablets are letters and dispatches from allies in Northern Syria, and from tributary princes and governors in Palestine, to the Egyptian kings Amenophis III and Amenophis IV, whose reigns are calculated to have extended from about 1412 to 1362 B. C. A few of them are inscribed with mythological legends of an interesting character.

The site of the ancient city of Akhetaten, which was built by Amenophis IV, was on the east bank of the Nile, about 180 miles south of Memphis; and it was during the decadence of the Egyptian power in Western Asia under the weak administration of that king that most of the dispatches in the collection were written.

The tablet represented in this plate is one of four dispatches addressed to the king by Abi-milki, the governor of Tyre, urgently appealing for assistance. The country was disorganized by rival factions, and Zimrida, governor of Sidon, had laid siege to the island-fortress of Tyre, first capturing the positions on the mainland and cutting off Abi-milki's supply of wood and water. 'To the king, my lord, my god, my sun, thus saith Abi-milki, thy servant: I prostrate myself at the feet of the king, my lord, seven times and seven times; I am the dust under the feet of the king, my lord, the Sun-god, who riseth upon the world daily by the decree of the Sun-god, his loving father.' If the king had not appointed him to the command, Tyre would have been lost, and the king's government and his name would have been blotted out from the land for ever. 'I will guard the city of Tyre, the great city, for the king, my lord, and I will hold it until the king shall send forth his power to help me, to give me water to drink and wood to warm myself withal.'

b. ASSYRIA AND BABYLONIA.

Plates LVI-LXXX. These plates illustrate the history of the Assyrian and later Babylonian empires. In the following brief historical account sufficient explanation of most of them will be found. Such as call for more detailed descriptions will be afterwards dealt with.

The line of development of the two great empires of Babylonia and Assyria, which played so great a part in the history of the ancient world, and which had such a vital influence on the fortunes and destiny of the Hebrews, was along the course of the Euphrates and the Tigris. The broad tract through which the Tigris and lower waters of the Euphrates flow, shut in, as it is, on the north-east by the mountain ranges of Kurdistan, and on the south-west by the great Arabian desert, formed a natural path for the progress of invaders marching northwards from the head of the Persian Gulf; and when the power of the more northern kingdom of Assyria was consolidated, and sought an outlet for further expansion, the natural direction again lay to the north-west. Contemporaneously, the Egyptian Pharaohs, now feeling their strength, and embarking on a course of foreign wars, chose the line which led them northwards into Syria. It was inevitable that the two chief powers of Western Asia and Northern Africa must sooner or later come into collision. It was also easy to foresee that in the end the tougher and more tenacious Semitic race of Mesopotamia must prove too strong for the Egyptian ; and, had not the vast sandy wastes of Arabia and Syria interposed and wedged asunder the two nations, curbing the expansion of Babylonia and Assyria on the west and extending the line of march round the northern apex of the desert lands, it is probable that Egypt would have fallen a prey to Western Asia far sooner than was actually the case. Syria and Canaan lay between the anvil and the hammer and suffered accordingly, now the subjects and again the allies of one or other of the contending powers ; and the catastrophe of the captivity of the children of Israel was inevitable.

Of the origin of the old Babylonian Empire we know various Sumerian traditions. The primeval inhabitants of the land were the Sumerians, settled in the country at the head of the Persian Gulf. At an early period an immigration of Semitic-speaking tribes took place, and these first gained the ascendancy under Sargon of Akkad, about 2650 B. C. ; hence the Semitic element was called 'Akkadian'. The Sumerian and Akkadian languages were used side by side until about 1700 B. C. ; thereafter Sumerian became a purely literary language. The earliest historical period revealed by excavations is a little before 3000 B. C. ; but some prehistoric remains must be dated much earlier.

In the north an invading tribe of Semitic tongue similarly settled amongst the Subaraean inhabitants of the Tigris valley. At first the local magistrates of the cities of Ashur and Nineveh were dependent on the great Babylonian kings, who treated the whole district as a province. Thus was created the kingdom of Assyria, which finally, about 1700 B. C., became strong enough to assert its independence. Four hundred years later it conquered its former suzerain, and from that time to the fall of Nineveh the history of Babylonia becomes of secondary importance. For centuries war was carried on with varying fortune between the two kingdoms, but the Assyrians were the more powerful, and nearly always held the Babylonians in subjection.

In the reign of Tiglath-Pileser I, 1100 B. C., Assyria was engaged in active war with the nations inhabiting the country to the north-west, along the upper course of the Euphrates and in Northern Syria, but was unable to maintain this position against the Aramaean migration, for after the death of that king her power declined, and she suffered severe defeats. It was not till the beginning of the ninth century B. C. that she began to recover under Tukulti-Ninurta II, a king who once more subdued Babylonia and passed on the kingdom in a prosperous condition to his son Ashur-nasir-pal in 884 B. C. From this time Assyria was ruled by a succession of enterprising kings who extended the boundaries of their empire, and who are brought more prominently under our notice by the wars with the western nations. Ashur-nasir-pal removed the seat of government from Assur some forty miles further north to Calah, the modern Nimrûd, where he built a great palace and carried out other works. From the remains of this palace we are enabled to judge of the knowledge of art and mechanical industries which the Assyrians possessed at this time. Their favourite form of sculpture was the bas-relief, in which they were not unsuccessful ; but in the higher artistic qualities required for rendering figures in the round they were wanting. The sculptured slabs from Nimrûd are executed in a broad style (Plate LXXXIV) ; but the Assyrian artist trusted more to ornamental detail than to grace of outline to produce an effect, his work being more mechanical than artistic. The subjects represented are for the most part scenes of war or the chase ; the conquest of enemies and the ruthless punishments inflicted on prisoners ; and lion-hunting, the favourite sport of the Assyrian kings. The conquests of Ashur-nasir-pal extended on every side, the chief line of progress being ever towards the west. His son Shalmaneser III (859-824 B.C.) was still more successful. His empire reached from the Persian Gulf to the mountains of Armenia, and from the frontiers of Media to the shores of the Mediterranean. His wars in Syria first brought the Assyrians and Hebrews into contact. When the Syrians of Damascus were crushed by an overwhelming defeat in 841 B.C., and Shalmaneser became undisputed master of the country, the surrounding nations hastened to submit, and among them Jehu, king of Israel, paid tribute (Plate LXIII). The submission of the Hebrews can be traced a little later in the records of the reign of king Adad-nirari III, who levied contributions on 'Omri', i. e. Israel. But greater evils befell them in the days of Tiglath-Pileser III, who reigned from 745 to 727 B.C. The wars which he waged are a repetition of the wars of his predecessors. Again he subdued Babylonia, and again he overran Syria, pushing forward even to the confines of Egypt. Since his identification with Pul of the Bible account has been proved correct, it was he to whom Menahem the usurper turned for support on the throne of Israel, and to whom he gave 'a thousand talents of silver, that his hand might be with him to confirm the kingdom in his hand' (2 Kings 15^{19}). It was also to Tiglath-Pileser that Ahaz, king of Judah, appealed for help when beset by Rezin of Damascus and Pekah, king of Israel (2 Kings 16$^{5-9}$). Rezin was slain, Damascus fell before the conqueror, and the Israelite tribes of Reuben and Gad and the half-tribe of Manasseh were led into captivity. Hoshea, the new king of Israel, who 'made a conspiracy against Pekah, the son of Remaliah, and smote him, and slew him, and reigned in his stead' (2 Kings 15^{30}), could only hold power on sufferance of the king of Assyria. With the death of Tiglath-Pileser he seems to have thought that his opportunity had come. But the new Assyrian king, Shalmaneser V (727-722 B.C.), was prompt. He came up against Israel, 'and Hoshea became his servant, and gave him presents'. Then Hoshea looked to Egypt: 'and the king of Assyria found conspiracy in Hoshea: for he had sent messengers to So, king of Egypt, and brought no present to the king of Assyria, as he had done year by year; therefore the king of Assyria shut him up, and bound him in prison' (2 Kings 17^{3,4}). Hoshea's personal captivity only preceded the fall of his kingdom. The country was invaded and Samaria was besieged (B.C. 724), but held out for two years. Before its fall, however, a sudden revolution drove Shalmaneser from his throne; and the usurper Sargon, of a junior branch, succeeded to the empire. Now Samaria was taken, and the second captivity of Israel was accomplished. Sargon 'carried Israel away into Assyria, and placed them in Halah and in Habor by the river of Gozan, and in the cities of the Medes'; and he 'brought men from Babylon, and from Cuthah, and from Ava, and from Hamath, and from Sepharvaim, and placed them in the cities of Samaria instead of the children of Israel' (2 Kings 17^{6,24}). Then he turned his arms against Egypt, and in a great battle overthrew an Egyptian army which, in alliance with the Philistines, met him at Raphia, near the frontier of Egypt.

This appears to have been the first actual conflict between the armies of the great rival powers. But, however severe the defeat that he had inflicted, Sargon appears not to have had the strength to follow it up, and we hear of no further operations against Egypt in his reign. Among his other campaigns, the one which he undertook against Azuri, king of Ashdod (Isa. 20^1), is known to us in his own account of it recorded on a clay cylinder in the British Museum. For eighteen years he reigned in almost ceaseless warfare, suppressing also with a firm hand the subject kingdom of Babylonia, and deposing the restless Merodach-baladan II, of whom we read as intriguing with Hezekiah of Judah (2 Kings 20¹²). The remains of his palace at Khorsabad attest the magnificence of his buildings. In 705 B. C. he was succeeded by his son Sennacherib.

This king's reign lasted longer than that of his father (705–681 B. C.), and was as eventful. Continual wars and great building operations fill up the outlines of the picture of each succeeding reign of this later period of Assyrian history, and the repetition tends to monotony. In the case of Sennacherib, however, the prominence given to his campaigns in Palestine by the Bible narrative at a critical moment in the history of the Jews, has invested him with a more than general interest for us. After first putting down revolt in Babylonia, where the accession of a new monarch to the Assyrian throne was almost always the signal for an attempt to throw off the yoke, he marched in 700 B. C. into Syria, and, first subduing the king of Sidon and the neighbouring petty states, he moved south and recovered the revolted city of Askalon. His next object was the city of Ekron, but, before its capture, he fought a great battle and defeated an Egyptian army which was marching to its relief. Then he turned to punish Hezekiah, who was even at that moment sheltering the fugitive king of Ekron. From the great cylinder of Sennacherib (Plate LXVI), which records the details of this campaign, we learn how the Assyrian king came up against Judah, and took six-and-forty of the fenced cities, enslaved two hundred thousand of the inhabitants, and laid siege to Jerusalem ; ' and Hezekiah gave him all the silver that was found in the house of the Lord, and in the treasures of the king's house. At that time did Hezekiah cut off the gold from the doors of the temple of the Lord, and from the pillars which Hezekiah king of Judah had overlaid, and gave it to the king of Assyria' (2 Kings 18¹⁵,¹⁶). Thus did Hezekiah purchase safety, and he brought his tribute to the Assyrian army, engaged in the siege of Lachish (Plate LXVII). There is a well-supported tradition of a great disaster, perhaps a sudden attack of the plague, which overtook the Assyrian host : ' the angel of the Lord went out, and smote in the camp of the Assyrians an hundred and fourscore and five thousand : and when they arose early in the morning, behold, they were all dead corpses ' (2 Kings 19³⁵). This disaster cannot have occurred during the campaign of 700 B. C., and it is probable that a later campaign is referred to.

Sennacherib's later wars were chiefly against the stubborn Babylonians and their allies, the Elamites. Their resistance was only quelled after a succession of campaigns, in the course of which the city of Babylon was destroyed. Towards the end of his reign he carried his arms into Cilicia, and defeated the Greeks : and the tradition that he founded the city of Tarsus refers to his making that city a provincial capital.

The important position which the city of Nineveh attained may be set down in great measure to Sennacherib, for he was the first Assyrian monarch to restore that ancient city for many centuries. The remains of his palace and of those of his immediate successors have yielded not only an extensive series of sculptures, but also an invaluable collection of inscribed tablets, dealing with literature and history and science, being a part of the great library of Nineveh, the collection of which was commenced by this enlightened king. ' And it came to pass, as he was worshipping in the house of Nisroch his god, that Adrammelech and Sharezer his sons smote him with the sword. And Esar-haddon his son reigned in his stead' (2 Kings 19³⁷). This passage is fully in accord with the cuneiform accounts, but the names have not been identified.

Again, Esar-haddon's reign (681–669 B. C.) is a long story of warfare.

Phoenicia, Cilicia, Edom, Babylonia, Arabia, Media, are all in turn the scenes of his campaigns. But the most important event was the final subjugation of the great rival power of Egypt, which fell before his arms. Lower Egypt was occupied by the Assyrians in 671 B. C. Manasseh, king of Judah, paid the penalty of revolt by the reduction of his kingdom and his own captivity. ' The Lord brought upon them the captains of the host of the king of Assyria, which took Manasseh among the thorns, and bound him with fetters, and carried him to Babylon' (2 Chron. 33[11]). But the Assyrian king, of a milder nature than most of his line, restored him afterwards to freedom, and let him return to Jerusalem. Esar-haddon's reign closed in the midst of war in Egypt. That country had broken into armed revolt, which required all the energy of the new king, Esar-haddon's son, Ashur-bani-pal, to subdue. But the empire of the Assyrians had now become too extended for its strength ; with the result that, while rebellion was being suppressed in one direction, the flame of revolt would break out in another. Ashur-bani-pal's long reign (668–632 (?) B. C.) saw a further increase of the northern limits of his empire ; Elam on the south-east was subjugated ; and Babylonia, again in revolt, was again crushed. But Lydia, which had become a vassal state, was with difficulty retained ; and Egypt broke loose and maintained her independence.

The closing years of Ashur-bani-pal's reign were years of decline, and the great empire was already tottering to its fall. The growing power of the Medes had become threatening ; but their advance was stayed for a few years by the irruption of the Scythian hordes which swept across Western Asia in their march of destruction. At length Cyaxares of Media and Nabopolassar, a Chaldean who claimed the kingship in Babylonia, joined their forces and invaded Assyria. Nineveh was captured in 612 B. C., and the great empire was divided among the conquerors, Babylonia falling to the share of Nabopolassar, who is thus the founder of the new Babylonian Empire.

This Empire was short-lived, lasting only some seventy years, the best-known king of the dynasty which ruled over it being Nebuchadnezzar II, who succeeded his father Nabopolassar in 604 B. C. He had just defeated Necho, king of Egypt, when he was called to the throne, an occurrence which seems to have prevented the invasion of Egypt, with which he would have followed up his victory. Of his wars generally we know best the details of those against Judah. After a first campaign Jehoiakim submitted and became tributary for three years. Then he rebelled, and only his death saved him from the punishment which fell upon his son Jehoiachin. In 597 B. C. the Babylonians took Jerusalem, and most of the inhabitants were led into captivity with their king ; ' none remained, save the poorest sort of the people of the land ' (2 Kings 24[14]). Zedekiah, who was set up as king in place of Jehoiachin, a mere vassal of the Babylonians, brought down, by his rebellion, the last act of vengeance on his country. In 586 B. C. Jerusalem was again taken, and practically destroyed, and the captivity of the people was accomplished : ' So Judah was carried away out of their land.' Nebuchadnezzar's reign lasted till the year 562 B. C. He has left behind him records of great works in Babylon ; the wall and temples were rebuilt, and the city was otherwise improved and beautified. But his successors were weak sovereigns, who could not withstand the advancing power of the Persians. In the reign of the last king, Nabonidus, the city of Babylon, which during the king's long absence in Arabia was under the command of his son Belshazzar, was captured by Cyrus in 539 B. C., and the kingdom was absorbed into the empire of the conqueror.

Names of Assyrian, Babylonian, and Persian Kings, &c. mentioned in the Bible. Like many Hebrew proper names, each name forms a sentence, thus :

Tiglath-pileser (2 Kings 15^{29}) = ' My help is the Son of Esharra ' (i.e. the god Ashur).

Shalmaneser (2 Kings 17^3) = ' Shalmanu is chief.'

Sargon (Isa. 20^1) = ' The legitimate king.'

Sennacherib (2 Kings 18^{13}) = ' The Moon-god hath increased brethren.'

Esar-haddon (2 Kings 19^{37}) = ' Assur hath given a brother.'

Asnapper, i. e. Ashur-bani-pal (Ezra 4^{10}) = ' Assur creates an heir.'

Merodach-baladan (Isa. 39^1) = ' Marduk hath given an heir.'

Belshazzar (Dan. 5^1) = ' Bel, protect the king ! '

Nebuchadnezzar (2 Kings 24^1) = ' Nebo, protect the boundary ! '

Evil-merodach (2 Kings 25^{27}) = ' The man (i. e. the worshipper) of Marduk.'

Nergal-sharezer (Jer. 39^3) = ' Nergal, protect the king ! '

The names Cyrus, Darius, and Artaxerxes are of Persian origin.

The king named Pul (2 Kings 15^{19}) has been identified with Tiglath-pileser III, who reigned from 745 B. C. to 727 B. C., and to whom Menahem paid tribute.

Plates LVI-LIX. Ur of the Chaldees, according to Genesis 11$^{28-31}$, was the original home of Terah, Abram's father. The site of the city of Ur was first discovered by Captain Taylor, who carried out excavations at Tall al Muqayyar for the Trustees of the British Museum in 1854. This site lies about 2 miles away from the most westerly branch of the Euphrates, just north of the point where that river begins to lose itself in the marshes at the head of the Persian Gulf. Its name, Tall al Muqayyar, 'the pitched ruin', seems to have been given to it because the Arabs found pitch, or rather bitumen, between the bricks which still stand in walls built four thousand years ago. The excavations conducted by Mr. Campbell Thompson and Dr. Hall for the British Museum in 1918–19 and by the Joint Expedition of the British Museum and University Museum of Pennsylvania since 1922 have uncovered a large part of the sacred precinct which contains the great temple of Sin or Nannar, the Moon-God. Since Harran, the city in northern Syria to which Abram went from Ur, was also devoted to the worship of the god Sin, it has been supposed that Abram's emigration from Ur took place at a time when the practice of religion had fallen into decay. The history of Ur, accounted by the Sumerians one of the earliest cities in Babylonia, does in fact accord with this view. Tradition stated that, after the Flood, Babylonia was ruled in turn from Kish (Tall al Uhaimir), excavated by Rassam for the British Museum, by the Abbé Genouillac for the French, and by the Weld-Blundell Expedition for Oxford), Erech (Warka, excavated by Loftus for the British Museum and by the Germans), and Ur. Mr. C. L. Woolley, working for the joint Anglo-American expedition at Ur, has discovered there early Sumerian royal tombs (dating before 3000 B.C.) with rich treasures of gold, found with the bodies of the royal dead and large numbers of retainers, chiefly women, apparently slain and buried with them. In Plates **LVI, LVII** are shown the gold dagger and open-work sheath of the prince Meskalamshar (Baghdad), his gold 'wig-helm' (a helmet, probably worn in life, in the form of a wig or actual coiffure of two plaits round the head and a small catogan at the back), also at Baghdad, and two beautifully chased and fluted gold vases, a beaker (Philadelphia) and a spouted cup of elliptical shape (British Museum). In Plate **LVIII** is illustrated the **Mosaic ' Standard' from Ur.** This shows one side of the most important relic (apart from intrinsic value) found at Ur, and in all respects the most interesting one : the so-called 'standard' of mosaic-work in lapis-lazuli and shell (British Museum). This object, the precise use of which is uncertain, shows in an oblong wooden framework a mosaic picture on each side ; on one is represented a prince and his court in war, and on the other in peace. In the warlike scene he is seen directing his soldiers, who capture prisoners, and drives in his four-wheeled chariot, drawn by asses in the usual Sumerian manner, over the bodies of the slain ; four pictures in succession show the chariot going first at a walking pace and then accelerating to a gallop. In the peaceful scene, here illustrated, he is seen feasting with his courtiers, while a musician with a lyre and a singing or dancing girl entertains them. Below, peasants bring animals and loads to the court. At each end are uncertain representations of some animals in the hills. The date of this priceless illustration of early Babylonian life, which is for the Sumerians what the Luttrell Psalter is for the medieval English, is before 3000 B.C. Dr. Hall discovered at Tall al 'Ubaid a remarkable shrine to the goddess of the Underworld, of which the principal remains date from this First Dynasty of Ur, which must have ruled a little before 3000 B.C. After this dynasty fell, the rule of Babylonia was disputed by different cities, but yet another dynasty arose at Ur which assumed universal sovereignty, and much later, about 2300 B.C., a powerful line of kings ruled from Ur to Elam, and as far north as Assyria, for over a century. After their time kings of other cities paid great attention to rebuilding the city and the temple ; but when the Amorite dynasty established Babylon as the capital of the country, Ur fell into neglect, and from this time never regained its old importance. A little rebuilding was done about 1600 B.C. by the Cassite king Kurigalzu, but the city must have been nearly a ruin when Nebuchadnezzar and Nabonidus, at the time of the New Babylonian Empire, rebuilt the temple of the Moon-god. The destruction of Ur took place in the reign of Samsu-iluna, the successor of Hammurabi, about 2020 B.C. (?)

The temple tower, called by the Babylonians a *ziggurat*, was a feature of all important Babylonian temples. At Ur, it stood at the west end of the sacred precinct, and the photograph shows the most complete extant remains of such a tower (Pl. LIX). This building only consisted of four stages, and coloured bricks prove that the four stages were different colours, to consort with certain astrological beliefs. Other *ziggurats* had seven stages, as had the **temple tower at Babylon** which is referred to in Genesis 11[4–9]. The significance of the temple tower is nowhere explained in extant Babylonian texts ; Herodotus says that a priestess went up to the shrine at the top to be with the god every night ; and other Greek writers describe it as the tomb of the god. The temple tower at Ur was first built by the founder of the Third Dynasty of Ur, about 2300 B.C., and was restored by Nabonidus about 550 B.C.

Plate LX. Hammurabi's Stele of Laws was discovered on the site of Susa (Shushan, Neh. 1[1], Esther 2[8], 3[15]) by M. J. de Morgan, in his excavations for the French Government. The stele, of black diorite, was originally erected and inscribed at Babylon, but was carried away from that city by an Elamite king at some unknown date, and part of the inscription was erased, for a new inscription, which, for some unknown reason, was never added. Hammurabi was the sixth king of the first or Amorite Dynasty of Babylon, when the city first became the capital of the whole country. He was the most powerful king of the dynasty, and ruled from the Persian Gulf to Assyria, after conquering his rival, Rim-Sin, king of Larsa (Sinkarah). The inscription on the stele falls into three parts, (1) a **prooemium,** describing the pious restoration of temples in many cities of the empire, (2) the laws, 282 in number, which formed a **codex** for legal administration, (3) an **epilogue** invoking blessings on those who observed the laws, and curses on those who might break or abrogate them. Earlier rulers had formulated codes of law in Babylonia, and some sections of a very early code in the Sumerian language have been recovered. Hammurabi's code followed the provisions of the earlier codes to a great extent, but he altered many details, and in general seems to have introduced an administration responsible directly to the king in place of the administrations by independent bodies of priests attached to different temples. Later codes of law have been discovered, that of the Assyrians on tablets from the city of Ashur (Qal'ah Sharqāt), and from the capital of the Hittites (Boghaz Keui), and laws of the New Babylonian period are known on a tablet in the British Museum. These differ, more or less, from Hammurabi's code, and it is clear that the social arrangements in Assyria and among the Hittites were different from those in Babylonia ; but it is known from tablets that Hammurabi's code was known and studied in all these countries until the sixth century B. C. All of these codes have points of similarity to, and difference from, the priestly code included in the Torah.

The scene in relief at the top of the stele represents Hammurabi receiving the laws from the Sun-god Shamash, who was considered by the Babylonians the god of Truth and Uprightness.

Plate LXI. Captives from Qarqara. This scene is depicted in repoussé work on a bronze band from a gate erected by Shalmaneser III, king of Assyria 859–824 B. C. This king engaged in a long struggle with the powerful king of Damascus, Adad-idri, who had vainly supported enemies of the Assyrians in Mesopotamia and at Hamath. In 853 the Assyrian army set out to face a great confederacy, which included all the most important independent princes, and was supported by Egypt. Marching by way of Aleppo, Shalmaneser delivered his first attack on Irkhuleni, prince of Hamath, by assaulting the city of Qarqara, and was then faced by the troops of the confederacy. These consisted, according to an Assyrian inscription, of the following detachments : 1,200 chariots, 1,200 cavalry, 20,000 infantry of Adadidri (Hadadezer) of Damascus, 700 chariots, 700 cavalry, 10,000 infantry of Irkhuleni of Hamath, 2,000 chariots, 10,000 infantry of **Akhabu (Ahab) of the Sir'lai (Israelites)**, 500 infantry of Que (a district round the Gulf of Issus), 1,000 infantry of the Egyptians, 10 chariots, 10,000 infantry of the Irkanatai (an unknown tribe), 200 infantry of Matinu-ba'al of Arvad, 200 infantry of the Usanatai (an unknown tribe), 30 chariots, 10,000 infantry of Adunu-ba'al of the Shianai (an unknown tribe), 10,000 camels of Gindibu' the Arabian (from the North Syrian desert), 10,000 infantry of Ba'asa of Ammon. Shalmaneser claimed a great victory ; but in actual fact he was unable to make immediate head against the allies, and retired. There is no mention of Ahab's alliance with Hadadezer against the Assyrians in the O.T. ; it seems most probable that this Hadadezer came to the throne at Damascus through the deposition of Ben-Hadad, whom Ahab had defeated, 1 Kings 20. The scene depicted on the bronze band from Shalmaneser's gates shows the captives being brought away from the city of Qarqara immediately before the battle.

Plates LXII, LXIII. The 'Black Obelisk' was set up at Nimrûd (Calah) by Shalmaneser III, king of Assyria, 859–824 B. C. On the lower part of the four sides are 190 lines of cuneiform writing detailing the principal events of Shalmaneser's campaigns, and on the upper part are cut bas-reliefs illustrating the historical narrative. The text relates that Shalmaneser conducted thirty-one expeditions against the peoples of various countries ; his sway extended to the shores of the Mediterranean on the west, to Cilicia on the north-west, to Babylonia and the Persian Gulf on the south and south-east, and to Media on the east. At certain places he set up memorial tablets sculptured with figures of his majesty and inscribed with his warlike deeds. In the Black Obelisk he records two wars against Hazael of Damascus in the eighteenth and twenty-first years of his reign, 841 and 838 B. C., and it appears from another inscription that the payment of tribute by 'Jehu, the son of Omri', as represented in one of the bas-reliefs on this monument, took place after the first of these campaigns. The words 'son of Omri' are probably not intended literally, but denote his origin and position as king over what had been Omri's realm.

The cuneiform text which describes the submission of Jehu begins as follows:—

ma - da - tu	sha D.P.* Ya - u - a	mār
Tribute	*of* *Jehu*	*the son of*

D.P. Khu - um - ri - i
Omri

The winged disk, the emblem of the presence of the god Ashur, is seen above the Assyrian king.

Plate LXIV. Tiglath-Pileser III. This king appears to have been a usurper; he ruled in Assyria 745–727 B.C., and in Babylonia, under the name of Pulu, 729–727 B.C. Mention is made in his inscriptions of the tribute he received from Menahem, king of Israel, and Ahaz, king of Judah, and of his conquest of Pekah, king of Israel, and appointment of Ausi' (Hosea) as king in Samaria. At the end of his reign he began the last siege of Samaria, which was captured shortly after his death by his successor, Shalmaneser V. The illustration, taken from a frieze in his palace at the city of Calah (Nimrûd), excavated by Sir Henry Layard and Rassam for the Trustees of the British Museum), shows the king standing in his war chariot with a driver and an attendant.

Plate LXV. Sargon invests an official. Sargon, king of Assyria, 722–705 B.C., is mentioned in Isaiah 20[1] as having conducted a campaign against Ashdod. It appears from Sargon's own inscriptions that this Philistine city rebelled from Assyria; the Assyrians deposed the king, Azuri, and appointed his brother, Akhi-miti. But the people of Ashdod, led by a Greek from Cyprus who was called 'the Ionian', again rebelled, and in 711 B.C. Sargon sent troops to quell the rebellion and instal an Assyrian governor. The illustration, taken from a large slab in Sargon's palace at 'Sargon's city' (Khorsabad, excavated by the French), shows the king appointing one of his high officials by striking his hands, a symbol of investiture with authority.

Plate LXVI. Prism of Sennacherib, king of Assyria, 705–681 B.C. This is one of the finest and most perfect objects of its class ever discovered, and its importance as an historical document can hardly be overrated. It contains 487 lines of closely written but legible cuneiform text, inscribed in the eponymy of Belimuranni, prefect of Carchemish, 686 B.C. The text records eight expeditions of Sennacherib, viz. the defeat of Merodach-baladan, king of Babylon, and sack of the city; the conquest of Ellipi and subjugation of the Medes; an invasion of Palestine and siege of Jerusalem; a second campaign against Merodach-baladan, who was deposed in favour of Sennacherib's son Ashur-nadin-shum; a campaign in the countries to the north-west

* Determinative prefix.

of Assyria ; an expedition to the Persian Gulf and defeat of the Elamites ; and a final expedition to Elam and the conquest of the allied Babylonians and Elamites.

The passage which describes the siege of Jerusalem in the reign of Hezekiah, king of Judah (2 Kings 18) in 700 B. C. reads as follows :—

Col. III. 11. 'And of Hezekiah [king of the]
12. Jews, who had not submitted to my yoke,
13. forty-six of his fenced cities, fortresses, and the smaller cities
14. in their environs, which were without number,
15. by treading down ramps, and by the attack of engines,
16. and by the assault of foot-soldiers, and . . . .*
17. I besieged, I captured, 200,150 people, small and great, male and female,
18. horses, and mules, and asses, and camels, and oxen,
19. and sheep innumerable from their midst I brought out and
20. I reckoned [them] as spoil. [Hezekiah] himself like a caged bird within Jerusalem,
21. his royal city, I shut in. Banks against him.
22. I threw up, and whosoever came forth from the gate of his city I turned back
23. to his disgust. His cities which I had despoiled from his dominions
24. I cut off, and to Mitinti, king of Ashdod,
25. to Padi, king of Ekron, and to Sillibel,
26. king of Gaza, I gave, and I cut short his borders.
27. Besides the old tribute, which they paid yearly,
28. tribute and gifts to my sovereignty I added and
29. laid upon them. As for Hezekiah himself,
30. the fear of the majesty of my lordship overwhelmed him ; and
31. the Arabs and his trusty warriors,
32. whom, in order to strengthen Jerusalem, his royal city,
33. he had brought in, left him.
34. Thirty talents of gold, and 800 talents of silver, and precious stones,
35. And stibium, and . . . . and great ' red stones ',
36. and couches of ivory, and seats of ivory, and elephant hide,
37. and ivory, and ebony, and box-wood, and divers things,
38. and great treasure,
39. and [his] daughters, and the women of his palace, and the male musicians,
40. and the female musicians, into the midst of Nineveh, the city of my sovereignty,
41. after me he brought ; and to give tribute
42. and to make submission he sent his envoy.'

Plate LXVII. Sennacherib at Lachish. This scene, depicted on a great alabaster frieze which ran round a whole room of Sennacherib's palace at Nineveh, shows Sennacherib seated on a hill overlooking the assault and capture of the city of Lachish. Behind him is the military camp he constructed there (not shown in the illustration), where perhaps Hezekiah sent the tribute he ultimately paid to the Assyrians. The sculptor has made an attempt to illustrate the hilly countryside by a conventional ornament which

* The three words which end this line denote a method of assault.

[43]

resembles scales; but he has represented various trees in a more natural manner.

Plate LXVIII. Esar-haddon and his Egyptian and Phoenician captives. Esar-haddon, king of Assyria 681–669 B.C., was engaged in a long struggle with Ba'al, king of Tyre, and undertook the conquest of Egypt, in which country he undertook three campaigns. He was engaged upon the fourth when he died. The illustration, taken from a great stele found at the city of Sam'al (Sinjirli, excavated by the Germans) in North Syria, shows Esar-haddon leading two captives, one of whom, Ushana-Khuru (= Horus), was an Egyptian notable; the other may be Ba'al of Tyre, but more probably is Abdi-Milkutti of Sidon, who was captured after the fall of his city in 677 B.C. and was executed in the following year. The captives are led by a string, hooked through their noses.

Plate LXIX. Darius at Behistun (Bisūtūn). Darius the Great, king of the Medes and Persians from 522 to 486–485 B.C., was opposed by many rivals, usurpers, and pretenders after the death of Cambyses. To record his ultimate victory he inscribed on the great rock of Behistun (or, perhaps more correctly, Bisūtūn) an inscription in the three most important languages of his empire, Old Persian (an early form of the modern language), Susian or Elamite, the last form of a language spoken in the district of Susa from prehistoric times, and Babylonian. All three languages were written in a cuneiform or wedge-shaped writing; but whereas the Babylonian and Susian or Elamite characters remained ideograms or picture-signs, and syllables, the Persian characters were for the most part of an alphabetic nature. A large relief was also carved on the rock which shows Darius triumphing over his rivals.

Plate LXX. Persian Seals. Seals were in common use among the Babylonians. They were cylindrical in shape, and were bored through the centre longitudinally, for the insertion of a string or wire whereby they might be secured. Made of hard stone of various kinds, they were engraved with mythological or other subjects, the impression being obtained by rolling the seal on a soft surface. Fig. 1 is a seal inscribed with the name of Darius. It is a small cylinder of chalcedony measuring $1\frac{7}{16}$ inches, with a diameter of $\frac{11}{16}$ of an inch. The design represents the king engaged in a lion hunt. Above is the emblem of the visible presence of the god Ahuramazda, the good god of the Zoroastrian faith. The symbol is identical with that of the old pagan god Ashur. The three lines of cuneiform characters are in Persian, Susian (Elamite), and Babylonian:

adam   Dārayavaush   khshāyathiya

u   Ta - ri - ya - ma - ush   zunkuk

ana-ku   Da - ri - ya - mush   sharru rabu

I AM   DARIUS   THE GREAT KING.

There is nothing in the inscription to identify the king, but he is probably Darius the Great, who reigned from 522 to 486 B.C.

Fig. 2. The Persian king was represented not only in the events of daily life: in certain instances he is also represented in attitudes which were well known long before the period of the Persians, engaged for instance in combats with lions and bulls as the Babylonians had once depicted a divine hero of their own stories. That means that the Persian king was identified with an old pagan half-god, half-hero, and shows the manner in which stories were adopted and adapted in the course of ages. The process continued, and some of the incidents once told of Gilgamish were finally attributed to Alexander the Great.

Fig. 3. In addition to these old stories which they adapted, the Persians seem to have been in possession of various stories not now known which gave rise to striking pictorial representations, the fore-runners of types which had a long history. Thus the Persian horseman striking down an animal, assisted by his dog, is the early type of the St. George and the dragon theme. The adaptation of old themes to new conditions was thus accompanied by new creative work which made the fifth century one of the turning-points in the history of the East.

Plates LXXI–LXXIII illustrate the site or appearance of three ancient cities mentioned in the O.T.

Plate LXXI. The Ishtar gate at Babylon. Nebuchadnezzar II, king of Babylon 605–562 B.C., who carried the people of Judaea into captivity, very largely rebuilt Babylon, his capital, and the 'great city' intended in most passages of the O.T. is the Babylon he restored. Apart from the great works of fortification on the east side of Babylon, intended to defend his city from attacks by the Medes and Persians, the principal feature of Babylon was a complex of temple buildings dedicated to the various gods of the pantheon, all of which were considered subordinate 'houses' of the great temple of Marduk (Merodach), 'the king of the gods', and were linked up by a great Processional Way, which led from the sacred enclosure out of the city by way of the Ishtar Gate. This gate was a great brick structure containing rooms within the walls ; the facing was of enamelled bricks, the moulds for the bricks being made in such a way that when properly set they formed figures of fantastic animals, associated in Babylonian religion with certain constellations. These fantastic creatures were among the 'spawn of Tiamat' which Marduk conquered.

Plate LXXII. The site of Nineveh. The photograph shows part of the edge of the great mound of Kuyūnjik, the site of the ancient Nineveh. The stream in front is the *Khosr*, which bears the same name now as it did in Assyrian times : the bridge is of course modern. This very ancient city was the capital of Assyria at various times, but the Nineveh of the O.T. is always the city as restored by Sennacherib and beautified by Esar-haddon and Ashur-bani-pal. After the death of the latter, Assyria was attacked in the reign of Sin-shar-ishkun, by the Babylonians and Medes, and finally by the Scythians, in alliance, and Nineveh fell in 612 B.C. The city was so thoroughly sacked that even the site of the place was deserted, and the principal mound, marking the place where Sennacherib's palace and Ashur-bani-pal's library had stood, has remained ever since in much the same condition. A vivid description of this destruction is given in the book of Nahum.

Plate LXXIII. Basalt figure from the gateway at Carchemish. Carchemish, a very ancient Mesopotamian city, has been continuously inhabited, if slight shifts be allowed for, down to the present. The history of the place is typical of the great mixture of races and tongues in Syria, for while Babylonia was in constant intercourse with the city, and much of the civilization is typically Babylonian, the Hittites formed a considerable element in the population, and as conquerors, intermarried freely with a subordinate stock of Semitic speech. In the tenth-ninth centuries B. C. Carchemish was an independent principality, but thereafter it became an Assyrian province, and subsequently was claimed by Babylonia. In 605 B. C. Nebuchadnezzar, the crown-prince of Babylon, fought Necho there (Jer. 46²). The illustration shows a basalt statue which may perhaps be a type of the Syrian weather-god Adad. It was recovered by the excavations for the British Museum, and was found near a gateway, through which a kind of Sacred Processional Way led.

Plates LXXIV–LXXXIII are intended to illustrate some of the racial types mentioned in the historical sections.

Plate LXXIV. A Sumerian figure. This alabaster statuette belongs to a period before 2600 B. C., and shows a normal type of the non-Semitic population of Babylonia called 'Sumerians'.

Plate LXXV. A king or priest of Carchemish. Part of north Syria was occupied by the mixed population called by the Assyrians 'Hittites'. They seem to have arisen from an admixture of 'Hittites' from Asia Minor with an indigenous people, and used a form of hieroglyph writing which has not yet been successfully deciphered. It is probably men of this type, who retained several features of the 'Hittites' of Asia Minor, who are intended by 'Hittites' in the O.T.

Plate LXXVI. An Aramaean king. This illustration is taken from a bas-relief of Bar-Rekub, a king of Sam'al, found at Sinjirli in Syria by the German excavators. The city of Sam'al was an independent principality, torn by civil faction, until the time of Tiglath-Pileser III of Assyria. Inhabited by Aramaeans, the inscriptions are in the Aramaic language, and the physical type represented is distinct from that of the 'Hittite' element in North Syria. From the middle of the eighth century the Aramaeans followed Assyrian fashion and artistic style, and it is probable that both races were originally closely related.

Plate LXXVII. Ambassadors from Urartu. In the ninth century B.C. there arose in eastern Asia Minor the important kingdom of Urartu, which centred about the city Turushpa, the modern Wān on the S.E. corner of Lake Wān. For two centuries the kings of Urartu were able to contest successfully Assyrian supremacy in northern Media, and at times in Syria. The people seem to have been known to the Greeks subsequently as Χαλδοί. It is generally believed that the name of Mt. Ararat is derived from this kingdom and so designates one of the peaks in Armenia. In the Babylonian legend of the flood the boat came to rest on a peak in Media called Mt. Niṣir. The people of Urartu seem to have had some features in common with the Carians; they spoke a debased language which included many elements, they used the Assyrian form of cuneiform writing, and seem to have borrowed some of their religious beliefs from one of the Indo-European tribes with whom they must have been in contact. The illustration shows some ambassadors who came to Ashur-bani-pal at the time of his successful war in Elam.

Plate LXXVIII. Assyrian officers installing an Elamite king. Elam, the highlands on the eastern side of the head of the Persian gulf, was inhabited from before 3000 B. C. to the seventh century by a people who spoke a non-Semitic, non-Indo-European tongue. In origin their civilization was closely connected with that of the Sumerians, and it is uncertain whether their earliest script was the origin of Sumerian writing, or was borrowed from it. Subsequently they borrowed Babylonian cuneiform characters. In the reign of Ashur-bani-pal the Assyrians, after long wars, reduced and destroyed the Elamite power, and nothing more is heard of the Elamites, who became subject to Persian conquerors, and lost their separate existence. The illustration, taken from a frieze in Ashur-bani-pal's palace, shows the Assyrian officers installing an Elamite prince as the creature of Ashur-bani-pal.

Plate LXXIX. Ships of Tyre. This illustration, taken from the bronze bands on the gates of Shalmaneser III, shows typical Phoenician ships of the ninth century B. C. bringing tribute to the Assyrian king. The sea-power of the Phoenicians steadily increased from the ninth to the sixth century, and by means of it Palestine and the neigbouring countries came into commercial contact with the nations of the western Mediterranean.

Plate LXXX. Phoenician Women. (*a*) An ivory plaque found in a palace at Nimrûd depicts a woman in Egyptian costume locking through a window. It is doubtful whether the object belongs to the reign of Ashurnasirpal (ninth century) or Sargon (late eighth century), but it is of Phoenician workmanship. Throughout the second millennium the Phoenicians were under the influence of Egypt, and followed the fashions of Egypt in dress and art, rather than those of Asia, while in religion they retained their own Semitic beliefs. The wealth and extravagance of the Phoenician women was displayed to the Israelites by Jezebel, and earned the denunciation of the religious teachers.

(*b, c*) The elaborate Egyptian toilette adopted by Phoenician ladies, illustrated by the lady at the window, was accompanied by an imitation of Egyptian artistic style : but there was another style in Syria, more representative of Asiatic art and dress, including hair-dressing, which is well represented by *c* as against *b*. Ivory figurines of the Asiatic class have been found over a large area, as far west as Ephesus, as far east as Assyria, and it is probable that in the mixed population of Palestine some followers of either style might be found.

Philistines are illustrated on Pl. XLI, *ante*. The invasion of Palestine, the land to which they gave their name, by the Philistines, was part of the general movement of the 'Peoples of the Sea'. Rameses III, who was the Pharaoh of Egypt about 1200–1170 B.C., recorded a great movement which started in the Mediterranean islands and the west of Asia Minor. A great horde of mixed peoples, including some apparently called Danaans and Achaeans, that is Greeks, marched along the south coast of Asia Minor and overwhelmed the Hittites, then turned southwards through the Cilician gates and marched along the coast with their fleet to Egypt. Rameses defeated them, but some settled in Syria, and the Philistines, called by the Egyptians Pulesati, settled in the Shephelah, the great plain. The illustrations are taken from the sculptures on Rameses III's building at Medinet Habu in Egypt, and show the Philistines engaged in battle with the Egyptians, and also a head-dress which recalls the plumed helmet of the Carian mercenaries. It is uncertain whether the Philistines came originally from western Asia Minor or still further west ; but they were strangers among their new neighbours in Palestine, and brought with them arts and crafts not previously practised there. The pottery is very closely connected with the elegant painted pottery made in the Aegean islands.

Plate LXXXI. A Median noble. The Medes appear to have pushed westward at the end of the second millennium as far as the Zagros hills, while retaining their power further east, and from the ninth century onwards the Assyrians were continually in contact with the westernmost tribes, and succeeded in exacting regular tribute and imposing provincial resident governors on them, except when Urarṭu asserted a temporary supremacy.

The 'distant Medes' mentioned by Sennacherib, that is the Medes further east, appear always to have remained independent. The Medes were organized in small tribes, and each tribal princeling was continually at variance with his equals, until, according to Herodotus, the first rule of Deioces united them all under one ruler. Nothing is known of the language of the Medes, and little of their civilization ; but they learnt much from the Assyrians. The illustration, taken from a frieze in Sargon's palace at Khorsabad, shows a Median noble presenting a model of a building in the Assyrian style for approval by his suzerain. The British Museum possesses part of such a model in bronze.

Plate LXXXII. Persian archers. This is taken from a coloured frieze found in a palace of Darius at Susa by M. Dieulafoy. The Achaemenian kings seem to have modelled their administration and their court on the Assyrian model, and the Persian artists directly imitated Assyrian rather than Babylonian work. Thus the Indo-European Persians assumed an appearance very similar to that of their neighbours, though certain elements are distinctively Persian.

Plate LXXXIII. A Sasanian king. The Sasanian dynasty, which claimed descent from the old Achaemenian kings, came to power originally as vassals of the Parthian kings. Ardeshir revolted from the Parthians, and after a long struggle secured the independence of Persia at the battle of Hormuz, A. D. 226, and subsequently the Sasanian dynasty won back the greater part of the old Persian Empire. The illustration is a medallion which belonged to an Ardeshir. The legend on this gem reads, ' To Ardeshir, of divine race, be Peace'. In Sasanian times Pahlavi, a form of Persian written in characters perhaps derived from Syriac, was in general use. The Sasanian dynasty remained the greatest power in the East until overthrown by Sa'd, the general of Caliph Omar, at the battle of Qadisia, A. D. 636. It was therefore during the rule of these kings that the Jewish schools in Babylonia flourished, whence came the Babylonian Talmud, and that the Christian churches of the East were founded.

Plates LXXXIV–XC illustrate features of Babylonian and Assyrian religion common in ancient times to most of the people of Western Asia, to which there are references in the O. T.

Plate LXXXIV. Tree Worship. This shows King Ashurnasirpal, with a priest wearing wings to represent a minor deity, engaged in magical ceremony. At the New Year festival in Assyria a bare tree-trunk was bound with metal bands and then ornamented with fillets ; the king and the priests, who were dressed to represent various divinities, then sprinkled a mixture of oily substances on the tree, each other, and on other objects, to promote the rebirth associated with spring. Ritual of this type was commonly practised in Syria and Asia Minor even after the advent of Alexander the Great. Though trees were regarded as sacred, they were not themselves divine, and the worship is not directed to the tree, but to the divine power which makes the tree fruitful. Similar notions about trees have been noted by travellers in the East in modern times.

Plate LXXXV. Stone Worship. The story of Jacob contains an instance of the belief in a sacred stone, the *bethel* or *baityl*. The illustration shows scenes depicted on (1) an Assyrian seal of cone shape, of the seventh century B. C. ; (2) a coin of Septimius Severus, from Harran, depicting the temple of the Moon-god there. In both may be seen a sacred stone, set up for worship, with an altar before it. The stone is surmounted (1) by a star, representing Ishtar, the star of Venus, (2) by a crescent moon, the symbol of Sin.

Plate LXXXVI. Types of Mesopotamian gods. This scene, which is carved high up in the rocks of a place called Maltai in the extreme north of Iraq, shows an Assyrian king worshipping the principal gods. Each of the gods stands on an animal : this custom of representing the gods was very popular among the Hittites but it is possible that it goes back to a very early date and was derived from Sumerian beliefs. The first god, Ashur, the national god of the Assyrians, holds in his left hand the measuring rod and line, to symbolize justice ; in his right hand is a curved weapon of which the exact use is not known. Behind Ashur comes his consort, Ninlil, holding the ring wherewith she bestows sovereignty. Next comes Enlil, 'the lord of the lands', in the same attitude and with the same attributes as Ashur. He was a god of an older generation than Ashur or Marduk (the city god of Babylon) according to the priestly view, and he was on the whole ill-disposed towards mankind. The last figure in the illustration shows Sin, the moon-god, whose name is written with the number 30, from the days of the month. These gods were not only Babylonian or Assyrian ; their worship extended right across to Mesopotamia and Syria, and the Amarnah letters prove that the inhabitants of Palestine in the second millennium knew the names of these gods.

Plate LXXXVII. Worship of the Babylonian Sun-god. This plate is taken from a stone tablet of Nabu-apal-iddin, king of Babylon about 900 B. C., which was found deposited in an earthenware coffer among the ruins of the city of Sippar. The Sun-god is seated within a shrine, holding in his right hand objects emblematic, probably, of royalty. Before him, on an altar, is a disk which is kept in its place with cords held by two figures surmounting the roof of the shrine. The three human figures are probably those of a priest, the king who is being led into the presence of the Sun-god, and an attendant. The cuneiform inscription above them is : 'The image of the Sun-god, the mighty lord, who dwelleth in E-barra, within Sippara.' In the shrine are three astronomical emblems of the gods Sin, Shamash, and Ishtar.

There is a long inscription on the tablet which describes the restoration of the temple of the Sun-god and the setting up of a new statue by Nabu-apal-iddin, the temple having been in ancient days wrecked by the enemy, and the old statue having been carried away. Nabu-apal-iddin also re-established the worship of the god and endowed the temple. Nearly three hundred years after, about 620 B. C., the contents of the coffer were examined by Nabo-polassar, king of Babylon, who, knowing that the scene on the tablet had been copied from an ancient original, protected it with a covering of clay, on the back of which he described the repairs which he himself carried out in the temple of the Sun-god. The coffer was once more opened in the reign of Nabonidus, king of Babylon, 556–539 B. C., who deposited in it two clay cylinders inscribed with an account of further work upon the temple.

Plate LXXXVIII. Combat between Tiāmat and Marduk (Mero-dach). The story of this combat is told in one of the tablets belonging to the 'Creation series'. Marduk, the god of light, endowed by the gods with a throne, a sceptre, and a ring, armed himself, and went forth to do battle with the dragon Tiāmat or Chaos. He made a lightning flash charged with blazing fire, and a net in which were the winds of the four quarters of heaven ; he also created a hurricane, a whirlwind, a storm, and winds. He cast his net over the monster, and let loose the hurricane, and drove the wind down her throat to burst her body. He ripped her up with his sickle-shaped sword and cut her skin into two parts, with one of which he made the vault of heaven.

The illustration (1) is taken from a Babylonian cylinder seal of uncertain date and shows Marduk advancing to slay Tiāmat, as described above in the Babylonian Account of Creation. The weapons he holds seem to be the thunderbolt and the lightning fork, but this is not certain. He is accompanied by another god, while a goddess faces Tiāmat, seemingly attempting to close the monster's jaws. Illustration (2) is taken from the top of a black stone, inscribed by King Esar-haddon with his account of the restoration of Babylon, destroyed by his father. Each of the symbols has an astrological meaning. The horned head-dress on a seat is the symbol of Anu; the pile of triangles below represents a 'great mountain', the god Enlil or Ellil. These two gods had 'ways' in the sky to which different stars belonged. The symbols of two, 'the labourer' and 'the bull', may be found in the top register, and of another two, 'the plough' and 'the chariot', in the bottom. The significance of the trees depicted is not certain. Esar-haddon says that these symbols constitute the writing of his own name, but we are not certain as to how this is to be interpreted.

Plates LXXXIX, XC. Babylonian Devils. The Babylonians believed in a number of beings, not gods and not men, whose mission it was alternately to plague and protect mankind. To secure immunity from their evil attentions was the chief object of magical incantations. Of these, Lamashtu was a female monster who wandered about the desert and in lonely streets, destroying the virility of men and the fertility of young girls: she is constantly represented with a lion's head, being carried away by a horse or ass, as she suckles animals, as in illustration (1), and resembles in character the Biblical Lilith, also known to the Babylonians. The winged, human-headed bull colossus depicted in (2) was a favourite architectural ornament for gateways in Assyria, and was called *shēdu*. The being had two aspects; he might be regarded as an evil demon, to avert whose influence recourse must be had to magic; or, if his favour be obtained, his protection would secure immunity from the attacks of enemies. Pazuzu was a god of sickness, particularly connected with the west wind, a cold blizzard which frequently causes fever; his figure or head was a frequent subject for amulets intended to be worn, on the principle that like drives away like. Such a head is figured in (3). Humbaba was a devil to overcome whom Gilgamish and his friend Enkidu entered on their adventures: the face of Humbaba consisted of a single line, as shown in (4), and it was considered that the entrails of sacrificial victims might resemble it.

The Babylonian Account of the Creation. A poem of epic character which was recited at the New Year Festival in Babylon was inscribed on seven tablets. The copies which have come down to us are of the time of Ashur-bani-pal, king of Assyria 668–626 B.C., and of the New Babylonian Empire, but the period of composition must have been far more ancient. The story of the Creation as told in this poem is as follows:—When the heaven above was not named, and when the earth beneath bore no name; when as yet Apsu, the sweet waters, who begat them, and Tiāmat, the bitter waters, who bare them, mingled their waters; when no land was formed; when no reed was to be seen; when as yet the gods had called nothing into being; when no name was named; when no fate was fixed; then were created the gods. Lakhmu and Lakhamu were called into being. Ages passed away, and then Anshar and Kishar were created. Long were the days, then came forth other gods. Afterwards, Apsu rebelled against the rule of the newly-born gods, and was overcome by Ea, henceforth the water-god; and Tiāmat to avenge him gave birth to a brood of monsters to wage war against the gods. This news was carried to the chief of the gods, who bade them go forth against Tiâmat and her brood, but they would not. At length Marduk (Merodach) came forward, and was endowed with great power and invincible weapons. He met Tiâmat in combat and slew her, and of one half of her skin he made the heavens ; then he established the earth and the underworld. Next he made the stars, the abodes of the gods, and the signs of the Zodiac, and he marked out the year into twelve months, and set the moon in the sky to fix times and seasons. The creation of the beasts of the field and of creeping things followed.

The Babylonian Account of the Deluge is found in the eleventh tablet of the series of legends of the mythical hero Gilgamish. It is in the form of a story told to Gilgamish by Utanapishtim or Khasistra, the Assyrian Noah. The tablet was found in the Library of Ashur-bani-pal. An earlier, but identical version of the story is extant on tablets of the First Dynasty of Babylon, about 2000 B. C., included in a poem in which it is connected with the creation of man. In this earlier account, after the creation of man, the wrath of Enlil was excited by ' the noise ', and he sent diseases, famine, and finally a flood.

According to the version in the Gilgamish epic, the great gods within Shurippak, the ancient city on the river Puratti (Euphrates), took counsel to bring a flood upon the earth. There was Anu, their father ; and there was Enlil, the warrior ; Ninurta their messenger, and Ennugi who directed them; and there was also Ea, the lord of wisdom. And Ea spake unto Utanapishtim and said, 'Thou man of Shurippak, son of Ubaratutu, build thee a ship, and forsake thy possessions and take heed for thy life, and bring into the ship living seed of every kind.' Therefore Utanapishtim built him a ship of six storeys, and an hundred and twenty cubits was the breadth thereof ; and he pitched it within and without with pitch. And with all that he had of silver and of gold, and with living seed of every kind, he filled it ; and he brought into it his family and his household, and cattle and the beasts of the field. Then, at even, the ruler of darkness sent a heavy rain ; and Utanapishtim feared to look upon it. And he entered into the ship and he shut the door; and the guidance of the ship he gave into the hands of Puzur-Bêl, the mariner. And at dawn a black cloud came up, and Adad thundered in the midst thereof ; and before it went Nebo and Sharru, even as messengers went they over mountain and over plain ; and Uragal tore up the anchor ; and Ninurta went forth, and the storm followed after. The Annunaki lifted aloft their torches and lighted up all the land with their brightness. The whirlwind of Adad reached unto heaven ; and day was turned into night, so that no man might behold his fellow. The gods were afraid, and they drew back into the heaven of Anu ; they crouched like hounds and sat cowering in heaven. Ishtar cried as a woman in travail, and with loud lamentation she bewailed the destruction of her people, which filled the sea like the spawn of fishes ; and with her wept the gods, they were bowed down, their tears flowed, their lips were pressed together. For six days and for six nights the tempest blew and the flood covered the earth ; but on the seventh day the storm and deluge, which had fought like a great host, were abated, the sea sank to rest, and the hurricane was spent. Utanapishtim looked forth upon the waters and called aloud ; but the race of man was turned again to earth, and their habitations had become a swamp. He opened the window, and the light of day fell upon his face ; and he bowed him down and wept, for lo ! all was sea. After twelve days the dry land appeared. To the land of Nisir the ship floated, and the mountain of Nisir held it fast. For six days the ship rested, and, when the seventh day drew nigh, Utanapishtim sent forth a dove. And the dove flew this way and that ; but she found no resting-place, and she returned. Then sent he forth a swallow. And the swallow flew this way and that ; but she found no resting-place, and she returned. Then sent he forth a raven, which flew away and, for that the waters were abated, came not back again. Then Utanapishtim went forth out of the ship, and offered up sacrifice and poured out a drink-offering on the mountain-top ; and the gods smelled the sweet savour, and like flies they gathered round the sacrifice. And Ishtar, the lady of the gods, drew near, and she said : ' Never shall I forget these days. Now let the gods come unto the offering ; but let not Enlil come, for he was ill-advised and sent the flood and gave my people to destruction.' But when Enlil saw the ship, then was he wroth and filled with anger against the gods, and he cried : ' Who then hath come forth with life ? Surely no man shall escape destruction.' Then Ninurta opened his mouth and spake : ' Who but Ea could do this thing, since Ea knoweth all things ?' Then spake Ea and said unto Enlil : ' Ill-advised wast thou, O counsellor of the gods, that thou didst send the flood. On the sinner lay his sin; and on the transgressor lay his transgression ; but let not all be destroyed. Let the lion and the leopard, let famine and pestilence, slay mankind ; but let there be no flood again. I divulged not the counsel of the gods in words ; but in a dream did Utanapishtim learn it.' Then went Enlil into the ship, and he took Utanapishtim by the hand and led him forth ; and he blessed him and his wife, and he said : ' Now let Utanapishtim and his wife be as we, who are gods ; and let them dwell afar off at the mouth of the rivers.' And the gods led them away and gave them a dwelling-place even at the mouth of the rivers.

NEW TESTAMENT ILLUSTRATIONS

No attempt has been made in this section to provide a comprehensive survey of the Graeco-Roman world of Our Lord's time. Its civilization was extremely diverse and complex and the mass of its extant remains is enormous. The purpose of this section is therefore merely to illustrate one or two aspects of that world which have a direct bearing upon the New Testament narrative.

Plates XCI–XCIII. These three plates illustrate the Roman Emperors from Augustus to Domitian (27 B.C.–A.D. 96), with the exception of the unimportant three Emperors of the year A.D. 69, Galba, Otho, and Vitellius, and of Titus (A. D. 79–81), whose triumphal arch forms the subject of Plate XCIV. Our Lord was born in or soon after 8 B.C. His Ministry, Death, and Resurrection fell in the latter part of the reign of Tiberius. St. Paul's first and second missionary journeys were undertaken in the reign of Claudius (A.D. 41–54) ; and it is conjectured that the Christian Narcissus mentioned in Rom. 16[11] was the famous freed slave who rose to the position of Secretary of State to this Emperor. The Caesar to whose tribunal St. Paul appealed was Nero, and it was under Nero that he seems to have met his death about A.D. 64, during the persecution of Christians which followed the great fire of that year. Nero was driven from power by a revolt of the army in A.D. 68 ; he had himself killed, and a year of confusion followed, during which Galba, Otho, Vitellius, and finally Vespasian were in succession acclaimed as Emperor by different groups of legions. Vespasian was at the time in chief command against the Jews, who had revolted in A.D. 66. He marched immediately on Rome, leaving his son Titus to continue the campaign in Judea; overthrew the last claimant, Vitellius ; established himself securely ; and, ruling for ten years, brought back order to the government, and more particularly to the finances of the Empire. He was succeeded by Titus, who, dying prematurely in A.D. 81, gave place to his younger brother Domitian, under whom took place for the second time what may be regarded as a systematic persecution of Christians. It is very probable that among the victims on this occasion were Domitian's own cousin and niece, Flavius Clemens and his wife Flavia Domitilla, the former of whom was put to death and the latter banished for 'having run after the customs of the Jews' (Cassius Dio, lxvii. 14).

In **Plate XCI** Augustus is shown as an *Imperator* in the act of haranguing troops. It is well to remember that the term 'Emperor', which is derived from *Imperator*, has not quite the same meaning when applied to Augustus and his earliest successors, as when applied to medieval or modern rulers, such as the Holy Roman Emperors or Tsars or Kaisers. What Augustus professed to do, when he assumed supreme power in Rome, was to restore the old Roman republican constitution, which had collapsed under the pressure of a long series of political disturbances culminating in the dictatorial government of the Triumvirs, Antony, Lepidus, and Augustus (then called Octavian) himself. Nominally therefore Augustus was no more than the first citizen in a restored republic; exceptional powers were granted to him, but they were constitutional powers, and granted in due form. The title of *Imperator* was not new; it belonged to the Consuls and to any Roman general placed by the Senate in supreme military and judicial command, within a limited area and for a limited period. What distinguished Augustus from previous *Imperatores* was that the area in which he was supreme was the entire Roman Empire, and the period was, in effect, his lifetime. He thus gained command of the whole Roman Army, and was free to govern in person any or all of the provinces of the Empire. In practice neither he nor his successors attempted to do the latter. Augustus handed back to the Senate the more peaceful provinces of the Empire, and the Senate appointed governors in the old manner, called 'proconsuls'. Gallio was appointed in this way to be governor of the senatorial province of Achaia, and accordingly in Acts 18^{12} is styled ἀνθύπατος, the Greek translation of 'pro consule'. Syria, on the other hand, was one of the provinces reserved by Augustus for direct administration by the Emperor, and he appointed a legate (*legatus*) as governor directly responsible to himself as *Imperator*, and not to the Senate. To administer the revenue and, on occasion, to look after small districts of a province, the Emperor appointed procurators, of inferior rank to the legate, but partially independent of him. Quirinius (Luke 2^2) was such a legate; Pontius Pilate, Festus, and Felix were procurators.

In **Plate XCII** Tiberius is seen wearing the robe of the *Pontifex maximus*, the chief priest of the Roman religion. Augustus and his successors regularly assumed the pontificate, which gave them a certain spiritual prestige as the central figures of the ceremonial worship conducted by the State. This had a consequence of great historical interest; when Christianity became the official religion of the Empire, the title passed to the Bishop of Rome, and came to be the official designation of the Pope. When the Western Empire broke up in the fifth century, it was largely the political prestige of a title which had for so long been held only by the Emperor that enabled the Pope to establish himself, amid the general confusion, as a temporal ruler in Italy.

Plate XCIII. The Flavian Emperors. Vespasian and his sons were Flavii, an Italian family of good standing in the professional and financial world of Rome. They were not aristocrats like the Emperors from Augustus to Nero, who were drawn from the old senatorial families of the

Julii and the Claudii. The change marks the decline of the older, purely Roman, governing classes, and their gradual displacement by a wider aristocracy drawn from families of Italy as a whole and of the provinces of the Empire. The contrast between the strong but coarse features of Vespasian, and the sensual or weak but delicate features of Caligula, Claudius, and Nero is significant.

Plate XCIV. Scenes from the Arch of Titus. Jerusalem was captured after a long siege by Titus in A.D. 70. A triumphal arch in honour of this victory was subsequently erected in Rome on the Sacred Way, just outside the limits of the Forum. The reliefs here illustrated show scenes from Titus's triumphal entry into Rome : in Fig. 1 are seen the Seven Branched Candlestick and other trophies from the siege ; in Fig. 2 Titus himself appears (the head defaced), riding in his chariot, and surrounded by his bodyguard.

Plate XCV. Fig. 1. **The Roman Citizen's right of Appeal.** This coin was struck in 90 B.C. to commemorate the passing of a law (*Lex Porcia de provocatione*) which gave Roman citizens in the provinces who were accused on a criminal charge, the right to appeal from the jurisdiction of Roman magistrates to the Senate and People of Rome. On the left is seen the citizen dressed in a toga ; he replies with the word PROVOCO, 'I appeal', to the magistrate who, wearing a cuirass and sword, menaces him with raised arm. The figure on the right is that of a lictor with the *fasces*, the emblem of the magistrate's authority. Compare the dress of the magistrate with that of Augustus (Plate LXXXVIII) ; it is that of the military commander, the holder of the *imperium*. The coin illustrates the inviolability which, nearly 150 years before the time of St. Paul, had been accorded to the person of a Roman citizen. It was the absolute respect felt for the privileges of a citizen which caused the dismay of the Roman officials who scourged Paul, when they found him to be a Roman citizen, and the insistence of the procurator Festus that St. Paul must go to Rome since he had chosen to appeal to Caesar. (British Museum.)

Fig. 2. **The Gallio Inscription.** Four fragments of a letter from the Emperor Claudius to the town of Delphi, about some disturbance ' which my friend Lucius Junius Gallio, the proconsul of Achaia, has reported to me '. The date is A.D. 52, or within a few months of St. Paul's appearance before Gallio. The words [ΙΟΥ] ΝΙΟΣ ΓΑΛΛΙΩΝ Ο Φ[ΙΛΟΣ] ΜΟΥ Κ[ΑΙ ΑΝΘΥ] ΠΑΤΟΣ can be read in the fourth line of the largest fragment and the last lines of the two fragments to the right of it. Achaia was a senatorial province ; therefore Gallio was ἀνθύπατος or proconsul, a governor appointed by the Senate and a man of senatorial rank himself, whereas procurators in Judea were direct agents of the Emperor and generally men of a lower social standing. (Adolf Deissmann, *Paul*, Revised Edition, 1926.)

Plate XCVI. Types of Roman Soldiers. These three reliefs are from tombstones, the last two belonging to the first century A. D., the other to the second.

Fig. 1. A Centurion, Marcus Favonius by name. He holds the *vitis*, or vine staff, in his right hand as a badge of his rank. (Colchester Museum.)

Fig. 2. A common soldier, Gaius Valerius Berta ; he is armed with the heavy javelin and shield (*pilum* and *scutum*). (Wiesbaden Museum.)

Fig. 3. A standard bearer, Gnaeus Musius. The rings on his chest are *phalarae*, long service decorations awarded to non-commissioned officers. The inscription beneath states that Cn. Musius died at the age of 32, after 15 years' service. (Mainz Museum.)

These three soldiers all belonged to the legions, which formed the backbone of the regular army and in the days of the Empire were stationed upon the frontiers. Palestine was garrisoned by the other branch of the army, the auxiliaries, troops raised from among the provincials and the tribes near the frontiers. Their organization was similar to that of the legions, however, and the three soldiers here illustrated may be taken as fairly representative of both divisions of the Roman army.

Plate XCVII. Fig. 1 shows a fragment of an altar of the second century from Pergamum. It bore the words θεοῖς ἀγνώστοις δᾳδοῦχος 'Torchbearer to the unknown Gods'. Compare Acts 17²³, 'I found also an altar with this inscription, TO AN UNKNOWN GOD' (θεῷ ἀγνώστῳ). (Adolf Deissmann, *Paul*, Revised edition, 1926.)

Fig. 2. **The Temple of Diana** (Artemis) at Ephesus. A drawing taken from the reverse side of an imperial coin of Ephesus of the time of Hadrian, A.D. 117–38. It is of some value as a contemporary though conventional design, which may be accepted as generally faithful to the original. It is not improbable that these conventional representations may have been modelled from some of the silver shrines which were made in large numbers and 'brought no small gain unto the craftsmen' (Acts 19²⁴). On the coin is the word ΕΦΕCΙΩΝ, 'Of the Ephesians'; and it shows clearly the sculptured bases of the columns which were a feature of the building, and of which considerable remains are now preserved in the British Museum. Excavations carried out in 1904 and 1905 by the British Museum have shown that at least four temples preceded this one on the same spot, the earliest of which was a small shrine built not later than about 700 B.C. and destroyed perhaps half a century afterwards. Two other temples were raised during the next hundred years; their successor, the fourth temple of which excavation has revealed the remains, was built about the middle of the sixth century, during the reign of the Lydian King Croesus, and was far larger and more splendid than its predecessors. It stood for nearly two hundred years; was burned down by an incendiary, Herostratus, on the night of the birth of Alexander the Great, and was succeeded by the temple represented in this illustration.

Plate XCVIII. Fig. 1, **A Roman Road in Syria,** shows a good example of the enduring construction of the road system which spread a network over the whole Roman Empire. (Photograph by Sir Aurel Stein.)

Fig. 2. **The ruins of Ephesus.** In the foreground, at the foot of the hill, is seen the Theatre where the demonstration took place against Paul and his followers, as described in Acts 19²³. The street to the right of the Theatre ran for 650 yards to the harbour, now silted up, but distinguishable in the photograph as a semicircular area lighter in colour than the surrounding hills and plain. The market place lay to the left of the Theatre, out of the picture. The ruins in the distance, near the harbour side, are those of baths. The Artemision, where the Temple of Diana stood, was over a mile away from this part of the city; it lay behind and to the right of the point where this photograph was taken.

Plate XCIX. **Ostia,** the seaport of Rome, presents a striking contrast in the character of its architecture to the better known Pompeii. Instead of one-storey houses built round a courtyard, there were large buildings of two or more storeys with shops on the ground floor and sets of living rooms, approached by separate staircases from the street, above. They must have resembled the commercial and tenement architecture of the modern world; and while Fig. 1 shows a street in Ostia as it is to-day, with the remains of two upper storeys visible above the shops and offices opening into the street, Fig. 2 shows an architect's conjectural restoration of one of these tenement buildings. These several-storeyed houses at Ostia were mostly built in the second and third centuries A.D., but both at Ostia and at Rome itself this type of building was already common in the first century A.D.

Plates C, CI. Coins.

1. Gold Daric. The *obverse* alone bears a design : the Persian king kneeling, armed with bow and spear.

2. Bronze half-shekel of Simon Maccabaeus : *Obverse*: citron (*ethrog*) between two bundles of twigs. Hebrew inscription. 'In the fourth year (i. e. 124 B.C.)', 'one half.' *Reverse* : palm-tree between two baskets of fruits : ' of the redemption of Zion'.

3. Bronze coin of Herod Agrippa I. *Obverse* : An umbrella ; BACIΛEWC AΓPIΠA, ' Of King Agrippa'. *Reverse* : Three ears of corn ; L (= ἔτους) ϛ, 'Year 6'.

4. Large bronze coin of Agrippa II. *Obverse* : Head of Vespasian ; AYTO-KPA[TOPI] OYEC[ΠACIANΩ] KAICAPI C[E]BACTΩ, 'To the Emperor Vespasian Caesar Augustus'. *Reverse* : Fortune with cornucopia ; ET[OYC] ΔI BA[CIΛEΩC] AΓPIΠΠA, 'Year 14 of King Agrippa'.

5. Silver Stater of Augustus, or Tetradrachm of Antioch. *Obverse* : Head of Augustus ; KAIΣAPOΣ ΣEBAΣTOY, ' Of Caesar Augustus'. *Reverse* : Female personifying Antioch, with figure at her feet personifying the river Orontes ; ETOYΣ ϛK NIKHΣ, 'Year 26 of Victory [of Actium]' (= 5 B.C.); monogram YΠA[TOY] IB, 'Consul 12, i.e. the twelfth consulate of Augustus'; monogram ANTX (Antioch).

6. Silver Denarius of Tiberius (*Penny*). *Obverse* : Head of Tiberius ; TI-[BERIVS] CAESAR DIVI AVG[VSTI] F[ILIVS [AVGVSTVS. *Reverse* : Seated figure of Livia, as Ceres, PONTIF[EX] MAXIM[VS].

7. Bronze Assarion (*farthing*) of Antioch. *Obverse* : Head of Tiberius : TI. CAESAR . AVG . TR . POT . XXXIII. *Reverse* : S.C. within wreath.

8. Bronze Lepton (*Mite*). *Obverse* : A chalice or cup ; TIBEPIOY KAICA-POC, ' Of Tiberius Caesar'. *Reverse* : Three ears of corn tied together ; IOYΛIA KAICAPOC, 'Julia [widow] of Caesar', i.e. Julia [Livia], mother of Tiberius and widow of Augustus.

9. Silver Shekel of the First Revolt. *Obverse :* A chalice or cup, with inscription in early Hebrew letters, ' Shekel of Israel ' ; and, above the cup, 'Year 3 '. *Reverse* : Triple lily, or Aaron's rod ; 'Jerusalem the Holy '.

Plates CII–CIV. These three plates illustrate scenes in the Holy Land.

Plate CII. Jerusalem, looking eastward across the city. The famous Moslem shrine, the ' Dome of the Rock ' (Qubbet-es-Sakhrah), is seen in the middle distance, upon the site of the Temple area. Behind it is the valley of the Brook Kedron, with the Mount of Olives in the background. The traditional site of the garden of Gethsemane, a white church with a grove of trees, is visible on the slope of the Mount of Olives, a little to the left of the Dome of the Rock. The Dead Sea lies below the hills in the far distance, upon the right of the picture.

Plate CIII. Fig. 1. **The Sea of Galilee,** with the snow-covered Mt. Hermon beyond. Fig. 2. The lower reaches of the Jordan.

Plate CIV. The Dead Sea, looking across to the Mountains of Moab.

PLATES

PLATES

PLATE I

Early Phœnician	Moabite Stone	Siloam Inscription	Square Hebrew	Phonetic Equivalent
ꓘꓘꓘꓘ	ꓘ	ꛜꛜ	א	
ꔰ	ꔰ	ꗷꗷ	ב	b, bh
ꀊꄑ	ꀊ	ꓤ	ג	g, gh
◁	◁	ꟼꟼ	ד	d, dh
ꘓꘓ	ꘓ	ꟼꟼ	ה	h
ꌕꌕ	ꌕ	ꛜꛜ	ו	w, v
ꀤ	ꀤ	ꞁ	ז	z
꒐꒐	꒐	꒐꒐	ח	ḥ (hard)
⊕	⊗	·	ט	ṭ (explosive)
꒒	꒒	꒒꒒	י	y, i
ꝟ	ꝟ	ꝟꝟ	כ	k, kh
꒒	꒒	꒒꒒	ל	l
꒓꒓	꒓	꒓꒓	מ	m
꒔	꒔	꒔꒔	נ	n
ꘘ	ꘘ		ס	s
○	○	○	ע	' (Arabic ʿAyin)
꒕	꒕	꒕	פ	p, ph (f)
꒖	꒖	ꞈ	צ	ṣ (ts)
	ꝗ	ꝗꝗ	ק	q
ꝗ	ꝗ	ꞁꞁ	ר	r
ꟺ	ꟺ	ꟺꟺ	ש	ś, š, (sh)
✛	✕	✕✕	ת	t, th

EARLY PHOENICIAN, ARAMAIC AND LATE HEBREW ALPHABETS

PLATE I

Present-day square-script	Square Hebrew	Siloam Inscription	Moabite Stone	Early Phoenician
'	א			
b, bh	ב			
g, gh	ג			
d, dh	ד			
h	ה			
w, v	ו			
z	ז			
ḥ (ḥeth)	ח			
ṭ (ṭeth)	ט			
y, î				
k, kh	כ			
l	ל			
m	מ			
n	נ			
s	ס			
' (ʿayin)	ע			
p, ph (f)	פ			
ṣ (ts)	צ			
q	ק			
r	ר			
s, ś (sh)	ש			
t, th	ת			

EARLY PHOENICIAN, MOABITE, AND THE HEBREW ALPHABET

PLATE II

	GREEK		LATIN		
	Eastern	Western	Etruscan	Latin	
alpha	A	A	A	A	a
beta	ß B	ß B	B	B	b
gamma	Γ C Γ	Γ C ‹ Γ	Γ ‹ C	C	c
delta	D D Δ	D D Δ	D	D	d
epsilon	⋖ E	⋵ E	⋵	E Il	e
digamma		Ϲ Ϝ F	Ϝ	F Iᶩ	f
zeta	I	I	I		
				G A new letter formed from C	g
eta	⊟ H	⊟ H	⊟	H	h
theta	⊗ ⊕ ⊙	⊗ ⊕ ⊙	⊗		
iota	I	ϟ I	I	I	i
kappa	K K	K K	K	K	k
lambda	Γ Λ	Γ Λ L	L	↳ L	l
mu	M M	M M	M	M	m
nu	N N	N N	N	N	n
xi	Ⱶ		⊞		
omikron	O	O	O	O	o
pi	Γ	Γ Π Γ	Γ	Γ P	p
san(ss)	[T]	M M	M		
koppa	φ	φ	φ	Q	q
rho	D R P	D R P	P R	R R	r
sigma	ϟ ϟ ϟ	ϟ ϟ ϟ	ϟ ϟ	ϟ S	s
tau	T	T	T	T	t
upsilon	V Y Y	V Y Y	Y	V	uv
xi	[see above]	+ X	X	X	x
phi	Φ Φ φ	Φ φ	Φ		
chi	+ X	Ψ Ψ Y	Ψ		
psi	Ψ Ψ	[✳]		Y Adapted at a later period	y
omega	Ω Ω	[Ω]		Z as foreign letters	z

GREEK AND LATIN ALPHABETS

The Greek alphabet was derived from that of the Phoenicians, which consisted of twenty-two signs. The early Greek alphabets fall into two main groups, viz. the Eastern or Ionian, used in Asia Minor and in certain states of Greece, both insular and mainland, and the Western, used in most of the states of mainland Greece and in the majority of the Greek colonies in Italy and Sicily. Of the Italian alphabets, which are derived from the Western Greek, the Etruscan is the earliest. From this the Latin developed, rejecting certain letters as superfluous and later introducing others.

PLATE III

CEREMONIAL PALETTE OF NA'RMERZA

c. 3300 B.C. Cairo Museum.

PLATE IV

DOORWAY OF A TOMB AT GÎZEH

The inscriptions are cut in the style of hieroglyphic characters
in vogue at the time of the Pyramid builders.
c. 2800 B.C.

PLATE V

THE ROSETTA STONE

Inscription in honour of Ptolemy V. Epiphanes, king of Egypt, in the Egyptian and Greek languages; the Egyptian portion being in hieroglyphics or writing of the priests, and in demotic or writing of the people. The key to the decipherment of the Egyptian hieroglyphics and the interpretation of the Egyptian language was obtained from this inscription.

195 B.C. British Museum.

PLATE VI

CRETAN WRITING

Clay Tablets from Knossos, c. 1600 B.C.
British Museum.

PLATE VII

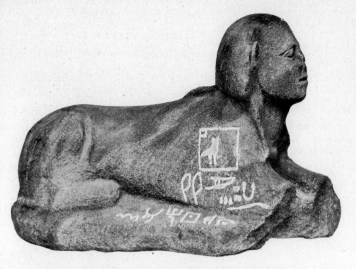

EARLY SEMITIC AND ALPHABETIC WRITING

(1) A Sphinx from Sinai. It bears Egyptian hieroglyphs and a
non-Egyptian, semi-hieroglyphic script.
c. 2000 B.C. British Museum.

(2) Inscription of Ahiram, king of Byblos.
c. 1000 B.C. *Orientalistisches Literaturzeitung*, 1925, 3.

PLATE VII

EARLY SCRIPT AND ALPHABETIC WRITING

PLATE VIII

THE MOABITE STONE

Monument dedicated to the god Kemôsh by Mesha', king
of Moab, to record his victory over the Israelites in the days
of Ahab: found at Dibhân in the land of Moab in 1868. The
inscription is in the Phoenician character.

c. 850 B.C. Paris, Museum of the Louvre.

PLATE VIII

THE MOABITE STONE

Monument designed to shew and J.B. crack by Mesha, king
of Moab, found at Dhibân in the land of Moab in 1868. The
inscription is in the Phoenician character.

c.850 B.C. Paris, Museum of the Louvre.

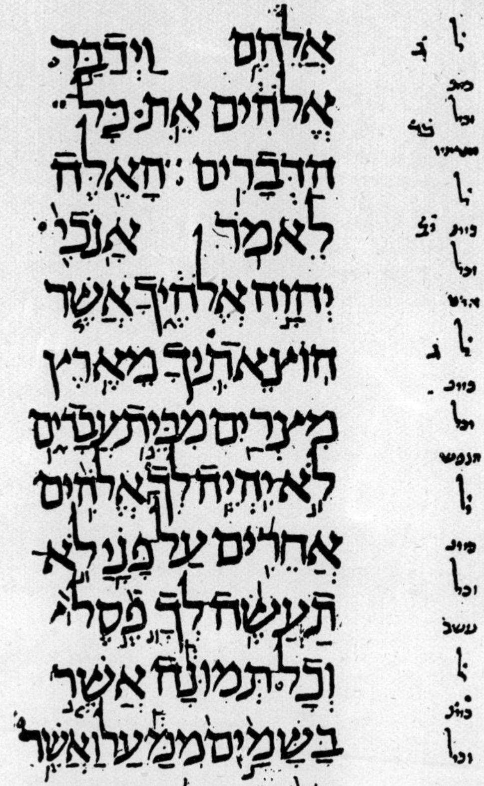
אלהם וידבר
אלהים את כל
הדברים האלה
לאמר אנכי
יהוה אלהיך אשר
הוצאתיך מארץ
מצרים מבית עבדים
לא יהיה לך אלהים
אחרים על פני לא
תעשה לך פסל
וכל תמונה אשר
בשמים ממעל ואשר
בארץ מתחת ואשר
במים מתחת לארץ
לא תשתחוה להם

HEBREW PENTATEUCH (Exodus xx. 1–5)

The text is arranged in three columns to the page, and is accompanied by the Massorah Magna and Parva.

9th century. British Museum, Oriental MS. 4445.

PLATE 12

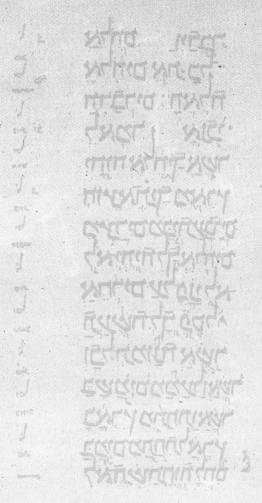

HEBREW PENTATEUCH (Exodus xxi. 1–5)

The text is arranged in three columns to the page, and is accompanied by the Masorah Magna and Parva.

9th century. British Museum, Oriental MS. 4445.

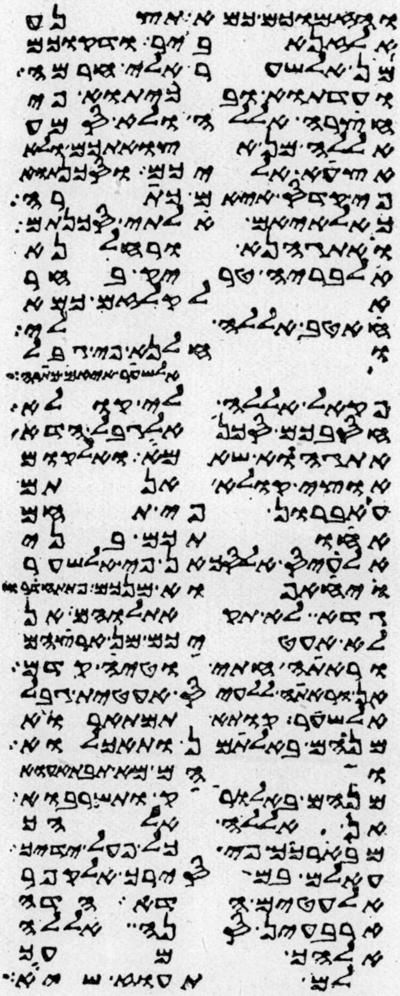

SAMARITAN PENTATEUCH
(Deut. i. 44–ii. 7)

The manuscript is bi-lingual, Hebrew
and Arabic, in Samaritan characters,
written in parallel double columns. This
plate represents the Arabic text.

PLATE X

A.D. 1219. Cambridge, University
Library, Add. 714.

PLATE XI

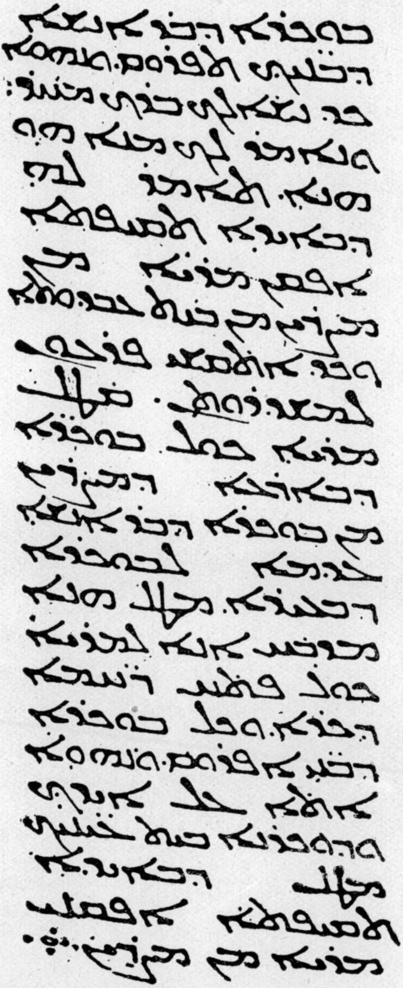

ܟܘܒܟܢ ܕܗܝ ܐܝܟ ܕܟܠܘܐ
ܕܚܠܘܝ ܠܦܪܘܟ. ܘܡܠܘܪܐܘ
ܟܕ ܢܫܐܠܟ ܟܪܟ ܡܚܪ ܡܢܘܗܝ:
ܘܐܝܠܗܢܐ ܠܟ ܝܗܒܟ ܡܢ ܠܗ
ܡܠܐܝ. ܐܠܗܝܐܪܘ ܠܗ
ܕܗܟܢܐܟܐ ܠܦܫܘܩܘܗ
ܐܦܩܢ ܡܪܝܢܟ ܡܢ
ܕܢܝܪܝܢ ܡܢ ܚܒܛ ܒܕܪܘܬܗܕ
ܘܗܘܐ ܐܘܬܝܒ ܡܫܘܐܐ ܦܪܥܗ
ܠܒܕܪ ܘܕܗܡܦ. ܡܛܠ
ܕܩܫܝܐ ܟܒܛ ܟܘܒܟܢ
ܕܗܟܐܝܬܗܟܐ ܕܡܠܪܝܢ
ܡܢ ܒܘܒܟܐ ܕܟܒܪ ܐܝܟܪܝܟ
ܠܐܕܟܐ ܠܒܘܬܦܟܪ
ܕܚܠܒܬܟܐ. ܘܟܠ ܡܢܐ
ܟܘܒܪ ܐܢܐ ܠܓܒܪܝܟܐ
ܒܗܕ ܦܗܒܪ ܕܢܫܒܟܐ
ܕܚܠܩܟܐ.ܝܗܒ ܟܘܒܟܐ
ܕܗܒܪ ܐܦܪܘܦ.ܘܢܘܡܗܘܐ
ܦܗܝܢ ܐܠ ܐܦܪܝܢ
ܘܕܗܕܟܒܕܗܟ ܡܢ ܟܝܡܝܢ
ܕܗܟܐܢܝܟܐ ܟܓܠ
ܐܦܩܘܡܠܟܐ ܐܝܟܘܡܠܪܘ
ܕܝܢܘܟܐ ܡܢ ܗܣ̈ܪܝܢ ܟܝܝܦ̈ܝܢ.

SYRIAC BOOKS OF THE PENTATEUCH (Exodus xiii. 14–16)

Four books of the Pentateuch, viz. Genesis, Exodus, Numbers, and
Deuteronomy, according to the Peshitta, in the Estrangela-Syriac character.
The oldest *dated* Biblical manuscript in existence.

A.D. 464. British Museum, Add. MS. 14425.

PLATE XII

PLATE XII

CINETШNЄBΔOMHK·
ᾱΡΤΑΒΑCIΛЄ⳾ONTOCKΥΡ·
ΠЄΡCШNЄTOYCΠPШ
TOYЄICCYNTЄΛЄIAN
ΡΗΜΑTOCKYЄNCTOMA
TIΙЄΡЄΜΙΟΥΗΓЄIPЄN
Κ̄C̄TOΠNЄΥΜΑΚΥΡΟΥ
ΒΑCIΛЄШCΠЄΡCШNΚΑΙ
ЄΚΗΡΥΞЄNΟΛΗΤΗΒΑCΙ
ΛЄΙΑΑΥΤΟΥΚΑΙΑΜΑΔΙΑ
ΓΡΑΠΤШNΛЄΓШN ΤΑ
ΔЄΛЄΓЄΙΟΒΑCIΛЄΥCΠЄΡ
CШNΚΥΡΟCЄΜЄΛNЄΛH
ΞЄNΒΑCIΛЄΑΤΗCΟΙΚΥ
ΜЄNΗCΟΚΥΡΙΟCTΟΥΙⲥ
ΡΑΗΛΚΟΥΨΙCTOCΚΑΙ
ЄCΗΜΗNЄNΜΟΙΟΙΚΟ
ΔΟΜΗCΑΙΑΥΤШΟΙΚΟN
ЄNΙЄΡΟΥCΑΛΗΜΤΗЄN
ΤΗΙΟΥΔΑΙΑЄΙΤΙCЄCTI
ΟΥΝΥΜШNЄΚΤΟΥЄΘΝ·Γ⳾
ΑΥΤΟΥЄCTШΟΚC̄ΑΥΤΥ
ΜЄΤΑΥΤΟΥΚΑΙΑΝΑΒΑ⳽
ЄICΤΗNΙЄΡΟΥCΑΛΗΜ
ΤΗNЄNΤΗΙΟΥΔΑΙΑΟΙΚ⳽
ΔΟΜЄΙΤШΤΟNΟΙΚΟNΤῩ
ΚῩΤΟΥΙⲥΡΑΗΛΟΥΤΟC
ΟΚC̄ΟΚΑΤΑCΚΗNШCΑN
ЄNΙЄΡΟΥCΑΛΗΜΟCΟΙ
ΟΥΝΚⳤΤΑΤΟΥCΤΟΠⲟⳡ⳽
ΟΙΚΟΥCΙNΒΟΗΘЄΙΤШCΑ
ΑΥΤШΟΙЄNΤШΤΟΠШ
ΑΥΤΟΥЄNΧΡΥCΙШΚΑΙ
ЄNΑΡΓΥΡΙШΚΑΙЄNΔΟ⳽
CЄCΙΗΜЄΘΙΠΠШNΚΑΙ
ΚΤΗNШNCΥNΤΟΙCΑΛ
ΛΟΙCΤΟΙCΚΑΤЄΥΧΑC
ΠΡΟCΤЄΘЄΙΜЄNΟΙCЄIC
ΤΟΙЄΡΟNΤΟΥΚῩΤΟЄNΙ
ЄΡΟΥCΑΛΗΜΚΑΙΚΑΤΑΤΗ
CΑΝΤЄCΟΙΑΡΧΙΦΥΛΟΙ
ΤШNΠΑΤΡΙШNΤΗCΙΟΥΔΑ

CODEX VATICANUS (1 Esdras ii. 1–8)

The Bible in Greek, written in uncial letters. The MS. was
already in the Vatican library in Rome in the fifteenth
century, but nothing is known of its previous history.
4th century.   Rome, Vatican Library.

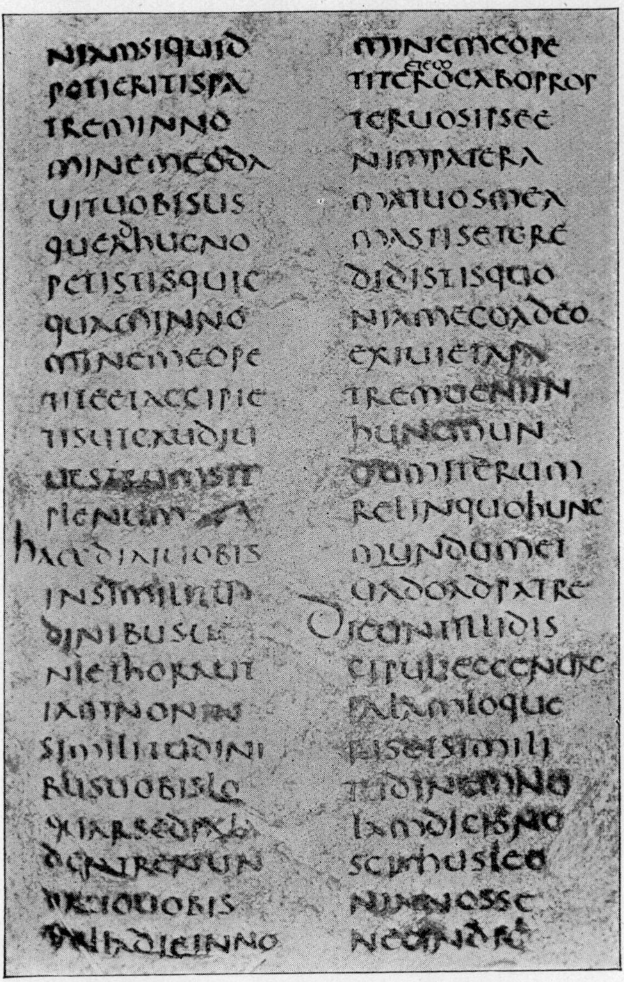

PLATE XIII

OLD LATIN GOSPELS (St. John xvi. 23–30)

Portions of the Gospels, partly 'European' and partly of a mixed
type, written in uncial letters in silver on purple vellum.
Late 4th century. Vercelli.

PLATE XIV

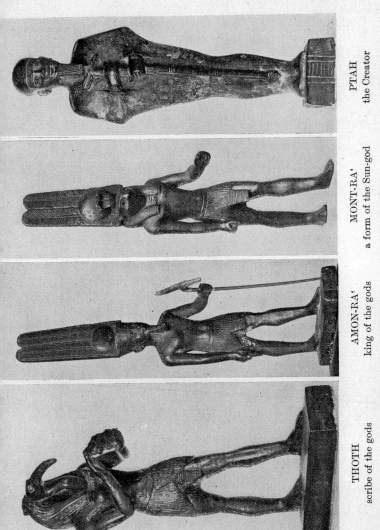

THOTH
scribe of the gods

AMON-RA'
king of the gods

MONT-RA'
a form of the Sun-god

PTAH
the Creator

EGYPTIAN GODS AND GODDESSES

(By permission of the Trustees of the British Museum.)

PLATE XV

ISIS (suckling HORUS) The goddess NEITH OSIRIS BAST
Consort of Osiris the weaver judge of the dead the cat-goddess

EGYPTIAN GODS AND GODDESSES (*continued*)

(By permission of the Trustees of the British Museum.)

PLATE XVI

'THE GOLDEN CALF'

The cow-goddess Hathor, from the temple of Dair-al-bahri.
XVIIIth Dynasty, *c.* 1450 B.C. Cairo Museum.

PLOUGH OF KALE

The one fashion of its kind, from the temple of Hat-shepsut, XVIIIth Dynasty. (Harris Cairo Museum.)

PLATE XVII

PROCESSION OF AN ARK

Amen-hetep III, king of Egypt about 1400 B.C., offering incense before the Ark
of the god Amen-Ra', the king of the gods.

From a bas-relief at Thebes.

PLATE XVII.

PLATE XVIII

MASKED DANCER
WITH A COBRA IN EACH HAND.
Ramesseum, Thebes.   XII dynasty.

(1) A masked dancer holding
two serpents.
XIIth Dynasty. *c.* 2000 B.C.
Manchester Museum.

(2) Kha'muese, son of Rameses II
and famous as a magician.
c. 1250 B.C. British Museum.

EGYPTIAN MAGICIANS AND SERPENT CHARMING

PLATE XIX

CEDAR-WOOD COFFIN OF THE IXth–XIIth DYNASTY

It was probably in coffins of this type that the bodies of Jacob and Joseph were placed after embalmment. c. 2400–2000 B.C. British Museum.

PLATE XX

(1) Of a king of the XIVth Dynasty.
c. 1750 B.C.

(2) Of a private lady of the
XIXth Dynasty.
c. 1300 B.C. British Museum.

ANTHROPOID COFFINS

PLATE XXI

(1) Egyptian embalmers bandaging a mummy.

(2) Egyptian embalmers painting a mummy.

EMBALMERS AT WORK
From an Egyptian wall-painting.

PLATE XVI

(1.) Egyptian embalmers bandaging a mummy.

(2.) Egyptian embalmers bandaging a mummy.

EMBALMERS AT WORK

From an ancient Egyptian painting

PLATE XXII

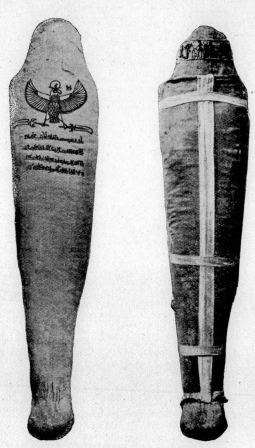

A ROYAL MUMMY

(1) With the outer covering, and (2) with the outer
covering removed and showing the bandages.
c. 1000 B.C. Cairo Museum.

PLATE XXIII

EGYPTIAN FUNERAL SCENE

Mourners crossing the Nile.

(From a wall-painting at Thebes, reproduced from the original by Mrs. N. de Garis Davies.
By permission of A. H. Gardiner, Esq., D.Litt., and Mrs. N. de Garis Davies.)

PLATE XXIV

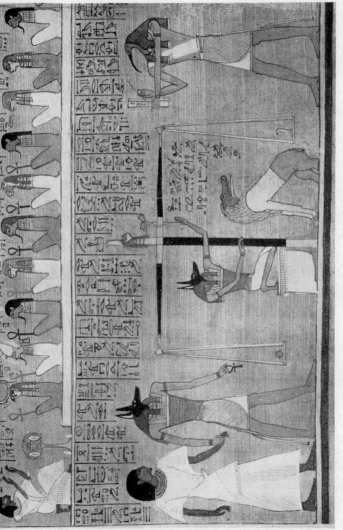

JUDGEMENT SCENE FROM THE PAPYRUS OF HUNEFER

The weighing of the heart in the Hall of Double Truth in the presence of Osiris (see Pl. XXV), the judge of the dead.
c. 1300 B.C. British Museum papyrus, No. 9901. (By permission of the Trustees of the British Museum.)

PLATE XXV

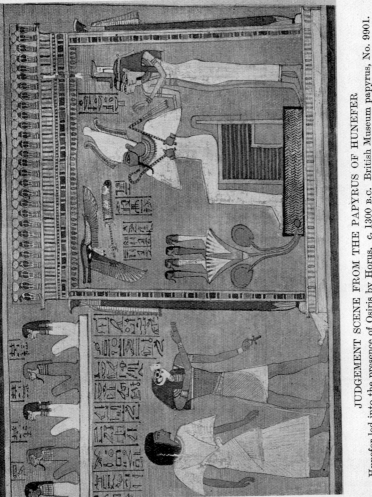

JUDGEMENT SCENE FROM THE PAPYRUS OF HUNEFER

Hunefer led into the presence of Osiris by Horus. c. 1300 b.c. British Museum papyrus, No. 9901.

(By permission of the Trustees of the British Museum.)

PLATE XXVI

THE SOUL REVISITING THE BODY

Vignette from the papyrus of Nekht, showing Nekht's soul in the form of a human-headed bird, revisiting the
mummied body on a bier in the tomb. *c.* 1350 B.C. British Museum papyrus, No. 10471.

(By permission of the Trustees of the British Museum.)

PLATE XXVII

'THE FIELDS OF SATISFACTION' OF THE EGYPTIAN LIFE AFTER DEATH

Vignette from the papyrus of Nekht. c. 1350 B.C. British Museum papyrus, No. 10471.

PLATE XXVIII

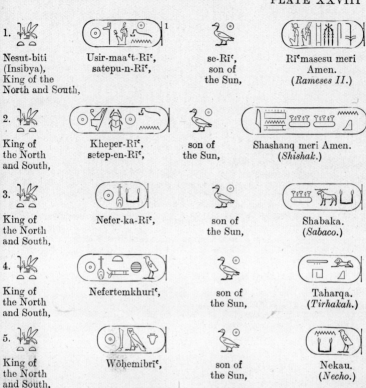

1. Nesut-biti (Insibya), King of the North and South, — Usir-maaʿt-Rīʿ, satepu-n-Rīʿ, — se-Rīʿ, son of the Sun, — Rīʿmasesu meri Amen. (*Rameses II.*)

2. King of the North and South, — Kheper-Rīʿ, setep-en-Rīʿ, — son of the Sun, — Shashanq meri Amen. (*Shishak.*)

3. King of the North and South, — Nefer-ka-Rīʿ, — son of the Sun, — Shabaka. (*Sabaco.*)

4. King of the North and South, — Nefertemkhurīʿ, — son of the Sun, — Taharqa. (*Tirhakah.*)

5. King of the North and South, — Wöhemibrīʿ, — son of the Sun, — Nekau. (*Necho.*)

6. King of the North and South. — Ḥaʿaʿibrīʿ, — son of the Sun, — Waḥibrīʿ. (*Hophra.*)

[1] The group of characters in this oval forms the *prenomen*.
[2] The group of characters in this oval forms the *nomen*.

NAMES OF EGYPTIAN KINGS mentioned in the Bible

PLATE XXIX

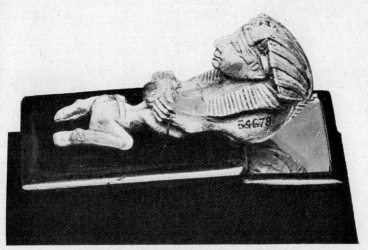

(1) PORTRAIT OF A 'HYKSOS' OR 'SHEPHERD'
KING OF EGYPT. From Abydos.
The period of the Hyksos kings is that of the Middle Kingdom,
between the XIIth and the XVIIIth Dynasties.
British Museum.

(2) HEAD OF THE MUMMY OF KING
IAʿHMASE (AMOSIS)
The expeller of the Hyksos.
XVIIIth Dynasty. *c.* 1580 B.C. Cairo Museum.

PLATE LXIX

PLATE XXX

THUTMASE III (THOTHMES, TUTHMOSIS)
c. 1510–1447 B.C. Cairo Museum.

PLATE XXXI

KING AKHENATEN AND QUEEN NEFRETITI

1376–1362 B.C. Berlin Museum.

PLATE XXXII

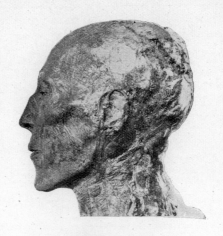

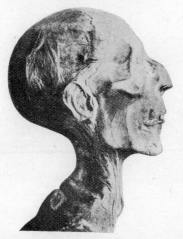

MUMMIED HEADS OF KING SETI I AND HIS
SON RĪ'MASESU (RAMESES) II
1320–1234 B.C. Cairo Museum.

PLATE XXXIII

(1) RAMESES II AS A
YOUNG MAN
British Museum.

(2) A RAMESSIDE KING
Possibly Rameses II or Meneptah.
This statue was found in Phoenicia.
c. 1250 B.C. British Museum.

PLATE XXXIII.

PLATE XXXIV

RAMESES IN BATTLE

Rameses II, king of Egypt, about 1280 B.C., attacking the Hittite forces before a fortified city. From the Ramesseum at Thebes.

PLATE XXXIV

PLATE XXXV

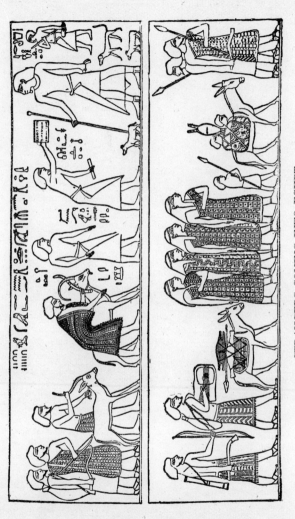

STRANGERS COMING INTO EGYPT

From a tomb of the XIIth Dynasty, about 2000 B.C., at Beni-Hasan in Upper Egypt.

PLATE XXXV.

PLATE XXXVI

SEMITES FROM PALESTINE OR SYRIA BRINGING
TRIBUTE TO THE EGYPTIAN COURT
XVIIIth Dynasty. *c.* 1400 B.C. British Museum.

PLATE XXXVII

(1) AN ANCIENT EGYPTIAN MODEL OF A GRANARY
XIth–XIIth Dynasty. *c.* 2000 B.C. British Museum.

(2) BRICKMAKERS AT WORK IN MODERN EGYPT
(Photograph by Gaddis & Seif, Luxor)

PLATE XXXVIII

EGYPTIAN FORCED LABOUR

Slaves making bricks and hauling stone. From the tomb of Rekhmira' at Thebes. c. 1470 B.C.
(By permission of the Metropolitan Museum, New York, and Mr. N. de G. Davies.)

PLATE XXXIX

UNBAKED BRICK made of Nile mud and
chopped straw, stamped with the prenomen of
Rameses (Rī'masesu) II, king of Egypt.
Usir-maaʿt-Rīʿ, Setep-en-Rīʿ, *c.* 1270 B.C.
From brick No. 6020, in the British Museum.

PLATE XXXIX

(1) King or god guarding the entrance to a palace: Boghaz Kyöi.

(2) Rock relief showing a priest king (?) under the protection of a god: Yasili Kayā.

(3) Procession of warriors: Yasili Kayā.

HITTITE RELIEF MONUMENTS

c. XVIIIth Dynasty of Egypt.
R. C. Thompson, *Proc. Soc. Bibl. Arch.*, 1910.
(By permission of the Royal Asiatic Society.)

PLATE XLI

TYPES OF HITTITES AND PHILISTINES
showing typical facial characteristics. From
the temple of Rameses III at Medinet Habu,
Thebes.
(By permission of Dr. H. R. Hall.)

PLATE XLII

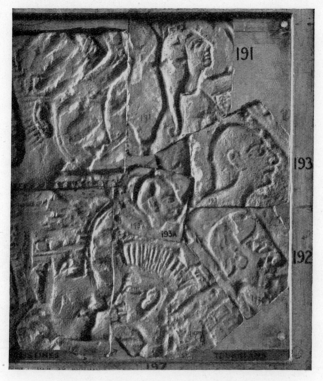

HITTITES AND PHILISTINES FROM MEDINET HABU
(By permission of Dr. H. R. Hall.)

PLATE XLIII

A PHILISTINE KNEELING BEFORE THE ROYAL
NAME OF RAMESES III.   Medinet Habu.

(By permission of Dr. H. R. Hall and the Royal Asiatic Society
Proc. Soc. Bibl. Arch. 1909, pl. xxxi.)

PLATE XLIV

AMBASSADORS FROM MINOAN CRETE

Egyptian representations of Greeks of the Bronze Age from
Crete and the Aegean.
From wall-paintings in the tombs of Sennemut and Rekhmira' at Thebes.
c. 1500–1450 B.C.
(Reproduced from the original by Mrs. N. de Garis Davies. By permission of A. H. Gardiner, Esq., D.Litt., and Mrs. N. de Garis Davies.)

PLATE XLV

MINOAN CRETE: THE 'CUPBEARER' FRESCO FROM
THE PALACE OF KNOSSOS. *c.* 1600 B.C.

The fainter outlines and shading indicate a modern
restoration of the figures, based on the evidence of the
darker portions, which represent the fresco as it is to-day.

(By permission of Sir Arthur Evans and the Candia Museum.)

PLATE XLVI

MINOAN PRINCE RECEIVING OR BIDDING
FAREWELL TO A WARRIOR

From a stone cup found at Hagia Trinda.
c. 1600 B.C. The original is in the Candia Museum.
Hall: *Civilization of Greece in the Bronze Age,* Fig. 195.
(By permission of Dr. H. R. Hall and Messrs. Methuens.)

PLATE XLVI.

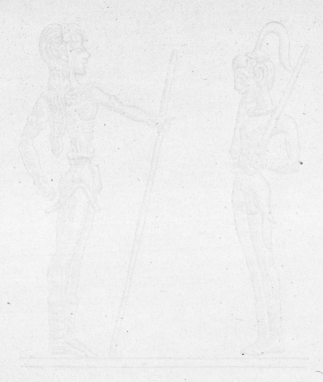

PLATE XLVII

(1) A gold cup with repoussé work. It is of the same type as the
cups represented in the wall-paintings in Plate XLIV.
Found at Vaphio, in the Peloponnese. *c.* 1600 B.C.

(2) A gold mask from the burial of a prince at Mycenae.
c. 1600 B.C.
National Museum, Athens.

THE ART OF 'THE ISLES'

PLATE XLVIII

PORTRAIT HEAD OF A THEBAN NOBLE
of VIIIth–VIIth centuries B.C.
British Museum.

PORTRAIT HEAD OF TIRHAKAH
689–663 B.C.   Cairo Museum.

PLATE XLIX

PORTRAIT OF APRIES (PHARAOH HOPHRA)
588–566 B.C. British Museum.

PORTRAIT OF PSAMMETICHUS
663–609 B.C. British Museum.

PLATE L

AN EGYPTIAN FOWLING SCENE

From a wall-painting in an XVIIIth Dynasty tomb at Thebes.
British Museum.

PLATE LI

DOCUMENT ON PAPYRUS, FROM EGYPT

In the form of a roll bound round with strips of
papyrus and sealed with two clay seals.
British Museum.

PLATE LII

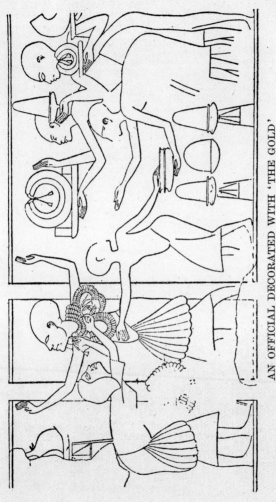

AN OFFICIAL DECORATED WITH 'THE GOLD'

From N. de G. Davies, *Rock Tombs of el-Amarna*, vol. VI, pl. IV.
From a tomb at el-'Amarna. c. 1360 B.C.

PLATE LIII

VI. OBJECTS DESCRIBED HALL (PL. XIV)

PLATE LIII

EGYPTIAN HARPER

From a painted wooden model in the British Museum,
No. 48658. *c.* 1300–1200 B.C.

(By permission of the Trustees of the British Museum.)

PLATE LIV

EGYPTIAN MUSICAL INSTRUMENTS. (1) Sistrum. (2) Bell. (3) Cymbals. (4) Flute.
British Museum, Nos. 12742, 6374, 6365, 6373. (By permission of the Trustees of the British Museum.)

PLATE LII.

PLATE LV

CLAY TABLET FROM TELL EL-ʿAMARNA
discovered on the site of the ancient
city of Akhet-Aten.
c. 14th century B.C. British Museum.

PLATE LVI

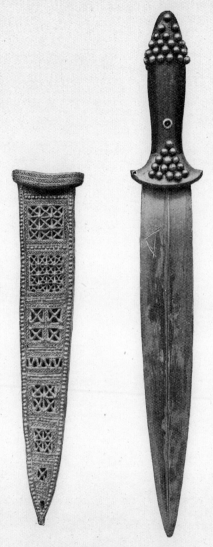

GOLD DAGGER with lapis-lazuli hilt
and open-work gold sheath.
Ur: before 3000 B.C.
(Baghdad.)

PLATE LVII

TWO GOLD VASES, AND GOLD HELMET OF MESKALAMSHAR
in form of wig.   Ur: before 3000 B.C.
(Philadelphia: London: Baghdad.)

PLATE LVI

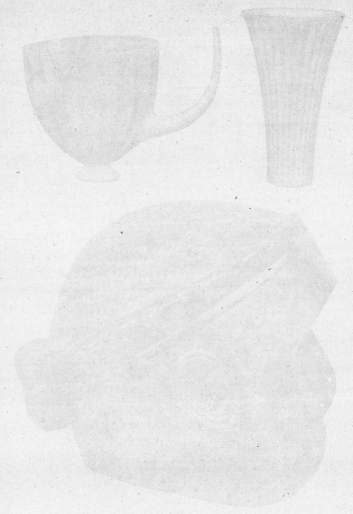

PLATE LVIII

One side of the MOSAIC 'STANDARD' from Ur: The Royal Court in peace.
Before 3000 B.C.   London.

PLATE XIII.

PLATE LIX

A ZIGGURAT AT UR

The tower was built at the west end of the sacred precincts : it consisted of four stages constructed of different coloured bricks to consort with certain astrological beliefs. Ur of the Chaldees was the original home of Terah, the father of Abram.

PLATE LIX

PLATE LX

HAMMURABI'S STELE OF LAWS

The scene in relief on the upper part of the
stele shows Hammurabi receiving the laws
from the Sun-god Shamshu.

First or Amorite Dynasty of Babylon, *c.* 1950 B.C.
Paris, Museum of the Louvre.

PLATE LXI

CAPTIVES FROM QARQARA BEING BROUGHT AWAY FROM THE
CITY BEFORE THE BATTLE

From a bronze band on a gate erected by Shalmaneser III, king of Assyria 859–824 B.C.
British Museum.

PLATE LXII

THE BLACK OBELISK

Set up at Nimrûd by Shalmaneser III, king of Assyria
859–824 B.C.   British Museum.

PLATE LXIII

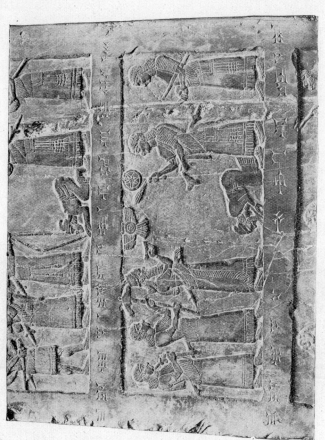

THE PAYMENT OF TRIBUTE BY JEHU, SON OF OMRI

From a bas-relief on the Black Obelisk (Plate LXII). The winged disk, the emblem of the presence of the god Ashur, is seen above the Assyrian king. British Museum.

3 A

PLATE XLIII.

PLATE LXIV

TIGLATH-PILESER III STANDING IN HIS WAR-CHARIOT WITH A DRIVER
AND AN ATTENDANT

From a frieze in his palace at Calah (Nimrúd).
c. 745–727 B.C. British Museum.

PLATE LXV

AN ASSYRIAN KING PROBABLY SARGON IN CONFERENCE WITH HIS COMMANDER IN CHIEF
824
KHORSABAD

KING SARGON INVESTING ONE OF HIS HIGH
OFFICIALS WITH AUTHORITY

c. 722–705 B.C. British Museum.

PLATE LXVI

PRISM OF SENNACHERIB

This records, in cuneiform writing, eight
campaigns of Sennacherib, king of Assyria.
705–681 B.C. British Museum.

PLATE LXVII

SENNACHERIB SEATED ON A HILL OVERLOOKING THE
ASSAULT AND CAPTURE OF LACHISH

From an alabaster frieze in a room of Sennacherib's
palace at Nineveh. British Museum.

PLATE LXVIII

ESARHADDON, KING OF ASSYRIA, LEADING
TWO OF HIS CAPTIVES BY A STRING HOOKED
THROUGH THEIR NOSES

From a great stele found at Sam'al (Sinjirli), in
North Syria. 681–669 B.C. Berlin Museum.

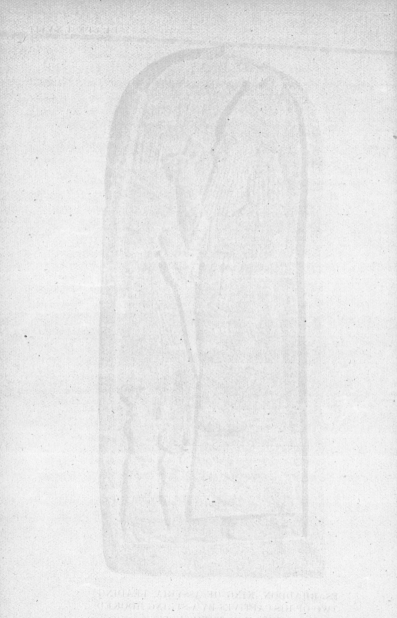

PLATE LXIX

DARIUS THE GREAT, KING OF THE MEDES AND
PERSIANS

Depicted triumphing over his rivals.
From a great rock relief at Behistun (Bisūtūn). 522–485 B.C.

PLATE LXX

(1) An impression of a Persian Seal showing
a king (probably Darius the Great) engaged
in a lion hunt. Above is the symbol of the
presence of the god Ahuramazda.

(2) Darius the Great represented as engaged in combat
with a lion.

(3) A Persian, assisted by his dog, striking
down an animal. An early type of the
St. George and the Dragon theme.
British Museum.

PERSIAN SEALS

PLATE LXXI.

PLATE LXXI

THE ISHTAR GATE, BABYLON
built by Nebuchadnezzar II, 605–562 B.C.

PLATE LXXII

THE SITE OF NINEVEH
Photograph by Dr. Campbell Thompson.

PLATE CXVII

PLATE LXXIII

BASALT FIGURE FROM THE GATEWAY AT CARCHEMISH
Possibly a type of the Syrian weather-god Adad.

PLATE LXXIV

AN ALABASTER STATUETTE
OF A SUMERIAN

Before 2600 B.C. British Museum.

PLATE LXXIV

PLATE LXXV

A KING OR PRIEST OF CARCHEMISH
A type of the 'Hittites' of the Old Testament.

PLATE LXXVI

AN ARAMAEAN KING
From a bas-relief of Bar-Rekub, found at Sinjirli, in Syria.
Berlin Museum.

PLATE LXXVII

PLATE LXXVII

AMBASSADORS FROM URARTU BEFORE ASHURBANIPAL, KING OF ASSYRIA

7th century B.C.   British Museum.

PLATE LXXVIII

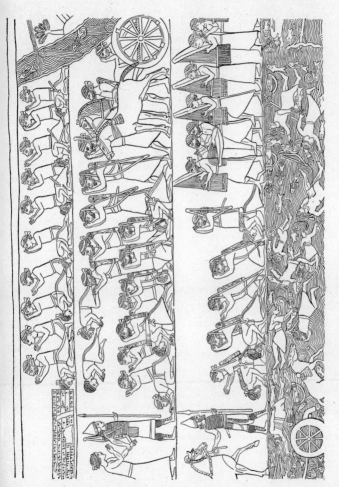

ASSYRIAN OFFICERS INSTALLING A KING OF ELAM, tributary to Ashurbanipal. From a frieze in the palace of Ashurbanipal. British Museum.

PLATE LXXVII.

PLATE LXXIX

PHOENICIAN SHIPS BRINGING TRIBUTE TO THE ASSYRIAN KING

From the bronze bands on the gates of Shalmaneser III.
9th century B.C. British Museum.

3 c

PLATE LXXX

(1) An ivory plaque of Phoenician workmanship depicting a woman in Egyptian
costume looking through a window.
c. 9th or 8th century B.C.

(2) An Egyptian style of
treatment.

(3) An Asiatic style of
treatment.

PHOENICIAN WOMEN

British Museum.

PLATE LXXXI

A MEDIAN NOBLE PRESENTING A MODEL OF A
BUILDING FOR THE APPROVAL OF HIS SUZERAIN

From a frieze in Sargon's palace at Khorsabad.

PLATE LXXXII

PERSIAN ARCHERS

From a coloured frieze found in a palace of Darius at Susa.
From Perrot and Chipiez: *Histoire de l'Art*, vol. v.

(By permission of Messrs. Chapman & Hall.)

PLATE LXXXIII

MEDALLION OF A SASANIAN KING
The legend reads, 'To Ardeshir, of divine
race, be Peace'.
c. 226 A.D. British Museum.

PLATE LXXXIV

TREE WORSHIP

King Ashurnasirpal with a priest wearing wings, engaged in a magical ritual.
British Museum.

PLATE LXXXV

(1) An Assyrian Seal, showing the sacred stone surmounted by a star, representing
Ishtar, the star of Venus.
British Museum.

(2) A coin of Septimus Severus,
depicting the temple of the moon-
god. The sacred stone is here surmounted by a crescent moon, the
symbol of Sin.

STONE WORSHIP

PLATE LXXXVI

TYPES OF MESOPOTAMIAN GODS

The illustration shows an Assyrian king worshipping the gods, Ashur, the national
god of the Assyrians, his consort Ninlil, Enlil, 'the lord of the lands',
and Sin, the moon-god.   Rock sculpture at Maltai.

PLATE LXXXVII

214   91000
TABLET SCULPTURED with a SCENE REPRESENTING the WORSHIP
of the SUN-GOD in the TEMPLE of SIPPARA and INSCRIBED with a RECORD
of the RESTORATION of the TEMPLE by NABU-PAL-IDDINA, KING of BABYLONIA,
about B.C. 870. THE TEXT DESCRIBES the RESTORATIONS CARRIED OUT by
the FORMER KINGS SIMMASH-SHIKHU (about B.C. 1050) and E-ULBAR-

THE SUN-GOD SHAMASH SEATED WITHIN HIS SHRINE

Found deposited in an earthenware coffer among the ruins of the
city of Sippur. 900 B.C. British Museum.

PLATE LXXXVIII

(1) An impression from a Babylonian cylindrical seal
showing Marduk advancing to slay Tiāmat.

(2) An impression taken from the top of a black stone inscribed by
Esarhaddon with an account of his restoration of Babylon. Each of
the symbols has an astrological significance.
British Museum.

PLATE LXXXIX

(2) Shēdu, a winged human-headed bull colossus, a favourite architectural decoration for gates in Assyria.

(1) Lamashtu, a female monster represented with a lion's head, being carried away by a horse as she suckles animals

BABYLONIAN DEVILS

PLATE XC

(1) Humbaba, a devil whose face consisted of a single line.

(2) Pazuzu, a god of sickness connected with the west wind, a cold blizzard which frequently caused fevers.

BABYLONIAN DEVILS (*continued*).   British Museum.

PLATE XCI

THE ROMAN EMPERORS

AUGUSTUS (63 B.C.–A.D. 14), as *imperator*, haranguing his troops.
From the villa of Livia, Prima Porta near Rome.
Vatican Museum.

PLATE XVI

PLATE XCII

a

c

b

d

THE ROMAN EMPERORS

a. TIBERIUS (42 B.C.–A.D. 37), as *Pontifex Maximus*.
   Museum of Fine Arts, Boston, Mass.
b. CALIGULA (A.D. 12–41). (Courtesy of the Metropolitan Museum of Art, New York.)
c. CLAUDIUS (10 B.C.–A.D. 54), represented as Jupiter
   with crown of oak leaves. Vatican Museum.
d. NERO (A.D. 37–68). Museo delle Terme, Rome.

(Photographs of c and d by Anderson)

PLATE XCIII

THE ROMAN EMPERORS

a. VESPASIAN (A.D. 9–79). Ny Carlsberg Glyptothek, Copenhagen. Tryde Photo.
b. DOMITIAN (A.D. 51–96). Museo Comunale, Rome. Alinari Photo.

PLATE XCIV

(1) A seven-branched candlestick and silver trumpets taken at
the capture of Jerusalem borne in procession.

(2) Titus in his triumphal chariot. The face is mutilated.

RELIEFS FROM THE ARCH OF TITUS

Photographs by Anderson.

PLATE XCV

1. THE RIGHT OF APPEAL OF A ROMAN CITIZEN

A coin with the word PROVOCO ('I appeal'), struck to commemorate the
passing of the law establishing this right in certain cases. 90 B.C.
British Museum.

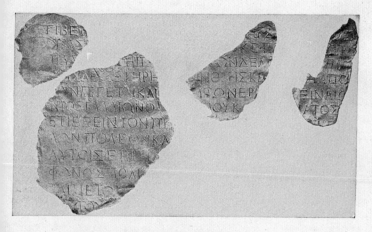

2. THE GALLIO INSCRIPTION

Fragment of a letter from the Emperor Claudius to the city of Delphi;
in which Gallio is mentioned as governor of Achaia. 52 B.C. (Adolf Deissmann: *Paul, A Study in Social and Religious History.* Revised edition 1926.
(By permission of Adolf Deissmann and Messrs. Hodder & Stoughton, Ltd.)

PLATE XCVI

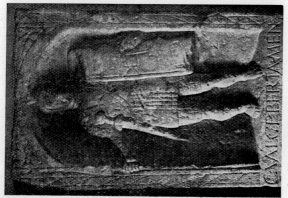

1. A centurion. 2nd century. (Colchester Museum.)

2. A private soldier. 1st century A.D. (Landes-Museum, Wiesbaden.)

3. A standard bearer. 1st century A.D. (Museum, Mainz.)

TYPES OF ROMAN SOLDIERS

PLATE XVI

1. ALTAR FROM PERGAMUM, inscribed 'To the unknown gods'. (Cf. Acts xvii. 23.) (Adolf Deissmann : *Paul, A Study in Social and Religious History*. Revised edition 1926. By permission of Adolf Deissmann and Messrs. Hodder & Stoughton, Ltd.)

2. THE TEMPLE OF DIANA AT EPHESUS showing the image of the goddess which was supposed to have fallen from heaven. From a Roman coin. 2nd century A.D.

PLATE XCVIII

1. A ROMAN ROAD IN SYRIA. (Sir Aurel Stein.)

2. THE RUINS OF EPHESUS, showing the theatre, and the street leading to the harbour (now dry land).

PLATE XCIX

1. A street corner in the ruins visible to-day, showing the 'Casa dei Dipinti' with traces of upper storeys above ground-floor shops. From *Architettura ed Arti Decorative*, 3 (1923). Besetti & Tumminelli.

2. A restoration of the 'House of Diana'.

OSTIA

1. A Phœnician In the after middle hundred; showing the Phœnician house, with tower; three objects above; probable house above. (From the Monumenti, &c. in Rome, Sossetti & Gregoratti.)

2. A restoration of the House of Minos.

CRETA.

PLATE C

GOLD DARIC

BRONZE HALF-SHEKEL OF SIMON MACCABAEUS

BRONZE COIN OF HEROD AGRIPPA I

LARGE BRONZE COIN OF AGRIPPA II

PLATE C

GOLD DARIC

BRONZE HALF-SHEKEL OF SIMON MACCABAEUS

BRONZE COIN OF HEROD AGRIPPA I

LARGE BRONZE COIN OF AGRIPPA II

PLATE CI

SILVER STATER OF AUGUSTUS, or
Tetradrachm of Antioch (Matt. xvii. 27).

SILVER DENARIUS OF TIBERIUS
(*Penny*, Matt. xviii. 28, &c.).

BRONZE ASSARION (*Farthing*, Matt. x. 29).

BRONZE LEPTON (*Mite*, Mark xii. 42).

SILVER SHEKEL OF THE FIRST REVOLT

PLATE CII

JERUSALEM

Looking across the city to the Temple area (now occupied by the Dome of the Rock) and the Mount of Olives.

(Photograph by Dr. M. J. Rendall)

PLATE CIII

1. The Sea of Galilee, with Mount Hermon in the distance.
(Photograph by the American Colony, Jerusalem.)

2. The lower reaches of the river Jordan.

PLATE CIV

THE DEAD SEA, looking across to the mountains of Moab.
(Photograph by the American Colony, Jerusalem.)

THE
INDEXED ATLAS TO THE HOLY BIBLE.

List of Maps.

List of Biblical Names,
WITH FIGURES AND LETTERS INDICATING THE SITUATION OF THE PLACES ON THE MAP.

NOTE.—*The figure preceding a hyphen denotes the number of the map, and the letter and figure following the hyphen indicate the square in which the name will be found ; thus Accho (3, 5 – B 3 ; 4 – B 5) will be found on Maps 3 and 5 in the square B 3, and on Map 4 in the square B 5.*

Plate 1.

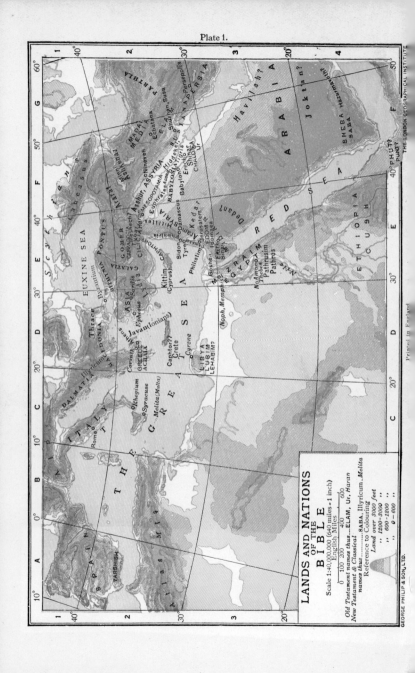

LANDS AND NATIONS
OF THE
BIBLE

Scale 1:40,000,000 (640 miles = 1 inch)
English Miles
0   100 200   400   600

Old Testament names thus....ELAM, Ur, Haran
New Testament & Classical
names thus........SABA, Illyricum, Melita

Reference to Colouring

Land over 3000 feet
" 1200-3000 "
" 600-1200 "
" 0 - 600 "

GEORGE PHILIP & SON, LTD.

THE LONDON GEOGRAPHICAL INSTITUTE

Printed in England

Plate 2.

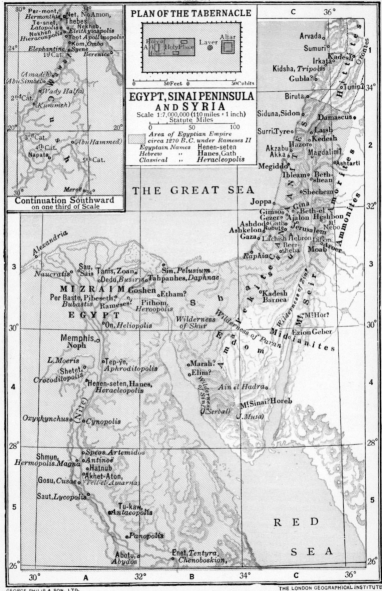

PLAN OF THE TABERNACLE

Holy of
Holies | Holy Place | Laver | Altar
Ark

0   50 Feet   50 Cubits

EGYPT, SINAI PENINSULA
AND SYRIA

Scale 1:7,000,000 (110 miles = 1 inch)
Statute Miles
0   50   100

Area of Egyptian Empire
circa 1220 B.C. under Rameses II
Egyptian Names   Henen-seten
Hebrew   „   Hanes, Gath
Classical   „   Heracleopolis

Continental inset (left):

80° Per-mont, 34°
Hermonthis, Net, No Amon,
Te-snet,   Thebes
Latopolis   Nekheb,
Nekhen   Eileithyiaspolis
Hieraconpolis Tbot Apollinopolis
          Kom Ombo
24° Elephantine, Syene
1st Cat.   Berenice
Berenice

(Amada?)
Abu Simbel

2nd Cat.
(Wady Halfa)
(Kuunneh)

20°   20°

3rd Cat.
4th Cat.   Abu Hammed
Napata

30° Meroë 34°

Continuation Southward
on one third of Scale

Main map labels:

C   36°

Arvada
Sumuri
Irkata Kadesh
Kidsha, Tripolis
Gubla?   Tunip?

Biruta   34°

Siduna, Sidon   Damascus
Surri, Tyre   Laish
Akzabu Hazor Kedesh
Akka   Magdalim?
Megiddo   Ashtarti
Ibleam   Beth-
          shean

THE GREAT SEA

Joppa   Gina
          Gimsoo Beth-el
          Gezer   Ajalon Heshbon
Ashdod   Gath Nebo
Ashkelon   Jerusalem
Gaza   Lachish Hebron Dibon
          Beer- Moab Aroer
          sheba
Raphia   Kadesh
              Barnea

Alexandria
Sau, Tanis, Zoan, Sin, Pelusium
Naucratis Sais Oedu, Busiris, Tahpanhes, Daphnae
MIZRAIM Goshen
Per Baste, Pibeseth? Etham?
Bubastis Rameses? Pithom,
EGYPT   Heroopolis
          Wilderness
          of Shur
On, Heliopolis
Memphis,
Noph

L. Moeris Tep-ye,
Shetet, Aphroditopolis Marah?
Crocodilopolis   Elim?
Henen-seten, Hanes,
Heracleopolis   Ain el Hadra
Oxyrhynchus   M! Sinai? Horeb
Cynopolis   (J. Serbal) (J. Musa)

Kadesh
Barnea

M! Hor?
Midianites
Ezion Geber

Shmun,   Speos Artemidos
Hermopolis Magna Antinoë
Hatnub
Gosu, Cusae Akhet-Aton
          (Tell-el-Amarna)
Saut, Lycopolis

Tu-kaw,
Antaeopolis

Panopolis   RED

Abotu, Enet, Tentyra,   SEA
Abydos Chenoboskion,

GEORGE PHILIP & SON, LTD.   THE LONDON GEOGRAPHICAL INSTITUTE

Plate 3.

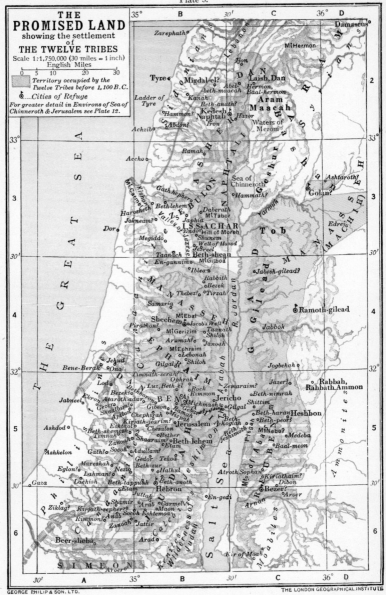

THE
PROMISED LAND
showing the settlement
of
THE TWELVE TRIBES
Scale 1:1,750,000 (30 miles = 1 inch)
English Miles
0   5   10   20   30
Territory occupied by the
Twelve Tribes before 1,100 B.C.
⊚....Cities of Refuge
For greater detail in Environs of Sea of
Chinneroth & Jerusalem see Plate 12.

Damascus

Zarephath

Mt Hermon

Tyre
Migdal-el?
Abel-
beth-maacah
Laish, Dan
Hermon,
Baal-hermon

Sidon

Ladder of
Tyre
Kanah
Beth-anath?
Kedesh

Aram
Maacah

Hammon?
Abdon?
Naphtali
Iron

Hazor

Geshur

Achzib

Waters of
Merom

THE   GREAT   SEA

Ramah

Accho

Sea of
Chinneroth

Ashtaroth?

Gath-hepher?
Bethlehem
Zebulun
Valley of Jezreel
Daberath
Mt Tabor
Japhia
Hammath?

Golan

Mt Carmel
Kishon

Harosheth?
Jokneam?

Issachar
Endor
Shunem
Well of Harod
Jezreel

Tob

Edrei?

Dor

Megiddo

Hill of Moreh

Taanach
Beth-shean

Manasseh
Machir

En-gannim
Ibleam
Mt Gilboa

Rabbith

Jabesh-gilead?

Thebez?
Bezek
Tirzah

Samaria

Gilead

Ramoth-gilead

Manasseh
Shechem
Mt Ebal
Jacob's Well
Mt Gerizim
Taanath
Shiloh
Janoah

Pirathon?
Arumah?
Ephraim
Mt Ephraim
Lebonah
Shiloh

Jordan

Jabbok

Jogbehah

Bene-Berak
Jehud
Ono

Gilgal?

Jabbok

Timnath-serah
Ophrah

Lod?
Bezek?
Bethhoron
Luz, Beth-el
Rock
Rimmon
Zemaraim?

Jabneel?
Ekron?
Ataroth-adar
Benjamin
Ai
Michmash
Jericho
Beth-nimrah
Rabbah,
Rabbath Ammon

Gezer?
Shaalbim?
Ajalon
Gibeon
Ramah
Mizpah
Gilgal
Shittim

Beth-haran
Heshbon

Esh-taol?
Chephirah
Kirjath-jearim?
Chesalon
Jerusalem
Beth-hoglah
Beth-jeshimoth
Mt Nebo?

Ashdod
Beth-shemesh?
Timnah?
Zanoah
Bether
Shaaraim?
Beth-lehem
Etam

Medeba

Ammonites

Gath?
Socoh?
Adullam?
Tekoa

Baal-meon

Ashkelon
Mareshah?
Nezib
Gedor
Beth-zur

Eglon?
Lahman?
Halhul

Atroth Sophan?
Kiriathaim?
Dibon

Gaza
Lachish
Beth-tappuah
Beth-anoth

Bezer?
Aroer

Etam
Hebron
En-gedi

Ziklag?
Shamir?
Kirjath-sepher?
Juttah
Arab
Carmel?
Maon

Arnon

Rimmon?
Anab
Socoh
Eshtemoa?

Moabites

Kir of Moab

Beer-sheba
Zanoah?
Jattir
Arad

Kenites

Wilderness of Judah

Judah

Salt Sea

SIMEON
Aroer

GEORGE PHILIP & SON, LTD.

THE LONDON GEOGRAPHICAL INSTITUTE

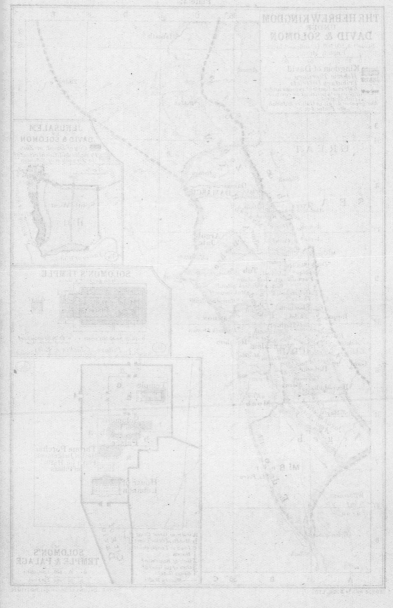

Plate 4.

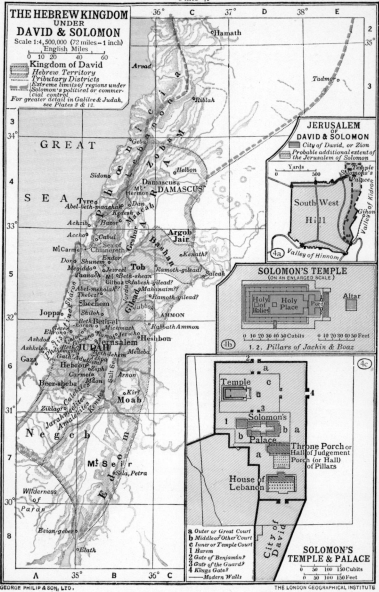

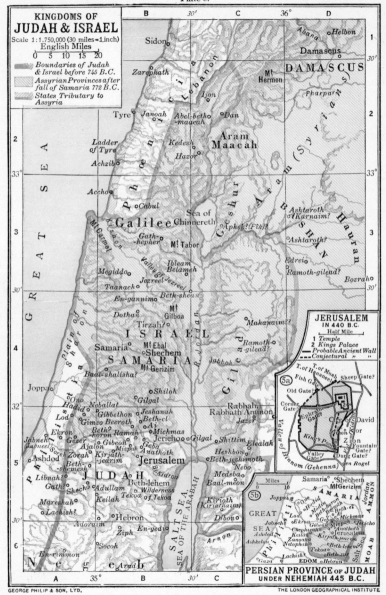

Plate 5.

Plate 6.

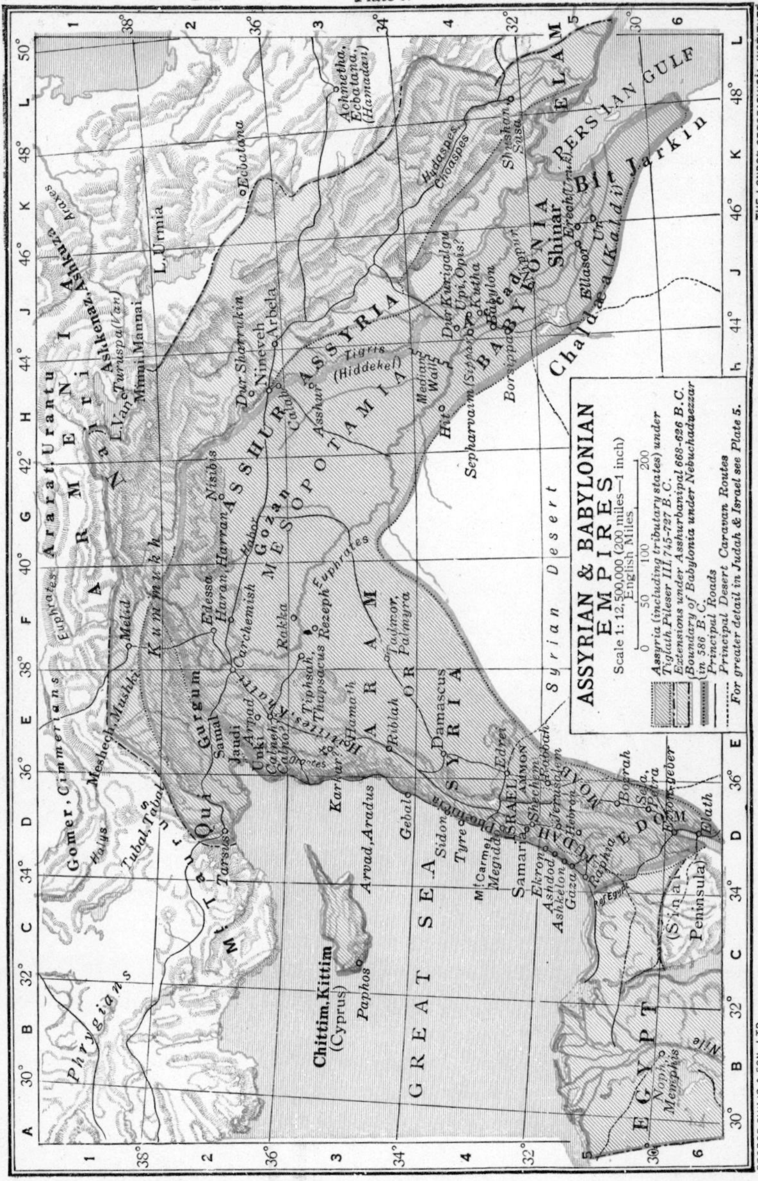
ASSYRIAN & BABYLONIAN EMPIRES
Scale 1: 12,500,000 (200 miles—1 inch)
0 50 100 200
English Miles
Assyria (including tributary states) under Tiglath Pileser III, 745-727 B.C.
Extensions under Asshurbanipal 668-626 B.C.
Boundary of Babylonia under Nebuchadnezzar in 586 B.C.
Principal Roads
Principal Desert Caravan Routes
For greater detail in Judah & Israel see Plate 5.
GREAT SEA
PERSIAN GULF
Chittim, Kittim (Cyprus)
Paphos
Arvad, Aradus
ASSYRIA
ASSHUR
MESOPOTAMIA
BABYLONIA
Shinar
Chaldaea (Kaldi)
Bit Jarkin
ELAM
ARAM
SYRIA
EGYPT
EDOM
MOAB
JUDAH
ISRAEL
AMMON
Syrian Desert
Mt Taurus
Phrygians
Gomer, Cimmerians
Meshech, Mushki
Tubal, Tabal
Kummukh
Gurgum
Ararat, Urantu
Armenia
Askkenaz, Ashkuza
Minni, Mannai
L. Van
L. Urmia
Euphrates
Tigris (Hiddekel)
Nile
Halys
Araxes
Orontes
Hydaspes
Choaspes
Melid
Edessa
Haran, Harran
Carchemish
Samal
Jaudi
Arpad
Unki
Calneh, Calno
Tiphsah, Thapsacus
Hamath
Riblah
Rakka
Rezeph
Tadmor, Palmyra
Damascus
Edrei
Rabbah
Bozrah
Sela, Petra
Ezion-geber
Elath
Gebal
Sidon
Tyre
Mt Carmel
Megiddo
Samaria
Shechem
Jerusalem
Hebron
Ekron
Ashdod
Ashkelon
Gaza
Raphia
R. of Egypt
(Sinai) Peninsula
Noph, Memphis
Tarsus
Nisibis
Gozan
Habor
Dur Sharrukin
Nineveh
Calah
Asshur
Arbela
Ecbatana
Achmetha, Ecbatana, (Hamadan)
Turuspa (Van)
Hit
Median Wall
Sepharvaim (Sippar)
Dur Kurigalzu
Upi, Opis?
Kutha
Babylon
Borsippa
Nippur
Erech (Uruk)
Ellasar
Ur
Shushan, Susa
Akkad

GEORGE PHILIP & SON, LTD.

THE LONDON GEOGRAPHICAL INSTITUTE

Plate 7.

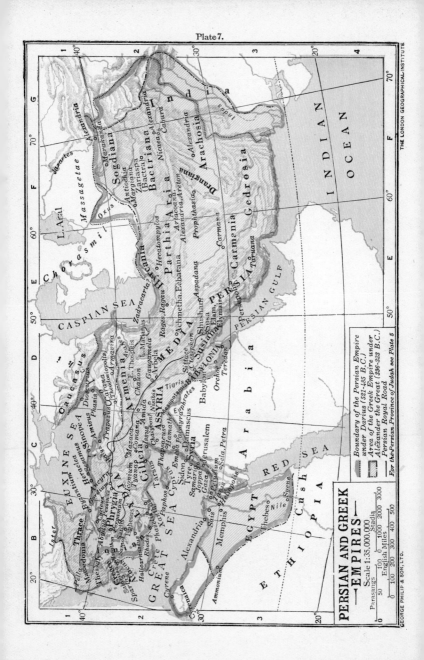

PERSIAN AND GREEK
—EMPIRES—
Scale 1:35,000,000

Parasangs 0 50 100 150
Stadia 0 1000 2000 3000
English Miles
0 100 200 300 400 500

.... Boundary of the Persian Empire
under Darius (521-485 B.C.)
▓▓ Area of the Greek Empire under
Alexander the Great (336-323 B.C.)
- - - Persian Royal Road
For the Persian Province of Judah see Plate 5

THE LONDON GEOGRAPHICAL INSTITUTE

GEORGE PHILIP & SON, LTD.

Plate 8.

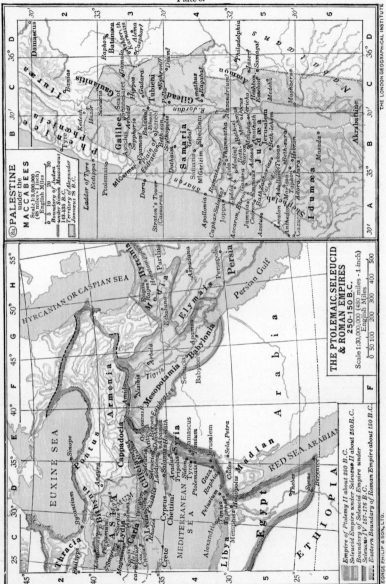

THE LONDON GEOGRAPHICAL INSTITUTE

PALESTINE under the MACCABEES

Scale 1:3,000,000
(48 miles = 1 inch)
English Miles

0 5 10 20 30

Boundary of Judæa
under Simon Maccabæus
143-135 B.C.
Territory of Alexander
Jannæus 78 B.C.

THE PTOLEMAIC, SELEUCID & ROMAN EMPIRES
250-150 B.C.

Scale 1:30,000,000 (480 miles = 1 inch)
English Miles

0 50 100 200 300 400 500

Empire of Ptolemy II about 250 B.C.
Seleucid Empire under Seleucus II about 250 B.C.
Seleucid Empire under
Seleucus IV 187-176 B.C.
Eastern Boundary of Roman Empire about 150 B.C.

GEORGE PHILIP & SON, LTD.

Plate 9.

PALESTINE IN THE TIME OF CHRIST

TEMPLE OF HEROD

North Cloister

West Cloister

Solomon's Porch

Court of the Gentiles

Royal Cloister

Cubits
300
Feet
200 400 600

1 Women's Court
2 Israelites' Court
3 Priests' Court

9a

Roman Miles
0   5   10   20
English Miles
0   5   10   20
Roman Province under
Pontius Pilate. Brown tint
Cities of the Decapolis
Principal Roman Roads

JERUSALEM before 70 A.D.

Ancient Walls — Do. (Conjectural)
Modern Wall

9b

TETRARCHY OF LYSANIAS
Mt Hermon
Damascus
Caesarea Philippi
Ituræa
TETRARCHY OF PHILIP
Sarepta Zarephath
Leontes
Tyre
Ladder of Tyre
Ecdippa
Semechonitis
Ptolemais
Gischala
Capernaum
Bethsaida Julias
Gergesa
Gaulanitis
Batanæa
Jotapata
Sephoris
Magdala
Sea of Galilee
Hippos
Abila
GALILEE
TETRARCHY OF
Nazareth
Cana?
Tiberias
Tarichæa
Mt Tabor
Nain
Plain of Esdraelon
Gadara
Dora
Megiddo
Cæsarea
Strato's Tower
Ginaea
Scythopolis
(Makhadet Abara)
Pella
DECAPOLIS
Dion
THE GREAT SEA
Samaria
Mt Ebal Ænon?
Sychem
Jacob's Well
Sychar
Salim?
Archelais?
Gerasa
SAMARIA
Apollonia
Antipatris
Joppa
Phasaelis
Peraea
Philadelphia
Lydda
Gophna
Ephraim?
HEROD ANTIPAS
Bethel
Jamnia
Ekron
Nicopolis
Ramah?
or Ram?
Jericho
Azotus
Jerusalem
Bethany
Makhadet Hajlah
Livias
Ascalon
Bethlehem
Herodium
Eleutheropolis
Callirhoe
Machaerus
Marisa?
Idumæa
Wilderness of Judea
SALT SEA (L. Asphaltitis)
Gaza
Hebron
Beer-sheba

JERUSALEM before 70 A.D.

Robinson
Calvary
Bezetha
Antonia
Pool of Bethesda
Gethsemane
Temple
Hippicus Herod's Palace
Upper City
Lower City
Pool of Siloam
Valley of Hinnom
Valley of Kidron
Mile

George Philip & Son, Ltd.

THE LONDON GEOGRAPHICAL INSTITUTE

Plate 10.

THE LONDON GEOGRAPHICAL INSTITUTE

MEDITERRANEAN LANDS
ILLUSTRATING THE
ACTS & EPISTLES

Scale 1:12,000,000 (192 miles=1 inch)
Statute Miles

50   0   100   200

The 7 Churches of ASIA thus...**Sardis**✝
Roman Empire...................
States Tributary to Rome.......
For greater detail in Palestine see Plate 9.

St Paul's Missionary Journeys
1st Journey........
2nd Journey....... } according to
3rd Journey....... Paul's 2nd Journey
Paul's 3rd Journey N. Galatian theory
Voyage to Rome....

GEORGE PHILIP & SON, LTD.